AF819597

Recommended by **Teachers**
Trusted by **Toppers**

All in One®

PHYSICS
Class 12

EVERYTHING YOU NEED TO SCORE

- Simplified NCERT Theory
- Chapter & In-text Exercises
- CBQs; MCQs, A-R, Case Based
- Board Questions Upto 2025
- Sample Question Papers

CBSE Exams 2026

Author
Keshav Mohan (M.Sc.)

arihant
SUCCESS AND NOTHING LESS

ARIHANT PRAKASHAN
(School Division Series)

卐 *ADMINISTRATIVE & PRODUCTION OFFICES*

Regd. Office

'Ramchhaya' 4577/15, Agarwal Road, Darya Ganj, New Delhi -110002
Tele: 011- 47630600, 43518550; Fax: 011- 23280316

卐 *Head Office*

Kalindi, TP Nagar, Meerut (UP) - 250002, Tel: 0121-7156203, 7156204

卐 *SALES & SUPPORT OFFICES*

Agra, Ahmedabad, Bengaluru, Bareilly, Chennai, Delhi, Guwahati, Hyderabad, Jaipur, Jhansi, Kolkata, Lucknow, Nagpur & Pune.

PO No : TXT-XX-XXXXXXX-X-XX

Published By Arihant Publications (India) Ltd.

For further information about the books published by Arihant, log on to www.arihantbooks.com or e-mail at info@arihantbooks.com

Follow us on

卐 *PRICE* ₹ 525.00

PRODUCTION TEAM

Publishing Managers	*Cover Designer*	*Inner Designer*
Mahendra Singh Rawat & Keshav Mohan	Salman Shaikh	Ankit Tyagi
Project Head	*Page Layouting*	*Proof Readers*
Yojna Sharma	Rajbhasker Rana, Subhash Chaprana	Ishan Khan, Mansi Tomar

Index *cum* Study Planner

Studied | Revised | Exam ready

One Book- Endless Features

to Help you Succeed

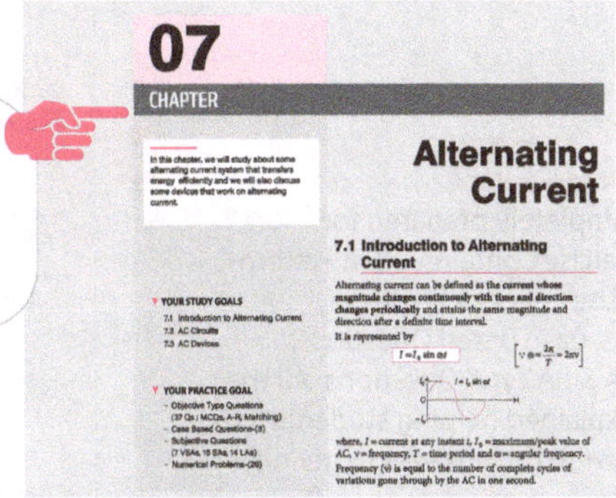

In This Chapter

At the start of each chapter, all the chapter topics have been listed , so that students may know what they are going to study.

Simplified Theory

It contains the necessary study material well supported by Definitions, Facts, Figures, Flow Charts, etc.

7.1 Introduction to Alternating Current

Alternating current can be defined as **the current whose magnitude changes continuously with time and direction changes periodically** and attains the same magnitude and direction after a definite time interval.

It is represented by

$$I = I_0 \sin \omega t \qquad \left[\because \omega = \frac{2\pi}{T} = 2\pi\nu\right]$$

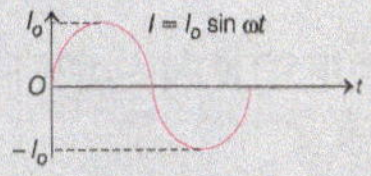

where, I = current at any instant t, I_0 = maximum/peak value of AC, ν = frequency, T = time period and ω = angular frequency.

Frequency (ν) is equal to the number of complete cycles of variations gone through by the AC in one second.

The inductive reactance opposes the current in a purely inductive circuit in the same way as the resistance opposes the current in a purely resistive circuit. It is also directly proportional to the inductance and to the frequency of the AC.

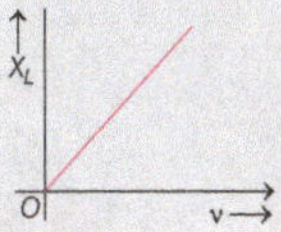

Thus, if the frequency of AC increases, its inductive reactance also increases.

If inductor is connected to DC source

$$\nu = 0 \qquad \left[\because \nu = \frac{1}{T}\right]$$

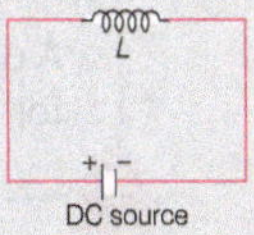

Here, ν is frequency. So, from Eq. (i)

$X_L = 0$.

Therefore, inductor passes DC and blocks AC of very high frequency.

Boxed Matter

Additional but informational matter related to given concept. It helps students to bring focus on important points.

Topical Exercises

To make students understand the chapter in a smooth part-by-part manner, Topical Exercises have been given in each chapter. These Exercises help students to assess the understanding of related concepts at regular interval.

Quick Test 1

Conceptual Questions

1. In many European homes and offices, the rms voltage available from a wall socket is 240 V. What is the maximum voltage in this case?
2. An AC current, $I = I_0 \sin \omega t$ produces certain heat H in a resistor R over a time $T = 2\pi/\omega$. Write the value of the DC current that would produce the same heat in the same resistor in the same time.
3. An alternating current is given by $I = I_1 \cos \omega t + I_2 \sin \omega t$. Determine the rms value of current through the circuit.
4. The current through an AC circuit is $I_t = I_0(t/\tau)$ for sometime. Determine the rms current through the circuit over time interval $t = 0$ to $t = \tau$.
5. Show that heat produced in a cycle of AC is same as the heat produced by DC with $I = I_{rms}$.
6. Both alternating current and direct current are measured in amperes. But how is the ampere defined for an alternating current? *NCERT Exemplar*

One Book- Endless Features

to Help you Succeed

Exam Pattern Exercise

To make students completely prepared for examination, this Exercise contains Exam Pattern Questions. This exercise covers all types of questions, like; MCQs, Case Based Questions, Assertion-Reason, SA & LA Type Questions. All the questions are fully explained helping students to understand, how to write the answers to get full marks in the exam.

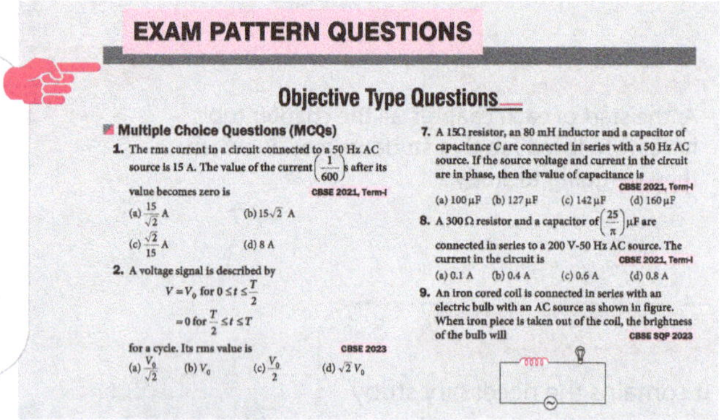

Mind Map

A quick revision visual tool for the complete chapter.

Sample Question Papers

To make students practice of examination in real sense, there are 3 Sample Question Papers at the end. All these Sample Questions Papers are exactly prepared on the latest syllabus & pattern of examination.

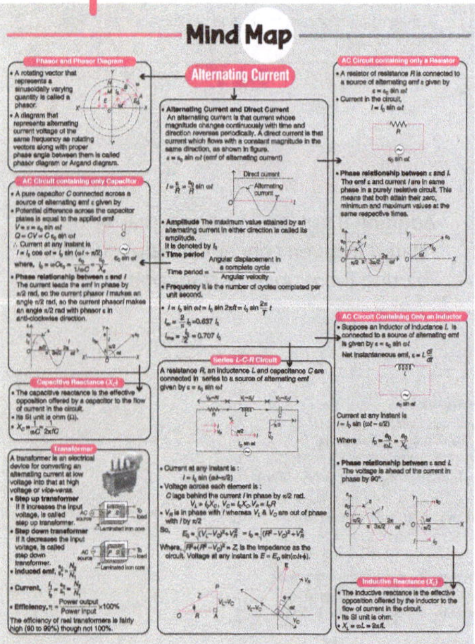

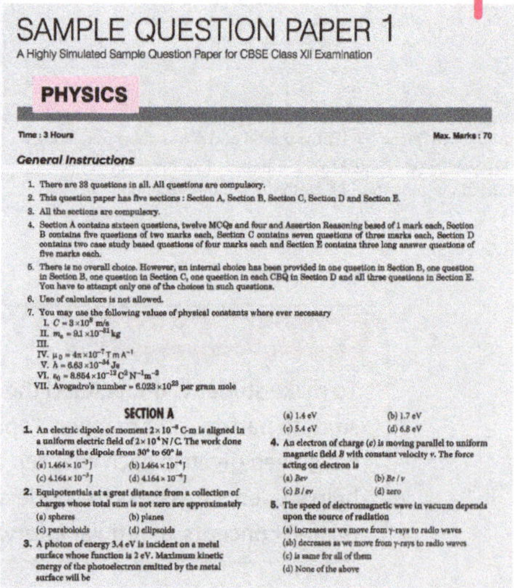

Latest Course Structure

Time: 3 Hrs **Max. Marks : 70**

Units		Marks
I	**Electrostatics** Chapter 1: Electric Charges and Fields Chapter 2: Electrostatic Potential and Capacitance	16
II	**Current Electricity** Chapter 3: Current Electricity	
III	**Magnetic Effects of Current and Magnetism** Chapter 4: Moving Charges and Magnetism Chapter 5: Magnetism and Matter	17
IV	**Electromagnetic Induction and Alternating Currents** Chapter 6: Electromagnetic Induction Chapter 7: Alternating Current	
V	**Electromagnetic Waves** Chapter 8: Electromagnetic Waves	18
VI	**Optics** Chapter 9: Ray Optics and Optical Instruments Chapter 10: Wave Optics	
VII	**Dual Nature of Radiation and Matter** Chapter 11: Dual Nature of Radiation and Matter	12
VIII	**Atoms and Nuclei** Chapter 12: Atoms Chapter 13: Nuclei	
IX	**Electronic Devices** Chapter 14: Semiconductor Electronics: Materials, Devices and Simple Circuits	7
	Total	70

UNIT I Electrostatics

Chapter 1 : Electric Charges and Fields

Electric charges, Conservation of charge, Coulomb's law-force between two-point charges, forces between multiple charges; superposition principle and continuous charge distribution.

Electric field, electric field due to a point charge, electric field lines, electric dipole, electric field due to a dipole, torque on a dipole in uniform electric field.

Electric flux, statement of Gauss's theorem and its applications to find field due to infinitely long straight wire, uniformly charged infinite plane sheet and uniformly charged thin spherical shell (field inside and outside).

Chapter 2 : Electrostatic Potential and Capacitance

Electric potential, potential difference, electric potential due to a point charge, a dipole and system of charges; equipotential surfaces, electrical potential energy of a system of two-point charges and of electric dipole in an electrostatic field.

Conductors and insulators, free charges and bound charges inside a conductor. Dielectrics and electric polarization, capacitors and capacitance, combination of capacitors in series and in parallel, capacitance of a parallel plate capacitor with and without dielectric medium between the plates, energy stored in a capacitor (no derivation, formulae only).

UNIT II Current Electricity

Chapter 3 : Current Electricity

Electric current, flow of electric charges in a metallic conductor, drift velocity, mobility and their relation with electric current; Ohm's law, V-I characteristics (linear and non-linear), electrical energy and power, electrical resistivity and conductivity, temperature dependence of resistance, Internal resistance of a cell, potential difference and emf of a cell, combination of cells in series and in parallel, Kirchhoff's rules, Wheatstone bridge.

UNIT III Magnetic Effects of Current and Magnetism

Chapter 4 : Moving Charges and Magnetism

Concept of magnetic field, Oersted's experiment.

Biot - Savart law and its application to current carrying circular loop.

Ampere's law and its applications to infinitely long straight wire. Straight solenoid (only qualitative treatment), force on a moving charge in uniform magnetic and electric fields.

Force on a current-carrying conductor in a uniform magnetic field, force between two parallel current-carrying conductors-definition of ampere, torque experienced by a current loop in uniform magnetic field; Current loop as a magnetic dipole and its magnetic dipole moment, moving coil galvanometer-its current sensitivity and conversion to ammeter and voltmeter.

Chapter 5 : Magnetism and Matter

Bar magnet, bar magnet as an equivalent solenoid (qualitative treatment only), magnetic field intensity due to a magnetic dipole (bar magnet) along its axis and perpendicular to its axis (qualitative treatment only), torque on a magnetic dipole (bar magnet) in a uniform magnetic field (qualitative treatment only), magnetic field lines.

Magnetic properties of materials- Para-, dia- and ferro - magnetic substances with examples, Magnetization of materials, effect of temperature on magnetic properties.

UNIT IV Electromagnetic Induction and Alternating Currents

Chapter 6 : Electromagnetic Induction

Electromagnetic induction; Faraday's laws, induced EMF and current; Lenz's Law, Self and mutual induction.

Chapter 7 : Alternating Current

Alternating currents, peak and RMS value of alternating current/voltage; reactance and impedance; LCR series circuit (phasors only), resonance, power in AC circuits, power factor, wattless current.

AC generator, Transformer.

UNIT V Electromagnetic Waves

Chapter 8 : Electromagnetic Waves

Basic idea of displacement current, Electromagnetic waves, their characteristics, their transverse nature (qualitative idea only).

Electromagnetic spectrum (radio waves, microwaves, infrared, visible, ultraviolet, X-rays, gamma rays) including elementary facts about their uses.

UNIT VI Optics

Chapter 9 : Ray Optics and Optical Instruments

Ray Optics: Reflection of light, spherical mirrors, mirror formula, refraction of light, total internal reflection and optical fibers, refraction at spherical surfaces, lenses, thin lens formula, lens maker's formula, magnification, power of a lens, combination of thin lenses in contact, refraction of light through a prism.

Optical instruments: Microscopes and astronomical telescopes (reflecting and refracting) and their magnifying powers.

Chapter 10 : Wave Optics

Wave optics: Wave front and Huygen's principle, reflection and refraction of plane wave at a plane surface using wave fronts. Proof of laws of reflection and refraction using Huygen's principle. Interference, Young's double slit experiment and expression for fringe width (No derivation final expression only), coherent sources and sustained interference of light, diffraction due to a single slit, width of central maxima (qualitative treatment only).

UNIT VII Dual Nature of Radiation and Matter

Chapter 11 : Dual Nature of Radiation and Matter

Dual nature of radiation, Photoelectric effect, Hertz and Lenard's observations; Einstein's photoelectric equation-particle nature of light.

Experimental study of photoelectric effect Matter waves-wave nature of particles, de-Broglie relation.

UNIT VIII Atoms and Nuclei

Chapter 12 : Atoms

Alpha-particle scattering experiment; Rutherford's model of atom; Bohr model of hydrogen atom, Expression for radius of nth possible orbit, velocity and energy of electron in nth orbit, hydrogen line spectra (qualitative treatment only).

Chapter 13 : Nuclei

Composition and size of nucleus, nuclear force Mass-energy relation, mass defect; binding energy per nucleon and its variation with mass number; nuclear fission, nuclear fusion.

UNIT IX Electronic Devices

Chapter 14 : Semiconductor Electronics: Materials, Devices and Simple Circuits

Energy bands in conductors, semiconductors and insulators (qualitative ideas only) Intrinsic and extrinsic semiconductors- p and n type, p-n junction Semiconductor diode - I-V characteristics in forward and reverse bias, application of junction diode - diode as a rectifier.

01

CHAPTER

Electrostatics deals with the study of forces, fields and its effects arising from static charges or charges at rest. In this chapter, we will discuss below topics in detail.

YOUR STUDY GOALS

1.1 Electric Charge
1.2 Coulomb's Law and Electrostatic Field
1.3 Electrostatic Force due to Continuous Charge Distribution
1.4 Electric Field
1.5 Electric Field Lines
1.6 Electric Dipole
1.7 Dipole in a Uniform External Field
1.8 Electric Flux
1.9 Applications of Gauss' Theorem

YOUR PRACTICE GOAL

- Objective Type Questions (35 Qs ; MCQs, A-R, Statements, Matching)
- Case Based Questions-3
- Subjective Questions (10 VSAs, 17 SAs, 8 LAs)
- Numerical Problems-10

Electric Charges and Fields

1.1 Electric Charge

Charge is an intrinsic property of matter associated with its elementary particles due to which it produces and experiences electric and magnetic effects. It is a **scalar quantity** and its SI unit is **Coulomb (C)** named after French physicist Charles Augustin de Coulomb.

Types of Charges

There are two types of electric charge : Positive and Negative.

An object can attain positive charge by loosing electrons while other can attain negative charge by gaining electrons.

Charges with same sign are known as **like charges** and they repel each other. On the other hand, charges with opposite sign are called **unlike charges** and they attract each other.

Detection of Charge

An **electroscope** is a scientific instrument used to detect the presence and magnitude of electric charge on a body.

It consists of a brass rod with a brass disc at the top, and at the bottom. There are two thin gold leaves in the form of foils. In order to keep the rod in place, the rod travels through the insulator. The charges move from the disc to the leaves through

the rod. The object that needs to be tested is touched with the metal cap.
If the leaves diverge, the body is said to be **charged,** if there is no change in the leaves of the electroscope, then the body is said to be **uncharged.**

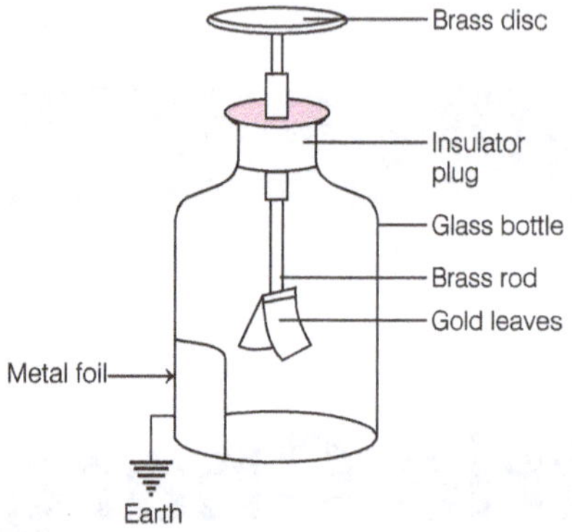

Gold-leaf electroscope

Conductor and Insulator

Conductors are those substances which can be used to carry or conduct electric charge/electron from one point to other. They allow electricity to pass through them easily. e.g. Silver, copper, iron, aluminium, etc.

Insulators are those substances which cannot conduct electricity. They are also called as **dielectrics.** They offer high resistance to the passage of electricity through them. e.g. Glass, rubber, plastic, ebonite, mica, etc.

Difference between Dielectrics and Conductors

Dielectrics are **non-conductors** and they do not have free electrons at all, while conductors have free electrons which allows electricity to pass through them. Therefore, dielectrics can be defined as the insulators which transmit electric effects without conducting.

Basic Properties of Electric Charge

Some basic properties of electric charge are given below.

- **Additive nature of charge** According to this, if a system has multiple charges, the total or **net charge** of the system is the **algebraic sum** of individual charges.
  i.e. If a system consists of n charges, $q_1, q_2, q_3 \ldots q_n$, then total charge $Q = q_1 + q_2 + q_3 + \ldots + q_n$.
- **Quantisation of charge** The electric charge on any body is always an integral multiple of basic unit of charge.
  i.e. $q = \pm ne$, where n is any integer (n = 0, 1, 2, 3......) and the value of $e = 1.6 \times 10^{-19}$ C.
- **Conservation of charge** The total electric charge of an isolated system always remains constant. It implies that charge can neither be created nor destroyed, it can only be transferred from one body to another, i.e. **the net charge will always be conserved.**

Example 1. **A polythene piece when rubbed with wool is found to have a negative charge of 3×10^{-7} C.** NCERT

(i) Estimate the number of electrons transferred from which to which?

(ii) Is there a transfer of mass from wool to polythene?

Sol. (i) Here, $q = -3 \times 10^{-7}$C

Charge on one electron, $e = -1.6 \times 10^{-19}$C

Therefore, number of electrons transferred from wool to polythene piece,

$$n = \frac{q}{e} = \frac{-3 \times 10^{-7}}{-1.6 \times 10^{-19}} = 1.875 \times 10^{12}$$

(ii) Yes, there is a transfer of mass from wool to polythene. As, mass of each electron,

$$m_e = 9 \times 10^{-31} \text{ kg}$$

Therefore, mass transferred from wool to polythene,

$$m = n \times m_e = 1.687 \times 10^{-18} \text{ kg}$$

When polythene is rubbed with wool, some amount of electron get transferred. So, a negligible amount of mass is transferred.

Example 2. **A copper slab of mass 2 g contains 2×10^{22} atoms. The charge on the nucleus of each atom is 29 e. What fraction of the electrons must be removed from the sphere to give it a charge of +2 μC?**

Sol. Total number of electrons in the slab = $29 \times 2 \times 10^{22}$

Number of electrons removed $= \frac{q}{e}$

$$= \frac{2 \times 10^{-6}}{1.6 \times 10^{-19}} = 1.25 \times 10^{13}$$

The fraction of electrons removed

$$= \frac{1.25 \times 10^{13}}{29 \times 2 \times 10^{22}} = 2.16 \times 10^{-11}$$

1.2 Coulomb's Law and Electrostatic Field

Coulomb's Law

According to **Coulomb's law,** "the force of interaction (attraction or repulsion) between two stationary point charges in vacuum is **directly proportional to the product of the charges and inversely proportional to the square of distance between them".**

Mathematically, electrostatic force between two stationary charges is given by

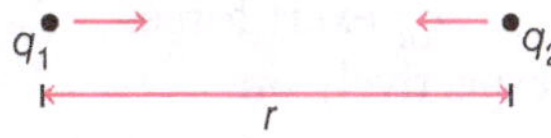

$$F=\frac{k|q_1q_2|}{r^2} \qquad \text{...(i)}$$

where, k is a **proportionality constant** and is given by

$$k=\frac{1}{4\pi\varepsilon_0}=9\times 10^9\ \text{N-m}^2\text{C}^{-2}$$

where, $\varepsilon_0=8.85\times 10^{-12}\ \text{C}^2\text{N}^{-1}\text{m}^{-2}$ and is called the **permittivity of free space.**

Its **dimensional formula** is $[\text{M}^{-1}\text{L}^{-3}\text{T}^4\text{A}^2]$.

If $\quad q_1=q_2=1\,\text{C}$ and $r=1\,\text{m}$

Then, $\quad F=9\times 10^9\times\dfrac{1\times 1}{(1)^2}$ [from Eq. (i)]

$$F=9\times 10^9\ \text{N}$$

One coulomb is the quantity of charge which exerts a force of 9×10^9N on an equal charge placed at a distance of 1m from it.

- The CGS unit of charge is **esu** or **stat-coulomb.** If we substitute $q_1=q_2=q, r=1$ cm and $F=1$ dyne, we get $q=\pm 1$ stat-coulomb.

TEACHER TIP

- Coulomb force of interaction is a two body interaction, hence it is not affected by the presence or absence of other charges.
- Coulomb's law holds good for stationary point charges.

Absolute Permittivity of Medium (Dielectric Constant)

The force between two charges q_1 and q_2 located at a distance r apart in a medium may be expressed as

$$F_{\text{medium}}=\frac{1}{4\pi\varepsilon}\frac{|q_1q_2|}{r^2}$$

where, ε is **absolute permittivity of the medium.**

Now, $$\frac{F_{\text{vacuum}}}{F_{\text{medium}}}=\frac{\dfrac{1}{4\pi\varepsilon_0}\dfrac{|q_1q_2|}{r^2}}{\dfrac{1}{4\pi\varepsilon}\dfrac{|q_1q_2|}{r^2}}=\frac{\varepsilon}{\varepsilon_0}$$

The ratio $\varepsilon/\varepsilon_0$ is called **relative permittivity** or **dielectric constant** (K) of the medium. Being a ratio, **it has no unit.**

We can also write it as

$$K=\varepsilon_r=\frac{\varepsilon}{\varepsilon_0}=\frac{F_{\text{vacuum}}}{F_{\text{medium}}}$$

$\therefore \quad \varepsilon=K\varepsilon_0 \qquad [\because \varepsilon_r=K]$

Coulomb's Law in Vector Form

Consider two like charges q_1 and q_2 are present at points A and B respectively in vacuum at a distance r apart.

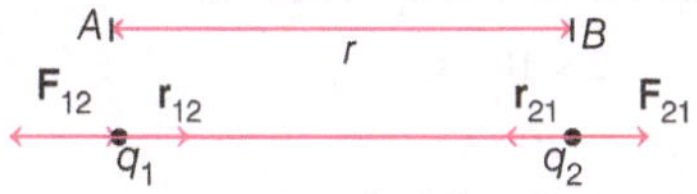

Coulomb force between two charges

According to Coulomb's law, the magnitude of force on charge q_1 due to q_2 (or on charge q_2 due to q_1) is given by

$$|\mathbf{F}_{12}|=|\mathbf{F}_{21}|=\frac{1}{4\pi\varepsilon_0}\cdot\frac{q_1q_2}{r^2} \qquad \text{...(i)}$$

Let $\mathbf{r}_{12}$ be the unit vector pointing from charge q_1 to q_2.

$$\mathbf{F}_{12}=\frac{1}{4\pi\varepsilon_0}\cdot\frac{q_1q_2}{r^2}\hat{\mathbf{r}}_{21} \qquad \text{...(ii)}$$

[$\because$ $\mathbf{F}_{12}$ is along the direction of unit vector $\mathbf{r}_{21}$]

Also, $\mathbf{r}_{21}$ be the unit vector pointing from charge q_2 to q_1.

$$\therefore \quad \mathbf{F}_{21}=\frac{1}{4\pi\varepsilon_0}\cdot\frac{q_1q_2}{r^2}\hat{\mathbf{r}}_{12} \qquad \text{...(iii)}$$

[$\because$ $\mathbf{F}_{21}$ is along the direction of unit vector $\mathbf{r}_{12}$]

$\because \quad \hat{\mathbf{r}}_{21}=-\hat{\mathbf{r}}_{12}$

Eq. (ii) becomes,

$$\mathbf{F}_{12}=\frac{-1}{4\pi\varepsilon_0}\cdot\frac{q_1q_2}{r^2}\hat{\mathbf{r}}_{12} \qquad \text{...(iv)}$$

On comparing Eq. (iii) with Eq. (iv), we get

$$\mathbf{F}_{12}=-\mathbf{F}_{21}$$

i.e. **Coulomb's law agrees with Newton's third law.**

Comparison of Coulomb's Law with Gravitational Law

Both the Coulomb's and Newton's laws follow inverse square law. According to Newton's universal law of gravitation,

$$F_G=\frac{Gm_1m_2}{r^2} \quad (\text{Here, } G=6.67\times 10^{-11}\ \text{Nm}^2/\text{kg}^2)$$

As discussed earlier, according to Coulomb's law,

$$F_E = \frac{k q_1 q_2}{r^2} \qquad \text{(Here, } k = 9\times10^9 \text{ Nm}^2/\text{C}^2\text{)}$$

From the equations, it is clear that **electrostatic force is much stronger than the gravitational force between a proton and an electron.**

i.e. $$\boxed{F_E = 10^{39} F_G}$$

Example 3. **What is the force between two small charged spheres having charges of 2×10^{-7} C and 3×10^{-7} C placed 30 cm apart in air?** *NCERT*

Sol. Given, $q_1 = 2\times10^{-7}$ C

$q_2 = 3\times10^{-7}$ C

$r = 30$ cm $= 0.3$ m

$k = 9\times10^9$ N-m^{2}C^{-2}

$F = ?$

We have, $$F = \frac{1}{4\pi\varepsilon_0}\frac{|q_1q_2|}{r^2} = \frac{k|q_1q_2|}{r^2} \qquad \left[\because \frac{1}{4\pi\varepsilon_0} = k\right] \quad \ldots\text{(i)}$$

Substituting the given values in Eq. (i), we get

$$F = \frac{(9\times10^9)(2\times10^{-7})\times(3\times10^{-7})}{(0.3)^2}$$

$\therefore \quad F = 6\times10^{-3}$ N

This force is repulsive, since the spheres have same type of charges.

Example 4. **The sum of two point charges is 7 μC. They repel each other with a force of 1 N when kept 30 cm apart in free space. Calculate the value of each charge.**

Sol. Let one of two charges be x μC. Therefore, other charge will be $(7-x)$ μC.

By Coulomb's law, $$F = \frac{1}{4\pi\varepsilon_0}\cdot\frac{q_1q_2}{r^2}$$

$$\Rightarrow 1 = 9\times10^9\times\frac{(x\times10^{-6})\times(7-x)\times10^{-6}}{(0.3)^2}$$

$$\Rightarrow \quad 9\times10^{-2} = 9\times10^{9-12}x(7-x)$$

$$\Rightarrow \quad 10 = x(7-x)$$

$$\Rightarrow \quad x^2 - 7x + 10 = 0 \Rightarrow (x-2)(x-5) = 0$$

$\therefore \quad x = 2$ μC or 5 μC

Therefore, charges are 2 μC and 5 μC.

Forces between Multiple Charges: Superposition Principle

This principle states that the net electric force experienced by a charge due to a system of charges is equal to the vector sum of all the forces exerted on it individually. Force between two charges is not affected by other charges.

Consider a system of n point charges $q_1, q_2, q_3, \ldots, q_n$ be distributed in space in a discrete manner. Let the charges be $q_2, q_3, \ldots, q_n$ exert forces $\mathbf{F}_{12}, \mathbf{F}_{13}, \ldots, \mathbf{F}_{1n}$, respectively on charge q_1.

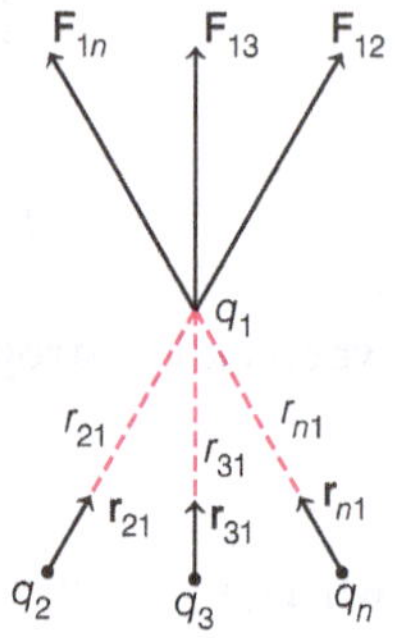

Then, according to the principle of superposition, the total force on charge q_1 is given by

$$\mathbf{F}_1 = \mathbf{F}_{12} + \mathbf{F}_{13} + \ldots + \mathbf{F}_{1n} \quad \ldots\text{(i)}$$

If the distance between the charges q_1 and q_2 is denoted as r_{21} and $\hat{\mathbf{r}}_{21}$ is unit vector from charge q_2 to q_1, then

$$\mathbf{F}_{12} = \frac{1}{4\pi\varepsilon_0}\cdot\frac{q_1q_2}{r_{21}^2}\hat{\mathbf{r}}_{21}$$

Similarly, the force on charge q_1 due to other charges is given by

$$\mathbf{F}_{13} = \frac{1}{4\pi\varepsilon_0}\cdot\frac{q_1q_3}{r_{31}^2}\hat{\mathbf{r}}_{31}$$

$$\mathbf{F}_{1n} = \frac{1}{4\pi\varepsilon_0}\cdot\frac{q_1q_n}{r_{n1}^2}\hat{\mathbf{r}}_{n1}$$

Substituting these values in Eq.(i), we get

$$\mathbf{F}_1 = \frac{1}{4\pi\varepsilon_0}\left(\frac{q_1q_2}{r_{21}^2}\hat{\mathbf{r}}_{21} + \frac{q_1q_3}{r_{31}^2}\hat{\mathbf{r}}_{31} + \cdots + \frac{q_1q_n}{r_{n1}^2}\hat{\mathbf{r}}_{n1}\right)$$

$$\Rightarrow \quad \boxed{\mathbf{F}_{1i} = \frac{q_1}{4\pi\varepsilon_0}\sum_{i=2}^{n}\frac{q_i}{r_{i1}^2}\hat{\mathbf{r}}_{i1}}$$

This force is on the charge q_1 due to impact of forces exerted by other charges.

Example 5. **Two charges each of $+Q$ Coulomb are separated by a distance r. A third charge $-q$ is placed between them. At what position of $-q$, will the system be in equilibrium?**

Sol.

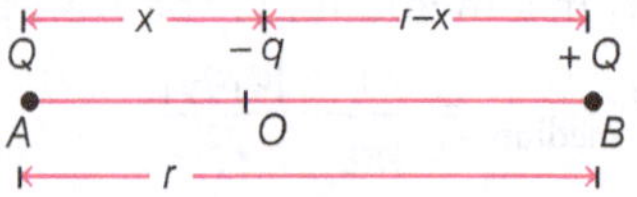

For charge $-q$ to be in equilibrium, force on the charge $-q$ at point O due to the charge $+Q$ at point A should be equal and opposite to that due to the charge $+Q$ at the point B, i.e. $$\frac{1}{4\pi\varepsilon_0}\frac{Qq}{x^2} = \frac{1}{4\pi\varepsilon_0}\frac{Qq}{(r-x)^2}$$

$$\Rightarrow \quad x^2 = (r-x)^2 \text{ or } x = r - x$$

$$\therefore \quad x = \frac{r}{2}$$

Hence, for equilibrium, the charge $-q$ should be kept at the middle of the line joining the points A and B.

Example 6. **Two equal positive charges, each of $2\,\mu C$ interact with a third positive charge of $3\,\mu C$ situated as shown in figure. Calculate the magnitude and direction of the force on the $3\,\mu C$ charge.**

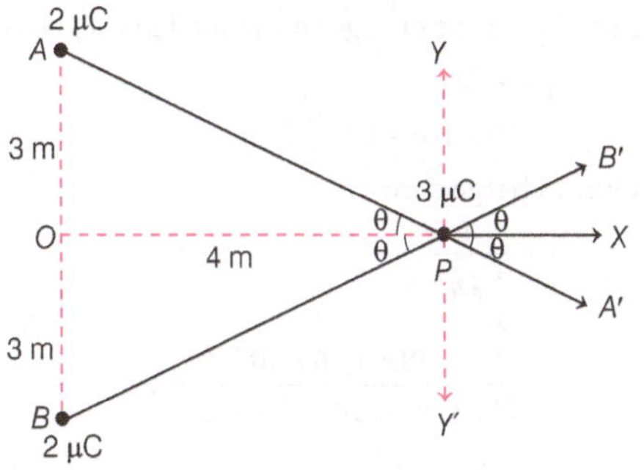

Sol. In the figure, $OA = OB = 3$ m, $OP = 4$ m

$\therefore \quad AP = BP = \sqrt{3^2 + 4^2} = 5$ m

According to Coulomb's law,

Force on charge at P due to charge at A,

$$F_1 = \frac{1}{4\pi\varepsilon_0}\frac{q_1 q_2}{(AP)^2}$$

$$= \frac{9\times 10^9 \times (2\times 10^{-6})\times(3\times 10^{-6})}{5^2}$$

$$= \frac{54}{25}\times 10^{-3}$$

$= 2.16\times 10^{-3}$ N, along PA'.

It has two rectangular components, i.e. $F_1 \cos\theta$ along PX and $F_1 \sin\theta$ along PY'.

Similarly, force on charge at P due to charge at B, $F_2 = F_1$ (in magnitude). It is along PB'. It also has two rectangular components, i.e. $F_2 \cos\theta$ along PX and $F_2 \sin\theta$ along PY.

The components along PY and PY' get cancelled. The components along PX add up.

$\therefore$ Total force on $3\,\mu C$ charge,

$$F = 2F_1 \cos\theta$$

$$= 2\times 2.16\times 10^{-3}\times\frac{4}{5}$$

$= 3.5\times 10^{-3}$ N, along PX.

1.3 Electrostatic Force due to Continuous Charge Distribution

The region where charges are closely spaced in continuous manner is said to have **continuous distribution of charge.**

Continuous charge distribution is of three types

Linear Charge Density

It is defined as the **charge per unit length** of linear charge distribution.

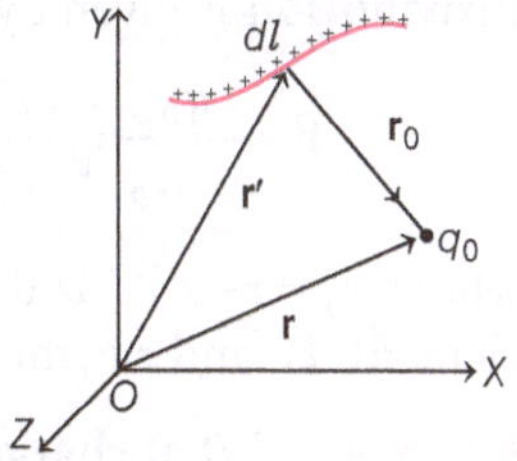

i.e. $\quad \lambda = \dfrac{dq}{dl} \Rightarrow dq = \lambda\, dl$

Its SI unit is **coulomb/metre.**

Electrostatic force at a point due to a **linear charge distribution** is given by

$$\mathbf{F} = \frac{q_0}{4\pi\varepsilon_0}\int_l \frac{\lambda dl}{r_0^2}\,\hat{\mathbf{r}}_0$$

where, $\mathbf{r}_0 = \mathbf{r} - \mathbf{r}'$, $\mathbf{r}'$ is the position vector of length element dl and $\mathbf{r}$ is the position vector of charge q_0.

Surface Charge Density

It is defined as the **charge per unit surface area** of surface charge distribution.

i.e. $\quad \sigma = \dfrac{dq}{dS} \Rightarrow dq = \sigma\, dS$

Its SI unit is **coulomb/metre^2.**

Electrostatic force at a point due to a **surface charge** distribution is given by

$$\mathbf{F} = \frac{q_0}{4\pi\varepsilon_0}\int_S \frac{\sigma\, dS}{r_0^2}\,\hat{\mathbf{r}}_0$$

where, $\mathbf{r}_0 = \mathbf{r} - \mathbf{r}'$, $\mathbf{r}'$ is the position vector of surface element dS and $\mathbf{r}$ is the position vector of charge q_0.

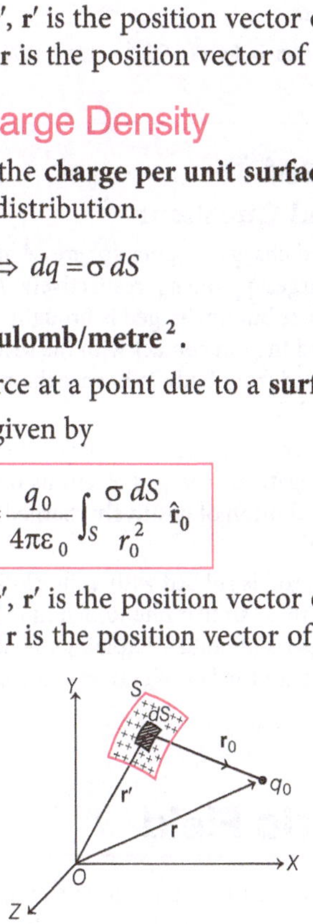

Volume Charge Density

It is defined as the **charge per unit volume** of volume charge distribution.

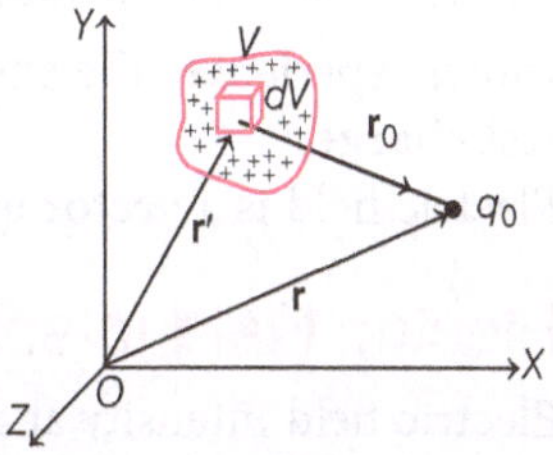

i.e. $\quad \rho = \dfrac{dq}{dV} \Rightarrow dq = \rho\, dV$

Its SI unit is **coulomb/metre^3.**

Electrostatic force at a point due to **volume charge distribution** is given by

$$\mathbf{F} = \frac{q_0}{4\pi\varepsilon_0} \int_V \frac{\rho dV}{r_0^2} \hat{\mathbf{r}}_0$$

where, $\mathbf{r}_0 = \mathbf{r} - \mathbf{r}'$, $\mathbf{r}'$ is the position vector of volume element dV and $\mathbf{r}$ is the position vector of charge q_0.

Example 7. **What charge would be required to electrify a sphere of radius 25 cm, so as to get a surface charge density of $3/\pi$ Cm^{-2}?**

Sol. Here, $r = 25$ cm $= 0.25$ m, $\sigma = 3/\pi$ Cm^{-2}

As, $\sigma = \dfrac{q}{4\pi r^2}$

$\therefore \quad q = 4\pi r^2 \sigma = 4\pi \times (0.25)^2 \times 3/\pi = 0.75$ C

Example 8. **The radius of gold nucleus ($Z = 79$) is about 7.0×10^{-15} m. Assuming that the positive charge is distributed uniformly throughout the nuclear volume, find the volume charge density.**

Sol. The total positive charge in the nucleus is given by

$$q = +Ze$$
$$= 79 \times 1.6 \times 10^{-19} \text{C}$$

$\therefore$ Volume charge density,

$$\rho = \frac{q}{\frac{4}{3}\pi R^3}$$
$$= \frac{79 \times 1.6 \times 10^{-19}}{(4/3) \times 3.14 \times (7.0 \times 10^{-15})^3}$$
$$= 0.088 \times 10^{26}$$
$$= 8.8 \times 10^{24} \text{ Cm}^{-3}$$

Quick Test 1

Conceptual Questions

1. Two insulated charged copper spheres A and B of identical size have charges q_A and q_B, respectively. A third sphere C of the same size but uncharged is brought in contact with the first A and then in contact with the second B and finally removed from both. What are the new charges on spheres A and B?
2. "An object becomes positively charged through the removal of negatively charged electrons rather than through the addition of positively charged protons". Explain, why?
3. When a glass rod is rubbed with a silk cloth, charges appear on both. A similar phenomenon is observed with many other pairs of bodies. Explain, how this observation is consistent with the law of conservation of charge? NCERT
4. If the distance between two equal point charges is doubled and their individual charges are also doubled, then what would happen to the force between them?

Numerical Questions

5. What is the total charge of a system containing five charges $+1, +2, -3, +4$ and -5 in some arbitrary unit?
6. How many electrons are there in one coulomb of negative charge?
7. A metal sphere has a charge of $-6\,\mu$C. When 5×10^{12} electrons are removed from the sphere, what would be net charge on it?

Answers

5. -1 6. 6.25×10^{18} electrons 7. $-5.2\,\mu$C

For Solutions, See QR Code on Pg. 40

1.4 Electric Field

The **electric field** can be defined as the space around a charge Q, where its effect of force can be experienced by the other charge q. The charge Q which produces the electric field is called **source charge** and the charge q which experiences the effect of source charge is called **test charge.**

Electric field is a **vector quantity.**

Electric Field Intensity

Electric field intensity at a point due to source charge is defined as the force experienced by a unit positive test charge placed at that point without disturbing the source charge. It is expressed as

$$\mathbf{E} = \frac{\mathbf{F}}{q_0}$$

or

$$\mathbf{E} = \lim_{q_0 \to 0} \frac{\mathbf{F}}{q_0}$$

where, E = electric field intensity

and $\quad F$ = force experienced by the test charge q_0.

- It is a **vector quantity** and its SI unit is **NC^{-1}** or **V/m.**
- Its dimensional formula is $[\text{MLT}^{-3}\text{A}^{-1}]$.

Direction of Electric Field

- Electric field due to a **positive charge** ($+q$) is **always away from the charge** as shown in Fig. (a).

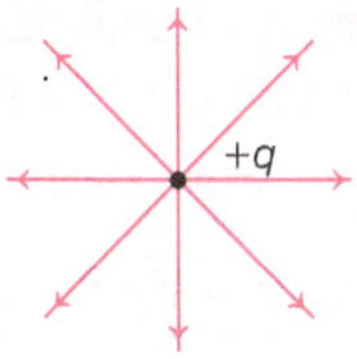

(a)

- Electric field due to **negative charge** ($-q$) is **always towards the charge** as shown in Fig. (b).

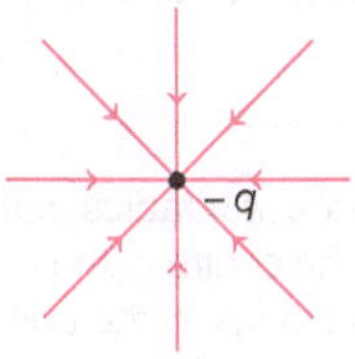

(b)

Physical Significance of Electric Field

We can readily calculate the magnitude and direction of force experienced by any charge q_0 placed at a point by knowing the electric field intensity at that point.

Electric Field due to a Point Charge

We have to find the electric field at a point P due to a point charge $+q$ placed at the origin such that $\mathbf{OP} = \mathbf{r}$.

We have to find the electric force on a test charge q_0 placed at point P, due to source charge q.

Force on the test charge q_0 due to charge q is given by

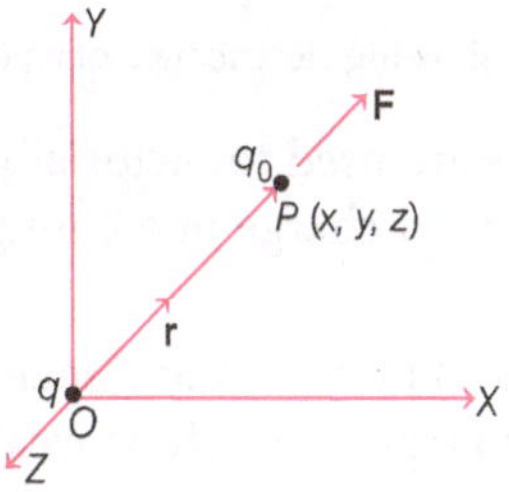

$$\mathbf{F} = \frac{1}{4\pi\varepsilon_0}\frac{qq_0}{r^2}\hat{\mathbf{r}}$$

If $\mathbf{E}$ is the electric field at a point P, then

$$\mathbf{E} = \lim_{q_0 \to 0}\frac{\mathbf{F}}{q_0} = \lim_{q_0 \to 0}\left(\frac{1}{q_0}\cdot\frac{1}{4\pi\varepsilon_0}\frac{qq_0}{r^2}\hat{\mathbf{r}}\right)$$

$$\Rightarrow \quad \boxed{\mathbf{E} = \frac{1}{4\pi\varepsilon_0}\cdot\frac{q}{r^2}\hat{\mathbf{r}}} \quad \ldots(i)$$

The magnitude of the electric field at a point P is given by

$$\boxed{E = \frac{1}{4\pi\varepsilon_0}\cdot\frac{q}{r^2}}$$

The electric field at any point in space due to a charge depends only on the distance. That means, the magnitude of electric field due to point charge is same at all the points of sphere, i.e. it has spherical symmetry.

Example 9. **A conducting sphere of radius 10 cm has an unknown charge. If the electric field at 20 cm from the centre of the sphere is 1.5×10^3 N/C and points radially inwards, then what is the net charge on the sphere?** *NCERT*

Sol. Let the value of unknown charge be q.

Electric field at 20 cm away, $E = 1.5 \times 10^3$ N/C

From the formula, electric field,

$$E = \frac{1}{4\pi\varepsilon_0}\cdot\frac{q}{r^2} \Rightarrow 1.5 \times 10^3 = \frac{9 \times 10^9 \times q}{(20 \times 10^{-2})^2}$$

$$\therefore \quad q = \frac{1.5 \times 10^3 \times 20 \times 20 \times 10^{-4}}{9 \times 10^9} = 6.67 \times 10^{-9}\text{C}$$

As the electric field is radially inwards which shows that the nature of unknown charge q is negative.

Electric Field due to System of Charges

Consider that n point charges $q_1, q_2, q_3, \ldots, q_n$ exert forces $\mathbf{F}_1, \mathbf{F}_2, \mathbf{F}_3, \ldots, \mathbf{F}_n$ on a test charge q_0 placed at origin O.

Let $\mathbf{F}_i$ be the force due to ith charge q_i on q_0, then

$$\mathbf{F}_i = \frac{1}{4\pi\varepsilon_0}\frac{q_iq_0}{r_i^2}\hat{\mathbf{r}}_i$$

where, r_i is the distance of the test charge q_0 from q_i.

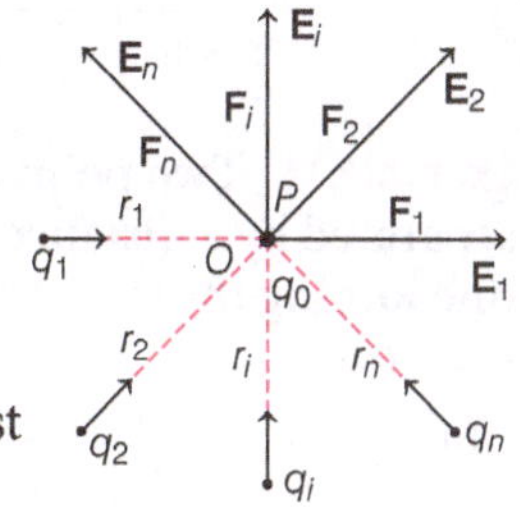

The electric field at the observation point P is given by

$$\mathbf{E}_i = \lim_{q_0 \to 0}\frac{\mathbf{F}_i}{q_0} = \lim_{q_0 \to 0}\left[\frac{1}{q_0}\left(\frac{1}{4\pi\varepsilon_0}\cdot\frac{q_iq_0}{r_i^2}\hat{\mathbf{r}}_i\right)\right]$$

$$\boxed{\mathbf{E}_i = \frac{1}{4\pi\varepsilon_0}\cdot\frac{q_i}{r_i^2}\hat{\mathbf{r}}_i} \quad \ldots(i)$$

If E is electric field at point P due to the system of charges, then by principle of superposition of electric fields, $\mathbf{E} = \mathbf{E}_1 + \mathbf{E}_2 + \mathbf{E}_3 + \cdots + \mathbf{E}_n = \sum_{i=1}^{n} \mathbf{E}_i$

Using Eq. (i), we get $\mathbf{E} = \sum_{i=1}^{n} \frac{1}{4\pi\varepsilon_0} \cdot \frac{q_i}{r_i^2} \hat{\mathbf{r}}_i$

or
$$\mathbf{E} = \frac{1}{4\pi\varepsilon_0} \sum_{i=1}^{n} \frac{q_i}{r_i^2} \hat{\mathbf{r}}_i$$

Example 10. **Two charges $+Q$ and $-Q$ are kept at points $(-x_2, 0)$ and $(x_1, 0)$ respectively, in the XY-plane. Find the magnitude and direction of the net electric field at the origin $(0, 0)$.**

Sol.

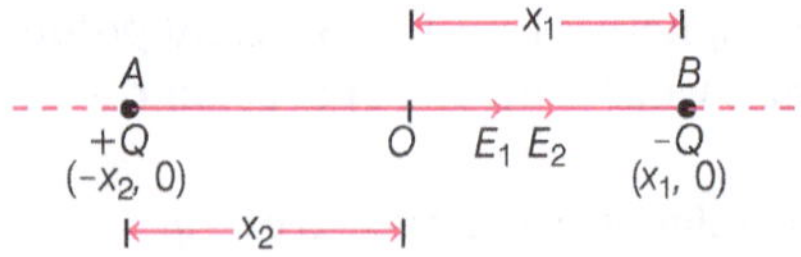

Electric field intensity at point O due to $+Q$ charge,

$$E_1 = \frac{1}{4\pi\varepsilon_0} \times \frac{Q}{(x_2)^2} \text{ (towards } B) \quad \ldots\text{(i)}$$

Electric field intensity at point O due to $-Q$ charge,

$$E_2 = \frac{1}{4\pi\varepsilon_0} \times \frac{Q}{(x_1)^2} \text{ (towards } B) \quad \ldots\text{(ii)}$$

$\because E_1$ and E_2 act along the same direction.

$\therefore$ Net electric field intensity at point O is given by

$$E = E_1 + E_2$$
$$= \frac{1}{4\pi\varepsilon_0} \times \frac{Q}{(x_2)^2} + \frac{1}{4\pi\varepsilon_0} \times \frac{Q}{(x_1)^2} \text{ (towards } B)$$
$$E = \frac{Q}{4\pi\varepsilon_0}\left[\frac{1}{x_2^2} + \frac{1}{x_1^2}\right]$$

Example 11. **Two point charges $+Q$ and $+4Q$ are separated by a distance of $6a$. Find the point on the line joining the two charges where the electric field is zero.**

Sol. The electric field is zero at point P only, if the field due to charge $+Q$ balances the field due to charge $+4Q$.

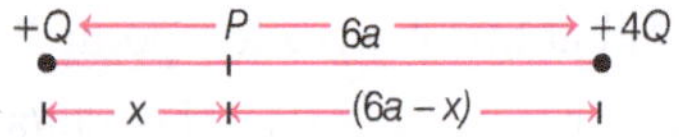

$$\therefore \frac{1}{4\pi\varepsilon_0} \cdot \frac{Q}{x^2} = \frac{1}{4\pi\varepsilon_0} \cdot \frac{4Q}{(6a - x)^2}$$

$$\Rightarrow \frac{1}{x^2} = \frac{4}{(6a - x)^2}$$

$$\Rightarrow \frac{1}{x} = \frac{2}{(6a - x)}$$

$$\Rightarrow 2x = 6a - x \Rightarrow x = 2a$$

$\therefore$ The required point is at a distance of $2a$ to the right of $+Q$.

Electric Field Intensity at any Point on the Axis of Uniformly Charged Ring

The electric field intensity at any point Q on the axis is given by

$$E = \frac{qr}{4\pi\varepsilon_0 (r^2 + a^2)^{3/2}}$$

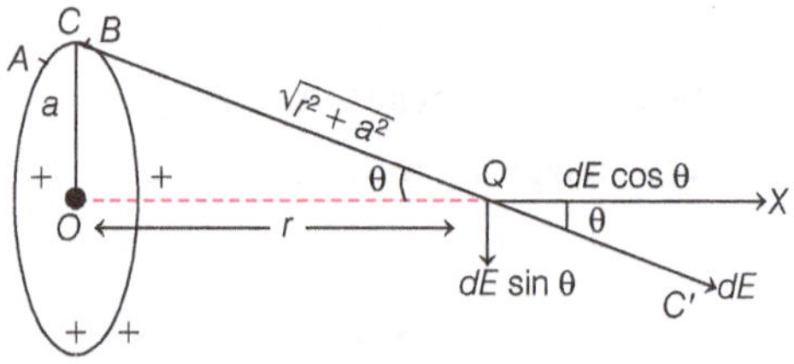

where, q = total charge, a = radius of the ring and r = distance of the point Q from the centre of the ring.
The direction of E is along QX, the axis of the loop.

1.5 Electric Field Lines

An **electric field line** is a curve drawn in such a way that the tangent to it at each point is in the direction of the electric field at that point. A field line is a space curve, i.e. a curve in three dimensions.

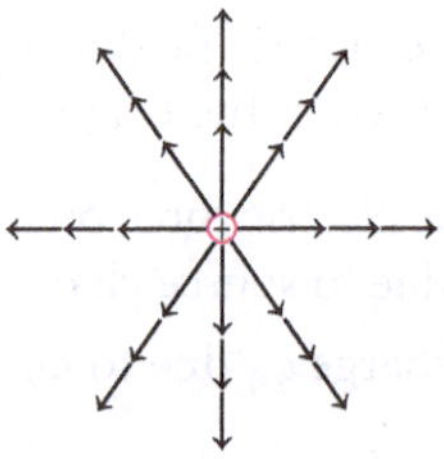

Field lines showing electric field of a point charge

Electric field lines are used to pictorially map the electric field around a charge or a configuration of charges.

The density of field lines is more near the charge. Away from the charge, the field is weak, so the density of field lines is less.

Properties of Electric Field Lines

Electric field lines follow some important properties which are discussed below

(i) Electric field lines are imaginary lines which **start from positive charges and end at negative charges.**

In the case of a single charge, they may start or end at infinity, as shown in figure.

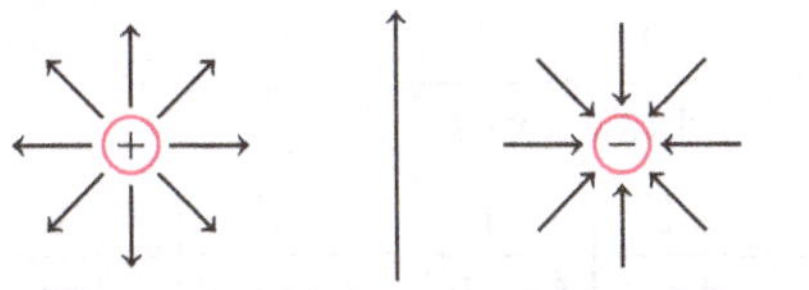

Direction is away from the positive charge | Direction is towards the negative charge

(ii) **Two field lines can never intersect each other** because if they intersect, then two tangents drawn at that point will represent two directions of field at that point, which is not possible.

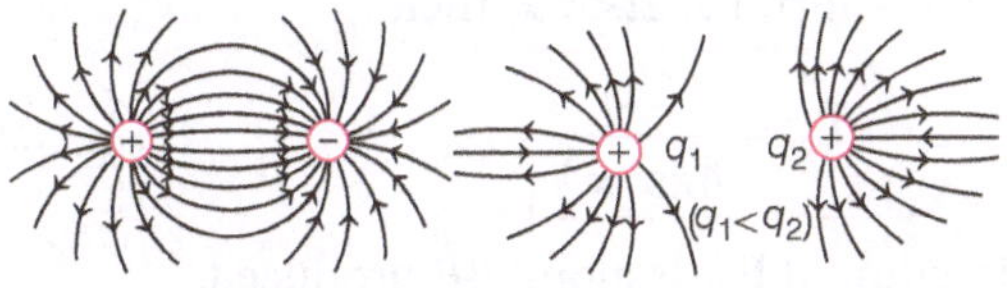

(a) (b)

(iii) In a charge free region, electric field lines can be taken to be continuous curves without any breaks.

(iv) Electric field lines do not form closed loops (because of the conservative nature of electric field).

(v) Electric field lines are perpendicular to the surface of a charged conductor.

(vi) Electric field lines contract lengthwise to represent attraction.

(vii) Electric field lines exert sideways pressure to represent repulsion.

(ix) Electric field lines (a) for uniform field and (b) for non-uniform field are shown below.

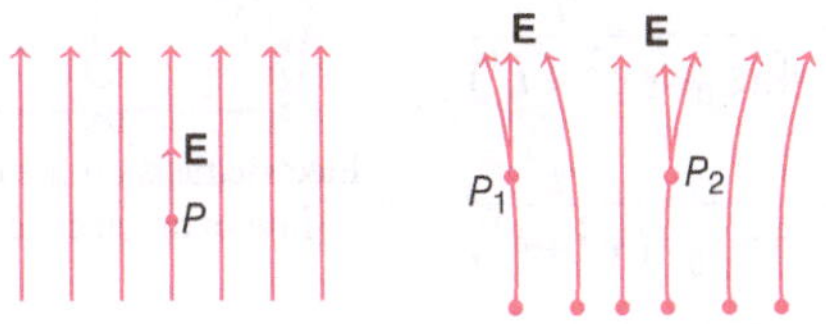

(a) Electric field lines for a uniform field | (b) Electric field lines for a non-uniform field

(x) Electric field lines do not pass through a conductor. Hence, the interior of a conductor is free from the influence of the electric field.

TEACHER TIP

It is a common misconception that the path traced by a positive charge is a field line. The path traced by a unit positive test charge represents a field line only when it moves along a straight line.

Quick Test 2

Conceptual Questions

1. The test charge used to measure electric field at a point should be vanishingly small. Why?
2. Why electrostatic field must be normal to the surface at every point of a charged conductor?
3. Sketch the electric field lines for two point charges q_1 and q_2 for $q_1 = q_2$ and $q_1 > q_2$ separated by distance d. CBSE 2019
4. Explain, why the following curves cannot possibly represent electrostatic field lines?

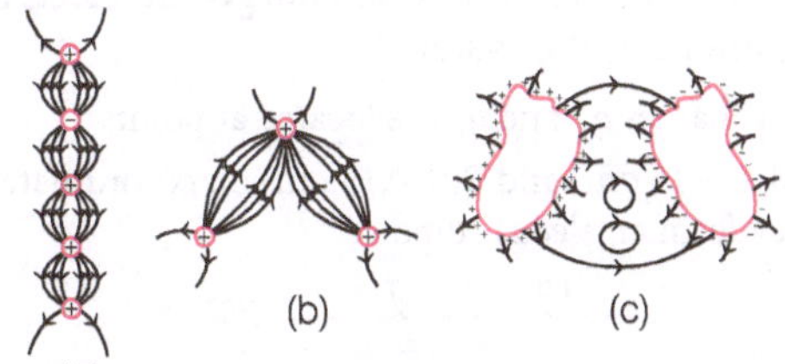

(a) (b) (c)

Numerical Questions

5. The dielectric constant of water is 80. What is its permittivity?
6. Two point charges having equal charges separated by 1 m distance experience a force of 8 N. What will be the force experienced by them, if they are held in water, at the same distance? (Given, $K_{water} = 80$)

Answers

5. $7.08 \times 10^{-10} C^2N^{-1}m^{-2}$ 6. $\frac{1}{10}$ N

For Solutions, See QR Code on Pg. 40

1.6 Electric Dipole

An **electric dipole** is a pair of point charges with equal magnitude and opposite in sign separated by a very small distance.

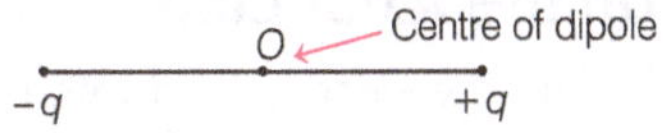

Electric Dipole Moment

The strength of an electric dipole is measured by a vector quantity known as **electric dipole moment (p),** which is the product of the charge (q) and separation between the charges ($2l$).

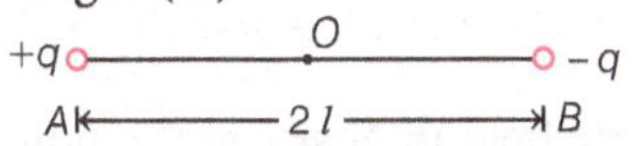

i.e. $p = q \times 2l$ or $|\mathbf{p}| = q(2l)$

It is a **vector quantity** and its direction is always from **negative charge to positive charge.** The SI unit of dipole moment is **coulomb-metre** (C-m).

If charge q increases and the distance $2l$ becomes very small while keeping the product $|\mathbf{p}| = q \times 2l =$ constant, we get an **ideal dipole** or **point dipole**. Thus, **an ideal dipole is the smallest dipole having almost no size.**

Example 12. **A system has two charges $q_A = 2.5 \times 10^{-7}$ C and $q_B = -2.5 \times 10^{-7}$ C located at points $A(0, 0, -15 \text{ cm})$ and $B(0, 0, +15 \text{ cm})$, respectively. What are the total charge and electric dipole moment of the system?** NCERT

Sol. Two charges q_A and q_B are located at points $A(0, 0, -15 \text{ cm})$ and $B(0, 0, 15 \text{ cm})$ on co-ordinate axis. They form an electric dipole.

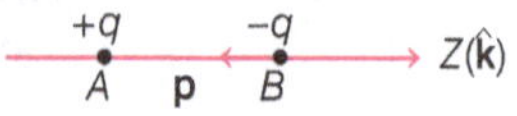

Total charge, $q = q_A + q_B$

$= 2.5 \times 10^{-7} - 2.5 \times 10^{-7}$

$\Rightarrow \quad q = 0$

Also, $\quad AB = 15 + 15$

$= 30$ cm

or $\quad AB = 30 \times 10^{-2}$ m

Electric dipole moment,

$\mathbf{p} =$ Either charge $\times$ $\mathbf{BA}$

$= 2.5 \times 10^{-7} \times (30 \times 10^{-2})(-\hat{\mathbf{k}})$

$= -7.5 \times 10^{-8} \hat{\mathbf{k}}$ C-m

Electric Field Intensity Due to an Electric Dipole

Electric field of an electric dipole is the space around the dipole in which the electric field effect of the dipole can be experienced.

At a Point on the Axial Line

We have to calculate the electric field intensity (E) at a point P on the axial line of the dipole and at a distance $OP = x$ from the centre O of the dipole.

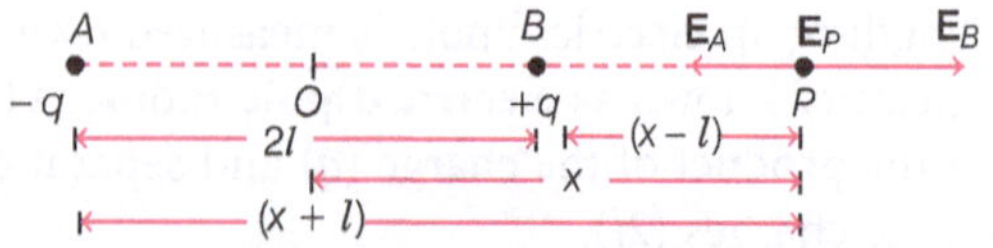

Electric field on axial line of an electric dipole

Resultant electric field intensity at the point P,

$$\mathbf{E}_P = \mathbf{E}_A + \mathbf{E}_B$$

The vectors $\mathbf{E}_A$ and $\mathbf{E}_B$ are collinear and opposite.

$$\therefore \quad E_P = E_B - E_A$$

Here, $E_A = \dfrac{1}{4\pi\varepsilon_0} \cdot \dfrac{q}{(x+l)^2}$

and $\quad E_B = \dfrac{1}{4\pi\varepsilon_0} \cdot \dfrac{q}{(x-l)^2}$

$$\therefore \quad E_P = \frac{1}{4\pi\varepsilon_0}\left[\frac{q}{(x-l)^2} - \frac{q}{(x+l)^2}\right] = \frac{1}{4\pi\varepsilon_0} \cdot \frac{4qlx}{(x^2 - l^2)^2}$$

Hence, $E_P = \dfrac{1}{4\pi\varepsilon_0} \cdot \dfrac{2px}{(x^2 - l^2)^2}$ $\quad [\because p = q \times 2l]$

In vector form, $\mathbf{E}_P = \dfrac{1}{4\pi\varepsilon_0} \cdot \dfrac{2\mathbf{p}x}{(x^2 - l^2)^2}$

If dipole is short, i.e. $2l << x$, then

$$E_P = \frac{2|\mathbf{p}|}{4\pi\varepsilon_0 x^3} \quad \text{...(i)}$$

The direction of $\mathbf{E}_P$ is along BP produced.

Clearly, $\quad E_P \propto \dfrac{1}{x^3}$

At a Point on the Equatorial Line

Consider an electric dipole consisting of two point charges $+q$ and $-q$ separated by a small distance $AB = 2l$ with centre at O and dipole moment, $p = q(2l)$ as shown in the figure below.

Resultant electric field intensity at the point Q,

$$\mathbf{E}_Q = \mathbf{E}_A + \mathbf{E}_B$$

The vectors $\mathbf{E}_A$ and $\mathbf{E}_B$ are acting at an angle 2θ.

Here, $E_A = \dfrac{1}{4\pi\varepsilon_0} \cdot \dfrac{q}{(x^2 + l^2)}$

and $\quad E_B = \dfrac{1}{4\pi\varepsilon_0} \cdot \dfrac{q}{(x^2 + l^2)}$

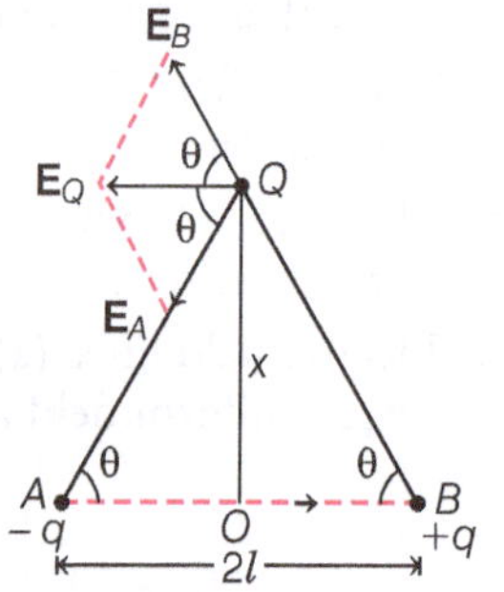

Electric field on the equatorial line of an electric dipole

On resolving $\mathbf{E}_A$ and $\mathbf{E}_B$, the vectors $E_A \sin\theta$ and $E_B \sin\theta$ are equal in magnitude and opposite to each other and hence cancel each other.

The vectors $E_A \cos\theta$ and $E_B \cos\theta$ are acting along the same direction and hence add up.

$$\therefore \quad E_Q = E_A \cos\theta + E_B \cos\theta = 2E_A \cos\theta \quad [\because E_A = E_B]$$

$$= \frac{2}{4\pi\varepsilon_0} \cdot \frac{q}{(x^2 + l^2)} \cdot \frac{l}{(x^2 + l^2)^{1/2}} \quad \left[\because \cos\theta = \frac{l}{(x^2 + l^2)^{1/2}}\right]$$

$$= \frac{1}{4\pi\varepsilon_0} \cdot \frac{2ql}{(x^2 + l^2)^{3/2}}$$

But $q \times 2l = |\mathbf{p}|$, the dipole moment,

$$E_Q = \frac{1}{4\pi\varepsilon_0} \cdot \frac{|\mathbf{p}|}{(x^2 + l^2)^{3/2}}$$

The direction of E is opposite to AB. In vector form, we can rewrite as $\mathbf{E}_Q = \frac{-\mathbf{p}}{4\pi\varepsilon_0 (x^2 + l^2)^{3/2}}$

If the dipole is short, i.e. $2l << x$, then

$$\therefore \quad E_Q = \frac{1}{4\pi\varepsilon_0} \cdot \frac{|\mathbf{p}|}{x^3} \quad \text{...(ii)}$$

Clearly, $E_Q \propto \frac{1}{x^3}$

From Eqs. (i) and (ii), we get

$$\frac{E_{\text{axial}}}{E_{\text{equatorial}}} = 2$$

IMPORTANT RESULT

The magnitude and the direction of dipole field depend on the distance r, as well as the angle between the position vector **r** and dipole moment $\mathbf{p}$.

The electric field due to a dipole falls off at large distances as $\left(\propto \frac{1}{r^3}\right)$ than the electric field due to a single charge $\left(\propto \frac{1}{r^2}\right)$.

$$E_{\text{axial}} = 2\,E_{\text{equatorial}}$$

Example 13. **Two charges $\pm 5\ \mu C$ are placed 5 mm apart. Determine the electric field at**

(i) a point X on the axis of dipole 10 cm away from its centre O on the side of the positive charge as shown in Fig. (a).

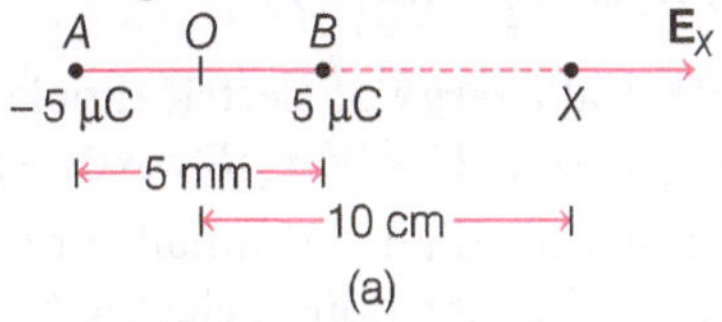

(a)

(ii) a point Y, 10 cm away from centre O on a line passing through O and normal to the axis of the dipole as shown in Fig.(b).

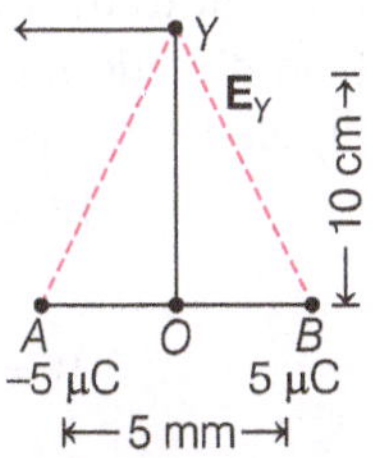

(b)

Sol. Given, $q = \pm 5\ \mu C = \pm 5 \times 10^{-6}$ C,

$$2l = 5 \text{ mm} = 5 \times 10^{-3} \text{ m}$$

$$x = OX = OY = 10 \text{ cm}$$
$$= 10 \times 10^{-2} \text{ m}$$
$$E_X = ? \text{ and } E_Y = ?$$

Dipole moment, $p = q \times 2l$

$$= 5 \times 10^{-6} \times 5 \times 10^{-3}$$
$$= 25 \times 10^{-9} \text{C-m}$$

(i) Now, find out the electric field at point X on the axial line of dipole.

$$\mathbf{E}_X = \frac{2px}{4\pi\varepsilon_0 (x^2 - l^2)^2}, \text{ along } BX \text{ produced}$$

Since, $l << x$, therefore

$$\mathbf{E}_X = \frac{2\mathbf{p}}{4\pi\varepsilon_0 x^3}$$
$$= \frac{2 \times 25 \times 10^{-9} \times 9 \times 10^9}{(10 \times 10^{-2})^3}$$
$$= 4.5 \times 10^5 \text{ NC}^{-1}, \text{ along } BX \text{ produced.}$$

(ii) Now, find out the electric field at point Y on equatorial line of dipole.

$$\mathbf{E}_Y = \frac{\mathbf{p}}{4\pi\varepsilon_0 (x^2 + l^2)^{3/2}}, \text{ along a line parallel to } BA$$

Since, $l << x$, therefore

$$\mathbf{E}_Y = \frac{\mathbf{p}}{4\pi\varepsilon_0 x^3}$$

$$\therefore \quad \mathbf{E}_Y = \frac{25 \times 10^{-9} \times 9 \times 10^9}{(10 \times 10^{-2})^3}$$
$$= 2.25 \times 10^5 \text{NC}^{-1}, \text{ along a line parallel to } BA$$

Physical Significance of Dipole

The significance of dipole can be understood from the fact that electric dipole is not only prominent in electrostatics but also in chemistry.

In most molecules, the centres of positive charges and negative charges lie at the same place, hence their dipole moment is zero, e.g. CO_2, CH_4.

However, they develop a dipole moment when an electric field is applied. But some molecules have permanent dipole moment, e.g. H_2O which are called **polar molecules.**

If the centre of mass of positive charges coincides with the centre of mass of negative charges, the molecule behaves as a **non-polar molecule**. Therefore, **dipole moment is the measure of the polarity of a bond.** It is used to differentiate between polar and non-polar molecules.

Electric field intesity at any point (K) due to a short electric dipole. It is given by

$$E = \frac{1}{4\pi\varepsilon_0}\frac{p}{r^3}\sqrt{3\cos^2\theta + 1}$$

***Case* I** K lies on the axial line of dipole, then θ = 0°

$$E = \frac{1}{4\pi\varepsilon_0}\frac{p}{r^3}\sqrt{3\cos^2 0° + 1} = \frac{1}{4\pi\varepsilon_0}\frac{2p}{r^3}$$

$$\Rightarrow \tan\alpha = \frac{\tan 0°}{2} = 0 \Rightarrow \alpha = 0$$

***Case* II** K lies on the equatorial line of dipole, then θ = 90°

$$E = \frac{1}{4\pi\varepsilon_0}\frac{p}{r^3}\sqrt{3\cos^2 90° + 1} = \frac{1}{4\pi\varepsilon_0}\frac{p}{r^3}$$

1.7 Dipole in a Uniform External Field

Torque on an Electric Dipole in a Uniform Electric Field

Consider an electric dipole of charges $-q$ and $+q$, and length $2l$ placed in a uniform external electric field of intensity **E**.

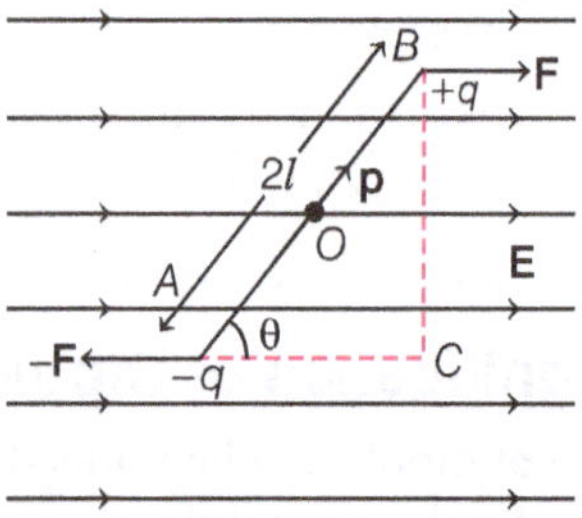

The dipole moment **p** makes an angle θ with the direction of the electric field. Two forces **F** and −**F** which are equal in magnitude and opposite in directions act on the dipole.

$$|\mathbf{F}| = |-\mathbf{F}| = qE$$

Thus, the net force will be zero, therefore they constitute a **couple.** A net torque τ acts on the dipole about an axis passing through the mid-point of the dipole.

Now, torque, τ = either force × perpendicular distance (BC) between the parallel forces $= qE(2l\sin\theta)$

$$\tau = (q\times 2l)E\sin\theta \quad \text{or} \quad \boxed{\tau = pE\sin\theta}$$

In vector notation, $\boxed{\boldsymbol{\tau} = \mathbf{p}\times\mathbf{E}}$

Special Cases

***Case* I** If θ = 0°, then τ = 0.

The dipole is in **stable equilibrium.**

***Case* II** If θ = 90°, then τ = pE **(maximum value).**

The torque acting on dipole will be **maximum.**

***Case* III** If θ = 180°, then τ = 0.

The dipole is in **unstable equilibrium.**

Example 14. **An electric dipole consists of two charges of 0.1 μC separated by a distance of 2.0 cm. The dipole is placed in an external field of 10^5 N/C. What maximum torque does the field exert on the dipole?**

Sol. Here, $q = 0.1\ \mu C = 10^{-7} C$, $2l = 2.0\text{ cm} = 2\times 10^{-2}$ m,

$$E = 10^5\ \text{N/C}$$

$$\Rightarrow \quad \tau = pE\sin\theta = q\times 2l\times E\sin\theta$$

$$\therefore \quad \tau_{max} = 10^{-7}\times 2\times 10^{-2}\times 10^5\times 1 \qquad [\because \sin 90° = 1]$$

$$= 2\times 10^{-4}\ \text{N-m}$$

Work Done on a Dipole in a Uniform Electric Field

When an electric dipole is placed in a uniform electric field, it experiences **torque** and tends to align it in such a way to attain stable equilibrium. Small amount of work done in rotating the dipole through a small angle $d\theta$ against the torque is given by

$$dW = \tau\, d\theta = pE\sin\theta\, d\theta$$

∴ Total work done in rotating the dipole from orientation θ_1 to θ_2, $W = \int_{\theta_1}^{\theta_2} pE\sin\theta\, d\theta = pE(\cos\theta_1 - \cos\theta_2)$

$$\Rightarrow \quad \boxed{W = pE(\cos\theta_1 - \cos\theta_2)}$$

Similarly, **potential energy** of electric dipole, when it rotates from θ_1 to θ_2, $U = W = pE(\cos\theta_1 - \cos\theta_2)$

Let us assume that the dipole is initially oriented perpendicular to the direction of electric field and brought to the orientation making an angle θ with the field direction, then the work done in rotating the dipole from $\theta_1 = 90°$ to $\theta_2 = \theta$,

$$W = pE(\cos 90° - \cos\theta)$$

$$= -pE\cos\theta = -\mathbf{p}\cdot\mathbf{E}$$

$$W = -\mathbf{p}\cdot\mathbf{E}$$

Quick Test 3

Conceptual Questions

1. What do you mean by an "ideal electric dipole"?
2. If an electric dipole is placed in a uniform electric field, then state whether it always experiences a torque or not?
3. What is meant by the statement, "the electric field of a point charge has spherical symmetry, whereas that of an electric dipole is cylindrically symmetric"?
4. Depict the orientation of the dipole in (i) stable (ii) unstable equilibrium in a uniform electric field. *CBSE 2017*

Numerical Questions

5. Two charges of $+25\times10^{-9}$ C and -25×10^{-9} C are placed 6 m apart. Find the electric field at a point 4 m from the centre of the electric dipole (i) on axial line and (ii) on equatorial line.
6. An electric dipole with dipole moment 4×10^{-9}C-m is aligned at 30° with the direction of a uniform electric field of magnitude 5×10^4 N / C. Calculate the magnitude of the torque acting on the dipole.
7. Two charges $\pm 10\,\mu$C are placed 5 mm apart. Determine the electric field at
   (i) a point P, on the axis of dipole 15 cm away from its centre O on the side of the positive charge

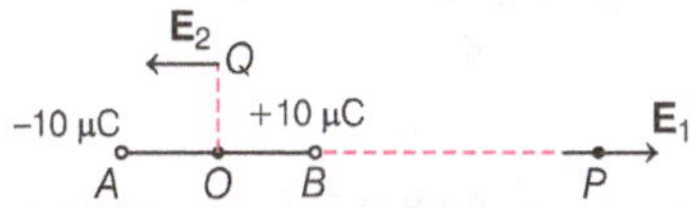

   (ii) a point Q, 15 cm away from centre O on a line passing through centre O and normal to axis of the dipole. *NCERT*

8. The electric field at a point on the axial line at a distance of 10 cm from the centre of an electric dipole is 3.75×10^5 N/C in air, while at a distance of 20 cm, the electric field is 3×10^4 N/C. Calculate the length of an electric dipole.

Answers

5. (i) 220.4 NC^{-1} (ii) 10.8 NC^{-1} 6. 10^{-4} N-m
7. (i) 6×10^6 NC^{-1} (ii) 3×10^6 NC^{-1} 8. 0.1 m

For Solutions, See QR Code on Pg. 40

1.8 Electric Flux

Area Vector

It is the vector associated with every area element of a closed surface, and is taken to be in the direction of the outward normal. Thus, the area element vector ΔS at a point on a closed surface is equal to $\Delta S\,\hat{n}$, where ΔS is the magnitude of the area element and $\hat{n}$ is a unit vector in the direction of outward normal at the point.

$$\Delta \mathbf{S} = \hat{n}(\Delta S)$$

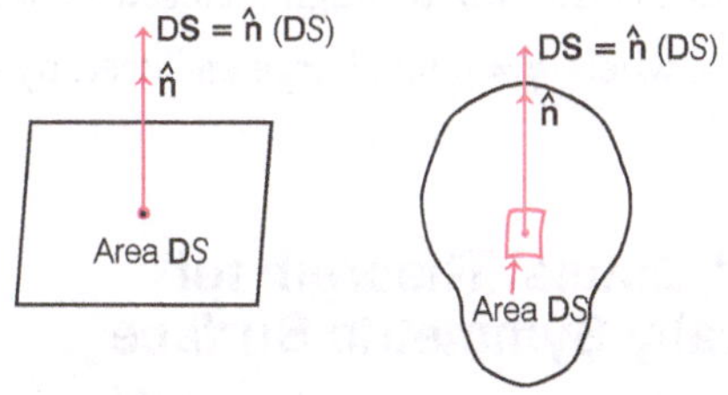

Electric Flux

Electric flux linked with any surface is defined as the **total number of electric field lines crossing or diverging normally through that surface.**

Electric flux $d\phi$ through a small area element $d\mathbf{S}$ due to an electric field $\mathbf{E}$ at an angle θ with $d\mathbf{S}$,

$$d\phi = \mathbf{E}\cdot d\mathbf{S} = E\,dS\cos\theta$$

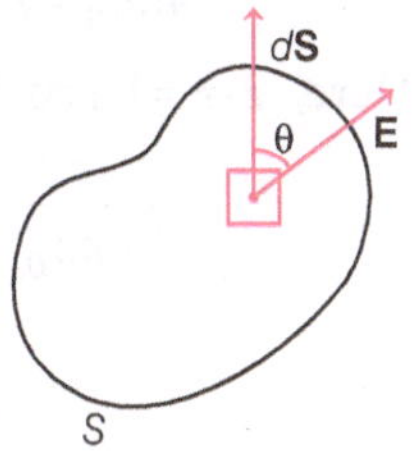

which is proportional to the number of field lines cutting the area element.

Total electric flux ϕ over the whole surface S due to an electric field $\mathbf{E}$,

$$\phi = \oint_S \mathbf{E}\cdot d\mathbf{S} = \oint_S E\,dS\cos\theta$$

Special Cases

(i) For $0° < \theta < 90°$, ϕ is **positive.**

(ii) For $\theta = 90°$, ϕ is **zero.**

(iii) For $90° < \theta < 180°$, ϕ is **negative.**

- Electric flux is a **scalar quantity** but it is a property of vector field.
- SI unit of electric flux is $\mathbf{N\text{-}m^2C^{-1}}$ or **volt-metre**. Its dimensional formula is

$$\phi = [MLT^{-2}][L^2][AT]^{-1} = [ML^3T^{-3}A^{-1}].$$

Gauss' Theorem

The surface integral of the electric field intensity over any closed surface (Gaussian surface) in free space is equal to $\frac{1}{\varepsilon_0}$ times the net charge enclosed within the surface.

$$\phi_E = \oint_S \mathbf{E}\cdot d\mathbf{S} = \frac{1}{\varepsilon_0}\sum_{i=1}^{n} q_i = \frac{q}{\varepsilon_0}$$

where, $q = \sum_{i=1}^{n} q_i$ is the algebraic sum of all the charges inside the closed surface.

Hence, total electric flux through a closed surface is equal to $\frac{q}{\varepsilon_0}$, where q = total charge enclosed by the surface.

Proof of Gauss' Theorem for Spherically Symmetric Surface

Electric flux through a surface element dS is given by

$$d\phi_E = \mathbf{E} \cdot d\mathbf{S} = \frac{1}{4\pi\varepsilon_0} \cdot \frac{q}{r^2} \hat{\mathbf{r}} \cdot (dS \hat{\mathbf{n}})$$

$$\Rightarrow d\phi_E = \frac{1}{4\pi\varepsilon_0} \cdot \frac{q\,dS}{r^2} \hat{\mathbf{r}} \cdot \hat{\mathbf{r}} \qquad [\because \hat{\mathbf{n}} = \hat{\mathbf{r}}]$$

Here, $\hat{\mathbf{r}} \cdot \hat{\mathbf{r}} = 1 \cdot 1 \cos 0° = 1$

$$\therefore \quad d\phi_E = \frac{1}{4\pi\varepsilon_0} \cdot \frac{q\,dS}{r^2}$$

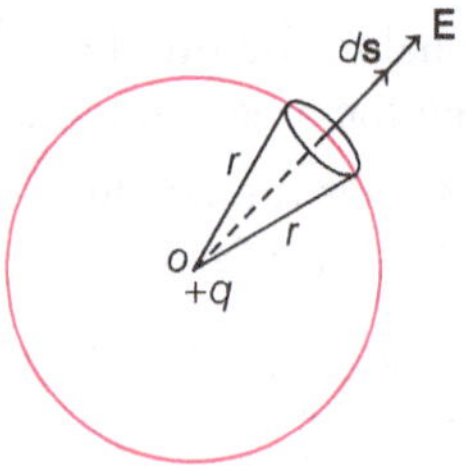

Total electric flux through the spherical surface,

$$\phi_E = \oint_S d\phi_E = \frac{1}{4\pi\varepsilon_0} \cdot \frac{q}{r^2} \oint_S dS$$

$$= \frac{1}{4\pi\varepsilon_0} \cdot \frac{q}{r^2} \cdot 4\pi r^2 = \frac{q}{\varepsilon_0} \Rightarrow \boxed{\phi_E = \frac{q}{\varepsilon_0}}$$

If there is no net charge within the closed surface, i.e. when $q = 0$, then $\phi_E = 0$.

$\therefore$ The total electric flux through a closed surface is zero, if no charge is enclosed by the surface.

It can be said that the charges situated outside the closed surface make no contribution to total electric flux over the surface.

Some Features of Gauss' Law

(i) Gauss' law is true for any closed surface, no matter what its shape or size be.

(ii) The electric field on a Gaussian surface is the result of all the charges inside and outside the surface.

(iii) Gauss' law is often useful when the system has some symmetry. This is facilitated by the choice of a suitable Gaussian surface.

Deduction of Coulomb's Law from Gauss' Theorem

Consider a sphere of radius r with centre O.

Suppose there is an isolated positive point charge at O. The magnitude of electric field intensity $\mathbf{E}$ is same at every point on the surface and is directed radially outwards. In the figure, it can be seen that direction of $d\mathbf{S}$ is along $\mathbf{E}$. It means $\theta = 0°$.

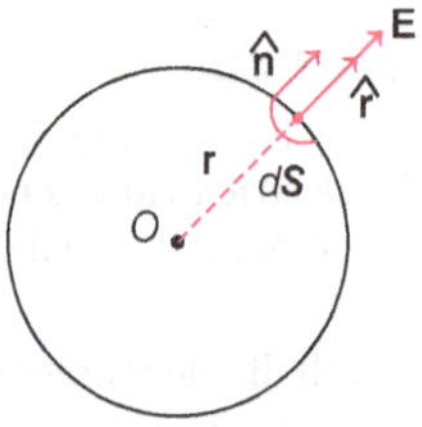

$\because$ According to Gauss' theorem, $\oint \mathbf{E} \cdot d\mathbf{S} = \frac{q}{\varepsilon_0}$

$$\Rightarrow \quad \oint E \cdot dS \cos 0° = \frac{q}{\varepsilon_0} \Rightarrow E \oint dS = \frac{q}{\varepsilon_0}$$

$$\Rightarrow \quad E(4\pi r^2) = \frac{q}{\varepsilon_0}$$

$$\Rightarrow \quad E = \frac{q}{4\pi\varepsilon_0 r^2} \qquad \text{...(i)}$$

$$\because \quad F = E \times q_0 \qquad \text{... (ii)}$$

$\therefore$ From Eqs. (i) and (ii), we get

$\boxed{F = \frac{q q_0}{4\pi\varepsilon_0 r^2}}$, which is Coulomb's law.

Example 15. **Figure shows three point charges $+2q$, $-q$ and $+3q$. Two charges $+2q$ and $-q$ are enclosed within a surface S. What is the electric flux due to this configuration through the surface S?**

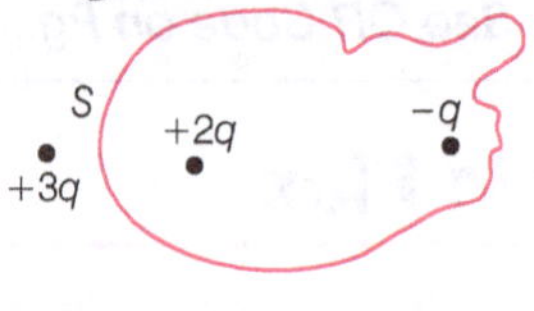

Sol. Electric flux through the closed surface S,

$$\phi_S = \frac{\Sigma q}{\varepsilon_0} = \frac{+2q - q}{\varepsilon_0} = \frac{q}{\varepsilon_0}$$

Charge $+3q$ is outside the closed surface S, therefore it would not be taken into consideration in applying Gauss' theorem.

1.9 Applications of Gauss' Theorem

The electric field due to some symmetric charge configurations can be obtained using Gauss' law.

Field due to an Infinitely Long Thin Straight Charged Wire

Consider an infinitely long thin straight wire with uniform linear charge density (λ).

From symmetry, the electric field is everywhere radial in the plane cutting the wire normally and its magnitude only depends on the radial distance (r).

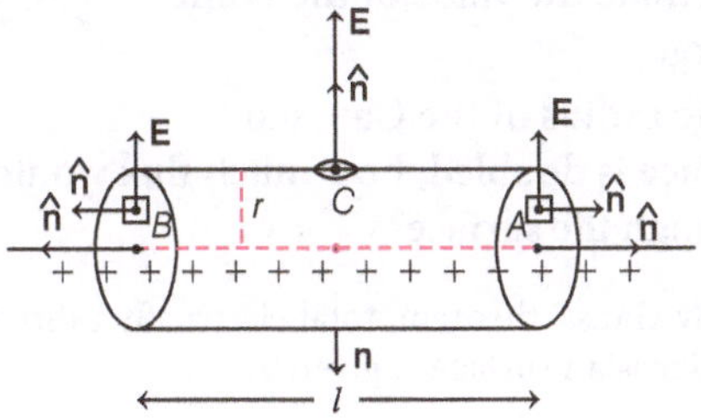

From Gauss' law, $\phi_E = \oint_S \mathbf{E}\cdot d\mathbf{S} = \dfrac{q}{\varepsilon_0}$

Now, $\phi_E = \oint_S \mathbf{E}\cdot dS = \oint_S \mathbf{E}\cdot\hat{\mathbf{n}}\, dS$

$$= \oint_A \mathbf{E}\cdot\hat{\mathbf{n}}\, dS + \oint_B \mathbf{E}\cdot\hat{\mathbf{n}}\, dS + \oint_C \mathbf{E}\cdot\hat{\mathbf{n}}\, dS$$

$$\therefore \oint_S \mathbf{E}\cdot dS = \oint_A E\, dS\cos 90^\circ + \oint_B E\, dS\cos 90^\circ + \oint_C E\, dS\cos 0^\circ$$

$$= \oint_C E\, dS = E(2\pi r l)$$

Charge enclosed in the cylinder, $q = \lambda l$

$$\therefore \quad E(2\pi r l) = \frac{\lambda l}{\varepsilon_0} \quad \text{or} \quad \boxed{E = \frac{\lambda}{2\pi\varepsilon_0 r}}$$

Vectorially, $\mathbf{E} = \dfrac{\lambda}{2\pi\varepsilon_0 r}\hat{\mathbf{r}}$ $\quad [\because \hat{\mathbf{n}} = \hat{\mathbf{r}}]$

- The direction of the electric field is radially outward from the positive line charge. For negative line charge, it will be radially inward.
- Thus, **electric field (E) due to the linear charge is inversely proportional to the distance (r).** The variation of electric field (E) with distance (r) is shown in figure.

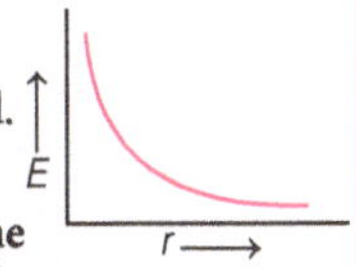

$\because \quad E = \dfrac{\lambda}{2\pi\varepsilon_0 r} \Rightarrow E \propto \dfrac{1}{r}$. It means

(i) if $\lambda > 0$, the direction of electric field at every point is radially outwards.

(ii) if $\lambda < 0$, the direction of electric field at every point is radially inwards.

Field due to a Uniformly Charged Thin Infinite Plane Sheet

Let σ be the surface charge density of the sheet. From symmetry, E on either side of the sheet must be perpendicular to the plane of the sheet, having same magnitude at all points equidistant from the sheet.

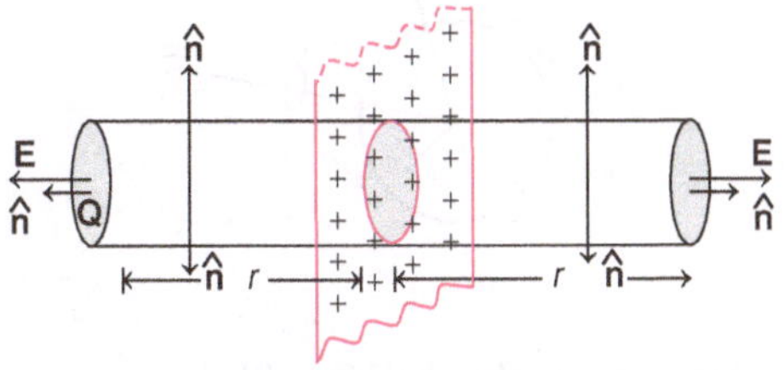

We take a cylindrical cross-sectional area A and length $2r$ as the Gaussian surface.

On the curved surface of the cylinder, E and $\hat{\mathbf{n}}$ are perpendicular to each other. Therefore, flux through curved surface $= 0$.

Flux through the flat surfaces $= EA + EA = 2EA$

$\therefore$ Total electric flux over the entire surface of cylinder,

$$\phi_E = 2EA$$

Total charge enclosed by the cylinder, $q = \sigma A$

According to Gauss' law, $\phi_E = \dfrac{q}{\varepsilon_0}$

$$\therefore \quad 2EA = \frac{\sigma A}{\varepsilon_0} \quad \text{or} \quad E = \frac{\sigma}{2\varepsilon_0}$$

***E* is independent of *r*, the distance of the point from the plane charged sheet.**

Field due to a Non-Conducting Charged Solid Sphere

- At **external point**, $E = \dfrac{q}{4\pi\varepsilon r^2}$
- At **internal point**, $E = \dfrac{r\rho}{3\varepsilon}$
- At **centre of sphere** ($r = 0$), $E = 0$
- At the **surface of sphere**,

$$r = R \Rightarrow E = \frac{R\rho}{3\varepsilon}, \text{i.e. maximum.}$$

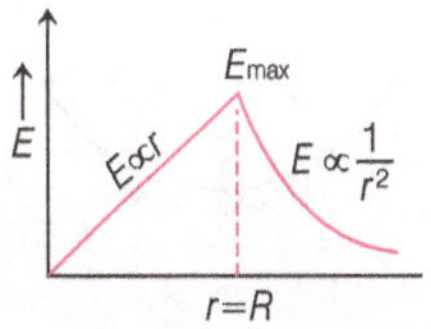

Field due to a Uniformly Charged Thin Spherical Shell

Let σ be the uniform surface charge density of a thin spherical shell of radius (R). The Gaussian surface will be a spherical surface centered at the centre of shell.

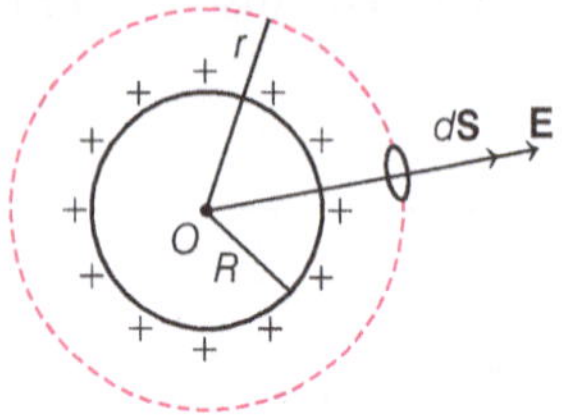

- **At a point outside the shell** ($r > R$)

  Since, E and dS are in the same direction.

$$\therefore \quad \phi_E = \oint_S \mathbf{E}\cdot d\mathbf{S} = \frac{q}{\varepsilon_0} \text{ or } E(4\pi r^2) = \frac{q}{\varepsilon_0}$$

$$\therefore \quad E = \frac{q}{4\pi\varepsilon_0 r^2}$$

Since, $q = \sigma \times 4\pi R^2$

$$\therefore \quad E = \frac{\sigma R^2}{\varepsilon_0 r^2}$$

Vectorially, $$\mathbf{E} = \frac{\sigma R^2}{\varepsilon_0 r^2}\hat{\mathbf{r}}$$

- **At a point on the surface of the shell** ($r = R$)

$$\boxed{E = \frac{q}{4\pi\varepsilon_0 R^2}} \text{ and } \boxed{E = \frac{\sigma}{\varepsilon_0}}$$

- **At a point inside the shell** ($r < R$)

Here, the charge inside the Gaussian surface shell,

$$q = 0$$

$$\therefore \quad E(4\pi r^2) = 0$$

$$\therefore \quad \boxed{E = 0}$$

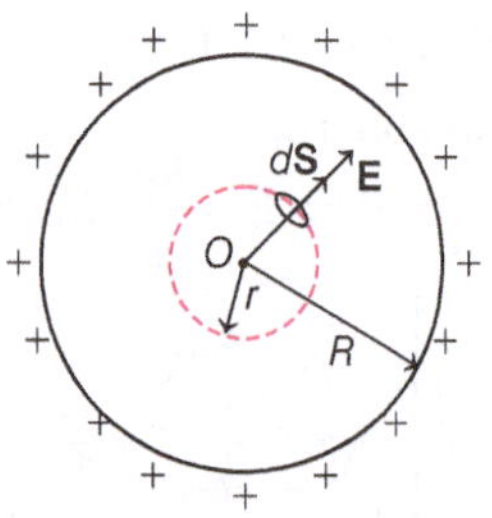

This important result is a direct consequence of Gauss' law which follows from Coulomb's law.

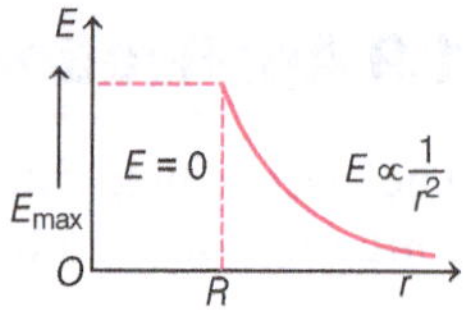

The **variation of electric field intensity (E) with distance from the centre of a uniformly charged spherical shell** is as shown in the following figure.

Example 16. **A point charge causes an electric flux -3×10^{-14} N - m^2 /C to pass through a spherical Gaussian surface.**

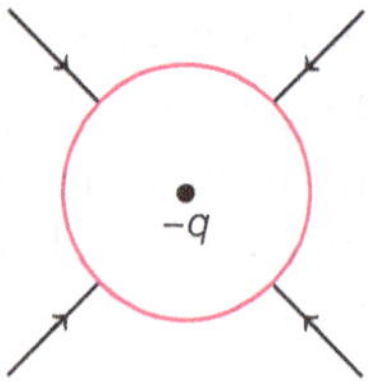

(i) Calculate the value of the point charge.

(ii) If the radius of the Gaussian surface is doubled, how much flux would pass through the surface?

Sol. (i) By Gauss' theorem, total electric flux through closed Gaussian surface is given by

$$\phi = \frac{q}{\varepsilon_0}$$

$$\therefore \quad q = \phi\varepsilon_0$$

But electric flux passing through the surface is

$$\phi = -3\times10^{-14}\text{N-m}^2/\text{C}$$

$$\therefore \quad q = (-3\times10^{-14})\times 8.85\times10^{-12}$$
$$= -26.55\times10^{-26}\text{C}$$
$$= -2.655\times10^{-25}\text{C}$$

(ii) Electric flux passing through the surface remains unchanged because it depends only on charge enclosed by the surface and is independent of its size.

Field due to Two Thin Infinite Parallel Sheets of Charge

Suppose P and Q are two thin infinite plane charged sheets placed parallel to each other.

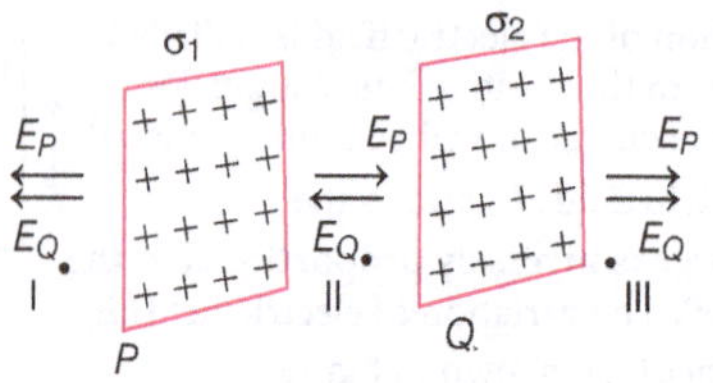

σ_1 = Uniform surface density of charge on P,

σ_2 = Uniform surface density of charge on Q.

$\because E_1 = \dfrac{\sigma_1}{2\varepsilon_0}$ and $E_2 = \dfrac{\sigma_2}{2\varepsilon_0}$. Consider $\sigma_1 > \sigma_2 > 0$

In region I $E_I = -E_1 - E_2$

$$= -\frac{\sigma_1}{2\varepsilon_0} - \frac{\sigma_2}{2\varepsilon_0} = -\frac{1}{2\varepsilon_0}(\sigma_1 + \sigma_2)$$

In region II $E_{II} = E_1 - E_2 = \dfrac{\sigma_1}{2\varepsilon_0} - \dfrac{\sigma_2}{2\varepsilon_0} = \dfrac{1}{2\varepsilon_0}(\sigma_1 - \sigma_2)$

In region III $E_{III} = E_1 + E_2 = \dfrac{\sigma_1}{2\varepsilon_0} + \dfrac{\sigma_2}{2\varepsilon_0} = \dfrac{1}{2\varepsilon_0}(\sigma_1 + \sigma_2)$

Quick Test 4

Conceptual Questions

1. Can Gauss' law in electrostatics tell us exactly where the charge is located within the Gaussian surface?

2. An arbitrary surface encloses a dipole. What is the electric flux through this surface? *NCERT Exemplar*

3. What is the net flux of the uniform electric field through a cube of side 20 cm oriented, so that its faces are parallel to the coordinate planes? *NCERT*

4. How does the electric flux due to a point charge enclosed by a spherical Gaussian surface get affected when its radius is increased? *Delhi 2016*

5. Consider two hollow concentric spheres S_1 and S_2 enclosing charges 2Q and 4Q respectively, as shown in the figure.

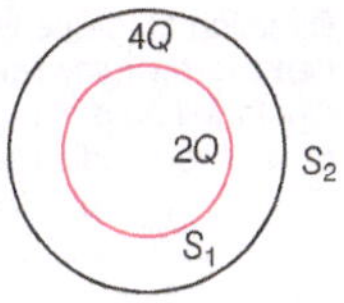

(i) Find out the ratio of the electric flux through them.

(ii) How will the electric flux through the sphere S_1 change, if a medium of dielectric constant ε_r is introduced in the space inside S_1 in place of air? Deduce the necessary expression.

Numerical Questions

6. A point charge of 2.0 μC is at the centre of a cubic Gaussian surface 9.0 cm on edge. What is the net electric flux through the surface? *NCERT*

7. Given a uniform electric field $\mathbf{E} = 5 \times 10^3 \hat{\mathbf{i}}$ N/C, find the flux of this field through a square of 10 cm on a side whose plane is parallel to the *YZ*-plane. What would be the flux through the same square, if the plane makes an angle of 30° with the *X*-axis? *Delhi 2014*

8. A uniformly charged conducting sphere of diameter 2.4 m has a surface charge density of 80.0 $\mu C/m^2$.

(i) Find the charge on the sphere.

(ii) What is the total electric flux leaving the surface of the sphere? *NCERT*

9. An infinite line charge produces a field of 9×10^4 N / C at a distance of 2 cm. Calculate the linear charge density. *NCERT*

10. Two large thin metal plates are parallel and close to each other. On their inner faces, the plates have surface charge densities of opposite signs and of magnitude $17.0 \times 10^{-22}\, Cm^{-2}$. What is the electric field

(i) to the left of the plates, (ii) to the right of the plates and

(iii) in between the plates? *NCERT*

Answers

5. (i) 1:3 *6.* 2.26×10^5 N-m^2/C *7.* 25N-m^2/C

8. (i) 1.45×10^{-3}C (ii) 1.637×10^{-8}N-m^2/C *9.* 10^{-7} cm^{-1}

10. (i) Zero (ii) Zero (iii) 1.9×10^{-10} NC^{-1}

For Solutions, See QR Code on Pg. 40

Mind Map

Electric Charges and Fields

Electric Charge

- Electric charge is an intrinsic property of elementary particles of matter.
- It is a scalar quantity.
- Its SI unit is coulomb (C).
- Charge can be divided into two types
  Positive due to loss of electron
  Negative due to gain of electron

Properties of Charge

- **Charge is always conserved**

(i) The total charge of an isolated system remains constant.

(ii) The electric charge can neither be created nor be destroyed, they can only be transferred from one body to another.

- **Additive in nature** The total charge of a system is the algebraic sum of all the individual charges inside the system.
- **It is always quantised** The total charge(q) of a body is always an integral multiple of a basic quantum of charge (e), i.e. $q = ne$, where, $n = 0, \pm 1, \pm 2, \pm 3...$

The Superposition Principle

- The total force acting on a charged particle due to the presence of other charged particles is the vector sum of the individual sources acting on the charge due to each of the other charges.

$$\mathbf{F}(r) = \sum_{i=1}^{n} \mathbf{F}_i(r_i)$$

- The force between two charges is not affected by the presence of other charge.

Continuous Distribution of Charge

- **Linear charge distribution** Charge is distributed along a line, like a charged wire. $\lambda = dq/dL$
  The SI unit for λ is Cm^{-1}.
- **Surface charge distribution** Charge is spread over a surface, like a charged sheet. $\sigma = dq/dS$
  The SI unit for σ is Cm^{-2}.
- **Volume charge distribution** Charge is distributed throughout a volume, like a charged sphere.
  $\rho = dq/dV$
  The SI unit is Cm^{-3}.

Charges at rest produce Electric Field

$$E = \frac{F}{q_0} = \frac{kq}{r^2}$$

$$\text{SI unit} = \frac{\text{newton}}{\text{coulomb}} = \frac{\text{volt}}{\text{metre}}$$

Basic Characteristics of Electric Field Lines

- Field lines start from positive charge and end at negative charge.
- Electrostatic field lines do not form any closed loop.
- Two field lines can never cross each other.

Electric field intensity
Electrostatic force per unit charge

$$E = F/q$$

SI unit - N/C or V/m

Coulomb's Law

The force of interaction between two charges is directly proportional to the product of two charges and inversely proportional to the square of the distance between them.

$$F \propto \frac{q_1 q_2}{r^2}$$

Electric Dipole

The arrangement of two equal and opposite charges separated by small distance. The dipole moment is given by $p = 2qa$

Axial Point

Electric field at any axial point of the dipole acts along the dipole axis from negative to positive charge, i.e. in the direction of dipole moment **p**.

$$\mathbf{E}_{axial} = \frac{1}{4\pi\varepsilon_0} \cdot \frac{2\mathbf{p}}{r^3}$$

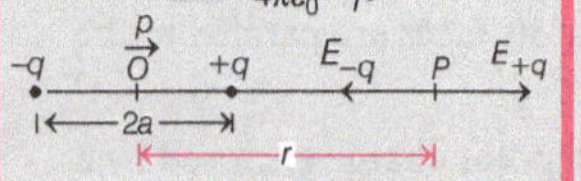

Equatorial Point

The direction of electric field at any point on the equatorial line will be anti-parallel to the dipole moment **p**.

$$\mathbf{E}_{eq} = \frac{-1}{4\pi\varepsilon_0} \cdot \frac{\mathbf{p}}{r^3}$$

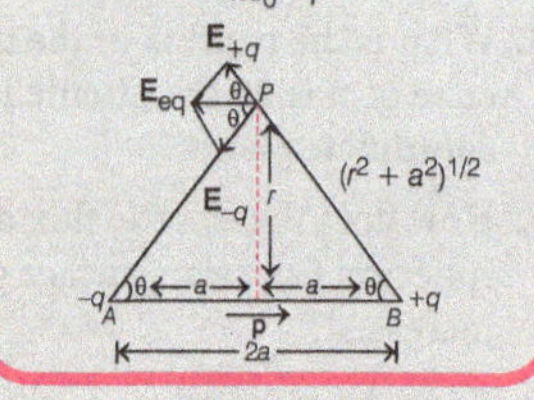

Torque

Direction of torque is given by right hand screw rule. The torque on the dipole will be maximum when the dipole is held perpendicular to **E**.

Thus, $\tau_{max} = pE \sin 90° = pE$

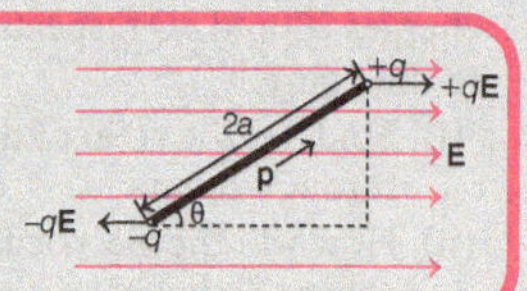

Electric Flux

The total number of electric lines of force passing normally through that area. If an electric field **E** passes normally through an areal element ΔS, then the electric flux through this area is $\Delta\phi_E = E\Delta S$.

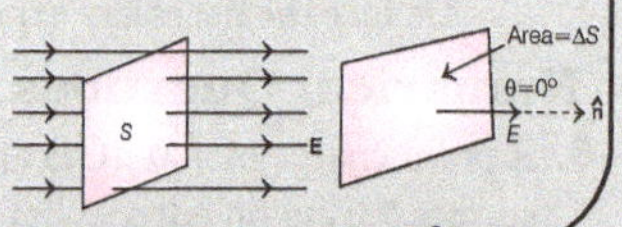

Gauss's Law

The total flux through a closed surface is $1/\varepsilon_0$ times the net charge enclosed by the closed surface.

Mathematically, it can be expressed as $\phi_E = \oint_S \mathbf{E} \cdot d\mathbf{S} = \frac{q}{\varepsilon_0}$

Applications of Gauss's Law

Field Due to an Infinitely Long Charged Wire

The electric field of a line charge is inversely proportional to the distance from the line charge.

Vectorially, $\mathbf{E} = \frac{\lambda}{2\pi\varepsilon_0 r} \hat{\mathbf{n}}$

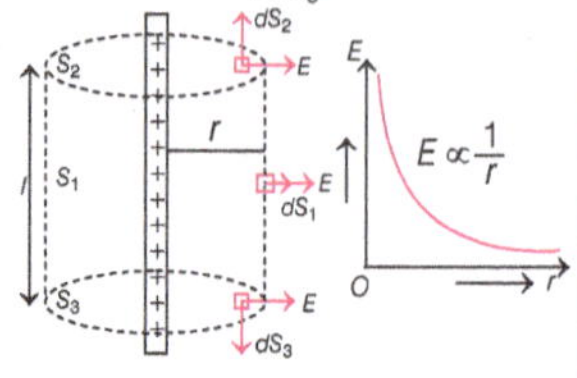

Uniformly Charged Thin Spherical Shell

For spherical shell, $E = \frac{1}{4\pi\varepsilon_0} \cdot \frac{q}{r^2}$

Vectorially, $\mathbf{E} = \frac{q\hat{\mathbf{r}}}{4\pi\varepsilon_0 r^2}$

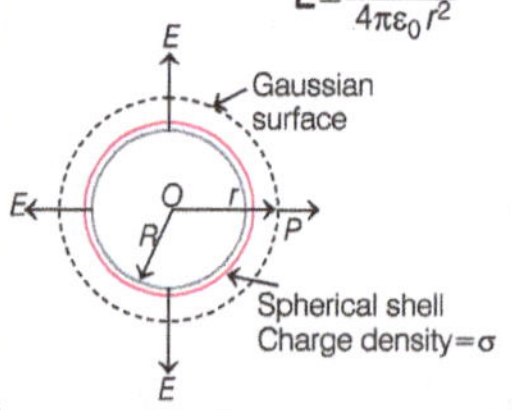

Uniformly Charged Infinite Plane Sheet

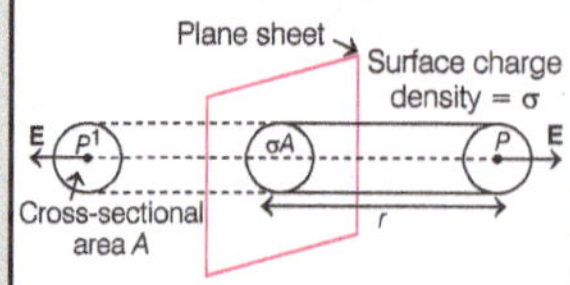

According to Gauss's theorem,

$$2EA = \frac{\sigma A}{\varepsilon_0} \text{ or } E = \frac{\sigma}{2\varepsilon_0}$$

$\therefore$ Vector form, $\mathbf{E} = \frac{\sigma}{2\varepsilon_0} \hat{\mathbf{n}}$

EXAM PATTERN QUESTIONS

Objective Type Questions

Multiple Choice Questions (MCQs)

1. Two identical small conducting balls B_1 and B_2 are given −7pC and +4 pC charges, respectively. They are brought in contact with a third identical ball B_3 and then separated. If the final charge on each ball is −2 pC, the initial charge on B_3 was **CBSE 2024**

(a) −2 pC (b) −3 pC (c) −5 pC (d) −15 pC

2. An isolated point charge particle produces an electric field E at a point 3 m away from it. The distance of the point at which the field is $\frac{E}{4}$ will be **CBSE 2023**

(a) 2 m (b) 3 m (c) 4 m (d) 6 m

3. Two identical point charges are placed at the two vertices A and B of an equilateral triangle of side l. The magnitude of the electric field at the third vertex P is E. If a hollow conducting sphere of radius $\left(\frac{1}{4}\right)$ is placed at P, the magnitude of the electric field at point P now becomes **CBSE 2025**

(a) $>E$ (b) E (c) $\frac{E}{2}$ (d) zero

4. Which one of the following statements is correct? Electric field due to static charges is **CBSE 2025**

(a) conservative and field lines do not form closed loops.
(b) conservative and field lines form closed loops.
(c) non-conservative and field lines do not form closed loops.
(d) non-conservative and field lines form closed loops.

5. Two charges $-q$ each are placed at the vertices A and B of an equilateral triangle ABC. If M is the mid-point of AB, the net electric field at C will point along **CBSE 2025**

(a) CA (b) CB (c) MC (d) CM

6. A charge Q is placed at the centre of a cube. The electric flux through one if its face is **CBSE 2023**

(a) $\frac{Q}{\varepsilon_0}$ (b) $\frac{Q}{6\varepsilon_0}$

(c) $\frac{Q}{8\varepsilon_0}$ (d) $\frac{Q}{3\varepsilon_0}$

7. Electric field lines are pictorial representations of electric fields due to static charges on the plane of a paper.

Study the given electric field representation and identify one incorrect qualitative impression given by this representation.

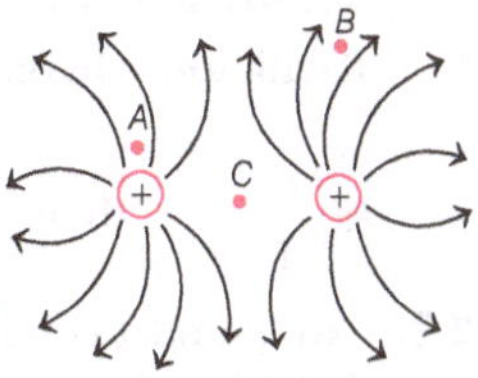

Competency Based Que

(a) The electric field at point A is stronger than at point B.
(b) The electric field distribution is two dimensional.
(c) The electric field at point C is zero.
(d) The electric field always points away from a positive charge.

8. Four objects W, X, Y and Z each with charge $+q$ are held fixed at four points of a square of side d as shown in the figure. Objects X and Z are on the mid-points of the sides of the square. The electrostatic force exerted by object W on object X is F, then the magnitude of the force exerted by object W on Z is **CBSE SQP, Term-I**

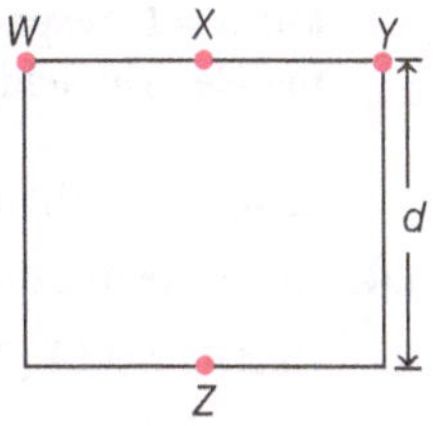

(a) $\frac{F}{7}$ (b) $\frac{F}{5}$ (c) $\frac{F}{3}$ (d) $\frac{F}{2}$

9. Three charges q, $-q$ and q_0 are placed as shown in figure. The magnitude of the net force on the charge q_0 at point O is $\left(\text{Take, } K = \frac{1}{4\pi\varepsilon_0}\right)$ **CBSE 2021, Term-I**

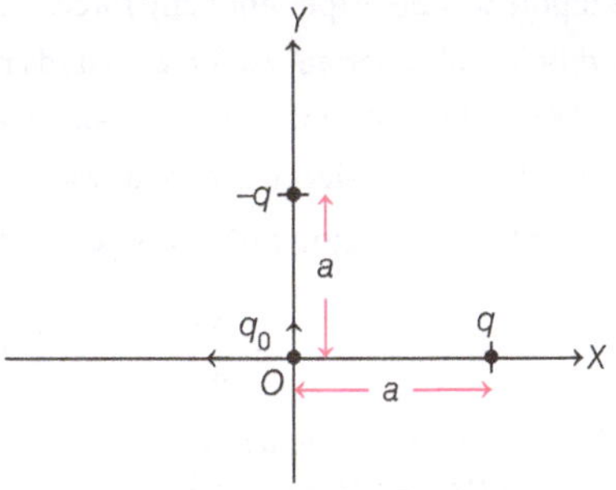

(a) 0 (b) $\frac{2Kqq_0}{a^2}$

(c) $\frac{\sqrt{2}Kqq_0}{a^2}$ (d) $\frac{1}{\sqrt{2}}\frac{Kqq_0}{a^2}$

10. An electric dipole of dipole moment p is kept in a uniform electric field E. The amount of work done to rotate it from the position of stable equilibrium to that of unstable equilibrium will be **CBSE 2024**

(a) $2pE$ (b) $-2pE$ (c) pE (d) zero

11. The magnitude of electric field due to a point charge $2q$, at distance r is E. Then, the magnitude of electric field due to a uniformly charged thin spherical shell of radius R with total charge q at a distance $\frac{r}{2}$ $(r >> R)$ will be **CBSE SQP, Term-I**

(a) $\frac{E}{4}$ (b) 0 (c) $2E$ (d) $4E$

12. Two parallel large thin metal sheets have equal surface densities 26.4×10^{-12} C/m^2 of opposite signs. The electric field between these sheets is **CBSE SQP, Term-I**

(a) 1.5 N/C (b) 1.5×10^{-16} N/C
(c) 3×10^{-10} N/C (d) 3 N/C

13. Two point charges $+8q$ and $-2q$ are located at $x = 0$ and $x = L$, respectively. The point on X-axis at which net electric field is zero due to these charges is **CBSE SQP, Term-1**

(a) $8L$ (b) $4L$ (c) $2L$ (d) L

14. An electron experiences a force $(1.6 \times 10^{-16}\ \text{N})\ \hat{i}$ in an electric field E. The electric field E is **CBSE 2023**

(a) $(1.0 \times 10^3\ \text{NC}^{-1})\hat{i}$ (b) $-(1.0 \times 10^3\ \text{NC}^{-1})\hat{i}$
(c) $(1.0 \times 10^{-3}\ \text{NC}^{-1})\hat{i}$ (d) $-(1.0 \times 10^{-3}\ \text{NC}^{-1})\hat{i}$

15. Figure shows electric field lines in which an electric dipole p is placed as shown. Which of the following statements is correct? **NCERT Exemplar**

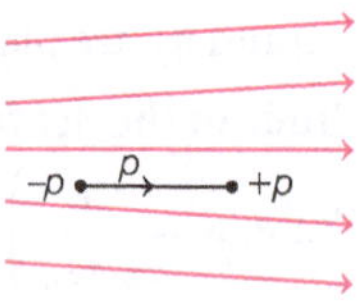

(a) The dipole will not experience any force.
(b) The dipole will experience a force towards right.
(c) The dipole will experience a force towards left.
(d) The dipole will experience a force upwards.

16. The electric flux emerging out from 1C charge is **CBSE 2020**

(a) $\frac{1}{\varepsilon_0}$ (b) 4π (c) $\frac{4\pi}{\varepsilon_0}$ (d) ε_0

17. A small object with charge q and weight mg is attached to one end of a string of length L attached to a stationary support. The system is placed in a uniform horizontal electric field E, as shown in the given figure. In the presence of the field, the string makes a constant angle θ with the vertical. What will be the sign and magnitude of q.

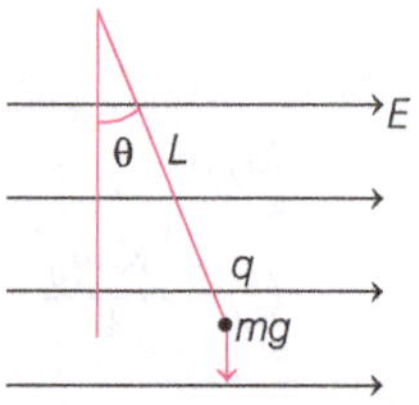

CBSE SQP, Term-I

(a) Positive with magnitude mg / E
(b) Positive with magnitude $(mg / E) \tan\theta$
(c) Negative with magnitude $(mg / E) \tan\theta$
(d) Positive with magnitude $E \tan\theta / mg$

18. An electric dipole of moment p is placed parallel to the uniform electric field. The amount of work done in rotating the dipole by 90° is **CBSE SQP, Term-I**

(a) $2pE$ (b) pE
(c) $pE/2$ (d) zero

19. A conducting wire connects two charged conducting spheres such that they attain equilibrium with respect to each other. The distance of separation between the both spheres is very large as compared to either of their radii.
The ratio of the magnitudes of the electric fields at the surfaces of the two spheres is

(a) $\frac{r_1}{r_2}$ (b) $\frac{r_2}{r_1}$ (c) $\frac{r_2^2}{r_1^2}$ (d) $\frac{r_1^2}{r_2^2}$

20. A square sheet of side a is lying parallel to XY-plane at $z = a$. The electric field in the region is $\mathbf{E} = cz^2\hat{\mathbf{k}}$. The electric flux through the sheet is **CBSE SQP, Term-I**

(a) a^4c (b) $\frac{1}{3}a^3c$
(c) $\frac{1}{3}a^4c$ (d) 0

21. Which statement is true for Gauss law? **CBSE SPQ, Term-1**

(a) All the charges whether inside or outside the Gaussian surface contribute to the electric flux.
(b) Electric flux depends upon the geometry of the Gaussian surface.
(c) Gauss theorem can be applied to non-uniform electric field.
(d) The electric field over the Gaussian surface remains continuous and uniform at every point.

22. For a given surface, the $\oint \mathbf{E} \cdot d\mathbf{S} = 0$. From this, we can conclude that

(a) E is necessarily zero on the surface
(b) E is perpendicular to the surface at every point
(c) the total flux through the surface is zero
(d) the flux is only going out of the surface

23. An electric dipole of length 2 cm is placed at angle of 30° with an electric field 2×10^5 N/C. If the dipole experiences a torque of 8×10^{-3} N-m, the magnitude of either charge of the dipole is

(a) 4 μC (b) 7 μC
(c) 8 μC (d) 2 μC

24. Match the Column I with Column II.

Column I (Concept/ Theories)		Column II (Advance Description/ Application)
1. Total number of field lines of force passing through the area normally.	(A)	$\frac{\sigma}{2\varepsilon_0}$
2. Electric field intensity due to a thin infinite plane sheet charge	(B)	$\frac{2px}{4\pi\varepsilon_0(x^2-l^2)^2}$
3. The field of an electric dipole for point on the axis	(C)	Electric flux
4. All charges must be integral multiple of charge $(e), Q = \pm ne$	(D)	Quantisation of charge

(a) 1-(C), 2-(B), 3-(A), 4-(D)
(b) 1-(C), 2-(A), 3-(B), 4-(D)
(c) 1-(D), 2-(A), 3-(B), 4-(C)
(d) 1-(B), 2-(D), 3-(A), 4-(C)

25. Match the Column I with Column II.

Column I (Concept/ Theories)		Column II (Advance Description/ Application)
1. Electric force between an electron and a proton at a distance r apart	(A)	$E=\frac{F}{q}$
2. A charge Q experiences an electrical force due to q	(B)	$F=-\frac{1}{4\pi\varepsilon_0}\frac{e^2}{r^2}$
3. Field due to an infinitely long straight uniformly charged wire	(C)	$\frac{dq}{dS}$
4. Surface charge density	(D)	$\frac{\lambda}{2\pi\varepsilon_0 r}$

(a) 1-(B), 2-(A), 3-(D), 4-(C) (b) 1-(B), 2-(C), 3-(A), 4-(D)
(c) 1-(A), 2-(C), 3-(D), 4-(B) (d) 1-(C), 2-(D), 3-(A), 4-(B)

Assertion-Reason

Directions (Q. Nos. 26-35) *In the following questions, two statements are given- one labelled Assertion* (A) *and the other labelled Reason* (R). *Select the correct answer to these questions from the codes* (a), (b), (c) *and* (d) *as given below*

(a) Both Assertion and Reason are true and Reason is the correct explanation of Assertion.
(b) Both Assertion and Reason are true but Reason is not the correct explanation of Assertion.
(c) Assertion is true but Reason is false.
(d) Assertion is false but Reason is true.

26. **Assertion (A)** Electric force between two charges always acts along the line joining the two charges
Reason (R) Electric force is a conservative force.

27. **Assertion (A)** When a neutral body acquires positive charge, its mass decreases.
Reason (R) A body acquires positive charge when it loses electrons.

28. **Assertion (A)** In a non-uniform electric field, a dipole will have translatory as well as rotatory motion.
Reason (R) In a non-uniform electric field, a dipole experiences a force as well as torque.

29. **Assertion (A)** A negative charge in an electric field moves along the direction of the electric field.
Reason (R) On a negative charge, a force acts in the opposite direction of the electric field.

30. **Assertion (A)** If a proton and an electron are placed in the same uniform electric field, they experience different acceleration.
Reason (R) Electric force on a test charge is dependent on its mass.

31. **Assertion (A)** All the charges in a conductor get distributed on whole of its outer surface.
Reason (R) In a dynamic system, charges try to keep their potential energy minimum.

32. **Assertion (A)** An electric dipole is in stable equilibrium when it is placed in a uniform electric field with its dipole moment opposite to the field.
Reason (R) No torque acts on an electric dipole when its dipole moment is in a direction opposite to the field.

33. **Assertion (A)** If Gaussian surface does not enclose any charge, then **E** at any point on the Gaussian surface must be zero.
Reason (R) No net charge is enclosed by Gaussian surface, so net flux passing through the surface is zero.

34. **Assertion (A)** Surface charge density of an irregularly shaped conductor is non-uniform.
Reason (R) Surface charge density is defined as charge per unit area.

35. **Assertion (A)** Total flux through a closed surface is zero, if no charge is enclosed by the surface.
Reason(R) Gauss' law is true for any closed surface, no matter what its shape or size is.

Case Based Questions

Directions (Q.Nos. 36-38) *These questions are case study based questions. Read the following paragraphs and answer the questions on the basis of same.*

36. Surface charge density is defined as the charge per unit surface area of surface charge distribution

i.e. $\sigma = \dfrac{dq}{dS}$

Two large, thin metal plates are parallel and close to each other. On their inner faces, the plates have surface charge densities of opposite signs having magnitude of 17.0×10^{-22} Cm^{-2} as shown.

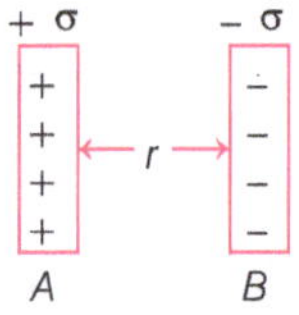

The intensity of electric field at a point is $E = \dfrac{\sigma}{\varepsilon_0}$

where, ε_0 = permittivity of free space.

(i) E in the outer region of the first plate is
(a) 17×10^{-22} N/C
(b) 1.5×10^{-15} N/C
(c) 1.9×10^{-10} N/C
(d) zero

(ii) E in the outer region of the second plate is
(a) 17×10^{-22} N/C (b) 1.5×10^{-15} N/C
(c) 1.9×10^{-10} N/C (d) zero

(iii) E between the plates is
(a) 17×10^{-22} N/C (b) 1.5×10^{-15} N/C
(c) 1.92×10^{-10} N/C (d) zero

(iv) The ratio of E from right side of B at distances 2 cm and 4 cm respectively, is
(a) 1 : 2 (b) 2 : 1 (c) 1 : 1 (d) $1 : \sqrt{2}$

(v) In order to estimate the electric field due to a thin finite plane metal plate, the gaussian surface considered is
(a) spherical (b) cylindrical
(c) straight line (d) None of these

37. The nuclear charge (*Ze*) is non-uniformly distributed within a nucleus of radius *R*. The charge density $\rho(r)$ [charge per unit volume is dependent only on the radial distance *r* from the centre of the nucleus as shown in figure. The electric field is only along the radial direction.

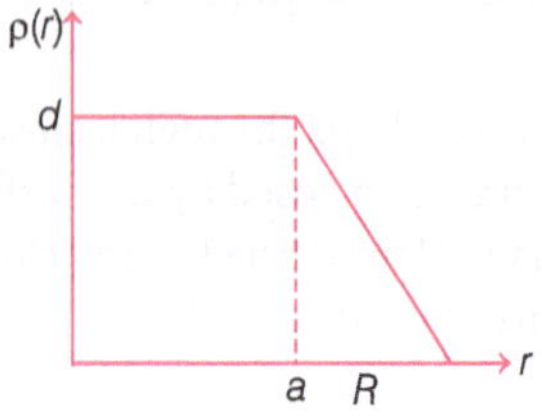

(i) The electric field at $r = R$ is
(a) independent of *a*
(b) directly proportional to *a*
(c) directly proportional to a^2
(d) inversely proportional to *a*

(ii) Net charge on given system is
(a) $Q = \int \rho_r (4\pi r^2) dr$
(b) $Q = \int \rho_r (\pi r^2) dr$
(c) $Q = \int \rho_r \dfrac{r^2}{2} dr$
(d) $Q = \int \rho_r (4\pi r) dr$

(iii) For $a = 0$, the value of *d* (maximum value of ρ as shown in the figure) is
(a) $\dfrac{3Ze^2}{4\pi R^3}$ (b) $\dfrac{3Ze}{\pi R^3}$
(c) $\dfrac{4Ze}{3\pi R^3}$ (d) $\dfrac{Ze}{3\pi R^3}$

(iv) The correct graph representing the variation of *E* with *r* is

(a)
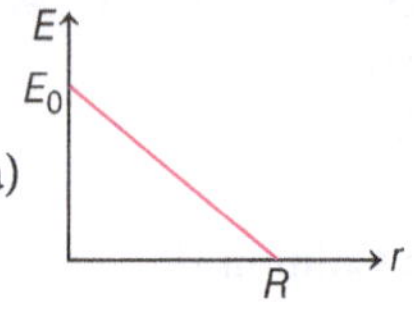

(b)
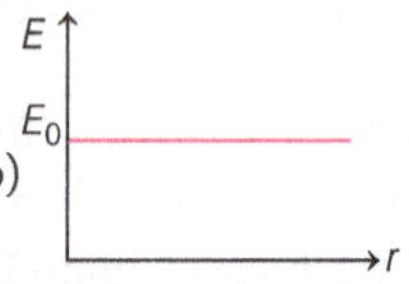

(c)

(d)
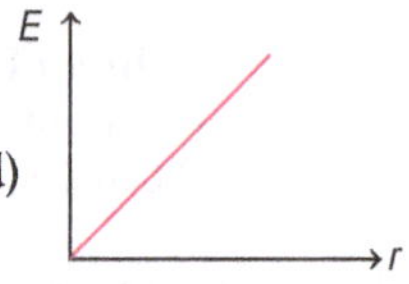

(v) The electric field within the nucleus is generally observed to be linearly dependent on *r*. This implies
(a) $a = 0$ (b) $a = \dfrac{R}{2}$
(c) $a = R$ (d) $a = \dfrac{2R}{3}$

38. The electric field due to a charge at a point in space may be defined as the force that a unit positive charge would experience, if placed at that point. It is a vector quantity and its SI unit is N/C.

The magnitude of the electric field at a point is given by $E = \dfrac{1}{4\pi\varepsilon_0} \cdot \dfrac{q}{r^2}$

Electric field lines start from positive charges and end at negative charges. In case of a single charge, they may start or end at infinity.

Two field lines can never intersect each other because, if they intersect, then two tangents drawn at that point will represent two directions of field at that point, which is not possible. Electric field lines do not pass through a conductor.

(i) Four point charges are placed at the corners of a square of side a cm as shown in figure. Find the magnitude and direction of the electric field at the centre O of the square.

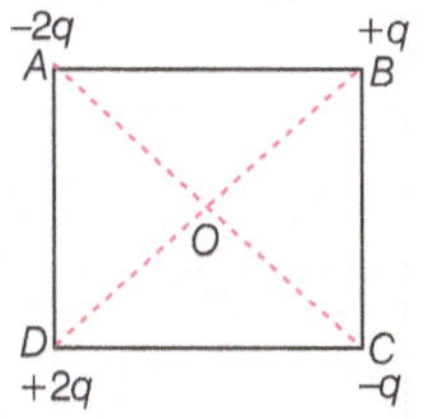

(ii) The dimensions of an atom are of the order of an angstrom, thus there must be large electric fields between the protons and electrons. Why there is the electrostatic field inside a conductor zero?

(iii) A charged particle is free to move in an electric field. Will it always be along a line of force? Explain.

(iv) Sketch the electric field lines for a uniformly charged hollow cylinder as shown in the figure.

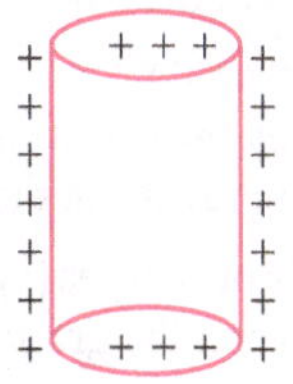

Subjective Questions

Very Short Answer Type Questions

1. (i) A glass rod when rubbed with silk cloth, acquires a charge 1.6×10^{-13} C. What is the charge on the silk cloth? **[1]**

(ii) Does the Coulomb force that one charge exerts on another charge changes, if other charge is brought nearby? **[1]**

2. Two identical balls having same positive charge q coulomb are suspended by two insulating strings of equal length. What would be the effect on the force when a plastic sheet is inserted between the two?

3. The dimensions of an atom are of the order of an angstrom. Thus, there must be large electric fields between the protons and electrons why? When is the electrostatic field inside a conductor zero?

4. Draw the pattern of electric field lines, when a point charge $-Q$ is kept near an uncharged conducting plate. **Delhi 2019**

5. Draw the pattern of electric field lines due to two positive charges placed at distance d apart. **All India 2019**

6. The work done in moving a charge particle between two points in a uniform electric field does not depend on the path followed by the particle. Why? **CBSE 2020**

7. Two point charges of 3 μC and 4 μC are kept in air at (0.3 m, 0) and (0, 0.3 m) in xy-plane. Find the magnitude and direction of the net electric field produced at the origin (0, 0). **CBSE 2024C**

8. Define electric flux and write its SI unit. **CBSE SQP 2024-25**

9. (i) An electrostatic field line is a continuous curve. That is, a field line cannot have sudden breaks. Why not?

(ii) Explain, why two field lines never cross each other at any point?

10. (i) State Gauss' theorem in electrostatics. **CBSE SQP 2024-25**

(ii) Torque acting on an electric dipole placed in a uniform electric field is maximum when the angle between the electric field and the dipole moment is .... **All India 2020**

Short Answer Type Questions

11. (i) Explain the meaning of the statement 'electric charge of a body is quantised'. **[1½]**

(ii) Why can one ignore quantisation of electric charge when dealing with macroscopic, i.e. large scale charges? **[1½]**

12. A point charge + 10μC is at a distance 5 cm directly above the centre of a square of side 10 cm, as shown in figure. What is the magnitude of the electric flux through the square?

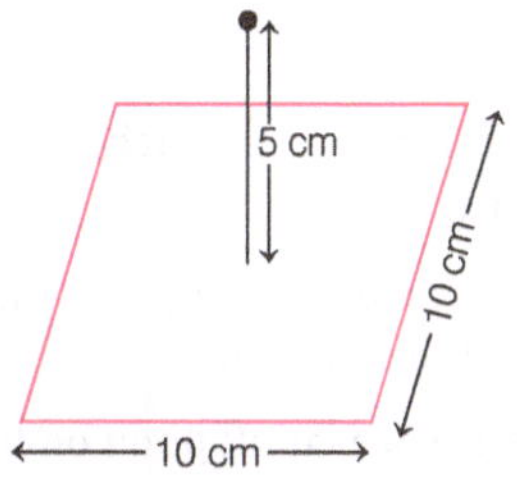

13. "Electrostatic forces are much stronger than the gravitational forces". Give one example to justify this statement.

14. An uncharged metallic ball is suspended in the region between two vertical metal plates. If the two plates are charged, one positively and one negatively, then describe the motion of the ball after it is brought into contact with one of the plates.

15. Plot a graph showing the variation of Coulomb's force (F) *versus* $(1/r^2)$, where r is the distance between the two charges of each pair of charges $(1\,\mu C,\ 2\,\mu C)$ and $(1\,\mu C,\ -3\,\mu C)$. Interpret the graphs obtained.

16. A charge q is placed at the centre of the line joining two equal charges (Q). Show that the system of three charges will be in equilibrium, if $q = -\frac{Q}{4}$.

17. Two positive charges q_1 and q_2 lie along a straight line separated by a distance of 2 m as shown.

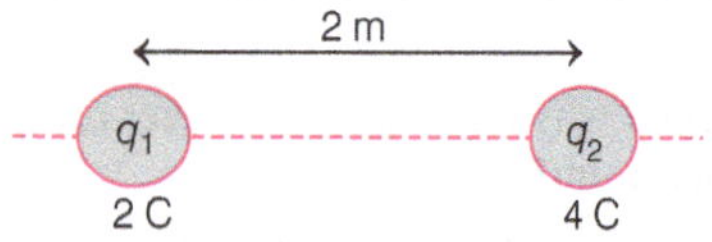

(i) Find a location along the straight line joining the two charges, where if a positive charge q_3 is placed, it experiences a zero resultant force. **[1½]**

(ii) Will the resultant force on q_3 placed at the location of part (i) still be zero, if it is negatively charged? Explain. **[1½]**

18. A thin metallic spherical shell of radius R carries a charge Q on its surface. A point charge $\frac{Q}{2}$ is placed at the centre C and another charge $+2Q$ is placed outside the shell at A at a distance x from the centre as shown in the figure.

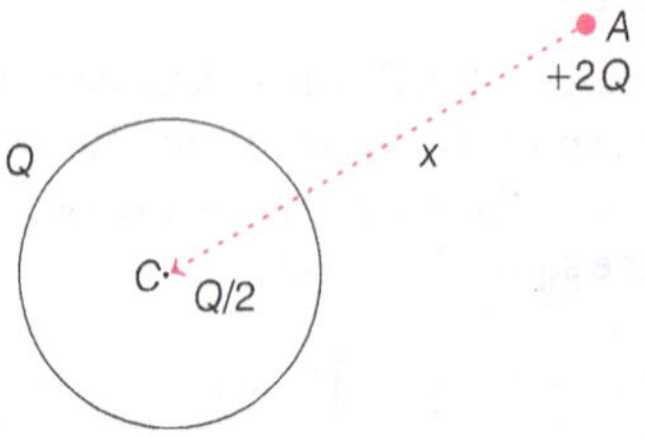

(i) Find the electric flux through the shell. **[1]**

(ii) State the law used. **[1]**

(iii) Find the force on the charges at the centre C of the shell and at the point A. **[1]**

19. (i) The distance of a far off point on the equatorial plane of an electric dipole is halved. How will the electric field be affected for the dipole? **[1½]**

(ii) Two identical electric dipoles are placed along the diagonals of a square $ABCD$ of side $\sqrt{2}$ m as shown in the figure. Obtain the magnitude and direction of the net electric field at the centre O of the square. **CBSE 2023** **[1½]**

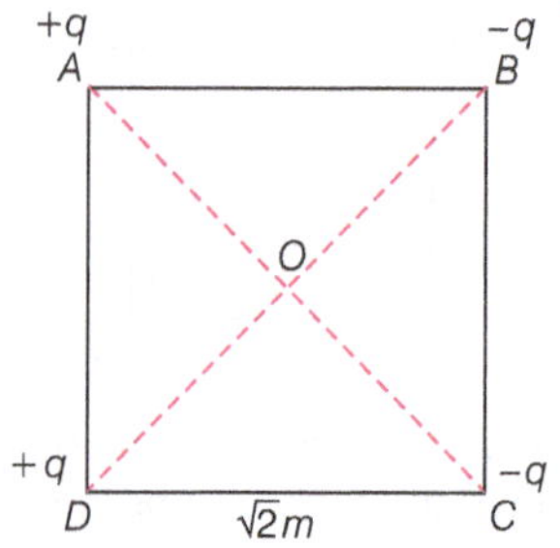

20. Two charged conducting spheres of radii a and b are connected to each other by a wire. Find the ratio of the electric fields at their surfaces. **CBSE 2023**

21. Given a line of charge of uniform linear density. A charge $+q$ is distributed uniformly between $y = 0$ and $y = a$ and charge $-q$ is distributed uniformly between $y = 0$ and $y = -a$.
Explain, how the direction of the resultant electric field at point P can be obtained. Represent using a vector diagram.

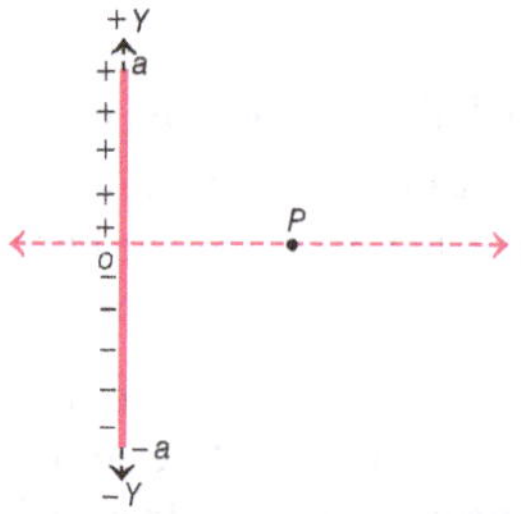

22. Derive the expression for the torque acting on an electric dipole, when it is held in a uniform electric field. Identify the orientation of the dipole in the electric field, in which it attains a stable equilibrium. **CBSE 2020**

23. (i) A point charge is placed at the centre of a hollow conducting sphere of internal radius r and outer radius $2r$. The ratio of the surface charge density of the inner surface to that of the outer surface will be .... **CBSE 2020** **[1½]**

(ii) Rank the Gaussian surfaces as shown in the figure, in order of increasing electric flux, starting with the most negative. **[1½]**

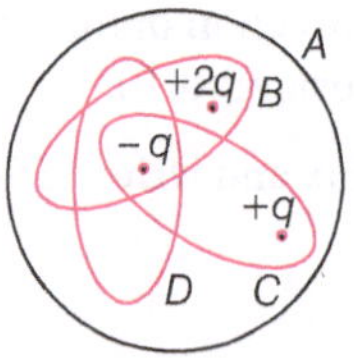

24. Two large plane sheets P_1 and P_2 having charge densities $+\sigma$ and -3σ respectively are arranged parallel to each other as shown in the figure. Find the net electric field (E) at points A, B and C. **CBSE 2024C**

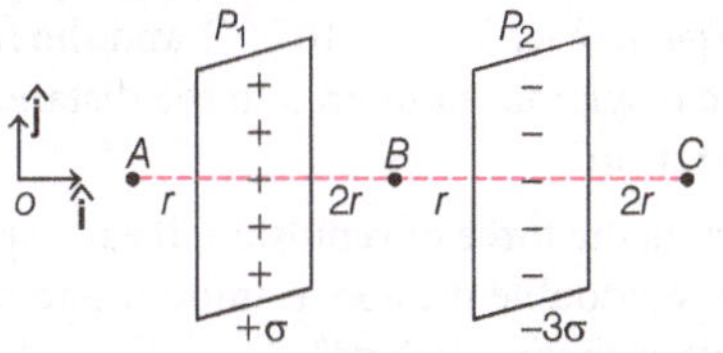

25. (i) A thin straight infinitely long conducting wire having charge density λ is enclosed by a cylindrical surface of radius r and length l, its axis coinciding with the length of the wire. Find the expression for the electric flux through the surface of the cylinder. **[1½]**

(ii) A square surface of side l metre is in the plane of paper. A uniform electric field E (V/m), also in the plane of the paper, is limited only to the lower half of the square surface, (see figure). What is the electric flux associated with this surface? **[1½]**

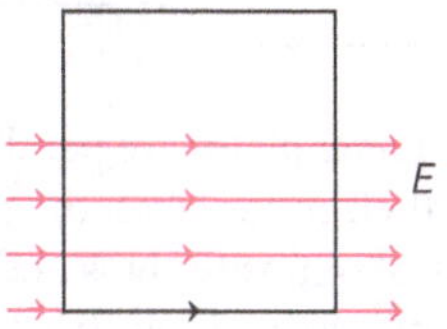

26. Two point charges q_1 and q_2 of $+10^{-8}$ C and -10^{-8} C, respectively are placed 0.1 m apart.

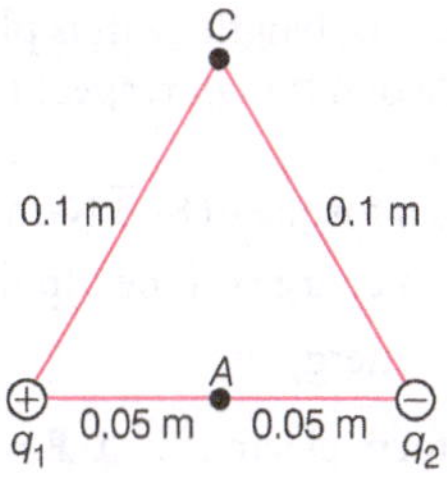

Then, find the magnitudes of electric fields at points A and C. **[3]**

27. Four point charges Q, q, Q and q are placed at the corners of a square of side a as shown in the figure. Find the resultant electric force on a charge Q.

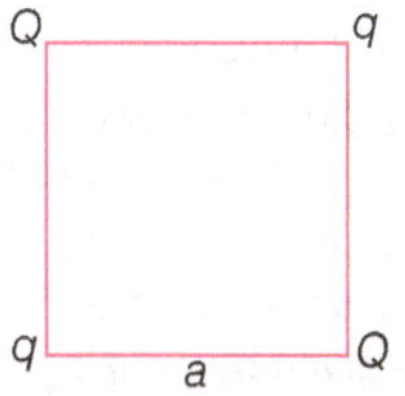

Long Answer Type Questions

28. (i) Three charges $-q, Q$ and $-q$ are placed at equal distances on a straight line. If the potential energy of the system of these charges is zero, then what is the ratio $Q:q$? **[2]**

(ii) (a) Obtain the expression for the electric field intensity due to a uniformly charged spherical shell of radius R at a point distant r from the centre of the shell outside it. **[2]**

(b) Draw a graph showing the variation of electric field intensity E with r, for $r > R$ and $r < R$ **CBSE 2023** **[1]**

29. (A) A spherical conducting shell of inner radius r_1 and outer radius r_2 has a charge Q. A charge q is placed at the centre of the shell.

(i) What is the surface charge density on the

(a) inner surface? **[1½]**

(b) outer surface of the shell? **[1½]**

(ii) Write the expression for the electric field at a point $r > r_2$ from the centre of the shell.

(B) Two large charged plane sheets of charge densities σ and -2σ C/m^2 are arranged vertically with a separation of d between them. Deduce expressions for the electric field at points (i) to the left of the first sheet, (ii) to the right of the second sheet and (iii) between the two sheets. **CBSE 2019** **[2]**

30. Total charge $-Q$ is uniformly spread along length of a ring of radius R. A small test charge $+q$ of mass m is kept at the centre of the ring and is given a gentle push along the axis of the ring.

(i) Show that the particle executes a simple harmonic oscillation. **[3]**

(ii) Obtain its time period. **[2]**

31. (i) A point charge is placed at the centre of spherical gaussian surface. How will the electric flux ϕ change, if

(a) the sphere is replaced by a cube of same or different volume? **[1]**

(b) a second charge is placed near and outside the original sphere? **[1]**

(c) the original charge is replaced by an electric dipole? **[1]**

(ii) Two point charges $q_A = 3\mu$C and $q_B = -3\mu$C are located 20 cm apart in vacuum. What is the electric field and its direction at the mid-point O of the line AB joining the two charges? **[2]**

32. (i) State Gauss' law. Using this law, obtain the expression for the electric field due to an infinitely long straight conductor of linear charge density λ. **[3]**

(ii) A wire AB of length L has linear charge density $\lambda = kx$, where x is measured from the end A of the wire. This wire is enclosed by a Gaussian hollow surface.

Find an expression for the electric flux through this surface. **[2]**

33. Two charges $-q$ each are fixed separated by distance $2d$. A third charge q of mass m placed at the mid-point is displaced slightly by $x(x << d)$ perpendicular to the line joining the two fixed charged as shown in figure.

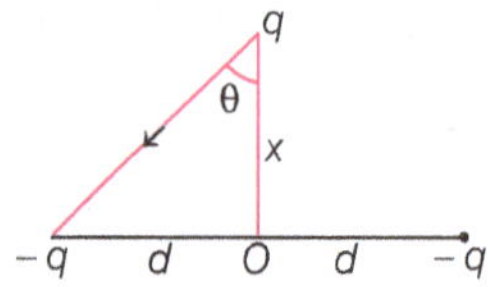

Show that q will perform simple harmonic oscillation of time period.

$$T = \left[\frac{8\pi^3 \varepsilon_0 m d^3}{q^2}\right]^{1/2}$$

34. (i) Use Gauss' law to obtain an expression for the electric field due to an infinitely long thin straight wire with uniform linear charge density λ. **[2]**

(ii) An infinitely long positively charged straight wire has a linear charge density λ. An electron is revolving in a circle with a constant speed v such that the wire passes through the centre, and is perpendicular to the plane of the circle. Find the kinetic energy of the electron in terms of magnitudes of its charge and linear charge density λ on the wire. **[2]**

(iii) Draw a graph of kinetic energy as a function of linear charge density λ. **CBSE 2023** **[1]**

35. (i) What is difference between an open surface and a closed surface? Draw elementary surface vector $d\mathbf{S}$ for a spherical surface **S**. **[2]**

(ii) Define electric flux through a surface. Give the significance of a Gaussian surface. A charge outside a Gaussian surface does not contribute to total electric flux through the surface. Why? **[1½]**

(iii) A small spherical shell S_1 has point charges $q_1 = -3\ \mu C$, $q_2 = -2\ \mu C$ and $q_3 = 9\ \mu C$ inside it. This shell is enclosed by another big spherical shell S_2. A point charge Q is placed in between the two surfaces S_1 and S_2. If the electric flux through the surface S_2 is four times the flux through surface S_1 find charge Q. **CBSE 2025** **[1½]**

Numerical Problems

36. (i) Two insulated charged copper spheres A and B have their centres separated by a distance of 50 cm. What is the mutual force of electrostatic repulsion, if the charge on each is 6.5×10^{-7} C and the radii of A and B are negligible compared to the distance of separation? **[1½]**

(ii) What is the force of repulsion, if each sphere is charged double the above amount and the distance between them is halved? **NCERT** **[1½]**

37. In the figure given below, the electric field lines on the left have twice the separation of those on the right.

(i) If the magnitude of the field of A is 40 N / C, then what force acts on a proton at A? **[1½]**

(ii) What is the magnitude of the field at B? **[1½]**

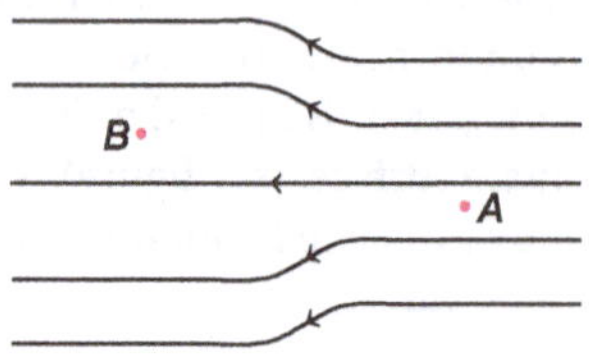

38. Two large, thin metal plates are parallel and close to each other. On their inner faces, the plates have surface charge densities of opposite signs and of magnitude 17.0×10^{-22} C / m^2. What is electric field intensity E

(i) in the outer region of the first plate, and **[1½]**

(ii) between the plates? **CBSE 2023** **[1½]**

39. An electric dipole of length 2 cm is placed with its axis making an angle of 60° with respect to uniform electric field of 10^5 N/C.

If it experiences a torque of $8\sqrt{3}$ N-m, calculate the

(i) magnitude of charge on the dipole and **[1½]**

(ii) its potential energy. **[1½]**

40. Consider a uniform electric field $\mathbf{E} = 3 \times 10^3\ \hat{\mathbf{i}}$ N/C.

(i) What is the flux of this field through a square of 10 cm on a side whose plane is parallel to the YZ-plane? **[1½]**

(ii) What is the flux through the same square, if the normal to its plane makes an angle 60° with the X-axis? **NCERT** **[1½]**

41. A point charge of 2.0 μC is at the centre of a cubic Gaussian surface 9.0 cm on edge. What is the net electric flux through the surface? Electric flux linked with a surface can be calculated using Gauss' theorem according to which total electric flux linked with a closed surface is given by $\phi = q/\varepsilon_0$.

42. A point charge causes an electric flux of -3.1×10^4 N-m^2/C to pass through a spherical Gaussian surface.

(i) Find the value of the point charge.

(ii) If the radius of the Gaussian surface is doubled, how much flux would pass through the surface?

43. (i) Using Gauss' law, show that the electric field $\mathbf{E}$ at a point due to a uniformly charged infinite plane sheet is given by $\mathbf{E} = \frac{\sigma}{2\varepsilon_0}\hat{\mathbf{n}}$, where symbols have their usual meanings. **[2]**

(ii) Electric field $\mathbf{E}$ in a region is given by $\mathbf{E} = (5x^2 + 2)\hat{\mathbf{i}}$, where E is in N/C and x is in metre.

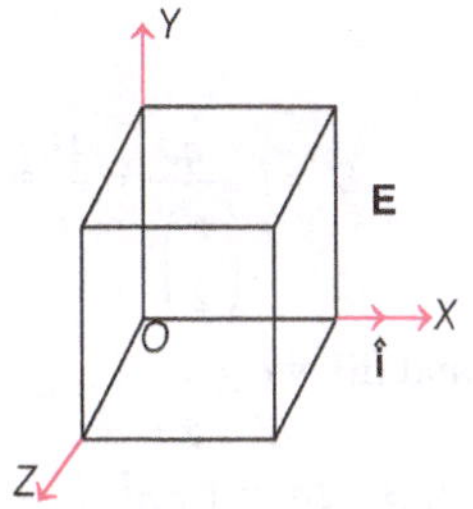

A cube of side 10 cm is placed in the region as shown in figure.

Calculate (a) the electric flux through cube and (b) the net charge enclosed by the cube. **CBSE 2024** **[3]**

44. Two point charges q_1 and q_2 of magnitude 10^{-7} C and -10^{-7} C, respectively are placed 0.2 m apart. Calculate the electric fields at points A, B and C as shown in the figure.

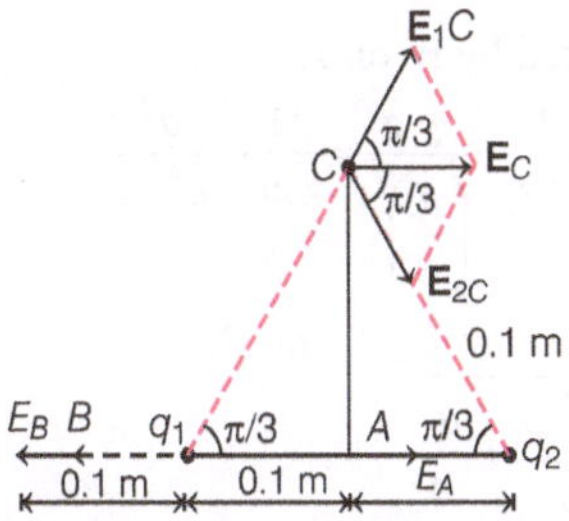

45. (i) Calculate the maximum torque experienced by a water molecule whose electric dipole moment is 6.2×10^{-30} C-m, when it is placed in an electric field of intensity 10^6 N / C. **[1½]**

(ii) Determine the work that must be done to take a water molecule aligned with the above field and set it anti-parallel to the field. **[1½]**

Hints & Solutions

Objective Type Questions

1. (*b*) Let the charge of ball B_3 is x, then according to conservation of charge,

$$-7\,\text{pC} + x + 4\,\text{pC} = -2\,\text{pC} \times 3$$
$$x - 3\,\text{pC} = -6\,\text{pC}$$
$$x = -3\,\text{pC}$$

2. (*d*) Electric field produced by charge particle at a distance of 3 m,

$$E = \frac{1}{4\pi\varepsilon_0} \cdot \frac{q}{3^2} \quad \text{...(i)}$$

Let x be the distance from point charge where electric field is $\frac{E}{4}$.

$$\therefore \quad \frac{E}{4} = \frac{1}{4\pi\varepsilon_0} \cdot \frac{q}{x^2} \quad \text{...(ii)}$$

Dividing Eq. (i) by Eq. (ii), we get

$$4 = \frac{x^2}{3^2}$$
$$x = 2 \times 3 = 6\,\text{m}$$

3. (*d*) Zero

Since, the sphere is hollow and conducting.
So, the charge will be distributed in such a way that there will be no electric field at the centre of point P.

4. (*a*)

5. (*d*)

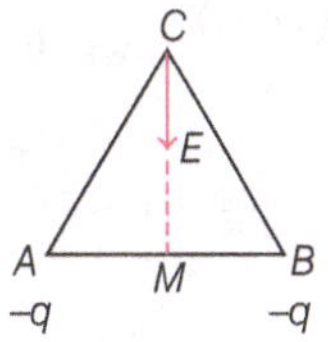

The net electric field E will be along CM.

6. (*b*) As the charge is at the centre of the cube, the flux through each face is same. By using Gauss' law,

$$6\phi = \frac{Q}{\varepsilon_0} \Rightarrow \phi = \frac{Q}{6\varepsilon_0}$$

7. (*b*) Electric field lines in the diagram are often represented in two dimensions for simplicity, even though electric fields are three dimensional in reality. Therefore, the incorrect qualitative impression given by the representation is the electric field distribution is two dimensional.

8. (*b*)

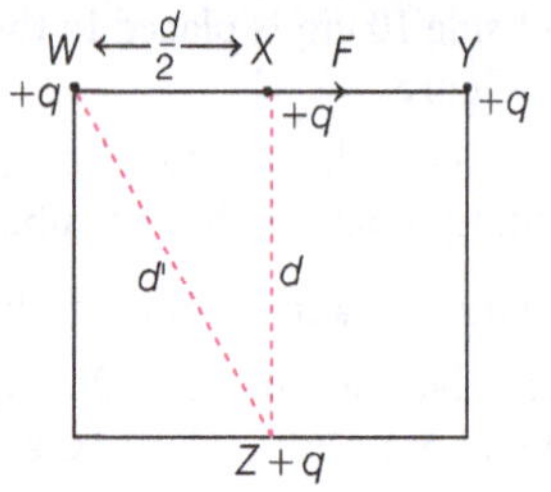

Force exerted by W on X,

$$F = \frac{1}{4\pi\varepsilon_0} \cdot \frac{q \cdot q}{\left(\frac{d}{2}\right)^2} = \frac{1}{4\pi\varepsilon_0} \frac{q^2}{d^2/4} \quad \text{... (i)}$$

Separation between W and Z,

$$d' = \sqrt{d^2 + \frac{d^2}{4}}$$

$$\Rightarrow \quad d' = \sqrt{\frac{5}{4}d^2}$$

Force exerted by W on Z,

$$F' = \frac{1}{4\pi\varepsilon_0} \cdot \frac{q \cdot q}{d'^2} = \frac{1}{4\pi\varepsilon_0} \frac{q^2}{\left(\sqrt{\frac{5}{4}d^2}\right)^2}$$

$$= \frac{1}{4\pi\varepsilon_0} \cdot \frac{q^2}{\frac{5}{4}d^2} = \frac{4}{5} \frac{1}{4\pi\varepsilon_0} \frac{q^2}{d^2}$$

$$= \frac{F}{5} \quad \left[\because F = \frac{4q^2}{4\pi\varepsilon_0 d^2}\right]$$

9. (c) The force on charge q_0 due to $-q$,

$$F_1 = K\frac{(-q)(q_0)}{a^2}, \text{ towards } +Y\text{-axis} \quad \text{... (i)}$$

Force on q_0 due to q,

$$F_2 = K\frac{(q)(q_0)}{a^2}, \text{ towards } -X\text{-axis} \quad \text{...(ii)}$$

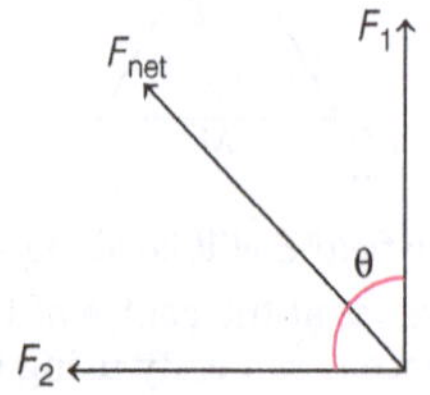

So, the resultant or net force on the charge at point O,

$$F_{\text{net}} = \sqrt{F_1^2 + F_2^2 + 2F_1F_2 \cos\theta}$$

Since, $F_1 = -F_2$

$$\therefore \quad F_{\text{net}} = \sqrt{F_2^2 + F_2^2 + 2(-F_2)(F_2)\cos 90^\circ} = \sqrt{2}F_2$$

$$= \frac{\sqrt{2}Kqq_0}{a^2}$$

10. (*a*) The amount of work done to rotate an electric dipole from an angle θ_1 to θ_2 is given by

$$W = pE(\cos\theta_1 - \cos\theta_2)$$

The dipole is rotated from the position of stable equilibrium, i.e. $\theta_1 = 0°$ to that of unstable equilibrium, i.e. $\theta_2 = 180°$

$\therefore$ Work done,

$$W = pE(\cos 0° - \cos 180°)$$

$$W = pE[1 - (-1)] = pE(2)$$

$$\Rightarrow \quad W = 2pE$$

11. (*c*) The electric field due to a point charge $2q$ at a distance r,

$$E = k\frac{(2q)}{r^2} \quad \text{...(i)}$$

The electric field due to a uniformly charged thin spherical shell of charge q and of radius R at distance $\frac{r}{2}(r >> R)$,

$$E' = k\frac{q}{\left(\frac{r}{2}\right)^2} = \frac{4kq}{r^2} \quad \text{...(ii)}$$

From Eqs. (i) and (ii), we get

$$E' = 2E$$

12. (*d*) Given, $\sigma = 26.4 \times 10^{-12}\ \text{C/m}^2$

The electric field between the sheets is

$$E = \frac{\sigma}{\varepsilon_0} = \frac{26.4 \times 10^{-12}}{8.85 \times 10^{-12}} = 2.983 \approx 3\ \text{N/C}$$

13. (*c*) **14.** (*b*)

15. (*c*) **16.** (*a*)

17. (*b*) From given figure,

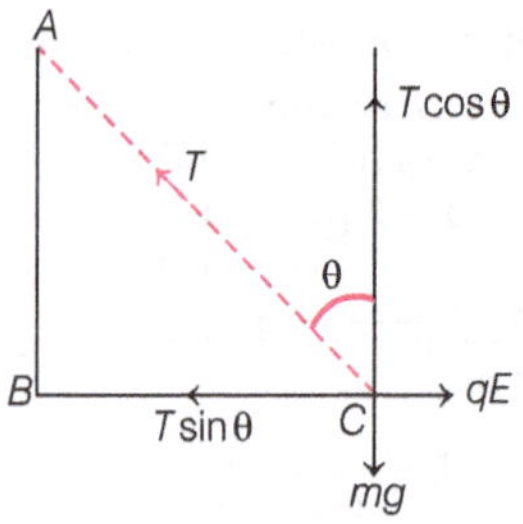

$$\cos\theta = mg \quad \text{... (i)}$$

$$T\sin\theta = qE \quad \text{... (ii)}$$

Dividing Eq. (ii) by Eq. (i),

$$qE = mg\tan\theta \Rightarrow q = \left(\frac{mg}{E}\right)\tan\theta$$

$$\tan\theta = \frac{F_e}{mg} \quad [\because F_e = qE]$$

$\because$ Direction of force and field is same.

Hence, the charge q is positive with magnitude $(mg/E)\tan\theta$.

18. (b)

19. (b) In the state of equilibrium, the potential on the surface of a large sphere = potential on the surface of a smaller sphere, $V = \frac{kq_1}{r_1} = \frac{kq_2}{r_2} \Rightarrow \frac{q_1}{q_2} = \frac{r_1}{r_2}$

Since, both spheres are very far from each other, the electric field on the surface of the both spheres will be

$$E_1 = \frac{kq_1}{r_1^2} \text{ and } E_2 = \frac{kq_2}{r_2^2}$$

The ratio of electric fields is $\frac{E_1}{E_2} = \frac{r_2}{r_1}$

20. (a) Area vector for the sheet, $\mathbf{A} = a^2\hat{\mathbf{k}}$

Electric field at $z = a$ is, $\mathbf{E} = c(a)^2\hat{\mathbf{k}}$

Electric flux through the sheet is

$$\phi = \mathbf{E} \cdot \mathbf{A} = c(a^2)\hat{\mathbf{k}} \cdot a^2\hat{\mathbf{k}} = a^4 c$$

21. (d) 22. (c)

23. (a) Given, $\theta = 30°$

$E = 2 \times 10^5$ N/C

$\tau = 8 \times 10^{-3}$ N-m

Dipole length, $2l = 2$ cm $= 2 \times 10^{-2}$ m

$\because \quad \tau = pE\sin\theta$

As, $\quad p = q \times 2l$

$$\therefore \quad q = \frac{\tau}{2lE\sin\theta} = \frac{8 \times 10^{-3}}{2 \times 10^{-2} \times 2 \times 10^5 \times \frac{1}{2}}$$

$$= \frac{8 \times 10^{-3} \times 2 \times 10^2}{2 \times 2 \times 10^5} = 4 \times 10^{-6} = 4\mu C$$

24. (b) 25. (a) 26. (b) 27. (a) 28. (a)

29. (d) 30. (a) 31. (a)

32. (d) A is false but R is true.
An electric dipole is placed in a uniform electric field and its equilibrium will be stable when the dipole is set along the direction of the electric field. When the dipole moment p is either parallel or anti-parallel to the electric field E, the angle θ between p and E is 0° or 180°. In both case, torque will be zero.

$$\tau = pE\sin\theta = pE\sin 0° \text{ or } pE\sin 180°$$

$$\tau = 0$$

33. (b) 34. (b) 35. (a)

36. (i) (d) There are two plates A and B having surface charge densities $\sigma_A = 17.0 \times 10^{-22}$ C/m² on A and $\sigma_B = -17.0 \times 10^{-22}$ C/m² on B, respectively.

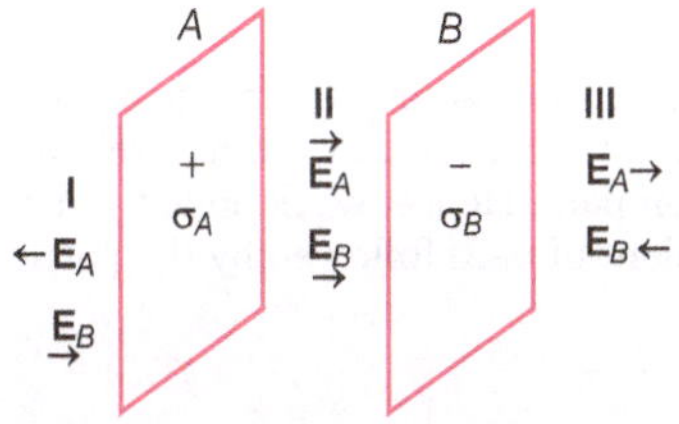

According to Gauss' theorem, if the plates have same surface charge density but having opposite signs, then the electric field in region I is zero.

$$\mathbf{E}_{\text{I}} = \mathbf{E}_A + \mathbf{E}_B = \frac{\sigma}{2\varepsilon_0} + \left(-\frac{\sigma}{2\varepsilon_0}\right) = 0$$

(ii) (d) The electric field in region III is also zero.

$$\mathbf{E}_{\text{III}} = \mathbf{E}_A + \mathbf{E}_B$$

$$= \frac{\sigma}{2\varepsilon_0} + \left(-\frac{\sigma}{2\varepsilon_0}\right) = 0$$

(iii) (c) In region II, the electric field

$$\mathbf{E}_{\text{II}} = \mathbf{E}_A - \mathbf{E}_B = \frac{\sigma}{2\varepsilon_0} + \frac{\sigma}{2\varepsilon_0}$$

$$= \frac{\sigma}{\varepsilon_0} = \frac{\sigma_A \text{ or } \sigma_B}{\varepsilon_0} = \frac{17.0 \times 10^{-22}}{8.85 \times 10^{-12}}$$

$$E = 1.92 \times 10^{-10} \text{ NC}^{-1}$$

(iv) (c) Since, electric field due to an infinite plane sheet of charge does not depend on the distance of observation point from the plane sheet of charge, so for the given distances, the ratio of **E** will be 1 : 1.

(v) (b) In order to estimate the electric field due to a thin finite plane metal plate, we take a cylindrical cross-sectional area A and length $2r$ as the gaussian surface.

37. (i) (a) Electric field at $r = R$

$$E = \frac{KQ}{R^2}; Q = \text{Total charge within the nucleus} = Ze$$

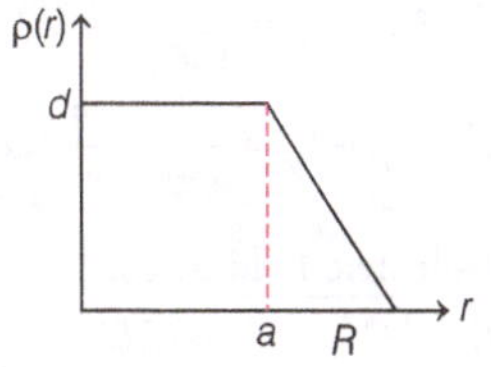

So, $\quad E = \frac{KZe}{R^2}$

So, electric field is independent of a.

(ii) (a) Net charge, $Q = \int \rho_r (4\pi r^2)\, dr$

(iii) (b) As, $\frac{d}{R} = \frac{\rho_r}{R - r}$

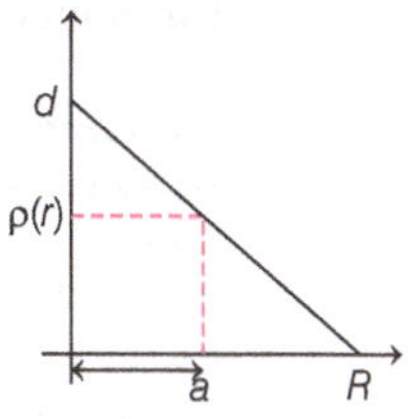

$$Q = \int_0^R \frac{d}{R}(R - r) 4\pi r^2 dr$$

$$= \frac{4\pi d}{R}\left(R\int_0^R r^2 dr - \int_0^R r^3 dr\right)$$

$$= \frac{4\pi d}{R}\left(\frac{R^4}{3} - \frac{R^4}{4}\right) = \frac{\pi d R^3}{3}$$

$$Q = Ze = \frac{\pi d R^3}{3}$$

$$\Rightarrow \quad d = \frac{3Ze}{\pi R^3}$$

(iv) (*d*) From the formula of uniformly (volume) charged sphere $E = \dfrac{\rho r}{3\varepsilon_0}$

$\Rightarrow E \propto r$, so correct graph is as shown.

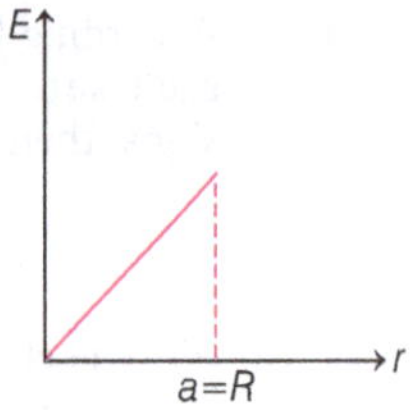

(v) (*c*) For $E \propto r, \rho$ should be constant throughout the nucleus. This will be possible only when $a = R$.

38. (i)

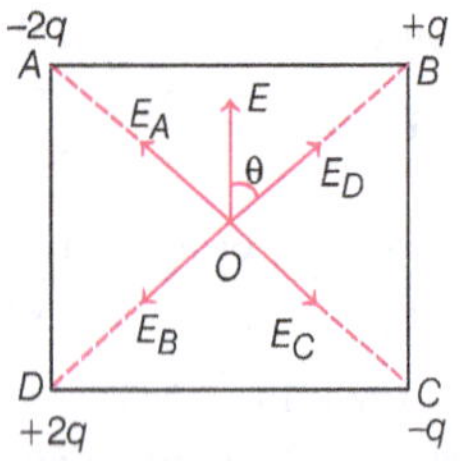

The side of square is a.

Let $OA = OC = OB = OD = r$, then

$$(2r)^2 = a^2 + a^2 \text{ or } r = \frac{a}{\sqrt{2}}$$

Consider a unit charge placed at O, then

$$E_A = E_D = \frac{1}{4\pi\varepsilon_0} \cdot \frac{2q}{r^2}$$

$$E_B = E_C = \frac{1}{4\pi\varepsilon_0} \cdot \frac{q}{r^2}$$

$$E' = E_A - E_C = \frac{1}{4\pi\varepsilon_0} \cdot \frac{q}{r^2} (O \to A)$$

$$E'' = E_D - E_B = \frac{1}{4\pi\varepsilon_0} \cdot \frac{q}{r^2} (O \to B)$$

Resultant electric field at O,

$$E = \sqrt{E'^2 + E''^2} = \sqrt{2}E'$$

$$= \frac{1}{4\pi\varepsilon_0} \cdot \frac{\sqrt{2}q}{r^2} = \frac{1}{4\pi\varepsilon_0} \cdot \frac{\sqrt{2}q}{a^2/2}$$

$$= \frac{1}{4\pi\varepsilon_0} \cdot \frac{2\sqrt{2}q}{a^2}$$

Direction of field, $\theta = \tan^{-1}\left(\dfrac{E''}{E'}\right) = \tan^{-1}(1) = 45°$

(ii) The electric fields find the atoms to be neutral entities. As it is known that, electrostatic fields are caused by excess charges. However, there is no excess charge on the inner surface of an isolated conductor. Therefore, electrostatic field inside a conductor is zero.

(iii) The electric force on the particle will always act in the direction of a line of force. Hence, if the particle is initially at rest, then it will be accelerated along the line of force. But if it enters with accelerated motion at an angle with the direction of the field, then its path will not be along the line of force.

(iv) Here, the hollow cylinder is positively charged.

We know that the electric field lines appear to come out from the conductor. Thus, the field lines for a uniformly positive charged hollow cylinder is shown in the figure.

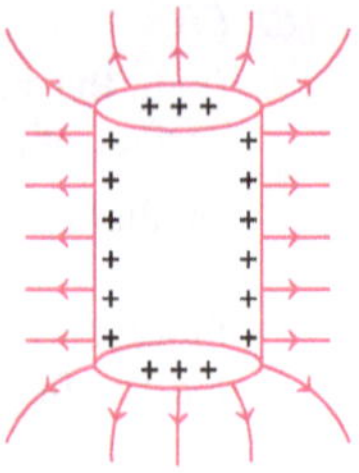

Subjective Questions

1. (i) Silk cloth will also acquire a charge 1.6×10^{-13} C. However, it will be negative in nature.

(ii) Yes, it changes as the distance becomes less.

2. According to the question, both the balls have same charge q. Let the balls are separated by a distance r. Hence, according to Coulomb's law, if F and F' are the force of attraction between balls in air and in medium respectively.

Then, $$F = \frac{1}{4\pi\varepsilon_0} \frac{q^2}{r^2}$$

In medium, $$F' = \frac{1}{4\pi K\varepsilon_0} \frac{q^2}{r^2}$$

$$\therefore \quad F' = F/K$$

where, K is dielectric constant of material and $K > 1$ for insulators, hence the force is reduced, when a plastic sheet is inserted.

3. The protons and electrons are bound into an atom with distinct and independent existence and neutral in charge. Electrostatic fields are caused by the presence of excess charges.

But there can be no excess charge inside an isolated conductor. So, the electrostatic fields inside a conductor is zero despite the fact that the dimensions of an atom are of the order of an angstrom.

4.

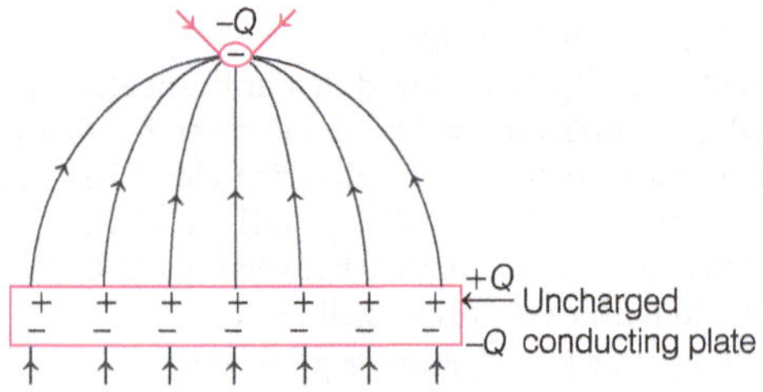

5.

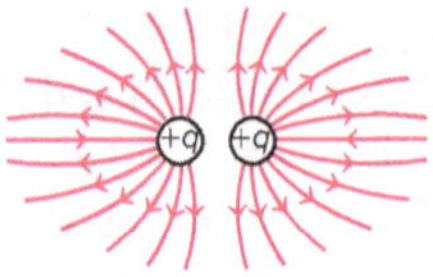

6. It is because force acting on charge particle in an electric field is conservative in nature which does not depend on path. Hence, work done by electric force is independent of path followed by the particle.

7. Electric field at O due to 3 μC,

$$\mathbf{E}_1 = \frac{kq_1}{r_1^2}(-\hat{\mathbf{i}})$$

$$\mathbf{E}_1 = \frac{9 \times 10^9 \times 3 \times 10^{-6}}{(0.3)^2}(-\hat{\mathbf{i}})$$

$$\mathbf{E}_1 = 3 \times 10^5 (-\hat{\mathbf{i}})\,\text{NC}^{-1}$$

Electric field at O due to 4 μC,

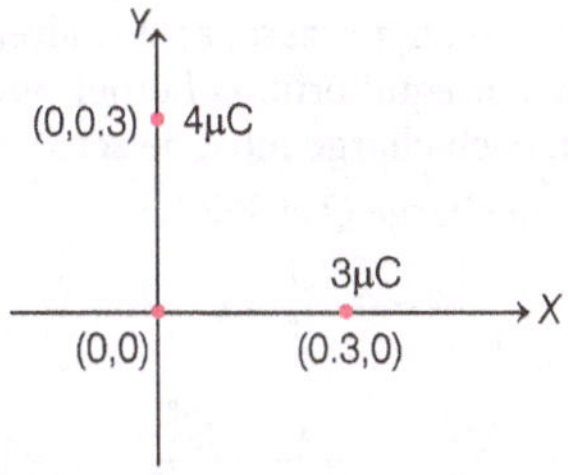

$$\mathbf{E}_2 = \frac{kq_2}{r_2^2}(-\hat{\mathbf{j}})$$

$$\mathbf{E}_2 = \frac{9 \times 10^9 \times 4 \times 10^{-6}}{(0.3)^2}(-\hat{\mathbf{j}})$$

$$\mathbf{E}_2 = 4 \times 10^5 (-\hat{\mathbf{j}})\,\text{NC}^{-1}$$

Net electric field, $\mathbf{E} = \mathbf{E}_1 + \mathbf{E}_2$

and $$E = \sqrt{E_1^2 + E_2^2}$$

$$E = 5 \times 10^5\,\text{NC}^{-1}$$

and for direction, $\tan\theta = \frac{4}{3}$

$$\theta = \tan^{-1}\left(\frac{4}{3}\right)$$

Inclination with respect to the X-axis (in III quadrant).

8. Electric flux through a surface in an electric field is defined as the total number of electric lines of force crossing the surface in a direction normal to the surface. Its SI unit is $\text{N-m}^2\text{C}^{-1}$

9. (i) An electrostatic field line represents the actual path travelled by a unit positive charge in an electric field. If the line have sudden breaks it means the unit positive test charge jumps from one place to another which is not possible. It also means that electric field becomes zero suddenly at the breaks which is not possible. So, the field line cannot have any sudden breaks.

(ii) If two field lines cross each other, then we can draw two tangents at the point of intersection which indicates that (as tangent drawn at any point on electric line of force gives the direction of electric field at that point) there are two directions of electric field at a particular point, which is not possible at the same instant. Thus, two field lines never cross each other at any point.

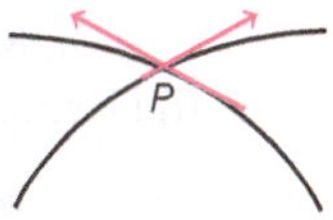

10. (i) The flux of electric field through any closed surface is $\frac{1}{\varepsilon_0}$ times the total charge enclosed by the closed surface.

i.e., $\phi_E = \frac{q}{\varepsilon_0}$

(ii) 90° or $\frac{\pi}{2}$.

11. (i) The electric charge of a body is quantised means that the charge on a body can occur in some particular values only. Charge on any body is the integral multiple of charge on an electron because the charge of an electron is the elementary charge in nature. The charge on any body can be expressed by the formula, $q = \pm ne$

where, n= number of electrons transferred

and e = charge on one electron.

The cause of quantisation is that only integral number of electrons can be transferred from one body to other.

(ii) We can ignore the quantisation of electric charge when dealing with macroscopic charges because the charge on one electron is 1.6×10^{-19}C in magnitude, which is very small as compared to the large scale charges.

12. A point charge +10μC is at a dsitance 5 cm above the centre of a square of side 10 cm is shown below.

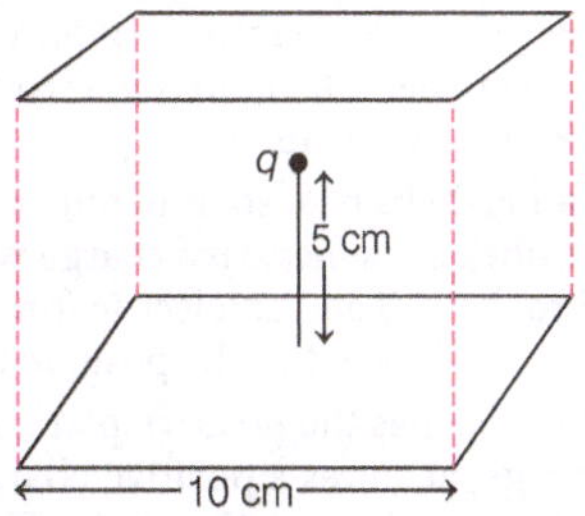

Given, $q = 10\mu\text{C} = 10 \times 10^{-6}$ C

According to Gauss' theorem, the total flux enclosed,

$$\phi = \frac{q}{\varepsilon_0} \quad \text{... (i)}$$

The flux enclosed by one face of square is 1/6 of total flux (because the cube has six square shaped faces).

The flux linked with each face,

$$\phi' = \frac{\phi}{6} = \frac{1}{6}\cdot\frac{q}{\varepsilon_0} \quad \text{[From Eq. (i)]}$$

$$\phi' = \frac{1}{6} \times \frac{10 \times 10^{-6}}{8.854 \times 10^{-12}}$$

$$= 1.88 \times 10^5\,\text{N-m}^2\text{C}^{-1}$$

Thus, the flux linked with the square is $1.88 \times 10^5\,\text{N-m}^2\text{C}^{-1}$.

13. This statement can be proved by taking comparison of electric and magnetic forces between two protons.

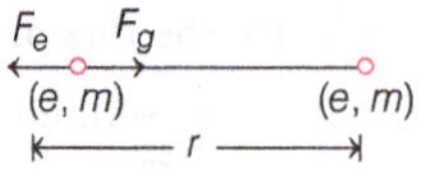

Let the two protons having charge $+e$ and mass m be placed at a distance r from each other as shown in figure.

$$\therefore \quad F_e = \frac{1}{4\pi\varepsilon_0}\frac{q_1 q_2}{r^2} \quad \text{[Coulomb's law]}$$

$$= \frac{1}{4\pi\,\varepsilon_0}\frac{e \times e}{r^2}$$

$$\Rightarrow \quad F_g = G\frac{m_1 m_2}{r^2} \text{ (gravitation law)} = G\frac{m \times m}{r^2}$$

where, F_e and F_g are electric and gravitational force respectively. On putting the values, we get

$$\frac{F_e}{F_g} = \frac{\frac{1}{4\pi\varepsilon_0}\frac{e^2}{r^2}}{\frac{Gm^2}{r^2}} = \frac{1}{4\pi\varepsilon_0}\frac{e^2}{m^2}\cdot\frac{1}{G}$$

$$= \frac{(9\times10^9)(1.6\times10^{-19})^2}{(1.67\times10^{-27})^2} \times \frac{1}{(6.67\times10^{-11})}$$

$$= 1.2\times10^{36} \simeq 10^{36}$$

$$\Rightarrow \quad F_e >> F_g$$

Hence, the electrostatic force is much stronger than the gravitational force.

14. The two charged plates create a region with a uniform electric field between them, directed from the positive towards the negative plate.

Once the ball is disturbed, so as to touch one plate (say, the negative one), some negative charge will be transferred to the ball and an electric force will act on the ball, that will accelerate it to the positive plate.

Once the ball touches the positive plate, it releases its negative charge, acquires a positive charge and accelerates back to the negative plate. The metallic ball continues to move back and forth between the plates until it has transferred all their net charges, thereby making both the plates neutral.

15. According to Coulomb's law, the magnitude of force acting between two stationary point charges is given by

$$F = \left(\frac{q_1 q_2}{4\pi\varepsilon_0}\right)\left(\frac{1}{r^2}\right)$$

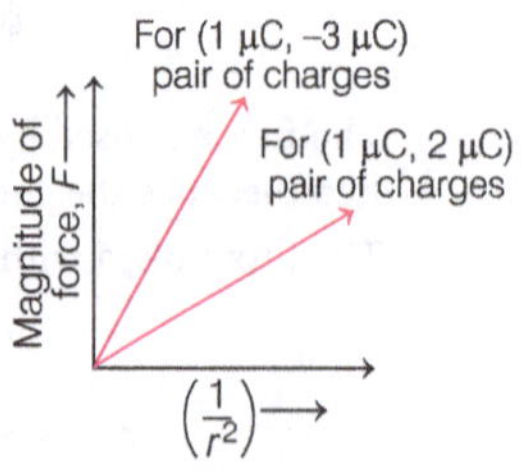

For given $q_1 q_2$, $F \propto \left(\frac{1}{r^2}\right)$

The slope of $F - \frac{1}{r^2}$, graph depends on q_1 and q_2.

Magnitude of $q_1 q_2$ is higher for second pair.

$\therefore$ Slope of $F - \frac{1}{r^2}$ graph, corresponding to second pair $(1\,\mu\text{C}, -3\,\mu\text{C})$ is greater. Higher the magnitude of product of charges q_1 and q_2, higher will be the slope.

16. Suppose the three charges be placed as shown in the figure.

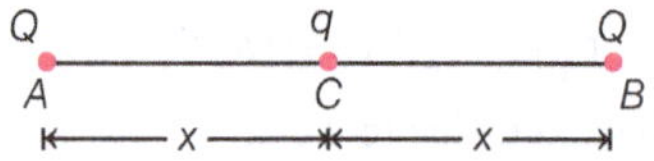

As the net force on q is zero, so it is already in equilibrium. For equilibrium of other two charges, the net force on each charge must be zero.

Total force on charge Q at B is

$$\frac{1}{4\pi\varepsilon_0}\cdot\frac{Qq}{x^2} + \frac{1}{4\pi\varepsilon_0}\cdot\frac{Q\cdot Q}{(2x)^2} = 0$$

$$\Rightarrow \quad \frac{1}{4\pi\varepsilon_0}\cdot\frac{Qq}{x^2} = -\frac{1}{4\pi\varepsilon_0}\cdot\frac{Q^2}{4x^2}$$

$$\therefore \quad q = -\frac{Q}{4}$$

17. (i) For a resultant force at the location of q_3 to be zero, the net electrostatic force on q_3 due to q_1 and q_2 has to be zero.

Since, q_3 is positive, it will be under the effect of repulsive force by both q_1 and q_2 as represented by F_{13} and F_{23}.

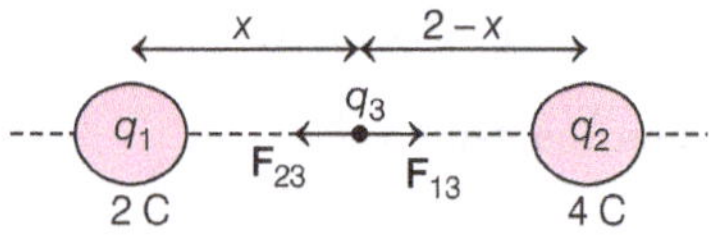

i.e., $F_{13} = F_{23}$

$$\frac{kq_1 q_3}{x^2} = \frac{kq_2 q_3}{(2-x)^2}$$

Substituting values of $q_1 = 2$ C, $q_2 = 4$ C, we get

$$(2-x)^2 = 2x^2$$

$$\therefore \quad x = \frac{2}{\sqrt{2}+1} = 0.83 \text{ m}$$

So, q_3 placed at 0.83 m away from q_1 along the straight line joining q_1 and q_2 experiences a zero resultant force.

(ii) Yes, the negative charge at the location of q_3 will still experience zero resultant force. The forces on the negative charge due to q_1 and q_2 will get reversed.

18. (i) Electric flux through a Gaussian surface,

$$\phi = \frac{\text{Total enclosed charge}}{\varepsilon_0}$$

Net charge enclosed inside the shell, $q = Q/2$

$\therefore$ Electric flux through the shell, $\phi = \frac{q}{\varepsilon_0} = \frac{Q}{2\varepsilon_0}$

(ii) **Gauss' Law** Electric flux through a Gaussian surface is $\frac{1}{\varepsilon_0}$ times the net charge enclosed within it.

Mathematically, $\oint \mathbf{E} \cdot d\mathbf{S} = \frac{1}{\varepsilon_0} \times q$

(iii) We know that, electric field or net charge inside the spherical conducting shell is zero. Hence, the force at centre C of the shell on charge $\frac{Q}{2}$ is zero.

Force on charge at A,

$$F_A = \frac{1}{4\pi\varepsilon_0} \frac{2Q\left(Q + \frac{Q}{2}\right)}{x^2} = \frac{1}{4\pi\varepsilon_0} \frac{3Q^2}{x^2}$$

19. (i) If $r' = \frac{r}{2}$

Then, $E'_{eq} = \frac{kp}{(r')^3} = \frac{kp}{\left(\frac{r}{2}\right)^3} = \frac{8kp}{r^3} = 8E_{eq}$

Hence, electric field at new position at equatorial line becomes 8 times of its initial value.

(ii) Here, $AB = BC = CD = AD = \sqrt{2}$ m and

$q_A = q_D = +q$, $q_B = q_C = -q$

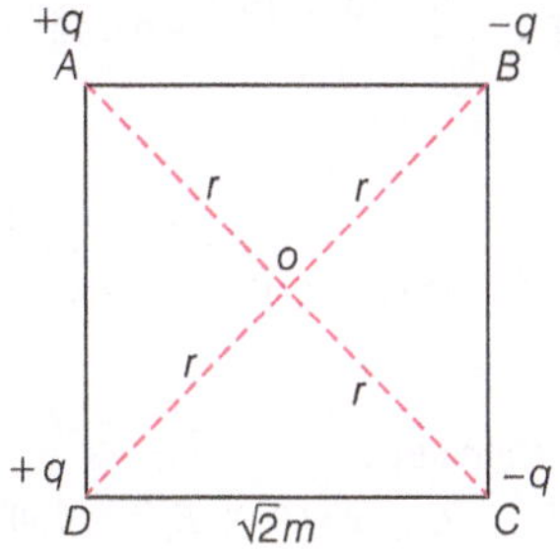

Electric field due to A and C at O,

$$E_1 = E_A + E_C = \frac{kq}{r^2} + \frac{kq}{r^2}$$

$$= \frac{kq}{(1)^2} + \frac{kq}{(1)^2} = 2kq \text{ NC}^{-1}$$

$$\left[r = \sqrt{2} \sin 45° = \frac{\sqrt{2}}{\sqrt{2}} = 1 \text{ m}\right]$$

Again, electric field due to D and B,

$$E_2 = E_D + E_B = \frac{kq}{(r)^2} + \frac{kq}{(r)^2}$$

$$= \frac{kq}{(1)^2} + \frac{kq}{(1)^2} = 2kq \text{ NC}^{-1}.$$

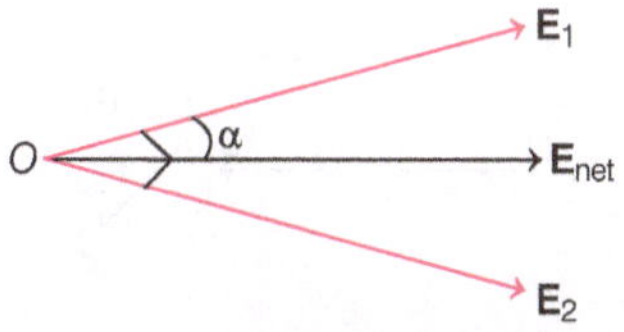

So, $E_{net} = \sqrt{E_1^2 + E_2^2} = \sqrt{(2kq)^2 + (2kq)^2}$

$= 2\sqrt{2}\, kq \text{ NC}^{-1}$

For direction, $\alpha = \tan^{-1}\left(\frac{2\,kq}{2\,kq}\right) = \tan^{-1}(1) = 45°$

So, E_{net} is along 45° from E_1 or E_2.

20. Two charged conducting spheres are connected to a wire, then their potential on the surfaces are same.

i.e., $V_1 = V_2$

$$\frac{kq_a}{a} = \frac{kq_b}{b} \Rightarrow \frac{q_a}{q_b} = \frac{a}{b} \qquad \left[\text{Since, } V = \frac{kq}{r}\right]$$

Also, we know, $E = \frac{kq}{r^2}$ (for point charge)

then, $E_a = \frac{kq_a}{a^2}$, and $E_b = \frac{kq_b}{b^2}$

Ratio, $$\frac{E_a}{E_b} = \frac{\frac{kq_a}{a^2}}{\frac{kq_b}{b^2}} = \frac{b^2}{a^2} \times \frac{q_a}{q_b} = \frac{b}{a}$$

21. The x-components of E_1 and E_2, due to two equidistant points on either side of O, cancel each other.

The resultant electric field is due to the superposition of the y-components of E_1 and E_2.

The direction of the net electric field is along the negative Y-axis.

This is true for all pairs of equidistant points on either side of O.

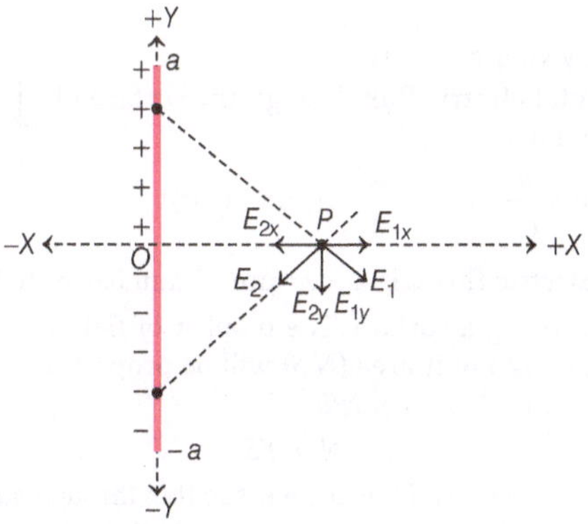

22. Refer to text on page 12.

23. (i) Surface charge density on inner surface,

$\sigma_1 = \frac{q}{4\pi r^2}$ and that on the outer surface,

$$\sigma_2 = \frac{q}{4\pi(2r)^2} = \frac{q}{16\pi r^2} \Rightarrow \frac{\sigma_1}{\sigma_2} = \frac{4}{1}$$

$\therefore \quad \sigma_1 : \sigma_2 = 4 : 1$

(ii) Since, surface D encloses negative charge, hence it has least flux, which is negative in nature.

In parts C, there is zero net charge, hence flux is zero. Surface B has a net charge as $+q$ hence its flux is more than C but less than surface A.

Surface A has most flux, which is positive in nature, since it consists positive charge, i.e. $+2q$.

24. Electric field at A $(\mathbf{E}_A)$,

$$\mathbf{E}_A = \mathbf{E}_1 + \mathbf{E}_2 = \frac{\sigma}{2\varepsilon_0}(-\hat{\mathbf{i}}) + \frac{3\sigma}{2\varepsilon_0}(\hat{\mathbf{i}})$$

$$\mathbf{E}_A = \frac{\sigma}{\varepsilon_0}\hat{\mathbf{i}}$$

Electric field at B $(\mathbf{E}_B)$,

$$\mathbf{E}_B = \mathbf{E}_1 + \mathbf{E}_2 = \frac{\sigma}{2\varepsilon_0}\hat{\mathbf{i}} + \frac{3\sigma}{2\varepsilon_0}\hat{\mathbf{i}}$$

$$\mathbf{E}_B = \frac{2\sigma}{\varepsilon_0}\hat{\mathbf{i}}$$

Electric field at C $(\mathbf{E}_C)$,

$$\mathbf{E}_C = \mathbf{E}_1 + \mathbf{E}_2 = \frac{\sigma}{2\varepsilon_0}\hat{\mathbf{i}} + \frac{3\sigma}{2\varepsilon_0}(-\hat{\mathbf{i}})$$

$$\mathbf{E}_C = \frac{\sigma}{\varepsilon_0}(-\hat{\mathbf{i}})$$

25. (i) Let q charge be enclosed by the cylindrical surface.

$\therefore$ Linear charge density, $\lambda = \frac{q}{l}$

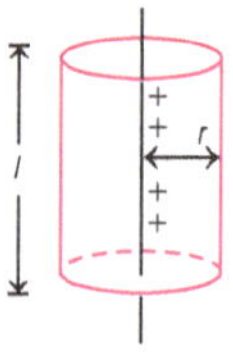

$\Rightarrow \quad q = \lambda l \quad$ ...(i)

By Gauss' theorem,

total electric flux through the surface of cylinder,

$$\phi = \frac{q}{\varepsilon_0} \quad \therefore \quad \phi = \frac{\lambda l}{\varepsilon_0} \quad \text{[from Eq. (i)]}$$

(ii) Electric flux ϕ is a measure of number of field lines crossing a surface. The number of field lines passing through unit area (N/S) will be proportional to the electric field, i.e. $N/S \propto E$

$\Rightarrow \quad N \propto ES$

The quantity ES is the electric flux through surface S. As in the given question, the field lines that enter the closed surface leave the surface immediately, so the net electric flux is bound to the system. Thus, electric flux is zero.

26. Electric field at A,

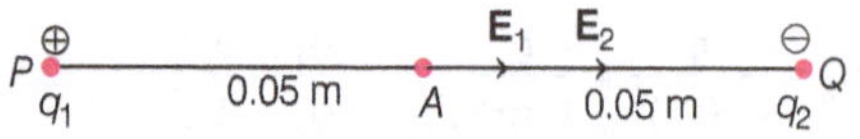

due to q_1

$$E_1 = \frac{1}{4\pi\varepsilon_0}\frac{q}{(PA)^2}$$

$$E_1 = \frac{9 \times 10^9 \times 10^{-8}}{(0.05)^2} = 36000 \text{ N/C}$$

due to q_2

$$E_2 = \frac{1}{4\pi\varepsilon_0}\frac{q_2}{(AQ)^2}$$

$$E_2 = \frac{9 \times 10^9 \times 10^{-8}}{(0.05)^2}$$

$$E_2 = 36000 \text{ N/C}$$

Net electric field on A,

$$(E_{\text{net}})_A = (36000 + 36000) \text{ N/C}$$

$$(E_{\text{net}})_A = 72000 \text{ N/C}$$

Electric field at C due to q_1,

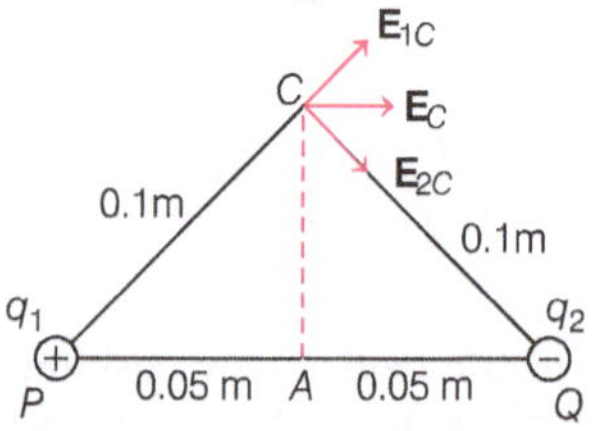

$$E_{C_1} = \frac{1}{4\pi\varepsilon_0}\frac{q}{(PC)^2}$$

$$E_{C_1} = \frac{9 \times 10^9 \times 10^{-8}}{(0.1)^2} = 9 \times 10^3 \text{ N/C}$$

due to q_2,

$$E_{C_2} = \frac{1}{4\pi\varepsilon_0}\frac{q}{(CQ)^2} = \frac{9 \times 10^9 \times 10^{-8}}{(0.1)^2}$$

$$E_{C_2} = 9 \times 10^3$$

Net electric field at C,

$$E_C = E_{C_1}\cos 60^\circ + E_{C_2}\cos 60^\circ$$

$$E_C = 9 \times 10^3 \times \frac{1}{2} + 9 \times 10^3 \times \frac{1}{2}$$

$$E_C = 9 \times 10^3 \text{ N/C}$$

27. Let us find the force on the charge Q at the point C.

Force due to the other charge Q,

$$F_1 = \frac{1}{4\pi\varepsilon_0}\frac{Q^2}{(a\sqrt{2})^2} = \frac{1}{4\pi\varepsilon_0}\left(\frac{Q^2}{2a^2}\right) \text{(along } AC\text{)}$$

Force due to the charge q (at B),

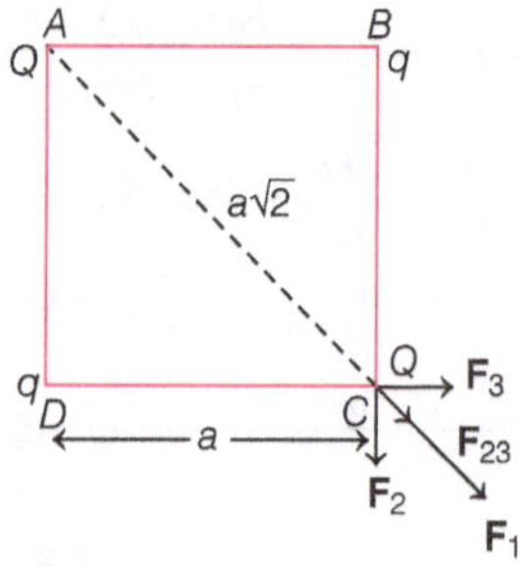

$$F_2 = \frac{1}{4\pi\varepsilon_0}\frac{qQ}{a^2} \text{ (along } BC)$$

Force due to the charge q (at D),

$$F_3 = \frac{1}{4\pi\varepsilon_0}\frac{qQ}{a^2} \text{ (along } DC)$$

Resultant of these two equal forces,

$$F_{23} = \frac{1}{4\pi\varepsilon_0}\frac{qQ(\sqrt{2})}{a^2} \text{ (along } AC)$$

∴Net force on charge Q (at point C),

$$F = F_1 + F_{23} = \frac{1}{4\pi\varepsilon_0}\frac{Q}{a^2}\left[\frac{Q}{2} + \sqrt{2}q\right]$$

This force is directed along AC. (For the charge Q, at the point A, the force will have the same magnitude but will be directed along CA).

28. (i) The potential energy between the charged particles is given as $U = K\frac{Q_1Q_2}{d}$, where $K = \frac{1}{4\pi\varepsilon_0}$

The following figure depicts the pictorial representation of the placement of the charged particles.

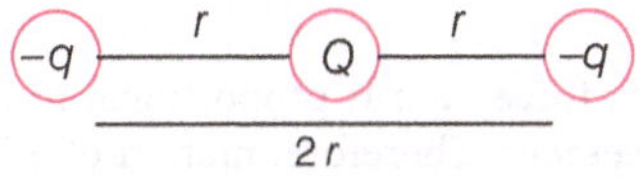

Net U = (Potential energy due to $-q$ and Q)+ (Potential energy due to Q and $-q$)+ (Potential energy due to $-q$ and $-q$)

$$U_{net} = K\left(\frac{-qQ}{r}\right) + K\left(\frac{-qQ}{r}\right) + K\left(\frac{(-q)^2}{2r}\right)$$

According to the question, the net potential energy of the combination is zero. So, $U_{net} = 0$

$$\Rightarrow K\left(\frac{-qQ}{r}\right) + K\left(\frac{-qQ}{r}\right) + K\left(\frac{(-q)^2}{2r}\right) = 0$$

$$\Rightarrow \frac{Kq}{r}\left(-Q - Q + \frac{q}{2}\right) = 0$$

$$\Rightarrow -2Q + \frac{q}{2} = 0 \Rightarrow -2Q = -\frac{q}{2}$$

$$\therefore \quad \frac{Q}{q} = \frac{1}{4}$$

(ii) (a) Electric field due to a uniformly charged thin spherical shell

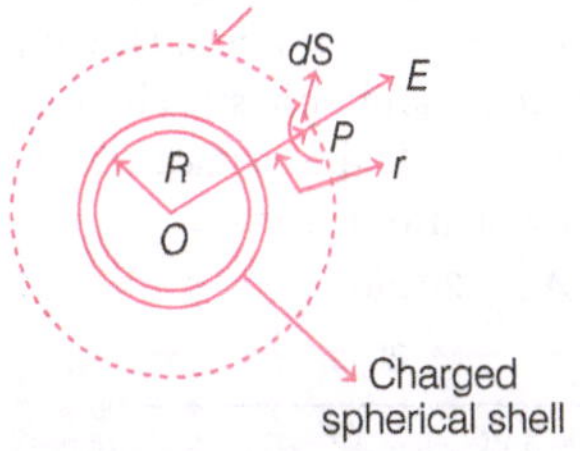

When point P lies outside the spherical shell

Suppose that we have to calculate the field at point P at a distance $r (r > R)$ from its centre. The Gaussian surface through point P so as to enclose the charged spherical shell. The gaussian surface is a spherical surface of radius r and centre O.

Let $\mathbf{E}$ be the electric field at point P, then the electric flux through the area element of area dS is given by $d\phi = \mathbf{E} \cdot d\mathbf{S}$

Since, dS is also along normal to the surface

$d\phi = E \cdot dS$

∴ Total electric flux through the Gaussian surface is given by $\phi = \oint EdS = E\oint dS$

Now, $\oint dS = 4\pi r^2$ ...(i)

$= E \times 4\pi r^2$

Since, the charge enclosed by the Gaussian surface is q, according to Gauss's theorem,

$$\phi = \frac{q}{\varepsilon_0} \quad \text{...(ii)}$$

From Eqs. (i) and (ii), we obtain

$$E \times 4\pi r^2 = \frac{q}{\varepsilon_0}$$

$$E = \frac{1}{4\pi\varepsilon_0} \cdot \frac{q}{r^2} \quad \text{(For } r > R)$$

For $r < R$

$q = 0 \qquad \phi = 0$

So, $E = 0 \quad (r < R)$

(b) The graph of electric field intensity E with r shows that $E = 0$ for $r < R$ and decreases as $\frac{1}{r^2}$ for $r > R$.

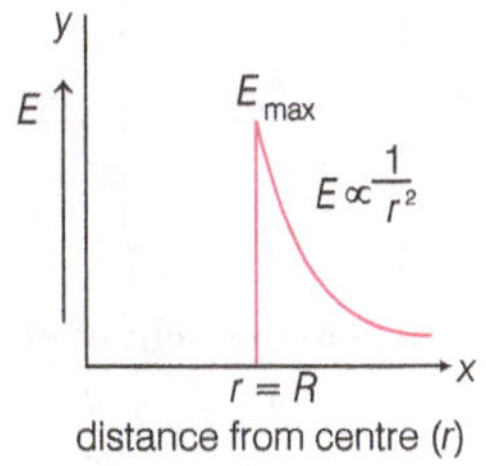

29. (A) (i) When a charge $-q$ is placed at the centre of the hollow conducting sphere, the charge induced on the inner surface is $+q$ and on outer surface is $-q$. But charge Q is already present on its outer surface. So, net charge on outer surface is $(Q - q)$ as shown below.

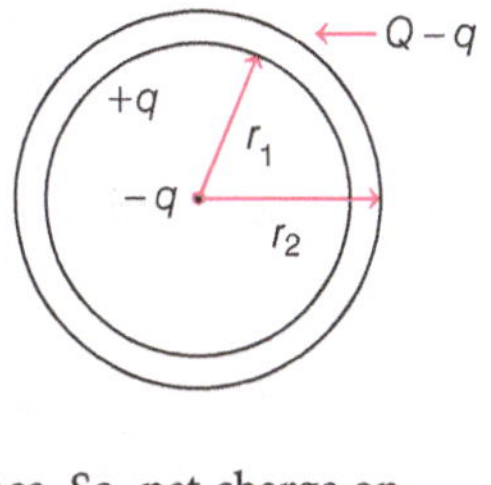

Therefore, surface charge density on

(a) inner surface is $\dfrac{q}{4\pi r_1^2}$

(b) and on outer surface is $\dfrac{Q-q}{4\pi r_2^2}$.

(ii) At a point lying outside the sphere by Gauss' law, the electric flux is given by

$$\phi_E = \oint_s \mathbf{E}\cdot d\mathbf{S} = \frac{q}{\varepsilon_0}$$

where, q is the net charge enclosed.

As $\mathbf{E}$ and $d\mathbf{S}$ are in same direction as shown below.

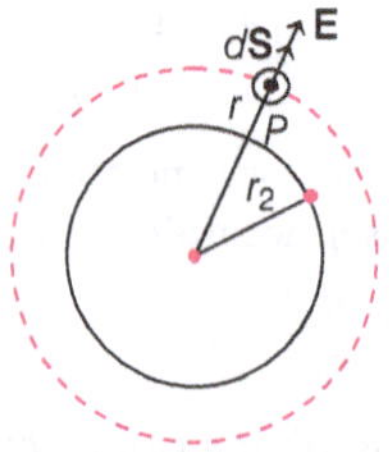

$$\therefore \quad E(4\pi r^2) = \frac{Q-q}{\varepsilon_0}$$

$\Rightarrow$ Electric field, $E = \dfrac{Q-q}{4\pi\varepsilon_0 r^2}$

(B) (i) Electric field to the left of plate 1 (region I)

$$E_I = E_1 + E_2 = \frac{-\sigma}{2\varepsilon_0}\hat{\mathbf{r}} + \frac{2\sigma}{2\varepsilon_0}\hat{\mathbf{r}} = \frac{\sigma}{2\varepsilon_0}$$

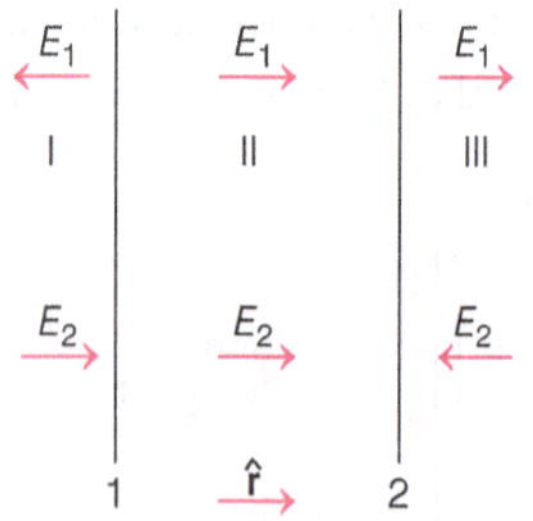

(ii) Electric field to the right of plate 2 (region III)

$$E_{III} = \frac{\sigma}{2\varepsilon_0}\hat{\mathbf{r}} + \frac{2\sigma}{2\varepsilon_0}\hat{\mathbf{r}} = 3\frac{\sigma}{2\varepsilon_0}$$

(iii) Electric field between two plates (region II)

$$E_{II} = \frac{\sigma}{2\varepsilon_0}\hat{\mathbf{r}} - \frac{2\sigma}{2\varepsilon_0}\hat{\mathbf{r}} = -\frac{\sigma}{2\varepsilon_0}$$

30. (i) Let us draw the figure according to question,

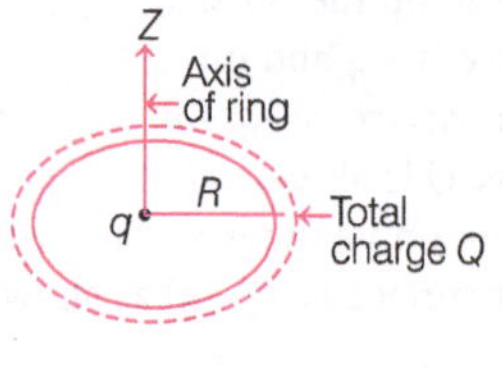

A gentle push on q along the axis of the ring gives rise to the situation shown in the figure below.

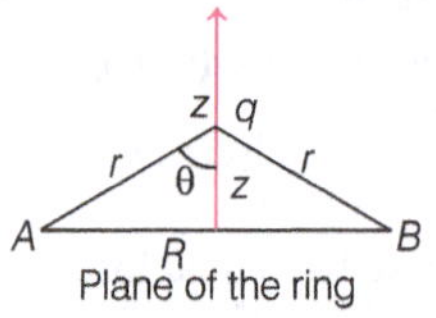

Taking line elements of charge at A and B, having unit length, then force on each element,

$$dF = 2\left(-\frac{Q}{2\pi R}\right)q \times \frac{1}{4\pi\varepsilon_0}\frac{1}{r^2}\cos\theta\cdot dl$$

Total force on the charge q, due to entire ring

$$F = -\frac{Qq}{\pi R}(\pi R)\cdot\frac{1}{4\pi\varepsilon_0}\frac{1}{r^2}\cdot\frac{z}{r}$$

$$F = -\frac{Qqz}{4\pi\varepsilon_0 (z^2+R^2)^{3/2}}$$

Here, $z << R$, $\quad F = -\dfrac{Qqz}{4\pi\varepsilon_0 R^3} = -Kz$

where, $\quad \dfrac{Qq}{4\pi\varepsilon_0 R^3} = \text{constant} \Rightarrow F \propto -z$

Clearly, force on q is proportional to negative of its displacement. Therefore, motion of q is simple harmonic.

(ii) $\omega = \sqrt{\dfrac{K}{m}}$ and $T = \dfrac{2\pi}{\omega} = 2\pi\sqrt{\dfrac{m}{K}}$

$$T = 2\pi\sqrt{\frac{m\,4\pi\varepsilon_0 R^3}{Qq}}$$

$$\Rightarrow \quad T = 2\pi\sqrt{\frac{4\pi\varepsilon_0\, m\, R^3}{Qq}}$$

31. (i) By Gauss' law, electric flux passing through closed surface is given by $\phi = \oint \mathbf{E}\cdot d\mathbf{S} = \dfrac{q}{\varepsilon_0}$

where, q is the net charge enclosed in the Gaussian surface.

(a) ϕ does not change because it depends only on the total charge enclosed by the gaussian surface and not on its shape or size.

(b) ϕ will not change because the total flux is determined by the charge inside the surface, not on the charge outside.

(c) ϕ will become zero because a dipole consists of two equal and opposite charges. So, the net charge inside the surface will be zero. Thus, the flux will also be zero.

(ii) Given, $AB = 20$ cm

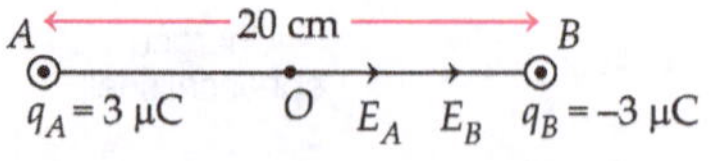

$$AO = OB = 10 \text{ cm} = 0.1 \text{ m}$$
$$q_A = 3\,\mu\text{C} = 3 \times 10^{-6} \text{ C}$$
$$q_B = -3\,\mu\text{C} = -3 \times 10^{-6} \text{ C}$$

The electric field at a point due to a charge q,

$$E = \frac{1}{4\pi\varepsilon_0} \cdot \frac{q}{r^2}$$

where, r is the distance between charge and the point.

Electric field due to q_A at O,

$$E_A = \frac{1}{4\pi\varepsilon_0} \cdot \frac{|q_A|}{(AO)^2}$$
$$= \frac{9 \times 10^9 \times 3 \times 10^{-6}}{(0.1)^2} = \frac{27 \times 10^3}{0.1 \times 0.1} = 2.7 \times 10^6 \text{ N/C}$$

The direction of E_A is A to O, i.e. towards O or towards OB as the electric field is always directed away from positive charge.

Electric field due to q_B at O,

$$E_B = \frac{1}{4\pi\varepsilon_0} \cdot \frac{|q_B|}{(OB)^2} = \frac{9 \times 10^9 \times 3 \times 10^{-6}}{(0.1)^2}$$
$$= \frac{27 \times 10^3}{0.1 \times 0.1} = 2.7 \times 10^6 \text{ N/C}$$

The direction of E_B is O to B, i.e. towards B or towards OB as the electric field is always directed towards the negative charge.

Now, we see that both E_A and E_B are in same direction. So, the resultant electric field at O is E. Hence,

$$E = E_A + E_B$$
$$= 2.7 \times 10^6 + 2.7 \times 10^6 = 5.4 \times 10^6 \text{ N/C}$$

The direction of E (resultant electric field) will be from O to B or towards B.

32. (i) Refer to text on pages 13, 14 and 15.

(ii) Use $dQ = \lambda \cdot dl$ and Gauss' theorem $\phi = \frac{Q}{\varepsilon_0}$

33. The force between $-q$ and q placed at A and C respectively is F_1.

$$F_1 = \frac{1}{4\pi\varepsilon_0} \cdot \frac{qq}{(AC)^2}$$

$$F_1 = \frac{1}{4\pi\varepsilon_0} \cdot \frac{q^2}{(d^2 + x^2)} \quad \text{(along } C \text{ to } A) \quad \text{...(i)}$$

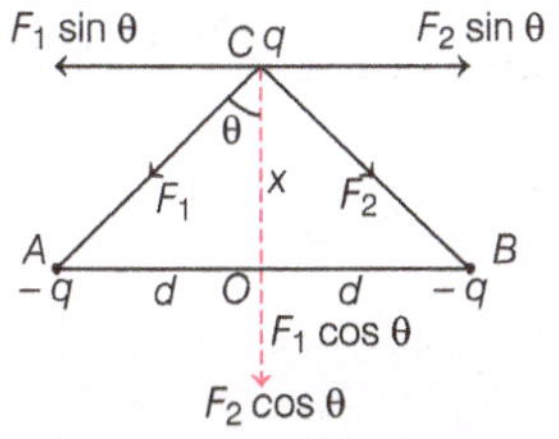

$\because \quad AC = \sqrt{d^2 + x^2} = BC$ (By Pythagoras theorem)

The force between $-q$ and q placed at B and C respectively is F_2.

$$\therefore \quad F_2 = \frac{1}{4\pi\varepsilon_0} \cdot \frac{qq}{(BC)^2} = \frac{1}{4\pi\varepsilon_0} \cdot \frac{q^2}{d^2 + x^2} \quad \text{...(ii)}$$

Now, resolve the components of F_1 and F_2.

Forces along C to O is $F_1 \cos\theta$ and $F_2 \cos\theta$, they both are in the same direction. Forces along perpendicular to CO is $F_1 \sin\theta$ and $F_2 \sin\theta$, these components are opposite to each other and the values of F_1 and F_2 are same. So, they balance each other.

So, net force on q is

$$F = F_1 \cos\theta + F_2 \cos\theta$$
$$F = 2F_1 \cos\theta = 2 \cdot \frac{1}{4\pi\varepsilon_0} \cdot \frac{q^2}{(d^2 + x^2)} \cdot \cos\theta$$

$(\because F_1 = F_2)$

In ΔACO, $\quad \cos\theta = \frac{x}{\sqrt{d^2 + x^2}}$

$$F = \frac{1}{4\pi\varepsilon_0} \cdot \frac{2q^2}{(d^2 + x^2)^{3/2}} x$$

This force is attractive in nature, so

$$F = -\frac{1}{4\pi\varepsilon_0} \cdot \frac{2q^2 . x}{(d^2 + x^2)^{3/2}}$$

According to question, $x << d$, so neglect x^2 as compared to d^2.

$$F = -\frac{1}{4\pi\varepsilon_0} \cdot \frac{2q^2}{d^3} \cdot x \quad \text{...(iii)}$$

Here, $F \propto -x$ or $F = -\omega^2 x$, $\quad$ ...(iv)

So, the motion is simple harmonic, where ω is the angular frequency.

By comparing Eqs. (iii) and (iv), we get

$$\omega = \sqrt{\frac{2q^2}{4\pi\varepsilon_0 d^3 m}} = \sqrt{\frac{2q^2}{4\pi\varepsilon_0 d^3 m}} = \sqrt{\frac{k \text{ (Spring factor)}}{m \text{ (Inertia factor)}}}$$

$$\omega = \frac{2\pi}{T} = \sqrt{\frac{2q^2}{4\pi\varepsilon_0 d^3 m}}$$

where, T is the time period of the charged particle of mass m.

$$T = \left(\frac{8\pi^3 \varepsilon_0 m d^3}{q^2}\right)^{1/2}$$

34. (i) Refer to text on page 15.

(ii) Infinitely long charged wire produces a radial electric field,

$$E = \frac{\lambda}{2\pi\varepsilon_0 r} \quad \text{...(i)}$$

The revolving electron experiences an electrostatic force and provides necessarily centripetal force,

$$eE = \frac{mv^2}{r} \quad ...(ii)$$

From Eq. (i), we can write

$$\frac{e\lambda}{2\pi\varepsilon_0 r} = \frac{mv^2}{r}$$

$$\Rightarrow \quad mv^2 = \frac{e\lambda}{2\pi\varepsilon_0}$$

Therefore, kinetic energy of the electron,

$$K = \frac{1}{2}mv^2 = \frac{e\lambda}{4\pi\varepsilon_0}$$

(iii) The graph is as follows

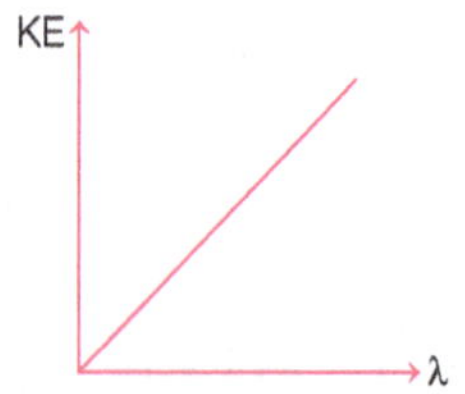

35. (i) Open surfaces are surfaces having edges or boundaries. It is affected by the charges present outside the boundary and the electric flux can change if the position of any charge within the boundary of the surface is changed.

Closed surfaces are those which doesn't have an edge as such. The flux through the surface depends only upon the charges enclosed by the closed surface and is not dependent upon the location of the charges present inside the surface.

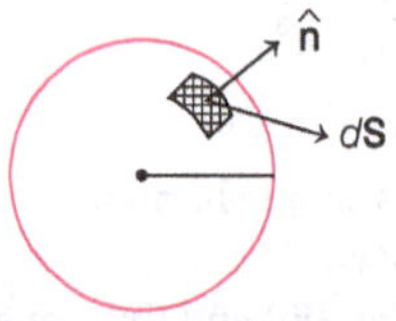

The normal $\hat{\mathbf{n}}$ is along the radial direction of the sphere and dS is the magnitude of the small elementary area on the surface of the sphere.

$\therefore \quad \mathbf{dS} = dS\ \hat{\mathbf{n}}$.

(ii) Refer to the text on page 13
(Electric Flux)
Refer to the text on page 14.
(Some Features of Gauss' Law).

From the mathematical expression of Gauss' law we see that, ϕ_E (Flux through any closed surface)

$$= \frac{Q_{\text{enclosed}}}{\varepsilon_0}$$

$\therefore$ Only the charges enclosed by a closed surface contribute to the electric flux passing through the surface.

(iii)

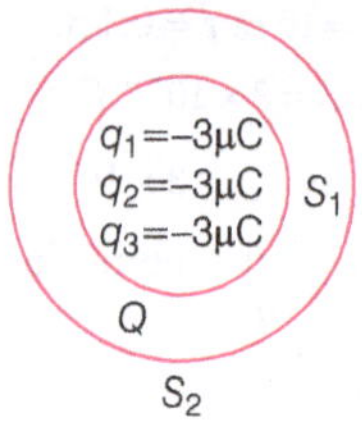

By Gauss' theorem, total flux passing through the surface S_2 is

$$\phi_2 = \frac{Q_{\text{enclosed}}}{\varepsilon_0} = \frac{q_1 + q_2 + q_3 + Q}{\varepsilon_0} \quad ...(i)$$

(iii) The total flux passing through the surface S_1 is

$$\phi_1 = \frac{q_1 + q_2 + q_3}{\varepsilon_0} \quad ...(ii)$$

Now, it is given that $\phi_2 = 4\phi_1$

$\therefore$ Equating Eqs. (i) and (ii), we get

$$\frac{q_1 + q_2 + q_3 + Q}{\varepsilon_0} = \frac{4(q_1 + q_2 + q_3)}{\varepsilon_0}$$

$$\Rightarrow \quad Q = 4(q_1 + q_2 + q_3) - (q_1 + q_2 + q_3)$$

$$\Rightarrow \quad Q = 3 \times (-3 - 2 + 9)\ \mu\text{C}$$

$$= (3 \times 4)\ \mu\text{C}$$

$$\Rightarrow \quad Q = 12\ \mu\text{C}$$

36. (i) Here, $q_1 = q_2 = 6.5 \times 10^{-7}$ C, $r = 50$ cm $= 0.5$ m

Electrostatic force of repulsion,

$$F = \frac{1}{4\pi\varepsilon_0}\frac{q_1 q_2}{r^2} = \frac{9 \times 10^9 \times (6.5 \times 10^{-7})^2}{(0.5)^2}$$

$$= 1.521 \times 10^{-2}\ \text{N}$$

(ii) Now, q_1, q_2 both are doubled and r is halved. So,

$$F = \frac{1}{4\pi\varepsilon_0}\frac{q_1 q_2}{r^2}, \text{ then}$$

$$F = \frac{(2q_1)(2q_2)}{4\pi\varepsilon_0\left(\frac{r}{2}\right)^2} = 16\left(\frac{q_1 q_2}{4\pi\varepsilon_0 r^2}\right)$$

F becomes 16 times, i.e. $F' = 16\ F$.

$F' = 16 \times 1.521 \times 10^{-2}$ N or $F' = 0.24$ N

37. (i) Charge of proton, $q = 1.6 \times 10^{-19}$ C

Force on proton at A, $F = qE_A$

$$= (1.6 \times 10^{-19}\ \text{C})(40\ \text{N/C})$$

$$= 6.4 \times 10^{-18}\ \text{N}$$

(ii) Since, electric field, $E \propto \frac{\text{Number of electric field lines}}{\text{Area}}$

Hence, $E_B = \frac{1}{2} \times E_A = \frac{1}{2}(40\ \text{N/C}) = 20\ \text{N/C}$

38. The situation is represented as follows

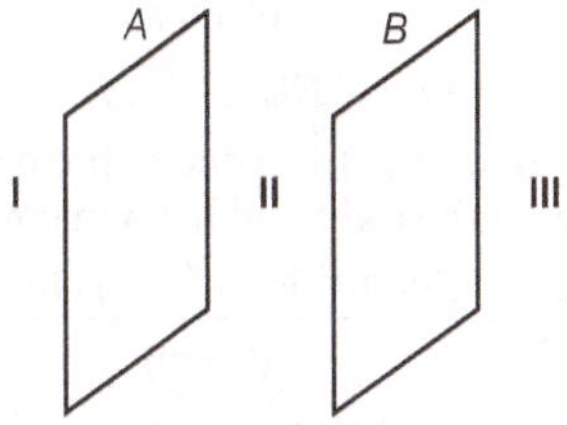

A and B are two parallel plates close to each other. Outer region of plate A is labelled as I, outer region of plate B is labelled as III, and the region between the plates A and B, is labelled as II.

Charge density of plate A, $\sigma = 17.0 \times 10^{-22}\ \text{C/m}^2$

Charge density of plate B, $\sigma = -17.0 \times 10^{-22}\ \text{C/m}^2$

(i) In the regions, I and III, electric field E is zero. This is because charge is not enclosed by the respective plates.

(ii) Electric field E in region II is given by the relation,

$$E = \frac{\sigma}{\varepsilon_0}$$

where, ε_0 = permittivity of free space $= 8.854 \times 10^{-12}\ \text{N}^{-1}\text{C}^2\text{m}^{-2}$

$$E = \frac{17.0 \times 10^{-22}}{8.854 \times 10^{-12}} = 1.92 \times 10^{-10}\ \text{N/C}$$

Therefore, electric field between the plates is 1.92×10^{-10} N/C.

39. Given, length of electric dipole, $2l = 2\ \text{cm} = 2 \times 10^{-2}$ m

$$\theta = 60°$$
$$E = 10^5\ \text{N/C}$$

(i) $\because$ $\tau = pE\sin\theta$

$$p = \frac{\tau}{E\sin\theta}$$

$$\Rightarrow \quad 2lq = \frac{\tau}{E\sin\theta}$$

$$\Rightarrow \quad q = \frac{\tau}{(2l)E\sin\theta}$$

$$= \frac{8\sqrt{3}}{2 \times 10^{-2} \times 10^5 \times \sin 60°} = 8 \times 10^{-3}\ \text{C}$$

(ii) Potential energy $= -pE\cos\theta$

$$= -(2l \times q)E\cos 60°$$
$$= -2 \times 10^{-2} \times 8 \times 10^{-3} \times 10^5 \times \frac{1}{2}$$
$$= -8\ \text{J}$$

40. Electric field $\mathbf{E} = 3 \times 10^3\ \hat{\mathbf{i}}$ N/C, *i.e.*, electric field is directed towards X-axis (due to involvement of $\hat{\mathbf{i}}$).

(i) As the surface is in YZ- plane, so the area vector (normal to the square) is along X-axis.

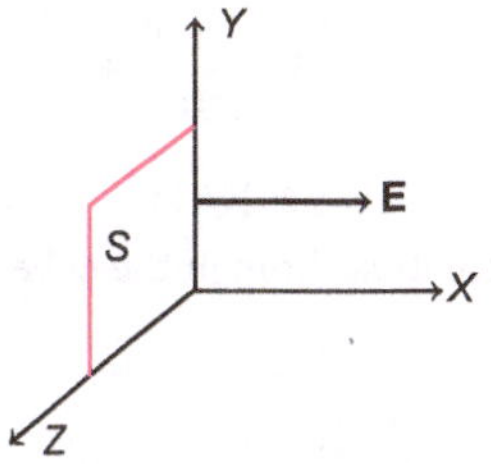

Area, $S = 10 \times 10 = 100\ \text{cm}^2 = 10^{-2}\ \text{m}^2$

Area vector, $\mathbf{S} = 10^{-2}\ \hat{\mathbf{i}}\ \text{m}^2$

Using the formula of electric flux,

$$\phi = \mathbf{E} \cdot \mathbf{S} = ES\cos\theta$$
$$= ES \quad [\because \text{angle between } \mathbf{E} \text{ and } \mathbf{S} \text{ is } 0°]$$
$$\phi = 3 \times 10^3 \times 10^{-2} = 30\ \text{N-m}^2/\text{C}$$

(ii) Now, the area vector makes an angle of 60° with X-axis.

$$\mathbf{E} = 3 \times 10^3\ \hat{\mathbf{i}}\ \text{N/C}$$
$$\mathbf{S} = 100\ \text{cm}^2 = 10^{-2}\ \text{m}^2, \theta = 60°$$

Using the formula of electric flux, $\phi = \mathbf{E} \cdot \mathbf{S}$

$$\phi = ES\cos\theta = 3 \times 10^3 \times 10^{-2}\cos 60°$$
$$= 3 \times 10 \times \frac{1}{2}$$
$$= 15\ \text{N-m}^2/\text{C}$$

41. Let us consider a charge q is placed at the centre of a cubic Gaussian surface.

As per the question, $q = 2\mu\text{C} = 2 \times 10^{-6}\text{C}$

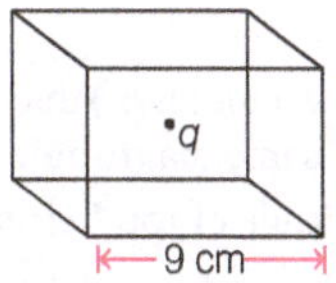

Length of edge = 9 cm

According to Gauss' theorem, the net electric flux (ϕ) through the surface is

$$\phi = \frac{q}{\varepsilon_0} = \frac{2 \times 10^{-6}}{8.85 \times 10^{-12}} = 2.26 \times 10^5\ \text{N-m}^2/\text{C}$$

Thus, the net electric flux through the surface is 2.26×10^5 N-m²/C.

42. Refer to example 16 on page 16.

43. (i) Refer to text on page 15.

(ii) Here, $x = 10\ \text{cm} = \frac{10}{100}\ \text{m} = \frac{1}{10}\ \text{m}$

The magnitude of the electric field at the left face,

$$(5x^2 + 2)\hat{\mathbf{i}} = 5 \times (0)^2 + 2)\hat{\mathbf{i}} = 2\hat{\mathbf{i}}$$

The magnitude of the electric field at the right face,

$$E_R = (5x^2 + 2)\hat{\mathbf{i}}$$

$$= \left(5 \times \left(\frac{1}{10}\right)^2 + 2\right) = \left(\frac{5}{100} + 2\right)$$

$$E_R = 2.05 \text{ N/C}$$

(a) Net electric flux through the cube,

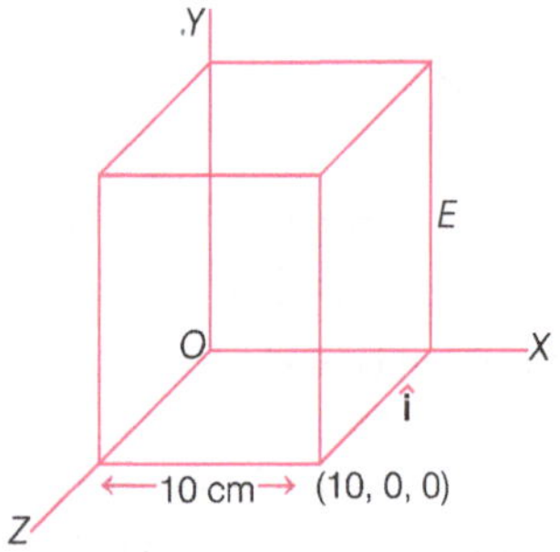

$$\phi = \phi_L + \phi_R$$
$$= E_L dS \cos 180° + E_R dS \cos 0°$$
$$= 2 \times \left(\frac{1}{10}\right)^2 + 2.05 \times \left(\frac{1}{10}\right)^2$$
$$= 5 \times 10^{-4} \text{ N-m}^2\text{C}^{-1}$$

(b) Charge, $q = \phi\varepsilon_0 = 5 \times 10^{-4} \times 8.85 \times 10^{-12}$
$$= 4.425 \times 10^{-15} \text{C}$$

44. The electric field vector $(\mathbf{E}_{1A})$ at A due to the positive charge q_1 points towards the right. Its magnitude,

$$E_{1A} = \frac{(9 \times 10^9 \text{N-m}^2\text{C}^{-2})(10^{-7}\text{C})}{(0.1 \text{ m})^2}$$
$$= 9 \times 10^4 \text{N C}^{-1}$$

The electric field vector $(\mathbf{E}_{2A})$ due to q_2 points to the right and has the same magnitude.

Hence, the magnitude of total electric field $\mathbf{E}_A$ at A,

$$E_A = E_{1A} + E_{2A} = 18 \times 10^4 \text{NC}^{-1}$$

i.e. $(\mathbf{E}_A)$ is directed towards right.

The electric field $(\mathbf{E}_{1B})$ at B due to q_1 points towards the left and has a magnitude,

$$E_{1B} = \frac{(9 \times 10^9 \text{N-m}^2\text{C}^{-2})(10^{-7}\text{C})}{(0.1 \text{ m})^2}$$
$$= 9 \times 10^4 \text{NC}^{-1}$$

The electric field $(\mathbf{E}_{2B})$ at B due to the negative charge q_2 points towards the right and has a magnitude

$$E_{2B} = \frac{(9 \times 10^9 \text{ N-m}^2\text{C}^{-2})(10^{-7}\text{C})}{(0.3 \text{ m})^2}$$
$$= 1 \times 10^4 \text{NC}^{-1}$$

The magnitude of the total electric field at B,

$$E_B = E_{1B} - E_{2B} = 8 \times 10^4 \text{NC}^{-1}$$

i.e. $\mathbf{E}_B$ is directed towards the left.

The magnitude of each electric field vector at point C due to charge q_1 and q_2,

$$E_{1C} = E_{2C} = \frac{(9 \times 10^9 \text{N - m}^2\text{C}^{-2})(10^{-7}\text{C})}{(0.2 \text{ m})^2}$$
$$= 2.25 \times 10^4 \text{ NC}^{-1}$$

The resultant of these two vectors,

$$\mathbf{E}_C = E_{1C} \cos \frac{\pi}{3} + E_{2C} \cos \frac{\pi}{3}$$
$$= 2.25 \times 10^4 \text{NC}^{-1}$$

i.e. $\mathbf{E}_C$ points towards the right.

45. (i) Here, $p = 6.2 \times 10^{-30}$ C-m and $E = 10^6$ N/C

$\therefore \quad \tau = pE \sin\theta \quad$ [for maximum value, $\theta = 90°$]

$$\tau_{\text{max}} = pE \sin 90° = 6.2 \times 10^{-30} \times 10^6 \times 1$$
$$= 6.2 \times 10^{-24} \text{ N-m}$$

(ii) When dipole is aligned anti-parallel to the field, $\theta = 180°$.

$\therefore \quad W = pE(1 - \cos\theta)$

$$= 6.2 \times 10^{-30} \times 10^6 (1 - \cos 180°) \quad [\because \cos 180° = -1]$$
$$= 6.2 \times 10^{-30} \times 10^6 (1 - (-1))$$
$$= 6.2 \times 10^{-30} \times 10^6 \times 2$$
$$= 1.24 \times 10^{-23} \text{ J}$$

QR Code for Quick Test 1	QR Code for Quick Test 2	QR Code for Quick Test 3	QR Code for Quick Test 4

SELF ASSESSMENT TEST

Multiple Choice Questions (MCQs)

1. Two point charges of magnitudes $+10\ \mu C$ and $-10\ \mu C$ are placed 1 m apart in a vacuum. The potential energy of the system is

(a) 0 J (b) 9×10^{-2} J
(c) -9×10^{-1} J (d) -9×10^{-3} J

2. A spherical conductor of radius 10 cm carries a charge of $+1\ \mu C$. The electric field just outside the surface of the conductor is

(a) 900 N/C (b) 9000 N/C
(c) 9×10^5 N/C (d) 9×10^7 N/C

3. Two point charges, each of $+q$, are placed on the X-axis at $x = +a$ and $x = -a$. The net electric field at a point on the Y-axis at a distance y from the origin is

(a) $\dfrac{kq}{(a^2 + y^2)^{3/2}}$ (b) $\dfrac{2kq \cdot a}{(a^2 + y^2)^{3/2}}$

(c) $\dfrac{2kq.y}{(a^2 + y^2)^{3/2}}$ (d) zero

4. According to Gauss' law, the net electric flux through any closed surface depends upon

(a) the distribution of charges inside the surface
(b) the net charge enclosed within the surface
(c) the shape of the surface
(d) the distribution of charge on the surface

5. An electric dipole of dipole moment 2×10^{-8} C-m in a uniform electric field experiences a maximum torque of 6×10^{-1} N-m. The magnitude of electric field is

(a) $2.2 \times 10^3\ Vm^{-1}$ (b) $1.2 \times 10^4\ Vm^{-1}$
(c) $3.0 \times 10^7\ Vm^{-1}$ (d) $4.2 \times 10^3\ Vm^{-1}$

Assertion-Reason

Direction *(Q. Nos. 6-8) In the following questions, two statements are given-one labelled Assertion (A) and the other labelled Reason (R). Select the correct answer to these questions from the codes (a), (b), (c) and (d) as given below.*

(a) Both Assertion and Reason are true and Reason is the correct explanation of Assertion.
(b) Both Assertion and Reason are true but Reason is not the correct explanation of Assertion.
(c) Assertion is true but Reason is false.
(d) Assertion is false but Reason is true.

6. **Assertion** (A) The electric field lines contain information about the direction as well as magnitude of the field.
Reason (R) Electric field lines do not form closed loops.

7. **Assertion** (A) In a region where uniform electric field exists, the net charge within volume of any size is zero.
Reason (R) The electric flux within any closed surface in region of uniform electric field is zero.

8. **Assertion** (A) When charges are shared between any two bodies, then no charge is really lost but some loss of energy does occur.
Reason (R) Some energy disappears in the form of heat, sparking, etc.

Case Based Question

Directions *(Q.Nos. 9) This question is case study based question. Read the following paragraph and answer the questions on the basis of same.*

9. A Faraday cage or Faraday shield is an enclosure made of a conducting material. The fields within a conductor cancel out with any external fields, so the electric field within the enclosure is zero. These Faraday cages act as big hollow conductors you can put things in to shield them from electrical fields. Any electrical shocks the cage receives, pass harmlessly around the outside of the cage.

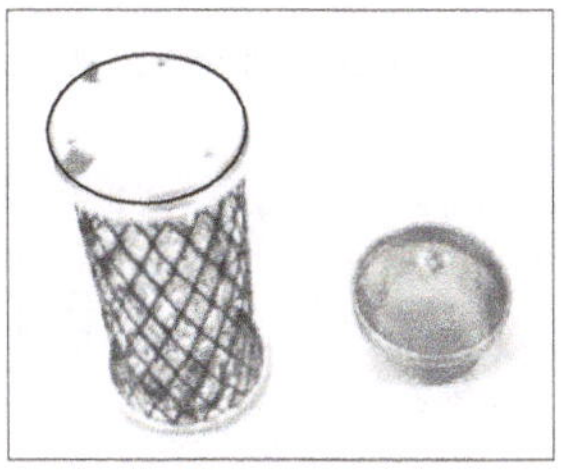

(i) Which of the following materials can be used to make a Faraday cage?

(a) Plastic (b) Glass
(c) Copper (d) Wood

(ii) Example of a real-word Faraday cage is

(a) car (b) plastic box
(c) lightning rod (d) metal rod

(iii) What is the electrical force inside a Faraday cage when it is struck by lightning?

(a) The same as the lightning
(b) Half that of the lightning
(c) Zero
(d) A quarter of the lightning

(iv) An isolated point charge $+q$ is placed inside the Faraday cage. Its surface must have charge equal to
(a) zero (b) $+q$
(c) $-q$ (d) $+2q$

(v) A point charge of $2\mu C$ is placed at centre of Faraday cage in the shape of cube with surface of 9 cm edge. The number of electric field lines passing through the cube normally will be
(a) $1.91 \times 10^5 \, Nm^2/C$, entering the surface
(b) $1.91 \times 10^5 \, Nm^2/C$, leaving the surface
(c) $2.25 \times 10^5 \, Nm^2/C$, leaving the surface
(d) $2.25 \times 10^5 \, Nm^2/C$, entering the surface

Very Short Answer Type Question

10. Two charges, $+3 \times 10^{-6}$ C and -3×10^{-6} C, are separated by 0.4 m in air. Calculate the electric field intensity at the mid-point between the charges.

Short Answer Type Questions

11. The electric field components in the figure shown are $E_x = \alpha x, E_y = 0, E_z = 0$, where $\alpha = \frac{100 N}{Cm}$. Calculate the charge within the cube, assuming $a = 0.1$ m.

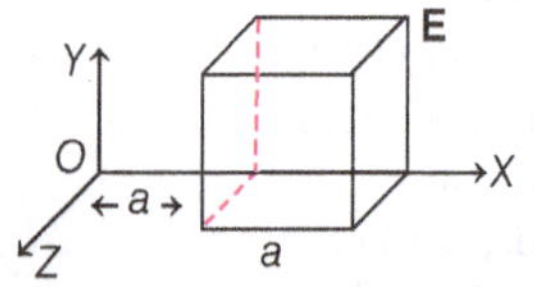

12. A hollow cylindrical box of length 1 m and area of cross-section 25 cm^2 is placed in a three-dimensional coordinate system as shown in the figure. The electric field in the region is given by $\mathbf{E} = 50 \, x\hat{\mathbf{i}}$, where E is in NC^{-1} and x is in metre.

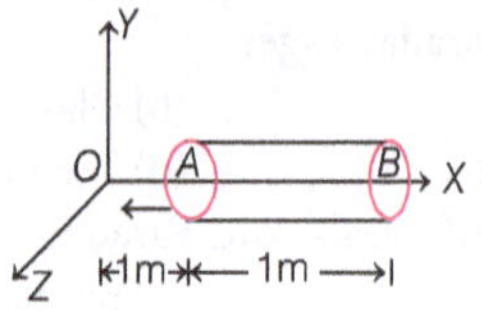

Find
(i) net flux through the cylinder.
(ii) charge enclosed by the cylinder.

Long Answer Type Questions

13. (A) Given the electric field in the region $\mathbf{E} = 2 \times \hat{\mathbf{i}}$, find the net electric flux through the cube and the charge enclosed by it.

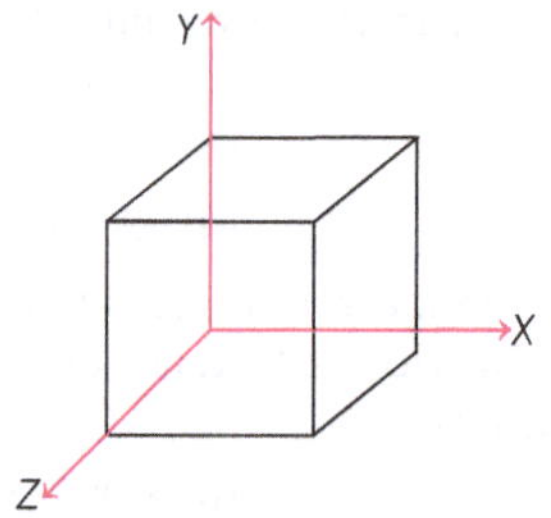

(B) A small charged particle is placed in a uniform electric field of intensity 500 N/C, directed along the positive X-axis. The particle experiences a force of 2.5×10^{-7} N due to the field.
(i) What is the charge on the particle?
(ii) If the particle is released from rest, which direction will it move?
(iii) If the charge is negative, what will be the direction of the force experienced by the particle?

14. (i) Define an ideal electric dipole. Give an example. **[1]**
(ii) Derive an expression for the torque experienced by an electric dipole in a uniform electric field. What is net force acting on this dipole. **[2]**
(iii) An electric dipole of length 2 cm is placed with its axis making an angle of $60°$ with respect to uniform electric field of 10^5 N/C.
If it experiences a torque of $8\sqrt{3}$ Nm, calculate the magnitude of charge on the dipole, and its potential energy. **[2]**

Answers

1. (c) *2.* (c) *3.* (c) *4.* (b) *5.* (c)
6. (b) *7.* (a) *8.* (a)
9. (i) (c), (ii) (a), (iii) (c), (iv) (c), (v) (c)
10. 1.35×10^6 N/C.

02

CHAPTER

This Chapter explores electrostatic potential, its relation to electric fields, and its applications in capacitors and circuits, providing a clear overview of its role in electromagnetism.

Electrostatic Potential and Capacitance

▼ **YOUR STUDY GOALS**

2.1 Electrostatic Potential
2.2 Electrostatic Potential Energy of a System of Charges
2.3 Electrostatics of Conductor
2.4 Capacitors and Capacitance
2.5 Combination of Capacitors

▼ **YOUR PRACTICE GOAL**

- Objective Type Questions (37 Qs ; MCQs, A-R, Matching)
- Case Based Questions-3
- Subjective Questions (10 VSAs, 17 SAs, 19 LAs)
- Numerical Problems-16

2.1 Electrostatic Potential

The **electrostatic potential** at any point in the region of electric field is equal to the amount of work done in bringing a unit positive test charge from infinity to that point without acceleration. If W is work done in bringing a unit positive test charge q_0 from infinity to a given point, then electric potential is given by

$$\text{Electrostatic potential } (V) = \frac{\text{Work done } (W)}{\text{Charge } (q_0)}$$

- It is a **scalar quantity** and its dimensional formula is $[\mathrm{M\,L^2T^{-3}A^{-1}}]$
- Its SI unit is **volt** (V).

1 volt is simply the electrostatic potential at a point when 1 joule of work is done in bringing 1 coulomb of positive charge from infinity to that point.

$$1\,\mathrm{V} = \frac{1\,\mathrm{J}}{1\,\mathrm{C}} = 1\,\mathrm{Nm\,C^{-1}}$$

TEACHER TIP

Electric potential at any point is also defined as the negative line integral of electric field from infinity to given point,

i.e. $$V = -\int_{\infty}^{r} \mathbf{E} \cdot d\mathbf{l}$$

Electrostatic Potential Difference

The **electrostatic potential difference** between two points in an electric field is defined as the amount of work done in moving a unit positive test charge from one point to the other point.

If V_Q and V_P are the electrostatic potentials at Q and P respectively, then electrostatic potential difference between points Q and P,

$$\Delta V = V_P - V_Q$$

Thus, $$\boxed{\Delta V = \frac{W_{QP}}{q_0}}$$

The **unit of potential difference** is same as that of electrostatic potential, i.e. **volt.**

> **One electron-volt** (1 eV) is the energy equal to the work required to move a single elementary charge e such as an electron or a proton through a potential difference of exactly one volt (1 V).
>
> $\therefore$ $1\text{ eV} = e(1\text{ V}) = (1.6\times 10^{-19}\text{ C})(1\text{ J/C})$
> $= 1.6\times 10^{-19}\text{ J}$

Conservative Nature of Electrostatic Forces

The work done by electrostatic forces does not depend upon the path along which a charge is moved.

Let us consider the following figure.

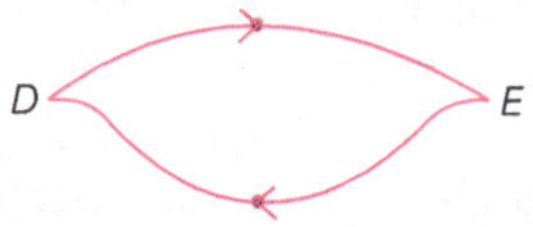

$\therefore$ Work done in moving a positive charge q_0 from D to E,

$$W_{DE} = (V_E - V_D)q_0 \quad \dots \text{(i)}$$

Similarly, work done in moving a positive charge q_0 from E to D, $W_{ED} = (V_D - V_E)q_0 \quad \dots$ (ii)

If we add Eqs. (i) and (ii), we will get the total work done in moving a unit positive charge over a closed path.

$\therefore$ On adding Eqs. (i) and (ii), we get

$$W_{DE} + W_{ED} = (V_E - V_D)q_0 + (V_D - V_E)q_0 = 0$$

It means that **work done in moving a unit positive charge over a closed path in an electric field is zero. Hence, electrostatic forces are conservative in nature.**

Example 1. **Potential at a point P in space is given as 3×10^5 V. Find the work done in bringing a charge of 2×10^{-6} C from infinity to the point P. Does the answer depend on the path along which the charge is brought?**

Sol. Given, potential at the point P,

$$V = 3\times 10^5\text{ V},$$

Charge, $q_0 = 2\times 10^{-6}$ C

Work done in bringing the charge from infinity to the point P,

$$W_{\infty\to P} = q_0 V = 2\times 10^{-6}\times 3\times 10^5$$
$$= 6\times 10^{-1} = 0.6\text{ J}$$

No, the work done is path independent.

Example 2. **The potential difference between two points is 20 V. How much work will be done in carrying a charge of 400 μC from one point to the another?**

Sol. Given, $\Delta V = 20$ V and $q = 400\ \mu\text{C} = 400\times 10^{-6}$ C

Since, we know,

$$\text{Electrostatic potential difference} = \frac{\text{Work done}}{\text{Charge}}$$

$$\Rightarrow \quad \Delta V = \frac{W}{q}$$

$$\Rightarrow \quad W = \Delta V q$$

$$\therefore \quad W = 20\times 400\times 10^{-6} = 8\times 10^{-3}\text{ J}$$

Electrostatic Potential due to a Point Charge

Let P be the point at a distance r from a charge q placed at origin O.

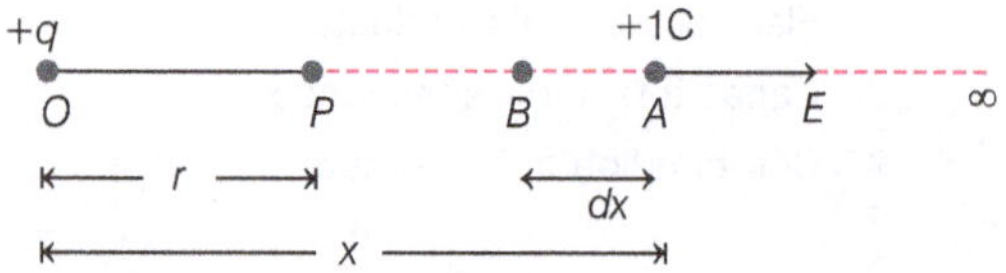

The electric potential at point P is the amount of work done in carrying a unit positive charge from infinity to P without acceleration.

Let A be an intermediate point on this path where $OA = x$. The electrostatic force on a unit positive charge at A is given by

$$F = \frac{1}{4\pi\varepsilon_0}\cdot\frac{q\times 1}{x^2} \quad \text{[along } OA] \quad \dots \text{(i)}$$

Small work done in moving the charge through a distance dx from A to B is given by

$$dW = \mathbf{F}\cdot d\mathbf{x}$$

$$= Fdx\cos 180° = -Fdx \qquad [\because \cos 180° = -1]$$

$$\Rightarrow \quad dW = -Fdx \qquad \ldots\text{(ii)}$$

Total work done in moving a unit positive charge from ∞ to the point P is given by

$$W = \int_{\infty}^{r} -Fdx = \int_{\infty}^{r} -\frac{1}{4\pi\varepsilon_0}\cdot\frac{q}{x^2}dx$$

$$= -\frac{q}{4\pi\varepsilon_0}\int_{\infty}^{r} x^{-2}dx$$

$$= -\frac{q}{4\pi\varepsilon_0}\left[\frac{-1}{x}\right]_{\infty}^{r} \qquad \left[\because \int x^{-2}\,dx = -\frac{1}{x}\right]$$

$$= \frac{q}{4\pi\varepsilon_0}\left[\frac{1}{r} - \frac{1}{\infty}\right]$$

$$\Rightarrow \quad W = \frac{q}{4\pi\varepsilon_0 r} \qquad \ldots\text{(iii)}$$

From the definition of electric potential, this work is equal to the potential at point P.

$$V = \frac{q}{4\pi\varepsilon_0 r} \qquad \ldots\text{(iv)}$$

- When q is **positive,** the electrostatic potential V is **positive** and when q is **negative**, electrostatic potential is **negative**.
- Electrostatic potential due to a single charge is **spherically symmetric.**

Variation of Electric Potential with Distance

Figure given below shows the variation of electrostatic potential with distance, i.e. $V \propto \frac{1}{r}$ and also the variation of electrostatic field with distance, i.e. $E \propto \frac{1}{r^2}$.

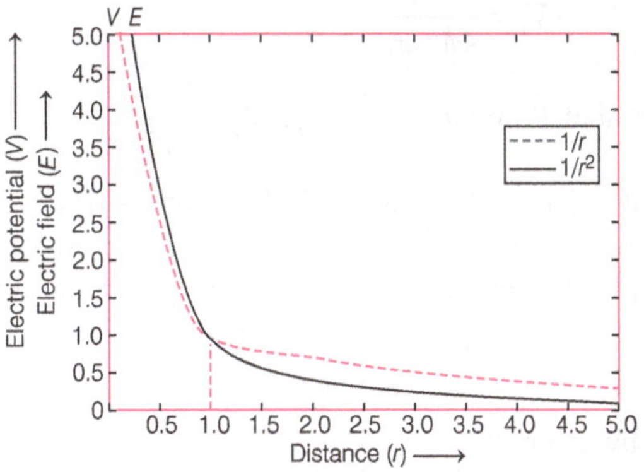

Variation of electrostatic potential V and electric field E with distance r

Example 3. **What is the electrostatic potential at the surface of a silver nucleus of diameter 12.4 fm? Atomic number (Z) for silver is 47.**

Sol. Given, $r = \frac{12.4}{2} = 6.2\text{ fm} = 6.2\times10^{-15}\text{ m}$ and $Z = 47$

$\therefore$ Charge of the nucleus, $q = Ze = 47\times1.6\times10^{-19}$ C $[\because e = 1.6\times10^{-19}\text{C}]$

$\therefore$ Electrostatic potential at the surface,

$$V = \frac{q}{4\pi\varepsilon_0 r} = \frac{9\times10^9\times47\times1.6\times10^{-19}}{6.2\times10^{-15}} = 1.09\times10^7\text{V}$$

Example 4. **A point charge Q is placed at point O as shown in the figure. Is the potential difference $(V_A - V_B)$ positive, negative or zero, if Q is**

(i) positive? (ii) negative?

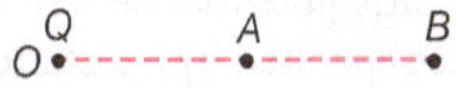

All India 2011

Sol. Let the distance of points A and B from charge Q be r_A and r_B, respectively.

$\therefore$ Potential difference between points A and B,

$$V_A - V_B = \frac{Q}{4\pi\varepsilon_0}\left[\frac{1}{r_A} - \frac{1}{r_B}\right]$$

As, $\quad r_A = OA,\ r_B = OB$ and $r_A < r_B$

$$\Rightarrow \quad \frac{1}{r_A} > \frac{1}{r_B}$$

Therefore, $\left[\frac{1}{r_A} - \frac{1}{r_B}\right]$ has positive value.

$\therefore$ $(V_A - V_B)$ depends on the nature of charge Q.

(i) $(V_A - V_B)$ is positive when $Q > 0$ and

(ii) $(V_A - V_B)$ is negative when $Q < 0$.

Electrostatic Potential due to a System of Charges

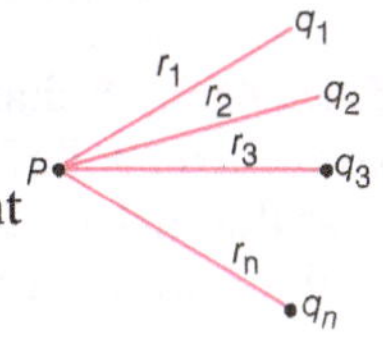

Let there be a number of point charges $q_1, q_2, q_3, \ldots\ldots q_n$ located at distances $r_1, r_2, r_3 \ldots\ldots r_n$ respectively, from a point P where the electric potential is to be calculated.

The potential at point P due to each charge is

$$V_1 = \frac{1}{4\pi\varepsilon_0}\times\frac{q_1}{r_1},\ V_2 = \frac{1}{4\pi\varepsilon_0}\times\frac{q_2}{r_2},\ldots\ldots$$

$$V_n = \frac{1}{4\pi\varepsilon_o}\times\frac{q_n}{r_n}$$

The resultant potential at P is

$$V = V_1 + V_2 + V_3 + \ldots. + V_n$$

$$V = \frac{1}{4\pi\varepsilon_0}\left(\frac{q_1}{r_1}+\frac{q_2}{r_2}+\frac{q_3}{r_3}+\ldots\ldots\ldots+\frac{q_n}{r_n}\right)$$

The net electrostatic potential at a point due to multiple charges is equal to the algebraic sum of potentials due to individual charges at that particular point.

$$\therefore \quad V_{\text{net}} = \sum_{i=1}^{n} V_i$$

Example 5. Two point charges of 4 μC and −2 μC are separated by a distance of 1 m in air. Find the location of a point on the line joining the two charges, where the electric potential is zero.

Sol. Let the electrostatic potential be zero at point P between the two charges separated by a distance x metre.

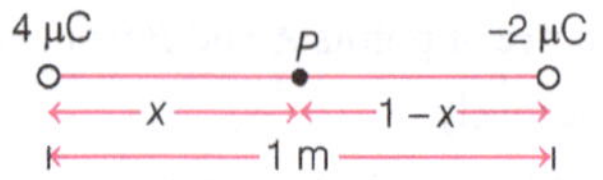

At point P, $\quad V_P = V_1 + V_2 = 0$

$$\Rightarrow \quad \frac{1}{4\pi\varepsilon_0}\cdot\frac{q_1}{r_1} + \frac{1}{4\pi\varepsilon_0}\cdot\frac{q_2}{r_2} = 0$$

$$\Rightarrow \quad \frac{1}{4\pi\varepsilon_0}\cdot\frac{4\times10^{-6}}{x} + \frac{1}{4\pi\varepsilon_0}\cdot\frac{(-2\times10^{-6})}{(1-x)} = 0$$

$$\Rightarrow \quad \frac{4\times10^{-6}}{x} = \frac{2\times10^{-6}}{(1-x)}$$

$$\Rightarrow \quad \frac{4}{x} = \frac{2}{(1-x)}$$

$$\Rightarrow \quad 2(1-x) = x$$

$$\Rightarrow \quad 2 = 3x \text{ or } x = \frac{2}{3}$$

∴ Electrostatic potential is zero at a distance 2/3 m from charge 4μC between the two charges.

Example 6. A charge Q is distributed over two concentric hollow spheres of radii r and R (>r) such that the surface densities are equal. Find the potential at the common centre.

Sol. Let q_1 and q_2 be the charges on them.

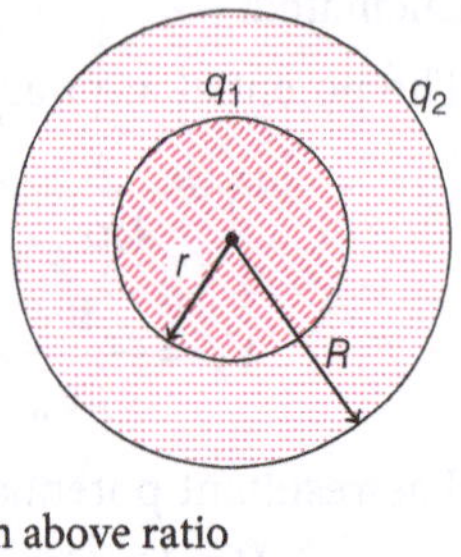

$$\sigma_1 = \sigma_2$$

$$\therefore \quad \frac{q_1}{4\pi r^2} = \frac{q_2}{4\pi R^2}$$

$$\therefore \quad \frac{q_1}{q_2} = \frac{r^2}{R^2}$$

i.e. charge on them is distributed in above ratio

or $\quad q_1 = \frac{r^2}{r^2+R^2}Q$ and $q_2 = \frac{R^2}{r^2+R^2}Q$

∴ Potential at centre,

V = Potential due to q_1 + Potential due to q_2

$$\Rightarrow \quad V = \frac{1}{4\pi\varepsilon_0}\cdot\frac{q_1}{r} + \frac{1}{4\pi\varepsilon_0}\cdot\frac{q_2}{R} = \frac{Q(R+r)}{4\pi\varepsilon_0(r^2+R^2)}$$

Electrostatic Potential due to an Electric Dipole

An **electric dipole** is defined as a couple of opposite charges q and $-q$ which are separated by a distance $2a$.

Now, let us consider an electric dipole consisting of charges $+q$ and $-q$ separated by a distance $2a$.

The dipole moment $|\mathbf{p}| = q \times 2a$.

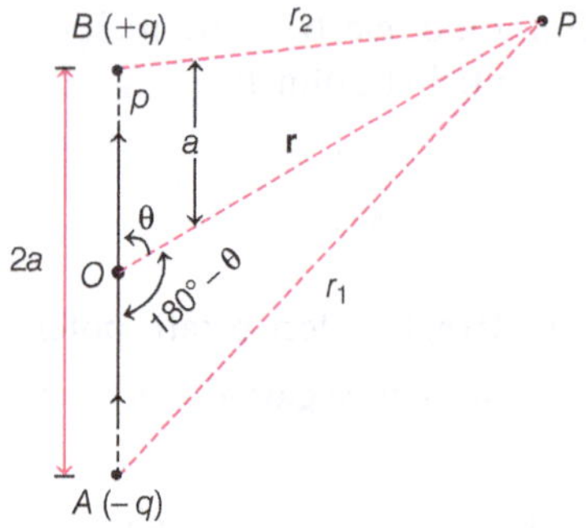

Electric potential at point P due to electric dipole

Let O be the centre of the dipole, P be any point near the electric dipole inclined at an angle θ as shown in the figure.

Let P be the point at which electric potential is required. Potential at P due to $-q$ charge,

$$V_1 = \frac{-q}{4\pi\varepsilon_0 r_1}$$

Potential at P due to $+q$ charge, $V_2 = \frac{q}{4\pi\varepsilon_0 r_2}$

As, potential is related to work done by the field, electrostatic potential also follows the superposition principle. Therefore, potential at P due to the dipole,

$$V_P = V_1 + V_2 = \frac{q}{4\pi\varepsilon_0}\left[\frac{1}{r_2} - \frac{1}{r_1}\right] \quad \ldots\text{(i)}$$

Now, by geometry,

$$r_1^2 = r^2 + a^2 + 2ar\cos\theta$$

Similarly, $\quad r_2^2 = r^2 + a^2 + 2ar\cos(180° - \theta)$

or $$r_2^2 = r^2 + a^2 - 2ar\cos\theta$$
$[\because \cos(180°-\theta) = -\cos\theta]$

and $$r_1^2 = r^2\left(1 + \frac{a^2}{r^2} + \frac{2a}{r}\cos\theta\right)$$

If $r >> a$, $\frac{a}{r}$ is small.

Therefore, $\frac{a^2}{r^2}$ can be neglected.

$$r_1^2 = r^2\left(1 + \frac{2a}{r}\cos\theta\right)$$

$$\Rightarrow \quad r_1 = r\left(1 + \frac{2a}{r}\cos\theta\right)^{1/2}$$

or $$\frac{1}{r_1} = \frac{1}{r}\left(1 + \frac{2a}{r}\cos\theta\right)^{-1/2}$$

Similarly, $$\frac{1}{r_2} = \frac{1}{r}\left(1 - \frac{2a}{r}\cos\theta\right)^{-1/2}$$

Putting these values in Eq. (i), we obtain

$$V_P = \frac{q}{4\pi\varepsilon_0}\left[\frac{1}{r}\left(1 - \frac{2a}{r}\cos\theta\right)^{-\frac{1}{2}} - \frac{1}{r}\left(1 + \frac{2a}{r}\cos\theta\right)^{-\frac{1}{2}}\right]$$

Using Binomial theorem, $[(1+x)^n = 1 + nx, x << 1]$ and retaining terms upto the first order in $\frac{a}{r}$, we get

$$V_P = \frac{q}{4\pi\varepsilon_0 r}\left[\left(1 + \frac{a}{r}\cos\theta\right) - \left(1 - \frac{a}{r}\cos\theta\right)\right]$$

$$= \frac{q}{4\pi\varepsilon_0 r}\left[1 + \frac{a}{r}\cos\theta - 1 + \frac{a}{r}\cos\theta\right]$$

$$= \frac{q}{4\pi\varepsilon_0 r}\left(\frac{2a\cos\theta}{r}\right) = \frac{q \times 2a\cos\theta}{4\pi\varepsilon_0 r^2}$$

$$\Rightarrow \quad \boxed{V_P = \frac{p\cos\theta}{4\pi\varepsilon_0 r^2}} \quad [\because p = q \times 2a] \quad \ldots\text{(i)}$$

As, $p\cos\theta = \mathbf{p} \cdot \hat{\mathbf{r}}$

where, $\hat{\mathbf{r}}$ is a unit vector along the position vector $\mathbf{OP} = \mathbf{r}$.

$\therefore$ Electrostatic potential at point P due to a short dipole

$(a << r)$ is given by $$\boxed{V = \frac{\mathbf{p} \cdot \hat{\mathbf{r}}}{4\pi\varepsilon_0 r^2}} \quad \ldots\text{(ii)}$$

The electric potential due to an electric dipole at point P varies inversely with square of r, i.e. the distance of point P from the centre of the dipole.

(i) **On the dipole axis** ($\theta = 0$ or π)

$$V = \pm\frac{p}{4\pi\varepsilon_0 r^2} \quad \text{[from Eq. (i)]}$$

Positive sign for $\theta = 0°$ and negative sign for $\theta = \pi$.

(ii) **On the equatorial plane** $\left(\theta = \frac{\pi}{2}; \cos\frac{\pi}{2} = 0\right)$

$$V = 0 \quad \text{[from Eq. (ii)]}$$

So, electrostatic potential at any point in the equatorial plane of dipole is zero.

Differences between electric potential due to an electric dipole and due to a single charge

- The potential due to a dipole depends not just on r but also on the angle between the position vector **r** and dipole moment vector **p**.
- The electric potential due to dipole falls off at a distance r as $1/r^2$ not as $1/r$, which is a characteristic of the potential due to single charge.

Example 7. **An electric dipole consists of two charges of equal magnitude and opposite signs separated by a distance $2a$ as shown in figure. The dipole is along the X-axis and is centred at the origin.**

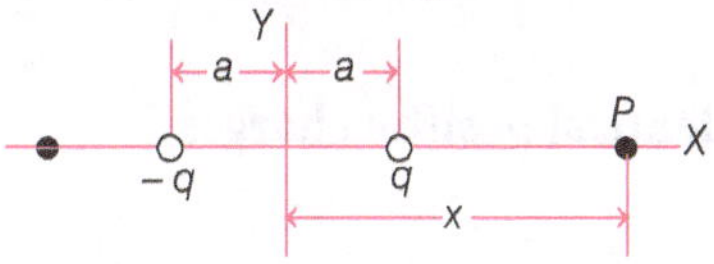

(i) Calculate the electric potential at point P.

(ii) Calculate V at a point far from the dipole.

Sol. (i) For the point P in figure,

$$V = k\Sigma\frac{q_i}{r_1} = k_e\left(\frac{q}{x-a} - \frac{q}{x+a}\right) = \frac{2kqa}{x^2 - a^2}$$

(ii) If point P is far from the dipole, such that $x >> a$, then a^2 can be neglected in the terms $x^2 - a^2$ and V becomes $V = \frac{2kqa}{x^2}$ $[\because x >> a]$

Equipotential Surfaces

Any surface which has same electrostatic potential at every point is called **equipotential surfaces.**

The **properties** of equipotential surfaces are given below

(i) No work is done in moving a test charge from one point to another point on equipotential surface.

(ii) The electric field is always perpendicular to the equipotential surface.

(iii) No two equipotential surfaces intersect each other.

(iv) Equipotential surfaces are closer in regions of strong electric field and they are farther apart in the region of weak electric fields.

Some Equipotential Surfaces are given below

- **For a point chage**

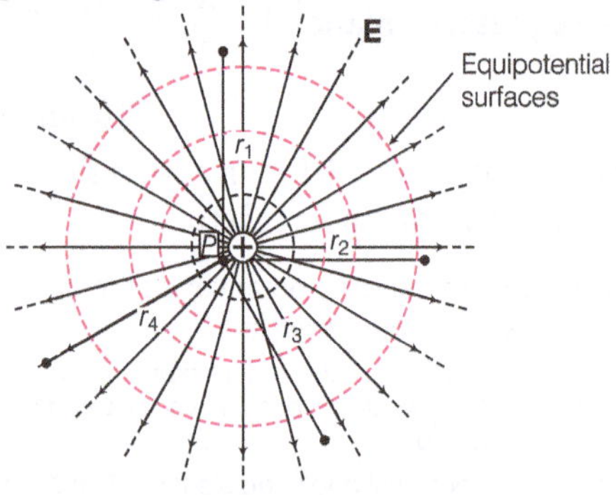

- **For uniform electric field**

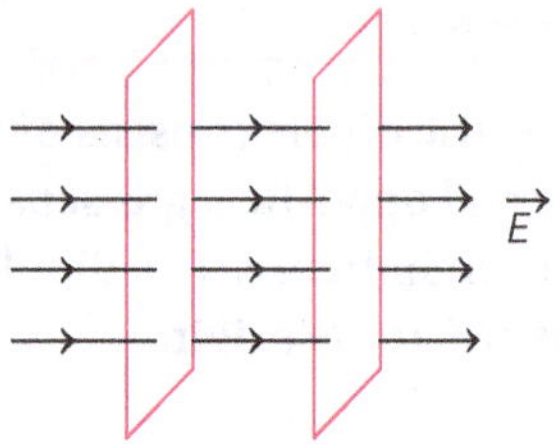

- **For two identical positive charges**

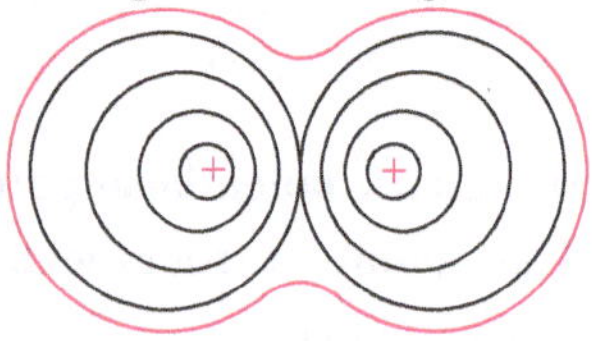

- **For an electric dipole**

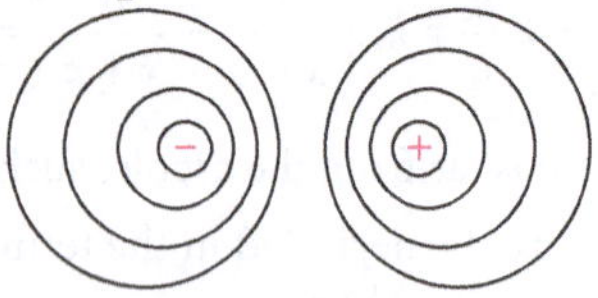

- **For non-uniform electric field**

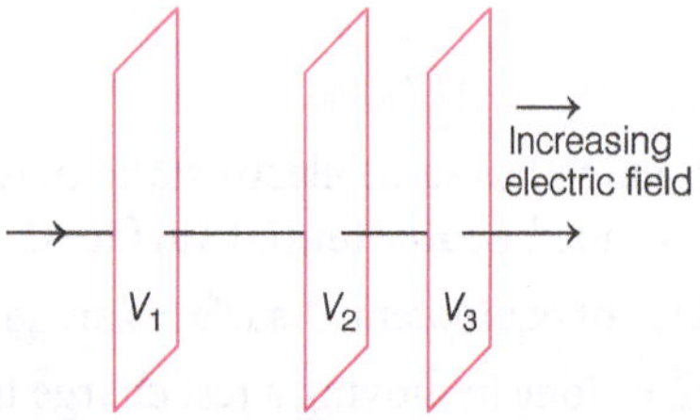

TEACHER TIP

The shape of equipotential surface due to a line charge is **cylindrical** and point charge is **spherical**.

Example 8. **Two charges 2 μC and – 2 μC are placed at points *A* and *B*, 5 cm apart. Depict an equipotential surface of the system.** Delhi 2013

Sol. Equipotential surface means the surface where potential remains the same at each point. Here, this is the system of two equal and opposite charges.

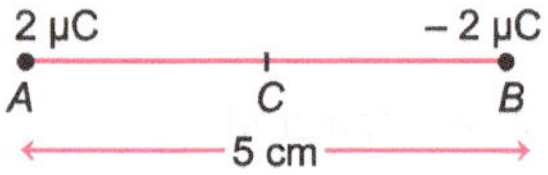

∴ The potential at *C* (mid-point of *AB*),

$$V = \frac{1}{4\pi\varepsilon_0}\left(\frac{q_1}{r_1} + \frac{q_2}{r_2}\right)$$

$$= \frac{1}{4\pi\varepsilon_0}\left[\frac{2\times10^{-6}}{2.5\times10^{-2}} + \frac{(-2\times10^{-6})}{2.5\times10^{-2}}\right] = 0$$

Thus, potential is zero at each point on the line which passes through the mid-point of *AB* and perpendicular to it, so a plane passing through the mid-point *C* of *AB* is an equipotential surface.

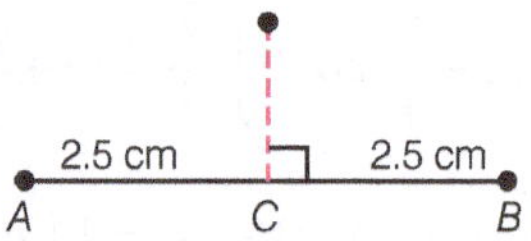

Relation between Electric Field and Electric Potential

Relation between *E* and *V* is given as

$$E = -\frac{dV}{dx}$$

where, *dx* is the perpendicular distance between two equipotential surfaces and *dV* is the change in *V* in the direction of *E*.

For a three-dimensional potential function,

$$\mathbf{E} = -\Delta V$$

$$\mathbf{E} = -\left(\frac{\partial V}{\partial x}\hat{\mathbf{i}} + \frac{\partial V}{\partial y}\hat{\mathbf{j}} + \frac{\partial V}{\partial z}\hat{\mathbf{k}}\right)$$

This means that electric potential *V* decreases in direction of electric field *E*.

Example 9. **A small particle carrying a negative charge of 1.6×10^{-19} C is suspended in equilibrium between the horizontal metal plates 5 cm apart, having a potential difference of 3000 V across them. Find the mass of the particle.**

Sol. Here, $q = -1.6 \times 10^{-19}$ C, $dr = 5\text{ cm} = 5 \times 10^{-2}$ m

and $dV = 3000$ V

$$\therefore \quad E = -\frac{dV}{dr} = \frac{-3000}{5 \times 10^{-2}}$$

$$= -6 \times 10^{4}\ \text{Vm}^{-1}$$

As, the charged particle remains suspended in equilibrium, therefore

$$F = mg = qE$$

$$\therefore \quad m = \frac{qE}{g} = \frac{(-1.6 \times 10^{-19}) \times (-6 \times 10^{4})}{9.8}$$

$$= 9.8 \times 10^{-16}\ \text{kg}$$

Example 10. The electric potential in a region is represented as

$$V = 2x + 3y - z$$

Obtain expression for electric field strength.

Sol. As, $\mathbf{E} = -\left[\frac{\partial V}{\partial x}\hat{\mathbf{i}} + \frac{\partial V}{\partial y}\hat{\mathbf{j}} + \frac{\partial V}{\partial z}\hat{\mathbf{k}}\right]$

Here, $\frac{\partial V}{\partial x} = \frac{\partial}{\partial x}(2x + 3y - z) = 2$

$\frac{\partial V}{\partial y} = \frac{\partial}{\partial y}(2x + 3y - z) = 3$

and $\frac{\partial V}{\partial z} = \frac{\partial}{\partial z}(2x + 3y - z) = -1$

$\therefore$ Electric field, $\mathbf{E} = -2\hat{\mathbf{i}} - 3\hat{\mathbf{j}} + \hat{\mathbf{k}}$

Example 11. In uniform electric field, $\mathbf{E} = 10\ \text{NC}^{-1}$ as shown in figure.

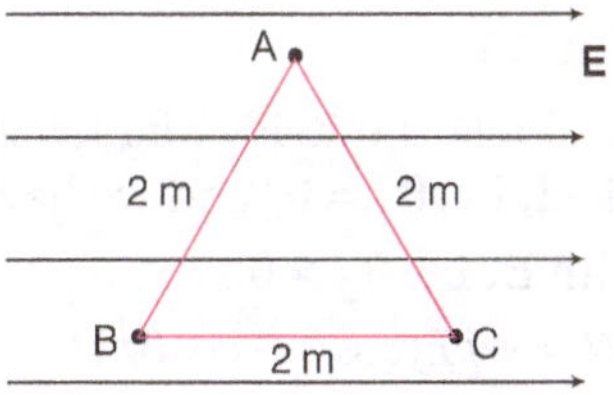

Find

(i) $V_A - V_B$ **(ii) $V_B - V_C$**

Sol. Since, electric field is directed from higher electric potential to lower electric potential,

(i) Thus, $V_B > V_A$, so $V_A - V_B$ will be negative.

Further, $d_{AB} = 2 \cos 60° = 1$ m

$$\therefore \quad V_A - V_B = -Ed_{AB} = (-10)(1) = -10\ \text{V}$$

(ii) As, $V_B > V_C$, so $V_B - V_C$ will be positive.

Further, $d_{BC} = 2$ m

$$\therefore \quad V_B - V_C = (10)(2) = 20\ \text{V}$$

2.2 Electrostatic Potential Energy of a System of Charges

It is defined as the total amount of work done in bringing the different charges to their respective positions from infinitely large mutual separations.

- The SI unit of **electrostatic potential energy** is **joule (J).** Another convenient unit of energy is electron-volt (eV).
- Electrostatic potential energy is a **scalar quantity**.

Electrostatic Potential Energy of a System of Two Point Charges

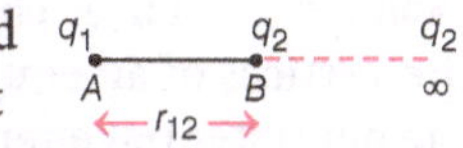

Let us consider q_1 is placed at A and another point charge q_2 is placed at ∞ distance from q_1.

q_2 is brought from ∞ to the point B.

Potential at B due to q_1, $V = \frac{q_1}{4\pi\varepsilon_0 r_{12}}$

Work done in carrying a charge q_2 from ∞ to B, $U = W =$ Potential × Charge

Potential energy at $B = W = \frac{q_1 q_2}{4\pi\varepsilon_0 r_{12}}$

(The values of q_1 and q_2 must be with proper signs)

Special cases

Case	**Potential energy**
$q_1 q_2 > 0$	Potential energy is +ve and increases on bringing $q_1 q_2$ closer.
$q_1 q_2 < 0$	Potential energy is −ve and decreases on bringing $q_1 q_2$ closer.

Note For n charges, the potential energy of a system at $\mathbf{r}_1, \mathbf{r}_2 \ldots\ldots \mathbf{r}_n$.

$$U = \frac{1}{4\pi\varepsilon_0} \Sigma \frac{q_j q_k}{r_{jk}}$$

Example 12. In a hydrogen atom, the electron and proton are bound at a distance of about 0.53 Å. Estimate the potential energy of the system (in eV), taking the zero of the potential energy at infinite separation of the electron from proton.

Sol. Charge on electron, $q_e = -1.6 \times 10^{-19}$ C and charge on proton, $q_p = 1.6 \times 10^{-19}$ C

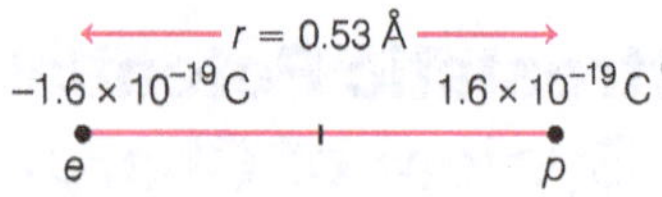

Potential energy of the system

= Potential energy at infinity

− Potential energy at a distance of 0.53 Å

$$= 0 - \frac{1}{4\pi\varepsilon_0} \cdot \frac{q_e q_p}{r}$$

$$= 0 - \frac{9 \times 10^9 \times (-1.6 \times 10^{-19}) \times 1.6 \times 10^{-19}}{0.53 \times 10^{-10}}$$

$$= -43.47 \times 10^{-19} \text{ J} \quad [\because 1 \text{ eV} = 1.6 \times 10^{-19} \text{ J}]$$

$$= -\frac{43.47 \times 10^{-19}}{1.6 \times 10^{-19}} = -27.16 \text{ eV}$$

Example 13. **Three charges (all $q = 10\text{ C}$) are placed at the vertices of an equilateral triangle of side 2 m. Find the net potential energy of the system.**

Sol. Given, charge, $q = 10$ C $(q_1 = q_2 = q)$

Each side of equilateral triangle, $r = 2$ m

Potential energy (PE) = ?

Potential energy between two charges is given by

$$\text{PE} = \frac{kq_1q_2}{r} \quad [\because r = \text{distance between } q_1 \text{ and } q_2]$$

∴ PE of system will be three times the potential energy between the two charges as the equal charge is placed at the vertices of an equilateral triangle.

$$\text{So, PE}_{\text{net}} = \frac{3 \times kqq}{r} = \frac{3\,kq^2}{r}$$

$$= \frac{3 \times 9 \times 10^9 \times 10 \times 10}{2} = 1.35 \times 10^{12} \text{ J}$$

Potential Energy in an External Field

A single charge or a system of charges possess electrostatic potential energy in the presence of an external electric field, these are discussed as follows.

(i) **Potential energy due to single charge in an external field**

Potential energy of a charge q at a position **r** in an external field is $\boxed{U = qV(r)}$

(ii) **Potential energy due to two charges in an external field**

Potential energy of two charges q_1 and q_2 at positions r_1 and r_2 in an external field is

$$\boxed{U = q_1V(r_1) + q_2V(r_2) + \frac{1}{4\pi\varepsilon_0}\frac{q_1q_2}{r_{12}}}$$

Potential Energy of a Dipole in an External Field

Consider a dipole with charges $+q$ and $-q$ placed in a uniform external electric field as shown in the figure. In a uniform electric field, the dipole experiences no force but experiences a torque τ given by $\tau = \mathbf{p} \times \mathbf{E} = pE\sin\theta$

This torque will tend to rotate the dipole. Suppose an external torque τ_{ext} is applied to the dipole, so that it rotates from angle θ_1 to θ_2 with respect to the electric field (**E**).

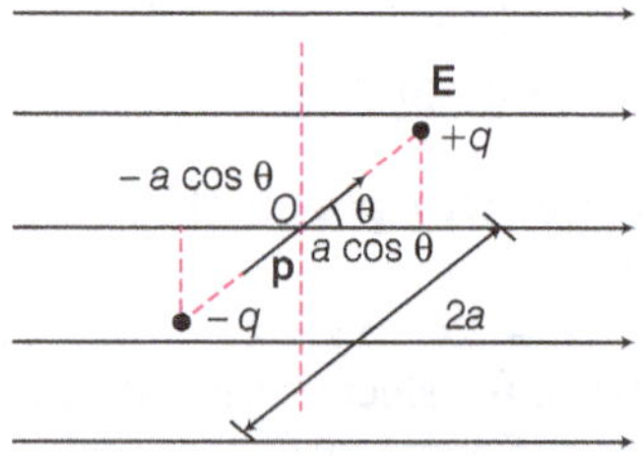

Dipole in a uniform external field

The amount of work done by the external torque is given by

$$W = \int_{\theta_1}^{\theta_2} \tau_{\text{ext}}\, d\theta = \int_{\theta_1}^{\theta_2} pE\sin\theta\, d\theta$$

$$= pE[-\cos\theta]_{\theta_1}^{\theta_2}$$

$$W = pE(\cos\theta_1 - \cos\theta)_2$$

The work done W is stored as the potential energy of the system. Therefore, the potential energy of the dipole placed in external field **E** is given by

$$\boxed{U(\theta) = pE(\cos\theta_1 - \cos\theta_2)}$$

Particular Cases

(i) When the dipole is initially **aligned along the electric field, i.e. $\theta_1 = 0°$** and we have to set it at angle θ with **E**, i.e. $\theta_2 = \theta$.

$$\therefore \quad W = -pE(\cos\theta - \cos 0°)$$

$$= -pE(\cos\theta - 1)$$

This **work done is stored in the dipole in the form of potential energy.**

(ii) When the dipole is initially at right angle to **E**, i.e. $\theta_1 = 90°$ and we have to set it at angle θ with **E**,

i.e. $\theta_2 = \theta$.

$$\therefore \quad W = -pE(\cos\theta - \cos 90°) = -pE\cos\theta$$

∴ Potential energy of dipole, $U = W = -pE\cos\theta$

$$\boxed{U = -\mathbf{p} \cdot \mathbf{E}}$$

Hence, potential energy of an electric dipole is a **scalar quantity.** It is measured in **joule.**

Example 14. **An electric dipole of length 4 cm, when placed with its axis making an angle of 60° with a uniform electric field, experiences a torque of $4\sqrt{3}$ N-m. Calculate the potential energy of the dipole, if it has charge ± 8 nC.**

Sol. Given, length, $2a = 4\text{ cm} = 4\times 10^{-2}$ m

Angle, $\theta = 60°$

Torque, $\tau = 4\sqrt{3}$ N-m

Charge, $q = 8\times 10^{-9}$ C

We know that, $\tau = pE\sin\theta$

$\Rightarrow$ Electric field, $E = \dfrac{\tau}{p\sin\theta}$ ... (i)

$\because$ Potential energy,

$$U = -\mathbf{p}\cdot\mathbf{E} = -pE\cos\theta$$

On solving, we get

$$U = -\frac{p\cdot\tau}{p\cdot\sin\theta}\cdot\cos\theta$$

$$= -\tau\cot\theta$$

$$= -4\sqrt{3}\cdot\cot 60°$$

$$= -4\sqrt{3}\times\frac{1}{\sqrt{3}} \qquad \left(\because \cot 60° = \frac{1}{\sqrt{3}}\right)$$

$$= -4\text{ J}$$

Example 15. **A point charge q is fixed at origin. A dipole with a dipole moment p is placed along the X-axis far away from the origin with p pointing along positive X-axis. Find**

(i) the kinetic energy of the dipole when it reaches a distance d from the origin.

(ii) the force experienced by the charge q at this moment.

Sol. (i) Applying energy conservation principle,

Increase in kinetic energy of the dipole = Decrease in electrostatic potential energy of the dipole

$\therefore$ Kinetic energy of dipole at distance d from origin

$$= U_i - U_f = 0 - (-\mathbf{p}\cdot\mathbf{E}) = \mathbf{p}\cdot\mathbf{E}$$

$$= (p\hat{\mathbf{i}})\cdot\left(\frac{1}{4\pi\varepsilon_0}\frac{q}{d^2}\hat{\mathbf{i}}\right)$$

$$= \frac{qp}{4\pi\varepsilon_0 d^2}$$

(ii) Electric field at origin due to the dipole,

$$\mathbf{E} = \frac{1}{4\pi\varepsilon_0}\frac{2p}{d^3}\hat{\mathbf{i}} \qquad [\because \mathbf{E}_{\text{axis}} \uparrow\uparrow \mathbf{p}]$$

$\therefore$ Force on charge q,

$$\mathbf{F} = q\mathbf{E} = \frac{pq}{2\pi\varepsilon_0 d^3}\hat{\mathbf{i}}$$

Quick Test 1

Conceptual Questions

1. A charge q is moved from a point A above a dipole of dipole moment p to a point B below the dipole in equatorial plane without acceleration. Find the work done in this process.

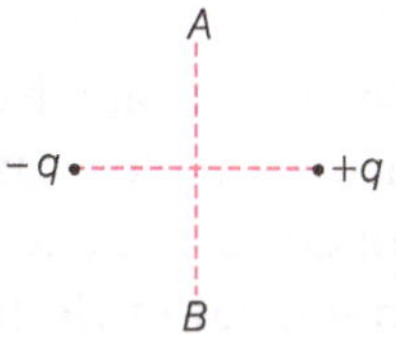

2. A point charge Q is placed at point O as shown in the figure. Is the potential at point A, i.e., V_A greater, smaller or equal to potential, V_B, at point B, when Q is (i) positive and (ii) negative charge ?

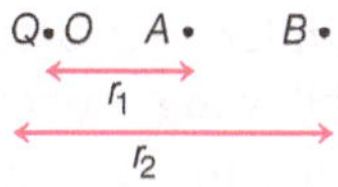

3. For a uniform electric field given as shown below, at what point will the electric potential be maximum?

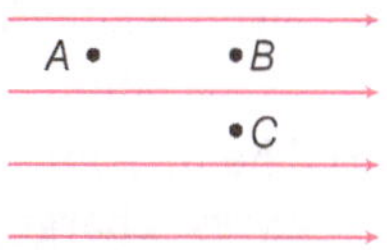

4. A thin spherical conducting shell of radius R has a charge q. A point charge Q is placed at the centre of the shell. Find

(i) the charge density on the outer surface of the shell and

(ii) the potential at a distance $(R/2)$ from the centre of the shell. *CBSE 2024*

5. Name the shape of the equipotential surface at a great distance from a collection of charges whose total sum is not zero.

6. If a point charge $+q$ is taken from A to C and then from C to B. Points A and B lie on a circle drawn with another charge $+q$ at its centre, then along which path more work will be done?

7. Do free electrons travel to region of higher potential or lower potential? *NCERT Exemplar*

Numerical Questions

8. Two identical metallic plate surfaces A and B are kept parallel to each other in air, separated by a distance of 1 cm, surface A is given a positive potential of 10 V and the outer surface of B is earthed.

(i) What is the magnitude and direction of the electric field between the surfaces A and B?

(ii) What is the work done in moving a charge of 20 μC from surface A to surface B ?

9. Two charges 5×10^{-8} C and -3×10^{-8} C are located 16 cm apart. At what point(s) on the line joining the two charges is the electric potential zero? Take the potential at infinity to be zero. *NCERT*

10. A regular hexagon of side 10 cm has a charge 5 μC at each of its vertices. Calculate the potential at the centre of the hexagon. *NCERT*

Answers

8. (i) 10^3 V/m (ii) -20×10^{-5} J *9.* 6 cm, -3×10^{-8} C

10. 2.7×10^6 V

For Solutions, See QR Code on Pg. 85

2.3 Electrostatics of Conductor

Conductors

Conductors are the materials through which electric charge can flow easily. Most of the metals are conductors of electric charge. **Silver is the best conductor of electric charge.**

Under electrostatic conditions, the conductors have following properties

(i) Inside a conductor, electrostatic field is zero.

(ii) At the surface of a charged conductor, electrostatic field must be normal to the surface at every point.

(iii) The interior of a conductor does not have any excess charge in the static situation.

(iv) Electrostatic potential is constant throughout the volume of the conductor and has the same value (as inside) on its surface.

(v) Surface charge density of a conductor could be different at different points.

(vi) Electric field at the surface of a charged conductor is $\mathbf{E} = \dfrac{\sigma}{\varepsilon_0}\hat{\mathbf{n}}$, where σ is the surface charge density and $\hat{\mathbf{n}}$ is a unit vector normal to the surface in the outward direction.

Electrostatic Shielding

The phenomenon of protecting a certain region of space from external electric field is called **electrostatic shielding.**

We know that inside a conductor, electric field is zero, so to protect some instruments from external field, they are enclosed in hollow conductors.

For e.g. It is always advisable that when lightning strikes, we should be inside a bus or car. This is because cars and buses are conductors which stop the electric current flow, as there is no electric field inside them.

Insulators

Insulators are those substances which contain practically no free charge carriers and do not allow the flow of current. **Examples** Plastic and glass.

Free Charges and Bound Charges Inside the Conductors

- **Free charges** In a metal, the outer (valence) electrons part away from their atoms and are free to move, these electrons are called **free electrons** or **conduction electrons.**
- **Bound charges** When an electron leaves an atom, atom becomes positively charged ion. The positively charged ions and bound electrons remain held in their fixed positions and are called bound charges.

Dielectrics

Dielectrics are insulating materials which transmit electric effects without actually conducting electricity.

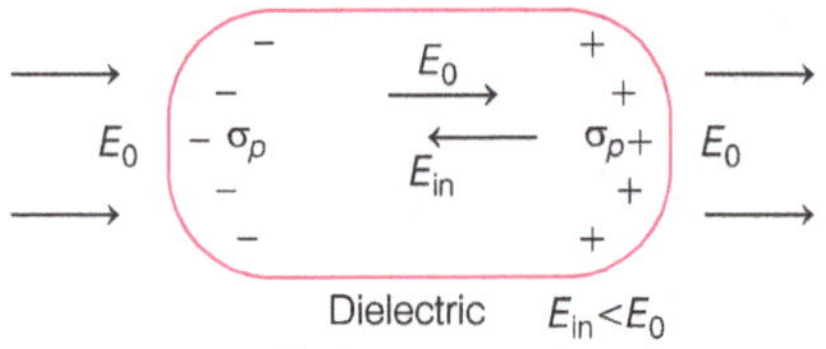

Polarised dielectric slab

$$\mathbf{E} = \mathbf{E}_0 + \mathbf{E}_{in}$$

where, $\mathbf{E}$ = resultant electric field inside the dielectric.

$\mathbf{E}_0$ = external electric field

and $\mathbf{E}_{in}$ = electric field inside the dielectric.

Dielectrics are of two types

(a) **Polar dielectrics** Polar dielectrics (H_2O, CO_2, NH_3, etc.) are made up of polar atoms / molecules in which the centre of positive charge does not coincide with the centre of negative charge of the atom.

(b) **Non-polar dielectrics** Non-polar dielectrics (H_2O, CO_2, NH_3, etc) are made up of polar atoms / molecules in which the centre of positive charge coincides with the centre of negative charge of the atom/molecule.

Dielectric Constant

Dielectric constant is defined as the ratio of the electric permittivity of the material to the electric permittivity of the free space.

It is also known as **relative permittivity** or **dielectric constant** and is denoted by K(or ε_r).

Therefore, dielectric constant of a dielectric medium is given by

$$K = \frac{\varepsilon}{\varepsilon_0}$$

The value of K is always greater than 1.

Polarisation

- The induced dipole moment developed per unit volume in a dielectric slab on placing it in an electric field is called polarisation. It is denoted by P.

If p is induced dipole moment acquired by an atom of the dielectric and N is the number of atoms per unit volume, then **polarisation** is given by

$$\boxed{P = Np}$$

- The induced dipole moment (p) acquired by the atom is found to be directly proportional to the reduced value of electric field (E) and is given by

$$\boxed{\mathrm{p} = \alpha \varepsilon_0 \mathrm{E}}$$

where, α is constant of proportionality and is called **atomic polarisability.**

Electric Susceptibility

The **polarisation density** of a dielectric slab is directly proportional to the reduced value of the electric field and may be expressed as

$$\boxed{P = \chi \varepsilon_0 E}$$

The constant of proportionality χ is called **electric susceptibility** of the dielectric slab. It is a dimensionless constant. It describes the electrical behaviour of a dielectric.

It has different values for different dielectrics.
For vacuum, $\chi = 0$

Relation between dielectric constant and electric susceptibility can be given as

$$\boxed{K = 1 + \chi}$$

Dielectric Strength

The maximum electric field that a dielectric can withstand without breakdown (of its insulating property), is called its dielectric strength. For air, it is about 3×10^6 V/m.

2.4 Capacitors and Capacitance

A **capacitor** is a system of the conductors separated by an insulator. It is an arrangement for storing large amounts of electric charge and hence electric energy in a small space.

The **electric charges** stored between plates of capacitor is directly proportional to potential differences,

i.e. $Q \propto V$

or $Q = CV$

$\Rightarrow$ $\boxed{C = \dfrac{Q}{V}}$

- The constant C is called the capacitance of the capacitor. Capacitance C is defined as the ratio of charge given to the conductor to the rise in its potential. It depends on shape, size and separation of the system of two conductors.
- The **SI unit** of capacitance is **farad** (F).
- Its **dimensional formula** is $[M^{-1}L^{-2}T^4A^2]$.
  1 farad = 1 coulomb/volt
- A capacitor with fixed capacitance is symbolically shown as —| |—, while the one with variable capacitance is shown as —|/|—. In practice, farad is a very big unit, the most common units are its sub-multiples.

$$1\ \mu\text{F} = 10^{-6}\text{F},\ 1\ \text{nF} = 10^{-9}\ \text{F},\ 1\ \text{pF} = 10^{-12}\text{F}$$

Parallel Plate Capacitor

A parallel plate capacitor is made up of two thin conducting plates, labelled 1 and 2, each having an area A and positioned parallel to each other at a distance d apart.

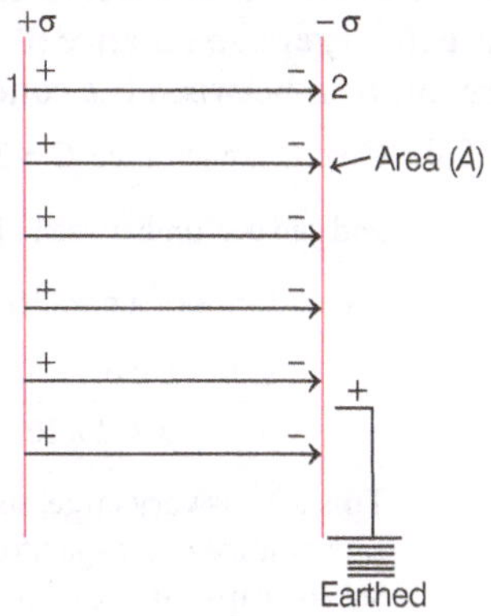

The plates are separated by a non-conducting material (dielectric) such as air, paper, mica or glass.

When a charge $+Q$ is placed on plate 1, an equal but opposite charge $-Q$ is induced on plate 2, creating surface charge densities of $+\sigma$ on plate 1 and $-\sigma$ on plate 2.

The electric field intensity E between the plates, assuming air or vacuum as the medium is given by

$$E = \frac{\sigma}{\varepsilon_0} = \frac{Q}{\varepsilon_0 A}$$

If E is the electric field between the plates, then the potential difference V between the plates is

$$V = E \times d = \frac{1}{\varepsilon_0} \times \frac{Q}{A} d$$

So, the capacity of parallel plate capacitor,

$$C = \frac{Q}{V} \Rightarrow C = \frac{Q}{\dfrac{1}{\varepsilon_0} \times \dfrac{Q}{A} d}$$

$$C = \frac{\varepsilon_0 A}{d}$$

where, $\varepsilon_0 = 8.85 \times 10^{-12}$ F/m

It is clear from this formula that in order to obtain high capacitance :

(i) **A should be large,** i.e. the plates of large area should be taken.

(ii) **d should be small,** i.e. the plates should be kept close to each other.

TEACHER TIP

The force between the two plates of capacitor can be given as $F = \dfrac{q^2}{2\varepsilon_0 A}$

Example 16. **What is the area of the plates of a 2 F parallel plate capacitor, given that the separation between the plates is 0.5 cm? [You will realise from your answer why ordinary capacitors are in the range of μF or less. However, electrolytic capacitors do have a much larger capacitance (0.1 F) because of very minute separation between the conductors].**

Sol. Given, capacitance, $C = 2$ F

and separation between plates, $d = 0.5$ cm $= 0.5 \times 10^{-2}$ m

Capacitance of a parallel plate capacitor, $C = \dfrac{\varepsilon_0 A}{d}$

or $A = \dfrac{Cd}{\varepsilon_0} = \dfrac{2 \times 0.5 \times 10^{-2}}{8.854 \times 10^{-12}} = 1.13 \times 10^9 \text{ m}^2 = 1130 \text{ km}^2$

This area is very large, so it is not possible that the capacitance of a capacitor is as large as 2 F.

So, the capacitance of any capacitor should be in order of μF.

Example 17. **A parallel plate capacitor has plate area 25 cm^2 and a separation of 2 mm between the plates. The capacitor is connected to a battery of 12 V.**

(i) Find the charge on the capacitor.

(ii) If the plate separation is decreased to 1.0 mm, then find the extra charge given by the battery to the positive plate.

Sol. Given, area of plate, $A = 25 \text{ cm}^2 = 25 \times 10^{-4} \text{m}^2$

Distance between the plates, $d = 2 \text{ mm} = 2 \times 10^{-3}$ m

Potential difference, $V = 12$ V

(i) Charge on the capacitor, $q = CV$

$$q = \frac{\varepsilon_0 A}{d} V = \frac{8.85 \times 10^{-12} \times 25 \times 10^{-4} \times 12}{2 \times 10^{-3}}$$

$= 1.33 \times 10^{-10}$C

(ii) If the plate separation is decreased to half, the capacity becomes twice. Then, charge becomes twice as battery is still connected.

∴ Extra charge given by the battery $= q' - q$

$= 2q - q = q = 1.33 \times 10^{-10}$C

Effect of Dielectric on Parallel Plate Capacitor

The capacitance C with dielectric between the plates is given by

$$C = \frac{q}{V} = \frac{\varepsilon_0 KA}{d}$$

The product $\varepsilon_0 K$ is called the **permittivity of the medium** and is denoted by ε.

$$\varepsilon = \varepsilon_0 K$$

For vacuum, $K = 1$ and $\varepsilon = \varepsilon_0$, where ε_0 is called the **permittivity of the vacuum.**

The dimensionless ratio, $K = \dfrac{\varepsilon}{\varepsilon_0}$ is called the **dielectric constant** of the substance.

Similarly, $K = \dfrac{C}{C_0}$

Thus, the **dielectric constant of a substance is the factor ($K > 1$) by which the capacitance increases when the dielectric is inserted fully between the plates of a capacitor.**

- When a dielectric slab of thickness t is inserted between the plates, then

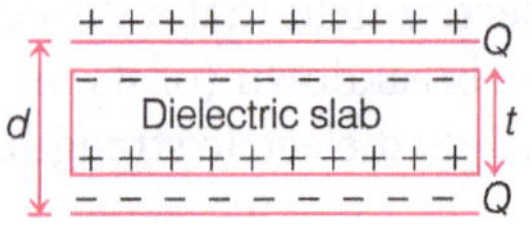

Capacitance, $C = \dfrac{\varepsilon_0 A}{d - t + \dfrac{t}{K}}$

- If several slabs of dielectric constants $K_1, K_2, K_3, \ldots$ and respective thicknesses $t_1, t_2, t_3, \ldots$ are placed in between the plates of a capacitor, then capacitance,

$$C = \frac{\varepsilon_0 A}{d - (t_1 + t_2 + t_3 + \ldots) + \dfrac{t_1}{K_1} + \dfrac{t_2}{K_2} + \dfrac{t_3}{K_3} + \ldots}$$

- If a metallic slab ($K = \infty$) of thickness t is placed between the plates of capacitor, then

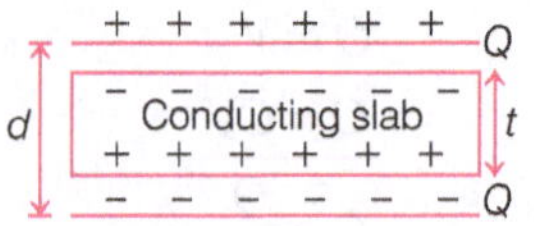

Capacitance, $C = \dfrac{\varepsilon_0 A}{d - t}$

If metallic slab fills the entire space between the plates (i.e. $d = t$), then capacitance will become infinite.

- The capacity of cylindrical air capacitor,
$$C = \frac{2\pi\varepsilon_0 L}{\log_e (r_y / r_x)}$$
- Capacity of an isolated spherical conductor,
$$C = 4\pi\varepsilon_0 r$$
where, r = radius of the sphere.
- The capacity of spherical capacitor, $C = \dfrac{4\pi\varepsilon_0 r_x r_y}{r_y - r_x}$

Example 18. In a parallel plate capacitor with air between the plates, each plate has an area of $6 \times 10^{-3}\,\text{m}^2$ and the separation between the plates is 3 mm.

(i) Calculate the capacitance of the capacitor.

(ii) If this capacitor is connected to 100 V supply, what would be the charge on each plate?

(iii) How would charge on the plates be affected, if a 3 mm thick mica sheet of $K = 6$ is inserted between the plates while the voltage supply remains connected? *(Foreign 2014)*

Sol. Given, area of each plate, $A = 6 \times 10^{-3}\,\text{m}^2$

Distance between the plates, $d = 3\text{ mm} = 3 \times 10^{-3}\,\text{m}$

(i) Capacitance of parallel plate capacitor is given by
$$C = \frac{\varepsilon_0 A}{d} = \frac{8.85 \times 10^{-12} \times 6 \times 10^{-3}}{3 \times 10^{-3}}$$
$$\therefore \quad C = 1.77 \times 10^{-11}\text{F}$$

(ii) Charge on parallel plate capacitor is given by
$$Q = CV = 1.77 \times 10^{-11} \times 100 = 1.77 \times 10^{-9}\text{C}$$

(iii) Given, $K = 6$

Now, $C' = KC \Rightarrow \dfrac{Q'}{V} = \dfrac{KQ}{V}$
$$\therefore \quad Q' = KQ = 6 \times 1.77 \times 10^{-9} = 10.62 \times 10^{-9}\text{C}$$

Example 19. An air-cored capacitor of plate area A and separation d has a capacity C. Two dielectric slabs are inserted between its plates in two different manners as shown. Calculate the capacitance in it.

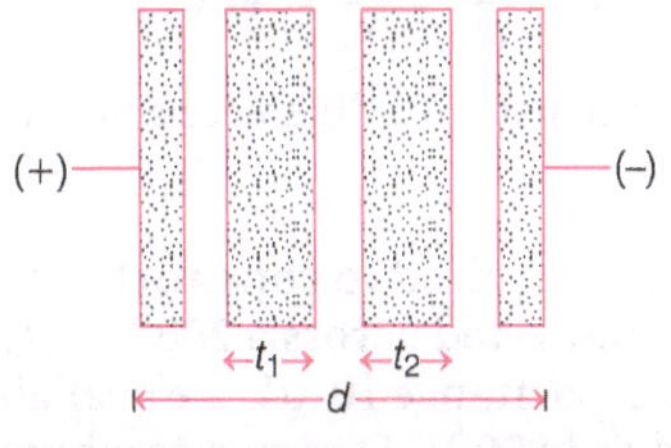

Sol. Let the charges on the plates are q and $-q$.

Electric field in free space, $E_0 = \dfrac{\sigma}{\varepsilon_0} = \dfrac{q}{A\varepsilon_0}$

Electric field in first slab, $E_1 = \dfrac{E_0}{K_1} = \dfrac{q}{A\varepsilon_0 K_1}$

Electric field in second slab, $E_2 = \dfrac{E_0}{K_2} = \dfrac{q}{A\varepsilon_0 K_2}$

The potential difference between the plates,
$$V = E_0(d - t_1 - t_2) + E_1 t_1 + E_2 t_2$$
$$\Rightarrow \quad V = E_0\left(d - t_1 - t_2 + \frac{t_1}{K_1} + \frac{t_2}{K_2}\right)$$
$$\left[\because E_1 = \frac{E_0}{K_1} \text{ and } E_2 = \frac{E_0}{K_2}\right]$$
$$\therefore \quad V = \frac{q}{A\varepsilon_0}\left(d - t_1 - t_2 + \frac{t_1}{K_1} + \frac{t_2}{K_2}\right)$$
$$\therefore \quad C = \frac{\varepsilon_0 A}{d - t_1 - t_2 + \dfrac{t_1}{K_1} + \dfrac{t_2}{K_2}}$$

2.5. Combination of Capacitors

Two or more capacitors can be connected by two different ways.

Capacitors in series

In series combination, capacitors are connected end-to-end.

Here a potential difference (V) is applied across several capacitors connected end-to-end in such a way that, **sum of potential differences across all the capacitors is equal to the applied potential difference V** and each capacitor's plates have the same charges $\pm q$.

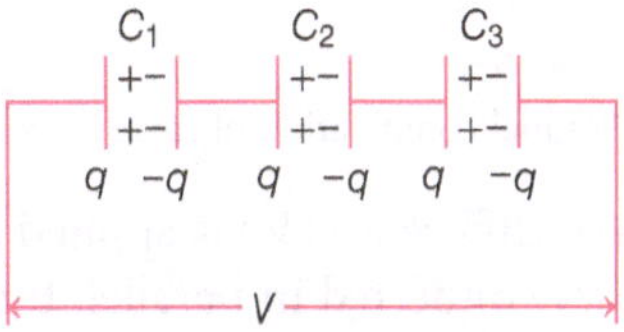

Series combination of capacitors

The potential difference across the each capacitors are given by
$$V_1 = \frac{q}{C_1},\ V_2 = \frac{q}{C_2} \text{ and } V_3 = \frac{q}{C_3}$$

However, the potential difference across the series combination of capacitors is V volt

where, $V = V_1 + V_2 + V_3$ ...(i)

Let C_s represents the equivalent capacitance, then
$$V = \frac{q}{C_s} \qquad \text{...(ii)}$$

Combining Eqs. (i) and (ii), we get

$$\frac{q}{C_s} = \frac{q}{C_1} + \frac{q}{C_2} + \frac{q}{C_3}$$

$$\Rightarrow \quad \frac{1}{C_s} = \frac{1}{C_1} + \frac{1}{C_2} + \frac{1}{C_3}$$

The **equivalent capacitance** of n capacitors are connected in series is equal to the sum of the reciprocals of individual capacitances of the capacitors.

Mathematically, it is expressed as,

$$\boxed{\frac{1}{C_{eq}} = \frac{1}{C_1} + \frac{1}{C_2} + \frac{1}{C_3} + \ldots + \frac{1}{C_n}}$$

All the capacitors connected in series have same amount of charge, but potential difference between their plates are inversely proportional to their capacitances.

Capacitors in Parallel

In parallel combination, all the positive plates of capacitors are connected to one point and all the negative plates are connected to other.

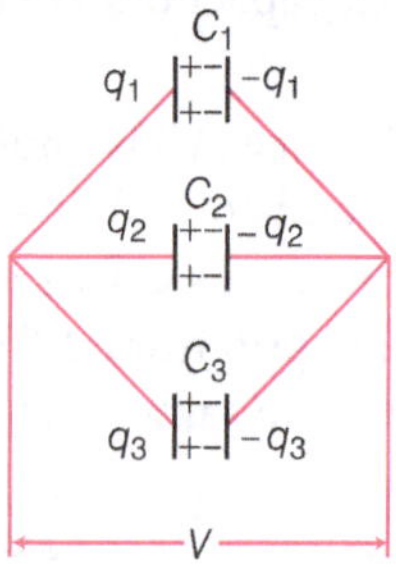

Parallel combination of capacitors

When a potential difference (V) is applied across several capacitors connected in parallel, the same potential difference (V) exists across each capacitor. **The total charge (q) stored on the capacitor is the sum of the charges stored on all the capacitors.**

If q is the total charge on the parallel network, then

$$q = q_1 + q_2 + q_3 \quad \ldots\text{(i)}$$

Let C_p be the equivalent capacitance of the parallel combination, then

$$q = C_pV, \; q_1 = C_1V, \; q_2 = C_2V$$

and $\quad q_3 = C_3V \quad \ldots\text{(ii)}$

Combining Eqs. (i) and (ii), we get

$$C_pV = C_1V + C_2V + C_3V$$

$$\boxed{C_p = C_1 + C_2 + C_3}$$

The **equivalent capacitance** of n number of capacitors in parallel is equal to the algebraic sum of the individual capacitances of the capacitors.

Mathematically, it is expressed as,

$$\boxed{C_{eq} = C_1 + C_2 + C_3 + \ldots + C_n}$$

All the capacitors connected in parallel have same potential difference between their plates but the charge is distributed proportionally to their capacitances.

Example 20. **Three capacitors each of capacitance 9 pF are connected in series.**

(i) What is the total capacitance of the combination?

(ii) What is the potential difference across each capacitor, if the combination is connected to a 120 V supply? NCERT

Sol. There are three capacitors each of capacitance 9 pF.

$\therefore \quad C_1 = C_2 = C_3 = 9$ pF

and voltage, $V = 120$ V

(i) The total capacitance in series combination,

$$\frac{1}{C_s} = \frac{1}{C_1} + \frac{1}{C_2} + \frac{1}{C_3} = \frac{1}{9} + \frac{1}{9} + \frac{1}{9}$$

$$\Rightarrow \quad \frac{1}{C_s} = \frac{3}{9} \Rightarrow C_s = 3 \text{ pF}$$

(ii) Let the charge across the system be q and potentials across C_1, C_2 and C_3 be V_1, V_2 and V_3, respectively.

Charge, $q = C_s \cdot V = 3 \times 120 = 360$ pC

Potential difference across C_1,

$$V_1 = \frac{q}{C_1} = \frac{360}{9} = 40 \text{ V}$$

Potential difference across C_2,

$$V_2 = \frac{q}{C_2} = \frac{360}{9} = 40 \text{ V}$$

Potential difference across C_3,

$$V_3 = \frac{q}{C_3} = \frac{360}{9} = 40 \text{ V}$$

Thus, the potential difference across each capacitor is 40 V.

Example 21. **It is required to construct a 10 μF capacitor which can be connected across a 200 V battery. Capacitors of capacitance 10 μF are available but they can withstand only 50 V. Design a combination which can yield the desired result.**

Sol. Capacitor of $10\mu F$ can withstand only 50 V, therefore to be connected across a 200 V battery, four capacitors must be connected in series in a row. Capacitor C_1 of each row of four capacitors is

$$\frac{1}{C_1}=\frac{1}{10}+\frac{1}{10}+\frac{1}{10}+\frac{1}{10}=\frac{4}{10}$$

$$\Rightarrow \quad C_1=\frac{10}{4}=2.5\mu F$$

For a total capacity of 10 μF, four such rows of capacitors must be connected in parallel, so that

$$C_P = 4\,C_1 = 4\times 2.5 = 10\,\mu F$$

Hence, we need 16 capacitors, with 4 capacitors in series in each row and 4 such rows in parallel.

Example 22. In the circuit shown in figure, find

(i) the equivalent capacitance and

(ii) the charge stored in each capacitor.

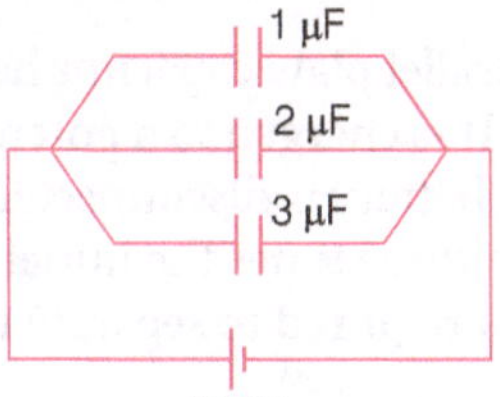

Sol. (i) The capacitors are in parallel. Hence, the equivalent capacitance,

$$C=C_1+C_2+C_3=(1+2+3)=6\mu F$$

(ii) Total charge drawn from the battery,

$$q=CV=6\times 100=600\,\mu C$$

This charge will be distributed in the ratio of their capacities. Hence,

$$q_1:q_2:q_3=C_1:C_2:C_3=1:2:3$$

$$\therefore \quad q_1=\left(\frac{1}{1+2+3}\right)\times 600=100\,\mu C$$

$$q_2=\left(\frac{2}{1+2+3}\right)\times 600=200\,\mu C$$

and $$q_3=\left(\frac{3}{1+2+3}\right)\times 600=300\,\mu C$$

Example 23. Three capacitors of 1 μF 2 μF and 3 μF are joined in series.

(i) How many times will the capacity become when they are joined in parallel ?

(ii) Determine the charge supplied by the battery of 100 V to the maximum resultant capacitor among both the arrangements.

Sol. (i) Given, $C_1=1\,\mu F, C_2=2\,\mu F, C_3=3\,\mu F$

The combined capacity (C_s) in series combination is given by

$$\frac{1}{C_s}=\frac{1}{C_1}+\frac{1}{C_2}+\frac{1}{C_3}=\frac{1}{1}+\frac{1}{2}+\frac{1}{3}=\frac{11}{6}$$

$$\Rightarrow \quad C_s=\frac{6}{11}\mu F$$

The combined capacity (C_P) in parallel combination is given by

$$C_P=C_1+C_2+C_3=1+2+3=6\,\mu F$$

$$\Rightarrow \quad C_P=11C_s$$

(ii) As, $\quad C_P>C_s$

∴ The charge supplied by 100 V battery,

$$q_P=C_pV=6\,\mu F\times 100$$
$$=6\times 10^{-6}\times 100$$

$$\Rightarrow \quad q_P=6\times 10^{-4}C=600\mu C$$

Example 24. Find the equivalent capacitance between *A* and *B* given in Figs. (i) and (ii). Given area of each plate = *A* and separation between plates = *d*.

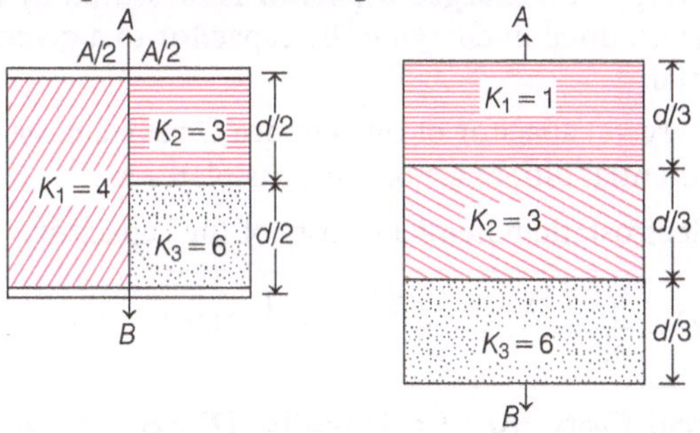

Sol. (i)

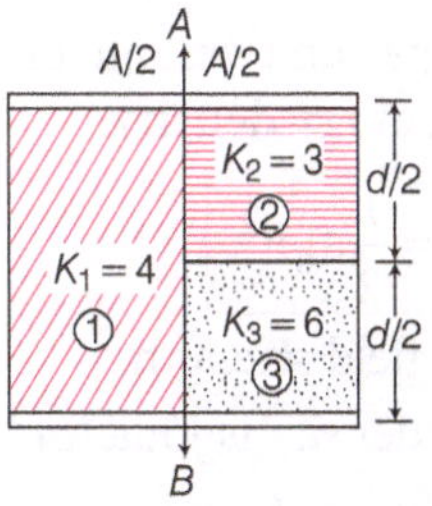

$$\text{Capacitance, } C_1=\frac{K_1\frac{A}{2}\varepsilon_0}{d}=\frac{4\frac{A}{2}\varepsilon_0}{d}=\frac{2A\varepsilon_0}{d}$$

$$\left[\because C=\frac{KA\varepsilon_0}{d}\right]$$

$$\text{Capacitance, } C_2=\frac{K_2\frac{A}{2}\varepsilon_0}{\frac{d}{2}}=\frac{3A\varepsilon_0}{d}$$

$$\text{Capacitance, } C_3=\frac{K_3\frac{A}{2}\varepsilon_0}{\frac{d}{2}}=\frac{6A\varepsilon_0}{d}$$

C_2 and C_3 are in series, $C' = \dfrac{C_2C_3}{C_2 + C_3} = \dfrac{2A\varepsilon_0}{d}$

C' and C_1 are in parallel $= \dfrac{4A\varepsilon_0}{d}$

(ii) Capacitance, $C_1 = \dfrac{K_1 A\varepsilon_0}{d/3} = \dfrac{3A\varepsilon_0}{d}$,

$$C_2 = \frac{K_2 A\varepsilon_0}{d/3} = \frac{9A\varepsilon_0}{d}$$

and $$C_3 = \frac{K_3 A\varepsilon_0}{d/3} = \frac{18A\varepsilon_0}{d}$$

$\because C_1, C_2$ and C_3 are in series,

$$\frac{1}{C_{eq}} = \frac{1}{C_1} + \frac{1}{C_2} + \frac{1}{C_3}$$

$\therefore$ Equivalent capacitance, $C_{eq} = \dfrac{2A\varepsilon_0}{d}$

Energy Stored in a Capacitor

The **energy of a charged capacitor** is measured by the total work done in charging the capacitor to a given potential.

If a charged capacitor of capacitance C have charge q and potential difference between its plates is V.

The electrostatic potential energy of the capacitor,

$$U = \frac{q^2}{2C} = \frac{1}{2}qV = \frac{(CV)^2}{2C} = \frac{1}{2}CV^2 \qquad [\because q = CV]$$

Energy Density of a Parallel Plate Capacitor

The energy stored per unit volume of space in a capacitor is called **energy density**.

Energy density, $u = \dfrac{1}{2}\varepsilon_0 E^2$

where, E is electric field strength.

The unit of energy density is joule/m^3.

Total Energy Stored in a combination of Capacitors

Total energy stored in series combination or parallel combination of capacitors is equal to the sum of energies stored in individual capacitors,

i.e. $U = U_1 + U_2 + U_3 + \ldots$

Example 25. **A capacitor of capacity 10 μF is subjected to charge by a battery of 10 V. Calculate the energy stored in the capacitor.**

Sol. Given, capacity, $C = 10\,\mu F = 10 \times 10^{-6}$ F

Voltage, $V = 10$ V

$\therefore$ Energy stored in the capacitor, $U = \dfrac{1}{2}CV^2$

$$U = \frac{1}{2} \times 10 \times 10^{-6} \times 10 \times 10 = 5 \times 10^{-4}\,\text{J}$$

Change in Energy on Introducing a Dielectric Slab

(i) When a dielectric slab is inserted between the plates of a charged capacitor, with battery connected to its plates, the capacitance becomes K (dielectric constant) times and the energy stored in the capacitor becomes KU_0.

(ii) When a dielectric slab is inserted between the plates of a charged capacitor and battery is disconnected, the charge on the plates remains unchanged and the energy stored in the capacitor becomes $\dfrac{U_0}{K}$, i.e. energy decreases.

Example 26. **A parallel plate capacitor has plate area A and separation d. It is charged to a potential difference V_0. This charging battery is disconnected and the plates are pulled apart to three times the initial separation. Calculate the work required to separate the plates.**

Sol. $\therefore$ Capacitance, $C = \dfrac{\varepsilon_0 A}{d}$

Charge on plate, $q = CV = \dfrac{\varepsilon_0 A}{d}V_0$

Energy stored, $U = q^2/2C$

As d is increased 3 times, so C decreases 3 times.

Battery is disconnected, so q remains the same. The difference in the energy is equal to the work done.

Change in potential energy, $\Delta U = U_i - U_f$

$$= \frac{q^2}{2}\left[\frac{1}{C_i} - \frac{1}{C_f}\right] = \left(\frac{\varepsilon_0 A V_0}{d}\right)^2 \times \frac{1}{2}\left[\frac{1}{C} - \frac{1}{C/3}\right]$$

$$= -\frac{1}{2} \times \left(\frac{\varepsilon_0 A V_0}{d}\right)^2 \times \frac{2}{C} = -\left(\frac{\varepsilon_0 A V_0}{d}\right)^2 \times \frac{d}{\varepsilon_0 A V_0}$$

$$= -\frac{\varepsilon_0 A V_0}{d}$$

$\therefore$ Work done, $\Delta W = -\Delta U = \dfrac{\varepsilon_0 A V_0}{d}$

Example 27. **A 2 μF capacitor is charged as shown in the figure. Find the percentage of its stored energy dissipated after the switch S is turned to position 2.**

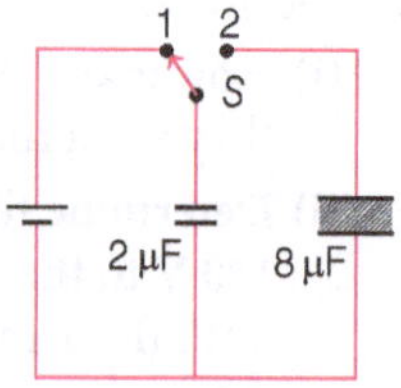

Sol. Initially, charge on the capacitor,

$$q_i = C_i V = 2V = q$$

This charge will remain constant after switch is shifted from position 1 to position 2.

$$U_i = \frac{1}{2}\frac{q^2}{C_i} = \frac{q^2}{2\times 2} = \frac{q^2}{4}$$

$$U_f = \frac{1}{2}\frac{q^2}{C_f} = \frac{q^2}{2\times 10} = \frac{q^2}{20}$$

$\therefore$ Energy dissipated $= U_i - U_f = \dfrac{q^2}{5}$

This energy dissipated $\left(=\dfrac{q^2}{5}\right)$ is 80% of the initial stored energy $\left(=\dfrac{q^2}{4}\right)$.

Common Potential

When two capacitors of different potentials are connected by a conducting wire, then **charge flows from capacitor at higher potential to the capacitor at lower potential.** This flow of charge continues till their potentials become equal, this equal potential is called **common potential.**

$$\text{Common potential} = \frac{\text{Total charge}}{\text{Total capacitance}}$$

$$\text{Common potential } V = \frac{C_1V_1 + C_2V_2}{C_1 + C_2}$$

where, C_1 and C_2 are capacities of two capacitors charged to potentials V_1 and V_2, respectively.

$\therefore \quad C_1V_1 + C_2V_2 = C_1V + C_2V$

or $\quad C_1V_1 - C_1V = C_2V - C_2V_2$

i.e. Charge lost by one capacitor

= Charge gained by the other capacitor

TEACHER TIP

Above concept is not true for potential, i.e. potential lost by one is not equal to potential gained by the other, as their capacities are different.

Example 28. A 600 pF capacitor is charged by a 200 V supply. It is then disconnected from the supply and is connected to another uncharged 600 pF capacitor. How much electrostatic energy is lost in this process? (NCERT)

Sol. Given, $C_1 = C_2 = 600 \text{ pF} = 600\times10^{-12}\text{F} = 6\times10^{-10}\text{F}$

$V_1 = 200 \text{ V}, V_2 = 0$

$$\therefore \text{Energy lost} = \frac{C_1C_2(V_1 - V_2)^2}{2(C_1 + C_2)} = \frac{(6\times10^{-10})^2(200-0)^2}{2\times12\times10^{-10}}$$

$= 6\times10^{-6}\text{J}$

Quick Test 2

Conceptual Questions

1. The given graph shows the variation of charge q *versus* potential difference V for two capacitors C_1 and C_2. Both the capacitors have same plate separation but plate area of C_2 is greater than that of C_1. Which line (A or B) corresponds to C_1 and why?

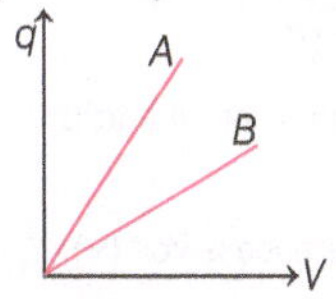

2. A spherical shell of radius b with charge Q is expanded to a radius a. Find the work done by the electrical forces in the process.

3. A sensitive instrument is to be shifted from the strong electrostatic field in its environment. Suggest a possible way.

4. Can the potential function have a maximum or minimum in free space? NCERT Exemplar

5. Guess a possible reason, why water has a much greater dielectric constant (= 80) than mica (= 6)?

6. A 2 m insulating slab with a large aluminium sheet of area 1 m^2 on its top is fixed by a man outside his house one evening. Will he get an electric shock, if he touches the metal sheet next morning?

Numerical Questions

7. A technician has only two capacitors. By using them in series or in parallel, he is able to obtain the capacitance of 4 μF, 5μF, 20 μF and 25 μF. What is the capacitance of both capacitors?

8. In the circuit shown below, initially K_1 is closed and K_2 is opened, what are the charges on each of the capacitors? If K_1 was opened and K_2 was closed (order is important), what will be the charge on each capacitor now? [Given, $C = 1\mu\text{F}$] NCERT Exemplar

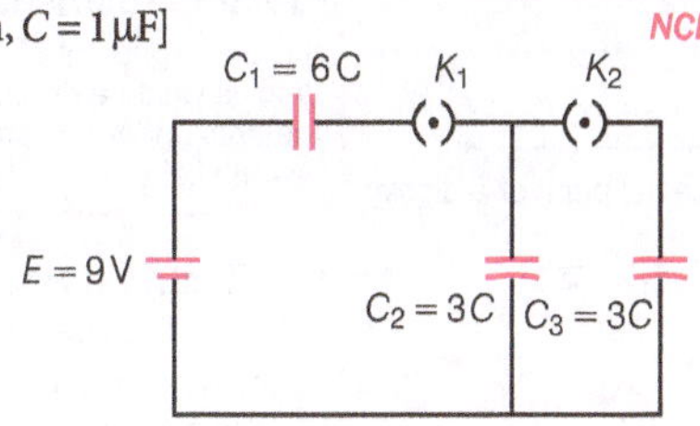

9. A 12 pF capacitor is connected to a 50 V battery. How much electrostatic energy is stored in the capacitor? If another capacitor of 6 pF is connected in series with it with the same battery connected across the combination, find the charge stored and potential difference across each capacitor. Delhi 2017

Answers

7. 5μF and 20μF *8.* 18μC, 18μC, 0

9. 15×10^{-9} J, 2×10^{-10} C, 16.67V, 33.33V

For Solutions, See QR Code on Pg. 85

Mind Map

Electrostatic Potential and Capacitance

Electric Potential
The work done per unit charge in bringing a charge from infinity to a point in an electric field.

Potential Difference
The work done per unit charge in moving a charge between two points in an electric field.

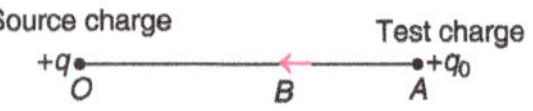

Potential difference between points A and B

$$V = V_B - V_A = \frac{W_{AB}}{q_0}$$

The SI unit of potential difference is volt (V).

Electric Potential due to a Point Charge
It is the amount of work done in bringing a unit positive charge from infinity to a point in the electric field without acceleration.

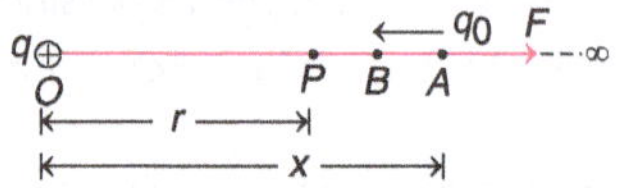

Electric potential due to a point charge at point P

$$V = \frac{W}{q_0} \text{ or } V = \frac{1}{4\pi\varepsilon_0}\cdot\frac{q}{r}$$

Conductors Materials that allow free movement of electric charges due to presence of free charges(usually electrons) distributed on the surface to cancel the internal electric field (e.g. metals).

Insulators Materials that do not allow free movement of charges due to presence of bound charges (e.g. rubber, glass). But they may get polarised in an electric field.

Dielectrics are insulators which gets polarised in response to an applied electric field which induces an internal electric field that opposes the applied electric field.

Uniformly Charged Thin Spherical Shell
(i) When the point P lies outside the shell, $V = \frac{1}{4\pi\varepsilon_0}\frac{q}{r}$ $[r > R]$

(ii) When point P lies on the surface of the shell $V = \frac{1}{4\pi\varepsilon_0}\frac{q}{R}$ $[r = R]$

(iii) When point P lies inside the shell $V = \frac{1}{4\pi\varepsilon_0}\frac{q}{R}$ $[r < R]$

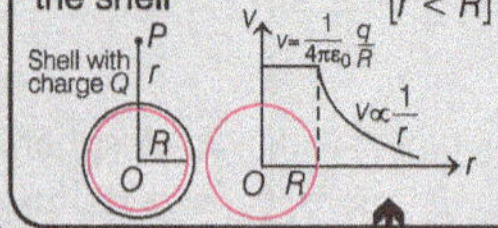

Electrostatic Potential Energy
It is the energy stored in a system of charges due to their positions in an electrostatic field for two point charges.

Potential energy of the system of charges

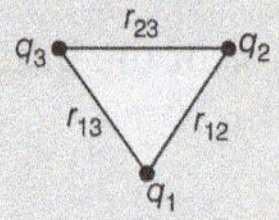

$$U = \frac{1}{4\pi\varepsilon_0}\left(\frac{q_1 q_2}{r_{12}} + \frac{q_1 q_3}{r_{13}} + \frac{q_2 q_3}{r_{23}}\right)$$

Potential Energy of System of Charges

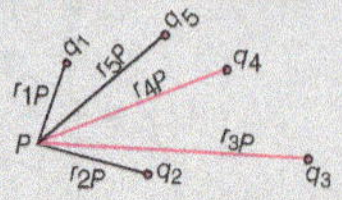

Potential at a point due to a system of N point charges

$$V = \frac{1}{4\pi\varepsilon_0}\sum_{i=1}^{N}\frac{q_i}{r_i}$$

The electric potential at a point whose position vector is r, would be

$$V = \frac{1}{4\pi\varepsilon_0}\sum_{i=1}^{N}\frac{q_i}{|\mathbf{r} - \mathbf{r}_i|}$$

Equipotential Surfaces
These are imaginary surfaces where all points have the same electric potential i.e., no work is done in moving a charge along the surface.

Properties of Equipotential Surface
1. No work is done in moving a test charge between two points on an equipotential surface.
2. Electric field is always normal to the equipotential surface at every point.
3. Equipotential surfaces are closer together in the regions of strong field and farther apart in the regions of weak fields.
4. No two equipotential surfaces can intersect each other.

Capacitor
It is a device that stores electrical energy by accumulating electric charges on two closely spaced surfaces insulated from each other.

Capacitance
Capacitance is the measure of a capacitor's ability to store charge per unit voltage, given by $C = Q/V$.

Dielectric Slab
The capacitance of the capacitor on introduction of dielectric slab becomes,

$$C = \frac{Q}{V} = \frac{\varepsilon_0 A}{\left(d - t + \frac{t}{k}\right)}$$

Capacitors in Series The reciprocal of the equivalent capacitance is the sum of the reciprocals of individual capacitances $\frac{1}{C_{eq}} = \frac{1}{C_1} + \frac{1}{C_2} + \ldots$

Capacitors in Parallel The equivalent capacitance is the sum of the individual capacitances $C_{eq} = C_1 + C_2 + \ldots$

Capacitance of a Parallel Plate Capacitor

Without dielectric	With dielectric
$C = \frac{\varepsilon_0 A}{d}$	$C = \frac{\varepsilon_r \varepsilon_0 A}{d}$

Conducting Slab
Capacitance of the capacitor in the presence of conducting slab becomes

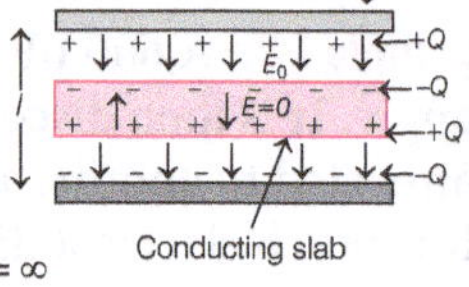

$$C = \frac{\varepsilon_0 A}{d - t}, \text{ since } K = \infty$$

If $t = d$, $C = \infty$

Air filled Parallel Plate Capacitor $C_0 = \frac{A\varepsilon_0}{d}$
- **Energy density of capacitor** $u = \frac{U}{V} = \frac{1}{2}\varepsilon_0 E^2$
- **Energy stored in a capacitor** $U = \frac{1}{2}CV^2 = \frac{1}{2}QV = \frac{1}{2}\frac{Q^2}{C}$

At an Axial Point

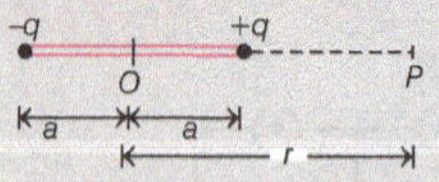

Potential at an axial point of a dipole is

$$V = \frac{1}{4\pi\varepsilon_0}\cdot\frac{p}{r^2}$$

Electric Polarisation
It is the alignment of dipoles within a dielectric material under an external electric field.

Electrical Potential Energy of an Electric Dipole in an Electrostatic Field.
The potential energy U of an electric dipole with dipole moment p in a uniform electric field E is

$$U = -\mathbf{p}\cdot\mathbf{E} = -pE\cos\theta$$

At an Equatorial Point

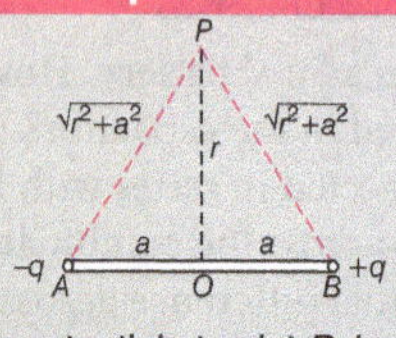

Electric potential at point P due to the dipole is

$$V = V_1 + V_2 = \frac{1}{4\pi\varepsilon_0}\cdot\frac{-q}{AP} + \frac{1}{4\pi\varepsilon_0}\cdot\frac{q}{BP}$$

$$= -\frac{1}{4\pi\varepsilon_0}\cdot\frac{q}{\sqrt{r^2 + a^2}} + \frac{1}{4\pi\varepsilon_0}\cdot\frac{q}{\sqrt{r^2 + a^2}} = 0$$

Torque Acting on Dipole
The magnitude of torque will be given as; $\tau = qE \times 2a \sin\theta = pE\sin\theta$

where, $q \times 2a = p$, is the dipole moment.

∴ The torque due to an electric dipole is given as

$\Rightarrow \tau = pE\sin\theta\,\hat{n}$

$\tau = \mathbf{p} \times \mathbf{E}$

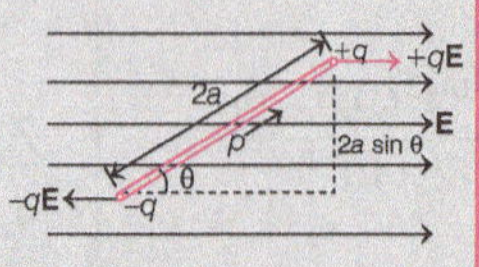

EXAM PATTERN QUESTIONS

Objective Type Questions

Multiple Choice Questions (MCQs)

1. A car battery is charged by a 12 V supply and energy stored in it is 7.20×10^5 J. The charge passed through the battery is **CBSE 2021, Term-I**

(a) 6.0×10^4 C (b) 5.8×10^3 J
(c) 8.64×10^6 J (d) 1.6×10^5 C

2. Four charges $-q, -q, +q$ and $+q$ are placed at the corners of a square of side $2L$ is shown in figure. The electric potential at point A mid-way between the two charges $+q$ and $+q$ is

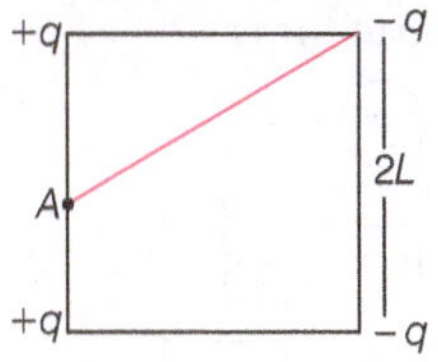

CBSE 2021, Term-I

(a) $\frac{1}{4\pi\varepsilon_0}\frac{2q}{L}\left(1-\frac{1}{\sqrt{5}}\right)$ (b) $\frac{1}{4\pi\varepsilon_0}\frac{2q}{L}\left(1+\frac{1}{\sqrt{5}}\right)$

(c) $\frac{1}{4\pi\varepsilon_0}\frac{q}{2L}\left(1-\frac{1}{\sqrt{5}}\right)$ (d) zero

3. The electric potential V at any point (x, y, z) is given by $V = 3x^2$, where x is in metres and V in volts. The electric field at the point (1 m, 0, 2 m) is **CBSE 2021, Term-I**

(a) 6 V/m along $-X$-axis
(b) 6 V/m along $+X$-axis
(c) 1.5 V/m along $-X$-axis
(d) 1.5 V/m along $+X$-axis

4. In the case of a charged metallic sphere, potential (V) changes with respect to distance (r) from the centre as

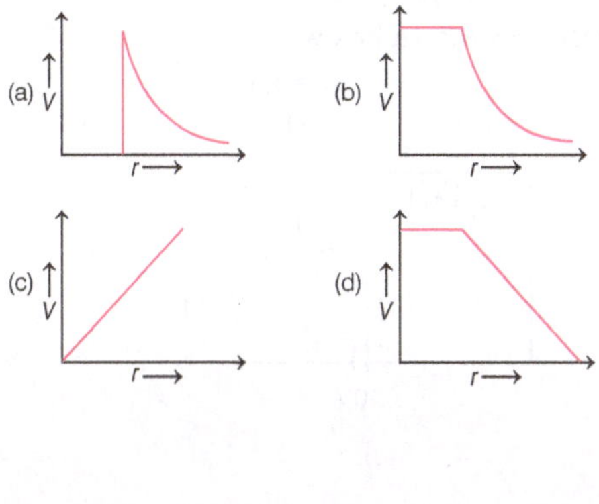

5. The variation in potential V with r and electric field E with r for a point charge is correctly shown in the graph.

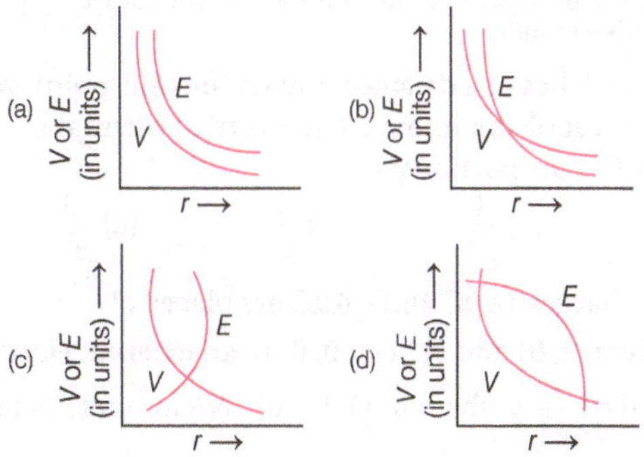

6. Which of the following is not the property of equipotential surface? **CBSE SQP, Term-I**

(a) They do not cross each other.
(b) The rate of change of potential with distance on them is zero.
(c) For a uniform electric field, they are concentric spheres.
(d) They can be imaginary spheres.

7. Three equipotential surfaces are shown in figure. Which of the following is correct one for the corresponding field lines?

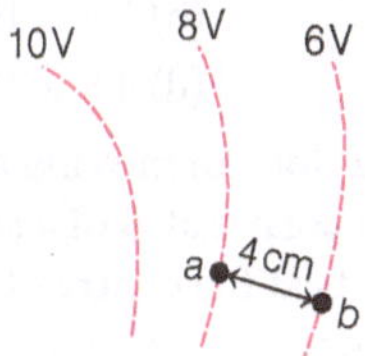

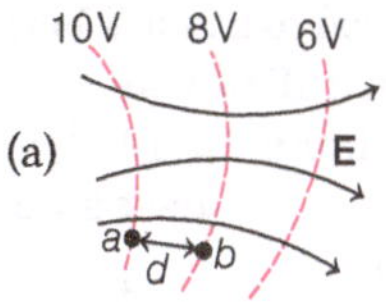

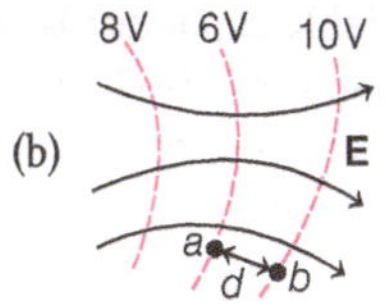

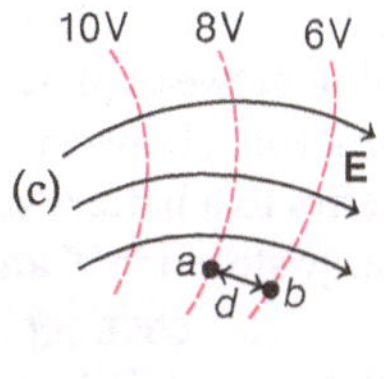

(d) None of these

8. The electrostatic potential on the surface of a charged conducting sphere is 100V. Two statements are made in this regard

S_1 : At any point inside the sphere, electric intensity is zero.

S_2 : At any point inside the sphere, the electrostatic potential is 100V.

Which of the following is a correct statement? **NCERT Exemplar**

(a) S_1 is true but S_2 is false.
(b) Both S_1 and S_2 are false.
(c) S_1 is true, S_2 is also true and S_1 is the cause of S_2.
(d) S_1 is true, S_2 is also true but the statements are independent.

9. A point *P* lies at a distance *x* from the mid-point of an electric dipole on its axis. The electric potential at point *P* is proportional to

(a) $\frac{1}{x^2}$ (b) $\frac{1}{x^3}$ (c) $\frac{1}{x^4}$ (d) $\frac{1}{x^{1/2}}$

10. Two charges 14 μC and − 4 μC are placed at (− 12 cm, 0, 0) and (12 cm, 0, 0) in an external electric field $E = \left(\frac{B}{r^2}\right)$, where $B = 1.2 \times 10^6$ N/cm^2 and *r* is in m.

The electrostatic potential energy of the configuration is **CBSE 2021, Term-I**

(a) 97.9 J (b) 102.1 J
(c) 2.1 J (d) − 97.9 J

11. A + 3.0 nC charge *Q* is initially at a distance of $r_1 = 10$ cm from a + 5.0 nC charge *q* fixed at the origin. The charge *Q* is moved away from *q* to a new position at $r_2 = 15$ cm. In this process, work done by the field is **CBSE 2021, Term-I**

(a) 1.29×10^{-5} J (b) 3.6×10^5 J
(c) -4.5×10^{-7} J (d) 4.5×10^{-7} J

12. What is the work done in moving a 5 μC point charge from corner *A* to corner at *B* of a square *ABCD*, when a 20 μC charge exists at the centre of square?

(a) 100 J (b) 25 J (c) 0 J (d) 5 J

13. A variable capacitor is connected to a 200 V battery. If its capacitance is changed from 2 μF to *x* μF, the decrease in energy of the capacitor is 2×10^{-2} J. The value of *x* is **CBSE 2021, Term-I**

(a) 1 μF (b) 2 μF (c) 3 μF (d) 4 μF

14. Two parallel plate capacitors *X* and *Y*, have the same area of plates and same separation between plates. *X* has air and *Y* with dielectric constant 2, between its plates. They are connected in series to a battery of 12 V. The ratio of electrostatic energy stored in *X* and *Y* is **CBSE SQP, Term-I**

(a) 4 : 1 (b) 1 : 4 (c) 2 : 1 (d) 1 : 2

15. If the charge on each plate of a capacitor of 60 μF is 3×10^{-8} C, then energy stored in the capacitor will be

(a) 2.5×10^{-15} J (b) 1.5×10^{-14} J
(c) 3.5×10^{-13} J (d) 7.5×10^{-12} J

16. Three capacitors 2 μF, 3 μF and 6 μF are joined in series with each other. The equivalent capacitance is **CBSE SQP, Term-I**

(a) 1 / 2 μF (b) 1 μF
(c) 2 μF (d) 11 μF

17. The capacitors of capacitances C_1 and C_2 are connected in parallel. If a charge *Q* is given to the combination, the ratio of the charge on the capacitor C_1 to the charge on C_2 will be **CBSE 2020**

(a) $\frac{C_1}{C_2}$ (b) $\sqrt{\frac{C_1}{C_2}}$ (c) $\sqrt{\frac{C_2}{C_1}}$ (d) $\frac{C_2}{C_1}$

18. Four capacitors, each 50 μF are connected as shown. The DC voltmeter *V* reads 100 V. The charge on each plate of each capacitor is

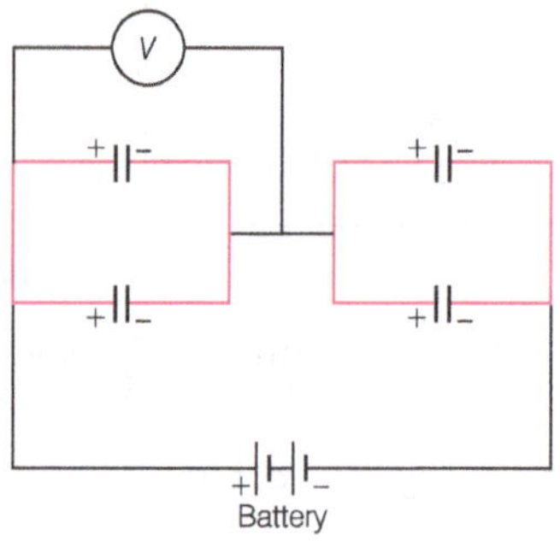

(a) 2×10^{-3} C (b) 5×10^{-3} C
(c) 0.2 C (d) 0.5 C

19. A capacitor's plates are charged by a battery with *V* volts. After charging, battery is disconnected and a dielectric slab with dielectric constant *K* is inserted between its plates, the potential across the plates of a capacitor will become **CBSE SQP, Term-I**

(a) zero (b) *V* / 2
(c) *V* / *K* (d) *KV*

20. Three capacitors C_1, C_2 and C_3 are connected in a combination as shown below.

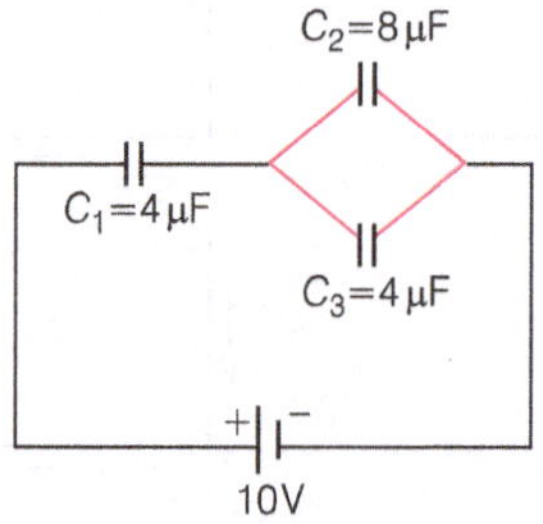

Identify the correct statement(s).

I. The charge on capacitor C_1 is greater than that on capacitor C_2.

II. The charge on capacitor C_1 is the same as that on capacitor C_3.

III. The charge on capacitor C_1 is 30 μC.

Competency Based Que.

(a) Only (I) is correct.
(b) Only (III) is correct.
(c) Both (I) and (III) are correct.
(d) Both (I) and (II) are correct.

21. **In a given region, electric potential varies with position as $V(x) = 3 + 2x^2$. Identify which of the following statements is correct.** **Competency Based Que.**

(a) Potential difference between the two points $x = 2$ and $x = -2$ is 2 V.
(b) A charge of 1 C placed at $x = 2$ experiences a force of 6 N.
(c) The force experienced by the above charge is along $+X$-axis.
(d) The electric field in the given region is non-uniform along X-axis.

22. **A parallel plate capacitor is made of two dielectric blocks in series. One of the blocks has thickness d_1 and dielectric constant K_1 and the other has thickness d_2 and dielectric constant K_2 as shown in figure. This arrangement can be thought as a dielectric slab of thickness $d\ (= d_1 + d_2)$ and effective dielectric constant K. The K is`** **NCERT Exemplar**

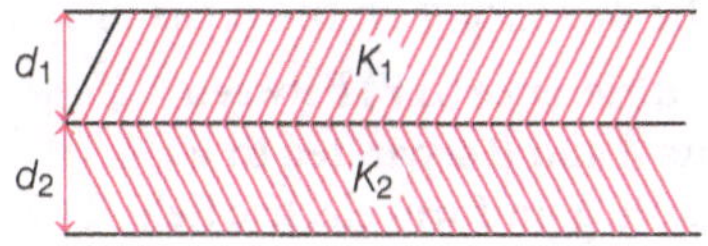

(a) $\dfrac{K_1d_1 + K_2d_2}{d_1 + d_2}$ (b) $\dfrac{K_1d_1 + K_2d_2}{K_1 + K_2}$

(c) $\dfrac{K_1K_2(d_1 + d_2)}{(K_1d_2 + K_2d_1)}$ (d) $\dfrac{2K_1K_2}{K_1 + K_2}$

23. **A capacitor consists of two parallel plates, with an area of cross-section of 0.001 m^2, separated by a distance of 0.0001 m. If the voltage across the plates varies at the rate of 10^8 V/s, then the value of displacement current through the capacitor is**

(a) 8.85×10^{-3} A (b) 8.85×10^{-4} A
(c) 7.85×10^{-3} A (d) 9.85×10^{-3} A

24. **Two charges $+q$ each are kept $2a$ distance apart. A third charge $-2q$ is placed mid-way between them. The potential energy of the system is**

(a) $\dfrac{q^2}{8\pi\varepsilon_0 a}$ (b) $-\dfrac{6q^2}{8\pi\varepsilon_0 a}$ (c) $\dfrac{-7q^2}{8\pi\varepsilon_0 a}$ (d) $\dfrac{9q^2}{8\pi\varepsilon_0 a}$

25. **Three point charges, each of charge q are placed on vertices of a triangle ABC, with $AB = AC = 5L$, $BC = 6L$. The electrostatic potential at mid-point of side BC will be** **CBSE 2024**

(a) $\dfrac{11}{48}\dfrac{q}{\pi\varepsilon_0 L}$ (b) $\dfrac{8q}{36\pi\varepsilon_0 L}$

(c) $\dfrac{5q}{24\pi\varepsilon_0 L}$ (d) $\dfrac{1}{16}\dfrac{q}{\pi\varepsilon_0 L}$

26. **Match the Column I with Column II and choose the correct option.**

Column I (Concept)		Column II (Formulae)	
A.	Potential due to a point charge	P.	$\dfrac{1}{4\pi\varepsilon_0}\dfrac{p\cos\theta}{r^2}$
B.	Work done in bringing a charge from infinity to a point	Q.	$W = q(V_f - V_i)$
C	Potential due to an electric dipole at an axial point	R.	Concentric spheres with centre at the charge
D.	Equipotential surface near a point charge	S.	$\dfrac{1}{4\pi\varepsilon_0}\cdot\dfrac{q}{r}$

Codes

	A	B	C	D		A	B	C	D
(a)	S	Q	P	R	(b)	P	Q	R	S
(c)	R	Q	P	S	(d)	Q	P	R	S

27. **Match the Column I with Column II and choose the correct option.**

Column I		Column II	
A.	Equipotential surface	P.	The work done in moving a unit positive charge between two points in an electric field.
B.	Electrostatic potential energy	Q.	Zero at the mid-point between the two charges of a dipole along the axial line.
C	Potential due to an electric dipole	R.	The energy stored in a system of charges
D.	Electric potential difference	S.	Surface where electric potential is constant everywhere

Codes

	A	B	C	D		A	B	C	D
(a)	P	Q	R	S	(b)	P	R	S	Q
(c)	S	R	Q	P	(d)	R	P	S	Q

Assertion-Reason

Directions *(Q. Nos. 28-37) In the following questions, two statements are given- one labelled Assertion (A) and the other labelled Reason (R). Select the correct answer to these questions from the codes (a), (b), (c) and (d) as given below.*

(a) Both Assertion and Reason are true and Reason is the correct explanation of Assertion.
(b) Both Assertion and Reason are true but Reason is not the correct explanation of Assertion.
(c) Assertion is true but Reason is false.
(d) Assertion is false but Reason is true.

28. Assertion (A) Work done by the electrostatic force in bringing the unit positive charge from infinity to the point P is positive.

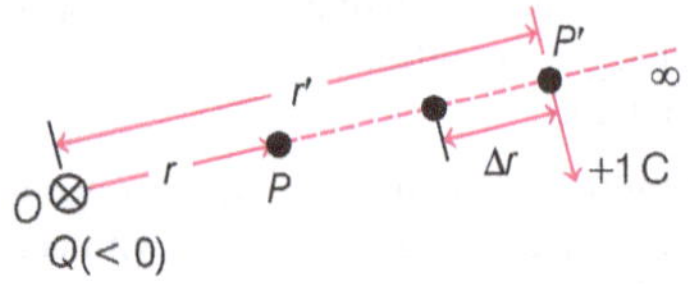

Reason (R) For $Q < 0$, the force on unit positive charge is attractive, so that the electrostatic force and the displacement (from infinity to P) are in the same direction.

29. Assertion (A) A and B are two conducting spheres of same radius. A being solid and B hollow. Both are charged to the same potential. Then, charge on A = charge on B.

Reason (R) Potential on both are same.

30. Assertion (A) An electron has a high potential energy when it is at a location associated with a more negative value of potential, and a low potential energy when at a location associated with a more positive potential.

Reason (R) Electrons move from a higher potential region to lower potential region. **CBSE SQP, Term-I**

31. Assertion (A) In the absence of an external electric field, the dipole moment per unit volume of a polar dielectric is zero.

Reason (R) The dipoles of a polar dielectric are randomly oriented.

32. Assertion (A) Polar molecules have permanent dipole moment.

Reason (R) In polar molecules, the centres of positive and negative charges coincide even when there is no external field.

33. Assertion (A) Charge on all the condensers connected in series is the same.

Reason (R) Capacitance of capacitor is directly proportional to charge on it.

34. Assertion (A) An electron moves from a region of lower potential to a region of higher potential.

Reason (R) An electron has a negative charge.

35. Assertion (A) A parallel plate capacitor is connected across a battery through a key. A dielectric slab of dielectric constant K is introduced between the plates. The energy which is stored becomes K times.

Reason (R) The surface density of charge on the plate remains constant or unchanged.

36. Assertion (A) If three capacitors of capacitances $C_1 < C_2 < C_3$ are connected in parallel, and in series, then their equivalent capacitances, $C_p > C_s$

Reason (R) $\dfrac{1}{C_p} = \dfrac{1}{C_1} + \dfrac{1}{C_2} + \dfrac{1}{C_3}$

37. Assertion (A) The electric potential is constant everywhere inside a charged conductor and is equal to its value at the surface.

Reason (R) A constant work has to be done to move a test charge from the interior of a charged conductor to its surface. **CBSE QB**

Case Based Questions

Directions *(Q.Nos. 38-40) These questions are case study based questions. Read the following paragraph and answer the questions on the basis of same.*

38. **Potential difference (ΔV) between two points A and B separated by a distance x, in a uniform electric field E is given by $\Delta V = -Ex$, where x is measured parallel to the field lines.**

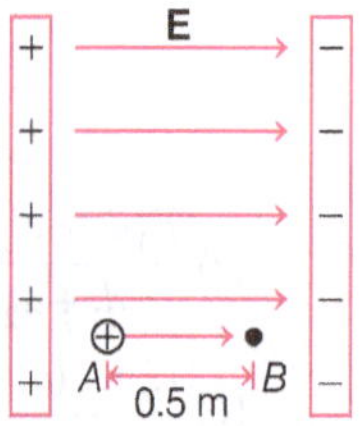

If a charge q_0 moves from A to B, the change in potential energy (ΔU) is given as $\Delta U = q_0 \Delta V$. A proton is released from rest in uniform electric field of magnitude 8.0×10^4 Vm^{-1} directed along the positive X-axis. The proton undergoes a displacement of 0.50 m in the direction of E.

Mass of a proton = 1.66×10^{-27} kg
and charge on a proton = 1.6×10^{-19} C.

With the help of the given passage, choose the most appropriate alternative for each of the following questions.

(i) As the proton moves from A to B, then
(a) the potential energy of proton decreases
(b) the potential energy of proton increases
(c) the proton loses kinetic energy
(d) total energy of the proton increases

(ii) The change in electric potential of the proton between the points A and B is
(a) 4.0×10^{4} V (b) -4.0×10^{4} V
(c) 6.4×10^{-19} V (d) -6.4×10^{-19} V

(iii) The change in electric potential energy of the proton for displacement from A to B is
(a) -6.4×10^{-19} J (b) 6.4×10^{-19} J
(c) -6.4×10^{-15} J (d) 6.4×10^{-15} J

(iv) The velocity (v_B) of the proton after it has moved 0.50 m starting from rest is
(a) 1.6×10^{8} ms^{-1} (b) 2.77×10^{6} ms^{-1}
(c) 2.77×10^{4} ms^{-1} (d) 1.6×10^{6} ms^{-1}

(v) If in place of charged plates, two similar point charges of 1 μC are kept in air at 1 m distance from each other. Then, potential energy is
(a) 1 J (b) 1 eV
(c) 9×10^{-3}J (d) zero

39. **Electrostatic potential energy of a system of point charges is defined as the total amount of work done in bringing the different charges to their respective positions from infinitely large mutual separations.**

By definition, work done in carrying charge from infinity to any point is W = Potential × Charge

This work is stored in the system of two point charges in the form of electrostatic potential energy U of the system.

(i) Work done in moving a charge from one point to other inside a uniformly charged conducting sphere is
(a) always zero (b) non-zero
(c) may be zero (d) None of these

(ii) A positively charged particle is released from rest in a uniform electric field. The electric potential energy of the charge
(a) remains a constant because the electric field is uniform
(b) increases because the charge moves along the electric field
(c) decreases because the charge moves along the electric field
(d) decreases because the charge moves opposite to the electric field

(iii) Three charges are placed at the vertices of an equilateral triangle of side l as shown in figure. For what value of Q, the electrostatic potential energy of the system is zero?

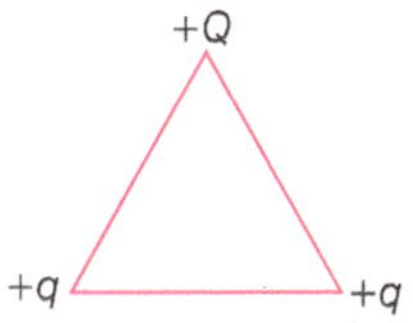

(a) $-q$ (b) $q/2$
(c) $-2q$ (d) $-q/2$

(iv) In the figure, proton moves a distance d in a uniform electric field E as shown in the figure. The work done on the proton by electric field is

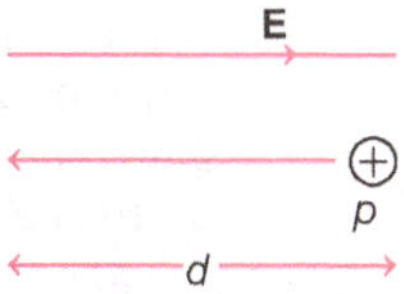

(a) negative (b) positive
(c) zero (d) None of these

(v) Two similar positive point charges each of 2 μC have been kept in air at 3m distance from each other. What will be the potential energy?
(a) 1 J (b) 1 eV (c) 12×10^{-3} J (d) Zero

40. **A parallel plate capacitor has two parallel plates which are separated by an insulating medium like air, mica, etc. When the plates are connected to the terminals of a battery, they get equal and opposite charges and an electric field is set up in between them. This electric field between the two plates depends upon the potential difference applied, the separation of the plates and nature of the medium between the plates.** **CBSE 2025**

(i) The electric field between the plates of a parallel plate capacitor is E. Now, the separation between the plates is doubled and simultaneously the applied potential difference between the plates is reduced to half of its initial value. The new value of the electric field between the plates will be
(a) E (b) $2E$ (c) $\frac{E}{4}$ (d) $\frac{E}{2}$

(ii) A constant electric field is to be maintained between the two plates of a capacitor whose separation d changes with time. Which of the graphs correctly depict the potential difference (V) to be applied between the plates as a function of separation between the plates (d) to maintain the constant electric field?

(a)
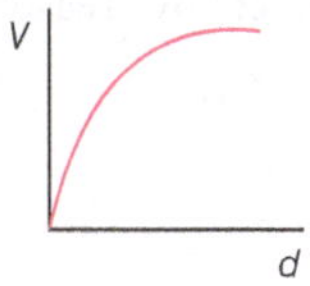

(b)
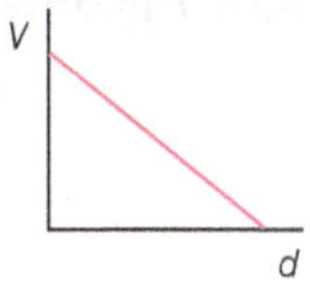

(c)
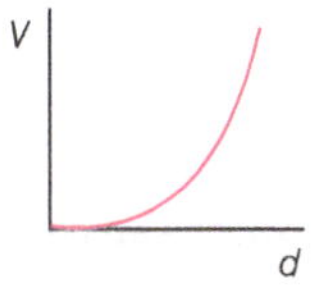

(d)
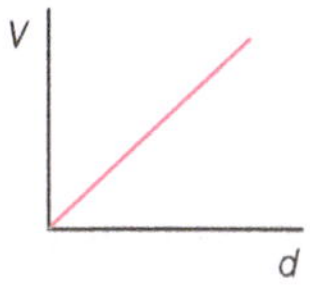

(iii)
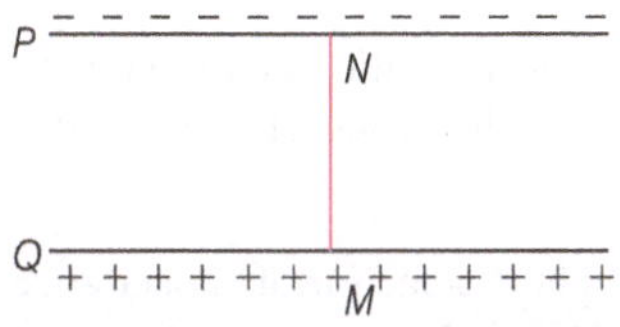

In the above figure P, Q are the two parallel plates of a capacitor. Plate Q is at positive potential with respect to plate P. MN is an imaginary line drawn perpendicular to the plates. Which of the graphs shows correctly the variations of the magnitude of electric field strength E along the line MN?

(a) 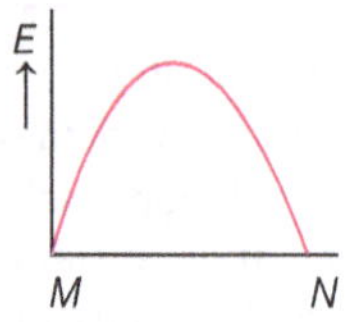

(b) 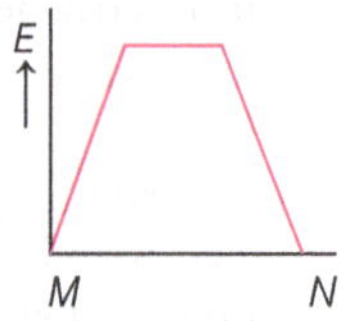

(c) 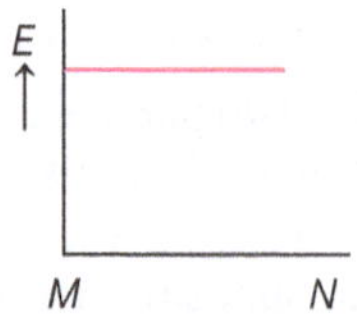

(d) 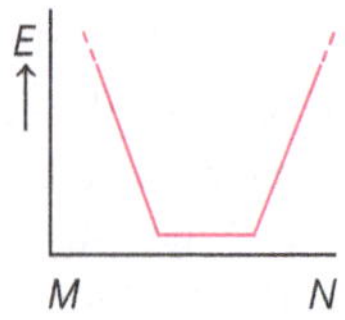

(iv) Three parallel plates are placed above each other with equal displacement $\mathbf{d}$ between neighbouring plates. The electric field between the first pair of the plates is $\mathbf{E}_1$ and the electric field between the second pair of the plates is $\mathbf{E}_2$. The potential difference between the third and the first plate is

(a) $(\mathbf{E}_1 + \mathbf{E}_2) \cdot \mathbf{d}$
(b) $(\mathbf{E}_1 - \mathbf{E}_2) \cdot \mathbf{d}$
(c) $(\mathbf{E}_2 - \mathbf{E}_1) \cdot \mathbf{d}$
(d) $\frac{d(E_1 + E_2)}{2}$

Or

(iv) A material of dielectric constant K is filled in a parallel plate capacitor of capacitance C. The new value of its capacitance becomes

(a) C (b) $\frac{C}{K}$
(c) CK (d) $C\left(1+\frac{1}{K}\right)$

Subjective Questions

Very Short Answer Type Questions

1. Define electric potential at a point and write its SI unit. **CBSE 2023**

2. A proton released from rest in an electric field, will start moving towards a region of .... potential in the field. **CBSE 2020**

3. Why there is no work done in moving a charge from one point to another on an equipotential surface?

4. Draw the equipotential surfaces due to an isolated point charge.

5. Figure shows the field lines on a positive charge. Is the work done by the field in moving a small positive charge from Q to P positive or negative? Give reason.

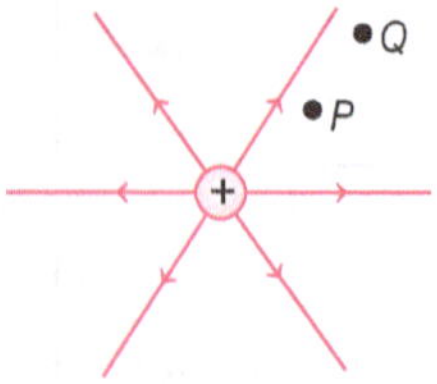

6. Depict equipotential surfaces due to an electric dipole. **CBSE 2020**

7. Why is the electrostatic potential inside a charged conducting shell constant throughout the volume of the conductor? **CBSE 2019**

8. A parallel plate capacitor of capacitance C is charged to a potential V. It is then connected to another uncharged capacitor having the same capacitance. Find out the ratio of the energy stored in the combined system to that stored initially in the single capacitor.

9. Net capacitance of three identical capacitors in series is 1 μF. What will be their net capacitance if connected in parallel? Find the ratio of energy stored in these two configurations if both are connected to the same source.

10. A charge particle $(+q)$ moves in a uniform electric field E in the direction opposite to E. What will be the effect on its electrostatic potential energy during its motion? **CBSE 2020**

Short Answer Type Questions

11. Two capacitors are connected in series. Derive an expression of the equivalent capacitance of the combination. **CBSE 2023**

12. The figure shows the variation of potential V with $\frac{1}{r}$ for two point charges Q_1 and Q_2, where V is the potential at a distance r due to a point charge. Find $\frac{Q_1}{Q_2}$ **CBSE 2023**

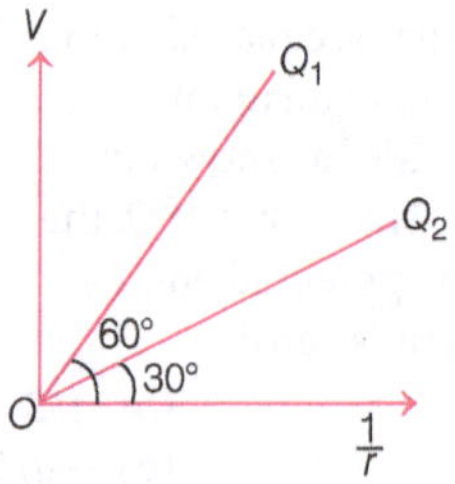

13. Two point charges 5 μC and –5 μC are placed at points *A* and *B*, 5 cm apart.

(i) Draw the equipotential surface of the system. **[2]**

(ii) What is the direction of electric field at every point on this surface? **[1]**

14. Deduce an expression for the potential energy of a system of two point charges q_1 and q_2 located at positions r_1 and r_2 respectively, in an external field (**E**). **CBSE SQP, Term-I**

15. The plates in a parallel plate capacitor are separated by a distance *d* with air as the medium between the plates. In order to increase the capacity by 66%, a dielectric slab of dielectric constant 5 is introduced between the plates. What is the thickness of dielectric slab?

16. A slab of material of a dielectric constant *K* has the same area as that of plates of a parallel plate capacitor but has the thickness $2d/3$, where *d* is separation between the plates. Find the expression of the capacitance when the slab is inserted between the plates of the capacitor.

17. Find the expression for the capacitance of a parallel plate capacitor of plate area *A* and plate separation *d* when (I) a dielectric slab of thickness *t* and (II) a metallic slab of thickness *t*, where $(t < d)$ are introduced one by one between the plates of the capacitor. In which case would the capacitance be more and why?

18. A conducting wire connects two charged conducting spheres such that they attain equilibrium with respect to each other. The distance of separation between the two spheres is very large as compared to either of their radii. **Competency Based Que**

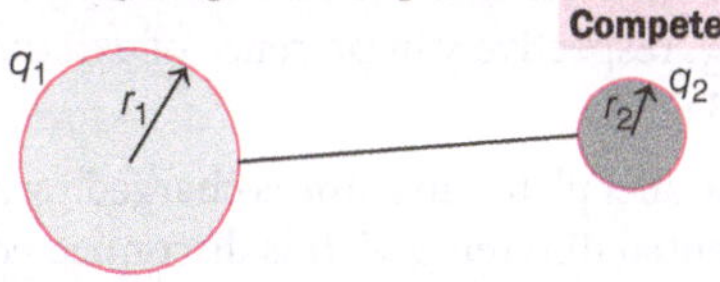

Find the ratio of the magnitudes of the electric fields at the surfaces of the two spheres.

19. A parallel plate capacitor is given as in the diagram. A small ball is suspended by an insulated thread in the space between the plates of the capacitor. The thread makes an angle θ with the vertical at equilibrium. **Competency Based Que**

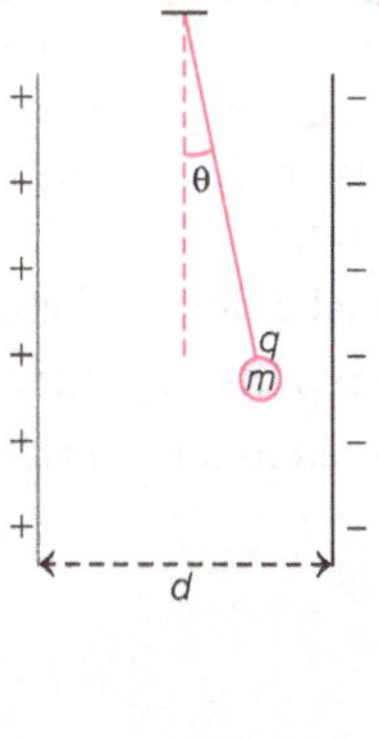

What is the potential difference between the capacitor plates?

20. A test charge *q* moves along a path $P \to Q \to R \to S$ in a uniform electric field region directed along +*X*-axis. The coordinates of the points are as follows $P(a,b,0)$, $Q(2a,0,0)$, $R(a,-b,0)$ and $S(0,0,0)$.

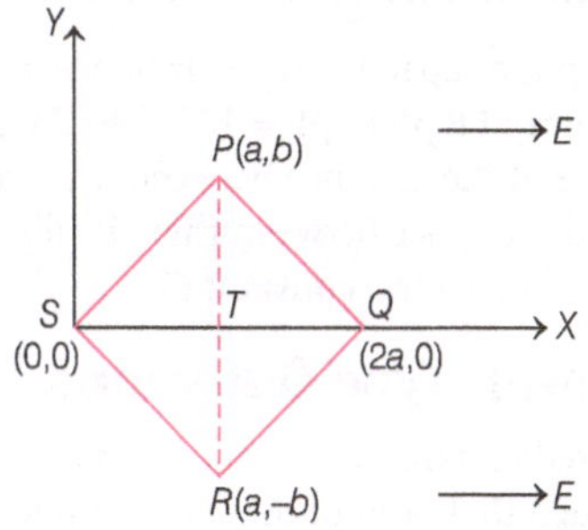

(i) Identify the plane of motion of the test charge. **[1]**

(ii) Determine the work done by the electric field as the test charge moves from *P* to *S*. Use diagram, if necessary. **[2]**

21. An electric dipole is held in a uniform electric field **E**.

(i) Show that the net force acting on it is zero. **[1]**

(ii) The dipole is aligned with its dipole moment **p** parallel to the field **E** Find .

(a) the work done in turning the dipole till its dipole moment points in the direction opposite to **E**. **[1]**

(b) the orientation of the dipole for which the torque acting on it becomes maximum. **[1]**

22. The electric field inside a parallel plate capacitor is *E*. Find the amount of work done in moving a charge *q* over a closed rectangular loop *abcda*.

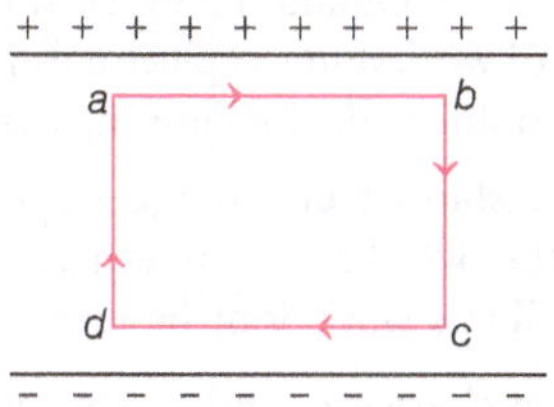

23. Obtain an expression for electrostatic potential energy of a system of three charges *q*, 2*q* and –3*q* placed at the vertices of an equilateral triangle of side *a*.

24. Calculate potential energy of a point charge –*q* placed along the axis due to a charge +*Q* uniformly distributed along a ring of radius *R*.

25. A capacitor has some dielectric between its plates and the capacitor is connected to a DC source. The battery is now disconnected and then the dielectric is removed. State whether the capacitance, the energy stored in it, electric field, charge stored and the voltage will increase, decrease or remain constant.

26. A spherical conductor of radius 12 cm has a charge of 1.6×10^{-7} C distributed uniformly on its surface. What is the electric field

(i) inside the sphere? **[1]**

(ii) just outside the sphere? **[1]**

(iii) at a point 18 cm from the centre of the sphere? **[1]**

27. A parallel plate capacitor with air between the plates has a capacitance of 8 pF (1 pF = 10^{-12} F). What will be the capacitance, if the distance between the plates is reduced by half and the space between them is filled with a substance of dielectric constant 6?

Long Answer Type Questions

28. Two isolated metallic solid spheres of radii R and $2R$ are charged such that both of these have same charge density σ. The spheres are located far away from each other and connected by a thin wire. Find the new charge density on the bigger sphere.

29. (i) Draw the equipotential surfaces corresponding to a uniform electric field in the z-direction. **[1]**

(ii) Derive an expression for the electric potential at any point along the axial line of an electric dipole. **[4]**

CBSE 2019

30. (i) Draw equipotential surfaces corresponding to the electric field that uniformly increases in magnitude along with the z-direction. **[2]**

(ii) Two charges $-q$ and $+q$ are located at points $(0, 0, -a)$ and $(0, 0, a)$. What is the electrostatic potential at the points $(0, 0, z)$ and $(x, y, 0)$? **CBSE 2019 [3]**

31. (i) Two point charges $+q_1$ and $-q_2$ are placed r distance apart. Obtain the expression for the amount of work done to place a third charge q_3 at the mid-point of the line joining the two charges. **[3]**

(ii) At what distance from charge $+q_1$ on the line joining the two charges (in terms of q_1, q_2 and r) will this work done be zero? **CBSE 2020 [2]**

32. (i) Two point charges q_1 and q_2 are kept at a distance of r_{12} in air. Deduce the expression for the electrostatic potential energy of this system. **[3]**

(ii) If an external electric field (E) is applied on the system, write the expression for the total energy of this system. **CBSE 2020 [2]**

33. Derive an expression for the capacitance of a parallel plate capacitor when a dielectric slab of dielectric constant K and thickness $t = d/2$ but of same area as that of the plates is inserted between the capacitor plates. (d = separation between the plates).

34. (i) Compare the individual dipole moment and the specimen dipole moment for H_2O molecule and O_2 molecule when placed in

(a) absence of external electric field and **[1½]**

(b) presence of external electric field. Justify your answer. **[1½]**

(ii) Given two parallel conducting plates of area A and charge densities $+\sigma$ and $-\sigma$. A dielectric slab of constant K and a conducting slab of thickness d each are inserted in between them as shown.

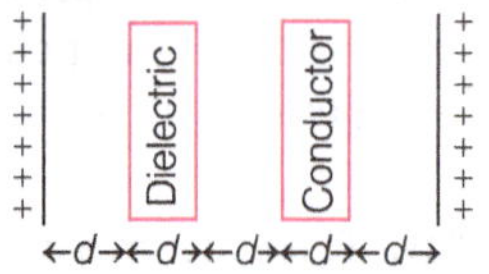

(a) Find the potential difference between the plates. **[1]**

(b) Plot E *versus* x graph, taking $x = 0$ at positive plate and $x = 5d$ at negative plate. **[1]**

35. (i) Establish the relation between electric field and electric potential at a point. **[3]**

(ii) Draw the equipotential surface for an electric field pointing in $+z$-direction with its magnitude increasing at constant rate along $-z$-direction. **CBSE SQP, Term-I [2]**

36. (i) (a) Depict the equipotential surfaces for a system of two identical positive point charges placed at distance d apart.

(b) Deduce the expression for the potential energy of a system of two point charges q_1 and q_2 brought from infinity to the points with positions r_1 and r_2, respectively in presence of external electric field **E**. **[2]**

(ii) A parallel plate capacitor is charged by a battery to a potential difference V. It is disconnected from battery and then connected to another uncharged capacitor of the same capacitance. Calculate the ratio of the energy stored in the combination to the initial energy on the single capacitor. **CBSE 2019 [3]**

37. (i) Obtain an expression for the capacitance of a parallel plate capacitor. **[2]**

(ii) Two identical plates, each of area A having surface charge densities $+\sigma$ and $-\sigma$ respectively, are separated by a distance d in air and a dielectric of dielectric constant K is filled between them. Write the expression for

(a) the potential difference between the plates

(b) capacitance of the capacitor so formed

(c) energy stored in this capacitor **CBSE 2024C [3]**

38. Three concentric metal shells A, B and C of radius a, b and c $(a < b < c)$ have surface charge densities $+\sigma$, $-\sigma$ and $+\sigma$, respectively.

(i) Find the potential of three shells at A, B and C. **CBSE 2019** [3]

(ii) If the shells A and C are at the same potential, obtain the relation between the radii a, b and c. [2]

39. Two metal spheres, one of radius R and the other of radius $2R$, both have same surface charge density σ. They are brought in contact and separated. What will be new surface charge densities on them? **NCERT Exemplar**

40. A parallel plate capacitor of capacitance C is charged to a potential V by a battery. Without disconnecting the battery, the distance between the plates is tripled and a dielectric medium of $K = 10$ is introduced between the plates of the capacitor. Explain giving reasons, how will the following be affected **All India 2017**

(i) capacitance of the capacitor, [1]

(ii) charge on the capacitor and [2]

(iii) energy density of the capacitor? [2]

41. Two identical parallel plate capacitors A and B are connected to a battery of V volts with the switch S is closed. The switch is now opened and the free space between the plates of the capacitors is filled with a dielectric of dielectric constant K. Find the ratio of the total electrostatic energy stored in both capacitors before and after the introduction of the dielectric. **All India 2017**

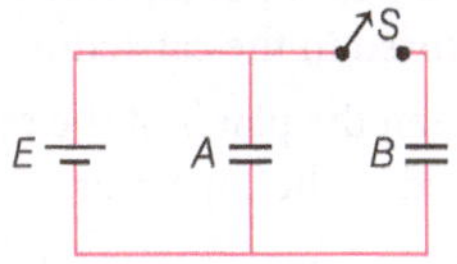

42. (i) Explain using suitable diagram, the difference in the behaviour of a

(a) conductor and [1]

(b) dielectric in the presence of external electric field. Define the terms polarisation of a dielectric and write its relation with susceptibility. [2]

(ii) A thin metallic spherical shell of radius R carries a charge Q on its surface. A point charge $Q/2$ is placed at its centre C and an another charge $+2Q$ is placed outside the shell at a distance x from the centre as shown in figure. Find (a) the force on the charge at the centre of the shell and at point A, (b) the electric flux through the shell. [2]

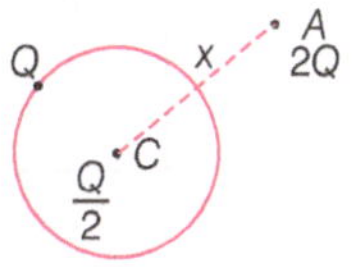

43. (i) If two similar large plates, each of area A having surface charge densities $+\sigma$ and $-\sigma$ are separated by a distance d in air, find the expression for

(a) field at points between the two plates and on outer side of the plates. Specify the direction of the field in each case. [1]

(b) the potential difference between the plates. [1]

(c) the capacitance of the capacitor so formed. [1]

(ii) Two metallic spheres of radii R and $2R$ are charged, so that both of these have same surface charge density σ. If they are connected to each other with a conducting wire, in which direction will the charge flow and why? [2]

44. Find the equation of the equipotentials for an infinite cylinder of radius r_0 carrying charge of linear density λ.

45. Two charges $-q$ each are separated by distance $2d$. A third charge $+q$ is kept at mid-point O. Find potential energy of $+q$ as a function of small distance x from O due to $-q$ charges. Sketch PE *versus* x and convince yourself that the charge at O is in an unstable equilibrium. **NCERT Exemplar**

46. (i) A dielectric slab of dielectric constant K and thickness t is inserted between plates of a parallel plate capacitor of plate separation d and plate area A. Obtain an expression for its capacitance. [2]

(ii) Two capacitors of different capacitances are connected first (1) in series and then (2) in parallel across a DC source of 100 V. If the total energy stored in the combination in the two cases are 40 mJ and 250 mJ respectively, find the capacitance of the capacitors. **CBSE 2024** [3]

Numerical Problems

Electrostatic Potential

47. What is the work done in moving a 2 μC point charge from corner A to corner B of a square $ABCD$, when a 10 μC charge exists at the centre of the square?

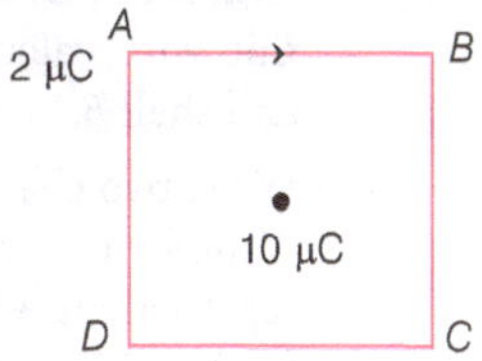

48. Calculate the work done to dissociate the system of three charges placed on the vertices of a triangle as shown in the figure. (Here, $q = 1.6 \times 10^{-10}$ C) **CBSE 2020**

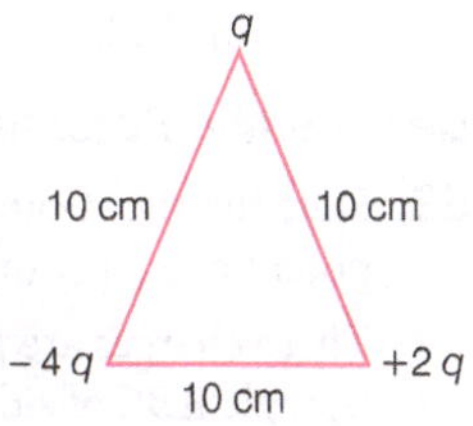

Electrostatic Potential Difference

49. A test charge q is moved without acceleration from A to C along the path from A to B and then from B to C in electric field E as shown in the figure.

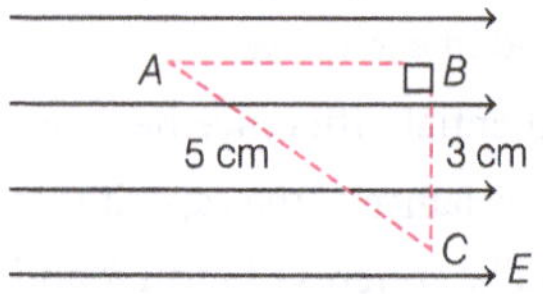

(i) Calculate the potential difference between A and C. **[1½]**

(ii) At which point (of the two) is the electric potential more and why? **[1½]**

Electrostatic Potential due to Point Charge

50. The electric potential at 0.1 m from a point charge is + 50 V. What is the magnitude and sign of the charge?

51. The circular arc shown in the figure, has a uniform charge per unit length of 1×10^{-8} C / m. Find the potential at the centre O of the arc.

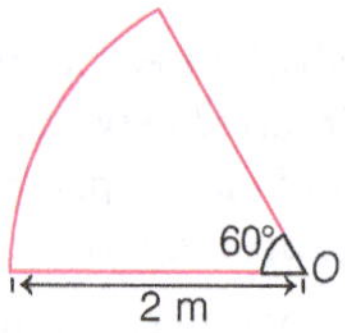

52. Calculate the potential at a point P due to a charge of 5×10^{-7} C located 11 cm away.

53. A hollow metal sphere of radius 7 cm is charged, such that potential on its surface is 20 V. What is the potential at the centre of the sphere?

54. (i) A small conducting sphere A of radius r charged to a potential V, is enclosed by a spherical conducting shell B of radius R. If A and B are connected by a thin wire, calculate the final potential on sphere A and shell B. **[1½]**

(ii) Write two characteristics of equipotential surfaces. A uniform electric field of 50 NC^{-1} is set up in a region along $+X$ axis. If the potential at the origin (0, 0) is 220 V, find the potential at a point (4m, 3m). **CBSE 2025** **[1½]**

Electrostatic Potential due to System of Charges

55. State the significance of negative value of electrostatic potential energy of a system of charges.

Three charges are placed at the corners of an equilateral triangle ABC of side 2.0 m as shown in figure. Calculate the electric potential energy of the system of three charges. **CBSE 2023**

Relation between Electric Field and Electric Potential

56. When reaching for door handle often sliding across a car seat on a dry winter day, you get a spark when your finger tip is 5 mm away from the handle. What was the potential difference between you and the door handle just before the spark? Given that dielectric strength of air $= 3\times10^{6}$ V/m.

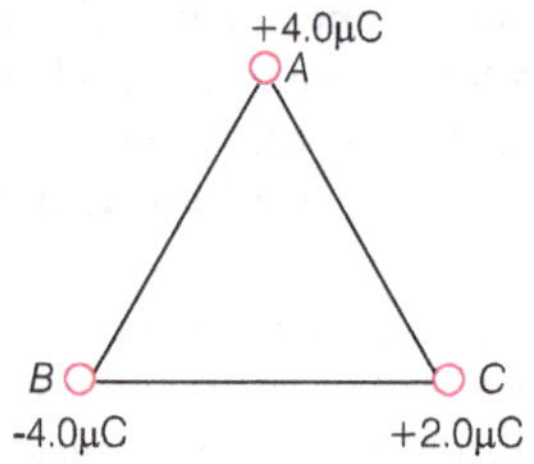

Parallel Plate Capacitor

57. A 200 μF parallel plate capacitor having plate separation of 5 mm is charged by a 100 V DC source. It remains connected to the source. Using an insulated handle, the distance between the plates is doubled and a dielectric slab of thickness 5 mm and dielectric constant 10 is introduced between the plates. Explain with reason, how the (i) capacitance, (ii) electric field between the plates and (iii) energy density of the capacitor will change. **CBSE 2019**

58 A capacitor of 4μF is charged by a battery of 12 V. The battery is disconnected and a dielectric slab of dielectric constant 8 is inserted in between the plates of the capacitor to fill the space completely. Find the change in the (i) charge stored in the capacitor, (ii) potential difference between the plates of the capacitor, and (iii) energy stored in the capacitor. **CBSE 2019**

Combination of Capacitors

59. In a network, four capacitors C_1,C_2,C_3 and C_4 are connected as shown in the figure.

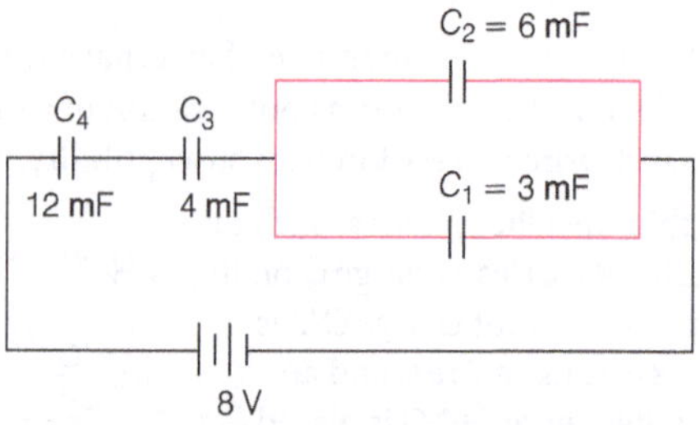

(i) Find the net capacitance of the circuit. **[2]**

(ii) If the charge on the capacitor C_1 is 6 μC,
(a) calculate the charge on the capacitors C_3 and C_4 and (b) net energy stored in the capacitors C_3 and C_4 connected in series. **CBSE 2019** **[3]**

60. Find the total charge stored in the network of capacitors connected between A and B as shown in figure.

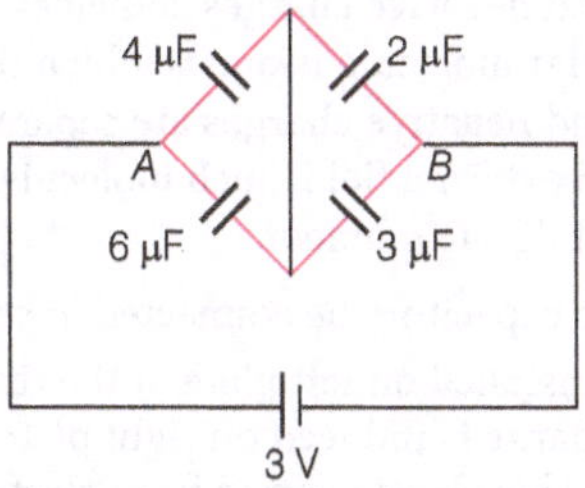

CBSE 2020

61. You are given three capacitors of 2 μF, 3 μF, 4 μF, respectively.

(i) Form a combination of all these capacitors of equivalent capacitance $\frac{13}{3}$ μF.

(ii) What is the maximum and minimum value of the equivalent capacitance that can be obtained by connecting these capacitors? **CBSE 2020**

62. A network of four 10 μF capacitors is connected to a 500 V supply as shown in the figure. Determine the equivalent capacitance of the network along AD.

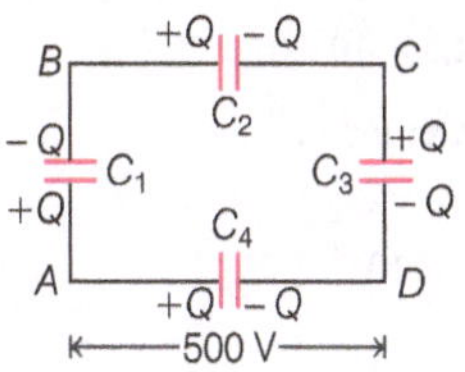

Hints & Solutions

Objective Type Questions

4. (b)	5. (b)	6. (c)	7. (c)	8. (c)
9. (a)	10. (a)	12. (c)	14. (c)	16. (b)
17. (a)	18. (b)	19. (c)	20. (c)	21. (d)
22. (c)	23. (a)	24. (c)	25. (a)	26. (a)
27. (c)	28. (a)	29. (a)	37. (c)	

1. (*a*) We know that,

$$U = qV$$
$$7.2 \times 10^5 = q \times 12$$
$$q = \frac{7.2 \times 10^5}{12}$$
$$q = 6.0 \times 10^{14} \text{ C}$$

2. (*a*)

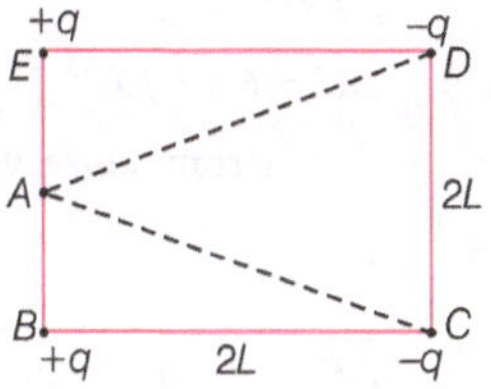

Potential at A,

$$V_A = \frac{1}{4\pi\varepsilon_0}\left[\frac{q}{AB} + \frac{(-q)}{AC} + \frac{(-q)}{AD} + \frac{q}{AE}\right]$$

$\because$ $AB = AE = L$

$$AC = AD = \sqrt{(AB)^2 + (BC)^2}$$
$$= \sqrt{L^2 + (2L)^2} = \sqrt{5}\,L$$

So, $$V_A = \frac{1}{4\pi\varepsilon_0}\left[\frac{q}{L} - \frac{q}{\sqrt{5}L} - \frac{q}{\sqrt{5}L} + \frac{q}{L}\right]$$
$$= \frac{2q}{4\pi\varepsilon_0 L}\left[1 - \frac{1}{\sqrt{5}}\right]$$

3. (*a*) We know that,

$$\mathbf{E} = -\nabla V$$

and $$V = 3x^2$$

$$\mathbf{E} = -\left[\frac{\partial V}{\partial x}\hat{\mathbf{i}} + \frac{\partial V}{\partial y}\hat{\mathbf{j}} + \frac{\partial V}{\partial z}\hat{\mathbf{k}}\right]$$
$$\mathbf{E} = -[6x\hat{\mathbf{i}} + 0 + 0]$$
$$\mathbf{E} = -6x\hat{\mathbf{i}}$$

at point (1m, 0, 2m)

$$\mathbf{E} = -6(1)\,\hat{\mathbf{i}}$$
$$\mathbf{E} = -6\hat{\mathbf{i}}$$

So, $|\mathbf{E}| = 6$ V/m and direction $= -\hat{\mathbf{i}}$

11. (*d*)

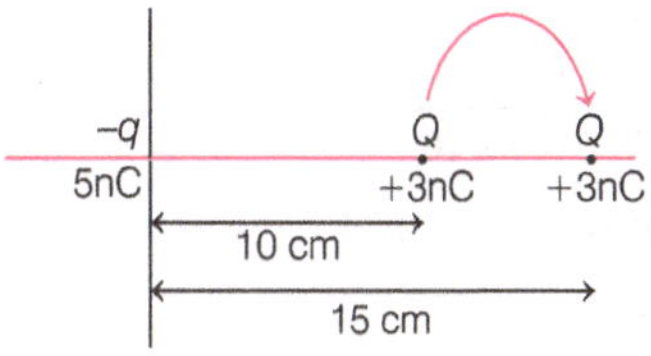

Work done in this process,

$$W = U_i - U_f$$
$$W = \frac{kq_1q_2}{r_1} - \frac{kq_1q_2}{r_2}$$

$$W = \frac{9\times10^9\times5\times10^{-9}\times3\times10^{-9}}{10\times10^{-2}} - \frac{9\times10^9\times5\times10^{-9}\times3\times10^{-9}}{15\times10^{-2}}$$

$$W = \frac{135\times10^{-9}}{0.1} - \frac{135\times10^{-9}}{0.15}$$

$$W = 4.5\times10^{-7}\text{ J}$$

13. (*a*) Change in energy,

$$U = U_1 - U_2 \quad \text{...(i)}$$

$$U = 2\times10^{-2}$$

$$U_1 = \frac{1}{2}C_1V^2$$

$$= \frac{1}{2}\times2\times10^{-6}\times(200)^2$$

$$E_1 = 4\times10^{-2}\text{ J}$$

From Eq. (i)

$$U_2 = U_1 - U$$

$$= (4\times10^{-2} - 2\times10^{-2})\text{ J}$$

$$U_2 = 2\times10^{-2}\text{ J}$$

$$\because \quad U_2 = \frac{1}{2}C_2V^2$$

$$2\times10^{-2} = \frac{1}{2}\times(x\times10^{-6})\times(200)^2$$

$$2\times10^{-2} = 2\times10^{-2}\times x$$

$$x = 1$$

15. (*d*) Given, $C = 60\,\mu\text{F}$

$$q = 3\times10^{-8}\text{ C}$$

Energy stored in the capacitor, $U = \frac{1}{2}CV^2$

$$\therefore \quad C = \frac{q}{V}$$

$$\Rightarrow \quad V = \frac{q}{C}$$

$$U = \frac{1}{2}\frac{q^2}{C}$$

$$U = \frac{1}{2}\times\frac{(3\times10^{-8})^2}{60\times10^{-6}}$$

$$U = 0.075\times10^{-10}\text{ J}$$

$$U = 7.5\times10^{-12}\text{ J}$$

30. (*c*) Electrons move from a lower potential region to higher potential region.

31. (*a*) There are polar and non-polar dielectric materials. The molecules of a polar dielectric have a permanent dipole moment. However, due to random orientations, net dipole moment is zero. If there is no external electric field, there is no polarisation.

32. (*c*) The molecules of a substance may be polar or non-polar. In a non-polar molecule, the centre of positive and negative charges coincides. On the other hand, a polar molecule is one is which the centres of positive and negative charges are separated, even when there is no external field. Such molecules have a permanent dipole moment.

33. (*b*) Let two capacitors be connected in series. If $+q$ charge is installed on left plate of the first capacitor, then $-q$ charge is induced on right plate of this capacitor. This charge comes from electron drawn from the left plate of second capacitor. There will be equal charge $+q$ on the left plate of second capacitor and $-q$ charge induced on the right plate of second capacitor. Thus, each capacitor has same charge q when connected in series. Capacitance is quantity dependent on the construction of capacitor and independent of charge.

34. (*a*) Electric field is set-up from higher potential to lower potential. An electron is negatively charged and moves opposite to the direction of electric field, i.e. from lower potential to higher potential.

35. (*c*) The Reason is false as

$$\sigma' = \frac{q'}{A} = \frac{C'V'}{A} = \frac{(KC)V}{A}$$

$$= \frac{Kq}{A} = K\sigma$$

(as $C' = KC$, $V' = V$ and $CV = q$)

36. (*c*) Assertion is true as capacitance in parallel is greater than capacitance is series. Reason is false as

$$C_p = C_1 + C_2 + C_3$$

38. (i) (*a*) Potential energy of the proton decreases as it moves in the direction of the electric field.

(ii) (*b*) $\Delta V = -E\Delta x = -(8.0\times10^4\text{ V/m})(0.50\text{ m})$

$$= -4\times10^4\text{ V}$$

(iii) (*c*) $\Delta U = q_0\Delta V = (1.6\times10^{-19}\text{ C})(-4.0\times10^4\text{ V})$

$$= -6.4\times10^{-15}\text{ J}$$

(iv) (*b*) As, $\Delta K = -\Delta U = 6.4\times10^{-15}$ J

(from conservation of energy)

$$\Delta K = \frac{1}{2}mv_B^2$$

or $$v_B = \sqrt{\frac{2\Delta K}{m}} = \sqrt{\frac{2(6.4\times10^{-15}\text{ J})}{(1.66\times10^{-27}\text{ kg})}}$$

$$= 2.77\times10^6\text{ ms}^{-1}$$

(v) (*c*) Electrostatic potential energy of the system,

$$U = \frac{1}{4\pi\varepsilon_0}\frac{q_1q_2}{r}$$

$$= \frac{9\times10^9\times1\times10^{-6}\times1\times10^{-6}}{1}$$

$$= 9\times10^{-3}\text{ J}$$

39. (i) (*a*) Since, $E = 0$ inside the conductor and has no tangential component on the surface, so no work is done in moving a small test charge within the conductor and on its surface.

(ii) (*c*) The positively charged particle experiences electrostatic force along the direction of electric field, i.e. from high electrostatic potential to low electrostatic potential. Thus, the work is done by the electric field on the positive charge, hence electrostatic potential energy of the positive charge decreases.

(iii) (*d*) Potential energy of the system,

$$U = \frac{KQq}{l} + \frac{Kq^2}{l} + \frac{KqQ}{l} = 0$$

$$\Rightarrow \quad \frac{Kq}{l} \times [(Q + q + Q)] = 0$$

$$\Rightarrow \quad Q = -q/2$$

(iv) (*a*) Since, the proton is moving against the direction of electric field, so work is done on the proton against electric field. It implies that electric field does negative work on the proton.

(v) (*c*) Electric potential energy of the system,

$$U = \frac{1}{4\pi\varepsilon_0} \cdot \frac{q_1 q_2}{r}$$

Here, $q_1 = q_2 = 2\,\mu\text{C} = 2 \times 10^{-6}$ C,

$r = 3$ m and $\frac{1}{4\pi\varepsilon_0} = 9 \times 10^9\ \text{N-m}^2/\text{C}^2$

$$\therefore \quad U = \frac{9 \times 10^9 \times 2 \times 10^{-6} \times 2 \times 10^{-6}}{3}$$

$$= 12 \times 10^{-3}\ \text{J}$$

40. (i) (*c*) $E = \frac{V}{d}$, when d is doubled and V is reduced to half, new electric field is

$$E' = \frac{V}{2} \times \frac{1}{2d} = \frac{V}{4d} = \frac{E}{4}$$

(ii) (*d*) Since, $E = \frac{V}{d}$ so E gives the slope of V-d curve.

In option (d), since the graph is a straight line. So, E is constant in this case.

(iii) (*c*)

(iv) (*a*)

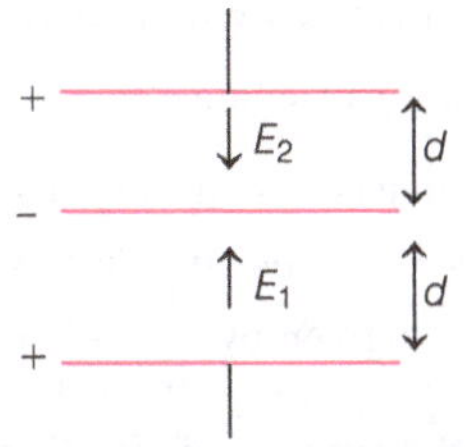

Potential difference, $V = \mathbf{E}_1 \cdot \mathbf{d} + \mathbf{E}_2 \cdot \mathbf{d}$

$\Rightarrow V = (\mathbf{E}_1 + \mathbf{E}_2) \cdot \mathbf{d}$

Or

(*c*) When a dielectric of dielectric constant K is filled in between a parallel plate capacitor, the new value of capacitance becomes CK.

Subjective Questions

1. Refer to page 43.
2. As, electric field lines starts from higher potential and ends at lower potential, so when a proton is released from rest in the field, then it moves towards the region of decreasing potential in the field.
3. Change in potential is zero on an equipotential surface.
4. Refer to text and diagram on page 48.
5. The work done by the field is negative. This is because the charge is moved against the force exerted by the field.
6. Refer to text on page 48.
7. $E = 0$ inside the conductor and has no tangential component on the surface.
   $\therefore$ No work is done in moving charge inside or on the surface of the conductor, potential is constant.
8. Let q be the charge on the charged capacitor.
   $\therefore$ Energy stored in it is given by $U = q^2/2C$
   When another uncharged similar capacitor is connected, then the net capacitance of the system is given by $C' = 2C$.
   The charge on the system remains constant, so the energy stored in the system is given by

$$U' = \frac{q^2}{2C'} = \frac{q^2}{4C} \qquad [\because C' = 2C]$$

Thus, the required ratio is given by

$$\frac{U'}{U} = \frac{q^2/4C}{q^2/2C} = \frac{1}{2}$$

9. Given, net capacitance of three identical capacitor in series $C_s = 1\mu\text{F}$

$$\frac{1}{1} = \frac{1}{C_1} + \frac{1}{C_2} + \frac{1}{C_3}$$

$$C_1 = C_2 = C_3 = C$$

After solving $1 = \frac{3}{C}$

$$C = 3\mu\text{F}$$

When connected in parallel

$$C_P = C_1 + C_2 + C_3$$

$$C_P = 9\mu\text{F}$$

Ratio of energy stored,

$$\frac{U_s}{U_P} = \frac{\frac{1}{2}C_s V^2}{\frac{1}{2}C_P V^2} = \frac{C_s}{C_P}$$

$$U_s : U_P = 1:9$$

10. When a positive charge q moves in a direction opposite to the direction of electric field, the work done by field is negative and electrostatic potential energy increases.

11. Refer to pages 55 and 56.

12. Since, we know, $V = \frac{1}{4\pi\varepsilon_0} \cdot \frac{q}{r}$

From the given graph, we have

$$\frac{V}{1/r} = \tan\theta = \frac{1}{4\pi\varepsilon_0} q$$

$$\therefore \quad \frac{Q_1}{Q_2} = \frac{\tan\theta_1}{\tan\theta_2} = \frac{\tan 60^\circ}{\tan 30^\circ} = \frac{\sqrt{3}}{1/\sqrt{3}} = 3$$

$$\left(\because \tan 30^\circ = \frac{1}{\sqrt{3}}, \tan 60^\circ = \sqrt{3}\right)$$

13. (i) Refer to Example 8 on page 48.

(ii) The direction of electric field is normal to the plane in the AB direction.

14. Suppose q_1 and q_2 charges are brought from infinity at locations r_1 and r_2 respectively, in an external electric field.

Let $V(\mathbf{r}_1)$ and $V(\mathbf{r}_2)$ be the potentials at positions r_1 and r_2 due to external electric field E. In this case, work is done in bringing these charges against their own electric fields and external electric field.

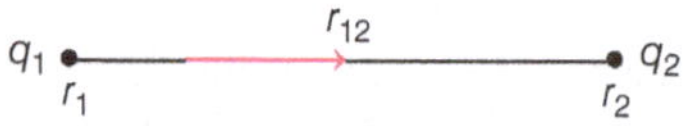

Work done in bringing q_1 from infinity to r_1,

$$W_1 = q_1 V(\mathbf{r}_1)$$

Similarly, for q_2, work done, $W_2 = q_2 V(\mathbf{r}_2)$

Work done on q_2 against the electric field due to q_1,

$$W_3 = \int_{\infty}^{r_{12}} \mathbf{F}_{12} \cdot d\mathbf{r} = \frac{1}{4\pi\varepsilon_0} \int_{\infty}^{r_{12}} \frac{q_1 q_2}{r^2} (-d\mathbf{r})$$

$$= -\frac{q_1 q_2}{4\pi\varepsilon_0} \int_{\infty}^{r_{12}} \frac{1}{r^2} dr = \frac{1}{4\pi\varepsilon_0} \frac{q_1 q_2}{\mathbf{r}_{12}}$$

where, $\mathbf{r}_{12} = |\mathbf{r}_2 - \mathbf{r}_1|$.

$\therefore$ Potential energy of system U = Work done in assembling the configuration $= W_1 + W_2 + W_3$

$$U = q_1 V(\mathbf{r}_1) + q_2 V(\mathbf{r}_2) + \frac{1}{4\pi\varepsilon_0} \frac{q_1 q_2}{\mathbf{r}_{12}}$$

15. The capacity in air, $C = \frac{\varepsilon_0 A}{d}$

The capacity when dielectric slab of dielectric constant 5 is introduced between the plates

$$C' = \frac{\varepsilon_0 A}{d - t + \frac{t}{5}}$$

$$\frac{C}{C'} = \frac{d - t + \frac{t}{5}}{d} \quad \text{...(i)}$$

Capacity is increased by 66%

So, new capacity is $\quad C' = \frac{166}{100} C$

$$\frac{C'}{C} = \frac{166}{100} \quad \text{...(ii)}$$

From Eqs. (i) and (ii), we get

$$\frac{100}{166} = \frac{d - t + \frac{t}{5}}{d} = \frac{d - \frac{4t}{5}}{d}$$

$$100d = 166d - 166\left(\frac{4t}{5}\right)$$

$$166\left(\frac{4t}{5}\right) = 66d$$

$$t = \frac{66d \times 5}{166 \times 4} = \frac{d}{2}$$

16. Capacitance of parallel plate capacitor filled with dielectric, $\quad C = \frac{\varepsilon_0 A}{(d - t) + \frac{t}{k}}$

Since, thickness, $t = \frac{2d}{3}$

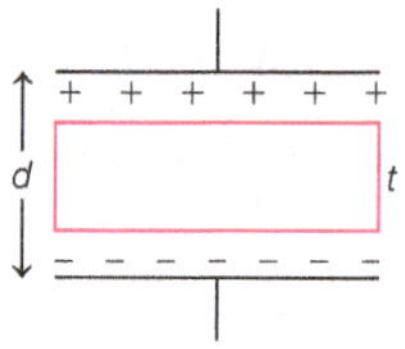

$$\therefore C = \frac{\varepsilon_0 A}{\left(d - \frac{2d}{3}\right) + \frac{2d}{3k}} = \frac{\varepsilon_0 A}{\frac{d}{3} + \frac{2d}{3k}} = \frac{3k\varepsilon_0 A}{d(k+2)}$$

17. When dielectric material is introduced between the plates, electric field between plates is reduced which increases the capacitance.

The system can be treated as two capacitors in series

I. One capacitor with air in the space $(d - t)$, with separation and one capacitor with the dielectric in the space t, with separation t for a capacitor filled with air (or vacuum), the capacitance is $C_1 = \frac{\varepsilon_0 A}{d - t}$

For a capacitor filled with a dielectric slab of thickness, the capacitance is $C_2 = \frac{k\varepsilon_0 A}{t}$

where k = dielectric constant of slab.

Since, these two capacitors are in series, the total capacitance is given by $\frac{1}{C} = \frac{1}{C_1} + \frac{1}{C_2}$

Substitute the expressions for C_1 and C_2,

$$\frac{1}{C} = \frac{d - t}{\varepsilon_0 A} + \frac{t}{k\varepsilon_0 A}$$

$$\Rightarrow \quad \frac{1}{C} = \frac{1}{\varepsilon_0 A}\left[(d-t)+\frac{t}{k}\right]$$

$$\Rightarrow \quad C = \frac{\varepsilon_0 A}{d-t+\frac{t}{k}}$$

II. **Metallic slab of thickness *t*** When a metallic slab is introduced between the plates, the slab behaves as a conductor and effectively reduces the distance between the plates.The metallic slab does not affect the electric field but shortens the effective separation between the plates. The effective distance between the plates decreases because the metallic slab completely cancels the electric field inside it.

Capacitance with metallic slab

If the separation between the plates is $d - t$, then

$$C = \frac{\varepsilon_0 A}{d-t}$$

The capacitance is greater when a metallic slab of thickness is introduced, because the effective distance between the plates is reduced to $(d-t)$ leading to a larger capacitance compared to the dielectric case.

18. At equilibrium,

The potential on the surface of a larger sphere = potential on the surface of a smaller sphere

$$V = \frac{kq_1}{r_1} = \frac{kq_2}{r_2}$$

So, $\frac{q_1}{q_2} = \frac{r_1}{r_2}$

Since, the two charges are very far from each other, the electric fields on the surfaces of the two spheres will be

$$E_1 = \frac{kq_1}{r_1^2} \text{ and } E_2 = \frac{kq_2}{r_2^2}$$

The ratio of the electric fields is

$$\frac{E_1}{E_2} = \frac{kq_1/r_1^2}{kq_2/r_2^2} = \frac{q_1}{q_2}\left(\frac{r_2}{r_1}\right)^2 = \frac{r_1}{r_2}\left(\frac{r_2}{r_1}\right)^2 \quad \left[\because \frac{q_1}{q_2} = \frac{r_1}{r_2}\right]$$

$$\frac{E_1}{E_2} = \frac{r_2}{r_1}$$

19. At equilibrium, the forces on the ball are balanced along X-axis and Y-axis. Let T be the tension in the thread.

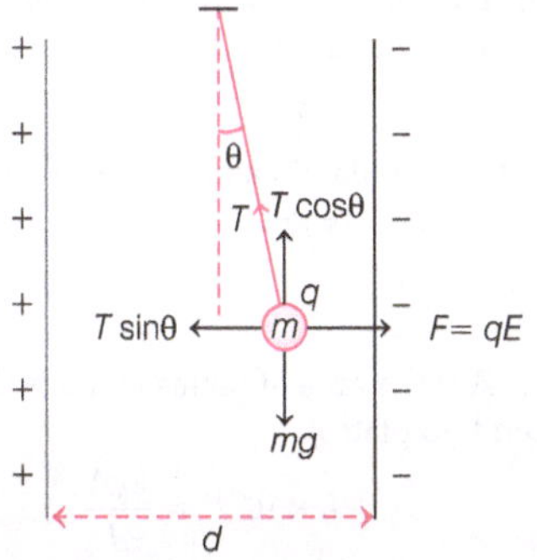

$$\Sigma F_y = 0, \text{ so } T\cos\theta = mg$$
$$\Sigma F_x = 0, \text{ so } T\sin\theta = qE$$

Dividing both equations, $\tan\theta = qE/mg$

$$E = mg\tan\theta/q$$

Potential difference,

$$V = Ed = mgd\tan\theta/q$$

20. (i) As the z-coordinate of each of the point is zero, the plane of motion from P to Q to R to S is in XY-plane.

(ii) Since, E is conservative, the work done is path independent, so replace the path $P \to Q \to R \to S$ with a simpler path as $P \to T \to S$.

Work done along $P \to T = 0$, as the path is perpendicular to the direction of E.

Work done along $T \to S = -qEa$

So, total work done $= 0 - qEa = -qEa$

Or

Since, E is conservative, the work done is path independent, so replace the path $P \to Q \to R \to S$ with a simpler path $P \to S$.

$$W = qE \cdot PS \cdot \cos(90+\theta)$$

Here, $(90+\theta)$ is the angle between the electric field E and displacement vector PS.θ is the $\angle SPT$.

$$W = -qE\sqrt{a^2+b^2}\sin\theta$$

$$W = -qE\sqrt{a^2+b^2}\cdot\frac{a}{\sqrt{a^2+b^2}}$$

$$W = -qEa$$

21. (i) $F = qE - qE = 0$

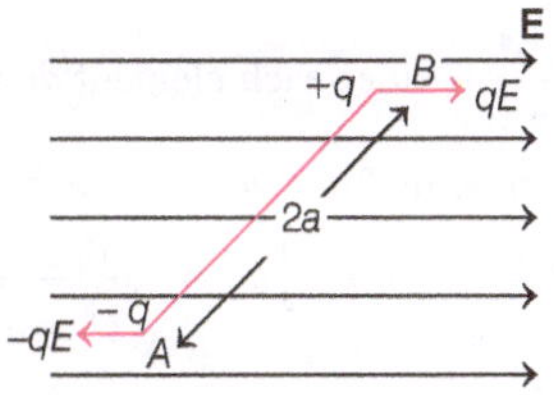

(ii) (a) $W = \int_0^{\pi}\tau d = \int_0^{\pi} pE\sin\theta = pE(\cos 0° - \cos\pi) = 2pE$

(b) As $\tau = pE\sin\theta$

It is maximum when $\theta = 90$,

$$\tau_{max} = pE\sin 90° = pE$$

22. Work done in moving a charge q from a to $b = 0$.

Work done in moving a charge q from c to $d = 0$.

This is because the electric field is perpendicular to the displacement.

Now, work done from b to $c = -$ work done from d to a, as work done in opposite direction cancel out each other resulting in zero work done.

Therefore, total work done in moving a charge q over a closed loop $abcda = 0$

23. For the system of three charges at vertices of an equilateral triangle,

PE of each pair of charges, $U = \dfrac{kq_1q_2}{r}$

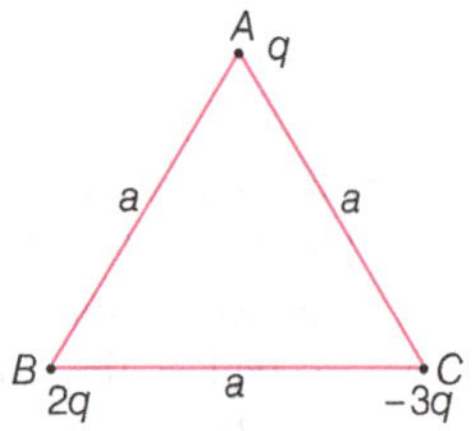

then, $U_{AB} = \dfrac{k(q)(2q)}{a} = \dfrac{2kq^2}{a}$

And $U_{BC} = \dfrac{k(2q)(-3q)}{a} = \dfrac{-6kq^2}{a}$

$U_{CA} = \dfrac{k(q)(-3q)}{r} = \dfrac{-3kq^2}{a}$

$\therefore$ Total energy, $U = U_{AB} + U_{BC} + U_{CA}$

$$= \frac{kq^2}{a}[2-6-3] = -\frac{7kq^2}{a}$$

$$= -\frac{1}{4\pi\varepsilon_0}\left(\frac{7q^2}{a}\right) \qquad \left[k = \frac{1}{4\pi\varepsilon_0}\right]$$

24. Let us take point P to be at a distance z from the centre of the ring, as shown in figure. The charge element dq is at a distance x from point P. Therefore, V can be written as

$$V = k_e\int\frac{dq}{r} = k_e\int\frac{dq}{\sqrt{z^2+a^2}}$$

where, $k = \dfrac{1}{4\pi\varepsilon_0}$, since each element dq is at the same distance from point P, so we have net potential,

$$V = \frac{k_e}{\sqrt{Z^2+a^2}}\int dq = \frac{k_eQ}{\sqrt{Z^2+a^2}}$$

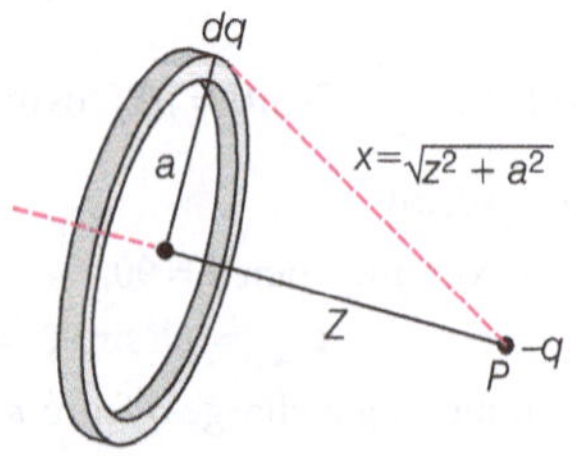

Considering $-q$ charge at P, the potential energy is given by

$$U = W = q \times \text{potential difference}$$

$$U = \frac{k_eQ(-q)}{\sqrt{Z^2+a^2}}$$

25. The capacitance of the parallel plate capacitor, filled with dielectric medium of dielectric constant K is given by

$$C = \frac{K\varepsilon_0 A}{d}, \text{ where signs are as usual.}$$

The capacitance of the parallel plate capacitor decreases with the removal of dielectric medium as for air or vacuum $K = 1$.

After disconnection from battery, charge stored will remain the same due to conservation of charge.

The energy stored in an isolated charge capacitor $= \dfrac{q^2}{2C}$,

as q is constant, energy stored $\propto 1/C$ and C decreases with the removal of dielectric medium, therefore energy stored increases. Since, q is constant and $V = q/C$ and C decreases which in turn increases V and therefore E increases as $E = V/d$.

26. Radius of spherical conductor $(r) = 12$ cm $= 0.12$ m and charge on conductor $(q) = 1.6 \times 10^{-7}$ C.

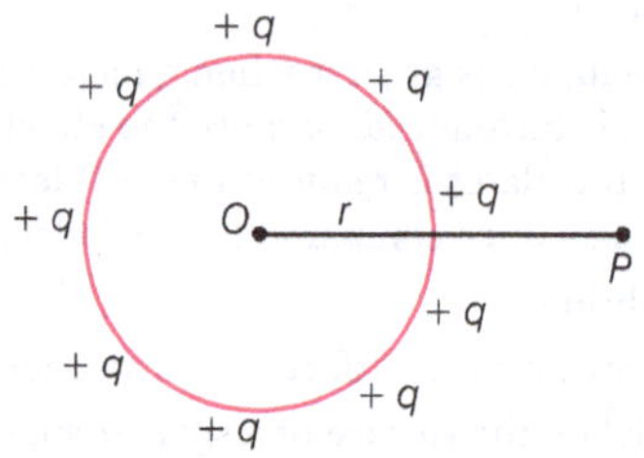

(i) According to the property of electric field, inside the conductor it is zero. So, the electric field inside the sphere is zero.

(ii) For a point just outside the sphere, i.e. for a point lying on the surface of the sphere, the charge may be supposed to be cancentrated on the centre of the sphere. By using the formula of electric field,

$$E = \frac{1}{4\pi\varepsilon_0}\cdot\frac{q}{r^2} = \frac{9\times10^9\times1.6\times10^{-7}}{0.12\times0.12} = 1\times10^5 \text{ N/C}$$

(iii) Now, we have to find the electric field at point P, where $OP = 18$ cm $= 0.18$ m

Using the formula of electric field,

$$E = \frac{1}{4\pi\varepsilon_0}\cdot\frac{q}{(OP)^2} = \frac{9\times10^9\times1.6\times10^{-7}}{0.18\times0.18}$$

$$= 4.4\times10^4 \text{ N/C}$$

27. Let initially the distance between the plates be d and air be filled between the plates. Now, the capacitance is C_0.

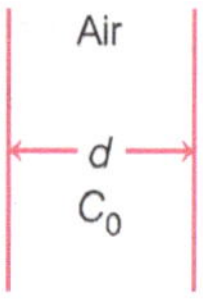

$$C_0 = 8 \text{ pF} = 8\times10^{-12} \text{ F}$$

Using the formula of capacitance of a parallel plate capacitor, we get

$$C_0 = \frac{\varepsilon_0 A}{d}$$

(where, A is the area of plates and d is the distance between two plates)

$$8\times10^{-12} = \frac{\varepsilon_0 A}{d} \qquad \text{...(i)}$$

Now, the distance between the plates is reduced to half, $d' = \frac{d}{2}$ and the space between the plates is filled with a dielectric of dielectric constant 6. Now, let the new capacitance be C. In this condition, area remains same.

$$\therefore \qquad C = \frac{K\varepsilon_0 A}{d'}$$

(where K is the dielectric constant)

$$C = 6.\frac{\varepsilon_0 A}{d}\cdot 2$$

or $\quad C = 12 \times 8 \times 10^{-12}$ [From Eq. (i)]

or $\quad C = 96 \times 10^{-12}\text{ F} = 96\text{ pF}$

The capacitance becomes 96 pF.

28. Charge on the sphere of radius R, $q_1 = 4\pi R^2\sigma$

Charge on the sphere of radius $2R$, $q_2 = 4\pi\,(2R)^2\sigma$

$C_1 = 4\pi\varepsilon_0 R$ and $C_2 = 4\pi\varepsilon_0(2R)$

$\therefore$ Common potential, $V = \dfrac{C_1V_1 + C_2V_2}{C_1 + C_2} = \dfrac{q_1 + q_2}{C_1 + C_2}$

$$= \frac{4\pi R^2\sigma + 4\pi\,(2R)^2\sigma}{4\pi\varepsilon_0 R + 4\pi\varepsilon_0 2R}$$

$$= \frac{5\sigma R}{3\varepsilon_0} \quad \text{... (i)}$$

So, new charge on bigger sphere,

$$q_2 = C_2V = 4\pi\varepsilon_0\,(2R) \times \frac{5\sigma R}{3\varepsilon_0} \quad \text{[from Eq. (i)]}$$

$$= \frac{40\pi R^2\sigma}{3}$$

New charge density of bigger sphere,

$$\sigma_2' = \frac{q_2'}{A_2} = \frac{\frac{40\pi R^2\sigma}{3}}{4\pi\,(2R)^2} = \frac{5}{6}\sigma$$

29. (i) Refer to text on page 48.

(ii) Refer to text on pages 46 and 47.

30. (i) The equipotential surface are plane parallel to XY-plane. As the field is increasing in magnitude, the spacing between surfaces decreases.

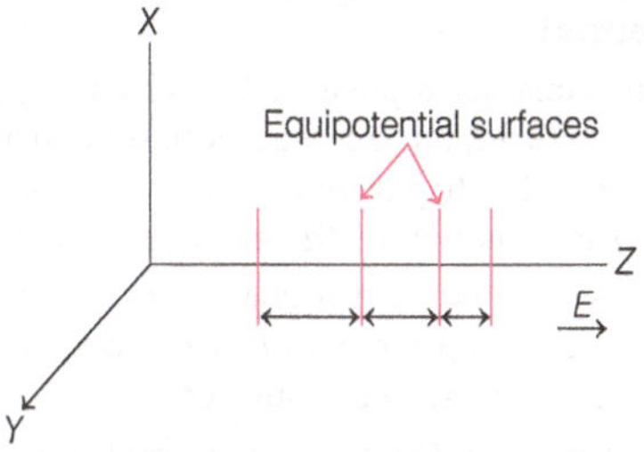

(ii) Let $P(0, 0, z)$ and $Q(x, y, 0)$ are two points on which electric potential are to be calculated.

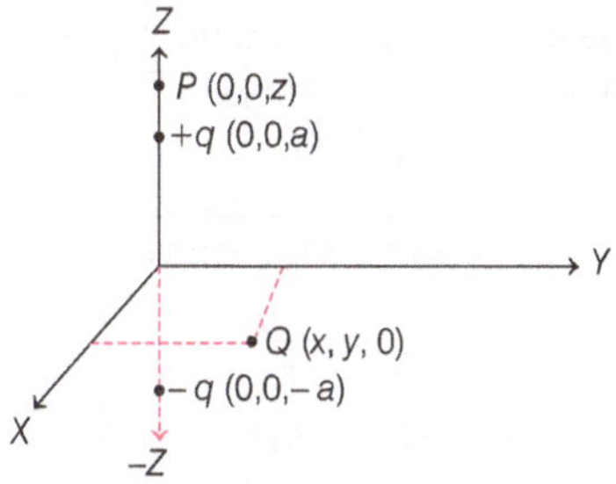

Then, electrostatic potential at P,

$$V_P = \frac{1}{4\pi\varepsilon_0}\left[\frac{q}{(z-a)} - \frac{q}{(z+a)}\right]$$

$$= \frac{1}{4\pi\varepsilon_0}\left[\frac{q \times 2a}{(z^2 - a^2)}\right]$$

$$= \frac{1}{4\pi\varepsilon_0}\frac{p}{(z^2 - a^2)} \qquad [\because p = q \times 2a]$$

The electrostatic potential at Q,

$$V_Q = \frac{1}{4\pi\varepsilon_0}\left[\frac{q}{\sqrt{x^2 + y^2 + a^2}} - \frac{q}{\sqrt{x^2 + y^2 + a^2}}\right]$$

$$= 0$$

31. (i) The charges $+q_1$ and $-q_2$ are placed at A and B respectively, as shown below

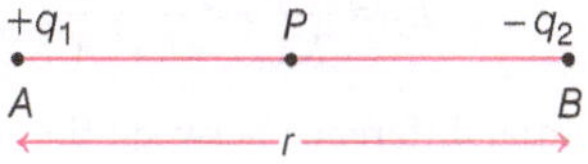

Let P be the mid-point of line joining A and B. The potential at P due to charge $+q_1$,

$$V_1 = \frac{q_1}{4\pi\varepsilon_0 r/2}$$

and due to charge $-q_2$,

$$V_2 = \frac{-q_2}{4\pi\varepsilon_0 r/2}$$

The net potential at P,

$$V = V_1 + V_2 = \frac{q_1}{4\pi\varepsilon_0 r/2} - \frac{q_2}{4\pi\varepsilon_0 r/2}$$

$$= \frac{2}{4\pi\varepsilon_0 r}(q_1 - q_2)$$

The work done to place a charge q_3 at P,

$$W = q_3V = \frac{2q_3(q_1 - q_2)}{4\pi\varepsilon_0 r} \text{ or } W = \frac{q_3\,(q_1 - q_2)}{2\pi\varepsilon_0 r}$$

(ii) Let x be the distance from charge $+q_1$ on the line joining the two charges, at which the work done will be zero as shown.

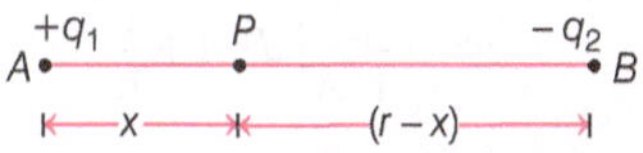

So, the potential due to charge $+q_1$ at A is equal to potential due to charge $-q_2$ at B at point P,

i.e $\quad V_{q_1} = V_{q_2}$

$$\frac{q_1}{4\pi\varepsilon_0 x} = \frac{-q_2}{4\pi\varepsilon_0 (r-x)}$$

$$\Rightarrow \quad \frac{q_1}{x} = -\frac{q_2}{r-x}$$

$$\Rightarrow \quad rq_1 - xq_1 = -q_2 x$$

$$\text{or} \quad x = \frac{rq_1}{(q_1 - q_2)}$$

32. (i) Refer to text on page 49.

(ii) Refer to text on page 50.

33. Consider a parallel plate capacitor, area of each plate being A, the separation between the plates being d. Let a dielectric slab of dielectric constant K and thickness $t < d$ be placed between the plates. The thickness of air between the plates is $(d-t)$. If charges on plates are $+Q$ and $-Q$, then surface charge density $\sigma = \frac{Q}{A}$

The electric field between the plates in air,

$$E_1 = \frac{\sigma}{\varepsilon_0} = \frac{Q}{\varepsilon_0 A}$$

The electric field between the plates in slab,

$$E_2 = \frac{\sigma}{K\varepsilon_0} = \frac{Q}{K\varepsilon_0 A}$$

$\therefore$ The potential difference between the plates,

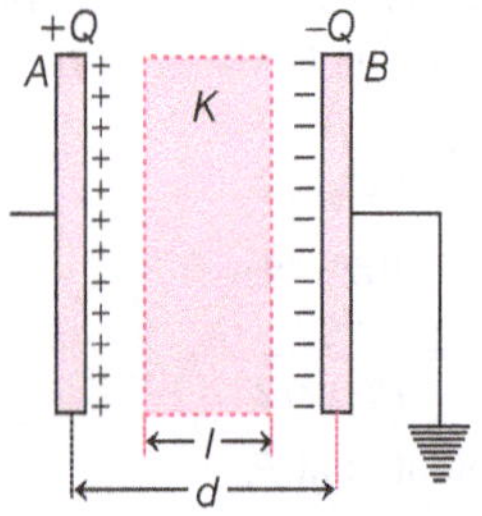

V_{AB} = work done in carrying unit positive charge from one plate to another

$= \Sigma Ex$ (as field between the plates is not constant).

$$= E_1(d-t) + E_2 t = \frac{Q}{\varepsilon_0 A}(d-t) + \frac{Q}{K\varepsilon_0 A}t$$

$$\therefore \quad V_{AB} = \frac{Q}{\varepsilon_0 A}\left|d - t + \frac{t}{K}\right|$$

$\therefore$ Capacitance of capacitor,

$$C = \frac{Q}{V_{AB}} = \frac{Q}{\frac{Q}{\varepsilon_0 A}\left(d - t + \frac{t}{K}\right)}$$

$$\text{or,} \quad C = \frac{\varepsilon_0 A}{d - t + \frac{t}{K}} = \frac{\varepsilon_0 A}{d - t\left(1 - \frac{1}{K}\right)} = \frac{\varepsilon_0 A}{\frac{d}{2}\left(1 + \frac{1}{K}\right)}$$

Here, $t = \frac{d}{2}$

$$\therefore \quad C = \frac{\varepsilon_0 A}{d - \frac{d}{2}\left(1 - \frac{1}{K}\right)} = \frac{\varepsilon_0 A}{\frac{d}{2}\left(1 + \frac{1}{k}\right)}$$

34. (i)

	Non-polar (O_2)	Polar (H_2O)
(a) Absence of electric field		
Individual	No dipole moment exists	Dipole moment exists
Specimen	No dipole moment exists	Dipoles are randomly oriented. Net $\mathbf{p} = 0$
(b) Presence of electric field		
Individual	Dipole moment exists (molecules become polarised)	Torque acts on the molecules to align them parallel to $\mathbf{E}$
Specimen	Dipole moment exists	Net dipole moment exists parallel to $\mathbf{E}$

(ii) (a) The potential difference between the plates is given by

$$V = E_0 d + \frac{E_0}{K}d + E_0 d + 0 + E_0 d \Rightarrow V = 3E_0 d + \frac{E_0}{K}d$$

(b) E versus x graph

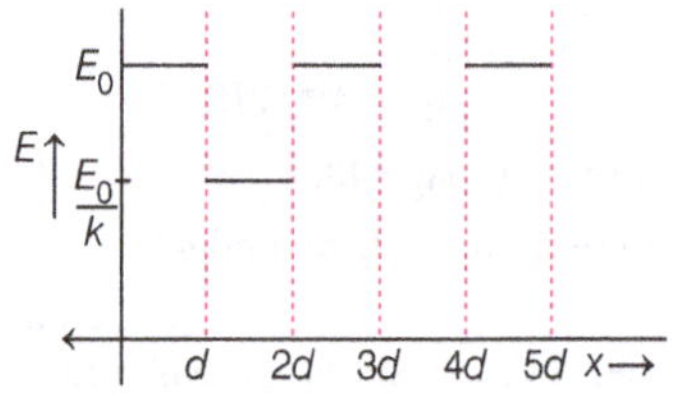

35. (i) **Relation between Electric Field and Electric Potential**

Let us consider a positive test charge (q_0) moves a distance (ds) from one equipotential surface to another. The displacement (ds) makes an angle (θ) with the direction of the electric field $(\mathbf{E})$.

Suppose a positive test charge (q_0) moves through a differential displacement ds from one equipotential surface to the adjacent surface.

We know that, the work done by the electric field on the test charge during its movement is $-q_0\, dV$. We see that, the work done by the electric field may also be written as the scalar product ($q_0 \mathbf{E} \cdot ds$) or $q_0 E \cos\theta\, ds$.

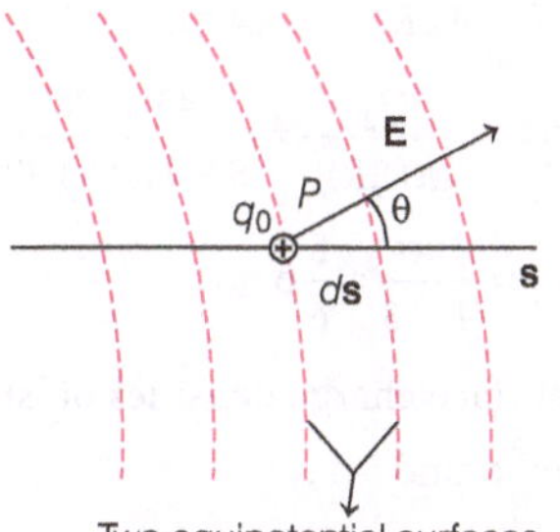

Equating these two expressions for the work yields

$$-q_0 dV = q_0 E \cos\theta\, ds$$

$$\Rightarrow \quad E\cos\theta = -\frac{dV}{ds}$$

Since, $E\cos\theta$ is the component of E in the direction of ds, therefore $E_s = -\frac{\partial V}{\partial s}$

$$\mathbf{E} = E_x\hat{\mathbf{i}} + E_y\hat{\mathbf{j}} + E_z\hat{\mathbf{k}}$$

where, E_x, E_y and E_z are the x, y and z-components of E at any point.

$$\because \quad E_x = -\frac{\partial V}{\partial x},$$

$$E_y = -\frac{\partial V}{\partial y}, \quad E_z = -\frac{\partial V}{\partial z}$$

$$\therefore \quad \mathbf{E} = -\left[\frac{\partial V}{\partial x}\hat{\mathbf{i}} + \frac{\partial V}{\partial y}\hat{\mathbf{j}} + \frac{\partial V}{\partial z}\hat{\mathbf{k}}\right]$$

For the simple situation in which the electric field **E** is uniform.

$$\mathbf{E} = -\Delta V$$

Negative sign shows that the direction of electric field **E** is in the direction of decreasing potential.

(ii) The equipotential surfaces for an electric field in + z-direction are shown below.

As the distance between the surfaces is decreasing towards − z-direction, this means the electric field is increasing in magnitude towards − z-direction at a constant rate.

36. (i) (a) Refer to text on page 48.

(b) Refer to text on page 49.

(ii) $\because U_f = \frac{CV^2}{4}$ and $U_i = \frac{1}{2}CV^2$

$$\therefore \quad \frac{U_f}{U_i} = \frac{1}{2}$$

37. (i) Refer to text on pages 53 and 54.

(ii) (a) Refer to text on pagse 53 and 54.

(b) Refer to text on pages 53 and 54.

(c) Refer to text on page 58.

38. (i) Potential of three shells

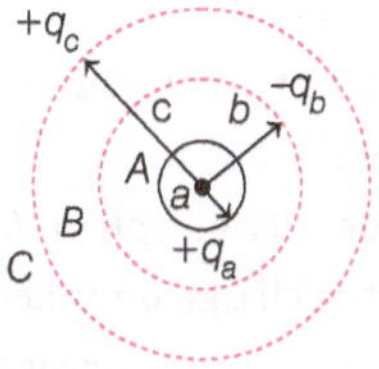

At shell *A*,

$$\text{Potential, } V_A = \frac{1}{4\pi\varepsilon_0}\left(\frac{q_a}{a} - \frac{q_b}{b} + \frac{q_c}{c}\right)$$

$$= \frac{1}{4\pi\varepsilon_0}\left(\frac{4\pi a^2\sigma}{a} - \frac{4\pi b^2\sigma}{b} + \frac{4\pi c^2\sigma}{c}\right)$$

$$\left[\because \sigma = \frac{q}{4\pi r^2}\right]$$

$$= \frac{\sigma}{\varepsilon_0}(a - b + c)$$

At shell *B*,

$$\text{Potential, } V_B = \frac{1}{4\pi\varepsilon_0}\left(\frac{q_a}{b} - \frac{q_b}{b} + \frac{q_c}{c}\right)$$

$$= \frac{1}{4\pi\varepsilon_0}\left(\frac{4\pi a^2\sigma}{b} - \frac{4\pi b^2\sigma}{b} + \frac{4\pi c^2\sigma}{c}\right)$$

$$\left[\because \sigma = \frac{q}{4\pi r^2}\right]$$

$$= \frac{\sigma}{\varepsilon_0}\left(\frac{a^2 - b^2}{b} + c\right)$$

At shell *C*,

$$\text{Potential, } V_C = \frac{1}{4\pi\varepsilon_0}\left(\frac{q_a}{c} - \frac{q_b}{c} + \frac{q_c}{c}\right)$$

$$= \frac{1}{4\pi\varepsilon_0}\left(\frac{4\pi a^2\sigma}{c} - \frac{4\pi b^2\sigma}{c} + \frac{4\pi c^2\sigma}{c}\right)$$

$$\left[\because \sigma = \frac{q}{4\pi r^2}\right]$$

$$= \frac{\sigma}{\varepsilon_0}\left(\frac{a^2 - b^2 + c^2}{c}\right)$$

(ii) Relation between the radii

Now, $V_A = V_C$ (given)

$$\frac{\sigma}{\varepsilon_0}(a - b + c) = \frac{\sigma}{\varepsilon_0}\frac{(a^2 - b^2 + c^2)}{c}$$

$$a - b + c = \frac{a^2 - b^2 + c^2}{c} = \frac{a^2 - b^2}{c} + c$$

$$c(a - b) = a^2 - b^2$$

$$\Rightarrow \quad c = a + b$$

$$[\because (a^2 - b^2) = (a - b)(a + b)]$$

39. Radius of sphere $A = R$

Surface charge density on sphere $A = \sigma$

Radius of sphere $B = 2R$

Surface charge density on sphere $B = \sigma$

Before contact, the charge on sphere A is

Q_1 = Surface charge density × Surface area

$$\Rightarrow \quad Q_1 = \sigma \cdot 4\pi R^2 \qquad \text{...(i)}$$

Before contact, the charge on sphere B is

Q_2 = Surface charge density × Surface area

$$Q_2 = \sigma \cdot 4\pi(2R)^2 = \sigma \cdot 16\pi R^2 \qquad \text{...(ii)}$$

Let after the contact, the charge on A be Q_1' and the charge on B be Q_2'.

According to the conservation of charge, the charge before contact is equal to charge after contact.

$$Q_1' + Q_2' = Q_1 + Q_2$$

Now, from Eqs. (i) and (ii), we get

$$Q_1' + Q_2' = 4\pi R^2\sigma + 16\pi R^2\sigma = 20\pi R^2\sigma \qquad \text{...(iii)}$$

As they are in contact, so they have same potential.

Potential on sphere A, $V_A = \frac{1}{4\pi\varepsilon_0}\cdot\frac{Q_1'}{R}$

Potential on sphere B, $V_B = \frac{1}{4\pi\varepsilon_0}\cdot\frac{Q_2'}{2R}$

So, $V_A = V_B$

$$\Rightarrow \quad \frac{1}{4\pi\varepsilon_0}\cdot\frac{Q_1'}{R} = \frac{1}{4\pi\varepsilon_0}\cdot\frac{Q_2'}{2R}$$

$$\Rightarrow \quad \frac{Q_1'}{R} = \frac{Q_2'}{2R}$$

$$\Rightarrow \quad 2Q_1' = Q_2' \qquad \text{...(iv)}$$

Putting the value of Q_2' in Eq. (iii), we get

$$Q_1' + 2Q_1' = 20\pi R^2\sigma \Rightarrow 3Q_1' = 20\pi R^2\sigma$$

$$\Rightarrow \quad Q_1' = \frac{20}{3}\pi R^2\sigma$$

and $$Q_2' = \frac{40}{3}\pi R^2\sigma \qquad \text{[from Eq. (iv)]}$$

Let the new charge densities be σ_1 and σ_2.

$$\sigma_1 = \frac{Q_1'}{4\pi R^2} = \frac{20\pi R^2\sigma}{3\times 4\pi R^2} = \frac{5}{3}\sigma$$

$$\sigma_2 = \frac{Q_2'}{4\pi(2R)^2} = \frac{40\pi R^2\sigma}{3\times 4\pi\times 4R^2} = \frac{40\sigma}{16\times 3}$$

$$\sigma_2 = \frac{10\sigma}{4\times 3} = \frac{5}{6}\sigma$$

Thus, the surface charge densities on spheres after contact are $\frac{5}{3}\sigma$ and $\frac{5}{6}\sigma$.

40. On introducing the dielectric slab to fill the gap between plates of capacitor completely when capacitor is connected with battery, i.e.,

(i) The capacitance of capacitor becomes K times of original capacitor.

$$C' = KC = 10C$$

(ii) The potential difference V between capacitors is same due to connectivity with battery and hence, charge q' becomes K times of original charge as

$$q' = C'V' = (KC)(V) = K(CV)$$
$$= Kq = 10CV$$

(iii) The energy density of the capacitor,

$$u = \frac{1}{2}\varepsilon_0 E^2$$

$$u' = \frac{1}{2}k\varepsilon_0 E'^2 = \frac{1}{2}\times 10\varepsilon_0\left(\frac{V^2}{l^2}\right)$$

$$= \frac{1}{2}\times 10\times\varepsilon_0\left(\frac{V^2}{(3d)^2}\right) = \frac{10}{9}\left(\frac{1}{2}\varepsilon_0\frac{V^2}{d^2}\right) = \frac{10}{9}\times\frac{1}{2}\varepsilon_0 E^2$$

$$u' = \frac{10}{9}u$$

41. The given figure is shown below.

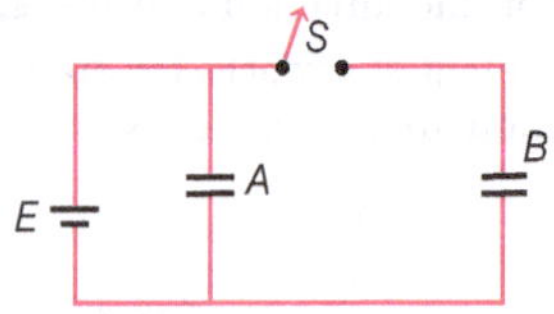

When switch S is closed, the potential difference across capacitors A and B are same,

i.e. $$V = \frac{Q_A}{C} = \frac{Q_B}{C}$$

Initial charges on capacitors,

$$Q_A = Q_B = CV$$

When the dielectric is introduced, the new capacitance of either capacitor,

$$C' = KC$$

As switch S is opened, the potential difference across capacitor A remains same (V volts).

Let potential difference across capacitor B be V'. When dielectric is introduced with switch S opened (i.e. battery disconnected), the charges on capacitor B remains unchanged, so

$$Q_B = CV = C'V'$$

$$\Rightarrow \quad V' = \frac{C}{C'}V = \frac{V}{K}$$

Initial energy of both capacitors,

$$U_i = \frac{1}{2}CV^2 + \frac{1}{2}CV^2 = CV^2$$

Final energy of both capacitors,

$$U_f = \frac{1}{2}C'V^2 + \frac{1}{2}C'V'^2$$

$$= \frac{1}{2}(KC)V^2 + \frac{1}{2}(KC)\left(\frac{V}{K}\right)^2$$

$$= \frac{1}{2}CV^2\left[K + \frac{1}{K}\right] = \frac{1}{2}CV^2\left(\frac{K^2+1}{K}\right)$$

$$\Rightarrow \quad \frac{U_i}{U_f} = \frac{CV^2}{\frac{1}{2}CV^2\left(\frac{K^2+1}{K}\right)} = \frac{2K}{K^2+1}$$

42. (i) (a) When a conductor is placed in an external electric field, the free charges present inside the conductor redistribute themselves in such a manner that the electric field due to induced charges opposes the external field within the conductor.

This happens until a static situation is achieved, i.e. when the two fields cancel each other and the net electrostatic field in the conductor becomes zero.

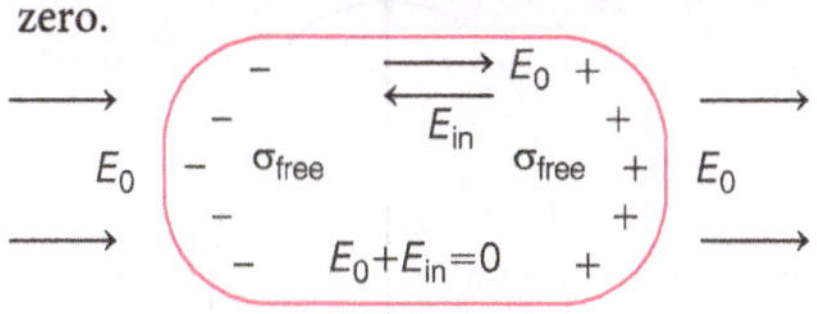

Conductor

(b) In contrast to conductors, dielectrics are non-conducting substances, i.e. they have no charge carriers. Thus, in a dielectric, free movement of charges in not possible. It turns out that the external field induces dipole moment by stretching molecules of the dielectric.

The collective effect of all the molecular dipole moments is the net charge on the surface of the dielectric which produces a field that opposes the external field. However, the opposing field is so induced that does not exactly cancel the external field. It only reduces it. The extent of the effect depends on the nature of dielectric.

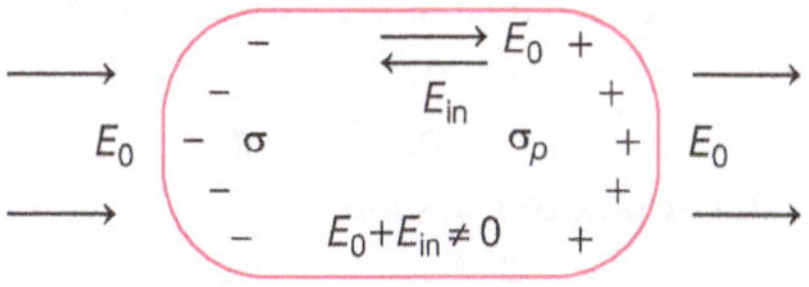

Dielectric

Both polar and non-polar dielectrics develop net dipole moment in the presence of an external field. The dipole moment per unit volume is called polarisation and is denoted by P for linear isotropic dielectrics.

$$P = \chi E$$

where, χ is constant of proportionality and is called electric susceptibility of the electric slab.

(ii) (a) At point C, inside the spherical shell, electric field is zero.

Thus, the force experienced by charge at centre C will also be zero.

$$\because \quad F_C = qE \; (E_{\text{inside the shell}} = 0)$$

$$\therefore \quad F_C = 0$$

At point A, $|F_A| = 2Q\left[\frac{1}{4\pi\varepsilon_0} \cdot \frac{3Q/2}{x^2}\right]$

$$F = \frac{3Q^2}{4\pi\varepsilon_0 x^2}, \text{ away from shell.}$$

(b) Electric flux through the shell,

$$\phi = \frac{1}{\varepsilon_0} \times \text{magnitude of charge enclosed by shell}$$

$$= \frac{1}{\varepsilon_0} \times \frac{Q}{2} = \frac{Q}{2\varepsilon_0}$$

43. (i) According to the question,

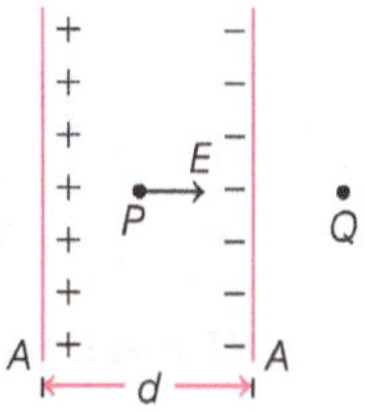

(a) Electric field due to a plate of positive charge at point P,

$$E_P = \frac{\sigma}{2\varepsilon_0}$$

Electric field due to other plate $= \dfrac{\sigma}{2\varepsilon_0}$

Since, they have same direction, so

$$E_{net} = \frac{\sigma}{2\varepsilon_0} + \frac{\sigma}{2\varepsilon_0} = \frac{\sigma}{\varepsilon_0}$$

Outside the plate, electric field will be zero because of opposite directions.

(b) Potential difference between the plates is given by

$$V = Ed = \frac{\sigma d}{\varepsilon_0} \qquad \left[\because E = \frac{\sigma}{\varepsilon_0}\right]$$

(c) Capacitance of the capacitor is given by

$$C = \frac{Q}{V} = \frac{\sigma A}{\sigma d}\varepsilon_0 = \frac{\varepsilon_0 A}{d}$$

(ii) According to question,

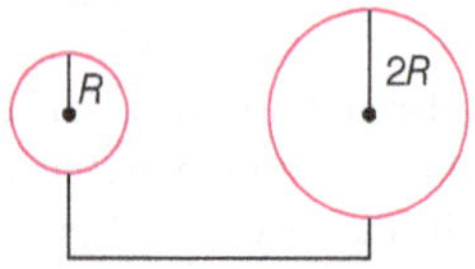

Potential at the surface of radius R,

$$V = \frac{kq}{R} = \frac{k\sigma 4\pi R^2}{R} \quad [\because q = \sigma \times 4\pi R^2]$$
$$= 4k\sigma\pi R$$

Potential at the surface of radius $2R$,

$$V' = \frac{kq}{2R}$$

So, $$V' = \frac{k\sigma 16\pi R^2}{2R} = 8k\sigma\pi R$$
$$[\because q = \sigma \times 4\pi(2R)^2 = 16\sigma\pi R^2]$$

Since, the potential of bigger sphere is more, so charge will flow from sphere of radius $2R$ to sphere of radius R.

44. Draw a cylindrical Gaussian surface of radius r and length l, then by applying Gauss' theorem,

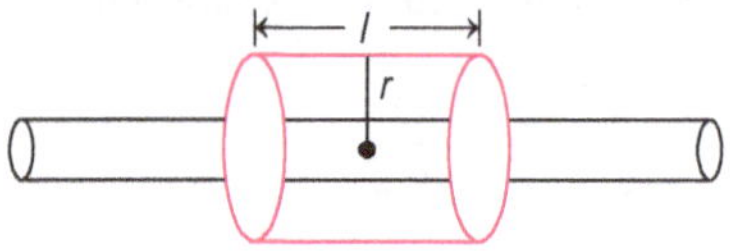

$$\int \mathbf{E} \cdot d\mathbf{S} = \frac{1}{\varepsilon_0}\lambda l$$

or $$E_r\, 2\pi r l = \frac{1}{\varepsilon_0}\lambda l \Rightarrow E_r = \frac{\lambda}{2\pi\varepsilon_0 r}$$

Hence, if r_0 is the radius,

$$V(r) - V(r_0) = -\int_{r_0}^{r} \mathbf{E} \cdot d\mathbf{l} = \frac{\lambda}{2\pi\varepsilon_0}\ln\frac{r_0}{r}$$

Since, $$\int_{r_0}^{r} \frac{\lambda}{2\pi\varepsilon_0 r}dr = \frac{\lambda}{2\pi\varepsilon_0}\int_{r_0}^{r}\frac{1}{r}dr = \frac{\lambda}{2\pi\varepsilon_0}\ln\frac{r}{r_0}$$

For a given V,

$$\ln\frac{r}{r_0} = -\frac{2\pi\varepsilon_0}{\lambda}[V(r) - V(r_0)]$$

$$\Rightarrow \quad r = r_0 e^{-2\pi\varepsilon_0 [V(r) - V(r_0)]/\lambda}$$

The equipotential surfaces are cylinders of radius

$$r = r_0 e^{-2\pi\varepsilon_0 [V(r) - V(r_0)]/\lambda}$$

45. Let third charge $+q$ is slightly displaced from mean position towards first charge, so the total potential energy of the system is given by

$$U = \frac{1}{4\pi\varepsilon_0}\left\{\frac{-q^2}{(d-x)} + \frac{-q^2}{(d+x)}\right\}$$

$$U = \frac{-q^2}{4\pi\varepsilon_0}\frac{2d}{(d^2 - x^2)}$$

$$\frac{dU}{dx} = \frac{-q^2 . 2d}{4\pi\varepsilon_0}\cdot\frac{2x}{(d^2 - x^2)^2}$$

The system will be in equilibrium, if $F = -\frac{dU}{dx} = 0$

On solving, $x = 0$. So, for $+q$ charge to be in stable/unstable equilibrium, finding second derivative of PE.

$$\frac{d^2U}{dx^2} = \left(\frac{-2dq^2}{4\pi\varepsilon_0}\right)\left[\frac{2}{(d^2 - x^2)^2} - \frac{8x^2}{(d^2 - x^2)^3}\right]$$
$$= \left(\frac{-2dq^2}{4\pi\varepsilon_0}\right)\frac{1}{(d^2 - x^2)^3}[2(d^2 - x^2)^2 - 8x^2]$$

At $x = 0$

$$\frac{d^2U}{dx^2} = \left(\frac{-2dq^2}{4\pi\varepsilon_0}\right)\left(\frac{1}{d^6}\right)(2d^2), \text{ which is } < 0$$

This shows that system will be in unstable equilibrium.

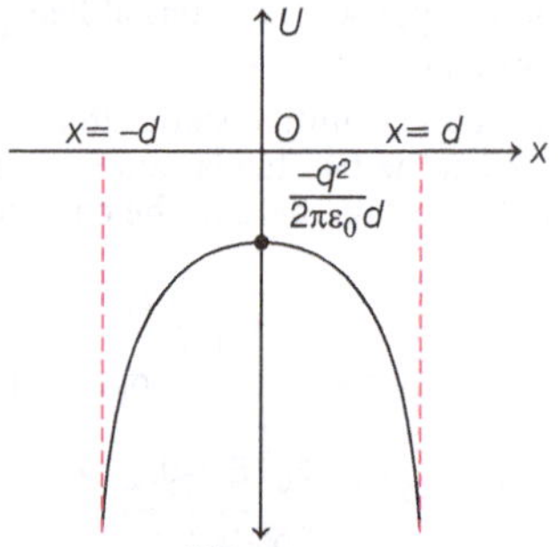

PE *versus* x

46. (i) A dielectric material of thickness $t (t < d)$ and dielectric constant K is inserted between the plates. In the remaining space $(d - t)$ there is air.

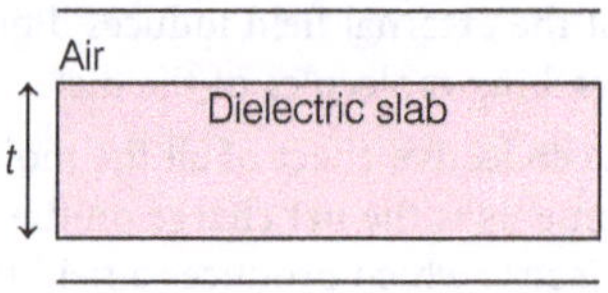

The electric field in the dielectric-filled portion

$$E_1 = \frac{\sigma}{\varepsilon_0 K}.$$

The electric field in the air-filled portion

$$E_2 = \frac{\sigma}{\varepsilon_0}$$

The potential difference between the plates = V

$$V = E_2 \times (d - t) + E_1 \times t$$

or $$V = \frac{\sigma}{2\varepsilon_0} \times (d - t) + \frac{\sigma}{\varepsilon_0 K} \times t$$

or $$V = \frac{q}{A\varepsilon_0} \times \left[(d - t) + \frac{t}{K}\right]$$

Now, capacitance $C = \frac{q}{V}$

or $$C = \frac{\varepsilon_0 A}{(d - t) + \frac{t}{K}}$$

(ii) When the capacitors are connected in parallel, equivalent capacitance $C_p = C_1 + C_2$.

The energy stored in the combination of capacitor,

$$E_p = \frac{1}{2} C_p V^2$$

$$\Rightarrow \quad E_p = \frac{1}{2}(C_1 + C_2)(100)^2 = 0.25\,\text{J}$$

$$(C_1 + C_2) = 5 \times 10^{-5} \quad \text{..(i)}$$

When the capacitors are connected in series equivalent capacitance,

$$C_s = \frac{C_1 C_2}{C_1 + C_2}$$

The energy stored in the combination of the capacitance,

$$E_s = \frac{1}{2} C_s V^2$$

$$= \frac{1}{2} \frac{C_1 C_2}{C_1 + C_2}(100)^2 = 0.040\,\text{J}$$

$$\frac{1}{2} \times \frac{C_1 C_2}{5 \times 10^{-5}}(100)^2 = 0.040\,\text{J}$$

$$C_1 C_2 = 0.040 \times 10^{-4} \times 5 \times 10^{-5} \times 2 = 4 \times 10^{-10}$$

Now, $(C_1 - C_2)^2 = (C_1 + C_2)^2 - 4C_1 C_2$

$$(C_1 - C_2)^2 = 25 \times 10^{-10} - 4 \times 4 \times 10^{-10} = 9 \times 10^{-10}$$

$$C_1 - C_2 = \sqrt{9 \times 10^{-10}}$$

$$C_1 - C_2 = 3 \times 10^{-5} \quad \text{...(ii)}$$

By solving Eqs. (i) and (ii), we get

$$C_1 = 45\,\mu\text{F and } C_2 = 15\,\mu\text{F}$$

47. Work done, $W = q \times \Delta V$

But $\Delta V = 0$, as the two diagonally opposite points are at the same potential due to 10 μC charge.

$\therefore \quad W = 2\,\mu\text{C} \times 0 = 0$

Work done $W = 0$

48. Initial potential energy of system,

$$= \frac{1}{4\pi\varepsilon_0}\frac{q_1 q_2}{r} + \frac{1}{4\pi\varepsilon_0}\frac{q_2 q_3}{r} + \frac{1}{4\pi\varepsilon_0}\frac{q_3 q_1}{r}$$

$$= \frac{1}{4\pi\varepsilon_0 r}[q(-4q) + (-4q)(2q) + (2q)(q)]$$

$$= \frac{1}{4\pi\varepsilon_0 r}[-10q^2]$$

$$= \frac{9 \times 10^9 \times [-10 \times (1.6 \times 10^{-10})^2]}{10 \times 10^{-2}} = -2.30 \times 10^{-8}\,\text{J}$$

Final potential energy of system, $U_f = 0$

The work done to dissociate the system of charges is $W = U_f - U_i = 2.304 \times 10^{-6}$ J

49. (i) ∵ Electric field intensity and potential difference are related as, $E = -\Delta V / \Delta r$

$$\Delta V = -\mathbf{E}\cdot\Delta\mathbf{r} = -\mathbf{E}\cdot\Delta\mathbf{r}_{AB} - \mathbf{E}\cdot\Delta\mathbf{r}_{BC}$$

$$\Rightarrow \quad V_C - V_A = -4E + 0$$

$$\left[\because \text{By Pythagoras theorem}, AC^2 = AB^2 + BC^2 \Rightarrow AB^2 = 5^2 - 3^2 \Rightarrow \Delta r = \sqrt{16} \Rightarrow \Delta r = 4\right]$$

(ii) As $V_C - V_A = -4E$, which is negative

$\therefore \quad V_C < V_A$

Potential at point A is greater than potential at point C, as potential decreases along the direction of electric field.

50. Given, $r = 0.1$ m, $V = +50$ V and $q = ?$

As, $$V = \frac{1}{4\pi\varepsilon_0}\cdot\frac{q}{r} \Rightarrow 50 = 9 \times 10^9 \times \frac{q}{0.1}$$

$$\therefore \quad q = \frac{50 \times 0.1}{9 \times 10^9} = 5.6 \times 10^{-10}\,\text{C}$$

As, V is positive, therefore q must be positive.

51. Potential at the centre,

$$V = \frac{1}{4\pi\varepsilon_0}\left(\frac{q}{r}\right) = 9 \times 10^9 \times 10^{-8} \times \frac{60}{360} \times 2\pi r$$

$$= 9 \times 10^9 \times 10^{-8} \times \frac{2 \times 3.14 \times 2}{6} = 188.4\,\text{V}$$

52. $$V = \frac{q}{4\pi\varepsilon_0 r} = \frac{9 \times 10^9 \times 5 \times 10^{-7}}{11 \times 10^{-2}} = 40.9\,\text{kV}$$

53. Potential is same in the sphere, so potential at the centre of the sphere will be 20V.

54. (i) Let us consider the figure below.

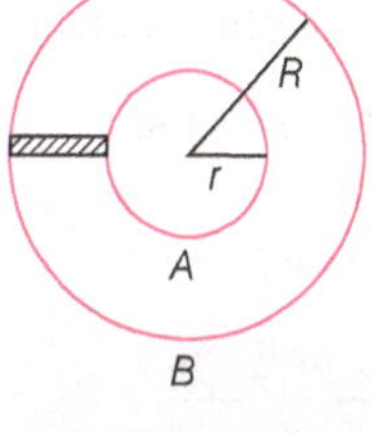

Initial potential of sphere A is $V = \frac{kQ_A}{r}$

where Q_A is the charge on sphere A.

Now, when shell B is connected to A by a wire, the entire charge Q_A flows to sphere B.

$\therefore$ The final potential on shell B will be

$$V_B = \frac{kQ_A}{R} = \frac{k}{R} \times \frac{Vr}{K} = \frac{r}{R}V$$

Since, shell A is inside shell B so the final potential of both the spheres will be same which is

$$V_f = \frac{rV}{R}$$

(ii) Refer to text on pages 47 and 48. (Equipotential surfaces)

Let us draw a diagram.

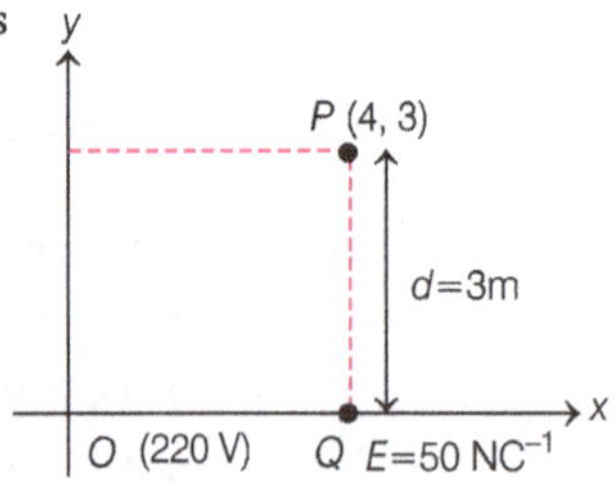

Since E is constant along the X-axis so it is an equipotential surface with the potential of 220V.

Let us consider a point Q on the X-axis which , when extended point $P(4, 3)$, forms a straight line parallel to the Y-axis. The distance between P and Q is $d = 3$ m.

$\therefore$ The potential at point P will be V_P, which is

$$V_P - V_Q = Ed$$

$$\Rightarrow \quad V_P = (50 \times 3 + 220)\ V = 370\text{V}$$

55. A negative value of electrostatic potential energy of a system signifies a stable system.

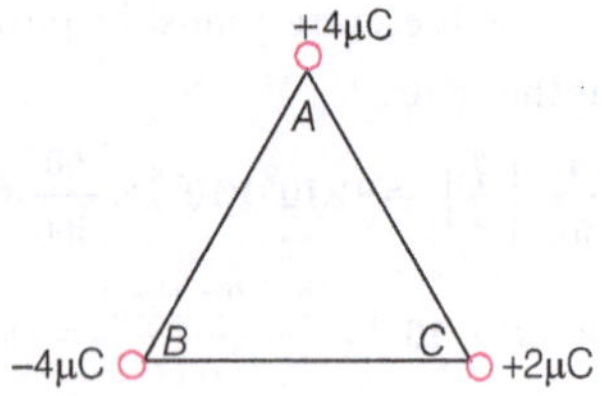

$$U = \frac{KQ_AQ_B}{r} + \frac{KQ_BQ_C}{r} + \frac{KQ_CQ_A}{r}$$

$$U = \frac{K}{r}[Q_AQ_B + Q_BQ_C + Q_CQ_A]$$

$$U = \frac{K}{r} \times [4 \times 40^{-6} \times -4 \times 10^{-6}]$$

$$+[-4 \times 10^{-6} \times 2 \times 10^{-6}] + [2 \times 10^{-6} \times 4 \times 10^{-6}]$$

$$U = \frac{K}{r} \times 10^{-12}[-16 - 8 + 8]$$

$$U = \frac{K}{r} \times 10^{-12}(-16)$$

$$U = \frac{-9 \times 10^9 \times 10^{-12} \times 16}{2}$$

$$U = -72 \times 10^{-3}\ \text{J}$$

$$U = -7.2 \times 10^{-2}\ \text{J}$$

56. As, $\quad E = \frac{dV}{dr}$

$$\Rightarrow \quad 3 \times 10^6 = \frac{\Delta V}{5 \times 10^{-3}}$$

$$\Rightarrow \quad \Delta V = 15000\,\text{V}$$

57. Given, $C = 200\,\mu\text{F}$, $d = 5$ mm, $t = 5$ mm, $V = 100$ V

(i) $C = \frac{\varepsilon_0 A}{d} \Rightarrow A = \frac{Cd}{\varepsilon_0}$

$$A = \frac{200 \times 10^{-6} \times 5 \times 10^{-3}}{8.85 \times 10^{-12}} = 112.99 \times 10^3\ \text{m}^2$$

When $d' = 2d$, then $C' = \frac{\varepsilon_0 A}{2d - t + \frac{t}{K}}$

$$= \frac{8.85 \times 10^{-12} \times 112.99 \times 10^3}{\left(10 - 5 + \frac{5}{10}\right) \times 10^{-3}}$$

$$= 181.8 \times 10^{-6} = 181.8\,\mu\text{F}$$

(ii) Charge on capacitor, $q = C_0V_0$

$$= 200 \times 10^{-6} \times 100 = 2 \times 10^{-2}\ \text{C}$$

$$\Rightarrow \quad C_0V_0 = C'V'$$

or $\quad V' = \frac{C_0V_0}{C'} = \frac{2 \times 10^{-2}}{181.8 \times 10^{-6}} = 110\ \text{V}$

$$E_0 = \frac{V_0}{d} = \frac{100}{5 \times 10^{-3}} = 20 \times 10^3\ \text{V/m}$$

$$E' = \frac{V'}{2d} = \frac{110}{10 \times 10^{-3}} = 11 \times 10^3\ \text{V/m}$$

(iii) $\overline{U} = \frac{1}{2}\varepsilon_0 E_0^2 = \frac{1}{2} \times 8.85 \times 10^{-12} \times (20 \times 10^3)^2$

$$= 1770 \times 10^{-6}\ \text{J/m}^3$$

$$(\overline{U})' = \frac{1}{2} \times \varepsilon_0 (E')^2$$

$$= \frac{1}{2} \times 8.85 \times 10^{-12} \times (11 \times 10^3)^2$$

$$= 535.42 \times 10^{-6}\ \text{J/m}^3$$

58. (i) Charge, $q = CV = 48 \times 10^{-6}\,\text{C}$

After battery is disconnected, from charge conservation. Charge remains same or no change.

(ii) Initial potential difference, $V_0 = 12\text{V}$

After battery is removed, $V = \frac{V_0}{K} = \frac{12}{8} = 1.5$ volt

Decrease in potential difference $= 12 - 1.5 = 10.5\text{V}$

(iii) Energy stored initially.

$$U_0 = \frac{1}{2}C_0V_0^2 = \frac{1}{2} \times 4 \times 10^{-6} \times 12 \times 12$$

$= 288 \times 10^{-6}$ J

Final energy stored,

$$U = \frac{1}{2}CV^2 = \frac{1}{2}C_0\frac{V_0^2}{K}$$

$$= \frac{1}{2}\times\frac{4\times10^{-6}\times12\times12}{8} = 36\times10^{-6}\text{ J}$$

∴ Energy reduces,

$$\Delta U = U_0 - U = (288-36)\times10^{-6}\text{ J} = 252\times10^{-6}\text{ J}$$

59. (i) C_1 and C_2 are in parallel combination, so

$$C' = C_1 + C_2 = 3 + 6 = 9\,\mu\text{F}$$

Now, C', C_3 and C_4 are in series, so net capacitance,

$$\frac{1}{C} = \frac{1}{C'} + \frac{1}{C_3} + \frac{1}{C_4} = \frac{1}{9} + \frac{1}{4} + \frac{1}{12} = \frac{16}{36} \Rightarrow C = \frac{9}{4}\,\mu\text{F}$$

(ii) (a) Given, $Q_1 = 6\,\mu$C

Now, potential across C_1,

$$V = \frac{Q_1}{C_1} = \frac{6}{3} = 2\text{ V}$$

Thus charge on C_2,

$$Q_1 = C_2V = 6\times2 = 12\,\mu\text{C}$$

Total charge on C_1 and C_2,

$$Q = 12 + 6 = 18\,\mu\text{C}$$

As charge is same in series combination,

∴ Charge on C_3 and C_4 is 18 μC each.

(b) Total capacitance, $\frac{1}{C''} = \frac{1}{4} + \frac{1}{12} = \frac{1}{3} \Rightarrow C'' = 3\,\mu\text{F}$

Thus, total energy stored in them is

$$U = \frac{1}{2}\frac{Q^2}{C''} = \frac{1}{2}\frac{(18)^2}{3}\times10^{-6} = 54\times10^{-6}\text{ J}$$

60. As the given network is like a balanced Wheatstone bridge, so no current flows through the middle wire and the network becomes as shown below.

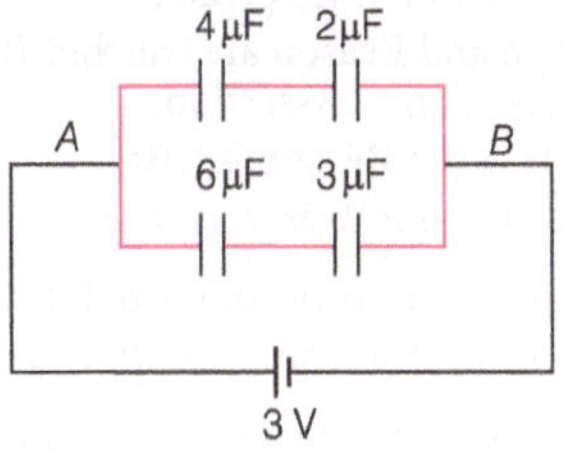

So, equivalent capacitance of upper arm (series combination), $C_1 = \frac{4\times2}{4+2} = \frac{8}{6} = \frac{4}{3}\,\mu$F

and of lower arm, $C_2 = \frac{6\times3}{6+3} = \frac{18}{9} = 2\,\mu$F

The net capacitance of the network,

$$C_{net} = C_1 + C_2 \text{ (for parallel combination)}$$

$$= \frac{4}{3} + 2 = \frac{10}{3}\,\mu\text{F}$$

∴ Total charge, $Q = C_{net}\times V = \frac{10}{3}\times3 = 10\,\mu$F

61. (i) When C_1 and C_3 are in series and C_2 is in parallel as shown, then

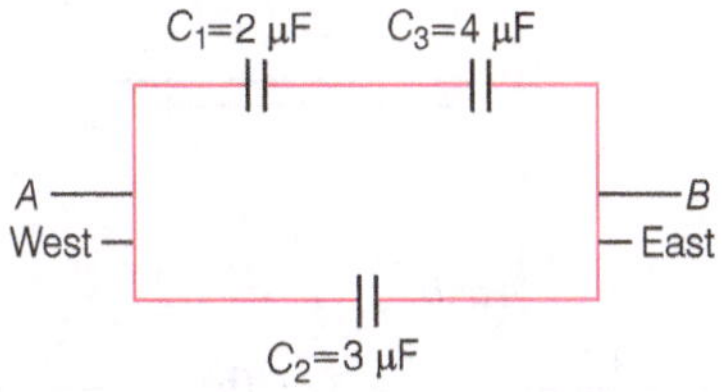

$$C_{eq} = \frac{2\times4}{2+4} + 3 = \frac{4}{3} + 3 = \frac{13}{3}\,\mu\text{F}$$

(ii) Maximum value of the equivalent capacitance is obtained when all capacitors are connected in parallel combination.

i.e. $C_{eq} = C_1 + C_2 + C_3 = 2+3+4 = 9\,\mu$F

or $C_{eq} = C_{max} = 9\,\mu$F

and minimum value is obtained, when all capacitors are connected in series combination,

i.e. $C_{eq} = \frac{C_1\times C_2\times C_3}{C_1C_2 + C_2C_3 + C_3C_1} = \frac{2\times3\times4}{2\times3+3\times4+4\times2}$

or $C_{eq} = C_{min} = \frac{12}{13}\,\mu$F

62. $\frac{1}{C'} = \frac{1}{C_1} + \frac{1}{C_2} + \frac{1}{C_3}$

$$\frac{1}{C'} = \frac{1}{10} + \frac{1}{10} + \frac{1}{10}$$

$$C' = \frac{10}{3}\,\mu\text{F},\ C_{eq} = C' + C_4$$

$$C_{eq} = \frac{10}{3} + 10$$

$$C_{eq} = 13.3\,\mu\text{F}$$

QR Code for Quick Test 1

QR Code for Quick Test 2

SELF ASSESSMENT TEST

Multiple Choice Questions (MCQs)

1. Two point charges of magnitude $+q$ are located along the Y-axis as shown. The potential at a point P on the X-axis at a distance x from the origin is

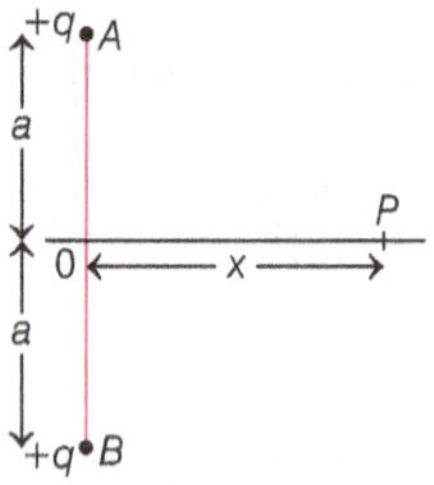

(a) $\frac{q}{4\pi\varepsilon_0\sqrt{x^2+a^2}}$ (b) $\frac{2q}{4\pi\varepsilon_0\sqrt{x^2+a^2}}$

(c) zero (d) $\frac{2qx}{4\pi\varepsilon_0(x^2+a^2)}$

2. Two charges q and $-4q$ are placed a distance apart. At what distance from the charge of smaller magnitude will the electrostatic potential be zero?

(a) $\frac{a}{5}$ (b) a

(c) $\frac{a}{2}$ (d) $\frac{a}{4}$

3. A free electron and a free proton are placed between two oppositely charged parallel plates. Both are closer to the positive plate than the negative plate.

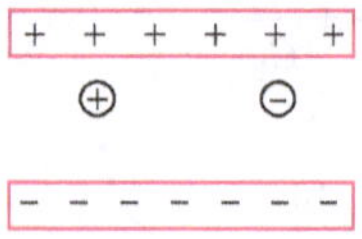

Which of the following statements is true?

I. The force on the proton is greater than the force on the electron.

II. The potential energy of the proton is greater than that of the electron.

III. The potential energy of the proton and the electron is the same.

(a) I only (b) II only

(c) III and I only (d) II and I only

4. Three charges $2q, -q$ and $-q$ lie at the vertices of a triangle. The value of E and V at centroid of triangle will be **CBSE 2022**

(a) $E \neq 0$ and $V \neq 0$ (b) $E = 0$ and $V = 0$

(c) $E \neq 0$ and $V = 0$ (d) $E = 0$ and $V \neq 0$

5. Consider a dipole of length a made of charges q and $-q$. Three points A, B and C placed at equal distance r away from the dipole are shown. Which of the following relations is correct with respect to the potential at these points?

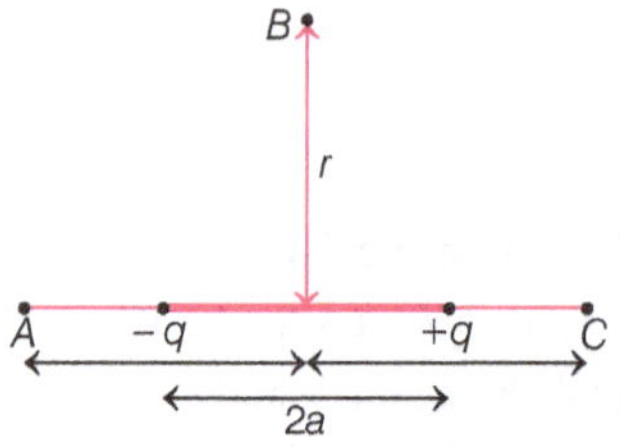

(a) $V_A = V_C, V_B = 0$ (b) $V_A = -V_C, V_B = 0$

(c) $V_A = V_B = V_C$ (d) $V_A = V_B = 0$

Assertion-Reason

Directions (Q. Nos. 6-7) *In the following questions, two statements are given- one labelled Assertion (A) and the other labelled Reason (R). Select the correct answer to these questions from the codes (a), (b), (c) and (d) as given below*

(a) Both Assertion and Reason are true and Reason is the correct explanation of Assertion.

(b) Both Assertion and Reason are true but Reason is not the correct explanation of Assertion.

(c) Assertion is true but Reason is false.

(d) Assertion is false but Reason is true.

6. Assertion (A) There is no potential difference between any two points on the equipotential surface.

Reason (R) No work is required to move a test charge on the equipotential surface from one point to other.

7. Assertion (A) Five charges $+q$ each are placed at five vertices of a regular pentagon. A sixth charge $-Q$ is placed at the centre of pentagon, then net electrostatic force on $-Q$ is zero.

Reason (R) Net electrostatic potential at the centre is zero.

Case Based Question

Directions (Q. No. 8) *This question is case study based question. Read the following paragraph and answer the questions on the basis of same.*

8. Electrostatics deals with the study of forces, fields and potentials arising from static charges. Force and electric field, due to a point charge is basically determined by Coulomb's law. For symmetric charge configurations, Gauss's law, which is also based on Coulomb's law, helps us to find the electric field. A charge a system of charges like a dipole experience a force/torque in an electric field. Work is required to be done to provide a specific orientation to a dipole with respect to an electric field.

(i) Consider a uniformly charged thin conducting shell of radius R. Which of the following graph showing the variation of $|\mathbf{E}|$ with distance r from the centre, for points $0 \le r \le 3r$.

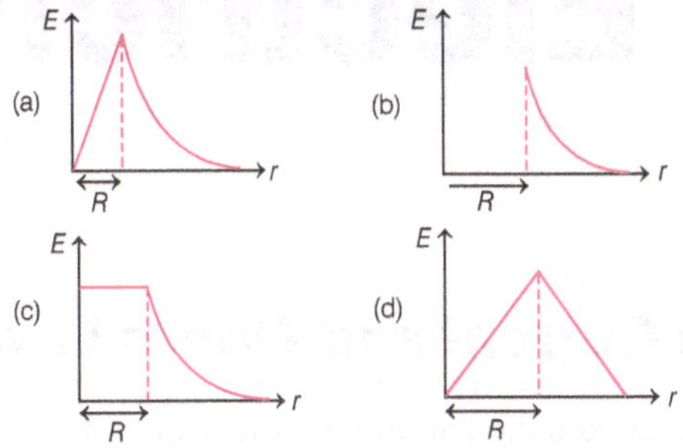

(ii) An electric dipole of dipole moment of 6×10^{-7} C-m is kept in a uniform electric field of 10^4 N/C such that the dipole moment and the electric field are parallel. The potential energy of the dipole will be

(a) 2×10^3 J (b) -2×10^3 J
(c) -6×10^{-3} J (d) 6×10^{-3} J

(iii) A dipole is placed parallel to electric field. If W is the work done in rotating the dipole from 0° to 60°, then work done in rotating it from 0° to 180° is

(a) $2W$ (b) $3W$
(c) $4W$ (d) $\frac{W}{2}$

(iv) The electric potential V at any point x, y, z (all in metres) in space is given by $V = 4x^2$ volt. The electric field at the point (1 m, 0, 2 m) in volt/metre is

(a) 8 along negative X-axis
(b) 8 along positive X-axis
(c) 16 along negative X-axis
(d) 16 along positive Z-axis

Very Short Answer Type Questions

9. A charged particle $(+q)$ moves in a uniform electric field $(\mathbf{E})$ in the direction opposite to $\mathbf{E}$. What will be the effect on its electrostatic potential energy during its motion? **CBSE 2020**

10. Consider two identical point charges located at points (0, 0) and $(a, 0)$.

(i) Is there a point on the line joining them at which the electric field is zero?

(ii) Is there a point on the line joining them at which the electric potential is zero?

Justify your answers for each case. **CBSE 2023**

11. A proton is released at rest in a uniform electric field. Does the proton's electric potential energy increase or decrease? Does the poroton move towards a location with a higher or lower electric potential?

Short Answer Type Questions

12. In the following arrangement of capacitors, the energy stored in the 6 μF capacitor is E. Find the value of the following.

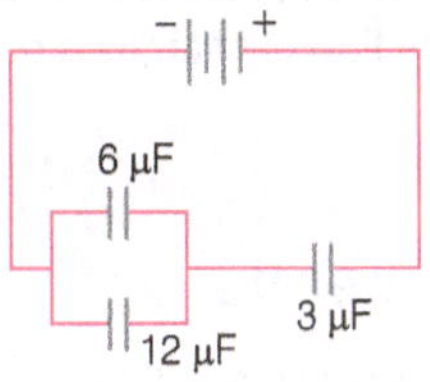

(i) Energy stored in 12μF capacitor. **[3]**

(ii) Energy stored in 3μF capacitor. **[1]**

(iii) Total energy drawn from the battery. **[1]**

Foreign 2016

13. Figure shows two identical capacitors C_1 and C_2 each of 2μF capacitance connected to a battery of 5 V. Initially, switch S is closed. After sometime, S is left open and dielectric slabs of dielectric constant $K = 5$ are inserted to fill completely the space between the plates of the two capacitors. How will the (i) charge and (ii) potential difference between the plates of the capacitors be affected after the slabs are inserted?

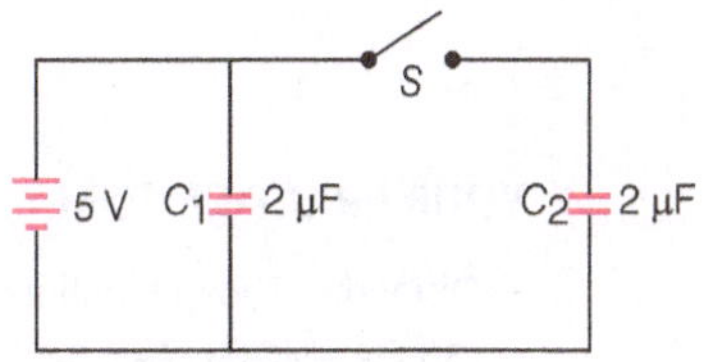

Answers

1. (b) *2.* (a) *3.* (b) *4.* (c) *5.* (b) *6.* (a)
7. (c) *8.* (i) (b) (ii) (c) (iii) (c) (iv) (a)

03

CHAPTER

In electrostatics, we have studied about the charges at rest. Here, we will study about the charges in motion which constitute an electric current. Such electric currents occur naturally in many situations, e.g. in lightning, charges flow from the clouds to the earth through the atmosphere, which sometimes becomes disastrous, as the flow of charges is not steady.

YOUR STUDY GOALS

3.1 Electric Current and Ohm's Law
3.2 Electrical Energy
3.3 Cells, EMF and Internal Resistance
3.4 Kirchhoff's Laws and its Applications

YOUR PRACTICE GOAL

- Objective Type Questions (36 Qs ; MCQs, A-R, Matching)
- Case Based Questions-4
- Subjective Questions (9 VSAs, 14 SAs, 18 LAs)
- Numerical Problems-9

Current Electricity

3.1 Electric Current and Ohm's Law

The flow of charge in metallic conductor constitutes electric current. If we maintain a constant potential difference between the two conductors, we get a constant flow of charge in a metallic wire connecting the two conductors.

The branch of Physics which deals with the charges in motion is called **current electricity**.

Electric Current

It is defined as the rate of flow of electric charge through any cross-section of a conductor. It is denoted by I.

Electric current can be expressed by

$$I = \frac{\text{Total charge flowing } (q)}{\text{Time taken } (t)} = \frac{ne}{t}$$

where, n = number of free electrons

and e = electronic charge

If the rate of flow of charge varies with time, then current at any time (instantaneous current) is given by

$$I = \frac{dq}{dt}$$

Conventionally, the direction of electric current is along the direction of motion of positive charges and opposite to the direction of motion of negative charges.

- It is a **scalar quantity.**
- Its SI unit is **Ampere (A) or Cs^{-1}**

1 Ampere

The current through a wire is said to be 1 ampere, if one coulomb of charge is flowing per second through any cross-section of wire.

$$1 \text{ ampere (A)} = \frac{1 \text{ coulomb (C)}}{1 \text{ second (s)}} = 1 \text{ C/s}$$

Example 1. How many electrons pass through a lamp in 1 min, if the current is 300 mA? Given, the charge on an electron is 1.6×10^{-19} C.

Sol. Given, current, $I = 300 \text{ mA} = 300 \times 10^{-3}$ A

Charge on one electron, $e = 1.6 \times 10^{-19}$ C

Time, $t = 1 \text{ min} = 60 \text{ s}$

Charge passing through a lamp in 1 min, $q = I \times t$

$$= 300 \times 10^{-3} \times 60$$

Let n electrons pass through the lamp in 1 min.

$$\therefore \quad q = ne \Rightarrow n = \frac{q}{e} = \frac{300 \times 10^{-3} \times 60}{1.6 \times 10^{-19}}$$

$$= 1.125 \times 10^{20} \text{ C}$$

Note
- The direction of flow of positive charge gives the direction of current. This is called conventional current.
- The direction of flow of electrons gives the direction of electric current. Therefore, the direction of electronic current is opposite to the conventional current.

Current Density

The current density at a point in a conductor is defined as the amount of current flowing normally through unit area around that point of conductor.

If a current I is distributed uniformly over the cross-section area A of a conductor, then the current density at that point is

$$J = \frac{I}{A}$$

It is a characteristic property of a point inside the conductor. It is a **vector quantity**. Its direction at a point is the direction of flow of positive charge at that point.

The **SI unit of current density is Am^{-2}.**

Example 2. An aluminium wire of diameter 0.24 cm is connected in series to a copper wire of diameter 0.16 cm. The wires carry an electric current of 10 A. Determine the current density in aluminium wire.

Sol. Given, diameter = 0.24 cm,

$$\text{radius, } r = \frac{0.24 \times 10^{-2}}{2} = 0.12 \times 10^{-2} \text{ m}$$

and current, $I = 10$ A

$$\therefore \text{Current density, } J = \frac{I}{A} = \frac{I}{\pi r^2}$$

$$= \frac{10}{3.14 \times (0.12 \times 10^{-2})^2} = 2.2 \times 10^6 \text{ Am}^{-2}$$

Electric Current in Conductors

- The electric current in a conductor can be explained by electron theory. Free electrons or conduction electrons carry the charge in the conductor from one place to the other.
- Therefore, the electrical conductivity of a solid substance depends upon the number of free electrons in it.
- Electrolytic solutions are the type of conductors in which electric current flows due to the movement of both positive and negative charges.
- When no electric field is applied on a solid conductor, the free electrons in the them move like molecules in a gas due to their thermal velocities. There is no preferential direction for the velocities of the electrons. The average thermal random velocity is zero. Due to this, there is no net flow of electric charge in a particular direction inside the conductor and hence no current flows in it.

Ohm's Law

It states that the current I flowing through a conductor is directly proportional to the potential difference V across the ends of the conductor, provided that the physical conditions (temperature, mechanical strain, etc.) are kept constant. Mathematically, $I \propto V$

or $\quad V \propto I$ or $V = IR$

$$\text{or} \quad \frac{V}{I} = R = \text{constant}$$

where, R is resistance of the conductor.

Resistance depends on the length, shape and the nature of the material of the conductor. It is independent of the values of V and I. Such conductors are said to obey Ohm's law.

Linear characteristics : Ohmic and Non-ohmic conductors

(a) **Ohmic conductors** The conductors or circuit elements for which *V-I* graph is linear are called ohmic conductors.

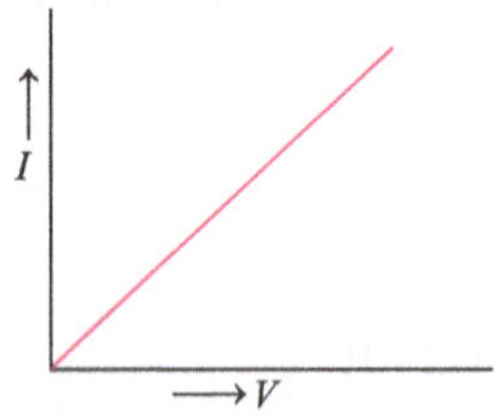

(b) **Non-ohmic conductors** The conductors or circuit elements for which *V-I* graph is non-linear are called non-ohmic conductors.

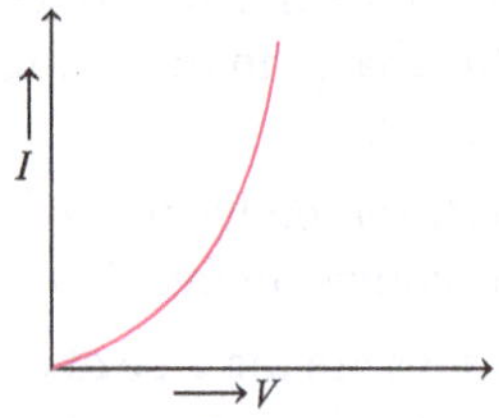

Ohm's law is not applicable to all types of conductor. It is applicable only for those conducting materials for which *V-I* graph is linear.

Example 3. A potential difference of 3 V is applied across a conductor through which 5 A of current is flowing. Determine the resistance of the conductor.

Sol. Given, potential difference, $V = 3$ V

Current, $I = 5$A

According to Ohm's law, $R = \frac{V}{I} \Rightarrow R = \frac{3}{5} = 0.6\Omega$

Resistance of a Conductor

It is defined as the ratio of the potential difference applied across the ends of the conductor to the current flowing through it.

Mathematically, $R = V/I$

The **SI unit of resistance is ohm** and denoted by Ω.

$$1 \text{ ohm } (\Omega) = \frac{1 \text{ volt (V)}}{1 \text{ ampere (A)}} = 1 \text{ volt/ampere (or V/A)}$$

Dimensional formula of electrical resistance is $[ML^2T^{-3}A^{-2}]$.

The resistance of a conductor is said to be one ohm, if one ampere of current flows, when a potential difference of one volt is applied across the ends of the conductor.

The resistance of the conductor depends on the following factors :

(i) It is directly proportional to the length of the conductor,

i.e. $R \propto l$ ...(i)

(ii) It is inversely proportional to the area of the cross-section of the conductor,

i.e. $R \propto \frac{1}{A}$ ...(ii)

From Eqs. (i) and (ii), we get

$$R \propto \frac{l}{A} \quad \text{or} \quad \boxed{R = \rho\frac{l}{A}}$$

where, ρ is the constant of proportionality known as resistivity or specific resistance of the conductor.

(iii) It depends on the nature of the material and temperature of the conductor.

Example 4. A negligible small current is passed through a wire of length 15 m and uniform cross-section 6×10^{-7} m^2 and its resistance is measured to be 5 Ω. What is the resistivity of the material at the temperature of the experiment? NCERT

Sol. Given, $R = 5\Omega$, $A = 6 \times 10^{-7} m^2$ and $l = 15$ m

Let the resistivity of the material be ρ.

$\therefore$ Resistance of wire, $R = \rho\frac{l}{A}$

$$\Rightarrow \rho = \frac{RA}{l} = \frac{5 \times 6 \times 10^{-7}}{15}$$

$$= 2 \times 10^{-7} \Omega\text{-m}$$

Thus, the resistivity of the material at the temperature of the experiment is $2 \times 10^{-7} \Omega$-m.

Effect of Temperature on Resistance

Resistance of a metallic conductor at temperature t °C is given as

$$\boxed{R_t = R_0 (1 + \alpha t + \beta t^2)} \quad ...(i)$$

where, R_0 = resistance of conductor at 0°C and α, β are the temperature coefficients of resistance.

If the temperature t °C is not sufficiently large which is so in most of the practical cases, then Eq. (i) can be written as

$$R_t = R_0(1+\alpha t) \text{ or } \alpha = \frac{R_t - R_0}{R_0 \times t}$$

$$\alpha = \frac{\text{Change in resistance}}{\text{Original resistance} \times \text{Rise of temperature}}$$

Therefore, **temperature coefficient of resistance is defined as the increase in resistance per unit original resistance per degree celsius or kelvin rise of temperature.**

- **For metals like silver, copper, etc.,** the value of α is positive, therefore **resistance of the metal increases with the rise in temperature.**
- **For insulators and semiconductors,** the value of α is negative, therefore **resistance decreases with the rise in temperature.**
- **For alloys like manganin, constantan, etc.,** the value of α is very small as compared to metals. The value of α is different at different temperatures.

Temperature coefficient of resistance averaged over the temperature range t_1°C to t_2°C is given by

$$\alpha = \frac{R_2 - R_1}{R_1(t_2 - t_1)}$$

where, R_1 and R_2 are the resistances at t_1°C and t_2°C, respectively.
Due to high resistivity and low temperature coefficient, alloys are used to make standard resistance coils.

Example 5. **A silver wire has a resistance of 2.1 Ω at 27.5 °C and a resistance of 2.7 Ω at 100 °C. Determine the temperature coefficient of resistivity of silver.** NCERT

Sol. Given, $t_1 = 27.5$ °C, $t_2 = 100$ °C

$$R_1 = R_{27.5} = 2.1\,\Omega \text{ and } R_2 = R_{100} = 2.7\,\Omega$$

∴ Temperature coefficient of silver is given by

$$\alpha = \frac{R_2 - R_1}{R_1(t_2 - t_1)} = \frac{2.7 - 2.1}{2.1\,(100 - 27.5)} = 0.0039\ ^\circ\text{C}^{-1}$$

Limitations of Ohm's Law

The limitations of Ohm's law are given below.

(i) Potential difference may vary non-linearly with current.

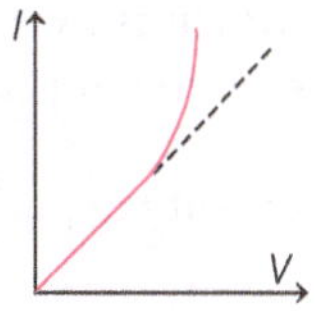

Variation of potential difference with current

(ii) The variation of current with potential difference may depend on the sign of potential difference applied.

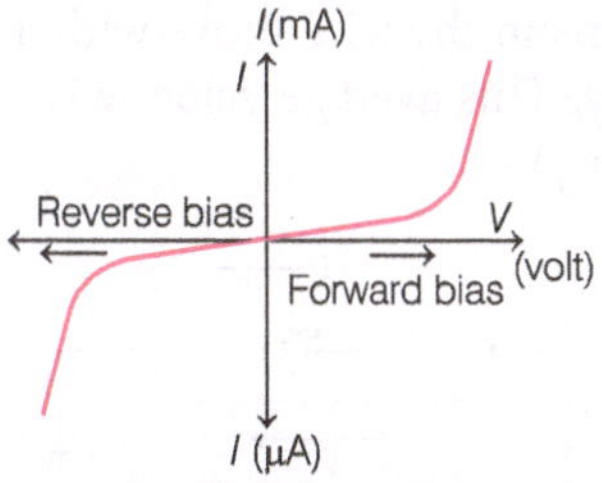

Variation of current according to the sign of potential difference

(iii) The relation between potential difference and current is not unique, i.e. there is more than one value of V for the same current I.

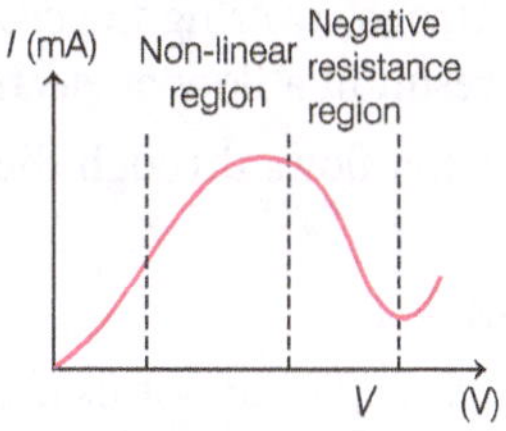

Graph of current *versus* potential difference for GaAs

Drift Velocity

It is defined as "the average velocity with which the free electrons in a conductor get drifted towards the positive end of the conductor under the influence of an electric field applied across the conductor".

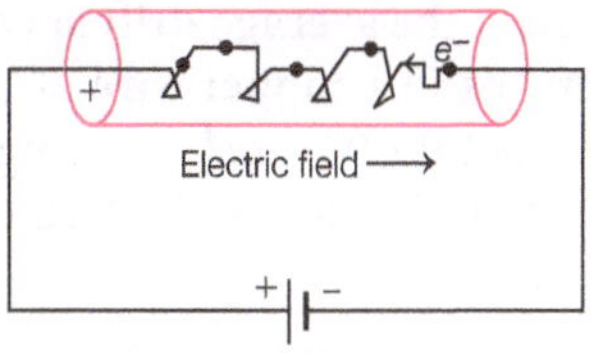

Let E be the strength of applied electric field, then the force on electron due to applied field is

$$F = -eE$$

If m is the mass of electron, then the acceleration produced is given by

$$a = -\frac{eE}{m} \qquad \left[\because a = \frac{F}{m}\right]$$

If τ is relaxation time, which is average time that an electron spends between two collisions, then

$$\text{Average drift velocity, } v_d = \frac{eE}{m}\tau$$

Relation between Drift Velocity and Current

Consider a conducting wire of length l and uniform cross-section area A, placed in an electric field E. Then, the free electrons in the wire move with a certain average velocity. This average velocity is called as the **drift velocity** (v_d).

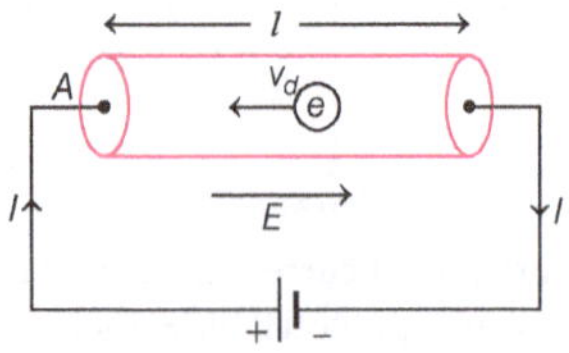

Let the number of free electrons per unit volume in the wire be n. Each electron carries a charge e.

In a time t, the electrons covering the cross-sectional area A of the wire will result in a flow of electric charge.

The total charge Q that flows through the wire in time t is

$$Q = nAev_d t$$

The current I, which is the rate of flow of charge is

$$I = \frac{Q}{t} = nAev_d$$

Thus, the current I in the wire is directly proportional to the drift velocity v_d.

or $$I = \frac{Ane^2\tau E}{m} \qquad \left[\text{Putting } v_d = \frac{eE\tau}{m}\right]$$

Example 6. **Estimate the average drift speed of conduction electrons in a copper wire of cross-sectional area 1.0×10^{-7} m^2 carrying a current of 1.5 A. Assume the density of conduction electrons to be 9×10^{28} m^{-3}.**

Sol. Given, cross-sectional area, $A = 1.0 \times 10^{-7}$ m^2

Current, $I = 1.5$ A

Electron density, $n = 9 \times 10^{28}$ m^{-3}

Drift velocity, $v_d = ?$

We know that, $I = neAv_d$

$$\Rightarrow \quad v_d = \frac{I}{neA} = \frac{1.5}{9 \times 10^{28} \times 1.6 \times 10^{-19} \times 1.0 \times 10^{-7}}$$

$$= 1.042 \times 10^{-3} \text{ m/s}$$

Example 7. **Calculate the drift velocity of electrons in a copper wire having cross-sectional area 3.14×10^{-6} m^2 and carrying a current of 16A.**

Avogadro's number $= 6.023 \times 10^{23}$

Atomic weight of copper = 64 u,

Density of copper $= 8.96 \times 10^3$ kgm^{-3},

$e = 1.6 \times 10^{-19}$ C

Sol. Given, $A = 3.14 \times 10^{-6}$ m^2, $I = 16$ A

$\therefore$ Number of moles of Cu $= \dfrac{m}{M}$

$\therefore$ Number of Cu atoms $= \dfrac{m}{M} \times N_A$

$\therefore$ Number of electrons in Cu atoms $= \dfrac{m}{M} \times N_A \times 2$

($\because$ 1 Cu atom gives 2 electrons)

$\therefore$ Number of electrons per unit volume,

$$n = \frac{m}{M} \times N_A \times 2 \times \frac{1}{V} = \frac{N_A \times 2 \times \rho}{M}$$

$$= \frac{6.023 \times 10^{23} \times 2 \times 8.96 \times 10^3}{64}$$

$\therefore$ Drift velocity, $v_d = \dfrac{I}{neA}$

$$= \frac{16 \times 64}{1.6 \times 10^{-19} \times 3.14 \times 10^{-6} \times 6.023 \times 10^{23} \times 2 \times 8.96 \times 10^3}$$

$$= 1.88 \times 10^{-3} \text{ m/s}$$

Mobility

It is defined as the magnitude of drift velocity of charge per unit electric field applied. It is expressed as

$$\mu = \frac{\text{Drift velocity } (v_d)}{\text{Electric field } (E)} = \frac{qE\tau / m}{E} = \frac{q\tau}{m}$$

Mobility of electrons, $\mu_e = \dfrac{e\tau_e}{m_e}$

and **mobility of holes,** $\mu_h = \dfrac{e\tau_h}{m_h}$

where, τ_e and τ_h are average relaxation time for electrons and holes, respectively. m_e and m_h refer to mass of electrons and holes, respectively (either electron or hole).

The **SI unit of mobility is m^{2}s^{-1}V^{-1} or m s^{-1}N^{-1}C** and it is in the order of 10^4 in practical units (cm^{2}s^{-1}V^{-1}).

Therefore, **mobility is positive for both positive current carriers and negative current carriers.**

Example 8. **Find the current flow through a copper wire of length 0.2 m, area of cross-section 1 mm^2, when it's connected to a battery of 4 V. Given that, electron mobility is $4.5\times10^{-6}\ m^2s^{-1}V^{-1}$ and charge on an electron is 1.6×10^{-19} C. The number density of electrons in copper wire is $8.5\times10^{28}\ m^{-3}$.**

Sol. Given, length of copper wire, $l = 0.2$ m

Cross-sectional area, $A = 1\ mm^2 = 10^{-6}\ m^2$

Potential difference, $V = 4$ V

Electron mobility, $\mu = 4.5\times10^{-6}\ m^2s^{-1}V^{-1}$

Charge of an electron, $e = 1.6\times10^{-19}$ C

Number density of electrons, $n = 8.5\times10^{28}\ m^{-3}$

We know that electric field set up across the conductor,

$$E = \frac{V}{l} = \frac{4}{0.2} = 20\ V/m$$

$\therefore$ Current through the wire, $I = nAev_d = nAe\mu E$ $[\because \mu = v_d/E]$

$$= 8.5\times10^{28}\times10^{-6}\times1.6\times10^{-19}\times4.5\times10^{-6}\times20 = 1.22\ A$$

Resistivity of Various Materials

Specific resistance or resistivity of the material of a conductor is defined as the resistance of a unit length with unit area of cross-section of the material of the conductor, i.e. it is also defined as the resistance of unit cube of a material of the given conductor.

The **SI unit of resistivity is ohm-metre** or Ω-m and its dimensional formula is $[ML^3T^{-3}A^{-2}]$.

- Materials are classified as conductors, semiconductors and insulators depending on their resistivities.
- Metals have low resistivities in the range of $10^{-8}\ \Omega$-m to $10^{-6}\ \Omega$-m.
- Resistivity of insulators; like ceramic, rubber and plastic have 10^8 times greater than metals or more.
- The resistivities of semiconductors lie between the resistivities of metals and insulators.

Temperature Dependence of Resistivity

Resistivity of a metal conductor is given by

$$\rho = \rho_0[1+\alpha(T-T_0)] \text{ where,}$$

ρ = resistivity at temperature T

and ρ_0 = resistivity at temperature T_0

$$\Rightarrow \quad \alpha = \frac{\rho-\rho_0}{\rho_0(T-T_0)} = \frac{d\rho}{\rho_0}\cdot\frac{1}{dT}$$

Thus, temperature coefficient of electrical resistivity is also defined as the fractional change in electrical resistivity $\frac{d\rho}{\rho_0}$ per unit change in temperature dT.

- **For metals**, the value of α is **positive**, therefore resistivity of metal increases with increase in temperature.

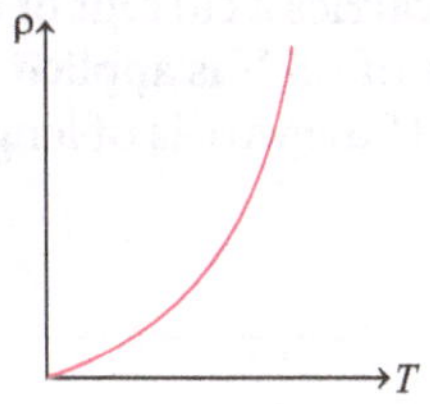

Resistivity as a function of temperature for metals

- **For semiconductors**, the resistivity decreases with increase in temperature.

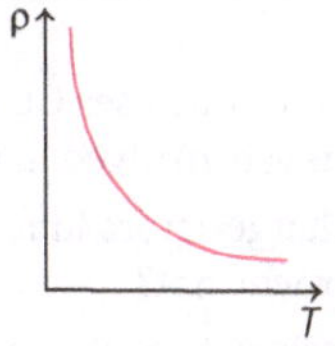

Resistivity as a function of temperature for semiconductors

- **For alloys**, the resistivity is very large, but has weak dependence on temperature.

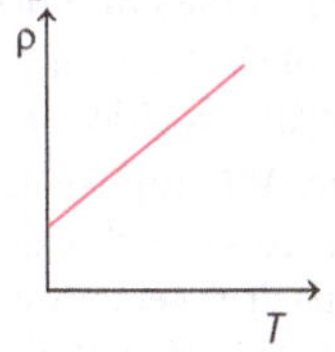

Resistivity as a function of temperature for alloys

Conductance and Conductivity

Conductance

It is defined as the reciprocal of resistance of a conductor. It is expressed as $G = \frac{1}{R}$

Its SI **unit is mho** (Ω^{-1}) or **siemen** (S).

The dimensional formula of conductance is $[M^{-1}L^{-2}T^3A^2]$.

Conductivity

It is defined as the reciprocal of resistivity of a conductor. It is expressed as $\sigma = \frac{1}{\rho}$

Its **SI unit is mho per metre** ($\Omega^{-1}\,m^{-1}$) or siemen per metre (S/m).

The dimensional formula of conductivity is $[M^{-1}L^{-3}T^3A^2]$.

Note Relation between J, σ and E is $J = \sigma E$

Example 9. **A wire carries a current of 0.5 A when a potential difference of 1.5 V is applied across it. What is its conductance? If the wire is of length 3 m and area of cross-section is 5.4 mm^2, then calculate its conductivity.**

Sol. Here, $I = 0.5$ A, $V = 1.5$ V, $l = 3$ m,

$$A = 5.4\,\text{mm}^2 = 5.4 \times 10^{-6}\,\text{m}^2$$

$\therefore$ New resistance, $R = \dfrac{V}{I} = \dfrac{1.5}{0.5} = 3\Omega$

$\therefore$ Conductance, $G = \dfrac{1}{R} = \dfrac{1}{3} = 0.33$ S

and electrical conductivity,

$$\sigma = \frac{1}{\rho} = \frac{l}{RA} = \frac{3}{3 \times 5.4 \times 10^{-6}} = 1.85 \times 10^5\,\text{Sm}^{-1}$$

Quick Test 1

Conceptual Questions

1. Why are alloys used for making standard resistance coils? NCERT Exemplar
2. For wiring in the home, one uses Cu wires or Al wires. What considerations are involved in this? NCERT Exemplar
3. Is the motion of a charge across junction momentum conserving? Why or why not? NCERT Exemplar
4. Describe how the resistivity of the conductor depends on
   (i) number density (n) of free electrons and
   (ii) relaxation time (τ).
5. Two conducting wires A and B of the same length but of different materials are joined in series across a battery. If the number density of electrons in A is twice than that in B, find the ratio of drift velocities of electrons in two wires.
6. A potential difference V is applied across a conductor of length l and uniform cross-section area A. How will the (i) electric field E, (ii) drift velocity v_d and (iii) current density J be affected when V is doubled and l is halved (keeping other factors constant)? CBSE 2023

Numerical Questions

7. Find the temperature at which the resistance of a conductor increases by 25% of its value at 27°C. The temperature coefficient of resistance of the conductor is $2.0 \times 10^{-4}\,°C^{-1}$. CBSE 2024
8. Two conductors are made of the same material and have the same length. Conductor A is a solid wire of diameter 1 mm. Conductor B is a hollow tube of outer diameter 2 mm and inner diameter 1 mm. Find the ratio of resistance R_A to R_B. NCERT Exemplar
9. The circuit in given figure shows two cells connected in opposition to each other. Cell E_1 is of emf 6 V and internal resistance 2 Ω, the cell E_2 is of emf 4 V and internal resistance 8 Ω. Find the potential difference between the points A and B.

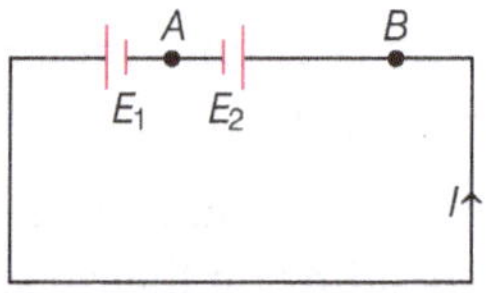

10. A wire is stretched to increase its length by 5%. Calculate percentage change in its resistance.

Answers

7. 1550 K *8.* 3 : 1 *9.* 3.6 V *10.* 10.25%

For Solutions, See QR Code on Pg. 127

3.2 Electrical Energy

Joule's Law of Heating

When an electric current is passed through a conductor, it becomes hot after some time. This effect is called heating effect of current or **Joule's law of heating.**

Mathematically, amount of heat produced is proportional to the square of amount of current flowing through conductor, electrical resistance of wire and the time of current flow through it, i.e.

$$H \propto I^2Rt$$

Derivation of Joule's heating law

The work done in an electric circuit is given by

$$W = Q \times V$$

where, $Q = It$

$V = IR$ (From Ohm's law)

Substituting these values in the equation, we get

$$W = I \times t \times I \times R$$

Simplifying, we get $\boxed{W = I^2Rt}$

This work done is converted into heat energy, so the equation becomes

$$\boxed{H = I^2Rt \text{ (in joule)} = \frac{I^2Rt}{4.2} \text{ cal}}$$

Electrical Energy and Power

Electrical energy

- It is the total work done by the source of emf in maintaining the electric current in the given circuit for a specified time.
- It is given by $\boxed{E = W = VIt = V^2t/R}$
- Its **SI unit** is **joule (J)** or **watt-second.**
- To express electrical energy consumed commercially, a special unit kilowatt-hour is used in place of joule.
- It is also called 1 unit of electrical energy.

$$1 \text{ kilowatt hour (kWh)} = 3.6 \times 10^6 \text{ joule}$$

Example 10. **A resistance coil is made by joining two resistances each of 10 Ω in parallel. An emf of 1 V is applied between the two ends of coil for 5 min. Calculate the heat produced in calories.**

Sol. Given, resistance, $R_1 = 10\Omega$, $R_2 = 10\Omega$

Voltage, $V = 1\text{V}$

and time, $t = 5 \text{ min} = 5 \times 60 = 300 \text{ s}$

Since, effective resistance in parallel combination will be

$$R_p = \frac{R_1R_2}{R_1 + R_2} = \frac{10 \times 10}{10 + 10} = 5\Omega$$

$$\therefore \text{Heat produced} = \frac{V^2t}{R_p} = \frac{1^2}{5} \times 300 = \frac{60}{4.2} \text{ cal} = 14.3 \text{ cal}$$

Electrical Power

It is defined as the rate of electrical energy supplied per unit time to maintain the flow of electric current through a conductor.

Mathematically, $\boxed{P = \frac{W}{t} = VI = I^2R = \frac{V^2}{R}}$ $[\because W = VIt]$

The **SI unit of power is watt (W).**

1 watt = 1 volt × 1 ampere = 1 ampere-volt

Power of an electric circuit is said to be one watt, if one ampere current flows in it against a potential difference of one volt. The bigger units of electrical power are **kilowatt** (kW) and **megawatt** (MW).

where, 1 kW = 1000 W and 1 MW = 10^6 W

Commercial unit of electrical power is **horse power (HP),**

where, $\boxed{1 \text{ HP} = 746 \text{ W}}$

Example 11. **Two bulbs are marked 220 V-100 W and 220 V-50 W, respectively. They are connected in series to 220 V mains. Determine the ratio of heat generated in them.**

Sol. $P_1 = 100$ W, $P_2 = 50$ W, $V = 220$ V

$\because$ $R_1 = V^2/P_1 = (220)^2/100 = 484\Omega$,

$R_2 = V^2/P_2 = (220)^2/50 = 968\Omega$

When bulbs are connected in series to mains, there will be current I in each bulb.

$\Rightarrow$ $H_1 = I^2R_1t = I^2 \times 484t$,

$H_2 = I^2R_2t = I^2 \times 968t$

$\therefore$ $H_1/H_2 = 484/968 = 1/2 \Rightarrow H_1 : H_2 = 1:2$

Example 12. **A 60 W bulb and a 100 W bulb are designed to operate on 220 V. They are connected in series across a 220 V supply. Calculate :**

(a) The total power consumed by the combination.

(b) The voltage drop across each bulb.

Sol. **Calculating resistance of each bulb**

For the 60 W bulb;

$$R_1 = \frac{V^2}{P} = \frac{220^2}{60} = \frac{48400}{60} \approx 806.67\Omega$$

For the 100 W bulb;

$$R_2 = \frac{V^2}{P} = \frac{220^2}{100} = \frac{48400}{100} = 484\Omega$$

Total resistance in series,

$$R_{\text{total}} = R_1 + R_2 = 806.67 + 484 = 1290.67\Omega$$

Total power consumed (using the total voltage and resistance)

$$P_{\text{total}} = \frac{V^2}{R_{\text{total}}} = \frac{220^2}{1290.67} = \frac{48400}{1290.67} \approx 37.5\text{W}$$

Voltage drop across each bulb

For the 60 W bulb,

$$V_1 = I \times R_1, \text{ where } I = \frac{V}{R_{\text{total}}} = \frac{220}{1290.67} \approx 0.17 \text{ A}$$

$$V_1 = 0.17 \times 806.67 \approx 137.1 \text{ V}$$

For the 100 W bulb,

$$V_2 = I \times R_2 = 0.17 \times 484 \approx 82.3 \text{V}$$

Quick Test 2

Conceptual Questions

1. Nichrome and copper wires of same length and same radius are connected in series. Current I is passed through them. Which wire gets heated up more? Justify your answer.

2. The potential difference applied across a given resistor is altered, so that the heat produced per second increases by a factor of 9. By what factor does the applied potential difference change?

3. Power P is to be delivered to a device *via* transmission cables having resistance R_c. If V is the voltage across R and I is the current through it, find the power wasted and how can it be reduced. *NCERT Exemplar*

4. When is more power delivered to a light bulb, just after it is turned ON and the glow of the filament is increasing or after it has been ON for a few seconds and the glow is steady?

5. Two identical slabs of a given metal are joined together in two different ways as shown in figures (a) and (b).

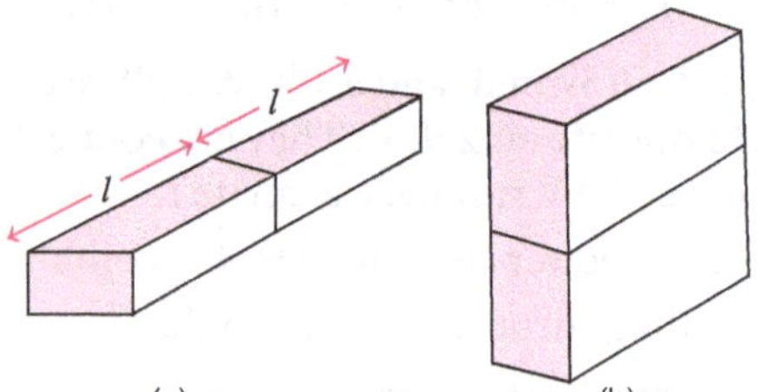

(a) (b)

What is the ratio of the resistances of these two combinations?

Numerical Questions

6. A heater is made from a wire of resistance 18.0 Ω and is connected to a power supply of 240 V. The heater is switched ON for 2.60 ms. Calculate
(i) the power transferred in the heater and
(ii) the current in the heater and
(iii) the number of electrons per second passing a given point in the heater.

7. Two bars of radius r and $2r$ are kept in contact as shown in the figure. An electric current I is passed through the bars.

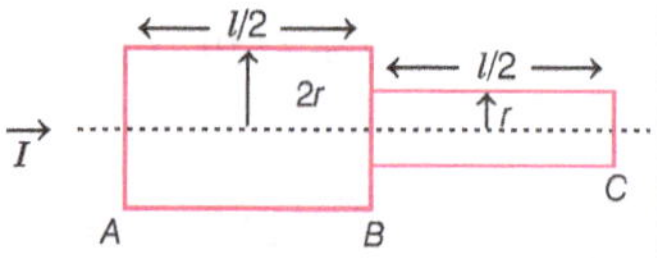

Find the ratio of heat produced in bars AB and BC.

8. Two electric bulbs P and Q have their resistances in the ratio of 1 : 2. They are connected in series across a battery. Find the ratio of the power dissipation in these bulbs.

9. Calculate the current in given figure of the circuit shown below. What is the terminal potential of each cell?

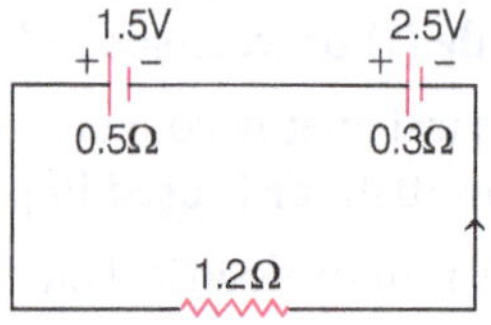

Answers

6. (i) 3200 W (ii) 13.3 A (iii) 2.16×10^{17}

7. 1 : 4 **8.** 1 : 2 **9.** 1.9 V

For Solutions, See QR Code on Pg. 127

3.3 Cells, EMF and Internal Resistance

Cells

It is a device which converts chemical energy into electrical energy.

Electromotive Force (EMF) of a Cell (E)

Emf of a cell is the maximum potential difference between two electrodes of the cell when no current is drawn from the cell.

It is denoted by E.

If during the flow of q coulomb of charge in an electric circuit, the work done by the cell is W, then

emf of the cell, $$E = \frac{W}{q}$$

Its unit is joule/coulomb or volt.

Internal Resistance (r)

Internal resistance of a cell is defined as the resistance offered by the electrolyte and electrodes of the cell to the flow of current through it.

- It is denoted by r.
- Its unit is ohm.

Internal resistance of a cell depends on the following factors

(i) It is directly proportional to the separation between the two plates of the cell.

(ii) It is inversely proportional to the area of plate dipped into the electrolyte.

(iii) It depends on the nature, concentration and temperature of the electrolyte and increases with increase in concentration.

Terminal Potential Difference (V)

Terminal potential difference of a cell is defined as the potential difference between the two terminals of the cell in a closed circuit (i.e. when current is drawn from the cell). It is represented by V and its unit is volt.

Thus, in a closed circuit, there is some fall in emf of the cell due to current flow through its internal resistance.

Note The terminal potential difference of a cell is always less than the emf of the cell.

Relation between Terminal Potential Difference, emf of a Cell and Internal Resistance of a Cell

(i) If no current is drawn from the cell, i.e. the cell is in open circuit, then emf of the cell will be equal to the terminal potential difference of the cell.

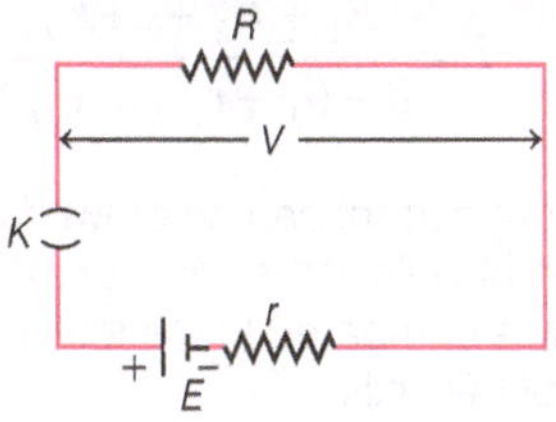

$$I = 0 \quad \text{or} \quad V = E$$

(ii) Consider a cell of emf E and internal resistance r is connected across an external resistance R.

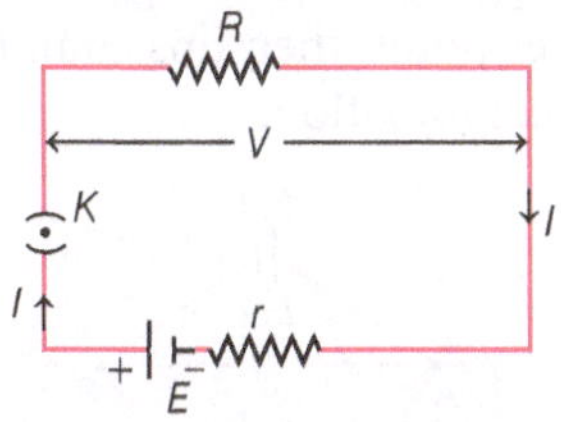

Current drawn from the cell, $I = \dfrac{E}{R+r}$ ...(i)

where, E = emf of the cell,

R = external resistance

and r = internal resistance of the cell.

Now, from Ohm's law, $V = IR$

$\Rightarrow \quad I = \dfrac{V}{R}$ ...(ii)

From Eqs. (i) and (ii), we get

$$\frac{V}{R} = \frac{E}{R+r}$$

$$\Rightarrow \quad \boxed{r = \left(\frac{E}{V} - 1\right)R}$$

From definition of terminal potential difference,

$$\boxed{V = E - Ir}$$

Note At the time of charging of a cell, the terminal potential difference across the cell is

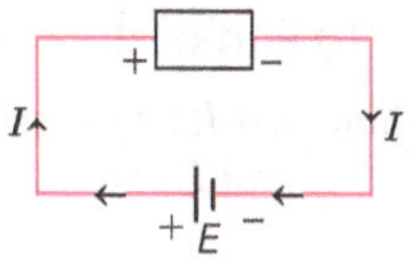

$$V = E + Ir$$

Difference between EMF and Terminal Potential Difference of a Cell

EMF	Terminal potential difference
The emf of a cell is the maximum potential difference between the two electrodes (terminals) of a cell, when the cell is in the open circuit.	The terminal potential difference of a cell is the potential difference between the two terminals of the cell in a closed circuit.
It is independent of the resistance of the circuit and depends upon the nature of electrodes and electrolyte of the cell.	It depends upon the resistance of the circuit and current flowing through it.
The term emf is used for the source of electric current.	The potential difference is measured between any two points of the electric circuit.

Example 13. **The reading on a high resistance voltmeter, when a cell is connected across it, is 2.2 V. When the terminals of the cell are connected to a resistance of 5 Ω as shown in figure, the voltmeter reading drops to 1.8 V. Find the internal resistance of the cell.**

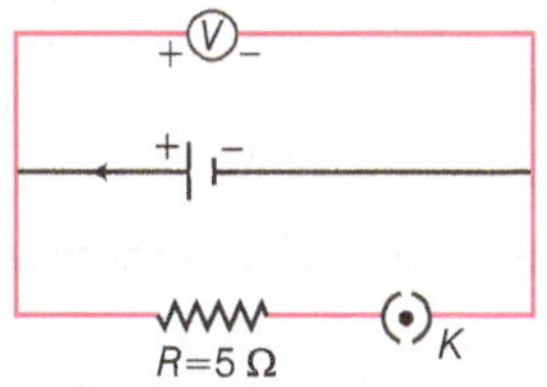

Sol. Given, emf, $E = 2.2$ V

Terminal potential difference,

$V = 1.8$ V

External resistance,

$R = 5\Omega$

∴ Internal resistance,

$$r = \left(\frac{E-V}{V}\right)R = \left(\frac{2.2-1.8}{1.8}\right) \times 5 = \frac{10}{9}\,\Omega$$

Example 14. **A cell of emf E and internal resistance r gives a current of 0.5 A with an external resistance of 12 Ω and a current of 0.25 A with an external resistance of 25 Ω. Calculate the**

(i) internal resistance of the cell and

(ii) emf of the cell.

Sol. Let R be the external resistance in series with the cell of emf E and internal resistance r. The current in circuit is

$$I = \frac{E}{R+r}$$

***Case* I** $I = 0.5\,\text{A}, R = 12\,\Omega$, then

$$0.5 = \frac{E}{12+r} \Rightarrow E = 0.5\,(12+r)$$

$$\Rightarrow \quad E = 6.0 + 0.5r \quad \text{...(i)}$$

***Case* II** $I = 0.25\,\text{A}, R = 25\Omega$, then

$$0.25 = \frac{E}{25+r} \Rightarrow E = 0.25\,(25+r)$$

$$\Rightarrow \quad E = 6.25 + 0.25r \quad \text{...(ii)}$$

From Eqs. (i) and (ii), we get

$$6.0 + 0.5\,r = 6.25 + 0.25\,r \Rightarrow r = 1\Omega$$

From Eq. (i), we get

$$E = 6.0 + 0.5 \times (1) = 6.5\,\text{V}$$

Hence, (i) internal resistance of the cell is 1 Ω and (ii) emf of the cell is 6.5 V.

Cells in Series

When the negative terminal of one cell is connected to the positive terminal of the other cell, then this combination of cells is called series combination.

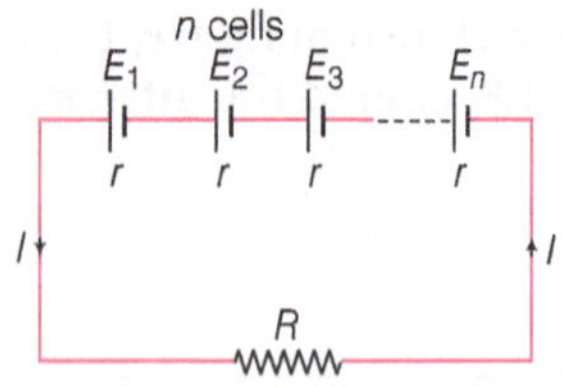

Points to remember for series combination of cells

(i) The equivalent emf of a series combination of n cells is equal to the sum of their individual emfs.

(ii) The equivalent internal resistance of a series combination of n cells is equal to sum of their individual internal resistances.

Equivalent emf of n cells in series,

$$E_{eq} = E_1 + E_2 + \ldots + \text{upto } n \text{ terms} = nE$$

Equivalent internal resistance of n cells in series,

$$r_{eq} = r_1 + r_2 + \ldots + \text{upto } n \text{ terms} = nr$$

Total resistance of the circuit $= nr + R$

∴ Current in the resistance R is given by

$$\boxed{I = \frac{nE}{R+nr}}$$

where, n = number of cells,
r = internal resistance,
R = external resistance,
E = emf of cell
and I = current flowing.

***Case* I** When $R << nr$, then

$$I = \frac{E}{r} = \text{current due to a single cell}$$

***Case* II** When $R >> nr$, then

$$I = \frac{nE}{R} = n \text{ times the current due to a single cell}$$
$$= \text{maximum current}$$

***Case* III** When cells are of different emfs and different internal resistances, then

$$I = \frac{E_1 + E_2 + \ldots + E_n}{R + (r_1 + r_2 + \ldots + r_n)}$$

Note The maximum current can be drawn from the series combination of cells, if the value of external resistance is very high as compared to the total internal resistance of the cells.

Cells in Parallel

When the positive terminals of all the cells are connected to one point and the negative terminals are connected to other point, then this combination of cells is called parallel combination.

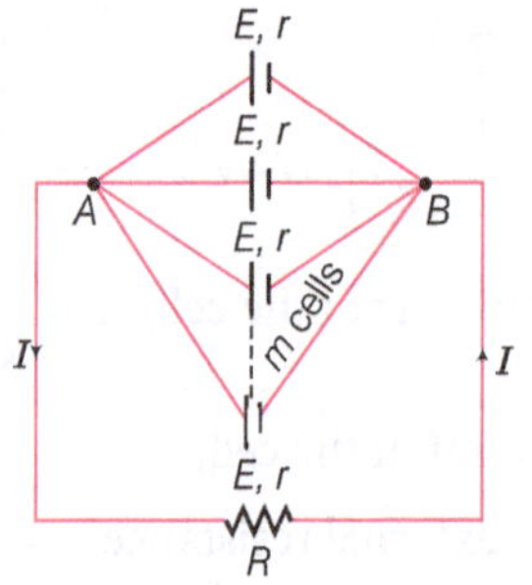

Points to remember for parallel combination of cells

(i) The equivalent emf of parallel combination of cells of same emfs is equal to emf of one cell.

(ii) The reciprocal of equivalent internal resistance of parallel combination of cells is equal to the sum of the reciprocals of the internal resistance of each cell.

$$\therefore \quad \frac{1}{r_p} = \frac{1}{r_1} + \frac{1}{r_2} + \dots \text{ upto } m \text{ terms} = \frac{m}{r}$$

or $\quad r_p = \dfrac{r}{m}$

As, R and r_p are in series, so total resistance in the circuit $= R + \dfrac{r}{m}$

$\therefore$ Current in the resistance R is given by

$$I = \frac{E}{R + \frac{r}{m}}$$

***Case* I** When $R >> \dfrac{r}{m}$, then

$I = \dfrac{E}{R}$ = current due to a single cell

***Case* II** When $R << \dfrac{r}{m}$, then $I = \dfrac{E}{r/m}$

$= \dfrac{mE}{r} = m$ times current due to a single cell

= maximum current

***Case* III** When cells are of same emf and different internal resistances, then

$I = \dfrac{E}{R + r'} \quad [\because E_1 = E_2 = \dots E_n = E]$

where, $\dfrac{1}{r'} = \dfrac{1}{r_1} + \dfrac{1}{r_2} + \dfrac{1}{r_3} + \dots + \dfrac{1}{r_n}$ and E is emf of each cell.

TEACHER TIP

The maximum current can be drawn from the parallel combination of cells, if the external resistance is very low as compared to the total internal resistance of the cells.

Example 15. Two identical cells, when joined together in series or in parallel give the same current when connected to external resistance of 2 Ω. Find the internal resistance of each cell.

Sol. Let E, r be the emf and internal resistance of each cell respectively.

External resistance, $R = 2\Omega$

If both cells are connected in series, then

Total emf of cells $= E + E = 2E$

Total resistance of circuit $= R + r + r = 2 + 2r$

Current in the circuit, $I_1 = \dfrac{2E}{2 + 2r}$

If both cells are connected in parallel, effective emf of two cells = emf of single cell $= E$

Total internal resistance of two cells $= \dfrac{r \times r}{r + r} = \dfrac{r}{2}$

Total resistance of the circuit $= R + \dfrac{r}{2} = 2 + \dfrac{r}{2}$

Current in the circuit,

$$I_2 = \frac{E}{2 + \frac{r}{2}} = \frac{2E}{4 + r}$$

As per question, $I_1 = I_2$

$$\Rightarrow \quad \frac{2E}{2 + 2r} = \frac{2E}{4 + r}$$

$$\Rightarrow \quad 2 + 2r = 4 + r$$

$$\therefore \quad r = 2\Omega$$

Example 16. When 14 cells in series are connected to the ends of a resistance of 82.6 Ω, then the current is found to be 0.25A. When same cells after being connected in parallel are joined to the ends of a resistance of 0.053Ω, then the current is 25A. Calculate the internal resistance and the emf of each cell.

Sol. Let E and r be the emf and internal resistance of each cell respectively.

***Case* I** When the cells are in series.

Total emf of cells $= 14E$

Total resistance of circuit $= 82.6 + 14r$

$\therefore$ Current in the circuit is given by

$$\frac{14E}{82.6 + 14r} = 0.25 \text{ A} \quad \dots\text{(i)}$$

***Case* II** When the cells are in parallel.

Total emf of cells $= E$

Total resistance of circuit $= 0.053 + \dfrac{r}{14}$

$\therefore$ Current in the circuit is given by

$$\frac{E}{0.053 + \frac{r}{14}} = 25 \text{ A} \quad \dots\text{(ii)}$$

Dividing Eq. (i) by Eq. (ii), we get

$$14 \times \frac{\left(0.053 + \frac{r}{14}\right)}{(82.6 + 14r)} = 10^{-2}$$

$$\Rightarrow \quad 14 \times \frac{14 \times 0.053 + r}{14} \times 10^2 = 82.6 + 14r$$

$$\Rightarrow \quad 5.3 \times 14 + 100r = 82.6 + 14r$$

Solving, we get

$$r = 0.097\Omega \approx 0.1\Omega$$

Substituting the value of r in Eq. (i), we get

$$E = 1.5 \text{ V}$$

Mixed Combination of Cells

When a certain number of cells are connected in various series and all such series are mutually connected in parallel, then this combination of cells is called mixed combination.

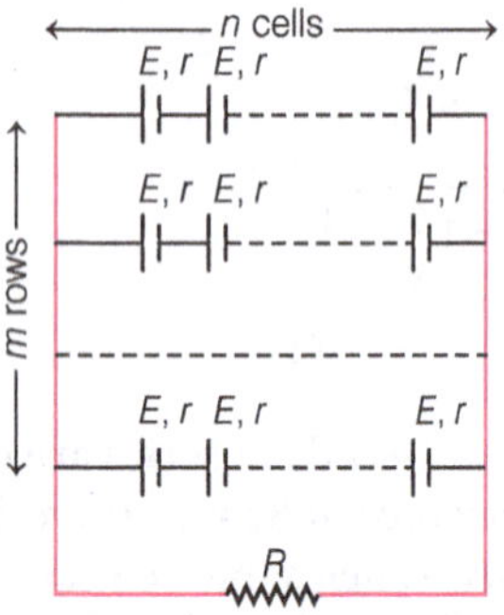

Let there be n cells in series in one row and m rows of cells in parallel.

Suppose all the cells are identical. Let each cell be of emf E and internal resistance r.

Equivalent emf of each row $= nE$

Equivalent internal resistance of each row $= nr$

Total emf of combination $= nE$

Total internal resistance of combination,

$$\frac{1}{r'} = \frac{1}{nr} + \frac{1}{nr} + \dots \text{ upto } m \text{ times}$$

$$\frac{1}{r'} = \frac{m}{nr} \text{ or } r' = \frac{nr}{m}$$

Total resistance of the circuit

$$= r' + R = \frac{nr}{m} + R$$

Current in the resistance R is given by

$$I = \frac{nE}{\frac{nr}{m} + R}$$

Thus, we get the maximum current in mixed grouping of cells, if the value of external resistance is equal to the total internal resistance of all the cells, i.e. external resistance = total internal resistance of all the cells $\left(R = \frac{nr}{m}\right)$.

Example 17. **36 cells, each of internal resistance 0.5 Ω and emf 1.5 V are used to send current through an external circuit of 2 Ω resistance. Find the best mode of grouping them and the current through the external circuit.**

Sol. Here, $E = 1.5\text{ V}, r = 0.5\,\Omega, R = 2\,\Omega$

Total number of cells, $mn = 36$ ...(i)

For maximum current in the mixed grouping,

$$\frac{nr}{m} = R$$

$$\Rightarrow \frac{n \times 0.5}{m} = 2 \quad \text{... (ii)}$$

Multiplying Eqs. (i) and (ii), we get

$$0.5n^2 = 72 \Rightarrow n^2 = 144$$

$$\therefore n = 12 \text{ and } m = \frac{36}{12} = 3$$

Thus, for maximum current, there should be three rows in parallel, each containing 12 cells in series.

$$\therefore \text{ Maximum current} = \frac{mnE}{mR + nr} = \frac{36 \times 1.5}{3 \times 2 + 12 \times 0.5} = 4.5\text{ A}$$

Example 18. **12 cells, each of emf 1.5 V and internal resistance of 0.5 Ω are arranged in m rows each containing n cells connected in series, as shown in the figure. Calculate the values of n and m for which this combination would send maximum current through an external resistance of 1.5 Ω.**

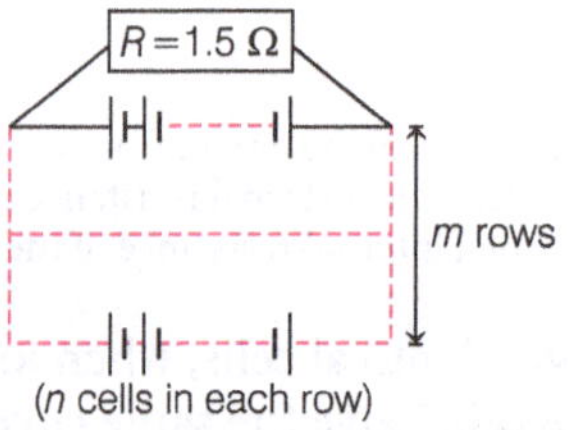

Sol. For maximum current through the external resistance,

external resistance = total internal resistance of cells

or $$R = \frac{nr}{m}$$

$$\therefore 1.5 = \frac{n \times 0.5}{\frac{12}{n}} \quad [\because mn = 12]$$

or $$36 = n^2$$

$$\therefore n = 6 \text{ and } m = 2$$

Quick Test 3

Conceptual Questions

1. A cell of emf E and internal resistance r is connected across an external resistance R. Plot a graph showing the variation of potential difference V across R, *versus* R. *NCERT Exemplar*

2. Which of the two, emf E or potential difference V of a cell, is greater and by how much?

3. What is the difference between the values of potential difference across the two terminals of a cell in an open circuit and closed circuit?

4. A low voltage supply from which one needs high currents must have very low internal resistance. Why?

5. Under what condition will the current in a wire be the same when connected in series and in parallel of n identical cells having internal resistance r and external resistance R ? *CBSE 2019*

Numerical Questions

6. First a set of n equal resistors of R each are connected in series to a battery of emf E and internal resistance R and current I is observed to flow. Then, the resistors are connected in parallel to the same battery.

It is observed that the current is increased 10 times. What is n? *NCERT Exemplar*

7. A battery of emf 10 V and internal resistance 3Ω is connected to a resistor. If the current in the circuit is 0.5 A, what is the resistance of resistor? What is the terminal voltage of the battery when the circuit is closed? *NCERT*

8. A voltmeter of resistance 998 Ω is connected across a cell of emf 2V and internal resistance 2Ω. Find the potential difference across the voltmeter and also across the terminals of the cell. Estimate the percentage error in the reading of the voltmeter.

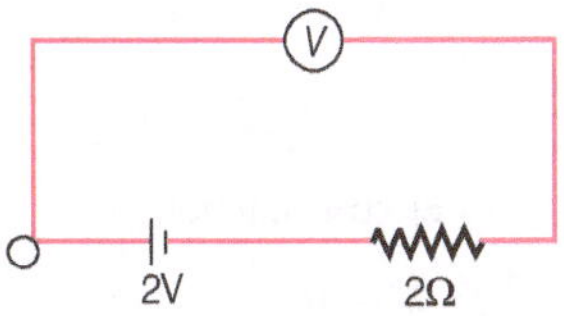

9. Eva needs a 3V power supply for her electronic circuit experiment. There is a 10 V battery in the lab that she can use. Eva decides to make a voltage divider using this battery and two different resistors, the larger value resistor being 300 Ω. What value of the smaller resistor should Eva use to make the desired voltage divider?

10. A battery of emf 12 V and internal resistance 2 Ω is connected to a 4 Ω resistor as shown in the figure.

(i) Show that a voltmeter when placed across the cell and across the resistor, in turn, gives the same reading.

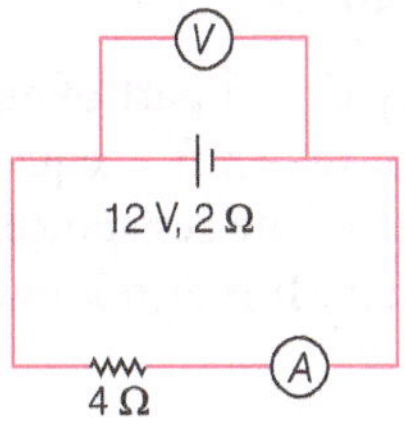

(ii) To record the voltage and the current in the circuit, why is voltmeter placed in parallel and ammeter in series in the circuit?

Answers

6. 10 7. 8.5 V 8. 1.996 V, 0.2% 9. 128.6 Ω 10. (i) 8 V

For Solutions, See QR Code on Pg. 127

3.4 Kirchhoff's Laws and its Applications

Kirchhoff's Rules or Laws

Many complex electrical circuits cannot be reduced to simple series and parallel combinations.

However, such circuits can be analysed by applying two rules, devised by Kirchhoff's which are as follows

First Law (Kirchhoff's Junction Rule)

This law states that the **algebraic sum of the currents meeting at a point in an electrical circuit is always zero.** It is also known as **Kirchhoff's junction rule** or **Kirchhoff's current rule.**

i.e. $$\Sigma I = 0$$

Sign Convention (First Law)

1. The incoming currents towards the junction are taken positive.
2. The outgoing currents away from the junction are taken negative.

By Kirchhoff's current law,

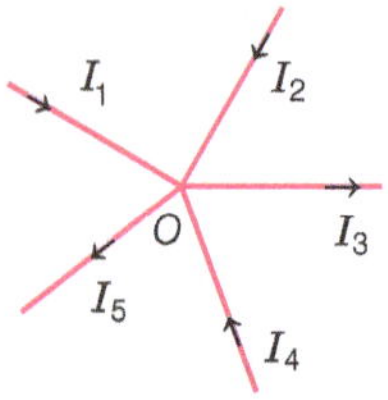

Electric junction

$$I_2 + I_4 + I_1 - I_3 - I_5 = 0$$

So, junction rule can be stated as **the sum of currents entering the junction is equal to the sum of currents leaving the junction.**

Second Law (Kirchhoff's Voltage Rule)

This law states that the **algebraic sum of changes in potential around any closed loop involving resistors and cells in the loop is zero.**

i.e. $$\boxed{\Sigma \Delta V = 0}$$

It means that in any closed part of an electrical circuit, the algebraic sum of the emfs is equal to the algebraic sum of the products of the resistances and currents flowing through them. It is also known as **Kirchhoff's loop rule.**

Sign Convention (Second Law)

1. The emf is taken positive when we traverse from positive to negative terminal of the cell.
2. The emf is taken negative when we traverse from negative to positive terminal of the cell.
3. If the resistor is being traversed in the direction opposite to the current, then potential difference across it is taken positive, i.e. *IR*.

If the resistor is being traversed in the direction of circuit, then potential difference across it, is taken negative, i.e. $-IR$.

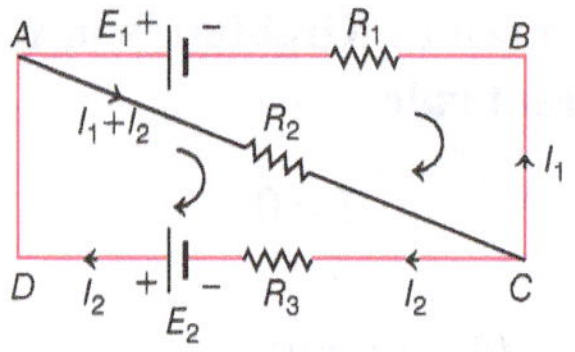

For loop *ABCA*

$$-E_1 + I_1R_1 (I_1 + I_2)R_2 = 0$$

For loop *ACDA*

$$-(I_1 + I_2)R_2 - I_3R_3 + E_2 = 0$$

Example 19. **Find currents in different branches of the electric circuit shown in figure.**

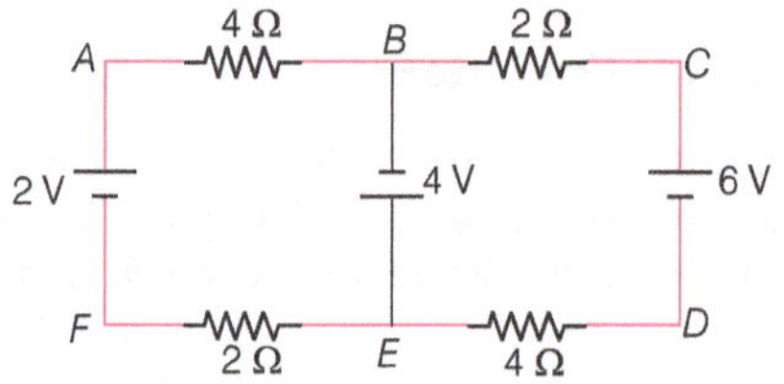

Sol.

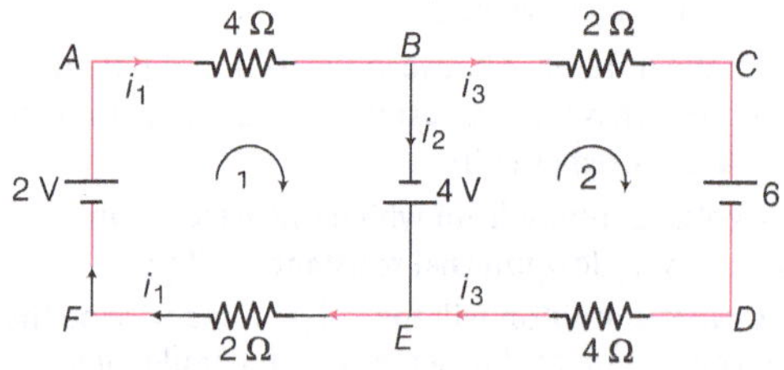

Applying Kirchhoff's first law (junction law) at junction *B*,

$$i_1 = i_2 + i_3 \quad \text{...(i)}$$

Applying Kirchhoff's second law in loop 1 (*ABEFA*),

$$-4i_1 + 4 - 2i_1 + 2 = 0 \quad \text{...(ii)}$$

Applying Kirchhoff's second law in loop 2 (*BCDEB*),

$$-2i_3 - 6 - 4i_3 - 4 = 0 \quad \text{...(iii)}$$

Solving Eqs. (i), (ii) and (iii), we get

$$i_1 = 1\,\text{A}, i_2 = \frac{8}{3}\,\text{A}$$

and $$i_3 = -\frac{5}{3}\,\text{A}$$

Here, negative sign of i_3 implies that current i_3 is in the opposite direction of what we have assumed.

Example 20. **In the circuit shown in figure *E, F, G, H* are cells of emf 2, 1, 3 and 1 V respectively, and their internal resistances are 2, 1, 3 and 1 Ω, respectively. Calculate**

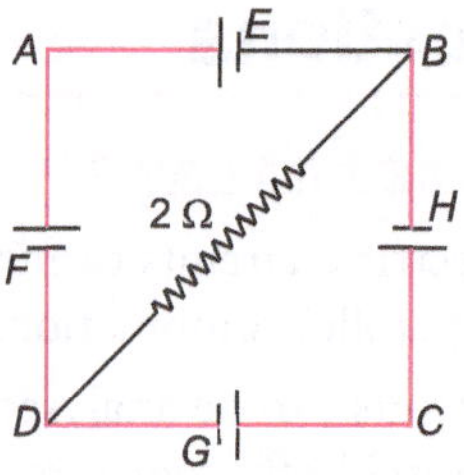

(i) the potential difference between *B* and *D*, and

(ii) the potential difference across the terminals of each cells *G* and *H*.

Sol.

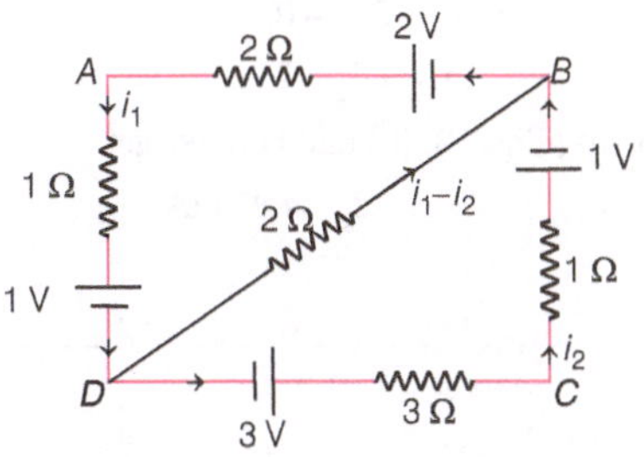

Applying Kirchhoff's second law in loop *BADB*,

$$2-2i_1-i_1-1-2(i_1-i_2)=0 \quad \text{...(i)}$$

Similarly, applying Kirchhoff's second law in loop *BDCB*,

$$2(i_1-i_2)+3-3i_2-i_2-1=0 \quad \text{...(ii)}$$

Solving Eqs. (i) and (ii), we get

$$i_1=\frac{5}{13}, i_2=\frac{6}{13} \text{ and } i_1-i_2=-\frac{1}{13}$$

(i) Potential difference between *B* and *D*,

$$V_B+2(i_1-i_2)=V_D$$

$$\therefore \quad V_B-V_D=-2(i_1-i_2)=\frac{2}{13}\text{ V}$$

(ii) $V_G=E_G-i_2r_G=3-\frac{6}{13}\times 3=\frac{21}{13}\text{ V}$

$$V_H=E_H-i_2r_H=1-\frac{6}{13}\times 1=\frac{7}{13}\text{ V}$$

Wheatstone Bridge

It is an arrangement of four resistances in a parallelogram which is used to measure one resistance in terms of the other three.

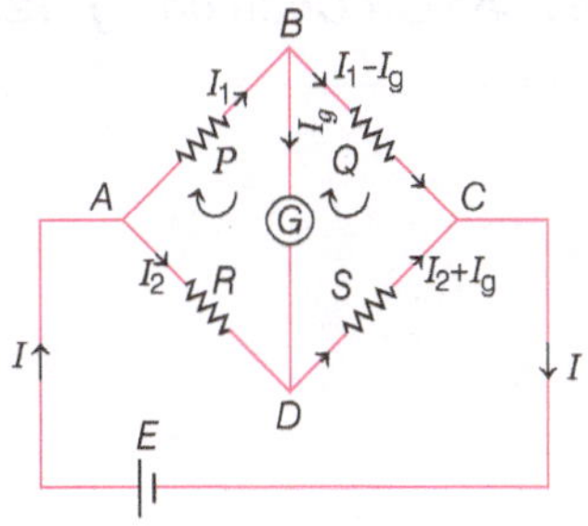

Let four resistances *P*,*Q*,*R* and *S* connected to form the arms of a quadrilateral *ABCD*.

$G \rightarrow$ resistance of galvanometer

Applying Kirchhoff's second law to loop *ABDA*,

$$-I_1P-I_gG+I_2R=0 \quad \text{...(i)}$$

Again applying Kirchhoff's second law to loop *BCDB*,

$$-(I_1-I_g)Q+(I_2+I_g)S+GI_g=0 \quad \text{...(ii)}$$

The bridge is said to be balanced when no current passes through galvanometer, i.e. $I_g=0$.

From. Eq (i),

$$-I_1P+0+I_2R=0 \quad (\because I_g=0)$$

$$I_1P=I_2R \quad \text{...(iii)}$$

From Eq. (ii),

$$-(I_1-I_g)+Q(I_2+I_g)S-GI_g=0$$

$$-(I_1-0)Q+(I_2+0)S-0=0 \quad (\because I_g=0)$$

$$-I_1Q+I_2S=0$$

$$I_1Q=I_2S \quad \text{...(iv)}$$

Dividing Eq. (iii) by Eq. (iv), we get

$$\frac{I_1P}{I_1Q}=\frac{I_2R}{I_2S}$$

or

$$\boxed{\frac{P}{Q}=\frac{R}{S}}$$

This equation gives the condition for the balanced Wheatstone bridge.

Example 21. **In a Wheatstone bridge circuit, $P=7\,\Omega$, $Q=8\,\Omega$, $R=12\ \Omega$ and $S=7\,\Omega$. Find the additional resistance to be used in series with *S*, so that the bridge is balanced.**

Sol. Let the bridge be balanced when additional resistance *x* is put in series with *S*.

Then, $(S+x)=\frac{Q}{P}R$ or $x=\frac{Q}{P}R-S$

$$=\frac{8}{7}\times 12-7=6.72\,\Omega$$

Example 22. **The Wheatstone bridge circuit have the resistances in various arms as shown in figure. Calculate the current through the galvanometer.**

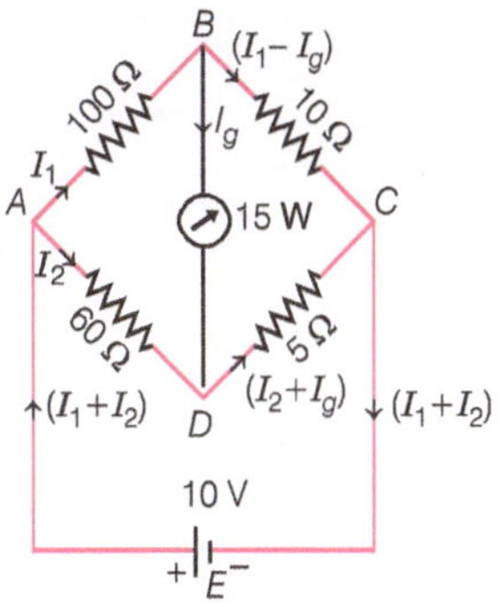

Sol. In the closed loop *ABDA*,

$$-100I_1-15I_g+60I_2=0$$

$$-20I_1-3I_g+12I_2=0 \quad \text{... (i)}$$

$$-10(I_1-I_g)+5(I_2+I_g)+15I_g=0$$

$\Rightarrow \quad -10I_1 + 30I_g + 5I_2 = 0$

$\Rightarrow \quad -2I_1 + 6I_g + I_2 = 0 \quad \ldots \text{(ii)}$

In the closed loop *ADCEA*,

$$-60I_2 - 5(I_2 + I_g) + 10 = 0$$

$$65I_2 + 5I_g = 10$$

$$13I_2 + I_g = 2 \quad \ldots \text{(iii)}$$

On solving Eqs. (i), (ii) and (iii), we get

$$I_g = 4.87 \text{ mA}$$

Quick Test 4

1. Use Kirchhoff's rules to obtain the balance condition in a Wheatstone bridge.

2. On what basic conservation laws, are Kirchhoff's laws based?

3. Using Kirchhoff's rules in the given circuit, determine

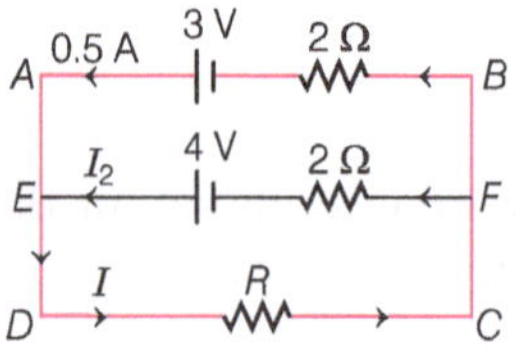

(i) the voltage drop across the unknown resistor *R*.

(ii) the current *I* in the arm *EF*.

4. Calculate the value of the resistance *R* in the circuit shown in the figure, so that the current in the circuit is 0.2 A. What would be the potential difference between points *A* and *B*?

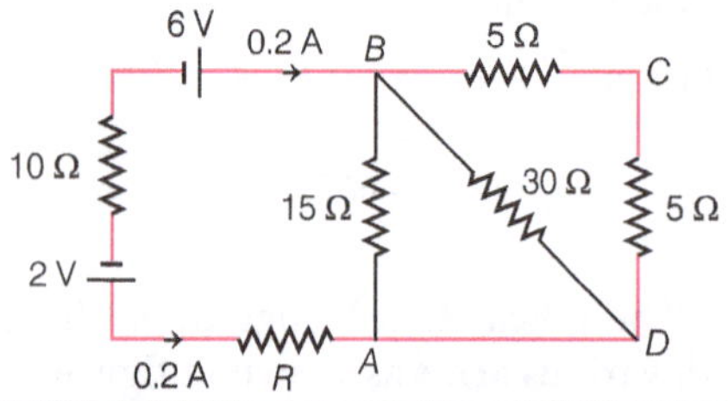

5. A battery of 10 V and negligible internal resistance are connected across the diagonally opposite corners of a cubical network consisting of 12 resistors each of 1 Ω resistance. Use Kirchhoff's rules to determine

(i) the equivalent resistance of the network.

(ii) the total current in the network.

6. Calculate the current drawn from the battery in the given network.

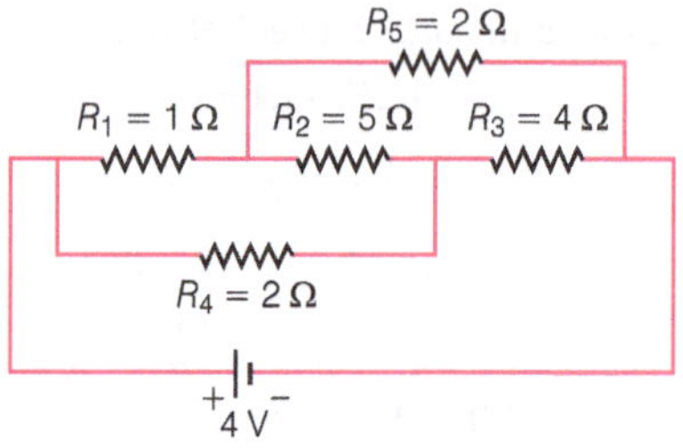

Answers

3. (i) 2 V (ii) 1 A

4. 5Ω, −1 V

5. (i) $\frac{5}{6}$Ω (ii) 12 A

6. 2 A

For Solutions, See QR Code on Pg. 127

Mind Map

Current Density

Current Density The amount of charge flowing per second through a unit area held normal to the direction of the flow of charge at that point. $j = I/A$

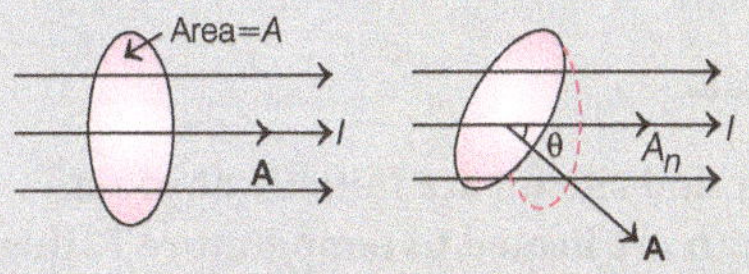

Mobility

It is the ease with which charge carriers move in a material, directly influencing the electric current by increasing drift velocity under an electric field.

Mobility, $\mu = \frac{v_d}{E} = \frac{q\tau}{m}$

Drift Velocity

The average velocity gained by the free electrons of a conductor in the opposite direction of the externally applied electric field is called drift velocity.

$v_d = a\tau = \frac{eE\tau}{m}$

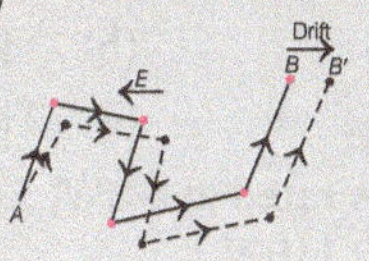

Relation between Drift Velocity and Electric Field

The relation between drift velocity (v_d) and the electric field (E) is given by $v_d = \mu E$

Electrical Conductivity

A measure of a material's ability to conduct electric current.

- It is the reciprocal of resistivity $\sigma = \frac{1}{\rho}$

V-I Characteristics

- For ohmic conductors, the *V-I* relationship is a straight line, indicating constant resistance.
- For non-ohmic components, the *V-I* relationship is curved, indicating varying resistance.

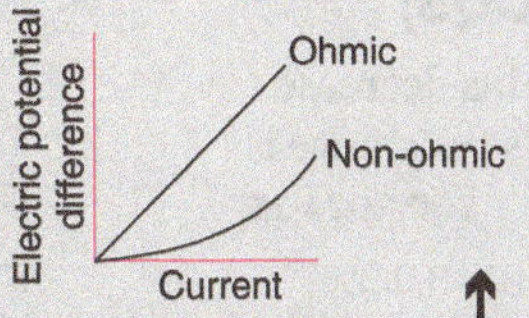

Ohm's Law

$V = IR$ or equivalently, $I = V/R$

where, R is the resistance of the circuit expressed in ohms (Ω).

Ohm's law states that, the electric current through a conductor is directly proportional to the voltage across the conductor.

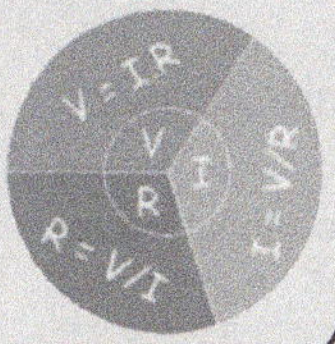

CURRENT ELECTRICITY

Resistance

Resistance is the opposition of a material or object offered to the flow of electric current, measured in ohms (Ω).

Factors Affecting the Resistance

- **Length** The resistance R of a conductor is directly proportional to its length, i.e. $R \propto l$.
- **Area of cross-section** The resistance R of a uniform conductor is inversely proportional to its area of cross-section A, i.e. $R \propto 1/A$.
- **Nature of the material** The resistance of a conductor also depends on the nature of its material. $R = \rho \frac{l}{A}$

Temperature Dependence of Resistance

- Resistance of most conductors increases with temperature.
- For some materials like semiconductors, resistance decreases as temperature rises.

Electrical Resistivity

Electrical Resistivity A measure of how strongly a material opposes the flow of electric current, typically measured in ohm-metres (Ω-m).

Relation between resistivity and relaxation time $\rho = \frac{m}{ne^2\tau}$

Temperature Dependence of Resistivity

The resistivity of any material depends on the number density n of free electrons and the mean collision time τ.

$\rho = \frac{m}{ne^2\tau}$

The resistivity of a metal ($r \propto 1/\tau$) increases and the conductivity decreases with the increase in temperature.

$\alpha = \frac{\rho - \rho_0}{\rho_0(T - T_0)} = \frac{1}{\rho_0} \cdot \frac{d\rho}{dT}$

Electrical Energy

The energy caused by the movement of electric charges, measured in joules (J) or kilowatt- hours (kWh).

Electrical power The rate at which electrical energy is transferred by an electric circuit. It is measured in watts (W) and calculated using $P = VI$.

Kirchhoff's Laws

Kirchhoff's Current Law (KCL)
The total current entering a junction equals the total current leaving the junction.

Kirchhoff's Voltage Law (KVL)
The sum of all voltages around a closed loop in a circuit equals zero.

$\Sigma\Delta V = 0$ or $\Sigma\varepsilon = \Sigma IR$

Internal Resistance of a Cell

It is the opposition to the flow of current within the cell itself, which causes a voltage drop when current flows.

EMF **(Electromotive Force)** The voltage generated by a cell or battery when no current is flowing, representing the energy provided per charge.

The relationship between **internal resistance** (r), EMF (E), **external resistance** (R) and **terminal voltage** (V) of a circuit is given by $V = E - Ir$.

Wheatstone Bridge

A wheatstone bridge is a circuit used to measure an unknown resistance by balancing two legs of a bridge circuit.

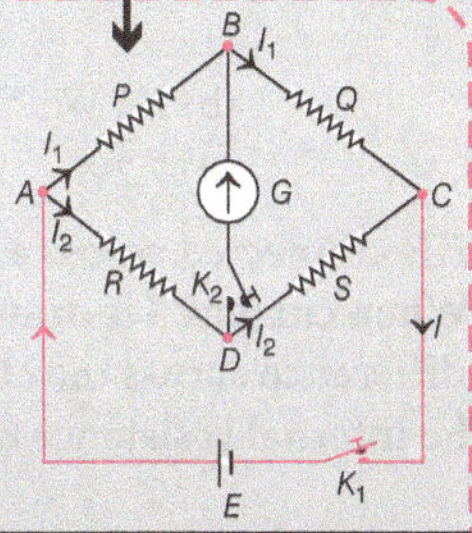

$\frac{P}{Q} = \frac{R}{S}$

Cells in Series

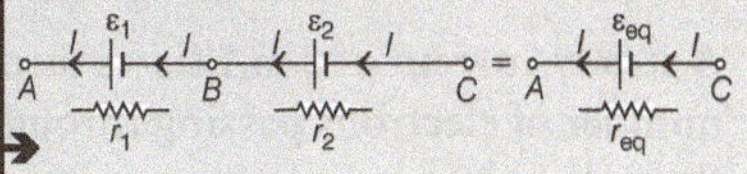

$\varepsilon_{eq} = \varepsilon_1 + \varepsilon_2$ and $r_{eq} = r_1 + r_2$

Cells in Parallel

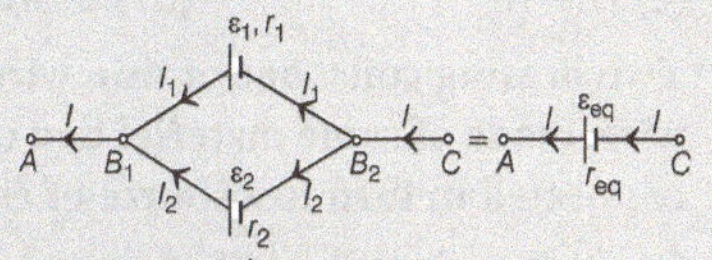

$\varepsilon_{eq} = \frac{\varepsilon_1 r_2 + \varepsilon_2 r_1}{r_1 + r_2}$ and

$r_{eq} = \frac{r_1 r_2}{r_1 + r_2}$

EXAM PATTERN QUESTIONS

Objective Type Questions

Multiple Choice Questions (MCQs)

1. **If copper wire is stretched to make its radius decrease by 0.1%, then the percentage change in its resistance is approximately** SQP 2024-25

(a) −0.4% (b) +0.8% (c) +0.4% (d) +0.2%

2. **A student has three resistors, each of resistance R. To obtain a resistance of $\frac{2}{3}R$, she should connect** CBSE 2025

(a) all the three resistors in series.
(b) all the three resistors in parallel.
(c) two resistors in series and then this combination in parallel with the third resistor.
(d) two resistors in parallel and then this combination in series with the third resistor.

3. **Three identical cells, each of 4 V and internal resistance r, are connected in series to a 6 ohm resistor. If the current flowing in the circuit is 2A. The internal resistance of each cell is** Diksha

(a) 0.11Ω (b) 0 (c) 0.12Ω (d) 1.1Ω

4. **The current density due to drift of electrons in a conductor is given by (symbols have their usual meanings)** CBSE 2023

(a) $neAv_d$ (b) $\frac{nAv_d}{e}$ (c) $\frac{nv_d}{eA}$ (d) nev_d

5. **For which of the following relation between drift velocity (v_d) and electric field (E), Ohm's law is obeyed?**

(a) $v_d \propto E^{1/2}$ (b) $v_d \propto E$
(c) $v_d \propto E^2$ (d) $v_d \propto E^{-1}$

6. **A steady current of 8 mA flows through a wire. The number of electrons passing through a cross-section of the wire in 10 s is** CBSE 2023

(a) 4.0×10^{16} (b) 5.0×10^{17}
(c) 1.6×10^{16} (d) 1.0×10^{17}

7. **Two heating coils, one of thin wire and other of thick wire, made of same material and of same length are connected in turn to a source of emf. Then,**

(a) thicker wire will produce more heat
(b) thinner wire will produce more heat
(c) both the wires will produce same heat
(d) no wire will produce heat

8. **Pieces of copper and silicon are initially at room temperature. Both are heated to temperature T, then conduction of** CBSE 2023

(a) both increases
(b) both decreases
(c) copper increases and silicon decreases
(d) copper decreases and silicon increases

9. **A current of 2 A flows in a wire offering a resistance of 10 ohm. Calculate the energy dissipated by the wire in 0.5 hours.**

(a) 72 W-h (b) 72 kJ
(c) 7200 J (d) 72 k J-h

10. **A light bulb is rated at 44 W, 220 V and a table fan is rated at 60 W, 110 V.**

Which statement is correct if each of the two devices is connected to a power supply of 220 V separately? Competency Based Que.

(a) The light bulb has a greater resistance and draws a greater current than the table fan.
(b) The light bulb has a greater resistance and draws a smaller current than the table fan.
(c) The light bulb has a smaller resistance and draws a greater current than the table fan.
(d) The light bulb has a smaller resistance and draws a smaller current than the table fan.

11. **A constant voltage is applied between the two ends of a uniform metallic wire, heat H is developed in it. If another wire of the same material, double the radius and twice the length as compared to original wire is used, then the heat developed in it will be** CBSE SQP, Term-I

(a) $H/2$ (b) H (c) $2H$ (d) $4H$

12. **A conductor of 10Ω is connected across a 6V ideal source. The power supplied by the source to the conductor is** CBSE 2023

(a) 1.8W (b) 2.4 W
(c) 3.6 W (d) 7.2W

13. **A cell of emf E is connected across an external resistance R. When current I is drawn from the cell, the potential difference across the electrodes of the cell drops to V. The internal resistance r of the cell is** CBSE 2023

(a) $\left(\frac{E-V}{E}\right)R$ (b) $\left(\frac{E-V}{R}\right)$

(c) $\frac{(E-V)R}{I}$ (d) $\left(\frac{E-V}{V}\right)R$

14. **The current in a device varies with time t as $I = 6t$, where I is in mA and t is in second. The amount of charge that passes through the device during $t = 0$s to $t = 3$s is** CBSE 2023

(a) 10 mC (b) 18 mC (c) 27 mC (d) 54 mC

15. **The radii of two metallic spheres are 10 cm and 15 cm and carrying charge of 75 μC each. If they are shorted, then the charge will be transferred**

(a) 15 μC from bigger to smaller sphere

(b) 15 μC from smaller to bigger sphere

(c) 25 μC from bigger to smaller sphere

(d) 25 μC from smaller to bigger sphere

16. **When no current is passed through a conductor,**

(i) the free electrons do not move.

(ii) the average speed of a free electron over a large period of time is not zero.

(iii) the average velocity of a free electron over a large period of time is zero.

(iv) the average velocities of all the free electrons at an instant is non-zero.

Which statement(s) is/are correct ?

(a) Only (iii) and (iv) (b) Only (i)

(c) Only (i) and (iii) (d) Only (ii) and (iii)

17. **In a DC circuit, the direction of current inside the battery and outside the battery respectively, are** CBSE 2021, Term-I

(a) positive to negative terminal and negative to positive terminal

(b) positive to negative terminal and positive to negative terminal

(c) negative to positive terminal and positive to negative terminal

(d) negative to positive terminal and negative to positive terminal

18. **Kirchhoff's first law, $\Sigma i = 0$ at a junction and second law $\Sigma V = 0$ in a closed loop are based on**

(a) conservation of charge and conservation of energy, respectively

(b) both on conservation of charge

(c) conservation of energy and conservation of charge, respectively

(d) both on conservation of energy

19. **A battery of emf 12 V and internal resistance 0.5 Ω is connected to a 9.5 Ω resistor through a key. The ratio of potential difference between the two terminals of the battery, when the key is open to that when the key is closed, is** CBSE 2025

(a) 1.05 (b) 1 (c) 0.95 (d) 1.1

20. **A cell of emf (E) and internal resistance (r) is connected across a variable external resistance R. The graph of terminal potential difference V as a function of R is** CBSE 2020

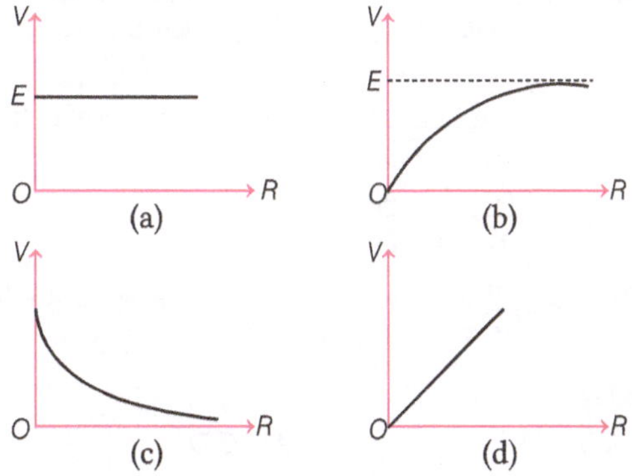

21. **If n identical cells each of emf E and identical resistance r are connected in parallel, then equivalent emf and equivalent resistance will be respectively,**

(a) $\frac{\varepsilon}{n}$ and $\frac{r}{n}$ (b) $n\varepsilon$ and nr

(c) ε and $\frac{r}{n}$ (d) ε and nr

22. **In the equation $A = BC$, A is the electric field, B is the current density, then C is**

(a) conductivity (b) resistivity

(c) conductance (d) resistance

23. **Five cells each of emf E and resistance r, are connected in series. Due to oversight, one cell is connected wrongly. Calcualte the equivalent emf of the combination?** Diksha

(a) $5E$ (b) $2E$ (c) $3E$ (d) $4E$

24. **Match the Column I with Column II.**

Column I		Column II	
A	Electric current	1.	Defined as the amount of current flowing per unit area of conductor
B	Current density	2.	The rate of flow of electric charge through any cross-section of a conductor
C	Ampere	3.	Responsible for electrical conduction in metals
D	Free electrons	4.	The SI unit of electric current

Codes

	A B C D		A B C D
(a)	1 2 3 4	(b)	2 1 4 3
(c)	3 4 1 2	(d)	1 2 4 3

25. Match the Coloumn I with Column II.

	Column I		Column II
(A)	$v_d = \frac{eE}{m}\tau$	1.	Resistivity of material
(B)	$\mu_h = \frac{eIh}{mh}$	2.	Temperature dependence of resistivity
(C)	$\alpha = \frac{\rho - \rho_o}{\rho_0(T - T_o)} = \frac{d\rho}{\rho_o} \cdot \frac{1}{dT} = \frac{d\rho}{\rho_o} \cdot \frac{1}{dT}$	3.	Mobility of holes
(D)	$\rho = \frac{m}{ne^2\tau}$	4.	Average drift velocity

Codes

	A B C D		A B C D
(a)	4 3 2 1	(b)	1 2 3 4
(c)	3 2 4 1	(d)	2 3 4 1

Assertion-Reason

Directions *(Q. Nos. 26-36) In the following questions, two statements are given- one labelled Assertion (A) and the other labelled Reason (R). Select the correct answer to these questions from the codes (a), (b), (c) and (d) as given below.*

(a) Both Assertion and Reason are true and Reason is the correct explanation of Assertion.
(b) Both Assertion and Reason are true but Reason is not the correct explanation of Assertion.
(c) Assertion is true but Reason is false.
(d) Assertion is false but Reason is true.

26. **Assertion (A)** The equivalent resistance between points *A* and *B* in the given network is 2*R*.

Reason (R) All the resistors are connected in parallel. **CBSE 2023**

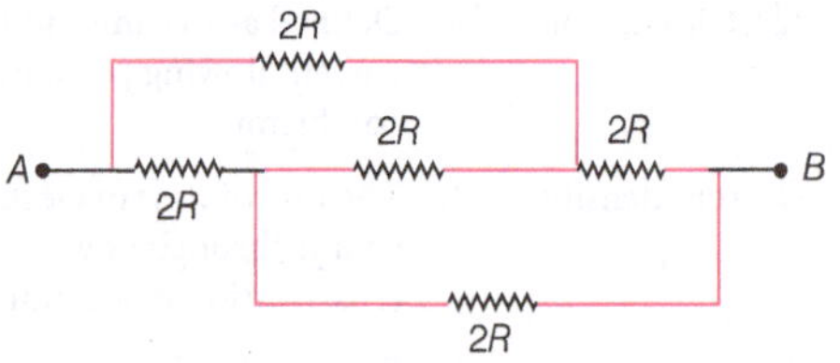

27. **Assertion (A)** As the temperature of a conducting wire increases, the drift velocity of the electrons also increases.

Reason (R) With an increase in temperature, the average time of collision decreases. **Competency Based Que.**

28. **Assertion (A)** The average time of collisions τ, decreases with increasing temperature.

Reason (R) With an increase in temperature, average speed of the electrons, which act as the carriers of current, increases, resulting in more frequent collisions.

29. **Assertion (A)** Charge carriers do not move with acceleration, but with a steady drift velocity.

Reason (R) Charge carriers undergo collisions with ions and atoms during transit.

30. **Assertion (A)** If we bend an insulated conducting wire, the resistance of the wire increases.

Reason (R) The drift velocity of electron in bended wire remains same.

31. **Assertion (A)** The drift velocity of electrons in a metallic wire decreases when temperature of the wire is increased.

Reason (R) On increasing temperature, conductivity of metallic wire decreases.

32. **Assertion (A)** Manganin and constantan are widely used in standard resistors.

Reason (R) Manganin and constantan resistance, values would change very little with temperature.

33. **Assertion (A)** Higher the range, lower is the resistance of an ammeter.

Reason (R) To increase the range of an ammeter, additional shunt is added in series to it. **CBSE 2021, Term-I**

34. **Assertion (A)** When electrons drift in a conductor, it does not mean that all free electrons in the conductor are moving in the same direction.

Reason (R) The drift velocity is superimposed over large random velocities of electrons. **CBSE 2024**

35. **Assertion (A)** If the charges are placed on an isolated conductor, it results in a zero electric field inside the conductor. On the other hand, a conductor connected to a source of emf, results in a steady current due to a constant electric field inside the conductor.

Reason (R) A conductor is always in an electrostatic equilibrium whether it is connected to a source of emf or not. **Competency Based Que.**

36. **Assertion (A)** The net current in an isolated conductor placed in a uniform electric field is zero.

Reason (R) There is no motion of electrons inside an isolated conductor placed in a uniform electric field as all charges reside on the surface of the conductor. **Competency Based Que.**

Case Based Questions

Directions *(Q.Nos. 37-40) These questions are case study based questions. Read the following paragraph and answer the questions on the basis of same.*

37. The potential difference (V) across a source in a circuit is not equal to its emf (ε). This is due to the reason that every source of electric energy has some internal resistance (r). Further, ε, V and r are related to each other as $V = \varepsilon - Ir$. A single battery shown in figure, consists of two cells of emfs ε_1 and ε_2 and internal resistances r_1 and r_2 respectively, in series.

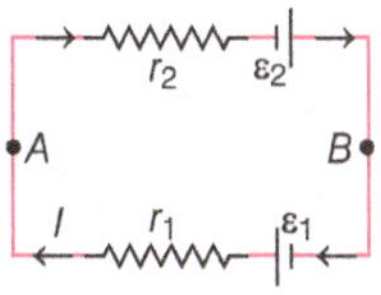

(i) The current in the internal circuit is
(a) zero (b) $\frac{\varepsilon_2 - \varepsilon_1}{r_1 + r_2}$
(c) $\frac{\varepsilon_1 + \varepsilon_2}{r_1 + r_2}$ (d) $\frac{\varepsilon_1 - \varepsilon_2}{r_1 + r_2}$

(ii) The equivalent emf of the battery is
(a) $(\varepsilon_1 + \varepsilon_2)$ (b) $(\varepsilon_1 - \varepsilon_2)$
(c) $(\varepsilon_2 - \varepsilon_1)$ (d) $\frac{(\varepsilon_1 r_2 - \varepsilon_2 r_1)}{r_1 + r_2}$

(iii) For the terminal A to be positive
(a) $\varepsilon_1 > \varepsilon_2$ (b) $\varepsilon_2 > \varepsilon_1$
(c) $\varepsilon_1 r_1 = \varepsilon_2 r_2$ (d) $\varepsilon_1 r_2 > \varepsilon_2 r_1$

(iv) The internal resistance of the battery is
(a) $(r_1 + r_2)$ (b) $\frac{(r_1 + r_2)}{r_1 r_2}$
(c) $\frac{r_1 r_2}{(r_1 + r_2)}$ (d) $\frac{r_2}{(r_1 + r_2)}$

(v) The algebraic sum of changes in potential around any closed loop involving resistor and cells in the loop is
(a) more than zero (b) less than zero
(c) zero (d) constant

38. An experiment was set-up with the circuit diagram shown in figure. Given that, $R_1 = 10\Omega$, $R_2 = R_3 = 5\Omega$, $r = 0\Omega$ and $E = 5$ V. **CBSE 2021, Term-I**

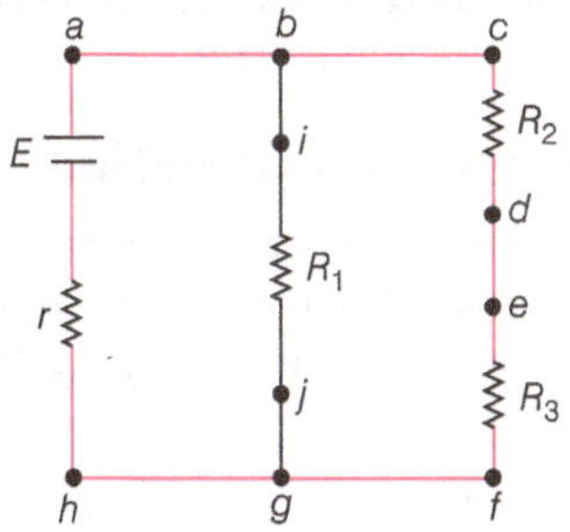

(i) The points with the same potential are
(a) b, c, d (b) $f, h,$
(c) d, e, f (d) a, b, j

(ii) The current through branch bg is
(a) 1 A (b) $\frac{1}{3}$ A
(c) $\frac{1}{2}$ A (d) $\frac{2}{3}$ A

(iii) The power dissipated in R_1 is
(a) 2 W (b) 2.5 W
(c) 3 W (d) 4.5 W

(iv) The potential difference across R_3 is
(a) 1.5 V (b) 2 V
(c) 2.5 V (d) 3 V

39. According to Ohm's law, the current flowing through a conductor is directly proportional to the potential difference across the ends of the conductor, i.e. $I \propto V$ or $\frac{V}{I} = R =$ constant, where R is known as resistance of the conductor. It is the obstruction possessed by the conductor to flow electric current through it. It depends upon lengths, area of cross-section, nature of material and temperature of a conductor. The expression for resistance of a conductor is given by $R = \rho\frac{l}{A}$, where ρ is the resistivity of the conductor.

(i) Write the dimensional formula of resistance of a conductor.
(ii) Draw the graph of V *versus* I for an ohmic conductor.
(iii) Write the factors on which resistance of a conductor depends.
(iv) If length of a conductor is increased by 2 times, then how much times the resistance of the conductor increases or decreases ?

40. In 1942, a German physicist Kirchhoff has given two rules to solve complicated electrical circuits. According to Kirchhoff's first rule, the algebraic sum of currents meeting at a junction in a closed electric circuit is zero. The incoming currents towards the junction is taken as positive and the outgoing currents away from the junction is taken as negative. So, Kirchhoff's first rule is on the basis of law of conservation of charge. According to Kirchhoff's second rule, the algebraic sum of potential drop across the resistors and the emfs of the cell in a closed loop is zero. So, Kirchhoff's second rule is based on conservation of energy.

(i) Write the principle on which Kirchhoff's first rule is based.
(ii) Write the principle on which Kirchhoff's second rule is based.

(iii) Find the potential difference between points A and B in the circuit given below.

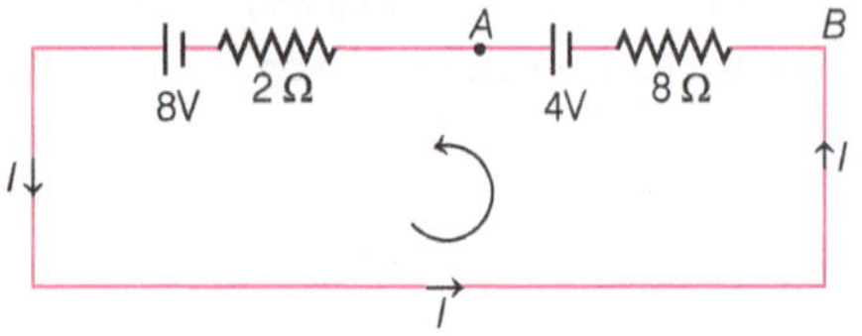

(iv) Find the value of current I in the following circuit.

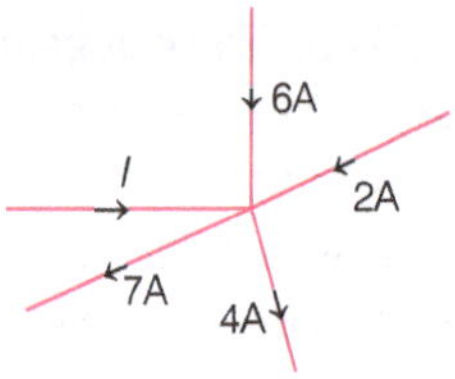

Subjective Questions

Very Short Answer Type Questions

1. The plot of the variation of potential difference across a combination of three identical cells in series, *versus* current is shown in figure.

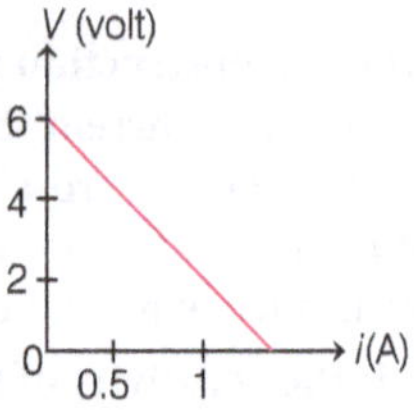

What is the emf and internal resistance of each cell?

2. Two wires of the same material and the same radius have their lengths in the ratio 2: 3. They are connected in parallel to a battery which supplies a current of 15 A. Find the current through the wires. **CBSE 2025**

Or

In the circuit three ideal cells of emf V, V and $2V$ are connected to a resistor of resistance R, a capacitor of capacitance C and another resistor of resistance $2R$ as shown in figure. In the steady state find (i) the potential difference between P and Q and (ii) potential difference across capacitor C. **CBSE 2025**

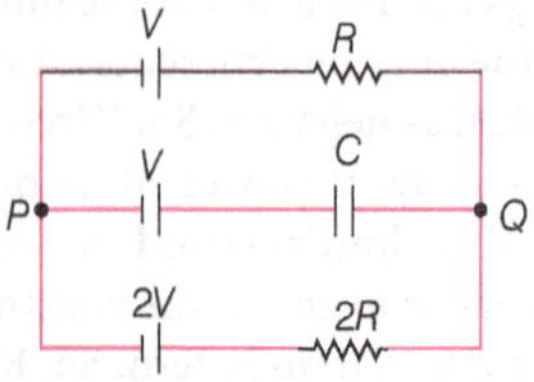

3. How does the mobility of electrons in a conductor change, if the potential difference applied across the conductor is doubled keeping the length and temperature of the conductor constant? **Delhi 2019**

4. When a potential difference is applied across the ends of a conductor, how is the drift velocity of the electrons related to the relaxation time? **Delhi 2019**

5. I-V graph for a metallic wire at two different temperatures T_1 and T_2 is as shown in the figure below. Which of the two temperatures is lower and why?

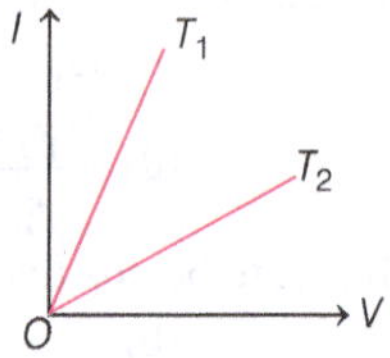

6. A potential difference (V) is applied across a conductor of length L and cross-sectional area A.
How will the drift velocity of electrons and the current density be affected, if another identical conductor of the same material were connected in series with the first conductor? Justify your answers.

7. Explain the statement temperature coefficient of resistance of metal is 4×10^{-3} / °C.

8. The relaxation time τ is nearly independent of applied field E whereas it changes significantly with temperature T. First fact is (in part) responsible for Ohm's law whereas the second fact leads to variation of ρ with temperature. Elaborate why?

9. What is the advantage of using thick metallic strips to join wires in a potentiometer?

Short Answer Type Questions

10. What are the advantages of the null-point method in a Wheatstone bridge? What additional measurements would be required to calculate $R_{unknown}$ by any other method?

11. Given figure shows a plot of current *versus* voltage for two different materials P and Q.

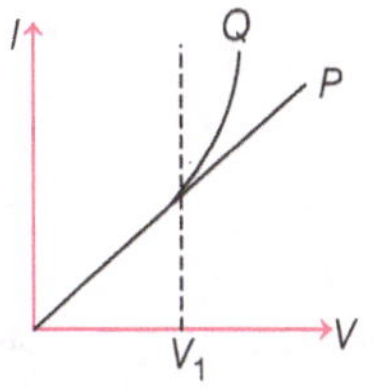

Which of the two materials satisfies Ohm's law? Explain.

12. Two cells of same emf E but internal resistances r_1 and r_2 are connected in series to an external resistor R (see figure). What should be the value of R, so that the potential difference across the terminals of the first cell becomes zero?

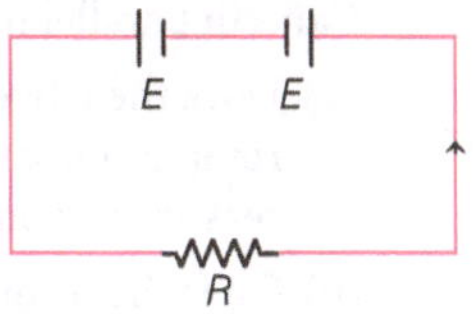

13. (i) A cell of emf E and internal resistance r is connected with a variable external resistance R and a voltmeter showing potential drop V across R. Obtain the relationship between V, E, R and r. **[1½]**

(ii) Draw the shape of the graph showing the variation of terminal voltage V of the cell as a function of current I drawn from it. How one can determine the emf of the cell and its internal resistance from this graph? **CSBE 2025** **[1½]**

14. (i) A wire of resistivity ρ is stretched to three times its length. What will be its new resistivity? **[1]**

(ii) In what manner does the relaxation time in the good conductor change when its temperature increases? **[2]**

15. A metal rod of square cross-sectional area A having length l has current I flowing through it when a potential difference of V volt is applied across its ends (Fig. I). Now, the rod is cut parallel to its length into two identical pieces and joined as shown in Fig. II. What potential difference must be maintained across the length of $2l$, so that the current in the rod is still I ?

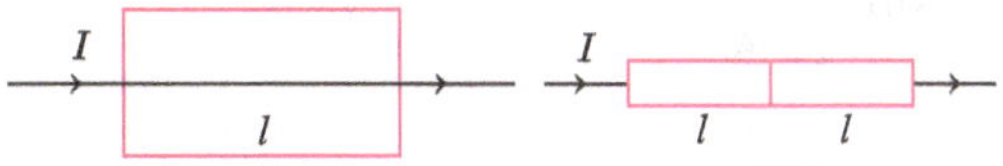

(I) (II)

16. (i) Define resistivity of a conductor. Discuss its dependence on temperature of the conductor and draw a plot of resistivity of copper as a function of temperature. **[1½]**

(ii) (a) A low voltage battery from which high current is required must have low internal resistance. Justify.

(b) A high voltage battery must have a large internal resistance. Justify. **CBSE 2025** **[1½]**

17. Write the expression for the resistivity of a metallic conductor showing its variation over a limited range of temperatures.

18. (i) Car batteries are often rated in unit ampere hours. Does this unit designate the amount of current, energy, power or charge that can be drawn from the battery? Explain. **[1½]**

(ii) Is there some net field inside the cell, when the circuit is closed and a steady current passes through it? Explain. **[1½]**

19. The radius of a conducting wire AB uniformly decreases from its one end A to another end B. It is connected across a battery. How will (i) electric field, (ii) current density, and (iii) mobility of electrons change from end A to end B ? Justify your answer in each case. **CBSE 2024C**

20. A wire of length L_0 has a resistance R_0. It is gradually stretched till its length becomes $2L_0$. **CBSE 2020**

(i) Plot a graph showing variation of its resistance R with its length L during stretching. **[2]**

(ii) What will be its resistance when its length becomes $2L_0$? **[1]**

21. A wire of length L_0 has a resistance R_0. It is gradually stretched till its length becomes $1.5\,L_0$.

(i) Plot a graph showing variation of its resistance R with its length L during stretching. **[2]**

(ii) What will be its resistance when its length becomes $1.5\,L_0$? **[1]**

22. A potential difference V is applied across a conductor of length l and cross-sectional area A. Briefly explain how the current density J in the conductor will be affected if **CBSE 2023**

(i) the potential difference V is doubled. **[1]**

(ii) the conductor were gradually stretched to reduce its cross-sectional area to $\frac{A}{2}$ and then the same potential difference V is applied across it. **[2]**

23. Find the currents flowing through the branches AB and BC in the network shown.

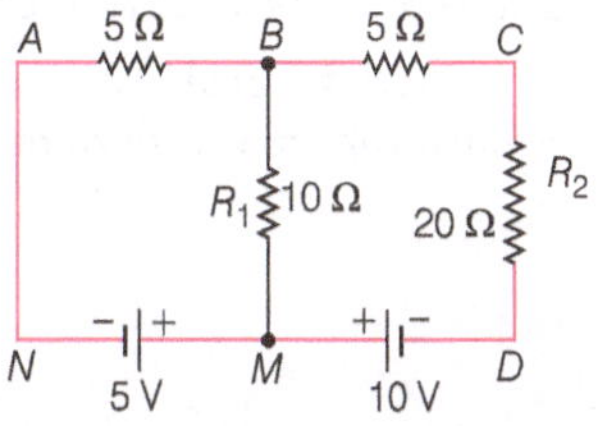

CBSE 2024

Long Answer Type Questions

24. Find the current in branch *BM* in the network shown. **CBSE 2024**

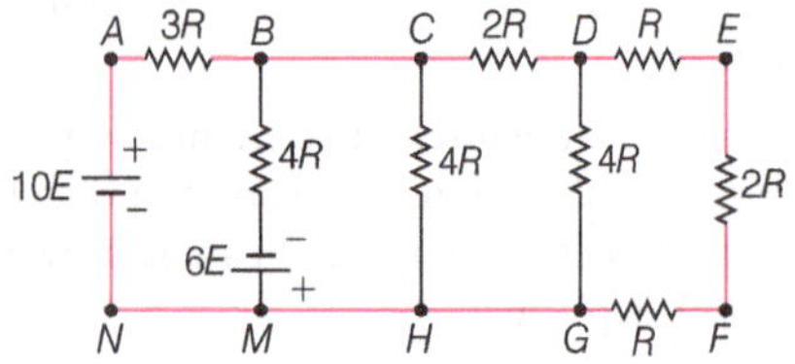

25. (i) Explain how electron mobility changes for a good conductor, when (a) the temperature of the conductor is decreased at constant potential difference and (b) applied potential difference is doubled at constant temperature. **Diksha** **[3]**

(ii) At transition temperature, what happens to the resistivity and conductivity of a superconductor? **[2]**

26. (i) A cell of emf (*E*) and internal resistance (*r*) is connected across a variable load resistance (*R*). Draw plots showing the variation of terminal voltage *V* with (a) *R* and (b) the current (*I*) in the load. **[2½]**

(ii) Three cells each of emf *E* but internal resistances 2*r*, 3*r* and 6*r* are connected in parallel across a resistor *R*. Obtain expressions for (a) current flowing in the circuit and (b) the terminal potential difference across the equivalent cell. **CBSE 2023** **[2½]**

27. In the given network, calculate

(i) effective resistance between points *A* and *M*. **[2½]**

(ii) power supplied by the battery. **CBSE 2024** **[2½]**

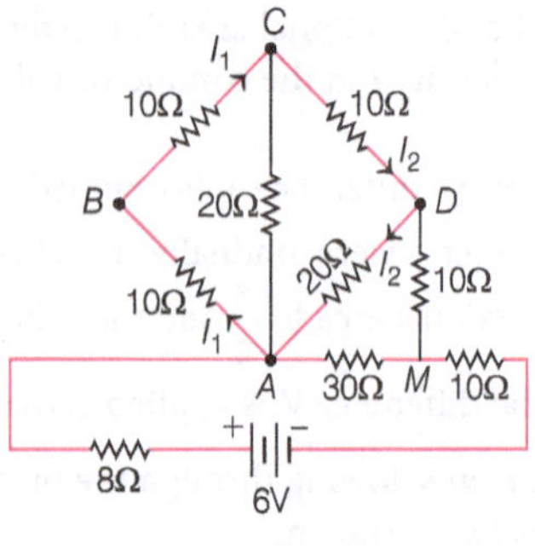

28. Given two resistors R_1 and R_2 are connected in series in circuit 1 and in parallel in circuit 2 across identical batteries of terminal voltage *V* with some internal resistance.

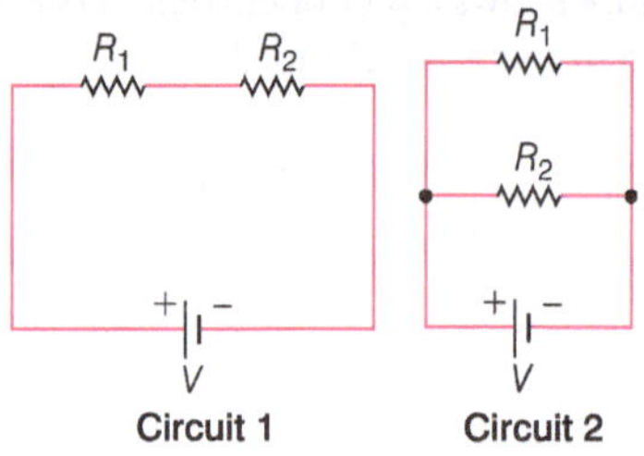

A third unknown resistor R_3 is added in series in circuit 1 and in parallel in circuit 2. **Competency Based Que.**

(i) Does the current in the battery increase, decrease, or remain the same in each of the two circuits? Give a reason for your answer. **[2½]**

(ii) Does the terminal voltage of the battery increase, decrease or remain the same in each of the two circuits? Give a reason for your answer. **[2½]**

29. In an electric circuit shown, a network of resistors is connected across a cell of emf 2V and internal resistance 0.5 Ω.

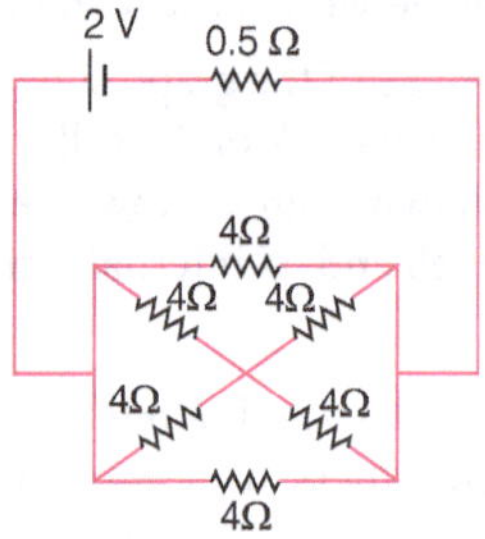

(i) What is the total current drawn from the battery by the circuit? **[3]**

(ii) What is the power consumed by the circuit from the battery? **Competency Based Que.** **[2]**

30. (i) Deduce the relation between current *I* flowing through a conductor and drift velocity v_d of the electrons. **[3]**

(ii) Figure shows a plot of current *I* flowing through the cross-section of a wire *versus* the time *t*. Use the plot to find the charge flowing in t_2 second through the wire. **[2]**

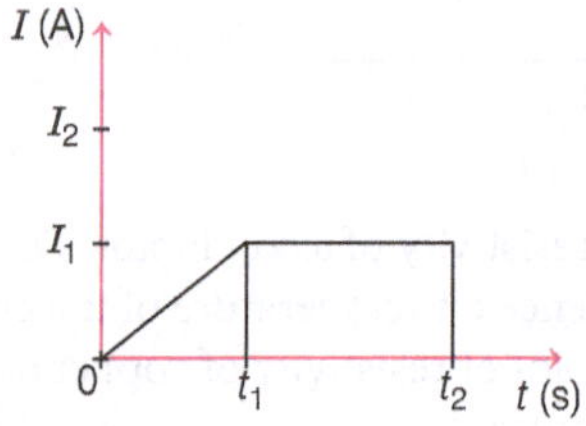

31. A variable resistor R is connected across a cell of emf E and internal resistance r.

(i) Draw the circuit diagram. **[2]**

(ii) Plot the graph showing variation of potential drop across R as function of R. **[2]**

(iii) At what value of R, current in circuit will be maximum? **[1]**

32. (i) Show on a plot, variation of resistivity of (a) a conductor and (b) a typical semiconductor as a function of temperature. **[2]**

(ii) Using the expression for the resistivity in terms of number density and relaxation time between the collisions, (a) explain how resistivity in the case of a conductor increases (b) while it decreases in a semiconductor, with the rise of temperature. **CBSE 2019** **[3]**

33. What do you mean by terminal potential difference of a cell? Under what conditions will the terminal potential difference of a cell be greater than its emf?

34. (i) The emf of a cell is always greater than its terminal voltage. Why? Give reason. **[1]**

(ii) Plot a graph showing the variation of terminal potential difference across a cell of emf E and internal resistance r with current drawn from it. Using this graph, how does one determine the emf of the cell? **[2]**

(iii) Three cells of emf E, $2E$ and $5E$ having internal resistances r, $2r$ and $3r$, variable resistance R as shown in the figure. Find the expression for the current. Plot a graph for variation of current with R. **[2]**

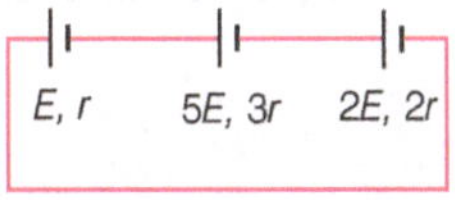

35. Which type of combination of cells is used in the following three cases?

(i) If the external resistance is much larger than the total internal resistance? **[2]**

(ii) If the external resistance is much smaller than the total internal resistance? **[1]**

(iii) If the external resistance is equal to the total internal resistance? **[2]**

36. (i) Explain the term drift velocity of electrons in a conductor. Hence, obtain the expression for the current through a conductor in terms of drift velocity. **[2]**

(ii) Two cells of emfs E_1 and E_2 and internal resistances r_1 and r_2 respectively, are connected in parallel as shown in the figure.

Deduce the expression for the

(a) equivalent emf of the combination

(b) equivalent internal resistance of the combination

(c) potential difference between the points A and B. **[3]**

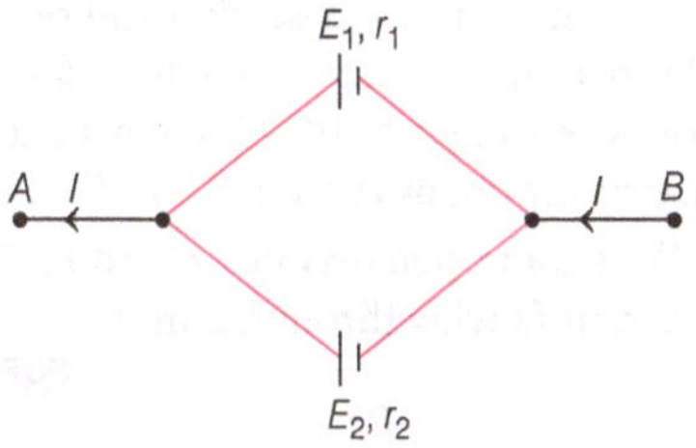

37. With the help of a suitable diagram, explain in brief about the sensitivity of Wheatstone bridge?

38. Two cells of voltages 10V and 2V and internal resistances 10Ω and 5Ω respectively, are connected in parallel with the positive end of 10V battery connected to negative pole of 2V battery (figure). Find the effective voltage and effective resistance of the combination. **NCERT Exemplar**

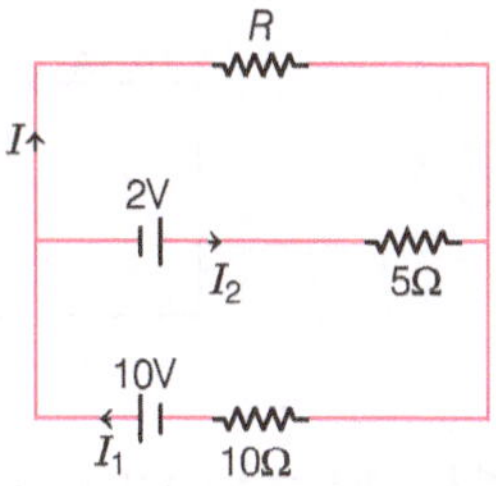

39. (i) Consider circuit in figure. How much energy is absorbed by electrons from the initial state of no current (Ignore thermal motion) to the state of drift velocity ? **[3]**

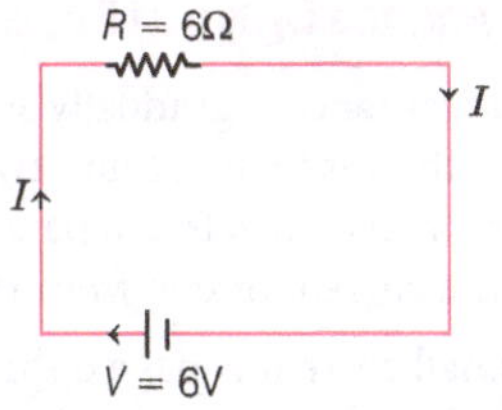

(ii) Electrons give up energy at the rate of RI^2 per second to the thermal energy. What time scale is associated with the power loss for the energy calculated in problem (i)? n = number of electron/volume $= 10^{29}\ /\ \text{m}^3$. Length of circuit $= 10$ cm, cross-section $= A = 1\ \text{mm}^2$. **[2]**

40. (a) Write two limitations of Ohm's law. Plot their I-V characteristics. **[2]**

(b) A heating element connected across a battery of 100 V having an internal resistance of 1 Ω draws an initial current of 10 A at room temperature 20.0 °C which settles after a few seconds to a steady value. What is the power consumed by battery itself after the steady temperature of 320.0 °C is attained?

Temperature coefficient of resistance averaged over the temperature range involved is $3.70 \times 10^{-4}\ °C^{-1}$. **[3]**

Or (a) Using Kirchhoff's laws, obtain the equation of the balanced state in Wheatstone bridge. **[2]**

(b) A wire of uniform cross-section and resistance of $12\ \Omega$ is bent in the shape of circle as shown in the figure. A resistance of $10\ \Omega$ is connected to diametrically opposite ends C and D. A battery of emf 8V is connected between A and B. Determine the current flowing through arm AD.

SQP 2024-25 [3]

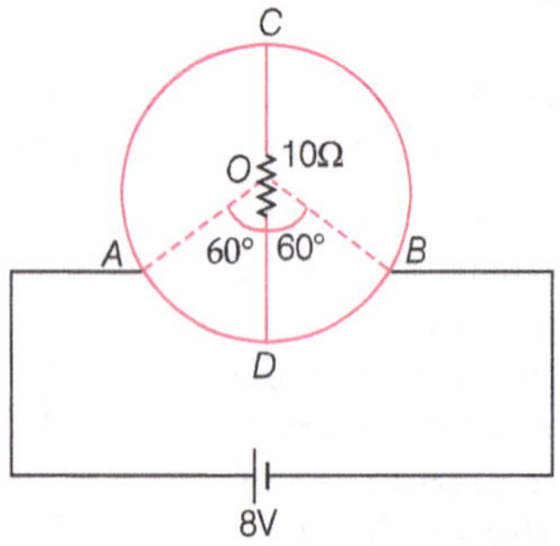

41. Define relaxation time of the free electrons drifting in a conductor. How is it related to the drift velocity of free electrons? Use this relation to deduce the expression for the electrical resistivity of the material. **Diksha**

Numerical Problems

Drift of Electrons and the Origin of Resistivity

42. A wire of 20Ω resistance is gradually stretched to double its original length. It is then cut into two equal parts. These parts are then connected in parallel across a 4.0 V battery. Find the current drawn from the battery.

43. A negligible small current is passed through a wire of length 30 m and uniform cross-section $6 \times 10^{-7}\ m^2$ and its resistance is measured to be 10Ω. What is the resistivity of the material at the temperature of the experiment?

Mobility

44. A semiconductor has electron concentration $0.45 \times 10^{12}\ m^{-3}$ and hole concentration $5 \times 10^{20}\ m^{-3}$. Find its conductivity. (Given, electron mobility $= 0.135\ m^2/Vs$, hole mobility $= 0.048\ m^2/Vs$ and $e = 1.6 \times 10^{-19}$ C)

Cells, EMF and Internal Resistance

45. A storage battery is of emf 8 V and internal resistance 0.5Ω is being charged by DC supply of 120 V using a resistor of $15.5\ \Omega$.

(i) Draw the circuit diagram.

(ii) Calculate the potential difference across the battery.

(iii) What is the purpose of having series resistance in this circuit?

46. When two identical batteries of internal resistance $1\ \Omega$ each are connected in series across a resistor R, the rate of heat produced is H_1. When the same batteries are connected in parallel across R, the rate of heat produced is H_2. If $H_1 = 2.25 H_2$, then what will be the value of R?

47. Write any two factors on which internal resistance of a cell depends. The reading on a high resistance voltmeter when a cell is connected across it is 2.2 V. When the terminals of the cell are also connected to a resistance of $5\ \Omega$ as shown in the figure, the voltmeter reading drops to 1.8 V. Find the internal resistance of the cell.

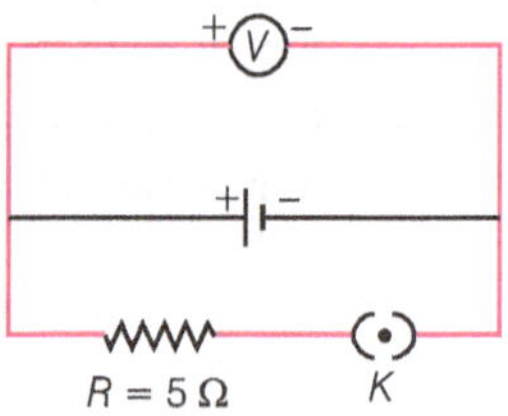

48. The emf of a battery is 2 V and its internal resistance is $2\ \Omega$. Its potential difference is measured by a voltmeter of resistance $998\ \Omega$. Calculate the percentage error in the reading of emf shown by the voltmeter.

Kirchhoff's Law

49. Using Kirchhoff's rules, calculate the current through the $40\ \Omega$ and $20\ \Omega$ resistors in the following circuit.

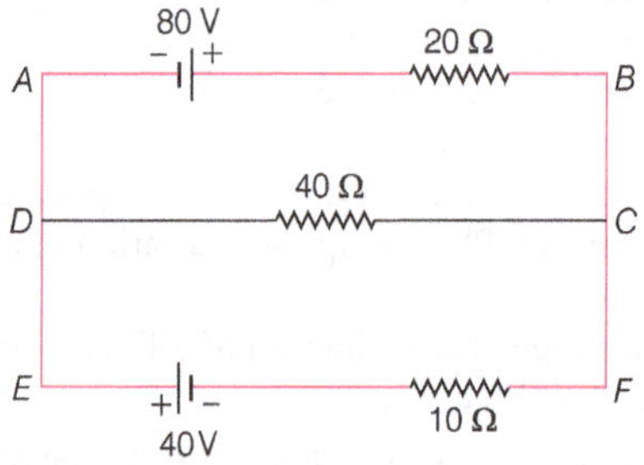

Wheatstone Bridge

50. For what value of unknown resistance y, the potential difference between A and B is zero in the arrangement as shown in figure given below?

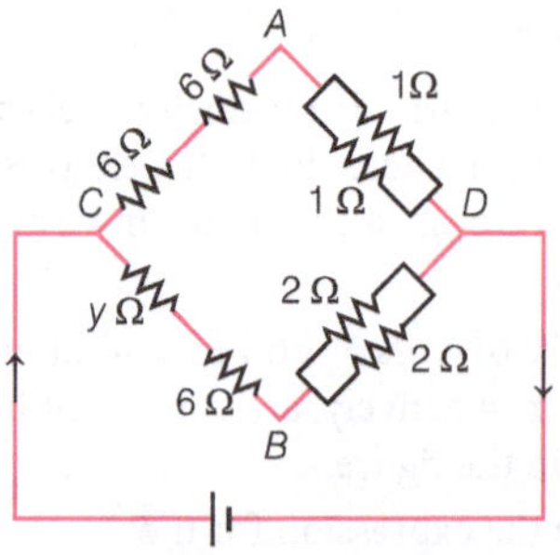

Hints & Solutions

Objective Type Questions

1. (c) When a wire is stretched it's volume remains constant

$$\because \qquad R = \rho \frac{L}{A}$$

$$R = \rho \frac{V}{A^2} = \rho \frac{V}{\pi^2 r^4}$$

$$R \propto \frac{1}{r^4}$$

$$\frac{R'}{R} = \left(\frac{r}{r'}\right)^4 = \left(\frac{r'}{r}\right)^{-4}$$

$$\because \qquad \frac{r'}{r} = \frac{r\left(1 - \frac{1}{100}\right)}{r}$$

$$\text{So, } \frac{R'}{R} = \left(1 - \frac{1}{100}\right)^{-4} \approx 1 + \frac{4}{100}$$

$$\frac{R'}{R} - 1 = \frac{4}{100}$$

$$\left(\frac{R' - R}{R}\right) \times 100 = \frac{4}{1000} \times 100 = 0.4\%$$

2. (c)

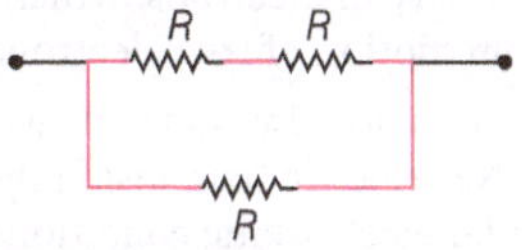

The net resistance in the circuit for the figure shown is

$$R_{\text{net}} = \frac{2R \times R}{2R + R} = \frac{2R}{3}$$

3. (b) Total emf $= 3 \times 4 = 12$V

Total resistance $= 6 + 3r$

Current in the circuit = 2A

Using Ohm's law,

$$2 = 12/(6 + 3r)$$
$$2(6 + 3r) = 12$$
$$12 + 6r = 12$$
$$6r = 12 - 12 = 0$$
$$r = 0/6 = 0$$

4. (d) $J = \frac{I}{A} = \frac{neAv_d}{A} = nev_d \qquad (\because I = nAev_d)$

5. (b) $\because I = neAv_d \qquad \dots \text{(i)}$

and $I = \frac{V}{R}$

$$I = \frac{E \times l}{R} \qquad (\because V = E \times l)$$

From Eq. (i), we get

$$\frac{E \times l}{R} = neAv_d$$

$$E \propto v_d$$

6. (b) $Q = It = (8 \times 10^{-3})(10) = 8 \times 10^{-2}$ C

We know, $Q = ne$

$$\Rightarrow \qquad n = \frac{Q}{e} = \frac{8 \times 10^{-2}}{1.6 \times 10^{-19}} = 5 \times 10^{17}$$

7. (a) Thicker wire will produce more heat.

8. (d) The resistance of copper wire increases with temperature, which causes a drop in conductivity, while the resistance of silicon wire reduces with temperature, which cause increase in conductivity.

9. (b) Here, current $(I) = 2$A and resistance $(R) = 10\,\Omega$

Power, $P = I^2R = (2)^2 \times 10 = 40$

Energy $= Pt = 40 \times 0.5 \times 60 \times 60 = 72000$ J = 72 kJ

10. (b) **For bulb,**

$$P = \frac{V^2}{R}$$

$$\Rightarrow \qquad R = \frac{V^2}{P} = \frac{(220)^2}{44} = \frac{48400}{44} = 1100\,\Omega$$

When connected to 220 V,

$$I = \frac{V}{R} = \frac{220}{1100} = 0.2 \text{ A}$$

For fan,

$$P = \frac{V^2}{R} \Rightarrow R = \frac{V^2}{P} = \frac{12100}{60} = 201.67\,\Omega$$

When connected to 220 V,

$$I = \frac{V}{R} = \frac{220}{201.67} = 1.09 \text{ A}$$

Now, comparison :

Resistance The light bulb has resistance of 1100 Ω which is greater than the table fan's resistance which is 201.67 Ω.

Current The light bulb draws 0.2 A which is smaller than the table fan's current drawn which is 1.09 A.

11. (c)

12. (c) Given, $R = 10\,\Omega$

$$V = 6\text{V}$$

We know, $P = \frac{V^2}{R} = \frac{(6)^2}{10} = \frac{36}{10} = 3.6$ W

13. (d)

14. (c) We know, $I = \frac{dq}{dt}$

$$q = \int_{t_1}^{t_2} I\,dt = \int_0^3 6t\,dt = 6\left[\frac{t^2}{2}\right]_0^3 = 3 \times 9 = 27 \text{ mC}$$

15. (*b*) 15 μC from smaller to bigger sphere.

16. (*a*) 17. (*c*)

18. (*a*)

19. (*a*) Emf of the cell, $E = 12$ V

Internal resistance, $r = 0.5\Omega$

External resistance, $R = 9.5\,\Omega$

Terminal voltage,

$$V = E\left(\frac{R}{R+r}\right)$$

$$V = 12\left(\frac{9.5}{9.5+0.5}\right)$$

$$V = 11.4\text{V}$$

The ratio will be

$$\frac{E}{V} = \frac{12}{11.4} = 1.05$$

20. (*b*)

21. (*c*)

22. (*b*) We know that, $J = \sigma E$

where, J = current density, σ = conductivity and E = electric field.

Also resistivity, $\rho = \frac{1}{\sigma}$

$\therefore \quad \frac{J}{\sigma} = E$

$\Rightarrow \quad J\rho = E$

Therefore, $C = \rho$

23. (*c*) Emf of the 5 identical cells of emf E are connected in series. Then, the net emf of the combination should be $5E$. But, one of them is wrongly connected, i.e. with its polarity reversed. This cell will cancel the emf of another cell.

Thus, equivalent number of cells in the combination

$$= E + E + E + E - E = 3E$$

Thus, the equivalent emf can be calcualted as

$$E_{eq} = 4E - E = 3E$$

24. (*b*) $A \to 2, B \to 1, C \to 4, D \to 3$

25. (*a*) $A \to 4, B \to 3, C \to 2, D \to 1$

26. (*c*) This is balanced Wheatstone bridge, so all resistance are not in parallel.

27. (*d*) As temperature of conducting wire increases, collison becomes more frequent, so average time of collison decreases. More collison means less drift velocity.

28. (*a*) With increase in temperature, average speed of the electrons, which acts as the carriers of current increases, resulting in more frequent collisions. The average time of collisions τ, thus decreases with temperature.

29. (*a*) Charge carriers do not move with acceleration, but with a steady drift velocity. This is because of the collisions with ions and atoms during transit.

30. (*d*) Bending will not increase the resistance of the conducting wire. Also, drift velocity of electron is independent of bending of conductor.

31. (*b*) Increasing the temperature of a conductor, the kinetic energy of free electrons increases.
On account of this, they collide more frequently with each other (and with the ions of the conductor) and consequently their drift velocity decreases.

On increasing temperature, conducitvity of wire decreases because of the same reason mentioned above but the statement itself is not the correct explanations of Assertion.

32. (*a*) Manganin and constantan have high resistivity and very low temperature coefficient of resistance.

33. (*c*) To increase the range of an ammeter, a shunt (a small resistance) is connected in parallel with the ammeter's coil. This shunt diverts a portion of the total current around the coil, allowing the device to measure larger currents without increasing its internal resistance.

34. (*a*) No, all the free electrons do not move in the same direction. The net movement of the electrons is from lower to higher potential. As a result, there is definite small drift velocity of electrons, which is superimposed on the random motion of free electrons.

35. (*c*) A conductor is not always in an electrostatic equilibrium. Net electric field inside the conductor is zero only under electrostatic conditions, i.e. charges are stationary. While in case of a conductor, free charges are present and they move constantly if an electric field exists inside.

36. (*c*) Since, current density is given as

$$J = \sigma E$$

and in an isolated conductor placed in a uniform electric field, $E = 0$.

So, $J = 0$ and current is zero.

Initially, when the conductor is placed in the electric field, electrons will move until they reach a state where the internal electric field cancels out the external field. Once equilibrium is reached, there will be no further motion of electrons.

37. (i) (*c*) Net current,

$$I = \frac{\text{Net emf}}{\text{Total resistance}} = \frac{\varepsilon_1 + \varepsilon_2}{r_1 + r_2}$$

(ii) (*d*) Equivalent emf of battery

$$\varepsilon = V_A - V_B = \varepsilon_1 - Ir_1$$

$$= \varepsilon_1 - \left(\frac{\varepsilon_1 + \varepsilon_2}{r_1 + r_2}\right)r_1$$

$$= \frac{(\varepsilon_1 r_2 - \varepsilon_2 r_1)}{(r_1 + r_2)}$$

(iii) (*d*) Terminal *A* is positive, if $V_A > V_B$ or $V_A - V_B > 0$

or $(\varepsilon_1 r_2 - \varepsilon_2 r_1) > 0$ or $\varepsilon_1 r_2 > \varepsilon_2 r_1$

(iv) (*a*) Since, r_1 and r_2 are in series, so resultant resistance is $r = r_1 + r_2$

(v) (*c*) **Loop Rule** The algebraic sum of changes in potential around any closed loop involving resistors and cells in the loop is zero. This rule is also obvious, since electric potential is dependent on the location of the point. Thus, starting with any point, if we come back to the same point, the total change must be zero. In a closed loop, we do come back to the starting point and hence the rule. $\Sigma Ir = \Sigma V$

38. (i) (*b*), (ii) (*c*), (iii) (*b*), (iv) (*c*)

39. (i) The dimensional formula of resistance is given by

$$R = \frac{V}{I} = \frac{W}{qI}$$

$$\therefore \quad [R] = \frac{[ML^2T^{-2}]}{[AT]\,[A]} = [ML^2T^{-3}A^{-2}]$$

(ii) The *V versus I* graph for an ohmic conductor is given by a straight line.

(iii) The resistance of a conductor depends on following factors

(a) It is directly proportional to length of the conductor.

(b) It is inversely proportional to the area of cross-section of the conductor.

(iv) The resistance of a condutor is given by

$$R = \rho \cdot \frac{l}{A} = \rho \frac{l^2}{V} \Rightarrow R \propto l^2$$

$\therefore$ If length of the conductor is increased by two times, then its resistance increases by four times.

40. (i) Kirchhoff's first rule is based on the conservation of charge principle.

(ii) Kirchhoff's second rule is based on the conservation of energy principle.

(iii) The given circuit is

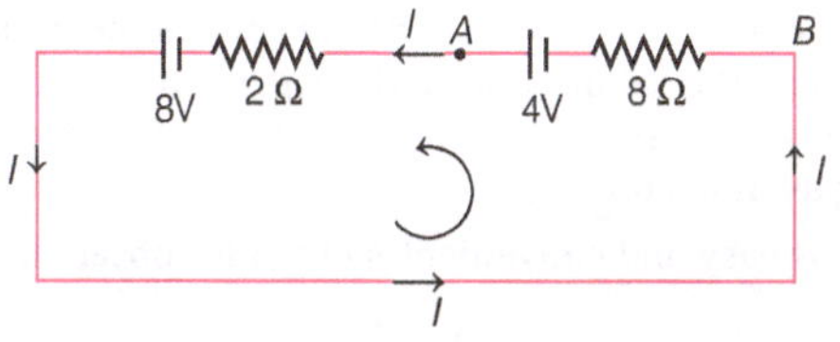

Applying Kirchhoff's second rule,

$$\Sigma \Delta V = 0$$

$$\Rightarrow \quad 8 - 8I + 4 - 2I = 0$$

$$I = 1.2 \text{ A}$$

$\therefore$ Potential difference between points *A* and *B* is

$$V_{AB} = 4 + 8I = 4 + 8 \times 1.2 = 13.6$$

(iv) The given circuit is

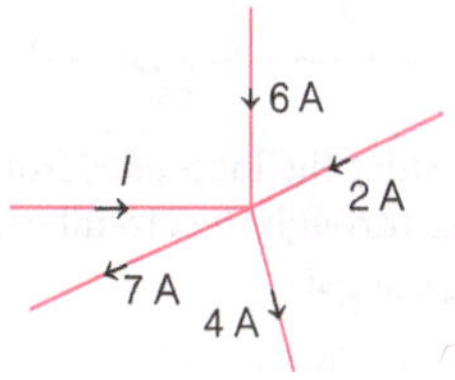

From Kirchhoff's junction rule,

$$\Sigma I_0 = 0$$

$$\Rightarrow \quad I + 6 + 2 - 7 - 4 = 0$$

$$\therefore \quad I = 3\text{A}$$

Subjective Questions

1. Three identical cells are connected in series,

$E' = E_1 + E_2 + E_3 = 3E = 6$ V, when *I* is zero.

Hence, $E = 2$ V

The internal resistance of each cell, $Ir = E - V$

or $r = \frac{E - V}{I} = \frac{2 - 0}{1} = 2\Omega$

2. Resistance of the 1st wire, $R_1 = \frac{\rho \times 2l}{A} = 2R$

Resistance of the 2nd wire, $R_2 = \frac{\rho \times 3l}{A} = 3R$

They are connected in parallel as shown in the circuit below.

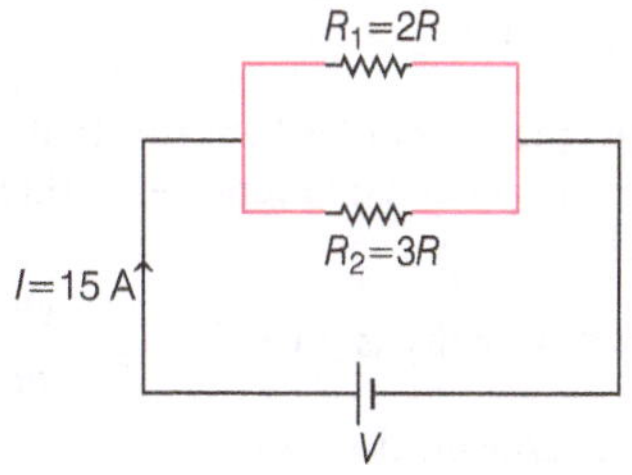

Let the voltage across the circuit be *V* volts.

Current $I = 15$A

Equivalent resistance, $R_{eq} = \frac{2R \times 3R}{2R + 3R} = \frac{6R}{5}$

$$\therefore \quad V = I \times R_{eq} = 15 \times \frac{6R}{5} = 18\,R$$

$\therefore$ Current through $R_1 = \frac{V}{2R} = \frac{18R}{2R} = 9\text{A}$

Current through $R_2 = \frac{V}{3R} = \frac{18R}{3R} = 6\text{A}$

Or

The circuit is redrawn as shown in the figure below.

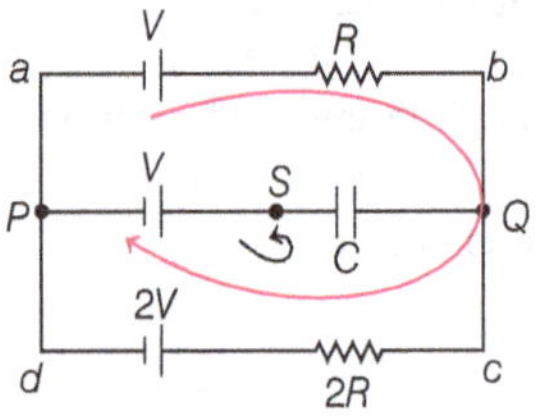

Let us first consider the loop *abcd* from which the net current flowing through the circuit can be found.

Applying KVL, we get

$$V + IR + 2IR - 2V = 0$$

$$\Rightarrow \quad I = \frac{V}{3R}$$

Now, considering loop *dcPQ*, and applying KVL

$$2V + (V_Q - V_P) - I \times 2R = 0$$

$$\Rightarrow \quad V_P - V_Q = V_{PQ}$$

$$= 2V - I \times 2R = 2V - \frac{V}{3R} \times 2R$$

$$\Rightarrow \quad V_{PQ} = \frac{4V}{3}$$

Again looking into the wire *PQ*, we see that

$$V_{PS} = V, V_{SQ} = V_C = V_{PQ} - V_{PS} = \frac{4}{3}V - V = \frac{V}{3}$$

3. The mobility of electrons in a conductor is given by

$$\mu = \frac{e\tau}{m}$$

where, e = charge on electron,

m = mass of electron

and τ = relaxation time.

Also, $\tau \propto \frac{1}{T}$

But here temperature (T) is kept constant. As mobility is independent of potential difference, so there is no change in it.

4. Average drift velocity is given by $v_d = \frac{eE}{m}\tau$

where, e = charge on electron,

m = mass of electron,

E = electric potential or field across conductor

and τ = relaxation time.

5. Consider the figure.

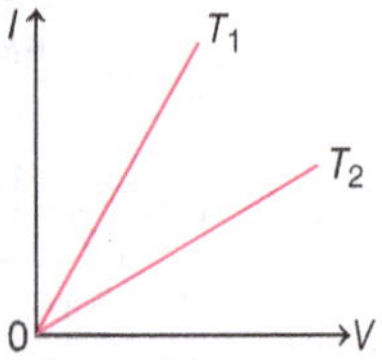

Since, slope of 1 > slope of 2

$$I_1 / V_1 > \frac{I_2}{V_2}$$

$$\Rightarrow \quad V_2 / I_2 > V_1 / I_1$$

$$\therefore \quad R_2 > R_1 \qquad (\because V/I = R)$$

Also, we know that resistance is directly proportional to the temperature.

Therefore, $T_2 > T_1$.

6. The drift velocity when a potential difference (V) is applied to a single conductor of length L,

$$v_d = \frac{e\tau}{m}E = \frac{e\tau}{m}\cdot\frac{V}{L} \qquad \left[\because E = \frac{V}{L}\right]$$

$$\therefore \quad v_d \propto \frac{1}{L}$$

Also, $J = nev_d$

$\Rightarrow$ $J \propto v_d$

When a same conductor is connected in series with first conductor, then $L' = 2L$

$$\therefore \quad \frac{v'_d}{v_d} = \frac{L}{L'} = \frac{L}{2L}$$

$$\therefore \quad v'_d = \frac{v_d}{2}$$

Hence, drift velocity as well as current density will become half of original value.

7. As given temperature coefficient of resistance of a metal is 4×10^{-3}/°C, it represents the increase in resistance by $4 \times 10^{-3}\,\Omega$ for rise of temperature by unit degree celsius (1°C).

8. Relaxation time is inversely proportional to the velocities of electrons and ions. The applied electric field produces the insignificant change in velocities of electrons at the order of 1mm/s, whereas the change in temperature (T), affects velocities at the order of 10^2 m/s.

This decreases the relaxation time considerably in metals and consequently resistivity of metal or conductor increases as

$$\rho = \frac{1}{\sigma} = \frac{m}{ne^2\tau}$$

9. In a potentiometer, the thick metallic strips are used as they have negligible resistance and need not to be counted in the length l_1 of the null point of potentiometer.

10. The advantage of null-point method in a Wheatstone bridge is that the resistance of galvanometer does not affect the balance point, there is no need to determine current in resistances and the internal resistance of a galvanometer.

It is easy and convenient method for observer.

The $R_{unknown}$ can be calculated applying Kirchhoff's rules to the circuit. We would need additional accurate measurement of all the currents in resistances and galvanometer and internal resistance of the galvanometer.

11. The plot of V *versus* I is a straight line for materials that obey Ohm's law. So, from the figure, material P obeys Ohm's law.

12. Applying Ohm's law,
Effective resistance $= R + r_1 + r_2$ and effective emf of two cells $= E + E = 2E$, so the electric current is given by

$$I = \frac{E + E}{R + r_1 + r_2}$$

The potential difference across the terminals of the first cell and putting it equal to zero.

$$V_1 = E - Ir_1$$

$$E - \left(\frac{2E}{r_1 + r_2 + R}\right) r_1 = 0$$

or $$E = \frac{2Er_1}{r_1 + r_2 + R}$$

$\Rightarrow$ $$1 = \frac{2r_1}{r_1 + r_2 + R}$$

$$r_1 + r_2 + R = 2r_1$$

$\Rightarrow$ $$R = r_1 - r_2$$

This is the required relation.

13. (i) Refer to theory on page 97 (Relation between Terminal Potential Difference, emf of a cell and Internal Resistance of a cell).

(ii) From the definition of terminal potential difference,

$$V = E - I_r$$

where, E is the emf of the cell, I is the current drawn and r is the internal resistance of the cell.

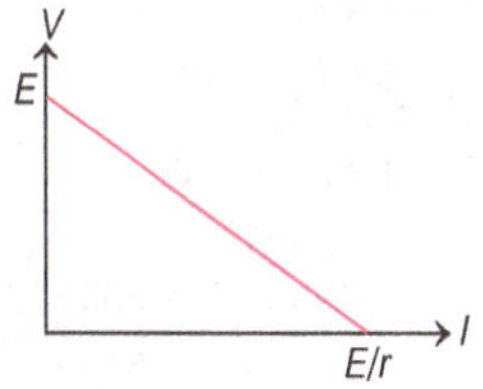

Slope of the curve is $-r$.

when current drawn is zero, then the terminal voltage becomes equal to the emf of the cell.

Again when the terminal voltage becomes zero, then the internal resistance is given by the ratio of the emf of the cell to the current drawn.

14. (i) Resistivity is a property of the material, it does not depend on the dimensions of the wire. Thus, when the wire is stretched, then its resistivity remains same.

(ii) We know that, $R = \dfrac{ml}{ne^2\tau A}$

or relaxation time, $\tau = \dfrac{ml}{ne^2RA}$

If temperature increases, the resistance (R) of a good conductor increases and hence relaxation time decreases.

15. From Ohm's law, we have

$$V = IR$$

$\Rightarrow$ $$V = I\rho\frac{l}{A} \qquad \left[\because R = \rho\frac{l}{A}\right] \quad ...(i)$$

When the rod is cut parallel and rejoined by length, the length of the conductor becomes $2l$, whereas the area decreases to $\dfrac{A}{2}$. If the current remains the same, then the potential changes as

$$V' = I\rho\frac{2l}{A/2}$$

$$= 4 \times I\rho\frac{l}{A} = 4V \qquad \text{[using Eq. (i)]}$$

The new potential applied across the metal rod will be four times the original potential (V).

16. (i) Resistivity is defined as the electrical resistance of a conductor of unit cross-section area and unit length.

The resistivity variation with temperature

$$\rho_T = \rho_0[1 + \alpha(T - T_0)]$$

For the conductor, the resistivity increases with increasing temperature. As the temperature increases, metal atoms vibrate which obstructs the flow of electric current.

Plot of resistivity of copper as a function of temperature is shown below.

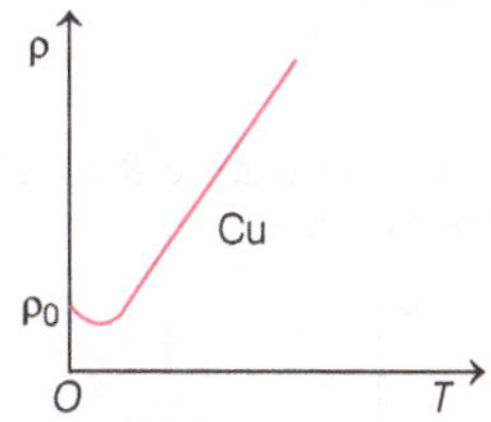

(ii) (a) If the internal resistance is high, then current drawn for external circuit will be minimum. Therefore, for the low voltage battery internal resistance should be minimum. So, we can drawn high current from the cell.

Mathematically

$$I = \frac{E}{R + r}$$

(b) For the safe value of current to pass through a circuit, a high voltage battery must have a large internal resistance. So, if the circuit is accidentally shorted, then the current drawn will not exceed safety limits.

17. Refer to text on page 93.

18. (i) An ampere hours is the unit of charge as ampere is the unit of current and hours is the unit of time.

Charge = Current × Time

(ii) Yes, there is some electric field inside a cell from positive end of the battery to negative end when the circuit is closed. This electric field is produced due to electrode potential between positive and negative terminals.

19. Given, the radius of a conducting wire AB uniformly decreases from its one end A to another end B.

(i) $\because$ Electric field from, $J = \sigma E \Rightarrow E = \frac{\tau}{\sigma}$

and $$J = \frac{I}{A}$$

$$E = \frac{I}{A\sigma}$$

$$\Rightarrow \quad E \propto \frac{1}{A}$$

Since, the area gradually decreases, so the field increases from A to B.

(ii) Current density (J)

$$J = \frac{I}{A}$$

(iii) The mobility of elecron (μ) is an intrinsic property of the material and is not affected by the change in wire geometry.

So, mobility remains constant from A to B.

20. (i) Initially, the resistance R_0 of a wire of length L_0 is given by

$$R_0 = \rho \frac{L_0}{A_0} \quad \text{...(i)}$$

$$\Rightarrow \quad R_0 \propto L_0$$

The variation of resistance R with length L during stretching is shown as

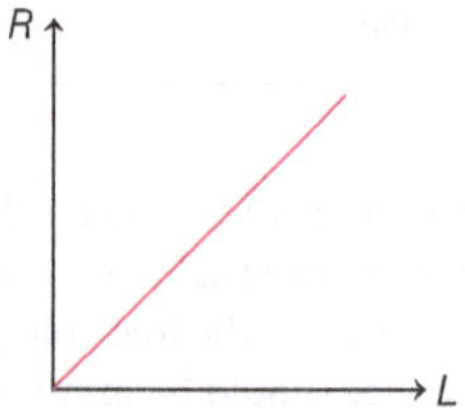

(ii) When a wire is stretched to $2L_0$, the area of wire becomes $\frac{A_0}{2}$. So, the new resistance will be

$$R = \frac{\rho 2L_0}{A_0/2} = 4\rho \frac{L_0}{A_0} = 4R_0 \quad \text{[using Eq. (i)]}$$

$\therefore$ The resistance of wire becomes 4 times of previous.

21. (i) Refer to the (i) part of pervious solution.

(ii) 2.25 R_0; Refer to (ii) part of previous solution.

22. (i) The current density in a conductor is

$$J = n e v_d = ne \cdot \frac{e\tau}{m} E = ne \cdot \frac{e\tau}{m} \cdot \frac{V}{l}$$

$$\Rightarrow \quad J \propto V$$

Hence, when V is doubled, then current density will be also doubled.

(ii) As, $\quad J \propto \frac{1}{l}$

When the conductor is stretched, then volume remains constant.

i.e. $\quad A_1 l_1 = A_2 l_2$

$$\Rightarrow \quad A \cdot l_1 = \frac{A}{2} \cdot l_2$$

$$\therefore \quad l_2 = 2l_1$$

$$\therefore \quad \frac{J_2}{J_1} = \frac{l_1}{l_2} = \frac{l_1}{2l_1} \Rightarrow J_2 = \frac{J_1}{2}$$

Hence, the current density becomes half of its original value.

23.

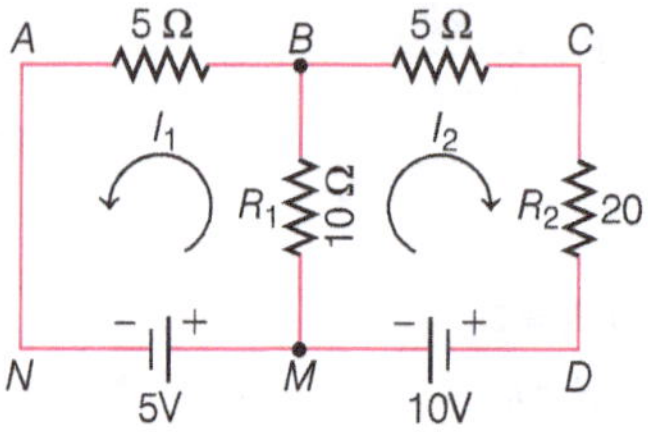

Applying Kirchhoff's second law in mesh $ANMBA$,

$$(I_1 + I_2)10 + 5(I_1) - 5 = 0$$

$$\Rightarrow \quad 15I_1 + 10I_2 = 5 \quad \text{...(i)}$$

Applying Kirchhoff''s second law in mesh $BCDMB$,

$$-10(I_1 + I_2) - 5I_2 - 20I_2 + 10 = 0$$

$$\Rightarrow \quad 35I_2 + 10I_1 = 10 \quad \text{... (ii)}$$

Solving Eqs. (i) and (ii), we get (Eq. (i) × 10 − Eq. (ii) × 15)

$$\Rightarrow \quad 150I_1 + 100I_2 = 50$$

$$\underline{\underset{-}{}150I_1 \underset{-}{+} 525I_2 \underset{-}{=} 150}$$

$$-425I_2 = -100$$

$$I_2 = 0.23 \text{ A}$$

From Eq. (i) $I_1 = \frac{5 - 10\, I_2}{15} = \frac{5 - 2.35}{15} = 0.17$ A

Thus, $I_1 = 0.17$ A and $I_2 = 0.23$A in the branch AB and BC, respectively.

24. In the network, resistors R, $2R$ and R in the $DEFG$ branch are in series combination,

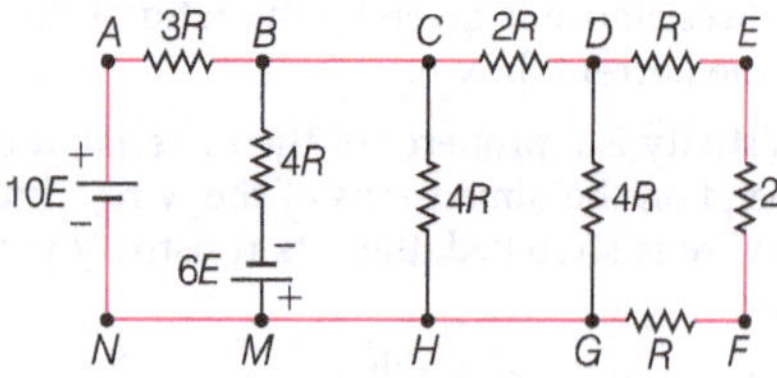

$\therefore \quad R' = R + 2R + R = 4R$

and R' and $4R$ are in parallel combination,

$$R'' = \frac{4R \times 4R}{8R} = \frac{16R^2}{8R} = 2R$$

$\Rightarrow R''$ and $2R$ are in series combination,

$$R''' = R'' + 2R = 2R + 2R = 4R$$

and R''' and $4R$ are in parallel combination,

$$r = \frac{R''' \times 4R}{R''' + 4R} = \frac{4R \times 4R}{4R + 4R} = \frac{16R^2}{8R} = 2R$$

Simplified network of resistors will be

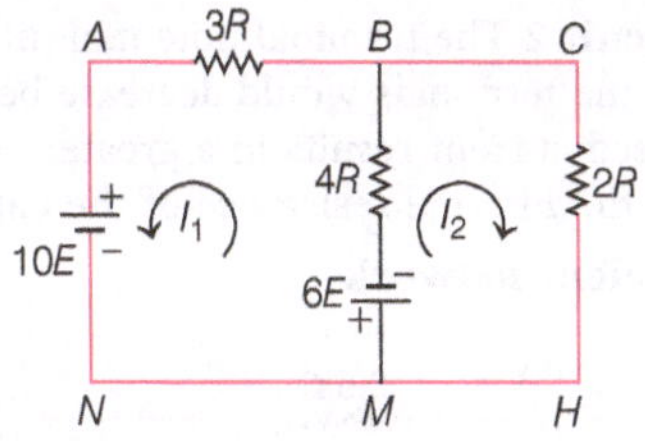

In loop $NMBAN$,

$$-6E - 4R(I_1 + I_2) - 3RI_1 - 10E = 0$$

$$4RI_2 + 7RI_1 = -16E \quad \text{...(i)}$$

In loop $BCHMB$,

$$-6E - 4R(I_1 + I_2) - 2RI_2 = 0$$

$$4RI_1 + 6RI_2 = -6E \quad \text{...(ii)}$$

$7 \times$ Eq. (ii) $- 4 \times$ Eq. (i), we get

$$(28RI_1 + 42RI_2) - (28RI_1 + 16RI_2) = -42E - (-64E)$$

$$\Rightarrow \quad 42RI_2 - 16RI_2 = -42E + 64E$$

$$\Rightarrow \quad 26RI_2 = 22E$$

$$I_2 = \frac{22E}{26R} = 0.84\frac{E}{R}$$

Put this value of I_2 in Eq. (ii), we get

$$4RI_1 = -6E - 6R\left(\frac{22E}{26R}\right)$$

$$= -6E\left(1 + \frac{22}{26}\right)$$

$$= -6E \times \frac{48}{26} = -11.07E$$

$$I_1 = \frac{-11.07}{4}\frac{E}{R} = -2.76\frac{E}{R}$$

Hence, current in the branch BM is

$$I = I_1 + I_2$$

$$= -2.76\frac{E}{R} + 0.84\frac{E}{R} = -1.92\frac{E}{R}$$

Negative sign indicates direction of current is opposite, it flows from M to B in the branch BM.

25. (i) Electron mobility in conductor is given by

$$\mu = \frac{v_d}{E} = \frac{\left(\frac{eE\tau}{m}\right)}{E} = \frac{e\tau}{m}$$

(a) When temperature of the conductor decreases, the relaxation time τ of the electrons in the conductor increases, so mobility μ increases.

(b) Mobility μ is independent of applied potential difference.

(ii) For the superconductors, at transition temperature, the resistivity becomes zero and conductivity becomes infinity.

26. (i) $\because$ Terminal voltage, $V = E - ir$ ... (i)

and current, $i = \frac{E}{R + r}$

So, $V = E - \frac{Er}{R + r} = \frac{ER}{R + r}$

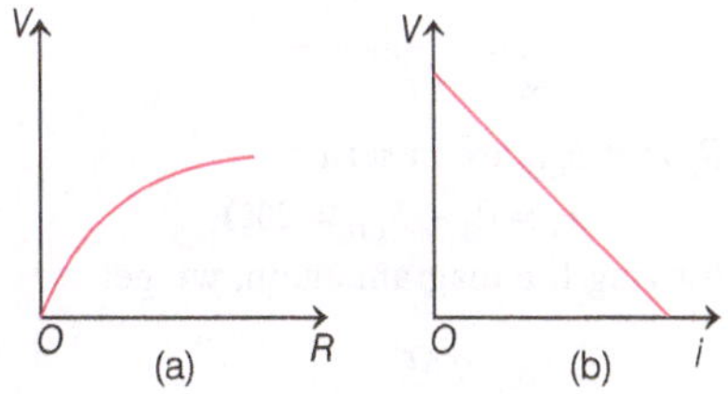

(ii)

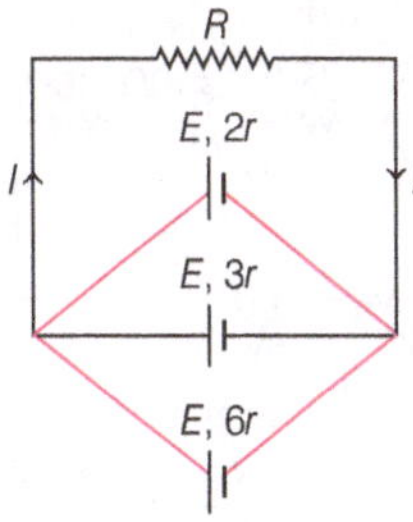

(a) Equivalent resistance across the cells is given by

$$\frac{1}{r_{eq}} = \frac{1}{2r} + \frac{1}{3r} + \frac{1}{6r}$$

$$\therefore \quad r_{eq} = r, \; E_{eq} = \frac{\frac{E}{2r} + \frac{E}{3r} + \frac{E}{6r}}{\frac{1}{2r} + \frac{1}{3r} + \frac{1}{6r}} = E$$

$\therefore$ Current through the circuit, $I = \frac{E_{eq}}{R + r_{eq}} = \frac{E}{R + r}$

(b) The terminal potential difference across the equivalent cell is $V = IR = \frac{E \cdot R}{R + r}$

27. (i)

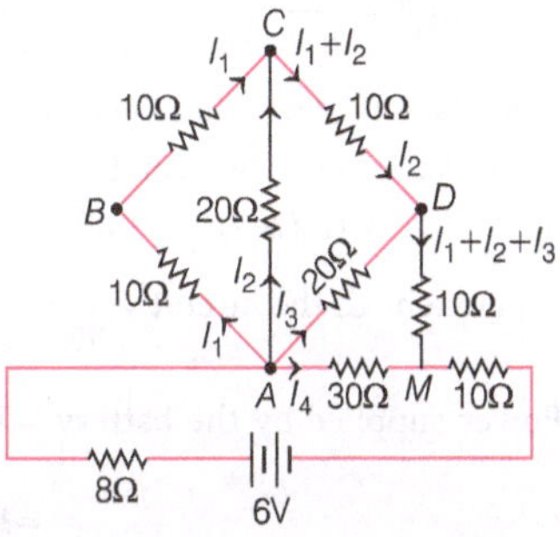

R_{AB} and R_{BC} are in series combination, then equivalent resistance,

$$R_1 = R_{AB} + R_{BC} = 10\Omega + 10\Omega = 20\Omega$$

$\Rightarrow R_1$ and R_{AC} are in parallel combination, then equivalent resistance,

$$R_2 = \frac{R_1 \times R_{AC}}{R_1 + R_{AC}} = \frac{20 \times 20}{40} = 10\Omega$$

Redrawing the diagram, we get

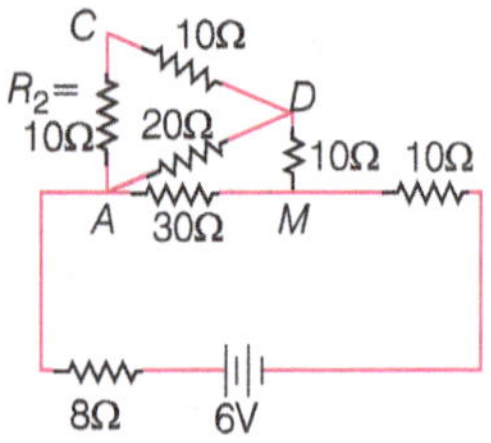

$\Rightarrow R_2$ and R_{CD} are in series.

$\therefore \quad R_3 = R_2 + R_{CD} = 20\Omega$

Redrawing the diagram again, we get

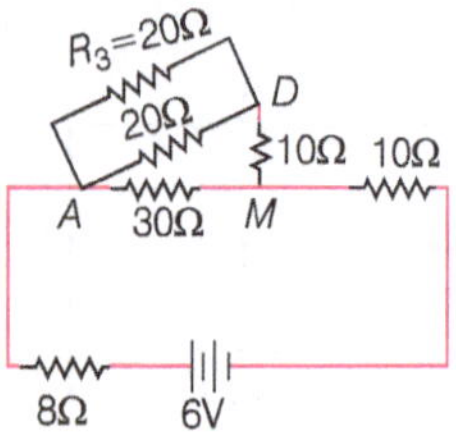

$\Rightarrow R_3$ and R_{AD} are in parallel.

$$\therefore \quad R_4 = \frac{R_3 \times R_{AD}}{R_3 + R_{AD}} = \frac{20 \times 20}{20 + 20} = \frac{400}{40} = 10\Omega$$

Redrawing the diagram agin, we get

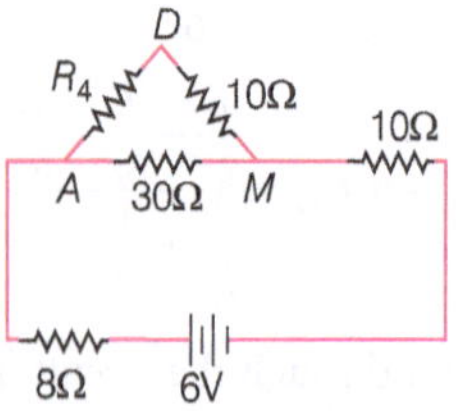

$\therefore R_4$ and R_{DM} are in series.

$\therefore \quad R_5 = R_4 + R_{DM} = 10 + 10 = 20\Omega$

Now, R_5 and R_{AM} are in parallel.

$$\therefore \quad R_{EQ}^{AM} = \frac{R_5 \times R_{AM}}{R_5 + R_{AM}} = \frac{20 \times 30}{20 + 30} = \frac{600}{50} = 12\Omega$$

$\therefore$Equivalent reistance between A and M is 12Ω.

(ii) Total resistance of the circuit

$$= (12\Omega + 10\Omega + 8\Omega) = 30\Omega$$

$\therefore$Net current in the circuit $= \frac{6}{30} = \frac{1}{5}$ A

$\therefore$ Power supplied by the battery $= VI = \left(6 \times \frac{1}{5}\right)$W

$$= 1.2 \text{ W}$$

28. (i) **In circuit 1** Adding another series resistor R_3 increases the total resistance of the circuit 1 and thus reduces the current in the battery.

In circuit 2 If another resistor R_3 is connected in parallel, the total resistance of the circuit 2 would decrease, and the current in the battery would increase.

(ii) **In circuit 1** The terminal potential difference ($V = E - Ir$) across the battery terminals increases because the reduced current results in a smaller voltage drop across the internal resistance of the battery.

In circuit 2 The terminal potential difference across the terminals would decrease because the increased current results in a greater voltage drop across the internal resistance of the battery.

29. (i) **Equivalent network**

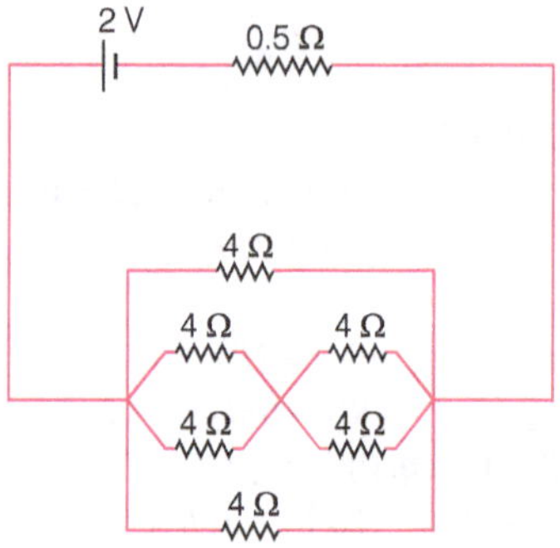

Applying the principle of resistors in parallel and series, $R_{eq} = \frac{4}{3}\Omega$

Current is drawn from the cell due to total resistance

$$= \frac{4}{3}\Omega + 0.5\,\Omega \text{ in series} = \frac{11}{6}\Omega$$

$$V = RI$$

So, current drawn from the cell,

$$I = 2 \times \frac{6}{11} = \frac{12}{11} \text{ A}$$

(ii) Power consumed by the circuit

$$= I^2 R = \left(\frac{12}{11}\right)^2 \cdot \left(\frac{11}{6}\right) = \frac{24}{11} = 2.2 \text{ W}$$

30. (i) Refer to the text on page 92.

(ii) Charge flowing $= \Sigma I \Delta t$

$= $ area under the curve

$$= \left[\frac{1}{2} \times t_1 \times I_1 + (t_2 - t_1)(I_1 - 0)\right]$$

$$= \frac{1}{2} t_1 I_1 + t_2 I_1 - t_1 I_1$$

$$= \left(t_2 - \frac{t_1}{2}\right) I_1$$

31. (i) Circuit diagram

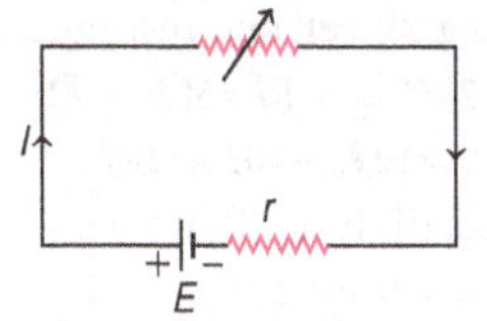

(ii) Variation of potential drop across R as function of R is

$$\left[\because V = E\left(1 - \frac{1}{1 + r/R}\right)\right]$$

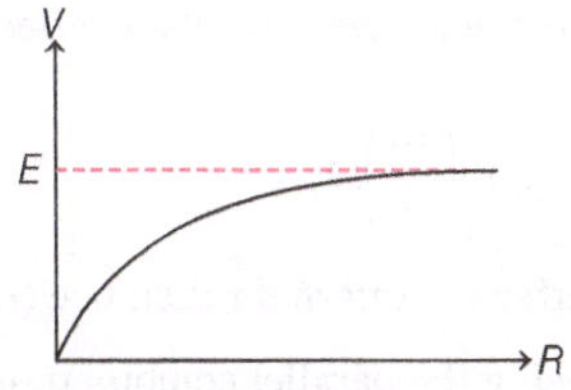

(iii) The maximum value of current is obtained, when external resistance R is zero,

i.e. $$I_{max} = \frac{E}{r}$$

32. (i) Refer to the text on page 93.

(ii) $\because \rho = \dfrac{m}{ne^2\tau}$

(a) In case of conductor the number of free electrons are almost independent of temperature increases. The thermal speed of free electrons increases and due to this, the mean collision time (τ) decreases. Hence the resistivity of conductor increases and the conductivity decreases with increase in temperature.

(b) In case of semiconductor, τ does not change with temperature but number density of free electron increases exponentially. So, the condcutivity increase with the increase in temperature.

33. Refer to text on page 97 (Terminal potential difference).

The terminal potential difference of the cell becomes greater than the emf of the cell during charging of the cell. In this process, current flows from positive electrode to negative electrode of the cell.

Hence, $V = E + Ir$.

34. (i) The emf of a cell is greater than its terminal voltage because there is some potential drop across the cell due to its small internal resistance.

(ii) $\because$ $$V = \left(\frac{E}{R + r}\right)R = \frac{E}{1 + r/R}$$

i.e. with the increase of R, V increases.

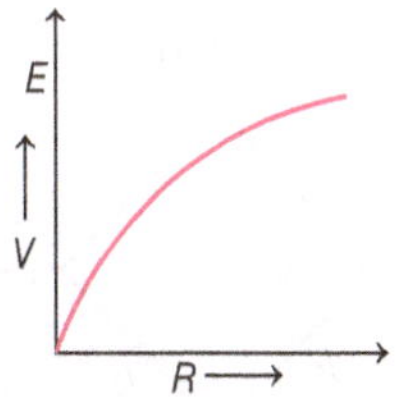

One can determine the emf of cell by finding terminal potential difference when current I becomes zero.

(iii) In these type of questions, we have to look out the connections of different cells, if the opposite terminals of all the cells are connected, then they support each other, i.e. these individual emfs are added up. If the same terminals of the cells are connected, then the equivalent emf is obtained by taking the difference of emfs.

Net emf of combination $= E + 2E + 5E = 8E$

Net resistance of current $= r + 2r + 3r + R = 6r + R$

$\therefore$ Current, $I = \dfrac{V}{R}$ (from Ohm's law)

$$\Rightarrow \qquad I = \frac{4E}{6r + R}$$

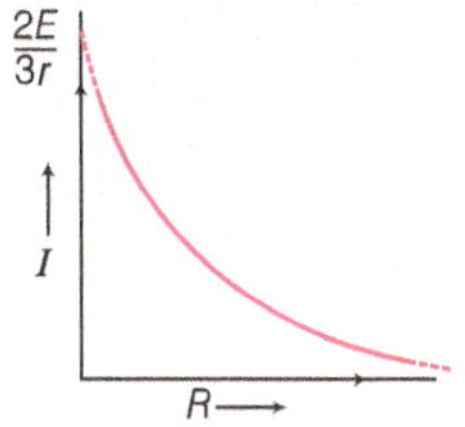

35. (i) Current in series combination of n cell,

$$I = \frac{n\varepsilon}{R + nr}$$

If $R >> nr$, then $I = \dfrac{n\varepsilon}{R}$

If R is much higher than total internal resistance, then cell should be connected in series to get maximum current.

(ii) $$I = \frac{n\varepsilon}{R + nr}$$

If $R << nr$, then $I = \dfrac{n\varepsilon}{nr} = \dfrac{\varepsilon}{r}$

Current in the series arrangement due to the number of cells is equal to the current due to one cell.

(iii) If external resistance is equal to total internal resistance, then current in the series arrangement will be minimum.

36. (i) Refer to text on pages 91 and 92 (Drift velocity).

(ii) Let V = Potential difference between points A and B

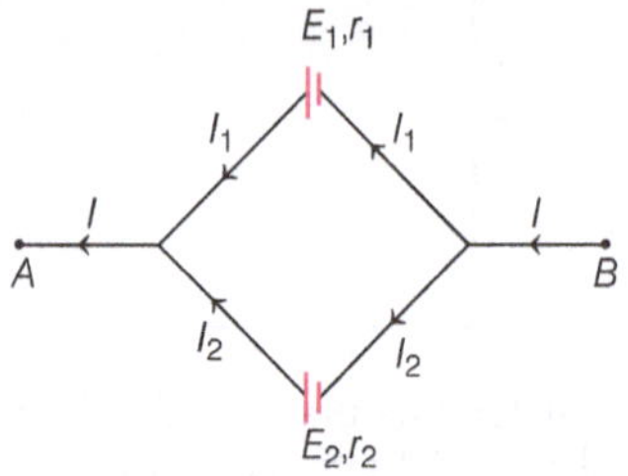

Here, $I = I_1 + I_2$ ...(i)

For cell E_1, $V = E_1 - I_1 r_1$

$\therefore \quad I_1 = \dfrac{E_1 - V}{r_1}$ ...(ii)

For cell E_2, $V = E_2 - I_2 r_2$

$\therefore \quad I_2 = \dfrac{E_2 - V}{r_2}$ ...(iii)

From Eqs. (i), (ii) and (iii), we get

$$I = \frac{E_1 - V}{r_1} + \frac{E_2 - V}{r_2}$$

$$= \left(\frac{E_1}{r_1} + \frac{E_2}{r_2}\right) - V\left(\frac{1}{r_1} + \frac{1}{r_2}\right)$$

$$\Rightarrow V\left(\frac{r_1 + r_2}{r_1 r_2}\right) = \left(\frac{E_1 r_2 + E_2 r_1}{r_1 r_2}\right) - I$$

$$\Rightarrow V = \left(\frac{E_1 r_2 + E_2 r_1}{r_1 + r_2}\right) - I\left(\frac{r_1 r_2}{r_1 + r_2}\right) \quad ...(iv)$$

Also, the potential difference between points A and B is $V = E_{eq} - Ir_{eq}$ ...(v)

From Eqs. (iv) and (v), we get

(a) Equivalent emf of the combination is given by

$$E_{eq} = \frac{E_1 r_2 + E_2 r_1}{r_1 + r_2} = \frac{\left(\frac{E_1}{r_1} + \frac{E_2}{r_2}\right)}{\left(\frac{1}{r_1} + \frac{1}{r_2}\right)}$$

(b) The equivalent internal resistance of the combination is given by

$$r_{eq} = \frac{r_1 r_2}{r_1 + r_2} = \frac{1}{\frac{1}{r_1} + \frac{1}{r_2}}$$

(c) The potential difference between points A and B is given by

$$V = E_{eq} - Ir_{eq}$$

37. Refer to text on page 103.

38. Applying Kirchhoff's junction rule, $I_1 = I + I_2$

Applying Kirchhoff's II law / loop rule applied in outer loop containing 10V cell and resistance R, we have

$$10 = IR + 10I_1 \quad ...(i)$$

Applying Kirchhoff II law / loop rule applied in outer loop containing 2V cell and resistance R, we have

$$2 = 5I_2 - RI = 5(I_1 - I) - RI$$

or $\quad 4 = 10I_1 - 10I - 2RI$ ...(ii)

Subtracting Eq. (ii) from (i), we get

$\Rightarrow \quad 6 = 3RI + 10I$

$$2 = I\left(R + \frac{10}{3}\right)$$

Also, the external resistance is R. The Ohm's law states that

$$V = I(R + R_{eff})$$

On comparing, we have $V = 2V$ and effective internal resistance,

$$(R_{eff}) = \left(\frac{10}{3}\right)\Omega$$

Since, the effective internal resistance (R_{eff}) of two cells is $\left(\frac{10}{3}\right)\Omega$, being the parallel combination of 5Ω and 10Ω.

The equivalent circuit is given below

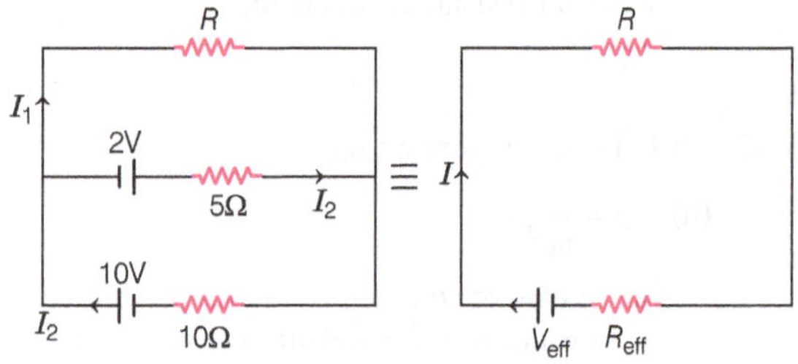

39. (i) By Ohm's law, current is given by

$$I = 6\text{ V}/6\Omega = 1\text{ A}$$

But, $\quad I = neAv_d$

or $\quad v_d = \dfrac{I}{neA}$

On substituting the values

For, n = number of electron/volume $= 10^{29}/\text{m}^3$

length of circuit (l) = 10 cm, cross-section $= A = (1\text{ mm})^2$

$$v_d = \frac{1}{10^{29} \times 1.6 \times 10^{-19} \times 10^{-6}} = \frac{1}{1.6} \times 10^{-4}\text{ m/s}$$

Therefore, the energy absorbed in the form of KE as given by all electrons

$$\text{KE} = \frac{1}{2} m_e v_d^2 \times nAl$$

$$= \frac{1}{2} \times 9.1 \times 10^{-31} \times \frac{1}{2.56} \times 10^{-8} \times 10^{29} \times 10^{-6} \times 10^{-1}$$

$$= 1.78 \times 10^{-17}\text{ J}$$

(ii) Power loss is given by

$$P = I^2 R = 6 \times 1^2 = 6\text{ W} = 6\text{ J/s}$$

Since, $P = \frac{E}{t}$

Therefore, $E = P \times t$

or $t = \frac{E}{P} = \frac{1.78 \times 10^{-17}}{6} = 2.9 \times 10^{-18}\,s \approx 10^{-18}\,s$

40. (a) **Limitations of Ohm's law**

1. **Non-linear conductors**

(i) Ohm's law is not applicable to non-linear conductors where the current does not vary linearly with the applied voltage.
For example, semiconductors like diodes, thermistors and other materials that exhibit non-ohmic behaviour.

(ii) In such materials, the *I-V* graph is not a straight line.

2. **Temperature dependence**

(i) Ohm's law is valid only if the temperature of the conductor remains constant. For materials where the resistance changes significantly with temperature (like metals at very high temperatures), the law is not applicable.

***I-V* Characteristics**

For ohmic conductors The *I-V* graph is a straight line, showing a direct proportionality between current and voltage.

For non-ohmic conductors The *I-V* graph is a curve, indicating that the current does not increase proportionally with the voltage.

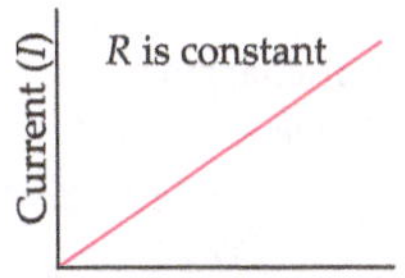

Ohmic graph

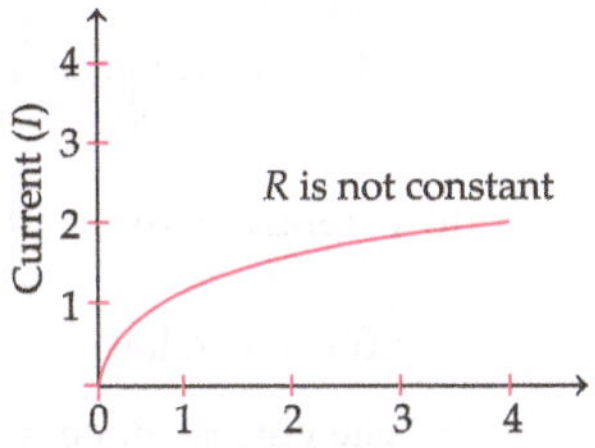

Non-ohmic graph

(b) **Initial resistance at room temperature**

The initial current is 10 A and the voltage is 100 V.

Using Ohm's law,

$$R_{total} = \frac{V}{I} = \frac{100}{10} = 10\ \Omega$$

The total resistance includes the internal resistance of the battery $R_{internal} = 1\Omega$, so the resistance of the heating element at 20°C is

$$R_{element\ at\ 20°C} = R_{total} - R_{internal} = 10 - 1 = 9\Omega$$

Resistance at 320°C

The resistance of the heating element increases with temperature. The resistance at 320°C can be calculated using the formula

$$R_{T_2} = R_{T_1}(1 + \alpha \Delta T)$$

where, $R_{T_1} = 9\Omega$ (resistance at 20°C),

$\alpha = 3.70 \times 10^{-4}\,°C^{-1}$,

$\Delta T = 320°C - 20°C = 300°C$ (change in temperature).

Substituting the values,

$$R_{320°C} = 9 \times (1 + 3.70 \times 10^{-4} \times 300)$$

$$\Rightarrow \quad R_{320°C} = 9 \times (1 + 0.111) = 9 \times 1.111 = 9.999\Omega \approx 10\Omega$$

Total resistance after heating

The total resistance at 320°C includes the resistance of the element and the internal resistance of the battery,

$$R_{total\ at\ 320°C} = R_{320°C} + R_{internal} = 10 + 1 = 11\Omega$$

Current after heating

The current drawn at 320°C can be calculated using Ohm's law, $I = \frac{V}{R_{total\ at\ 320°C}} = \frac{100}{11} \approx 9.09\,A$

Power consumed by the battery

The power consumed by the battery's internal resistance is $P_{battery} = I^2 R_{internal}$

Substituting the values,

$$P_{battery} = (9.09)^2 \times 1 = 82.64\ W$$

The power consumed by the battery after the steady temperature of 320°C is attained is approximately 82.6 W.

Or

(a) The Wheatstone bridge is as shown in the figure.

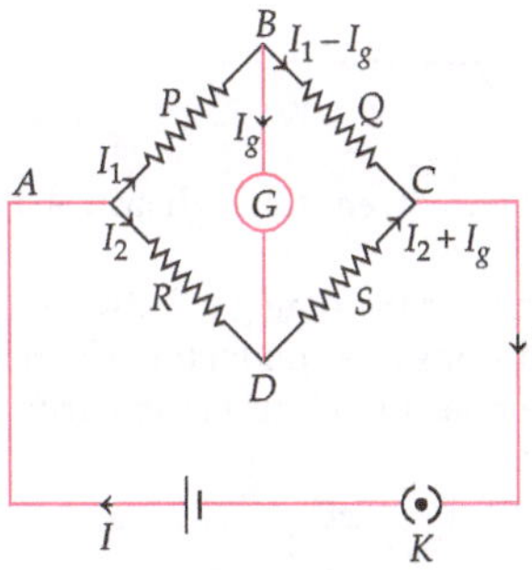

Applying Kirchhoff's second law to mesh *ABDA*,

$$-I_1P - I_gG + I_2R = 0 \qquad \text{... (i)}$$

For the mesh *BCDB*,

$$-(I_1 - I_g)Q + [(I_2 + I_g)S] + [I_gG] = 0 \qquad \text{... (ii)}$$

When the bridge is balanced, no current flows through the galvanometer,

i.e. $I_g = 0$ ...(iii)

From Eqs. (i), (ii) and (iii), we get

$$I_1P = I_2R \qquad \text{... (iv)}$$

$$I_1Q = I_2S \qquad \text{... (v)}$$

From Eqs. (iv) and (v), we get $\frac{P}{Q} = \frac{R}{S}$

(b) Given circuit is balanced Wheatstone bridge that can be drawn as below.

Resistance across the junction AC

$$= \frac{120^\circ}{360^\circ} \times 12\Omega = 4\Omega$$

Resistance across the junction CB

$$= \frac{120^\circ}{360^\circ} \times 12\Omega = 4\Omega$$

Similarly, resistaance across the junction AD and BD

$$= \frac{60^\circ}{360^\circ} \times 12\Omega = 2\Omega$$

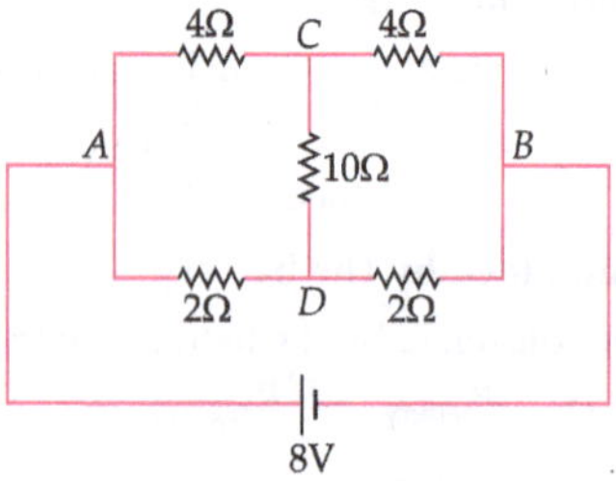

As it is balanced Wheatstone bridge, so circuit will be as below.

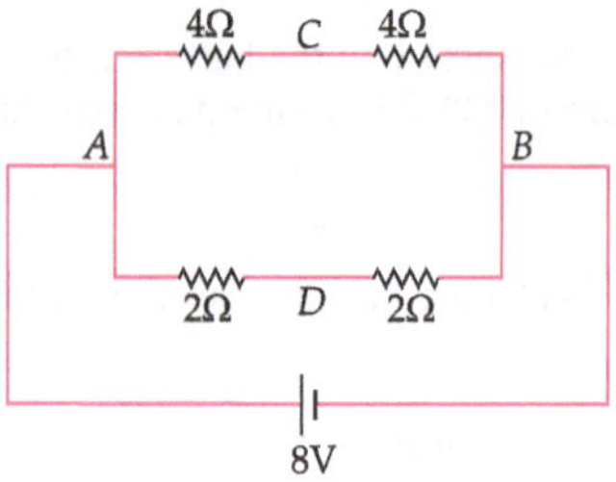

$V_{AB} = 8\text{V}$, hence current through arm $AD = \frac{8}{4} = 2\text{A}$

41. Relaxation time is the time gap between two successive electron collisions in a conductor. The relationship between the relaxation time (τ) and drift velocity (v_d) is given below.

$$v_d = \frac{eE}{m}\tau$$

Current flowing through the conductor, $I = neAv_d$

$$I = neA\left(\frac{eE}{m}\tau\right) = \frac{ne^2EA}{m}\tau$$

Field can be expressed as $E = \frac{V}{l}$

Then, current flowing through the conductor becomes

$$I = \frac{ne^2VA}{ml}\tau = \frac{ml}{ne^2\tau A}$$

From Ohm's law, $V = IR \Rightarrow R = \frac{V}{I}$

$$R = \left(\frac{m}{ne^2\tau}\right)\frac{l}{A} = \rho\frac{l}{A}, \ \rho = \frac{m}{ne^2\tau}$$

42. When a wire is stretched to double its length, the new resistance is given by $R' = (2)^2 R$

where, R is the original resistance $= 20\Omega$

$$R' = 4 \times 20 = 80\ \Omega$$

When this wire is cut into two parts, each part has a resistance $= \frac{80}{2}\Omega = 40\ \Omega$.

When these two pieces are connected in parallel,

$$R_{eq} = \frac{40}{2} = 20\Omega \Rightarrow V = 4\text{V}$$

$$\therefore \quad I = \frac{V}{R_{eq}} = \frac{4}{20} = \frac{1}{5}\text{A}$$

43. Refer to Example 4 page 90.

44. Total conductivity of semiconductor

$$\sigma = \sigma_e + \sigma_h = n_e e\mu_e + n_n e\mu_h$$

As per given, n_e is negligible as compared to n_h, so that we can write

$$\sigma = en_h\mu_h$$

$$\sigma = (1.6 \times 10^{-19})(5.0 \times 10^{20})(0.048)$$

$$\sigma = 3.84\ \Omega^{-1}\text{m}^{-1}$$

$$\sigma = 3.84\ \text{Sm}^{-1}$$

45. Given, $E = 8\text{ V}$, $r = 0.5\Omega$,

$$V = 120\text{ V and } R = 15.5\Omega$$

(i)

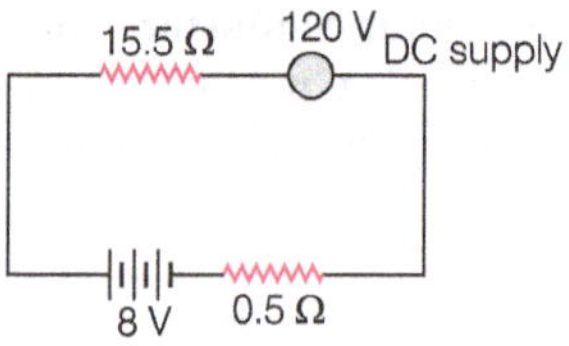

(ii) Potential across battery in charging,

$$V = E + Ir$$

Effective voltage, $V' = V_{DC} - E = 120 - 8 = 112\text{ V}$

The current in circuit, $I = \frac{112}{15.5 + 0.5} = 7\text{ A}$

$$\Rightarrow \quad V = 8 + 7 \times 0.5 = 8 + 3.5 = 11.5\text{ V}$$

(iii) Series resistor in the charging circuit limits the current drawn from the external source.

46. When batteries are connected in series.

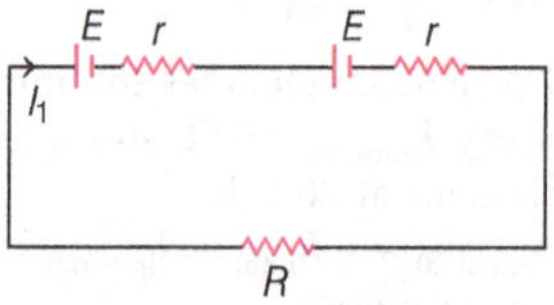

Current, $I_1 = \frac{2E}{2r + R}$

and heat produce, $H_1 = I_1^2Rt$

$$H_1 = \left(\frac{2E}{2r + R}\right)^2 Rt$$

When batteries are connected in parallel.

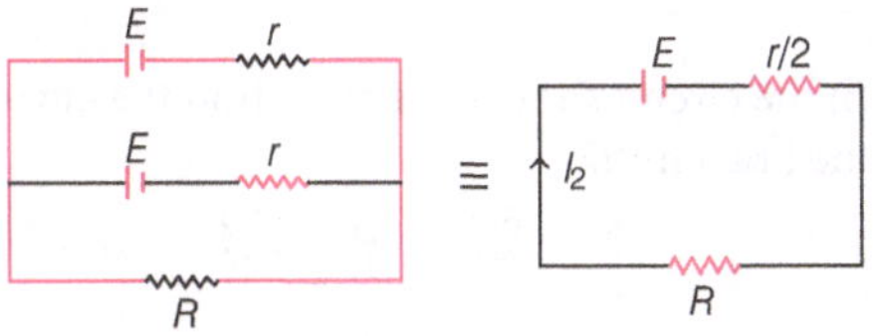

Current, $I_2 = \frac{E}{\left(\frac{r}{2} + R\right)} = \left(\frac{2E}{r + 2R}\right)$

and heat produce $H_2 = I_2^2 RT$

$$H_2 = \left(\frac{2E}{r + 2R}\right)^2 Rt$$

Given, $H_1 = 2.25 H_2$

$$\left(\frac{2E}{2r + R}\right)^2 Rt = \frac{225}{100}\left(\frac{2E}{r + 2R}\right)^2 Rt$$

$$\left(\frac{2E}{2r + R}\right)^2 = \frac{9}{4}\left(\frac{2E}{r + 2R}\right)^2$$

$$2(r + 2R) = 3(2r + R)$$

$$R = 4r$$

$\because \quad r = 1\Omega$

$\therefore \quad R = 4\Omega$

47. The internal resistance of cell depends on

(i) The concentration of electrolyte and

(ii) distance between the two electrodes.

Internal resistance, $r = R\left(\frac{E}{V} - 1\right)$

Given, $R = 5\Omega$

$E = 2.2\,V$

$V = 1.8\,V$

$r = 5\left(\frac{2.2}{1.8} - 1\right)$

$r = \frac{10}{9}\Omega$

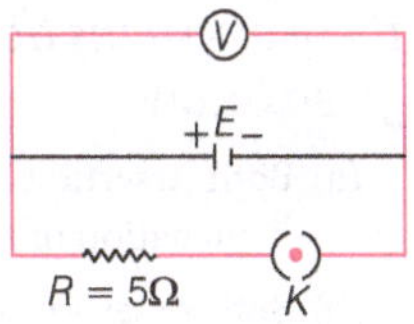

48. Given, $E = 2\,V$, $\quad r = 2\Omega$

From the diagram,

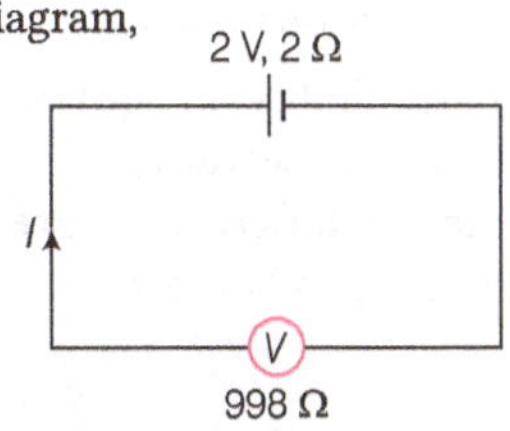

$$I = \frac{2}{2 + 998} = \frac{2}{1000}\,A$$

$$V = E - Ir = 2 - \frac{2}{1000} \times 2 = 2 - 0.004 = 1.996\,V$$

$$\therefore \% \text{ error} = \frac{0.004}{2} \times 100 = 0.2\%$$

49. Taking loops clockwise as shown in figure.

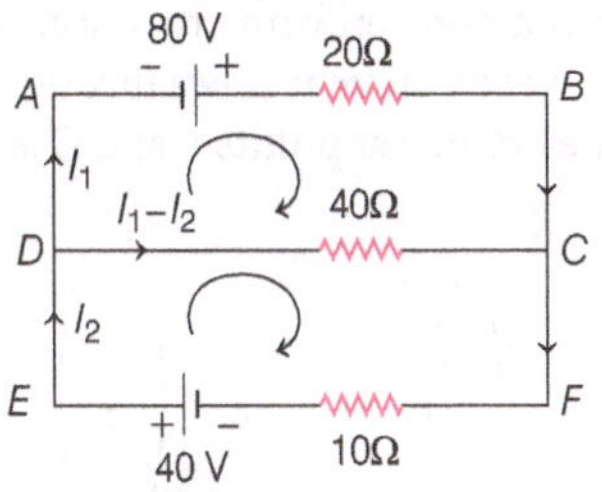

Using KVL in $ABCDA$,

$$80 - 20I_1 + 40(I_1 - I_2) = 0$$

$\Rightarrow \quad 3I_1 - 2I_2 = 4 \quad$ ...(i)

Using KVL in $DCFED$,

$$-40(I_1 - I_2) + 10I_2 - 40 = 0$$

$\Rightarrow \quad -4I_1 + 5I_2 = 4 \quad$ ...(ii)

From Eqs. (i) and (ii), we get

$$I_1 = 4\text{ A and } I_2 = 4\text{ A}$$

Thus, $\quad I_{40} = I_1 - I_2 = 0\text{ A}$

$$I_{20} = I_1 = 4\text{ A}$$

50. As $V_A - V_B = 0$

Thus, it is a balanced Wheatstone bridge.

$\frac{P}{Q} = \frac{R}{S} \quad$ ...(i)

where, $P = 6\Omega + 6\Omega = 12\Omega$

$Q = 6\Omega + y\Omega = (6 + y)\Omega$

So, $\quad \frac{1}{R} = \frac{1}{1} + \frac{1}{1} \Rightarrow R = \frac{1}{2}\Omega$

$\frac{1}{S} = \frac{1}{2} + \frac{1}{2} \Rightarrow S = 1\Omega$

From Eq. (i)

$\frac{12}{6 + y} = \frac{1}{2} \Rightarrow 24 = 6 + y$

$\Rightarrow \quad y = 18\Omega$

QR Code for Quick Test 1 | QR Code for Quick Test 2 | QR Code for Quick Test 3 | QR Code for Quick Test 4

SELF ASSESSMENT TEST

Multiple Choice Questions (MCQs)

1. A wire has a non-uniform cross-section as shown in figure. A steady current flows through it. The drift speed of electrons at points P and Q is v_P and v_Q, then

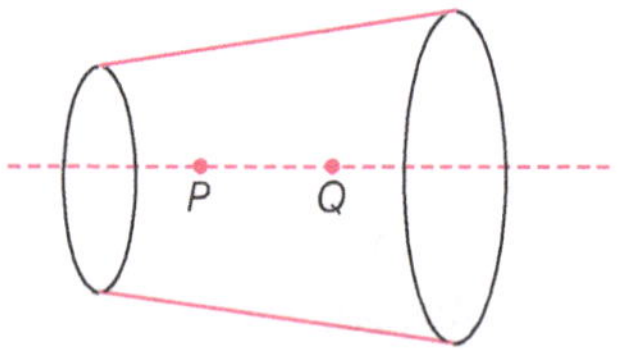

(a) $v_P = v_Q$ (b) $v_P < v_Q$
(c) $v_P > v_Q$ (d) Data is insufficient

2. If the ammeter reading in the given circuit is zero, find the value of the resistance R.

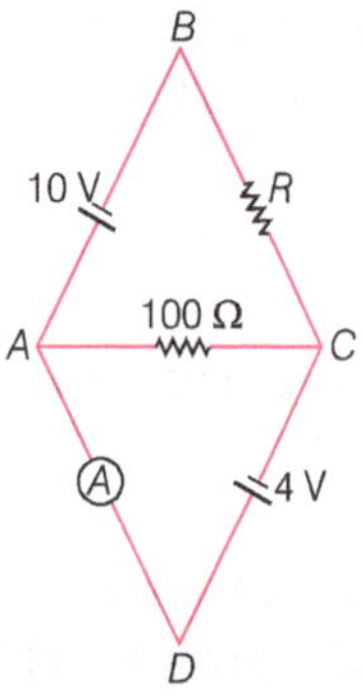

(a) 50 Ω (b) 100 Ω (c) 150 Ω (d) 200 Ω

3. Find the potential of J with respect to G.

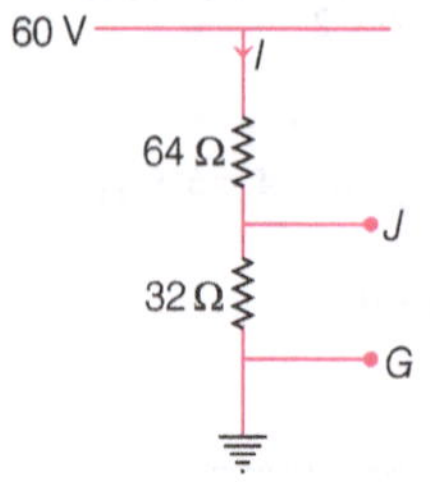

(a) 40 V (b) 60 V
(c) 20 V (d) 30 V

4. In the circuit shown in figure, find the current through the branch BD.

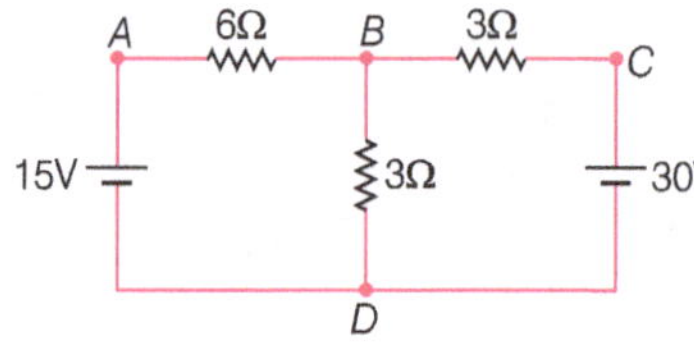

(a) 1 A (b) 5 A (c) 3 A (d) 7 A

5. If the voltmeter in the given circuit reads 8 V, what is the resistance of the voltmeter?

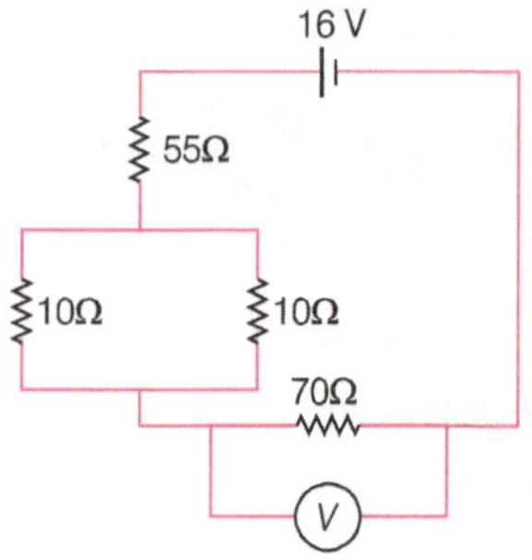

(a) $\frac{70}{4119}\,\Omega$ (b) 70 Ω (c) 420 Ω (d) 4200 Ω

Assertion-Reason

Directions (Q. Nos. 6-8) *In the following questions, two statements are given- one labelled Assertion (A) and the other labelled Reason (R). Select the correct answer to these questions from the codes (a), (b), (c) and (d) as given below.*

(a) Both Assertion and Reason are true and Reason is the correct explanation of Assertion.

(b) Both Assertion and Reason are true but Reason is not the correct explanation of Assertion.

(c) Assertion is true but Reason is false.

(d) Assertion is false but Reason is true.

6. **Assertion** (A) Kirchhoff's voltage law indicates that electrostatic field is conservative.
Reason (R) Potential difference between two points in a circuit does not depend on path.

7. **Assertion** (A) The internal resistance of a cell is constant.

Reason (R) Ionic concentration of the electrolyte changes during use of a cell.

8. **Assertion** (A) Resistivity of a conductor increases with increase in temperature.

Reason (R) When temperature increases, the random motion of free electrons increases and vibration of ions increases which decreases the relaxation time.

Very Short Answer Type Questions

9. How does one explain increase in resistivity of a metal with increase of temperature?

10. Write a relation between current and drift velocity of electrons in a conductor. Use this relation to explain how the resistance of a conductor changes with the rise in temperature?

11. When electrons drift in a metal from lower to higher potential, does it mean that all the free electrons of the metal are moving in the same direction?

Short Answer Type Questions

12. The following table gives the length of three copper wires, their diameters and the applied potential difference across their ends. Arrange the wires in increasing order according to the following

(i) The magnitude of the electric field within them **[1]**

(ii) The drift velocity of electrons through them, and **[1]**

(iii) The current density within them. **[1]**

Length	Diameter	Potential Difference
L	$3d$	V
$2L$	d	V
$3L$	$2d$	$2V$

13. (i) Define the term of drift velocity. **[1]**

(ii) Why alloys like constantan and manganin are used for making standard resistors? **[1]**

Long Answer Type Questions

14. A conductor of length l is connected to a DC source of potential V. If the length of the conductor is tripled by gradually stretching it, keeping V constant, how will

(i) drift speed of electrons and

(ii) resistance of the conductor be affected? Justify your answer.

15. On the basis of electron drift, derive an expression for resistivity of a conductor in terms of number density of free electrons and relaxation time. On what factors does resistivity of a conductor depend?

Answers

1. (c)	*2.* (c)	*3.* (c)	*4.* (b)	*5.* (c)
6. (a)	*7.* (d)	*8.* (a)		

04

CHAPTER

Moving Charges and Magnetism

When charged particles such as electrons move through a conductor, they generate a magnetic field around the path of motion. The direction of magnetic field can be determined by right hand rule. The relationship between electricity and magnetism is the basis of electromagnetism, leading to technologies like motors, generator and transformers.

YOUR STUDY GOALS

YOUR PRACTICE GOAL

- Objective Type Questions (34 Qs ; MCQs, A-R, Matching)
- Case Based Questions-2
- Subjective Questions (9 VSAs, 19 SAs, 15 LAs)
- Numerical Problems-16

4.1 Magnetic Field and Its Applications

In this chapter, we will study about magnetism produced by a moving charge and further we will proceed with Ampere's circuital law and its applications and at last, the chapter will be ended with magnetic force and torque between two parallel conductors.

Magnetic Field

The space in the surroundings of a magnet or a current-carrying conductor in which its magnetic influence can be experienced is called magnetic field.

The SI unit of magnetic field is **tesla** (T) or **weber/metre^2** (Wbm^{-2}) or $\mathbf{NA^{-1}m^{-1}}$ and its **CGS unit is gauss (G)**.

$$1 \text{ tesla} = 10^4 \text{ gauss}$$

Dimensions of $B = [MT^{-2}A^{-1}]$

Oersted's Experiment

In 1820 HC Oersted discovered that an electric current creates a magnetic field. He showed this by placing a magnetic compass near a current-carrying wire.

When the current flowed through the wire, the needle of the compass gets **deflected, proving that moving charges produce a magnetic field around them.** This experiment was a key set up in understanding the relationship between electricity and magnetism.

Magnetic Field due to a Current Element : Biot-Savart's Law

Biot-Savart's law is an experimental law predicted by Biot and Savart. This law deals with the magnetic field induction at a point due to a small current element (a part of any current-carrying conductor).

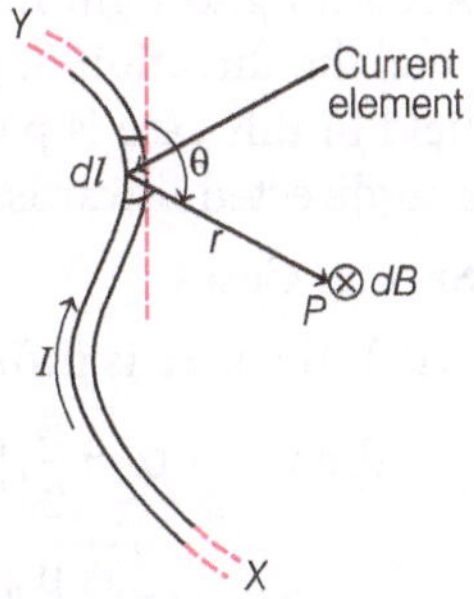

Let XY be the current-carrying conductor, I be the current in the conductor, dl be infinitesimal small element of the conductor, dB be the magnetic field at point P at a distance r from the current element.

Here, θ is the angle between the current element and the line joining the current element with point P.

According to Biot-Savart's law, the magnitude of magnetic field induction (dB) at a point P due to a current element depends on the following factors

(i) $dB \propto I$ (ii) $dB \propto dl$

(iii) $dB \propto \sin\theta$ (iv) $dB \propto \frac{1}{r^2}$

Combining all the above relations, $dB \propto \frac{Idl\sin\theta}{r^2}$

This relation is called Biot-Savart's law.

- **If conductor is placed in air or vacuum, then magnetic field is given by**

$$dB = \frac{\mu_0}{4\pi}\cdot\frac{Idl\sin\theta}{r^2}$$

where, $\frac{\mu_0}{4\pi}$ is a proportionality constant, $\mu_0 = 4\pi \times 10^{-7}$ Tm/A (or Wb/A-m) is the permeability of free space. , its dimensions are $[MLT^{-2}A^{-2}]$.

- **In vector form, Biot-Savart's law** can be written as

$$d\mathbf{B} = \frac{\mu_0}{4\pi}\cdot\frac{Id\mathbf{l}\times\mathbf{r}}{r^3} \quad \text{...(i)}$$

or $$B = \int \frac{\mu_0}{4\pi}\cdot\frac{I\,dl\sin\theta}{r^2}$$

From Eq. (i), the direction of $d\mathbf{B}$ would be the direction of the cross-product vector ($d\mathbf{l} \times \mathbf{r}$), which is represented by the right handed screw rule or right hand thumb rule.

Here, $d\mathbf{B}$ is perpendicular to the plane containing $d\mathbf{l}$ and $\mathbf{r}$ is directed inwards (since, point P is to the right of the current element).

Example 1. **Find the magnitude of the magnetic field at the centre of an equilateral triangular loop of side 1 m which is carrying a current of 10 A. [Take $\mu_0 = 4\pi \times 10^{-7}$ NA^{-2}]**

Sol. For a current carrying wire, from result obtained by Biot-Savart's law magnetic field at a distance r is given by

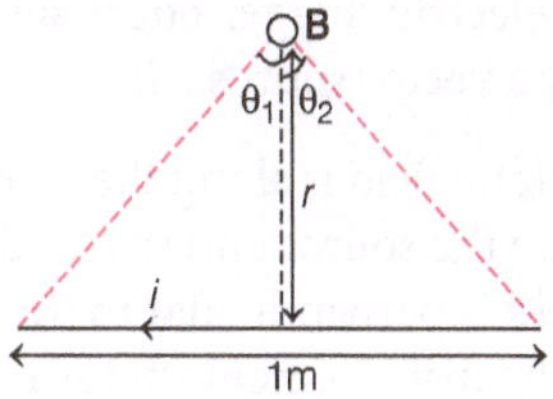

$$B = \frac{\mu_0 i}{4\pi r}(\sin\theta_1 + \sin\theta_2)$$

Now, in given case,

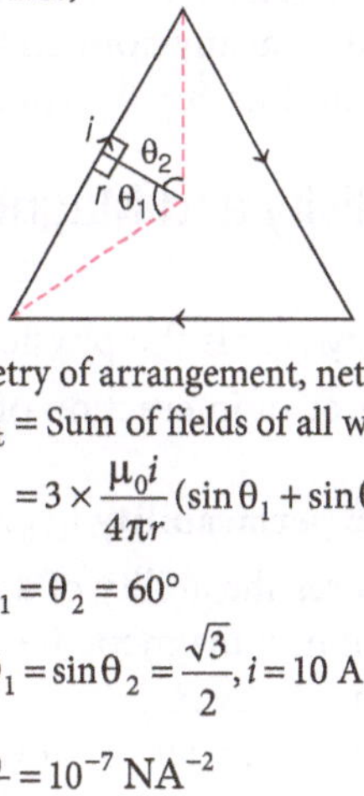

Due to symmetry of arrangement, net field at centre of triangle is B_{net} = Sum of fields of all wires (sides)

$$= 3 \times \frac{\mu_0 i}{4\pi r}(\sin\theta_1 + \sin\theta_2)$$

Here, $\theta_1 = \theta_2 = 60^\circ$

$\therefore$ $\sin\theta_1 = \sin\theta_2 = \frac{\sqrt{3}}{2}, i = 10$ A,

$$\frac{\mu_0}{4\pi} = 10^{-7}\ \text{NA}^{-2}$$

and $r = \frac{1}{3} \times \text{altitude} = \frac{1}{3} \times \frac{\sqrt{3}}{2} \times \text{side length}$

$$= \frac{1}{2\sqrt{3}} \times 1 = \frac{1}{2\sqrt{3}}\ \text{m}$$

So, $$B_{net} = \frac{3 \times 10^{-7} \times 10 \times 2\left(\frac{\sqrt{3}}{2}\right)}{\left(\frac{1}{2\sqrt{3}}\right)} = 18 \times 10^{-6}\ \text{T}$$

$\Rightarrow$ $B_{net} = 18\,\mu\text{T}$

Similarities and Differences between Biot-Savart's Law and Coulomb's Law

The Biot-Savart's law for the magnetic field has certain similarities as well as differences with the Coulomb's law for the electrostatic field. Some of these are as follows

(i) Both are long range, since both depend inversely on the square of distance from the source to the point of interest. The principle of superposition applies to both fields. (In this connection, note that the magnetic field is directly proportional to source Idl just as the electrostatic field is directly proportional to its source, the electric charge.)

(ii) The electrostatic field is produced by a scalar source, namely, the electric charge. The magnetic field is produced by a vector source Idl.

(iii) The electrostatic field is along the displacement vector joining the source and the field point. The magnetic field is perpendicular to the plane containing the displacement vector **r** and the current element Idl.

(iv) There is an angle dependence in the Biot-Savart's law, which is not present in the electrostatic case. The magnetic field at any point in the direction of dl is zero. Along this line, $\theta = 0°$, $\sin 0° = 0$, so $|d\mathbf{B}| = 0$.

Electric Permittivity and Magnetic Permeability

Electric permittivity (ε_0) is the physical quantity that determines the degree of interaction of electric field with medium.

However, **magnetic permeability** (μ_0) is the physical quantity that measures the ability of a substance to acquire magnetisation in magnetic field, i.e. the degree of penetration of matter by B.

The relation between ε_0 and μ_0 is always a constant, i.e.

$$\mu_0 \varepsilon_0 = (4\pi\varepsilon_0) \times \left(\frac{\mu_0}{4\pi}\right)$$

$$= \frac{1 \times 10^{-7}}{9 \times 10^9}$$

$$= \frac{1}{(3 \times 10^8)^2} = \frac{1}{c^2}$$

$$\mu_0 \varepsilon_0 = \frac{1}{c^2}$$

Magnetic Field due to a Current Carrying Conductor

Magnetic field B for a straight wire of finite length is given by

$$B = \frac{\mu_0 I}{4\pi R}(\sin\alpha + \sin\beta)$$

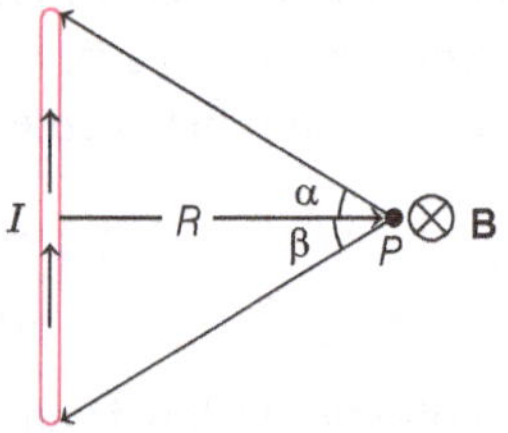

According to right hand thumb rule, the direction of magnetic field in this case is perpendicular to the plane of paper and directed inwards.

Special Cases

(i) If the **wire is infinitely long,**

then $\alpha = \frac{\pi}{2}, \beta = \frac{\pi}{2}$

$$B = \frac{\mu_0 I}{2\pi R}$$

The direction of the magnetic field associated with current-carrying conductor can be determined by **right hand thumb rule** or **Maxwell's cork screw rule.**

(ii) **If point is near one end of a long wire,**

$\left(\alpha = \frac{\pi}{2}, \beta = 0\right)$ then, $B = \frac{\mu_0 I}{4\pi R}$

Right Hand Thumb Rule

If a straight current-carrying conductor is held in the right hand such that the thumb of the hand represents the direction of current flow, then the direction of the folding fingers will represent the direction of magnetic field lines of force.

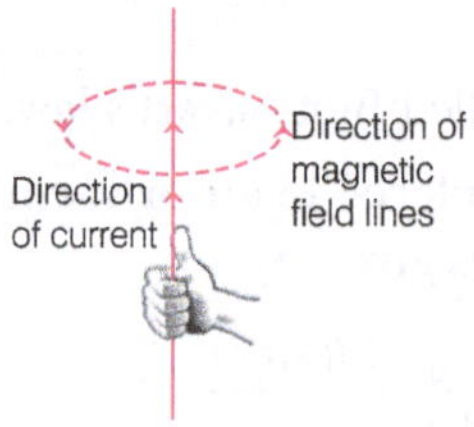

Maxwell's Cork Screw Rule

According to this rule, if we imagine a right handed cork screw placed along the current carrying wire conductor, rotated such that the screw moves in the direction of current, then the direction of rotation of the screw gives the direction of magnetic field lines.

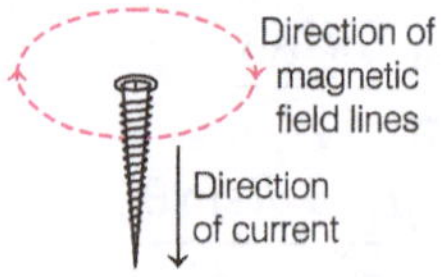

Example 2. **A current 10 A is flowing east to west in a long wire kept horizontally in the east-west direction. Find the magnitude and direction of magnetic field in a horizontal plane at a distance of 10 cm north.**

Sol. Given, current, $I = 10$ A (east to west)

Distance, $r = 10\text{cm} = 10 \times 10^{-2}$ m

Magnetic field, $|\mathbf{B}| = ?$

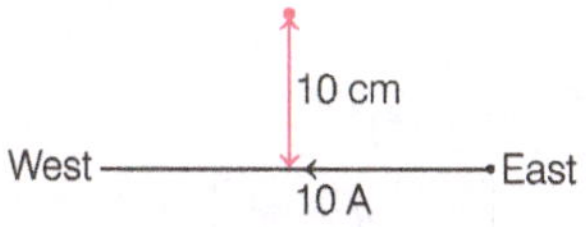

The magnitude of magnetic field $|\mathbf{B}|$ for infinite length of wire $= \dfrac{\mu_0 I}{2\pi r}$

$$\Rightarrow \quad |\mathbf{B}| = \frac{4\pi \times 10^{-7} \times 10}{2 \times \pi \times 10 \times 10^{-2}} = 2 \times 10^{-5}\,\text{T}$$

The direction of magnetic field is given by right hand thumb rule or Maxwell's cork screw rule. So, the direction of magnetic field at point 10 cm north due to flowing current is perpendicularly inwards to the plane of paper.

Example 3. **Find an expression for the magnetic field at the centre of a coil bent in the form of square of side 2*a*, carrying current *I* as shown in the figure.**

Sol. Given, $\theta_1 = 45°, \theta_2 = 45°$

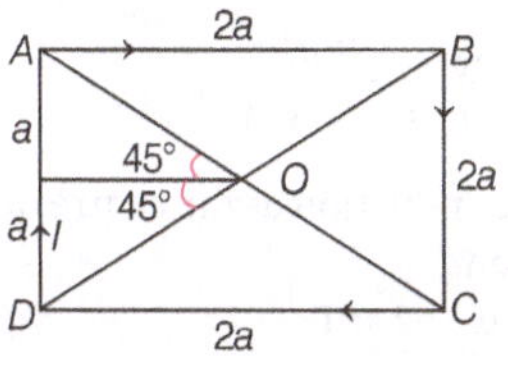

Magnetic field at point O due to each side is given by

$$B' = \frac{\mu_0 I}{4\pi a}(\sin\theta_1 + \sin\theta_2)$$

Now, total magnetic field due to all sides at point O is given by

$$B = 4\frac{\mu_0 I}{4\pi a}(\sin\theta_1 + \sin\theta_2)$$

$$= 4\frac{\mu_0 I}{4\pi a}(\sin 45° + \sin 45°)$$

$$= \frac{\mu_0 I}{\pi a}\left(\frac{1}{\sqrt{2}} + \frac{1}{\sqrt{2}}\right) = \frac{\sqrt{2}\mu_0 I}{\pi a}$$

Magnetic Field on the Axis of a Current Carrying Circular Loop

Let us consider a circular loop of radius a with centre C. Let the plane of the coil be perpendicular to the plane of the paper and current I be flowing in the direction shown. Suppose P is any point on the axis of a coil at a distance r from the centre C.

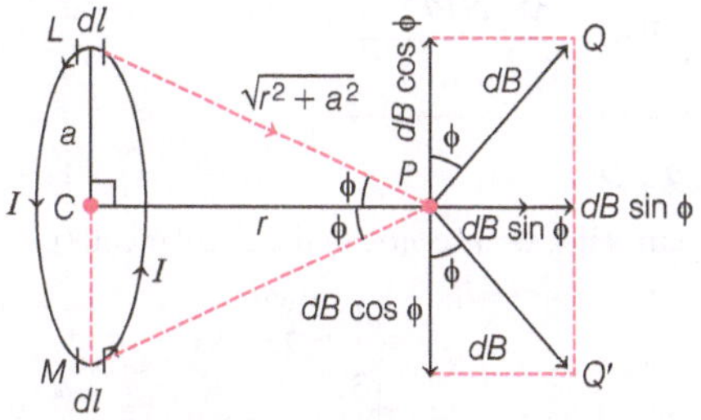

Now, consider a current element Idl on top (L), where current comes out of paper normally, whereas at bottom (M), current enters into the plane of paper normally.

$\because \quad LP \perp dl$

Also, $\quad MP \perp dl$

$\therefore \quad LP = MP = \sqrt{r^2 + a^2}$

The magnetic field at point P due to the current element Idl, according to Biot-Savart's law is given by

$$dB = \frac{\mu_0}{4\pi} \cdot \frac{Idl \sin 90°}{(r^2 + a^2)} = \frac{\mu_0}{4\pi} \cdot \frac{Idl}{(r^2 + a^2)}$$

where, $a =$ radius of circular loop

and $\quad r =$ distance of point P from the centre C along the axis.

According to right hand screw rule, the direction of dB is perpendicular to LP and along PQ, where $PQ \perp LP$. Similarly, the same magnitude of magnetic field is obtained due to current element Idl at the bottom and direction is along PQ', where $PQ' \perp MP$.

Now, resolving dB due to current element at L and M. So, $dB \cos\phi$ components balance each other and net magnetic field is given by

$$B = \oint dB \sin\phi = \oint \frac{\mu_0}{4\pi}\left(\frac{Idl}{r^2 + a^2}\right) \cdot \frac{a}{\sqrt{r^2 + a^2}}$$

$$\left[\because \text{In } \Delta PCL, \sin\phi = \frac{a}{\sqrt{r^2 + a^2}}\right]$$

$$= \frac{\mu_0}{4\pi} \frac{Ia}{(r^2 + a^2)^{3/2}} \oint dl$$

$$= \frac{\mu_0}{4\pi} \frac{Ia}{(r^2 + a^2)^{3/2}} (2\pi a)$$

or $$\boxed{B = \frac{\mu_0 I a^2}{2(r^2 + a^2)^{3/2}}}$$

For N turns, the net magnetic field is given by

$$B = \frac{\mu_0 N I a^2}{2(r^2 + a^2)^{3/2}}$$

TEACHER TIP

When point P lies at the centre of the circular coil (i.e. $x = 0$)

$$B = \frac{\mu_0 n I}{2a}$$

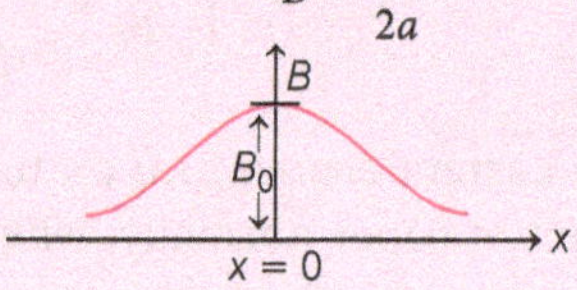

Example 4. **A circular coil of 120 turns has a radius of 18 cm and carries a current of 3A. What is the magnitude of the magnetic field at a point on the axis of the coil at a distance from the centre equal to the radius of the circular coil?**

Sol. Given, number of turns $N = 120$, current $I = 3$ A, radius of coil, $r = 18$ cm $= 0.18$ m and distance from the centre to a point on axis, $a = r = 0.18$ m

As, $B = \dfrac{\mu_0 N I a^2}{2(a^2 + r^2)^{3/2}}$

$$= \frac{4\pi \times 10^{-7} \times 120 \times 3 \times (0.18)^2}{2[(0.18)^2 + (0.18)^2]^{3/2}}$$

$\Rightarrow \quad B = 4.4 \times 10^{-4}$ T

Example 5. **A circular coil of wire consisting of 100 turns, each of radius 8.0 cm carries a current of 0.40 A. What is the magnitude of the magnetic field B at the centre of the coil?** NCERT

Sol. Here, $n = 100$, $r = 8$ cm $= 8 \times 10^{-2}$ m and $I = 0.40$ A

$\therefore$ Magnetic field B at the centre,

$$B = \frac{\mu_0}{4\pi} \cdot \frac{2\pi I n}{r}$$

$$= \frac{10^{-7} \times 2 \times 3.14 \times 0.40 \times 100}{8 \times 10^{-2}}$$

$$= 3.1 \times 10^{-4}\,\text{T}$$

Example 6. **The magnetic field B due to a current carrying circular loop of radius 12 cm at its centre is 0.5×10^{-4} T. Find the magnetic field due to this loop at a point on the axis at a distance of 5.0 cm from the centre.**

Sol. Magnetic field at the centre of a circular loop,

$$B_1 = \frac{\mu_0 I}{2R}$$

and that at an axial point,

$$B_2 = \frac{\mu_0 I R^2}{2(R^2 + x^2)^{3/2}}$$

Thus, $\dfrac{B_2}{B_1} = \dfrac{R^3}{(R^2 + x^2)^{3/2}}$

or $B_2 = B_1 \left[\dfrac{R^3}{(R^2 + x^2)^{3/2}}\right]$

Substituting the values, we have

$$B_2 = (0.5 \times 10^{-4}) \left[\frac{(12 \times 10^{-2})^3}{\{(144 + 25) \times 10^{-2}\}^{3/2}}\right]$$

$$= 3.9 \times 10^{-8}\ \text{T}$$

Example 7. **An electric current is flowing in a circular coil of radius a. At what distance from the centre on the axis of the coil will the magnetic field be $\frac{1}{8}$ th of its value at the centre?**

Sol. Magnetic field induction at a point on the axis at distance x from the centre of the circular coil carrying current,

$$B_1 = \frac{\mu_0}{4\pi} \cdot \frac{2\pi n I a^2}{(a^2 + x^2)^{3/2}}$$

Magnetic field induction at the centre of the circular coil carrying current,

$$B_2 = \frac{\mu_0}{4\pi} \cdot \frac{2\pi n I}{a}$$

But as per question,

$$B_1 = \frac{B_2}{8}$$

$$\Rightarrow \quad \frac{\mu_0}{4\pi} \cdot \frac{2\pi n I a^2}{(a^2 + x^2)^{3/2}} = \frac{\mu_0}{4\pi} \cdot \frac{2\pi n I}{a} \times \frac{1}{8}$$

$$\Rightarrow \quad \frac{a^2}{(a^2 + x^2)^{3/2}} = \frac{1}{8a}$$

$$\Rightarrow \quad 8a^3 = (a^2 + x^2)^{3/2}$$

$$\Rightarrow \quad 2a = (a^2 + x^2)^{1/2}$$

$$\Rightarrow \quad 4a^2 = a^2 + x^2 \Rightarrow x = \sqrt{3}a$$

Quick Test 1

Theoretical Questions

1. An electron is revolving around a circular loop as shown in the figure. What will be the direction of magnetic field at the point A?

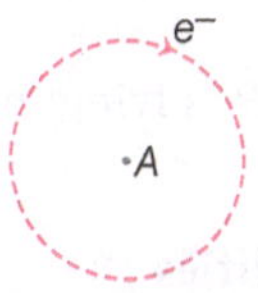

2. There is a circuit given below, where APB and AQB are semi-circles. What will be the magnetic field at the centre C of the circular loop?

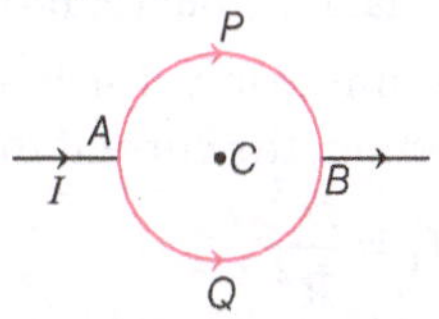

3. Find the magnetic field at point P due to the current carrying conductor of current I as shown in the figure.

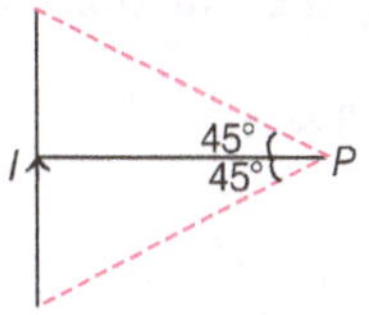

4. If a current loop of radius R carrying an anti-clockwise current I is placed in a plane parallel to YZ-plane, then what will be the magnetic field at a point on the axis of the loop?

5. What will be the magnetic field at the centre of a circular coil carrying current when the current through the coil is doubled and the radius of the coil is halved?

Numerical Questions

6. A tightly wound 100 turns coil of radius 10 cm is carrying a current of 1 A. What is the magnitude of the magnetic field at the centre of the coil? NCERT

7. Two wires A and B have the same length equal to 44 cm and carry a current of 10 A each. Wire A is bent into a circle and wire B is bent into a square.
(i) Obtain the magnitudes of the fields at the centres of the two wires.
(ii) Which wire produces a greater magnetic field at its centre?

8. An element $d\mathbf{l} = dx\,\hat{\mathbf{i}}$ (where, $dx = 1$ cm) is placed at the origin and carries a large current $I = 10$ A. What is the magnetic field on the Y-axis at a distance of 0.5 m? NCERT

9. A long straight wire in the horizontal plane carries a current of 50 A in north to south direction. Give the magnitude and direction of B at a point 2.5 m east of the wire. NCERT

10. A straight wire carrying a current of 10 A is bent into a semi-circular arc of radius 2.0 cm as shown in the figure. What is the magnetic field at O due to
(i) straight segments and
(ii) the semi-circular arc?

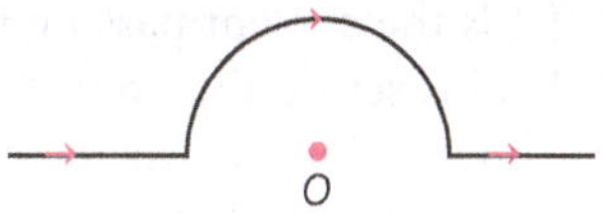

Answers

6. 6.28×10^{-4} T *7.* (i) Circle : 8.9×10^{-5}T square : 10.3×10^{-5}T
8. $4 \times 10^{-8}\,\hat{\mathbf{k}}$T *9.* 4×10^{-6}T *10.* (i) zero (ii) $5\pi \times 10^{-5}$T

For Solutions, See QR Code on Pg. 166

4.2 Ampere's Circuital Law and Moving Charges

Ampere's Circuital Law

According to this law, the line integral of a magnetic field **B** around any closed path in vacuum is μ_0 times the net current I_{net} enclosed by the curve.

Mathematically, $\oint \mathbf{B} \cdot dl = \mu_0 I_{net}$

Ampere's law is applicable only for an Amperian loop as the Gauss' law is used for Gaussian surface in electrostatics.

The choice of an Amperian loop has to be such that, at each point of the loop either

(i) **B** is tangential to the loop and is a non-zero constant
(ii) **B** is normal to the loop
(iii) **B** vanishes

Magnitude of Magnetic Field of a Long Straight Thin Wire using Ampere's Law

Magnetic field at a point P at a distance (r) due to a long straight wire carrying current I is in the form of a circle of radius (r) which is taken as closed path for Amperian loop.

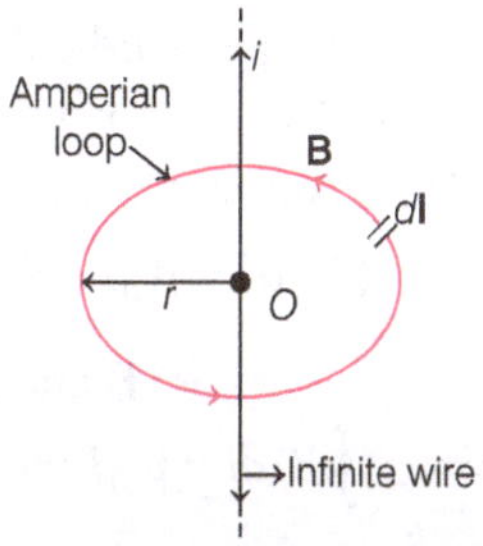

Angle between **B** and dl is zero, everywhere in this path. Hence, on applying Ampere's law to this closed path, we get

$$\oint \mathbf{B} \cdot d\mathbf{l} = \mu_0 I \quad \text{or} \quad \oint B\, dl \cos 0° = \mu_0 I$$

$$\Rightarrow \quad B \oint dl = \mu_0 I$$

$$\Rightarrow \quad B \times 2\pi r = \mu_0 I$$

or

$$\boxed{B = \frac{\mu_0 I}{2\pi r}}$$

From the result, some important points can be derived.

(i) The field direction at any point on this circle is tangential to it. The lines of constant magnitude of magnetic field forms concentric circles. The circular lines are called **magnetic field lines.**

(ii) Even though the wire is of infinite length, the field due to it at a non-zero distance is not infinite.

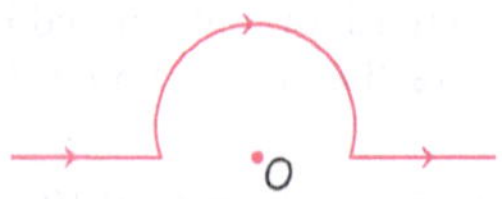

Magnetic field due to a Infinitely Long Current-Carrying Straight Wire

Suppose there is an infinte long straight wire of radius R with axis AB. If I is the current passing through wire, then a magnetic field is set-up due to it. Due to this, circular magnetic lines of force starts forming with their centres lying on the axis of cylinder. These lines of force are perpendicular to the cylinder length.

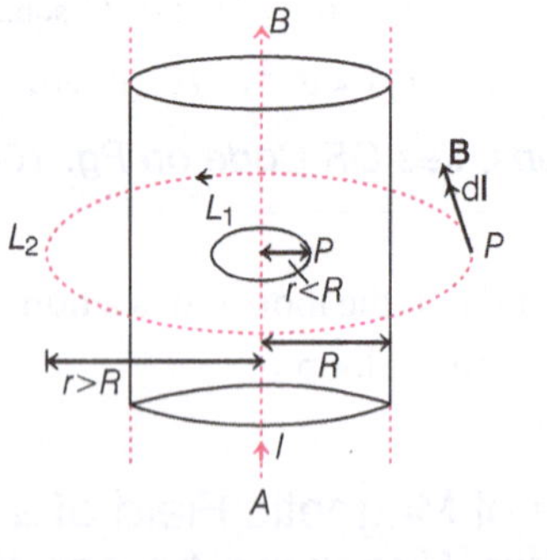

Case I When point P is lying outside the wire.

$\because r$ is the perpendicular distance of point P from the axis of the wire, where $r > R$.

Using Ampere's circuital law,

$$\oint \mathbf{B} \cdot d\mathbf{l} = \mu_0 I = \oint B \cdot dl \cos\theta = \mu_0 I$$

[$\because$ **B** and $d\mathbf{l}$ are in same direction. $\therefore \theta = 0°$]

$$\Rightarrow \quad \oint B \cdot dl = \mu_0 I \Rightarrow B \times 2\pi r = \mu_0 I$$

$$\Rightarrow \quad \boxed{B = \frac{\mu_0 I}{2\pi r}} \Rightarrow B \propto \frac{1}{r}$$

Case II When point P is lying on the surface of the wire, where $r = R$.

$$\therefore \quad \boxed{B = \frac{\mu_0 I}{2\pi R}}$$

Case III When point P is lying inside the wire, where $r < R$.

There are two possibilities

(a) If the current flows along the surface of the wire, the current through the closed path will be zero (using Ampere's circuital law) hence, $B = 0$.

(b) If the current is uniformly distributed across the wire's cross-section, the current thrugh the path is

$$I_1 = \frac{Ir^2}{R^2}$$

Using Ampere's law $\quad 2\pi B = \mu_0 I_1$

After simplifying the equation $\quad B = \dfrac{\mu_0 I r}{2\pi R^2}$

This shows that $B \propto r$.

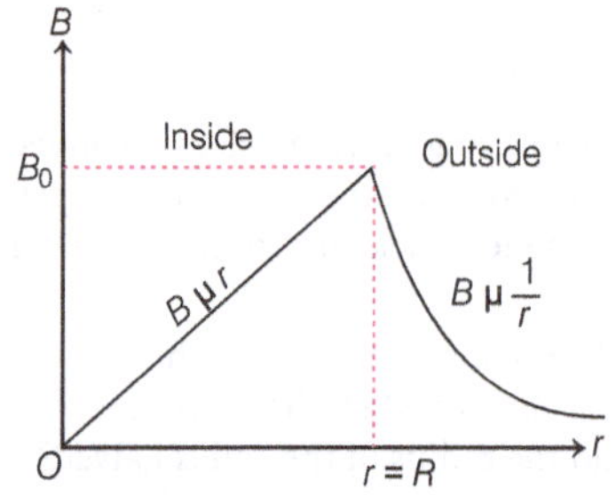

Example 8. **A straight wire carries a current of 3 A. Calculate the magnitude of the magnetic field at a point 15 cm away from the wire.**

Sol. Here, current, $I = 3\,\text{A}$, point where magnetic field is to be determined, $a = 15\text{ cm} = 0.15\,\text{m}$

$\therefore$ Magnitude of magnetic field,

$$B = \frac{\mu_0 2I}{4\pi a} = \frac{10^{-7} \times 2 \times 3}{0.15} = 4 \times 10^{-6}\,\text{T}$$

Solenoid

A solenoid is an insulated long wire closely wound in the form of a helix. Its length is very long as compared to its diameter. The solenoid is an equipment which is used to produce magnetic fields.

Magnetic Field of a Solenoid

When current passes through solenoid its magnetic field resembles that of a bar magnet of south(S) and north(N) poles as shown in the figure given below.

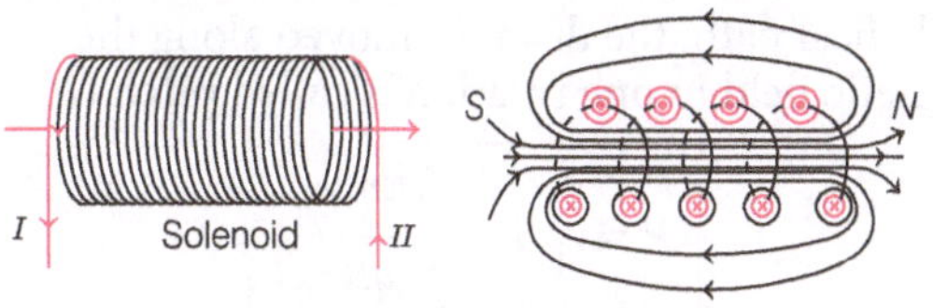

Magnetic field of a solenoid

Inside the solenoid, magnetic field is uniform and parallel to the solenoid axis. Outside the solenoid, magnetic field is assumed to be zero.

Consider an air cored solenoid having closely packed coils in which I is current, n is number of turns per unit length and B is magnetic field inside the solenoid.

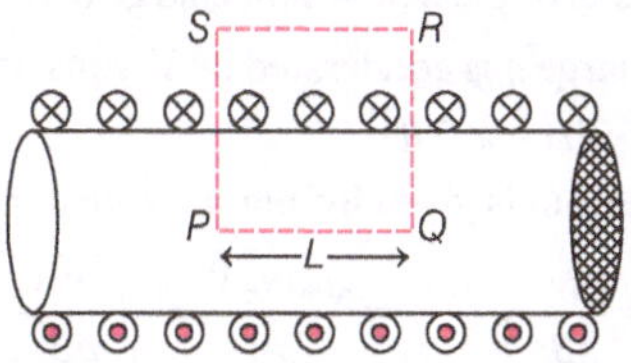

Applying Ampere's circuital law to determine magnetic field ($\mathbf{B}$) inside the solenoid, we choose rectangular closed path $PQRS$, where $PQ = L$.

Along transverse section QR and SP, the field component is zero, Thus, these three sections makes no contribution.

The number of turns in length L is nL. The current in each turn is I, so net current enclosed by the loop is nLI.

Total current, $I_{net} = nLI$

$$\therefore \quad \oint_{PQRS} \mathbf{B} \cdot d\mathbf{l} = \mu_0 \times I_{net} \Rightarrow BL = \mu_0 nIL$$

$$\Rightarrow \quad \boxed{B = \mu_0 nI}$$

From the expression, it is clear that B is independent of the length and diameter of the solenoid and is uniform over the cross-section of the solenoid.

Note The formula for magnetic field $B = \mu_0 nI$ is only valid, when length of the solenoid (l) is much larger than its radius (r), i.e. $l >> r$.

Example 9. **A solenoid of length 0.5 m has a radius of 1 cm and is made up of 500 turns. It carries a current of 5 A. What is the magnitude of magnetic field inside the solenoid?** *NCERT*

Sol. Given, total number of turns, $N = 500$

Length of solenoid, $l = 0.5$ m

Current, $I = 5$ A Radius, $r = 1\text{ cm} = 10^{-2}$ m

Here, $\dfrac{l}{r} = \dfrac{0.5}{10^{-2}} = 50 \Rightarrow l >> r$

$$\therefore \quad B = \mu_0 nI = \frac{\mu_0 NI}{l}$$

$$= 4\pi \times 10^{-7} \times \frac{500}{0.5} \times 5 = 6.28 \times 10^{-3}\text{ T}$$

Force on a Moving Charge Particle in a Uniform Magnetic Field

- When a charged particle (q) moves with velocity ($\mathbf{v}$) inside a uniform magnetic field $\mathbf{B}$, then force acting on it is $\boxed{\mathbf{F} = q(\mathbf{v} \times \mathbf{B}) = qvB\sin\theta}$

  Force due to magnetic field depends on $q, \mathbf{v}, \mathbf{B}$.
- The magnetic force will be zero, if the particle is at rest.
- The magnetic force is at its maximum value, when $\mathbf{v}$ and $\mathbf{B}$ are perpendicular to each other and the maximum force will be

  $$F_{max} = qvB\sin 90° = qvB \qquad [\because \sin 90° = 1]$$
- The magnetic force includes the cross product of velocity ($\mathbf{v}$) of the particle and magnetic field ($\mathbf{B}$). Thus, the magnetic force will be zero, if the velocity vector and magnetic field vector are either parallel or anti-parallel to each other.
- The force ($F_{magnetic}$) acting on a charged particle moving with velocity ($\mathbf{v}$) through a magnetic field ($\mathbf{B}$) is always perpendicular to $\mathbf{v}$ and $\mathbf{B}$.
- From right hand thumb rule, the force F is perpendicular to velocity ($\mathbf{v}$) and magnetic field ($\mathbf{B}$). Hence, it changes its path continuously.

Motion of a Charged Particle in Uniform Magnetic Field

In case of motion of a charged particle in a magnetic field, the magnetic force is perpendicular to the velocity of the particle. So, no work is done hence, according to work-energy theorem, change in kinetic energy is zero. Thus, no change in the magnitude of the velocity is produced.

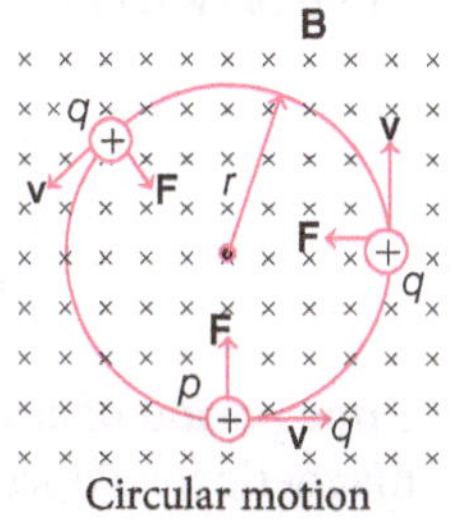

Circular motion

Magnetic force acts as a centripetal force and produces a circular motion perpendicular to the magnetic field. If **v and B are perpendicular to each other, then particle will describe a circle.**

- If a charged particle has a velocity not perpendicular to **B**, then the component of velocity along **B** remains unchanged.
- Then, **the motion of the particle in a plane perpendicular to B is as before a circular one, thereby producing a helical motion.**

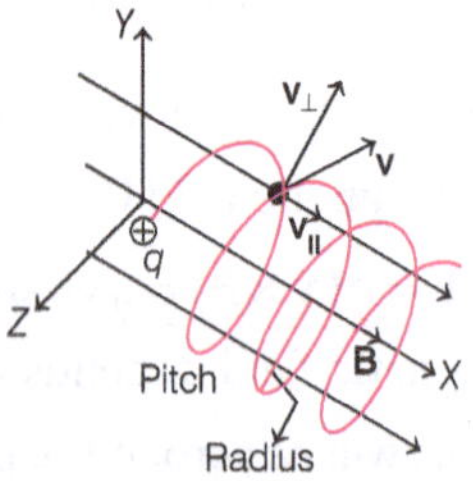

Helical motion of a charge particle in magnetic field

- As, **centripetal force** required for circular motion is provided by magnetic force, so

$$\frac{mv_\perp^2}{r} = qBv_\perp \text{ or } \boxed{r = \frac{mv_\perp}{qB} = \frac{p}{qB}} \quad ...(i)$$

where, m = mass of charged particle

and r = radius of circular path.

where, $v_\perp$ and $v_\parallel$ are perpendicular and parallel components of the velocity v.

- **Radius** of the path of charged particle is proportional to the momentum ($p = mv$) of the particle and inversely proportional to the magnitude of charge (q) and magnetic field (B).
- In **terms of kinetic energy (K), the equation may** be expressed as $\boxed{r = \frac{\sqrt{2mK}}{qB}}$ $[\because p = \sqrt{2mK}]$
- **Time period** (T) of the motion is given by

$$T = \frac{2\pi r}{v} = \frac{2\pi}{v} \times \frac{mv}{qB}$$

or $$\boxed{T = \frac{2\pi m}{qB}}$$

- **Time period** of circular path of charged particle in magnetic field does not depend on its velocity.
- **Angular frequency,** $\omega = \frac{2\pi}{T} = \frac{Bq}{m}$
- **Frequency,** $\boxed{\nu = \frac{Bq}{2\pi m}}$ $[\because \omega = 2\pi\nu]$
- The **angular speed** ω of the particle is given by

$$\omega = v/r \text{ or } \boxed{\omega = (qB)/m}$$

- For helical path, the distance moved along the magnetic field in one rotation is called **pitch** (P).

$$\boxed{P = v_\parallel T = \frac{2\pi m v_\parallel}{qB}}$$

Example 10. A proton and an α-particle, accelerated through same potential difference, enter in a region of uniform magnetic field with their velocities perpendicular to the field. Compare the radii of circular paths followed by them.

Sol. Let mass of proton = m, charge of proton = e

Now, mass of α-particle = $4m$, charge of α-particle = $2e$

When a charge q is accelerated by V volts, it acquires a kinetic energy, $E_K = qV$

$\therefore$ Momentum is given by $mv = \sqrt{2mE_K} = \sqrt{2mqV}$

Radius, $r = \frac{mv}{qB}$ or $r = \frac{\sqrt{2mqV}}{qB} = \sqrt{\frac{2mV}{qB^2}}$

Thus, $\frac{r_p}{r_\alpha} = \sqrt{\frac{2mV}{eB^2}} \times \sqrt{\frac{2eB^2}{2(4m)V}} = \frac{1}{\sqrt{2}}$

Example 11. A beam of protons with a velocity of 4×10^5 ms^{-1} enters in a region of uniform magnetic field of 0.3 T. The velocity makes an angle of 60° with the magnetic field. Find the radius of the helical path taken by the proton beam and the pitch of the helix.

Sol. Velocity component along the field,

$$v_\parallel = 4 \times 10^5 \times \cos 60° = 2 \times 10^5 \text{ ms}^{-1}$$

and velocity component perpendicular to the field,

$$v_\perp = (4 \times 10^5) \sin 60° = 2\sqrt{3} \times 10^5 \text{ ms}^{-1}$$

Proton will describe a circle in plane perpendicular to magnetic field with radius,

$$r = \frac{mv_\perp}{qB} = \frac{(1.67 \times 10^{-27} \text{ kg}) \times (2\sqrt{3} \times 10^5 \text{ ms}^{-1})}{(1.6 \times 10^{-19} \text{C}) \times (0.3 \text{ T})} = 1.2 \text{ cm}$$

Time taken to complete one revolution,

$$T = \frac{2\pi r}{v_\perp} = \frac{2 \times 3.14 \times 0.012}{2\sqrt{3} \times 10^5} \text{ s}$$

Because of $v_\parallel$ protons will also move in the direction of magnetic field.

$\therefore$ Pitch of helix $= v_\parallel \times T = \frac{2 \times 10^5 \times 2 \times 3.14 \times 0.012}{2\sqrt{3} \times 10^5}$ m

$= 0.044$ m $= 4.4$ cm

Force on a Moving Charge Particle in a Uniform Magnetic and Electric Field (Lorentz Force)

Suppose a point charge (q) is moving in the presence of both electric and magnetic fields. Let q be the magnitude of the charge, **v** be velocity of the point charge, **B** be the magnetic field and **E** be the electric field.

The electric force is given by $\mathbf{F} = q\mathbf{E}$ and the magnetic force is $\mathbf{F} = q(\mathbf{v} \times \mathbf{B})$.

The sum of these forces represents the net force that can be exerted on the charged particle due to presence of electric and magnetic field. This net force is called the **Lorentz force** and is given by

$$\mathbf{F}_{\text{Lorentz}} = \mathbf{F}_{\text{Electric}} + \mathbf{F}_{\text{Magnetic}}$$
$$= q\mathbf{E} + q(\mathbf{v} \times \mathbf{B})$$

$$\boxed{F_{\text{Lorentz}} = q[\mathbf{E} + (\mathbf{v} \times \mathbf{B})]}$$

Force on negative charge is opposite to that of positive charge.

Quick Test 2

Conceptual Questions

1. A solenoid tends to contract when a current passes through it. Justify the given statement.
2. A charged particle moving in a straight line parallel to a uniform magnetic field enters the field. What will be its path in the field? Will there be any change in its speed or direction of motion?
3. A loop of irregular shape carrying-current is located in an external magnetic field. If the wire is flexible, why does it change to a circular shape?
4. An electron moves along $+x$-direction. It enters into a region of uniform magnetic field **B** directed along $-z$-direction as shown in figure. Draw the shape of trajectory followed by the electron after entering the field. CBSE 2020

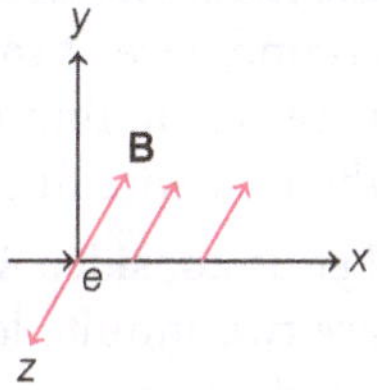

5. An electron beam projected along $+X$-axis experiences a force due to a magnetic field along the $+Y$-axis. What is the direction of the magnetic field?

Numerical Questions

6. The length of a solenoid is 0.2 m and it has 120 turns. Find the magnetic field in its interior, if a current of 2.5 A is flowing through it.
7. A copper coil of 100 turns, radius 8×10^{-2} m carries a current of 0.40 A. What will be the magnitude of magnetic field at the centre of coil?
8. Two circular loops A and B, each of radius 3 m, are placed co-axially at a distance of 4 m. They carry currents of 3 A and 2 A in opposite directions, respectively. Find the net magnetic field at the centre of loop A. CBSE 2023

Answers

6. 1.85×10^{-3} T 7. 3.1×10^{-4}T 8. 5.38×10^{-7}T

For Solutions, See QR Code on Pg. 166

4.3 Magnetic Force and Torque Experienced by a Current Loop

Force on a Current-Carrying Conductor Placed in a Uniform Magnetic Field

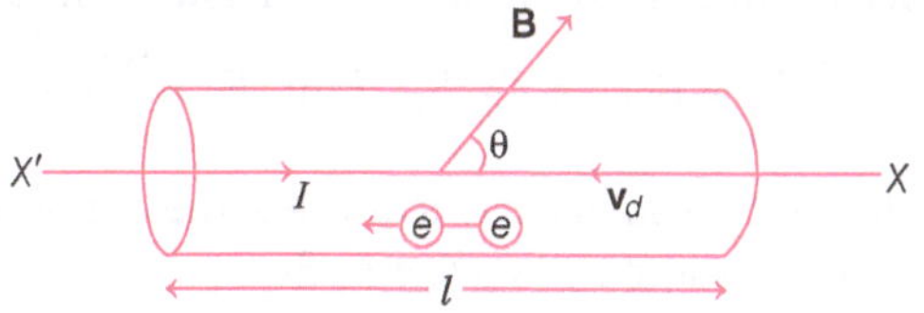

Current carrying conductor in a uniform magnetic field

Let us consider a portion of length l and cross-sectional area A of a straight conductor carrying a current I.

Let n be the number of free electrons per unit volume in the conductor and v_d be the drift velocity of the electrons. From the relation $\mathbf{F} = q(\mathbf{v} \times \mathbf{B})$, where ($q = e$) is the charge of an electron. The magnitude of the force on each electron is

$$F' = ev_d B \sin\theta$$

The number of electrons in the length l of the conductor is $N = nAl$

The total force F on the free electrons and hence on the length l of the conductor is, therefore

$$F = F' \times N = (ev_d B \sin\theta)(nAl)$$
$$= (neAv_d)Bl\sin\theta$$

But current flowing through a conductor, $I = neAv_d$

$$\therefore \quad F = IBl\sin\theta \quad \text{or} \quad \boxed{\mathbf{F} = I(\mathbf{l} \times \mathbf{B})}$$

Special Cases

- If $\theta = 0°$ or $180°$, then $F = IBl \sin 0° = 0$

$[\because \sin 0° = 0 \text{ and } \sin 180° = 0]$

- If $\theta = 90°$, then **force is maximum.**

$$F_{max} = IBl \sin 90° = IBl \quad [\because \sin 90° = 1]$$

Rules to Find Out the Direction of Force

The direction of the force acting on a current-carrying conductor in a magnetic field can be found by any of the following two rules.

(i) **Right Hand Palm Rule** If we stretch our right hand palm such that the thumb points in the direction of the current I and the stretched fingers in the direction of the magnetic field **B**, then the force **F** on the conductor will be perpendicular to the palm in the direction of pushing by the palm as shown in the Fig. (a).

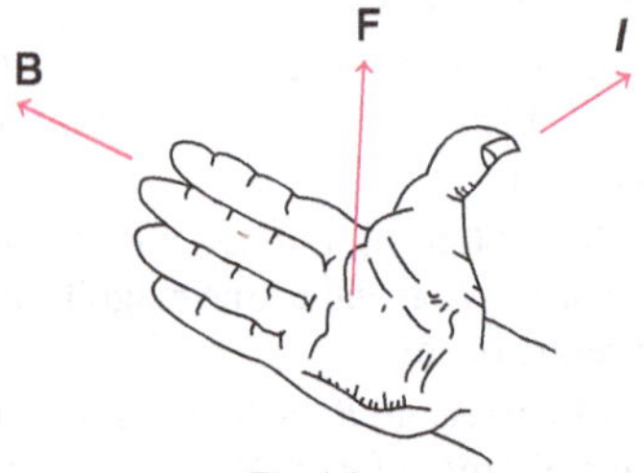

Fig.(a)

(ii) **Fleming's Left Hand Rule** If the fore-finger, the middle-finger and the thumb of the left hand are stretched mutually at right angles to one another such that the fore-finger points in the direction of the magnetic field **B** and the middle-finger in the direction of the current I, then the thumb will point in the direction of the force **F** on the conductor as shown in the Fig. (b).

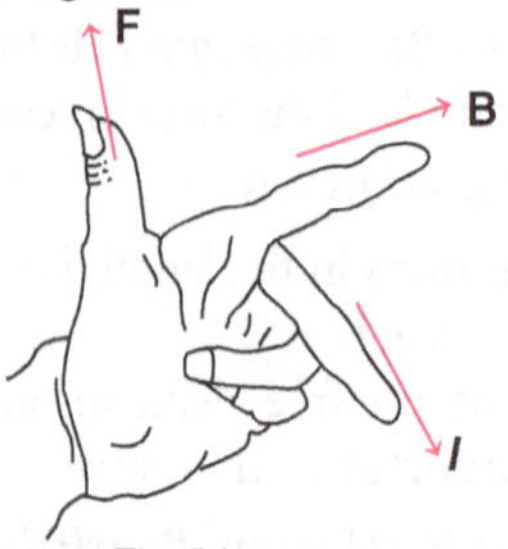

Fig.(b)

Example 12. **A 3.0 cm wire carrying a current of 10 A is placed inside a solenoid perpendicular to its axis. The magnetic field inside the solenoid is given to be 0.27 T. What is the magnetic force on the wire?**

Sol. Magnetic force on the wire,

$$F = BIl \sin\theta = BIl \sin 90° \quad [\because \theta = 90°]$$

$$= 0.27 \times 10 \times 3 \times 10^{-2} \times 1 = 8.1 \times 10^{-2} \text{N}$$

Example 13. **A straight wire of mass 200 g and length 1.5 m carries a current of 4 A. It is suspended in mid-air by a uniform horizontal magnetic field B. What is the magnitude of the magnetic field?**

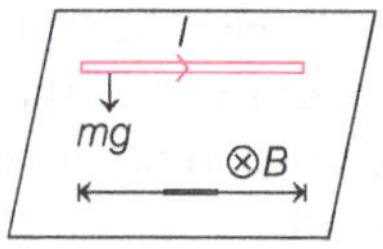

Sol. Applying Fleming's left hand rule, we find that upward force F of magnitude IlB acts. For mid-air suspension, this must be balanced by the force due to gravity.

$$\therefore \quad mg = IlB \Rightarrow B = \frac{mg}{Il}$$

Given, $m = 200\text{g} = 0.2 \text{ kg}$, $g = 9.8 \text{ ms}^{-2}$, $I = 4 \text{ A}$, $l = 1.5 \text{ m}$

We have, $$B = \frac{0.2 \times 9.8}{4 \times 1.5} = 0.325 \text{ T}$$

Force between Two Parallel Current Carrying Conductors

To find the force on a current carrying wire due to a second current carrying wire, first find the magnetic field due to second wire at the site of first wire. Then, find the force on the first wire due to that field.

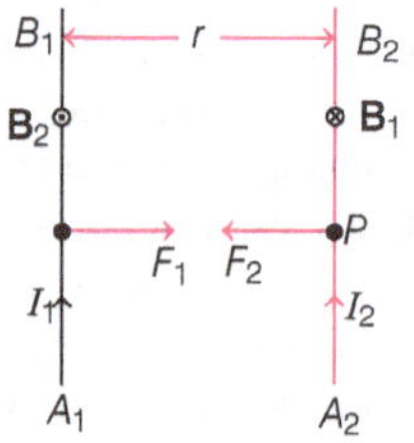

Two parallel current carrying conductors

Let us consider A_1B_1 and A_2B_2 are two infinite long straight conductors.

I_1 and I_2 are the currents flowing through them and these are at r distance apart.

Magnetic field induction at a point P on conductor A_2B_2 due to current I_1 passing through A_1B_1,

$$B_1 = \frac{\mu_0 2I_1}{4\pi r}$$

The l metre length of A_2B_2 will experience a force as

$$F_2 = B_1 I_2 \times l = B_1 I_2 l \quad \text{or} \quad F_2 = \frac{\mu_0}{4\pi} \cdot \frac{2I_1 I_2}{r} \cdot l$$

Conductor A_1B_1 also experiences the same amount of force, directed towards the wire A_2B_2.

Therefore, force between two current-carrying parallel conductors per unit length is

$$F = \frac{\mu_0}{4\pi} \cdot \frac{2I_1 I_2}{r}$$

Two linear parallel conductors carrying currents in the same direction attracts each other, while the conductors carrying currents in the opposite direction attracts each other.

Definition of Ampere (In terms of the force)

1 ampere is the current which flowing in each of the two parallel wires in vacuum at separation of 1m from each other exert a force of $\frac{\mu_0}{2\pi} = 2\times10^{7}$ N/m on each other.

Example 14. Calculate the force per unit length on a long straight wire carrying current of 4 A due to a parallel wire carrying 6 A current, if the distance between the wires is 3 cm.

Sol. Given, $I_1 = 4$ A, $I_2 = 6$ A, $r = 3$ cm $= 0.03$ m

$$F = \frac{\mu_0}{4\pi}\cdot\frac{2I_1I_2}{r} = \frac{10^{-7}\times2\times4\times6}{0.03} = 1.6\times10^{-4}\text{N/m}$$

Example 15. A short conductor of length 5 cm is placed parallel to a long conductor of length 1.5 m near its centre. The conductors carry currents 4 A and 3 A respectively, in the same direction. What is the total force experienced by the long conductor when they are 3 cm apart?

Sol. Force on long conductor is equal and opposite to the force on small conductor $= \frac{\mu_0}{4\pi}\cdot\frac{2I_1I_2l}{r}$

Given, $I_1 = 4$ A, $I_2 = 3$ A, $r = 3\times10^{-2}$m, $l = 5\times10^{-2}$ m

$$\Rightarrow \quad F = \frac{10^{-7}\times2\times4\times3\times5\times10^{-2}}{3\times10^{-2}} = 4\times10^{-6}\text{ N}$$

Torque Experienced by a Current Loop in Uniform Magnetic Field (Magnetic Dipole)

Consider a rectangular loop $ABCD$ be suspended in a uniform magnetic field **B**. Let $AB = CD = b$ and $AD = BC = a$. Let I be the current flowing through the loop.

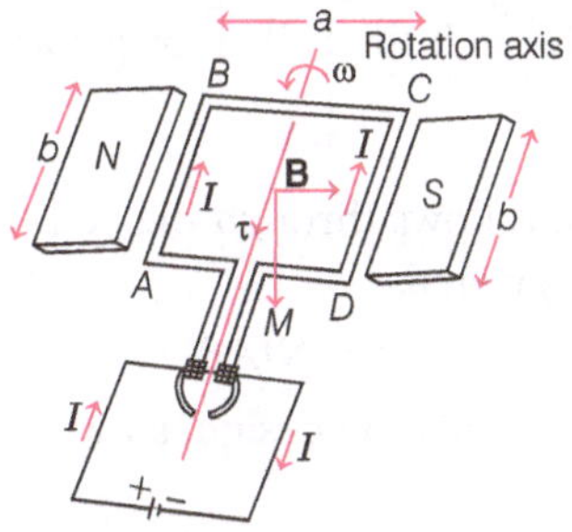

A rectangular current carrying coil in uniform magnetic field

***Case* I** The rectangular loop is placed such that the uniform magnetic field B is in the plane of loop.

$F_{AD} = F_{BC} = 0$ ($\because$ they are parallel to the magnetic field)

Magnetic field exerts a force F_1 on arm AB,

$$F_1 = IbB$$

Magnetic field exerts a force F_2 on arm CD,

$$F_2 = IbB = F_1$$

$$F_1 = -F_2 \quad \therefore \quad F_{\text{loop}} = 0$$

But line of action of F_1 and F_2 are opposite and parallel, so they form a couple.

The torque produced due to couple on the loop rotates the loop in anti-clockwise direction.

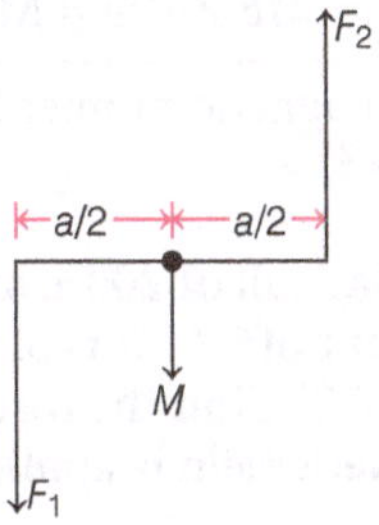

Torque, $\tau = \mathbf{r}\times\mathbf{F}$

($\because$ Torque = Force × Perpendicular distance of line of action)

So, $\quad \tau = F_1\frac{a}{2} + F_2\frac{a}{2} \quad [\because \sin 90° = 1]$

$$\Rightarrow \quad \tau = IbB\frac{a}{2} + IbB\frac{a}{2} = I(ab)B = IAB$$

where, b be breadth of the rectangular coil, a be length of the rectangular coil and $A = ab$ (area of the coil).

***Case* II** The plane of the loop is not along the magnetic field, but makes an angle with it.

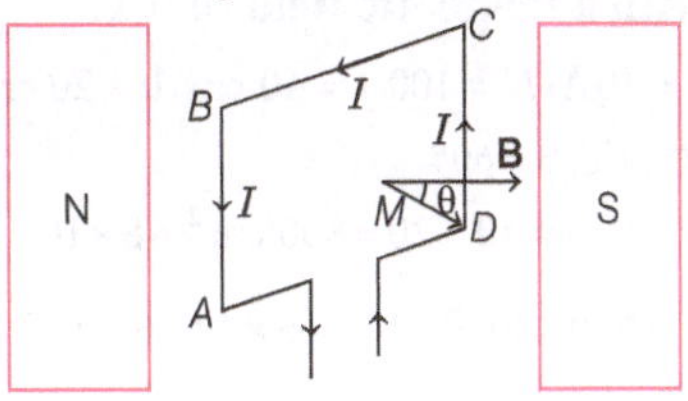

The area vector of the loop $ABCD$ makes an arbitrary angle θ with the magnetic field

$$F_{BC} = -F_{DA}$$

Force on AB is F_1 and force on CD is F_2.

and $\quad F_1 = F_2 = IbB$

Magnitude of torque on the loop is as shown in figure

$$\tau = F_1\frac{a}{2}\sin\theta + F_2\frac{a}{2}\sin\theta$$

$$\tau = IabB\sin\theta = IAB\sin\theta$$

where, $A = ab$ (area of coil)

The torque on the loop can be represented by

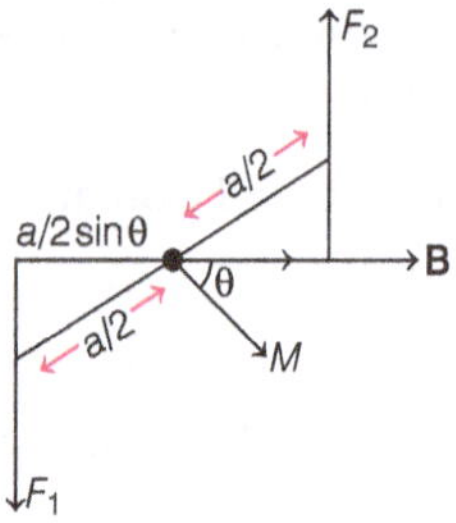

Top view of the loop. The forces F_1 and F_2 acting on the area AB and CD are indicated.

$$\boxed{\tau = MB\sin\theta\hat{n} = \mathbf{M}\times\mathbf{B}}$$

where, $\mathbf{M} = NI\mathbf{A}$ is magnetic moment of the loop, its unit is ampere-metre^2.

Example 16. **A circular coil of 20 turns and radius 10 cm carries a current of 5 A. It is placed in a uniform magnetic field of 0.10 T. Find the torque acting on the coil, when the magnetic field is applied in the plane of coil.**

Sol. Given, total number of turns, $N = 20$

Radius, $r = 10\ \text{cm} = 10\times 10^{-2}\ \text{m}$

Current, $I = 5\ \text{A}$

Angle, $\theta = 90°$

External uniform magnetic field, $B = 0.10\ \text{T}$

As, torque, $\tau = BINA\sin\theta$

$\Rightarrow \quad = 0.10\times 5\times 20\times 0.0314\times \sin 90° = 0.314\ \text{N - m}$

Example 17. **Calculate the torque of a 100 turns rectangular coil of length 40 cm and breadth 20 cm, carrying a current of 10 A, when placed making an angle of 60° with a magnetic field of 5 T.**

Sol. Given, $I = 10\text{A}, N = 100, l = 40\ \text{cm}, b = 20\ \text{cm}$

$B = 5\ \text{T}, \theta = 60°$

$A = l\times b = 40\times 20 = 800\ \text{cm}^2 = 8\times 10^{-2}\ \text{m}^2$

$\because \quad \tau = NBIA\sin\theta = 100\times 5\times 10\times 8\times 10^{-2}\times \frac{\sqrt{3}}{2}$

$$\left[\because \sin 60° = \frac{\sqrt{3}}{2}\right]$$

$= 346.41\ \text{N-m}$

Example 18. **Find the magnitude of magnetic moment of the current carrying loop *ABCDEFA*. Each side of the loop is 10 cm long and current in the loop is *I* = 2.0 A.**

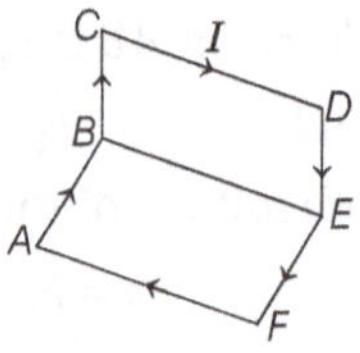

Sol. By assuming two equal and opposite currents in *BE*, two current-carrying loops (*ABEFA* and *BCDEB*) are formed. Their magnetic moments are equal in magnitude but perpendicular to each other, hence

$$M_{\text{net}} = \sqrt{M^2 + M^2} = \sqrt{2}M$$

$\because \quad M = IA = I\times(l\times b) \qquad [\because A = l\times b]$

$= 2\times(0.1)(0.1) = 0.02\ \text{A-m}^2$

$\therefore \quad M_{\text{net}} = (\sqrt{2})(0.02) = 0.028\ \text{A-m}^2$

Moving Coil Galvanometer

Moving coil galvanometer is an instrument which is used for detection and measurement of small electric current and voltage.

Principle

Its working is based on the fact that when a current carrying coil is placed in a magnetic field, it experiences a torque.

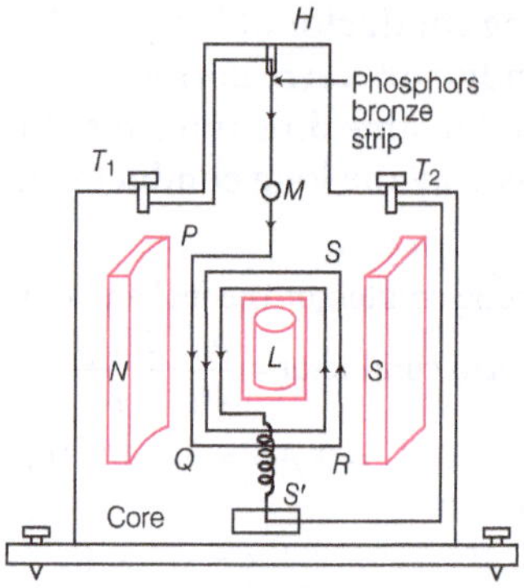

Schematic arrangement of moving coil galvanometer

Construction

The moving coil galvanometer consists of a coil with many turns free to rotate about a fixed axis, in a uniform radial magnetic field. There is a cylindrical soft iron core which not only makes the field radial but also increases the strength of the magnetic field. When a current flows through the coil, a torque acts on it.

Working

When the current flows through the coil torque acts on it which can be given as

$$\tau = NIAB$$

Since, the field is radial by design, so we have taken $\sin\theta = 1$.

This magnetic torque tends to rotate the coil.

The spring S' provides a counter torque $K\theta$ that balance the magnetic torque $NIAB$ and results in steady angular deflection ϕ,

In equilibrium, $K\theta = NIAB$

where K is the torsional constant of the spring i.e., restoring torque per unit twist.

The deflection θ is indicated on the scale by a pointer attached to the spring.

We have, $\theta = \left(\frac{NBA}{K}\right) I$

Hence, deflection produced is proportional to the current flowing through the galvanometer.

Current Sensitivity

Current sensitivity of the galvanometer is the deflection produced per unit current flowing through it.

It is given by $I_S = \frac{\theta}{I} = \frac{NAB}{k}$

Its unit is rad/A or div/A.

Voltage Sensitivity

Voltage sensitivity is the deflection per unit voltage.

It is given by $V_S = \frac{\theta}{V} = \left(\frac{NAB}{k}\right)\frac{I}{V}$

or $V_S = \frac{NAB}{k} \times \frac{I}{IR} = \frac{NAB}{kR}$

[$\because$ according to Ohm's law, $V = IR$]

Its unit is rad/V or div/V.

Note **Dead beat galvanometer** is one in which the coil comes to rest at once after the passage of current through it. The deflection can be noted in no time.

Example 19. In order to increase the current sensitivity of a moving coil galvanometer by 50%, its resistance is increased so that the new resistance becomes twice its initial resistance. By what factor does its voltage sensitivity change?

Sol. Increased current sensitivity,

$$I'_S = I_S + \frac{50\, I_S}{100} = \frac{150\, I_S}{100} = \frac{3\, I_S}{2},\ R' = 2R$$

Initial voltage sensitivity, $V_S = \frac{I_S}{R}$ ...(i)

New voltage sensitivity, $V'_S = \frac{I'_S}{R'} = \frac{\frac{3}{2} I_S}{2R}$

$\Rightarrow \quad V'_S = \frac{3}{4} V_S$ [from Eq. (i)]

$\therefore$ % decrease in voltage sensitivity

$$= \frac{V_S - V'_S}{V_S} \times 100 = \left(1 - \frac{3}{4}\right) \times 100 = 25\%$$

Conversion of a Galvanometer into Ammeter

A low resistance galvanometer is known as an **ammeter.** An ammeter is used to measure the current in a circuit in amperes.

To convert a galvanometer into ammeter, its resistance needs to be lowered, so that maximum current can pass through it and it can give exact reading.

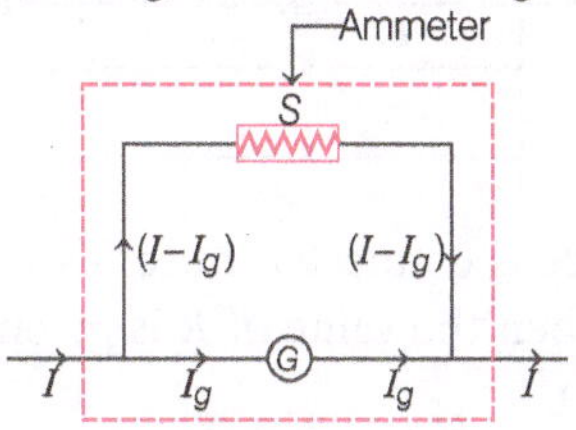

A shunt (low resistance) is connected in parallel with the galvanometer.

$$S = \left(\frac{I_g}{I - I_g}\right) G$$

where, I = total current in circuit,

G = resistance of the galvanometer,

S = resistance of the shunt (low resistance)

and I_g = current through the galvanometer. (full scale deflection current)

The effective resistance of shunted galvanometer, i.e. ammeter will be

$$R_P = \frac{GS}{G+S}$$

The resistance of an ideal ammeter is zero.

Example 20. A galvanometer of resistance 15 Ω gives full scale deflection for a current of 2 mA. Calculate the shunt resistance needed to convert it to an ammeter of range 0 to 5 A.

Sol. Given, $G = 15\,\Omega, I_g = 2\text{ mA} = 2 \times 10^{-3}\text{ A}, I = 5\text{ A}$

$\therefore$ Shunt resistance,

$$S = \frac{I_g G}{I - I_g} = \frac{2 \times 10^{-3} \times 15}{5 - 2 \times 10^{-3}} = 0.006\,\Omega$$

This resistance, $S = 0.006\,\Omega$ is connected in parallel with the galvanometer. The small resistance is connected in parallel, because we have to decrease the resistance of the galvanometer, so that most of the current passes through it and it gives the exact value of the current.

Conversion of a Galvanometer into Voltmeter

The high resistance galvanometer which is used to measure the potential difference between two points of a circuit is known as **voltmeter.**

To convert a galvanometer into voltmeter, its resistance needs to be increased, so that there is no potential drop across it because with high resistance no current passes through it.

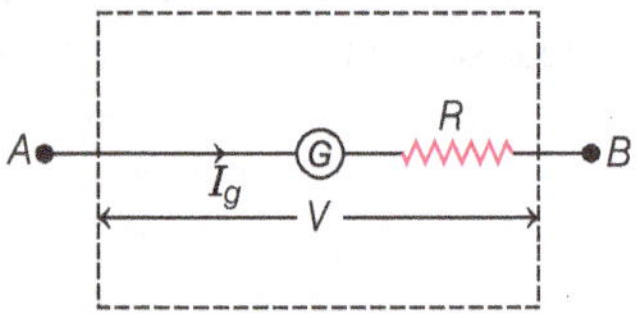

A high resistance is connected in series with the galvanometer, then the value of R is given by

$$R = \frac{V}{I_g} - G$$

where, V = potential difference across the terminals A and B,

I_g = current through the galvanometer (full scale deflection current),

R = high resistance

and G = resistance of the galvanometer.

Effective resistance R_S of converted galvanometer into voltmeter is $R_S = G + R$

Note The resistance of an ideal voltmeter is infinity.

Example 21. **The full scale deflection current of a galvanometer of resistance 1 Ω is 5 mA. How will you convert it into a voltmeter of range 5 V?**

Sol. From the relation, $V = I_g (G + R)$, we have

$$R = \frac{V}{I_g} - G = \left(\frac{5}{5 \times 10^{-3}}\right) - 1 = 999\,\Omega$$

i.e. A resistance of 999 Ω should be connected in series with the galvanometer to convert it into a voltmeter of desired range.

Quick Test 3

Conceptual Questions

1. Briefly describe how the current sensitivity of a moving coil galvanometer can be increased.

2. A galvanometer shows full scale deflection for current I. A resistance R_1 is required to convert it into a voltmeter of range (0-1V) and a resistance R_2, to convert it into a voltmeter of range (0-2V). Find the resistance of the galvanometer. *CBSE 2023*

3. A conducting loop carrying a current I is placed in a uniform magnetic field, pointing into the plane of the paper as shown in the figure, then the loop will have a tendency to expand. Explain.

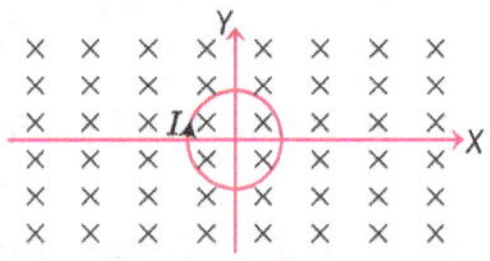

4. Two long wires carrying currents I_1 and I_2 are arranged as shown in the figure. One carrying current I_1 is along the X-axis. The other carrying current I_2 is along a line parallel to Y-axis, given by $x = 0$ and $z = d$. Find the force exerted at point O_2 because of the wire along the X-axis. *NCERT Exemplar*

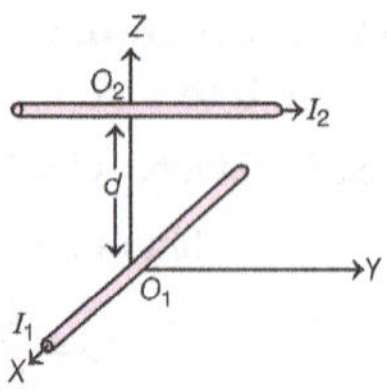

5. Two long parallel wires carrying a current I, separated by a distance r are exerting a force F on each other. If the distance between them is increased to $2r$ and current in each wire is reduced from I to $I/2$, then what will be the force between them?

Numerical Questions

6. What is the magnitude of magnetic force per unit length on a wire carrying a current of 8 A making an angle of 30° with the direction of a uniform magnetic field of 0.15 T? *NCERT*

7. A 3.0 cm wire carrying a current of 10 A is placed inside a solenoid perpendicular to its axis. The magnetic field inside the solenoid is given to be 0.27 T. What is the magnetic force on the wire? *NCERT*

8. Two long and parallel straight wires A and B carrying currents of 8.0 A and 5.0 A in the same direction are separated by a distance of 4.0 cm. Estimate the force on a 10 cm section of wire A. *NCERT*

9. A square coil of side 10 cm consists of 20 turns and carries current of 12 A. The coil is suspended vertically and normal to the plane of the coil makes an angle of 30° with the direction of a uniform horizontal magnetic field of magnitude 0.80 T. What is the magnitude of torque experienced by the coil? *NCERT*

Answers

6. 0.6 Nm^{-1} *7.* 8.1×10^{-2} N *8.* 2×10^{-5} N

9. 0.96 N-m

For Solutions, See QR Code on Pg. 166

Mind Map

Moving Charges and Magnetism

Oersted's Experiment

It demonstrated that an electric current flowing through a wire produces a magnetic field around it.

Biot-Savart's Law The magnetic field generated by a steady current is proportional to the current and inversely proportional to the distance.

$$dB = \frac{\mu_0}{4\pi} \frac{I dl \times r}{r^3}$$

Ampere's Circuital Law

The line integral of the magnetic field around a closed loop is equal to the permeability of free space times the total current enclosed by the loop.

$$\oint \mathbf{B}.dl = \mu_0 I$$

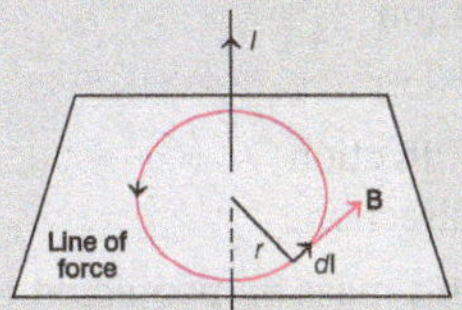

The force between two parallel current-carrying conductors is described by Ampere's force law

$$\frac{F}{L} = \frac{\mu_0 I_1 I_2}{2\pi d}$$

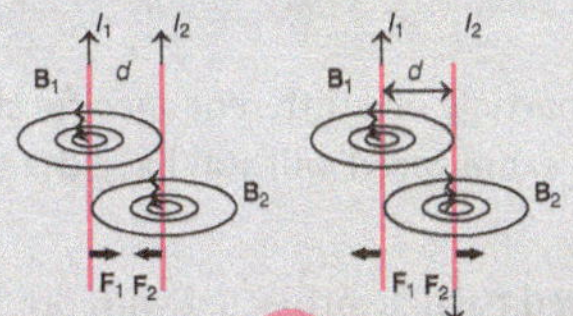

The torque τ experienced by a current loop in a uniform magnetic field is given by

Torque, τ = force × perpendicular distance

If the rectangular loop has N turns, the torque increases N times, i.e.

$$\tau = NIBA \sin \theta$$

$$\tau = \mathbf{m} \times \mathbf{B}$$

The direction of the torque τ is such that it rotates the loop anti-clockwise about the axis of suspension.

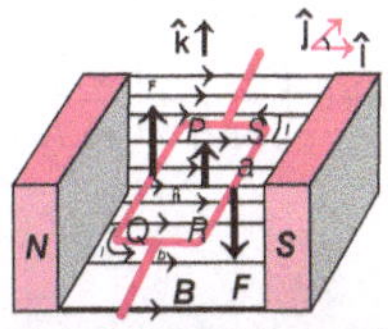

Magnetic Field

A region around a magnetic material or a moving electric charge where the force of magnetism acts. Solenoid is a long, cylindrical coil of wire that generates a uniform magnetic field inside it when an electric current passes through it. The magnetic field inside a straight solenoid is $B = \mu_0 nI$

- **At the Centre of Circular Current Loop**

$$B = \frac{\mu_0 I}{2r}$$

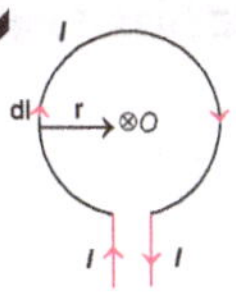

- **A Long Straight Current Carrying Conductor**

$$B = \frac{\mu_0 I}{4\pi a}[\sin \phi_1 + \sin \phi_2]$$

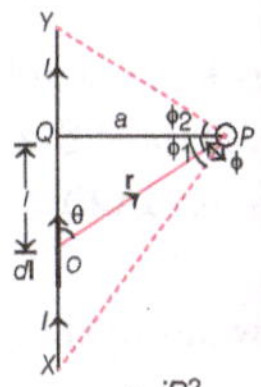

- **The Axis of a Circular Current Loop**

Field **B** at an axial point P at a distance r from the centre C.

$$B = \frac{\mu_0 IR^2}{2(x^2+R^2)^{3/2}}$$

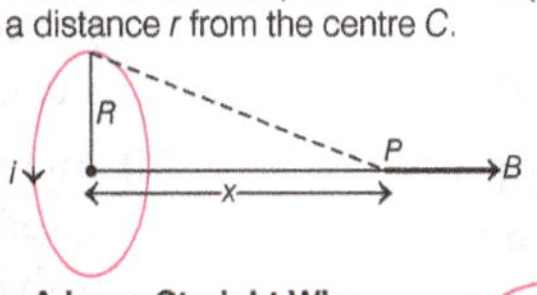

- **A Long Straight Wire**

$$\therefore B = \frac{\mu_0 I}{2\pi r}$$

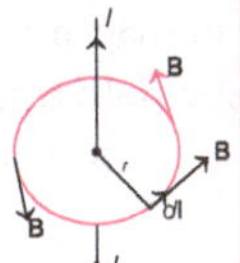

Current Loop as a Magnetic Dipole

A current loop generates a magnetic field similar to that of a bar magnet with a north and south pole, acting as a magnetic dipole.

- The magnetic dipole moment m of a current loop is given by $m = IA$
- This determines the strength and direction of the magnetic field produced by the loop.

Force on a moving charge in uniform magnetic Fields

$$F = q(\mathbf{v} \times \mathbf{B})$$

Lorentz force Force on a moving charge in uniform magnetic and electric fields.

$$F = q(E + \mathbf{v} \times \mathbf{B})$$

The force on a current-carrying conductor in a uniform magnetic field is given by

$$F = I(\mathbf{L} \times \mathbf{B})$$

where, L is the length of the conductor.

Right Hand Thumb Rule

If we hold the straight conductor in the grip of our right hand in such a way that the extended thumb points in the direction of current, then the direction of the curl of the fingers will give the direction of the magnetic field.

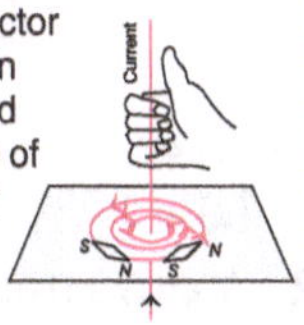

Fleming's Left Hand Rule

Fleming's left-hand rule review It is possible to predict the direction of the force acting on a wire, if the direction of the current or the magnetic field are known. Fleming's left hand rule is used to do this.

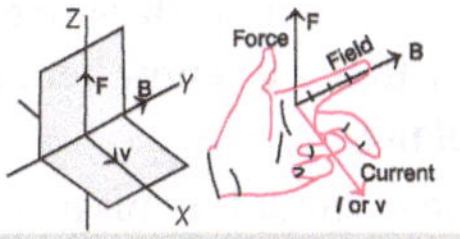

Moving Coil Galvanometer An instrument used to detect and measure small electric currents by deflecting a needle in response to the current passing through a coil in a magnetic field.

Current Sensitivity

The deflection per unit current, $S = \frac{NBA}{k}$

Conversion to Ammeter By connecting a low resistance (shunt) in parallel with the galvanometer, it can measure larger currents.

Conversion to Voltmeter By connecting a high resistance in series with the galvanometer, it can measure higher voltages.

- **Galvanometer into Ammeter**

$$S = \frac{I_g}{I - I_g} \times G$$

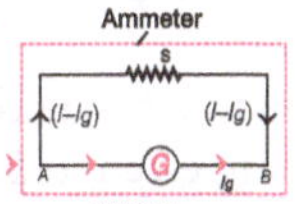

- **Galvanometer into Voltmeter**

$$R = \frac{V}{I_g} - G$$

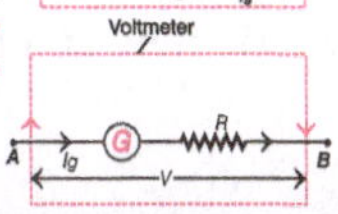

EXAM PATTERN QUESTIONS

Objective Type Questions

Multiple Choice Questions (MCQs)

1. **A long straight wire of circular cross-section of radius a carries a steady current I. The current is uniformly distributed across its cross-section. The ratio of magnitudes of the magnetic field at a point $\frac{a}{2}$ above the surface of wire to that of a point $\frac{a}{2}$ below its surface is** SQP 2024-25

(a) 4:1 (b) 1:1
(c) 4: 3 (d) 3 : 4

2. **A current-carrying wire kept in a uniform magnetic field will experience a maximum force, when it is** CBSE 2021, Term-I

(a) perpendicular to the magnetic field
(b) parallel to the magnetic field
(c) at an angle of 45° to the magnetic field
(d) at an angle of 60° to the magnetic field

3. **A current-carrying circular loop of radius R is placed in the XY-plane with centre at the origin. Half of the loop with $x > 0$ is now bent so that it now lies in the YZ- plane.**

(a) The magnitude of magnetic moment now diminishes
(b) The magnetic moment does not change
(c) The magnitude of **B** at $(0,0,z), z > R$ increases
(d) The magnitude of **B** at $(0,0,z), z >> R$ is unchanged

4. **A 1 cm straight segment of a conductor carrying 1 A current in x-direction lies symmetrically at origin of Cartesian coordinate system. The magnetic field due to this segment at point (1m, 1m, 0) is** CBSE 2025

(a) $1.0 \times 10^{-9} \hat{\mathbf{k}}$ T
(b) $-1.0 \times 10^{-9} \hat{\mathbf{k}}$ T
(c) $\frac{5.0}{\sqrt{2}} \times 10^{-10} \hat{\mathbf{k}}$ T
(d) $-\frac{5.0}{\sqrt{2}} \times 10^{-10} \hat{\mathbf{k}}$ T

5. **The magnetic field at the centre of a current carrying circular loop of radius R is B_1. The magnetic field at a point on its axis at a distance R from the centre of the loop is B_2, then the ratio of $\frac{B_1}{B_2}$ is** CBSE 2021, Term-I

(a) $2\sqrt{2}$ (b) $\frac{1}{\sqrt{2}}$ (c) $\sqrt{2}$ (d) 2

6. **Two concentric and coplanar circular loops P and Q have their radii in the ratio 2 : 3. Loop Q carries a current 9 A in the anti-clockwise direction. For the magnetic field to be zero at the common centre, loop P must carry**

(a) 3 A in clockwise direction
(b) 9 A in clockwise direction
(c) 6 A in anti-clockwise direction
(d) 6 A in the clockwise direction

7. **A particle of charge q and mass m projected with a speed v into a uniform magnetic field B undergoes circular motion under the effect of magnetic force. Identify an incorrect statement.** Competency Based Que.

(a) Both KE and PE of this charged particle remain constant, so no work is done by the magnetic field on it.
(b) An identical charged particle projected at an angle other than 90° with magnetic field B will undergo helical motion.
(c) Another charged particle of a different specific charge, projected with the same speed will still have the same angular frequency.
(d) An identical charged particle projected with double the speed in the same magnetic field will follow a circular path of larger circumference than the earlier one but with the same time period.

8. **Two charged particles traverse identical helical paths in a completely opposite sense in a uniform magnetic field $\mathbf{B} = B_0 \hat{\mathbf{k}}$.** NCERT Exemplar

(a) They have equal z-components of momenta
(b) They must have equal charges
(c) They necessarily represent a particle, anti-particle pair
(d) The charge to mass ratio satisfy $\left(\frac{e}{m}\right)_1 + \left(\frac{e}{m}\right)_2 = 0$

9. For a cylindrical conductor of radius *a*, which of the following graphs shows a correct relationship of *B* *versus r*?

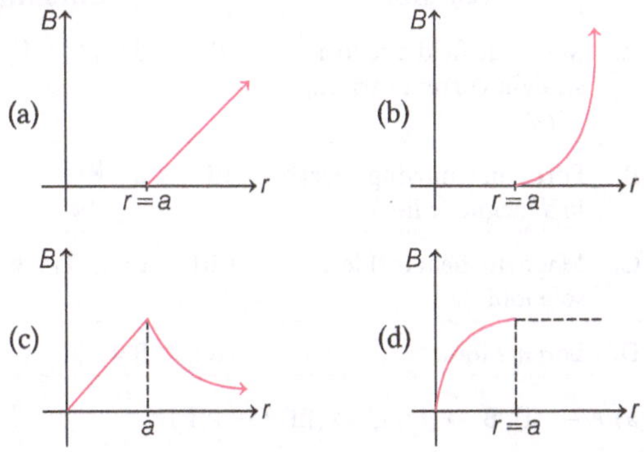

10. An electron enters in a uniform magnetic field with speed *v*. It describes a semi-circular path and comes out of the field. The final speed of the electron is **CBSE 2023**

(a) zero (b) v (c) $\frac{v}{2}$ (d) $2v$

11. A proton and an alpha particle move in circular orbits in a uniform magnetic field. Their speeds are in the ratio of 9 : 4. The ratio of radii of their circular orbits $\left(\frac{r_p}{r_\alpha}\right)$ is **CBSE 2021, Term-I**

(a) $\frac{3}{4}$ (b) $\frac{4}{3}$ (c) $\frac{8}{9}$ (d) $\frac{9}{8}$

12. The wire which connects the battery of a car to its starter motor carries current of 300 A during starting. Force per unit length between wires (wires are 0.7 m long and 0.015 m distant apart) is **Competency Based Que.**

(a) $1.2\ Nm^{-1}$, repulsive
(b) $1.2\ Nm^{-1}$, attractive
(c) $2.4\ Nm^{-1}$, repulsive
(d) $2.4\ Nm^{-1}$, attractive

13. A straight conducting rod of length *l* and mass *m* is suspended in a horizontal plane by a pair of flexible strings in a magnetic field of magnitude *B*. To remove the tension in the supporting strings, the magnitude of the current in the wire is **CBSE 2021, Term-I**

(a) $\frac{mgB}{l}$ (b) $\frac{mgl}{B}$ (c) $\frac{mg}{lB}$ (d) $\frac{lB}{mg}$

14. A current of 5A is flowing in a wire of length 1.5 cm. A force of 7.5 mN acts on it when it is placed in a uniform magnetic field of 0.2 T. The angle between the magnetic field and the direction of current is **CBSE 2024C**

(a) 30° (b) 45°
(c) 60° (d) 90°

15. Two wires carrying currents I_1 and I_2 lie, one slightly above the other, in a horizontal plane as shown in figure. The region of vertically upward strongest magnetic field is **CBSE 2021, Term-I**

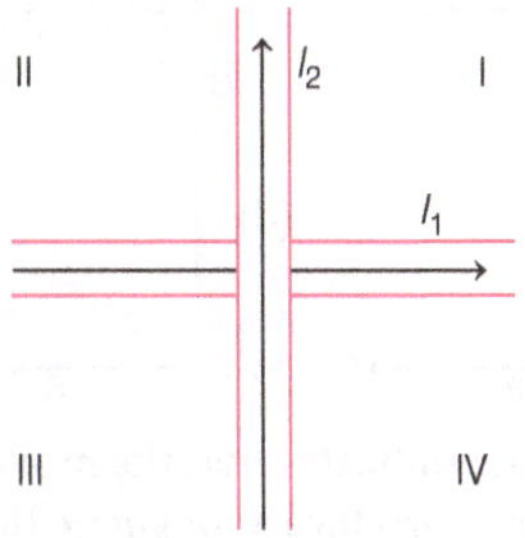

(a) I (b) II
(c) III (d) IV

16. Beams of electrons and protons move parallel to each other in the same direction. They **CBSE 2023**

(a) attract each other
(b) repel each other
(c) neither attract nor repel
(d) Force of attraction or repulsion depends upon speed of beams

17. Two circular loops of areas *A* and 4 A carry currents 2*I* and *I* respectively. The magnetic fields at their centres will be in the ratio of **CBSE 2024C**

(a) 3 : 1 (b) 4 : 1
(c) 1 : 1 (d) 1 : 2

18. A current of 5 A is flowing from east to west in a long straight wire kept on a horizontal table. The magnetic field developed at a distance of 10 cm due south on the table is **CBSE 2020**

(a) 1×10^{-5} T, acting downwards
(b) 1×10^{-5} T, acting upwards
(c) 2×10^{-5} T, acting downwards
(d) 2×10^{-5} T, acting upwards

19. A particle of mass *m* and charge *q* is moving with velocity $\mathbf{v} = v_x\hat{\mathbf{i}} + v_y\hat{\mathbf{j}}$. If it is subjected to a magnetic field $\mathbf{B} = B_0\hat{\mathbf{i}}$, it will move in a **CBSE 2024**

(a) straight line path (b) circular path
(c) helical path (d) parabolic path

20. Which of the following graphs correctly represents the variation of the magnitude of the magnetic field outside a straight infinite current-carrying wire of radius a, as a funciton of distance r from the centre of the wire? **CBSE 2023**

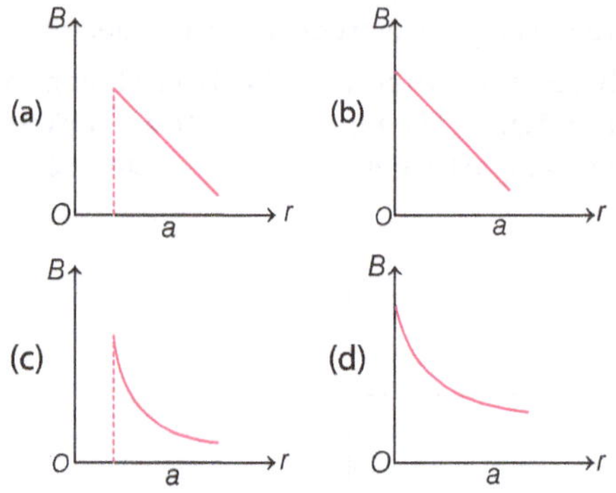

21. Biot-Savart law indicates that the moving electrons with (velocity v) produce a magnetic field B such that **NCERT Exampler**

(a) **B** is perpendicular to **v**

(b) **B** is parallel to **v**

(c) it obeys inverse cube law

(d) it is along the line joining the electron and point of observation.

22. A galvanometer of resistance 100 Ω is converted into an ammeter of range (0-1A) using a resistance of 0.1 Ω. The ammeter will show full scale deflection for a current of about **CBSE 2024**

(a) 0.1 mA (b) 1 mA (c) 10 mA (d) 0.1 A

23. The current sensitivity of a galvanometer increases by 20%. If its resistance also increases by 25%, the voltage sensitivity will **CBSE SQP 2021-22**

(a) decrease by 1% (b) increase by 5%

(c) increase by 10% (d) decrease by 4%

24. Match the Column I with Column II and choose the correct option.

	Column I		Column II
A.	Biot-Savart law	(i)	Method to find the direction of the magnetic field around a current-carrying conductor
B.	Lorentz force	(ii)	Magnetic field produced by a current element
C.	Ampere's circuital law	(iii)	Force on a moving charge in both electric and magnetic fields
D.	Right hand thumb rule	(iv)	Derives the expression for the magnetic field due to current using symmetry

(a) A → (ii) B → (iii) C → (iv) D → (i)

(b) A → (i) B → (ii) C → (iii) D → (iv)

(c) A → (i) B → (ii) C → (iv) D → (iii)

(d) A → (iii) B → (iv) C → (ii) D → (i)

25. Match the Column I with Column II and choose the correct option.

	Column I		Column II
A.	Magnetic field due to a straight current carrying wire	(i)	$\mathbf{F} = q(\mathbf{v} \times \mathbf{B})$
B.	Force on a moving charge in a magnetic field	(ii)	$B = \frac{\mu_0 I}{2\pi r}$
C.	Magnetic field inside a solenoid	(iii)	$\mathbf{F} = q(\mathbf{E} + \mathbf{v} \times \mathbf{B})$
D.	Lorentz force	(iv)	$B = \mu_0 n I$

(a) A → (i) B → (iv) C → (iii) D → (ii)

(b) A → (ii) B → (i) C → (iv) D → (iii)

(c) A → (ii) B → (iv) C → (iii) D → (i)

(d) A → (i) B → (ii) C → (iv) D → (iii)

Assertion-Reason

Directions *(Q. Nos. 26-34) In the following questions, two statements are given- one labelled Assertion (A) and the other labelled Reason (R). Select the correct answer to these questions from the codes (a), (b), (c) and (d) as given below.*

(a) Both Assertion and Reason are true and Reason is the correct explanation of Assertion.

(b) Both Assertion and Reason are true but Reason is not the correct explanation of Assertion.

(c) Assertion is true but Reason is false.

(d) Assertion is false but Reason is true.

26. **Assertion (A)** Magnetic field lines always form closed loops.

Reason (R) Moving charges or current produce a magnetic field.

27. **Assertion (A)** The magnetic field produced by a current-carrying solenoid is independent of its length and cross-sectional area.

Reason (R) The magnetic field inside the solenoid is uniform.

28. **Assertion (A)** An electron moving along the direction of magnetic field experiences no force.

Reason (R) The force on electron moving along the direction of magnetic field is $F = qvB \sin 0° = 0$

29. **Assertion (A)** An electron and a proton enter a magnetic field with equal velocities, then the force experienced by the proton will be more than electron.

Reason (R) The mass of proton is 1837 times more than that of electron.

30. **Assertion (A)** A proton and an electron, with same momenta, enter in a magnetic field in a direction at right angles to the lines of the force. The radius of the paths followed by them will be same.
Reason (R) Electron has less mass than the proton. **CBSE SQP, Term-1**

31. **Assertion (A)** When radius of a current carrying loop is doubled, its magnetic moment becomes four times.
Reason (R) The magnetic moment of a current-carrying loop is directly proportional to the area of the loop. **CBSE 2021, Term-1**

32. **Assertion (A)** On increasing the current sensitivity of a galvanometer by increasing the number of turns, may not necessarily increase its voltage sensitivity.
Reason (R) The resistance of the coil of the galvanometer increases on increasing the number of turns. **SQP 2024-25, Competency Based Que.**

33. **Assertion (A)** Higher the range, lower is the resistance of an ammeter.
Reason (R) To increase the range of an ammeter, additional shunt is added in series to it.

34. **Assertion (A)** A galvanometer can be used as an ammeter to measure the current across a given section of the circuit.
Reason (R) For this, it must be connected in series with the circuit.

Case Based Questions

Directions *(Q.Nos. 35-36) These questions are case study based questions. Read the following paragraph and answer the questions on the basis of same.*

35. **An electron with speed $v_0 << c$ moves in a circle of radius r_0 in a uniform magnetic field. This electron is able to traverse a circular path as the magnetic force acting on the electron is perpendicular to both v_0 and B as shown in the figure. This force continuously deflects the particle sideways without changing its speed and the particle will move along a circle perpendicular to the field. The time required for one revolution of the electron is T_0.** **CBSE SQP 2024-25**

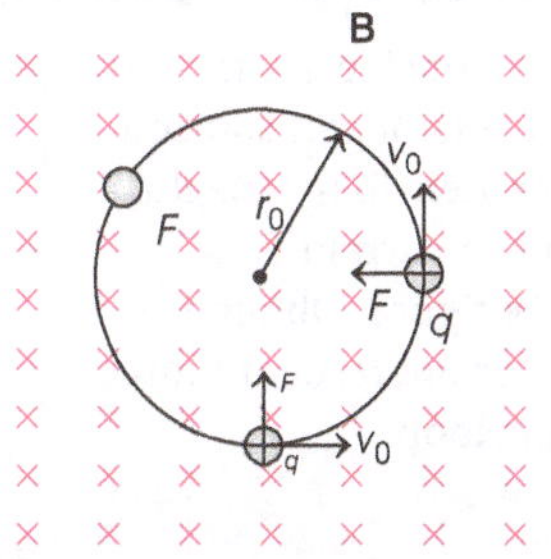

(i) If the speed of the electron is now changed to $2v_0$, then the radius of the circle will change to
(a) $4r_0$ (b) $2r_0$
(c) r_0 (d) $r_0 / 2$

(ii) If $v = 2v_0$, then the time required for one revolution of the electron (T_0) will change to
(a) $4\,T_0$ (b) $2\,T_0$
(c) T_0 (d) $T_0 / 2$

(iii) A charged particle is projected in a magnetic field $\mathbf{B} = (2\hat{\mathbf{i}} + 4\hat{\mathbf{j}}) \times 10^2\ \mathrm{T}$. The acceleration of the particle is found to be $\mathbf{a} = (x\hat{\mathbf{i}} + 2\hat{\mathbf{j}})\ \mathrm{m/s^2}$. The value of x is
(a) $4\ \mathrm{ms^{-2}}$ (b) $-4\ \mathrm{ms^{-2}}$
(c) $-2\ \mathrm{ms^{-2}}$ (d) $2\ \mathrm{ms^{-2}}$

(iv) If the given electron has a velocity not perpendicular to *B*, then trajectory of the electron is
(a) straight line (b) circular
(c) helical (d) *zig-zag*

Or

(iv) If the electron of charge (*e*) is moving parallel to uniform magnetic field with constant velocity *v*, the force acting on the electron is **Competency Based Que**
(a) *Bev* (b) *Be/v*
(c) *B/ev* (d) zero

36. **Moving coil galvanometer operates on Permanent Magnet Moving Coil (PMMC) mechanism and was designed by the scientist D'Arsonval.**
Moving coil galvanometers are of two types
(i) Suspended coil galvanometer
(ii) Pivoted coil type or tangent galvanometer.
Its working is based on the fact that when a current carrying coil is placed in a magnetic field, it experiences a torque.
This torque tends to rotate the coil about its axis of suspension in such a way that the magnetic flux passing through the coil is maximum.

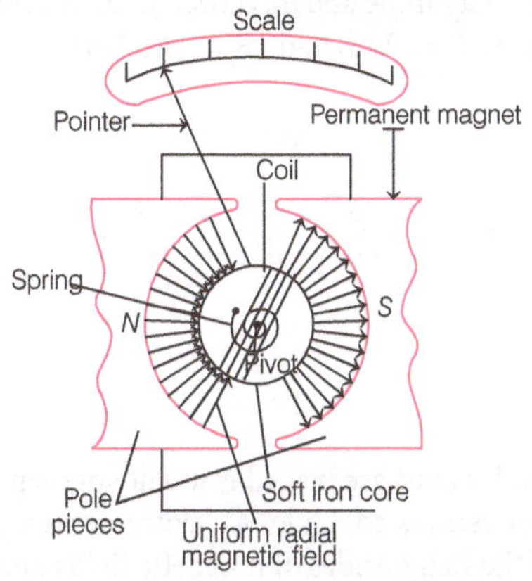

(i) A moving coil galvanometer is an instrument which
   (a) is used to measure emf
   (b) is used to measure potential difference
   (c) is used to measure resistance
   (d) is a deflection instrument which gives a deflection when a current flows through its coil

(ii) To make the field radial in a moving coil galvanometer,
   (a) number of turns of coil is kept small
   (b) magnet is taken in the form of horse-shoe
   (c) poles are of very strong magnets
   (d) poles are cylindrically cut

(iii) The deflection in a moving coil galvanometer is
   (a) directly proportional to torsional constant of spring
   (b) directly proportional to the number of turns in the coil
   (c) inversely proportional to the area of the coil
   (d) inversely proportional to the current in the coil

(iv) In a moving coil galvanometer, having a coil of N turns, area A and carrying-current I is placed in a radial field of strength B.
   The torque acting on the coil is
   (a) NA^2B^2I (b) $NABI^2$
   (c) N^2ABI (d) $NABI$

Or

To increase the current sensitivity of a moving coil galvanometer, we should decrease
   (a) strength of magnet
   (b) torsional constant of spring
   (c) number of turns in coil
   (d) area of coil

Subjective Questions

Very Short Answer Type Questions

1. If a charged particle is moving perpendicular to the magnetic field, what is the work done? Explain. **Diksha**

2. The magnetic force depends on v which depends on the inertial frame of reference. Does then the magnetic force differ from inertial frame to frame? Is it reasonable that the net acceleration has a different value in different frames of reference? **NCERT Exemplar**

3. What is the nature of the force acting on the two parallel current-carrying conductors?
   (i) If the current flows in the same direction. **[1]**
   (ii) If the current flows in the opposite direction. **[1]**

4. Two long insulated straight wires carrying currents of 3 A and 5 A are arranged in XY-plane as shown in figure. Find the magnitude and direction of the net magnetic field at points $P_1(2\text{ m}, 2\text{ m})$ and $P_2(-1\text{ m}, 1\text{m})$. **CBSE 2024**

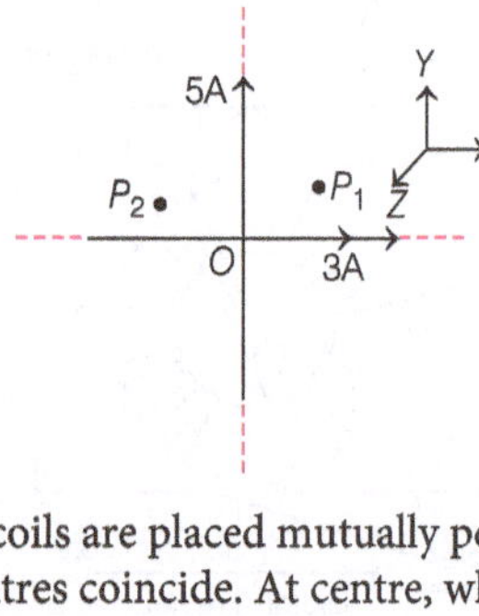

5. Two similar coils are placed mutually perpendicular such that their centres coincide. At centre, what will be the ratio of the magnitudes of magnetic fields due to one coil and the resultant magnetic field?

6. Write the expression for the Lorentz force on a particle of charge q moving with a velocity $\mathbf{v}$ in a magnetic field $\mathbf{B}$. When is the magnitude of this force maximum? Show that no work is done by this force on the particle during its motion from a point $\mathbf{r}_1$ to point $\mathbf{r}_2$. **CBSE 2023**

7. A square coil of side 10 cm has 20 turns and carries a current of 12 A. The coil is suspended vertically and normal to the plane of the coil, makes an angle θ with the direction of a uniform horizontal magnetic field of 0.8 T. If the torque experienced by the coil equals 0.96 N-m, find the value of θ. **Competency Based Que.**

8. Increasing the number of turns increases the current sensitivity and not the voltage sensitivity. Why?

9. Define current sensitivity and voltage sensitivity of galvanometer. Increasing the current sensitivity may not necessarily increase the voltage sensitivity of a galvanometer. Justify your answer.

Short Answer Type Questions

10. A square loop of side a carrying a current I_2 is kept at distance x from an infinitely long straight wire carrying a current I_1 as shown in the figure. Obtain the expression for the resultant force acting on the loop.

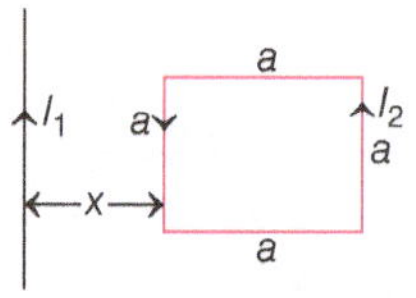

Delhi 2019

11. P and Q are two identical charged particles each of mass 4×10^{-26} kg and charge 4.8×10^{-19} C, each moving with the same speed of 2.4×10^{5} m/s as shown in the figure. The two particles are equidistant (0.5 m) from the vertical Y-axis. At some instant, a magnetic field B is switched ON, so that the two particles undergo head-on collision.

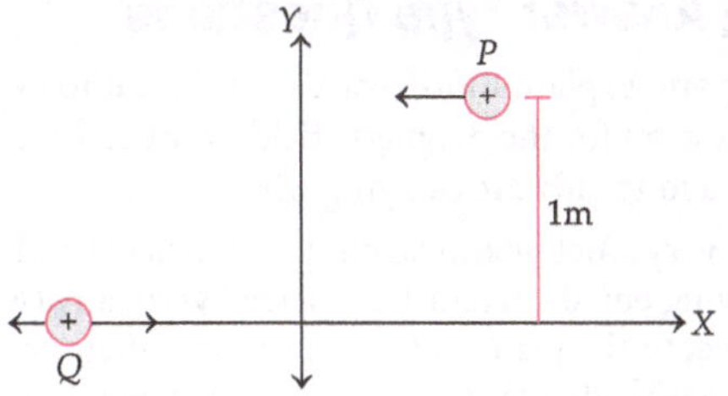

Find

(i) the direction of the magnetic field and **[2]**

(ii) its magnitude. **Competency Based Que** **[1]**

12. A stream of singly charged particles of mass $m_1 = 0.8 \times 10^{-26}$ kg accelerated through a potential difference V are projected into a uniform magnetic field $B_1 = 0.2$ T. The stream deflects along a curved path under the effect of the magnetic field and strikes the detector.

Another stream of singly charged particles of mass $m_2 = 0.2 \times 10^{-26}$ kg, projected through the same accelerating potential and into the same magnetic field B_1, fail to reach the detector.

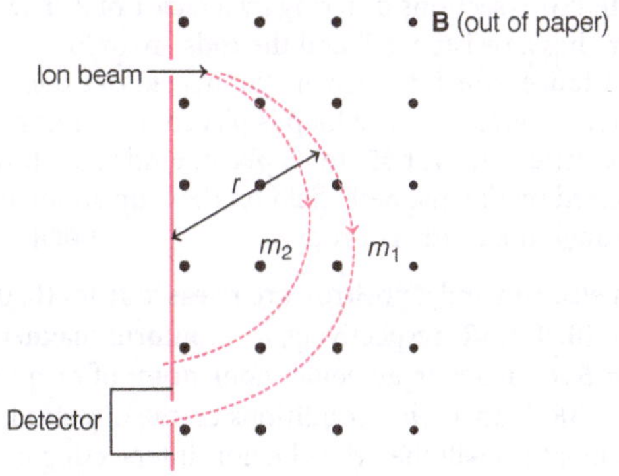

To what value should the magnetic field be changed, so that this stream of particles strikes the detector?

Competency Based Que

13. (i) Write the expression for the magnetic force acting on a charged particle moving with velocity v in the presence of magnetic field **B**. **[1½]**

(ii) A neutron, an electron and an alpha particle moving with equal velocities, enter a uniform magnetic field going into the plane of the paper as shown in the figure. Trace their paths in the field and justify your answer. **Competency Based Que.** **[1½]**

14. A current-carrying loop consists of 3 identical quarter circles of radius R, lying in the positive quadrants of the XY, YZ and ZX-planes with their centres at the origin, joined together. Find the direction and magnitude of **B** at the origin.

15. A wire of length l is in the form of a circular loop A of one turn. This loop is reshaped into loop B of three turns. Find the ratio of the magnetic fields at the centres of loop A and loop B for the same current through them. **CBSE 2023**

16. An α-particle and a proton of the same kinetic energy are in turn allowed to pass through a magnetic field **B**, acting normal to the direction of motion of the particles. Calculate the ratio of radii of the circular paths described by them. **CBSE 2019**

17. A circular loop of radius 10 cm carrying-current of 1.0 A lies in XY-plane. A long straight wire lies in the same plane parallel to X-axis at a distance of 20 cm as shown in figure.

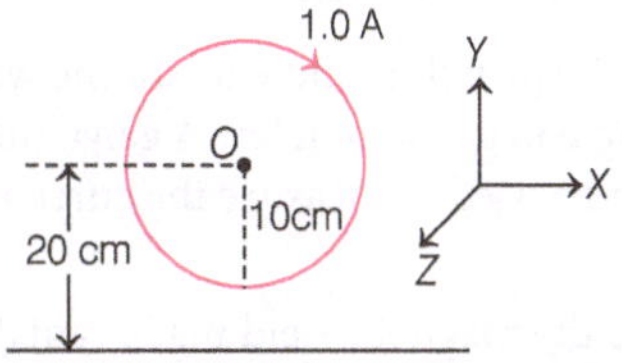

Find the direction and value of current that has to be maintained in the wire, so that the net magnetic field at O is zero. **CBSE 2024**

18. An infinite straight conductor is kept along $X'X$-axis and carries a current I. A charge q at point $P(0, r)$ starts moving with velocity $\mathbf{v} = v_0\hat{\mathbf{j}}$ as shown in figure. Find the direction and magnitude of force initially experienced by the charge. **CBSE 2024**

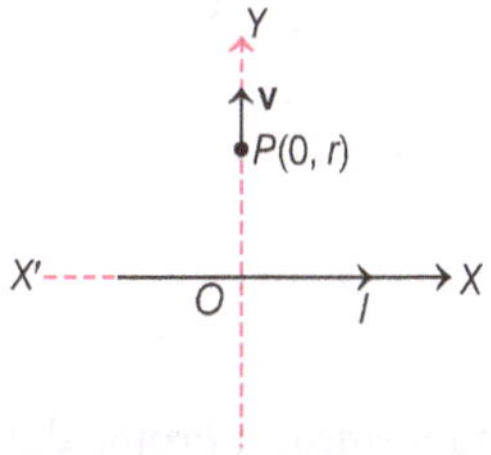

19. A long straight wire carrying current of 25A rests on a table as shown in figure. Another wire PQ of length 1m, mass 2.5 g carries the same current but in the opposite direction. The wire PQ is free to slide up and down. To what height will PQ rise? **Competency Based Que.**

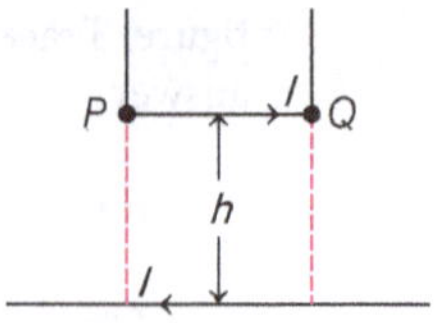

20. A charged particle q is moving in the presence of a magnetic field B which is inclined to an angle 30° with the direction of the motion of the particle. Draw the trajectory followed by the particle in the presence of the field and explain how the particle describes this path.

21. A deuteron and an alpha particle having same momentum are in turn allowed to pass through a magnetic field **B**, acting normal to the direction of motion of the particles. Calculate the ratio of the radii of the circular paths described by them. **Competency Based Que**

22. Deduce an expression for the torque on a current carrying loop suspended in a uniform magnetic field.

23. In a moving coil galvanometer having a coil of N turns of area A and carrying current I and is placed in a radial field of strength B. What will be the torque acting on the coil?

24. Briefly explain why and how a galvanometer is converted into an ammeter? **CBSE 2023**

25. (i) Write the principle and explain the working of a moving coil galvanometer. A galvanometer as such cannot be used to measure the current in a circuit. Why? **[1½]**

(ii) Why is the magnetic field made radial in a moving coil galvanometer? How is it achieved? **CBSE 2023** **[1½]**

26. A point charge is moving with a constant velocity perpendicular to a uniform magnetic field as shown in the figure. What should be magnitude and direction of the electric field so that the particle moves undeviated along the same path?

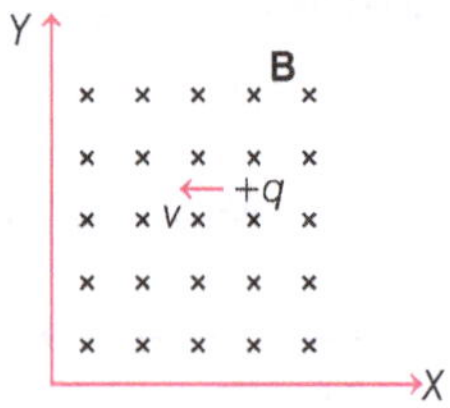

27. In a certain arrangement, a proton does not get deflected while passing through a magnetic field region. Under what condition, is it possible?

28. (i) Write two reasons why a galvanometer cannot be used as such to measure the current in a given circuit. Name any two factors on which the current sensitivity of a galvanometer depends.

(ii) Why is it necessary to introduce a cylindrical soft iron core inside the coil of a galvanometer?

Long Answer Type Questions

29. State and explain Biot-Savart's law. Use it to derive an expression for the magnetic field produced at a point near a long current-carrying wire.

30. Two very small identical circular loops (1) and (2) carrying equal current I are placed vertically (with respect to the plane of the paper) with their geometrical axes perpendicular to each other as shown in the figure. Find the magnitude and direction of the net magnetic field produced at the point O.

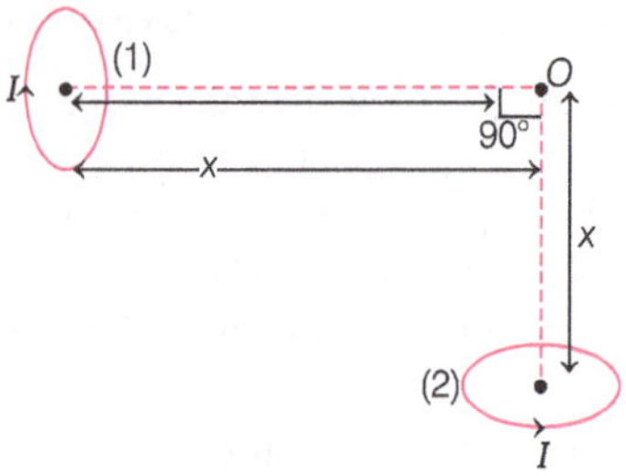

31. A rectangular conducting loop consists of two wires on two opposite sides of length l joined together by rods of length d. The wires are each of the same material but with cross-sections differing by a factor of 2. The thicker wire has a resistance R and the rods are of low resistance, which in turn are connected to a constant voltage source V_0. The loop is placed in a uniform magnetic field **B** at 45° to its plane. Find τ, the torque exerted by the magnetic field on the loop about an axis through the centres of rods. **NCERT Exemplar**

32. An electron and a positron are released from (0, 0, 0) and (0, 0, 1.5R) respectively, in a uniform magnetic field $\mathbf{B} = B_0\hat{\mathbf{i}}$, each with an equal momentum of magnitude $p = eBR$. Under what conditions on the direction of momentum will the orbits be non-intersecting circles? **NCERT Exemplar**

33. (i) In a region of a uniform electric field **E**, a negatively charged particle is moving with a constant velocity $\mathbf{v} = -v_0\hat{\mathbf{i}}$ near a long straight conductor coinciding with XX' axis and carrying current I towards $-X$ axis. The particle remains at a distance d from the conductor.

(a) Draw a diagram showing direction of electric and magnetic fields. **[1]**

(b) What are the various forces acting on the charged particle? **CBSE 2025** **[2]**

(c) Find the value of v_0 in terms of E, d and I. **[2]**

Or (ii) Two infinitely long conductors kept along XX' and YY' axes are carrying currents I_1 and I_2 along $-X$ and $-Y$ axes respectively. Find the magnitude and direction of the net magnetic field produced at point $P(X,Y)$. **CBSE 2025**

34. Two straight infinitely long wires are fixed in space, so that the current in the left wire is 2 A and directed out of the plane of the page and the current in the right wire is 3 A and directed into the plane of the page. In which region(s) is/are there a point on the X-axis, at which the magnetic field is equal to zero due to these current carrying wires? **CBSE SQP, Term-I**

Justify your answer.

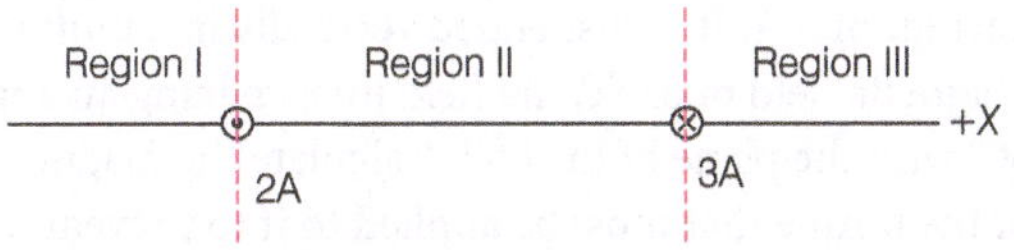

35. Explain, how Biot-Savart's law enables one to express the Ampere's circuital law in the integral form, *viz.*

$$\oint \mathbf{B} \cdot d\mathbf{l} = \mu_0 I$$

where, I is the total current passing through the surface.

36. (i) State Ampere's circuital law expressing it in the integral form. **[2]**

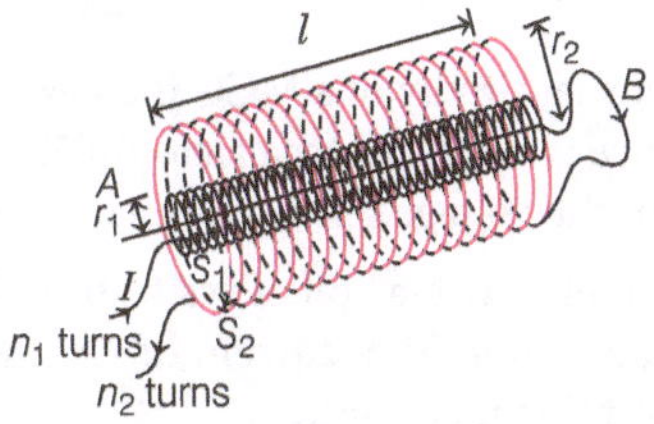

(ii) Two long coaxial insulated solenoids, S_1 and S_2 of equal lengths are wound one over the other as shown in the figure. A steady current I flows through the inner solenoid S_1 to the other end B, which is connected to the outer solenoid S_2 through which the same current I flows in the opposite direction, so as to come out at end A. If n_1 and n_2 are the number of turns per unit length, find the magnitude and direction of the net magnetic field at a point (a) inside on the axis and (b) outside the combined system. **[3]**

37. (i) What is the source of force acting on a current-carrying conductor placed in a magnetic field? Obtain the expression for force acting between two long straight parallel conductors carrying steady currents and hence define 'ampere'. **[2]**

(ii) A point charge q is moving with velocity **v** in a uniform magnetic field **B**. Find the work done by the magnetic force on the charge. **[1½]**

(iii) Explain the necessary conditions in which the trajectory of a charged particle is helical in a uniform magnetic field. **CBSE 2025** **[1½]**

38. (i) Show that a current- carrying solenoid behaves like a small bar magnet. Obtain the expression for the magnetic field at an external point lying on its axis. **[2]**

(ii) Derive the expression for the force acting between two long parallel current carrying conductors. Hence, define 1 A current. **[3]**

39. (i) Write the expression for the force **F** acting on a particle of mass m and charge q moving with velocity v in a magnetic field **B**. Under what conditions will it move in **[3]**

(a) a circular path and (b) a helical path?

(ii) Show that the kinetic energy of the particle moving in magnetic field remains constant. **[2]**

40. A uniform magnetic field **B** is set-up along the positive X-axis. A particle of charge q and mass m moving with a velocity v enters the field at the origin in XY-plane, such that it has velocity components both along and perpendicular to the magnetic field **B**. Trace, giving reason, the trajectory followed by the particle. Find out the expression for the distance moved by the particle along the magnetic field in one rotation.

41. A 100 turns rectangular coil $ABCD$ (in XY-plane) is hung from one arm of a balance figure. A mass 500 g is added to the other arm to balance the weight of the coil. A current 4.9 A passes through the coil and a constant magnetic field of 0.2 T acting inward (in XZ-plane) is switched ON such that only arm CD of length 1 cm lies in the field. How much additional mass m must be added to regain the balance?

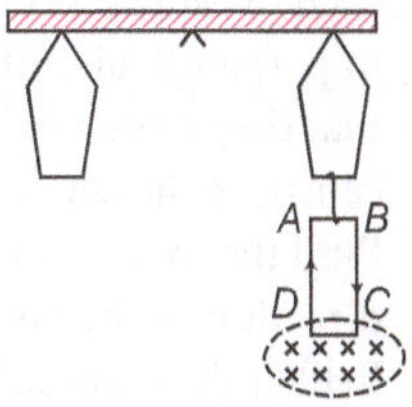

42. Three wires of equal lengths are bent into the form of three loops. One of the loops is square-shaped, second loop is equilateral triangular-shaped and third loop is circular. These are suspended in a uniform magnetic field and the same current is passed through them. Which loop will experience greater torque? Give reasons.

43. (i) Write the principle and explain the working of a moving coil galvanometer. A galvanometer as such cannot be used to measure the current in a circuit. Why? **[4]**

(ii) Why is the magnetic field made radial in a moving coil galvanometer? How is it achieved? **[1]**

CBSE 2023

Numerical Problems

Magnetic Field on the Axis of a Current-Carrying Circular Loop

44. Two concentric circular wire loops of radii 20 cm and 30 cm are located in an XY-plane, each carries a clockwise current of 7 A.

(i) Find the magnitude of the net magnetic dipole moment of the system.

(ii) Repeat for reversed current in the inner loop.

45. The wire shown in the figure carries a current of 10 A. Determine the magnitude of magnetic field induction at the centre O. Given the radius of bent coil is 3 cm.

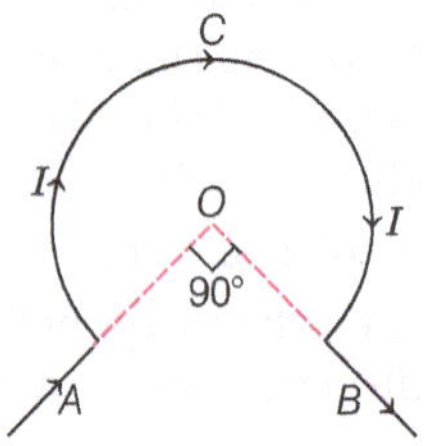

Competency Based Que.

46. Two identical circular coils, P and Q each of radius R, carrying currents 1 A and $\sqrt{3}$ A respectively, are placed concentrically and perpendicular to each other lying in the XY and YZ-planes. Find the magnitude and direction of the net magnetic field at the centre of the coils.

47. Two identical loops P and Q each of radius 5 cm are lying in perpendicular planes such that they have a common centre as shown in the figure. Find the magnitude and direction of the net magnetic field at the common centre of the two coils, if they carry currents equal to 3 A and 4 A, respectively. Competency Based Que

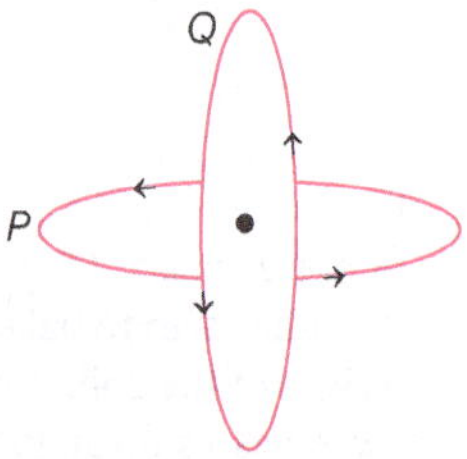

Solenoid

48. A closely wound solenoid 0.80 m long has 5 layers of windings of 400 turns each. The diameter of the solenoid is 1.8×10^{-2} m. If the current carried is 0.8 A, what will be the magnitude of field near the centre?

49. A solenoid of length 1.0 m and 3.0 cm diameter has 5 layers of windings of 850 turns each and carries a current of 5 A. What is the magnetic field at the centre of solenoid? Also, calculate the magnetic flux from a cross-section of the magnetic flux solenoid at the centre of solenoid. Competency Based Que

Magnetic Force and Torque Experienced by a Current Loop

50. A conductor of length 2 m carrying-current of 2 A is held parallel to an infinitely long conductor carrying current of 10 A at a distance of 100 mm. Find the force on a small conductor.

51. A wire AB is carrying a steady current of 12 A and is lying on the table. Another wire CD carrying 5 A is held directly above AB at a height of 1 mm. Find the mass per unit length of the wire CD, so that it remains suspended at its position when left free. Give the direction of the current flowing in CD with respect to that in AB. (Take, $g = 10\ \text{ms}^{-2}$)

52. A circular coil of 100 turns, radius 10 cm carries a current of 5 A. It is suspended vertically in a uniform magnetic field of 0.5 T, the field lines making an angle of 60° with the plane of the coil. Calculate the magnitude of the torque that must be applied to it to prevent it from turning. Competency Based Que

Galvanometer

53. The coil of galvanometer consists of 100 turns and effective area of 1 cm^2. The restoring couple is 10^{-8} N-m/rad. The magnetic field between poles is of 5 T. What will be the current sensitivity of galvanometer? Competency Based Que

54. The current sensitivity of a MCG increases by 20%, when its resistance is increased by a factor of 2. Calculate by what factor the voltage sensitivity changes ?

55. A galvanometer with a coil of resistance 12.0 Ω shows full scale deflection for a current of 2.5 mA. How will you convert this meter into

(i) an ammeter of range 0 to 7.5 A ? **[1]**

(ii) a voltmeter of range 0 to 10 V? Determine the net resistance of the meter in each case. When an ammeter is put in a circuit, does it read less or more than the actual current in the original circuit? When a voltmeter is put across a part of the circuit, does it read less or more than the required voltage drop? Explain. **[2]**

56. A galvanometer having 30 divisions has a current sensitivity of 20 μA/ div. It has a resistance of 25 Ω.

(i) How will you convert it into an ammeter of range 0 to 1 A? **[1]**

(ii) How will you convert this ammeter into a voltmeter of range 0 to 1 V? **[2]**

57. When a galvanometer having 30 division scale and 100 Ω resistance is connected in series to the battery of emf 3 V through a resistance of 200 Ω, shows full scale deflection. Find the figure of merit of the galvanometer (in microampere).

58. (i) A circular coil of 30 turns and radius 8.0 cm carrying a current of 6.0 A is suspended vertically in a uniform horizontal magnetic field of magnitude 1.0 T.
The field lines make an angle 60° with the normal of the coil. Calculate the magnitude of the counter torque that must be applied to prevent the coil from turning.
(ii) Would your answer change, if the circular coil were replaced by a planar coil of some irregular shape that encloses the same area? All other particulars are also unaltered. **NCERT**

59. A rectangular coil of area $2\times10^{-4}\ m^2$ and 40 turns is pivoted about one of its vertical sides. The coil is in a radial horizontal field of 60 G. What is the torsional constant of the hair springs connected to the coil, if a current of 4.0 mA produces an angular deflection of 16°?

Hints & Solutions

Objective Type Questions

1. (c) Magnetic field inside the wire, $B_{in} = \dfrac{\mu_0 I\cdot r}{2\pi a^2}$

Magnetic field outside the wire, $B_{out} = \dfrac{\mu_0 I}{2\pi r}$

We have to find the ratio of magnetic field at point $\dfrac{a}{2}$ above the surface (outside the wire) and $\dfrac{a}{2}$ below the surface.

$$r = a + \frac{a}{2} = \frac{3a}{2}$$

Then, $B_{outside} = \dfrac{\mu_0 I}{2\pi\left(\dfrac{3a}{2}\right)} = \dfrac{\mu_0 I}{3\pi a}$

Similarly, for below the surface,

$$r = \frac{a}{2}$$

$$B_{inside} = \frac{\mu_0 I \frac{a}{2}}{2\pi a^2} = \frac{\mu_0 I}{4\pi a}$$

$$\therefore \quad \frac{B_{outside}}{B_{inside}} = \frac{\dfrac{\mu_0 I}{3\pi a}}{\dfrac{\mu_0 I}{4\pi a}} = \frac{4}{3}$$

2. (a)

3. (a) The direction of magnetic moment of circular loop of radius R is placed in the XY-plane is along z-direction and given by $M = I(\pi r^2)$, when half of the loop with $x > 0$ is now bent so that it now lies in the YZ-plane, the magnitudes of magnetic moment of each semicircular loop of radius R lie in the XY-plane and the YZ-plane is $M' = I(\pi r^2)/4$ and the direction of magnetic moments are along z-direction and x-direction, respectively. Their resultant is

$$M_{net} = \sqrt{M'^2 + M'^2}$$
$$= \sqrt{2}\, M' = \sqrt{2}\, I(\pi r^2)/4$$

So, $M_{net} < M$ or M diminishes.

4. (c)

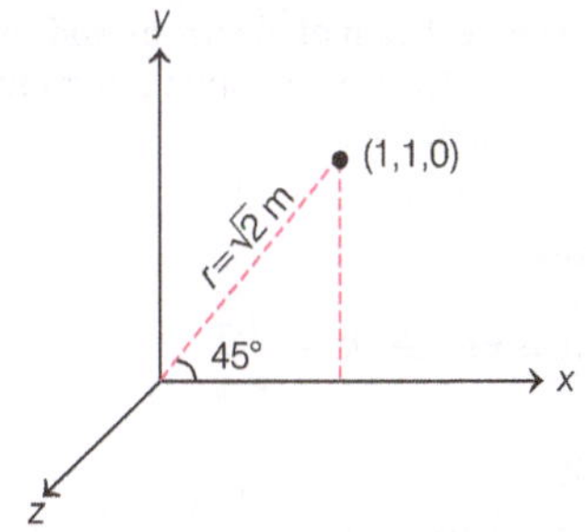

By Biot-Savart's law, $B = \dfrac{\mu_0 I\, dl \sin\theta}{4\pi\, r^2}$

$$\Rightarrow \quad B = \frac{10^{-7}\times1\times10^{-2}\sin45^\circ}{r^2}$$

$$\Rightarrow \quad B = \frac{10^{-7}\times1\times10^{-2}}{2}\times\frac{1}{\sqrt{2}}$$

$$\therefore \quad B = \frac{0.5}{\sqrt{2}}\times10^{-9}\,\hat{\mathbf{k}}\ T$$

$$= \frac{5}{\sqrt{2}}\times10^{-10}\,\hat{\mathbf{k}}\ T$$

5. (a) 6. (d)

7. (c) Statement c is incorrect. The angular frequency $\omega = \dfrac{qB}{m}$ depends on the specific charge. A particle with a different specific charge will have a different angular frequency.

8. (*d*) For given pitch d correspond to charge particle, we have

$$\frac{q}{m} = \frac{2\pi v \cos\theta}{qB} = \text{constant}$$

Since, charged particles traverse identical helical paths in a completely opposite sense in a uniform magnetic field **B**, LHS for two particles should be same and of opposite sign. Therefore,

$$\left(\frac{e}{m}\right)_1 + \left(\frac{e}{m}\right)_2 = 0$$

9. (*c*)

10. (*b*) Since, an electron moves on semi-circular path in magnetic field, therefore its speed remains constant during its entire motion in magnetic field. Hence, final speed of the electron will be same as its initial speed (v).

11. (*d*)

12. (*a*) 13. (*c*)

14. (*a*) Force, $F = IBl\sin\theta$

$$7.5 \times 10^{-3} = 5 \times 0.2 \times 1.5 \times 10^{-2} \sin\theta$$

$$\Rightarrow \quad \sin\theta = \frac{7.5}{2 \times 5 \times 1.5} = \frac{1}{2}$$

$$\theta = 30°$$

15. (*b*)

16. (*b*) Since, direction of current is taken in opposite direction of flow of electron or in the direction of flow of proton. Hence, beam of electrons and protons moving parallel to each other in the same direction produce current in opposite direction.

Therefore, they repel each other.

17. (*b*) For loop-I,

$$A = \pi R_1^2 \Rightarrow R_1 = \sqrt{\frac{A}{\pi}}$$

For loop-II,

$$4A = \pi R_2^2 \Rightarrow R_2 = \sqrt{\frac{4A}{\pi}}$$

Magnetic field at the centres of loop,

$$B = \frac{\mu_0 I}{2R} \Rightarrow B \propto \frac{I}{R}$$

$$\frac{B_1}{B_2} = \frac{I_1 R_2}{I_2 R_1} \Rightarrow \frac{B_1}{B_2} = \sqrt{\frac{4A}{\pi}} \times \sqrt{\frac{\pi}{A}} \times \frac{2I}{I}$$

$$\frac{B_1}{B_2} = \frac{4}{1}$$

$$B_1 : B_2 = 4:1$$

18. (*b*) The situation is as shown below.

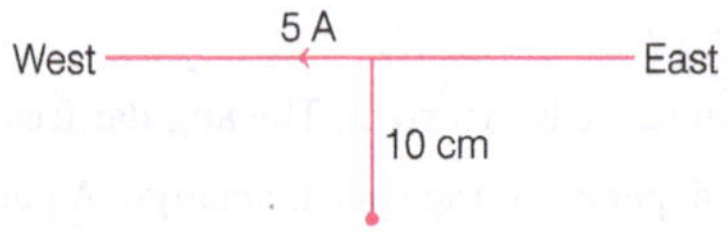

Magnetic field due to long straight wire, $B = \dfrac{\mu_0 I}{2\pi r}$

Here, $I = 5\text{A}$ and $r = 10\text{ cm} = 0.1\text{ m}$

$$\therefore \quad B = \frac{4\pi \times 10^{-7} \times 5}{2\pi \times 0.1} = 1 \times 10^{-5}\ \text{T}$$

The direction of magnetic field is given by right hand thumb rule. So, the direction of magnetic field of point 10 cm is upward due South on the table.

19. (*c*) When a charged particle moves in a magnetic field, it experiences a force called Lorentz force, which is given by $\mathbf{F} = q(\mathbf{v} \times \mathbf{B})$

In this case, the particles has a negative velocity in the y-direction and a magnetic field in the x-direction. The cross product of these two vectors point in the positive z-direction.

∴ The particle will experience a force in the positive z-direction which will cause it to move in a helical path.

20. (*d*) The magnetic field due to an infinitely long straight wire at a distance R is given by

$$B = \frac{\mu_0 I}{2\pi R}$$

For $\quad R = a$

$$B \propto \frac{1}{a}$$

21. (*a*) According to Biot-Savart's law,

$$\mathbf{B} = \frac{\mu_0}{4\pi} |q| \frac{(\mathbf{v} \times \mathbf{r})}{|r^3|} \hat{\mathbf{n}}$$

where, $\hat{\mathbf{n}}$ is direction of **B** which is the direction of cross product of **v** and **r**.

So, we can say that **B** is perpendicular to both **v** and **r**.

22. (*b*) A galvanometer can be converted into an ammeter of given range by connecting a suitable low resistance S called shunt in parallel to the given galvanometer, whose value is given by

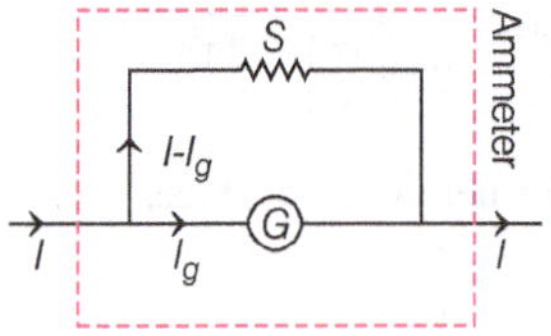

$$\Rightarrow \quad S = \left(\frac{I_g}{I - I_g}\right) G$$

$$\Rightarrow \quad I_g = \left(\frac{S}{S+G}\right) I$$

where, I_g is the current in circuit for which ammeter will show full scale deflection,

Here, $\quad G = 100\,\Omega$

$S = 0.1\,\Omega$

$I_g = 1\text{A}$

$$I_g = \left(\frac{S}{S+G}\right) I = \frac{0.1}{(0.1 + 100)} \times 1$$

$$= 9.9 \times 10^{-4} \simeq 10 \times 10^{-4} = 1 \times 10^{-3} = 1\text{ mA}$$

23. (*d*) Given that, $I'_g = I_g + \frac{20}{100} I_g$

$$I'_g = 1.2 I_g$$

and $R' = R + \frac{25}{100} R = 1.25R$

$$V'_g = ?$$

$$V'_g = \frac{I'_g}{R'} = \frac{1.2 I_g}{1.25R} = \frac{24}{25} V_g$$

$$\% \text{ Change } = \frac{V'_g - V_g}{V_g} \times 100$$

$$= \frac{\frac{24}{25} V_g - V_g}{V_g} \times 100$$

$$= -\frac{1}{25} \times 100$$

$$\% \text{ Change} = -4\%$$

24. (*a*) **25.** (*b*)

26 (*b*) **27.** (*b*)

28. (*a*) **29.** (*d*)

30. (*b*) **31.** (*a*)

32. (*a*) **33.** (*c*)

34. (*a*)

35. (i) (*b*) We know that, $r = \frac{mv}{qB}$

If the speed is double, i.e. $v = 2v_0$, then

$$r' = \frac{m(2v_0)}{qB} = 2 \times \frac{mv_0}{qB} = 2r_0$$

(ii) (*c*) The time period for one revolution T is given by

$$T = \frac{2\pi r}{v} = \frac{2\pi\left(\frac{mv}{qB}\right)}{v} = \frac{2\pi m}{qB}$$

The time period is independent of the speed v, therefore even when the speed is double, the time period remains the same.

(iii) (*b*) Given, $\mathbf{B} = (2\hat{i} + 4\hat{j}) \times 10^2 \text{T}$, $\mathbf{a} = (x\hat{i} + 2\hat{j}) \text{ ms}^{-2}$

We know that, magnetic field, $\mathbf{F} = q(\mathbf{v} \times \mathbf{B})$

where, $q =$ charge, $\mathbf{v} =$ velocity

and $\mathbf{B} =$ magnetic field.

Since, dot product of two perpendicular vectors is zero, i.e. $\mathbf{F} \cdot \mathbf{B} = 0$

$$\Rightarrow \quad m(\mathbf{a} \cdot \mathbf{B}) = 0 \qquad (\because \mathbf{F} = m\mathbf{a})$$

$$\Rightarrow \quad \mathbf{a} \cdot \mathbf{B} = 0 \Rightarrow (x\hat{i} + 2\hat{j}) \cdot (2\hat{i} + 4\hat{j}) \times 10^2 = 0$$

$$\Rightarrow \quad 2x + 8 = 0 \Rightarrow x = \frac{-8}{2} \Rightarrow x = -4 \text{ ms}^{-2}$$

(iv) (*c*) When the velocity of the charged particle is not perpendicular to the magnetic field, the component of velocity along the field will remain unaffected, while the perpendicular component will cause circular motion. As a result, the path of the electron becomes helical.

Or

(*d*) When the velocity of a charged particle is parallel or anti-parallel to the magnetic field, the magnetic force on the particle is zero, because the force is proportional to $\sin\theta$, where θ is the angle between v and B for parallel motion $\theta = 0°$ and $\sin 0° = 0$.

36. (i) (*d*) A moving coil galvanometer is a sensitive instrument which is used to measure a deflection when a current flows through its coil.

(ii) (*d*) Uniform field is made radial by cutting pole pieces cylindrically.

(iii) (*b*) The deflection in a moving coil galvanometer, $\phi = \frac{NAB}{k} \cdot I$ or $\phi \propto N$, where N is number of turns in a coil, B is magnetic field and A is area of cross-section.

(iv) (*d*) The deflecting torque acting on the coil,

$$\tau_{\text{deflection}} = NIAB$$

Or

(*b*) Current sensitivity of galvanometer,

$$\frac{\phi}{I} = S_i = \frac{NBA}{k}$$

Hence, to increase current sensitivity S_i, then torsional constant of spring k must be decreased.

Subjective Questions

1. The work done is zero because in a perpendicular magnetic field the charge will execute a circular path and the velocity of the particle and the force are perpendicular to each other.

2. Yes, the magnetic force differ from inertial frame to frame. The magnetic force is frame dependent.

The net acceleration which comes into existing out of this is however, frame independent (non -relativistic physics) for inertial frames.

3. (i) If the current flows in the same direction, then they will experience attractive force.

(ii) If the current flow in the opposite direction, then they will experience a repulsive force.

4. At point P_1 (2 m , 2 m),

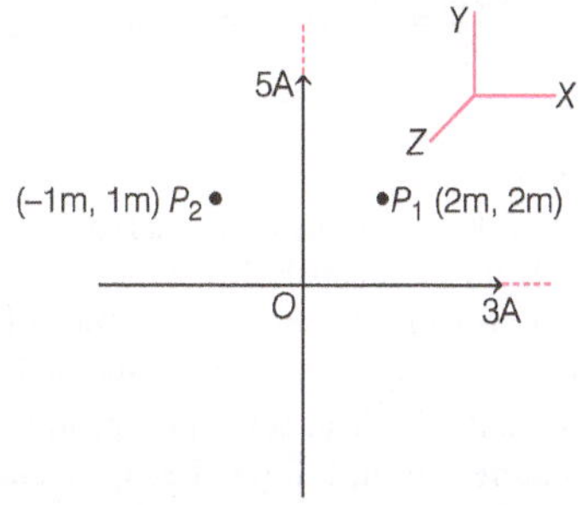

The net magnetic field, at point P_1 (2m, 2m)

$$\mathbf{B}_{\text{net}} = \mathbf{B}_X - \mathbf{B}_Y = \frac{\mu_0 I_1}{2\pi d} - \frac{\mu_0 I_2}{2\pi d}$$

$$= \frac{\mu_0(I_1 - I_2)}{2\pi d} = \frac{+\mu_0}{2\pi} \text{ (inward)}$$

At point $P_2(-1\text{m}, 1\text{m})$, the net magnetic field is

$$\mathbf{B}_{\text{net}} = \frac{\mu_0 \times 5}{2\pi \times 1} + \frac{\mu_0 \times 3}{2\pi \times 1} = \frac{4\mu_0}{\pi} \text{ (outward)}$$

The direction of magnetic field on point P_1 is inward whereas direction of magnetic field on point P_2 is outward.

5. Ratio $= \frac{B_1}{\sqrt{B_1^2 + B_2^2}} = \frac{B}{\sqrt{B^2 + B^2}} = \frac{1}{\sqrt{2}}$

6. Suppose a particle is moving in the presence of magnetic field. Consider q be the charge on the particle, v be the velocity of the particle and **B** be the magnitude of magnetic field.

Then, the magnitude of force is given by

$$\mathbf{F} = q(\mathbf{v} \times \mathbf{B})$$

This force is acting perpendicular to the plane containing **v** and **B** and is directed as given by right hand rule. Since, work done, $W = \mathbf{F} \cdot \mathbf{s} = F \cdot s \cos\theta$

Displacement of the charged particle,

$$s = (r_2 - r_1)$$

and angle, $\theta = 90°$

So, work done by this force on the particle during its motion.

$$W = F \cdot (r_2 - r_1) \cos 90°$$
$$W = 0$$

7. Here, area of coil, $A = 10 \times 10 = 100 \text{ cm}^2 = 10^{-2} \text{ m}^2$

Number of turns, $N = 20$ turns

Current, $I = 12$ A

Number of the coils make angle with magnetic field $= \theta = ?$

Magnetic field, $B = 0.8$ T

Torque, $\tau = 0.96$ N-m

$\because$ Torque (τ) experienced by current-carrying coil, the magnetic field,

$$\tau = NIAB \sin\theta$$
$$0.96 = 20 \times 12 \times 10^{-2} \times 0.8 \times \sin\theta$$
$$\Rightarrow \sin\theta = \frac{0.96}{1.92} = \frac{1}{2} \Rightarrow \theta = \frac{\pi}{6} \text{ rad}$$

8. $V_s = \frac{nBA}{(KR_g)}$.

According to the given formula, increasing the number of turns will simultaneously increase the length of the coil which in turn increase the resistance of the coil R_g. Therefore, the voltage sensitivity remains the same.

9. **Current sensitivity** The deflection produced in the coil of galvanometer per unit flow of electric current through it.

Current sensitivity, $I_g = \frac{\theta}{I} = \frac{NBA}{K}$

where, abbreviations are as usual.

Voltage sensitivity The deflection produced in the galvanometer per unit applied potential difference across it.

$\therefore$ Voltage sensitivity, $V_s = \frac{\theta}{V} = \frac{\theta}{IR} = \frac{NBA}{KR}$

where, abbreviations are as usual.

Its unit is $\frac{\text{rad}}{\text{V}}$ or $\frac{\text{div}}{\text{V}}$

Increasing the current sensitivity may not necessarily increase the voltage sensitivity because the current sensitivity increases with the increase of number of turns of the coil but the resistance of coil also increases which affect adversely on voltage sensitivity.

10. According to right-hand screw rule, force on AD is

$$F_1 = \frac{\mu_0 I_1 I_2 a}{2\pi x} \text{ (towards right)}$$

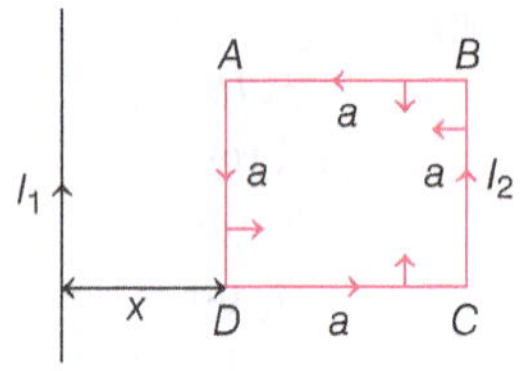

Force on BC is $F_2 = \frac{\mu_0 I_1 I_2 a}{2\pi(x + a)}$ (towards left)

The forces on AB and DC are equal and opposite, so they will cancel each other. Thus, net force on loop is

$$F_R = \frac{\mu_0 I_1 I_2 a}{2\pi}\left(\frac{1}{x} - \frac{1}{x + a}\right)$$
$$= \frac{\mu_0 I_1 I_2 a^2}{2\pi x(x + a)} \text{ (towards right)}$$

11. (i) Particle in magnetic field, $F_B = qvB$

Since, the particles have same charge undergo head-on collision, this implies that the magnetic field exert force on both particles in opposite direction. The magnetic forces on both particles must be directed towards each other. Hence, the magnetic field must be perpendicular to both their velocity and direction into the plane (i.e. along negative Z-axis).

(ii) For a head-on collision to take place, the radius of the path of each ion should be equal to 0.5m.

Given, $m = 4 \times 10^{-26}$ kg, $v = 2.4 \times 10^5$ m/s

$q = 4.8 \times 10^{-19}$ C, $r = 0.5$ m

$$\therefore \quad r = \frac{mv}{qB}$$
$$\Rightarrow B = \frac{mv}{qr} = \frac{4 \times 10^{-26} \times 2.4 \times 10^5}{4.8 \times 10^{-19} \times 0.5} \Rightarrow B = 0.04 \text{ T}$$

12. Equating the kinetic energy of charged particles to the energy gained due to accelerating potential V,

$$\frac{1}{2}mv^2 = qV$$

$$v = \sqrt{\frac{2qV}{m}}$$

Equating the magnetic force on the charged particle's to the centripetal force acting on them,

$$qvB = \frac{mv^2}{r}$$

$$B = \frac{1}{r}\sqrt{\frac{2mV}{q}}$$

For same accelerating potential V, radius r and charge q,

$$\frac{B_2}{B_1} = \sqrt{\frac{m_2}{m_1}} = \sqrt{\frac{0.2\times10^{-26}}{0.8\times10^{-26}}} = \sqrt{\frac{1}{4}} = \frac{1}{2}$$

$$B_2 = \frac{B_1}{2} = \frac{0.2}{2} = 0.1 \text{ T}$$

13. (i) Magnetic force on a charged particle is given by

$$\mathbf{F} = q(\mathbf{v}\times\mathbf{B})$$

(ii) The direction of force on the charged particle is given by $(\mathbf{v}\times\mathbf{B})$ with the sign of charged particle, i.e. for α-particle, charge is positive and direction of $\mathbf{v}$ is $+\hat{\mathbf{i}}$ and direction of $\mathbf{B}$ is $-\hat{\mathbf{k}}$.

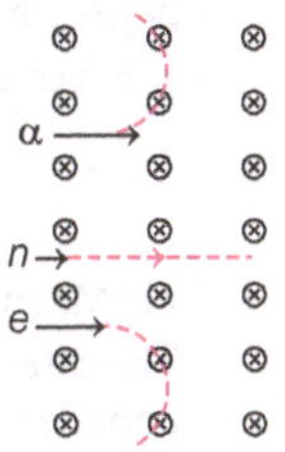

So, direction of force is $+\{(\hat{\mathbf{i}}\times-\hat{\mathbf{k}})\}$, i.e. $+\hat{\mathbf{j}}$.

It describes a circle with anti-clockwise motion.

For neutron

It is a neutral particle, so goes undeviated.

As, $\mathbf{F} = q(\mathbf{v}\times\mathbf{B}) = 0$

For electron

Force is given by $\mathbf{F} = -e(\mathbf{v}\times\mathbf{B})$

So, direction $= -\{(\hat{\mathbf{i}}\times-\hat{\mathbf{k}})\} = -\hat{\mathbf{j}}$

e^- describes a circle with clockwise motion

14. For the current-carrying loop quarter circles of radius R, lying in the positive quadrants of the XY-plane.

$$\mathbf{B}_1 = \frac{\mu_0}{4\pi}\frac{I(\pi/2)}{R}\hat{\mathbf{k}} = \frac{\mu_0}{4}\frac{I}{2R}\hat{\mathbf{k}}$$

For the current-carrying loop quarter circles of radius R, lying in the positive quadrants of the YZ-plane.

$$\mathbf{B}_2 = \frac{\mu_0}{4}\frac{I}{2R}\hat{\mathbf{i}}$$

For the current-carrying loop quarter circles of radius R, lying in the positive quadrants of the ZX-plane.

$$\mathbf{B}_3 = \frac{\mu_0}{4}\frac{I}{2R}\hat{\mathbf{j}}$$

Current-carrying loop consists of 3 identical quarter circles of radius R, lying in the positive quadrants of the XY, YZ and ZX-planes with their centres at the origin, joined together is equal to the vector sum of magnetic field due to each quarter and given by

$$\mathbf{B} = \frac{1}{4}(\hat{\mathbf{i}}+\hat{\mathbf{j}}+\hat{\mathbf{k}})\frac{\mu_0 I}{2R} = \frac{\mu_0 I}{8R}(\hat{\mathbf{i}}+\hat{\mathbf{j}}+\hat{\mathbf{k}})$$

$\therefore$ The magnitude of the resultant magnetic field is given as

$$|\mathbf{B}| = \sqrt{\left(\frac{\mu_0 I}{8R}\right)^2 + \left(\frac{\mu_0 I}{8R}\right)^2 + \left(\frac{\mu_0 I}{8R}\right)^2} = \frac{\sqrt{3}\mu_0 I}{8R}$$

The direction is given as

$$\hat{\mathbf{B}} = \mathbf{B}/|\mathbf{B}| = (\hat{\mathbf{i}}+\hat{\mathbf{j}}+\hat{\mathbf{k}})/\sqrt{3}$$

15. Length of circular loop $A = l$

If R_1 be the radius of circular loop A, then,

$$l = 2\pi r_1$$

$$\Rightarrow \quad r_1 = l/2\pi$$

$\therefore$ Magnetic field at the centre of the circular loop A.

$$B_1 = \frac{\mu_0 I_1}{2r_1} \quad \text{... (i)}$$

When the loop A is reshaped into loop B, then radius of circular loop B, is calculated as

$$3\times 2\pi r_B = l$$

$$\Rightarrow \quad r_B = \frac{l}{6\pi}$$

$\therefore$ Magnetic field at the centre of the circular loop B,

$$B_2 = \frac{\mu_0 I_2}{2r_2} \quad \text{... (ii)}$$

$\therefore$ From Eqs. (i) and (ii), we get

$$\therefore \quad \frac{B_1}{B_2} = \frac{I_1}{I_2}\times\frac{r_2}{r_1} = \frac{r_2}{r_1}$$

$$= \frac{l/6\pi}{l/2\pi} \quad [\because I_1 = I_2]$$

$$= \frac{2\pi}{6\pi} = \frac{1}{3}$$

$$\therefore \quad B_1 : B_2 = 1:3$$

16. Refer to sol. of Example 10 on page 138.

17. Given, a circular loop of radius 10 cm carrying-current of 1 A and a long straight wire at a distance of 20 cm from the centre of loop.

Magnetic field at point O due to the circular loop,

$B_1 = \frac{\mu_0 I_1}{2R}$, where R is the radius of circular loop,

$$B_1 = \frac{1\mu_0}{2(0.1)}$$

Magnetic field at point O due to the straight wire,

$B_2 = \frac{\mu_0 I_2}{2\pi r}$, where r is the distance of wire from the point O.

$$B_2 = \frac{\mu_0 I_2}{2\pi(0.2)}$$

For net magnetic field at O to be zero.

$$\Rightarrow \quad B_1 = B_2$$

$$\frac{1\,\mu_0}{2(0.1)} = \frac{-\mu_0 I_2}{2\pi(0.2)}$$

$$\Rightarrow \quad 1 = \frac{-I_2}{\pi(0.2)}$$

$$\Rightarrow \quad I_2 = -\pi(0.2)$$

$$\Rightarrow \quad I_2 = -6.28\text{ A}$$

Direction of current is from negative X-axis to positive X-axis.

18. Magnetic field due to an infinite straight conductor in the upper region of $X'X$-axis,

$$\mathbf{B} = \frac{\mu_0 I}{2\pi r}\hat{\mathbf{k}}$$

A charge q at point $P(0, r)$ starts moving with velocity $\mathbf{v} = v_0\hat{\mathbf{j}}$.

Force of charge q due to straight conductor wire,

$$\mathbf{F} = q\,(\mathbf{v} \times \mathbf{B})$$

$$\mathbf{F} = q\left[(v_0\hat{\mathbf{j}}) \times \left(\frac{\mu_0 I}{2\pi r}\hat{\mathbf{k}}\right)\right]$$

$$\Rightarrow \quad \mathbf{F} = q\left[\frac{\mu_0 v_0 I}{2\pi r}(\hat{\mathbf{j}} \times \hat{\mathbf{k}})\right]$$

$$\mathbf{F} = \frac{q\mu_0 v_0 I}{2\pi r}\hat{\mathbf{i}} \qquad (\because \hat{\mathbf{j}} \times \hat{\mathbf{k}} = \hat{\mathbf{i}})$$

19. The magnetic field produced by long straight wire carrying current of 25A rests on a table on small wire

$$B = \frac{\mu_0 I}{2\pi h}$$

The magnetic force on small conductor is

$$F = BIl \sin\theta = BIl$$

Force applied on PQ balance the weight of small current carrying wire.

$$F = mg = \frac{\mu_0 I^2 l}{2\pi h}$$

$$h = \frac{\mu_0 I^2 l}{2\pi mg} = \frac{4\pi \times 10^{-7} \times 25 \times 25 \times 1}{2\pi \times 2.5 \times 10^{-3} \times 9.8} = 51 \times 10^{-4}$$

$$h = 0.51\text{ cm}$$

20. When a charged particle q enters in a uniform magnetic field at an angle of 30°, then its path becomes helix of radius

$$r = \frac{mv \sin 30^\circ}{eB} = \frac{mv}{2eB}$$

For diagram and description Refer to text on pages 137 and 138 (Force on a Moving Charge particle in a Uniform Magnetic Field).

21. Mass on deuteron, $m_d = 2\,m$

Charge on deuteron, $q_d = e$

Mass on α-particle, $m_\alpha = 4\,m$

Charge on α-particle, $q_\alpha = 2e$

The radius of circular path is given by

$$r = \frac{mv}{qB}$$

Momentum of particle, $p = mv$

$$\therefore \quad r \propto \frac{1}{qB} \qquad [\because \text{momentum is same}]$$

$$\text{So,} \quad \frac{r_d}{r_\alpha} = \frac{q_\alpha}{q_d} = \frac{2e}{e} = \frac{2}{1} \text{ or } r_d : r_\alpha = 2:1$$

22. Refer to text on pages 141 and 142.

23. Refer to text on page 142.

24. Refer to text on page 143.

25. Refer the text on pages 142 and 143.

26. As, $\mathbf{v} = -v\hat{\mathbf{i}}$

[$\because$ the particle is moving along $-x$-direction]

$$\therefore \quad \mathbf{B} = -B\hat{\mathbf{k}}$$

[$\because$ the magnetic field is perpendicular to the plane of the paper directed inwards, i.e. negative z-direction]

$\therefore$ Force acting due to magnetic field,

$$\mathbf{F}_m = q\,(\mathbf{v} \times \mathbf{B}) = q\,[-v\hat{\mathbf{i}} \times (-B\hat{\mathbf{k}})]$$

$$\mathbf{F}_m = -qvB\hat{\mathbf{j}} \qquad [\because \hat{\mathbf{i}} \times \hat{\mathbf{k}} = -\hat{\mathbf{j}}]$$

$\Rightarrow$ Magnitude of $\mathbf{F}_m = |\mathbf{F}_m| = qvB$

The direction of $\mathbf{F}_m$ is along negative y-direction. For the undeflected motion of particle,

Force due to electric field = Force due to magnetic field,

$$q\mathbf{E} = q(\mathbf{v} \times \mathbf{B})$$

$$\therefore \quad \mathbf{E} = \mathbf{v} \times \mathbf{B}$$

Magnitude of electric field, $|E| = |\mathbf{v} \times \mathbf{B}|$ and direction of magnetic field will be perpendicular to both $\mathbf{v}$ and $\mathbf{B}$, i.e. along Y-axis.

27. Force on the proton in magnetic field

$$\mathbf{F} = q\,(\mathbf{v} \times \mathbf{B})$$

$\because$ Proton does not get deflected.

$$\mathbf{F} = 0$$

$$q\,(\mathbf{v} \times \mathbf{B}) = 0$$

$$qvB\sin\theta = 0$$

$$\sin\theta = 0$$

$$\theta = n\pi$$

$$\theta = 0, \pi$$

When a proton moves parallel or anti-parallel to the direction of magnetic field, it does not get deflected.

28. (i) The galvanometer cannot be used to measure the current because

(a) all the currents to be measured passes through coil and it gets damaged easily.

(b) its coil has considerable resistance because of length and it may affect original current.

Current sensitivity of galvanometer depends on

(I) the magnetic field

(II) the value of torsional constant.

(ii) It is necessary to introduce a cylindrical soft iron core inside the coil of a galvanometer because magnetic field is increased, so its sensitivity increases and magnetic field becomes radial. So, angle between the plane of coil and magnetic line of force is zero in all orientations of coil.

29. Refer to text on pages 131 and 132.

30. The magnetic field at a point due to a circular loop is given by

$$B = \frac{\mu_0}{4\pi} \cdot \frac{2\pi I a^2}{(a^2 + r^2)^{3/2}}$$

where, I = current through the loop,

a = radius of the loop

and r = distance of O from the centre of the loop.

Since I, a and $r = x$ are the same for both the loops, the magnitude of B will be the same and is given by

$$B_1 = B_2 = \frac{\mu_0}{4\pi} \cdot \frac{2\pi I a^2}{(a^2 + x^2)^{3/2}}$$

The direction of magnetic field due to loop (1) will be away from O and that of the magnetic field due to loop (2) will be towards O as shown. The direction of the net magnetic field will be as shown in figure.

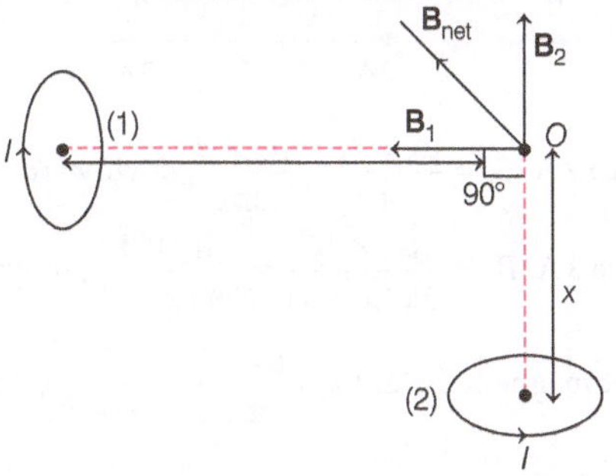

The magnitude of the net magnetic field is given by

$$B_{net} = \sqrt{B_1^2 + B_2^2} = \frac{\mu_0}{4\pi} \cdot \frac{2\pi \sqrt{2} I a^2}{(a^2 + x^2)^{3/2}}$$

31.

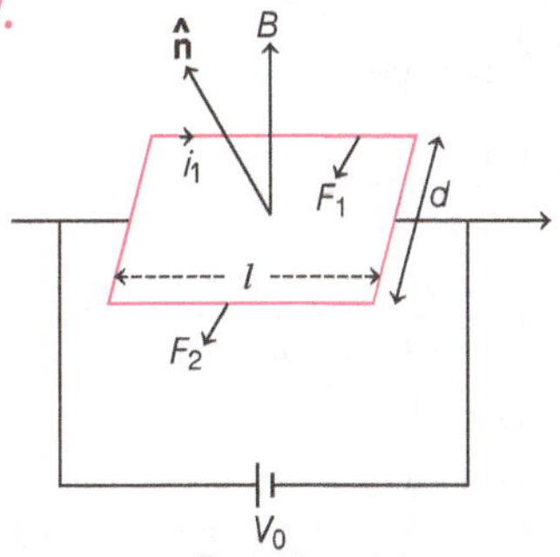

Front view

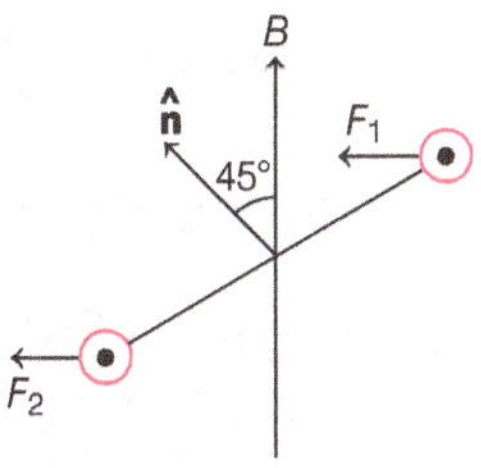

Side view

The thicker wire has a resistance R, then the other wire has a resistance $2R$ as the wires are of the same material but with cross-sections differing by a factor 2.

Now, the force and hence, torque on first wire is given by

$$F_1 = i_1 lB = \frac{V_0}{R} lB, \tau_1 = \frac{d}{2\sqrt{2}} F_1 = \frac{V_0 l dB}{2\sqrt{2}R}$$

Similarly, the force hence torque on other wire is given by

$$F_2 = i_2 lB = \frac{V_0}{2R} lB, \tau_2 = \frac{d}{2\sqrt{2}} F_2 = \frac{V_0 l dB}{4\sqrt{2}\, R}$$

So, net torque, $\tau = \tau_1 - \tau_2$

$$\tau = \frac{1}{4\sqrt{2}} \frac{V_0 l dB}{R}$$

32. Since, B is along the X-axis, for a circular orbit the momenta of the two particles are in the YZ-plane. Let p_1 and p_2 be the momenta of the electron and positron, respectively. Both traverse a circle of radius R of opposite sense. Let p_1 make an angle θ with the Y-axis p_2 must make the same angle.

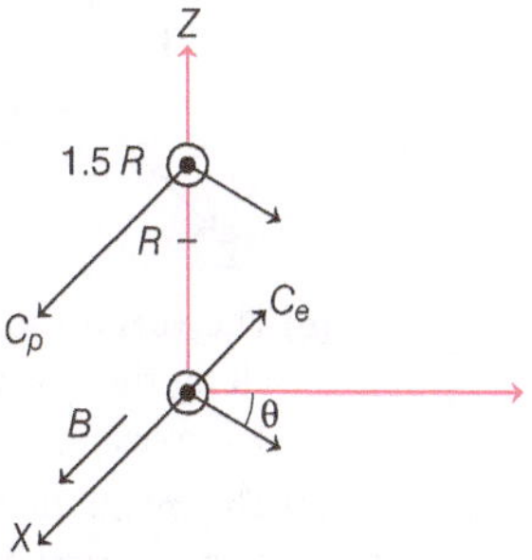

The centres of the respective circles must be perpendicular to the momenta and at a distance R. Let the centre of the electron be at C_e and of the positron at C_p. The coordinates of C_e is

$$C_e = (0, -R\sin\theta, R\cos\theta)$$

The coordinates of C_p is

$$C_p = (0, +R\sin\theta, \frac{3}{2}R - R\cos\theta)$$

The circles of the two shells will not overlap if the distance between the two centres are greater than $2R$.

Let d be the distance between C_p and C_e.

Then, $d^2 = (2R\sin\theta)^2 + \left(\frac{3}{2}R - 2R\cos\theta\right)^2$

$$= 4R^2\sin^2\theta + \frac{9}{4}R^2 - 6R^2\cos\theta + 4R^2\cos^2\theta$$

$$= 4R^2 + \frac{9}{4}R^2 - 6R^2\cos\theta$$

Since, d has to be greater than $2R$.

$\therefore \quad d^2 > 4R^2$

$$\Rightarrow 4R^2 + \frac{9}{4}R^2 - 6R^2\cos\theta > 4R^2 \Rightarrow \frac{9}{4} > 6\cos\theta$$

or $\cos\theta < \frac{3}{8}$

33. (i) Since the charged particle moves undeflected through the region, so the net force acting on the particle must be zero.

The Lorentz force acting on the particle is

$\mathbf{F} = -q[\mathbf{E} + (\mathbf{v} \times \mathbf{B})]$ {∵ charge is -ve}

(i) The conductor carries current I towards the X-axis and hence the magnetic field $\mathbf{B}$ will be towards the positive Z-axis given by the right hand thumb rule.

$\mathbf{v}$ is along the $-X$-axis and hence from the Lorentz force equation we can conclude that the electric field must be along the positive Y-axis.

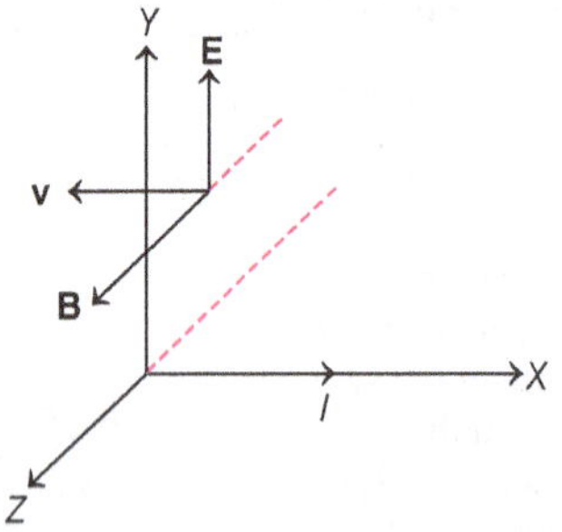

(b) The various forces acting are the magnetic force along the $-Y$-axis and electric force along the $+Y$-axis.

(c) The magnetic field at a distance d due to the current-carrying conductor is given as

$$\mathbf{B} = \frac{\mu_0 I}{2\pi d}\,\hat{\mathbf{Z}}.$$

Now, we know that the net force acting on the particle is zero,

$$\therefore\ -q(\mathbf{E} + \mathbf{v} \times \mathbf{B}) = 0$$

$$\Rightarrow \quad \mathbf{E} = -(\mathbf{v} \times \mathbf{B})$$

$$\Rightarrow \quad -\mathbf{E}\,\hat{\mathbf{j}} = -\left(-v_0\hat{\mathbf{i}} \times \frac{\mu_0 I}{2\pi d}\hat{\mathbf{Z}}\right)$$

$$\Rightarrow \quad -\mathbf{E}\hat{\mathbf{j}} = \frac{v_0 u_0 I}{2\pi d}(-\hat{\mathbf{j}})$$

$$\Rightarrow \quad E = \frac{v_0 \mu_0 I}{2\pi d}$$

$$\Rightarrow \quad v_0 = \frac{2\pi E d}{\mu_0 I}$$

Or

(ii)

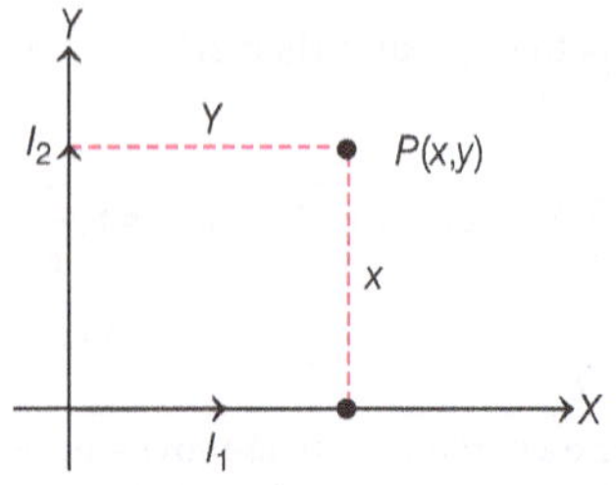

Let us assume that I_1 is greater than I_2. Also, let us consider the point P for which Y is at a greater distance than X.

Magnetic field at point P due to the conductor carrying current I_1 is

$$\mathbf{B}_1 = \frac{\mu_0 I_1}{2\pi X}\hat{\mathbf{k}} \text{ [along } +Z\text{-axis].}$$

Magnetic field at point P due to the conductor carrying current I_2 is

$$\mathbf{B}_2 = -\frac{\mu_0 I_2}{2\pi Y}\hat{\mathbf{k}} \text{ [along } -Z\text{-axis]}$$

∴ The direction of the net magnetic field will be along the $+Z$-axis.

The magnitude of the field will be

$$|\mathbf{B}_{\text{net}}| = |\mathbf{B}_1 - \mathbf{B}_2|$$

$$\Rightarrow \mathbf{B}_{\text{net}} = \frac{\mu_0}{2\pi}\left(\frac{I_1}{X} - \frac{I_2}{Y}\right)$$

Writing in the vector form we get,

$$B_{\text{net}} = \frac{\mu_0}{2\pi}\left(\frac{I_1}{X} - \frac{I_2}{Y}\right)\hat{\mathbf{k}}$$

34. Let d be the distance between two current-carrying wires, then the magnetic field in the region I at a point P at a distance x can be calculated using figure given below.

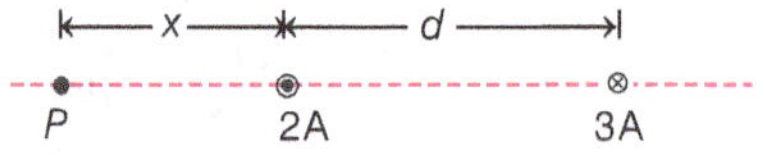

Due to 2 A, $B_1 = \dfrac{\mu_0 \times I_1}{2\pi x} = \dfrac{\mu_0 \times 2}{2\pi x}$, downward

Due to 3 A, $B_2 = \dfrac{\mu_0 \times I_2}{2\pi(x+d)} = \dfrac{\mu_0 \times 3}{2\pi(x+d)}$, upward

∴ Net magnetic field, $B_P = \dfrac{\mu_0}{2\pi}\left(\dfrac{2}{x} - \dfrac{3}{x+d}\right)$, downward ...(i)

The magnetic field in region II is

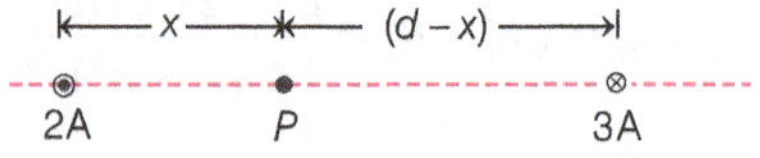

Due to 2 A, $B_1 = \dfrac{\mu_0 \times 2}{2\pi x}$, upward

Due to 3 A, $B_2 = \dfrac{\mu_0 \times 3}{2\pi(d-x)}$, upward

∴ Net magnetic field, $B_P = \dfrac{\mu_0}{2\pi}\left(\dfrac{2}{x} + \dfrac{3}{d-x}\right)$, upward

The magnetic field in region III is

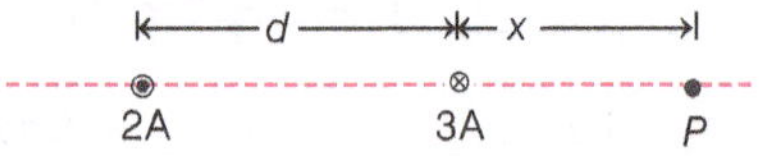

Due to 2 A, $B_1 = \dfrac{\mu_0 \times 2}{2\pi(x+d)}$, upward

Due to 3 A, $B_2 = \dfrac{\mu_0 \times 3}{2\pi d}$, downward

$\therefore$ Net magnetic field, $B_P = \dfrac{\mu_0}{2\pi}\left(\dfrac{3}{d} - \dfrac{2}{x+d}\right)$, downward

As, the current and hence the magnetic field, due to 2 A is less than that due to 3 A.

So, for zero magnetic field, $\dfrac{\mu_0}{2\pi}\left(\dfrac{2}{x} - \dfrac{3}{x+d}\right) = 0$

$\Rightarrow \qquad 2x + 2d = 3x$ or $x = 2d$

So, the point lies in region I.

35.

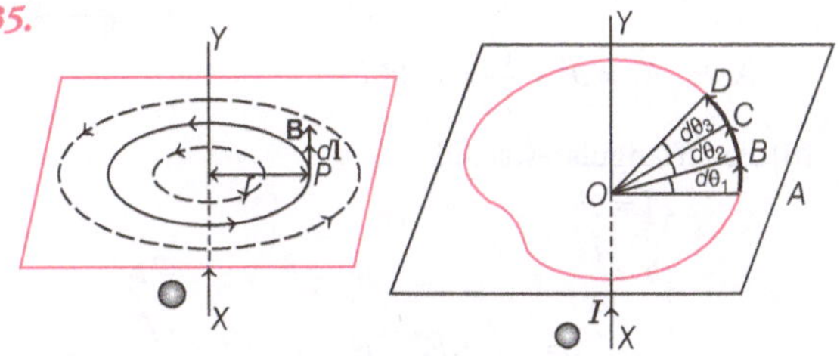

Consider any arbitrary closed path in the the plane of paper around a long straight conductor XY carrying current from X to Y, lying perpendicular to the plane of paper.

Let the closed path be made of large number of small elements, where

$$AB = dl_1,\ BC = dl_2,\ CD = dl_3$$

Let $d\theta_1$, $d\theta_2$ and $d\theta_3$ be the angles subtended by the various elements at point O through which conductor is passing. Then, $d\theta_1 + d\theta_2 + d\theta_3 + \ldots = 2\pi$

Suppose these small elements AB, BC, CD,...... are small circular arcs of radii r_1, r_2, r_3, ... respectively.

Then, $d\theta_1 = \dfrac{d\mathbf{l}_1}{r_1}$, $d\theta_2 = \dfrac{d\mathbf{l}_2}{r_2}$, $d\theta_3 = \dfrac{d\mathbf{l}_3}{r_3}$

If $\mathbf{B}_1, \mathbf{B}_2, \mathbf{B}_3$ are the magnetic field inductions at a point along the small elements $d\mathbf{l}_1, d\mathbf{l}_2, d\mathbf{l}_3$ ......, then from Biot-Savart's law, we know that for the conductor of infinite length, magnetic field is given by

$$B_1 = \frac{\mu_0}{4\pi}\cdot\frac{2I}{r_1},\ B_2 = \frac{\mu_0}{4\pi}\cdot\frac{2I}{r_2},\ B_3 = \frac{\mu_0}{4\pi}\cdot\frac{2I}{r_3}$$

In case of each element, the magnetic field induction $\mathbf{B}$ and current element vector $d\mathbf{l}$ are in the same direction.

Line integral of $\mathbf{B}$ around closed path is

$$\oint \mathbf{B}\cdot d\mathbf{l} = \mathbf{B}_1\cdot d\mathbf{l}_1 + \mathbf{B}_2\cdot d\mathbf{l}_2 + \mathbf{B}_3\cdot d\mathbf{l}_3 + \ldots$$

$$= B_1(dl_1) + B_2(dl_2) + B_3(dl_3) + \ldots$$

$$= \frac{\mu_0}{4\pi}\cdot\frac{2I}{r_1}dl_1 + \frac{\mu_0}{4\pi}\cdot\frac{2I}{r_2}dl_2 + \frac{\mu_0}{4\pi}\cdot\frac{2I}{r_3}dl_3 + \ldots$$

$$= \frac{\mu_0 2I}{4\pi}\left[\frac{dl_1}{r_1} + \frac{dl_2}{r_2} + \frac{dl_3}{r_3} + \ldots\right]$$

$$= \frac{\mu_0 2I}{4\pi}[d\theta_1 + d\theta_2 + d\theta_3 + \ldots]$$

$$= \frac{\mu_0}{4\pi}2I \times 2\pi = \mu_0 I$$

which is an expression of Ampere's circuital law.

36. (i) Refer to text on page 135.

(ii) According to Ampere's circuital law, the net field is given by $B = \mu_0 nI$

(a) The net magnetic field is given by

$$B_{net} = B_2 - B_1$$
$$= \mu_0 n_2 I - \mu_0 n_1 I \qquad [\because I_2 = I_1 = I]$$
$$= \mu_0 I(n_2 - n_1)$$

The direction is from B to A.

(b) As the magnetic fields due to S_1 is confined solely inside S_1 as the solenoids are assumed to be very long. So, there is no magnetic field outside S_1 due to current in S_1, similarly there is no field outside S_2.

$\therefore \qquad B_{net} = 0$

37. (i) When current passes through a conductor, a magnetic field is produced around the conductor which is the source of the force acting on a current carrying conductor.

Refer to text on pages 140 and 141. (Force between two parallel current-carrying conductors).

(ii) When a point charge q moves with a velocity $\mathbf{v}$ in a uniform magnetic field $\mathbf{B}$, the magnetic force acting on the particle is given by

$$\mathbf{F} = q(\mathbf{v} \times \mathbf{B})$$

From the expression, we can see that the direction of the force and the direction of velocity, hence the displacement is always mutually perpendicular. Therefore, the work done by a magnetic force is always zero.

(iii) If a charged particle has a velocity which is not perpendicular to $\mathbf{B}$, then the component of velocity along $\mathbf{B}$ remains unchanged as the motion along the magnetic field will not be affected by the magnetic field. Then, the motion of the particle in a plane perpendicular to $\mathbf{B}$ is a before a circular one, thereby producing a helical motion.

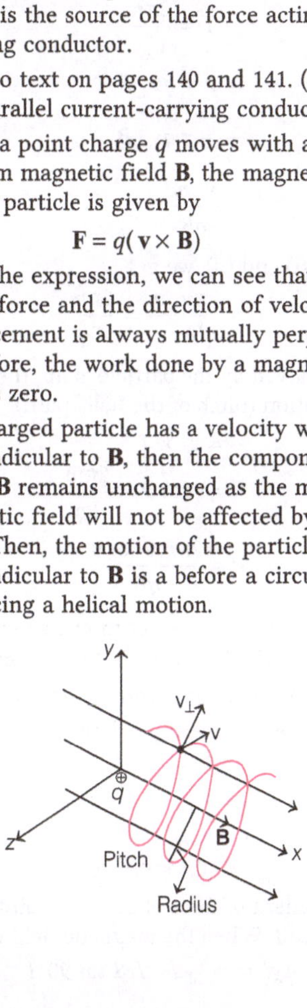

38. (i) Refer to text on page 136.

(ii) Refer to text on pages 140 and 141.

39. (i) Refer to text on pages 137 and 138.

(ii) Since, force always adjusts itself in a direction which becomes perpendicular to velocity, so only direction of velocity changes not the magnitude . Hence, the kinetic energy of the particle moving in magnetic field always remains constant.

40.

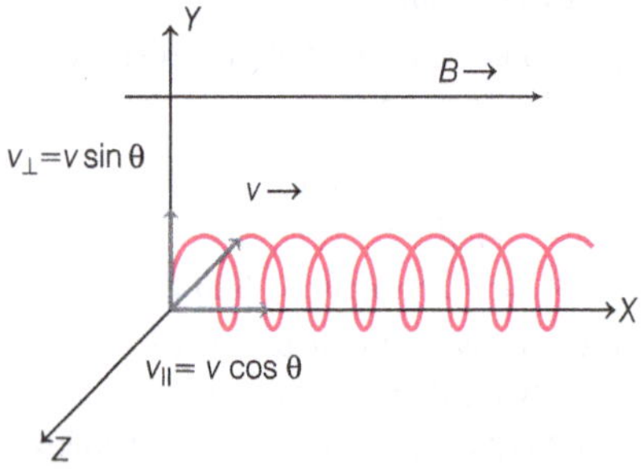

The path of the charged particle will be helix. As, the charge moves linearly in the direction of the magnetic field with velocity $v\cos\theta$ and also describe the circular path due to velocity $v\sin\theta$.

Time taken by the charge to complete one circular rotation, $\quad T = \dfrac{2\pi r}{v_\perp} \quad$ ...(i)

$\Rightarrow \quad F = qv_\perp B$

and $\quad \dfrac{mv_\perp^2}{r} = qv_\perp B$

$\Rightarrow \quad \dfrac{v_\perp m}{qB} = r \quad$ ...(ii)

From Eqs. (i) and (ii), we get

$\Rightarrow \quad T = \dfrac{2\pi v_\perp m}{qB\cdot v_\perp} = \dfrac{2\pi m}{Bq}$

Distance moved by the particle along the magnetic field in one rotation (pitch of the helix path)

$= v_\parallel \times T \quad [\because v_\parallel = v_{\text{parallel}}]$

$= v\cos\theta \times \dfrac{2\pi m}{Bq}$

$P = \dfrac{2\pi mv\cos\theta}{qB}$

41. For equilibrium balance, net torque should also be equal to zero.When the field is OFF $\Sigma\tau = 0$ considering the separation of each hung from mid-point be l.

$\because$ The magnetic force applied on CD by magnetic field must balance the weight.

$\therefore \quad Mgl = w_{\text{coil}}\, l$

$\Rightarrow \quad 500\, g\, l = w_{\text{coil}}\, l$

$\Rightarrow \quad w_{\text{coil}} = (0.5 \times 9.8)$ N

Taking moment of force about mid-point, we have the weight of coil. When the magnetic field is switched ON.

$Mgl + mgl = w_{\text{coil}}\, l + IBL\sin 90°\, l$

$\Rightarrow \quad mgl = BIL\, l$

$\therefore$ Additional mass,

$$m = \frac{BIL}{g} = \frac{0.2 \times 4.9 \times 1 \times 10^{-2}}{9.8} = 10^{-3}\text{ kg} = 1\text{ g}$$

Thus, 1 g of additional mass must be added to regain the balance.

42. $\because$ Torque $\tau = \mathbf{m} \times \mathbf{B}$

$\tau = iAB$

and let, length of wire = l

(i) For square

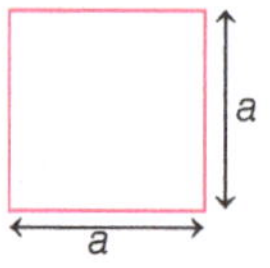

$l = 4a$

$a = \dfrac{l}{4}$

Area, $A_1 = a^2 = \dfrac{l^2}{16} = 0.625\, l^2$

(ii) For triangular-shaped

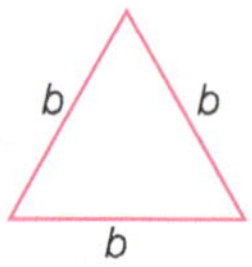

$l = 3b$

$b = \dfrac{l}{3}$

Area, $A_2 = \dfrac{\sqrt{3}}{4}b^2 = \dfrac{\sqrt{3}}{4} \times \dfrac{l^2}{9}$

$A_2 = 0.048\, l^2$

(iii) For circle, $l = 2\pi r$

$r = \dfrac{l}{2\pi}$

Area, $A_3 = \pi r^2 = \pi \times \dfrac{l^2}{4\pi^2} = \dfrac{l^2}{4\pi}$

$A_3 = 0.7958\, l^2$

Given that, these are suspended in a uniform magnetic field and same current.

So, $\quad \tau \propto A$

Circle has greater area, so it will experience greater torque.

43. (i) Refer to the text on pages 142 and 143.

(ii) The uniform radial magnetic field keeps the plane of the coil always parallel to the direction of the mangetic field i.e., the angle between the plane of the coil and the magnetic field is zero for all the orientations of the coil.

44. (i) $M_1 = N_1 I_1 A_1 \otimes$

$M_2 = N_2 I_2 A_2 \otimes$

$\therefore M = M_1 + M_2 = 2.86$ A-m^2

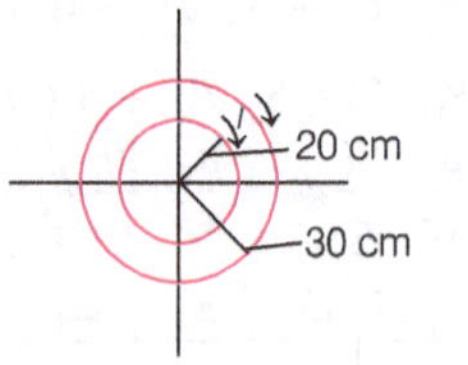

(ii) $M = |M_1 - M_2| = 1.10$ A-m^2

45. Here, $I = 10$ A, $r = 3$ cm $= 3 \times 10^{-2}$ m

Angle subtended by coil at the centre,

$$\theta = 360^\circ - 90^\circ = 270^\circ = \frac{3\pi}{2} \text{ rad}$$

Magnetic field induction at point O due to current through circular path ACB,

$$B = \frac{\mu_0}{4\pi} \cdot \frac{I}{r} \theta$$

$$= 10^{-7} \times \frac{10}{3 \times 10^{-2}} \times \frac{3\pi}{2}$$

$$= 1.57 \times 10^{-4} \text{ T}$$

46. Magnetic field due to circular wire P,

$$B_P = \frac{\mu_0}{4\pi} \times \frac{2\pi I_1}{R} \quad \text{[along vertically upwards]}$$

$$= \frac{\mu_0 I_1}{2R}$$

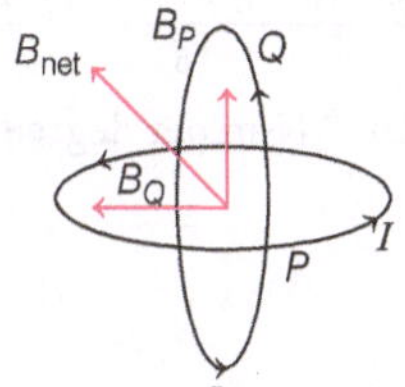

Magnetic field due to circular wire Q,

$$B_Q = \frac{\mu_0}{4\pi} \times \frac{2\pi I_2}{R} \quad \text{[along horizontal towards left]}$$

$$= \frac{\mu_0 I_2}{2R}$$

Net magnetic field at the common centre of the two coils,

$$B = \sqrt{B_P^2 + B_Q^2} = \sqrt{\left(\frac{\mu_0 I_1}{2R}\right)^2 + \left(\frac{\mu_0 I_2}{2R}\right)^2}$$

$$= \sqrt{\left(\frac{\mu_0}{2R}\right)^2 (I_1^2 + I_2^2)} = \frac{\mu_0}{2R}\sqrt{I_1^2 + I_2^2}$$

$$= \frac{4\pi \times 10^{-7}}{2 \times R}\sqrt{(1)^2 + (\sqrt{3})^2}$$

$$= \frac{4\pi \times 10^{-7}}{R} \text{ T}$$

Resultant magnetic field makes an angle θ with direction of B_Q, which is given by

$$\tan\theta = \frac{B_P}{B_Q} = \frac{1}{\sqrt{3}}$$

$$\therefore \quad \theta = 30^\circ$$

47. $B_{net} = \sqrt{B_P^2 + B_Q^2} = \sqrt{\left(\frac{\mu_0 i_P}{2r}\right)^2 + \left(\frac{\mu_0 I_Q}{2r}\right)^2}$

$$= \frac{\mu_0}{2r}\sqrt{I_P^2 + I_Q^2} = \frac{4\pi \times 10^{-7}}{2 \times 5 \times 10^{-2}} \times 5$$

$$= 2\pi \times 10^{-5} \text{ T}$$

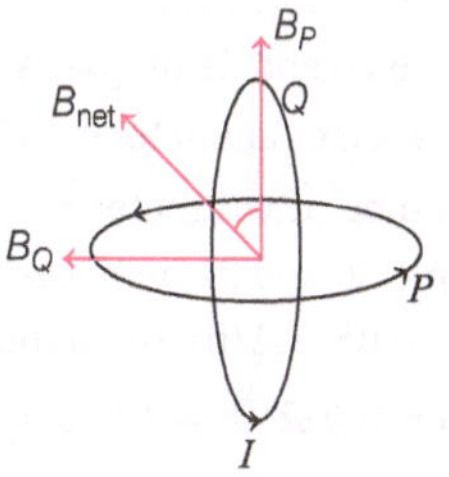

From the figure, it is clear that, resultant magnetic field makes an angle θ with B_Q which is given by

$$\tan\theta = \frac{B_P}{B_Q} = \frac{I_P}{I_Q} = \frac{3}{4}$$

48. Refer to Example 9 on page 137.

[**Ans.** $B = \mu_0 nI = 2.5 \times 10^{-3}$ T]

49. Number of turns, $N = 850 \times 5$, $l = 1$ m, $I = 5$ A

Area of cross-section, $A = \pi r^2 = \frac{22}{7}\left(\frac{3}{2} \times 10^{-2}\right)^2 \text{ m}^2$

Magnetic field at the centre of solenoid, $B = \mu_0 NI/l$

$$= 4\pi \times 10^{-7} \times (850 \times 5) \times 5/l$$

$$= 2.671 \times 10^{-2} \text{ T}$$

$\therefore$ Magnetic flux $= BA$

$$= 2.671 \times 10^{-2} \times \frac{22}{7} \times \left(\frac{3}{2} \times 10^{-2}\right)^2$$

$$= 1.89 \times 10^{-5} \text{ Wb}$$

50. 8×10^{-5} N ; refer to Example 15 on page 141.

51. Force per unit length between the current-carrying wires is given as $F = \frac{\mu_0}{4\pi} \cdot \frac{2I_1 I_2}{r}$

where, I_1 = current in wire $AB = 12$ A,

I_2 = current in wire $CD = 5$ A

and r = distance between wires

$= 1$ mm $= 1 \times 10^{-3}$ m

$$\therefore \quad \frac{\mu_0}{4\pi} \cdot \frac{2I_1 I_2}{r} = mg$$

where, m = mass per unit length.

$$\Rightarrow \quad 10^{-7} \times \frac{2 \times 12 \times 5}{1 \times 10^{-3}} = m \times 10$$

$$\Rightarrow \quad m = 10^{-7} \times \frac{2 \times 12 \times 5}{1 \times 10^{-3}} \times \frac{1}{10}$$

$$m = 1.2 \times 10^{-3} \text{ kg/m}$$

Current in CD should be in opposite direction to that in AB.

52. Refer to Example 16 on page 142. [**Ans.** 3.927 N-m]

53. Current sensitivity,

$$I_s = \frac{NAB}{k} = \frac{100 \times 1 \times 10^{-4} \times 5}{10^{-8}} = 5 \times 10^6 \text{ A}^{-1}$$

54. Refer to Example 19 on page 143.
[**Ans.** Decreased by a factor 0.4]

55. Refer to Example 20 and 21 on pages 143 and 144.
[**Ans.** (i) Resistance of ammeter $4 \times 10^{-3} \Omega$
(ii) Resistance of voltmeter = 4000 Ω

56. Refer to Example 20 and 21 on pages 143 and 144.
[**Ans.** (i) Shunt = 0.815 Ω (ii) Resistance in series 0.985 Ω]

57. Here, $n = 30$, $G = 100\ \Omega$, $E = 3\text{V}$, $R = 200\ \Omega$, $k = ?$

Total resistance $= G + R = 100 + 200 = 300\ \Omega$

$$I_g = \frac{E}{G+R} = \frac{3}{300} = \frac{1}{100}\text{ A}$$

$$k = \frac{I_g}{n} = \frac{1/100}{30} = \frac{1}{3} \times 10^{-3}\text{ A/div}$$

$$k = \frac{1}{3} \times 10^{-3} \times 10^6 \mu\text{A/div}$$

Figure of merit (Restoring torque per unit twist)

$$k = 333.3\ \mu\text{A/div}$$

58. Here, $N = 30$, $R = 8.0\text{ cm} = 8 \times 10^{-2}\text{m}$,

$I = 6.0\text{ A}$, $\theta = 60°$ and $B = 1.0\text{ T}$

(i) The magnitude of the counter torque

= magnitude of the deflecting torque

$= NAIB \sin\theta = N \cdot (\pi R^2)\, IB \sin\theta$

$= 30 \times 3.14 \times (8 \times 10^{-2})^2 \times 6.0 \times 1.0 \times \sin 60°$

$= 3.14\text{N-m}$

(ii) The answer would not change as area enclosed by the coil as well as all other particulars remain unaltered and the formula, $\tau = NAIB \sin\theta$ is true for planar coil for any shape.

59. Here, $B = 60\text{ G} = 60 \times 10^{-4}\text{ T}$,

$A = 2 \times 10^{-4}\text{ m}^2$, $N = 40$

$I = 4\text{ mA} = 4 \times 10^{-3}\text{ A}$, $\theta = 16°$

$\because \quad I = \frac{k}{NBA}\theta$

$\Rightarrow \quad k = \frac{NBAI}{\theta}$

$$= \frac{40 \times 60 \times 10^{-4} \times 2 \times 10^{-4} \times 4 \times 10^{-3}}{16}$$

$= 1.2 \times 10^{-8}$ N-m per degree

QR Code for Quick Test 1

QR Code for Quick Test 2

QR Code for Quick Test 3

SELF ASSESSMENT TEST

Multiple Choice Questions (MCQs)

1. Which one of the following is not correct about Lorentz force?

(a) In presence of electric field $\mathbf{E}(r)$ and magnetic field $\mathbf{B}(r)$ the force on a moving electric charge is $\mathbf{F} = q[\mathbf{E}(r) + \mathbf{v} \times \mathbf{B}(r)]$

(b) The force due to magnetic field on a negative charge is opposite to that on a positive charge.

(c) The force due to magnetic field becomes zero if velocity and magnetic field are parallel or anti-parallel.

(d) For a static charge the magnetic force is maximum.

2. A 2.5 m long straight wire having mass of 500 g is suspended in mid air by a uniform horizontal magnetic field *B*. If a current of 4 A is passing through the wire, then the magnitude of the field is (Take, $g = 10 \text{ ms}^{-1}$)

(a) 0.5 T (b) 0.6 T (c) 0.25 T (d) 0.8 T

3. A current *I* flows through a long straight conductor which is bent into a circular loop of radius *R* in the middle as shown in the figure. The magnitude of the net magnetic field at point *O* will be

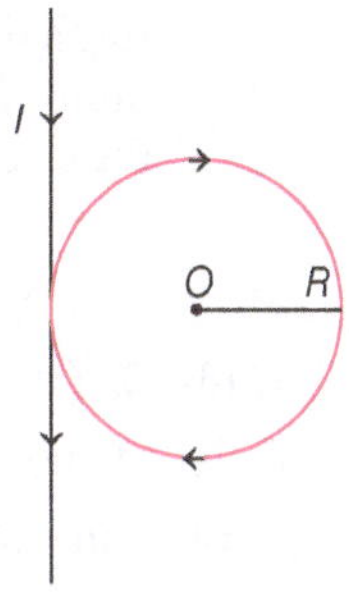

(a) zero

(b) $\frac{\mu_0 I}{2R}(1+\pi)$

(c) $\frac{\mu_0 I}{4\pi R}$

(d) $\frac{\mu_0 I}{2R}\left(1-\frac{1}{\pi}\right)$

4. A charge particle after being accelerated through a potential difference *V* enters in a uniform magnetic field and moves in a circle of radius *r*. If *V* is doubled, then the radius of the circle will becomes

(a) $2r$ (b) $\sqrt{2}r$ (c) $4r$ (d) $\frac{r}{\sqrt{2}}$

5. A current loop in a magnetic field

(a) can be in equilibrium in one orientation.

(b) can be in equilibrium in two orientations, both the equilibrium states are unstable.

(c) can be in equilibrium in two orientations, one stable while the other is unstable.

(d) experiences a torque whether the field is uniform or non-uniform in all orientations.

Assertion-Reason

Directions *(Q. Nos. 6-8) In the following questions, two statements are given- one labelled Assertion (A) and the other labelled Reason (R). Select the correct answer to these questions from the codes (a), (b), (c) and (d) as given below.*

(a) Both Assertion and Reason are true and Reason is the correct explanation of Assertion.

(b) Both Assertion and Reason are true but Reason is not the correct explanation of Assertion.

(c) Assertion is true but Reason is false.

(d) Assertion is false but Reason is true.

6. Assertion (A) Current-carrying solenoid behaves like a bar magnet.

Reason (R) The circular loop in which the direction of current is clockwise behaves like the south pole and the one having anti-clockwise current behaves like the north pole.

7. Assertion (A) A proton and an electron with same momenta, enter in a magnetic field in a direction at right angles to the lines of the force. The radius of the paths followed by them will be same.

Reason (R) Electron has less mass than the proton.

8. Assertion (A) The deflecting torque acting on a current-carrying loop is zero when its plane is perpendicular to the direction of magnetic field.

Reason (R) The deflecting torque acting on a loop of magnetic moment **M** in a magnetic field **B** is given by the cross-product of **M** and **B**.

Case Based Question

Directions *(Q.No. 9) This question is case study based question. Read the following paragraph and answer the questions on the basis of same.*

9. A magnetic field can be produced by moving charges or electric current. The basic equation of magnetic field due to a current distribution is governed by Biot-Savart law. According to this law, the magnetic field at a point due to a current element of length $d\mathbf{l}$ carrying current I, at a distance r from the element $d\mathbf{l}$ is, $d\mathbf{B} = \frac{\mu_0}{4\pi} \cdot \frac{I d\mathbf{l} \times \mathbf{r}}{r^3}$.

This law has certain similarities as well as differences with Coulomb's law of electrostatic. e.g. There is an angle dependence in Biot-Savart law which is absent in electrostatic case.

(i) Write the alternative way to express Biot-Savart law.

(ii) What is the difference between Biot-Savart law and Coulomb's law in electrostatic.

(iii) How magnetic field due to an infinitely long current carrying wire at a distance r on its perpendicular bisector is related with current?

(iv) What is the magnetic field at a point on a long current-carrying wire?

Very Short Answer Type Questions

10. What is the direction of the force acting on a charged particle q moving with a velocity $\mathbf{v}$ in a uniform magnetic field $\mathbf{B}$?

11. Depict the trajectory of a charged particle moving with velocity v as it enters in a uniform magnetic field perpendicular to the direction of its motion.

Short Answer Type Questions

12. A wire AB is carrying a steady current of 12 A and is lying on the table. Another wire CD carrying 5 A is held directly above AB at a height of 1 mm. Find the mass per unit length of the wire CD, so that it remains suspended at its position when left free. Give the direction of the current flowing in CD with respect to that in AB. [Take, the value of $g = 10 \text{ ms}^{-2}$]

13. A rectangular loop of wire of size 2.5 cm × 4 cm carries steady current of 1 A. A straight wire carrying 2 A current is kept near the loop as shown. If the loop and the wire are co-planar, then find the (i) torque acting on the loop and (ii) the magnitude and direction of the force on the loop due to the current-carrying wire.

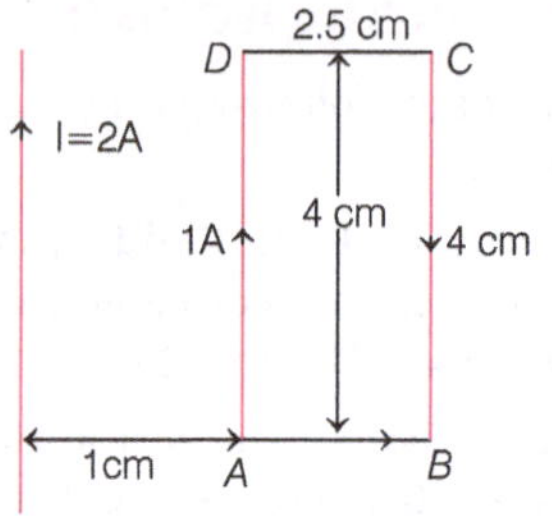

Long Answer Type Question

14. (i) A magnetic field that varies in magnitude from point-to-point but has a constant direction (east to west) is set-up in a chamber. A charged particle enters the chamber and travels undeflected along a straight path with constant speed. What can you say about the initial velocity of the particle?

(ii) An electron travelling west to east enters a chamber having a uniform electrostatic field in north to south direction. Specify the direction in which a uniform magnetic field should be set-up to prevent the electron from deflecting its straight line path.

Answers

1. (d) *2.* (a) *3.* (d) *4.* (b) *5.* (a) *6.* (a)
7. (b) *8.* (e) *12.* 1.2×10^{-3} kgm^{-1}
13. 4.44×10^{-7} N

05

CHAPTER

Magnetism and Matter

In this chapter, we'll learn about key ideas in magnetism, such as magnetic fields, forces and moments, and how different materials react to magnetic fields.
We'll also look at how electricity and magnetism are connected, leading to the concept of electromagnetism, which is important in modern technology and physics.

YOUR STUDY GOALS

YOUR PRACTICE GOAL

- Objective Type Questions (30 Qs ; MCQs, A-R, Matching)
- Case Based Questions-3
- Subjective Questions (7 VSAs, 8 SAs, 9 LAs)
- Numerical Problems-6

5.1 Bar Magnet and Magnetic Dipole

The phenomenon of attraction of small bits of iron, steel, cobalt, etc., towards the ore is called **magnetism.** The materials which exhibit this property are known as magnets.

A **magnet** is a material or an object that produces a magnetic field. The magnetic field is invisible but is responsible for the most notable property of a magnet.

Magnets are of two types

(i) Natural magnets

(ii) Artificial magnets

Natural magnets are generally irregular in shape and weak in strength. On the other hand, **artificial magnets** have desired shape and strength. A bar magnet, a horse shoe magnet, compass needle, etc., all are the examples of artificial magnets.

The Bar Magnet

- The bar magnet has two poles similar to the positive and negative charges of an electric dipole. One pole is designated as **North pole** (N) and the other as **South pole** (S).

- When a bar magnet is suspended freely, these poles point approximately towards the geographic North and South poles, respectively.
- If a bar magnet is dropped into a pile of iron-filings, then the maximum amount of filings get deposited near the ends of the magnet and almost nil in the middle.

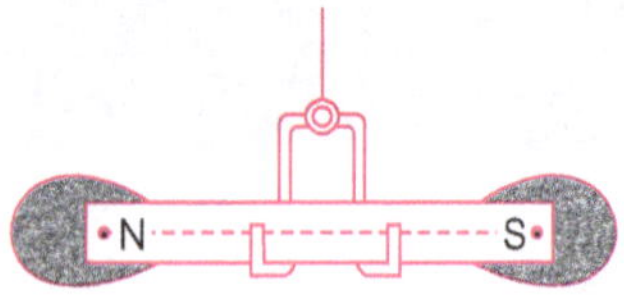

- The pattern suggests that attraction is maximum at the two ends of the bar magnet. These ends are called **poles** of the magnet.
- The poles of a magnet can never be separated.

Magnetic Length of a Bar Magnet

The distance between two poles of a bar magnet is known as **magnetic length** of a magnet. Its direction is from S-pole of the magnet to N-pole and is represented by $2l$. It is sometimes also known as effective length (L_e) of the magnet and is less than its geometric length (L_g).

For a bar magnet, $L_e = \left(\frac{5}{6}\right) L_g$

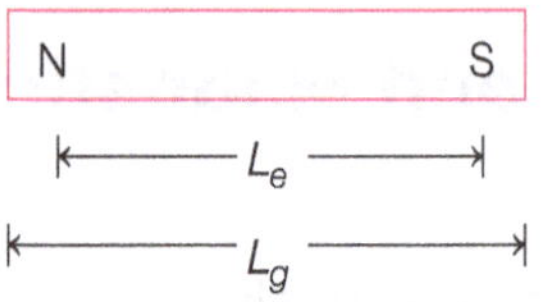

Properties of a Bar Magnet

(i) Every bar magnet attracts small pieces of magnetic substances like iron, cobalt, nickel and steel towards it.

(ii) When a magnet is suspended freely with the help of thread, then it comes to rest along the north-south direction.

The pole of the magnet which points towards geographic north is called **north pole** and the pole which points towards geographic south is called **south pole**.

(iii) The straight line passing through north and south pole of magnet is called **axial line** and the line passing through centre of the magnet in a direction perpendicular to the length of the magnet is called **equatorial line** of the magnet.

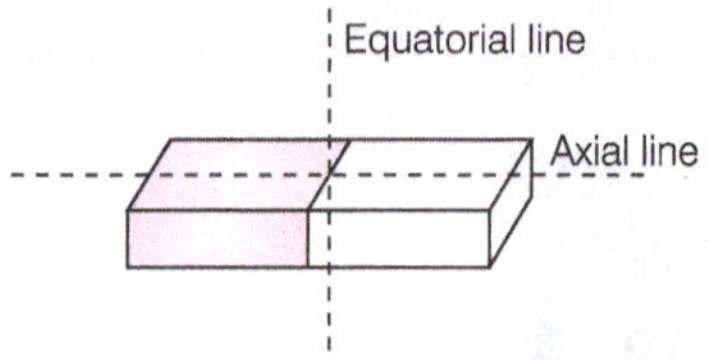

(iv) Like poles repel and unlike poles attract each other.

(v) **Inductive property** When a piece of a magnetic material like soft iron, cobalt, nickel, etc., is placed near a bar magnet, it acquires magnetism and this property of magnetism is called **inductive property.**

(vi) **Directive property** When a bar magnet is suspended freely, it points in the north-south direction. The tip of the magnet which points to the geographic north is called **north pole** and the tip which points to the geographic south is called **south pole**.

Magnetic Monopole does not exist

We cannot isolate the North or South pole of a magnet, i.e. magnetic poles exist in pairs. If a bar magnet is broken into two halves, we get two similar bar magnets with somewhat weaker properties.

Unlike electric charges, isolated magnetic North and South poles are known as magnetic monopoles which do not exist.

If a bar magnet is broken, each piece behaves as a small magnet

Example 1. **Consider a short magnetic dipole of magnetic length 20 cm. Find its geometric length.**

Sol. Geometric length of a magnet is $\frac{6}{5}$ times its magnetic length.

$\therefore$ Geometric length $= \frac{6}{5} \times 20 = 24\,\text{cm}$

Example 2. **A thin bar magnet of length $4L$ is bent at the mid-point, so that the angle between them is 60°. Find the new length of the bar magnet.**

Sol. On bending the bar magnet, the length of the bar magnet,

$$AC = AO + OC$$

$$= 2L\sin\left(\frac{60°}{2}\right) + 2L\sin\left(\frac{60°}{2}\right)$$

$$= 4L\sin 30° = 4L \times \frac{1}{2} = 2L$$

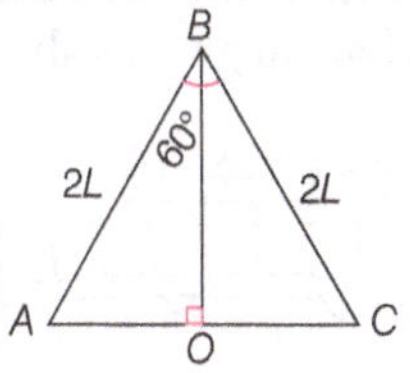

Magnetic Field Lines

The magnetic field lines are a visual and intuitive realisation of the magnetic field.

The magnetic field lines in a magnetic field are those continuous imaginary lines which represent the direction of the magnetic field.

The tangent drawn at any point on magnetic field line shows the direction of magnetic field at that point.

Properties of Magnetic Field Lines

(i) The magnetic field lines of a magnet (or of a solenoid) form closed continuous loops. The magnetic field lines extending through the magnet/solenoid from south pole to north.

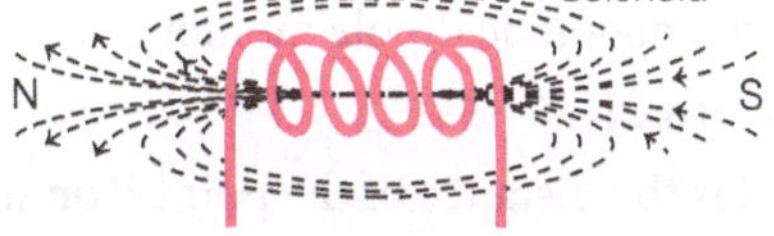

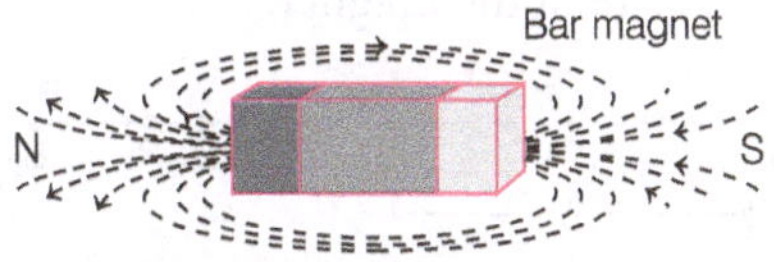

(ii) Outside the body of the magnet, the direction of magnetic field lines is from north pole to south pole.

(iii) The magnitude of magnetic field at any point is represented by the number of magnetic field lines passing normally through unit area around that point.

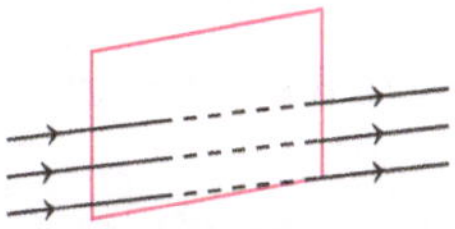

Weak magnetic field

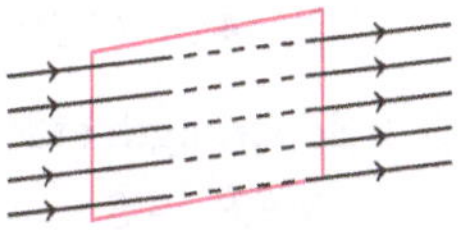

Strong magnetic field

(iv) Two magnetic field lines cannot intersect each other because at the point of intersection there will be two directions of magnetic field which is not possible.

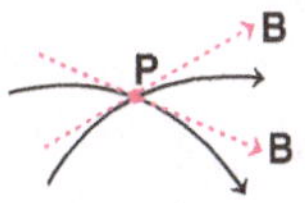

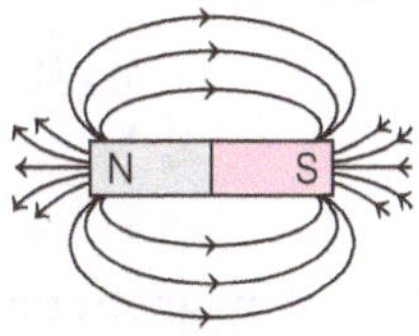

(v) Magnetic field lines exists inside every magnetised material.

TEACHER TIP

- The electric field lines are continuous curves which are not closed, whereas magnetic field lines are closed and continuous curves.

Pole Strength (m)

It is defined as the strength of a magnetic pole to attract magnetic materials towards itself.

It is a **scalar quantity** and its SI unit is **ampere-metre (A-m).**

The strength of N and S-poles of a magnet is conventionally represented by $+m$ and $-m$, respectively.

It depends on the nature of material and area of cross-section of the magnet.

Strength of N and S-poles of a magnet is always equal and opposite ($+m$ and $-m$).

Note • According to Coulomb's law of magnetic force, the force between two magnetic poles,

$$F = \frac{\mu_0}{4\pi} \cdot \frac{m_1 m_2}{r^2}$$

Strength of a magnetic pole is said to be one ampere-metre, if it repels an equal and similar pole, when placed in vacuum (or air) at a distance of one metre from it, with a force of 10^{-7} N.

Magnetic Dipole

A magnetic dipole is an arrangement of two magnetic poles of equal and opposite strengths ($-m$, $+m$) separated by a small distance. e.g. A bar magnet, a compass needle, etc., are magnetic dipoles.

The two poles of a magnetic dipole (or a magnet), called **North pole** and **South pole**, are always of equal strength and of opposite nature. Further, such two **magnetic poles always exist in pair.**

Magnetic Dipole Moment

It is the product of the strength of either pole and the magnetic length of the magnet.

It is represented by **M**.

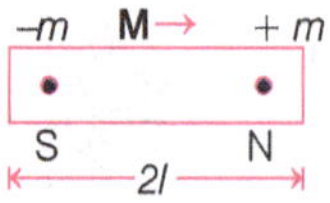

The direction of magnetic dipole moment is same as that of 2**l**. Therefore,

$$\mathbf{M} = m(2\mathbf{l})$$

SI unit of magnetic dipole moment is (joule/tesla) or ampere-metre^2 (A-m^2).

TEACHER TIP

When a magnet of pole strength m is cut into two equal parts

(a) along its axis (longitudinally), the pole strength of each half become $m/2$.

(b) perpendicular to its axis (transversely), the pole strength of each half still remains m (same).

Example 3. **A magnetic wire of dipole moment 4π A-m^2 is bent in the form of semicircle. Find the new magnetic moment.**

Sol. If length of wire is $2l$, then magnetic moment,

$$M = m \times 2l = 4\pi \text{ A-m}^2 \quad \text{[given]}$$

As wire is bent in the form of semicircle, effective distance between the ends is $2r$.

So, new dipole moment,

$$M' = m \times 2r = m \times 2 \times \frac{2l}{\pi} = \frac{2}{\pi}(m \times 2l) \quad [\because \pi r = 2l]$$

$$= \frac{2}{\pi} M = \frac{2}{\pi} 4\pi$$

$$= 8 \text{ A-m}^2$$

Bar Magnet as an Equivalent Solenoid

The magnetic field lines for a bar magnet and a current carrying solenoid resemble very closely. Therefore, a bar magnet can be thought as a large number of circulating currents in analogy with a solenoid.

The expression for the magnetic field due to a solenoid,

$$B = \frac{\mu_0}{4\pi} \cdot \frac{2M}{r^3}$$

where, r is the distance between the centre of solenoid to the required point.

This expression is same as the expression for magnetic field of a bar magnet at its axial point. Thus, a bar magnet and a solenoid produce similar magnetic fields. Therefore, magnetic field lines associated with a solenoid are also similar to a bar magnet as shown in the figure.

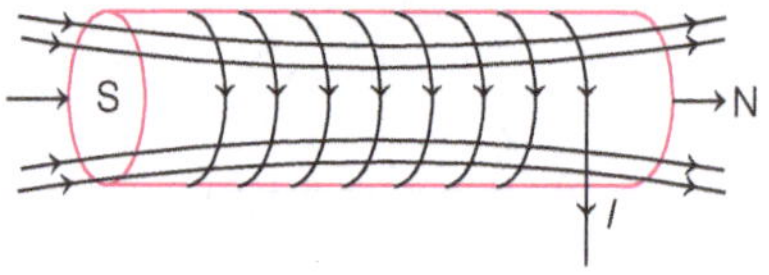

Magnetic field lines due to a solenoid carrying current

Magnetic Field Intensity at a Point due to a Bar Magnet

The **strength of magnetic field** at any point is defined as, the force experienced by a hypothetical unit North pole placed at that point.

It is a **vector** quantity.

The direction of magnetic field **B** is the direction along which hypothetical unit North pole would tend to move, if free to do so.

When Point Lies on Axial Line of a Bar Magnet

Let $2l$ be the magnetic length of a bar magnet with centre O and M is the magnetic dipole moment of the magnet.

where, $M = m \times 2l$

Here, $OP = d$ is the distance of the point P on the axial line from the centre of the magnet.

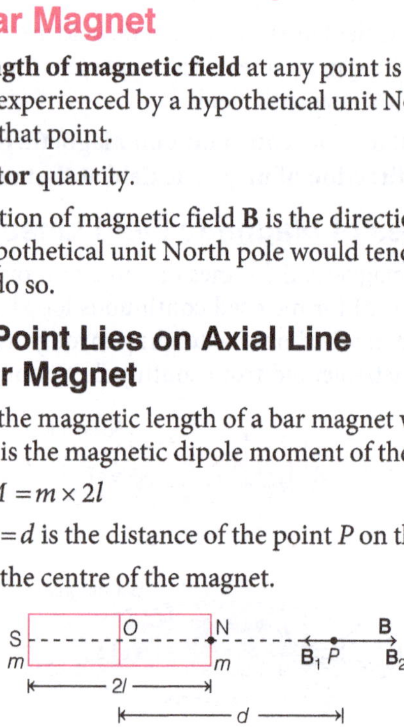

If m is the strength of each pole, then magnetic field strength at point P due to S-pole of magnet is

$$B_1 = \frac{\mu_0}{4\pi} \times \frac{m}{(SP)^2} = \frac{\mu_0 m}{4\pi(d+l)^2}$$

Magnetic field strength at P due to N-pole of magnet is

$$B_2 = \frac{\mu_0}{4\pi} \times \frac{m}{(NP)^2} = \frac{\mu_0 m}{4\pi(d-l)^2}$$

Magnetic field strength at P due to the bar magnet,

$$B = B_2 - B_1$$

$$B = \frac{\mu_0}{4\pi} \frac{m}{(d-l)^2} - \frac{\mu_0}{4\pi} \times \frac{m}{(d+l)^2}$$

$$= \frac{\mu_0}{4\pi} m \left[\frac{1}{(d-l)^2} - \frac{1}{(d+l)^2} \right]$$

$$= \frac{\mu_0}{4\pi} m \left[\frac{(d+l)^2 - (d-l)^2}{(d^2 - l^2)^2} \right]$$

$$B = \frac{\mu_0}{4\pi} m \cdot \frac{4ld}{(d^2 - l^2)^2}$$

$$\boxed{B = \frac{\mu_0}{4\pi} \frac{2Md}{(d^2 - l^2)^2}}$$

When the magnet is short ($l^2 << d^2$), so

$$B = \frac{\mu_0}{4\pi} \frac{2Md}{d^4}$$

or $$\boxed{B = \frac{\mu_0}{4\pi} \frac{2M}{d^3}} \quad \text{(along } NP\text{)}$$

Example 4. What is the magnitude of the axial fields due to a bar magnet of length 5 cm at a distance of 50 cm from its mid-point? The magnetic moment of the bar magnet is 0.40 A-m^2.

Sol. Given, magnetic length of bar magnet, $2l = 5$ cm

$\Rightarrow \quad l = 2.5 \text{ cm} = 2.5 \times 10^{-2}$ m

Distance, $d = 50$ cm $= 0.5$ m

Magnetic moment, $M = 0.40$ A-m^2

$$\therefore \quad B = \frac{\mu_0}{4\pi} \cdot \frac{2Md}{(d^2 - l^2)^2}$$

$$= \frac{\mu_0}{4\pi} \cdot \frac{2M}{d^3} \qquad [\because l << d]$$

$$= \frac{10^{-7} \times 2 \times 0.40}{(0.5)^3} = 6.4 \times 10^{-7} \text{ T}$$

When Point Lies on Equatorial Line of a Bar Magnet

In the given figure, the point P is shown on the equatorial line of the same bar magnet, where $OP = d$.

Magnetic field strength at P due to N-pole of magnet is

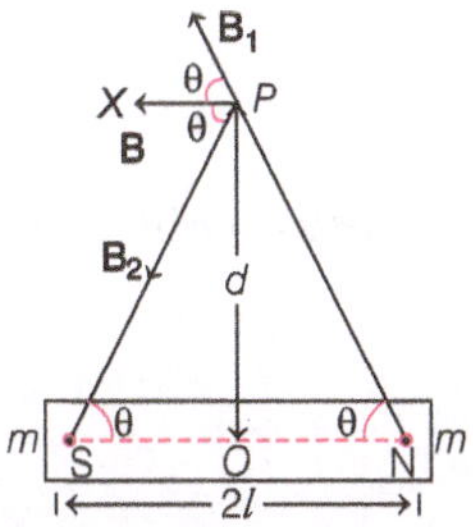

$$B_1 = \frac{\mu_0}{4\pi} \cdot \frac{m}{(NP)^2} = \frac{\mu_0}{4\pi} \cdot \frac{m}{(d^2 + l^2)}, \text{ along } NP \text{ produced.}$$

Magnetic field strength at P due to S-pole of magnet is

$$B_2 = \frac{\mu_0}{4\pi} \cdot \frac{m}{(SP)^2} = \frac{\mu_0}{4\pi} \cdot \frac{m}{(d^2 + l^2)}, \text{ along } PS \text{ produced.}$$

As $B_1 = B_2$ in magnitude, so their components $B_1 \sin\theta$ along OP produced and $B_2 \sin\theta$ along PO will cancel out. However, components along PX will add. Therefore, magnetic field strength at P due to the bar magnet, $B = B_1 \cos\theta + B_2 \cos\theta = 2 B_1 \cos\theta$, along PX.

$$B = 2 \cdot \frac{\mu_0}{4\pi} \cdot \frac{m}{(d^2 + l^2)} \times \frac{l}{\sqrt{d^2 + l^2}}$$

$$\left[\because \cos\theta = \frac{l}{\sqrt{d^2 + l^2}} \right]$$

$$= \frac{\mu_0}{4\pi} \cdot \frac{m \times 2l}{(d^2 + l^2)^{3/2}}$$

$$\Rightarrow \quad \boxed{B = \frac{\mu_0}{4\pi} \cdot \frac{M}{(d^2 + l^2)^{3/2}}}$$

If the magnet is short, $l^2 << d^2$, such that l^2 is neglected.

$$\therefore \quad B = \frac{\mu_0}{4\pi} \cdot \frac{M}{(d^2)^{3/2}} = \frac{\mu_0}{4\pi} \cdot \frac{M}{d^3}$$

$$\Rightarrow \quad \boxed{\mathbf{B} = \frac{\mu_0}{4\pi} \cdot \frac{\mathbf{M}}{d^3}}$$

The direction of B is along PX, a line parallel to NS.

Note Magnetic field due to a short bar magnet at any point on the axial line of magnet is twice the magnetic field at a point at the same distance on the equatorial line of the magnet.

Example 5. Determine the magnitude of the equatorial fields due to a bar magnet of length 6 cm at a distance of 60 cm from its mid-point. The magnetic moment of the bar magnet is 0.60 A-m^2.

Sol. Given, magnetic length of bar magnet, $2l = 6$ cm

$\Rightarrow \quad l = 3 \text{ cm} = 3 \times 10^{-2}$ m

Distance, $d = 60$ cm $= 0.6$ m

Magnetic moment, $M = 0.60$ A-m^2

$\therefore$ Magnetic field,

$$B = \frac{\mu_0}{4\pi} \times \frac{M}{(d^2 + l^2)^{3/2}} = \frac{\mu_0 M}{4\pi d^3} \qquad [\because l << d]$$

$$= \frac{4\pi \times 10^{-7} \times 0.60}{4\pi \times (0.6)^3}$$

$$= 2.7 \times 10^{-7} \text{ T}$$

Torque on a Magnetic Dipole in a Uniform Magnetic Field

Consider a bar magnet NS of length $2l$ placed in a uniform magnetic field **B** at an angle θ as shown below. The strength of each pole of the magnet is m.

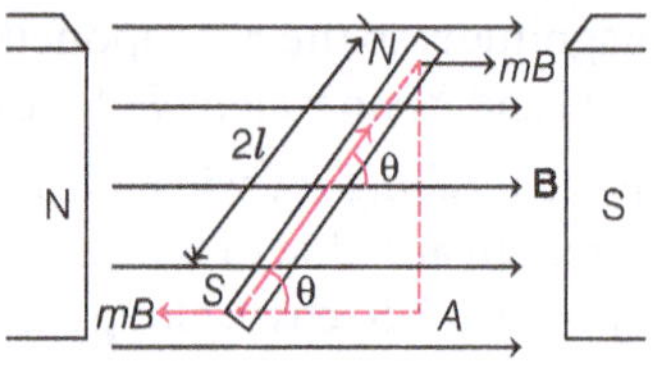

Bar magnet in a uniform magnetic field

Force on N-pole $= mB$, along **B**

Force on S-pole $= mB$, opposite to **B**

These equal and unlike forces form a couple which tends to rotate the magnet clockwise, so as to align it along **B**.

The torque on the dipole is

$$\tau = MB\sin\theta$$

In vector form, $\boldsymbol{\tau} = \mathbf{M} \times \mathbf{B}$

The direction of τ is perpendicular to the plane containing **M** and **B** and is given by right handed screw rule.

Note Circular current loop behaves as a magnetic dipole.
Magnetic field at a distance x on the axis of a circular loop is

$$B = \frac{\mu_0 M}{2\pi x^3}$$

where, $M = NIA$

Example 6. **A straight solenoid of length 50 cm has 1000 turns per metre and a mean cross-sectional area of 2×10^{-4} m^2. It is placed with its axis at 30°, with a uniform magnetic field of 0.32 T. Find the torque acting on the solenoid when a current of 2 A is passed through it.**

Sol. Given, $l = 50 \text{ cm} = \frac{1}{2}$ m

Number of turns per metre $= 1000$

$\therefore$ Total number of turns $(N) = 1000 \times \frac{1}{2} = 500$

Area, $A = 2 \times 10^{-4} \text{ m}^2$

Current, $I = 2\text{ A}$

Magnetic field, $B = 0.32\text{ T}$

$\therefore$ Torque, $\tau = MB\sin\theta = (NIA)B\sin\theta$

$$= 500 \times 2 \times (2 \times 10^{-4}) \times 0.32 \times \frac{1}{2}$$

$$= 0.032 \text{ N-m}$$

Example 7. **A bar magnet when suspended horizontally and perpendicular to the earth's magnetic field, experiences a torque of 3×10^{-4} N-m. What is the magnetic moment of the magnet? Horizontal component of earth's magnetic field at that place is 0.4×10^{-4} T.**

Sol. Given, $\theta = 90°, \tau = 3 \times 10^{-4}$ N-m

and $B = 0.4 \times 10^{-4}$ T

Since, torque $\tau = MB\sin\theta$

$$\therefore M = \frac{\tau}{B\sin\theta} = \frac{3 \times 10^{-4}}{0.4 \times 10^{-4} \sin 90°} = 7.5 \text{ JT}^{-1}$$

Potential Energy of a Magnetic Dipole in a uniform Magnetic Field

When a magnetic dipole of moment **M** is held at an angle θ with the direction of a uniform magnetic field **B**,
the magnitude of the torque acting on the dipole is given by

$$\tau = MB\sin\theta$$

Now, a small amount of work done in rotating the dipole through a small angle $d\theta$ is given by

$$dW = \tau\, d\theta = MB\sin\theta \cdot d\theta$$

Total work done in rotating the dipole from $\theta = \theta_0$ to $\theta = \theta$,

$$W = \int_{\theta_0}^{\theta} dW = \int_{\theta_0}^{\theta} MB\sin\theta d\theta = MB[-\cos\theta]_{\theta_0}^{\theta}$$

$$\Rightarrow \quad W = -MB[\cos\theta - \cos\theta_0]$$

$\therefore$ Potential energy of the dipole,

$$U = W = -MB(\cos\theta - \cos\theta_0)$$

If dipole is rotated from a direction perpendicular to the field, $\theta_0 = 90°$

$$U = W = -MB(\cos\theta - \cos 90°)$$

Therefore, $U = -MB\cos\theta$

In vector notation, we may rewrite this equation as

$$U = -\mathbf{M} \cdot \mathbf{B}$$

Particular Cases

(i) When $\theta = 90°$,

$$U = -MB\cos\theta = -MB\cos 90° = 0$$

i.e. **when the dipole is perpendicular to magnetic field, its potential energy is zero.**

(ii) When $\theta = 0°$, $U = -MB\cos\theta$

$$= -MB\cos 0° = -MB$$

i.e. when the magnetic dipole is aligned along the magnetic field, it is in **stable equilibrium** having minimum potential energy.

(iii) When $\theta = 180°$, $U = -MB\cos\theta$

$$= -MB\cos 180° = MB$$

which is maximum. This is the position of **unstable equilibrium.**

Example 8. **A circular coil of 100 turns and have an effective radius of 5 cm carries a current of 0.1 A. How much work is required to turn it in an external magnetic field of 1.5 Wb/m^2 through 180° about an axis perpendicular to the magnetic field? The plane of the coil is initially perpendicular to the magnetic field.**

Sol. Given, number of turns, $N = 100$

Radius, $r = 5 \text{ cm} = 0.05 \text{ m}$

Current, $I = 0.1 \text{ A}$

Magnetic field, $B = 1.5 \text{ Wb/m}^2$

$\theta_1 = 0°$, $\theta_2 = 180°$

Area, $A = \pi r^2 = 3.14(0.05)^2 \text{m}^2$

$\therefore$ Required work done, $W = -MB(\cos\theta_2 - \cos\theta_1)$

$$= -(NIA)B(\cos\theta_2 - \cos\theta_1)$$

$$= -100 \times 0.1 \times 3.14\,(0.05)^2 \times 1.5 \times (\cos 180° - \cos 0°)$$

$$= -10 \times 3.14(0.05)^2 \times 1.5(-1-1) = 0.24 \text{ J}$$

Electrostatic Analogy

The magnetic dipole is analogous to an electric dipole consisting of two equal charges of opposite signs ($\pm q$) separated by a certain distance ($2\mathbf{a}$). It has an electric dipole moment, i.e. $\mathbf{p} = q(2\mathbf{a})$

The equations for magnetic field **B** due to a magnetic dipole can be obtained from the equations of electric field **E** due to an electric dipole by making the following changes, $\mathbf{E} \to \mathbf{B}$, $\mathbf{p} \to \mathbf{M}$

$$\frac{1}{4\pi\varepsilon_0} \to \frac{\mu_0}{4\pi} \Rightarrow \frac{1}{\varepsilon_0} \to \mu_0$$

The table below shows the analogy between electric and magnetic dipoles.

The Dipole Analogy

	Electrostatics	Magnetism
Dipole moment	$\mathbf{p}$	$\mathbf{M}$
Equatorial field for a short dipole	$-\mathbf{p}/4\pi\varepsilon_0 r^3$	$-\mu_0\mathbf{M}/4\pi r^3$
Axial field for a short dipole	$2\mathbf{p}/4\pi\varepsilon_0 r^3$	$\mu_0 2\mathbf{M}/4\pi r^3$
External field : Torque	$\mathbf{p} \times \mathbf{E}$	$\mathbf{M} \times \mathbf{B}$
External field : Energy	$-\mathbf{p} \cdot \mathbf{E}$	$-\mathbf{M} \cdot \mathbf{B}$
At axial point	$\mathbf{E}_A = \frac{2k\mathbf{p}}{r^3}$	$\mathbf{B}_A = \frac{\mu_0}{4\pi} \cdot \frac{2\mathbf{M}}{d^3}$
At equatorial point	$\mathbf{E}_E = \frac{-k\mathbf{p}}{r^3}$	$\mathbf{B}_E = \frac{\mu_0 \mathbf{M}}{4\pi d^3}$

Magnetism and Gauss's Law

According to Gauss's law for magnetism, the net magnetic flux (ϕ_B) through any closed surface is always zero.

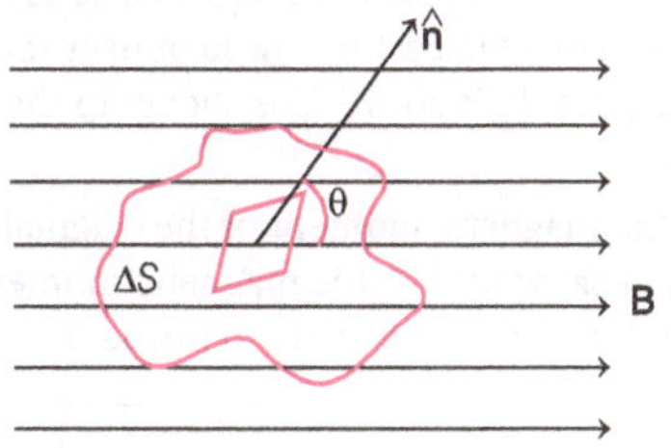

Consider a small vector area element $d\mathbf{S}$ of this surface. Magnetic flux through this area element is defined as

$$d\phi_B = \mathbf{B} \cdot d\mathbf{S}$$

Summing over all small area elements of the surface, we obtain according to Gauss's law for magnetism,

$$\phi_B = \oint_s \mathbf{B} \cdot d\mathbf{S} = 0$$

Comparing this with Gauss's law in electrostatics,

$$\phi_E = \oint \mathbf{E} \cdot d\mathbf{S} = \frac{q}{\varepsilon_0}$$

This difference between Gauss law of magnetism and electrostatics is a reflection of the fact that isolated magnetic poles (also called monopoles) do not exist.

Quick Test 1

Conceptual Questions

1. What is the basic difference between magnetic and electric field lines?

2. On what factors does the pole strength of a magnet depend?

3. A small magnetised needle P is placed at the origin of XY-plane with its magnetic moment pointing along the Y-axis. Another identical magnetised needle Q is placed in two positions, one by one,

Case I at $(a, 0)$ with its magnetic moment pointing along X-axis.

Case II at $(0, a)$ with its magnetic moment pointing along Y-axis.

(i) In which case the potential energy of P and Q is minimum?

(ii) In which case P and Q are not in equilibrium? Justify your answer. *CBSE 2023*

4. A bar magnet is cut into two equal parts as shown in the Fig. (a). One part is now kept over the other such that, the P_2 is above P_1 as shown in the Fig. (b).

If M is the magnetic moment of the original magnet, what would be the magnetic moment of new combination of magnets so formed?

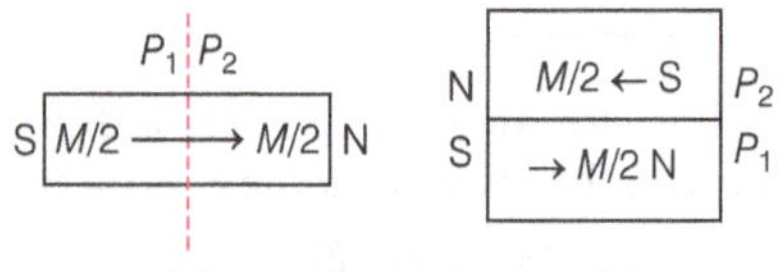

5. Three identical bar magnets are riveted together at centre in the same plane as shown in the figure. This system is placed at rest in a slowly varying magnetic field. It is found that the system of magnets does not show any motion.

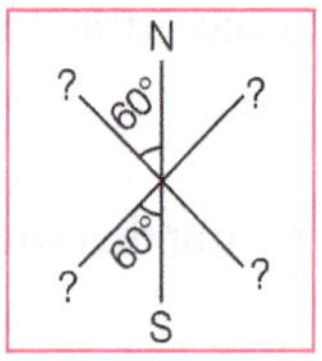

The N-S poles of one magnet is shown in the figure. Determine the poles of the remaining two. *NCERT Exemplar*

6. What happens to a bar magnet if it is cut into two pieces

(i) transverse to its length?

(ii) along its length?

7. Answer the following questions.

(i) Is it possibe to have a magnetic field configuration with three poles?

(ii) If magnetic monopoles existed, how would Gauss's law of magnetism be modified?

Numerical Questions

8. A short bar magnet has a magnetic moment of 0.48 J/T. Give the direction and magnitude of the magnetic field produced by the magnet at a distance of 10 cm from the centre of the magnet on

(i) the axis,

(ii) the equatorial lines (normal bisector) of the magnet. *NCERT*

9. If two magnets having magnetic moments M and $M\sqrt{3}$ are joined to form a cross (i.e.$\times$). The combination is suspended freely in a uniform magnetic field. In equilibrium position, the magnet having magnetic moment M makes an angle θ with the field. Calculate the value of θ.

10. A short bar magnet of magnetic moment $M = 0.32$ J/T is placed in a uniform magnetic field of 0.15 T. If the bar is free to rotate in the plane of the field, which orientation would correspond to its (i) stable and (ii) unstable equilibrium? What is the potential energy of the magnet in each case? *NCERT*

Answers

8. (i) 0.96 G, along S-N, (ii) 0.48 G, along N-S

9. 60° *10.* (i) -4.8×10^{-2} J, (ii) 4.8×10^{-2} J

For Solutions, See QR Code on Pg. 192

5.2 Various Terms Related to Magnetism

Magnetic Intensity (H)

The capability of magnetic field to magnetise the substance is measured in terms of magnetic intensity of the field.

The magnitude of **magnetic intensity** may be defined as the number of ampere turns flowing round the unit length of toroid to produce the magnetic induction B_0, in the toroid. It is denoted by H.

$$H = \frac{B_0}{\mu_0}$$

where, B_0 = magnetic field inside vacuum

and $\mu_0 = 4\pi \times 10^{-7}$ T-m A^{-1}

Its SI unit is Am^{-1}.

Magnetic intensity is also known as **magnetising force** and **magnetic field strength**.

Intensity of Magnetisation (I)

It is defined as the magnetic moment per unit volume of a magnetised material. It is denoted by I.

$$I = \frac{M}{V}$$

Its SI unit is Am^{-1}. Its dimension is $[L^{-1}A]$ and it is a **vector** quantity.

Magnetic Induction (B)

It is defined as the number of magnetic lines of induction crossing per unit area normally through the magnetic substance. It is denoted by B.

Magnetic induction B is the sum of the magnetic field B_0 and the magnetic field $\mu_0 I$ produced due to the magnetisation of the substance.

Thus, $B = B_0 + \mu_0 I = \mu_0 H + \mu_0 I \qquad (\because B_0 = \mu_0 H)$

$$B = \mu_0 (H + I)$$

Magnetic induction is also known as **magnetic flux density** or simply magnetic field.

Its SI unit is T or Wbm^{-2}.

Magnetic Susceptibility (χ_m)

It is a measure of how easily a substance is magnetised in a magnetising field.

The **magnetic susceptibility** of a magnetic substance is defined as the ratio of the intensity of magnetisation to the magnetic intensity.

It is denoted by χ_m.

$$\chi_m = \frac{I}{H}$$

As units of H and I are same (Am^{-1}), therefore it has no unit.

Magnetic Permeability (μ)

It is a measure of conduction of magnetic field lines through a substance. The **magnetic permeability** of a magnetic substance is defined as the ratio of the magnetic induction to the magnetic intensity. It is denoted by μ.

$$\mu = \frac{B}{H}$$

Its SI unit is TmA^{-1}.

The **relative magnetic permeability of a substance** is defined as the ratio of magnetic flux density B in that substance and flux density B_0 in vacuum in the same field.

$$\mu_r = \frac{B}{B_0}$$

Relation between Relative Magnetic Permeability (μ_r) and Magnetic Susceptibility (χ_m)

If a linear magnetic material is subjected to a magnetising field of intensity H, it develops a magnetisation I and magnetic induction B, the relationship is expressed as

$$B = \mu_0 (H + I)$$

But, $B = \mu H$

$$\mu H = \mu_0 (H + I)$$

$$\mu = \mu_0 \left(1 + \frac{I}{H}\right)$$

or $$\mu = \mu_0 (1 + \chi_m)$$

where, μ is the permeability and μ_0 is permeability in vacuum.

Thus, $\mu_r = 1 + \chi_m \qquad (\text{since } \mu_r = \mu/\mu_0)$

Example 9. **The magnetic field B and the magnetic intensity H in a material are found to be 1.6 T and 1000 Am^{-1}, respectively. Determine the relative permeability μ_r and the susceptibility χ_m of the material.**

Sol. Magnetic permeability,

$$\mu = \frac{B}{H} = \frac{1.6}{1000}$$

$$= 1.6 \times 10^{-3} \text{ T-mA}^{-1}$$

Since, relative magnetic permeability,

$$\mu_r = \frac{\mu}{\mu_0} = \frac{1.6 \times 10^{-3}}{4\pi \times 10^{-7}} = 0.127 \times 10^4$$

Therefore, susceptibility,

$$\chi_m = \mu_r - 1$$

$$= 1.27 \times 10^3 - 1$$

$$\Rightarrow \quad \chi_m \approx 1.27 \times 10^3$$

Example 10. **A solenoid of 600 turns per metre is carrying a current of 4 A. Its core is made of iron with relative permeability of 5000. Calculate the magnitudes of magnetic intensity, intensity of magnetisation and magnetic field inside the core.**

Sol. Given, current, $I = 4$ A

Number of turns per unit length, $n = 600$

Relative permeability, $\mu_r = 5000$

Since, magnetic intensity,

$$H = nI = 600 \times 4$$

$$= 2400 \text{ Am}^{-1}$$

Since, $\mu_r = 1 + \chi_m$

$$\Rightarrow \quad \chi_m = \mu_r - 1 = 5000 - 1$$

$$= 4999 \approx 5000$$

Here, χ_m = magnetic susceptibility.

Intensity of magnetisation can be given as

$$I = \chi_m H = 5000 \times 2400$$

$$= 1.2 \times 10^7 \text{ Am}^{-1}$$

Therefore, magnetic field, $B = \mu_r \mu_0 H$

$$= 5000 \times (4\pi \times 10^{-7}) \times 2400 = 15 \text{ T}$$

5.3 Magnetic Properties of Materials

There are several magnetism properties of matter such as diamagnetism, paramagnetism and ferromagnetism. Let's discuss these one by one in detail.

Diamagnetism

Diamagnetic substances are those substances which have a tendency to move from stronger to the weaker part of the external magnetic field.

When a bar of diamagnetic material is placed in an external magnetic field, the field lines are repelled or expelled and the field inside the material is reduced.

Explanation of Diamagnetism

Diamagnetic substances are those substances in which resultant magnetic moment in an atom is zero.

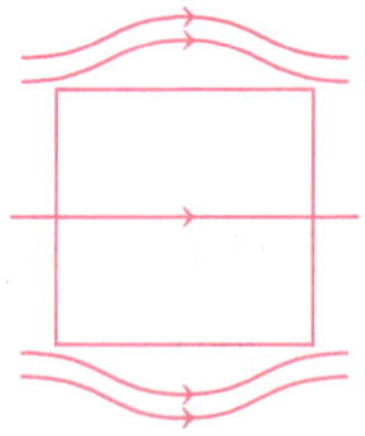

When magnetic field is applied, the electrons having orbital magnetic moment in the same direction slow down and those in opposite directions speed up. This happens due to induced current in accordance with Lenz's law.

Thus, the substance develops a net magnetic moment in the direction opposite to that of the applied field and hence, repels. e.g. Bismuth, copper, lead, silicon, nitrogen (at STP), water and sodium chloride.

> **Meissner Effect**
>
> Superconductors exhibit perfect diamagnetism.
> A superconductor repels a magnet and (by Newton's third law) is repelled by the magnet. This phenomenon of perfect diamagnetism in superconductors is called the **Meissner effect**. Superconducting magnets have been used for running magnetically levitated superfast trains.

Paramagnetism

The substances which get weakly magnetised in the direction of external field, when placed in an external magnetic field are called **paramagnetic substances.**

These substances have the tendency to move from a region of weak magnetic field to strong magnetic field, i.e. they get weakly attracted to a magnet.

Explanation of Paramagnetism

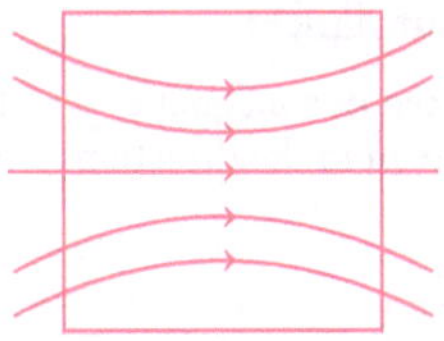

The atoms of a paramagnetic material possess a permanent magnetic dipole moment of their own.

On account of the ceaseless random motion of the atoms, no net magnetisation is seen. But in the presence of an external field B_0, which is strong enough and at low temperatures, the individual atomic dipole moment can be made to align and point in the same direction as B_0.

The field lines get concentrated inside the material and the field inside is enhanced.

When placed in a non-uniform magnetic field, the paramagnetic material tends to move from weaker part of the field to the stronger part. e.g. Aluminium, sodium, calcium, oxygen (at STP) and a copper chloride.

Ferromagnetism

The substances which get strongly magnetised when placed in an external magnetic field are called **ferromagnetic substances.**

They have strong tendency to move from a region of weak magnetic field to a region of strong magnetic field, i.e. they get strongly attracted to a magnet.

Explanation of Ferromagnetism

The atoms in a ferromagnetic material possess a dipole moment aligned in a common direction over a macroscopic volume called **domain**. Each domain has net magnetisation.

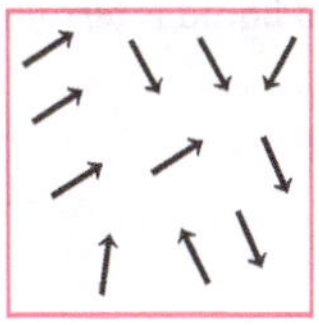

Randomly oriented domains

When we apply an external magnetic field B_0, the domains orient themselves in the direction of B_0 and simultaneously the domains grow in size.

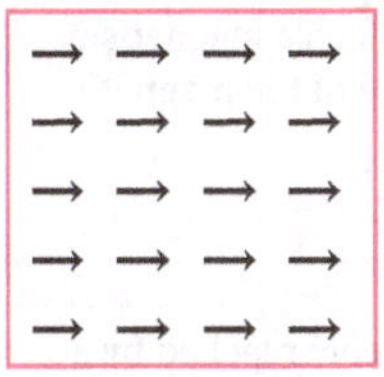

Aligned domains

In some ferromagnetic materials, the magnetisation persists on removal of external magnetic field. Such materials are called **hard magnetic materials** or **hard ferromagnets**, e.g. alnico (an alloy of iron, aluminium, nickel, cobalt and copper) is one such material which forms permanent magnets to be used among other things as a compass needle.

There are some ferromagnetic materials in which the magnetisation disappears on the removal of external magnetic field, e.g. soft iron. Such materials are called **soft magnetic materials or soft ferromagnets.** e.g. Iron, cobalt, nickel, gadolinium, etc.

The relative magnetic permeability of these substances is greater than 1000.

Materials can be classified as diamagnetic, paramagnetic and ferromagnetic on the basis of susceptibility (χ_m).

Diamagnetic	Paramagnetic	Ferromagnetic
$-1 \le \chi_m < 0$	$0 < \chi_m < \varepsilon$	$\chi_m >> 1$
$0 \le \mu_r < 1$	$1 < \mu_r < 1 + \varepsilon$	$\mu_r >> 1$
$\mu < \mu_0$	$\mu > \mu_0$	$\mu >> \mu_0$

Here, ε is a small positive number introduced to quantify paramagnetic materials.

Comparative Study of Magnetic Materials

Diamagnetic substances	Paramagnetic substances	Ferromagnetic substances
These substances when placed in a magnetic field, acquire feeble magnetism opposite to the direction of the magnetic field. 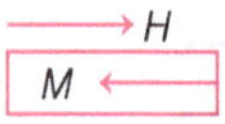	These substances when placed in a magnetic field, acquire feeble magnetism in the direction of the magnetic field. 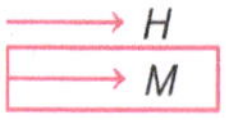	These substances when placed in a magnetic field are strongly magnetised in the direction of the field. 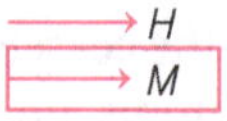
These substances are feebly repelled by a magnet.	These substances are feebly attracted by a magnet.	These substances are strongly attracted by a magnet.
When a diamagnetic solution is poured into a U-tube and one arm is placed between the poles of strong magnet, the level of solution in that arm is lowered. 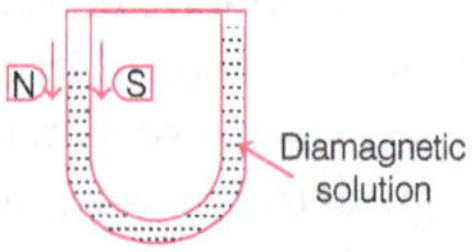	The level of the paramagnetic solution in that arm rises. 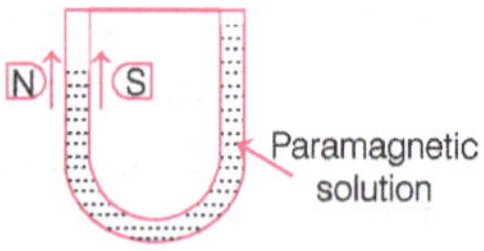	No liquid is ferromagnetic.
If a rod of diamagnetic material is suspended freely between two magnetic poles, its axis becomes perpendicular to the magnetic field. 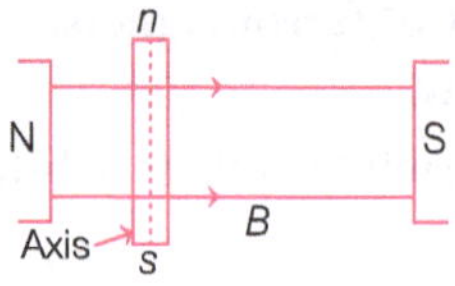	Paramagnetic rod becomes parallel to the magnetic field. 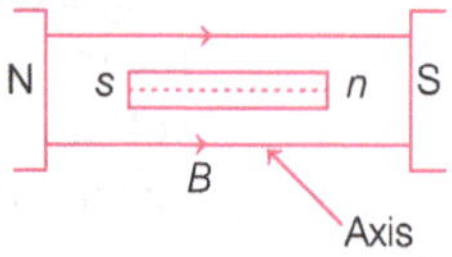	Ferromagnetic rod also becomes parallel to the magnetic field. 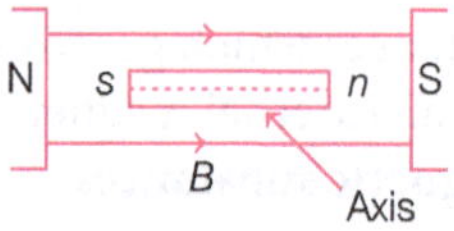
In non-uniform magnetic field, the diamagnetic substances are attracted towards the weaker fields, i.e. they move from stronger to weaker magnetic field.	In non-uniform magnetic field, paramagnetic substances move from weaker to stronger part of the magnetic field slowly.	In non-uniform magnetic field, ferromagnetic substances move from weaker to stronger magnetic field rapidly.
Their permeability is less than one ($\mu < 1$).	Their permeability is slightly greater than one ($\mu > 1$).	Their permeability is much greater than one ($\mu >> 1$).
Shape of diamagnetic liquid in a glass crucible and kept over two magnetic poles. 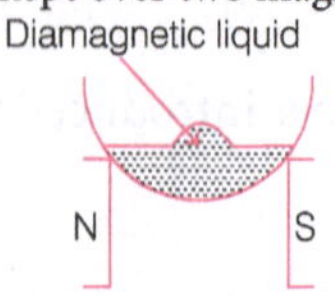	Shape of paramagnetic liquid in a glass crucible and kept over two magnetic poles. 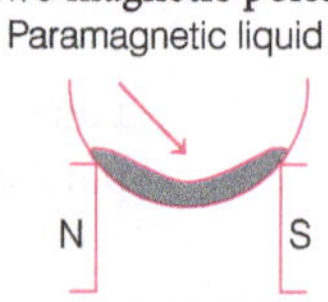	No liquid is ferromagnetic.
In these substances, the magnetic field lines are farther than in air.	In these substances, the magnetic field lines are closer than in air.	In these substances, the magnetic field lines are much closer than in air.
The resultant magnetic moment of these substances is zero.	These substances have a permanent magnetic moment.	These substances also have a permanent magnetic moment.

Quick Test 2

Conceptual Questions

1. In what way, the behaviour of a diamagnetic material is different from that of a paramagnetic, when kept in an external magnetic field? *All India 2016*
2. From molecular view point, discuss the temperature dependence of susceptibility for diamagnetism, paramagnetism and ferromagnetism. *NCERT Exemplar*
3. A ball of superconducting material is dipped in liquid nitrogen and placed near a bar magnet.
   (i) In which direction will it move?
   (ii) What will be the direction of its magnetic moment? *NCERT Exemplar*
4. One cannot write the proportionality $B = \mu H$ for the ferromagnets. Comment.
5. The magnetic susceptibility of χ of a given material is -0.5. Identify the magnetic material. *CBSE 2019*
6. The susceptibility of a magnetic material is 0.9853. Identify the type of magnetic material. Draw the modification of the field pattern on keeping a piece of this material in a uniform magnetic field. *CBSE 2018*
7. Out of the following, identify the materials which can be classified as
   (i) paramagnetic (ii) diamagnetic
   (a) Aluminium (b) Bismuth
   (c) Copper (d) Sodium

Numericals Questions

8. If relative permeability of iron is 5500, find its magnetic susceptibility.
9. When a piece of a ferromagnetic substance is put in a uniform magnetic field, the flux density inside it is four times the flux density away from the piece. Determine the relative magnetic permeability of the material.
10. An iron rod of volume 10^{-4} m^3 and relative permeability 1000 is placed inside a long solenoid wound with 5 turns/cm. If a current of 0.5 A is passed through the solenoid, find the magnetic moment of the rod.

Answers

8. 5499 *9.* 4 *10.* 25 Am^2

For Solutions, See QR Code on Pg. 192

Mind Map

Magnetism and Matter

Magnetic Dipole
An arrangement of two equal and opposite magnetic poles separated by a small distance is called a magnetic dipole.

Magnetic Dipole Moment
The product of its pole strength and magnetic length. It is a vector quantity, directed from S-pole to N-pole.

$$m = q_m \times 2l$$

Bar Magnet
A bar magnet is a rectangular piece of magnetised material that generates a magnetic field with a north and south poles.
Its magnetic fields resemble those of a solenoid with current flowing through it, creating a magnetic dipole.

Magnetic Field due to a Magnetic Dipole (Bar Magnet)

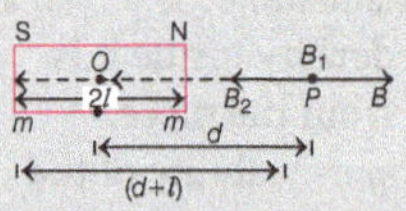

When point P lies on axial line of a bar magnet,

$$B = \frac{\mu_0}{4\pi}\frac{2N}{d^3}$$

for $d >> l$.

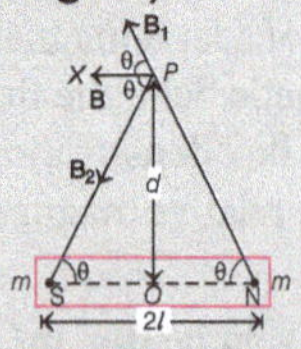

When point P lies on equilatorial line of a bar magnet,

$$B = \frac{\mu_0}{4\pi}\frac{M}{d^3}$$

for $d >> l$.

Solenoid as equivalent bar magnet
The magnetic field produced by a solenoid resembles that of a bar magnet, having a north pole and a south pole.
For a solenoid of length $2l$ and radius a consisting n per unit length, the magnetic field is given by

$$B = \frac{\mu_0 2M}{4\pi r^3}$$

(where, M = magnetic moment of solenoid $= n(2l)\, i\pi a^2$

Magnetic Field Lines These are imaginary lines representing the direction and strength of a magnetic field.

Properties of Magnetic Field Lines
They emerge from the north pole and enter the south pole of a magnet.
They form closed loops, with the density of the lines indicating the field's strength. They never intersects each other.

Magnetic Dipole in Uniform Magnetic Field
Torque on a magnetic dipole (bar magnet),
τ = force x perpendicular distance between coupled forces
$\tau = \mathbf{M}\times\mathbf{B} \Rightarrow |\tau| = MB\sin\theta$
Potential energy of magnetic dipole
$U = -\mathbf{M}\cdot\mathbf{B} = -MB\cos\theta$
When $\theta = 0$, $u = -MB$ (Minimum), so dipole is in stable equilibrium.
When $\theta = 180°$, $u = MB$ (Maximum), so dipole is in unstable equilibrium.

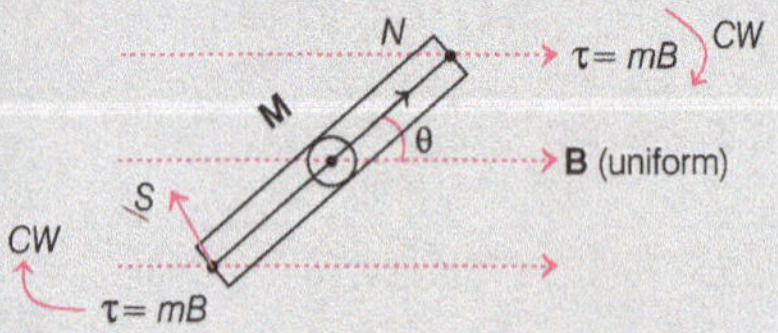

Intensity of Magnetisation (I)
It is the measure of the magnetic moment per unit volume of a material, indicating the extent to which a material is magnetized in response to an external magnetic field.

Magnetic Susceptibility (χ_m) It is a measure of how much a material becomes magnetised in response to an applied magnetic field.
It is a dimensionless quantity and defined as $\chi_m = I/H$

Magnetic Permeability (μ) It is a measure of a material's ability to support the formation of a magnetic field, defined by $\mu = B/H$ with units of henries per meter.

Relative magnetic permeability (μ_r)
It is the ratio of the magnetic permeability of a material (μ) to the magnetic permeability of free space (μ_0), i.e. $\mu_r = \mu/\mu_0$

Magnetic Field Intensity (H)
- It describes how strong and concentrated the magnetic field is due to the flow of electric current or magnetic sources.

Magnetic Induction (B)
- It is the measure of magnetic flux per unit area, given by $B = \mu H$ with unit tesla (T).

Effect of Temperature on Magnetic Properties
Temperature affects magnetic properties significantly
- Ferromagnetic materials becomes paramagnetic above the Curie temperature.
- Paramagnetic and diamagnetic materials show change in their magnetic susceptibility with temperature variations.

Magnetisation of Materials
Magnetisation is the vector field that expresses the density of permanent or induced magnetic dipole moments in a magnetic material.

Paramagnetic Substances
Weakly attracted by a magnetic field and do not retain magnetisation (e.g. aluminium, platinum).

Ferromagnetic Substances
Strongly attracted by a magnetic field and can retain magnetisation (e.g. iron, cobalt).

Diamagnetic Substances
Weakly repelled by a magnetic field and do not retain magnetisation (e.g. copper, gold).

EXAM PATTERN QUESTIONS

Objective Type Questions

Multiple Choice Questions (MCQs)

1. A bar magnet of length 3 cm has points A and B along axis at a distance of 24 cm and 48 cm on the opposite ends. Ratio of magnetic fields at these points will be

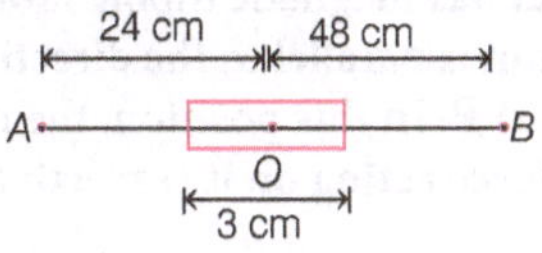

(a) 8 (b) 3 (c) 4 (d) $1/2\sqrt{2}$

2. Which of the following has its permeability less than that of free space? **CBSE 2023**

(a) Copper (b) Aluminium
(c) Copper chloride (d) Nickel

3. The magnetic field lines near a substance are as shown in the figure. The substance is **CBSE 2023**

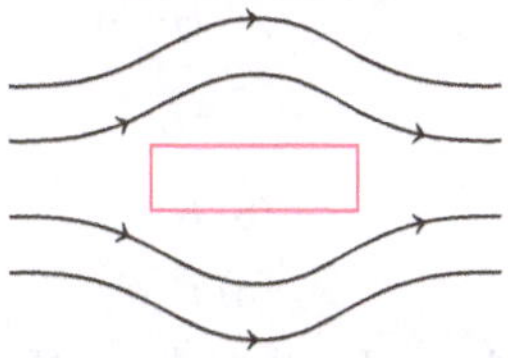

(a) Copper (b) Iron
(c) Sodium (d) Aluminium

4. Cutting a bar magnet in half is like cutting a solenoid, such that we get two smaller solenoids with

(a) weaker magnetic properties
(b) strong magnetic properties
(c) constant magnetic properties
(d) Both (a) and (b)

5. The relative permeability of a substance is 0.9999. The nature of substance will be

(a) diamagnetic
(b) paramagnetic
(c) magnetic moment
(d) intensity of magnetic field

6. Two blocks of different materials are placed in a uniform magnetic field B. The magnetic field lines passing through the two blocks are represented as follows. **Competency Based Que.**

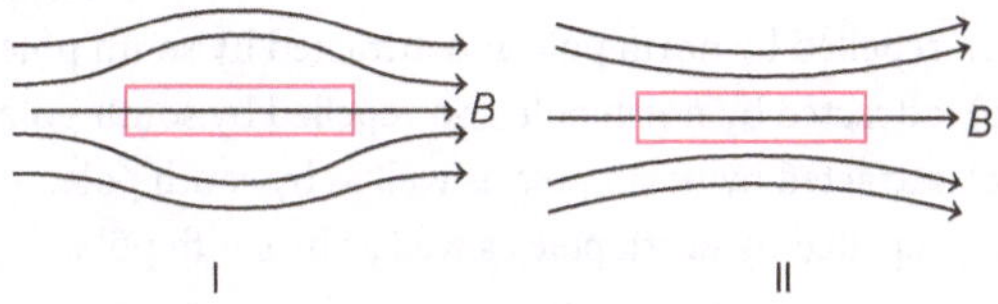

Identify the suitable values of relative permeability μ_r and magnetic susceptibility χ for the materials I and II.

(a) For I : $\mu_r > 1, \chi < 0$, For II : $\mu_r < 1, \chi > 0$
(b) For I : $\mu_r < 1, \chi = 0$, For II : $\mu_r > 1, \chi = 0$
(c) For I : $\mu_r = 0, \chi = 1$, For II : $\mu_r = 1, \chi = 0$
(d) For I : $\mu_r < 1, \chi < 0$, For II : $\mu_r > 1, \chi > 0$

7. The magnetic susceptibility for a diamagnetic material is **CBSE 2024**

(a) small and negative (b) small and positive
(c) large and negative (d) large and positive

8. The graph below represents the variation of intensity of magnetisation (M) with magnetic field strength (H) for substances P and Q. **Competency Based Que.**

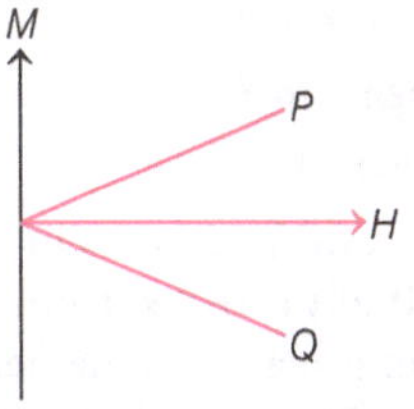

Which of the two substances is most likely to be attracted when taken near a magnet?

(a) Only P (b) Only Q
(c) Both P and Q (d) Neither P nor Q

9. The magnetic field due to a small magnetic dipole of dipole moment M at a distance r from the centre along the axis of the dipole is given by **CBSE 2025**

(a) $\frac{\mu_0}{4\pi} \times \frac{2M}{r^3}$ (b) $\frac{\mu_0}{4\pi} \times \frac{M}{r^3}$
(c) $\frac{\mu_0}{4\pi} \times \frac{M}{2r^3}$ (d) $\frac{\mu_0}{4\pi} \times \frac{2M}{r^2}$

10. A paramagnetic sample shows a net magnetisation of 8 Am^{-1} when placed in an external magnetic field of 0.6 T at a temperature of 4 K. When the same sample is placed in an external magnetic field of 0.2 T at a temperature of 16 K, the magnetisation will be **NCERT Exemplar**

(a) $\frac{32}{3}$ Am^{-1} (b) $\frac{2}{3}$ Am^{-1}

(c) 6 Am^{-1} (d) 2.4 Am^{-1}

11. **A diamagnetic substance is brought one by one near the north pole and the south pole of a bar magnet. It is** **CBSE 2025**

(a) repelled by north pole and attracted by south pole.

(b) attracted by north pole and repelled by south pole.

(c) attracted by north pole as well as by south pole.

(d) repelled by north pole as well as by south pole.

12. **In the figure, *X* is a coil wound over a hollow wooden pipe.** **CBSE 2025**

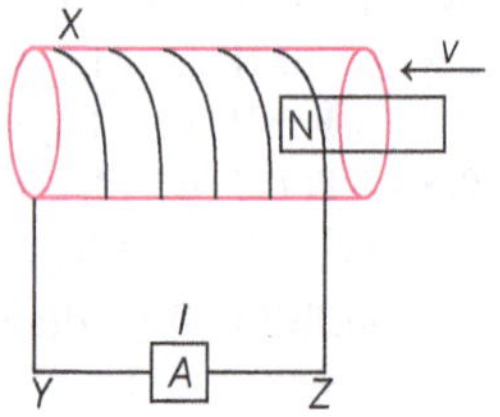

A permanent magnet is pushed at a constant speed *v* from the right into the pipe and it comes out at the left end of the pipe. During the entry and the exit of the magnet, the current in the wire *YZ* will be from

(a) *Y* to *Z* and then *Y* to *Z*

(b) *Z* to *Y* and then *Y* to *Z*

(c) *Y* to *Z* and then *Z* to *Y*

(d) *Z* to *Y* and then *Z* to *Y*

13. **A uniform magnetic field exists in space in the plane of paper and is initially directed from left to right. When a bar of soft iron is placed in the field parallel to it, the lines of force passing through it will be represented by**

(a) 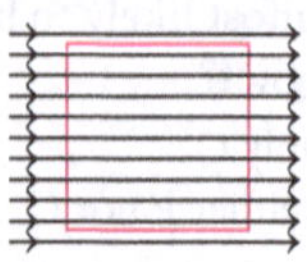

(b) 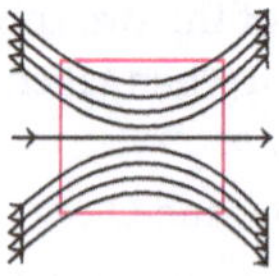

(c) 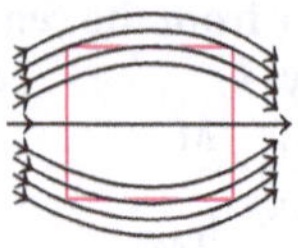

(d) 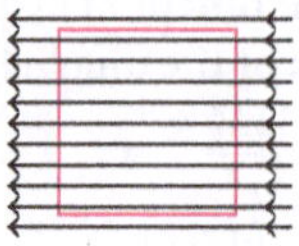

14. **Points *A* and *B* are situated perpendicular to the axis of a 2 cm long bar magnet at large distances *x* and 3*x* from its centre on opposite sides. The ratio of the magnetic fields at *A* and *B* will be approximately equal to**

(a) 1 : 9 (b) 2 : 9

(c) 27 : 1 (d) 9 : 1

15. **Electromagnets are made of soft iron because soft iron has**

(a) small susceptibility and small retentivity

(b) large susceptibility and small retentivity

(c) large permeability and large retentivity

(d) small permeability and large retentivity

16. **Above Curie temperature, a** **CBSE 2020**

(a) ferromagnetic material becomes diamagnetic.

(b) ferromagnetic material becomes paramagnetic.

(c) paramagnetic material becomes ferromagnetic.

(d) paramagnetic material becomes diamagnetic.

17. **A bar magnet has magnetic dipole moment M. Its initial position is parallel to the direction of uniform magnetic field B. In this position, the magnitudes of torque and force acting on it respectively are** **CBSE 2022, Term-1**

(a) 0 and *MB* (b) *MB* and *MB*

(c) 0 and 0 (d) $|\mathbf{M} \times \mathbf{B}|$ and 0

18. **The most appropriate *I*-*H* curve for a paramagnetic substance shown in figure is**

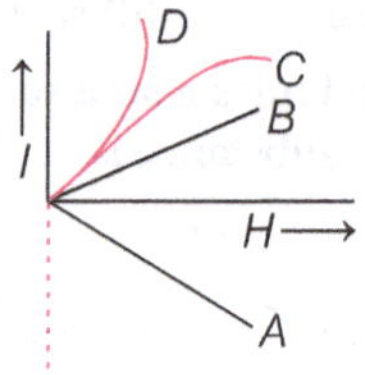

(a) *A* (b) *B*

(c) *C* (d) *D*

19. **Match the Column I with Column II and choose the correct option.**

Column I	Column II
A. Diamagnetic materials	P. Weakly repelled by a magnet
B. Paramagnetic materials	Q. Strongly attracted to a magnetic field lines
C. Ferromagnetic materials	R. It is a measure of conduction of magnetic field lines
D. Magnetic permeability	S. Weakly attracted to a magnetic field

Codes

	A	B	C	D
(a)	P	S	Q	R
(b)	P	Q	R	S
(c)	S	R	Q	P
(d)	R	Q	P	S

20. Match the Column I with Column II and choose the correct option.

Column I		Column II	
A.	Magnetic intensity (H)	P.	Tesla (T)
B.	Magnetic flux (ϕ)	Q.	Tm/A
C.	Magnetic permeability (μ)	R.	Weber (Wb)
D.	Magnetic field induction (B)	S.	Ampere per metre (A/m)

Codes

	A	B	C	D		A	B	C	D
(a)	P	Q	S	R	(b)	R	Q	S	P
(c)	P	Q	R	S	(d)	S	R	Q	P

Assertion-Reason

Directions *(Q.Nos. 21-30) In the following questions, two statements are given- one labelled Assertion (A) and the other labelled Reason (R). Select the correct answer to these questions from the codes (a), (b), (c) and (d) as given below.*

(a) Both Assertion and Reason are true and Reason is the correct explanation of Assertion.

(b) Both Assertion and Reason are true but Reason is not the correct explanation of Assertion.

(c) Assertion is true but Reason is false.

(d) Assertion is false but Reason is true.

21. Assertion (A) The poles of a bar magnet cannot be separated.
Reason (R) Magnetic monopoles do not exist.

22. Assertion (A) The poles of magnet cannot be separated by breaking into two pieces.
Reason (R) The magnetic moment will be reduced to half when a magnet is broken into two equal pieces.

23. Assertion (A) Susceptibility is defined as the ratio of intensity of magnetisation I to magnetic intensity H.
Reason (R) Greater the value of susceptibility, smaller the value of intensity of magnetisation I.

24. Assertion (A) When magnetic field is applied to a diamagnetic substance, those electrons having orbital magnetic moment in the same direction slow down and those in the opposite direction speed up.
Reason (R) This happens due to induced current in accordance with Lenz's law and the substance develops a net magnetic moment in direction opposite to that of the applied field and hence repulsion.

25. Assertion (A) Substances which at room temperature retain their ferromagnetic property for a long period of time are called permanent magnets.
Reason (R) Permanent magnet can be made by placing a ferromagnetic rod in a solenoid and passing current through it.

26. Assertion (A) Ferromagnetic substances are those which gets strongly magnetised when placed in an external magnetic field.
Reason (R) The individual atoms (or ions or molecules) in a ferromagnetic material possess a dipole moment as in a paramagnetic material.

27. Assertion (A) A paramagnetic sample displays greater magnetisation (for the same magnetising field) when cooled.
Reason (R) The magnetisation does not depend on temperature.

28. Assertion (A) Diamagnetic substances exhibit magnetism.
Reason (R) Diamagnetic materials do not have permanent magnetic dipole moment.

29. Assertion (A) Paramagnetic substances are weakly attracted to magnets.
Reason (R) The individual atoms of a paramagnetic substance do not possess a permanent magnetic dipole moment.

30. Assertion (A) When a bar of copper is placed in an external magnetic field, the field lines get concentrated inside the bar.
Reason (R) Copper is a diamagnetic substance.

Case Based Questions

Directions *(Q.Nos. 31-33) These questions are case study based questions. Read the following paragraph and answer the questions on the basis of same.*

31. When the atomic dipoles are aligned partially or fully, there is a net magnetic moment in the direction of field in any small volume of material. The actual magnetic field inside material placed in magnetic field is equal to the sum of the applied magnetic field and the magnetic field due to magnetisation. This field is called magnetising intensity (H), $H = B/\mu_0 - M$,

where M is the magnetisation of the material, μ_0 is the permittivity of vacuum and B is the total magnetic field. The measure that tells us how magnetic material responds to external field is given by a dimensionless quantity, known as magnetic susceptibility; for a certain class of magnetic materials, intensity of magnetisation is directly proportional to the magnetic intensity.

(i) **Magnetisation of a sample is**
(a) volume of sample per unit magnetic moment.
(b) net magnetic moment per unit volume.
(c) ratio of magnetic moment and pole strength
(d) ratio of pole strength the magnetic moment

(ii) **A bar magnet has length 3 cm, cross-sectional area 2 cm^2 and magnetic moment 3 Am^2. The intensity of magnetisation of bar magnet is**
(a) 2×10^5 A/m (b) 3×10^5 A/m
(c) 4×10^5 A/m (d) 5×10^5 A/m

(iii) **The relative permeability of iron is 6000. Its magnetic susceptibility is**
(a) 5999 (b) 6001
(c) 6000×10^{-7} (d) 6000×10^{-7}

32. **A magnetic dipole is an arrangement of two magnetic poles of equal and opposite strengths $+m$ and $-m$ separated by a small distance. The positive pole strength is north pole and the negative pole strength is south pole. A magnetic dipole is characterised by its magnetic dipole moment, $M = m\,(2l)$, where $2l$ is the distance between two poles. It is similar to electric dipole moment in electrostatics.**

(i) A bar magnet use dipole moment M. When it is bent to form a semicircular arc, then find its dipole moment.

(ii) The arrangement of two bar magnets each of dipole moment M is shown in figure.

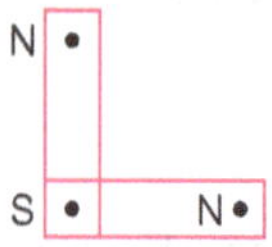

What will be the resultant dipole moment?

(iii) What is the direction of magnetic moment of a magnetic dipole?

(iv) How is the magnetic pole different from a charge?

33. **There are several magnetic materials like diamagnetic materials, paramagnetic materials and ferromagnetic materials. When a dimagnetic material is placed in a magnetising field, then it gets feebly magnetised in a direction opposite to the magnetising field. It is weakly repelled by magnetic field. The field (B) inside the diamagnetic material is less than magnetising field (H).**

A paramagnetic material is weakly attracted by the magnetic field. The field (B) inside the paramagnetic material is slighly greater than the magnetising field. A ferromagnetic material is a paramagnetic material which acquires very high magnetism in external magnetic field. It is strongly attracted by the magnetic field.

The relative permeability of magnetic material is given by $\mu_r = \chi + 1$, where χ is susceptibility of the material.

(i) When a diamagnetic material is placed in a magnetic field, then how it is oriented?

(ii) The value of magnetic field B and the magnetic intensity H in magnetic material are found to be 6.28×10^{-2} T and 100 Am^{-1}, respectively. Determine the value of relative permeability and magnetic susceptibility of the magnetic material.

(iii) Mention the three differences between diamagnetic substances and paramagnetic substances.

(iv) Which types of materials are called soft ferromagnets. Give any two examples of such materials.

Subjective Questions

Very Short Answer Type Questions

1. Differentiate between magnetisation and the susceptibility of a material. What can you say about the susceptibility of paramagnetic and diamagnetic materials? **CBSE 2024C**

2. Why is diamagnetism almost independent of temperature?

3. "Alkali halides are diamagnetic rather than paramagnetic". Explain why?

4. What are permanent magnets? Give one example.

5. Why is the core of an electromagnet made of ferromagnetic materials?

6. In what way is the behaviour of a diamagnetic material different from that of a paramagnetic, when kept in an external magnetic field?

7. Do the diamagnetic substances have resultant magnetic moment in an atom in the absence of external magnetic field? **CBSE 2019**

Short Answer Type Questions

8. What are the magnetic field lines? State their properties. Why two such lines do not intersect each other?

9. A ball of superconducting material is dipped in liquid nitrogen and placed near a bar magnet.

(i) In which direction will it move? **[2]**

(ii) What will be the direction of its magnetic moment? **[1]**

10. When two materials are placed in an external magnetic field, the behaviour of magnetic field lines is as shown in the figure. Identify the magnetic nature of each of these two materials.

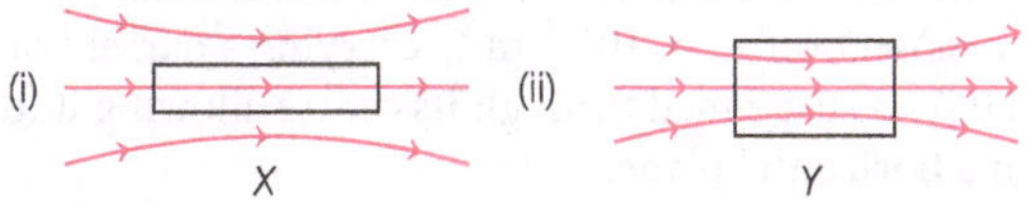

11. Suppose you have two bars of identical dimensions, one made of paramagnetic substance and the another of diamagnetic substance. If you place these bars along a uniform magnetic field, show diagrammatically, what modifications in the field pattern would take place in each case?

12. A bar magnet of magnetic moment 1.5 J/T lies aligned with the direction of a uniform magnetic field of 0.22 T.

(i) What is the amount of work required by an external torque to turn the magnet so as to align its magnetic moment: (a) normal to the field direction, (b) opposite to the field direction? **[2]**

(ii) What is the torque on the magnet in cases (a) and (b)? **[1]**

13. Three identical specimens of a magnetic material, nickel, antimony, aluminium are kept in a uniform magnetic field. Draw the modification in the field lines in each case. Justify your answer.

14. From molecular point of view, discuss the temperature evidence of susceptibility for diamagnetism, paramagnetism and ferromagnetism.

15. A proton has spin and magnetic moment just like an electron. Why its effect is neglected in magnetism of materials? **NCERT Exemplar**

Long Answer Type Questions

16. Verify the Gauss' law for magnetic field of a point dipole of dipole moment **M** at the origin for the surface which is a sphere of radius *R*. **NCERT Exemplar**

17. (i) State Gauss' law for magnetism. Explain its significance. **[2]**

(ii) Write the four important properties of the magnetic field lines due to a bar magnet. **[3]**

18. What are ferromagnetic materials? Explain ferromagnetism with the help of suitable diagrams, using the concept of magnetic domain. **CBSE 2024**

19. (i) Discuss briefly electron theory of magnetism for diamagnetic and paramagnetic materials. **[4]**

(ii) Give two methods to destroy the magnetism of a magnet. **[1]**

20. Define magnetic susceptibility of a material. Name two elements, one having positive susceptibility and the other having negative susceptibility. What does negative susceptibility signify?

21. Draw a plot showing the variation of intensity of magnetisation with the applied magnetic field intensity for bismuth. Under what condition does a diamagnetic material exhibit perfect conductivity and perfect diamagnetism?

22. Write three points of differences between para-, dia- and ferro-magnetic materials, giving one example for each. **CBSE 2019**

23. Each of the orbiting electrons in an atom contributes towards the orbital magnetic moment. In a diamagnetic material, the resultant magnetic moment of each atom is zero. When exposed to an external magnetic field, the diamagnetic substance experiences repulsion.

Competency Based Que.

(i) Why are diamagnetic materials repelled when placed in an external field? Give an explanation on the basis of the changes that occur to the orbital magnetic moment of the electrons. **[2]**

(ii) In contrast to a diamagnetic material, how does a material with each individual atom having a non-zero magnetic dipole moment but all atoms aligned in random directions, respond to an external magnetic field? What are such materials known as? **[1]**

(iii) In the material identified in (ii), what is the effect of fall in temperature and rise in applied magnetic field intensity? **[1]**

(iv) What does the value $\mu_r = 0$ signify in a magnetic material? Find χ of such materials. What are such materials known as? **[1]**

24. (i) A current carrying loop can be considered as a magnetic dipole placed along its axis. Explain.

(ii) Obtain the relation for magnetic dipole moment **M** of current carrying coil. Give the direction of **M**.

(iii) A current carrying coil is placed in an external uniform magnetic field. The coil is free to turn in the magnetic field. What is the net force acting on the coil? Obtain the orientation of the coil in stable equilibrium. Show that in this orientation the flux of the total field (field produced by the loop + external field) through the coil is maximum. **CBSE 2025**

Numerical Problems

25. What is the net magnetic moment of two identical magnets each of magnetic moment m_0 inclined at 60° with each other?

26. Calculate the magnetic induction at a point 4 cm from the centre and along the equatorial line of a bar magnet of length 6 cm and magnetic moment 0.26 A-m^2.

27. A short bar magnet placed with its axis at 30° with a uniform external magnetic field of 0.25 T experiences a torque of magnitude equal to 4.5×10^{-2} J. What is the magnitude of magnetic moment of the magnet?

28. A magnetic dipole of dipole moment m is aligned parallel to an external magnetic field B. Work of 0.25 J has to be done in order to turn it through angle of 60°. Find the external counter torque that is required in order to maintain the dipole at this angle. **Competency Based Que**

29. A closely wound solenoid of 800 turns and area of cross-section 2.5×10^{-4} m^2 carries a current of 3.0 A. Explain the sense in which the solenoid acts like a bar magnet. What is its associated magnetic moment? **NCERT**

30. A closely wound solenoid of 2000 turns and area of cross-section 1.6×10^{-4} m^2, carrying a current of 4.0 A, is suspended through its centre allowing it to turn in a horizontal plane.

(i) What is the magnetic moment associated with the solenoid? **[1]**

(ii) What are the force and torque on the solenoid, if a uniform horizontal magnetic field of 7.5×10^{-2} T is set up at an angle of 30° with the axis of the solenoid? **[2]**

Hints & Solutions

Objective Type Questions

1. (a) 2. (a) 3. (a)
4. (a) 5. (a) 6. (d)

7. (a) Magnetic susceptibility of the diamagnetic material is little less than unity.

$$\therefore \quad \mu_r = (1 + \chi_m) < 1 \quad \Rightarrow \quad \chi_m < 0$$

Thus, magnetic susceptibility for a diamagnetic material is small and negative.

8. (a) Ferromagnetic materials have a steep saturating curve, indicating strong attraction to a magnet. From the graph, it can be seen that the magnetic susceptibility of substance P is positive and shown by ferromagnetic substance. Therefore, substance P is more likely to be attracted to a magnet.

9. (a) Along the axis of the dipole,

$$B = \frac{\mu_0}{4\pi} \frac{2M}{r^3}$$

10. (b) As Curie law explains, we can deduce a formula for the relation between magnetic field induction, temperature and magnetisation,

i.e. $I \text{ (magnetisation)} \propto \dfrac{B \text{ (magnetic field induction)}}{t \text{ (temperature in kelvin)}}$

$$\Rightarrow \quad \frac{I_2}{I_1} = \frac{B_2}{B_1} \times \frac{t_1}{t_2}$$

Let us suppose, here $I_1 = 8$ Am^{-1}

$$B_1 = 0.6 \text{ T}, \; t_1 = 4 \text{ K}$$

$$B_2 = 0.2 \text{ T}, t_2 = 16 \text{ K}$$

$$I_2 = ?$$

$$\Rightarrow \quad \frac{0.2}{0.6} \times \frac{4}{16} = \frac{I_2}{8}$$

$$\Rightarrow \quad I_2 = 8 \times \frac{1}{12} = \frac{2}{3} \text{ Am}^{-1}$$

11. (d) 12. (c) 13. (b) 14. (c)
15. (b) 16. (b) 17. (c) 18. (b)
19. (a) 20. (d) 21. (a) 22. (b)

23. (c) From the relation, susceptibility of the material is

$$\chi_m = \frac{I}{H} \Rightarrow I = \chi_m H$$

Thus, it is obvious that greater the value of susceptibility of a material, greater will be the value of intensity of magnetisation, i.e. more easily it can be magnetised.

24. (a) 25. (b) 26. (a)
27. (c) 28. (b)

29. (c) A is correct but R is incorrect.

Paramagnetic substances are indeed weakly attracted to external magnetic fields due to presence of unpaired electrons that create a temporary magnetic dipole when an external field is applied.

The individual atoms or ions in a paramagnetic substance do possess a permanent magnetic dipole moment due to unpaired electrons.

30. (d)

31. (i) (b), (ii) (d), (iii) (a)

32. (i) Dipole moment of bar magnet $= M = m \cdot l$

When it is bent into semi-circular wire, then

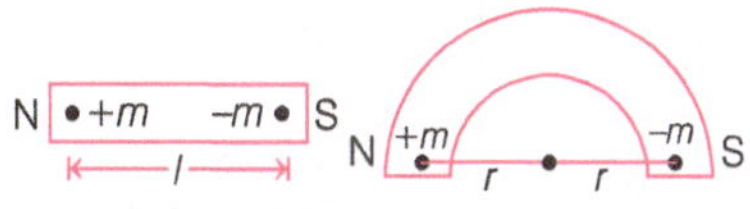

Radius of semi-circle, $r = \frac{l}{\pi}$

$\therefore$ Distance between the two poles is

$$l' = 2r = \frac{2l}{\pi}$$

$\therefore$ Dipole moment of semi-circle is

$$M' = m \cdot l' = \frac{2ml}{\pi} = \frac{2M}{\pi}$$

(ii) The dipole moment vector for the arrangement is shown.

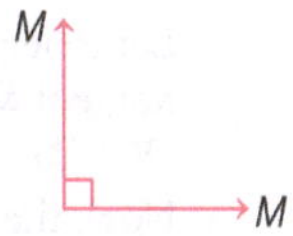

$\therefore$ The resultant dipole moment is given by

$$M' = \sqrt{M^2 + M^2} = \sqrt{2}M$$

(iii) The direction of magnetic dipole moment is from south pole to north pole of a magnetic dipole.

(iv) Unlike an electric charge, an isolated magnetic pole (either north or south pole) does not exist.

33. (i) Since, diamagnetic substances get magnetised in opposite direction, therefore it will try to reduce the magnetic field in the direction of magnetising field. Hence, diamagnetic material is oriented towards the region in which magnetising field is weaker.

(ii) Given, $B = 6.28 \times 10^{-2}$ T

$H = 100$ Am^{-1}

$\therefore$ Magnetic permeability,

$$\mu = \frac{B}{H} = \frac{6.28 \times 10^{-2}}{100}$$
$$= 6.28 \times 10^{-4} \text{ TmA}^{-1}$$

Relative permeability,

$$\mu_r = \frac{\mu}{\mu_0} = \frac{6.28 \times 10^{-4}}{4\pi \times 10^{-7}} = 5 \times 10^2 = 500$$

$\therefore$ Magnetic susceptibility,

$$\chi_m = \mu_r - 1 = 500 - 1 = 499$$

(iii) Refer the text on page 180.

(iv) Refer the text on page 179.

Subjective Questions

1. Refer the text on pages 177 and 179.

2. Since for a diamagnetic substance the net moment of an atom is zero, so the thermal motion of the atoms doesn't affect the diamagnetic property of the substance.

3. The alkali halides are all diamagnetic because of the absence of unpaired electrons. So, they do not show paramagnetism.

4. Substances that retain their attractive property for a long period of time at room temperature are called permanent magnets. e.g. Alnico magnets.

5. Ferromagnetic material has a high permeability. So, on passing current through windings, it gains sufficient magnetism immediately.

6. A diamagnetic specimen would move towards the weaker region of the field while a paramagnetic specimen would move towards the stronger region.

7. No, diamagnetic substances have no resultant magnetic moment in the absence of external magnetic field.

8. Refer to text on page 171.

9. When a diamagnetic material is dipped in liquid nitrogen, it again behaves as a diamagnetic material. Thus, superconducting material will again behave as a diamagnetic material. When this diamagnetic material is placed near a bar magnet, it will be feebly magnetised opposite to the direction of magnetising field.

(i) Thus, it will be repelled.

(ii) Its direction of magnetic moment will be opposite to the direction of magnetic field of magnet.

10. (i) Material X is paramagnetic substance. When a specimen of a paramagnetic substance is placed in a magnetising field, the lines of force prefer to pass through the specimen rather than through air.

Thus, magnetic induction inside the sample is more than the magnetic intensity.

(ii) Material Y is ferromagnetic substance. These are the substances in which a strong magnetism is produced in the same direction as the applied magnetic field, these are strongly attracted by a magnet, exhibits highly concentrated lines of force.

11. Refer to text on pages 178 and 179.

12. Given, magnetic moment of magnet $M = 1.5$ J/T

Uniform magnetic field, $B = 0.22$ T

(i) (a) Angle $\theta_1 = 0°$ ($\because$ The magnet lies aligned in the direction of field)

and $\theta_2 = 90°$ ($\because$ The magnet is to be aligned normal to the field direction)

Work done in rotating the magnet from angle θ_1 to θ_2

$$W = -MB(\cos\theta_2 - \cos\theta_1)$$
$$= -1.5 \times 0.22\,(\cos 90° - \cos 0°)$$
$$= 0.33 \text{ J}$$

(b) Angle $\theta_1 = 0°$ and $\theta_2 = 180°$ ($\because$ Magnet is to be aligned opposite to the direction of field)

Work done $= -MB(\cos\theta_2 - \cos\theta_1)$

$$= -1.5 \times 0.22\,(\cos 180° - \cos 0°) = 0.66 \text{ J}$$

(ii) Using the formula of torque,

$$\tau = MB \sin\theta$$

(a) $\theta = 90°$

(when magnetic moment normal to the field)

$$\tau = 1.5 \times 0.22 \sin 90° = 0.33 \text{ N-m}$$

(b) $\theta = 180°$

(when magnetic moment opposite to the field)

$$\tau = 1.5 \times 0.22 \sin 180° = 0$$

13.

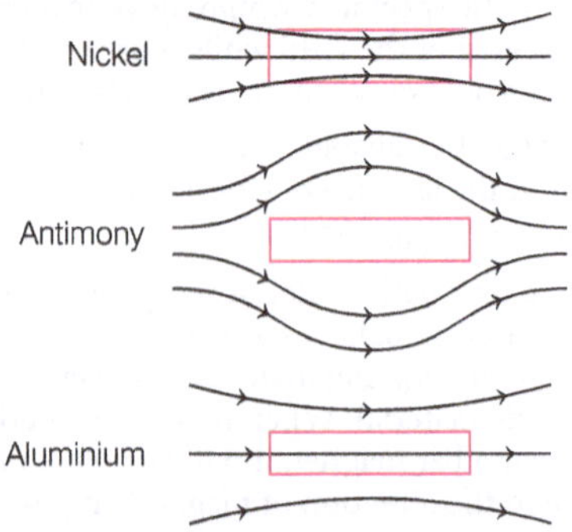

The modification in the field lines shown in the figure are as such because

(i) nickel is a ferromagnetic substance.

(ii) antimony is a diamagnetic substance.

(iii) aluminium is a paramagnetic substance.

14. Diamagnetism is due to the orbital motion of electrons in an atom developing magnetic moments opposite to applied field. Thus, the resultant magnetic moment of the diamagnetic material is zero and hence the susceptibility χ of diamagnetic material is not much affected by temperature.

Paramagnetism and ferromagnetism is due to alignments of atomic magnetic moments in the direction of the applied field. As temperature is raised, the alignment is disturbed, resulting decrease in susceptibility of both with increase in temperature.

15. The comparison between the spinning of a proton and an electron can be done by comparing their magnetic dipole moments which can be given by

$$M = \frac{eh}{4\pi m} \text{ or } M \propto \frac{1}{m} \qquad \left(\because \frac{eh}{4\pi} = \text{constant}\right)$$

$$\therefore \quad \frac{M_p}{M_e} = \frac{m_e}{m_p} = \frac{m_e}{1837 m_e} \qquad (\because M_p = 1837 m_e)$$

$$\Rightarrow \quad \frac{M_p}{M_e} = \frac{1}{1837} << 1$$

$$\Rightarrow \quad m_p << m_e$$

Thus, effect of magnetic moment of proton is neglected as compared to that of electron.

16. Let us draw the figure for given situation,

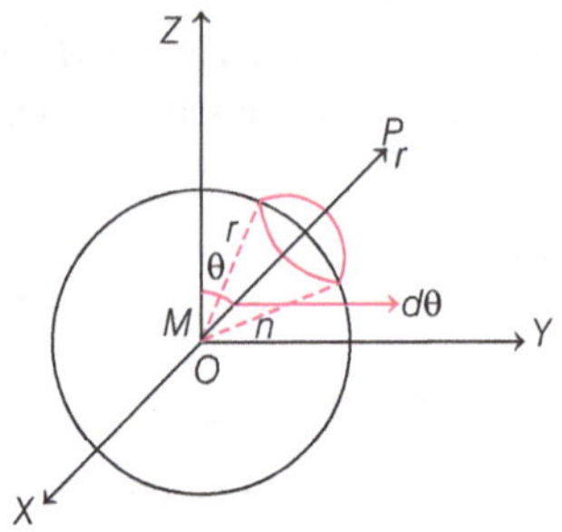

We have to prove that $\oint \mathbf{B} \cdot d\mathbf{S} = 0$. This is called Gauss's law in magnetisation.

According to the question,

Magnetic moment of dipole at origin O is $\mathbf{M} = M\hat{\mathbf{k}}$

Let P be a point at distance r from O and OP makes an angle θ with Z-axis. Component of $\mathbf{M}$ along $OP = M\cos\theta$.

Now, the magnetic field induction at P due to dipole of moment $M\cos\theta$ is $\mathbf{B} = \frac{\mu_0}{4\pi} \cdot \frac{2M\cos\theta}{r^3}\hat{\mathbf{r}}$

From the diagram, r is the radius of sphere with centre at O lying in YZ-plane. Take an elementary area $d\mathbf{S}$ of the surface at P. Then,

$$d\mathbf{S} = r(r\sin\theta \, d\theta)\hat{\mathbf{r}} = r^2 \sin\theta \, d\theta \hat{\mathbf{r}}$$

$$\therefore \oint \mathbf{B} \cdot d\mathbf{S} = \oint \frac{\mu_0}{4\pi} \cdot \frac{2M\cos\theta}{r^3}\hat{\mathbf{r}}(r^2 \sin\theta \, d\theta \hat{\mathbf{r}})$$

$$= \frac{\mu_0}{4\pi} \cdot \frac{M}{r} \int_0^{2\pi} 2\sin\theta . \cos\theta \, d\theta$$

$$= \frac{\mu_0}{4\pi} \cdot \frac{M}{r} \int_0^{2\pi} \sin 2\theta d\theta = \frac{\mu_0}{4\pi} \cdot \frac{M}{r}\left(\frac{-\cos 2\theta}{2}\right)_0^{2\pi}$$

$$= -\frac{\mu_0}{4\pi} \cdot \frac{M}{2r}[\cos 4\pi - \cos 0°]$$

$$= \frac{\mu_0}{4\pi} \cdot \frac{M}{2r}[1 - 1] = 0$$

17. (i) Refer to text on page 175.
(Magnetism and Gauss's Law)

(ii) Refer to text on page 171.
(Properties of Magnetic Field Lines)

18. The substances which get strongly magnetised when placed in an external magnetic field are called ferromagnetic substances. They have strong tendency to move from a region of weak magnetic field to a region of strong magnetic field, i.e. they get strongly attracted to a magnet.

Explanation of Ferromagnetism The atoms in a ferromagnetic material possess a dipole moment aligned in a common direction over a macroscopic volume called **domain**. Each domain has net magnetisation.

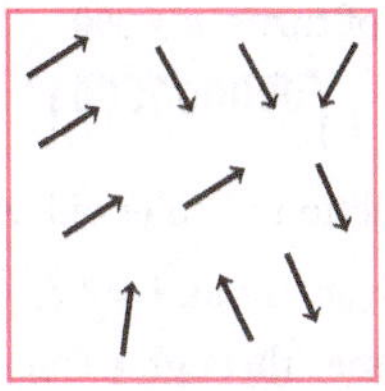

When we apply an external magnetic field B_0, the domains orient themselves in the direction of B_0 and simultaneously the domains grow in size.

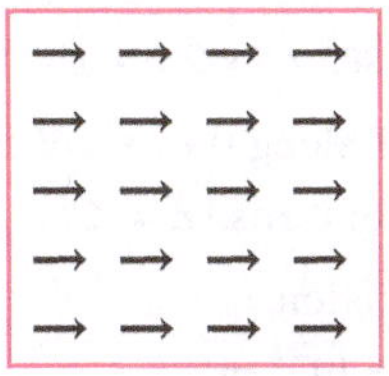

In some ferromagnetic materials, the magnetisation persists on removal of external magnetic field. Such materials are called **hard magnetic materials** or **hard ferromagnets**, e.g. alnico (an alloy of iron, aluminium, nickel, cobalt and copper) is one such material which forms permanent magnets to be used among other things as a compass needle.

19. (i) Refer to text on pages 178 and 179.

(ii) We can destroy the magnetism of a magnet

(a) by heating it.

(b) by applying magnetic field across it in reverse direction.

20. Refer to text on pages 177, 178 and 179.

21. Here, intensity of magnetisation varies inversely with magnetic field strength, i.e. $-I \propto H$ as shown in figure.

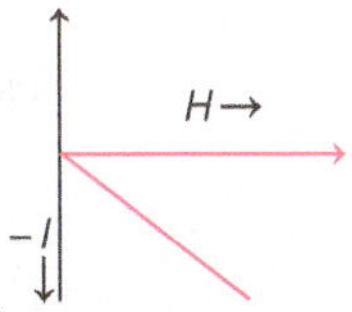

A diamagnetic substance exhibits perfect diamagnetism when it is in its superconducting state. This means that when it is cooled below a certain critical temperature, it expels all magnetic field form its interior. This is also known as meissner effect.

22. Refer to text on page 180.

(Comparative Study of Magnetic Materials)

23. (i) When an external magnetic field B is applied to a diamagnetic material, the electrons with an orbital magnetic moment in the direction same as B, slow down, whereas the ones in the direction opposite to B, speed up.

The diamagnetic material develops a net non-zero magnetic moment in the direction opposite to the applied B. This results in repulsion.

(ii) Each atom with a net non-zero magnetic moment aligns parallel to the applied magnetic field B. The material will experience attraction, so they are known as paramagnetic materials.

(iii) With the fall in temperature and rise in the applied magnetic field intensity B, the magnetisation intensity M of paramagnetic material increases until all dipole moments are perfectly aligned to B. The material is said to have reached its magnetic saturation.

(iv) As $\mu_r = 1 + \chi$, if $\mu_r = 0$, it implies $\chi = -1$. If such a material is placed in an external magnetic field, it will repel all the field lines.

The net magnetic field inside the material, i.e. $B = \mu H = \mu_0 \mu_r H = 0$.

Such materials are known as perfectly diamagnetic materials or superconductors.

24. (i) A current carrying loop produces a magnetic field inside the loop along the axis of the loop in which according to the right hand thumb rule, the direction of the thumb gives the direction of north pole of the magnetic field and hence the opposite end becomes the South Pole. Therefore, this entire configuration can be considered as a magnetic dipole placed along its axis.

(ii) Refer to the text on page 172 (Magnetic Dipole Moment)

(iii) A current carrying coil when placed in an external uniform magnetic field, acts as magnetic dipole of magnetic moment **M** acting perpendicular to the plane of the coil. Since the coil is free to rotate, so the magnetic dipole moment will orient itself along the direction of the magnetic field which means that the plane of the coil will be perpendicular to the direction of the magnetic field. This is because, the torque acting on the coil is $\tau = \mathbf{M} \times \mathbf{B} \Rightarrow$ $|\tau| = MB\sin\theta$ is zero when $\theta = 0°$ that is the angle between **M** and **B** is zero which is the position of the stable equilibrium of the coil.

The flux passing through the coil of area A (say) is given as

$$\phi = \mathbf{B} \cdot \mathbf{A} = BA\cos\theta$$

Since the angle between **B** and the area vector **A**, which is perpendicular to the plane of the loop is zero, so $\phi = BA$ which is the maximum amount of flux.

25. $M = \sqrt{M_1^2 + M_2^2 + 2M_1M_2 \cos\theta}$

$= \sqrt{m_0^2 + m_0^2 + 2m_0^2 \cos 60°} = \sqrt{3}m_0$

26. Refer to Sol. of Example 5 on page no. 173.

[**Ans.** 6.9×10^{-8}T]

27. Given, uniform magnetic field $B = 0.25$ T

The magnitude of torque $\tau = 4.5 \times 10^{-2}$ J

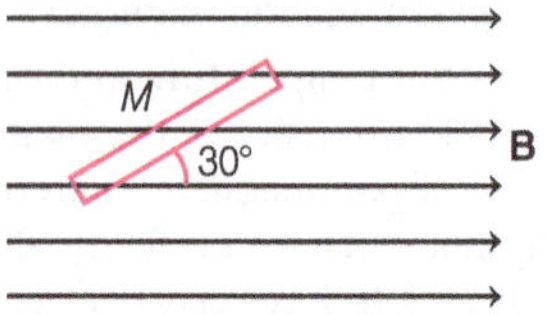

Angle between magnetic moment and magnetic field $\theta = 30°$

Torque experienced on a magnet placed in external magnetic field

$$\tau = \mathbf{M} \times \mathbf{B}$$

$$\tau = MB \sin \theta$$

$$4.5 \times 10^{-2} = M \times 0.25 \times \sin 30°$$

$$M = \frac{4.5 \times 10^{-2}}{0.25 \times \sin 30°}$$

$$= \frac{4.5 \times 10^{-2} \times 2}{0.25 \times 1} \quad \left(\because \sin 30° = \frac{1}{2}\right)$$

$$= 0.36 \text{ J/T}$$

Thus, the magnitude of magnetic moment of the magnet is 0.36 J/T.

28. Work done to rotate from parallel to 60°,

$$W = |\, mB(\cos\theta_2 - \cos\theta_1)\,|$$

$$= |\, mB(\cos 60° - \cos 0°)\,|$$

$$= \left| mB\left(\frac{1}{2} - 1\right) \right| = \frac{mB}{2}$$

Counter torque required to hold the dipole at angle 60°,

$$\tau = mB \sin\theta = mB \sin 60° = \sqrt{3}\,\frac{mB}{2}$$

$$\tau = \sqrt{3} \times W = \sqrt{3} \times 0.25 = \frac{\sqrt{3}}{4} \text{ N-m}$$

29. Given, number of turns, $n = 800$

Area of cross-section of solenoid, $A = 2.5 \times 10^{-4}$ m^2

Current through solenoid, $I = 3$ A

As a current passes through a solenoid, a magnetic field is produced. By the use of Maxwell's right hand grip rule, the magnetic field is along the axis of the solenoid. Using the formula of magnetic moment,

$$\mathbf{M} = n I \mathbf{A}$$

$$M = nIA = 800 \times 3 \times 2.5 \times 10^{-4}$$

$$= 0.6 \text{ J/T along the axis of the solenoid}$$

30. Given, number of turns, $n = 2000$

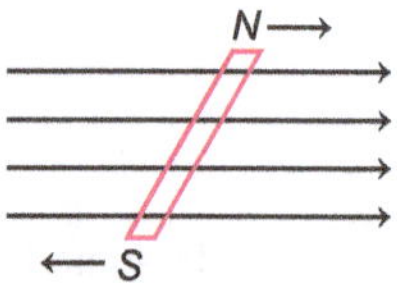

Area of cross-section,

$$A = 1.6 \times 10^{-4} \text{ m}^2$$

Current, $I = 4$ A

(i) Magnetic moment associated with solenoid,

$$M = nIA = 2000 \times 4 \times 1.6 \times 10^{-4} = 1.28 \text{ J/T}$$

(ii) The force (net) on the solenoid is zero, because two equal and opposite forces (on each of its poles) are acting, but their lines of action are parallel, so they form a couple, thus a torque (no force) is applied on it.

Torque on the solenoid

$$\tau = MB \sin\theta \quad (\text{given } \theta = 30°)$$

$$= 1.28 \times 7.5 \times 10^{-2} \sin 30°$$

$$= 1.28 \times 7.5 \times 10^{-2} \times \frac{1}{2}$$

$$= 4.8 \times 10^{-2} \text{ N-m}$$

QR Code for Quick Test 1

QR Code for Quick Test 2

SELF ASSESSMENT TEST

Multiple Choice Questions (MCQs)

1. What happens to the force between magnetic poles when their pole strength and the distance between them both get doubled?

(a) Force increases to two times the previous value

(b) No change

(c) Force decreases to half the previous value

(d) Force increases to four times the previous value

2. The mathematical equation for magnetic field lines of force is

(a) $\nabla \cdot \mathbf{B} = 0$ (b) $\nabla \cdot \mathbf{B} \neq 0$

(c) $\nabla \cdot \mathbf{B} > 0$ (d) $\nabla \cdot \mathbf{B} < 0$

3. The magnetic moment of a magnet of length 10 cm and pole strength 4.0 A-m will be

(a) 0.4 A-m^2 (b) 1.6 A-m^2

(c) 20 A-m^2 (d) 8.0 A-m^2

4. A magnet of magnetic moment M and pole strength m is cut in two equal parts along the axis of magnet, then magnetic moment of each part will be

(a) M (b) $M / 2$

(c) $M / 4$ (d) $2M$

5. A bar magnet of magnetic moment 3 A-m^2 is placed in a uniform magnetic field induction of 2×10^{-5} T. If each pole of the magnet experiences a force of 6×10^{-4} N, the length of the magnet is

(a) 0.5 m (b) 0.3 m

(c) 0.2 m (d) 0.1 m

Assertion-Reason

Directions *(Q.Nos. 6-8) In the following questions, two statements are given- one labelled Assertion (A) and the other labelled Reason (R). Select the correct answer to these questions from the codes (a), (b), (c) and (d) as given below.*

(a) Both Assertion and Reason are true and Reason is the correct explanation of Assertion.

(b) Both Assertion and Reason are true but Reason is not the correct explanation of Assertion.

(c) Assertion is true but Reason is false.

(d) Assertion is false but Reason is true.

6. Assertion (A) When radius of a current-carrying loop is doubled, its magnetic moment becomes four times.

Reason (R) The magnetic moment of a current carrying loop is directly proportional to the area of the loop.

7. Assertion (A) Relative magnetic permeability has no units and no dimensions.

Reason (R) $\mu_r = \frac{\mu}{\mu_0}$, where the symbols have their standard meaning.

8. Assertion (A) The net magnetic flux coming out of a closed surface is always zero.

Reason (R) Unlike poles of equal strength exist together.

Case Based Question

Directions *(Q.No. 9) This question is case study based question. Read the following paragraph and answer the questions on the basis of same.*

9. Before nineteenth century, scientists believed that magnetic properties were confined to a few materials like iron, cobalt and nickel. But in 1846, Curie and Faraday discovered that all the materials in the universe are magnetic to some extent. These magnetic substances are categorised into two groups. Weak magnetic materials are called diamagnetic and paramagnetic materials. Strong magnetic materials are called ferromagnetic materials. According to the modern theory of magnetism, the magnetic response of any material is due to circulating electrons in the atoms. Each such electron has a magnetic moment in a direction perpendicular to the plane of circulation. In magnetic materials, all these magnetic moments due to the orbital and spin motion of all the electrons in any atom, vectorially add upto a resultant magnetic moment. The magnitude and direction of these resultant magnetic moment is responsible for the behaviour of the materials. For diamagnetic materials, χ is small and negative and for paramagnetic materials, χ is small and positive. Ferromagnetic materials have large χ and are characterised by non-linear relation between B and H.

(i) The universal (or inherent) property among all substances is
(a) diamagnetism (b) paramagnetism
(c) ferromagnetism (d) Both (A) and (B)

(ii) When a bar is placed near a strong magnetic field and it is repelled, then the material of bar is
(a) diamagnetic
(b) ferromagnetic
(c) paramagnetic
(c) anti-ferromagnetic

(iii) Magnetic susceptibility of a diamagnetic substance
(a) decreases with temperature
(b) is not affected by temperature
(c) increases with temperature
(c) first increases then decreases with temperature

(iv) The value of the magnetic susceptibility for a superconductor is
(a) zero (c) infinity
(c) +1 (d) −1

(v) Which of the following is weakly repelled by a magnetic field ?
(a) Iron (b) Cobalt
(c) Steel (d) Copper

Very Short Answer Type Questions

10. The relative magnetic permeability of a magnetic material is 800. Identify the nature of magnetic material and state its two properties.

11. Out of the two magnetic materials, *A* has relative permeability slightly greater than unity while *B* has less than unity. Identify the nature of the materials *A* and *B*. Will their susceptibilities be positive or negative?

Short Answer Type Questions

12. Show diagrammatically the behaviour of magnetic field lines in the presence of
(i) diamagnetic and (ii) paramagnetic substances.
How does one explain this distinguishing feature?

13. (i) How does a diamagnetic material behave when it is cooled at very low temperature?
(ii) Why does a paramagnetic sample display greater magnetisation when cooled? Explain.

14. A bar magnet of dipole moment 3 A-m^2 rests with its centre on a frictionless pivot. A force *F* is applied at right angle to the axis of the magnet, 10 cm from the pivot. It is observed that an external magnetic field of 0.25 T is required to hold the magnet in equilibrium at an angle of 30° with the field. Calculate the value of *F*. How will the equilibrium be effected, if *F* is withdrawn?

Long Answer Type Question

15. A bar magnet of magnetic moment *m* and moment of inertia *I* are cut into two equal pieces, perpendicular to the length. Let *T* be the period of oscillations of the original magnet about an axis through the mid-point, perpendicular to the length, in a magnetic field *B*. What would be the similar period *T′* for each piece ?

Answers

1. (b) *2.* (a) *3.* (a) *4.* (b) *5.* (d)
6. (a) *7.* (a) *8.* (a)
9. (i)-(a), (ii)-(a), (iii)-(b), (iv)-(d), (v)-(d)
14. 3.75 N

06

CHAPTER

The phenomenon of generation of induced current in a coil due to change in magnetic field through the coil is called Electromagnetic Induction (EMI).
Power generator, dynamos, transformers, etc. are based upon the electromagnetic induction.

Electromagnetic Induction

YOUR STUDY GOALS

YOUR PRACTICE GOAL

- Objective Type Questions (35 Qs ; MCQs, A-R, Matching)
- Case Based Questions-3
- Subjective Questions (7 VSAs, 8 SAs, 12 LAs)
- Numerical Problems-6

6.1 Faraday's Laws and Motional Electromotive Force

The emf developed in the conductor by the process of EMI is known as **induced emf** and if the conductor is in the form of a closed loop, then the current flowing through the conductor is known as **induced current.**

It is the reverse process of magnetic field production by electric current.

Magnetic Flux (ϕ)

The total number of magnetic field line crossing through any surface normally, when it is placed in a magnetic field is known as the magnetic flux of that surface.

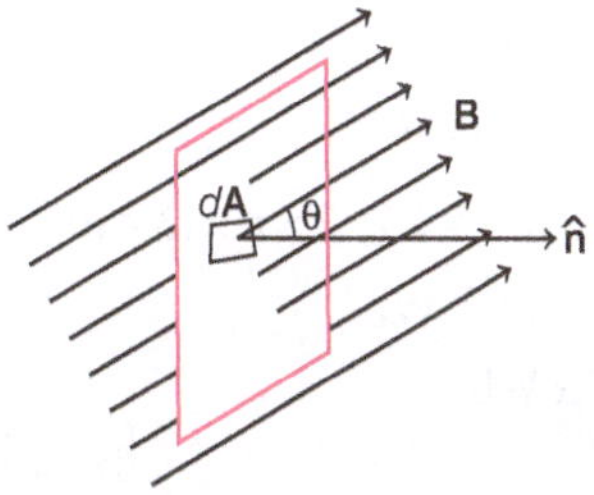

Suppose a loop enclosing an area **A** is placed in a uniform magnetic field **B**, then the magnetic flux through the loop is given by

$$\therefore \quad \phi = \mathbf{B} \cdot \mathbf{A} = BA\cos\theta$$

where, θ is the small angle between **B** and **A**.

Case I If $\theta = 90°$, then $\phi = 0$.

Case II If $\theta = 0°$, then $\phi = BA$ (maximum value).

- It is a **scalar quantity** and its dimensional formula is $[ML^2T^{-2}A^{-1}]$.
- SI unit of magnetic flux is **weber** and CGS unit is **Maxwell (Mx).**

Note 1 Weber is the amount of magnetic flux over an area of 1 m^2 held normal to a uniform magnetic field of 1 tesla (T).

$\therefore$ 1 weber = 1 T-m^2 = 10^8 maxwell

Example 1. A long solenoid of radius 4 cm, length 400 cm carries a current of 3 A. The total number of turns is 100. Assuming ideal solenoid, find the flux passing through a circular surface having centre on axis of solenoid of radius 3 cm and is perpendicular to the axis of solenoid (i) inside and (ii) at the end of solenoid.

Sol.

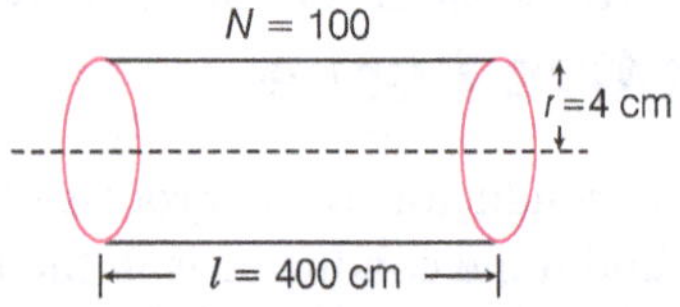

Number of turns per unit length is given by

$$n = \frac{N}{l} = \frac{100}{4} = 25 \text{ turns/m}$$

(i) Magnetic field of a solenoid at a point inside is

$$B = \mu_0 ni$$

Area of cross-section of the solenoid,

$$A = \pi r_1^2 \text{ and } \theta = 0°$$

Magnetic flux,

$$\phi_B = BA\cos\theta$$
$$= \mu_0 ni\, \pi r_1^2 \cos 0°$$
$$= 4\pi \times 10^{-7} \times 25 \times 3 \times \pi \times (3 \times 10^{-2})^2$$
$$= 0.27 \times 10^{-6} \text{ Wb}$$
$$= 0.27 \mu \text{ Wb}$$

(ii) At the end, magnetic field of solenoid is

$$B = \frac{1}{2}\mu_0 ni$$

$$\therefore \quad \phi_B = \frac{0.27}{2} = 0.135 \,\mu \text{ Wb}$$

Faraday's Laws of Electromagnetic Induction

On the basis of experiments carried out by Faraday and Henry, following are the two laws of Faraday's electromagnetic induction stated as below

Faraday's First Law

Whenever the amount of magnetic flux linked with a circuit changes, an emf and consequently a current is induced in the circuit. It lasts so long as the change in magnetic flux continues.

Faraday's Second Law

The magnitude of the induced emf in a circuit is equal to the rate of change of magnetic flux linked with the circuit. Mathematically, Faraday's second law can be expressed as,

Induced emf $\propto$ Rate of change of magnetic flux

i.e. $$e = \frac{-d\phi_B}{dt}$$

Negative sign represents that **induced emf always opposes to change in flux.**

In the case of a closely wound coil of N turns, the change of flux associated with each turn is same. Therefore, the expression for the total induced emf is given by

$$e = -N\frac{d\phi_B}{dt}$$

The induced emf can be increased by increasing the number of turns N of a closed coil.

Induced Emf and Current

If N is the number of turns and R is the resistance of a coil, and the magnetic flux linked with its each turn changes by $d\phi$ in short time interval dt, then

Induced emf in the coil, $e = -N\dfrac{d\phi_B}{dt}$

Induced current flowing through the coil,

$$I = \frac{e}{R} = -\frac{N}{R} \cdot \frac{d\phi_B}{dt} \qquad \left[\because I = \frac{V}{R}\right]$$

Electric charge flows due to induced current,

$$q = Idt = -\frac{N}{R} d\phi_B$$

Example 2. **A magnetic field of flux density 10 T acts normally to the coil of 50 turns having 100 cm^2 area. Find emf induced, if the coil is removed from the magnetic field in 0.15 s.**

Sol. Given, $B = 10$ T, $N = 50$ turns,

$A = 100 \text{ cm}^2 = 10^{-2} \text{ m}^2, dt = 0.15$ s

Magnetic flux linked with the coil initially,

$$\phi_1 = NBA = 50 \times 10 \times 10^{-2} = 5 \text{ Wb}$$

But magnetic flux linked with the coil finally, i.e. (when removed from the magnetic field), $\phi_2 = 0$.

$$\therefore \text{ Emf induced, } e = \frac{-d\phi}{dt} = -\left(\frac{\phi_2 - \phi_1}{dt}\right)$$

$$= -\left(\frac{0-5}{0.15}\right) = 33.33 \text{ V}$$

Example 3. **A square loop of side 10cm and resistance 0.5 Ω is placed vertically in the East-West plane. A uniform magnetic field of 0.10 T is set up across the plane in the North-East direction. The magnetic field is decreased to zero in 0.70 s at a steady rate. Determine the magnitudes of induced emf and current during this time interval.**

Sol. Given, $B = 0.10$ T, $A = 100 \text{ cm}^2 = 10^{-2} \text{ m}^2, \theta = 45°$ (as the angle made by area vector of the loop with magnetic field is 45°),

$R = 0.5\,\Omega,\ dt = 0.70$ s

Initial magnetic flux, $\phi_1 = BA\cos\theta$

$$= 0.10 \times 10^{-2} \times \cos 45° \qquad \left(\because \cos 45° = \frac{1}{\sqrt{2}}\right)$$

$$= \frac{10^{-3}}{\sqrt{2}} \text{ Wb}$$

As, final magnetic flux, $\phi_2 = 0$.

$\therefore$ Magnitude of induced emf is

$$e = -\frac{d\phi}{dt} = -\left(\frac{\phi_2 - \phi_1}{dt}\right) = -\left(\frac{0 - \frac{10^{-3}}{\sqrt{2}}}{0.70}\right)$$

$$\approx 10^{-3} \text{ V} = 1.0 \text{ mV}$$

$\therefore$ Magnitude of induced current,

$$I = \frac{e}{R} = \frac{10^{-3} \text{ V}}{0.5\,\Omega} = 2 \times 10^{-3} \text{ A} = 2 \text{ mA}$$

Lenz's Law

This law gives us the direction of induced current in the circuit.

According to Lenz's law, the polarity of emf induced is such that, it tends to produce a current which opposes the change in magnetic flux that produced it.

Explanation

When north pole of a bar magnet is being pushed towards the coil, the amount of magnetic flux linked with coil increases.

Current is induced in the coil in such a direction that it opposes the increase in flux. This is possible only when the current induced in the coil is in anticlockwise direction with respect to an observer on the side of the bar magnet.

Similarly, when north pole of the bar magnet is moved away from the coil the magnetic flux linked with the coil decreases. To oppose this decrease in magnetic flux, current induced in the coil is in clockwise so that its face towards the bar magnet becomes south pole.

This would result in an attractive force, which opposes the motion of the magnet and the corresponding decrease in magnetic flux.

Relative Motion between Loop and Magnet

If both the loop and magnet are in relative motion w.r.t. each other, the induced pole on the loop facing magnet is according to Lenz's law

(i) When $v_1 > v_2$, i.e. the loop is approaching towards N-pole, hence, induced pole in loop is N-pole.

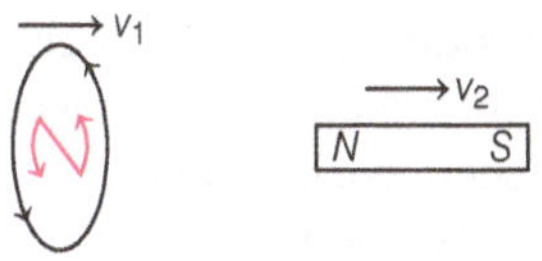

(ii) When $v_1 < v_2$, i.e. the loop is receding away from N-pole, hence induced pole in loop is S-pole.

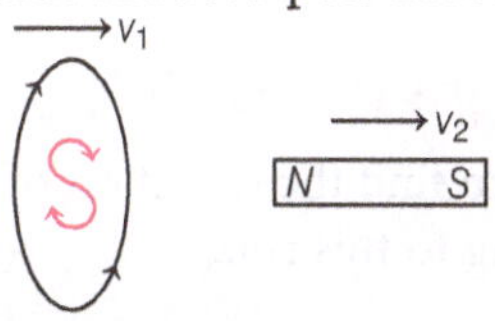

(iii) When loop and magnet have opposite directions of velocities, and loop is approaching towards N-pole, then, induced pole in loop is N-pole.

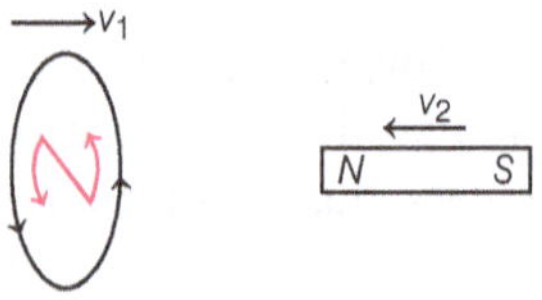

(iv) When loop and magnet have opposite directions of velocities and loop is receding away from N-pole, then induced pole in loop is S-pole.

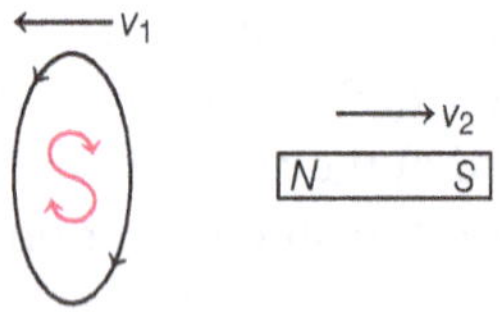

Thus, Lenz's law is used to find the direction of induced current in a closed circuit.

Lenz's Law and Conservation of Energy

Lenz's law is in accordance with the law of conservation of energy.

In the alongside circuit, when N-pole of magnet is moved towards the coil, the front face of the coil acquires North polarity. Thus, work has to be done against the force of repulsion in bringing the magnet closer to the coil.

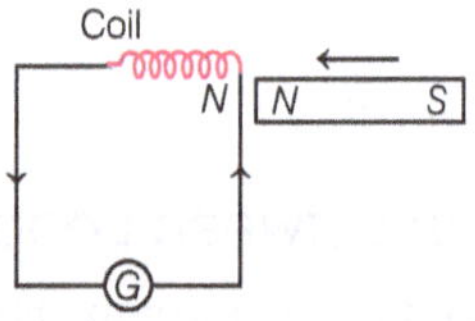

When N-pole of magnet is moved away, South pole develops on the front face of the coil. Therefore, work has to be done against the force of attraction in taking the magnet away from the coil. This mechanical work in moving the magnet w.r.t. the coil changes into electrical energy producing induced current.

Hence, energy transformation takes place.When we do not move the magnet, work done is zero. Therefore, induced current is also zero.

Hence, **Lenz's law obeys the law of conservation of energy**.

Fleming's Right Hand Rule

This rule is used to find the direction of induced current. According to this rule,

If we stretch the thumb, the forefinger and the central finger of right hand in such a way that all these three are mutually perpendicular to each other and if thumb represents the direction of motion of the conductor and the forefinger represents the direction of magnetic field, then central finger will represent the direction of induced current as shown below.

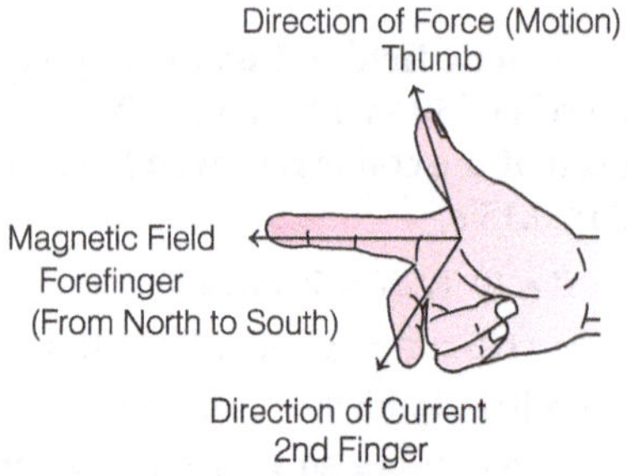

Motional Electromotive Force

Emf induced in a conductor due to its motion in magnetic field is called **motional emf**. Consider a uniform magnetic field **B** confined to the region $ABCD$ and a coil $PQRS$ is placed inside the magnetic field. At any time t, the part $P'Q = S'R = y$ of the coil is inside the magnetic field. Let l be the length of the arm of the coil.

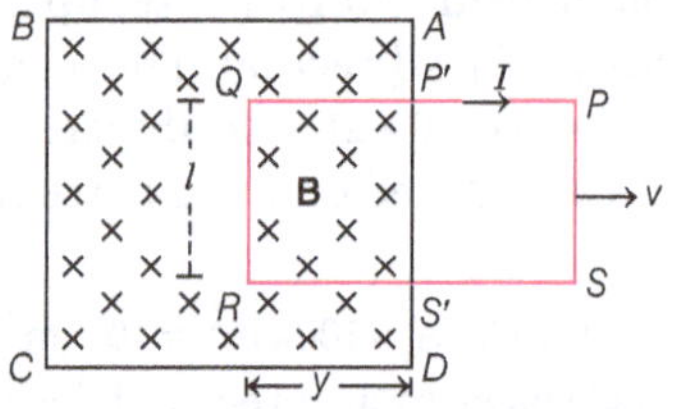

Inducing current by changing the area of the rectangular loop

Area of the coil inside the magnetic field at time t,

$$\Delta S = QR \times RS' = ly$$

Magnetic flux linked with the coil at any time t,

$$\phi = B\Delta S = Bly$$

If e is the induced emf, then according to Faraday's law,

$$e = -\frac{d\phi}{dt} = -\frac{d(Bly)}{dt} = Bl\left(\frac{-dy}{dt}\right)$$

or $\boxed{e = Blv}$

where, $-\dfrac{dy}{dt} = v$ is the velocity of the coil.

From Fleming's right hand rule, the current due to induced emf will flow from the end R to Q, i.e. along $SRQP$ in the coil. This induced electromotive force (emf) Blv is called **motional emf.**

TEACHER TIP

When a conducting rod of length l fixed at its one end moves on a circular path with angular velocity ω in a uniform magnetic field B normal to it, then induced emf produced in it is $e = \frac{1}{2} B\omega l^2$

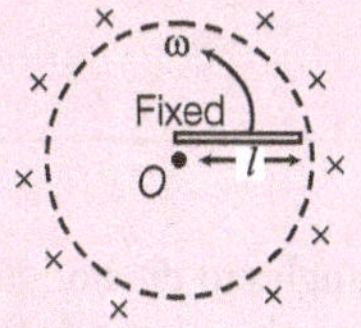

Example 4. **A wire of length 0.3 m moves with a speed of 20 m/s perpendicular to the magnetic field of induction 1 Wb/m^2 Calculate the induced emf.**

Sol. Given, velocity, $v = 20$ m/s

Length, $l = 0.3$ m

Angle, $\theta = 90°$

Magnetic field, $B = 1$ Wb/m^2

As, induced emf, $e = Blv = 1 \times 0.3 \times 20 = 6$ V

Example 5. **A wheel with 10 metallic spokes each 0.5 m long is rotated with a speed of 120 rev/min in a plane normal to the horizontal component of the earth's magnetic field H_E at a place. If $H_E = 0.4$ gauss at the place, what is the induced emf between the axle and the rim of the wheel? Take, 1 gauss = 10^{-4} T.**

Sol. Induced emf $= \frac{1}{2} B\omega l^2 = (1/2)\,\omega BR^2$

$$\left[\because \omega = 2\pi f = 2\pi \frac{120}{60} = 4\pi \text{ and } l = R\right]$$

$$= (1/2) \times 4\pi \times 0.4 \times 10^{-4} \times (0.5)^2 = 6.28 \times 10^{-5} \text{ V}$$

The number of spokes is immaterial because the emf's across the spokes are in parallel.

Methods of Producing Induced EMF

As we know that emf is induced in a circuit, whenever the amount of magnetic flux linked with circuit is changed.

$\because \phi = BA\cos\theta$, therefore the magnetic flux ϕ can be changed by changing the value of B, A or θ. So, **there are three methods of producing induced EMF**, i.e.,

(i) By changing the magnitude of magnetic field B

(ii) By changing the area

(iii) By changing angle θ between the direction of B and normal to the surface area A, *i.e.*, changing the relative orientation of the surface area and magnetic field.

The magnetic flux linked with a loop does not change when

(i) magnet and loop are moving with the same velocity.

(ii) magnet is rotated around its axis without changing its distance from the loop.

(iii) loop is moved in a uniform magnetic field and the whole of the loop remains in the field.

Induced Quantities and Their Formulae

S.No.	Name of the quantity	Formula	Circuit open/closed	Dependence upon resistance	SI unit
1.	Induced emf	$e = -\frac{d\phi}{dt}$	Open or closed	No	volt
2.	Induced current	$I = -\frac{d\phi}{Rdt}$	Closed	Yes	ampere
3.	Charge flown due to induced current	$dq = -\frac{d\phi}{R}$	Closed	Yes	coulomb

Induced Current in a Circuit

If R is the electrical resistance of the circuit, then induced current in the circuit is given by

$$I = \frac{e}{R}$$

If induced current is produced in a coil rotated in a uniform magnetic field, then

$$I = \frac{NBA\omega \sin\omega t}{R} = I_0 \sin\omega t$$

where, $I_0 = \frac{NBA\omega}{R}$ = peak value of induced current

N = number of turns in the coil,

B = magnetic field,

ω = angular velocity of rotation

and A = area of cross-section of the coil.

Example 6. **The rod shown below moves to the right on essentially zero-resistance rails at a speed of $v = 3.0$ m/s. If $B = 0.75$ T everywhere in the region, what is the current through the 5.0 Ω resistor ? Does the current circulate clockwise or counter clockwise?**

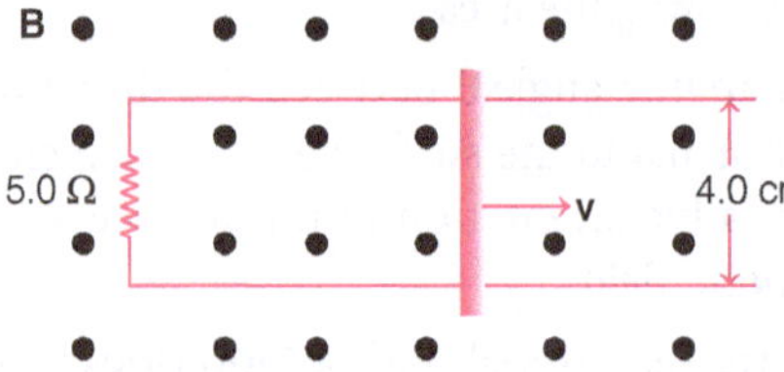

Sol. Given, $v = 3.0$ m/s, $B = 0.75\,T$, $R = 5.0\,\Omega$

Length, $l = 4.0$ cm $= 0.04$ m

We know that induced emf, $e = Bvl$

Induced current through resistor,

$$I = \frac{e}{R} = \frac{Bvl}{R}$$

$$= \frac{0.75 \times 3.0 \times 0.04}{5.0} = 0.018 \text{ A}$$

Since, the flux is increasing the induced current will be clockwise.

Quick Test 1

Conceptual Questions

1. Two coils of wire A and B are placed mutually perpendicular. When a current induced is changed in any one coil, will the current induced in another coil?
2. The closed loop $PQRS$ of wire is moved into a uniform magnetic field at right angles to the plane of the paper as shown in the figure. Predict the direction of the induced current in the loop.

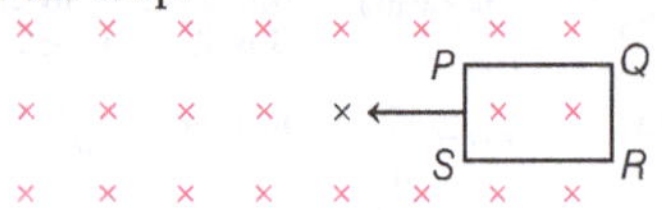

3. State Lenz's law. A metallic rod held horizontally along East-West direction, is allowed to fall under gravity. Will there be an emf induced at its ends? Justify your answer.
4. Will an induced emf develop in a conductor, when moved in a direction parallel to the magnetic field?
5. A wire in the form of tightly wound solenoid is connected to a DC source and carries a current I. If the coil is stretched, so that there are gaps between successive elements of the spiral coil, will the current increase or decrease? Explain. *NCERT Exemplar*
6. A solenoid is connected to a battery, so that a steady current flows through it. If an iron core is inserted into the solenoid, will the current increase or decrease? Explain. *NCERT Exemplar*

Numerical Questions

7. A horizontal straight wire 10 m long extending from East to West is falling with a speed of 5.0 m/s, at right angles to the horizontal component of the earth's magnetic field, 0.30×10^{-4} Wb/m^2.
   (i) What is the instantaneous value of the emf induced in the wire?
   (ii) What is the direction of the emf?
   (iii) Which end of the wire is at the higher electrical potential? *NCERT*
8. A 1 m long conducting rod rotates with an angular frequency of 400 rad/s about an axis normal to the rod passing through its one end. The other end of the rod is in contact with a circular metallic ring. A constant magnetic field of 0.5 T parallel to the axis exists everywhere. Calculate the emf developed between the centre and the ring. *NCERT*
9. A rectangular loop of sides 8 cm and 2 cm with a small cut is moving out of a region of a uniform magnetic field of magnitude 0.3 T directed normal to the loop. What is the voltage developed across the cut, if velocity of loop is 1 cms^{-1} in a direction normal to the
   (i) longer side?
   (ii) shorter side of the loop?
   For how long does the induced voltage last in each case? *NCERT*

Answers

7. (i) 1.5×10^{-3} V (ii) West to East (iii) West end
8. 100 V
9. (i) 2.4×10^{-4} V, 2 s (ii) 0.6×10^{-4} V, 8 s

For Solutions, See QR Code on Pg. 220

6.2 Self and Mutual Induction

Self-Inductance

- It is the property of a coil by virtue of which, the coil opposes any change in the strength of current flowing through it by inducing an emf in itself. This induced emf is also called **back emf**.
- When the current in a coil is switched ON, it opposes the growth of the current and when the current is switched OFF, the self-induction opposes the decay of the current. So, self-induction is also called the **inertia of electricity**.

Coefficient of Self-Induction

Let us consider a coil of N turns carrying a current I. Let ϕ_B be the magnetic flux linked with each turn of the coil. Then, the number of flux linked through the coil will be $N\phi_B$.

If no magnetic materials (iron, etc.) are present near the coil, then the number of flux linkages with the coil is proportional to the current I, i.e.

$$N\phi_B \propto I \text{ or } N\phi_B = LI$$

where, L is constant called the **coefficient of self-induction** or **self-inductance** of the coil.

By the above equation, we have

$$L = \frac{N\phi_B}{I} \qquad \text{...(i)}$$

If $I = 1$, then $L = N\phi_B$.

Hence, the coefficient of self-induction of a coil is numerically equal to the number of magnetic flux linkages with the coil when unit current is flowing through the coil.

If on changing the current through the coil, the back emf induced in the coil be e, then by Faraday's law, we have

$$e = -N\frac{d\phi_B}{dt} = -\frac{d(N\phi_B)}{dt}$$

where, $\frac{dN\phi_B}{dt}$ is the rate of change of magnetic flux (due to change of current) in the coil. But $N\phi_B = LI$.

$$\therefore \quad e = -\frac{d(LI)}{dt} = -L\frac{dI}{dt}$$

where, dI/dt is the rate of change of current in the coil. The negative sign indicates that the induced emf e is always in such a direction that it opposes the change of current in the coil. From the above formula, we have

$$L = -\frac{e}{dI/dt} \qquad \text{...(ii)}$$

If $dI/dt = 1$, then $L = e$ (numerically).

Hence, the coefficient of self-induction of a coil is numerically equal to the emf induced in the coil when the rate of change of current in the coil is unity.

The SI unit of the coefficient of self-induction is henry (H) and its dimensions are $[ML^2T^{-2}A^{-2}]$.

Thus, the self-inductance of a coil is 1 henry when an induced emf of 1volt is set up in the coil due to a current changing at the rate of 1 ampere per second in the coil, i.e.

$$1 \text{ henry} = \frac{1 \text{ volt}}{1 \text{ ampere/second}}$$

Thus, as before, $1 \text{ H} = 1 \text{ Vs A}^{-1}$

$$= 1 \text{ T-m}^2/\text{A}$$

$$= 1 \text{Wb A}^{-1}$$

But from Eq. (i), 1 henry = 1 weber/ampere.

The smaller units for L are millihenry (mH) and microhenry (μH).

$$1 \text{ mH} = 10^{-3} \text{ H}, 1\,\mu\text{H} = 10^{-6} \text{ H}$$

Self-Inductance of Long Solenoid

A long solenoid is one whose length is very large as compared to its area of cross-section. The magnetic field B at any point inside such a solenoid is practically constant and is given by

$$B = \frac{\mu_0 NI}{l} = \mu_0 nI \qquad \left[\because n = \frac{N}{l}\right] \qquad \text{...(i)}$$

where, μ_0 = magnetic permeability of free space,
N = total number of turns in the solenoid,
l = length of the solenoid
and n = number of turns per unit length.

$\therefore$ Magnetic flux through each turn of the solenoid,

$$\phi = B \times \text{area of the each turn}$$

$$\phi = \left(\mu_0 \frac{N}{l} I\right) A$$

Total magnetic flux linked with the solenoid

= Flux through each turn × Total number of turns

$$N\phi = \mu_0 \frac{N}{l} IA \times N \quad \ldots \text{(ii)}$$

If L is coefficient of self-inductance of the solenoid, then

$$N\phi = LI \quad \ldots \text{(iii)}$$

From Eqs. (ii) and (iii), we get

$$LI = \mu_0 \frac{N}{l} IA \times N \text{ or } \boxed{L = \frac{\mu_0 N^2 A}{l}}$$

If core of any other magnetic material μ is placed, then

$$\mu = \mu_0 \mu_r \quad [\mu_r = \text{relative magnetic permeability}]$$

$$\therefore \quad \boxed{L = \frac{\mu_0 \mu_r N^2 A}{l}}$$

Example 7. Current in a circuit falls steadily from 2.0 A to 0.0 A in 10 ms. If an average emf of 200 V is induced, calculate the self-inductance of the circuit.

Sol. Given, $\Delta I = -2\text{ A}$, $\Delta t = 10 \times 10^{-3}\text{ s}$

$e = 200\text{ V}$, $L = ?$

$\because$ Induced emf, $e = -L\dfrac{\Delta I}{\Delta t}$

$$\Rightarrow \quad 200 = -L\left(\frac{-2}{10 \times 10^{-3}}\right)$$

$$\Rightarrow \quad 200 = L \times 2 \times 10^2$$

$\therefore$ Self-induction, $L = 1\text{ H}$

Example 8. What is the self-inductance of a solenoid of length 40 cm, area of cross-section 20 cm^2 and total number of turns is 800 ?

Sol. Given, $l = 40\text{ cm} = 0.4\text{ m}$

$A = 20\text{ cm}^2 = 20 \times 10^{-4}\text{ m}^2$

$N = 800$, $L = ?$

$$\therefore \quad L = \frac{\mu_0 N^2 A}{l} = \frac{4\pi \times 10^{-7} \times (800)^2 \times 20 \times 10^{-4}}{0.4}$$

$$= 4.02 \times 10^{-3}\text{H}$$

Energy Stored in an Inductor

The energy of a capacitor is stored in the electric field between its plates. Similarly, an inductor has the capability of storing energy in its magnetic field.

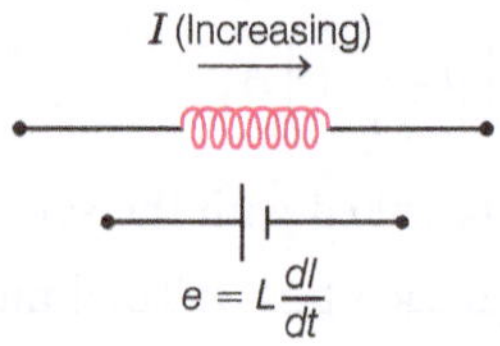

An increasing current in an inductor causes an emf between its terminals which is given by

$$\boxed{e = -L \cdot \frac{dI}{dt}}$$

Work required to move a charge dq against emf e is

$$dW = -edq = L \cdot \frac{dI}{dt} \cdot dq = L\left(\frac{dq}{dt}\right) \cdot dI = LIdI$$

$\therefore$ Total work to build up current from zero to maximum value I.

$$W = \int_0^W dW = \int_0^I L\,I\,dI = \frac{1}{2} L I^2$$

This work is stored as potential energy U in the inductor.

$$\therefore \quad \boxed{W = U = \frac{1}{2} LI^2}$$

Energy stored per unit volume(V) in magnetic field is known as **energy density.**

$$\therefore \quad \text{Energy density} = \frac{U}{V} = \frac{1}{2}\frac{B^2}{\mu_0}$$

Thus, if $I = 1$ A, then $2W = L$

Hence, the coefficient of self-inductance is equal to twice the work done in establishing a flow of one ampere current in the circuit.

Example 9. Two coils having self-inductances, $L_1 = 5$ mH and $L_2 = 1$ mH. The current in the coil is increasing at same constant rate at a certain instant and the power supplied to the coils is also same. Find the ratio of

(i) induced voltages

(ii) currents

(iii) energy stored in two coils at that instant.

Sol. Given, $L_1 = 5$ mH and $L_2 = 1$ mH

(i) As we know, induced voltage is given by

$$e = \frac{Ldi}{dt}$$

$$\Rightarrow \quad \frac{e_1}{e_2} = \frac{L_1(dI/dt)}{L_2(dI/dt)} = \frac{L_1}{L_2} = \frac{5}{1} = 5:1 \quad \ldots\text{(i)}$$

(ii) Power in the coil is given by $P = eI$

Here, $P_1 = P_2$

$$\Rightarrow \quad e_1 I_1 = e_2 I_2 \quad \Rightarrow \quad \frac{I_1}{I_2} = \frac{e_2}{e_1}$$

Using Eq. (i), we can write as, $\dfrac{i_1}{i_2} = \dfrac{1}{5} = 1:5$

(iii) Energy stored in a coil is given by $U = \frac{1}{2}Li^2$

$$\therefore \quad \frac{U_1}{U_2} = \frac{(1/2)L_1I_1^2}{(1/2)L_2I_2^2} = \frac{L_1}{L_2}\left(\frac{e_2}{e_1}\right)^2 = \frac{5}{1}\left(\frac{1}{5}\right)^2 = 1:5$$

Example 10. Suppose a cube of volume 2 mm^3 is placed at the centre of a circular loop of radius 5 cm carrying current 2 A. Find the magnetic energy stored inside the cube.

Sol. Magnetic field at the centre of the circular loop is given by $B = \frac{\mu_0 i}{2R}$.

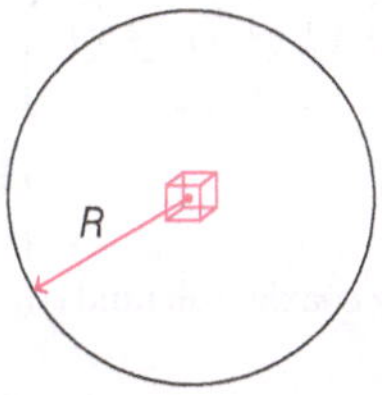

We know, energy density, $u = \frac{B^2}{2\mu_0}$ and energy stored in the cube will be given by

$$U = uV_0 = \frac{B^2}{2\mu_0}V_0$$

where, V_0 is the volume of the cube.

Substituting the values in the above equation,

$$= \frac{1}{2\mu_0} \times \left(\frac{\mu_0 I}{2R}\right)^2 V_0 = \frac{\mu_0 I^2 V_0}{8R^2}$$

$$= \frac{4\pi \times 10^{-7} \times 2^2 \times 2 \times 10^{-9}}{8 \times (0.05)^2}$$

$$= 16\,\pi \times 10^{-14}\text{ J}$$

Grouping of Coils

(a) **Coils in Series** Suppose the two coils of inductance L_1 and L_2 are connected in series and the coefficient of coupling $K = 0$.

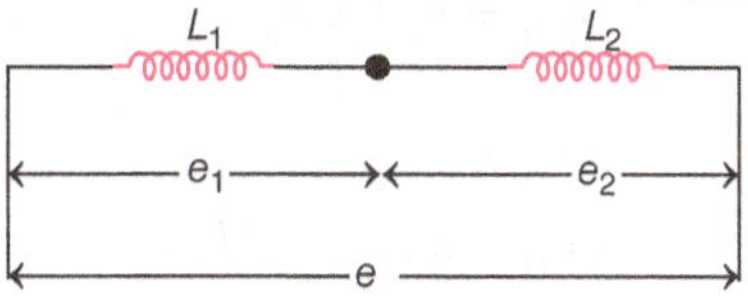

Since, current through each coil is same and potential divides, therefore, $e = e_1 + e_2$

$$\therefore \quad L_s\frac{dI}{dt} = L_1\frac{dI}{dt} + L_2\frac{dI}{dt}$$

$$\Rightarrow \quad \boxed{L_s = L_1 + L_2}$$

(b) **Coils in Parallel** Suppose two coils of inductance L_1 and L_2 are connected in parallel and the coefficient of coupling, $K = 0$.

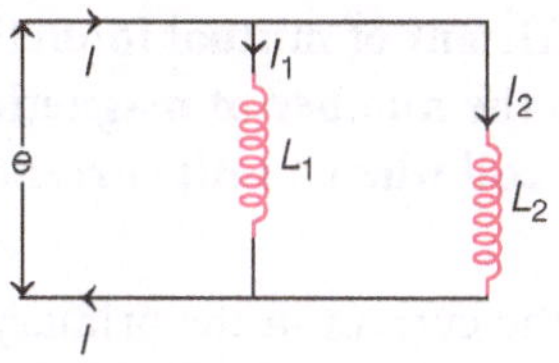

Since, potential remains the same in parallel and current divides.

$$I = I_1 + I_2$$

$$\therefore \quad \frac{dI}{dt} = \frac{dI_1}{dt} + \frac{dI_2}{dt}$$

Using $\quad e = \frac{LdI}{dt}, \frac{e}{L_p} = \frac{e_1}{L_1} + \frac{e_2}{L_2}$

$$\Rightarrow \quad \boxed{\frac{1}{L_P} = \frac{1}{L_1} + \frac{1}{L_2}} \qquad \{\because e_1 = e_2 = e\}$$

Mutual Inductance

The phenomenon according to which an opposing emf is produced in a coil (i.e. primary coil) as a result of change in current or magnetic flux linked with a neighbouring coil (i.e. secondary coil) is called **mutual induction.**

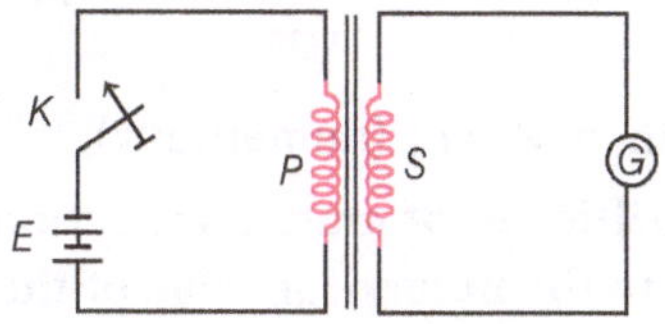

Mutual induction

Coefficient of Mutual Induction

Let a current of I_1 ampere flows in the primary coil (P). Due to this current, the magnetic flux linked with each turn of the secondary coil (S) be ϕ_2. If N_2 is the number of turns in the secondary coil, then the number of flux linkages in the coil will be $N_2\phi_2$. This number of flux linkages is proportional to the current I_1 flowing in the primary coil, i.e.

$$N_2\phi_2 \propto I_1 \quad \text{or} \quad N_2\phi_2 = MI_1$$

where, M is a constant called the **coefficient of mutual induction** or **mutual inductance** of the two coils. From the above equation, we have

$$M = \frac{N_2\phi_2}{I_1}$$

If $I_1 = 1$, then $M = N_2\phi_2$

Hence, the coefficient of mutual induction of two coils is equal to the number of magnetic flux linkages in one coil when a unit current flows in the other.

If on changing the current in the primary coil, the emf induced in the secondary coil is e_2, then according to Faraday's law, we have

$$e_2 = -N_2\frac{d\phi_2}{dt} = -\frac{d(N_2\,\phi_2)}{dt}$$

where, $d\phi_2/dt$ is the rate of change of magnetic flux in the secondary coil (due to change of current in the primary coil). But $N_2\phi_2 = MI_1$.

$$\therefore \quad e_2 = -\frac{d(MI_1)}{dt} = -M\frac{dI_1}{dt}$$

where, dI_1/dt is the rate of change of current in the primary coil. The negative sign indicates that the direction of emf induced in the secondary coil is always such that it opposes any change in current in the primary coil.

From the above expression, we have

$$\text{Mutual inductance, } M = -\frac{e_2}{dI_1/dt}$$

If $dI_1/dt = 1$, then $M = e_2$ (numerically).

Hence, the coefficient of mutual induction of two coils is equal to the numerical value of the induced emf in one coil when the rate of change of current in other coil is unity.

The SI unit of the coefficient of mutual inductance is henry (H). Thus, **the mutual inductance of two coils is 1 henry when an induced emf of 1 volt is set up in one of them due to a current changing at the rate of 1 ampere per second in the other.**

i.e. $$1\text{ henry} = \frac{1\text{volt}}{1\text{ ampere / second}}$$

or $$1\text{H} = 1\text{V s A}^{-1} = 1\text{ Wb A}^{-1}$$

The coefficient of mutual induction or mutual inductance of two coils depend on

(i) geometry of two coils, i.e. size of coils, their shape, number of turns, nature of material on which two coils are wound.

(ii) distance between two coils.

(iii) relative placement of two coils (i.e. orientation of the two coils).

Mutual Inductance of Two Long Coaxial Solenoids

Consider two long solenoids S_1 and S_2 of same length l, such that solenoid S_2 surrounds solenoid S_1 completely.

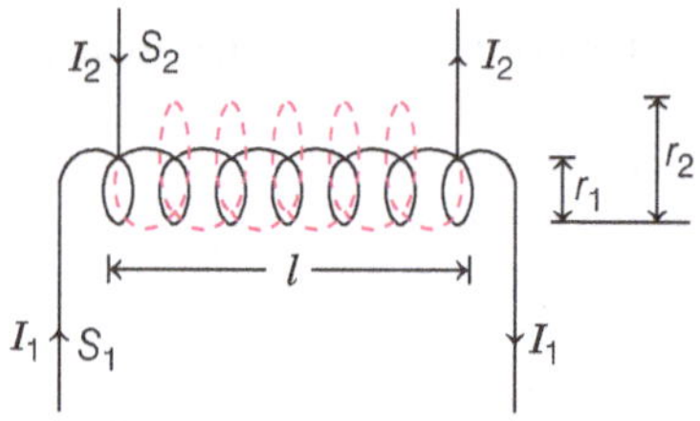

Two long coaxial solenoids of same length l

Let n_1 be the number of turns per unit length of S_1, n_2 be the number of turns per unit length of S_2, I_1 be current passed through solenoid S_1 and ϕ_{21} be the flux linked with S_2 due to current flowing through S_1.

$$\phi_{21} \propto I_1 \text{ or } \phi_{21} = M_{21}\,I_1$$

where, M_{21} is the coefficient of mutual induction of the solenoid S_2 w.r.t. solenoid S_1.

When current is passed through solenoid S_1, an emf is induced in solenoid S_2.Magnetic field produced inside solenoid S_1 on passing current through it.

$$B_1 = \mu_0 n_1 I_1$$

Magnetic flux linked with each turn of solenoid S_2 will be equal to B_1 times the area of cross-section of solenoid S_1.

Magnetic flux linked with each turn of the solenoid $S_2 = B_1 A$.

Therefore, total magnetic flux linked with the solenoid S_2 will be

$$\phi_{21} = B_1 A \times n_2 l$$
$$= \mu_0 n_1 I_1 \times A \times n_2 l$$
$$\phi_{21} = \mu_0 n_1 n_2 A I_1 l$$
$$M_{21} = \mu_0 n_1 n_2 A l \quad \text{...(i)}$$

Similarly, the mutual inductance between the two solenoids, when current is passed through solenoid S_2 and induced emf is produced in solenoid S_1 and is given by

$$M_{12} = \mu_0 n_1 n_2 A l$$
$$M_{12} = M_{21} = M \quad \text{(say)}$$

Hence, coefficient of mutual induction between two long solenoids, $M = \mu_0 n_1 n_2 A l$

We can rewrite Eq. (i) as,

$$M = \mu_0 \left(\frac{N_1}{l}\right)\left(\frac{N_2}{l}\right) \pi r_1^2 \times l = \frac{\mu_0 N_1 N_2 A}{l}$$

If core of any other magnetic material μ is placed, then

$$M = \frac{\mu_0 \mu_r N_1 N_2 A}{l}$$

where, l = length of longer solenoid (when two solenoids of different length)

A = Area of cross-section of inner solenoid

Example 11. **There are two coils, which have mutual inductance of 10 H. When the circuit is closed, current in the primary coil is raised to 3 A within a time range of 1 millisecond. Calculate the emf induced in secondary coil.**

Sol. Given, mutual inductance, $M = 10$ H

Change in current, $dI = 3$ A

Change in time, $dt = 1$ millisecond $= 10^{-3}$ s

emf induced, $e = ?$

emf induced in secondary coil is given by $e = \frac{M\,dI}{dt}$

$\therefore$ emf induced $= \frac{10 \times 3}{10^{-3}} = 3 \times 10^4$ V

Example 12. **A 1 m long solenoid with diameter 2 cm and 2000 turns has a secondary coil of 1000 turns wound closely near its mid-point. What will be the mutual inductance between the two coils?**

Sol. Given, $l = 1$ m, $r = \frac{2}{2}$ cm $= 1$ cm $= 10^{-2}$ m

$$N_1 = 2000, N_2 = 1000, A = \pi r^2 = \pi (10^{-2})^2 \text{ m}^2$$
$$= \pi \times 10^{-4} \text{m}^2, M = ?$$

$\therefore$ Mutual inductance between the two coils is given by

$$M = \frac{\mu_0 N_1 N_2 A}{l}$$
$$= \frac{4\pi \times 10^{-7} \times 2000 \times 1000 \times \pi \times 10^{-4}}{10^{-2}}$$
$$= 78.9 \times 10^{-3} \text{ H}$$

Example 13. **A circular wire loop of radius R is placed in the XY-plane centred at the origin O. A square loop of side a ($a << R$) having two turns is placed with its centre at $z = \sqrt{3}\,R$ along the axis of the circular wire loop, as shown in figure. The plane of the square loop makes an angle of 45° with respect to the Z-axis. If the mutual inductance between the loops is given by $\frac{\mu_0 a^2}{2^{p/2} R}$, then find the value of p.**

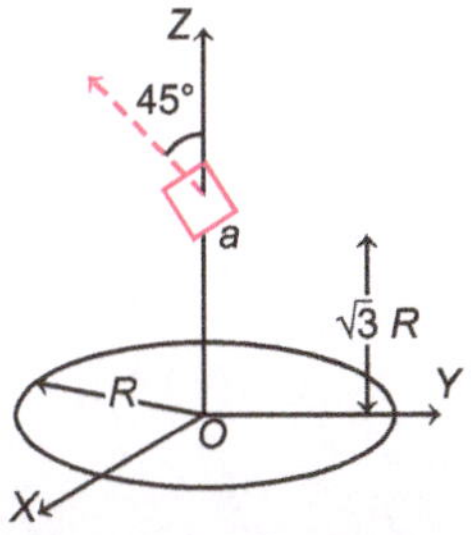

Sol. If I current flows through the circular loop, then magnetic field at the location of square loop is

$$B = \frac{\mu_0 I R^2}{2(R^2 + Z^2)^{3/2}}$$

Substituting the value of $Z = \sqrt{3}R$, we have

$$B = \frac{\mu_0 I}{16R}$$

Now, total flux through the square loop is

$$\phi_T = NBS\cos\theta = (2)\left(\frac{\mu_0 I}{16R}\right) a^2 \cos 45°$$

Mutual inductance,

$$M = \frac{\phi_T}{I} = \frac{\mu_0 a^2}{2^{7/2} R} \quad \ldots(i)$$

On comparing the Eq. (i) with given, $M = \frac{\mu_0 a^2}{2^{p/2} R}$

we get

$\therefore \quad p = 7$

AC Generator

It is a device which is used to convert mechanical energy into electrical energy.

Principle

An AC generator is based on the phenomenon of electromagnetic induction, which states that when a coil is rotated in uniform magnetic field, magnetic flux linked with a conductor (or coil) changes and an emf is induced in the coil.

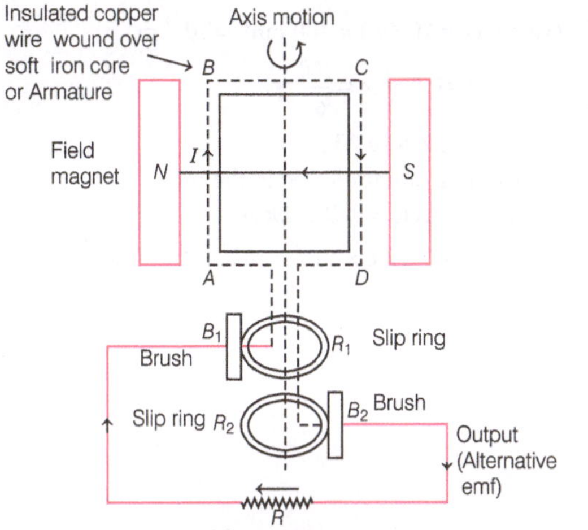

AC generator

Theory and Working

When the armature of the coil is rotated in uniform magnetic field, angle θ between the field and the normal to the coil changes continuously. Therefore, magnetic flux linked with the coil changes and an emf is induced in the coil. According to Fleming's right hand rule, current is induced in AB from A to B and it flows from C to D in CD. In the external circuit, current flows from B_2 to B_1.

If e is the emf induced in the coil, then

$$e = \frac{-Nd\phi}{dt}$$

or $e = -\frac{d}{dt}(NBA\cos\omega t)$ [by Faraday's flux rule]

$$\therefore \quad e = NBA\omega \sin \omega t$$

where, N = number of turns in the coil,

B = strength of magnetic field,

A = area of each turn of the coil,

ω = angular velocity of rotation of the coil

and $$I = \frac{e}{R} = \frac{NBA\omega}{R}\sin\omega t,$$

$$\therefore \quad e_0 = NBA\omega, \quad \frac{e_0}{R} = I_0$$

where, R = resistance of the coil.

$I = I_0 \sin \omega t$

Example 14. **An AC generator consists of a coil of 1000 turns and cross-sectional area of 100 cm^2, rotating at an angular speed of 100 rpm in a uniform magnetic field of 3.6×10^{-2} T. Calculate the maximum emf produced in the coil.**

Sol. Given, $N = 1000, A = 100 \text{ cm}^2 = 10^{-2} \text{ m}^2$,

$\nu = 100 \text{ rpm} = \frac{100}{60} \text{ rps}$,

$B = 3.6 \times 10^{-2}$ T, $e_0 = ?$

∴ Maximum emf produced in the coil is

$e_0 = NBA\omega = NBA(2\pi\nu)$

$= 1000 \times 3.6 \times 10^{-2} \times 10^{-2} \times 2 \times \frac{22}{7} \times \frac{100}{60} = 3.77$ V

Quick Test 2

Conceptual Questions

1. How can self-inductance of a given coil having N number of turns be changed, if N is doubled keeping other factors constant?
2. Two concentric circular coils, one of radius r and the other of radius R are placed coaxially with their centres coinciding. For $R >>> r$, give an expression for the mutual inductance of the arrangement.
3. A small square loop of wire of side l is placed inside a large square loop of wire of side $L (L >> l)$. The loops are coplanar and their centres coincide. Give the dependence of mutual inductance.
4. If two coils are very tightly wound over one another, will their mutual inductance increase or decrease as compared to the case when the coils are placed some distance apart?

Numerical Questions

5. A long solenoid with 15 turns per cm has a small loop of area 2.0 cm^2 placed inside, normal to the axis of solenoid. If the current carried by the solenoid changes steadily from 2 A to 4 A in 0.1 s, what is the induced voltage in the loop, while the current is changing? NCERT
6. Current in a circuit falls from 5.0 A to 0.0 A in 0.1 s. If an average emf of 200 V is induced, give an estimate of the self-inductance of the circuit. NCERT
7. A coil has a self-inductance of 10 mH. What is the maximum magnitude of the induced emf in the inductor, when a current $I = 0.1 \sin 200\, t$ ampere is sent through it?
8. There are two coils A and B separated by some distance. If a current of 2 A flows through A, a magnetic flux of 10^{-2} Wb passes through B (no current through B). If no current passes through A and a current of 1 A passes through B, what is the flux through A? NCERT Exemplar
9. An AC generator consists of coil of 100 turns and cross-sectional area of 3 m^2, rotating at a constant angular speed of 60 rad s^{-1} in a uniform magnetic field 0.04 T. The resistance of the coil is 500 Ω. Calculate (i) maximum current drawn from the generator and (ii) maximum power dissipation of the coil.

Answers

5. 7.5×10^{-6} V 6. 4 H 7. 0.2 V 8. 5 mWb

9. (i) 1.44 A (ii) 1036.8 W

For Solutions, See QR Code on Pg. 220

Mind Map

Electromagnetic Induction

Faraday's Law of Induction

It states that the induced electromotive force (EMF) in circuit is directly proportional to the rate of change of magnetic flux through the circuit, i.e.

$$\varepsilon = -\frac{d\phi_B}{dt}$$

(i) Whenever the magnetic flux linked with a conducting loop or coil changes, an emf is induced in it.
(ii) The induced emf is directly proportional to the rate of change of magnetic flux through the coil.

$$\varepsilon = -N \times \frac{d\phi}{dt}$$

The negative sign indicates that the induced emf opposes the cause that produces it.

Lenz's Law

Lenz's Law states that the direction of the induced current will oppose the change in the magnetic flux that caused it.
This is why the negative sign appears in Faraday's law.
Expression for induced charge

$$\Delta q = -\frac{\Delta\phi}{R}$$

It is a consequence of the law of conservation of energy.

Fleming's Right Hand Rule

Fleming's right hand rule states that if you align your right hand's thumb forefinger and middle finger perpendicular to each other, then
- thumb points in the direction of the motion of the conductor.
- forefinger points in the direction of the magnetic field.
- middle finger gives the direction of the induced current (EMF).

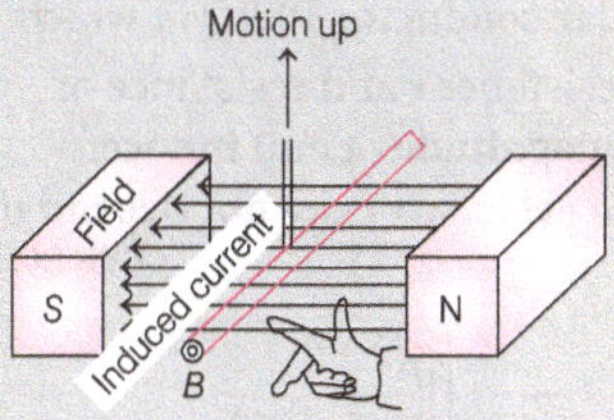

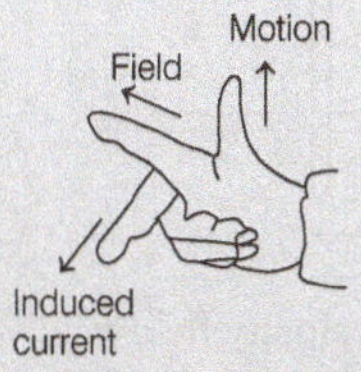

Motional EMF

It is the voltage induced in a conductor moving through a magnetic field, given by
$E = BvL$

Magnetic Flux

Magnetic flux is the measure of the total magnetic field passing through a given surface, defined as
$\phi = \mathbf{B}\cdot\mathbf{A}$ or $\phi = BA\cos\theta$

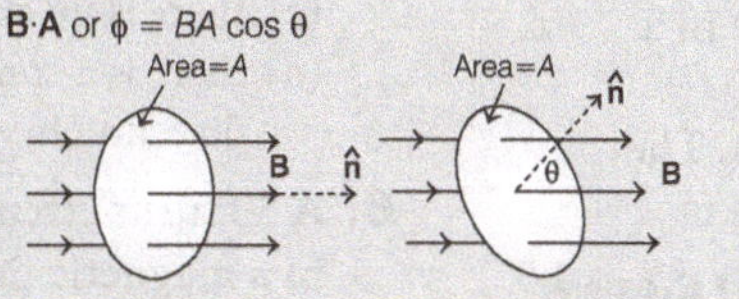

Induced EMF can be produced by changing the flux.

Self-Inductance

Self-inductance is the property of a circuit or coil to oppose changes in current by inducing an EMF in itself due to its own changing magnetic field.

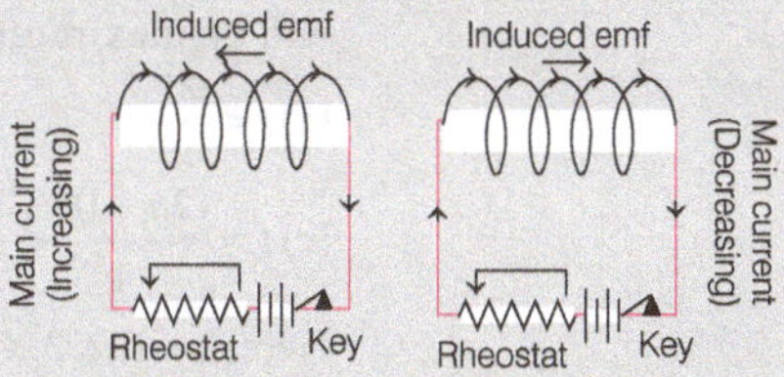

Main current increased | Main current decreased

Coefficient of self induction is the self inductance of a coil, measuring its ability to induce EMF in itself due to changes in current.
The magnetic flux ϕ linked with a coil is proportional to the current through it.
i.e, $\phi = LI$

$$\therefore \quad \varepsilon = -\frac{d\phi}{dt} = -L\frac{dI}{dt}$$

Self Induction of a Long Solenoid

Consider a long solenoid of length l and radius r with $r << l$ and having n turns per unit length.

$$B = \mu_0 nI$$

$\therefore$ Self-inductance of the long solenoid is

$$L = \mu_0 n^2 lA$$

$$\therefore \quad L = \frac{\mu_0 N^2 A}{l}$$

Mutual Inductance

Mutual inductance is the property of two coupled circuits, where a change in current in one induces an electromotive force in the other, measured in henry (H).

$$M = \frac{\phi_{21}}{I_1}$$

The coefficient of mutual induction of two coils is equal to the numerical value of the induced emf in one coil when the rate of change of current in other coil is unity.

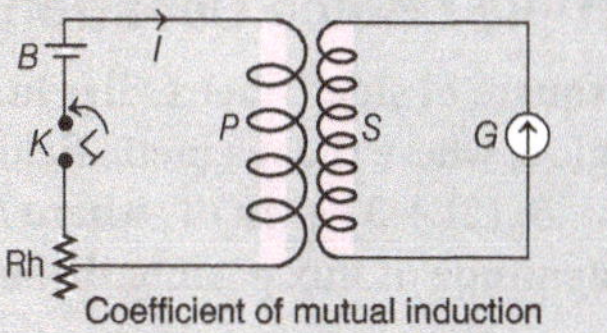

Coefficient of mutual induction
Here, $\varepsilon = -d\phi/dt = -MdI/dt$
where ε is the emf induced in coils

Factors Affecting Mutual Induction

Number of turns Larger the number of turns in the two solenoids, larger will be their mutual inductance.

$$M \propto N_1 N_2$$

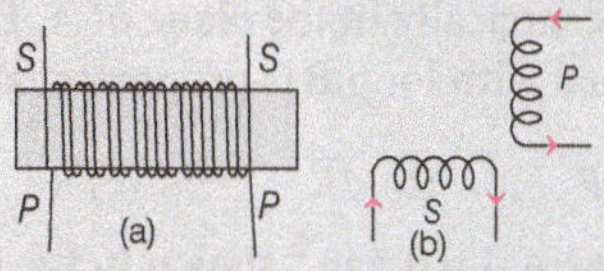

Relative separation Larger the distance between two solenoids, smaller will be the magnetic flux linked with secondary coil due to current in the primary coil.

Common cross-sectional area Larger the common cross-sectional area of two solenoids, larger will be their mutual inductance.

Relative orientation of the two coils Mutual inductance will be maximum, when they are placed coaxially to each other whereas minimum, when they are placed perpendicular to each other.

Mutual Inductance of Two Long Coaxial Solenoids

Mutual inductance of two long coaxial solenoids is given by

$$M = \frac{\mu_0 N_1 N_2 A}{l}$$

Factors Affecting Self-Induction

Number of turns
Larger the number of turns in the solenoid, larger is its self-inductance.

Area of cross-section
Larger the area of the cross-section of the solenoid, larger is its self-inductance.

Permeability of the core material
The self-inductance of a solenoid increases μ_r times, if it is wound over an iron core of relative permeability μ_r.

EXAM PATTERN QUESTIONS

Objective Type Questions

Multiple Choice Questions (MCQs)

1. A square of side L metres lies in the XY-plane in a region, where the magnetic field is given by $B = B_0(2\hat{i} + 3\hat{j} + 4\hat{k})$ T, where B_0 is constant. The magnitude of flux passing through the square is **NCERT Exemplar**

(a) $2B_0L^2$ Wb (b) $3B_0L^2$ Wb
(c) $4B_0L^2$ Wb (d) $\sqrt{29}B_0L^2$ Wb

2. A circular loop A of radius R carries a current I. Another circular loop B of radius $r\left(=\dfrac{R}{20}\right)$ is placed concentrically in the plane of A. The magnetic flux linked with loop B is proportional to **CBSE 2024**

(a) R (b) $\sqrt{R}$ (c) $R^{\frac{3}{2}}$ (d) R^2

3. An area $A = 0.5$ m^2 shown in the figure is situated in a uniform magnetic field $B = 4.9$ Wb/m^2 and its normal makes an angle of 60° with the field. The magnetic flux passing through the area A would be equal to

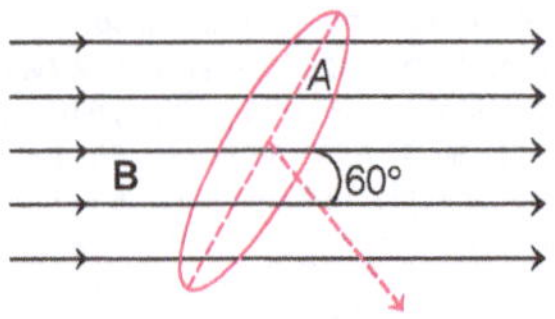

(a) 2.0 weber (b) 1.2 weber
(c) $\sqrt{3}$ weber (d) 0.5 weber

4. A circular loop of radius r, carrying a current I lies in YZ-plane with its centre at the origin. The net magnetic flux through the loop is **CBSE 2020**

(a) directly proportional to r (b) zero
(c) inversely proportional to r (d) directly proportional to I

5. There are two coils A and B as shown in the figure. A current starts flowing in B as shown, when A is moved towards B and stops when A stops moving. The current in A is counter clockwise. B is kept stationary when A moves. We can infer that **NCERT Exemplar**

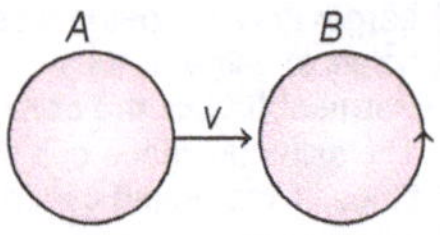

(a) there is a constant current in the clockwise direction in A
(b) there is a varying current in A
(c) there is no current in A
(d) there is a constant current in the counter clockwise direction in A

6. A 50 turns circular coil has a radius of 3 cm, it is kept in a magnetic field acting normal to the area of the coil. The magnetic field B increased from 0.10 T to 0.35 T in 2 ms. The average induced emf in the coil is

(a) 1.77 V (b) 17.7 V
(c) 1.77 V (d) 0.177 V

7. A coil of area 100 cm^2 is kept at an angle of 30° with a magnetic field of 10^{-1} T. The magnetic field is reduced to zero in 10^{-4} s. The induced emf in the coil is **CBSE 2022, Term-I**

(a) $5\sqrt{3}$ V (b) $50\sqrt{3}$ V (c) 5.0 V (d) 50.0 V

8. A coil of N turns is placed in a magnetic field **B** such that **B** is perpendicular to the plane of the coil. **B** changes with time as $B = B_0 \cos\left(\dfrac{2\pi}{T}t\right)$, where T is time period. The magnitude of emf induced in the coil will be maximum at **CBSE 2024**

(a) $t = \dfrac{nT}{8}$ (b) $t = \dfrac{nT}{4}$
(c) $t = \dfrac{(2n-1)T}{4}$ (d) $t = nT$

Here, $n = 1, 2, 3, 4, \ldots$

9. Figure shows a rectangular conductor $PSRQ$ in which movable arm PQ has a resistance r and resistance of $PSRQ$ is negligible. The magnitude of emf induced when PQ is moved with a velocity v does not depend on **CBSE 2020**

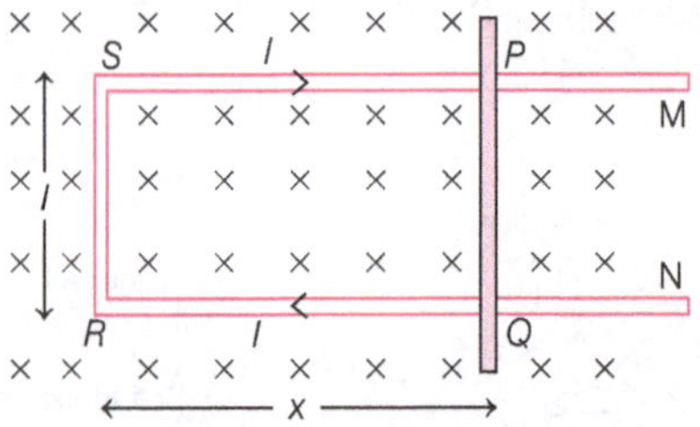

(a) magnetic field **B** (b) velocity field **v**
(c) resistance (r) (d) length of PQ

10. The direction of induced current in the loop *abc* is

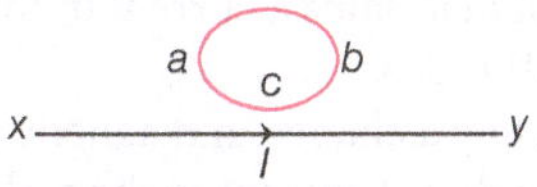

CBSE 2023

(a) along *abc* if *I* decreases (b) along *acb* if *I* increases
(c) along *abc* if *I* is constant (d) along *abc* if *I* increases

11. An electron moves along the line *PQ* which lies in the same plane as a circular loop of conducting wire as shown in figure. What will be the direction of the induced current in the loop?

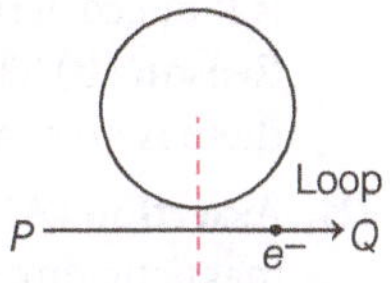

(a) Anti-clockwise (b) Clockwise
(c) Alternating (d) No current will be induced

12. A conducting square loop of side *L* and resistance *R* moves in its plane with the uniform velocity *v* perpendicular to one of its sides. A magnetic induction *B* constant in time and space pointing perpendicular and into the plane of the loop exists everywhere as shown in the figure. The current induced in the loop is CBSE SQP 2022. Term-I

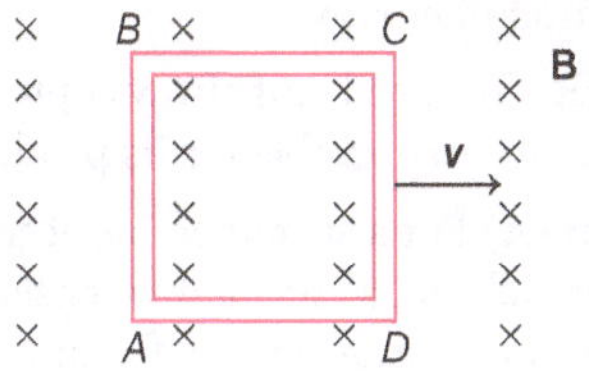

(a) BLv / R clockwise (b) BLv / R anti-clockwise
(c) $2BLv / R$ anti-clockwise (d) zero

13. A copper ring is held horizontally and a magnet is dropped through the ring with its length along the axis of the ring. The acceleration of the falling magnet is

(a) equal to that due to gravity
(b) less than that due to gravity
(c) more than that due to gravity
(d) depends on the diameter of the ring and the length of the magnet

14. A bar magnet is thrown from a distance into a closed loop with its north pole towards the loop and passes through it. The induced current in the loop is

(a) first clockwise and then anti-clockwise CBSE 2024C
(b) first anti-clockwise and then clockwise
(c) clockwise only
(d) anti-clockwise only

15. If both the number of turns and core length of an inductor is doubled keeping other factors constant, then its self-inductance will be CBSE SQP 2022, Term-I

(a) unaffected (b) doubled
(c) halved (d) quadrupled

16. The self inductance *L* of a solenoid of length *l* and area of cross section *A*, with a fixed number of turns *N* increases as NCERT Exemplar

(a) *l* and *A* increase.
(b) *l* decreases and *A* increases.
(c) *l* increases and *A* decreases.
(d) Both *l* and *A* decreases

17. The self-induced emf in a coil of 0.4H. The induced emf when current in it is changing at the rate of 50 As^{-1}, is

(a) 8×10^{-4} V (b) 8×10^{-3} V (c) 20 V (d) 500 V

18. A rectangular, a square, a circular and an elliptical loop, all in the *XY*-plane, are moving out of a uniform magnetic field with a constant velocity $\mathbf{v} = v\,\hat{\mathbf{i}}$. The magnetic field is directed along the negative *Z*-axis direction. The induced emf, during the passage of these loops, out of the field region, will not remain constant for CBSE SQP 2023

(a) any of the four loops
(b) the circular and elliptical loops
(c) the rectangular, circular and elliptical loops
(d) only the elliptical loops

19. The self-inductance of a solenoid of 600 turns is 108 mH. The self-inductance of a coil having 500 turns with the same length, the same radius and the same medium will be CBSE 2022, Term-I

(a) 95 mH (b) 90 mH (c) 85 mH (d) 75 mH

20. The current in the primary coil of a pair of coils changes from 7 A to 3 A in 0.04 s. The mutual inductance between the two coils is 0.5H. The induced emf in the secondary coil is CBSE 2022, Term-I

(a) 50 V (b) 75 V (c) 100 V (d) 220 V

21. Two coils are placed close to each other. The mutual inductance of the pair of coils depends upon the CBSE SQP 2022, Term-1

(a) rate at which current change in the two coils
(b) relative position and orientation of the coils
(c) rate at which voltage induced across two coils
(d) currents in the two coils

22. Two long solenoids of radii r_1 and $r_2 (> r_1)$ and number of turns per unit length n_1 and n_2 respectively are coaxially wrapped one over the other. The ratio of self-inductance of inner solenoid to their mutual inductance is CSBE 2025

(a) $\frac{n_1}{n_2}$ (b) $\frac{n_2}{n_1}$ (c) $\frac{n_1 r_1^2}{n_2 r_2^2}$ (d) $\frac{n_2 r_1^2}{n_1 r_2^2}$

23. There is a pair of concentric and coplanar conducting loops of radii R_1 and R_2 such that $R_2 = 0.01\, R_1$. To which of the following is the mutual inductance *M* for this pair directly proportional? Competency Based Que.

(a) $1 / R_1^2$ (b) R_1^2 (c) $1 / R_1$ (d) R_1

24. Match the Column I with Column II and Choose the correct option.

Column I	Column II
A. Lenz's law	P. Property of a coil to induced emf when the current in itself changes.
B. Faraday's law of induction	Q. The direction of induced emf opposes the change causing it.
C. Self- inductance	R. Induced emf in one coil due to change of current in another.
D. Mutual inductance	S. The induced emf is directly proportional to the rate of change of flux.

Codes

	A	B	C	D
(a)	R	P	S	Q
(b)	Q	S	P	R
(c)	S	R	Q	P
(d)	P	Q	R	S

25. Match the Column I with Column II and Choose the correct option.

Column I (Physical Quantities)	Column II (SI unit)
A. Magnetic flux	P. Volt (V)
B. Induced emf	Q. Henry (H)
C. Self-inductance	R. Ampere (A)
D. Current	S. Weber (Wb)

Codes

	A	B	C	D		A	B	C	D
(a)	S	P	Q	R	(b	R	Q	P	S
(c)	P	S	R	Q	(d)	P	Q	R	S

Assertion-Reason

Directions *(Q.No. 26-35) In the following questions, two statements are given- one labelled Assertion (A) and the other labelled Reason (R). Select the correct answer to these questions from the codes (a), (b), (c) and (d) as given below*

(a) Both Assertion and Reason are true and Reason is the correct explanation of Assertion.

(b) Both Assertion and Reason are true but Reason is not the correct explanation of Assertion.

(c) Assertion is true but Reason is false.

(d) Assertion is false but Reason is true.

26. Assertion (A) The presence of large magnetic flux through a coil maintains a current in the coil, if the circuit is continuous.
Reason (R) Only a change in magnetic flux will maintain an induced current in the coil.

27. Assertion (A) If the terminals of the primary of a transformer are connected across a battery then no emf is induced across the secondary in steady state.
Reason (R) The battery provides a steady current, so there is no change in flux linked with the secondary.

28. Assertion (A) An emf is induced in a closed loop where magnetic flux is varied. The induced field **E** is not a conservative field.
Reason (R) The line integral $\oint \mathbf{E}\cdot d\mathbf{l}$ around a closed path is non-zero.

29. Assertion (A) Faraday's law are consequence of conservation of energy.
Reason (R) The magnitude of the induced emf in a circuit is equal to the rate of change of magnetic flux linked with the circuit.

30. Assertion (A) Lenz's law violates the principle of conservation of energy.
Reason (R) Induced emf always opposes the change in magnetic flux responsible for its production.

31. Assertion (A) For a sustained induced motional emf across a metal rod, a constant work has to be done on the rod by an external agency for moving it with constant speed through the external magnetic field.
Reason (R) Work done by the external force keeps the charges in motion through the rod for a sustained induced current. **Competency Based Que.**

32. Assertion (A) If the inner solenoid was much shorter than (and placed well inside) the outer solenoid, then we could still have calculated the flux linkage $N_1\phi_1$.
Reason (R) The inner solenoid is effectively immersed in a uniform magnetic field due to the outer solenoid.

33. Assertion (A) Self-inductance is the electromagnetic analogue of mass in mechanics.
Reason (R) Work needs to be done against the back emf (ε) in establishing the current.

34. Assertion (A) The quantity L/R possesses dimensions of time.
Reason (R) To reduce the rate of increase of current through a solenoid, we should increase the time constant (L/R).

35. Assertion (A) An AC generator is based on the phenomenon of self-induction.
Reason (R) In single coil, we consider self-induction only.

Case Based Questions

Directions *(Q.Nos. 36-38) These questions are case study based questions. Read the following paragraph and answer the questions on the basis of same.*

36. **According the Faraday's first law, whenever the amount of magnetic flux linked with a circuit changes, an emf is induced in it. Induced current is determined by the rate at which the magnetic flux changes.**

Mathematically, the magnitude of the induced emf in a circuit is equal to the rate of change of magnetic flux through the circuit.

Induced emf $\propto$ Rate of change of magnetic flux

(i) On the basis of Faraday's law, current is larger in the coil

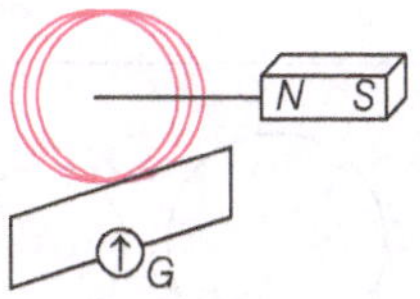

(a) when the magnet is pushed towards the coil faster
(b) when the magnet is pulled away the coil faster
(c) Both (a) and (b)
(d) Neither (a) nor (b)

(ii) The flux linked with a circuit is given by $\phi = t^3 + 3t - 7$. The graph between time (X-axis) and induced emf (Y-axis) will be a
(a) straight line through the origin
(b) straight line with positive intercept
(c) straight line with negative intercept
(d) parabola not through the origin

(iii) Wire loop is rotated in a magnetic field. The frequency of change of direction of the induced emf is
(a) once per revolution
(b) twice per revolution
(c) four times per revolution
(d) six times per revolution

(iv) The instantaneous magnetic flux linked with a coil is given by $\phi = (5t^3 - 100t + 300)$ Wb. The emf induced in the coil at time $t = 2$ s is
(a) -40 V (b) 40 V
(c) 140 V (d) 300 V

(v) A copper disc of radius 0.1 m is rotated about its centre with 20 rev/s in a uniform magnetic field of 0.1 T with its plane perpendicular to the field. The emf induced across the radius of the disc is
(a) $\frac{\pi}{20}$ V (b) $\frac{\pi}{10}$ V
(c) 20π mV (d) None of these

37. Lenz's law states that the direction of induced current in a circuit is such that it opposes the cause which produces it. Thus, if the magnetic flux linked with a closed circuit increases, then the induced current flows in the circuit in such a direction that the magnetic flux through the circuit decreases. It is based on conservation of energy principle in which mechanical energy is transformed into electrical energy.

(i) What is the conservation principle on which Lenz's law depends ?

(ii) A bar magnet is moved away from the coil as shown in figure

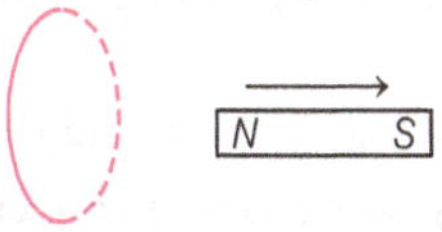

What is the direction of induced current in the coil when it is seen from magnet side.

(iii) A circular coil and a current carrying wire is arranged as shown in figure.
What is the direction of induced current in the coil ?

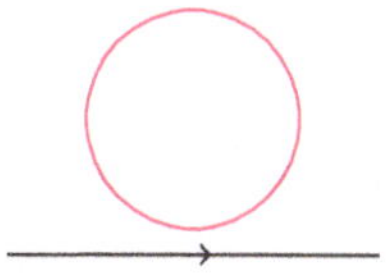

(iv) When a coil is placed facing a moving magnet towards it, then which rule is responsible to determine the polarity of magnetic dipole as a current carrying loop ?

38. Self-induction of a coil is a property by virtue of which it opposes any change in the strength of current through it by inducing an emf in the same coil. When a current I flow through the coil, then flux linked with it is given by $\phi = LI$, where L is a constant known as coefficient of self induction of the coil. The emf induced across an inductor carrying a current I is, $e = L \cdot \frac{dI}{dt}$. The Self inductance of a long solenoid is given by $L = \frac{\mu_0 N^2 A}{l}$

(i) Which property of the coil plays the same role as inertia in mechanics ?

(ii) Write the unit of coefficient of self induction in terms of tesla (T).

(iii) How the inductance of a solenoid depends on its radius ?

(iv) A current of 3A flows through a coil of inductance 5H. Find the magnetic flux linked with the coil ?

Subjective Questions

Very Short Answer Type Questions

1. A long straight current-carrying wire passes normally through the centre of circular loop. If the current through the wire increases, will there be an induced emf in the loop? Justify.

2. What is the direction of induced currents in metal rings 1 and 2, when current I in the wire is increasing steadily?

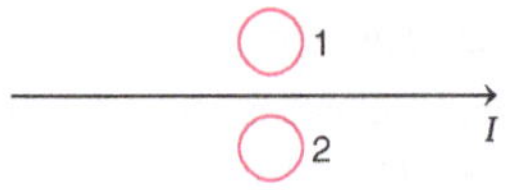

3. On what factors does the magnitude of induced emf in a coil depend?

4. Can a straight wire act as an inductor ?

5. A plot of magnetic flux (ϕ) *versus* current (I) is shown in the figure for two inductors A and B. Which of the two has larger value of self-inductance?

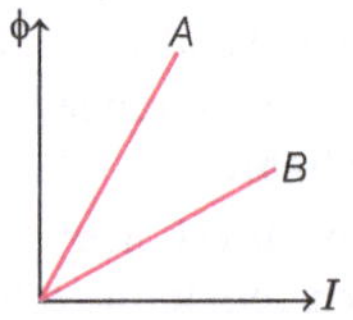

6. Self-induction is called the inertia of electricity. Why?

7. How can you increase the energy stored in an inductor by 4 times?

Short Answer Type Questions

8. A constant magnetic field $B = 1$ T acts perpendicularly on a static square copper coil of 100 turns with each side of 10 cm. The coil is removed from the magnetic field within 0.5 s and then replaced in another 0.5 s.

(i) Calculate an average emf that develops in the coil during the entire motion lasting for 1 s. **[2]**

(ii) Find the net thermal energy dissipated in the coil during the entire motion. Take, resistance of the coil as $1\,\Omega$. **Competency Based Que. [1]**

9. A rectangular frame of wire is placed in a uniform magnetic field directed outwards, normal to the paper. AB is connected to a spring which is stretched to $A'B'$ and then released at time $t = 0$. Explain qualitatively, how induced electromotive force in the coil would vary with time? (Neglect damping of oscillations of spring)

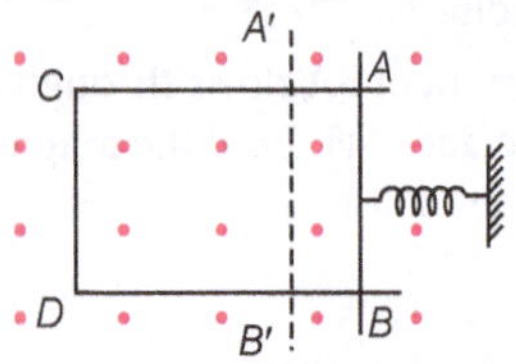

10. A conducting square loop of side L and resistance R moves in its plane with a uniform velocity v perpendicular to one of its sides. A magnetic induction B, constant in time and space, pointing perpendicular to the plane of the loop exists everywhere. What will be the induced emf?

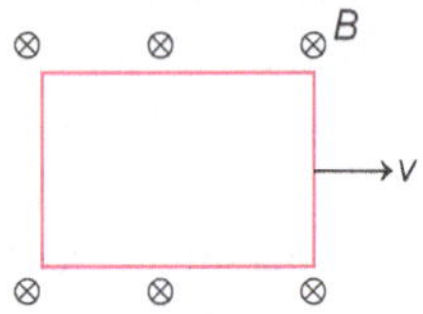

11. (i) Two static coils C_1 and C_2 are placed in the same plane in a region of uniform magnetic field B. If the magnetic field begins to increase at a constant rate, identify the directions of the induced currents in the two coils as seen from below.

Competency Based Que. [2]

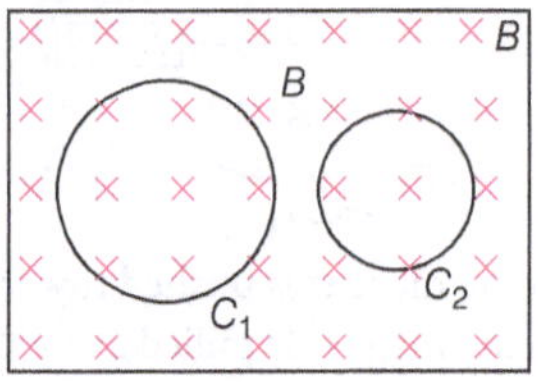

(ii) The two coils C_1 and C_2 of the above arrangement are now connected as shown below keeping all other conditions the same as earlier. **[1]**

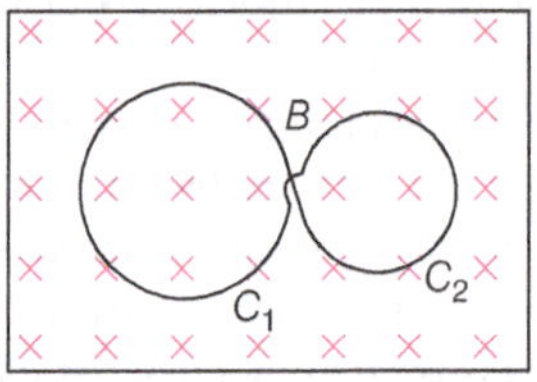

Identify the directions of the induced current through the coils C_1 and C_2 as seen from above. Give an appropriate reason for the answer.

Competency Based Que.

12. (i) State Lenz's law. **[1]**

(ii) In the given figure

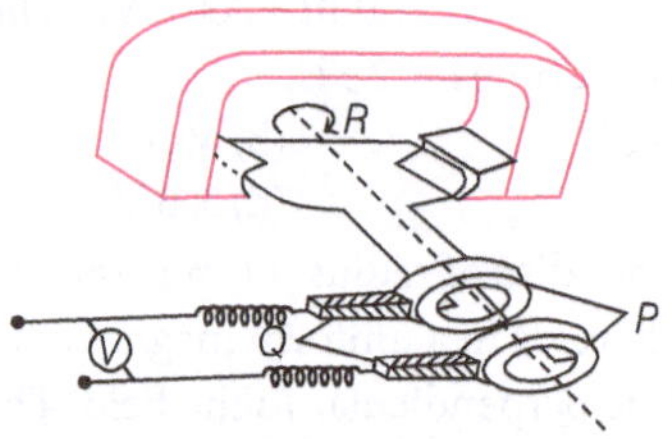

(a) Identify the machine. **[1/2]**

(b) Name the parts P and Q and R of the machine. **[1/2]**

(c) Give the polarities of the magnetic poles. **[1/2]**

(d) Write the two ways of increasing the output voltage. **CBSE 2025 [1/2]**

13. (i) The figure shows the variation of induced emf as a function of rate of change of current for two identical solenoids X and Y. One is air cored and the other is iron cored. Which one of them is iron cored? Why ? **[1]**

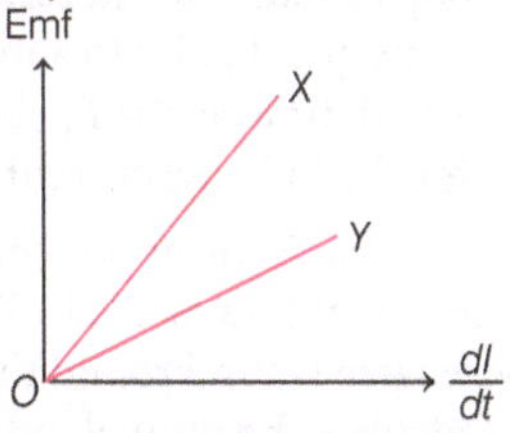

(ii) Obtain an expression for self-inductance of a long solenoid of length L and cross-sectional area A having N turns. **CBSE 2023** **[2]**

14. What is meant by the term mutual inductance of a pair of coils? Obtain an expression for the mutual inductance of two long coaxial solenoids, each of length l but having different number of turns N_1 and N_2 and radii r_1 and $r_2 (r_2 > r_1)$ **CBSE 2023**

15. A long solenoid of radius r consists of n turns per unit length. A current $I = I_0 \sin \omega t$ flows in the solenoid. A coil of N turns is wound tightly around it near its centre. What is

(i) the induced emf in the coil? **[2]**

(ii) the mutual inductance between the solenoid and the coil? **CBSE 2023** **[1]**

Long Answer Type Questions

16. (i) A bar magnet is moved in the direction indicated by the arrow between two coils PQ and CD. Predict the directions of induced current in each coil. **[2]**

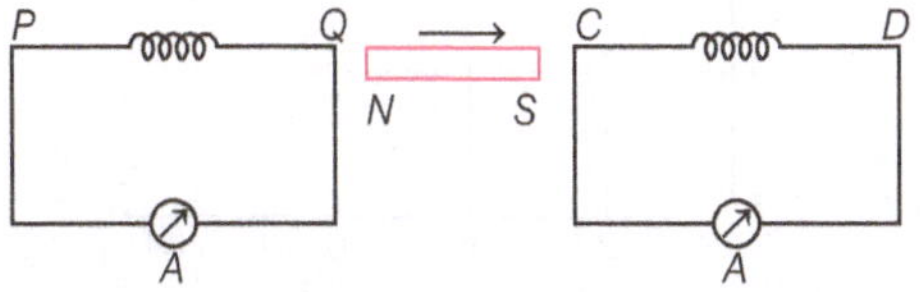

(ii) A source of emf e is used to establish a current I through a coil of self-inductance L. Show that the work done by the source to build up the current I is $\frac{1}{2}LI^2$. **[3]**

17. State and explain Faraday's law of electromagnetic induction.
A cylindrical bar magnet is placed along the axis of a circular coil. Will there be a current induced in the coil, if magnet is rotated about its axis?

18. (i) Describe a simple experiment (or activity) to show that the polarity of emf induced in a coil is always such that it tends to produce a current which opposes the change of magnetic flux that produces it. **[2]**

(ii) The current flowing through an inductor of self-inductance L is continuously increasing. Plot a graph showing the variation of **[3]**

(a) magnetic flux *versus* current.

(b) induced emf *versus* dI/dt.

(c) magnetic potential energy stored *versus* the current.

19. State Lenz's law. Give one example to illustrate this law. Lenz's law is a consequence of principle of energy conservation. Justify this statement.

20. Use Lenz's law to determine the direction of induced current in the situations described by figure.

(i) A wire of irregular shape turning into a circular shape. **[2½]**

(ii) A circular loop being deformed into a narrow straight wire. **NCERT** **[2½]**

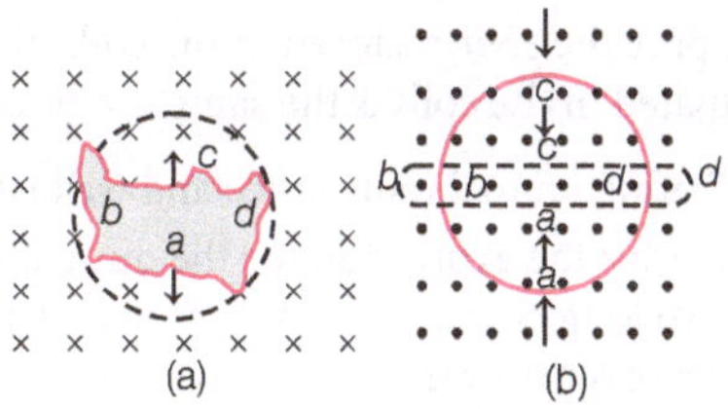

21. (i) A metallic rod of length l is moved perpendicular to its length with velocity v in a magnetic field B acting perpendicular to the plane in which rod moves. Derive the expression for the induced emf. **[2½]**

(ii) Starting from the expression for the energy, $W = \frac{1}{2}LI^2$, stored in a solenoid of self-inductance L to build up the current I, obtain the expression for the magnetic energy in terms of the magnetic field B, area A and length l of the solenoid having n number of turns per unit length. Hence, show that the energy density is given by $B^2/2\mu_0$. **[2½]**

22. Figure shows a metal rod PQ of length l, resting on the smooth horizontal rails AB positioned between the poles of a permanent magnet. The rails, rod and the magnetic field B are in three mutually perpendicular directions. A galvanometer G connects the rails through a key K. Assume the magnetic field to be uniform. Given the resistance of the closed loop containing the rod is R.

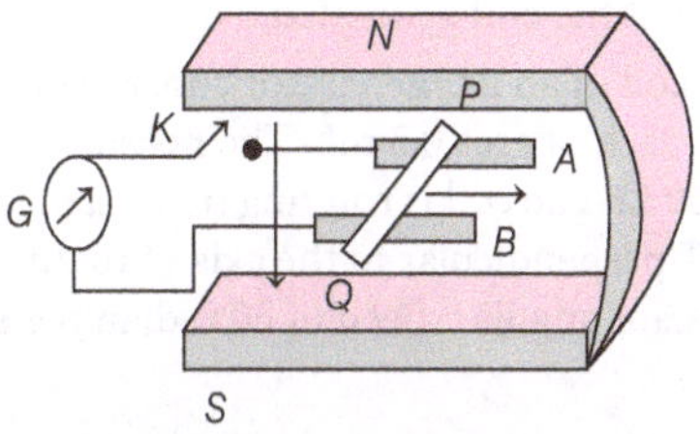

(i) Suppose K is open and the rod is moved with a speed v in the direction shown. Find the polarity and the magnitude of induced emf. **[2]**

(ii) With K open and the rod moving uniformly, there is no net force on the electrons in the rod PQ even though they do experience magnetic force due to the motion of the rod. Explain. **[1]**

(iii) What is the induced emf in the moving rod, if the magnetic field is parallel to the rails instead of being perpendicular? **CBSE SQP 2018** **[2]**

23. The current through two inductors of self-inductance 12 mH and 30 mH is increasing with time at the same rate. Draw graphs showing the variation of the

(i) emf induced with the rate of change of current in each inductor.

(ii) energy stored in each inductor with the current flowing through it.

Compare the energy stored in the coils, if the power dissipated in the coils is the same. **All India 2017 C**

24. (i) Define mutual inductance and write its SI units.

(ii) Derive the expression for the mutual inductance of two long coaxial solenoids of same length wound one over the other.

(iii) In an experiment, two coils C_1 and C_2 are placed close to each other. Find out the expression for the emf induced in the coil C_1 due to a change in the current through the coil C_2. **All India 2015**

25. (i) Explain the meaning of the term mutual inductance. Consider two concentric circular coils, one of the radius r_1 and the other of radius r_2 $(r_1 < r_2)$ placed coaxially with centres coinciding with each other. Obtain the expression for the mutual inductance of the arrangement.

(ii) A rectangular coil of area A, having number of turns N is rotated at f revolutions per second in a uniform magnetic field B, the field being perpendicular to the coil.

Prove that the maximum emf induced in the coil is $2\pi fNBA$.

26. (i) With the help of a labelled diagram, describe the principle and working of an AC generator.

Hence, obtain an expression for the instantaneous value of the emf generated.

(ii) The coil of an AC generator consists of 100 turns of wire each of area 0.5 m^2. The resistance of the wire is 100 Ω. The coil is rotating in a magnetic field of 0.8 T perpendicular to the axis of rotation, at a constant angular speed of 60 radian per second.

Calculate the maximum emf generated and power dissipated to the coil. **CBSE 2023**

27. (i) An induced emf has no direction of its own, justify. **[1]**

(ii) A circular loop of radius a and resistance R is placed with its plane perpendicular to a magnetic field which varies with time as $B = B_0 \sin \omega t$. Obtain the expression for the induced current in the loop. **[2]**

(iii) A solenoid coil has 50 turns per cm along its length and cross-sectional area of 4×10^{-4} m^2, 200 turns of another wire were wound round the first solenoid coaxially. Calculate the mutual inductance between the two coils.

Given, $\mu_0 = 4\pi \times 10^{-7}$ NA^{-2}, if two coils are insulated from each other. **[2]**

Numerical Questions

Faraday's law

28. A 0.5 m long solenoid of 10 turns/cm has area of cross-section 1 cm^2. Calculate the voltage induced across its ends, if the current in the solenoid is changed from 1A to 2A in 0.1s.

29. The magnetic field through a circular loop of wire, 12 cm in radius and 8.5Ω resistance, changes with time as shown in the figure. The magnetic field is perpendicular to the plane of the loop. Calculate the current induced in the loop and plot a graph showing induced current as function of time. **CBSE SQP 2023**

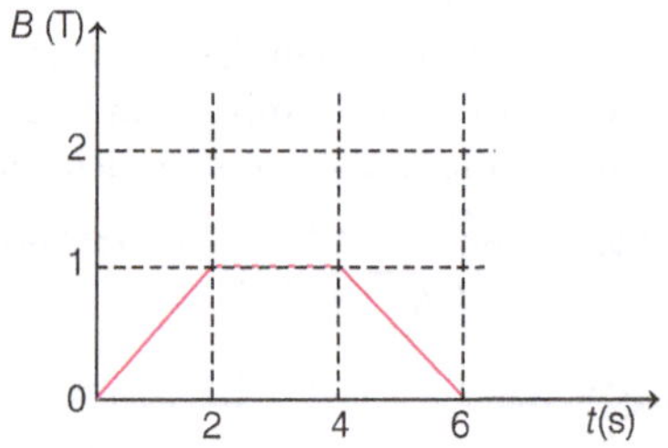

30 A jet plane is travelling towards West at a speed of 450 m/s. If the horizontal component of the earth's magnetic field at that place is 4×10^{-4} T and dip angle is 30°, calculate the emf induced between the ends of wings having a span of 30 m.

Inductance

31. A long solenoid of 10 turns/cm has a small loop of area 1 cm^2 placed inside with the normal of the loop parallel to the axis. Calculate the voltage across the small loop, if the current in the solenoid is changed from 1 A to 2 A in 0.1 s, during the duration of this change.

32. A solenoid of length 80 cm, area of cross-section 1 m^2 with 20 turns per cm completely surrounds another coaxial solenoid of the same length, area of cross-section 25 cm^2 with 20 turns per cm. Calculate the mutual inductance of the system.

33. A small flat search coil of area 5 cm^2 with 140 closely wound turns is placed between the poles of a poweful magnet producing magnetic field 0.09T and then quickly removed out of the field region. Calculate

(i) change of magnetic flux through the coil and

(ii) emf induced in the coil. **CBSE 2019**

Hints & Solutions

Objective Type Questions

1. (c)

2. (a) The magnetic field produced by the current through circular loop A of radius R and current I,

$$B_A = \frac{\mu_0 I}{2R}$$

The magnetic flux linked with loop B,

$$\phi_B = B_A A_B = \frac{\mu_0 I}{2R} \cdot \pi \left(\frac{R}{20}\right)^2 \quad \text{or} \quad \phi_B = \frac{\mu_0 I \pi R}{800}$$

$$\phi_B \propto R$$

Hence, option (a) is correct.

3. (b) 4. (b) 5. (d)

6. (b) 7. (a)

8. (c) Induced emf, $e = -NA \cdot \frac{dB}{dt} = -NA\frac{d}{dt}\left(B_0 \cos\frac{2\pi}{T}t\right)$

$$e = NAB_0 \frac{2\pi}{T} \sin\frac{2\pi}{T}t$$

For maximum magnitude of induced emf, $\sin\frac{2\pi t}{T} = \pm 1$

The value of sin will be maximum at $\frac{\pi}{2}, \frac{3\pi}{2}, \frac{5\pi}{2}, \frac{7\pi}{2}$.

Therefore, $\frac{2\pi}{T}t = \frac{(2n-1)\pi}{2}$ or $t = \frac{(2n-1)T}{4}$

where, $n = 1, 2, 3, 4$ ....

9. (c)

10. (d) The direction of induced current in the loop abc is along abc, if current increases.

11. (a) 12. (d) 13. (b) 14. (b)

15. (b) 16. (b) 17. (c) 18. (b)

19. (d) 20. (a) 21. (b)

22. (a) Self-inductance of inner solenoid,

$$L = \frac{\mu_0 N_1^2 A}{l}$$

Mutual inductance of co-axially cable,

$$M = \frac{\mu_0 N_1 N_2 A}{l}$$

The ratio will be $\frac{L}{M} = \frac{\frac{\mu_0 N_1^2 A}{l}}{\frac{\mu_0 N_1 N_2 A}{l}} = \frac{N_1}{N_2}$

In terms of number of turns per unit length,

$$\frac{N_1}{N_2} = \frac{n_1 l}{n_2 l} = \frac{n_1}{n_2}$$

23. (d)

24. (b) A-Q, B-S, C-P, D-R

25. (a) A-S, B-P, C-Q, D-R

26. (d) 27. (a) 28. (a)

29. (b) According to Faraday's law of the conservation mechanical energy into electrical energy is in accordance with the law of conservation of energy.

30. (d) Lenz's law is based on conservation of energy and induced emf always opposes the cause of it, change in magnetic flux.

31. (c) A is true but R is false.

No work is done by the external force to keep the charges in motion through the rod for a sustained induced current.

32. (a) If the inner solenoid was much shorter than (and placed well inside) the outer solenoid, then we could still have calculated the flux linkage $N_1\phi_1$ because the inner solenoid is effectively immersed in a uniform magnetic field due to the outer solenoid.

33. (a)

34. (b) The relation of induced emf is

$$e = \frac{Ldi}{dt} \text{ and current } i \text{ is given by}$$

$$i = \frac{e}{R} = \frac{1}{R}\frac{Ldi}{dt}$$

$$\Rightarrow \quad \frac{di}{dt} = i\frac{R}{L} = \frac{i}{L/R}$$

In order to decrease the rate of increase of current through solenoid we have to increase the time constant L/R.

35. (d)

36. (i) (*c*) Current will be larger, when the magnet is pushed faster towards the coil, also current is large when magnet is pulled faster away but now it is in opposite direction.

(ii) (*d*) $\phi = t^3 + 3t - 7$

$\therefore$ Induced emf,

$$e = -\frac{d\phi}{dt} = -(3t^2 + 3) = -3t^2 - 3$$

At $t = 0; e = -3$ V

Therefore, shape of graph will be a parabola not through origin ($\because e \propto t^2$).

(iii) (*b*) If a wire loop is rotated in a magnetic field, the frequency of change in the direction of the induced emf is twice per revolution.

(iv) (*b*) Given, $\phi = (5t^3 - 100t + 300)$, $t = 2$ s

Induced electromotive force,

$$e = -\frac{d\phi}{dt} = -\frac{d}{dt}(5t^3 - 100t + 300)$$

$$e = -5 \times 3t^2 + 100 = -5 \times 3(2)^2 + 100$$

$$= -5 \times 12 + 100 = -60 + 100 = 40 \text{ V}$$

(v) (*c*) Induced emf, $e = \frac{1}{2} B\omega l^2$

where, $B = 0.1$ T, $l = r = 0.1$ m,

$$\omega = 2\pi f = (2\pi \times 20) = 40\pi \text{ rad/s}$$

$\therefore$ $e = 20\pi$ mV

37. (i) The Lenz's law is based on principle of conservation of energy in which mechanical energy is transformed into electrical energy.

(ii) As, the bar magnet is moving away from the coil, so magnetic flux linked with the coil decreases. Hence, a current is induced in the coil in clockwise direction seen from the magnet side such that it increases the flux through the coil.

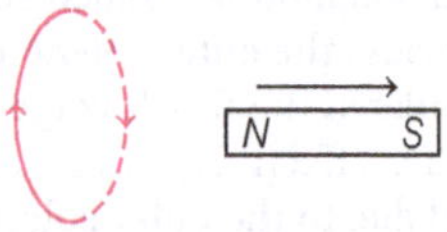

(iii) As, the magnetic flux through the coil due to current carrying wire is in upward direction containing the plane of paper. Hence, the direction of induced current in the coil is in clockwise direction such that it produces magnetic flux through it in downward direction.

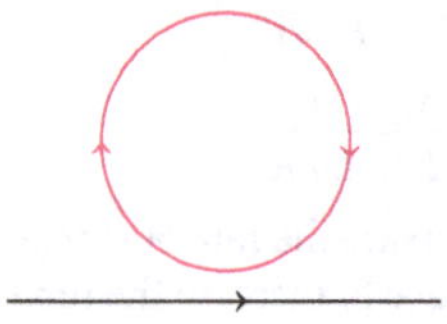

(iv) Lenz's law is used to determine the polarity of a magnetic dipole as a current carrying coil facing a moving magnet towards or away from it.

38. (i) Self induction is the property of a coil which plays same role as that of inertia in mechanics.

(ii) The unit of coefficient of self induction is given by

$$L = \frac{\phi}{I} = \frac{B \cdot A}{I} = \text{T-m}^2/\text{A}$$

(iii) The self inductance of a long solenoid is given by

$$L = \frac{\mu_0 N^2 A}{l} = \frac{\mu_0 N^2 \pi R^2}{l} \Rightarrow L \propto R^2$$

Hence, the self inductance of a solenoid is directly proportional to square of its radius.

(iv) Given, $I = 3$A, $L = 5$H

The magnetic flux through the coil is

$$\phi = LI = 5 \times 3 = 15 \text{ Wb}$$

Subjective Questions

1. The magnetic field created by straight current-carrying wire is circular along the perimeter of circular loop.

Hence, change in magnetic flux associated with the coil is zero due to increase of current through the wire.

As, induced emf (e) $\propto$ rate of change of magnetic flux (ϕ_B)
So, induced emf = 0.

Hence, a change in current of wire will not create any emf in the loop.

2. Current in the wire is steadily increasing, so the induced current in metal rings 1 and 2 will flow in such a way that it opposes the increase of current.
So, it will flow in same direction. Now, from the figure, it is clear that the direction of induced current in

(i) ring-1 is clockwise, (ii) ring-2 is anti-clockwise.

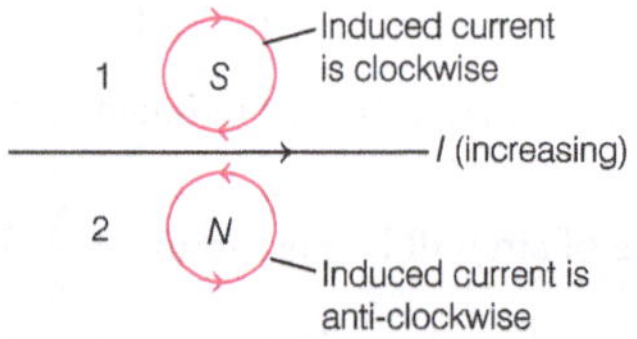

3. Induced emf in a coil depends on following factors

(i) Magnetic strength of the core in the coil of wire.

(ii) Number of turns of wire in the coil.

(iii) The cross-sectional area of the coil.

4. A straight wire cannot act as an inductor as the magnetic flux linked with the wire of negligible area of cross-section is zero. The wire has to be in the form of a coil to serve as an inductor.

5. Self-inductance of the inductor, $L = \phi/I$.

The slope of I-ϕ graph gives self-inductance of the coil.

Inductor A have got greater slope than inductor B, therefore self-inductance of A is greater than self-inductance of B.

6. Self-induction of coil is the property by virtue of which it tends to maintain the magnetic flux linked with it and opposes any change in the flux by inducing current in it.

This property of a coil is analogous to mechanical inertia, i.e. why self-induction is called the inertia of electricity.

7. Energy stored in an inductor is $E_i = \frac{1}{2}LI^2 \Rightarrow E \propto I^2$

Hence, when the current, I is doubled, the energy stored in the inductor becomes 4 times.

8. (i) Emf during removal,

$\phi_1 = nBA = 100 \times 1 \times 0.1 \times 0.1 = 1$ Wb

$\phi_2 = 0$

Time = 0.5 s

Induced emf, $\varepsilon = \frac{\Delta\phi}{\Delta t} = \frac{-1}{0.5} = -2$ V

Emf during return path

$\phi_1 = 0$

$\phi_2 = nBA = 100 \times 1 \times 0.1 \times 0.1 = 1$ Wb

Time = 0.5 s

Induced emf, $\varepsilon = \frac{\Delta\phi}{\Delta t} = \frac{1}{0.5} = 2$ V

Average emf during the entire motion = 0

Alternatively, $\phi_1 = nBA = 100 \times 1 \times 0.1 \times 0.1 = 1$ Wb

$\phi_2 = nBA = 100 \times 1 \times 0.1 \times 0.1 = 1$ Wb

Change in flux = 0, Time = 1 s

Average induced emf during the entire motion = 0

(ii) Thermal energy dissipated $= i^2rt = \frac{\varepsilon^2 t}{r}$

Energy dissipated during withdrawal

$$2^2 \times \frac{0.5}{2} = 2 \text{ J}$$

Energy dissipated during return path

$$2^2 \times \frac{0.5}{2} = 2 \text{ J}$$

Total energy dissipated during the entire motion = 4 J

9. According to figure, when wire AB is moved towards left at $A'B'$, then spring is stretched and provide a restoring force on wire, which starts moving towards right side, i.e. wire AB performs simple harmonic motion. In this case, magnetic flux linked with wire continuously changes. Therefore, an induced emf is produced across wire AB which is continuously decreases with time and finally becomes zero.

10. Refer to text on pagses 198 and 199 (Motional Electromotive Force).

11. (i) The direction of the induced current through C_1 = Anti-clockwise

The direction of the induced current through C_2 = Anti-clockwise

C_1 is a coil of a larger area, hence it will experience higher induced emf in comparison to the coil C_2 of a smaller area.

(ii) Since, coils C_1 and C_2 are connected to each other, the induced emf across coil C_1 will drive the current through the closed loop. So, the direction of the current in C_1 remains as anti-clockwise, whereas C_2 becomes clockwise.

12. (i) Refer to theory on page 197 (Lenz's Law).

(ii) (a) The machine is an AC generator.

(b) $P \rightarrow$ Slip Rings, $Q \rightarrow$ Brushes, $R \rightarrow$ Armature.

(c) The left side is the north pole and the right side is south pole.

(d) The output voltage can be increased by

I. increasing the number of turns in the armature.

II. increasing the strength of the field magnets.

13. (i) The magnitude of the induced emf depends on the rate of change of current, the number of turns in the coil and magnetic permeability of the core material. Iron bar has much higher the magnetic permeability than air. Hence, solenoid having iron core concentrates magnetic field lines and amplify their strength. Thus, induced emf is greater for solenoids (X) due to its iron cored.

(ii) Refer the text on pages 201 and 202.

14. Refer to text on pages 204 and 205.

15. Here, $I = I_0 \sin \omega t$

For solenoid, $B = \mu_0 nI$

Magnetic flux, $\phi = BA = \mu_0 nI \times \pi r^2 = \mu_0 n\pi r^2 I_0 \sin \omega t$.

(i) Emf induced, $e = -\frac{Nd\phi}{dt} = -\frac{Nd}{dt}(BA)$

$= -N\mu_0 n\pi r^2 \omega I_0 \cos \omega t$

$= -(\mu_0 I_0 \omega N n\pi r^2) \cos \omega t = -e_0 \cos \omega t$

where, peak emf, $e_0 = \mu_0 I_0 \omega N n\pi r^2$

(ii) Mutual inductance between the coil and solenoid,

$\phi = MI$

$\therefore \quad M = \frac{N\phi}{I} = \frac{\mu_0 N n\pi r^2 I_0 \sin \omega t}{I_0 \sin \omega t} = \mu_0 N n\pi r^2$

16. (i) From the figure, it is clear that North pole of the magnet is moving away from coil PQ, so the direction of current at end Q will flow in such a way that it will oppose the away movement of North pole, so it has to act as South pole. Hence, the direction of current will be clockwise.

Again, the South pole is approaching towards coil CD, so end C of the coil will act as South pole (to oppose the approaching South pole). Hence, the direction of current will be clockwise.

(ii) Refer to text on page 202.

17. Refer to text on page 196.

The current will not be induced in the coil.

18. (i) According to Lenz's law, the polarity of the induced emf is such that it opposes the change in magnetic flux responsible for its production.

Refer to text on page 197.

(ii) (a) **Magnetic flux *versus* current**

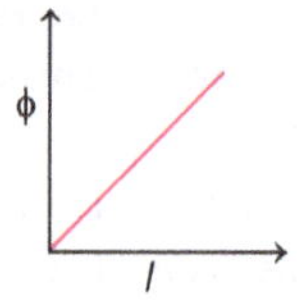

(b) **Induced emf *versus*** $\frac{dI}{dt} \Rightarrow e = -L\frac{dI}{dt}$

$\frac{dI}{dt}$ is positive, and e is negative and constant.

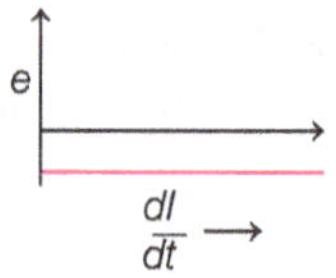

(c) **Magnetic potential energy stored *versus* current**

$$U = \frac{1}{2}LI^2$$

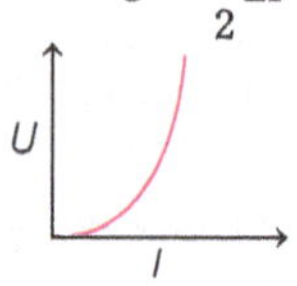

$$\Rightarrow \qquad U \propto I^2$$

19. Refer to text on pages 197 and 198.

20. (i) Here, the direction of magnetic field is perpendicularly inwards to the plane of paper. If a wire of irregular shape turns into a circular shape, then its area increases (therefore, the circular loop has greater area than the loop of irregular shape), so that the magnetic flux linked also increases.

Now, the induced current is produced in a direction such that it decreases the magnetic field, i.e. the current will flow in such a direction, so that the wire forming the loop is pulled inward in all directions (to decrease the area), i.e. current is in anti-clockwise direction, i.e. along *adcba*.

(ii) When a circular loop deforms into a narrow straight wire, the magnetic flux linked with it also decreases. The current induced due to change in flux will flow in such a direction that it will oppose the decrease in magnetic flux, so it will flow anti-clockwise, i.e. along *adcda* due to which the magnetic field produced will be out of the plane of paper.

21. (i) Refer to text on pages 198 and 199.

(ii) Energy stored in the magnetic field,

$$W = \frac{1}{2}LI^2 = \frac{1}{2}\cdot\frac{\mu_0 N^2 A}{l}\cdot\frac{B^2 l^2}{\mu_0^2 N^2}$$

$$= \frac{1}{2\mu_0}B^2\,Al \qquad \left[\because L = \frac{\mu_0 N^2 A}{l},\ B = \frac{\mu_0 NI}{l}\right]$$

Energy density,

$$u_B = \frac{\text{Energy}}{\text{Volume}} = \frac{\frac{1}{2\mu_0}B^2 Al}{Al} = \frac{B^2}{2\mu_0} \qquad [\because \text{volume} = Al]$$

22. (i) The magnitude of the induced emf is given by

$$|\varepsilon| = Blv \sin\theta$$

As the conductor *PQ* moves in the direction shown, the free electrons in it experience magnetic Lorentz force. By Fleming's left hand rule, the electrons move on the end *P* towards the end *Q*. Deficiency of electrons makes the end *P* positive while the excess of electrons makes the end *Q* negative.

(ii) The magnetic Lorentz force $[\mathbf{F}_m = -e(\mathbf{v}\times\mathbf{B})]$ is cancelled by the electric force force $[\mathbf{F}_m = e\mathbf{E}]$ exerted by the electric field set up by the opposite charges at its ends.

(iii) In this case, the angle θ made by the rod with the field **B** is zero.

$$\therefore \qquad \varepsilon = Blv \sin 0^\circ = 0$$

This is because the motion of the loop does not cut across the field lines. There is no change in magnetic flux. So the induced emf is zero.

23. Given, $L_1 = 12$ mH, $L_2 = 30$ mH

Also, $\frac{dI_1}{dt} = \frac{dI_2}{dt}$

(i) Induced emf in the inductors,

$$|e| = L\frac{dI}{dt}$$

As, $\frac{dI_1}{dt} = \frac{dI_2}{dt}$

$\Rightarrow \qquad e \propto L$

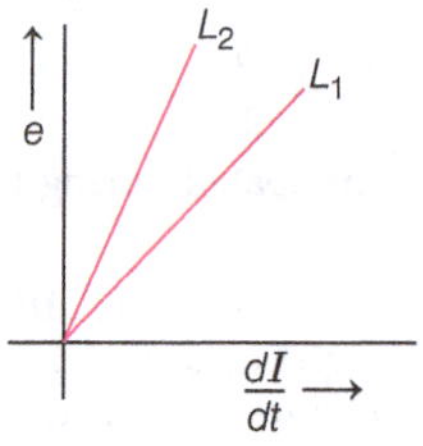

Thus, graph of e *versus* $\frac{dI}{dt}$ for two inductors is as shown in figure.

$\because \qquad L_2 > L_1$

$\therefore$ For the given $\frac{dI}{dt}$, $e_2 > e_1$.

(ii) Energy stored in inductor, $U = \frac{1}{2}LI^2$

For a given L, $U \propto I^2$

Thus, U *versus* I graph is curved as shown in the figure.

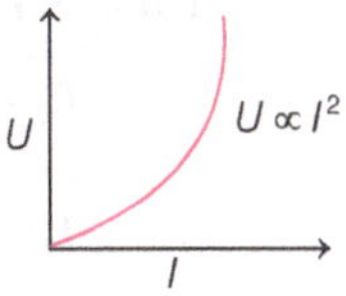

Given, $P_1 = P_2$

$$\Rightarrow \quad e_1 I_1 = e_2 I_2 \Rightarrow \frac{I_1}{I_2} = \frac{e_2}{e_1}$$

$$\therefore \frac{U_1}{U_2} = \frac{\frac{1}{2}(L_1 I_1^2)}{\frac{1}{2}(L_2 I_2^2)} = \frac{L_1}{L_2}\left(\frac{I_1}{I_2}\right)^2$$

$$= \frac{L_1}{L_2}\left(\frac{e_2}{e_1}\right)^2$$

$$= \frac{12}{30}\left[\frac{L_2\,(dI/dt)}{L_1\,(dI/dt)}\right]^2 = \left(\frac{12}{30}\right) \times \left(\frac{30}{12}\right)^2 = \frac{30}{12} = \frac{5}{2}$$

24. For parts (i) and (ii), refer to text on pages 203, 204 and 205.

(iii) Suppose that a current I is flowing through the coil C_2 at any instant. Flux linked with the coil C_1 is given by $\phi \propto I \Rightarrow \phi = MI$

where, M is the coefficient of mutual induction. If e is the induced emf produced in the coil C_1, then

$$e = -\frac{d\phi}{dt} = -\frac{d}{dt}(MI) = -M\frac{dI}{dt}$$

25. (i) Whenever the current passing through a coil or circuit changes, the magnetic flux linked with a neighbouring coil or circuit also changes. Hence, an emf is induced in the neighbouring coil or circuit. This phenomenon is called mutual induction.

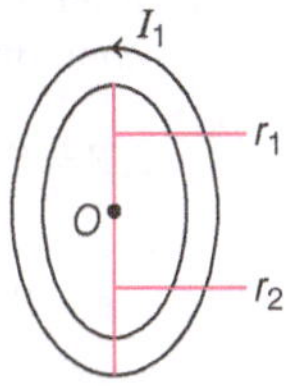

According to question, let the current in big coil of radius r_2 be I_1, so magnetic field at point O due to this coil will be $\frac{\mu_0 I_1}{2r_2}$.

Change in magnetic flux in the coil of radius r_1 is

$$\phi = BA = \frac{\mu_0 I_1}{2r_2} \times \pi r_1^2$$

Mutual inductance,

$$M = \frac{\phi}{I_1} = \frac{\mu_0 I_1 \pi r_1^2}{2r_2 \times I_1} = \frac{\mu_0 \pi r_1^2}{2r_2}$$

This is the required expression.

(ii) According to question, if the coil rotates with an angular velocity of ω and N turns through an angle θ in time t, thus $\theta = \omega t$.

$$\therefore \quad \phi = BA\cos\theta = BA\cos\omega t$$

As the coil rotates, the magnetic flux linked with it changes. An induced emf is set up in the coil which is given by

$$e = \frac{-d\phi}{dt} = \frac{-d}{dt}(BA\cos\omega t)$$

$$= BA\omega\sin\omega t$$

For N number of turns, $e = NBA\omega\sin\omega t$

For maximum value of emf ωt must be equals to 90°.

So, maximum emf induced is $= NBA\omega$

i.e. $\quad e = NBA\,2\pi f \quad [\because \omega = 2\pi f]$

26. (i) AC generator works on the principle of electromagnetic induction. Whenever amount of magnetic flux linked with a coil changes, an emf is induced in the coil. It lasts, so long as the change in magnetic flux through the coil continues.

Labelled diagram of an AC generator is shown below.

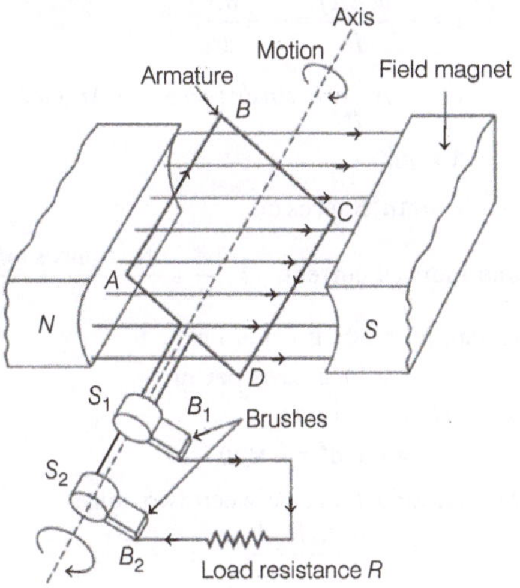

Working When a closed armature coil rotates in a uniform magnetic field with its axis perpendicular to the magnetic field, the magnetic flux linked with the loop changes and emf induces in the coil. Let initially angle between area vector of coil and magnetic field B is 0°. Thereafter, AB comes downward and CD upward then by Fleming's right hand rule induced current flows from B to A.

During the next half revolution, when CD comes downward and AB upward, then current flows from C to D. During the first half rotation, current flows through $BAS_2 B_2 RB_1 DC$ and during next half rotation along $CD\, B_1\, RB_2 S_2\, AB$. Hence,

$e = -Nd\phi/dt = NBA\omega\sin\omega t$, where $e_0 = NBA\omega$

$$i = \frac{e_0}{R}\sin\omega t = i_0\sin\omega t \quad \left[\text{Here, } \frac{e_0}{R} = i_0\right]$$

(ii) Given, number of turns, $N = 100$

Area, $A = 0.5\,\text{m}^2$

Resistance, $R = 100\,\Omega$

Magnetic field, $B = 0.8$ T

Angular speed, $\omega = 60$ rad/s

Induced emf $= NBA\omega$

$$= 100 \times 0.8 \times 0.5 \times 60$$

$$e_0 = 2400\text{ V} \quad \ldots\text{(i)}$$

Induced current (max), $I_0 = \frac{e_0}{R} = \frac{2400}{100} = 24$ A

Power dissipated, $P = e_0 \times I_0 = 2400 \times 24 = 57600$

$$P = 576 \times 10^2 \text{ W}$$

27. (i) The induced emf produced in a coil, always opposes the change in magnetic flux. So, direction of induced emf depends on the change of magnetic flux and hence has no direction of its own.

(ii) Given, $B = B_0 \sin \omega t$

$\because$ Induced emf, $e = -\frac{d\phi}{dt}$ and $\phi = BA$

$$e = -\frac{d(BA)}{dt} = -A\frac{dB}{dt}$$

$$e = -A\frac{d}{dt}(B_0 \sin \omega t) \Rightarrow e = -AB_0\omega\cos \omega t$$

$\because \quad A = \pi a^2$

so $|e| = \pi a^2 B_0 \omega \cos \omega t$

and induced current, $i = \frac{|e|}{R} = \frac{\pi a^2 B_0 \omega \cos \omega t}{R}$

(iii) Given, $N_1 = 50$ turns per cm

$= 5000$ turns per m

and $\quad N_2 = 200$ turns

$A = 4 \text{ cm}^2 = 4 \times 10^{-4} \text{ m}^2$

Mutual inductance between two coils,

$$M = \frac{\mu_0 N_1 N_2 A}{l}$$

$$M = \frac{4\pi \times 10^{-7} \times 5000 \times 200 \times 4 \times 10^{-4}}{1}$$

$$M = 5.03 \times 10^{-4} \text{ H}$$

28. $\because l = 0.5$ m, $n = 10$ turns/cm $= 1000$/m

$A = 1 \text{ cm}^2 = 1 \times 10^{-4} \text{ m}^2$

Change in current, $dI = (2-1) = 1$A, $dt = 0.1$ s

$\therefore$ Induced voltage, $|V| = \frac{LdI}{dt} = \mu_0 n^2 Al\frac{dI}{dt}$

$$= 4\pi \times 10^{-7} \times (1000)^2 \times 10^{-4} \times 0.5 \times \frac{1}{0.1}$$

$$= 20\pi \times 10^{-5} = 0.628 \text{ mV}$$

29. Given, for a circular coil,

Radius, $r = 12$ cm $= 0.12$ m,

Resistance, $R = 8.5\,\Omega$

$\therefore$ Area of the loop, $A = \pi r^2 = \pi \times (0.12)^2 = 4.5 \times 10^{-2} \text{m}^2$

Induced emf, $e = -\frac{\Delta\phi}{\Delta t} = -A \cdot \frac{B_2 - B_1}{t_2 - t_1}$

For $0 < t < 2$ s,

$$E_1 = -4.5 \times 10^{-2} \times \frac{1-0}{2-0} = -2.25 \times 10^{-2} \text{ V}$$

$$\therefore \quad I_1 = \frac{E_1}{R} = \frac{-2.25 \times 10^{-2}}{8.5}$$

$$= -2.6 \times 10^{-3} \text{ A} = -2.6 \text{ mA}$$

For $2\text{s} < t < 4$ s,

$$E_2 = -4.5 \times 10^{-2} \times \frac{1-1}{4-2} = 0$$

$$\therefore \quad I_2 = \frac{E_2}{R} = 0$$

For $4\text{s} < t < 6$ s,

$$E_3 = -4.5 \times 10^{-2} \times \frac{0-1}{6-4} = 2.25 \times 10^{-2} \text{ V}$$

$$\therefore \quad I_3 = \frac{E_3}{R} = \frac{2.25 \times 10^{-2}}{8.5} = 2.6 \text{ mA}$$

The graph of induced current *versus* time is given below.

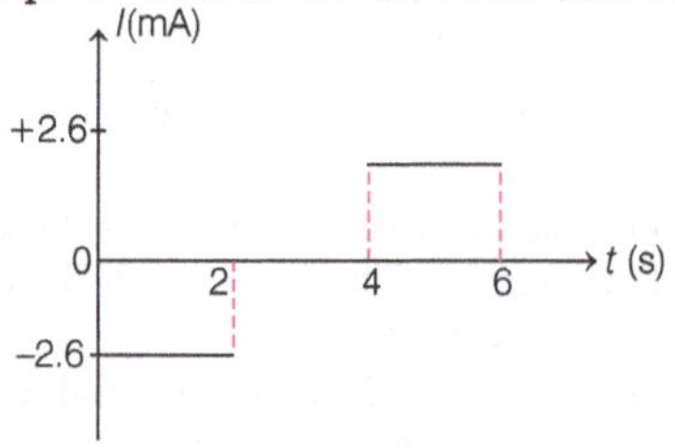

30. Given, $v = 450$ m/s, $H = 4 \times 10^{-4}$T

$\delta = 30°, l = 30$ m

A jet plane flying horizontally intercepts vertical component (V) of earth's magnetic field

$$\therefore B = V = H \tan \delta = 4 \times 10^{-4} \tan 30° = \frac{4 \times 10^{-4}}{\sqrt{3}}$$

$$e = Blv = \frac{4}{\sqrt{3}} \times 10^{-4} \times 30 \times 450 = 3.12 \text{ V}$$

31. Refer to Sol. as Q.28 on page 220.

Voltage $= 12.57 \times 10^{-7}$ V

32. Mutual inductance $= 10.05$ mH

Refer to Example 12 on page 205.

33. (i) Magnetic flux, $\phi_1 \hat{i} = N\mathbf{BA} \cos\theta$

$= NBA \cos 0° = NBA$

$= 140 \times 0.09 \times 5 \times 10^{-4} = 63 \times 10^{-4}$ Wb

$\phi_2 \hat{i} = NBA = 0 \qquad \{\because B = 0\}$

$\therefore$ Change in magnetic flux

$= \phi_2 - \phi_1 = -63 \times 10^{-2}$ Wb

(ii) Emf induced $= \frac{-\Delta\phi}{\Delta t} = \frac{-63 \times 10^{-4}}{\Delta t}$

QR Code for Quick Test 1

QR Code for Quick Test 2

SELF ASSESSMENT TEST

Multiple Choice Questions (MCQs)

1. The magnetic flux linked with the coil (in weber) is given by the equation **CBSE SQP 2021-22**

$$\phi = 5t^2 + 3t + 16$$

The induced emf in the coil at time, $t = 4$s will be

(a) –27 V (b) –43 V
(c) –108 V (d) 210 V

2. An air-cored solenoid with length 30 cm, area of cross-section 25 cm^2 and number of turns 800, carries current of 2.5 A. The current is suddenly switched OFF in a brief time of 10^{-3} s. Ignoring the variation in magnetic field near the ends of the solenoid, the average back emf induced across the ends of the open switch in the circuit would be **CBSE SQP 2021-22**

(a) zero (b) 3.125 V
(c) 6.54 V (d) 16.74 V

3. A square shaped coil of side 10 cm having 100 turns is placed perpendicular to a magnetic field which is increasing at 1 T/s. The induced emf in the coil is **CBSE 2023**

(a) 0.1 V (b) 0.5 V
(c) 0.75 V (d) 1.0 V

4. An iron cored coil is connected in series with an electric bulb with an AC source as shown in figure. When iron piece is taken out of coil, the brightness of the bulb will **CBSE SQP 2022-23**

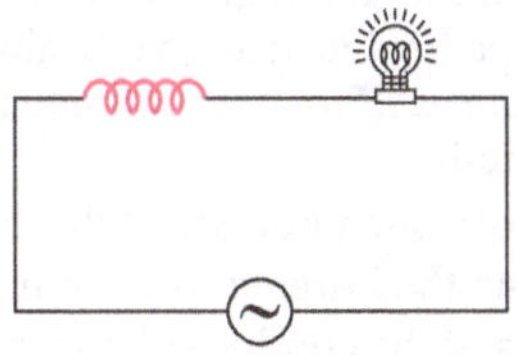

(a) decrease (b) increase
(c) remain unaffected (d) fluctuate

Assertion-Reason

Directions *(Q. Nos. 5-7) In the following questions, two statements are given-one labelled Assertion (A) and the other labelled Reason (R). Select the correct answer to these questions from the cods (a), (b), (c) and (d) as given below.*

(a) Both Assertion and Reason are true and Reason is the correct explanation of Assertion.
(b) Both Assertion and Reason are true but Reason is not the correct e xplanation of Assertion.
(c) Assertion is true but Reason is false.
(d) Assertion is false but Reason is true.

5. **Assertion (A)** A current carrying loop made of a wire of length L is placed in a magnetic field. It experiences a torque which is greater than the torque on a circular loop made of the same wire carrying the same current in the same magnetic field.

Reason (R) A circular loop occupies more area than a square loop, both made of wire of the same length.

6. **Assertion (A)** Magnetic flux of a magnetic field **B** passing through an area **A** is given by the relation $\phi = \mathbf{B} \cdot \mathbf{A}$.

Reason (R) Quantity obtained by product of two vectors is always scalar.

7. **Assertion (A)** Faraday's laws are consequence of conservation of energy.

Reason (R) Earth's magnetic field can induce emf.

Case Based Question

Directions *(Q. No. 8) This question is case based question. Read the following paragraph and answer the questions on the basis of same.*

8. The emf induced across the ends of a conductor due to its motion in a magnetic field is called motional emf. It is produced due to the magnetic Lorentz force acting on the free electrons of the conductor. For a circuit shown in figure, if a conductor of length l moves with velocity v in a magnetic field B perpendicular to both its length and the direction of the magnetic field, then induction is possible in the circuit.

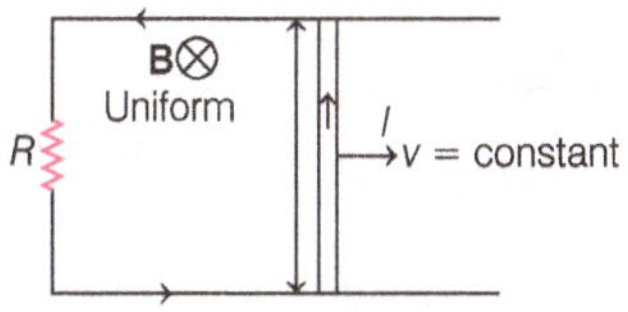

(i) Direction of current induced in a wire moving in a magnetic field is found using **[1]**
(a) Fleming's left hand rule
(b) Fleming's right hand rule
(c) Ampere's rule
(d) Right hand clasp rule

(ii) A conducting rod of length l is moving in a transverse magnetic field of strength B with velocity v. The resistance of the rod is R. The current in the rod is **[1]**
(a) $\frac{Blv}{R}$ (b) Blv (c) zero (d) $\frac{B^2v^2l^2}{R}$

(iii) A 0.1 m long conductor carrying a current of 50 A is held perpendicular to a magnetic field of 1.25 mT. The mechanical power required to move the conductor with a speed of $1 ms^{-1}$ is **[1]**
(a) 62.5 mW (b) 625 mW
(c) 6.25 mW (d) 12.5 mW

(iv) A bicycle generator creates 1.5 V at 15 km/h. The emf generated at 10 km/h is **[1]**
(a) 1.5 V (b) 2 V
(c) 0.5 V (d) 1 V

Short Answer Type Questions

9. A current is induced in coil C_1 due to the motion of current carrying coil C_2.

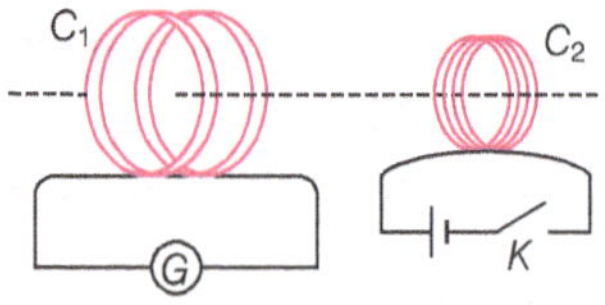

(i) Write any two ways by which a large deflection can be obtained in the galvanometer G.
(ii) Suggest an alternative device to demonstrate the induced current in place of a galvanometer.

10. A magnet is quickly moved in the direction indicated by an arrow between two coils C_1 and C_2 as shown in the figure.

What will be the direction of induced current in each coil as seen from the magnet? Justify your answer.

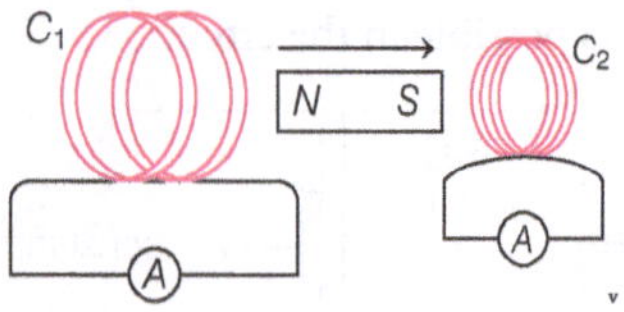

11. (i) When primary coil P is moved towards secondary coil S (as shown in the figure below), the galvanometer shows momentary deflection. What can be done to have larger deflection in the galvanometer with the same battery?

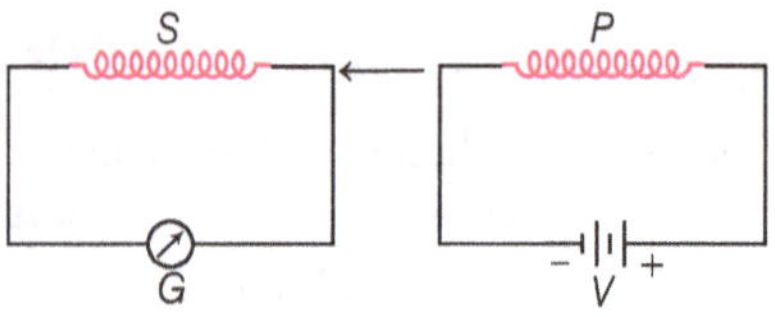

(ii) State the related law.

Long Answer Type Questions

12. A square loop of side 20 cm is initially kept 30 cm away from a region of uniform magnetic field of 0.1 T as shown in the figure. It is then moved towards the right with a velocity of $10 cms^{-1}$ till it goes out of the field. Plot a graph showing the variation of

(i) magnetic flux (ϕ) through the loop with time (t). **[2]**
(ii) induced emf (ε) in the loop with time t. **[2]**
(iii) induced current in the loop, if it has resistance of 0.1Ω **[1]**

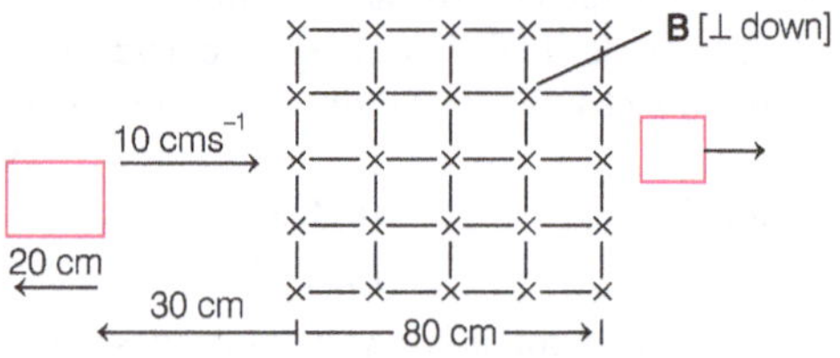

13. (i) A rod of length l is moved horizontally with a uniform velocity v in a direction perpendicular to its length through a region in which a uniform magnetic field is acting vertically downward. Derive the expression for the emf induced across the ends of the rod. **[3]**
(ii) How does one understand this motional emf by invoking the Lorentz force acting on the free charge carriers of the conductor? Explain. **[2]**

Answers

1. (b) *2.* (d) *3.* (d) *4.* (b) *5.* (d) *6.* (c) *7.* (b)
8. (i) (b), (ii) (a), (iii) (c), (iv) (d)
12. (i) 4×10^{-3} Wb (ii) 2×10^{-3} V (iii) 2×10^{-2} A

07

CHAPTER

In this chapter, we will study about some alternating current system that transfers energy efficiently and we will also discuss some devices that work on alternating current.

YOUR STUDY GOALS

7.1 Introduction to Alternating Current
7.2 AC Circuits
7.3 AC Devices

YOUR PRACTICE GOAL

- Objective Type Questions (37 Qs ; MCQs, A-R, Matching)
- Case Based Questions-3
- Subjective Questions (7 VSAs, 15 SAs, 14 LAs)
- Numerical Problems-26

Alternating Current

7.1 Introduction to Alternating Current

Alternating current can be defined as **the current whose magnitude changes continuously with time and direction changes periodically** and attains the same magnitude and direction after a definite time interval.

It is represented by

$$I = I_0 \sin \omega t \qquad \left[\because \omega = \frac{2\pi}{T} = 2\pi\nu \right]$$

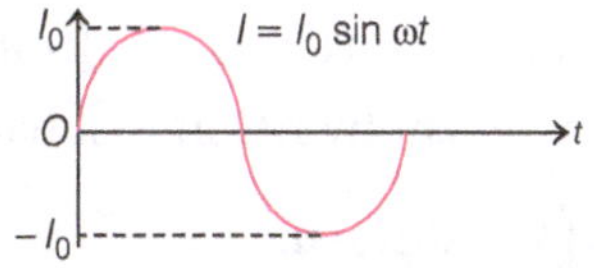

where, I = current at any instant t, I_0 = maximum/peak value of AC, ν = frequency, T = time period and ω = angular frequency.

Frequency (ν) is equal to the number of complete cycles of variations gone through by the AC in one second.

$$\nu = \frac{1}{T}$$

Similarly, the alternating emf can be represented as

$E = E_0 \sin \omega t$

where, E = voltage at time t, E_0 = maximum/peak value of alternating voltage and ω = angular frequency.

Note Current whose direction does not change with time through a load is known as **direct current (DC)**.

Advantages of AC over DC

- AC generation is easy and economical.
- It can be easily converted into DC with the help of rectifier.
- In AC, energy loss is minimum, so it can be transmitted over large distances.

Disadvantages of AC over DC

- AC shock is attractive, while DC shock is repulsive.
- 220 V AC is more dangerous than 220 V DC, because 220 V AC has peak value $E_0 = \sqrt{2} E_{rms} = 1.414 \times 220 \text{ V} = 331 \text{ V}$, but 220 V DC has fixed value 220 V only.
- AC cannot be used in electroplating process because here constant current with constant polarity is needed which is given by DC.

Mean or Average Value of AC

The mean or average value of AC over any half cycle is defined as the value of steady current which sends the same amount of charge through a circuit in half cycle time as sent by AC through the same circuit in same time. It is denoted by I_m or I_{av}.

Let the instantaneous value of alternating current is represented by

$$I = I_0 \sin \omega t \quad \text{... (i)}$$

Suppose current is kept constant for small time (dt). Then, small amount of charge (dq) in small time (dt) is given by

$$dq = I dt = I_0 \sin \omega t \, dt \quad \text{[from Eq. (i)]}$$

Let q be the total charge sent by AC in first half cycle

$$q = \int_0^{T/2} I dt = \int_0^{T/2} I_0 \sin \omega t \, dt$$

$$q = I_0 \left[-\frac{\cos \omega t}{\omega} \right]_0^{T/2} \quad [\omega T = 2\pi]$$

$$= -\frac{I_0}{\omega} \left[\cos \omega \frac{T}{2} - \cos 0° \right]$$

$$= -\frac{I_0}{\omega} [\cos \pi - \cos 0°]$$

$$\Rightarrow \quad q = \frac{2I_0}{\omega} \quad \text{...(ii)}$$

If I_m represents the mean or average value of AC over the 1st half cycle, then

$$q = I_m \times \frac{T}{2} \quad \text{...(iii)}$$

From Eqs. (ii) and (iii) we get

$$I_m \times \frac{T}{2} = \frac{2I_0}{\omega} = \frac{2I_0}{\frac{2\pi}{T}}$$

$$\boxed{I_m = \frac{2I_0}{\pi} = 0.637 I_0}$$

∴ **Mean or average value of AC over positive half cycle is 0.637 times the peak value of AC.**

Note For a complete cycle, the average value of AC is zero.

Root Mean Square (RMS) Value of AC

The root mean square (rms) value of AC is defined as the value of a steady current which would produce the same amount of heat in a given resistance in a given time as is produced by the AC through the same resistance in same time during complete cycle.

It is also called **virtual value** or **effective value** of AC.

It is represented by I_{rms} or I_{eff} or I_V.

Instantaneous value of AC,

$$I = I_0 \sin \omega t \quad \text{... (i)}$$

If dH is small amount of heat produced in time dt in resistor R, then

$$dH = I^2 R \, dt \quad [\because H = I^2 RT] \text{...(ii)}$$

In complete cycle $(0 \to T)$, the total heat produced is H.

$$H = \int_0^T I^2 R dt = \int_0^T (I_0^2 \sin^2 \omega t) R dt$$

$$H = I_0^2 R \int_0^T \frac{(1 - \cos 2\omega t)}{2} dt$$

$$H = \frac{I_0^2 R}{2} \left[\int_0^T 1 \cdot dt - \int_0^T \cos 2\omega t \, dt \right]$$

$$H = \frac{I_0^2 R}{2} \left[t - \frac{\sin 2\omega t}{2\omega} \right]_0^T$$

So, $\quad H = I_0^2 RT/2 \quad$ ...(iii)

If I_{rms} is rms value of alternating current and H is the heat produced by rms current (I_{rms}), then

$$H = I_{rms}^2 RT \quad \text{...(iv)}$$

On comparing Eqs. (iii) and (iv), we get

$$I_{rms}^2 RT = \frac{I_0^2 RT}{2}$$

$$\Rightarrow \quad I_{rms}^2 = \frac{I_0^2}{2}$$

$$\Rightarrow \quad \boxed{I_{rms} = \sqrt{\frac{I_0^2}{2}} = \frac{I_0}{\sqrt{2}} = 0.707 I_0}$$

$$\Rightarrow \quad \boxed{I_{rms} = 70.7\% \text{ of } I_0}$$

Hence, from the above equation, we conclude that **rms value of current is 70.7% of the peak value of current.**

Example 1 **The instantaneous current (in A) from an AC source is given by $I = 5\sin 314t$. What is the rms value of the current?**

Sol. Given, $I = 5\sin 314t$ ...(i)

We know that, $I = I_0 \sin \omega t$ ...(ii)

On comparing Eqs. (i) and (ii), we have

$$I_0 = 5\text{ A and } \omega = 314$$

$$\therefore \quad I_{rms} = \frac{I_0}{\sqrt{2}} = \frac{5}{\sqrt{2}} = 3.54\text{ A}$$

Example 2 **Calculate the instantaneous voltage for AC supply of 220 V and 50 Hz.**

Sol. Given, $E_V = 220\text{ V}$, $\nu = 50$ Hz and $E = ?$

Since, we know that for calculating the peak value of alternating voltage E_0, we can use the relation

$$E_0 = \sqrt{2}E_V = 1.414 \times 220 = 311\text{ V}$$

Therefore, instantaneous voltage (in V), $E = E_0 \sin \omega t$

$$E = E_0 \sin(2\pi\nu)t$$
$$= 311\sin(2\pi \times 50)t$$
$$= 311\sin 100\pi t$$

Example 3 **In an AC circuit, the rms voltage is $100\sqrt{2}$ V. Determine the peak value of voltage and its mean value during a positive half cycle.**

Sol. Given, $E_V = 100\sqrt{2}$ V

Peak value of voltage, $E_0 = ?$

Mean value of voltage, $E_m = ?$

$$\because \quad E_0 = \sqrt{2}E_V = \sqrt{2}(100\sqrt{2}) = 200\text{ V}$$

$\therefore$ During positive half cycle $(0 \to T/2)$,

$$E_m = \frac{2E_0}{\pi} = \frac{2 \times 200}{3.14} = 127.4\text{ V}$$

Quick Test 1

Conceptual Questions

1. In many European homes and offices, the rms voltage available from a wall socket is 240 V. What is the maximum voltage in this case?

2. An AC current, $I = I_0 \sin \omega t$ produces certain heat H in a resistor R over a time $T = 2\pi/\omega$. Write the value of the DC current that would produce the same heat in the same resistor in the same time.

3. An alternating current is given by $I = I_1 \cos \omega t + I_2 \sin \omega t$. Determine the rms value of current through the circuit.

4. The current through an AC circuit is $I_t = I_0(t/\tau)$ for sometime. Determine the rms current through the circuit over time interval $t = 0$ to $t = \tau$.

5. Show that heat produced in a cycle of AC is same as the heat produced by DC with $I = I_{rms}$.

6. Both alternating current and direct current are measured in amperes. But how is the ampere defined for an alternating current? *NCERT Exemplar*

Numerical Questions

7. The instantaneous value of current in an AC circuit is $I = 2\sin(100\pi t + \pi/3)$ A. At what first time, the current will be maximum ?

8. An alternating current in a circuit is given by $I = 20\sin(100\pi t + 0.05\pi)$ A. What is the rms value of current?

9. (i) The peak voltage of an AC supply is 300 V. What is its rms voltage?

(ii) The rms value of current in an AC circuit is 10 A. What is the peak current? *NCERT*

10. The alternating current in a circuit is described by the graph shown in the figure. Find the rms current in this graph. *NCERT Exemplar*

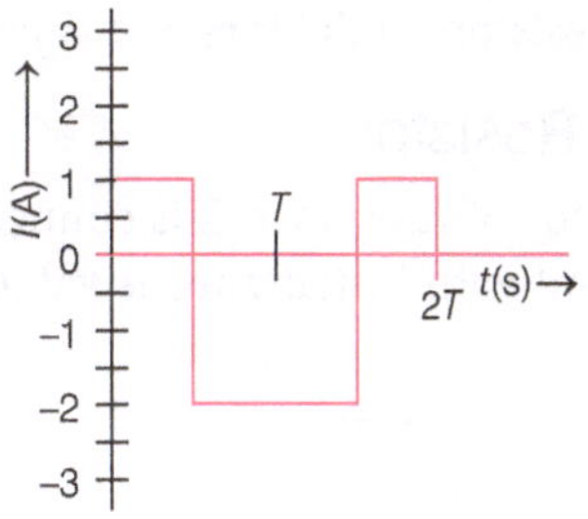

Answers

7. 1/200 s, 8. $10\sqrt{2}$ A 9. (i) 212.1V (ii) 14.14 A, 10. 1.6A

For Solutions, See QR Code on Pg. 258

7.2 AC Circuits

Phasor Diagrams

A rotating vector that represents a sinusoidally varying quantity is called **phasor**.

A diagram representing alternating current and alternating emf (of same frequency) as rotating vectors (phasors) with the phase angle between them is called **phasor diagram**.

The length of the vector represents the maximum or peak value, i.e. I_0 and E_0. The projection of the vector on fixed axis gives the instantaneous value of alternating current and alternating emf.

In sine form, ($I = I_0 \sin \omega t$ and $E = E_0 \sin \omega t$) projection is taken on Y-axis.

In cosine form ($I = I_0 \cos \omega t$ and $E = E_0 \cos \omega t$), projection is taken on X-axis.

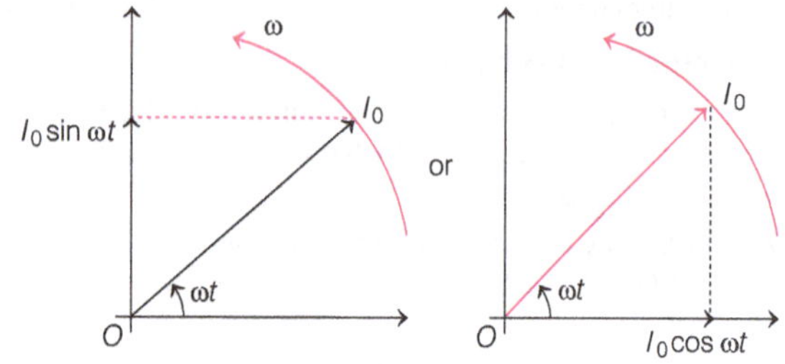

Phasor diagram

Different Types of AC circuit

In this section, we will derive voltage current relations for individual as well as combined circuit elements carrying a sinusoidal alternating current. Here, we will only consider resistors, inductors and capacitors.

AC through Resistor

Suppose a resistor of resistance R is connected to an AC source of emf with instantaneous value (E), which is given by

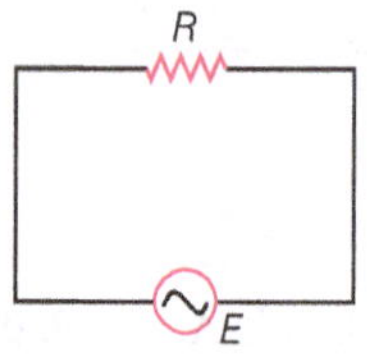

An AC voltage applied to a resistor

$$E = E_0 \sin \omega t \quad \ldots \text{(i)}$$

Let E be the potential drop across resistance (R), then $\quad E = IR \quad \ldots$(ii)

$\because$ Instantaneous emf = Instantaneous value of potential drop

From Eqs. (i) and (ii), we have

$$IR = E = E_0 \sin \omega t$$

$$\Rightarrow \quad I = \frac{E}{R} = \frac{E_0 \sin \omega t}{R}$$

$$\Rightarrow \quad \boxed{I = I_0 \sin \omega t} \quad \left[\because I_0 = \frac{E_0}{R}\right] \quad \ldots \text{(iii)}$$

Comparing $I_0 = E_0/R$ with Ohm's law, we find that resistors work equally well for both AC and DC voltages.

From Eqs. (i) and (iii), we get that in a **pure resistor, instantaneous alternating current and instantaneous alternating emf are in same phase (i.e. there is no phase difference).**

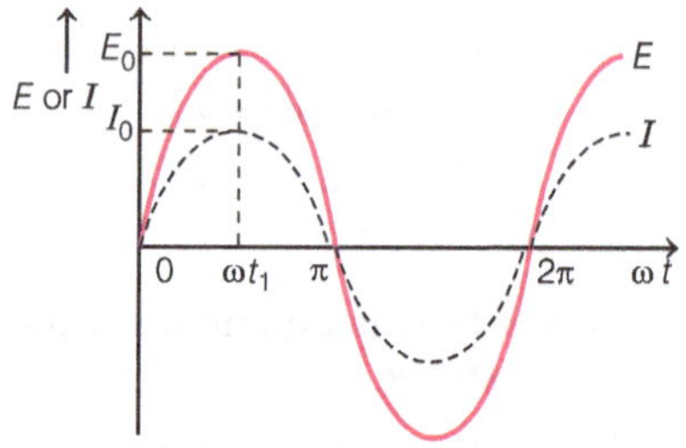

Graph of E and I *versus* ωt

Phasor Diagram

Here, peak values E_0 and I_0 are represented by vectors rotating with angular velocity ω with respect to horizontal reference axis. Their projections on vertical axis give their instantaneous values.

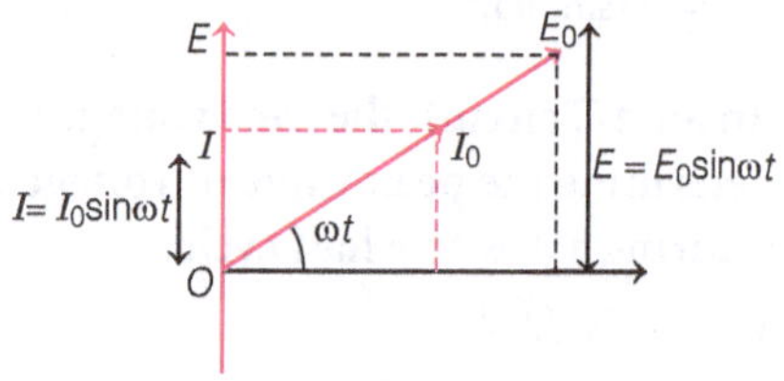

Phasor diagram for a purely resistive circuit

Example 4. **A resistance of 20 Ω is connected to a source of alternating current rated 110 V, 50 Hz. Find the**

(i) rms current.

(ii) maximum instantaneous current in the resistor.

(iii) time taken by the current to change from its maximum value to the rms value.

Sol. Given, resistance, $R = 20\Omega$

The rms value of voltage, $E_{rms} = 110\text{ V}$

Frequency, $\nu = 50\text{ Hz}$

(i) $I_{rms} = \dfrac{E_{rms}}{R} = \dfrac{110}{20} = 5.5\text{ A}$

(ii) $I_0 = \sqrt{2}\, I_{rms} = 1.414 \times 5.5 = 7.8\text{ A}$

(iii) Let the AC be represented by $I = I_0 \cos \omega t$

At $t = 0, I = I_0 \cos 0° = I_0(\max) = 7.8\text{ A}$

At $t = t$, let $I = I_V = \dfrac{I_0}{\sqrt{2}} = I_0 \cos \omega t$

$$\because \cos \omega t = \frac{1}{\sqrt{2}} = \cos \frac{\pi}{4} \Rightarrow \omega t = \frac{\pi}{4} \Rightarrow 2\pi \nu t = \frac{\pi}{4}$$

$$\therefore \quad t = \frac{1}{8\nu} = \frac{1}{8 \times 50} = 2.5 \times 10^{-3}\text{ s}$$

AC through Inductor

Suppose an inductor with self-inductance (L) is connected to an AC source with instantaneous emf (E), which is given by $\quad E = E_0 \sin \omega t \quad$ ...(i)

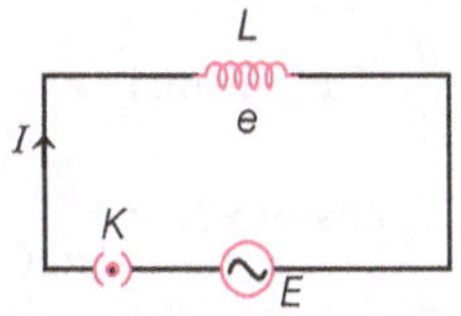

An AC voltage connected to an inductor

Such a circuit is known as **purely inductive circuit.**

When key K is closed, the current I begins to grow because magnetic flux linked with it changes and induced emf produces which opposes the applied emf. According to Lenz's law,

$$e = -L\frac{dI}{dt}$$

where, e is induced emf and $\dfrac{dI}{dt}$ is the rate of change of current.

The net instantaneous emf $= E - L\dfrac{dI}{dt}$

Since the circuit is purely inductive. Thus the resistance of the circuit is zero.

Therefore, we have,

$$E - L\frac{dI}{dt} = 0$$

$$\therefore \quad dI = \frac{E}{L}dt$$

Integrating the above equation on both sides, we get

$$\int dI = \int \frac{E}{L}dt$$

$$\Rightarrow \quad I = \int \frac{E_0 \sin \omega t}{L}dt \quad \text{[from Eq. (i)]}$$

$$\Rightarrow \quad I = \frac{E_0}{L}\left[\frac{-\cos \omega t}{\omega}\right] \Rightarrow I = -\frac{E_0}{\omega L}\sin(\pi/2 - \omega t)$$

$$\left[\because \sin\left(\frac{\pi}{2} - \omega t\right) = \cos \omega t\right]$$

$$\Rightarrow \quad I = \frac{E_0}{\omega L}\sin(\omega t - \pi/2) \quad \text{...(ii)}$$

If $\sin(\omega t - \pi/2) = \text{maximum} = 1$, then $I = I_0$

where, peak value of current, $I_0 = \dfrac{E_0}{\omega L}$

$$\therefore \quad \boxed{I = I_0 \sin(\omega t - \pi/2)} \quad \text{...(iii)}$$

From Eqs. (i) and (iii), it is clear that **in a pure inductor, the current lags behind the voltage by a phase angle of $\pi/2$ radians (90°) or the voltage leads the current by a phase angle of $\pi/2$ radians (90°).**

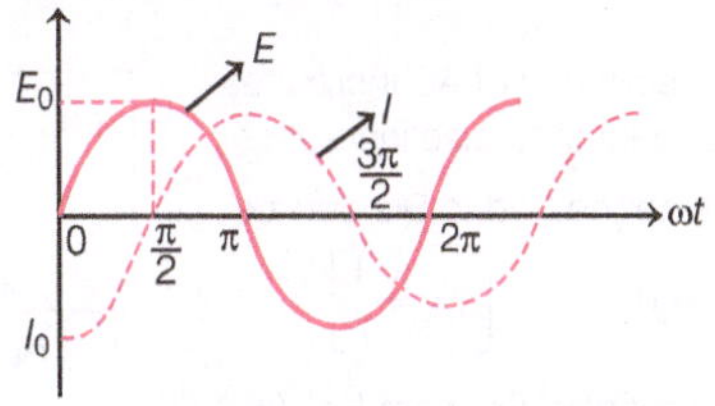

Graph of E and I *versus* ωt

Phasor Diagram

The phasor representing peak emf E_0 makes an angle ωt in anti-clockwise direction with horizontal axis. As current lags behind the voltage by 90°, so the phasor representing I_0 is turned 90° clockwise with the direction of E_0.

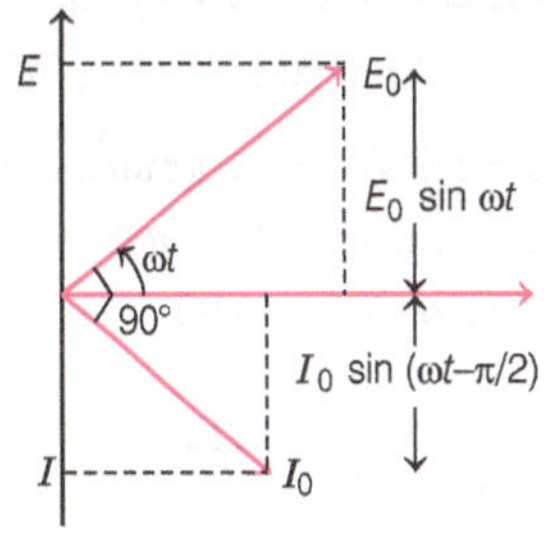

Phasor digram for purely inductive circuit

Inductive Reactance (X_L)

The opposing nature of inductor to the flow of alternating current is called **inductive reactance.**

It is denoted by X_L.

$$X_L = \omega L$$

where, X_L is called inductive reactance.
If ν is the frequency of AC source, then

$$X_L = \omega L = 2\pi\nu L \qquad \ldots\text{(i)} \left[\because \omega = \frac{2\pi}{T} = 2\pi\nu\right]$$

$\Rightarrow \qquad X_L \propto \nu$

The dimension of inductive reactance is the same as that of resistance and its SI unit is **ohm (Ω).**

The inductive reactance opposes the current in a purely inductive circuit in the same way as the resistance opposes the current in a purely resistive circuit. It is also directly proportional to the inductance and to the frequency of the AC.

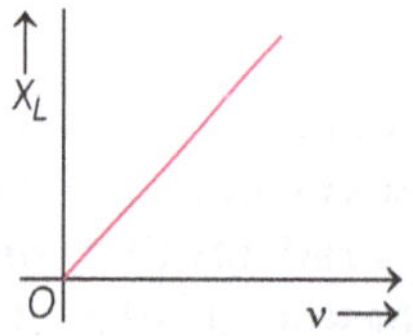

Thus, if the frequency of AC increases, its inductive reactance also increases.

If inductor is connected to DC source

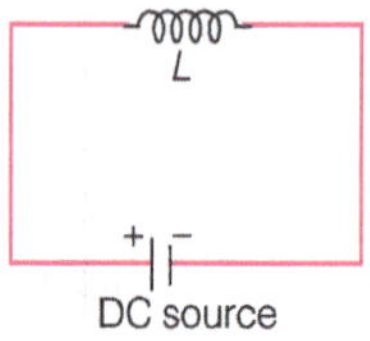

$$\nu = 0 \qquad \left[\because \nu = \frac{1}{T}\right]$$

Here, ν is frequency. So, from Eq. (i)
$X_L = 0$.

Therefore, inductor passes DC and blocks AC of very high frequency.

Example 5. **Alternating emf of $E = 220 \sin 100\pi t$ is applied to a circuit containing an inductance of $(1/\pi)$ H. Write equation for instantaneous current through the circuit. What will be the reading of AC galvanometer connected in the circuit?**

Sol. Given, $\quad E = 220 \sin 100\pi t$

$$E_0 = 220 \text{ V}, \omega = 100\pi \text{ rad/s}, L = (1/\pi) \text{ H}$$

Since, inductive reactance, $X_L = \omega L$

$$X_L = 100\pi \times \frac{1}{\pi} = 100\Omega$$

$$\therefore \quad I_0 = \frac{E_0}{X_L} = \frac{220}{100} = 2.2 \text{ A}$$

As current lags behind the emf by a phase angle of $\frac{\pi}{2}$.

$$\therefore \quad I = I_0 \sin(\omega t - \pi/2) = 2.2 \sin(100\pi t - \pi/2)$$

$\therefore$Reading of AC galvanometer, $I_V = \frac{I_0}{\sqrt{2}} = \frac{2.2}{\sqrt{2}} = 1.55$ A

AC through Capacitor

Let us consider a capacitor with capacitance C be connected to an AC source with an emf having instantaneous value,

$$E = E_0 \sin \omega t \qquad \ldots\text{(i)}$$

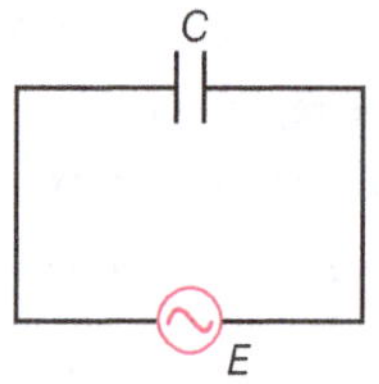

An AC source connected to a capacitor

At any instant t, suppose q is the charge on the capacitor. So, the potential difference across the plates of capacitor is $V = \frac{q}{C}$ or $q = CV$

The instantaneous value of current in the circuit,

$$I = \frac{dq}{dt} = \frac{d}{dt}(CE) \qquad [\because V = E]$$

$$I = \frac{d}{dt}(CE_0 \sin \omega t) \qquad \text{[from Eq. (i)]}$$

$$= CE_0 \cos \omega t \times \omega = \frac{E_0}{1/\omega C} \cos \omega t$$

$$\Rightarrow \quad I = \frac{E_0}{1/\omega C} \sin(\omega t + \pi/2) \qquad \ldots\text{(ii)}$$

$$[\because \cos \omega t = \sin(\pi/2 + \omega t)]$$

I will be maximum when $\sin(\omega t + \pi/2) = 1$, so that

$$I = I_0$$

where, peak value of current, $I_0 = \frac{E_0}{1/\omega C}$

$$\therefore \quad I = I_0 \sin(\omega t + \pi/2) \qquad \ldots\text{(iii)}$$

From Eqs. (i) and (iii), it is clear that **in a perfect capacitor, the current leads the voltage by a phase angle of $\pi/2$ radians (90°) or the voltage lags behind the current by a phase angle of $\pi/2$ radians (90°).**

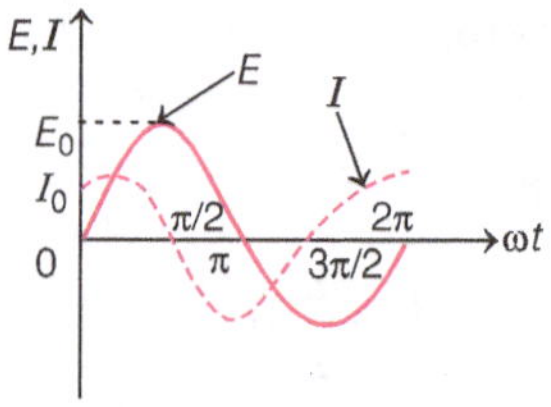

Graph of E and I ***versus*** ωt

Phasor Diagram

The phasor I_0 is turned anti-clockwise through 90° from the direction of phasor E_0. These projections on Y-axis gives the instantaneous values of E and I.

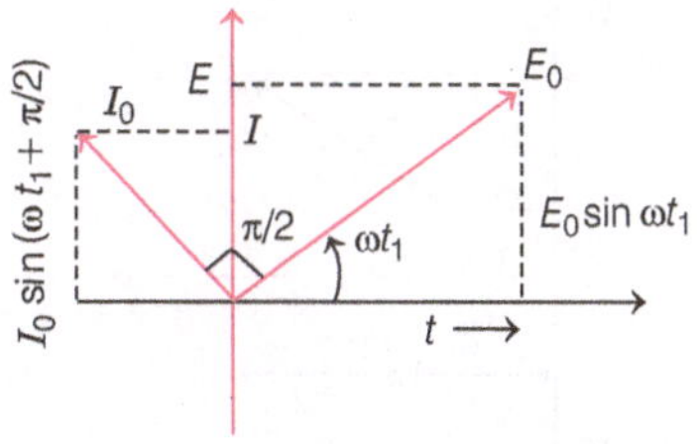

Phasor digram for purely capacitive circuit

Capacitive Reactance (X_C)

The opposing nature of capacitor to the flow of alternating current is called capacitive reactance. It is denoted by X_C.

$$X_C = \frac{1}{\omega C}$$

If ν is the frequency of the alternating current, then

$$X_C = \frac{1}{2\pi\nu C} \qquad \left[\because \omega = \frac{2\pi}{T} = 2\pi\nu\right]$$

$$\Rightarrow \qquad X_C \propto \frac{1}{\nu}$$

The dimension of capacitive reactance is same as that of resistance and its SI unit is **ohm** (Ω).

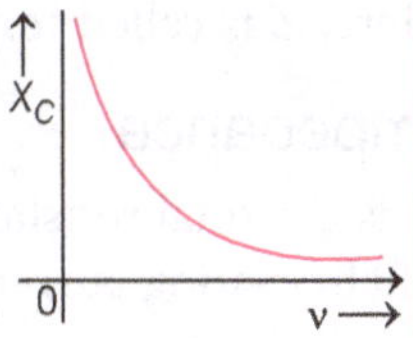

The capacitive reactance opposes the amplitude of the current in a purely capacitive circuit in the same way as the resistance opposes the current in a purely resistive circuit. It is inversely proportional to the capacitance and frequency of the current.

Thus, **if frequency of AC increases, then its capacitive reactance decreases.**

When capacitor is connected to DC source,

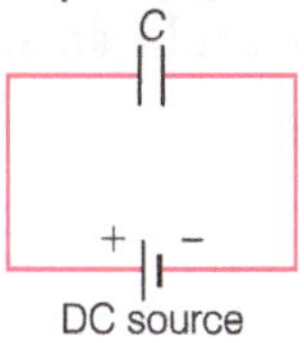

$$X_C = \frac{1}{\omega C} = \frac{1}{0} = \infty$$

[$\because$ for DC, $\omega = 2\pi\nu = 0$, as $\nu = 0$]

Thus, capacitor blocks DC and acts as open circuit, whereas it passes AC of high frequency.

Example 6. **A capacitor of 10 μF is connected to an AC source of emf $E = 220\sin(100\pi t)$V. Write the equation of instantaneous current through the circuit. What will be the reading of AC ammeter connected in the circuit?**

Sol. Given, capacitance, $C = 10\,\mu F = 10 \times 10^{-6}$F,

Emf, $E = 220 \sin 100\pi t = E_0 \sin \omega t$

$\therefore \quad E_0 = 220\,V, \omega = 2\pi\nu = 100\pi$

$\Rightarrow \quad \nu = 50$ Hz

Since, capacitive reactance,

$$X_C = \frac{1}{\omega C} = \frac{1}{2\pi\nu C} = \frac{1}{2 \times 3.14 \times 50 \times 10^{-5}} = 318.5\,\Omega$$

$$I_0 = \frac{E_0}{X_C} = \frac{220}{318.5} = 0.691\text{ A}$$

So, reading of AC ammeter,

$$I_V = \frac{I_0}{\sqrt{2}} = \frac{0.691}{1.414} = 0.489\text{ A}$$

AC Circuit Containing Resistance and Inductance

The circuit and phasor diagram can be represented as follows

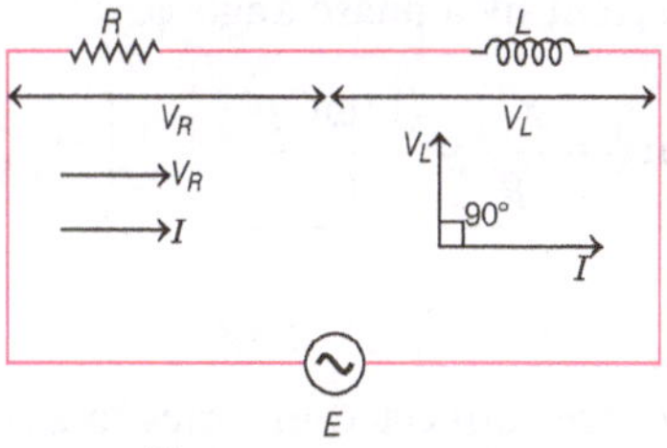

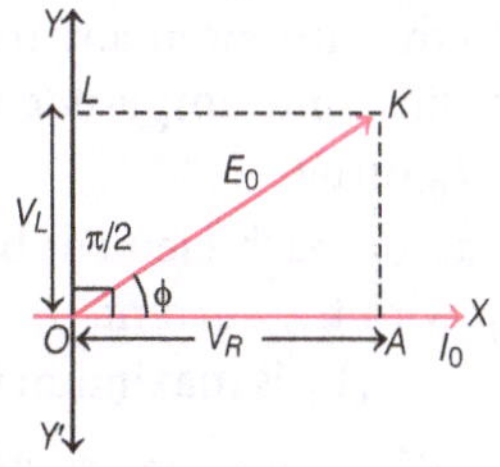

Impedance, $Z = \sqrt{R^2 + X_L^2}$

In the above R-L circuit, we noticed that voltage leads the current by a phase angle ϕ.

$$\tan\phi = \frac{X_L}{R} = \frac{\omega L}{R} \qquad (\because X_L = \omega L)$$

AC Circuit Containing Resistance and Capacitance

The circuit and phasor diagram can be represented as follows

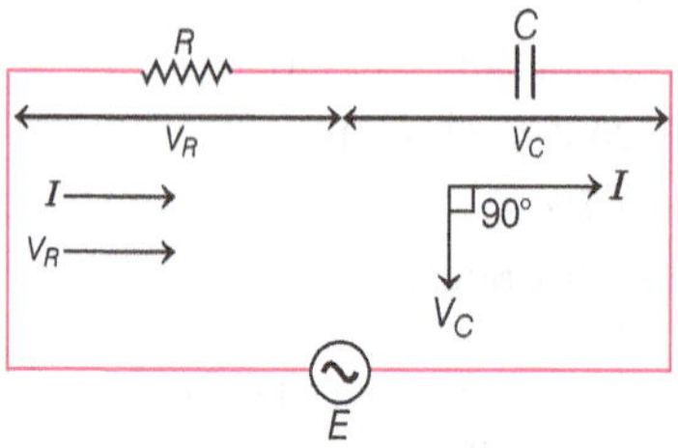

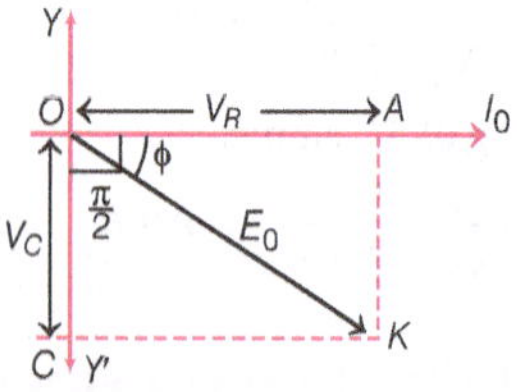

Impedance, $Z = \sqrt{R^2 + X_C^2}$

In the above *R-C* circuit, we noticed that voltage lags behind the current by a phase angle ϕ.

$$\tan \phi = \frac{X_C}{R} = \frac{(1/\omega C)}{R} \qquad \left(\because X_C = \frac{1}{\omega C}\right)$$

AC through *L-C-R* Circuit

Let *R*, *L* and *C* are connected in series to a source of alternating emf, so the current at any instant through the three elements has same amplitude and phase.

$$I = I_0 \sin \omega t$$

However, voltage across each element bears a different phase relationship with the current.

$V_L = I_0 X_L$ [V_L is maximum voltage across *L*]

$V_C = I_0 X_C$ [V_C is maximum voltage across *C*]

$V_R = I_0 R$ [V_R is maximum voltage across *R*]

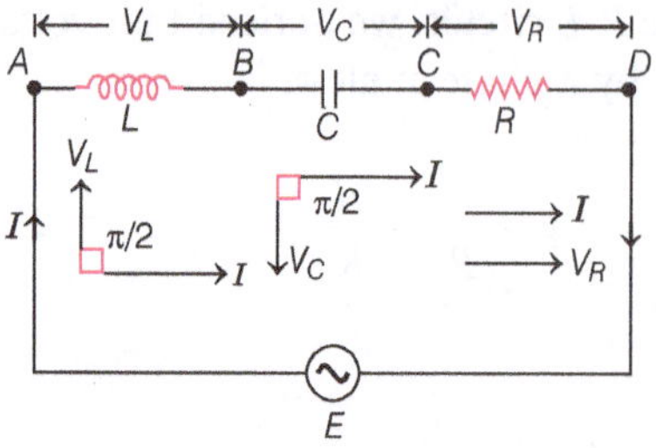

An AC source connected to *L-C-R* circuit

Inside the above figure for a *L-C-R* circuit, phasor diagrams of each *L*, *C* and *R* are given. To form phasor diagram for series *L-C-R* circuit, combine all these phasor diagrams.

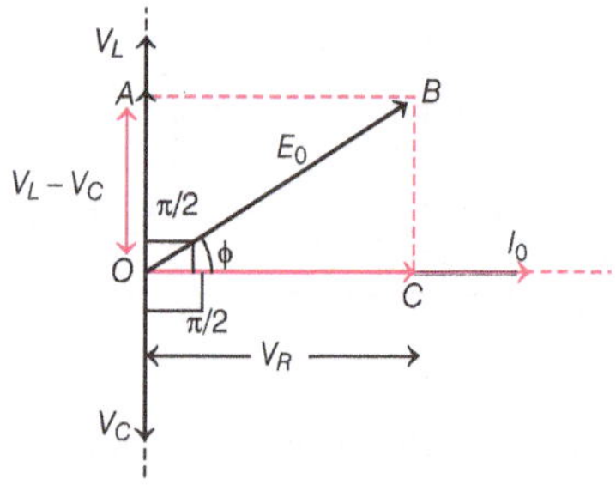

Phasor diagram for a series *L-C-R* circuit

Since, voltage (V_L) is in upward direction and voltage (V_C) in downward direction, so net voltage upto point *A* is $V_L - V_C$ (assuming $V_L > V_C$) and net maximum voltage is V_0.

From phasor diagram,

$$OB = \sqrt{(OC)^2 + (CB)^2} = \sqrt{V_R^2 + (V_L - V_C)^2}$$

$$\Rightarrow \quad E_0 = \sqrt{(I_0 R)^2 + (I_0 X_L - I_0 X_C)^2} \quad [\because OB = E_0]$$

$$\Rightarrow \quad E_0 = I_0 \sqrt{R^2 + (X_L - X_C)^2}$$

$$\therefore \quad Z = \frac{E_0}{I_0} = \sqrt{R^2 + (X_L - X_C)^2}$$

Here, *Z* is called **impedance**.

Impedance

It is the total resistance of a circuit applied in the path of alternating current. It is given by

$$Z = \sqrt{R^2 + (X_L - X_C)^2} \qquad \text{...(i)}$$

From phasor diagram, it is clear that voltage leads the current by an angle ϕ.

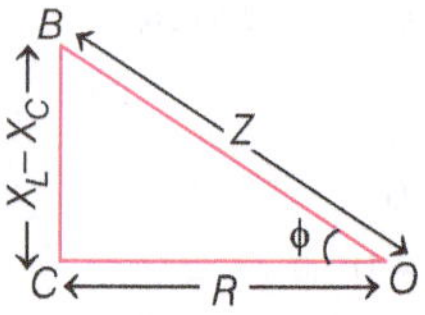

Impedance diagram of *L-C-R* circuit

The perpendicular, $BC = X_L - X_C$ is called **reactance** of the *L-C-R* circuit. It is represented by *X*.

i.e. $\quad X = X_L - X_C$

$\therefore$ From ΔOCB,

$$\tan\phi = \frac{CB}{OC} = \frac{V_L - V_C}{V_R} = \frac{I_0X_L - I_0X_C}{I_0R}$$

$$\Rightarrow \quad \boxed{\tan\phi = \frac{X_L - X_C}{R}} \quad \ldots\text{(ii)}$$

So, the alternating emf in the series *L-C-R* circuit would be represented by $E = E_0 \sin(\omega t + \phi)$.

Eqs. (i) and (ii) are graphically shown in the above graph. This is called **impedance diagram**, which is a right angled triangle with Z as its hypotenuse.

Special Cases

(i) When $X_L = X_C$, then $Z = R$ and $\tan\phi = 0$ $[\because \phi = 0°]$

(ii) When $X_L > X_C$, then $\tan\phi$ is positive.
Hence, **voltage leads the current by a phase angle ϕ. Therefore, the AC circuit is inductance dominated circuit.**

(iii) When $X_C > X_L$, then $\tan\phi$ is negative.
Hence, **voltage lags behind the current by a phase angle ϕ.**

A graph (given below) is showing variation of *E* and *I* with ωt for *L-C-R* circuit is

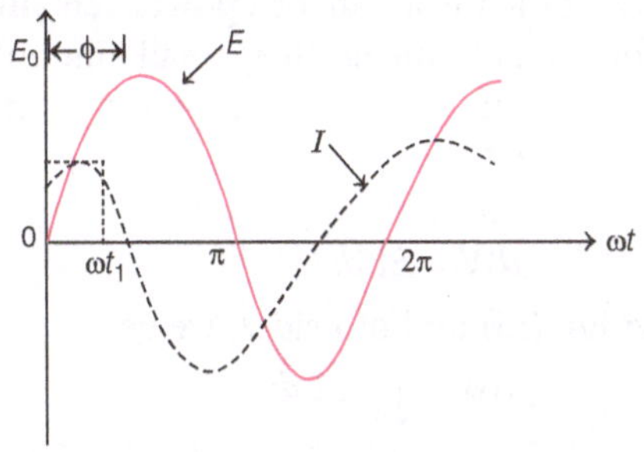

Graph of *E* and *I versus* ωt for series *L-C-R* circuit

$X_C > X_L$

The amplitude and phase of current in an *L-C-R* circuit can be analysed using phasors. However this method has drawbacks, particularly because the phasor diagram doesn't convey initial conditions. Phasors can assume arbitrary value and only depict the steady state solution by showing the relative phase angle.

Example 7. **A capacitor of 100 μF and a coil of resistance 50 Ω and inductance 0.5 H are connected in series with a 110 V - 50 Hz source. Calculate the rms value of current in the circuit.**

Sol. Given, capacitance, $C = 100\ \mu F = 100 \times 10^{-6}\ F = 10^{-4} F$

Resistance, $R = 50\ \Omega$

Inductance, $L = 0.5\ H$

rms value of voltage, $E_V = 110\ V$

Frequency, $\nu = 50$ Hz

Since, capacitive reactance,

$$X_C = \frac{1}{\omega C} = \frac{1}{2\pi\nu C} = \frac{1}{2 \times 3.14 \times 50 \times 10^{-4}}$$

$$X_C = 31.85\Omega$$

and inductive reactance,

$$X_L = \omega L = 2\pi\nu L = 2 \times 3.14 \times 50 \times 0.5 = 157\Omega$$

$\because$ Impedance, $Z = \sqrt{R^2 + (X_L - X_C)^2}$

$$= \sqrt{(50)^2 + (157 - 31.85)^2} = 134.77\Omega$$

$$\Rightarrow \quad I_V = \frac{E_V}{Z} = \frac{110}{134.77} = 0.816\ A$$

Example 8. **A coil of 0.01H inductance and 1 Ω resistance is connected to 200 V, 50 Hz AC supply. Find the impedance of the circuit and time lag between maximum alternating voltage and current.** *NCERT Exemplar*

Sol. Given, inductance, $L = 0.01$ H

Resistance, $R = 1\Omega$

Voltage, $V = 200$ V

Frequency, $\nu = 50$ Hz

Impedance of the circuit, $Z = \sqrt{R^2 + X_L^2}$

$$= \sqrt{R^2 + (2\pi\nu L)^2} = \sqrt{1^2 + (2 \times 3.14 \times 50 \times 0.01)^2}$$

$$= \sqrt{10.86} = 3.3\Omega$$

$$\tan\phi = \frac{\omega L}{R} = \frac{2\pi\nu L}{R} = \frac{2 \times 3.14 \times 50 \times 0.01}{1} = 3.14$$

$$\Rightarrow \quad \phi = \tan^{-1}(3.14) \approx 72°$$

Phase difference, $\phi = \dfrac{72 \times \pi}{180}$ rad

Time lag between maximum alternating voltage and current, $\Delta t = \dfrac{\phi}{\omega} = \dfrac{72\pi}{180 \times 2\pi \times 50} = \dfrac{1}{250}$ s

Resonance

In a series *L-C-R* circuit, when phase (ϕ) between current and voltage is zero, the circuit is said to be a **resonant circuit.**

As applied frequency increases, then

$X_L = \omega L$, X_L increases. Since, $X_C = \dfrac{1}{\omega C}$

$\therefore$ X_C decreases.

At some angular frequency (ω_r), $X_L = X_C$

where, $X_L = \omega_r L$, $X_C = \dfrac{1}{\omega_r C}$

The frequency at which X_C and X_L become equal, is called **resonant frequency**.

$$\Rightarrow \quad \omega_r L = \frac{1}{\omega_r C} \text{ or } \omega_r^2 = \frac{1}{LC}, \quad \boxed{\omega_r = \frac{1}{\sqrt{LC}}}$$

$$\Rightarrow \quad (2\pi\nu_r)^2 = \frac{1}{LC}$$

[$\because \omega_r = 2\pi\nu_r$, where ν_r is resonating frequency]

$$2\pi\nu_r = \frac{1}{\sqrt{LC}}$$

$$\therefore \quad \boxed{\nu_r = \frac{1}{2\pi\sqrt{LC}}}$$

At resonating frequency, the impedance is minimum i.e. $Z = R$.
So, the circuit behaves as purely resistive circuit.

$$\boxed{I_0 = \frac{E}{Z} = \text{Maximum}}$$

Since, Z is minimum, therefore I_0 will be maximum.

The variation of amplitude of current with angular frequency is shown below

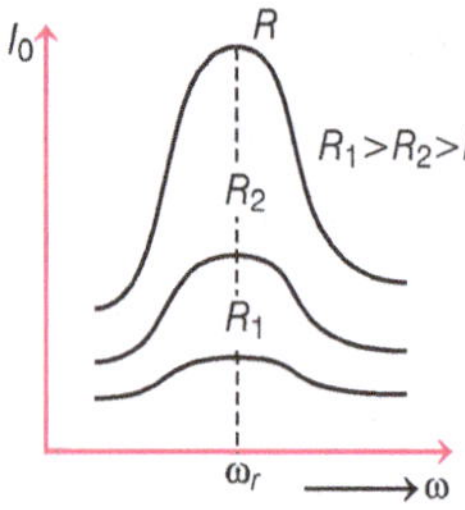

I_0 *versus* ω graph

Resonant circuits have a variety of applications, for example, in the tuning mechanism of a radio or TV set.

Example 9. **A 2 μF capacitor, 100 Ω resistor and 8 H inductor are connected in series with an AC source. What should be the frequency of source for which the current drawn in the circuit is maximum?**
If peak value of emf of source is 200 V, find the, inductive reactance, capacitive reactance, total impedance, peak value of current in the circuit.

Sol. Given, capacitance, $C = 2\ \mu\text{F} = 2 \times 10^{-6}$ F

Resistance, $R = 100\ \Omega$

Inductance, $L = 8$ H

Peak value of voltage, $E_0 = 200$ V

When frequency of AC source is equal to resonant frequency, then current drawn in the circuit is maximum.

$$\therefore \quad \nu = \nu_r = \frac{1}{2\pi\sqrt{LC}}$$

$$= \frac{1}{2 \times 3.14 \times \sqrt{8 \times 2 \times 10^{-6}}} = \frac{1000}{8 \times 3.14} = 39.8 \text{ Hz}$$

Peak value of current,

$$I_0 = \frac{E_0}{R} = \frac{200}{100} = 2 \text{ A}$$

$$\because \quad X_C = X_L = \omega L = 2\pi\nu L$$

$$= 2 \times 3.14 \times 39.8 \times 8 = 2000\ \Omega$$

$$\Rightarrow \quad Z = R = 100\Omega$$

Note The voltages across inductor and resistor differ in phase by 90° and the voltages across inductor and capacitor differ in phase by 180°.

Average Power Associated in AC Circuit

Power is defined as the rate of doing work.

$$P = \frac{dW}{dt} \quad \text{...(i)}$$

In AC circuit, both emf and current change continuously with respect to time. So in it, we have to calculate average power in complete cycle ($0 \to T$).

Instantaneous power, $P = EI$ ...(ii)

[$\because E = E_0 \sin \omega t, I = I_0 \sin(\omega t + \phi)$]

Here, E and I are instantaneous voltage and current, respectively. If the instantaneous power remains constant for a small time dt, then small amount of work done in maintaining the current for a small time dt is

$$\frac{dW}{dt} = EI$$

$$\Rightarrow \quad dW = EI\,dt \quad \text{...(iii)}$$

Integrating Eq. (iii) on both sides, we get

$$\int dW = \int_0^T EI\,dt$$

Total work done or energy spent in maintaining current over one full cycle,

$$W = \int_0^T E_0 \sin \omega t \cdot I_0 \sin(\omega t + \phi) dt$$

$$= E_0 I_0 \int_0^T \sin \omega t (\sin \omega t \cos \phi + \cos \omega t \sin \phi) dt$$

$$= E_0 I_0 \left[\cos\phi \int_0^T \sin^2 \omega t\,dt + \sin\phi \int_0^T \sin \omega t \cos \omega t\,dt\right]$$

$$= E_0 I_0 \left[\cos\phi \int_0^T \left(\frac{1 - \cos 2\omega t}{2}\right) dt + \frac{\sin\phi}{2} \int_0^T 2 \sin \omega t \cos \omega t\,dt\right]$$

$$= \frac{E_0 I_0}{2}\left[\cos\phi \left(\int_0^T dt - \int_0^T \cos 2\omega t\,dt\right) + \sin\phi \int_0^T \sin 2\omega t\,dt\right]$$

But $\int_0^T \cos 2\omega t\,dt = 0$ and $\int_0^T \sin 2\omega t\,dt = 0$

$\therefore \quad W = \dfrac{E_0 I_0 T}{2} \cos\phi$

Average power associated in AC circuit,

$$P_{av} = \frac{W}{T} = \frac{E_0 I_0 T \cos\phi}{2T} = \frac{E_0 I_0}{2} \cos\phi$$

$$\boxed{P_{av} = \frac{E_0}{\sqrt{2}} \cdot \frac{I_0}{\sqrt{2}} \cos\phi}$$

or $\boxed{P_{av} = E_{rms} I_{rms} \cos\phi = E_V I_V \cos\phi}$

As, $\quad E_{rms} = I_{rms} \cdot Z$

$\therefore P_{av}$ can also be written as

$$\boxed{P_{av} = I^2 Z \cos\phi}$$

Here, $\cos\phi$ **is power factor,** which is defined as the cosine of the phase difference between current and voltage.

If P_{av} is true power or average power, then power factor is given by,

$$\boxed{\cos\phi = \frac{P_{av}}{E_{rms} I_{rms}} = \frac{\text{True power}}{\text{Apparent power}}}$$

$$\boxed{\cos\phi = \frac{R}{Z}}$$

Here, ϕ is the phase difference between I_{rms} and E_{rms}.

Special Cases

(i) **AC circuit containing R**

When $\phi = 0°$, then $P_{av} = E_V I_V \cos 0°$

$P_{av} = E_V I_V$

So, average power in R is maximum.

(ii) **AC circuit containing L**

When $\phi = \dfrac{\pi}{2}$, then $P_{av} = E_V I_V \cos\dfrac{\pi}{2}$

$P_{av} = 0$

So, average power in L is zero.

(iii) **AC circuit containing C**

When $\phi = \dfrac{\pi}{2}$, then $P_{av} = E_V I_V \cos\dfrac{\pi}{2}$

$P_{av} = 0$

So, average power in C is zero.

(iv) **AC circuit containing L and R**

When $\tan\phi = \dfrac{\omega L}{R} \Rightarrow \cos\phi = \dfrac{R}{\sqrt{R^2 + \omega^2 L^2}}$,

then $\quad P_{av} = E_V I_V \cdot \dfrac{R}{\sqrt{R^2 + \omega^2 L^2}}$

(v) **AC circuit containing C and R**

When $\tan\phi = \dfrac{1/\omega C}{R} \Rightarrow \cos\phi = \dfrac{R}{\sqrt{R^2 + 1/\omega^2 C^2}}$

then $\quad P_{av} = E_V I_V \cdot \dfrac{R}{\sqrt{R^2 + 1/\omega^2 C^2}}$

(vi) **AC circuit containing L, C and R**

When $\tan\phi = \dfrac{\omega L - 1/\omega L}{R}$

$\Rightarrow \quad \cos\phi = \dfrac{R}{\sqrt{R^2 + (\omega L - 1/\omega C)^2}}$

then $\quad P_{av} = E_V I_V \cdot \dfrac{R}{\sqrt{R^2 + \left(\omega L - \dfrac{1}{\omega C}\right)^2}}$

Example 10. **A sinusoidal voltage of peak value 283 V and frequency 50 Hz is applied to a series L-C-R circuit in which $R = 3\,\Omega$, $L = 25.48$ mH and $C = 796\,\mu$. Find**

(i) the impedance of the circuit.

(ii) phase difference between the voltage across the source and current.

(iii) the power dissipated in the circuit.

(iv) the power factor. NCERT

Sol. Given, $E_0 = 283$ V, $\nu = 50$ Hz, $R = 3\,\Omega$,

$L = 25.48 \text{ mH} = 25.48 \times 10^{-3}$ H

and $C = 796\,\mu\text{F} = 796 \times 10^{-6}$ F

(i) Since, inductive reactance, $X_L = \omega L$

$\Rightarrow \quad X_L = 2\pi\nu L$

$= 2 \times 3.14 \times 50 \times 25.48 \times 10^{-3} \approx 8\,\Omega$

Since, capacitive reactance,

$X_C = \dfrac{1}{\omega C} = \dfrac{1}{2\pi\nu C} = \dfrac{1}{2 \times 3.14 \times 50 \times 796 \times 10^{-6}}$

$X_C = 4\,\Omega$

$\therefore$ Impedance, $Z = \sqrt{R^2 + (X_L - X_C)^2}$

$= \sqrt{3^2 + (8-4)^2} = 5\,\Omega$

(ii) Phase difference,

$\phi = \tan^{-1}\left(\dfrac{X_L - X_C}{R}\right) = \tan^{-1}\left(\dfrac{8-4}{3}\right) = 53.1°$

It means that the current in the circuit lags behind the voltage by 53.1°

(iii) Power dissipated in the circuit, $P = I_V^2 R$

$\because \quad I_V = \frac{I_0}{\sqrt{2}Z} = \frac{283}{1.414 \times 5} = 40\text{ A}$

$\therefore \quad P = I_V^2 R = (40)^2 \times 3 = 4800\ W$

(iv) Power factor, $\cos\phi = \cos 53.1° = 0.60$

Example 11. Suppose the frequency of the source in the above example can be varied.

(i) What is the frequency of the source at which resonance occurs ?

(ii) Calculate the impedance, the current and power dissipated of resonant condition. NCERT

Sol. (i) Resonant frequency,

$$\nu = \frac{1}{2\pi\sqrt{LC}}$$

$$= \frac{1}{2 \times 3.14 \times \sqrt{25.48 \times 10^{-3} \times 796 \times 10^{-6}}}$$

$$= 35.4\text{Hz}$$

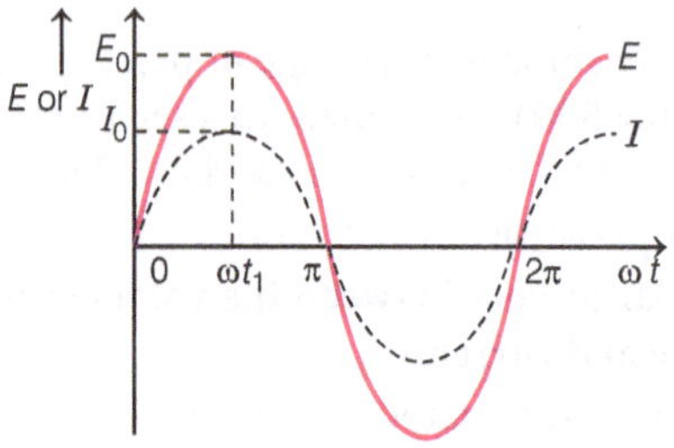

(ii) At resonance, $Z = R = 3\Omega$

$$\Rightarrow \quad I_V = \frac{E_V}{Z} = \frac{283}{\sqrt{2} \times 3} = 66.7\text{A} \qquad \left[\because E_V = \frac{E_0}{\sqrt{2}}\right]$$

$\therefore$ Power dissipated, $P = I_V^2 R$

$$= (66.7)^2 \times 3 \approx 13350\text{ W}$$

Wattless Current

The current which does not consume power for its flow in the circuit is called wattless current or **idle current**.

If the resistance in an AC circuit is zero, although current flows in the circuit, then the average power remains zero, i.e. there is no energy dissipation in the circuit, such a circuit is called **wattless circuit** and the current flowing is called wattless current.

If the circuit contains either inductance or capacitance only, then phase difference between current and voltage is 90°, i.e. $\phi = 90°$. The average power in such a circuit is

$$P_{av} = V_{rms} \times I_{rms} \times \cos\phi$$
$$= V_{rms} \times I_{rms} \times \cos 90° = 0$$

Quick Test 2

Conceptual Questions

1. How does the sign of the phase angle ϕ, by which the supply voltage leads the current in an L-C-R series circuit, change as the supply frequency is gradually increased from very low to very high values. *NCERT Exemplar*

2. Explain, why the reactance offered by an inductor increases with increasing frequency of an alternating voltage? *NCERT Exemplar*

3. Can the instantaneous power output of an AC source ever be negative? Can the average power output be negative? *NCERT Exemplar*

Numerical Questions

4. A coil of inductance 0.5 H and resistance 100 Ω is connected to a 240 V, 50 Hz AC supply.
   (i) What is the maximum current in the coil?
   (ii) What is the time lag between the voltage maximum and current maximum?

5. A 100 μF capacitor in series with a 40 Ω resistance is connected to a 110 V, 60 Hz supply.
   (i) What is the maximum current in the circuit?
   (ii) What is the time lag between the current maximum and the voltage maximum?

6. A 100 Ω resistor is connected to a 220 V, 50 Hz supply.
   (i) What is the rms value of current in the circuit?
   (ii) What is the net power consumed over a full cycle? *NCERT*

Answers

4. (i) 1.82 A (ii) 3.19×10^{-3} s 5. (i) 3.24 A (ii) 1.55×10^{-3} s
6. (i) 2.2 A (ii) 484 W

For Solutions, See QR Code on Pg. 258

7.3 AC Devices

Transformer

It is a device, which is used to increase or decrease the alternating voltage.

The transformers are of the following types

(i) Step-up transformer

(ii) Step-down transformer

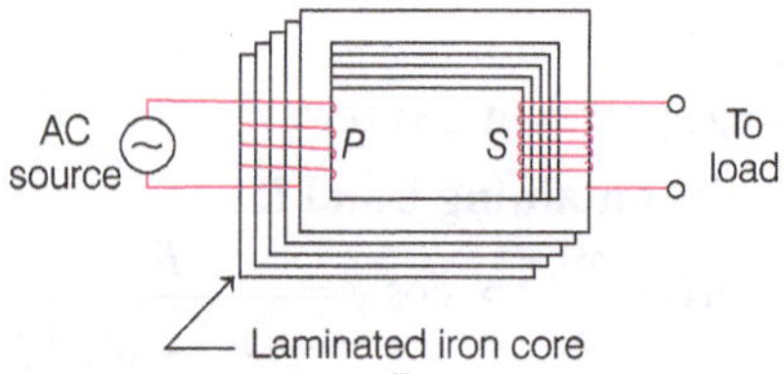

(i)

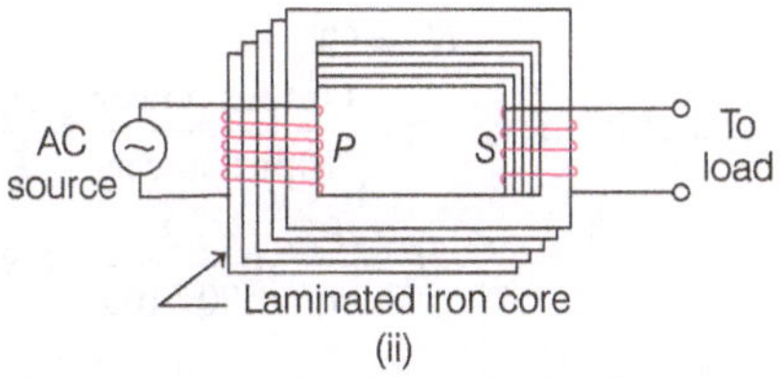

(i) Step-up and (ii) Step-down transformer

Principle

Transformer is based on the principle of **mutual induction.**

Construction

It consists of two coils, primary coil (p) and secondary coil (s), insulated from each other wounded on soft iron core. Often the primary coil is the input coil and secondary coil is the output coil. These soft iron cores are laminated to minimise eddy current loss.

Working and Theory

Let the alternating emf supplied by the AC source connected to primary is

$$E_p = E_0 \sin \omega t$$

The alternating primary current induces an alternating magnetic flux ϕ_B in the iron core because the core extends through the turns of secondary. So, the induced flux also extends through the secondary winding.

According to the **Faraday's law of electromagnetic induction,** the inducted emf per turn (E_{turn}) is same for both primary and secondary windings.

$$E_{\text{turn}} = \frac{d\phi_B}{dt} = \frac{E_p}{N_p} = \frac{E_s}{N_s}$$

Here, N_p, N_s represents the total number of turns in the primary and secondary coils respectively.

$$\frac{E_s}{E_p} = \frac{N_s}{N_p}$$

As we assume that no energy is lost along the way, conservation of energy requires that

$$\boxed{\text{Input power} = \text{Output power}}$$

$$I_p E_p = I_s E_s$$

$$\therefore \quad \frac{I_p}{I_s} = \frac{E_s}{E_p}$$

In general, $$\boxed{\frac{E_s}{E_p} = \frac{I_p}{I_s} = \frac{N_s}{N_p} = K}$$

Here, K = transformation ratio.

Note If $N_s > N_p$, then $E_s > E_p$, the transformer is called **step-up transformer**.
If $N_s < N_p$, then $E_S < E_P$, the transformer is called **step-down transformer**.

Efficiency of Transformer

The efficiency of a transformer is defined as,

$$\boxed{\eta = \frac{\text{Output power}}{\text{Input power}} \times 100\,\%}$$

In practical, the efficiency of a transformer is 90-99%.

Energy Losses in a Transformer

There are some energy losses in a transformer

(i) **Eddy Current Loss** Eddy current in iron core of transformer facilitate the loss of energy in the form of heat. It can be reduced by decreasing the thickness of the laminations.

(ii) **Flux Leakage** Total fluxes linked with the primary coil do not completely pass through the secondary coil which denotes the loss in the flux or flux leakage.

(iii) **Copper Loss** Due to heating, energy loss takes place in copper wires of primary and secondary coils.

(iv) **Hysteresis Loss** The energy loss takes place in magnetising and demagnetising the iron core over every cycle.

Uses of Transformers

Transformers are used in various AC applications including.

(i) **Induction Furnaces** Step-up or step-down voltage for melting materials.

(ii) **Voltage Regulators (TVs, computers, refrigerators)** Stabilize voltage for proper device operation.

(iii) **Welding** Step-down transformers reduce voltage and increase current for welding.

Transfromers are used for the large-scale transmission of electricity over long distances. The generator's voltage is stepped up to reduce current and minimize energy losses. It is then transmitted to a substation where the voltage is stepped down and further reduced at distribution points before reaching homes at 240 V.

This process ensures electricity is transmitted efficiently and safely to consumers.

Example 12. **How much current is drawn by the primary coil of a transformer which steps-down 220 V to 22 V to operate device with an impedance of 220 Ω?**

Sol. Given, $E_p = 220$ V, $E_s = 22$ V and $R_s = 220\,\Omega$

Since, $I_s = \frac{E_s}{R_s} = \frac{22}{220} = 0.1\text{A}$

In an ideal transformer, $\frac{I_p}{I_s} = \frac{E_s}{E_p}$

$$I_p = \frac{E_s}{E_p} \times I_s = \frac{22 \times 0.1}{220} = 10^{-2}\text{ A}$$

Example 13. **A step-down transformer converts a voltage of 2200 V into 220 V in the transmission line. Number of turns in primary coil is 5000. Efficiency of transformer is 90% and its output power is 8 kW. Determine**

(i) number of turns in the secondary coil.

(ii) input power.

Sol. Given, $E_p = 2200$ V, $E_s = 220$ V, $N_p = 5000$

Efficiency, $\eta = 90\%$

Output power, $P_o = 8$ kW

(i) Also, $\frac{N_s}{N_p} = \frac{E_s}{E_p}$

$$\Rightarrow \quad N_s = \frac{E_s}{E_p} N_p = \frac{220}{2200} \times 5000$$

$$\Rightarrow \quad N_s = 500$$

(ii) Since, efficiency, $\eta = \frac{\text{Output power}}{\text{Input power}} = \frac{P_o}{P_i}$

$$\Rightarrow \quad P_i = \frac{P_o}{\eta} = \frac{8}{90/100} = 8.9\text{ kW}$$

Quick Test 3

Conceptual Questions

1. A transformer is used to step-down AC voltage. What device do you use to step-down DC voltage?

2. What would happen if the primary winding of a transformer is connected to a battery?

Numerical Questions

3. The primary coil of an ideal step up transformer has 100 turns and transformation ratio is also 100. The input voltage and power are 220 V and 1100 W respectively. Calculate

(i) the number of turns in secondary.

(ii) the current in primary.

(iii) the voltage across secondary.

(iv) the current in secondary.

(v) the power in secondary.

4. A 60 W load is connected to the secondary of transformer whose primary draws line voltage. If current of 0.54 A flows in the load, what is the current in the primary coil? Comment on the type of transformer being used. *NCERT Exemplar*

Answers

3. (i) 10000 (ii) 5 A (iii) 22000 V (iv) 1/20 A (v) 1100 W

4. 0.27 A

For Solutions, See QR Code on Pg. 258

Mind Map

Alternating Current

Phasor and Phasor Diagram

- A rotating vector that represents a sinusoidally varying quantity is called a phasor.
- A diagram that represents alternating current voltage of the same frequency as rotating vectors along with proper phase angle between them is called phasor diagram or Argand diagram.

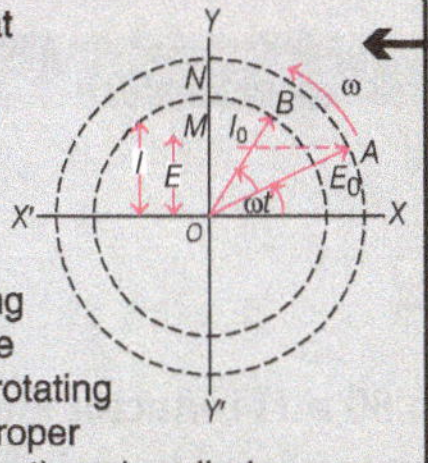

AC Circuit containing only Capacitor

- A pure capacitor C connected across a source of alternating emf ε given by
- Potential difference across the capacitor plates is equal to the applied emf

$V = \varepsilon = \varepsilon_0 \sin \omega t$

$Q = CV = C\varepsilon_0 \sin \omega t$

∴ Current at any instant is

$I = I_0 \cos \omega t = I_0 \sin(\omega t + \pi/2)$

where, $I_0 = \omega C\varepsilon_0 = \dfrac{\varepsilon_0}{1/\omega C} = \dfrac{\varepsilon_0}{X_C}$

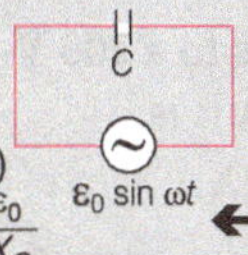

- **Phase relationship between ε and I**
  The current leads the emf in phase by $\pi/2$ rad, so the current phasor I makes an angle $\pi/2$ rad, so the current phasor I makes an angle $\pi/2$ rad with phasor ε in anti-clockwise direction.

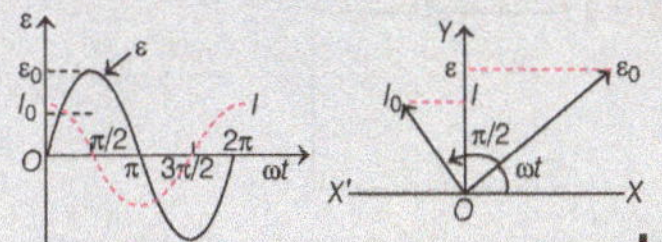

Capacitive Reactance (X_C)

- The capacitive reactance is the effective opposition offered by a capacitor to the flow of current in the circuit.
- Its SI unit is ohm (Ω).
- $X_C = \dfrac{1}{\omega C} = \dfrac{1}{2\pi fC}$

Transformer

A transformer is an electrical device for converting an alternating current at low voltage into that at high voltage or *vice-versa*.

- **Step up transformer**
  If it increases the input voltage, is called step up transformer.

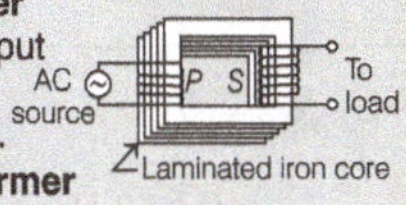

- **Step down transformer**
  If it decreases the input voltage, is called step down transformer.

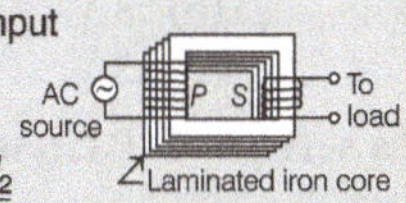

- **Induced emf,** $\dfrac{\varepsilon_2}{\varepsilon_1} = \dfrac{N_2}{N_1}$
- **Current,** $\dfrac{I_1}{I_2} = \dfrac{\varepsilon_2}{\varepsilon_1} = \dfrac{N_2}{N_1}$
- **Efficiency,** $\eta = \dfrac{\text{Power output}}{\text{Power input}} \times 100\%$

The efficiency of real transformers is fairly high (90 to 99%) though not 100%.

Alternating Current and Direct Current

- **Alternating Current and Direct Current**
  An alternating current is that current whose magnitude changes continuously with time and direction reverses periodically. A direct current is that current which flows with a constant magnitude in the same direction, as shown in figure.
  $\varepsilon = \varepsilon_0 \sin \omega t$ (emf of alternating current)

$I = \dfrac{\varepsilon}{R} = \dfrac{\varepsilon_0}{R} \sin \omega t$

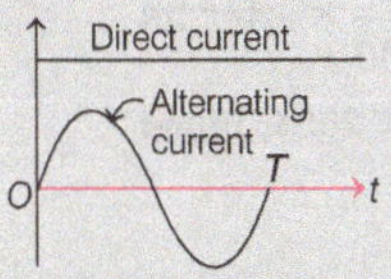

- **Amplitude** The maximum value attained by an alternating current in either direction is called its amplitude.
  It is denoted by I_0
- **Time period**

$$\text{Time period} = \frac{\text{Angular displacement in a complete cycle}}{\text{Angular velocity}}$$

- **Frequency** It is the number of cycles completed per unit second.
- $I = I_0 \sin \omega t = I_0 \sin 2\pi ft = I_0 \sin \dfrac{2\pi}{T} t$

$I_{av} = \dfrac{2}{\pi} I_0 = 0.637\, I_0$

$I_{rms} = \dfrac{I_0}{\sqrt{2}} = 0.707\, I_0$

Series *L-C-R* Circuit

A resistance R, an inductance L and capacitance C are connected in series to a source of alternating emf given by $\varepsilon = \varepsilon_0 \sin \omega t$

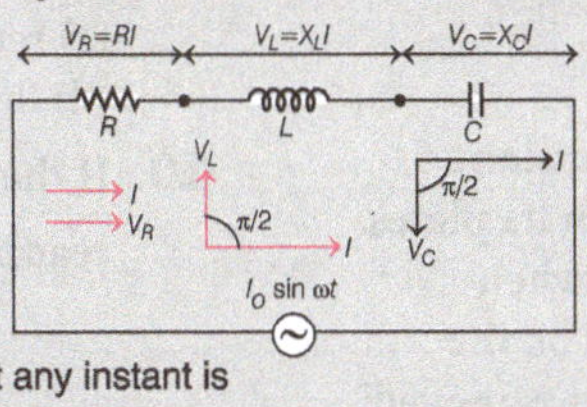

- Current at any instant is
  $I = I_0 \sin \omega t$
- Voltage across each element is
  C lags behind the current I in phase by $\pi/2$ rad.
  $V_L = X_0 X_L,\ V_C = I_0 X_C,\ V_R = I_0 R$
- V_R is in phase with I whereas V_L and V_C are out of phase with I by $\pi/2$.

So, $E_0 = \sqrt{(V_L - V_C)^2 + V_R^2} = I_0\sqrt{R^2 + (X_L - X_C)^2}$

where, $\sqrt{R^2 + (X_L - X_C)^2} = Z$ is the impedence of the circuit.

- Voltage at any instant is $E = E_0 \sin(\omega t \pm \phi)$

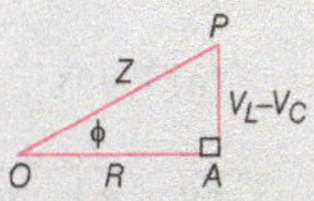

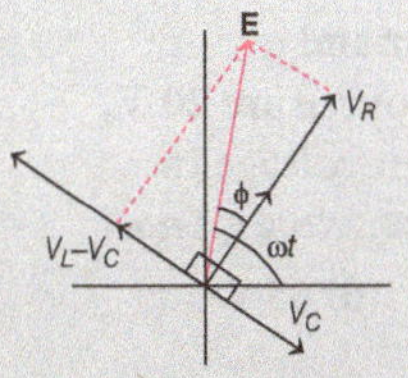

AC Circuit containing only a Resistor

- A resistor of resistance R is connected to a source of alternating emf ε given by
  $\varepsilon = \varepsilon_0 \sin \omega t$
- Current in the circuit,
  $I = I_0 \sin \omega t$

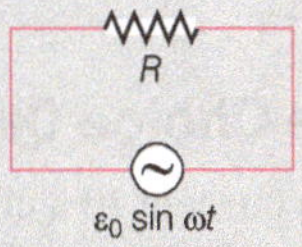

- **Phase relationship between ε and I.**
  The emf ε and current I are in same phase in a purely resistive circuit. This means that both attain their zero, minimum and maximum values at the same respective times.

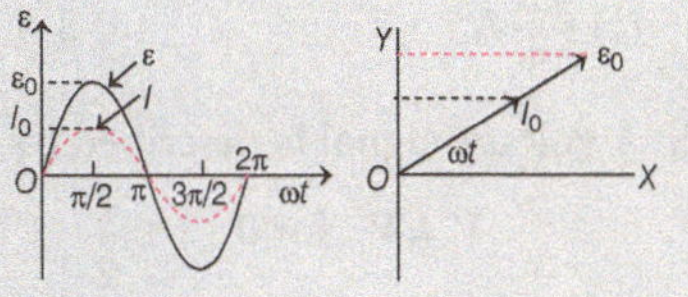

AC Circuit Containing Only an Inductor

- Suppose an inductor of inductance L is connected to a source of alternating emf is given by $\varepsilon = \varepsilon_0 \sin \omega t$
  Net instantaneous emf, $\varepsilon = L\dfrac{dI}{dt}$

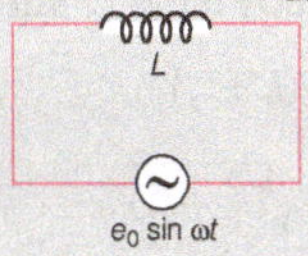

Current at any instant is

$I = I_0 \sin\left(\omega t - \dfrac{\pi}{2}\right)$

where

$I_0 = \dfrac{\varepsilon_0}{\omega L} = \dfrac{\varepsilon_0}{X_L}$

- **Phase relationship between ε and I.**
  The voltage is ahead of the current in phase by 90°.

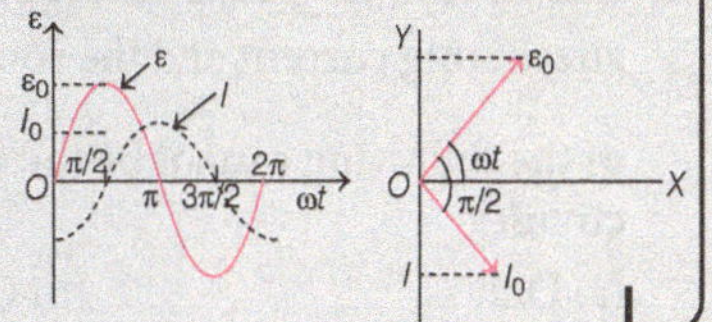

Inductive Reactance (X_L)

- The inductive reactance is the effective opposition offered by the inductor to the flow of current in the circuit.
- Its SI unit is ohm.
- $X_L = \omega L = 2\pi fL$

EXAM PATTERN QUESTIONS

Objective Type Questions

Multiple Choice Questions (MCQs)

1. The rms current in a circuit connected to a 50 Hz AC source is 15 A. The value of the current $\left(\frac{1}{600}\right)$s after its value becomes zero is **CBSE 2021, Term-I**

(a) $\frac{15}{\sqrt{2}}$ A (b) $15\sqrt{2}$ A

(c) $\frac{\sqrt{2}}{15}$ A (d) 8 A

2. A voltage signal is described by

$$V = V_0 \text{ for } 0 \le t \le \frac{T}{2}$$
$$= 0 \text{ for } \frac{T}{2} \le t \le T$$

for a cycle. Its rms value is **CBSE 2023**

(a) $\frac{V_0}{\sqrt{2}}$ (b) V_0 (c) $\frac{V_0}{2}$ (d) $\sqrt{2}\, V_0$

3. The rms value of a current given by $i = (i_1 \cos \omega t + i_2 \sin \omega t)$ is **CBSE 2024**

(a) $\frac{1}{\sqrt{2}}(i_1 + i_2)$ (b) $\frac{1}{\sqrt{2}}(i_1 - i_2)$

(c) $\frac{1}{\sqrt{2}}\sqrt{(i_1^2 + i_2^2)}$ (d) $\frac{1}{\sqrt{2}}(i_1^2 + i_2^2)$

4. A capacitor has a dielectric of dielectric constant 6, that completely occupies the space between its plates. If a current I flows through this capacitor when connected to an AC source, then what will be the current in the circuit when this dielectric is removed?

(a) $I/6$ (b) $I - 6$ (c) I (d) $6I$

5. In a circuit, the phase difference between the alternating current and the source voltage is $\frac{\pi}{2}$. Which of the following cannot be the element(s) of the circuit? **CBSE 2021, Term-I**

(a) Only C (b) Only L

(c) L and R (d) L or C

6. The voltage across a resistor, an inductor and a capacitor connected in series to an AC source are 20 V, 15 V and 30 V, respectively. The resultant voltage in the circuit is **CBSE 2021, Term-I**

(a) 5 V (b) 20 V (c) 25 V (d) 65 V

7. A 15Ω resistor, an 80 mH inductor and a capacitor of capacitance C are connected in series with a 50 Hz AC source. If the source voltage and current in the circuit are in phase, then the value of capacitance is **CBSE 2021, Term-I**

(a) 100 μF (b) 127 μF (c) 142 μF (d) 160 μF

8. A 300 Ω resistor and a capacitor of $\left(\frac{25}{\pi}\right)$μF are connected in series to a 200 V-50 Hz AC source. The current in the circuit is **CBSE 2021, Term-I**

(a) 0.1 A (b) 0.4 A (c) 0.6 A (d) 0.8 A

9. An iron cored coil is connected in series with an electric bulb with an AC source as shown in figure. When iron piece is taken out of the coil, the brightness of the bulb will **CBSE SQP 2023**

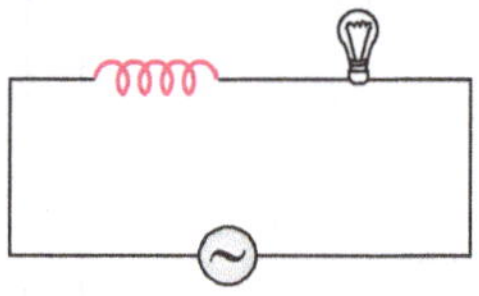

(a) decrease
(b) increase
(c) remain unaffected
(d) fluctuate

10. If the reading of the voltmeter V_1 is 40 V, then the reading of voltmeter V_2 is **CBSE SQP 2023**

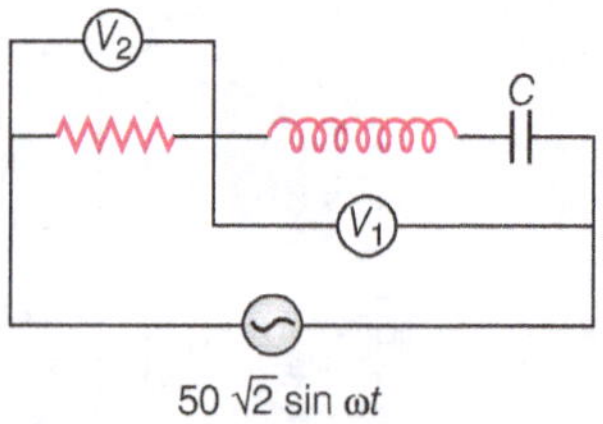

50 $\sqrt{2}$ sin ωt

(a) 30 V (b) 58 V

(c) 29 V (d) 15 V

11. The impedance of a series L-C-R circuit is **CBSE 2021, Term-I**

(a) $R + X_L + X_C$ (b) $\sqrt{\frac{1}{X_C^2} + \frac{1}{X_L^2} + R^2}$

(c) $\sqrt{X_L^2 - X_C^2 + R^2}$ (d) $\sqrt{R^2 + (X_L - X_C)^2}$

12. The L-C-R circuit is connected to source of an alternating current. At the resonance, the phase difference between current flowing in the circuit and potential difference will be

(a) zero (b) $\pi/4$ (c) $\pi/2$ (d) π

13. Which of the following graphs represent the variation of current (I) with frequency (f) in an AC circuit containing a pure capacitor? **CBSE SQP 2022, Term-I**

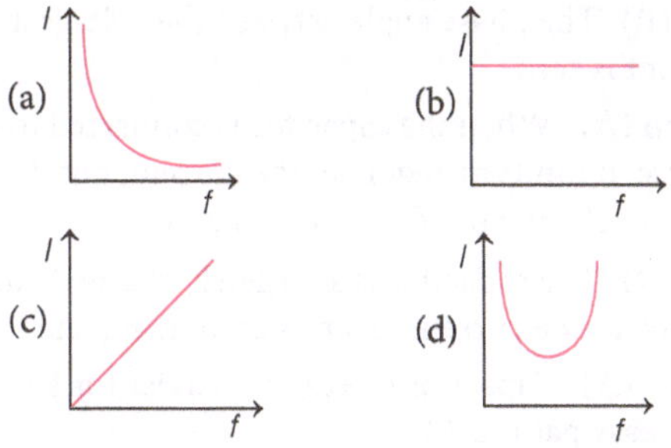

14. The alternating current I in an inductor is observed to vary with time t as shown in the graph for a cycle.

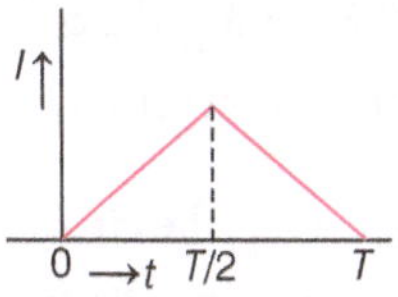

Which one of the following graphs is the correct representation of waveform of voltage V with time t? **CBSE 2025**

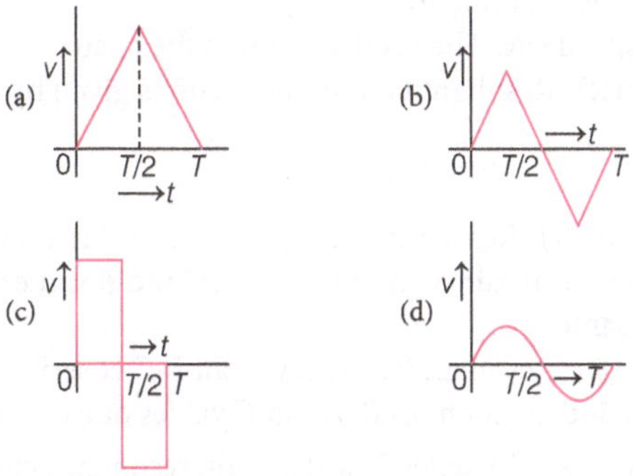

15. In an AC circuit, the power factor

(a) is zero when the circuit contains an ideal resistance only
(b) is unity when the circuit contains an ideal resistance only
(c) is unity when the circuit contains a capacitance only
(d) is unity when the circuit contains an ideal inductance only

16. If in an alternating circuit, the voltage is V and current is I, then the value of power dissipated in the circuit is

(a) VI (b) $VI/2$
(c) $VI/\sqrt{2}$
(d) depends upon the angle between V and I

17. The value of power factor is maximum in an alternating circuit, when circuit consists

(a) only inductive (b) only capacitive
(c) only L-C (d) only resistive

18. When an alternating voltage $E = E_0 \sin \omega t$ is applied to a circuit, a current $I = I_0 \sin\left(\omega t + \frac{\pi}{2}\right)$ flows through it. The average power dissipated in the circuit is **CBSE 2021, Term-I**

(a) $E_{rms} \cdot I_{rms}$ (b) $E_0 I_0$ (c) $\frac{E_0 I_0}{\sqrt{2}}$ (d) zero

19. An AC voltage $V = V_0 \sin \omega t$ is applied to a series combination of a resistor R and an element X. The instantaneous current in the circuit is $I = I_0 \sin\left(\omega t + \frac{\pi}{4}\right)$. Then, which of the following is correct? **CBSE 2023**

(a) X is a capacitor and $X_C = \sqrt{2} R$
(b) X is an inductor and $X_L = R$
(c) X is an inductor and $X_L = \sqrt{2} R$
(d) X is a capacitor and $X_C = R$

20. Which of the following statements about a series LCR circuit connected to an AC source is correct? **CBSE 2023**

(a) If the frequency of the source is incresed, the impedance of the circuit first decreases and then increases.
(b) If the net reactance $(X_L = X_C)$ of circuit becomes equal to its resistance, then the current leads the voltage by 45°.
(c) At resonance the voltage drop across the inductor is more than that across the capacitor.
(d) At resonance, the voltage drop across the capacitor is more than that across the inductor.

21. A conductor of $10\,\Omega$ is connected across a 6V ideal source. The power supplied by the source to the conductor is **CBSE 2023**

(a) 1.8 W (b) 2.4 W (c) 3.6 W (d) 7.2 W

22. An AC source $V = 282 \sin(100\,t)$ volt is connected across a 1 μF capacitor. The rms value of current in the circuit will be (take, $\sqrt{2} = 1.41$) **CBSE 2024**

(a) 10 mA (b) 20 mA (c) 40 mA (d) 80 mA

23. Figure shows the variation of inductive reactance X_L of two ideal inductors of inductances L_1 and L_2, with angular frequency ω. The value of $\frac{L_1}{L_2}$ is **CBSE 2024**

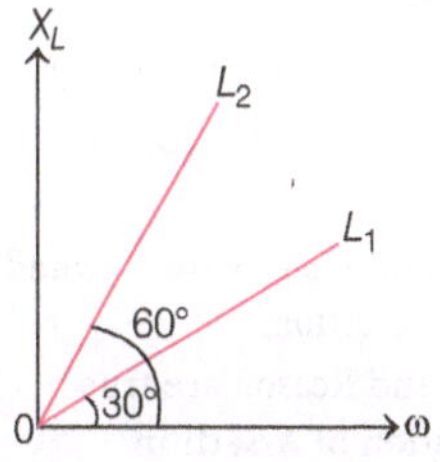

(a) $\sqrt{3}$ (b) $\frac{1}{\sqrt{3}}$ (c) 3 (d) $\frac{1}{3}$

24. The core of a transformer is laminated to reduce the effect of **CBSE 2021, Term-I**

(a) flux leakage (b) copper loss
(c) hysteresis loss (d) eddy current

25. A transformer is connected to a 200 V AC source. The transformer supplies 3000 V to a device. If the number of turns in the primary coil is 450, then the number of turns in its secondary coil is **CBSE 2025**

(a) 30 (b) 450 (c) 4500 (d) 6750

26. Match the Column I with Column II and choose the correct option.

	Column I		Column II
A.	Impedance (Z)	P.	$\frac{R}{Z}$
B.	Power factor ($\cos\phi$)	Q.	$\frac{1}{R^2+(X_L-X_C)^2}$
C.	Resonance frequency (f_0)	R.	$I_0 \times \frac{1}{\sqrt{2}}$
D.	rms value of current (I_{rms})	S.	$\frac{1}{2\pi\sqrt{LC}}$

	A	B	C	D
(a)	Q	P	S	R
(b)	P	Q	R	S
(c)	P	Q	S	R
(d)	R	S	Q	P

27. Match the Column I with Column II and choose the correct option.

	Column I		Column II
A.	Phase difference in pure inductor	P.	ωL
B.	Average power in pure capacitor	Q.	$\frac{\pi}{2}$
C.	Reactance of inductor	R.	Zero
D.	Voltage across a pure capacitor in a series L-C-R circuit	S.	$V_C = IX_C$

	A	B	C	D
(a)	S	R	Q	P
(b)	P	Q	R	S
(c)	Q	R	P	S
(d)	R	Q	S	P

Assertion-Reason

Directions (Q. Nos. 28-37) *In the following questions, two statements are given- one labelled Assertion and the other labelled Reason. Select the correct answer to these questions from the codes (a), (b), (c) and (d) as given below.*

(a) Both Assertion and Reason are true and Reason is the correct explanation of Assertion.
(b) Both Assertion and Reason are true but Reason is not the correct explanation of Assertion.
(c) Assertion is true but Reason is false.
(d) Assertion is false but Reason is true.

28. Assertion (A) Today, most of the electrical devices use/require AC voltage.
Reason (R) Most of the electrical energy sold by power companies is transmitted and distributed as alternating current.

29. Assertion (A) Phasors V and I for the case of a resistor are in the same direction.
Reason (R) The phase angle between the voltage and the current is zero.

30. Assertion (A) When the capacitor is connected to an AC source, it limits or regulates the current, but does not completely prevent the flow of charge.
Reason (R) The capacitor is alternately charged and discharged as the current reverses each half-cycle.

31. Assertion (A) Capacitor serves as a barrier for DC and offers an easy path to AC.
Reason (R) Capacitor reactance is inversely proportional to frequency.

32. Assertion (A) If $X_C > X_L$, the circuit is predominantly capacitive. The current in the circuit leads the source voltage.
Reason (R) If $X_C < X_L$, the circuit is predominantly inductive, the current in the circuit lags the source voltage.

33. Assertion (A) In a series R-L-C circuit, the voltages across resistor, inductor and capacitor are 8V, 16V and 10V, respectively. The resultant emf in the circuit is 10 V.
Reason (R) Resultant emf of the circuit is given by the relation.

$$E=\sqrt{V_R^2+(V_L-V_C)^2}$$

34. Assertion (A) Resonant frequencies of two different L-C-R series circuits with different L, C and R values may be same.
Reason (R) Resonant frequency of an L-C-R series circuit is independent of R, L and C values of a circuit.

35. Assertion (A) In series L-C-R circuit, resonance can take place.
Reason (R) Resonance takes place, if inductance and capacitive reactances are equal and opposite.

36. Assertion (A) The wire used for the windings of transformer has some resistance.
Reason (R) Energy is lost due to heat produced in the wire (I^2R).

37. Assertion (A) In an ideal step-down transformer, the electrical energy is not lost.
Reason (R) In a step-down transformer, voltage decreases but the current increases. **CBSE 2025**

Case Based Questions

Directions (Q.Nos. 38-40) *These questions are case study based questions. Read the following paragraph and answer the questions on the basis of same.*

38. **Transformer is a device, which is used to increase or decrease the alternating voltage. The transformers are of the following types**

1. Step-up transformer 2. Step-down transformer

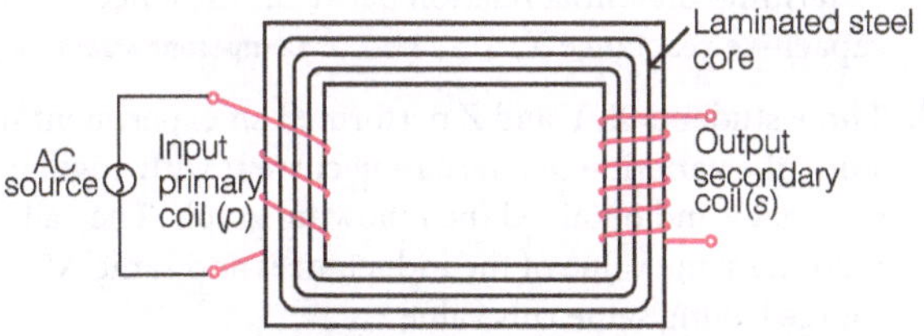

Transformer is based upon the principle of mutual induction. It consists of two coils, primary coil (*p*) and secondary coil (*s*), insulated from each other wounded on soft iron core. Often the primary coil is the input coil and secondary coil is the output coil. These soft iron cores are laminated to minimise eddy current loss.

(i) What is the cause of heating in a transformer?

(a) Eddy current (b) Direct current
(c) Alternating current (d) Induced current

(ii) Which quantities do not change during transformer operation?

(a) Power
(b) Frequency
(c) Voltage
(d) Both (a) and (b)

(iii) A transformer has 150 turns in its primary and 1000 in secondary. If the primary is connected to 440 V DC supply, what will be the induced voltage in the secondary side?

(a) 10 V (b) 3 V
(c) 5 V (d) Zero

(iv) The ratio of secondary to primary turns in an ideal transformer is 4 : 5. If power input is *P*, then the ratio of power output to power input is

(a) 4 : 9 (b) 9 : 4
(c) 5 : 4 (d) 1 : 1

(v) A power transmission line feeds input power at 2300 V to a step-down transformer with its primary windings having 4000 turns. What should be the number of turns in the secondary in order to get output power at 230 V?

(a) 600 (b) 550 (c) 400 (d) 375

39. Let an alternating source of emf $E = E_0 \sin \omega t$ is connected to a circuit having a pure inductance L. If I is the value of instantaneous current in the circuit, then $I = I_0 \sin\left(\omega t - \frac{\pi}{2}\right)$. The inductive reactance, $X_L = \omega L$ limits the current in a purely inductive circuit.

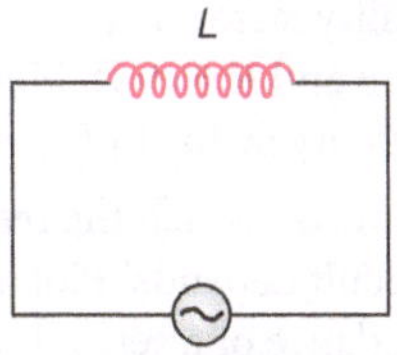

$E = E_0 \sin \omega t$

Answer the following questions based on above passage.

(i) What is the phase difference between E and I?

(ii) Draw the phasor diagram of the circuit containing pure inductor and connected to an AC voltage $E = E_0 \sin \omega t$.

(iii) What is the maximum value of current when inductance of 3 H is connected to 150 V - 50 Hz supply?

(iv) A 200 Hz AC is flowing in 15 mH coil. What is the value of reactance?

40. The average power over one full cycle of AC is given by $P_{av} = V_{rms} \cos \phi$ It is also known as true power. The term $\cos \phi$ is known as power factor, where ϕ is the phase difference between I_{rms} and E_{rms}.

Answer the following Questions based on above passage.

(i) What is the power factor of an AC circuit containing resistor and inductor?

(ii) What is the average power of an AC circuit containing purely inductance?

(iii) A resistor of 2Ω is connected to an AC supply 220 V- 150 Hz. What is the average power associated with the resistor?

(iv) A component X is connected to an AC supply $E = E_0 \sin \omega t$ such that maximum power factor is obtained. Identify the component X.

Subjective Questions

Very Short Answer Type Questions

1. In a series *L-C-R* circuit, the voltage across the resistance, capacitance and inductance is 10 V each. If the capacitance is short-circuited, what is the voltage across the inductance? **CBSE SQP 2024-25**

2. In a series *L-C-R* circuit, $V_L = V_C \neq V_R$. What is the value of power factor for this circuit?

3. Calculate the quality factor of a series *L-C-R* circuit with $L = 2.0$ H, $C = 2\,\mu$F and $R = 10\,\Omega$. Mention the significance of quality factor in *L-C-R* circuit.

4. Mention the factors on which the resonant frequency of a series *L-C-R* circuit depends. Plot a graph showing variation of impedance of a series *L-C-R* circuit with the frequency of the applied AC source. **CBSE 2024**

5. What happens to the impedance, current and phase difference between the voltage and current at resonant frequency in a series resonance *L-C-R* circuit? **Diksha**

6. With the help of a suitable diagram, explain the working of a step-up transformer. **CBSE 2024**

7. The primary of a transformer has 400 turns and the secondary has 2000 turns. If the power output from the secondary at 1000 V is 8 kW, calculate

(i) the primary voltage **[1]**

(ii) the heat loss in the primary coil, if the resistance of primary is 0.1 Ω and the efficiency of the transformer is 80%. **[1]**

Short Answer Type Questions

8. An alternating voltage $E = E_0 \sin \omega t$ is applied to a circuit containing a resistor *R* connected in series with a black box. The current in the circuit is found to be $I = I_0 \sin\left(\omega t + \frac{\pi}{4}\right)$.

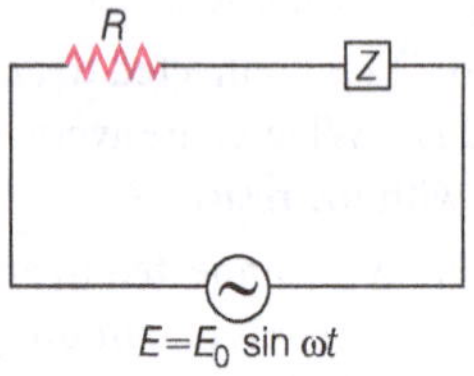

(i) State whether the element in the black box is a capacitor or inductor. **[1½]**

(ii) Draw the corresponding phasor diagram and find the impedance in terms of *R*. **[1½]**

9. An *L-C-R* circuit is connected to an AC voltage of fixed V_{max} and angular frequency. Current through the circuit is I_{max} and the resistance *R* equals the inductive reactance X_L in the circuit.
Now, if the distance of separation between the capacitor plates is doubled, the current I_{max} in the circuit is reduced to half.
Determine the initial relation between resistance *R* and capacitive reactance X_C. **Competency Based Que**

10. Three students *X*, *Y* and *Z* performed an experiment to study the variation of alternating current with angular frequency and obtained the following graph. They all used the same value of the inductances and same AC source having same rms value.

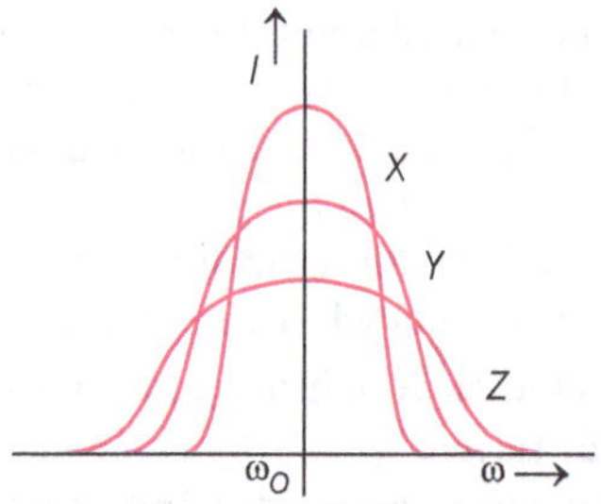

(i) What can be concluded (qualitatively) about the value of capacitance and resistance used by them? **[1]**

(ii) In which case, will the quality factor be maximum **[1]**

(iii) Comment on the nature of the impedance of the setup at the frequency ω_0. **Diksha [1]**

11. (i) An AC source $V = V_m \sin \omega t$ is connected across an ideal capacitor. Derive the expression for the

(a) current flowing in the circuit and **[1½]**

(b) reactance of the capacitor. Plot a graph of current *i versus* ωt. **[1½]**

Or

(ii) A series combination of an inductor *L*, a capacitor *C* and a resistor *R* is connected across an AC source of voltage in a circuit. Obtain an expression for the average power consumed by the circuit. Find power factor for (a) purely inductive circuit, and (b) purely resistive circuit. **CBSE 2023**

12. Prove mathematically that the average value of alternating current over one complete cycle is zero.

13. Draw the graph showing the variation of reactance of (i) a capacitor (ii) an inductor with the angular frequency of an AC circuit.

14. Distinguish between resistance, reactance and impedance for AC circuit.

15. An AC source generating a voltage $E = E_0 \sin \omega t$ is connected to a capacitor of capacitance C. Find the expression for the current I flowing through it. Plot graph of E *versus* I to show that the current is ahead of the voltage by $\pi/2$.

Or

An AC voltage $V = V_0 \sin \omega t$ is applied across a pure inductor of inductance L. Find an expression for the current I, flowing in the circuit and show mathematically that the current flowing through it lags behind the applied voltage by a phase angle of $\frac{\pi}{2}$. Also, draw graphs of V *versus* I for the circuit. **CBSE SQP 2023**

16. Show mathematically that an ideal inductor does not consume any power in an AC circuit.

17. Discuss the use of transformer for long distance transmission of electrical energy.

18. What are the factors which reduces the efficiency of the transformer?

19. An ideal resistor R, an ideal inductor L and an ideal capacitor C are connected one by one across the same source of AC voltage $V = V_0 \sin \omega t$. It is observed that the same current I flows in each case. **CBSE 2024C**

(i) What will be the instantaneous value of current that will flow through their series combination when connected across the same source? **[1½]**

(ii) How will the current in each case be affected, if the frequency of the source is increased ? **[1½]**

Justify your answers.

20. (i) When an AC source is connected to an ideal inductor, show that the average power supplied by the source over a complete cycle is zero. **[1½]**

(ii) A lamp is connected in series with an inductor and an AC source. What happens to the brightness of the lamp when the key is plugged in and an iron rod is inserted inside the inductor? Explain. **[1½]**

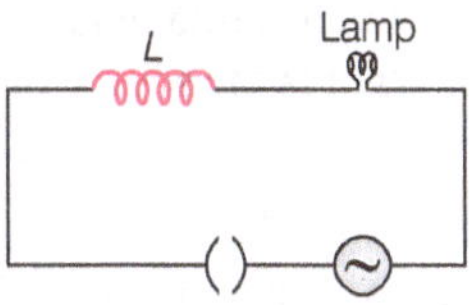

21. A capacitor C, a variable resistance R and a bulb B are connected in series to the AC mains in circuit as shown in the figure. The bulb glows with some brightness. How will the glow of the bulb change, if

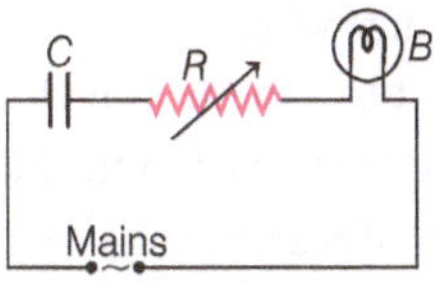

(i) a dielectric slab is introduced between the plates of the capacitor, keeping resistance R to be same ? **[1½]**

(ii) the resistance R is increased keeping the same capacitance? **[1½]**

22. (i) The graphs (a) and (b) represent the variation of the opposition offered by the circuit element to the flow of alternating current with frequency of the applied emf. Identify the circuit elements corresponding to each graph. **[1½]**

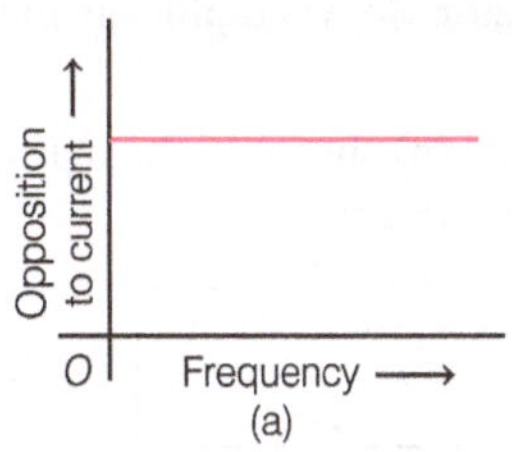

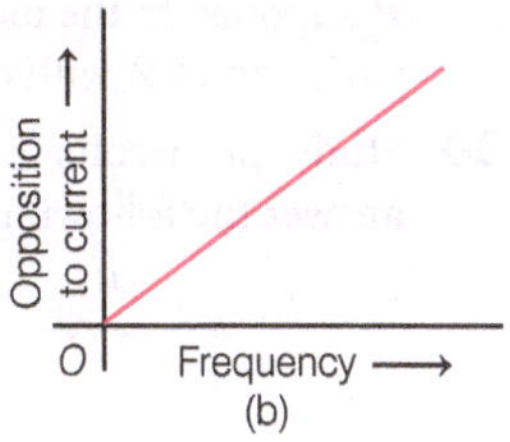

(ii) Write the expression for the impedance offered by the series combination of the above two elements connected across the AC source. Which will be ahead in phase in this circuit, voltage or current? **[1½]**

Long Answer Type Questions

23. Find the expression for the true power and apparent power in an AC circuit. Determine the condition so that current in the circuit may be wattless.

24. An AC source of voltage, $V = V_m \sin \omega t$, is applied across a series L-C-R circuit. Draw the phasor diagram for this circuit when the,

(i) capacitive impedance exceeds the inductive impedance. **[3]**

(ii) inductive impedance exceeds the capacitive impedance. **[2]**

25. Differentiate between the peak value and root mean square value of an alternating current. Derive the expression for the root mean square value of alternating current, in terms of its peak value. **CBSE 2025**

26. Obtain the expression for the average power consumed in a series L-C-R circuit connected to AC source for which the phase difference between the voltage and the current in the circuit is ϕ.

27. An inductor L of inductance X_L is connected in series with a bulb B and an AC source. How would brightness of the bulb change when

(i) number of turns in the inductor is reduced? **[2]**

(ii) an iron rod is inserted in the inductor? **[1½]**

(iii) a capacitor of reactance $X_C = X_L$ is inserted in series in the circuit? Justify your answer in each case. **[1½]**

28. Answer the following questions.

(i) What is the minimum value of the power factor of a circuit? Under what circumstances can it occur? **[2½]**

(ii) State the maximum value of the power factor? Under what circumstances can this occur? **[2½]**

29. An AC voltage $V = V_m \sin \omega t$ is applied across an inductor of inductance L. Find the instantaneous power P_i supplied to the inductor. Show graphically the variation of P_i with ωt.

30. Study the circuits (a) and (b) shown in the figure and answer the following questions:

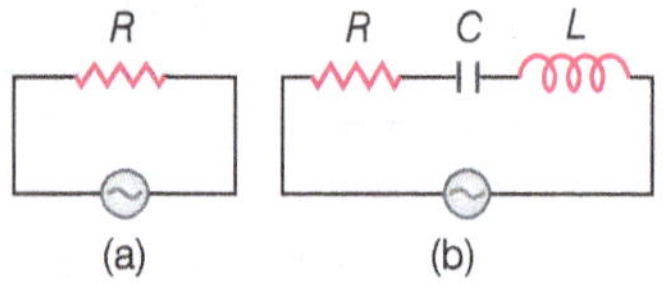

(i) Under which conditions would the rms currents in the two circuits be the same? **[2½]**

(ii) Can the rms current in circuit (b) be larger than that in (a)? **NCERT Exemplar** **[2½]**

31. In the L-C-R circuit, shown in the figure, the AC driving voltage is $V = V_m \sin \omega t$.

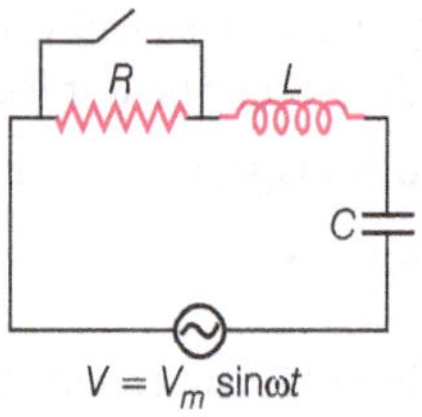

(i) Write down the equation of motion for $q(t)$. **[2]**

(ii) At $t = t_0$, the voltage source stops and R is short circuited. Now, write down how much energy is stored in each of L and C? **[1½]**

(iii) Describe subsequent motion of charges. **[1½]**

NCERT Exemplar

32. An AC source of voltage $V = V_0 \sin \omega t$ is connected to a series combination of L, C and R. Use the phasor diagram to obtain expressions for impedance of the circuit and phase angle between voltage and current. Find the condition when current will be in phase with the voltage. What is the circuit in the condition called?

33. (i) Show that a series L-C-R circuit at resonance behaves as a purely resistive circuit. Compare the phase relation between current and voltage in series L-C-R circuit for

(a) $X_L > X_C$ (b) $X_L = X_C$ using phasor diagrams. **[2½]**

(ii) What is an acceptor circuit and where it is used? **[2½]**

34. A device X is connected to an AC source, $V = V_0 \sin \omega t$. The variation of voltage, current and power in one cycle is shown in the following graph.

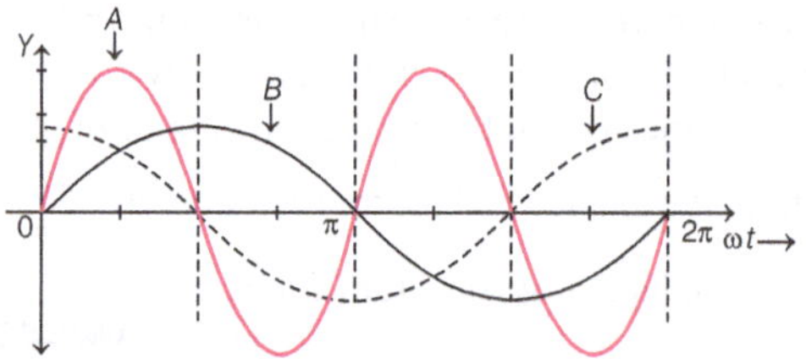

(i) Identify the device X. **[1]**

(ii) Which of the curves A, B and C represent the voltage, current and the power consumed in the circuit? Justify the answer. **[1]**

(iii) How does its impedance vary with frequency of the AC source? Show graphically. **[1]**

(iv) Obtain an expression for the current in the circuit and its phase relation with AC voltage. **[2]**

35. A device X is connected across an AC source of voltage $V = V_0 \sin \omega t$. The current through X is given as $I = I_0 \sin\left(\omega t + \frac{\pi}{2}\right)$.

(i) Identify the device X and write the expression for its reactance. **[1]**

(ii) Draw graphs showing variation of voltage and current with time over one cycle of AC, for X. **[1]**

(iii) How does the reactance of the device X vary with frequency of the AC? Show this variation graphically. **[1]**

(iv) Draw the phasor diagram for the device X. **[2]**

36. Explain briefly, with the help of a labelled diagram, the basic principle of the working of an AC generator. In an AC generator, coil of N turns and area A is rotated at an angular velocity ω in a uniform magnetic field B. Derive an expression for the instantaneous value of the emf induced in coil. What is the source of energy generation in this device?

Or

(i) With the help of a diagram, explain the principle of a device which changes a low AC voltage into a high voltage. **[3]**

Deduce the expression for the ratio of secondary voltage to the primary voltage in terms of the ratio of the number of turns of primary and secondary winding. For an ideal transformer, obtain the ratio of primary and secondary currents in terms of the ratio of the voltages in the secondary and primary coils.

(ii) Write any two sources of the energy losses which occur in actual transformers. **[1]**

(iii) A step-up transformer converts a low input voltage into a high output voltage. Does it violate law of conservation of energy? Explain.

CBSE SQP 2024-25 **[1]**

Numerical Problems

Alternating Current

37. An alternating voltage given by $E = 140 \sin 314t$ V is connected across a pure resistor of 50 Ω. Find

(i) the frequency of the source. **[1]**

(ii) the rms current through the resistor. **[1]**

38. A device X is connected to an AC source $V = V_0 \sin \omega t$. The variation of voltage, current and power in one complete cycle is shown in the following figure.

(i) Which curve shows power consumption over a full cycle? **[1]**

(ii) Identify the device X.

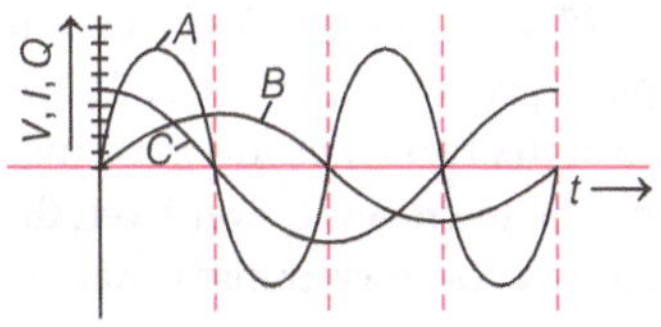

NCERT Exemplar **[1]**

39. A 60 μF capacitor is connected to a 110 V, 60 Hz AC supply. Determine the rms value of current in the circuit. What is the net power absorbed over a complete cycle? Explain. **NCERT**

Different Types of AC Circuit

40. A resistor of 30 Ω and a capacitor of $\frac{250}{\pi}$ μF are connected in series to a 200 V, 50 Hz AC source. Calculate (a) the current in the circuit and (b) voltage drops across the resistor and the capacitor (c) Is the algebraic sum of these voltages more than the source voltage? If yes, solve the paradox.

Or

A series L-C-R circuit with $R = 20\ \Omega$, $L = 2$ H and $C = 50$ μF is connected to a 200V AC source of variable frequency.

What is (a) the amplitude of the current and (b) the average power transferred to the circuit in one complete cycle, at resonance? (c) Calculate the potential drop across the capacitor. **CBSE 2023**

41. A resistor of 50 Ω, a capacitor of $\left(\frac{25}{\pi}\right)$ μF and an inductor of $\left(\frac{4}{\pi}\right)$ H are connected in series across an AC sources whose voltage (in volt) is given by $V = 70 \sin(100\ \pi t)$. Calculate

(i) the net reactance of the circuit. **[1]**

(ii) the impedance of the circuit. **[1]**

(iii) the effective value of current in the circuit. **CBSE 2023** **[1]**

42. A series RL circuit with $R = 10\ \Omega$ and $L = \left(\frac{100}{\pi}\right)$ mH is connected to an AC source of voltage $V = 141 \sin(100\ \pi\, t)$, where V is in volts and t is in seconds. Calculate

(i) impedance of the circuit, **[1]**

(ii) phase angle and **[1]**

(iii) voltage drop across the inductor **CBSE 2023** **[1]**

43. A series CR circuit with $R = 200\ \Omega$ and $C = (50 / \pi)$ μF is connected across an AC source of peak voltage $E_0 = 100$ V and frequency $\nu = 50$ Hz. Calculate (i) impedance of the circuit (Z), (ii) phase angle (ϕ) and (iii) voltage across the resistor. **CBSE 2023**

44. (i) Find the value of the phase difference between the current and the voltage in the series L-C-R circuit shown below. Which one leads in phase, current or voltage? **[2]**

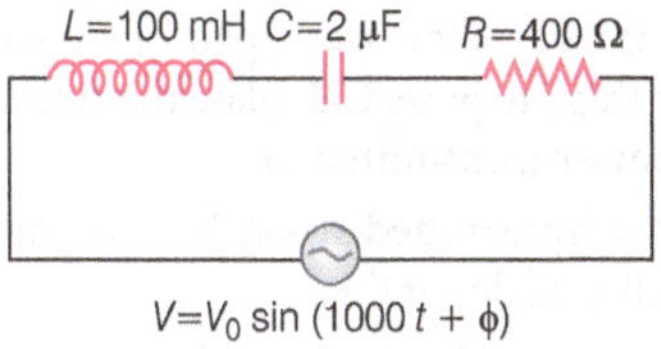

(ii) Without making any other change, find the value of the additional capacitor C', to be connected in parallel with the capacitor C, in order to make the power factor of the circuit unity. **[3]**

45. Determine the value of phase difference between the current and the voltage in the given series L-C-R circuit.

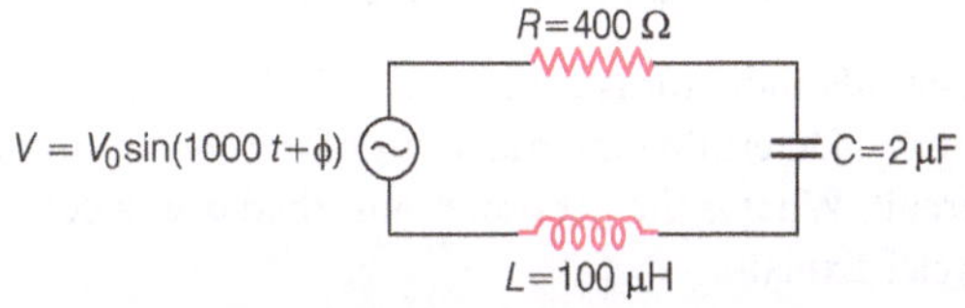

46. A 2 μF capacitor, 100 Ω resistor and 8 H inductor are connected in series with an AC source.

(i) What should be the frequency of the source such that current drawn in the circuit is maximum? What is this frequency called?

(ii) If the peak value of emf of the source is 200 V, find the maximum current.

47. A series *L-C-R* circuit connected to a variable frequency 230 V source has $L = 5.0$ H, $C = 80\ \mu$F, $R = 40\ \Omega$, as shown in the figure.

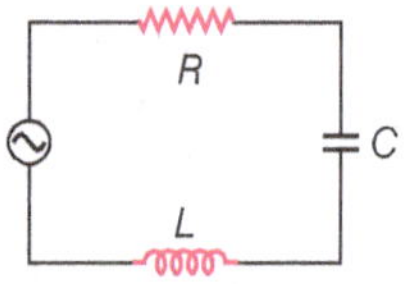

(i) Determine the source frequency which drives the circuit in resonance. [1]

(ii) Obtain the impedance of the circuit and amplitude of current at the resonant frequency. [1]

(iii) Determine the rms potential drop across the three elements of the circuit. Show that the potential drop across the *L-C* combination is zero at the resonating frequency. NCERT [1]

48. The electric mains in a house are marked 220 V, 50 Hz. Write down the equation for instantaneous voltage.

49. A series *L-C-R* circuit is connected to an AC source (200 V, 50 Hz). The voltages across the resistor, capacitor and inductor are respectively 200 V, 250 V and 250 V.

(i) The algebraic sum of the voltages across the three elements is greater than the voltage of the source. How is this paradox resolved? [3]

(ii) Given the value of the resistance of *R* is 40 Ω, calculate the current in the circuit. [2]

Average Power Circuit

50. 1 MW power is to be delivered from a power station to a town 10 km away. One uses a pair of Cu wires of radius 0.5 cm for this purpose. Calculate the fraction of ohmic losses to power transmitted, if

(i) power is transmitted at 220 V. Comment on the feasibility of doing this. [1½]

(ii) a step-up transformer is used to boost the voltage at 11000 V, power transmitted, then a step-up transformer is used to bring voltage is 220 V. (Take, $\rho_{Cu} = 1.7 \times 10^{-8}$ SI unit) NCERT Exemplar [1½]

51. What is the power dissipation in an AC circuit in which voltage and current are given by
$E = 300 \sin(\omega t + \pi/2)$ and $I = 5 \sin \omega t$?

52. A 44 mH inductor is connected to 220 V, 50 Hz AC supply. Determine the rms value of the current in the circuit. What is the net power absorbed over a complete cycle? Explain. NCERT

Transformer

53. How much current is drawn by the primary coil of a transformer, which step-down 220 V-44 V to operate a device with an impedance of 440 Ω?

54. A step-up transformer is operated on a 2.5 kV line. It supplies a load with 20 A. The ratio of the primary winding to the secondary is 10 : 1. If the transformer is 90% efficient, calculate

(i) the power output, [1]

(ii) the voltage and [1]

(iii) the current in the secondary. [1]

55. How much current is drawn by the primary of a transformer connected to 220 V supply when it delivers power to a 110 V-550 W refrigerator?

56. A power transmission line feeds input power at 2200 V to a step-down transformer with its primary winding having 3000 turns. Find the number of turns in the secondary windings to get the power output at 220 V.

57. A step-up transformer operates on a 220 V line and supplies a load of 2 A. The ratio of the primary to the secondary windings is 1:25. Determine the secondary voltage, primary current and power output. Assume efficiency to be 100%.

58. A small town with a demand of 800 kW of electric power at 220 V is situated 15 km away from an electric plant generating power at 440 V. The resistance of the two wires line carrying power is 0.5 Ω/km. The town gets power from the line through a 4000-220 V step-down transformer at a sub-station in the town.

(i) Estimate the line power of loss in the form of heat. [1]

(ii) How much power of the plant supply, assuming there is negligible power loss due to leakage? [1]

(iii) Characterise the step-up transformer at the plant. [1]

59. Do the same question as above with the replacement of the earlier transformer by a 40000-220 V step-down transformer (neglect, as before, leakage losses though this may not be a good assumption any longer because of the very high voltage transmission involved). Hence, explain why high voltage transmission is preferred?

60. A step-down transformer is used at 220 V to provide a current of 0.5 A to a 15 W bulb. If the secondary has 20 turns, find the number of turns in the primary coil and the current that flows in the primary coil.

61. A 100% efficient transformer has n_1 turns in its primary and n_2 turns in its secondary. If the power input to the transformer is W (watt), what is the power output?

62. A transformer has 150 turns in its primary and 1000 in secondary. If the primary is connected to 440 V DC supply, what will be the induced voltage in the secondary side?

Hints & Solutions

Objective Type Questions

1. (a)	2. (a)	5. (c)	6. (c)	7. (b)
8. (b)	9. (b)	10. (a)	11. (d)	12. (a)
15. (b)	16. (d)	17. (d)	18. (d)	19. (d)
20. (b)	21. (c)	24. (d)		

3. (c) The rms value of a current is given as follows

$$i_{\text{rms}} = \sqrt{\frac{i_0^{\,2}}{2}}, \text{ where } i_0 \text{ is the peak value of current}$$

Now $i = (i_1 \cos \omega t + i_2 \sin \omega t)$, then

$$i_{\text{rms}} = \sqrt{\frac{i_1^2 + i_2^2 + i_1\, i_2 \cos 90°}{2}}$$

$$i_{\text{rms}} = \sqrt{\frac{i_1^2}{2} + \frac{i_2^2}{2}} = \sqrt{\frac{i_1^2 + i_2^2}{2}}$$

$$i_{\text{rms}} = \frac{1}{\sqrt{2}}\sqrt{i_1^2 + i_2^2}$$

4. (a) Using Ohm's law for a capacitor, current in the capacitor,

$$I = C\left(\frac{dV}{dt}\right), \text{ where } C \text{ is the capacitance, then } C' = \frac{C}{6}$$

Hence, current in the circuit will be

$$I' = C'\left(\frac{dV}{dt}\right) = \left(\frac{C}{6}\right)\left(\frac{dV}{dt}\right) = \frac{1}{6}\left(C\frac{dV}{dt}\right) = \frac{I}{6}$$

14. (c) Instantaneous voltage, $V_0 \sin \omega t - L\dfrac{dI}{dt}$

Here $\omega t = 0$, since angular frequency is zero.

$$\therefore \quad |V| = L\frac{dI}{dt}$$

From 0 to $\dfrac{T}{2}$, slope of I is constant and positive.

$\therefore$ V is constant and positive.

from $\dfrac{T}{2}$ to T slope is negative and constant.

22. (b) Given, $V = 282 \sin(100t)$ V

$$C = 1\,\mu\text{F} = 10^{-6}\text{ F}$$

Pure capacitive, $X_C = \dfrac{1}{\omega C} = \dfrac{1}{100 \times 10^{-6}} = 10^4\,\Omega$

$$I_0 = \frac{V_0}{X_C} = \frac{282}{10^4} = 28.2\text{ mA}$$

$$I_{\text{rms}} = \frac{I_0}{\sqrt{2}} = \frac{28.2}{\sqrt{2}}$$

$$I_{\text{rms}} = 20\text{ mA}$$

23. (d) In the graph between inductive reactance X_L and angular frequency ω, slope gives the value of inductance. The slope is also given by tan θ, where θ is the angle between slope of X_L - ω graph and ω.

From the graph,

$$L_1 = \tan 30° = \frac{1}{\sqrt{3}} \text{ and } L_2 = \tan 60° = \sqrt{3}$$

So, $$\frac{L_1}{L_2} = \frac{\frac{1}{\sqrt{3}}}{\sqrt{3}} = \frac{1}{3}$$

25. (d) $\dfrac{V_S}{V_P} = \dfrac{N_S}{N_P} \Rightarrow \dfrac{3000}{200} = \dfrac{N_S}{450}$

$\Rightarrow N_S = 6750$

26. (a) $A \to Q, B \to P, C \to S, D \to R$.

27. (c) $A \to Q, B \to R, C \to P, D \to S$

28. (a) **29.** (a) **30.** (a)

31. (a) **32.** (b)

33. (a) The resultant emf in the L-C-R circuit is given by

$$E = \sqrt{V_R^2 + (V_L - V_C)^2}$$

$$\Rightarrow \quad E = \sqrt{(8)^2 + (16 - 10)^2}$$

$$\Rightarrow \quad E = \sqrt{64 + 36}$$

$$\Rightarrow \quad E = 10\text{ V}$$

34. (c) Resonant angular frequency is

$$\omega_r = \frac{1}{\sqrt{LC}} \Rightarrow \nu_r = \frac{1}{2\pi\sqrt{LC}}\text{ Hz}$$

For the case, $L_1C_1 = L_2C_2$, if product remains same for two values of L and C, then ω_r will be same in such case and resonant frequency of an L-C-R series circuit is independent of R only.

A is correct but R is incorrect.

35. (a) **36.** (b) **37.** (b)

38. (i) (a) The alternating magnetic flux in transformer casues eddy currents in its core which produce heating effect in the transformer.

(ii) (d) The power and frequency do not change in a transformer operation.

(iii) (d) As transformer works only in AC and in case of DC supply, there is no induced emf or voltage in secondary because there is no change in flux through the transformer circuit.

(iv) (d) In an ideal transformer, there is no energy loss and flux is completely confined with the magnetic core, i.e. perfectly coupled.

So, $\frac{P_{out}}{P_{in}} = 1$

(v) (c) Here, $\varepsilon_p = 2300$ V, $N_p = 4000$, $\varepsilon_s = 230$ V

Let N_s be the required number of turns in the secondary.

As, $\frac{\varepsilon_s}{\varepsilon_p} = \frac{N_s}{N_p}$

$$\Rightarrow \quad N_s = N_p\left(\frac{\varepsilon_s}{\varepsilon_p}\right) = 4000\left(\frac{230\text{ V}}{2300\text{ V}}\right) = 400$$

39. (i) The phase difference between E and I is $\frac{\pi}{2}$. The voltage E leads the current I by phase angle $\frac{\pi}{2}$.

(ii) The phasor diagram is given by

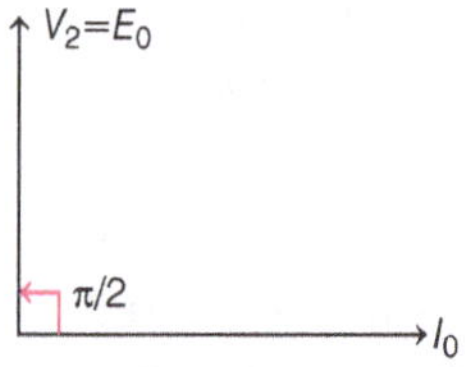

(iii) $L = 3$ H, $E_{rms} = 150$ V, $f = 50$ Hz

$$I_0 = \frac{E_0}{X_L} = \frac{\sqrt{2}\,E_{rms}}{2\pi f L} = \frac{\sqrt{2} \times 150}{2\pi \times 50 \times 3} = 0.225\text{ A}$$

(iv) $f = 200$ Hz, $L = 15$ mH $= 15 \times 10^{-3}$ H

$\therefore$ Inductive reactance, $X_L = \omega L = 2\pi f L$

$$= 2\pi \times 200 \times 15 \times 10^{-3}$$

$$= 18.84\ \Omega$$

40. (i) The power factor is given by

$$\cos\phi = \frac{R}{Z}$$

For a circuit containing resistor and inductor

$$Z = \sqrt{R^2 + (\omega L)^2}$$

$$\therefore \quad \cos\phi = \frac{R}{\sqrt{R^2 + (\omega L)^2}}$$

(ii) For purely inductive circuit, $\phi = \frac{\pi}{2}$

$$\therefore P_{av} = E_{rms} I_{rms} \cos\phi = E_{rms} I_{rms} \cos\frac{\pi}{2} = 0$$

(iii) $R = 2\,\Omega$, $E_{rms} = 220$ V, $f = 150$ Hz

$\therefore$ For a circuit containing only resistor

$\phi = 0° \Rightarrow \cos\phi = 0$

$$\therefore P_{av} = \frac{E_{rms}^2}{R} = \frac{(220)^2}{2} = 24200\text{ W}$$

(iv) For maximum power factor, $\cos\phi = 1$

$\therefore \phi = 0°$ (for purely resistive circuit)

$\Rightarrow X$ is resistance.

Subjective Questions

1. Given, voltage are equal, i.e. 10 V in each, then the impedance of all the elements is same.

$$R = X_L = X_C$$

Total voltage, $V = I\sqrt{R^2 + (X_L - X_C)^2} = IR = 10$ V

When capacitance is short-circuited, then the voltage across the inductance will be

$$I = \frac{V}{\sqrt{R^2 + X_L^2}} = \frac{10}{\sqrt{2}R} \Rightarrow IX_L = IR = \frac{10}{\sqrt{2}}\text{ V}$$

2. Power factor,

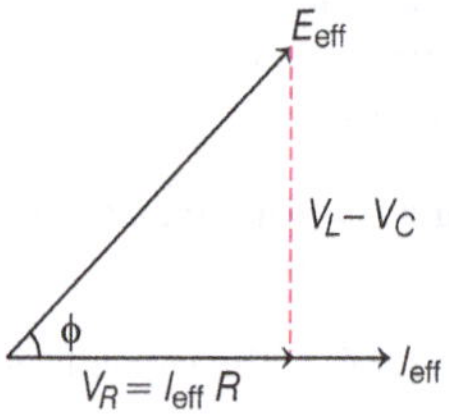

$$\cos\phi = \frac{V_R}{\sqrt{V_R^2 + (V_L - V_C)^2}}$$

Since $\quad V_L = V_C$

$$\therefore \quad \cos\phi = \frac{V_R}{V_R} = 1$$

The value of power factor is 1.

3. We have, $Q = \frac{1}{R}\sqrt{\frac{L}{C}} = \frac{1}{10}\sqrt{\frac{2}{2 \times 10^{-6}}} = 100$

It signifies the sharpness of resonance.

4. In a series LCR circuit, the resonant frequency is given as $f_0 = \frac{1}{2\pi\sqrt{LC}}$

From the above formula, it is clear that resonant frequency depends on the value of inductance L and capacitance C present in the circuit.

The graph between impedance and frequency is given below.

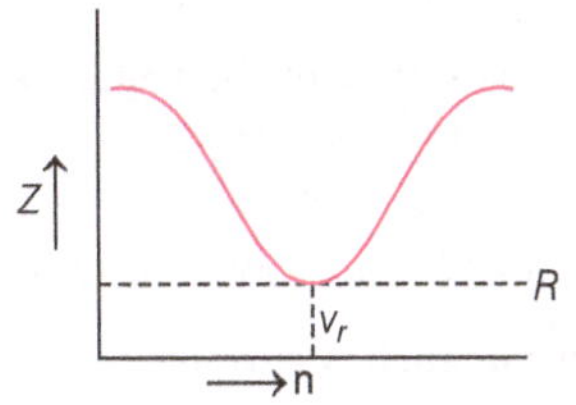

5. At resonant frequency, the capacitive reactance is equal to the inductive reactance. therefore the impedance of the circuit is reduced and it becomes ohmic resistance.

When the impedance is reduced, the current becomes maximum. The circuit now behaves as purely ohmic. Therefore, the phase difference between the voltage and current is zero, i.e. the voltage is in phase with the current.

6. The diagram of a step-up transformer is shown in the following figure.

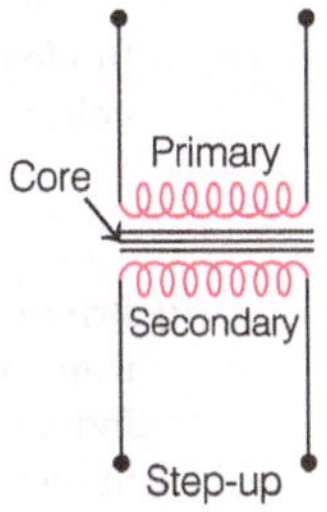

Working The given source of emf, say AC mains, is always connected to the primary coil. When alternating current flows through the primary coil, then in each cycle of current, the core is magnetised once in one direction and once in the opposite direction.

Hence, an alternating magnetic flux is produced in the core.

Since the secondary coil is also wound on the same core, the magnetic flux passing through it changes continuously due to the repeated magnetisation and demagnetisation of the core. Therefore, by mutual induction, an alternating emf of the same frequency is induced in the secondary coil.

7. (i) $E_1 = \frac{N_1 E_2}{N_2} = 400 \times \frac{1000}{2000} = 200$ V

(ii) Output power × 100/ Input power = 80

8000 × 100 / Input power = 80

Input power = 10000 W

Also, Input power $= E_1 I_1 = 10000$

$200 \times I_1 = 10000$

$I_1 = 50$ A

Heat loss in the primary coil

$= I_1^2 R_1 = 50 \times 50 \times 0.1 = 250$ W

8. Given, alternating voltage, $E = E_0 \sin \omega t$

Current in the circuit,

$$I = I_0 \sin\left(\omega t + \frac{\pi}{4}\right)$$

(i) $E = E_0 \sin \omega t$

$$I = I_0 \sin\left(\omega t + \frac{\pi}{4}\right)$$

Current is leading by $\frac{\pi}{4}$. Hence, box must be the capacitor.

(ii) Phasor diagram,

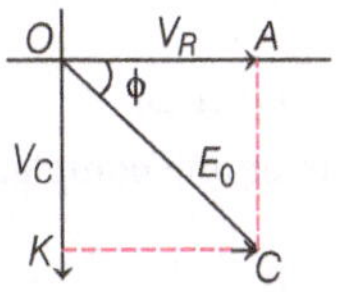

$$\tan \phi = \frac{OK}{OA} = \frac{AC}{OA} = \frac{V_C}{V_R} = \frac{-I_0 X_C}{I_0 R} = \frac{-X_C}{R}$$

From diagram, $AK^2 = OA^2 + OK^2$

$$= \sqrt{OA^2 + AC^2} = \sqrt{(I_0 R)^2 + (-I_0 X_C)^2}$$

Then, $E_0 = I_0 \sqrt{R^2 + X_C^2}$

$\therefore \quad Z = \frac{E_0}{I_0}$

Impedance, $Z = \sqrt{R^2 + X_C^2}$

9. For the distance between the plates doubled,

$$C' = \frac{kA}{2d} = \frac{C}{2}$$

So, capacitive reactance, $X'_C = 2X_C$

For the current I_{max} to be reduced to half,

impedance $Z' = 2Z$

$$\sqrt{R^2 + (X_L - X'_C)^2} = 2\sqrt{R^2 + (X_L - X_C)^2}$$

$$R^2 + (X_L - X'_C)^2 = 4\,[R^2 + (X_L - X_C)^2]$$

$$R^2 + (X_L - 2X_C)^2 = 4\,[R^2 + (X_L - X_C)^2]$$

Substituting $X_L = R$ and solving, we get.

$$X_C = \frac{3R}{2}$$

10. (i) $\omega_0 = \frac{1}{(LC)^{1/2}}$

$L_X = L_Y = L_Z$

Thus, $C_X = C_Y = C_Z$

Also, $I_0 = \frac{E_0}{R}$, i.e. $I_0 \propto R$

Since, $I_{0X} > I_{0Y} > I_{0Z}$

$R_X < R_Y < R_Z$

(ii) $Q = \frac{\omega L}{R}$

Since ω and L are same, $Q \propto \frac{1}{R}$

$Q_X > Q_Y > Q_Z$

(iii) At resonance, $Z = R$

Thus, the impedance is purely resistive in nature.

11. (i) Refer to text on pages no. 228 and 229.

Or

(ii) Refer to text on pages no. 232 and 233.

12. The instantaneous value of an alternating current is given by

$$I = I_0 \sin \omega t$$

Its average value over one complete cycle will be given as

$$I_{av} = \frac{\int_0^T I dt}{\int_0^T dt}$$

$$\text{or } I_{av} = \frac{\int_0^T I_0 \sin \omega t \, dt}{\int_0^T dt} = \frac{\frac{I_0}{\omega}[\cos \omega t]_0^T}{[t]_0^T}$$

$$= -\frac{\frac{I_0}{\omega}[\cos 2\pi - \cos 0]}{[T - 0]} \quad [\because \omega T = 2\pi]$$

$$= -\frac{I_0}{\omega}(1 - 1) = 0$$

13. (i)

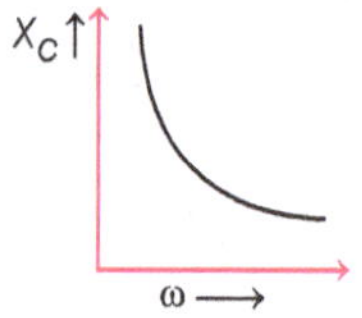

(ii)

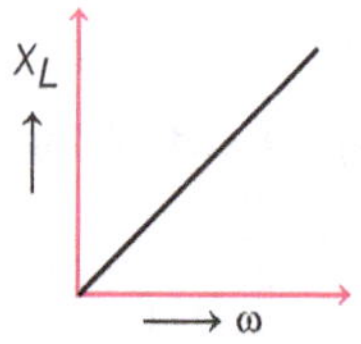

14. The basic function of the three is the same i.e. to oppose the flow of current through the circuit. But the difference lie in their expressions. As,

Resistance, $R = V/I$

Capacitive reactance, $X_C = \frac{1}{\omega C}$

Inductive reactance, $X_L = \omega L$

Impedance, $Z = \sqrt{R^2 + (X_L - X_C)^2}$

15. Refer to text on pages 227 and 228.

16. Refer to text on pages 232 and 233.

17. Refer to text on page 235.

18. Refer to text on page 235.

19. (i) Current, $I = \frac{V}{Z}$

$$= \frac{V_0 \sin \omega t}{\sqrt{R^2 + (X_L - X_C)^2}}$$

For the same source of AC voltage and current is same in all the three cases.

$$R = X_L = X_C$$

When L, R and C are joined in series $Z = R$.

Hence instantaneous current, $I = \frac{V_0}{R} \sin \omega t$

(ii) If frequency of the source is increased, current in pure resistive circuit will remain same as ohmic resistance is independent of frequency.

Current is pure inductive circuit will decreases

as $\quad X_L \propto V$

so, $\quad I \propto \frac{1}{V}$

Current in pure capacitive circuit will increase as

$$I \propto V$$

20. (i) As, $P_{av} = V_{rms} I_{rms} \cos \phi$

In ideal inductor, current I_{rms} lags behind applied voltage V_{rms} by $\pi/2$.

$\therefore \quad \phi = \pi/2$

Thus, $P_{av} = V_{rms} I_{rms} \cos \pi/2 = V_{rms} I_{rms} \times 0 = 0$

(ii) Brightness of the lamp decreases. It is because when iron rod is inserted inside the inductor, its inductance L increases, thereby increasing its inductive reactance X_L and hence impedance Z of the circuit. As $I_{rms} = \frac{V_{rms}}{Z}$, so this decreases the current I_{rms} in the circuit and hence the brightness of lamp.

21. (i) As the dielectric slab is introduced between the plates of the capacitor, its capacitance will increase. Hence, the potential drop across the capacitor will decrease, i.e. $V = \frac{Q}{C}$.

As a result, the potential drop across the bulb will increase as they are connected in series. Thus, its brightness will increase.

(ii) As the resistance R is increased, the potential drop across the resistor will increase. As a result, the potential drop across the bulb will decrease as they are connected in series. Thus, its brightness will decrease.

22. (i) From graph (a), it is clear that resistance (opposition to current) is not changing with frequency, i.e. resistance does not depend on frequency of applied voltage, so the circuit element here is pure resistive (R). From graph (b), it is clear that resistance increases linearly with frequency, so the circuit element here is inductive in nature.

Inductive resistance, $X_L = 2\pi \nu L \Rightarrow X_L \propto \nu$

(ii) Impedance offered by the series combination of resistance (R) and inductor (L).

$$Z=\sqrt{R^2+X_L^2}=\sqrt{R^2+(2\pi\nu L)^2}$$

In L-R circuit, the applied voltage leads the current by phase ϕ, where $\tan\phi=\frac{X_L}{R}$

23. Refer to text on pages 233 and 234.

24. Refer to text on page 230.

25. The peak value of the current is the maximum amplitude of the current in an AC circuit.

The root mean square value of AC current is defined as the value of the constant current which would produce the same amount of heat in a given resistance as is produced by the DC current through the same resistance in same time.

Refer pages 224 and 225.

(Root mean square value of AC)

26. Refer to text on pages 232 and 233.

27. (i) We know that if the number of turns in the inductor decreases, then inductance L decreases. So, the net resistance of the circuit decreases. Hence, the current through the circuit increases, increasing the brightness of the bulb.

(ii) Brightness of the bulb decreases.

Refer to the solution of Q.20 part (ii)

(iii) If the capacitor of reactance $X_C=X_L$ is connected in series with the circuit, then

$$Z=\sqrt{(X_L-X_C)^2+R^2}$$

$$\therefore \quad Z=R \qquad [\because X_L=X_C]$$

This is a case of resonance. In this case, the maximum current will flow through the circuit. Hence, the brightness of the bulb will increase.

28. Refer to the text on pages 232 and 233.

29. In an inductor, the current lags the voltage by 90°. If the source voltage is sinusoidal, then the current is also sinusoidal, but shifted in phase. The instantaneous power is defined as the product of the instantaneous voltage and current that can also be seen to be sinusoidal in time. However, in contrast to the resistive load, the instantaneous power in the inductor goes negative for part of the cycle of the source driving it.

As, $\quad V(t)=V_m\sin\omega t$

$\therefore \quad I(t)=-I_m\cos\omega t$

Instantaneous power, $P_i=V(t)\cdot I(t)$

$$=V_m\sin\omega t\times(-I_m\cos\omega t)$$

$$=-\frac{V_mI_m}{2}\times 2\sin\omega t\cos\omega t$$

$$=-\frac{V_mI_m}{2}[\sin 2\omega t]$$

$$P_i=-\frac{V_mI_m}{2}\sin 2\omega t$$

The variation of P_i with ωt is as given in the figure.

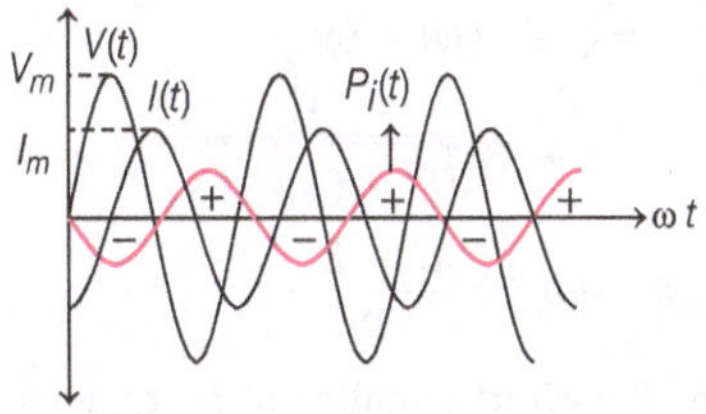

The instantaneous power alternates positive and negative at twice the frequency of source supplying it.

30. Let $(I_{rms})_a$ = rms current in circuit (a)

$(I_{rms})_b$ = rms current in circuit (b)

$$(I_{rms})_a=\frac{V_{rms}}{R}=\frac{V}{R}$$

$$(I_{rms})_b=\frac{V_{rms}}{Z}=\frac{V}{\sqrt{R^2+(X_L-X_C)^2}}$$

(i) When $(I_{rms})_a=(I_{rms})_b$

$$R=\sqrt{R^2+(X_L-X_C)^2}$$

$$\Rightarrow \quad X_L=X_C \text{ in resonance condition}$$

(ii) As, $Z\geq R$

$$\Rightarrow \quad \frac{(I_{rms})_a}{(I_{rms})_b}=\frac{\sqrt{R^2+(X_L-X_C)^2}}{R}=\frac{Z}{R}\geq 1$$

$$\Rightarrow \quad (I_{rms})_a\geq(I_{rms})_b$$

No, the rms current in circuit (b) cannot be larger than that in (a).

31. (i) Consider the R-L-C circuit as shown in the figure.

Given, $\quad V=V_m\sin\omega t$

Let current at any instant be i.

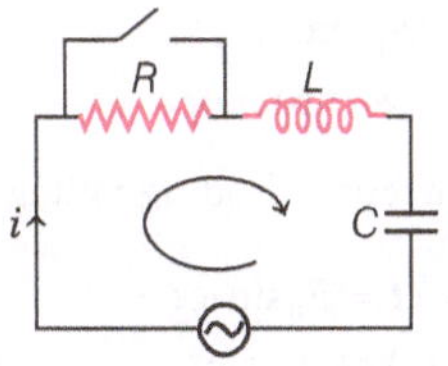

Applying KVL in the given circuit,

$$iR+L\frac{di}{dt}+\frac{q}{C}-V_m\sin\omega t=0 \qquad \text{...(i)}$$

Now, we can write, $i=\frac{dq}{dt}$

$$\Rightarrow \quad \frac{di}{dt}=\frac{d^2q}{dt^2}$$

From Eq. (i), we get

$$\frac{dq}{dt}R+L\frac{d^2q}{dt^2}+\frac{q}{C}=V_m\sin\omega t$$

$$\Rightarrow \quad L\frac{d^2q}{dt^2}+R\frac{dq}{dt}+\frac{q}{C}=V_m\sin\omega t$$

This is the required equation of variation motion of charge.

(ii) Let $i = i_m \sin(\omega t + \phi)$

$$i_m = \frac{V_m}{Z} = \frac{V_m}{\sqrt{R^2 + (X_C - X_L)^2}}$$

and $\phi = \tan^{-1}\left(\frac{X_C - X_L}{R}\right)$

When R is short circuited at $t = t_0$, energy is stored in L and C.

$$U_L = \frac{1}{2}Li^2 = \frac{1}{2}L\left[\frac{V_m}{\sqrt{R^2 + (X_C - X_L)^2}}\right]^2 \sin^2(\omega t_0 + \phi)$$

and $U_C = \frac{1}{2} \times \frac{q^2}{C} = \frac{1}{2C} \times \left(\frac{i_m}{\omega}\right)^2 \cos^2(\omega t_0 + \phi)$

$$= \frac{i_m^2}{2C\omega^2} \cos^2(\omega t_0 + \phi)$$

$$= \frac{1}{2C}\left[\frac{V_m}{\sqrt{R^2 + (X_C - X_L)^2}}\right]^2 \frac{\cos^2(\omega t_0 + \phi)}{\omega^2}$$

$$= \frac{1}{2C\omega^2}\left[\frac{V_m}{\sqrt{R^2 + (X_C - X_L)^2}}\right]^2 \cos^2(\omega t_0 + \phi)$$

(iii) When R is short circuited, it becomes an L-C oscillator. The capacitor will go on discharging and all energy will go to L.

Hence, there is an oscillation of energy from electrostatic to magnetic and again to electrostatic.

32. Refer to text on pages 230, 231 and 232.

33. (i) Refer to text on pages 230, 231 and 232.

(ii) Acceptor circuit is series L-C-R circuit. It is used to selectively pass current for a signal at only the specified frequency.

34. (i) Device X is a capacitor.

As, the current is leading voltage by $\frac{\pi}{2}$ radians.

(ii) As, $E(t) = E_0 \sin \omega t$

Current, $I(t) = I_0 \cos \omega t$

As, in the case of capacitor,

$I = I_0 \sin\left(\omega t + \frac{\pi}{2}\right)$ [current is leading voltage]

Average power, $P = E(t) I(t)$

$= E_0 I_0 \cos \phi / 2$

where, ϕ = phase difference

Hence, curve A represents power, curve B represents voltage and curve C represents current.

(iii) As, X_C = capacitive reactance $= \frac{1}{C\omega}$

where, ω is angular frequency.

So, reactance or impedance decreases with increase in frequency. Graph of X_C *versus* ω is shown below,

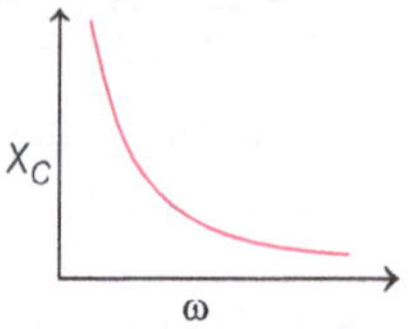

(iv) Refer to text on pages 230 and 231.

35. (i) Given, $V = V_0 \sin \omega t$

$$I = I_0 \sin\left(\omega t + \frac{\pi}{2}\right)$$

As it is clear that the current leads the voltage by a phase angle $\frac{\pi}{2}$.

$\therefore$ The device X is a capacitor.

(ii)

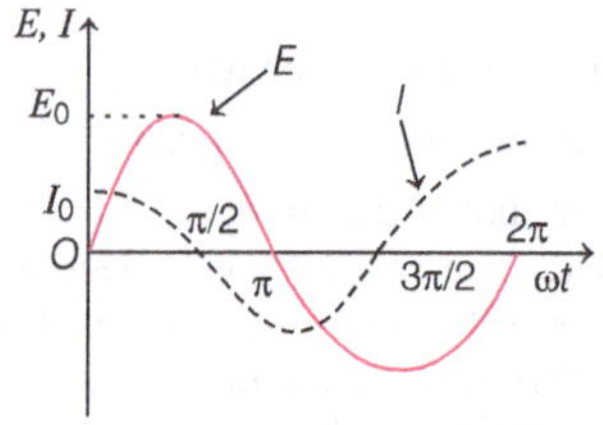

(iii) The reactance of the capacitance is given as

$$X_C = \frac{1}{\omega C}$$

where, ω = angular frequency

and C = capacitance of capacitor.

$\therefore$ $X_C = \frac{1}{2\pi \nu C}$

where, ν = frequency of AC or $X_C \propto \frac{1}{\nu}$

$\therefore$ The graphical representation between reactance of capacitance and frequency is given as

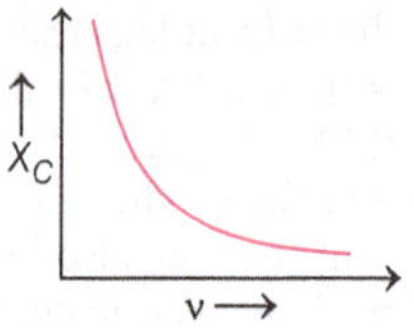

(iv) **Phasor diagram**

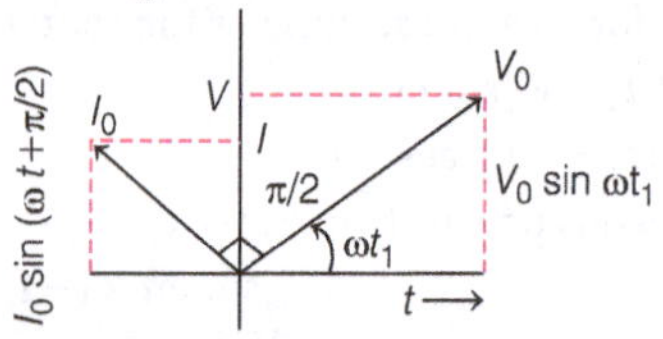

36. **AC generator** It is a device which is used to convert mechanical energy into electrical energy.

Principle It is based on the phenomenon of electromagnetic induction. The emf is induced in the rotating coil as flux is changing due to angle θ between **B** and **A** variation.

Main parts of an AC generator Main parts of an AC generator are shown in the figure and discussed as given below.

Armature A rectangular coil *ABCD* consisting of a large number of turns of copper wire wound over a soft iron core is called armature. The soft iron core is used to increase the magnetic flux.

Field magnets Two pole pieces of a strong electromagnet.

Slip rings The ends of the coil *ABCD* are connected to two hollow metallic rings R_1 and R_2.

Brushes B_1 and B_2 are two flexible metal plates or carbon rods. They are fixed and are kept in slight contact with R_1 and R_2.

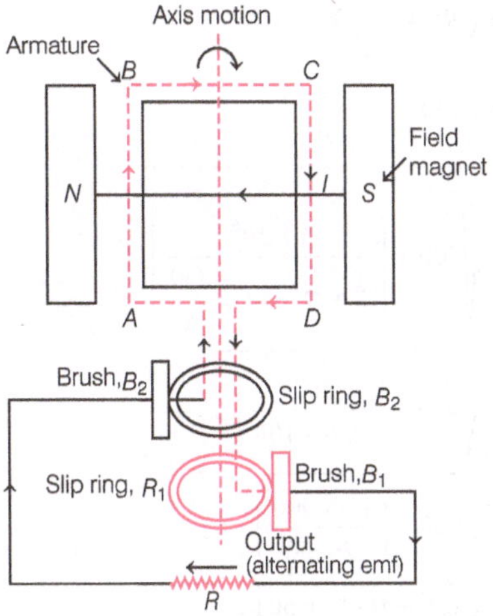

Theory and Working As the armature of coil is rotated in uniform magnetic field,the magnetic flux linked with the coil changes and an emf is induced in the coil. Hence current flow in it.

Suppose the coil is rotating clockwise and is horizontal of some instance of time. At this instant, the arm *AB* of the coil is moving up and the arm *CD* is moving down. According to Fleming's right hand rule, the current flows from *A* to *B* in the arm *AB* and *C* to *D* in the arm *CD*.

The brush B_1 at which the current is entering the external circuit is positive relative to the brush B_2 at which the current is leaving the external circuit.

During the time the coil rotates to the vertical position, the current in the armature will flow in the direction *ABCD*.

Now the coil *ABCD* reaches the vertical position, the arms *AD* and *CD* move momentarily parallel to the field. So, in vertical position, the induced emf (current) is zero.

After half the rotation of coil, the arm *AB* moves down and the arm *CD* moves up. The current flow from *B* to *A* in arm *AB* and *D* to *C* in the arm *CD*.

The brush B_2 is now positive relative to B_1 and remains so long as the coil reaches the vertical position again.

After this B_1 is again positive relative to B_2.

Hence, induced current in the external circuit changes direction after every half rotation of the coil. Hence the current induced is alternating in a nature.

Let N = number of turns in the coil,

ν = frequency of rotation,

A = area of coil

and B = is the magnetic induction.

Then, the induced emf is given by

$$e = \frac{-d\phi}{dt} = \frac{d}{dt}[NBA(\cos 2\pi\nu t)]$$

$$= 2\pi NBA\nu \sin 2\pi\nu t$$

We can see that the emf and current produced is alternating.

Current produced by an AC generator cannot measured by moving coil ammeter because the average value of AC over full cycle is zero.

The source of energy generation is the mechanical energy of rotation of armature coil.

Or (i) **Transformer** It is a device which converts low AC voltage at high current into high AC voltage at low current and *vice-versa.*

Principle It consists of two coils *P* and *S* wound on a closed soft iron core. The coil which is fed from the AC supply is called primary coil (*P*) and the other connected to the load is called secondary coil (*S*). The core of the transformer is made of soft iron to reduce hysteresis loss and is laminated to reduce eddy current losses.

Working When an alternating emf e_P is impressed on the primary winding, it sends an AC current through it which sets up an alternating magnetic flux in the core. This induces an alternating emf e_S in the secondary. If N_P and N_S are the number of turns in primary and secondary coil, their linkages with the flux are $\phi_P = N_P BA$, $\phi_S = N_S BA$

where, B = magnetic induction

and A = area of cross-section.

The magnitude of the emf induced in the secondary,

$$e_S = \frac{d\phi_S}{dt} = N_S A \frac{dB}{dt} \quad \text{... (i)}$$

The changing flux also induces an emf in the primary, whose magnitude

$$e_P = \frac{d\phi_P}{dt} = N_P A \frac{dB}{dt} \quad \text{... (ii)}$$

From Eqs (i) and (ii),

$$\frac{\text{emf induced in secondary}}{\text{voltage applied to primary}} = \frac{e_S}{e_P} = \frac{N_S}{N_P} \quad \text{... (iii)}$$

$\frac{N_S}{N_P}$ = turns ratio or transformation ratio.

If $N_S > N_P, e_S > e_P \rightarrow$ Such a transformer is called step-up transformer.

If $N_S < N_P, e_S < e_P \rightarrow$ Such a transformer is called step-down transformer.

In an ideal transformer;

Instantaneous output power = Instantaneous input power

$$e_S i_S = e_P i_P \quad \text{... (iv)}$$

From Eqs. (iii) and (iv),

$$\frac{e_S}{e_P} = \frac{i_P}{i_S} = \frac{N_S}{N_P}$$

In a step-up transformer, $N_S > N_P, e_S > e_P$ but $i_S < i_P$.

In a step-down transformer, $N_S < N_P, e_S < e_P$ but $i_S > i_P$.

At the generating station, a step-up transformer is used for stepping up the voltage and at the various receiving substations a step-down transformer is used.

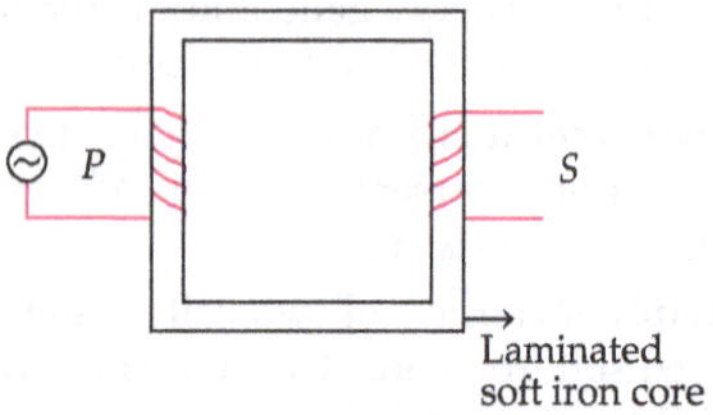

(ii) The two sources of energy losses are eddy current losses and flux leakage losses.

(iii) There is no violation of the principle of the conservation of energy in a step-up transformer. When output voltage increases, the output current decreases automatically keeping the power same.

37. (i) As given, $E = 140 \sin 314t$

On comparing with $E = E_0 \sin \omega t$, we have

$$\omega = 314, \; E_0 = 140 \text{ V}$$

$$\because \quad \omega = 2\pi\nu$$

$$\Rightarrow \quad \nu = \frac{\omega}{2\pi} = \frac{314}{2 \times 3.14} = 50 \text{ Hz}$$

(ii) $E_0 = 140$ V

$$E_{\text{rms}} = \frac{E_0}{\sqrt{2}} = \frac{140}{\sqrt{2}} = 99.29 \text{ V}$$

$$\therefore I_{\text{rms}} = \frac{E_{\text{rms}}}{R} = \frac{99.29}{50} = 1.98 \text{ A}$$

38. (i) Curve A shows power consumption over a full cycle.

(ii) Device X is a capacitor. As in a perfect capacitor, the current (curve C) leads the voltage (curve B) by a phase angle of $\frac{\pi}{2}$.

39. Given, $C = 60\,\mu\text{F} = 60 \times 10^{-6}$ F, $V_{\text{rms}} = 110$ V

and $\nu = 60$ Hz

$$\therefore \quad I_{\text{rms}} = \frac{V_{\text{rms}}}{X_C} = \frac{V_{\text{rms}}}{\frac{1}{2\pi\nu C}} \Rightarrow I_{\text{rms}} = V_{\text{rms}} \, 2\pi\nu C$$

$$= 110 \times 2 \times 3.14 \times 60 \times 60 \times 10^{-6}$$

$$= 2.5 \text{ A}$$

Power absorbed, $P = V_{\text{rms}} I_{\text{rms}} \cos \phi$

For pure capacitive circuit, $\phi = 90°$

$$\therefore \quad P = 0$$

Thus, power spent in one half cycle is retrieved in the other half cycle.

40. (a) $R = 30\,\Omega$

$$C = \frac{250}{\pi} \times 10^{-6} \text{ F}$$

$$V = 200 \text{ V}$$

$$f = 50 \text{ Hz}$$

$$Z = \sqrt{R^2 + (X_C)^2}$$

$$= \sqrt{(30)^2 + \left(\frac{1}{\omega C}\right)^2}$$

$$= \sqrt{900 + \left(\frac{1 \times 10^6}{2 \times \pi \times 50 \times \frac{250}{\pi}}\right)^2}$$

$$= \sqrt{900 + \left(\frac{10^6}{250 \times 100}\right)^2}$$

$$= \sqrt{900 + \left(\frac{1000000}{25000}\right)^2}$$

$$= \sqrt{900 + 1600} = 50\,\Omega$$

$$I = \frac{V}{Z} = \frac{200}{50} = 4 \text{ A}$$

(b) Voltage drops across the resistor = IR

$$= 4 \times 30 = 120 \text{ V}$$

Voltage drops across the capacitor

$$= I \times X_C$$

$$= 4 \times \frac{1 \times 10^6}{2 \times \pi \times 50 \times \frac{250}{\pi}}$$

$$= \frac{4 \times 10^6}{100 \times 250}$$

$$= \frac{4 \times 10^6}{25 \times 10^3} = \frac{4 \times 10^3}{25}$$

$$= \frac{4000}{25} = 160 \text{ V}$$

(c) Since, voltage drop across resistor (V_R) and voltage drop across capacitor (V_C) are out of phase by $\pi/2$. So, we cannot algebrically sum them up. The sum has to be obtained using triangle rule of addition, which gives

$$V = \sqrt{V_R^2 + V_C^2} = \sqrt{160^2 + 120^2} = 200 \text{ V}$$

(< source voltage)

Or

(a) $R = 20\,\Omega,\ L = 2\text{ H},\ C = 50\times10^{-6}\text{F}$

$$V_{rms} = 200\text{ V}$$

$$f_r = \frac{1}{2\pi\sqrt{LC}} = \frac{1}{2\pi\sqrt{2\times50\times10^{-6}}}$$

$$= \frac{1}{2\pi\sqrt{100\times10^{-6}}} = \frac{1}{2\pi\sqrt{10^{-4}}}$$

$$= \frac{1}{2\pi\sqrt{\frac{1}{100}\times\frac{1}{100}}} = \frac{1}{2\pi\times\frac{1}{100}} = \frac{50}{314}$$

$$= 15.92\text{ Hz} \approx 16\text{ Hz}$$

At resonance, the impedance of the circuit is minimum, and the current is maximum.

$$I_{rms} = V_{rms}/R = \frac{200}{20} = 10\text{A}$$

Amplitude of current is the peak value of current I_0 which is $I_{rms}\times\sqrt{2} = 14.14$ A

(b) Average power transferred to the circuit in one complete cycle.

$$P_{av} = I_{rms}\times V_{rms}\cos\phi$$

At resonance $\phi = 0°$

$$\Rightarrow \quad P_{av} = 10\times200 = 2000\text{ W}$$

(c) Potential drop across the capacitor, $V_C = \dfrac{I_{rms}}{2\pi fC}$

At resonance,

$$V_C = \frac{I_{rms}}{2\pi fC} = \frac{10\times10^6}{2\times3.14\times16\times50} = \frac{10^7}{314\times16} = \frac{10^7}{5024}$$

$$= 1990.4\text{ V}$$

41. $R = 50\,\Omega$

$$C = \frac{25}{\pi}\times10^{-6}\text{F}$$

$$L = \frac{4}{\pi}\text{H}$$

$\Rightarrow \quad V = 70\sin(100\,\pi t)$

$\Rightarrow \quad V_0 = 70\text{ V}$

$\therefore \quad \omega t = 100\pi t$

$\Rightarrow \quad \omega = 100\pi$

$\Rightarrow \quad 2\pi f = 100\pi$

$\Rightarrow \quad f = 50\text{ Hz}$

(i) Net reactance of the circuit,

$$X_L = \omega L = 2\pi fL = 2\times\pi\times50\times\frac{4}{\pi} = 8\times50 = 400\,\Omega$$

$$X_C = \frac{1}{\omega C} = \frac{1}{2\pi fC} = \frac{1}{2\times\pi\times50\times\frac{25}{\pi}\times10^{-6}}$$

$$= \frac{1\times10^6}{2\times50\times50} = \frac{10^6}{5000} = \frac{1000000}{5000} = 400\,\Omega$$

Net reactance of the circuit $= X_L - X_C$

$$= (400-400)\,\Omega = 0\,\Omega$$

(ii) Impedance, $Z = \sqrt{R^2 + (X_L - X_C)^2}$

$$= \sqrt{(50)^2 + (0)^2} = \sqrt{(50)^2} = 50\,\Omega$$

(iii) $V_{rms} = \dfrac{70}{\sqrt{2}}$

Effective value of current

$$I_{rms} = \frac{V_{rms}}{\text{Impedance}\,(Z)} = \frac{70/\sqrt{2}}{50} = \frac{49.5}{50} = 0.99\text{ A} = 1\text{ A}$$

42. $R = 10\,\Omega$

$$L = \left(\frac{100}{\pi}\right)\text{mH} = \frac{100}{\pi}\times10^{-3}\text{ H}$$

$$V = 141\sin(100\,\pi t)$$

$\therefore \quad V_0 = 141\text{ V}$

$\therefore \quad \omega t = 100\pi t \Rightarrow 2\pi f = 100\pi$

$\Rightarrow \quad f = 50\text{ Hz}$

(i) $Z = \sqrt{(X_L)^2 + R^2} = \sqrt{(10)^2 + (2\pi fL)^2}$

$$= \sqrt{100 + \left(2\times\pi\times50\times\frac{100}{\pi}\times10^{-3}\right)^2}$$

$$= \sqrt{100 + (100\times100\times10^{-3})^2}$$

$$= \sqrt{100 + (10^4\times10^{-3})^2}$$

$$= \sqrt{100 + (10)^2} = \sqrt{200} = 10\sqrt{2}\,\Omega$$

(ii) $\therefore \tan\phi = \dfrac{\omega L}{R} = \dfrac{2\times\pi\times50\times\frac{100}{\pi}\times10^{-3}}{10}$

$$= \frac{100\times100\times10^{-3}}{10} = 1$$

$\Rightarrow \quad \phi = 45°$

(iii) $V_L = I_0 X_L = \dfrac{V_0}{Z}\cdot\omega L$

$$= \frac{141}{10\sqrt{2}}\times100\pi\times\frac{100}{\pi}\times10^{-3} = 100\text{ V}$$

43. $R = 200\,\Omega$

$$C = \frac{50}{\pi}\times10^{-6}\text{F}$$

$$E_0 = 100\text{ V}$$

$$f = 50\text{ Hz}$$

(i) Capacitive reactance, $X_C = \dfrac{1}{\omega C} = \dfrac{1}{2\pi fC}$

$$= \frac{1}{2\times3.14\times50\times\frac{50}{\pi}\times10^{-6}}$$

$$= \frac{10^6}{2\times2500} = \frac{10^6}{5000} = \frac{1000000}{5000} = 200\,\Omega$$

$$Z = \sqrt{X_C^2 + R^2} = \sqrt{(200)^2 + (200)^2}$$

$$Z = \sqrt{40000 + 40000}$$

$$= \sqrt{80000} = 2\sqrt{2} \times 100 = 200\sqrt{2}\,\Omega$$

(ii) Phase angle, $\phi = \tan^{-1}\left(\frac{X_C}{R}\right) = \tan^{-1}\left(\frac{200}{200}\right)$

$$= \tan^{-1}(1) = 45°$$

(iii) $V_R = IR = \frac{E_0/\sqrt{2}}{Z} \times R = \frac{100}{\sqrt{2} \times 200\sqrt{2}} \times 200 = 50\text{ V}$

44. (i) Refer to Example 8 on page 231.

$$\phi = 135°$$

Since, $\omega L < \frac{1}{\omega C}$ or $X_L < X_C$

Therefore, current is leading in phase by a phase angle 135°.

(ii) For unit power factor, $\cos\phi = 1$

$$\Rightarrow \frac{R}{\sqrt{R^2 + \left(\omega L - \frac{1}{\omega C^T}\right)^2}} = 1$$

where, C^T is the total capacitance.

$$\Rightarrow R^2 + \left(\omega L - \frac{1}{\omega C^T}\right)^2 = R^2 \quad \Rightarrow \omega L = \frac{1}{\omega C^T}$$

$$\Rightarrow \omega L = 100 = \frac{1}{\omega C} = \frac{1}{1000} C^T$$

$$\Rightarrow C^T = \frac{1}{10^5} = 10^{-5}\text{ F} = 10\,\mu\text{F}$$

Additional capacitance C' required in parallel

$$= C^T - C = 10\,\mu\text{F} - 2\,\mu\text{F} = 8\,\mu\text{F}$$

45. Refer to Example 8 on page 231.

Phase difference, $\phi = \frac{-\pi}{4}$

46. (i) Refer to Example 9 on pages 232.

$$\nu = 39.80\text{ Hz}$$

(ii) $\therefore I_0 = \frac{E_0}{R} = \frac{200}{100} = 2\text{A}$

47. Given, $L = 5\text{ H}$,

$$C = 80\,\mu\text{F} = 80 \times 10^{-6}\text{F},$$

$$R = 40\,\Omega,\ V_{rms} = 230\text{ V}$$

(i) Resonance angular frequency,

$$\omega_r = \frac{1}{\sqrt{LC}} = \frac{1}{\sqrt{5 \times 80 \times 10^{-6}}} = 50\text{ rad/s}$$

(ii) Impedance, $Z = \sqrt{R^2 + \left(\omega L - \frac{1}{\omega C}\right)^2}$

At resonance, $\omega L = \frac{1}{\omega C}$

$\therefore \quad Z_r = R = 40\,\Omega$

Amplitude of current at resonance frequency,

$$I_0 = \frac{V_0}{Z_r} = \frac{\sqrt{2} \times 230}{40} = 8.13\text{ A}$$

(iii) $I_{rms} = \frac{I_0}{\sqrt{2}} = \frac{8.13}{\sqrt{2}} = 5.75\text{ A}$

Potential difference across L,

$$V_L = I_{rms} \times (\omega_r \times L)$$

$$= 5.75 \times 50 \times 5 = 1437.5\text{ V}$$

Potential difference across C,

$$V_C = I_{rms} \times \frac{1}{\omega_r C} = \frac{5.75}{50 \times 80 \times 10^{-6}}$$

$$= 1437.5\text{ V}$$

$\therefore$ Potential difference across L and C combination,

$$V_{LC} = I_{rms}\left(\omega_r L - \frac{1}{\omega_r C}\right) = 0$$

$\therefore$ Potential difference across R,

$$V_R = I_{rms} R = 5.75 \times 40 = 230\text{ V}$$

Potential drop across the L-C combination,

$$V_{LC} = I(X_L - X_C)$$

at resonance $X_L - X_C = V_{LC} = 0\text{V}$

48. Refer to Example 2 on page 225. [**Ans.** $220\sqrt{2}\sin 100\pi t$]

49. (i) Given

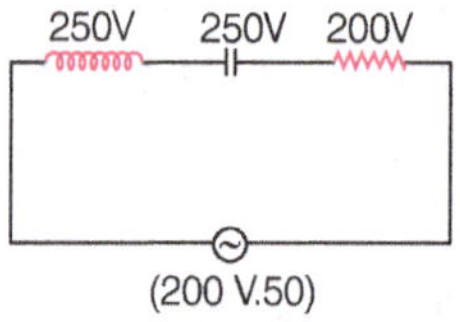

$V_R = 200\text{ V}$, $V_L = 250\text{ V}$ and $V_C = 250\text{ V}$

V_{eff} should be given as

$V_{eff} = V_R + V_L + V_C = 200\text{ V} + 250\text{ V} + 250\text{ V}$

$= 700\text{ V}$

However, $V_{eff} > 200\text{ V}$ of the AC source.

This paradox can be solved only be using phasor diagram, as given below

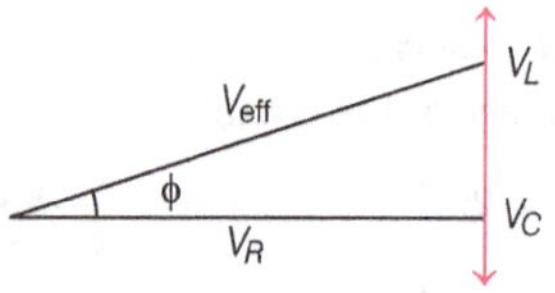

$$(V_{eff}) = \sqrt{V_R^2 + (V_L - V_C)^2}$$

Since, $V_L = V_C$, so $V_{eff} = V_R = 200\text{ V}$

(ii) Given $R = 40\,\Omega$. so current in the L-C-R circuit.

$$I_{eff} = \frac{V_{eff}}{R}\ [X_L = X_C \text{ or } Z = R]$$

$$= \frac{200}{40} = 5\text{ A}$$

50. (i) The town is 10 km away, length of pair of Cu wires used, l = 20 km = 20000 m.

Resistance of Cu wires,

$$R = \rho\frac{l}{A} = \rho\frac{l}{\pi(r)^2} = \frac{1.7\times 10^{-8}\times 20000}{3.14\,(0.5\times 10^{-2})^2} \approx 4\,\Omega$$

$$I \text{ at } 220\text{ V},\ VI = 10^6\text{ W};\ I = \frac{10^6}{220} = 0.45\times 10^4\text{ A}$$

$$RI^2 = \text{power loss} = 4\times(0.45)^2\times 10^8 > 10^6\text{ W}$$

Therefore, this method cannot be used for transmission.

(ii) When power, $P = 10^6$ W is transmitted at 11000 V.

$$V'I' = 10^6\text{ W} = 11000\,I'$$

Current drawn, $I' = \frac{1}{1.1}\times 10^2$

Power loss $= RI^2 = \frac{1}{121}\times 4\times 10^6 = 3.3\times 10^4$ W

$\therefore$ Fraction of power loss $= \frac{3.3\times 10^4}{10^6} = 3.3\%$

51. 0 W, $P_{av} = (E_0/\sqrt{2}_8)(I_0/\sqrt{2})\cos\theta$, [here, $\theta = 90°$]

52. Given, inductance, $L = 44\text{ mH} = 44\times 10^{-3}\text{ H}$, $V_{rms} = 220$ V

Frequency of inductor, $\nu = 50$ Hz

Inductive reactance, $X_L = 2\pi\nu L$

$$= 2\times 3.14\times 50\times 44\times 10^{-3} = 13.82\,\Omega$$

The rms value of current in the circuit,

$$I_{rms} = \frac{V_{rms}}{X_L} = \frac{220}{13.82} = 15.9\text{ A}$$

Power absorbed, $P = V_{rms}\,I_{rms}\cos\phi$

For pure inductive circuit, $\phi = 90°$

$\therefore \quad P = 0$

Thus, power spent in one half cycle is retrieved in the other half cycle.

53. We are given that,

$$E_P = 220\text{V}$$
$$E_s = 44\text{V}$$
$$Z = 440\Omega$$
$$I_P = ?$$

We know that, $I_s = \frac{E_s}{Z}$

$$I_s = \frac{44}{440} = \frac{1}{10} = 0.1\text{ A}$$

To find current drawn by primary coil to transformer, we have

$$E_P I_P = E_s I_s$$

$$I_P = \frac{E_s I_s}{E_P}$$

$$I_P = \frac{44\times 0.1}{220}$$

$$I_P = \frac{4.4}{220}$$

$$I_p = 0.02\text{ A}$$

0.02 A current is drawn by primary coil of the transformer.

54. Given, input voltage, $V_p = 2.5\times 10^3$ V

Input current, $I_p = 20$ A

Also, $\frac{N_p}{N_s} = \frac{10}{1} \Rightarrow \frac{N_s}{N_p} = \frac{1}{10}$ ...(i)

Percentage efficiency $= \frac{\text{Output power}}{\text{Input power}}\times 100$

$$\Rightarrow \frac{90}{100} = \frac{\text{Output power}}{V_p I_p}$$

(i) Output power $= \frac{90}{100}\times(V_p I_p)$

$$= \frac{90}{100}\times(2.5\times 10^3\text{ V})\times(20\text{ A})$$

$$= 4.5\times 10^4\text{ W}$$

(ii) $\because \quad \frac{V_s}{V_p} = \frac{N_s}{N_p} \Rightarrow V_s = \frac{N_s}{N_p}\times V_p$

Voltage, $V_s = \frac{1}{10}\times 2.5\times 10^3\text{ V} = 250$ V

(iii) $V_s I_s = 4.5\times 10^4$ W

Current, $I_s = \frac{4.5\times 10^4}{V_s} = \frac{4.5\times 10^4}{250} = 180$ A

55. $P_{in} = P_{out} = 550\text{ W} \Rightarrow \varepsilon_P I_P = 550$

$$220\times I_p = 550 \Rightarrow I_p = \frac{550}{220} = \frac{5}{2} = 2.5\text{ A}$$

56. Given, input voltage, $V_p = 2200$ V

Number of turns, $n_1 = 3000$

Output voltage, $V_s = 220$ V

As, $\frac{V_s}{V_p} = \frac{n_2}{n_1} \Rightarrow \frac{220}{2200} = \frac{n_2}{3000}$

$$\Rightarrow \quad n_2 = \frac{220}{2200}\times 3000$$

$\therefore$ Number of turns in the secondary winding,

$$n_2 = 300\text{ turns.}$$

57. In any transformer,

$$\frac{I_S}{I_P} = \frac{E_P}{E_S} = \frac{N_P}{N_S} = \frac{1}{K}$$

Here $E_P = 220$ V, $I_S = 2$ A.

$$\frac{N_P}{N_S} = \frac{1}{25}$$

$\therefore \quad I_P = \frac{N_S}{N_P} \times I_S = 25 \times 2 = 50 \text{ A}$

and $\quad E_S = \frac{N_S}{N_P} \times E_P = 25 \times 220$

$= 5500 \text{ V}$

Power output $= E_S \times I_S$

$= 5500 \times 2 = 11000 \text{ W}$

58. Generating power of electric plant = 800 kW at $V = 220$ V, resistance/length = 0.5Ω / km

Distance = 15 km, generating voltage = 440 V,

Primary voltage, $V_p = 4000$ V

Secondary voltage, $V_s = 220$ V

(i) Power $= I_p \cdot V_p$

$\Rightarrow \quad 800 \times 1000 = I_p \times 4000$

$\Rightarrow \quad I_p = 200$ A

Line power loss in form of heat

$= (I_p)^2 \times R \text{ (2 lines)} = (I_p)^2 \times 0.5 \times 15 \times 2$

$= (200)^2 \times 0.5 \times 15 \times 2 = 60 \times 10^4 \text{ W} = 600 \text{ kW}$

(ii) If there is no power loss due to leakage, then the power supply by plant = 800 + 600 = 1400 kW

(iii) Voltage drop across the line $= I_p \cdot R \text{(2 lines)}$

$= 200 \times 0.5 \times 15 \times 2 = 3000 \text{ V}$

Voltage from transmission = 3000 + 4000 = 7000 V

As, it is given that the power is generated at 440 V. So, the step-up transformer needed at the plant is 440V-7000 V.

59. Given, primary voltage, $V_p = 40000$ V

Let the current in primary be I_p.

$\therefore \quad V_p \cdot I_p = P$

$800 \times 1000 = 40000 \times I_p$

$I_p = 20$ A

(i) Line power loss $= I_P^2 \times R$ (2 lines)

$= (20)^2 \times 2 \times 0.5 \times 15 = 6000 \text{ W} = 6 \text{ kW}$

(ii) Power supply by plant = 800 + 6 = 806 kW

(iii) Voltage drop on line $= I_P \cdot R$ (2 lines)

$= 20 \times 2 \times 0.5 \times 15 = 300 \text{ V}$

Voltage for transmission = 40000 + 300 = 40300 V

Step-up transformer needed at the plant

= 440 V − 40.3 kV

Power loss at higher voltage $= \frac{6}{806} \times 100 = 0.74\%$

Power loss at lower voltage $= \frac{600}{1400} \times 100 = 42.8\%$

Hence, the power loss is minimum at higher voltage. So, the high voltage transmission is preferred.

60. Here, $E_P = 220$ V, $I_S = 0.5$ A, $P = 15$ W,

$n_S = 20, n_P = ?, I_P = ?$

$$E_S = \frac{P_S}{I_S} = \frac{15}{0.5} = 30 \text{ V}$$

As $\quad \frac{E_P}{E_S} = \frac{n_P}{n_S}$

$\therefore \quad n_P = \frac{E_P}{E_S} \times n_S = \frac{220}{30} \times 20 = 147$

Also, from $E_P I_P = E_S I_S$

$$I_P = \frac{E_S I_S}{E_P} = \frac{P_S}{E_P} = \frac{15}{220} = 0.068 \text{ A}$$

61. For 100% efficient transformer, $P_i = P_o$

$\therefore$ The power output is W (watt).

62. Zero, as transformer works only in AC and in case of DC supply, there is no induced emf in secondary because there is no change in flux through the transformer circuit.

QR Code for Quick Test 1

QR Code for Quick Test 2

QR Code for Quick Test 3

SELF ASSESSMENT TEST

Multiple Choice Questions (MCQs)

1. What happens to the inductive reactance when the frequency of the AC supply is increased?
   (a) Increases (b) Decreases
   (c) Remains the same (d) Decreases inversely

2. Which of the following statements is true about the L-C-R circuit connected to an AC source at resonance?
   (a) Voltage across R equals the applied voltage.
   (b) Voltage across R is zero.
   (c) Voltage across C is zero.
   (d) Voltage across L equals the applied voltage.

3. The core of a transformer is laminated to reduce the effect of **CBSE 2022 (Term-II)**
   (a) flux leakage (b) copper loss
   (c) hysteresis loss (d) eddy current

4. Which among the following, is not a cause for power loss in a transformer? **CBSE SQP 2021-22**
   (a) Eddy currents are produced in the soft iron core of a transformer.
   (b) Electric flux sharing is not properly done in primary and secondary coils.
   (c) Humming sound produced in the transformers due to magnetostriction.
   (d) Primary coil is made up of a very thick copper wire.

5. A sinusoidal voltage of peak value 283 V and frequency 50 Hz is applied to a series L-C-R circuit in which $R = 3\,\Omega$, $L = 25.48$ mH and $C = 796\,\mu$F, then the power dissipated at the resonant condition will be **CSBE SQP 2021-22**
   (a) 39.70 kW (b) 26.70 kW
   (c) 13.35 kW (d) zero

Assertion Reason

Directions *(Q. Nos. 6-8) In the following questions, two statements are given- one labelled Assertion and the other labelled Reason. Select the correct answer to these questions from the codes (a), (b), (c) and (d) as given below.*

(a) Both Assertion and Reason are true and Reason is the correct explanation of Assertion.
(b) Both Assertion and Reason are true but Reason is not the correct explanation of Assertion.
(c) Assertion is true but Reason is false.
(d) Assertion is false but Reason is true.

6. **Assertion (A)** The alternating current lags behind the emf by a phase angle of $\pi/2$, when AC flows through an inductor.
   Reason (R) The inductive reactance increases as the frequency of AC source decreases.

7. **Assertion (A)** Transformers are used only in alternating current source not in direct current.
   Reason (R) Only AC can be stepped up or down by means of transformers.

8. **Assertion (A)** In series LCR resonance circuit, the impedance is equal to the ohmic resistance.
   Reason (R) At resonance, the inductive reactance exceeds the capacitive reactance.

Case Based Question

Directions *(Q.No. 9) This question is case study based question. Read the following paragraph and answer the questions on the basis of same.*

9.

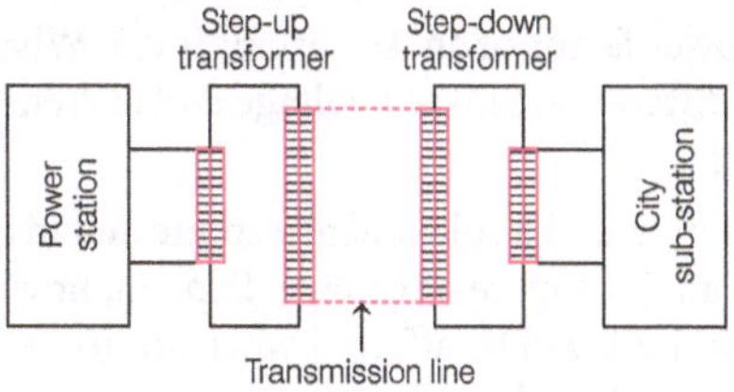

The large-scale transmission and distribution of electrical energy over long distances is done with the use of transformers. The voltage output of the generator is stepped-up. It is then transmitted over long distances to an area sub-station near the consumers. There the voltage is stepped down. It is further stepped down at distributing sub-stations and utility poles before a power supply of 240 V reaches our homes. **CBSE SQP 2021-22**

(i) Which of the following statement is true?
   (a) Energy is created when a transformer steps up the voltage.

(b) A transformer is designed to convert an AC voltage to DC voltage.
(c) Step-up transformer increases the power for transmission.
(d) Step-down transformer decreases the AC voltage.

(ii) If the secondary coil has a greater number of turns than the primary
(a) the voltage is stepped-up ($V_s > V_p$) and arrangement is called a step-up transformer
(b) the voltage is stepped-down ($V_s < V_p$) and arrangement is called a step-down transformer
(c) the current is stepped-up ($I_s > I_p$) and arrangement is called a step-up transformer
(d) the current is stepped-down ($I_s < I_p$) and arrangement is called a step-down transformer

(iii) We need to step-up the voltage for power transmission, so that
(a) the current is reduced and consequently, the I^2R loss is cut down
(b) the voltage is increased, the power losses are also increased
(c) the power is increased before transmission is done
(d) the voltage is decreased so V^2/R losses are reduced

(iv) A power transmission line feeds input power at 2300 V to a step down transformer with its primary windings having 4000 turns. The number of turns in the secondary in order to get output power at 230 V are
(a) 4 (b) 40 (c) 400 (d) 4000

Very Short Answer Type Questions

10. The power factor of an AC circuit is 0.5. What is the phase difference between voltage and current in this circuit?

11. A light bulb and a solenoid are connected in series across an AC source of voltage. Explain, how the glow of the light bulb will be affected when an iron rod is inserted in the solenoid.

Short Answer Type Questions

12. A resistor R and an element X are connected in series to an AC source of voltage. The voltage is found to lead the current in phase by $\pi/4$. If X is replaced by another element Y, the voltage lags behind the current by $\pi/4$.
(i) Identify elements X and Y.
(ii) When both X and Y are connected in series with R to the same source, will the power dissipated in the circuit be maximum or minimum?
Justify your answer.

13. Write the expression for the impedance offered by the series combination of resistor, inductor and capacitor connected to an AC source of voltage $V = V_0 \sin \omega t$. Show on a graph the variation of the voltage and the current with ωt in the circuit.

Long Answer Type Questions

14. An AC voltage $V = V_0 \sin \omega t$ is applied across a pure inductor of inductance L. Find an expression for the current i, flowing in the circuit and show mathematically that the current flowing through it lags behind the applied voltage by a phase angle of $\frac{\pi}{2}$. Also, draw graphs of V and i *versus* ωt for the circuit. **CBSE SQP 2022-23**

15. Find the value of the phase difference between the current and the voltage in the series L-C-R circuit shown below. Which one leads in phase : current or voltage?

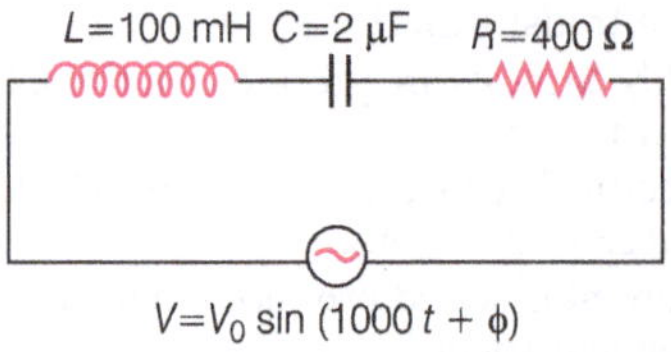

16. An electrical device draws 2 kW power from AC mains (voltage 223 V (rms) $= \sqrt{50000}$ V). The current differs (lags) in phase by $\phi \left(\tan \phi = \frac{-3}{4}\right)$ as compared to voltage. Find (a) R, (b) $X_C - X_L$ and (c) I_M. Another device has twice the values for R, X_C and X_L. How are the answers affected?

Answers

1. (a)	2. (a)	3. (d)	4. (d)	5. (c)
6. (c)	7. (a)	8. (c)		

9. (i) (d), (ii) (a), (iii) (a), (iv) (c)

08

CHAPTER

Electromagnetic Waves

In 1865, Maxwell predicted the existence of electromagnetic waves on the basis of his equations. He concluded that **variation of electric and magnetic field vectors perpendicular to each other leads to the generation of electromagnetic disturbances in space.** These disturbances possesses the properties of waves and can propagate in space without any medium. Thus, these waves are known as **electromagnetic waves.**

YOUR STUDY GOALS

YOUR PRACTICE GOAL

- Objective Type Questions (29 Qs ; MCQs, A-R, Matching)
- Case Based Question (1)
- Subjective Questions (8 VSAs, 11 SAs, 9 LAs)
- Numerical Problems (5)

8.1 Displacement Current

- **Ampere's circuital law** states that the line integral of magnetic field **B** around any closed path is equal to μ_0 times the total current threading the closed path,

$$\oint \mathbf{B} \cdot d\mathbf{l} = \mu_0 I \qquad \text{...(i)}$$

where, I is the net current threading the surface bounded by a closed path C.

- When a capacitor is allowed to charge in an electric circuit, the current flows through connecting wires. As capacitor charges, charge accumulates on the two plates of capacitor and as a result, a changing electric field is produced across between the two plates of the capacitor.
- According to Maxwell, changing electric field intensity is equivalent to a current through capacitor known as **displacement current** (I_d). The electric field between the plates is given by

$$E = \frac{\sigma}{\varepsilon_0} = \frac{q}{\varepsilon_0 A}$$

where, q is the charge on the plates and σ is the surface charge density.

- Change in electric field, $dE = \dfrac{dq}{\varepsilon_0 A} = \dfrac{I dt}{\varepsilon_0 A}$

$$\Rightarrow \qquad \frac{dE}{dt} = \frac{I}{\varepsilon_0 A}$$

$$I=\varepsilon_0 A\frac{dE}{dt} \Rightarrow \varepsilon_0=\frac{d}{dt}(EA)$$

$$=\varepsilon_0\frac{d\phi_E}{dt} \qquad (\because \phi_E=EA)$$

$$I_d=\varepsilon_0\frac{d\phi_E}{dt}$$

- The **conduction current** is the current due to the flow of charges in a conductor and it is denoted as I_c and **displacement current** is the current due to changing electric field between the plates of the capacitor and denoted as I_d, so the total current I is sum of I_c and I_d, i.e. $I=I_c+I_d$.
- **Modified Ampere's circuital** law can be written as

$$\oint \mathbf{B}\cdot d\mathbf{l}=\mu_0(I_c+I_d)$$

Maxwell's Equations in Vacuum

- **Gauss' law in electrostatics** $\oint \mathbf{E}\cdot d\mathbf{S}=\frac{q}{\varepsilon_0}$
- **Gauss' law in magnetism** $\oint \mathbf{B}\cdot d\mathbf{S}=0$
- **Faraday's law of electromagnetic induction**
  Emf $=\oint \mathbf{E}\cdot d\mathbf{l}=-\frac{d\phi_B}{dt}$
- **Maxwell-Ampere's circuital law**

$$\oint \mathbf{B}\cdot d\mathbf{l}=\mu_0\left[I_C+\varepsilon_0\frac{d\phi_E}{dt}\right]$$

Example 1. If voltage between the plates of a capacitor of capacitance 2.0 μF is changing at the rate of 10 Vs^{-1}. What is the displacement current in the capacitor?

Sol. Here, $C=2.0\,\mu\text{F}=2.0\times10^{-6}\text{F}$,

$$\frac{dV}{dt}=10\text{ Vs}^{-1}$$

Displacement current,

$$I_d=\varepsilon_0\frac{d\phi_E}{dt}=\varepsilon_0\frac{d}{dt}(EA)=\varepsilon_0\frac{d}{dt}\left(\frac{VA}{d}\right)$$

$$=\frac{\varepsilon_0 A}{d}\frac{dV}{dt}=C\frac{dV}{dt}=2.0\times10^{-6}\times10\text{ A}=20\,\mu\text{A}$$

Example 2. In which way you can establish an instantaneous displacement current of 1.0 A in the space between the parallel plates of 1 μF capacitor?

Sol. ∴Displacement current,

$$I_d=\varepsilon_0\frac{d\phi_E}{dt}=\varepsilon_0\frac{d}{dt}(EA) \qquad [\because \phi_E=EA]$$

$$=\varepsilon_0 A\frac{d}{dt}\left(\frac{V}{d}\right)$$

$$\Rightarrow \quad I_d=\frac{\varepsilon_0 A}{d}\times\frac{dV}{dt}=\frac{CdV}{dt} \qquad \left[\because C=\frac{\varepsilon_0 A}{d}\right]$$

$$\Rightarrow \quad \frac{dV}{dt}=\frac{I_d}{C}=\frac{1.0}{10^{-6}}=10^6\text{ Vs}^{-1}$$

Thus, an instantaneous displacement current of 1 A can be set up by changing the potential difference across the parallel plates of capacitor at the rate of 10^6 Vs^{-1}.

8.2 Electromagnetic Waves

The waves propagating in space through electric and magnetic fields varying in space and time simultaneously are called electromagnetic waves.

Source of Electromagnetic Waves

If a charge is moving with non-zero acceleration, the electric and magnetic fields will change with space and time, then it produces electromagnetic waves. So, the electromagnetic waves are produced by an accelerated or decelerated charge.

The frequency of EM wave is equal to the frequency of oscillation of charge, i.e.

$$\nu=\frac{1}{2\pi\sqrt{LC}}$$

where, L is inductance and C is capacitance.

Note Electromagnetic waves are also produced when fast moving electrons are suddenly stopped by metal target of high atomic number. These electromagnetic waves are called **X-rays.**

Transverse Nature of Electromagnetic Waves

Electromagnetic waves are transverse in nature i.e. electric and magnetic fields are perpendicular to each other and also perpendicular to the direction of wave propagation.

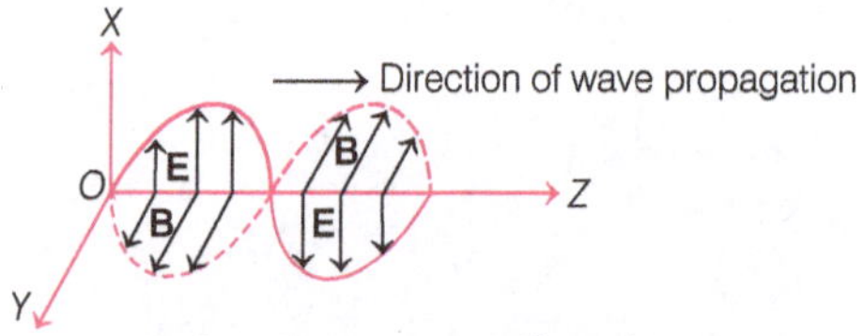

A plane EM wave travelling along Z-axis

E (electric field) and B (magnetic field) are in same phase.

The EM wave propagating in the positive z-direction may be represented by the following equations

Here, $E = E_x = E_0 \sin(kz - \omega t)$

$B = B_y = B_0 \sin(kz - \omega t)$

where, k = wave number $= \frac{2\pi}{\lambda}$ (λ = wavelength)

ω = angular frequency = $2\pi\nu$ (ν = frequency)

E_0 = amplitude of varying electric field

B_0 = amplitude of varying magnetic field.

Important Characteristics of Electromagnetic Waves

Important characteristics of EM waves are listed below

(i) The electromagnetic waves are produced by accelerated charge.

(ii) These waves do not require any material medium for propagation.

(iii) These waves travel in free space with the speed of light ($c = 3\times10^8 \text{ ms}^{-1}$), given by the relation

$$c = 1/\sqrt{\mu_0\varepsilon_0}$$

It means that light waves are electromagnetic in nature.

(iv) Speed of electromagnetic wave in a medium is given by $v = 1/\sqrt{\mu\varepsilon} = \frac{c}{\sqrt{\mu_r\varepsilon_r}} = \frac{c}{n}$

where, ε and μ are the permittivity and magnetic permeability of a material medium respectively, and n is refractive index. This means, the speed of EM wave in a medium depends on electric and magnetic properties of a medium.

(v) The direction of variations of electric and magnetic fields are perpendicular to each other and also perpendicular to the direction of wave propagation. Thus, **electromagnetic waves are transverse in nature.** So, they can be polarised.

(vi) In free space, the magnitudes of electric and magnetic fields in electromagnetic waves are related by $E_0/B_0 = c$

(vii) Electromagnetic waves follow the superposition principle. They show phenomena like reflection, refraction, interference, diffraction and polarisation.

(viii) In electromagnetic waves the average values of electric energy density and magnetic energy density are equal, i.e.

$$\left(\frac{1}{2}\varepsilon_0 E^2\right)_{av} = \left(\frac{B^2}{2\mu_0}\right)_{av}$$

(ix) The electric vector of electromagnetic wave is responsible for optical effects and is also called as the light vector.

(x) Electromagnetic waves carry energy and momentum.

$$E = \frac{hc}{\lambda}, p = \frac{U}{c} = mc$$

Example 3. An electromagnetic wave is travelling in vacuum with a speed of 3×10^8 m/s. Find its velocity in a medium having relative electric and magnetic permeability 2 and 1, respectively.

Sol. Given, velocity of electromagnetic wave in vacuum,

$$c = 3\times10^8 \text{m/s}$$

Relative electric permittivity, $\varepsilon_r = 2$

and relative magnetic permeability, $\mu_r = 1$

Since, velocity of electromagnetic wave in a medium can be calculated by

$$v = \frac{1}{\sqrt{\varepsilon_0\varepsilon_r\mu_0\mu_r}} = \frac{1}{\sqrt{\varepsilon_0\mu_0}\times\sqrt{\mu_r\varepsilon_r}}$$

where, $\frac{1}{\sqrt{\varepsilon_0\mu_0}} = c$

$$\Rightarrow \quad v = \frac{c}{\sqrt{\mu_r\varepsilon_r}}$$

Therefore, $v = \frac{3\times10^8}{\sqrt{2\times1}} = \frac{3}{\sqrt{2}}\times10^8$ m/s

Quick Test 1

Conceptual Questions

1. A variable frequency AC source is connected to a capacitor. How will the displacement current change with decrease in frequency? *NCERT Exemplar*

2. A charged particle oscillates about its mean position with frequency 10^9 Hz. What is the frequency of electromagnetic wave produced by the oscillators? *NCERT*

3. Show that the radiation pressure exerted by an EM wave of intensity I on a surface kept in vacuum is $\frac{I}{c}$. *NCERT Exemplar*

Numerical Questions

4. You are given a 2 μF parallel plate capacitor. How would you establish an instantaneous displacement current of 1 mA in the space between its plates? *NCERT Exemplar*

5. A radio can tune into any station in the 7.5 MHz to 12 MHz band. What is its corresponding wavelength? *NCERT*

6. The amplitude of the magnetic field part of a harmonic electromagnetic wave in vacuum is $B_0 = 510$ nT. What is the amplitude of the electric field part of the wave? *NCERT*

Answers

5. 25 m to 40 m *6.* 153 N/C

For Solutions, See QR Code on Pg. 275

8.3 Electromagnetic Spectrum

The orderly arrangement of EM waves in increasing or decreasing order of wavelength λ or frequency ν is called electromagnetic spectrum. The range varies from $\mathbf{10^{-12}}$ m **to** $\mathbf{10^4}$ m, i.e. from γ-rays to radio waves.

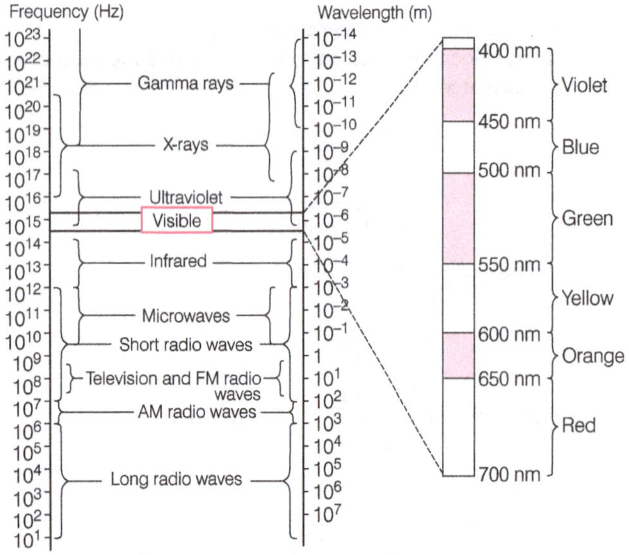

Electromagnetic spectrum with common names for various parts of it

The wavelength ranges, frequency ranges and use of various regions of electromagnetic spectrum are summarised below.

Radio waves

These waves are produced due to oscillating charge particles. The frequency varies from 500 kHz to 1000 MHz.

Uses of radio waves are given below

(i) These are used in AM (Amplitude Modulation) from 530 kHz to 1710 kHz. These are also used in ground wave propagation.

(ii) These are used in TV waves ranging from 54 MHz to 890 MHz.

(iii) These are used in FM (Frequency Modulation) ranging from 88 MHz to 108 MHz.

(iv) UHF (Ultra High Frequency) waves are used in cellular phones ranging from 300 MHz to 3GHz.

Microwaves

These waves are called **short wavelength radio waves** which are produced by vacuum tubes. Their frequency lies in the range of 1 GHz to 300 GHz (gigahertz).

Uses of microwaves are given below

(i) These are used in RADAR systems for aircraft navigation.

(ii) These are used in microwave oven for cooking purpose.

(iii) These are used in study of atomic and molecular structures.

(iv) These are used to measure the speed of vehicle, speed of cricket ball, etc.

Infrared Waves

These waves were discovered by Herschell. These waves are also called **heat waves**. These waves are produced from the heat radiating bodies and molecules.

They have high penetration power. Its frequency range is from 3×10^{11} Hz to 4×10^{14} Hz.

Uses of infrared waves are given below

(i) These are used in physical therapy.

(ii) These are used in satellite for defence purpose.

(iii) These are used in weather forecasting.

Visible Rays

It is that part of spectrum which is visible by naked human eye and its frequency range is from 4×10^{14} Hz to 7×10^{14} Hz. **Uses of visible rays** are given below

(i) Seeing things is the most important use of visible light.

(ii) Visible light is extensively used in photography, videography and imaging system.

(iii) It is also used medical imaging techniques such as endoscopy, microscopy and opthalmology.

Ultraviolet Rays

These rays were discovered by Ritter in 1801. These rays are produced by special lamps and very hot bodies.

The sun is an important source of UV-rays but most of these rays are absorbed by ozone layer at an altitude of about 40-50 km. Its frequency range is from 10^{14} Hz to 10^{16} Hz.

Uses of ultraviolet rays are given below

(i) These are used in burglar alarm.

(ii) These are used in checking mineral sample.

(iii) These are used to study molecular structures.

(iv) These are used to kill germs in minerals.

X-Rays

These rays were discovered by German professor Roentgen. Its frequency range is from 3×10^{16} Hz to 3×10^{21} Hz.

Uses of X-rays are given below

(i) These are used in surgery to detect the fracture, diseased organs, stones in the body, etc.

(ii) These are used in engineering to detect fault, crack on bridges, testing of welds.

(iii) These are used at metro station to detect metal or explosive material.

(iv) These are used in scientific research.

Gamma (γ) Rays

These rays were discovered by Rutherford. These waves have highest frequency range and lowest wavelength range. Thus, these waves have the highest penetrating power. The frequency range is from 3×10^{18} Hz to 5×10^{22} Hz.

Uses of gamma (γ) rays are given below

(i) These are used to produce nuclear reaction.

(ii) These are used in radio therapy for the treatment of tumor and cancer.

(iii) These are used in food industry to kill pathogenic microorganisms.

Different Types of Electromagnetic Waves

Type	Wavelength range	Production	Detection
Radio waves	> 0.1 m	Rapid acceleration and decelerations of electrons in aerials	Receiver's aerials
Microwave	0.1 m to 1 mm	Klystron valve or magnetron valve	Point contact diodes
Infrared waves	1 mm to 700 nm	Vibration of atoms and molecules	Thermopiles bolometer, Infrared photographic film
Light	700 nm to 400 nm	Electrons in atoms emit light when they move from higher energy level to a lower energy level	The eye, Photocells, Photographic film
Ultraviolet rays	400 nm to 1 nm	Inner shell electrons in atoms moving from higher energy level to a lower energy level	Photocells, Photographic film
X-rays	1 nm to 10^{-3} nm	X-ray tubes or inner shell electrons	Photographic film, Geiger tubes, Ionisation chamber
Gamma rays	$< 10^{-3}$ nm	Radioactive decay of the nucleus	Photographic film, ionisation chamber

Quick Test 2

1. Name the type of electromagnetic wave used in food industry to kill pathogenic microorganisms. Also write its frequency range.

2. Why does microwave oven heat up a food item containing water molecules most efficiently? *NCERT Exemplar*

3. A radio can tune into any station from 5.5 MHz to 16 MHz band. What is the corresponding wavelength band?

4. Use the formula, $\lambda_m T = 0.29$ cm-K to obtain the characteristic temperature ranges for different parts of the electromagnetic spectrum. What do the numbers that you obtain, tell you?

Answers

3. 54.5 m, 18.75 m *4.* 2900 K, 6000 K

For Solutions, See QR Code on Pg. 275

Mind Map

Displacment Current

When dealing with time varying electric fields, it represents a form of current that arises not from the motion of charges but from the changing electric field in a region.

Mathematically, $I_d = \varepsilon_0 \frac{d\phi}{dt}$

Maxwell's Equation

Maxwell's equations are the basic laws of electricity and magnetism.

1. Gauss's law in electrostatics

$$\oint \mathbf{E} \cdot d\mathbf{S} = \frac{q}{\varepsilon_0}$$

2. Gauss's law in magnetostatics

$$\oint \mathbf{B} \cdot d\mathbf{S} = 0$$

3. Faraday's law of electromagnetic Induction

$$\oint \mathbf{E} \cdot d\mathbf{l} = -\frac{d\phi_B}{dt}$$

4. Ampere-Maxwell's circuital law

$$\oint \mathbf{B} \cdot d\mathbf{l} = \mu_0 \left(I_c + \varepsilon_0 \frac{d\phi_E}{dt} \right)$$

Applications of Displacement Current

Charging a Capacitor
Displacement current flows through the dielectric of a capacitor when the electric field changes as it charges or discharges.

Electromagnetic Waves
Displacement current is crucial for the generation of electromagnetic waves, as it ensures the continuity of the magnetic field in regions without conduction current.

Significance
Displacement current bridges the gap in Ampere's law, ensuring that Maxwell's equations remain consistent and complete.

Electromagnetic Waves

Electromagnetic Waves (EM)

These are a form of radiation that propagate through space and consist of oscillating electric and magnetic fields that are perpendicular to each other and to the direction of wave propagation.

Transverse Nature (Qualitative Ideal)

The electric field vector oscillates up and down along the *Y*-axis, and the magnetic field vector oscillates along the *Z*-axis.
Both fields are perpendicular to each other and to the direction of propagation of wave, forming a 3D structure.
This transverse nature ensures the wave's ability to propagate even in the absence of a medium.
It also explains phenomena like polarisation, where the orientation of the electric field vector can be restricted to a single plane.

Characteristics of EM Waves

Transverse Nature EM waves are transverse waves, meaning the oscillations of the electric and magnetic fields are perpendicular to the direction of wave propagation.

Speed of Propagation In a vacuum, EM waves travel at the speed of light *c*. In mediums other than a vacuum, the speed decreases depending on the material's refractive index

Self-Sustaining Nature The oscillating electric field generates the magnetic field and *vice-versa*, making the wave self-sustaining.

Energy Transport EM waves carry energy in the form of oscillating electric and magnetic fields.

Spectrum EM waves cover a wide range of frequencies and wavelengths, collectively known as the electromagnetic spectrum. e.g. include radio waves, microwaves, infrared, visible light, ultraviolet, X-rays, and gamma rays.

Electromagnetic Spectrum

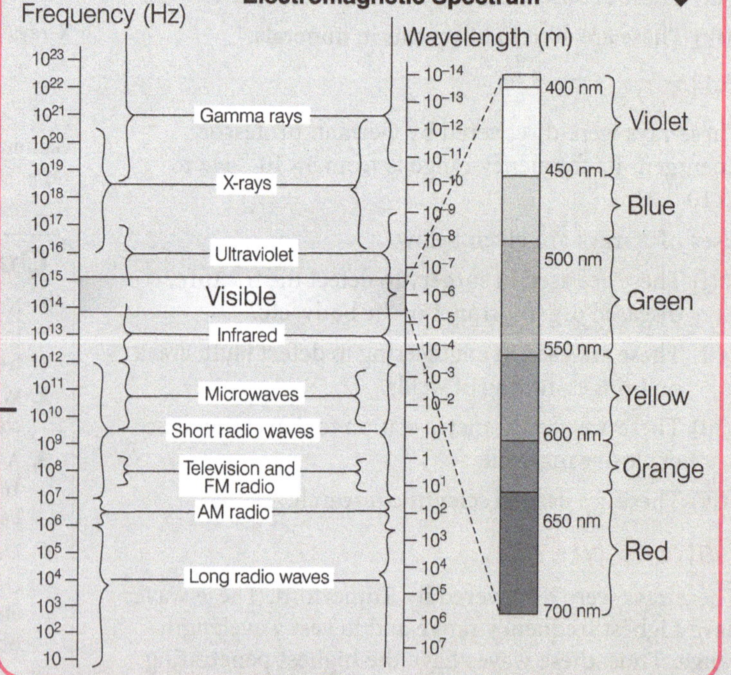

Radiowaves
- Used in AM and FM
- Used in cell phone communication

Microwaves
- Used in RADAR systems
- Used in microwave ovens for cooking

Infrared waves
- Used for weather forecasting.
- Used in physical therapy.

Visible Rays
- Used in photography.
- Used in fibre optic communications.

Ultraviolet Rays
- Used for studying molecular structure.
- Used in sterilising surgical instruments.

X-Rays
- Used to detect fractures in bones.
- Used in detecting metals on explosives.

Gamma rays
- Used in the treatment of cancer and tumor. Also used to initiate nuclear reaction.

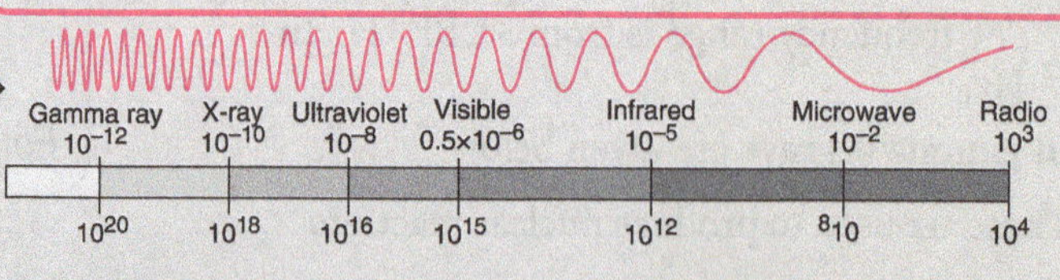

EXAM PATTERN QUESTIONS

Objective Type Questions

Multiple Choice Questions (MCQs)

1. **Which statement represents the symmetrical counterpart of Faraday's law and a consequence of the displacement current being a source of a magnetic field?**

(a) An electric field changing with time gives rise to a magnetic field.

(b) A magnetic field changing with time gives rise to an electric field.

(c) An emf changing with time gives rise to an electric field.

(d) A displacement current, changing with time gives rise to an electric field.

2. **A linearly polarised electromagnetic wave given as $\mathbf{E} = E_0 \hat{\mathbf{i}} \cos(kz - \omega t)$ is incident normally on a perfectly reflecting infinite wall at $z = a$. Assuming that the material of the wall is optically inactive, the reflected wave will be given as**

(a) $\mathbf{E}_r = E_0 \hat{\mathbf{i}}(kz - \omega t)$ (b) $\mathbf{E}_r = E_0 \hat{\mathbf{i}} \cos(kz + \omega t)$

(c) $\mathbf{E}_r = -E_0 \hat{\mathbf{i}} \cos(kz + \omega t)$ (d) $\mathbf{E}_r = E_0 \hat{\mathbf{i}} \sin(kz - \omega t)$

3. **Total energy density of electromagnetic waves in vacuum is given by the relation**

(a) $\frac{1}{2} \cdot \frac{E^2}{\varepsilon_0} + \frac{B^2}{2\mu_0}$ (b) $\frac{1}{2} \varepsilon_0 E^2 + \frac{1}{2} \mu_0 B^2$

(c) $\frac{E^2 + B^2}{c}$ (d) $\frac{1}{2} \varepsilon_0 E^2 + \frac{B^2}{2\mu_0}$

4. **The magnetic field of an electromagnetic wave is represented as**

$B_x = B_0 \sin(ky - \omega t)$. It means that the wave propagation direction and wave vector k are respectively. CBSE 2024C

(a) $+Z$-axis, $\frac{2\pi}{v}$ (b) $-Z$-axis, $\frac{2\pi}{T}$

(c) $+Y$-axis, $\frac{2\pi}{\lambda}$ (d) $-Z$-axis, $\frac{\lambda}{2\pi}$

5. **If E and B represent electric and magnetic field vectors of the electromagnetic wave, the direction of propagation of electromagnetic wave is along** NCERT Exemplar

(a) E (b) B (c) $\mathbf{B} \times \mathbf{E}$ (d) $\mathbf{E} \times \mathbf{B}$

6. **The ratio of contributions made by the electric field and magnetic field components to the intensity of an EM wave is** NCERT Exemplar

(a) $c:1$ (b) $c^2:1$ (c) $1:1$ (d) $\sqrt{c}:1$

7. **In the following waves, which is not electromagnetic wave?**

(a) α-rays (b) γ-rays

(c) Infrared rays (d) X-rays

8. **The largest wavelength of electromagnetic wave is**

(a) X-rays (b) radio waves

(c) ultraviolet rays (d) infrared rays

9. **A plane electromagnetic wave travelling along X-axis has a wavelength 10.0 mm. The electric field points along y-direction and has peak value of 30 V/m. Then the magnetic field in terms of x in metre and t in second may be expressed as**

(a) $30 \sin 200\pi(ct - x)$

(b) $10^{-7} \sin 200\pi(ct - x)$

(c) $30 \sin \frac{2\pi}{10}(ct - x)$

(d) $10^{-7} \sin \frac{2\pi}{10}(ct - x)$

10. **In the process of charging of a capacitor, the current produced between the plates of the capacitor is (where symbols have their usual meanings)** CBSE 2023

(a) $\mu_0 \frac{d\phi_E}{dt}$ (b) $\frac{1}{\mu_0} \frac{d\phi_E}{dt}$ (c) $\varepsilon_0 \frac{d\phi_E}{dt}$ (d) $\frac{1}{\varepsilon_0} \frac{d\phi_E}{dt}$

11. **If ε_0 and μ_0 are the electric permittivity and magnetic permeability of free space and ε and μ are the corresponding quantities in the medium, the index of refraction of the medium in terms of above parameter is**

(a) $\frac{\varepsilon\mu}{\varepsilon_0 \mu_0}$ (b) $\left(\frac{\varepsilon\mu}{\varepsilon_0 \mu_0}\right)^{1/2}$

(c) $\left(\frac{\varepsilon_0 \mu_0}{\varepsilon\mu}\right)$ (d) $\left(\frac{\varepsilon_0 \mu_0}{\varepsilon\mu}\right)^{1/2}$

12. **The electromagnetic radiations used to kill germs in water purifiers are called** CBSE 2023

(a) infrared waves (b) X-rays

(c) gamma rays (d) ultraviolet rays

13. **The phase difference between electric field E and magnetic field B in an electromagnetic wave propagating along Z-axis is** CBSE 2024

(a) zero (b) π (c) $\frac{\pi}{2}$ (d) $\frac{\pi}{4}$

14. **Study the following statements carefully.**

A. Electric and magnetic fields have zero average value in a plane EM wave.

B. For an EM wave, the ratio of k/ω is independent of wavelength.

C. In an EM wave, the **E** and **B** fields vary with the same frequency and are in opposite phase.

D. Since $E=cB$, the energy associated with the electric field is much greater than that associated with the magnetic field. **Competency Based Que.**

Identify the correct option.

(a) Only A and B are correct
(b) Only C and D are correct
(c) Only A and C are correct
(d) Only B and D are correct

15. **Light with an energy flux of 20 W/cm^2 falls on a non-reflecting surface at normal incidence. If the surface has an area of 30 cm^2, then the total momentum delivered (for complete absorption during 30 minutes) is**

(a) 3.6×10^{-3} kg m/s (b) 36×10^{-10} kg m/s
(c) 108×10^{-4} kg m/s (d) 1.08×10^{-7} kg m/s

16. **A 100 Ω resistance and a capacitor of 100 Ω reactance are connected in series across a 220 V source. When the capacitor is 50% charged, the peak value of the displacement current is**

(a) 2.2 A (b) 11 A
(c) 4.4 A (d) $11\sqrt{2}$ A

17. **An LC circuit contains inductance $L=1\,\mu$H and capacitance $C=0.01\,\mu$F. The wavelength of the electromagnetic wave generated is nearly**

(a) 0.5 m (b) 5 m
(c) 30 m (d) 188 m

18. **The radiowaves of wavelength 360 m are transmitted from a transmitter. The inductance of the coil which must be connected with capacitor of capacitance 3.6 μF in a resonant circuit to receive these waves will be nearly**

(a) 10^3 H (b) 10^2 H (c) 10^{-4} H (d) 10^{-8} H

19. **Correct match of Column I with Column II is**

Column I (Waves)		Column II (Production)	
A.	Infrared	P.	Rapid vibration of electrons in aerials
B.	Radio	Q.	Electrons in atoms emit light when they move from higher to lower energy level.
C.	Light	R.	Klystron valve
D.	Microwave	S.	Vibration of atoms and molecules

Codes

	A	B	C	D
(a)	P	R	S	Q
(b)	S	P	Q	R
(c)	Q	P	S	R
(d)	S	R	P	Q

20. **Match the following electromagnetic waves with their 20equency range.**

Column I		Column II	
A.	Visible light	P.	10^8 - 10^{11} Hz
B.	Ultraviolet radiation	Q.	10^{14} - 10^{15} Hz
C.	Gamma rays	R.	10^{19} - 10^{24} Hz
D.	Radio waves	S.	10^4 - 10^9 Hz

Codes

	A	B	C	D
(a)	Q	P	R	S
(b)	P	Q	R	S
(c)	S	R	Q	P
(d)	Q	R	P	S

Assertion-Reason

Directions *(Q.No. 21-29) In the following questions, two statements are given- one labelled Assertion (A) and the other labelled Reason (R). Select the correct answer to these questions from the codes (a), (b), (c) and (d) as given below.*

(a) Both Assertion and Reason are true and Reason is the correct explanation of Assertion.
(b) Both Assertion and Reason are true but Reason is not the correct explanation of Assertion.
(c) Assertion is true but Reason is false.
(d) Assertion is false but Reason is true.

21. **Assertion (A)** While applying Ampere's circuital law to given surfaces with same perimeter, the left hand side $\oint B\cdot dl=\mu_0 i(t)$ has not changed but the right hand side is zero.

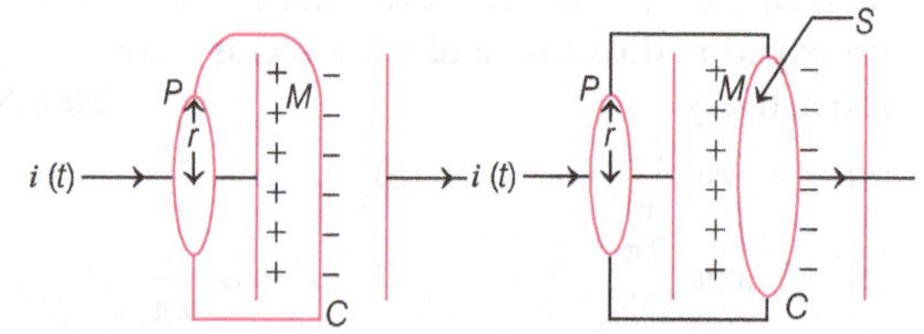

Reason (R) No current passes through the surface.

22. **Assertion (A)** An oscillating charge produces an electric field in space, which produces an oscillating magnetic field, which in turn, is a source of electric field and so on.

Reason (R) The oscillating electric and magnetic fields thus regnerate each other as a wave which propagates through space.

23. Assertion (A) When the sun shines on our hand, we feel the energy being absorbed from the electromagnetic waves (our hands get warm).
Reason (R) Electromagnetic waves also transfer momentum to our hand but because *c* is very large, the amount of momentum transferred is extremely small and we do not feel the pressure.

24. Assertion (A) In electromagnetic wave electric field vector and magnetic field vector are mutually perpendicular.
Reason (R) Electromagnetic waves are transverse in nature.

25. Assertion (A) An oscillating electric charge loses energy.
Reason (R) An oscillating electric charge radiates EM waves. **Competency Based Que.**

26. Assertion (A) Out of infrared and radiowaves, the radiowaves show more diffraction effect.
Reason (R) Radiowaves have greater frequency than infrared waves. **CBSE 2025**

27. Assertion (A) Optical waves are better carriers of signals than microwaves.
Reason (R) Microwaves move faster than optical waves.

28. Assertion (A) Gamma rays are more energetic than X-rays.
Reason (R) Gamma rays are of nuclear origin while X-rays originate from heavy atoms.

29. Assertion (A) UV radiation causes photo dissociation of ozone into O_2 and O, thus causing damage to the stratospheric ozone layer.
Reason (R) Ozone hole is resulting in global warming and climate change.

Case Based Questions

Directions *(Q.No. 30) This question is case study based question. Read the following paragraph and answer the questions on the basis of same.*

30. Electromagnetic waves are transverse in nature, *i.e.*, electric and magnetic fields are perpendicular to each other and to the direction of wave propagation. Electromagnetic waves are not deflected by electric and magnetic fields.

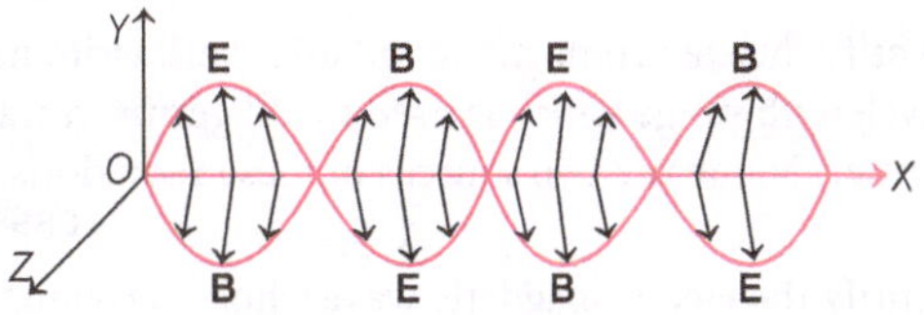

The magnetic field in a plane electromagnetic wave is given by $B_y = 2 \times 10^{-7} \sin(0.5 \times 10^3 x + 1.5 \times 10^{11} t)$ T.

(i) What is the angular frequency of wave?
(a) 0.5×10^3 rad s^{-1}
(b) 1.5×10^{11} rad s^{-1}
(c) 3×10^8 rad s^{-1}
(d) 2×10^{-7} rad s^{-1}

(ii) What is the wavelength of the wave?
(a) 12.6 cm (b) 1.26 cm (c) 1. 26 m (d) 6.12 m

(iii) What is the frequency of the wave?
(a) 2.39 GHz
(b) 23.9 MHz
(c) 23.9 GHz
(d) 20.3 MHz

(iv) The maximum value of electric field is
(a) 6×10^2 Vm^{-1}
(b) 6×10^3 Vm^{-1}
(c) 6×10^1 Vm^{-1}
(d) 6 Vm^{-1}

(v) Write an expression for the electric field?
(a) $E_y = 60 \sin(0.5 \times 10^3 x + 1.5 \times 10^{11} t)$ Vm^{-1}
(b) $E_x = 60 \sin(0.5 \times 10^3 x + 1.5 \times 10^{11} t)$ Vm^{-1}
(c) $E_z = 60 \sin(0.5 \times 10^3 x + 1.5 \times 10^{11} t)$ Vm^{-1}
(d) $E_y = 60 \cos(0.5 \times 10^3 x + 1.5 \times 10^{11} t)$ Vm^{-1}

Subjective Questions

Very Short Answer Type Questions

1. In which directions do the electric and magnetic field vectors oscillate in an electromagnetic wave propagating along the *X*-axis?

2. How is the speed of electromagnetic waves in vacuum determined by the electric and magnetic fields?

3. What physical quantity is the same for X-rays of wavelength 10^{-10} m, red light of wavelength 6800 Å and radiowaves of wavelength 500 m? **NCERT**

4. Even though an electric field *E* exerts a force *qE* on a charged particle yet electric field of an electromagnetic wave does not contribute to the radiation pressure (but transfers energy). Explain. **NCERT Exemplar**

5. Illustrate by giving suitable examples, how you can show that electromagnetic waves carry both energy and momentum. **CBSE 2019**

6. In which situation is there a displacement current but no conduction current?

7. The charging current for a capacitor is 0.25 A. What is the displacement current across its plates?

8. Differentiate between conduction current and displacement current. **CBSE 2020**

Short Answer Type Questions

9. How are infrared waves produced? Why are these referred to as 'heat waves'? Write their one important use. **Diksha**

10. Write any two characteristics of an electromagnetic wave. Why are microwave used in RADAR systems? **CBSE 2023**

11. How are X-rays produced? Give any two uses of these. **CBSE 2023**

12. Identify the electromagnetic radiation and write its wavelength range which is used to kill germs in water purifier. Name the two sources of these radiations. **CBSE 2023**

13. Identify the electromagnetic wave whose wavelengths range is from about

(i) 10^{-12} m to about 10^{-8} m

(ii) 10^{-3} m to about 10^{-1} m

Write one use of each. **CBSE 2023**

14. (i) How is an electromagnetic wave produced? **[1]**

(ii) An electromagnetic wave is travelling in vertically upward direction. At an instant, its electric field vector points in west direction. In which direction does the magnetic field vector point at that instant? **[1]**

(ii) Estimate the ratio of shortest wavelength of radiowaves to the longest wavelength of gamma waves. **CBSE 2025** **[1]**

15. What is meant by displacement current? How is this current different from the conduction current? A capacitor is being charged by a source of emf. Justify the continuity of current in the circuit. **CBSE 2024**

16. (i) The electric field **E** of an electromagnetic wave propagating in north direction is oscillating in up and down direction. Describe the direction of magnetic field **B** of the wave. **[1]**

(ii) Are the wavelength of radiowaves and microwaves longer or shorter than those detectable by human eyes? **[1]**

(iii) Write main use of each of the following in human life **CBSE 2025** **[1]**

(a) Infrared waves (b) Gamma rays

17. Explain the following giving reasons

(i) Electromagnetic waves differ considerably in their mode of interaction with matter. **[1]**

(ii) Food items to be heated in microwave oven must contain water. **[1]**

(iii) Welders wear face mask with glasses during welding. **CBSE 2024** **[1]**

18. Name the electromagnetic waves with their wavelength range which are used for **CBSE 2024** **[1]**

(i) FM radio broadcast.

(ii) detection of fracture in bones. **[1]**

(iii) treatment of muscular strain. **[1]**

19. Poynting vector is defined as a vector whose magnitude is equal to the wave intensity and whose direction is along the direction of wave propagation. Mathematically, it is given by $S = \frac{1}{\mu_0}(E \times B)$. Show the nature of S graph. **NCERT Exemplar**

Long Answer Type Questions

20. Name the constituent radiation of electromagnetic spectrum which

(i) is used in satellite communication. **[1]**

(ii) is used for studying crystal structure. **[1]**

(iii) is emitted during decay of radioactive nuclei.

Write two more uses of each. **[3]**

21. (i) How are infrared waves produced? Write their one important use. **[2]**

(ii) How are X-rays produced? Give any two uses of X-rays. **[3]**

22. (i) How is electromagnetic wave produced? What is the nature of electromagnetic waves? **[2]**

(ii) The magnetic field in a plane electromagnetic wave is given by

$$B_y = 8 \times 10^{-6} \sin[2 \times 10^{11} t + 300\pi]\text{T}$$

(a) What is the wavelength and frequency of the wave?

(b) Write an expression for the electric field. **[3]**

Diksha

23. How are X-rays different from γ-rays? Give a detailed description.

24. Answer the following questions.

(i) Name the electromagnetic waves which are used for the treatment of certain forms of cancer. Write their frequency range. **[2]**

(ii) Thin ozone layer on top of stratosphere is crucial for human survival. Why? **[1]**

(iii) Why is the amount of the momentum transferred by the electromagnetic waves incident on the surface so small? **[2]**

25. Answer the following questions.

(i) Name the electromagnetic waves which are produced during radioactive decay of a nucleus. Write their frequency range. **[2]**

(ii) Welders wear special glass goggles while working. Explain. Why? [1]

(iii) Why are infrared waves often called as heat waves? Give their one application. [2]

26. Name the parts of the electromagnetic spectrum which is

(i) suitable for RADAR systems in aircraft navigations. [1]

(ii) used to treat muscular strain. [1]

(iii) used as a diagnostic tool in medicine. [1]

Write in brief, how these waves can be produced? [2]

27. Name the following constituent radiations of electromagnetic spectrum which

(i) produce intense heating effect. [1½]

(ii) is absorbed by the ozone layer in the atmosphere. [1½]

(iii) is used for studying crystal structure. Write one more application for each of these radiations. [2]

28. (i) Which segment of electromagnetic waves has highest frequency? How are these waves produced? Give one use of these waves. [2]

(ii) Which EM waves lie near the high frequency end of visible part of EM spectrum?

Give its one use. In what way, this component of light has harmful effects on humans? [3]

Numerical Problems

Electromagnetic Wave

29. Green light of mercury has a wavelength 5×10^{-5} cm.

(i) What is the frequency (in MHz) and period (in second) in vacuum? [1]

(ii) What is the wavelength in glass, if refractive index of glass is 1.5? [2]

30. In a spaceship orbiting around the earth, two astronauts stationed 2 m apart are speaking to each other. The conversation is transmitted to earth *via* electromagnetic waves.

Given that the sound waves travel through the air between the two astronauts in exactly the same time as the EM waves take to reach the earth ground station.

Calculate the distance of the spaceship from the ground station. Take, speed of sound in the air between the two astronauts as 340 m/s. **Competency Based Que.**

31. A 2 mW laser beam is pointed on a 1 mm^2 area.

(i) What is the intensity of the beam in W/m^2?

(ii) If a 1 nC static charge is intercepted by this beam, what is the maximum electric force that the charge experiences?

(iii) What is the maximum magnetic force that acts on this charge, if it is set into a motion at 500 m/s?

(iv) Justify that the electric force exerted by the EM wave on the static charge is $\sim 10^6$ times the magnetic force on the moving charge as in the part (iii). **Competency Based Que.**

Electromagnetic Spectrum

32. There are some famous numbers associated with electromagnetic radiations in different contexts in Physics given below. State the part of the electromagnetic spectrum to which each belongs.

(i) 21 cm (wavelength emitted by atomic hydrogen in interstellar space).

(ii) 1057 MHz (frequency of radiation arising from two close energy levels in hydrogen, known as Lamb shift).

(iii) 2.7 K (temperature associated with the isotropic radiation filling all space thought to be a relic of the big-bang origin of the universe).

(iv) 5890 Å-5896 Å (double lines of sodium).

(v) 14.4 keV (energy of a particular transition in ^{57}Fe nucleus associated with a famous high resolution spectroscopic method (Mössbauer spectroscopy).

33. The terminology of different parts of the electromagnetic spectrum is given in the text. Use the formula $E = h\nu$ (for energy of a quantum of radiation: photon) and obtain the photon energy in units of eV for different parts of the electromagnetic spectrum. In what way are the different scales of photon energies that you obtain related to the sources of electromagnetic radiation? **NCERT**

Hints & Solutions

Objective Type Questions

1. (a) 2. (b) 3. (d) 4. (c) 5. (d)

6. (c) 7. (a) 8. (b) 9. (b) 10. (c)

11. (b) 12. (d)

13. (a) The phase difference between electric field **E** and magnetic field **B** in an electromagnetic wave propogating along Z-axis is zero.

14. (a) (i) In a plane electromagnetic wave, the electric field (E) and magnetic field (B) oscillate sinusoidally around zero. So, their average values over one complete cycle is zero.

$\therefore$ Statement (A) is correct.

(ii) The ratio of k/ω is called phase velocity $(v_p = \frac{\omega}{k})$. For electromagnetic waves in a vacuum, this is the speed of light c, which is constant and independent of the wavelength.

$\therefore$ Statement (B) is also correct.

15. (a) 16. (a) 17. (d) 18. (d)

19. (b) A $\rightarrow$ S, B $\rightarrow$ P, C $\rightarrow$ Q, D $\rightarrow$ R.

20. (d) A $\rightarrow$ Q, B $\rightarrow$ R, C $\rightarrow$ P, D $\rightarrow$ S.

21. (a) On applying Ampere's circuital law to such surfaces with the same perimeter, we find that the left hand side of equation $\oint B \cdot dl = \mu_0 i(t)$ has not changed but the right hand side is zero and not $\mu_0 i$. Since, no current passes through the surface.

22. (a) 23. (a) 24. (a)

25. (a) An oscillating electric charge produces an oscillating electric field and this induces a magnetic field. These two oscillating electric and magnetic fields regenerate each other. This causes the charge to lose energy in the form of EM waves.

26. (b) 27. (c) 28. (b) 29. (a)

30. (i) (b) Comparing with given equation, we get

$$\omega = 1.5 \times 10^{11} \text{ rad s}^{-1}$$

(ii) (b) Comparing the given equation with magnetic field in a plane

i.e., $$B_y = B_0 \sin\left[2\pi\left(\frac{x}{\lambda} + \frac{t}{T}\right)\right]$$

we get $$\lambda = \frac{2\pi}{0.5 \times 10^3} \text{ m} = 1.26 \text{ cm}$$

(iii) (c) As we know, frequency, $\nu = \frac{1}{\text{time taken}}$

$$\nu = \frac{1}{T} = \frac{\omega}{2\pi} = (1.5 \times 10^{11})/2\pi$$

$$= 23.9 \text{ GHz}$$

(iv) (c) According to Maxwell equation, electric field

i.e., $$E_0 = B_0 c = 2 \times 10^{-7} \times 3 \times 10^8 \text{ ms}^{-1}$$
$$= 6 \times 10^1 \text{ Vm}^{-1}$$

(v) (c) The electric field component is perpendicular to the direction of propagation and the direction of magnetic field. Therefore, the electric field component along the Z-axis is obtained as

$E_z = 60 \sin(0.5 \times 10^3 x + 1.5 \times 10^{11} t) \text{ Vm}^{-1}$

Subjective Questions

1. **E** and **B** are perpendicular to the direction of propagation of light. Also, direction of propagation is parallel to **E** $\times$ **B**.

Hence, **E** is along **j** or $+Y$-axis and **B** is along **k** or $+Z$-axis.

2. To determine speed of light in vacuum, we use the formula, $c = \frac{E_0}{B_0} = \frac{E_{rms}}{B_{rms}}$

where, E_0 and B_0 are maximum electric field and magnetic field components respectively, of electromagnetic waves.

3. Speed remains the same but wavelength differs.

4. Electric field of an electromagnetic wave is an oscillating field which causes force on the charged particle. This electric force averaged over an integral number of cycles is zero, because its direction changes with every half cycle. So, electric field is not responsible for radiation pressure.

5. When EM waves falls on charged particles, they set the charges into motion. This illustrates that the EM waves have energy and momentum.

Alternatively

When the sun shines on your hand, you feel energy being absorbed from the EM waves.

Alternatively

The radio and TV signals carry energy from one place to another (Give full marks if student explains on the basis of any one of above example)

Example Photoelectric effect

6. During charging or discharging there is a displacement current but no conduction current between plates of capacitor.

7. The displacement current is equal to the charging current. So, displacement current is also 0.25 A.

8. Conduction current is due to the flow of charges whereas the displacement current due to the change of electric field/ flux between the capacitor plates or due to changing electric field/ flux.

9. Infrared rays are produced by hot bodies and molecules. Infrared waves are sometimes referred to as heat waves because water molecules present in most materials readily absorb infrared waves. After absorption, their thermal motion increases, i.e., they heat up and heat their surroundings.

Infrared lamps are used in physical therapy.

10. Characteristics of an electromagnetic wave are

(a) The electromagnetic waves are produced by accelerated charge.

(b) These waves do not require any material medium of propagation.

Microwaves are used in radar system due to their short wavelengths.

11. X-rays are produced due to sudden deceleration of fast moving electrons when they collide and interact with target anode.

Uses of X-rays are

(a) They are used in engineering to detect faults, cracks on bridge, testing of welds.

(b) These are used in scientific research.

12. Ultraviolet rays are used to kill germs in water purifier. Its wavelength range is 400 nm to 1 nm.

The source of the ultra voilet rays are tanning booths and mercury vapor lamps.

13. Refer to text on pages 264 and 265.

14. (i) An accelerating charge produces an oscillating electric field in space, which produces an oscillating magnetic field, which inturn produces an oscillating electric field and so on. These oscillating electrical magnetic fields regenerate each other as a wave which propagates through space.

(ii) The magnetic field vector point in the South direction.

(iii) Shortest wavelength of radiowave, $\lambda_0 = 10^{-3}$m

Longest wavelength of gamma wave, $\lambda_g = 10^{-10}$ m

Their ratio will be

$$\frac{\lambda_r}{\lambda_g} = \frac{10^{-3}}{10^{-10}} = 10^7$$

15. Displacement current is that current which comes into play in the region in which the electric field and the electric flux is changing with time.

The displacement current arises due to rate of change of electric flux between the two plates of the capacitor and conduction current is due to flow of electrons.

When a capacitor is being charged by a source of emf, the conduction and displacement currents are individually discontinuous, but the currents together have the property of continuity through any closed electric circuit given by modified Ampere's law.

i.e. $$\oint \mathbf{B} \cdot d\mathbf{l} = \mu_0[I_c + I_d] = \mu_0\left[I_c + \varepsilon_0 \frac{d\phi_E}{dt}\right]$$

where, I_c = conduction current

and I_d = displacement current.

16. (i) We know that electromagnetic waves are transverse which are associated with both electric and magnetic fields. The electric and magnetic fields associated with the wave are mutually perpendicular as well as is perpendicular to the direction of propagation of the wave.

It is given that the electric field **E** is in the north direction and the wave oscillates in the up and down direction so the magnetic field will oscillate along the east-west direction.

(ii) The wavelength range of visible light is 400nm-700nm whereas the wavelength range of radiowaves is greater than 1m and that of microwaves is between 0.1m to 1 mm.

Human eyes can only detect wavelengths in the visible range. Hence microwaves and radiowaves are not detectable by human eyes.

(iii) (a) Infrared waves : Used in physical therapy.

(b) Gamma rays : Used in radio therapy to kill tumours and cancer.

17. (i) The basic difference between various types of electromagnetic waves lies in their wavelength of frequencies, since all of them travel through vacuum with the same speed. Consequently, the waves differ considerably in their mode of interaction with matter.

(ii) If there is no water present in the food material, then microwaves will not be able to generate heat in the food because the energy from the wave will transmit to the kinetic energy of the molecules. This raise the temperature of the food.

(iii) It is very necessary to wear special glass googles to welders while working, so that they can protect their eyes from harmful electromagnetic radiations.

18. (i) Radiowaves are used for broadcasting programmes to distant places like FM radio broadcast.

The wavelength range which is used is 10^{-1}m to 10^4 m.

(ii) X-rays are used in medical diagnosis to detect fractures in bones, etc.

The wavelength range in which it lies is 10^{-10}m to 10^{-8}m.

(iii) Infrared waves are used for the treatment of muscular strain.

The wavelength range in which it lies is 10^{-3}m to 7×10^{-7}m.

19. Consider an electromagnetic wave with **E** varying along Y-axis, **B** along Z-axis and propagation of wave along X-axis. Then, $\mathbf{E} \times \mathbf{B}$ will indicate the direction of propagation of energy flow in electromagnetic wave which will be along X-axis.

Let $\mathbf{E} = E_0 \sin(\omega t - kx)\hat{j}$

$$\mathbf{B} = B_0 \sin(\omega t - kx)\hat{k}$$

$$\mathbf{S} = \frac{1}{\mu_0}(\mathbf{E} \times \mathbf{B}) = \frac{1}{\mu_0} E_0 B_0 \sin^2(\omega t - kx)[\hat{j} \times \hat{k}]$$

$$= \frac{E_0 B_0}{\mu_0} \sin^2(\omega t - kx)\hat{i} \quad [\because \hat{j} \times \hat{k} = \hat{i}]$$

The variation of $|\mathbf{S}|$ with time t will be as given in the figure below.

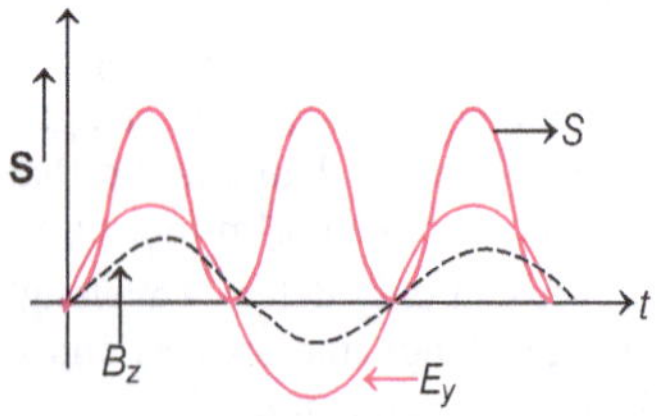

20. Refer to text on page 264 and 265.

21. (i) Infrared waves are produced by hot bodies and molecules.

Important uses of infrared waves are

(a) To treat muscular strains.

(b) To reveal the secret writings on ancient walls.

(ii) Refer to page no. 265.

22. (i) Electromagnetic waves are produced due to oscillating/accelerating charged particles.

Electromagnetic waves are transverse in nature, i.e. electric and magnetic fields are perpendicular to each other and to the direction of wave propagation. Electromagnetic waves are not deflected by electric and magnetic fields.

(ii) (a) Comparing the given equation with

$$B_y = B_0 \sin 2\pi\left(\frac{x}{\lambda} + \frac{t}{T}\right)$$

we get, $\lambda = \frac{2\pi}{300\pi}$ m $= 0.0067$ m

and $\nu = \frac{1}{T} = \frac{2 \times 10^{11}}{2\pi} = 3.18 \times 10^{10}$ Hz

(b) $E_0 = B_0 c = 8 \times 10^{-6} \times 3 \times 10^8$

$= 2400$ V/m

The electric field component is perpendicular to the direction of propagation and the direction of magnetic field. Therefore, the electric field component along the Z-axis is obtained

$$E_z = 2400 \sin(2 \times 10^{11} t + 300\pi x) \text{ V/m}$$

23. Refer to page no. 265.

24. (i) Refer to text on page no. 265.

(ii) Because sun emit harmful ultraviolet rays. The ozone layer acts as an invisible shield and protects us from these harmful rays.

(iii) Due to large value of speed of light (c), the amount of momentum transferred by the electromagatic waves incident on the surface so small.

25. (i) Refer to text on page no. 265.

(ii) Welders wear special goggles with glass windows to protect their eyes from ultraviolet rays.

(iii) Infrared waves are produced from heat radiating bodies and molecules. It has high penetration power. Its frequency range is from 3×10^{11} Hz to 4×10^{14} Hz. That's why infrared waves often called as heat waves. This wave is used in physical therapy.

26. (i) Microwave

(ii) Infrared waves are used to treat muscular strain.

(iii)
- X-rays are used as a diagnostic tool in medicine.
- Microwaves are produced by special vaccum tubes.
- Infrared waves are produced from the heat radiating bodies.
- X-rays are produced when high energy electrons strike a metal target and stopping them in targets.

27. (i) Infrared rays (ii) Ultraviolet rays

(iii) X-rays

Infrared rays are used in weather forecasting, Ultraviolet rays are used in burglar alarm and X-rays are used in scientific research.

28. (i) Gamma waves has highest frequency. This high frequency radiation is produced in nuclear reactions and also emitted by radioactive nuclie. Gamma rays are used in engineering to detect fault, crack on bridge.

(ii) Ultraviolet rays lie near the high frequency end of visible part of EM spectrum. They are used to sterilize surgical instrument. If ultraviolet rays directly come to humans, then it is harmful because of its high frequency.

29. (i) Frequency of the wave,

$$\nu = \frac{c}{\lambda} = \frac{3 \times 10^8 \text{ m/s}}{5 \times 10^{-5} \text{ cm}}$$

$$= \frac{3 \times 10^8 \text{ m/s}}{5 \times 10^{-7} \text{ m}} = 6 \times 10^{14} \text{ Hz}$$

or $\nu = 6 \times 10^8$ MHz

Time period, $T = \frac{1}{\nu} = \frac{1}{6 \times 10^{14} \text{ Hz}}$

$= 0.16 \times 10^{-14}$ s

(ii) Refractive index, $\mu = \frac{c}{v}$

$$\Rightarrow v = \frac{c}{\mu} = \frac{3 \times 10^8}{1.5} = 2 \times 10^8 \text{ m/s}$$

Also, $\nu = \dfrac{v}{\lambda}$

$$\Rightarrow \quad \lambda = \frac{v}{\nu} = \frac{2 \times 10^8}{6 \times 10^{14}} = 0.33 \times 10^{-6} \text{ m}$$

$$= 3.3 \times 10^{-7} \text{ m}$$

30. For the travel of sound waves between the two astronauts, $2/340 = t$ ...(i)

For the travel of EM waves from the spaceship of the earth station, $d/(3 \times 10^8) = t$. ...(ii)

Equating Eqs. (i) and (ii), we get

$$\frac{2}{340} = \frac{d}{3 \times 10^8}$$

$$d = 1764.7 \times 10^3 \approx 1765 \text{ km}$$

31. (i) Intensity of the EM beam, $I = \dfrac{\text{Power}}{\text{Area}}$

$$= \frac{2 \times 10^{-3}}{10^{-6}} = 2000 \text{ W/m}^2$$

(ii) Intensity I of the EM beam is also given as

$$= \frac{1}{2} c \varepsilon_0 E_0^2 \; (= \frac{1}{2} \text{ of electric field energy intensity} \times c)$$

$$E_0 = \sqrt{\frac{2I}{c \varepsilon_0}} = \sqrt{\frac{2 \times 2000}{3 \times 10^8 \times 8.85 \times 10^{-12}}}$$

$$\Rightarrow \quad E_0 = 1.22 \times 10^3 \text{ N/C}$$

Maximum force of the static charge,

$$F = qE_0 = 1 \times 10^{-9} \times 1.22 \times 10^3$$

$$= 1.22 \times 10^{-6} \text{ N}$$

(iii) Maximum magnetic force of a moving charge,

$$F_B = qvB_0 = \frac{qvE_0}{c}$$

$$= 1 \times 10^{-9} \times 500 \times \frac{1.22 \times 10^3}{3 \times 10^8} = 2 \times 10^{-12} \text{ N}$$

(iv) $\dfrac{F_E}{F_B} = \dfrac{1.22 \times 10^{-6}}{2 \times 10^{-12}} \sim 10^6$

So, the electric force exerted by the EM wave on the static charge is $\sim 10^6$ times, the magnetic force on the moving charge.

32. (i) This wavelength (21 cm) corresponds to the radio waves.

(ii) This frequency (1057 MHz) also corresponds to the radio waves (short wavelength).

(iii) As, $T = 2.7$ K

Using the formula, $\lambda_m T = b = 0.29$ cm-K

$$\lambda_m = \frac{0.29}{2.7} = 0.11 \text{ cm}$$

This wavelength corresponds to the microwaves region of the electromagnetic spectrum.

(iv) This wavelength lies in the visible region of the electromagnetic spectrum.

(v) Energy, $E = 14.4$ keV

$$= 14.4 \times 10^3 \times 1.6 \times 10^{-19} \text{ J}$$

Frequency of wave,

$$\nu = \frac{E}{h} = \frac{14.4 \times 1.6 \times 10^{-16}}{6.6 \times 10^{-34}} = 3.5 \times 10^{18} \text{ Hz}$$

This frequency lies in the X-ray region of the electromagnetic spectrum.

33. Given, energy of photon, $E = h\nu$

For γ-rays

Frequency of γ-rays, $\nu = 3 \times 10^{20}$ Hz

Energy of γ-rays, $E = h\nu = 6.6 \times 10^{-34} \times 3 \times 10^{20}$

$$= 19.8 \times 10^{-14} \text{ J}$$

$$\Rightarrow \quad E = \frac{19.8 \times 10^{-14}}{1.6 \times 10^{-19}}$$

$$= 1.24 \times 10^6 \text{ eV}$$

The source of γ-rays is nuclear origin.

For X-rays

Frequency of X-rays, $\nu = 3 \times 10^{18}$ Hz

Energy of X-rays, $E = h\nu = 6.6 \times 10^{-34} \times 3 \times 10^{18}$

$$= 19.8 \times 10^{-16} \text{ J}$$

$$\Rightarrow \quad E = \frac{19.8 \times 10^{-16}}{1.6 \times 10^{-19}} = 1.24 \times 10^4 \text{ eV}$$

The retardation of high energy electron produces X-rays. Similarly, we can find for ultraviolet rays, visible rays, infrared rays, microwaves and radio waves.

They originate by oscillating current

Types of radiation	Photon energy
γ-rays	1.24×10^6 eV
X-rays	1.24×10^4 eV
Ultraviolet rays	4.12 eV
Visible rays	2.475 eV
Infrared waves	4.125×10^{-2} eV
Microwaves	4.125×10^{-5} eV
Radio waves	1.24×10^{-6} eV

QR Code for Quick Test 1

QR Code for Quick Test 2

SELF ASSESSMENT TEST

Multiple Choice Questions (MCQs)

1. Which of the following statements is not true about the properties of electromagnetic waves?
   (a) These waves do not require any material medium for their propagation.
   (b) Both electric and magnetic field vectors attain the maxima and minima at the same time.
   (c) The energy in electromagnetic wave is divided equally between electric and magnetic fields.
   (d) Both electric and magnetic field vectors are parallel to each other.
2. An electromagnetic wave is produced by a charge
   (a) moving with a constant velocity
   (b) moving with a constant speed parallel to a magnetic field
   (c) moving with an acceleration
   (d) at rest
3. The ratio of the magnitude of the electric field and magnetic field of a plane electromagnetic wave is
   (a) 1 (b) $\frac{1}{c}$ (c) c (d) $\frac{1}{c^2}$
4. The electromagnetic waves used in RADAR systems are
   (a) Infrared waves
   (b) Ultraviolet rays
   (c) Microwaves
   (d) X-rays
5. Which one of the following electromagnetic radiation has the least wavelength?
   (a) Gamma rays (b) Microwave
   (c) Visible light (d) X-rays
6. The electric field E associated with an electromagnetic wave is represented by $E_y = E_0 \sin(kx - \omega t)$
   Which of the following statments is correct?
   (a) The wave is propagating along $+X$-axis
   (b) The wave is propagating along $+Z$-axis
   (c) The magnetic field $\mathbf{B}$ of the wave is acting along $+Y$-axis
   (d) The magnetic field $\mathbf{B}$ of the wave is acting along $-X$-axis

Directions *(Q.No. 7-8) In the following questions, two statements are given- one labelled Assertion (A) and the other labelled Reason (R). Select the correct answer to these questions from the codes (a), (b), (c) and (d) as given below.*

(a) Both Assertion and Reason are true and Reason is the correct explanation of Assertion.
(b) Both Assertion and Reason are true but Reason is not the correct explanation of Assertion.
(c) Assertion is true but Reason is false.
(d) Assertion is false but Reason is true.

7. **Assertion (A)** In electromagnetic wave, the direction of variations of electric and magnetic fields are perpendicular to each other and also perpendicular to the direction of wave propagation.
   Reason (R) Electromagnetic waves are transverse in nature.
8. **Assertion (A)** The frequency of the electromagnetic wave naturally equals the frequency of oscillations of the charge.
   Reason (R) The energy associated with the propagating wave comes at the expense of the energy of the source.

Case Based Questions

Directions *(Q.No. 9) This question is case study based question. Read the following paragraph and answer the questions on the basis of same.*

9. Wave Maxwell, in 1865, pointed out that when either an electric or a magnetic field is changing with time, a field of the other kind is induced in adjacent regions of space. From this Maxwell concluded that variation of electric and magnetic field vectors perpendicular to each other leads to the production of electromagnetic disturbances which show properties of waves and can travel in space even without any material medium. These waves are called electromagnetic waves.
   Electromagnetic waves with macroscopic wavelengths were first produced in the laboratory in 1887 by the

German physicist Heinrich Hertz. Seven years after Hertz, Jagdish Chandra Bose, working at Calcutta (now Kolkata) succeeded in producing and observing electromagnetic waves of much shorter wavelength (25 mm to 5 mm). At around the same time, Guglielmo Marconi in Italy followed Hertz's work and succeeded in transmitting electromagnetic waves over distances of many kilometers.

Electromagnetic waves have a broad frequency range 10^3 Hz to 10^{22} Hz. They can travel with speed of light (c) in vacuum. They obey the relation $c = \nu\lambda$, where ν is frequency and λ is wavelength.

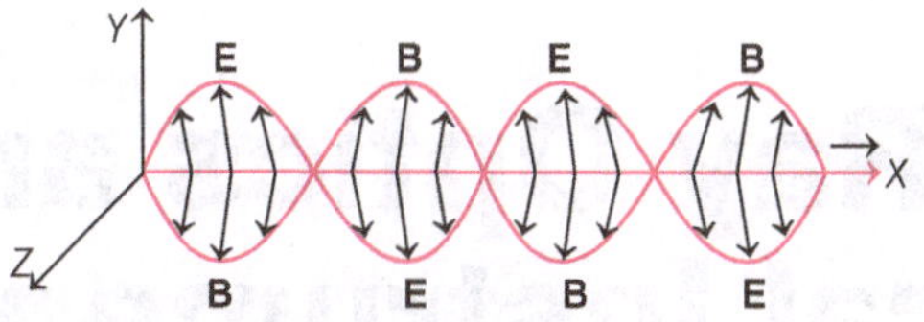

(i) Which of the following electromagnetic waves is in order of increasing frequency ?

(a) Microwave < Infrared < Ultraviolet < γ-rays
(b) γ-rays < Ultraviolet < Infrared < Microwave
(c) Ultraviolet < Infrared < Microwave < γ-rays
(d) γ-rays < Microwave < Infrared < Ultraviolet

(ii) Light wave constitutes

(a) electromagnetic waves
(b) longitudinal waves
(c) mechanical waves
(d) magnetic waves

(iii) If we want to produce electromagnetic waves of wavelength 500 km by an oscillating charge, then frequency of oscillating charge must be

(a) 600 Hz
(b) 500 Hz
(c) 167 Hz
(d) 15 Hz

(iv) The angle between **E** and **B** in an electromagnetic wave is

(a) 180° (b) 120°
(c) 90° (d) 45°

Or The electric field associated with an EM wave in vacuum is given by $\mathbf{E} = 40\cos(KZ - 6\times10^8 t)\hat{\mathbf{i}}$, where E, Z and t are in volt/m, metre and second respectively.

The value of vector K is

(a) $2\ \text{m}^{-1}$ (b) $0.5\ \text{m}^{-1}$ (c) $6\ \text{m}^{-1}$ (d) $3\ \text{m}^{-1}$

Very Short Answer Type Questions

10. (i) How are electromagnetic waves produced?

(ii) How do you convince yourself that electromagnetic waves carry energy and momentum?

11. (i) Arrange the following electromagnetic waves in the descending order of their wavelengths.

(a) Microwaves (b) Infrared rays
(c) Ultraviolet radiation (d) γ-rays

(ii) Write one use each of any two of them.

12. (i) Give one use of electromagnetic radiations obtained in nuclear disintegrations.

(ii) Give one example each to illustrate the situation where there is (a) displacement current but no conduction current and (b) only conduction current but no displacement current.

Short Answer Type Questions

13. (i) Depict a plane electromagnetic wave propagating along the X-axis. Write the expressions for its oscillating electric and magnetic fields.

(ii) Write three characteristics of electromagnetic waves.

14. Name the electromagnetic waves which are produced by the following

(i) Radioactive decays of nucleus
(ii) Welding arcs
(iii) Hot bodies

Write one use each of these waves.

Answers

1. (d) *2.* (c) *3.* (c) *4.* (c) *5.* (a)
6. (a) *7.* (a) *8.* (b)
9. (i) (a) (ii) (a) (iii) (a) (iv) (c) or (a)

09

CHAPTER

Ray optics is the study of light propagation in terms of rays, focusing on phenomena such as reflection, refraction and image formation, where light behaves as straight-line paths.

Ray Optics and Optical Instruments

YOUR STUDY GOALS

YOUR PRACTICE GOAL

- Objective Type Questions (29 Qs, MCQs, A-R)
- Case Based Questions (4)
- Subjective Questions (10 VSAs, 22 SAs, 15 LAs)
- Numerical Problems (14)

Ray Optics

The path trace by light along straight line is called **ray of light,** and bundle of such rays constitutes a **beam of light.**

The branch of study of light is called **optics.** Broadly, optics is divided into three groups

(i) Geometrical optics (Ray optics)

(ii) Wave optics

(iii) Quantum optics

9.1 Reflection of Light

The phenomenon of change in path of light (when light ray incident on a smooth surface) without change in the medium is called **reflection of light.**

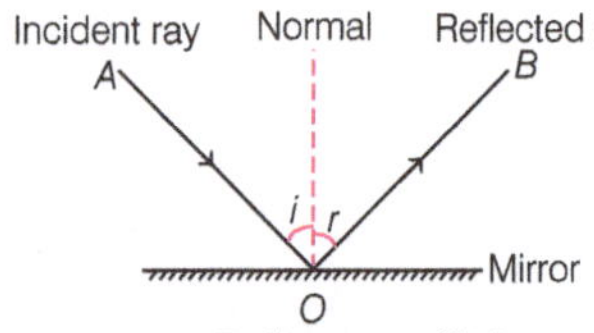

Reflection of light

Laws of Reflection

The laws of reflection are as given below

(i) The incident ray, the reflected ray and the normal to the reflecting surface all lie in the same plane.

(ii) The angle of reflection r is equal to the angle of incidence i, i.e. $i = r$.

- These laws are valid for any reflecting surface whether it is **plane** or **curved.**
- During reflection there is **no appreciable change in frequency and wavelength of light ray.**

Spherical Mirrors

Spherical mirror is a mirror whose reflecting surface is a part of a hollow sphere. Spherical mirrors are of two types

Concave Spherical Mirror A spherical mirror whose reflecting surface is towards the centre of the sphere is called concave spherical mirror.

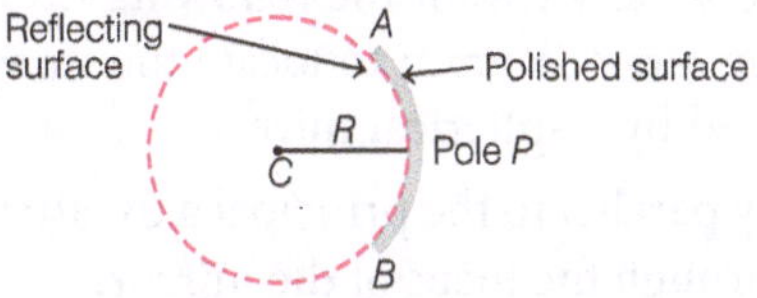

Concave mirror

Convex Spherical Mirror A spherical mirror whose reflecting surface is away from the centre of the sphere is called convex spherical mirror.

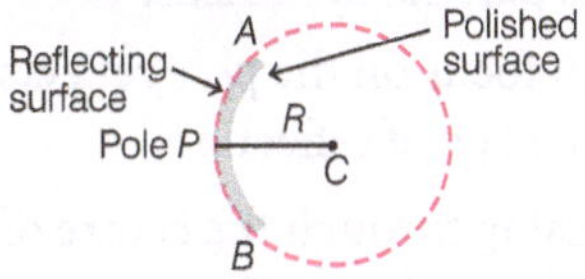

Convex mirror

Sign Convention

We must adopt sign convention for measuring distances, which are given below.

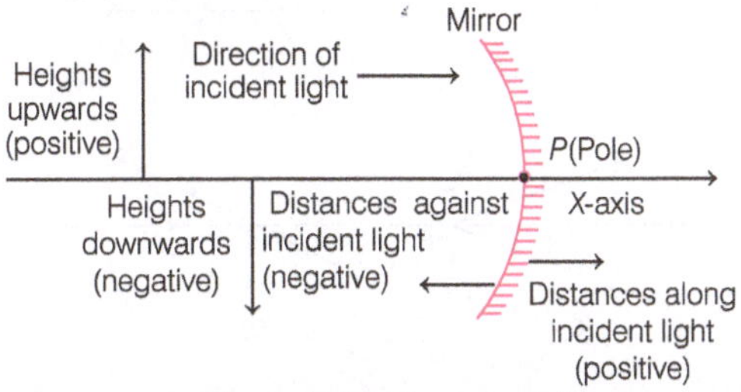

The cartesian sign convention

According to the cartesian sign convention

- All measurements should be taken from pole of mirror.
- All measurements along the direction of incident ray will be positive and opposite to incident ray are negative.
- All the measurements for the distances above the principal axis are taken as positive and below the principal axis are taken as negative.
- An object is always placed in front of a spherical mirror, so the **distance of the object** (u) is always **negative.**
- In a spherical mirror, **real image** is formed in front of the mirror. Therefore, its image distance (v) is taken as **negative**. However, **virtual image** is formed at the back of the mirror. So, its distance (v) is taken as **positive**, as per the new Cartesian sign convention.
- Similarly, focal length of a **concave mirror** is taken as **negative,** while that of **convex mirror** is taken as **positive.**

Focal Length of Spherical Mirrors

When a parallel beam of light is incident on a concave or convex mirror, the reflected rays **converge** or appear to **diverge** from a point F on principal axis called **principal focus** of the mirror.

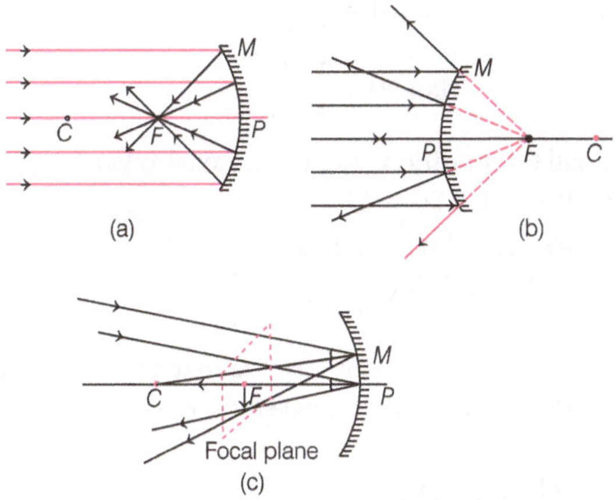

Focus of a concave and convex mirrors

The distance between the focus F and the pole P of the mirror is called **focal length.**

The Relation between Focal Length f and Radius of Curvature R

Focal length f and radius of curvature R are related as

$$\boxed{f = \frac{R}{2}}$$

Consider a ray parallel to the principal axis striking the mirror at point M, then CM will be perpendicular to the mirror at point M. Let θ be the angle of incidence and MD be perpendicular to the principal axis.

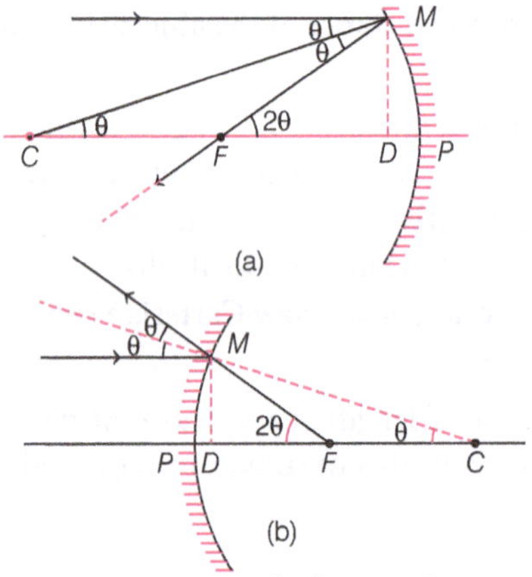

Geometry of reflection of an incident ray on
(a) concave spherical mirror

Then, $\angle MCP = \theta$

and $\angle MFP = 2\theta$

Now, $\tan\theta = \dfrac{MD}{CD}$

and $\tan 2\theta = \dfrac{MD}{FD}$ ...(i)

For small θ (condition true for paraxial rays), $\tan\theta \approx \theta$ and $\tan 2\theta \approx 2\theta$

Therefore, from Eq.(i), we get

$$\frac{MD}{FD} = 2\frac{MD}{CD} \quad \text{or} \quad FD = \frac{CD}{2} \qquad \text{...(ii)}$$

Again, for small θ, we can observe that the point D is very close to the point P. Therefore, $FD = f$ and $CD = R$.

From Eq.(ii), we have

$$\boxed{f = \frac{R}{2}}$$

Example 1 **Find the focal length of a convex mirror whose radius of curvature is 32 cm.**

Sol. Given,
Radius of curvature = 32 cm

From the relation between focal length (f) and radius of curvature (R)

We have $R = 2f$

$\therefore$ $f = \dfrac{R}{2}$ ...(i)

Now, putting the values in Eq. (i), we get

$$f = \frac{32}{2} = 16 \text{ cm}$$

Mirror Formula

Mirror formula (or equation) is a relation between focal length of the mirror, distances of object and image from the mirror.

Rules to Draw Image from Mirror

We can choose any two of the following rays when constructing a ray diagram to locate the **image** of an object formed by a spherical mirror.

(a) The ray parallel to the principal axis, after reflection goes through the focus of the mirror.

(b) The ray passing through the focus of the concave mirror or appearing to pass through (or directed towards) the focus of a convex mirror after reflection is parallel to the axis.

(c) The ray that focus on the pole reflects back by following the law of reflection.

(d) The ray passing through the centre of curvature of a concave mirror or appearing to pass through it for a convex mirror simply retraces the path.

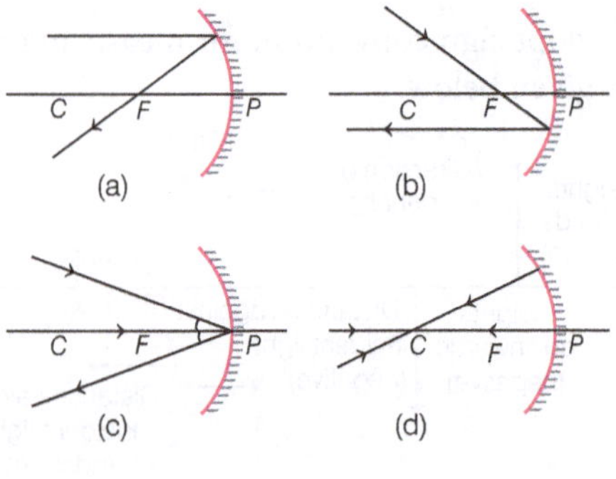

Derivation In the below figure, the ray diagram is considering three rays for image formation by a concave mirror.

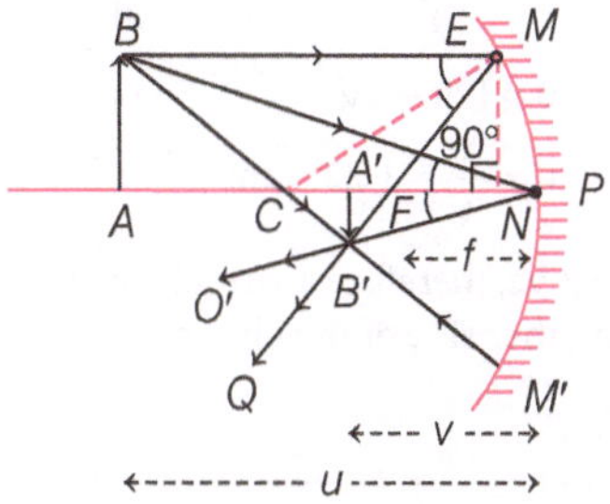

In the figure, triangles $A'B'F$ and NEF are similar.

Then, $$\frac{A'B'}{NM} = \frac{A'F}{NF}$$

As, the aperture of the concave mirror is small and the points N and P lie very close to each other, then

$$NF \approx PF \text{ and } NM = AB$$

$$\Rightarrow \quad \frac{A'B'}{AB} = \frac{A'F}{PF}$$

$$\therefore \quad \frac{A'B'}{AB} = \frac{PA' - PF}{PF} \qquad \ldots\text{(i)}$$

Also, triangles ABP and $A'B'P$ are similar, then

$$\frac{A'B'}{AB} = \frac{PA'}{PA} \qquad \ldots\text{(ii)}$$

From Eqs. (i) and (ii), we get

$$\frac{PA' - PF}{PF} = \frac{PA'}{PA} \qquad \ldots\text{(iii)}$$

Applying new Cartesian sign convention, we have

$$PA = -u$$

[∵ distance of object is measured against incident ray]

$$PA' = -v$$

[∵ distance of image is measured against incident ray]

$$PF = -f$$

[∵ focal length of concave mirror is measured against incident ray]

Substituting these values in Eq. (iii), we have

$$\frac{-v-(-f)}{-f} = \frac{-v}{-u} \Rightarrow \frac{v-f}{f} = \frac{v}{u} \Rightarrow \frac{v}{f} - 1 = \frac{v}{u}$$

Dividing both sides by v, we get

$$\therefore \quad \boxed{\frac{1}{f} = \frac{1}{u} + \frac{1}{v}}$$

The above relation is called **mirror formula.**

- **Relation between u, v and R**

∵ Focal length of the mirror, $f = \dfrac{R}{2}$

$$\therefore \quad \frac{1}{u} + \frac{1}{v} = \frac{1}{R/2} \Rightarrow \boxed{\frac{1}{u} + \frac{1}{v} = \frac{2}{R}}$$

Linear Magnification

The ratio of the height of the image (h') formed by a spherical mirror to the height of the object (h) is called the linear magnification of the spherical mirror.

It is denoted by m, i.e. $m = \dfrac{h'}{h}$

The above equation can be written as

$$\frac{h'}{h} = \frac{-v}{u} \qquad \ldots\text{(iv)}$$

∴ Linear magnification,

$$\boxed{m = \frac{h'}{h} = -\frac{v}{u} = -\frac{f}{u-f} = \frac{f-v}{f}}$$

The expression for magnification is the same for both the concave and convex mirrors.

- When $m > 1$, image formed is **enlarged.**
- When $m < 1$, image formed is **diminished.**
- When **m is positive,** image must be **erect, i.e. virtual.**
- When **m is negative,** image must be **inverted, i.e. real.**
- In case of **concave mirror,** m can be either positive or negative but in case of **convex mirror,** m is positive only.

Example 2. **A candle flame is held 3 cm away from a concave mirror of radius of curvature 24 cm. Where is the image formed? What is the nature of the image?**

Sol. Given, object distance, $u = -3$ cm

Radius of curvature, $R = -24$ cm

$$\therefore \quad f = \frac{R}{2} = \frac{-24}{2} = -12 \text{ cm}$$

From mirror formula, $\dfrac{1}{f} = \dfrac{1}{v} + \dfrac{1}{u}$

$$\Rightarrow \quad \frac{1}{v} = \frac{1}{f} - \frac{1}{u} = \frac{1}{(-12)} - \frac{1}{(-3)}$$

$$\Rightarrow \quad \frac{1}{v} = \frac{1}{-12} + \frac{1}{3} = \frac{-1+4}{12}$$

$$\Rightarrow \quad v = 4 \text{ cm}$$

∵ Magnification, $m = -\dfrac{v}{u} = \dfrac{-4}{-3} = +1.33$

i.e. The image formed is virtual, erect and magnified.

Example 3. **An object is placed in front of a convex mirror of focal length 30 cm. If the image is a quarter of the size of the object, find the position of the image.**

Sol. Given, focal length, $f = +30$ cm

Magnification, $m = \frac{1}{4}, v = ?$

From mirror's formula,

$$\frac{1}{f} = \frac{1}{u} + \frac{1}{v} \qquad \left[\because m = -\frac{v}{u} \Rightarrow u = -\frac{v}{m}\right]$$

$$\Rightarrow \frac{1}{f} = -\frac{m}{v} + \frac{1}{v}$$

$$\Rightarrow m = \frac{f - v}{f} \Rightarrow \frac{1}{4} = \frac{30 - v}{30}$$

$$\Rightarrow 30 = 120 - 4v$$

$$\Rightarrow v = \frac{90}{4} = +22.5 \text{ cm}$$

As, v is positive, therefore a virtual and erect image will be formed on other side of the object.

Quick Test 1

Conceptual Questions

1. A mirror is turned through 15°. With what angle will the reflected ray turn?
2. How can the real image of an object be obtained with a convex mirror?
3. The direction of ray of light incident on a concave mirror is shown by PQ while directions in which the ray would travel after reflection is shown by four rays marked as 1, 2, 3 and 4 in the figure? Which of the four rays correctly shows the direction of reflected rays?

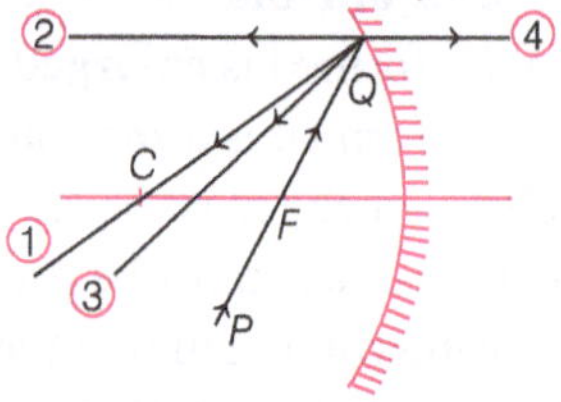

4. A concave mirror of small aperture forms a sharper image. Why?
5. An object AB is kept in front of a concave mirror as shown in the figure.
   (i) Complete the ray diagram showing the image formation of the object.
   (ii) How will the position and intensity of the image be affected, if the lower half of the mirror's reflecting surface is painted black?

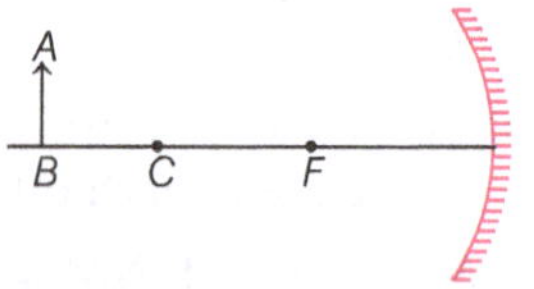

Numerical Questions

6. A square wire of side 3 cm is placed 25 cm away from a concave mirror of focal length 10 cm. What is the area enclosed by the image of the wire? Given, the centre of the wire is on the axis of the mirror, with its two sides normal to the axis.
7. An erect image 3 times the size of the object is obtained with a concave mirror of radius of curvature 36 cm. What is the position of the object?
8. A small candle, 2.5 cm in size is placed at 27 cm in front of a concave mirror of radius of curvature 36 cm. At what distance from the mirror should a screen be placed in order to obtain a sharp image? Describe the nature and size of the image. If the candle is moved closer to the mirror, how would the screen have to be moved? NCERT

Answers

6. 4 cm^2 *7.* −12 cm *8.* 54 cm, − 5 cm

For Solutions, See QR Code on Pg. 322

9.2 Refraction

When a ray of light enters from one transparent medium into another, there is a change in speed and direction of the ray in the second medium. This phenomena is called **refraction of light.**

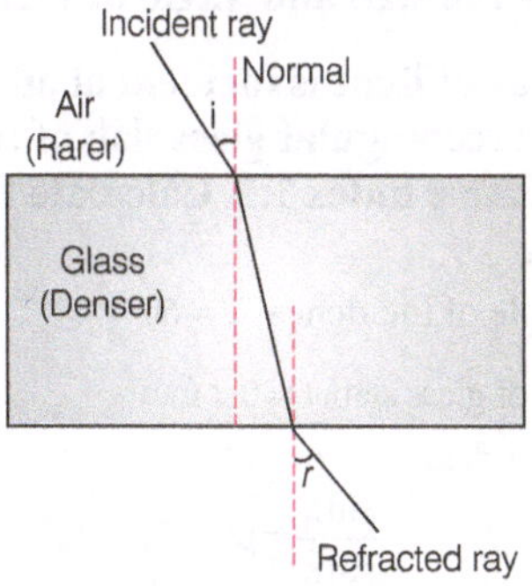

Laws of Refraction

(i) The incident ray, the refracted ray and the normal to the refracting surface (or interface) at the point of incidence, all lie in the same plane.

(ii) The ratio of the sine angle of incidence to the sine angle of refraction is constant for the two given media. This constant is denoted by ${}^a\mu_b$ and is called the **relative refractive index** of medium *b* with respect to medium *a*.

$$\therefore \quad \frac{\sin i}{\sin r} = {}^a\mu_b$$

This law is also called **Snell's law of refraction.**

Refractive Index

Mathematically, refractive index is given by the relation

$$\mu = \frac{\text{Speed of light in the vacuum}}{\text{Speed of light in the material}} = \frac{c}{v}$$

It is also called as **absolute refractive index of medium.**

- **Relative refractive index** is a measure of how much light bends, when it travels from one medium to another medium.

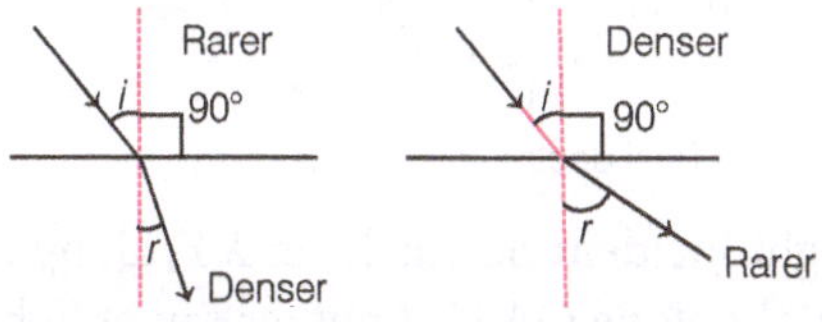

- **If light travels from rarer medium to denser medium, then it bends towards the normal, i.e. $i > r$.**
- **If light travels from denser medium to rarer medium, then light bends away from the normal, i.e. $i < r$.**
- The frequency of light remains unchanged while passing from one medium to the other.
- The medium in which the speed of light is higher with respect to other medium, is said to be **optically denser medium. Optical density** is the ratio of the speed of light in two media.

> **TEACHER TIP**
> **Optical density should not be confused with mass density,** which is mass per unit volume. It is possible that, mass density of an optically denser medium may be less than that of an optically rarer medium. e.g. Turpentine and water. Mass density of turpentine is less than that of water but its optical density is higher.

Principle of Reversibility of Light

This principle states that when final path of a light ray after suffering a number of reflection and refraction is reversed, then ray retraces its entire path.

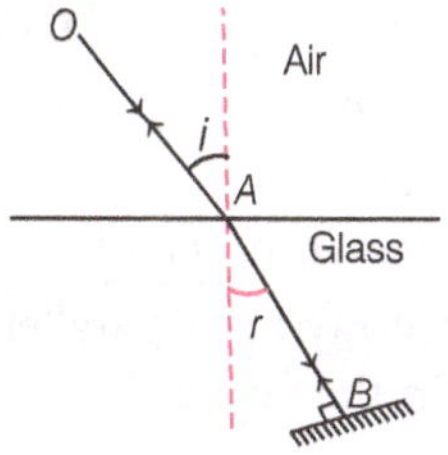

If ${}^a\mu_g$ is the refractive index of glass with respect to air and ${}^g\mu_a$ is the refractive index of air with respect to glass, then it should be clear that

$${}^a\mu_g = \frac{1}{{}^g\mu_a}$$

Thus, **the refractive index of glass relative to the air is equal to the reciprocal of the refractive index of air relative to the glass.**

9.3 Refraction of Light through a Rectangular Glass Slab

Let *ABCD* be a rectangular glass slab. A ray of light is incident along *MN* on the face *AB* of the rectangular slab at $\angle i_1$. It is refracted along *NK* with $\angle r_1$.

The refracted ray NK falls on face CD with $\angle i_2$ and emerges out along KL with $\angle r_2$.

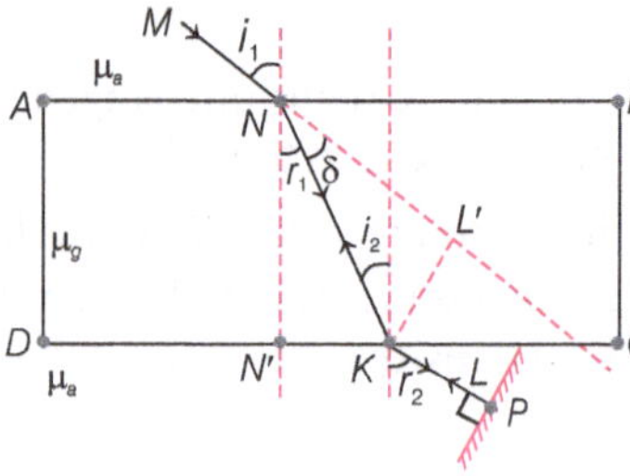

Applying Snell's law at N,

$$\mu_a \times \sin i_1 = \mu_g \times \sin r_1$$

or $$\frac{\sin i_1}{\sin r_1} = \frac{\mu_g}{\mu_a} = {}^a\mu_g \quad \text{...(i)}$$

Apply Snell's law at K,

$$\frac{\mu_g}{\mu_a} = \frac{\sin r_2}{\sin i_2} = {}^a\mu_g \quad \text{...(ii)}$$

From Eqs. (i) and (ii), we get

$$\frac{\sin i_1}{\sin r_1} = \frac{\sin r_2}{\sin i_2} \quad \text{...(iii)}$$

As, $i_2 = r_1$ [alternate angles]

$\therefore$ $\sin i_2 = \sin r_1$

From Eq. (iii), we get

$$\sin r_2 = \sin i_1 \text{ or } \boxed{r_2 = i_1}$$

Hence, the emergent ray KL is parallel to the incident ray MN as shown in the figure.

Expression for Lateral Displacement

We observe that the incident ray MN is displaced laterally, on suffering two refractions through a glass slab.

Now, from K, draw $KL' \perp MN$ produced.

$\therefore$ Lateral displacement of the ray on passing through the parallel slab = KL'.

Let $\angle KNL' = \delta$ = deviation on first refraction.

In $\Delta NKL'$, $\sin \delta = \dfrac{KL'}{NK}$

$$\therefore \quad KL' = NK \sin \delta \quad \text{...(iv)}$$

In $\Delta NN'K$, $\cos r_1 = \dfrac{NN'}{NK}$

$$\therefore \quad NK = \frac{NN'}{\cos r_1} = \frac{t}{\cos r_1}$$

where, $t = NN'$ = thickness of glass slab.

From Eq. (iv), we get, $KL' = \dfrac{t}{\cos r_1} \sin \delta$

or Lateral displacement $$KL' = \frac{t \sin(i_1 - r_1)}{\cos r_1} \quad \text{...(v)}$$

Lateral displacement (or shift) is proportional to the thickness (t) of the slab and angle of incidence (i_1).

Example 4. A ray of light is incident at an angle of 60° on one face of a rectangular glass slab of thickness 0.1 m and refractive index 1.5. Calculate the lateral shift produced.

Sol. Given, angle of incidence, $i_1 = 60°$

Thickness of glass slab, $t = 0.1$ m

Refractive index, $\mu = 1.5$

Since, $\dfrac{\sin i_1}{\sin r_1} = \mu$

$$\therefore \quad \sin r_1 = \frac{\sin i_1}{\mu} = \frac{\sin 60°}{1.5} = 0.5773$$

$$\left[\because \sin 60° = \frac{\sqrt{3}}{2} \text{ and } \sqrt{3} = 1.732\right]$$

$$r_1 = \sin^{-1}(0.5773) = 35.3°$$

$$\therefore \text{ Lateral shift } = \frac{t\sin(i_1 - r_1)}{\cos r_1} = \frac{0.1\sin(60° - 35.3°)}{\cos 35.3°}$$

$$= \frac{0.1 \sin 24.7°}{\cos 35.3°} = \frac{0.1 \times 0.418}{0.816} = 0.0513 \text{ m}$$

Apparent Depth and Normal Shift

The depth of an object immersed in water appears to be lesser than its actual depth. This happens due to the refraction of light. The apparent depth is less than the real depth.

Let see how real depth and apparent depth are related. Let O be a point object at an actual depth OA below the free surface of water XY.

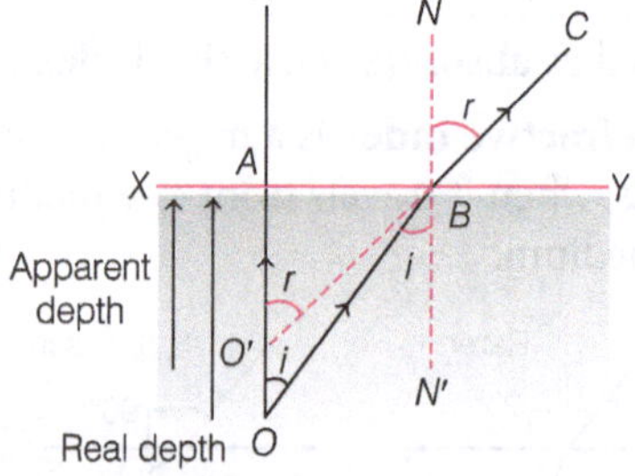

A ray of light incident normally on XY, along OA passes straight along OAA'. Another ray of light from O incident at $\angle i$ on surface XY along OB deviates away from normal. It is refracted at $\angle r$ along BC.

On producing backwards, BC meets OA at O'.
Therefore, O' is virtual image of O.

Apparent depth $= AO'$

Real depth $= OA$

Clearly, $AO' < OA$

Now, $\angle BOA = \angle OBN' = i$ [alternate angles]

$\angle AO'B = \angle CBN = r$ [corresponding angles]

In ΔOAB, $\sin i = \dfrac{AB}{OB}$

In $\Delta O'AB$, $\sin r = \dfrac{AB}{O'B}$

As, light ray is travelling from denser medium to rarer medium.

$$\therefore \quad {}^a\mu_w = \frac{\sin r}{\sin i} \quad \text{or} \quad {}^a\mu_w = \frac{AB}{O'B} \times \frac{OB}{AB} = \frac{OB}{O'B}$$

B is close to A (as angles are very small), so $OA \approx OB$ and $O'A \simeq O'B$

$$\therefore \quad {}^a\mu_w = \frac{OA}{O'A} = \frac{\text{Real depth}}{\text{Apparent depth}}$$

If x is the real depth of water surface and ${}^a\mu_w$ is the refractive index of water with respect to air, then the **normal shift** (d) in position of point object is given by

$d =$ Real depth $-$ Apparent depth

$$\therefore d = x - \frac{x}{{}^a\mu_w} \quad \left[\because \text{Apparent depth} = \frac{\text{Real depth}}{{}^a\mu_w} = \frac{x}{{}^a\mu_w}\right]$$

or

$$d = x\left(1 - \frac{1}{{}^a\mu_w}\right)$$

Note Consider a beaker filled with immiscible transparent liquids of refractive indices μ_1, μ_2, μ_3 and individual depth d_1, d_2, d_3 respectively, then apparent depth of beaker is given by

$$d_{app} = \frac{d_1}{\mu_1} + \frac{d_2}{\mu_2} + \frac{d_3}{\mu_3}$$

Example 5. Velocity of light in glass is 2×10^8 m/s and that in air is 3×10^8 m/s. By how much would an ink dot appear to be raised, when covered by a glass plate 6 cm thick?

Sol. Given, velocity of light in glass,

$$v = 2 \times 10^8 \text{ m/s}$$

Velocity of light in air, $c = 3 \times 10^8$ m/s

$\therefore$ Refractive index of glass with respect to air,

$${}^a\mu_g = \frac{c}{v} = \frac{3 \times 10^8}{2 \times 10^8} = 1.5$$

$\therefore$ Normal shift in the position of ink dot,

$$d = t\left(1 - \frac{1}{{}^a\mu_g}\right) \quad [\because t = 6 \text{ cm}]$$

$$= 6\left(1 - \frac{1}{1.5}\right) = \frac{6 \times 0.5}{1.5} = 2 \text{ cm}$$

Critical Angle

When angle of incident is increased, angle of refraction will also increase, and at a stage it becomes 90°

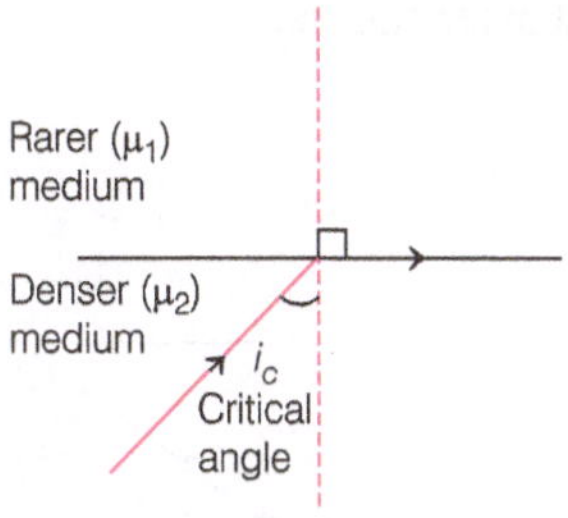

Critical angle for a pair of media in contact can be defined as, **"the angle of incidence in denser medium for which angle of refraction in rarer medium is 90°".**

The value of critical angle depends on the nature of two media in contact.

From Snell's law, $\mu_2 \times \sin i_c = \mu_1 \times \sin 90°$

$$\therefore \quad \frac{\mu_1}{\mu_2} = \frac{\sin i_c}{\sin 90°}$$

$$\Rightarrow \quad \frac{\mu_1}{\mu_2} = \sin i_c \quad [\because \sin 90° = 1]$$

$$\text{or} \quad \frac{\mu_2}{\mu_1} = \frac{1}{\sin i_c} \Rightarrow i_c = \sin^{-1}\left(\frac{\mu_1}{\mu_2}\right)$$

This is the expression for critical angle.

where, $\mu_1 =$ refractive index of rarer medium 1,

$\mu_2 =$ refractive index of denser medium 2

and $i_c =$ critical angle.

Example 6. If a ray of light travelling in air is incident on a glass surface with an angle of incidence 40°, it deviates through 15°. Determine the critical angle for a glass-air interface.

Sol. Given, angle of incidence, $i = 40°$

Angle of deviation, $\delta = 15°$

Since, ray deviates towards the normal, therefore

$$r = i - \delta = 40° - 15° = 25°$$

As we know that, $\mu = \dfrac{\sin i}{\sin r} = \dfrac{1}{\sin i_c}$

$$\Rightarrow \quad \sin i_c = \frac{\sin r}{\sin i} = \frac{\sin 25°}{\sin 40°} = \frac{0.4226}{0.6428}$$

$$\Rightarrow \quad \sin i_c = 0.6574$$

$$\therefore \quad i_c = \sin^{-1}(0.6574) = 41.1° \Rightarrow i_c = 41.1°$$

9.4 Total Internal Reflection (TIR)

The optical phenomenon observed when a ray of light travelling from denser to rarer medium strikes the boundary at an angle greater than the critical angle is called total internal reflection.
During TIR, the incident ray is reflected back to the denser media.

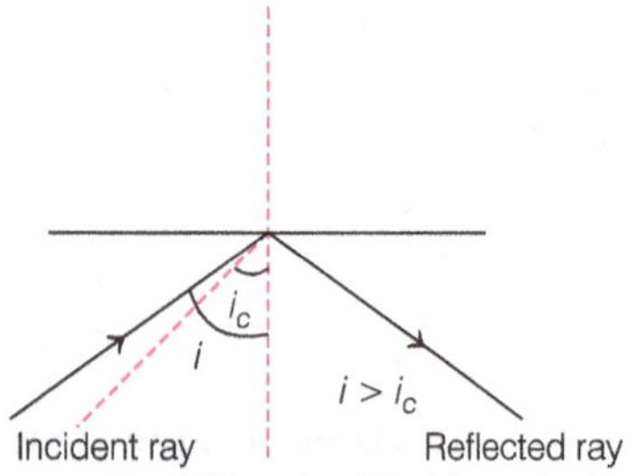

For TIR angle of incidence $i > i_c$

Necessary conditions for total internal reflection to take place are as follows

(i) The ray incident on the interface of two media should travel in the denser medium.

(ii) The angle of incidence should be greater than critical angle for the two media.

Application of TIR in Communication : Optical Fibres

An **optical fibre** is a thin tube of transparent material that allows light to pass through, without being refracted into the air or another external medium.

Optical fibres make use of total internal reflection to transmit signal in form of light. It is fabricated in such a way that light reflected at one side of the inner surface strikes at an angle greater than critical angle, it undergoes repeated total internal reflection along the length of the fibre and finally, comes out from other end.

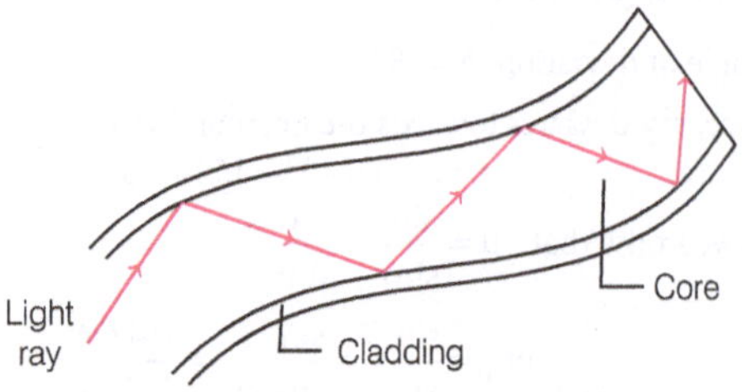

Typical structure of optical fibre

- Optical fibres are fabricated with high quality composite glass/quartz fibres.
- The refractive index of **core** is higher than that of the **cladding.**
- In signal transmission through optical fibres, there is no appreciable loss in the intensity of light signal due to TIR at each stage.

Uses of Optical Fibre

- In transmitting electrical and optical signals.
- In visual examination of internal organs like esophagus, stomach and intestine.
- In decorative lamps.

Multiple internal reflection in diamond ($i_c = 24.9°$), totally reflecting prism and mirage are some other examples of total internal reflection.

Prism

Prisms that are right-angled isosceles triangle, can turn the light ray by 90° or 180°. They are based on the phenomenon of **total internal reflection** of light.

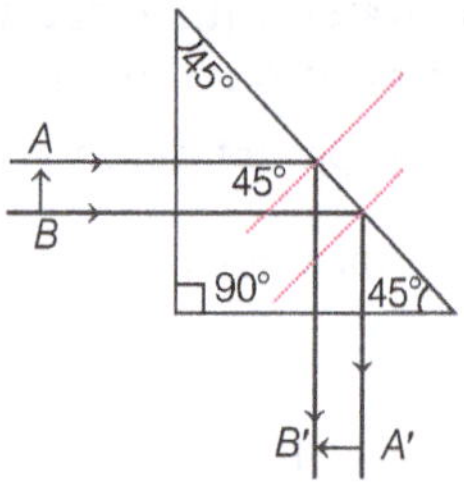

(a)

In totally reflecting glass prisms, angle of incidence is made 45°($> i_c$).

Prisms are designed to bend ray by 90° and 180° or to invert image without changing its size by the use of total internal reflection.

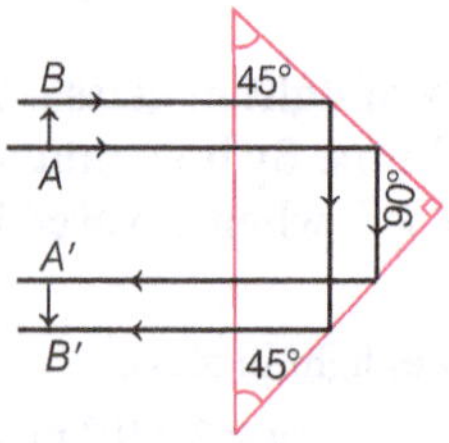

(b)

Quick Test 2

Conceptual Questions

1. For the same value of angle of incidence, the angles of refraction in three media *A*, *B* and *C* are 15°, 25° and 35°, respectively. In which medium, would the velocity of light be minimum?

2. When monochromatic light travels from a rarer to a denser medium, explain the following, giving reasons.
(i) Is the frequency of reflected and refracted light same as the frequency of incident light?
(ii) Does the decrease in speed imply a reduction in the energy carried by light wave?

3. Mention any two situations in which Snell's law of refraction fails.

4. A ray of light is incident at a glass-water interface at an angle of *i*. It emerges finally parallel to the surface water, then what will be the value of μ_g?

Numerical Questions

5. What is the critical angle for a material of refractive index $\sqrt{2}$?

6. A ray of light is incident at an angle of 45° on one face of a rectangular glass slab of thickness 10 cm and refractive index 1.5. Calculate the lateral shift produced.

7. What is the apparent position of an object below a rectangular block of glass 6 cm thick, if a layer of water 4 cm thick is on the top of the glass?
Given, $n_{ga} = 1.5$ and $n_{wa} = 1.33$.

8. The angle of incidence in air for a ray of light is 40°. If the ray travels through water of refractive index 4/3. Find the angle of refraction.

9. For a situation shown in figure, find the maximum angle *i* for which the light suffers total internal reflection at the vertical surface.

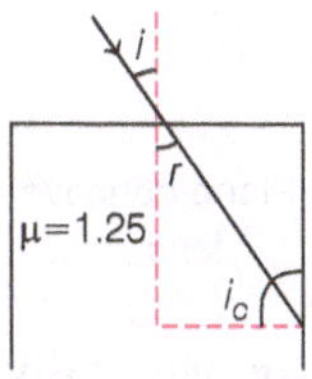

Answers

5. 45° 6. 0.033 m 7. 7 cm 8. 28.82° 9. 48.6°

For Solutions, See QR Code on Pg. 322

9.5 Refraction at Spherical Surfaces and Lenses

Refraction at a Spherical Surface

A refracting surface which is a part of a sphere of transparent refracting material is called a **spherical refracting surface.**

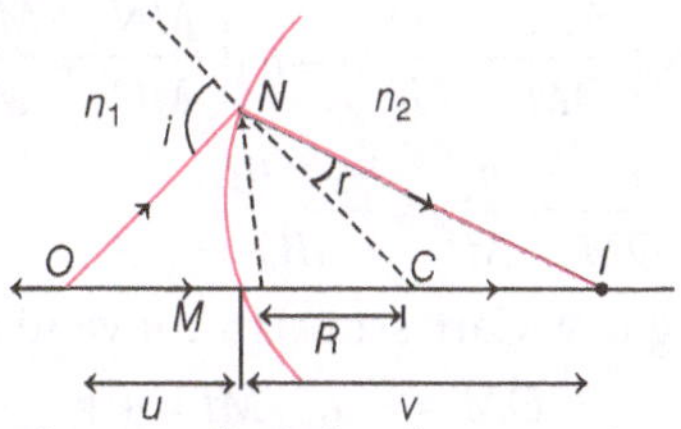

Refraction at a spherical surface separating two media

Derivation

(i) The aperture of the surface is small as compared to other distances involved.

(ii) *NM* will be taken to be nearly equal to the length of the perpendicular from the point *N* on the principal axis.

$$\tan NOM = \frac{MN}{OM}, \quad \tan NCM = \frac{MN}{MC},$$

$$\tan NIM = \frac{MN}{MI}$$

For small angles, $\tan\theta \approx \sin\theta \approx \theta$

So, $$\angle NOM = \frac{MN}{OM}$$

$$\angle NCM = \frac{MN}{MC}$$

$$\angle NIM = \frac{MN}{MI}$$

For ΔNOC, *i* is the exterior angle.

$$\therefore \quad i = \angle NOM + \angle NCM = \frac{MN}{OM} + \frac{MN}{MC} \quad \ldots\text{(i)}$$

For ΔNIC, $\angle NCM$ is the exterior angle.

$\therefore \quad \angle NCM = r + \angle NIM$

or $\quad r = \angle NCM - \angle NIM$

i.e. $$r = \frac{MN}{MC} - \frac{MN}{MI} \quad \ldots(\text{ii})$$

By Snell's law, $n_1 \sin i = n_2 \sin r$

For small angles, $n_1 i = n_2 r$

Substituting the values of i and r from Eqs. (i) and (ii), we get

$$n_1\left(\frac{MN}{OM} + \frac{MN}{MC}\right) = n_2\left(\frac{MN}{MC} - \frac{MN}{MI}\right)$$

or $$\frac{n_1}{OM} + \frac{n_2}{MI} = \frac{n_2 - n_1}{MC} \quad \ldots(\text{iii})$$

Applying new Cartesian sign conventions,

$$OM = -u, \quad MI = +v$$
$$MC = +R$$

Substituting these values in Eq. (iii), we get

$$\boxed{\frac{n_2}{v} - \frac{n_1}{u} = \frac{n_2 - n_1}{R}}$$

This equation holds for any curved spherical surface.

Example 7. Light from a point source in air falls on a spherical glass surface ($n = 1.5$ and radius of curvature = 20 cm). The distance of the light source from the glass surface is 100 cm. At what position, the image is formed? NCERT

Sol. Given, object distance, $u = -100$ cm,

$R = +20$ cm, $n_1 = 1, n_2 = 1.5$, image distance, $v = ?$

We know that, $\frac{n_2}{v} - \frac{n_1}{u} = \frac{n_2 - n_1}{R}$

$$\Rightarrow \quad \frac{1.5}{v} + \frac{1}{100} = \frac{1.5 - 1}{20}$$

$$\Rightarrow \quad \frac{1.5}{v} = \frac{0.5}{20} - \frac{1}{100} = \frac{2.5 - 1}{100} = \frac{1.5}{100}$$

$$v = +100 \text{ cm}$$

Thus, the image is formed at a distance of 100 cm from the glass surface in the direction of incident light.

Lens

Lens is a transparent medium bounded by two surfaces, out of which one or both surfaces are spherical.

Lenses are of two types

(i) Convex or converging lens

(ii) Concave or diverging lens

Convex or Converging Lens

A lens which is thicker at the centre and thinner at its ends is called **convex lens.** Convex lenses are of three types as shown below

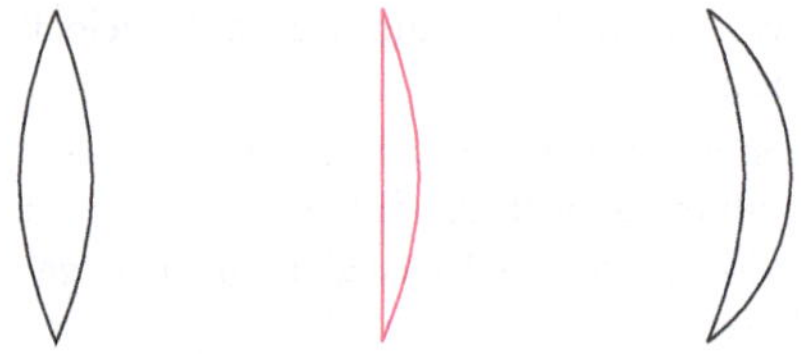

(a) Double convex lens (b) Plano-convex lens (c) Concavo-convex lens

A convex lens is also known as **converging lens** because it converges a parallel beam of light rays passing through it. A **double convex lens is simply called convex lens.**

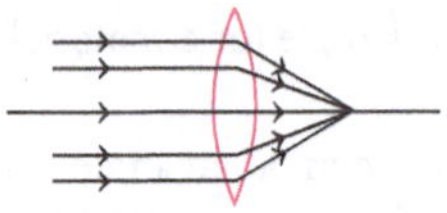

Converging lens

Concave or Diverging Lens

A lens which is thinner at the centre and thicker at its ends is called a **concave lens.** Concave lenses are of three types as shown below.

(a) Double concave lens (b) Plano-concave lens (c) Convexo-concave lens

A concave lens is also known as **diverging lens** because it diverges a parallel beam of light rays passing through it. **A double concave lens is simply called concave lens.**

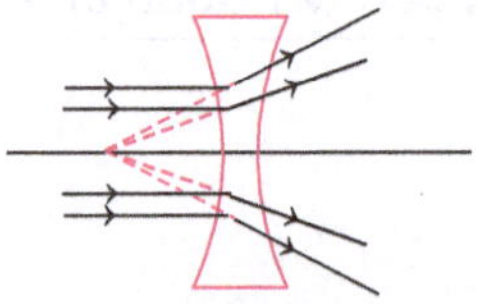

Diverging lens

Some Definitions Related to Lenses

(i) **Optical centre** It is a point lying on the principal axis of the lens, i.e. **the centre point of a lens is known as its optical centre.**

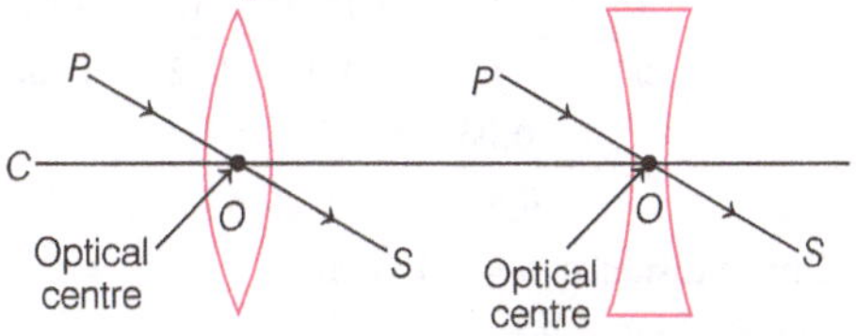

(ii) **Centre of curvature** The centres of the two imaginary spheres of which the lens is a part, are called centres of curvature of the lens. **A lens has two centres of curvature with respect to its two curved surfaces.**

(iii) **Radii of curvature** The radii of the two imaginary spheres of which the lens is a part are called radii of curvature of the lens. A lens has two radii of curvature. These may or may not be equal.

(iv) **Principal axis** The imaginary line joining the two centres of curvature is called principal axis of lens. It also passes through the optical centre.

(v) **Principal focus** Lens has two principal foci.

(a) **First principal focus** It is a point on the principal axis of lens, the rays starting from this point in convex lens or rays directed to this point in concave lens become parallel to principal axis after refraction.

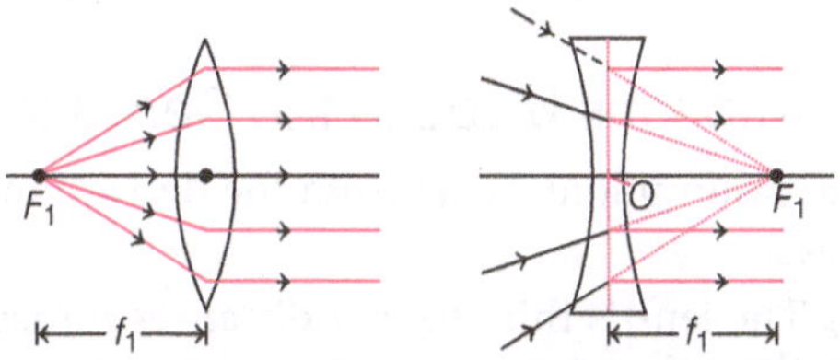

(b) **Second principal focus** It is a point on the principal axis at which the rays coming parallel to the principal axis converge (convex lens) or passing through it appear to diverge (concave lens) at this point after refraction from the lens.

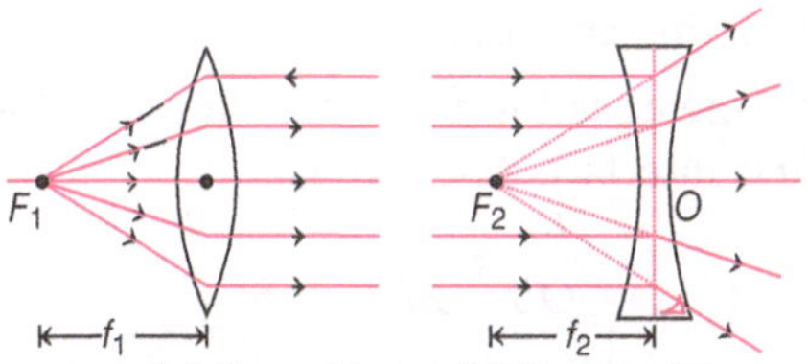

(a) Convex lens (b) Concave lens

Both the foci of convex lens are real, while that of concave lens are virtual.

(vi) **Aperture** The effective diameter of the circular outline of a spherical lens is called its aperture.

(vii) **Refractive axis** It is an imaginary axis at the optical centre perpendicular to the principal axis which represents the lens.

Image Formation in Lenses Using Ray Diagrams

We can represent image formation in lenses using ray diagrams. For drawing ray diagrams in lenses like spherical mirrors, we consider any two of the following rays.

(i) Rays which are parallel to the principal axis after refraction will pass through principal focus in case of convex lens and will appear to be coming from principal focus in case of concave lens.

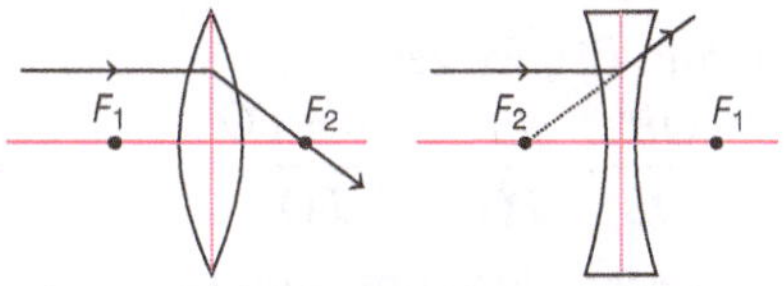

(ii) Rays passing through or directed to the focus will emerge parallel to the principal axis.

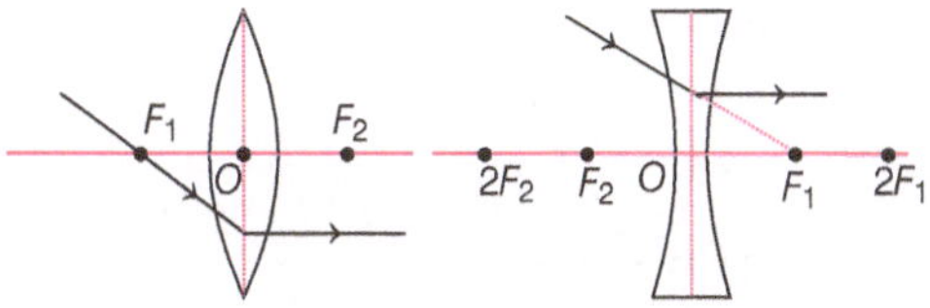

(iii) Rays directed to optical centre will emerge out undeviated.

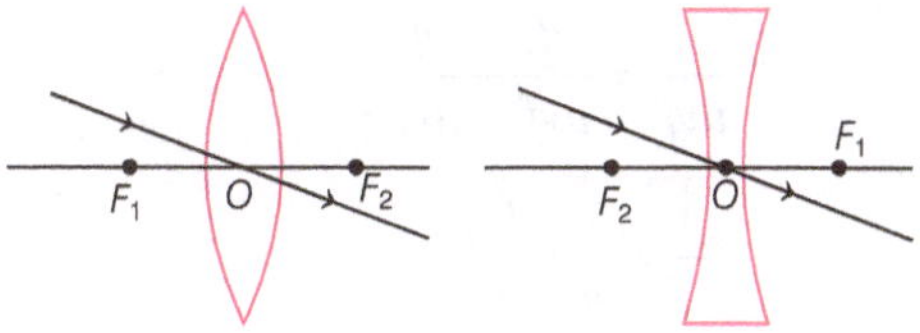

Thin Lens Formula

It is a relation between focal length of a lens, distances of object and image from optical centre of the lens.

Let O be the optical centre and f be the principal focus of a convex lens of focal length $OF = f$. AB is an object held perpendicular to the principal axis of the lens at a distance beyond focal length of the lens.

A real, inverted and magnified image $A'B'$ is formed as shown in the figure. As, $\Delta A'B'O$ and ΔABO are similar.

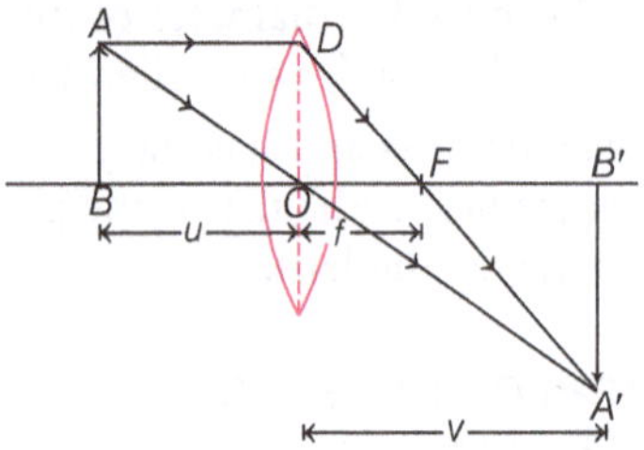

$$\therefore \quad \frac{A'B'}{AB} = \frac{OB'}{OB} \quad \text{...(i)}$$

Again, $\Delta A'B'F$ and ΔDOF are similar.

$$\therefore \quad \frac{A'B'}{DO} = \frac{FB'}{FO}$$

But $\quad DO = AB$

$$\therefore \quad \frac{A'B'}{AB} = \frac{FB'}{FO} \quad \text{...(ii)}$$

From Eqs. (i) and (ii), we get

$$\frac{OB'}{OB} = \frac{FB'}{FO} = \frac{OB' - FO}{FO}$$

Using new Cartesian sign conventions,

Let $\quad OB = -u, \quad OB' = +v,$

$$FO = +f$$

$$\therefore \quad \frac{v}{-u} = \frac{v-f}{f}$$

$$\Rightarrow \quad vf = -uv + uf$$

or $\quad uv = uf - vf$

Dividing both sides by uvf, we get

$$\frac{uv}{uvf} = \frac{uf}{uvf} - \frac{vf}{uvf}$$

$$\Rightarrow \quad \boxed{\frac{1}{f} = \frac{1}{v} - \frac{1}{u}}$$

This is the **thin lens formula.** This formula can also be proved for concave lens and for virtual images in the same way.

Example 8. A convergent beam of light passes through the diverging lens of focal length 0.2 m and comes to focus 0.3 m behind the lens. Find the position of the point at which the beams would converge in the absence of the lens.

Sol. Given, focal length, $f = 0.2$ m

Image distance, $v = -0.3$ m

Object distance, $u = ?$

From thin lens formula,

$$\frac{1}{v} - \frac{1}{u} = \frac{1}{f}$$

$$\Rightarrow \quad \frac{1}{u} = \frac{1}{v} - \frac{1}{f} = \frac{1}{-0.3} - \frac{1}{0.2} = \frac{-0.5}{0.06}$$

$$\Rightarrow \quad u = \frac{-0.06}{0.5}$$

$\therefore$ Object distance, $u = -0.12$ m

Refraction by a Lens : Lens Maker's Formula

The below figures show the image formation by a convex lens.

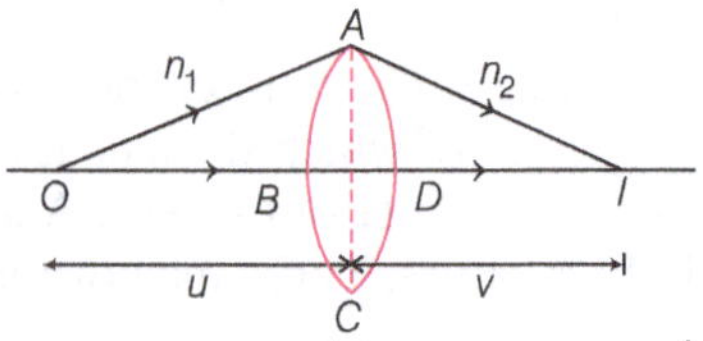

(a)

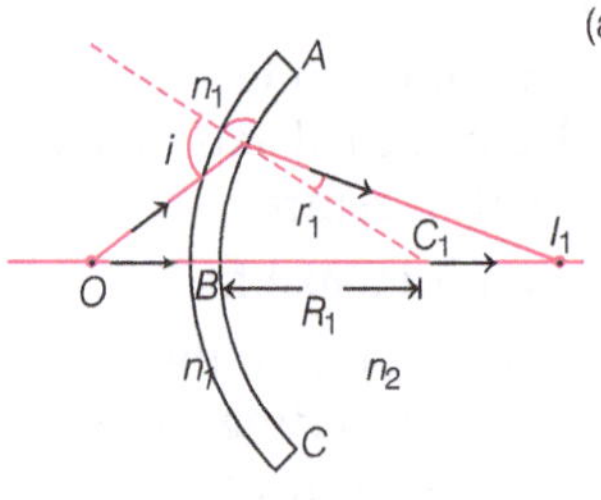

(b) The first refracting surface forms image I_1 of the object O.

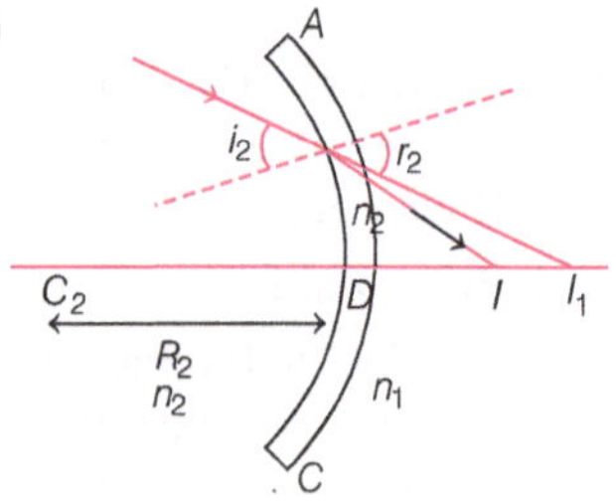

(c) Image I_1 acts as virtual object for the second surface that forms the image at I.

Assumptions Made in the Derivation

Some assumptions made from the derivation are follows

(i) The lens is thin, so that distances measured from the poles of its surfaces can be taken as equal to the distance from the optical centre of the lens.

(ii) The aperture of the lens is small.

(iii) The incident ray and refracted ray make small angles with the principal axis of the lens.

(iv) A convex lens is made up of two convex spherical refracting surfaces.

Applying the equation for spherical refracting surface to the first interface ABC, we get

$$\frac{n_1}{OB} + \frac{n_2}{BI_1} = \frac{n_2 - n_1}{BC_1} \quad \text{...(i)}$$

A similar procedure applied to the second interface ADC, we get

$$-\frac{n_2}{DI_1}+\frac{n_1}{DI}=\frac{n_2-n_1}{DC_2} \quad \text{...(ii)}$$

For a thin lens, $BI_1 = DI_1$

Adding Eqs. (i) and (ii), we get

$$\frac{n_1}{OB}+\frac{n_1}{DI}=(n_2-n_1)\left(\frac{1}{BC_1}+\frac{1}{DC_2}\right) \quad \text{...(iii)}$$

Suppose the object is at infinity, i.e.

$$OB \to \infty \quad \text{and} \quad DI \to f$$

So, Eq. (iii) can be written as

$$\frac{n_1}{f}=(n_2-n_1)\left(\frac{1}{BC_1}+\frac{1}{DC_2}\right) \quad \text{...(iv)}$$

The point where image of an object placed at infinity is formed is called the focus (f) of the lens and the distance f gives its focal length. A lens has two foci F and F' on either side of it by sign convention.

$$BC_1 = R_1$$

or $$DC_2 = -R_2$$

Therefore, Eq. (iv) can be written as

$$\boxed{\frac{1}{f}=({}_1n_2-1)\left(\frac{1}{R_1}-\frac{1}{R_2}\right)} \quad \left[\because {}_1n_2=\frac{n_2}{n_1}\right] \quad \text{...(v)}$$

Eq. (v) is known as the **lens Maker's formula.**

Putting $\frac{n_2}{n_1}=n$, refractive index of material of lens w.r.t. its surroundings, we get

$$\frac{1}{f}=(n-1)\left(\frac{1}{R_1}-\frac{1}{R_2}\right)$$

From Eqs. (iii) and (iv), we get

$$\frac{n_1}{OB}+\frac{n_1}{DI}=\frac{n_1}{f} \quad \text{...(vi)}$$

As, B and D both are close to the optical centre of the lens,

$OB = -u$, $DI = +v$, we get

$$\boxed{\frac{1}{v}-\frac{1}{u}=\frac{1}{f}} \quad \text{...(vii)}$$

Eq. (vii) is the **thin lens formula.**

From lens Maker's formula, it is clear that focal length of lens depends on the radii of curvature of lens and refractive index of material of lens w.r.t. its surroundings.

Dependence of Focal Length on Refractive Index

Refractive index of material of lens **depends on the medium in which it is kept.**

- If lens is immersed in a liquid whose refractive index with respect to air is less than the refractive index of material of lens with respect to air, then **focal length of the lens increases and power of lens decreases.** *i.e.*, The convergent lens becomes less convergent and divergent lens becomes less divergent.
- If lens is immersed in a liquid whose refractive index with respect to air is more than the refractive index of material of the lens with respect to air, then focal length will become negative. **This means that the nature of lens will change in such a medium and convex lens will behave like concave lens and concave lens will behave like convex lens.**
- If lens is immersed in a liquid whose refractive index with respect to air is equal to the refractive index of material of lens with respect to air, then focal length of the lens will become infinite and it will behave like plane glass sheet. Also, in such medium, **lens will become invisible.**

Dependence of Focal Length on the Radii of Curvature

From lens Maker's formula, it is clear that the focal length of a lens of large radii of curvature is large and that of a lens of small radii of curvature is small. In simple words, **the focal length of thin lens is large and that of thick lens is small.** For plano-convex or plano-concave lens, $R_1 = R$ and $R_2 = \infty$ (for plane surface).

Example 9. The radii of curvature of the surfaces of a double convex lens are 20 cm and 40 cm, respectively and its focal length is 20 cm. What is refractive index of the material of the lens?

Sol. Given, $R_1 = 20$ cm, $R_2 = -40$ cm, $f = 20$ cm, $n = ?$

We know that, $\frac{1}{f}=(n-1)\left(\frac{1}{R_1}-\frac{1}{R_2}\right)$

$$\Rightarrow \quad \frac{1}{20}=(n-1)\left(\frac{1}{20}+\frac{1}{40}\right)$$

$$\Rightarrow \quad \frac{1}{n-1}=20\left(\frac{2+1}{40}\right)=\frac{3}{2} \Rightarrow n-1=2/3$$

$$\Rightarrow \quad 3n=5 \Rightarrow n=5/3$$

Hence, the refractive index of the material of the lens is 5/3.

Linear Magnification Produced by a Lens (m)

Linear magnification of a lens is defined as **the ratio of the height of the image formed by the lens to height of the object.**

$$\text{Linear magnification } (m) = \frac{\text{Height of image } (I)}{\text{Height of object } (O)}$$

For Convex Lens

When image is real, $m = \frac{-I}{O} = \frac{v}{-u}$

When image is real, it is inverted and forms on the other side of object.

When image is virtual, $m = \frac{I}{O} = \frac{v}{u}$

When image is virtual, it is erect and forms on the same side of object. **Thus, it can be said that convex lens gives positive linear magnification for virtual image and negative linear magnification for real image.**

For Concave Lens

Concave lens always forms virtual image, so linear magnification of concave lens, $m = \frac{I}{O} = \frac{v}{u}$

Concave lens always gives positive linear magnification. Other formulae for linear magnification are

$$m = \frac{v}{u} = \frac{f-v}{f} = \frac{f}{f+u}$$

Example 10. **The focal length of a thin biconvex lens is 20 cm. When an object is moved from a distance of 25 cm in front of it to 50 cm, the magnification of its image changes from m_{25} to m_{50}. Find the ratio of $\frac{m_{25}}{m_{50}}$.**

Sol. Since, magnification, $m = \frac{f}{f+u}$

$\Rightarrow$ $m_{25} = \frac{20}{20-25} = -4$

Similarly, $m_{50} = \frac{20}{20-50} = \frac{-2}{3}$

Therefore, $\frac{m_{25}}{m_{50}} = (-4)\left(\frac{-3}{2}\right) = 6$

Power of a Lens

The ability of a lens to converge or diverge the rays of light incident on it is called the power of the lens.

Power of a lens is defined as the tangent of the angle by which it converges or diverges a beam of light falling at unit distance from the optical centre.

According to the figure,

$$\tan\delta = \frac{h}{f}, \quad \text{if } h = 1, \text{ then}$$

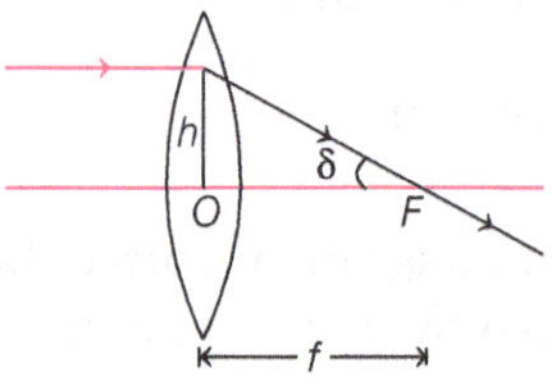

$$\tan\delta = \frac{1}{f}$$

For small values of δ, $\tan\delta \approx \delta$

$\therefore$ $\delta = \frac{1}{f}$

Thus, power of a lens, $P = \frac{1}{f}$

The SI unit of power of lens is **dioptre (D)**. The power of a lens is measured as the reciprocal of its focal length (in metre).

$$P = \frac{1}{f \text{ (in m)}}$$

If $f = 1$ m, then $P = 1\text{ m}^{-1} = 1$ dioptre (D)

- **For converging (convex) lens, power is positive and for diverging (concave) lens, power is negative.**

Example 11. **If the radii of curvature of the faces of a double convex lens are 9 cm and 15 cm, respectively and the refractive index of glass is 1.5, then determine the focal length and the power of the lens.**

Sol. Given, radii of curvature, $R_1 = 9$ cm, $R_2 = -15$ cm,

Refractive index, $\mu = 1.5$, $f = ?$, $P = ?$

According to lens Maker's formula,

$$\frac{1}{f} = (\mu - 1)\left(\frac{1}{R_1} - \frac{1}{R_2}\right)$$

$$\Rightarrow \frac{1}{f} = (1.5 - 1)\left[\frac{1}{9} - \left(\frac{-1}{15}\right)\right]$$

$$\Rightarrow \frac{1}{f} = (0.5)\left(\frac{1}{9} + \frac{1}{15}\right) = (0.5)\left(\frac{5+3}{45}\right)$$

$$\Rightarrow \quad \frac{1}{f} = 0.5 \times \frac{8}{45}$$

$$\Rightarrow \quad f = \frac{45}{4} = 11.25 \text{ cm}$$

$$\therefore \text{ Power, } P = \frac{1}{f} = \frac{1}{11.25 \times 10^{-2}}$$

$$= \frac{10000}{1125} = 8.88 \text{ D}$$

Combination of Thin Lenses in Contact

Consider two lenses A and B of focal lengths f_1 and f_2 placed in contact with each other. An object is placed at a point O beyond the focus of the first lens A. The first lens produces an image at I_1 (virtual image), which serves as a virtual object for the second lens B, producing the final image at I.

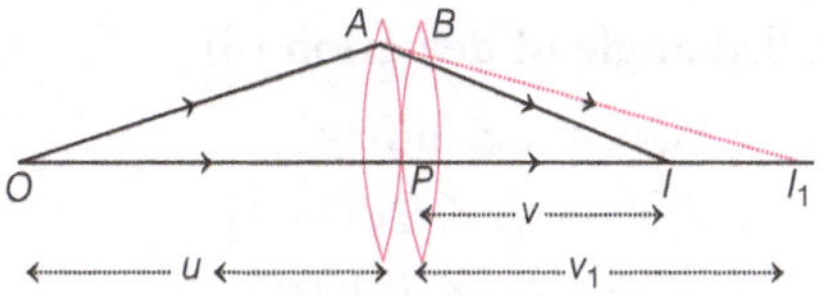

Since, the lenses are thin, we assume the optical centres (P) of the lenses to be co-incident.

For the image formed by the first lens A, we obtain

$$\frac{1}{v_1} - \frac{1}{u} = \frac{1}{f_1} \quad \ldots\text{(i)}$$

For the image formed by the second lens B, we get

$$\frac{1}{v} - \frac{1}{v_1} = \frac{1}{f_2} \quad \ldots\text{(ii)}$$

Adding Eqs. (i) and (ii), we get

$$\frac{1}{v} - \frac{1}{u} = \frac{1}{f_1} + \frac{1}{f_2} \quad \ldots\text{(iii)}$$

If the two lens system is regarded as equivalent to a single lens of focal length f. We have,

$$\frac{1}{v} - \frac{1}{u} = \frac{1}{f} \quad \ldots\text{(iv)}$$

From Eqs. (iii) and (iv), we get

$$\boxed{\frac{1}{f} = \frac{1}{f_1} + \frac{1}{f_2}} \quad \ldots\text{(v)}$$

For several thin lenses of focal lengths $f_1, f_2, f_3, \ldots$, the effective focal length,

$$\boxed{\frac{1}{f} = \frac{1}{f_1} + \frac{1}{f_2} + \frac{1}{f_3} + \ldots} \quad \ldots\text{(vi)}$$

In terms of power, Eq. (vi) can be written as

$$\boxed{P = P_1 + P_2 + P_3 + \ldots}$$

Example 12. **Two thin lenses are in contact and the focal length of the combination is 80 cm. If the focal length of one lens is 20 cm, then what would be the power of the another lens ?**

Sol. Given, combined focal length, $F = 80$ cm,

$$f_1 = 20 \text{ cm}, P_2 = ?$$

$$\therefore \quad P = \frac{100}{F(\text{cm})} = \frac{100}{80} = 1.25 \text{ D}$$

$$\Rightarrow \quad P_1 = \frac{100}{f_1} = \frac{100}{20} = 5 \text{ D}$$

We know that, $P_1 + P_2 = P$

$$\therefore \quad P_2 = P - P_1$$

$$= 1.25 - 5 = -3.75 \text{ D}$$

Magnification by Combination of Lenses

The image formed by the first lens becomes the object for second lens and so on. So, **the magnification of combination (m) is the product of magnification (m_1, m_2, m_3) of individual lenses.**

i.e., $$\boxed{m = m_1 \times m_2 \times m_3 \times \ldots}$$

(i) If combination of lenses consists of one convex lens (f_1) and one concave lens $(-f_2)$, then for combination of lenses,

$$\frac{1}{f} = \frac{1}{f_1} + \frac{1}{(-f_2)} = \frac{1}{f_1} - \frac{1}{f_2}$$

$$\Rightarrow \quad f = \frac{f_1 f_2}{f_2 - f_1}$$

(ii) If $f_1 > f_2$, then f **is negative,** i.e. combination will behave like **concave lens,** when focal length of convex lens is larger.

If $f_1 < f_2$, then f **is positive,** i.e. combination will behave like **convex lens,** when focal length of convex lens is smaller.

If $f_1 = f_2$, then f **is infinite,** i.e. combination will behave like **plane glass sheet.**

- If the lenses are placed d distance apart, then

$$\boxed{\frac{1}{f} = \frac{1}{f_1} + \frac{1}{f_2} - \frac{d}{f_1 f_2}}$$

Quick Test 3

Conceptual Questions

1. A concave lens of refractive index 1.5 is immersed in a medium of refractive index 1.65. What is the nature of the lens?
2. Show analytically from the lens equation that when the object is at the principal focus, the image is formed at infinity.
3. A student measures the focal length of a convex lens by putting an object pin at a distance u from the lens and measuring the distance v of the image pin. What will be the graph drawn between u and v?
4. A magician during a show makes a glass lens $n = 1.47$ disappear in a trough of liquid. What is the refractive index of the liquid? Could the liquid be water?
5. An equi-convex lens of focal length f is cut into two equal halves in thickness. What is the focal length of each half?

Numerical Questions

6. The radii of curvature of the faces of a double convex lens are 10 cm and 15 cm. If focal length of the lens is 12 cm, find the refractive index of the material of the lens.
7. What is the focal length of a convex lens of focal length 30 cm in contact with a concave lens of focal length 20 cm? Is the system, a converging or a diverging lens? Ignore thickness of the lenses. NCERT
8. (i) Monochromatic light of wavelength 589 nm is incident from air on a water surface. If μ for water is 1.33, find the wavelength, frequency and speed of the refracted light.
   (ii) A double convex lens is made of a glass of refractive index 1.55 with both faces of the same radius of curvature. Find the radius of curvature required, if the focal length is 20 cm.

Answers

6. 3/2   7. −60 cm
8. (i) 443 nm, $2.25 \times 10^8 \text{ ms}^{-1}$ (ii) 22 cm

For Solutions, See QR Code on Pg. 322

9.6 Prism and Optical Instruments

A **prism** is a portion of a transparent medium bounded by two plane faces inclined to each other at a suitable angle.

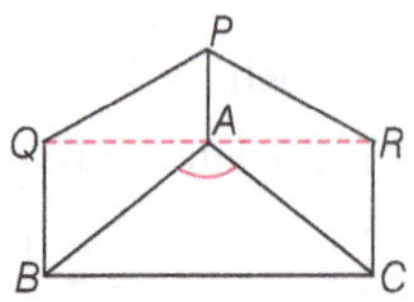

In the given figure, $ABQP$ and $ACRP$ are the two refracting faces and $\angle A$ is called **angle of prism**.

Refraction through a Prism

The figure below shows the passage of light through a triangular prism ABC.

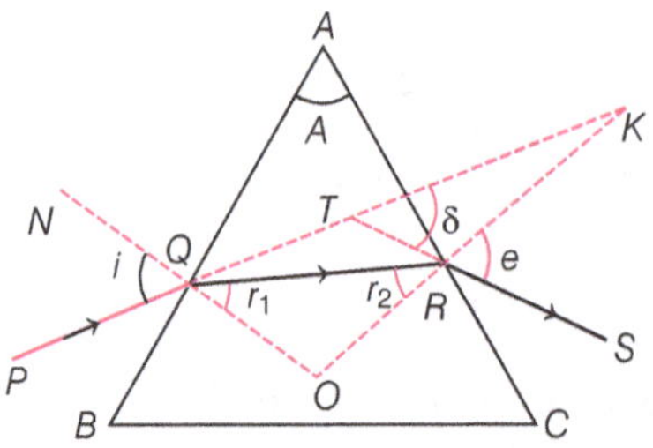

The angles of incidence and refraction at first face AB are i and r_1 and the second face AC is r_2 and the angle of emergence is e.

The angle between the emergent ray RS and incident ray PQ is called **angle of deviation** (δ).

Here, $\angle PQN = i$, $\angle SRK = e$

$\angle RQO = r_1$, $\angle QRO = r_2$

$\angle KTS = \delta$, $\angle TQO = i$

and $\angle TQR = i - r_1$ or $\angle TRQ = e - r_2$

In ΔTQR, the side QT has been produced outwards. Therefore, the exterior angle δ should be equal to the sum of the interior opposite angles.

i.e. $$\delta = \angle TQR + \angle TRQ$$
$$= (i - r_1) + (e - r_2)$$

$\Rightarrow$ $$\delta = (i + e) - (r_1 + r_2) \quad \text{...(i)}$$

In ΔQRO,
$$r_1 + r_2 + \angle ROQ = 180° \quad \text{...(ii)}$$

From quadrilateral $AROQ$, we have the sum of angles
$$\angle AQO + \angle ARO = 180°.$$

This means that the sum of the remaining two angles should be 180°.

i.e. $$\angle A + \angle ROQ = 180° \quad \text{...(iii)}$$

[$\angle A$ is called the angle of prism]

From Eqs. (ii) and (iii), we get
$$r_1 + r_2 = A \quad \text{...(iv)}$$

Substituting the value from Eq. (iv) in Eq. (i), we obtain
$$\boxed{\delta = (i + e) - A}$$

If μ is the refractive index of material of the prism, then according to Snell's law,

$$\mu = \frac{\sin i_1}{\sin r_1}$$

When angles are small, $\sin i_1 \approx i_1$ and $\sin r_1 \approx r_1$

$\therefore \quad \mu = \frac{i_1}{r_1} \Rightarrow i = \mu r_1 \quad$ [here, $i_1 = i$]

Similarly, $\quad \mu = \frac{i_2}{r_2}$ or $\mu = \frac{e}{r_2} \quad [\because i_2 = e]$

$\Rightarrow \quad e = \mu r_2$

$\therefore \quad \delta = i + e - A$

$= \mu r_1 + \mu r_2 - A$

$= \mu(r_1 + r_2) - A$

But $\quad r_1 + r_2 = A$

$\therefore \quad \delta = \mu A - A$

or $\quad \delta = (\mu - 1) A$

This is the angle through which a ray deviates on passing through a thin prism of small refracting angle *A*.

Prism Formula

If the angle of incidence is increased gradually, then the angle of deviation first decreases, then attains a minimum value (δ_m) and again starts increasing.

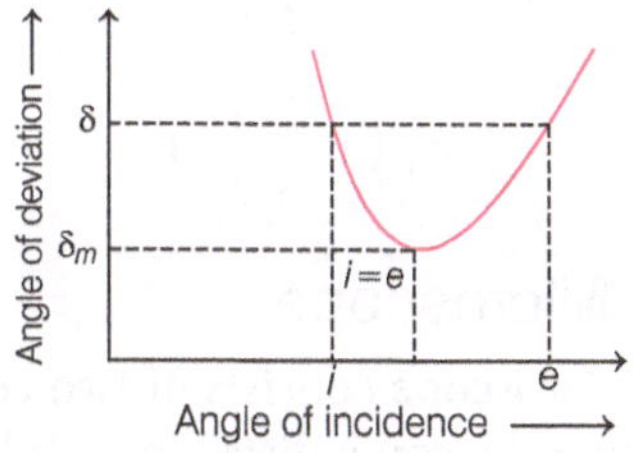

When angle of deviation is minimum, the prism is said to be placed in the **minimum deviation position.** There is only one angle of incidence for which the angle of deviation is minimum.

When $\quad \delta = \delta_m$ [prism in minimum deviation position]

$e = i$ and $r_2 = r_1 \quad$ ...(i)

$\because \quad r_1 + r_2 = A$

$\Rightarrow \quad r + r = A$ or $r = \frac{A}{2}$

Also, we have $\quad A + \delta = i + e \quad$ ...(ii)

Putting $\delta = \delta_m$ and $e = i$ in Eq. (ii), we get

$A + \delta_m = i + i$

$\Rightarrow \quad i = \left(\frac{A + \delta_m}{2}\right)$

From Snell's law, $\quad \mu = \frac{\sin i}{\sin r}$

$$\therefore \quad \mu = \frac{\sin\left(\frac{A + \delta_m}{2}\right)}{\sin \frac{A}{2}}$$

This relation is called a **prism formula.**

For thin prisms (i.e. A is very small), the value of δ_m is also very small.

So, $$\mu = \frac{\sin\left(\frac{A + \delta_m}{2}\right)}{\sin \frac{A}{2}} \approx \frac{\frac{A + \delta_m}{2}}{A/2}$$

$$\Rightarrow \quad \delta_m = (\mu - 1)A$$

Example 13. **A thin prism of 5° angle gives a deviation of 3.2°. What is the value of refractive index of the material of the prism?**

Sol. Given, $A = 5°, \delta = 3.2°, \mu = ?$

We know that, $\delta = A(\mu - 1)$

$\therefore \quad \mu = 1 + \frac{\delta}{A} = 1 + \frac{3.2°}{5°} = 1 + 0.64 = 1.64$

Example 14. **A ray of light suffers minimum deviation, while passing through a prism of refractive index 1.5 and refracting angle 60°. Calculate the angle of deviation and angle of incidence.**
(Given, $\sin^{-1}(0.75) = 48.6°$)

Sol. Given, refractive index, $\mu = 1.5$

Angle of prism, $A = 60°$, angle of deviation, $\delta_m = ?$

Angle of incidence, $i = ?$

We know that, $$\mu = \frac{\sin\left(\frac{A + \delta_m}{2}\right)}{\sin\left(\frac{A}{2}\right)}$$

$$\Rightarrow \quad 1.5 = \frac{\sin\left(\frac{60° + \delta_m}{2}\right)}{\sin\left(\frac{60°}{2}\right)}$$

$$\Rightarrow \quad 1.5 \sin 30° = \sin\left(\frac{60° + \delta_m}{2}\right)$$

$$\Rightarrow \quad 1.5 \times 0.5 = \sin\left(\frac{60° + \delta_m}{2}\right)$$

$$\Rightarrow \quad \frac{60° + \delta_m}{2} = \sin^{-1}(0.75)$$

$$\Rightarrow \quad \frac{60° + \delta_m}{2} = 48.6°$$

$$\delta_m = 48.6° \times 2 - 60° = 37.2°$$

Also, the angle of incidence,

$$i = \frac{(A + \delta_m)}{2} = \frac{60° + 37.2°}{2} = 48.6°$$

Optical Instruments

Using the reflecting and refracting properties of mirrors, lenses and prisms, many optical instruments have been designed like microscopes and telescopes. Our eye is a natural optical device.

Simple Microscope

Microscope is an optical instrument which forms large image of close and minute objects. A simple microscope is a converging lens of small focal length.

- **When an object is at a distance less than the focal length of the lens,** the image obtained is virtual, erect and magnified.
- **When the object is at a distance equal to the focal length of the lens,** the image is formed at infinity.

Case I **When the image is formed at the near point**

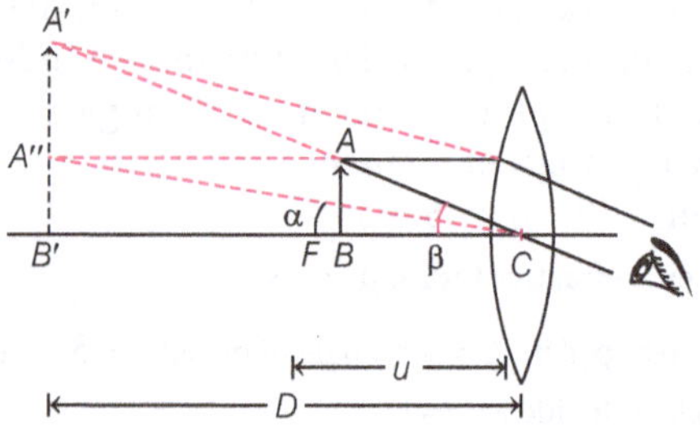

The **angular magnification** or **magnifying power** of a simple microscope is defined as the ratio of the angle subtended by the image and the object on the eye, when both are at the least distance of distinct vision from eye.

$$\therefore \quad \boxed{m = 1 + \frac{D}{f}}$$

It implies that smaller the focal length of the lens, greater is its magnifying power.

[$\because$ $v = -D$ because image is formed at near point]

In this case, the eye is placed behind the lens at a distance *a*, then

$$\boxed{m = 1 + \frac{D - a}{f}}$$

Case II **When the image is formed at infinity**

i.e. $v = \infty$

In this case, $\beta = \frac{AB}{f}$ and $\alpha = \frac{AB}{D}$

$$\therefore \quad m = \frac{AB}{f} \times \frac{D}{AB} = \frac{D}{f}$$

$$\boxed{m = \frac{D}{f}}$$

Example 15. A convex lens of focal length 5 cm is used as a simple microscope. What will be the magnifying power when the image is formed at the least distance of distinct vision?

Sol. Given, focal length, $f = 5$ cm

Least distance of distinct vision,

$$D = 25 \text{ cm}$$

$$\therefore \quad \text{Magnification, } m = \left(1 + \frac{D}{f}\right)$$

$$= \left(1 + \frac{25}{5}\right) = 6$$

Compound Microscope

A compound microscope consists of two convex lenses coaxially separated by some distance. The lens nearer to the object is called the **objective**. The lens through which the final image is viewed is called the **eyepiece**.

Working

The objective of compound microscope forms the real, inverted and magnified image of the object. This image serves as the object for the second lens, i.e. eyepiece which produces the final image, which is enlarged and virtual.

The first inverted image is thus near the focal plane of the eyepiece, at a distance appropriate for final image formation at infinity or a little closer for image formation at the near point. The final image is inverted with respect to the original object.

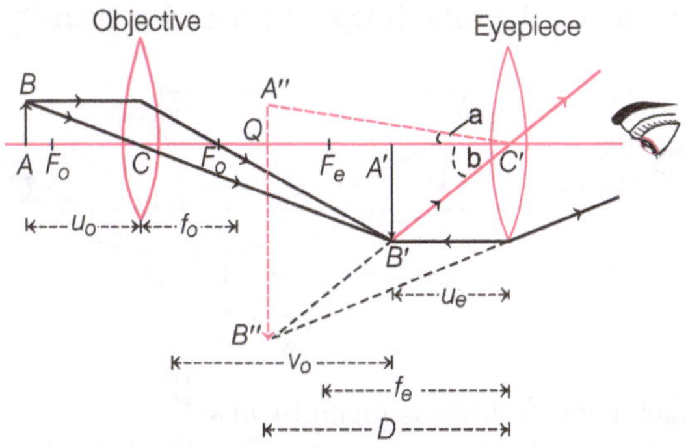

Angular magnification or **magnifying power** of a compound microscope is defined as the ratio of the angle β subtended by the final image at the eye to the angle α subtended by the object seen directly, when both are placed at least distance of distinct vision.

$\therefore$ Angular magnification, $m = \dfrac{\beta}{\alpha}$

Since, the angles are small, then

$$\alpha \approx \tan\alpha \quad \text{or} \quad \beta \approx \tan\beta$$

$$\therefore \qquad m = \frac{\tan\beta}{\tan\alpha} \qquad \text{...(i)}$$

From right angled $\Delta C'QB''$, we have

$$\tan\beta = \frac{B''Q}{C'Q} = \frac{B''Q}{D} = \frac{A''B''}{D}$$

Also, from right angled $\Delta C'A''Q$, we have

$$\tan\alpha = \frac{A''Q}{C'Q} = \frac{AB}{D} \qquad [\because A''Q = AB]$$

Substituting the values of $\tan\alpha$ and $\tan\beta$ in Eq. (i), we have

$$m = \frac{B''Q}{D} \times \frac{D}{AB} = \frac{B''Q}{AB}$$

$$\Rightarrow \qquad m = \frac{B''Q}{A'B'} \times \frac{A'B'}{AB}$$

Thus, **the magnification produced by the compound microscope is the product of the magnification produced by the eyepiece and objective.**

$$\therefore \qquad m = m_e \times m_o \qquad \text{...(ii)}$$

where, m_e and m_o are the magnifying powers of the eyepiece and objective, respectively.

The linear magnification of the real inverted image produced by the eyepiece is $\dfrac{A''B''}{A'B'}$.

***Case* I When the final image is formed at near point**

Linear magnification is given by

$$m_e = 1 + \frac{D}{f_e} \qquad \text{...(iii)}$$

where, f_e is focal length of the eyepiece

$\dfrac{A'B'}{AB}$ is the linear magnification of the object produced by the objective.

$$m_o = \frac{v_o}{u_o} \qquad \text{...(iv)}$$

From Eqs. (ii), (iii) and (iv), we have

$$m = \frac{v_o}{u_o}\left(1 + \frac{D}{f_e}\right) \qquad \text{...(v)}$$

We know that, $\dfrac{1}{v_o} - \dfrac{1}{u_o} = \dfrac{1}{f_o}$

Multiplying both sides by v_o, we have

$$\frac{v_o}{v_o} - \frac{v_o}{u_o} = \frac{v_o}{f_o}$$

$$\Rightarrow \qquad -\frac{v_o}{u_o} = -1 + \frac{v_o}{f_o} \Rightarrow \frac{v_o}{u_o} = 1 - \frac{v_o}{f_o}$$

Substituting the value of $\dfrac{v_o}{u_o}$ in Eq. (v), we have

$$m = \left(1 - \frac{v_o}{f_o}\right)\left(1 + \frac{D}{f_e}\right)$$

***Case* II When the final image is at infinity**

If u_o is the distance of the object from the objective and v_o is the distance of the image from the objective, then the magnifying power of the objective is

$$m_o = \frac{v_o}{u_o}$$

When the final image is at infinity, then angular magnification is given by

$$m_e = \frac{D}{f_e}$$

The total magnification when image is at infinity is given by

$$m = m_o \times m_e = \left(\frac{v_o}{u_o} \times \frac{D}{f_e}\right)$$

If the object is very close to the principal focus of the objective and the image formed by the objective is very close to the eyepiece, then

$$m = \frac{-L}{f_o} \cdot \frac{D}{f_e}$$

where, L = length of the tube of microscope

In this case, the microscope is said to be in normal adjustment.

Example 16. **A compound microscope has an objective of focal length 1 cm and an eyepiece of focal length 2.5 cm. An object has to be placed at a distance of 1.2 cm away from the objective for the normal adjustment. Determine the angular magnification and length of microscope tube.**

Sol. Given, focal length of objective, $f_o = 1$ cm

Focal length of eyepiece, $f_e = 2.5$ cm

Object distance, $u_o = -1.2$ cm

$$\because \quad \frac{1}{v_o} - \frac{1}{u_o} = \frac{1}{f_o} \Rightarrow \frac{1}{v_o} = \frac{1}{u_o} + \frac{1}{f_o}$$

$$\Rightarrow \quad \frac{1}{v_o} = 1 - \frac{1}{1.2} = \frac{0.2}{1.2} \Rightarrow v_o = \frac{1.2}{0.2}$$

$$\Rightarrow \quad v_o = 6 \text{ cm}$$

$$\because \text{ Angular magnification, } m = \frac{v_o}{|u_o|}\left(1 + \frac{D}{f_e}\right)$$

$$\Rightarrow \quad m = \frac{6}{|-1.2|}\left(1 + \frac{25}{2.5}\right) = 55$$

$\therefore$ Length of microscope tube,

$$L = v_o + f_e = (6 + 2.5) = 8.5 \text{ cm}$$

Astronomical (Refracting) Telescope

An **astronomical telescope** is an optical instrument which is used for observing distinct images of heavenly bodies like stars, planets, etc., when the final image is formed at infinity.

Astronomical telescope has two convex lenses coaxially separated by some distance. The lens towards the object is called **objective** and has much larger aperture than the eyepiece of the lens towards the eye.

Working

Light from the distant object enters the objective and real image is formed at second focal point of objective. The eyepiece magnifies this image producing a final inverted image.

Case I **When the final image is formed at infinity**

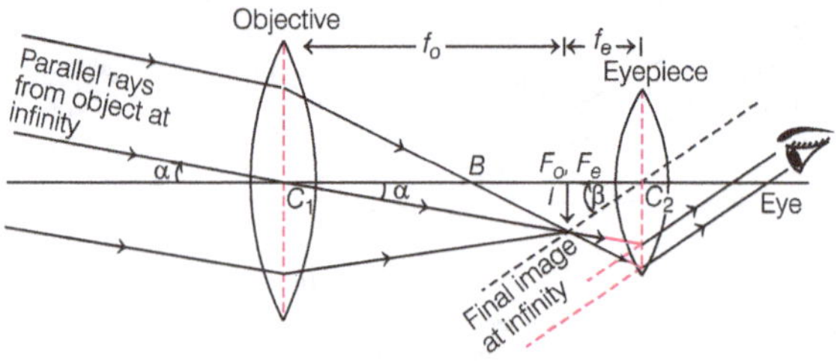

Angular magnification is given by $m = \dfrac{\beta}{\alpha}$

Since, β and α are very small.

$$\therefore \quad \beta \approx \tan\beta \quad \text{or} \quad \alpha \approx \tan\alpha$$

$$\Rightarrow \quad m = \frac{\tan\beta}{\tan\alpha} \qquad \text{...(i)}$$

Now, $\tan\alpha = \dfrac{I}{f_o}$ and $\tan\beta = \dfrac{I}{-f_e}$

where, I is the image formed by the objective, f_o and f_e are the focal lengths of objective and eyepiece, respectively.

Substituting the values of $\tan\alpha$ and $\tan\beta$ in Eq. (i), we get

$$m = \frac{-\frac{I}{f_e}}{\frac{I}{f_o}} \quad \text{or} \quad m = -\frac{f_o}{f_e}$$

Case II **When final image is formed at near point**

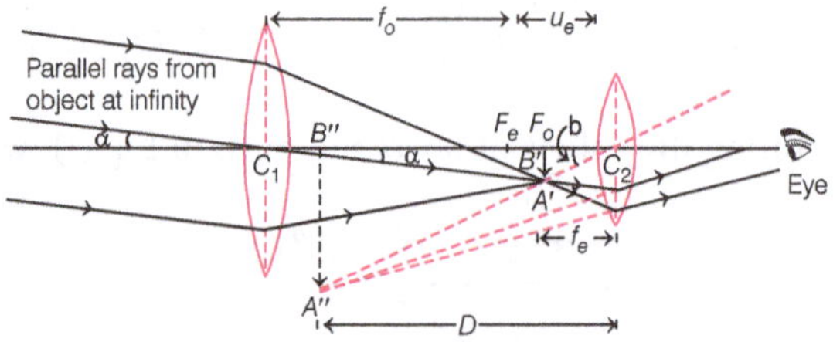

$$\text{Angular magnification, } m = \frac{\beta}{\alpha}$$

$$\Rightarrow \quad m = \frac{\tan\beta}{\tan\alpha} \quad [\because \beta \text{ and } \alpha \text{ are small}]$$

$$\Rightarrow \quad m = \frac{\frac{A'B'}{C_2B'}}{\frac{A'B'}{C_1B'}} = \frac{C_1B'}{C_2B'}$$

$$\Rightarrow \quad m = \frac{f_o}{-u_e} \qquad \text{...(i)}$$

Using lens formula $\left(\frac{1}{v}-\frac{1}{u}=\frac{1}{f}\right)$ for the eyepiece, we have

$$\frac{1}{-D}-\frac{1}{-u_e}=\frac{1}{f_e} \Rightarrow \frac{1}{u_e}=\frac{1}{f_e}+\frac{1}{D}=\frac{1}{f_e}\left(1+\frac{f_e}{D}\right)$$

Putting the value of $\frac{1}{u_e}$ in Eq. (i), we have

$$m=-\frac{f_o}{f_e}\left(1+\frac{f_e}{D}\right)$$

Example 17. A telescope consists of two lenses of focal lengths 20 cm and 5 cm. Obtain its magnifying power when the final image is (i) at infinity (ii) at 25 cm from the eye.

Sol. (i) When the final image is at infinity,

$$m=-\frac{f_o}{f_e}=\frac{-20}{5} \Rightarrow m=-4$$

(ii) When the final image is at 25 cm from the eye, i.e. $D = 25$ cm,

$$m=\frac{-f_o}{f_e}\left(1+\frac{f_e}{D}\right)=\frac{-20}{5}\left(1+\frac{5}{25}\right) \Rightarrow m=-4.8$$

Reflecting Telescope

Reflecting telescope is also known as **Cassegrain Telescope**, which was designed by Guillaume Cassegrain. Reflecting telescope is an improvement over refracting or astronomical telescope.

Working

To obtain a bright image of a distant star by refracting telescope, it is essential to have an objective of large aperture, so that it may collect more light coming from the object. But to deal with such a big lens is problem in terms of using and making and it is too costly. The same bright image of a distant object can be obtained by using a concave mirror of large aperture in place of objective.

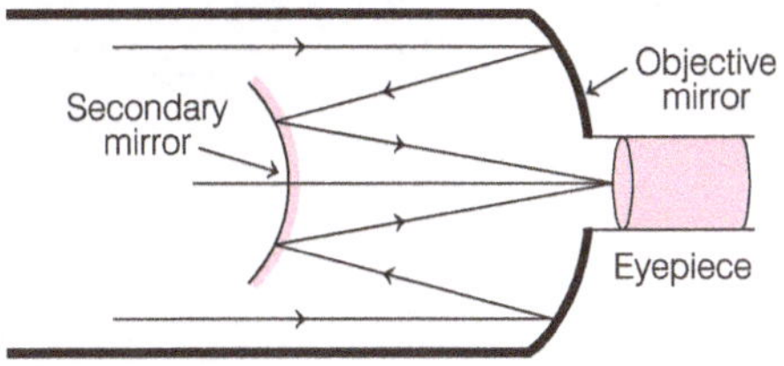

Reflecting telescope consists of concave mirror of large aperture and large focal length (objective). A convex mirror is placed between the concave mirror and its focus.

A small convex lens works as eyepiece In the reflecting telescope, parallel rays from a distant object are intercepted and focused by a reflecting concave mirror rather than a refracting lens.

One popular configuration of mirror and eyepiece is called the **Newtonian reflecting type telescope,** named after its designer Newton.

The parallel beam of light coming from the distant object (star) is reflected by concave parabolic mirror M_1, on the plane mirror M_2. The plane mirror M_2 is inclined at an angle of 45° to axis of the mirror M_1.

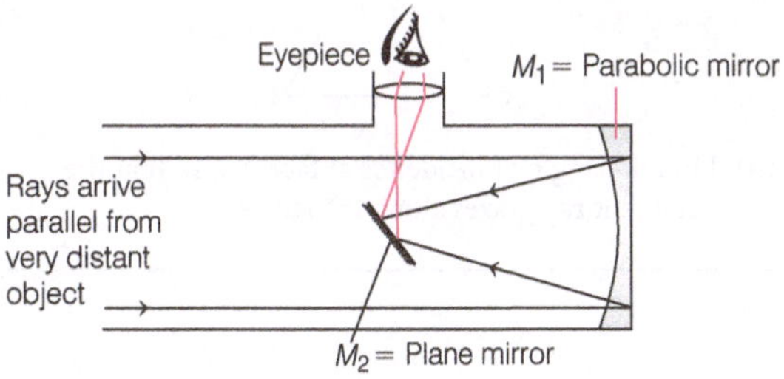

The plane mirror reflects the beam and a real image is formed in front of eyepiece. The eyepiece acts as a magnifier and the final magnified image of the distant object can be observed by the eye.

Advantages of Reflecting Telescope over Refracting Telescope

For astronomical telescope, the mirror affords several advantages over the objective lens.

- A mirror is easier to produce with a larger diameter, so that it can intercept rays crossing a larger area and direct them to the eyepiece.
- The mirror can be made parabolic to reduce spherical aberration.
- Aberration is further reduced because passage through one layer of glass (the objective lens) is eliminated.

Quick Test 4

Conceptual Questions

1. Write the relationship between angle of incidence i, angle of prism A and angle of minimum deviation δ_m for a triangular prism.

2. Why should the objective lens of a compound microscope have a small focal length?

3. Explain two advantages of a reflecting telescope over a refracting telescope.

Numerical Questions

4. (i) A ray of light incident of face AB of an equilateral glass prism, shows minimum deviation of 30°. Calculate the speed of light through the prism.

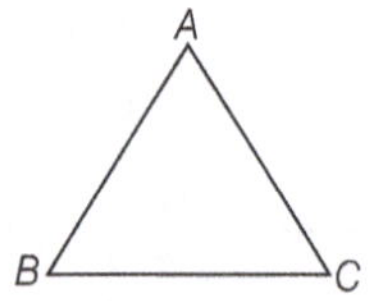

(ii) Find the angle of incidence at face AB, so that the emergent ray grazes along the face AC.

5. For a glass prism($\mu = \sqrt{3}$), the angle of minimum deviation is equal to the angle of the prism. Find the angle of the prism. *NCERT Exemplar*

6. You are given two converging lenses of focal length 1.25 cm and 5 cm to design a compound microscope. If it is desired to have a magnification of 30, then find out the separation between the objective and eyepiece.

7. A compound microscope uses an objective lens of focal length 4 cm and eyepiece lens of focal length 10 cm. An object is placed at 6 cm from the objective lens. Calculate the magnifying power of the compound microscope. Also, calculate the length of the microscope.

Answers

4. (i) $(3\times10^8/\sqrt{2})$ m/s (ii) $\sin^{-1}(\sqrt{2}\sin 15°)$

5. 60°

6. 7.5 cm

7. 19.14 cm

For Solutions, See QR Code on Pg. 322

Mind Map

Reflection

It is the phenomenon where light rays bounce off a surface and return to the same medium.

Laws of Reflection

- **First Law** The incident ray, reflected ray, and the normal, all lie in the same plane.
- **Second Law** The angle of incidence (i) is equal to the angle of reflection (r), i.e. $i = r$.

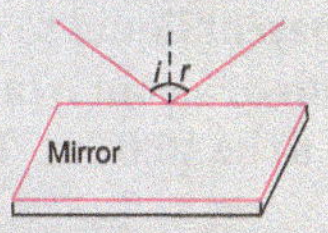

Sign Convention

- All the distances are measured from pole (P) of mirror.
- The distances measured in the direction of incident ray are taken positive, otherwise negative.
- Heights measured upward and perpendicular to the principal axis are +ve and otherwise –ve.

Spherical Mirrors

Spherical mirrors are curved mirrors with surfaces that form a part of a sphere. They are classified as

- **Concave Mirror** The reflecting surface is curved inward, like the inside of a bowl. It converges light rays.
- **Convex Mirror** The reflecting surface is curved outward, like the back of a spoon. It diverges light rays.

Mirror formula, $\frac{1}{u}+\frac{1}{v}=\frac{1}{f}=\frac{2}{R}$

Magnification, $m=-\frac{v}{u}=\frac{h_i}{h_o}$

If the image is upright or erect with respect to the object, then m is positive.

If the image is inverted with respect to the object, then m is negative.

Refraction of Light

The phenomenon of the change in the path of light as it passes obliquely from one transparent medium to another is called refraction of light.

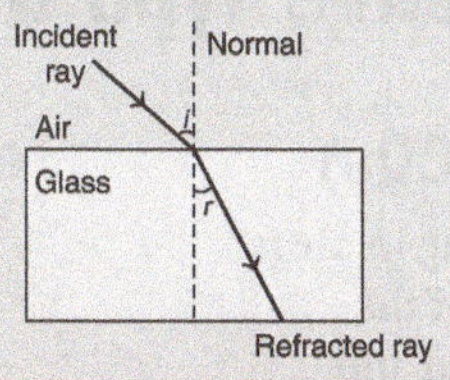

Laws of Refraction of Light

- **First Law** The incident ray, the refracted ray and the normal to the interface at the point of incidence all lie in the same plane.
- **Second Law** The ratio of the sine of the angle of incidence and the sine of the angle of refraction is constant for a given pair of media. Mathematically, $\frac{\sin i}{\sin r}={}^1\mu_2$

Refractive Index

The refractive index of a medium for a light of given wavelength may be defined as the ratio of the speed of light in vacuum to its speed in that medium.

$\mu=\frac{c}{v}$

Critical Angle

The angle of incidence in denser medium corresponds to which angle of refraction in rarer medium is 90°.

Total Internal Reflection (TIR)

It occurs when light gets reflected entirely within a denser medium after striking the boundary with a rarer medium at an angle greater than the critical angle.

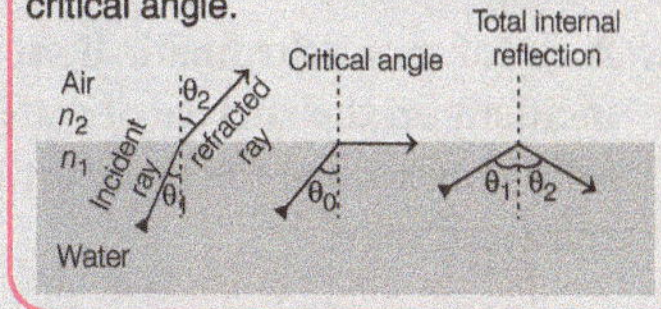

Optical Fibers

These are thin strands of glass or plastic that use TIR to transmit light efficiently over long distances.

Refraction through a Prism

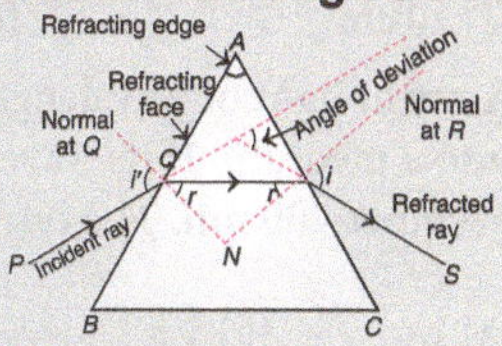

Angle of deviation,

$\delta = i + i' - A$ or $i + i' = A + \delta$

Refractive index of prism,

$$\mu=\frac{\sin\left(\frac{A+\delta_m}{2}\right)}{\sin\left(\frac{A}{2}\right)}$$

Ray Optics and optical Instruments

Refraction at Spherical Surfaces

The equation which holds good for any curved spherical surface is given by

$$\frac{n_2}{v}-\frac{n_1}{u}=\frac{n_2-n_1}{R}$$

Lens It is of two types

- **Convex Lens** is thicker at the centre and thinner at its ends.
- **Concave Lens** is thinner at the centre and thicker at its ends.

Thin lens formula, $\frac{1}{f}=\frac{1}{v}-\frac{1}{u}$

Magnification

Convex lens

- Where image formed is virtual, $m = -v/u$
- When image formed is real, $m = v/u$

Concave lens, $m = v/u$

Lens Maker's Formula

$$\frac{1}{f}=(\mu-1)\left[\frac{1}{R_1}-\frac{1}{R_2}\right]$$

Power of lens

$P=\frac{1}{f}$; unit → m^{-1} or Dioptre

Combination of thin lens in contact

For several thin lens of focal lengths $f_1, f_2, \ldots f_n$

$$\frac{1}{f}=\frac{1}{f_1}+\frac{1}{f_1}+\frac{1}{f_1}+\ldots-\frac{1}{f_n}$$

$$P = P_1 + P_2 + P_3 + \ldots + P_n$$

Magnification

$$m = m_1 \times m_2 \times m_3 \times \ldots$$

Optical Instrument

Simple Microscope

Magnifying power

- For final image formed at D (least distance),

$$m=\frac{\text{Angle subtended by the image at } D}{\text{Angle subtended by the object at infinity}}$$

$$=1+\frac{D}{f}$$

- For final image formed at infinity, $m=\frac{D}{f}$

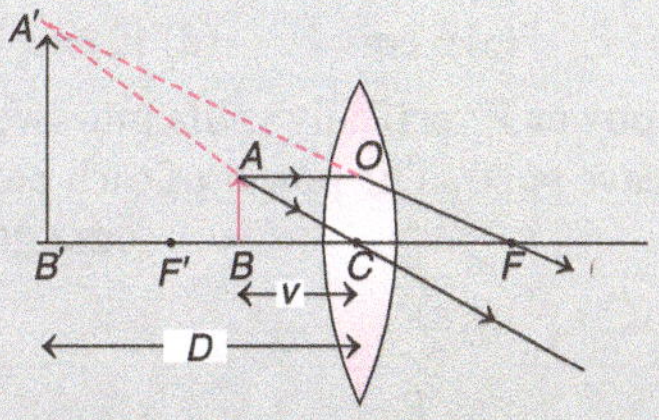

Astronomical Telescope

Magnifying power

- For final image formed at D (least distance),

$$m=\frac{\text{Angle subtended by the image at } D}{\text{Angle subtended by the object at infinity}}$$

$$=\frac{\beta}{\alpha}=\frac{-f_o}{f_e}\left(1+\frac{f_e}{D}\right)$$

- In normal adjustment, image formed at infinity, $m=-f_o/f_e$

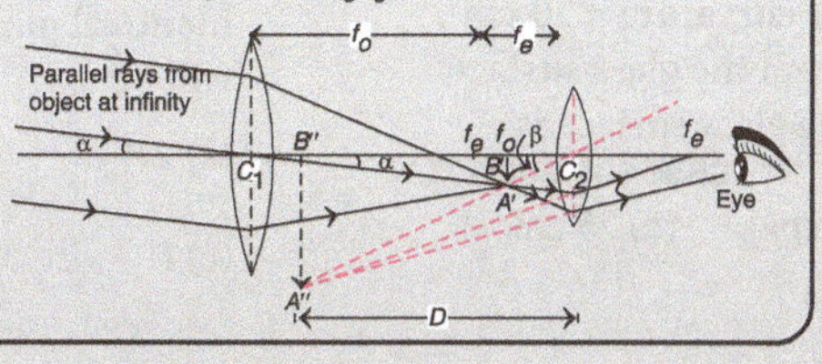

EXAM PATTERN QUESTIONS

Objective Type Questions

Multiple Choice Questions (MCQs)

1. A ray of monochromatic light propagating in air is incident on the surface of water. Which of the following will be the same for the reflected and refracted rays? **CBSE 2023**

(a) Energy carried (b) Speed
(c) Frequency (d) Wavelength

2. A convex mirror has focal length 20 cm. If an object is placed 20 cm away from the pole of mirror, then what is the distance between image formed and pole?

(a) 40 cm (b) 10 cm
(c) 20 cm (d) At infinity

3. A ray of light of wavelength 600 nm propagates from air into a medium. If its wavelength in the medium becomes 400 nm. The refractive index of the medium is **CBSE 2023**

(a) 1.4 (b) 1.5 (c) 1.6 (d) 1.8

4. A ray of light travels a distance of 12.0 m in a transparent sheet in 60 ns. The refractive index of the sheet is **CBSE 2023**

(a) 1.33 (b) 1.50 (c) 1.65 (d) 1.75

5. A beam of light travels from air into a medium. Its speed and wavelength in the medium are 1.5×10^8 ms^{-1} and 230 nm, respectively. The wavelength of light in air will be **CBSE 2023**

(a) 230 nm (b) 345 nm (c) 460 nm (d) 690 nm

6. Ray of light transmitted from glass ($n = 3/2$) to water ($n = 4/3$). What is the value of critical angle?

(a) $\sin^{-1}\left(\frac{1}{2}\right)$ (b) $\sin^{-1}\sqrt{\frac{8}{9}}$ (c) $\sin^{-1}\left(\frac{8}{9}\right)$ (d) $\sin^{-1}\left(\frac{5}{7}\right)$

7. Two convex and concave lenses are in contact and having focal lengths 12 cm and 18 cm, respectively. Focal length of joint lens will be

(a) 50 cm (b) 45 cm (c) 36 cm (d) 18 cm

8. Light from a point source in air falls on a spherical glass surface ($n = 1.5$ and radius of curvature = 20 cm). The distance of the light source from the glass surface is 100 cm. Image distance from the glass surface is **CBSE SQP 2020-21**

(a) 20 cm (b) 50 cm (c) 100 cm (d) 75 cm

9. A tub is filled with a transparent liquid to a height of 30.0 cm. The apparent depth of a coin lying at the bottom of the tub is found to be 16.0 cm. The speed of light in the liquid will be **CBSE 2025**

(a) 1.6×10^8 ms^{-1} (b) 2.0×10^8 ms^{-1}
(c) 3.0×10^8 ms^{-1} (d) 2.5×10^8 ms^{-1}

10. A plot of angle of deviation D *versus* angle of incidence for a triangular prism is shown below.

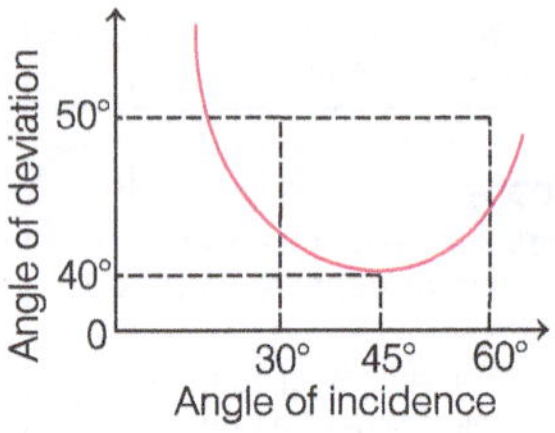

The angle of incidence for which the light ray travels parallel to the base is

(a) 30° (b) 60°
(c) 45° (d) Data insufficient

11. An equilateral prism is in condition of minimum deviation. If incidence angle is 4/5 times of prism angle, then minimum deviation angle is

(a) 72° (b) 60°
(c) 48° (d) 36°

12. When a wave undergoes reflection at an interface from rarer to denser medium, then change in its phase is **CBSE 2020**

(a) $\frac{\pi}{2}$ (b) zero
(c) π (d) $\frac{\pi}{4}$

13. A point object is placed at the centre of a glass sphere of radius 6 cm and refractive index 1.5. The distance of virtual image from the surface of the sphere is

(a) 2 cm (b) 4 cm (c) 6 cm (d) 12 cm

14. A biconcave lens of power P vertically splits into two identical plano-concave parts. The power of each part will be **CBSE 2020**

(a) $2P$ (b) $\frac{P}{2}$
(c) P (d) $\frac{P}{\sqrt{2}}$

15. Which of the following actions will lead to an increase in the magnifying power of an astronomical telescope? **Competency Based Que.**

(a) Increase in the length of the telescope tube.
(b) Interchange the objective and the eyepiece of the telescope.
(c) A small piece of paper on the objective of the telescope pointed towards the moon.
(d) Increase in the focal length of the objective and decrease in the focal length of the eyepiece.

16. The objective lens of an astronomical telescope must be of

(a) high power
(b) large focal length
(c) high refractive index
(d) low refractive index

17. An incident light ray falls on a glass prism at an angle of 60° and emerges with an angle of 30° with its initial incident direction. If the angle of the prism is 30°, then which of the following is an incorrect statement? **Competency Based Que.**

(a) Refractive index of the prism is $\sqrt{3}$.
(b) The light undergoes minimum deviation through the prism (i.e., $r_1 = r_2$).
(c) The emergent ray is perpendicular to the face from which it emerges.
(d) Angle of refraction r_1 at the incident face is same as angle of the prism.

18. Read the following statements carefully.

I. A drop of an oil in water or in a glass, both behave as convergent lens.
II. A water drop in air and a glass sphere in water, both behave as convergent lens.
III. An air bubble in water and a water bubble in glass, both behave as a divergent lens.
IV. A frozen ice crystal inside a glass sphere and a bromine liquid drop inside a glass sphere, behave as divergent lens. [Reference values of refractive indices of common substances: Air = 1.001, water = 1.33, ice = 1.31, glass = 1.51, oil = 1. 4, bromine = 1.66] **Competency Based Que.**

Select the correct option.

(a) Statements I and II are correct.
(b) Statements I and III are correct.
(c) Statements II and III are correct.
(d) Statements II and IV are correct.

19. If the focal length of the eyepiece of a telescope is doubled, its magnifying power m will be

(a) $2m$ (b) $3m$ (c) $\frac{m}{2}$ (d) $4m$

20. Match the corresponding entries of Column I with Column II where m is magnification produced by the mirror.

	Column I		Column II
A.	$m = -2$	p.	Convex mirror
B.	$m = -\frac{1}{2}$	q.	Concave mirror
C.	$m = +2$	r.	Real image
D.	$m = +\frac{1}{2}$	s.	Virtual image

(a) A-r, s; B-q, s; C-q, r; D-p, s
(b) A-q, r; B-q, r; C-q, s; D-p, s
(c) A-p, r; B-p, s; C-p, q; D-r, s
(d) A-p, s; B-q, r; C-q, s; D-q, r

Assertion-Reason

Directions *(Q. Nos. 21-29) In the following questions, two statements are given- one labelled Assertion (A) and the other labelled Reason (R). Select the correct answer to these questions from the codes (a), (b), (c) and (d) as given below.*

(a) Both Assertion and Reason are true and Reason is the correct explanation of Assertion.
(b) Both Assertion and Reason are true but Reason is not the correct explanation of Assertion.
(c) Assertion is true but Reason is false.
(d) Assertion is false but Reason is true.

21. **Assertion (A)** A ray of light incident along the normal to the plane mirror retraces its path after reflection from the mirror.
Reason (R) A ray of light along the normal has angle of incidence as $\pi/2$ and hence, it retraces its own path after reflection from mirror.

22. **Assertion (A)** A convex mirror cannot form real images.
Reason (R) Convex mirror converges the parallel rays that are incident on it. **CBSE SQP 2020-21**

23. **Assertion (A)** Propagation of light through an optical fibre is due to total internal reflection taking place at the core-clade interface.
Reason (R) Refractive index of the material of the core of the optical fibre is greater than that of air.

24. **Assertion (A)** Convergent property of converging lens remains same in mediums.
Reason (R) Property of lens whether the ray is diverging or converging depends on the surrounding medium.

25. **Assertion (A)** The focal length of the convex mirror will increase, if the mirror is placed in water.
Reason (R) The focal length of a convex mirror of radius R is equal to $f = \frac{R}{2}$. **CBSE SQP 2020-21**

26. **Assertion (A)** If a convex lens is kept in water, its convergence power decreases.
Reason (R) The refractive index of convex lens relative to water is less than that relative to air.

27. **Assertion (A)** In compound microscope, objective lens is taken as of small focal length.
Reason (R) This increases the magnifying power of microscope.

28. **Assertion (A)** The air bubble shines in water.
Reason (R) Air bubble in water shines due to refraction of light.

29. **Assertion (A)** If objective and eye lenses of a microscope are interchanged, then it can work as telescope.
Reason (R) The objective of telescope has small focal length.

Case Based Questions

Directions (Q.No. 30-33) *These questions are case study based questions. Read the following paragraph and answer the questions on the basis of same.*

30. **Refraction involves change in the path of light due to change in the medium.**

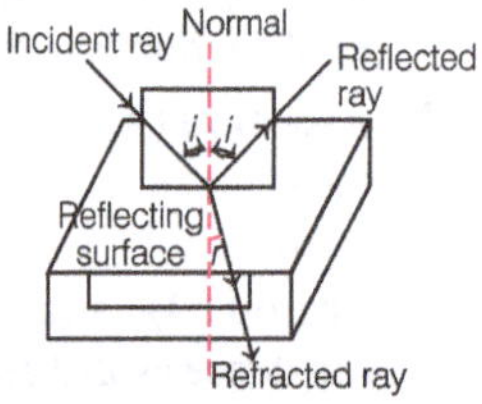

When a beam of light encounters another transparent medium, a part of light gets reflected back into the first medium while the rest enters the other. The direction of propagation of an obliquely incident ray of light, that enters the other medium, changes at the interface of two media. This phenomenon is called refraction of light.

(i) Which of the following quantity remains unchanged after refraction?
(a) Speed of light (b) Intensity of light
(c) Wavelength of light (d) Frequency of light

(ii) A ray of light strikes an air-glass interface at an angle of incidence ($i = 60°$) and gets refracted at an angle of refraction r. On increasing the angle of incidence ($i > 60°$), the angle of refraction r
(a) decreases (b) remains same
(c) is equal to 60° (d) increases

(iii) When an object lying in a denser medium is observed from rarer medium, then real depth of object is
(a) more than that observed
(b) less than that observed
(c) equals to observed depth
(d) depends on angle of vision

(iv) For the same angle of incidence, the angles of refraction in media P, Q and R are 35°, 25° and 15°, respectively. Which of the following relation hold true for the velocity of light in medium P, Q and R?
(a) $v_P < v_Q < v_R$ (b) $v_P < v_R < v_Q$
(c) $v_P > v_Q > v_R$ (d) $v_P > v_R > v_Q$

(v) A light ray enters from medium A to medium B as shown in figure. The refractive index of medium B relative to A will be

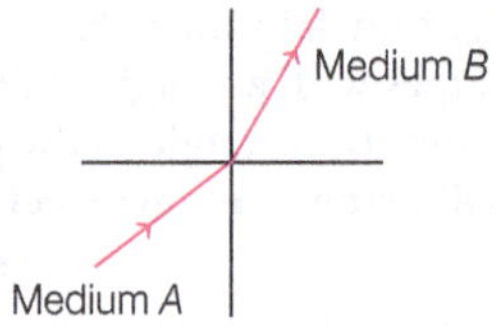

(a) greater than unity (b) less than unity
(c) equal to unity (d) zero

31. **A lens is a transparent optical medium bounded by two surfaces, at least one of which should be spherical. Applying the formula of image formation by a single spherical surface successively at the two surfaces of a thin lens, a formula known as lens Maker's formula and hence the basic lens formula can be obtained. The focal length (or power) of a lens depends on the radii of its surfaces and the refractive index of its material with respect to the surrounding medium. The refractive index of a material depends on the wavelength of light used. Combination of lenses helps us to obtain diverging or converging lenses of desired power and magnification.** **CBSE 2024**

(i) A thin converging lens of focal length 20 cm and a thin diverging lens of focal length 15 cm are placed coaxially in contact. The power of the combination is
(a) $\frac{-5}{6}$ D (b) $\frac{-5}{3}$ D
(c) $\frac{4}{3}$ D (d) $\frac{3}{2}$ D

(ii) The radii of curvature of two surfaces of a convex lens are R and $2R$. If the focal length of this lens is $\left(\frac{4}{3}\right)R$, the refractive index of the material of the lens is
(a) $\frac{5}{3}$ (b) $\frac{4}{3}$ (c) $\frac{3}{2}$ (d) $\frac{7}{5}$

(iii) The focal length of an equiconvex lens
(a) increases when the lens is dipped in water
(b) increases when the wavelength of incident light decreases
(c) increases with decrease in radius of curvature of its surface
(d) decreases when the lens is cut into two identical parts along its principal axis

(iv) A thin convex lens L of focal length 10 cm and a concave mirror M of focal length 15 cm are placed co-axially 40 cm apart as shown in figure. A beam of light coming parallel to the principal axis is incident on the lens. The final image will be formed at a distance of

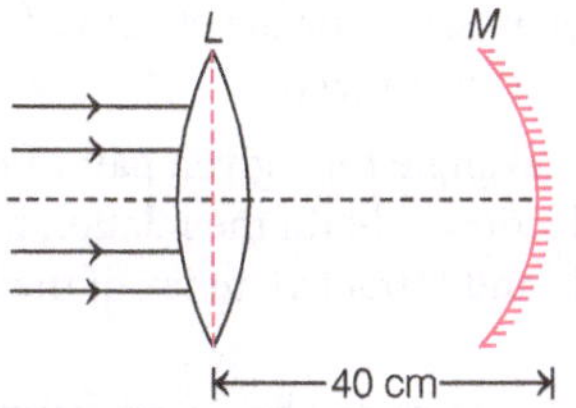

(a) 10 cm, left of lens (b) 19 cm, right of lens
(c) 20 cm, left of lens (d) 20 cm, right of lens

Or

A beam of light coming parallel to the principal axis of a convex lens L_1 of focal length 16 cm is incident on it. Another convex lens L_2 of focal length 12 cm is placed coaxially at a distance 40 cm from L_1. The nature and distance of the final image from L_2 will be
(a) real, 24 cm (b) virtual, 12 cm
(c) real, 32 cm (d) virtual, 18 cm

32. **The lens Maker's formula is useful to design lenses of desired focal lengths using surfaces of suitable radii of curvature. The focal length also depends on the refractive index of the material of the lens and the surrounding medium. The refractive index depends on the wavelength of the light used. The power of a lens is related to its focal length.** **CBSE 2023**

Answer the following questions based on the above.

(i) How will the power of a lens be affected with an increase of wavelength of light?

(ii) The radius of curvature of two surfaces of a convex lens is R each. For what value of μ of its material, will its focal length become equal to R?

(iii) The focal length of a concave lens of $\mu = 1.5$ is 20 cm in air. It is completely immersed in water of $\mu = \frac{4}{3}$. Calculate its focal length in water.

(iv) An object is placed in front of a lens which forms its erect image of magnification 3. The power of the lens is 5 D. Calculate the distance of the object and the image from the lens.

33. **When light travels from one transparent medium to another transparent medium, then in the second medium, its speed and direction of motion change. This is called refraction of light. The refraction of light takes place according to the following two laws, known as laws of refraction.**

(a) The incident ray, the refracted ray and the normal to the interface at the incident point all lie in the same plane.

(b) The ratio of the sine angle of incidence to the sine angle of refraction is constant for the two given media.

If the angle of incidence is i and the angle of refraction is r, then

$$\frac{\sin i}{\sin r} = {}_1\mu_2 \text{ (constant)}$$

${}_1\mu_2$ is called the refractive index.

The absolute refractive index of a material is the ratio of the speed of light (c) in vacuum to the speed of light in the medium (v).

The relation between refractive index and critical angle i_c is given by ${}_1\mu_2 = \frac{1}{\sin i_c}$

Answer the following questions based on the above.

(i) Refractive indices of water and glass are 4/3 and 3/2, respectively. A light ray travelling in water is incident on water-glass interface of 45°. What is angle of refraction?

(ii) Monochromatic light of wavelength 589 nm is incident from air on a water surface. If refractive index for water is 4/3, find the wavelength, frequency and speed of the refracted light.

(iii) A pin fixed on a table is viewed from above a distance of 50 cm. By what distance would the pin appear to be raised when viewed from the same point through a 15 cm thick glass ($n = 1.5$) slab held parallel to the table? Does the answer depend on the location of the slab?

(iv) Find the critical angle for glass-water interface, if the refractive indices of glass and water with respect to air are 3/2 and 4/3 respectively.

Subjective Questions

Very Short Answer Type Questions

1. Mention the laws of reflection.

2. A ray of light is incident on a medium with angle of incidence i and is refracted into a second medium with angle of refraction r. The graph of $\sin i$ *versus* $\sin r$ is as shown in figure. Find the ratio of the velocity of light in the first medium to the velocity of light in the second medium. **CBSE SQP 2018-19**

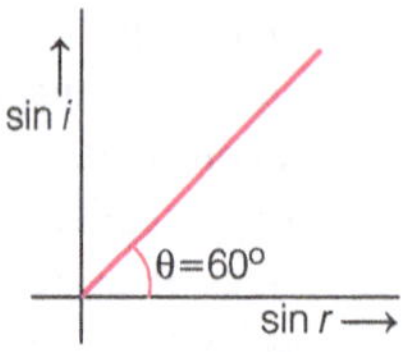

3. Sketch the emergent wavefront.

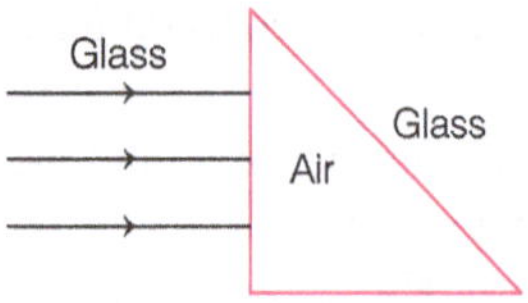

4. Under what condition, does a biconvex lens of glass having a certain refractive index act as a plane glass sheet when immersed in a liquid?

5. What is the focal length of a convex lens of focal length 30 cm in contact with a concave lens of focal length 20 cm? Is the system a converging or a diverging lens? Ignore thickness of the lenses.

6. Where should an object be placed from a convex lens to form an image of the same size? Can it happen in case of a concave lens?

7. Define the power of a lens. Write its SI unit.

8. Two lenses of focal lengths 6 cm and 50 cm are to be used for making a telescope. Which lens will be used as an objective and why?

9. Consider a telescope whose objective lens has a focal length of 100 cm and the eyepiece has focal length 1 cm. What will be the magnification of the given telescope?

10. A small telescope has an objective lens of focal length 144 cm and an eyepiece of focal length 6.0 cm. What is the magnifying power of the telescope? What is the separation between the objective and the eyepiece?

Short Answer Type Questions

11. Using the Snell's law of refraction, define the relative refractive index of a medium.

12. Why does a convex lens of glass $\mu = 1.5$ behave as a diverging lens when immersed in carbon disulphide of $\mu = 1.65$?

13 Show that for a material with refractive index $\mu \geq \sqrt{2}$, light incident at any angle shall be guided along a length perpendicular to the incident face. **NCERT Exemplar**

14. A ray of light is incident on a surface separating air from a denser medium A of refractive index μ_1. It is then made incident on the parallel surface of another medium B of refractive index μ_2 at the same angle of incidence. If the angle of refraction in the two media are 30° and 35° respectively, then in which one of the two media (A or B) will light travel faster and why ?

15. Derive the expression for the effective focal length of two thin lenses in contact.

16. Define critical angle for a given pair of media and total internal reflection. Obtain the relation between the critical angle and refractive index of the medium. **CBSE 2023**

17. A ray of light is refracted by a glass prism. Obtain an expression for the refractive index of the glass in terms of the angle of prism A and the angle of minimum deviation δ_m. **CBSE 2023**

18. The power of a thin lens is + 5D. When it is immersed in a liquid, it behaves like a concave lens of focal length 100 cm. Calculate the refractive index of the liquid. Given, refractive index of glass = 1.5. **CBSE 2023**

19. An air bubble is trapped at point B ($CB = 20$ cm) in a glass sphere of radius 40 cm and refractive index 1.5 as shown in figure. Find the nature and position of the image of the bubble as seen by an observer at point P. **CBSE 2024**

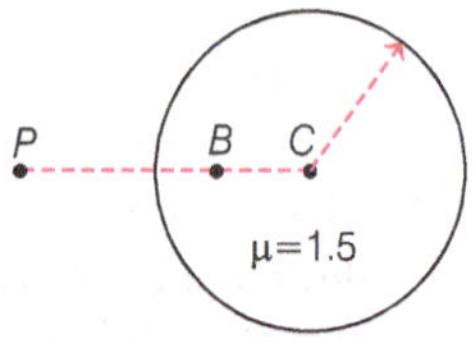

20. A ray of light is incident normally on one face of an equilateral glass prism of refractive index μ. When the prism is completely immersed in a transparent medium, it is observed that the emergent ray just grazes the adjacent face. Find the refractive index of the medium. **CBSE 2024**

21. (i) Why should the objective of a telescope have large focal length and large aperture? Justify your answer. **[1½]**

(ii) Two convex lenses of same focal length but of aperture A_1 and A_2 ($A_2 < A_1$), are used as the objective lenses in two astronomical telescopes having identical eyepieces. What is the ratio of their resolving power? Which telescope will you prefer and why? Give reason. **[1½]**

22. (i) Draw a ray diagram for the formation of image by a Cassegrain telescope. **[1½]**

(ii) Why these types of telescopes are preferred over refracting type telescopes. Write two point. **[1½]**

23. What are the uses of spherical mirrors?

24. A short object of length L is placed along the principal axis of a concave mirror away from focus. The object distance is u. If the mirror has a focal length f, what will be the length of the image? You may take $L << |v - f|$. **NCERT Exemplar**

25. A point object is placed at O in front of a glass sphere as shown in figure. Show the formation of image by the sphere. **CBSE 2022 Term-2**

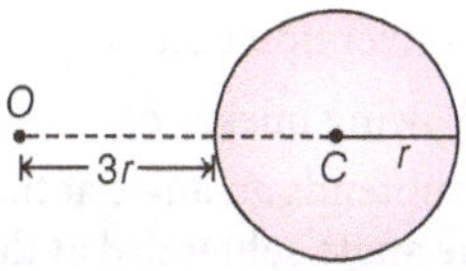

26. Write two characteristics of image formed when an object is placed between the optical centre and focus of a thin convex lens. Draw the graph showing variation of image distance v with object distance u in this case. **CBSE SQP 2021**

27. The refractive index of a material of a concave lens is n_1. It is immersed in a medium of refractive index n_2. A parallel beam of light is incident on the lens. Trace the path of emergent rays when (i) $n_2 = n_1$ (ii) $n_2 > n_1$ (iii) $n_2 < n_1$.

28. A convex lens made of a material of refractive index n_1 is kept in a medium of refractive index n_2. Parallel rays of light are incident on the lens. Complete the path of rays of light emerging from the convex lens if

(i) $n_1 > n_2$ (ii) $n_1 = n_2$ (iii) $n_1 < n_2$

29. In the given figure the radius of curvature of curved face in the plano-convex and the plano-concave lens is 15 cm each. The refractive index of the material of the lenses is 1.5. Find the final position of the image formed. **CBSE 2023**

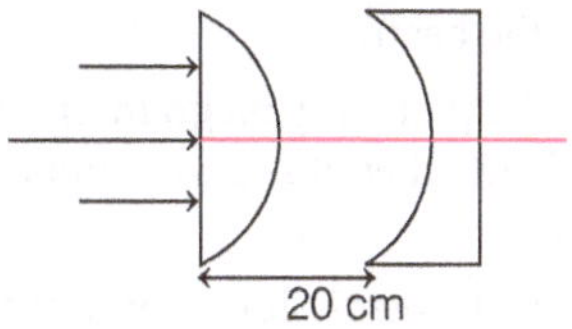

30. A symmetric biconvex lens of radius of curvature R and made of glass of refractive index 1.5, is placed on a layer of liquid placed on top of a plane mirror as shown in the figure. An optical needle with its tip on the principal axis of the lens is moved along the axis until its real, inverted image coincides with the needle itself. The distance of the needle from the lens is measured to be x. On removing the liquid layer and repeating the experiment, the distance is found to be y. Obtain the expression for the refractive index of the liquid in terms of x and y.

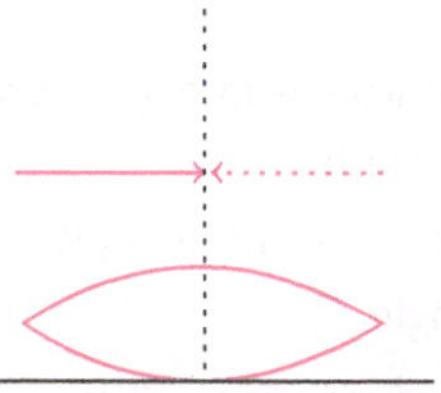

31. Figure shows a ray of light passing through a prism. If the refracted ray QR is parallel to the base BC, show that

(i) $r_1 = r_2 = \frac{A}{2}$, **[1½]**

(ii) angle of minimum deviation, $D_m = 2i - A$. **[1½]**

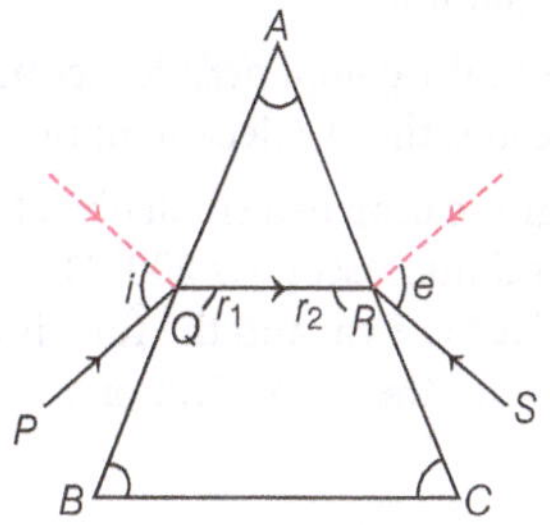

32. Three rays (1, 2, 3) of different colours fall normally on one of the sides of an isosceles right angled prism as shown. The refractive indices of prism for these rays are 1.39, 1.47 and 1.52 respectively. Find which of these rays get internally reflected and which get only refracted from AC. Trace the paths of rays. Justify your answer with the help of necessary calculations.

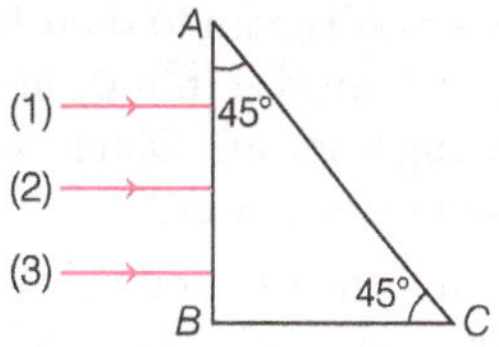

Long Answer Type Questions

33. Discuss refraction of monochromatic light through a prism and derive its relation.

34. Use the mirror equation to deduce that,

(i) an object placed between f and $2f$ of a concave mirror produces a real image beyond $2f$. **[2]**

(ii) a convex mirror always produces a virtual image independent of the location of the object. **[1]**

(iii) the virtual image produced by a convex mirror is always diminished in size and is located between the focus and the pole. **[1]**

(iv) an object placed between the pole and focus of a concave mirror produces a virtual and enlarged image. **NCERT [1]**

35. Define the following with required formula.

(i) Apparent depth **[2]**

(ii) Lateral displacement (or shift) **[2]**

(iii) Critical angle **[1]**

36. (i) Write the necessary conditions for the phenomenon of total internal reflection to occur. **[3]**

(ii) Write the relation between refractive index and critical angle for a given pair of optical media. **[2]**

37. (i) Draw a ray diagram for the formation of the image of an object by a convex mirror. Hence, obtain the mirror equation. **[2]**

(ii) Why are multi-component lenses used for both the objective and the eyepiece in optical instruments? **[2]**

(iii) The magnification of a small object produced by a compound microscope is 200. The focal length of the eyepiece is 2 cm and the final image is formed at infinity. Find the magnification produced by the objective. **CBSE 2024 [1]**

38. Draw a ray diagram showing the image formation by a compound microscope. Hence, obtain the expression for total magnification, when the image is formed at infinity.

39. Draw a labelled ray diagram on a refracting telescope. Define its magnifying power and write the expression for it. Write two important limitations of a refracting telescope over a reflecting type telescope.

40. (i) (a) Draw a ray diagram to show how the final image is formed at infinity in an astronomical refracting telescope. Obtain an expression for its magnifying power. **[1½]**

(b) Two thin lenses L_1 and L_2, L_1 being a convex lens of focal length 24 cm and L_2 a concave lens of focal length 18 cm are placed coaxially at a separation of 45 cm. A 1 cm tall object is placed in front of the lens L_1 at a distance of 36 cm. Find the location and height of the image formed by the combination. **CBSE 2023 [1½]**

Or (ii) (a) Explain the working principle of an optical fibre with the help of a diagram. Mention one use of a light pipe. **[1½]**

(b) A ray of light is incident at an angle of 60° on one face of a prism with the prism angle $A = 60°$. The ray passes symmetrically through the prism. Find the angle of minimum deviation (δ_m) and refractive index of the material of the prism. If the prism is immersed in water, how will δ_m be affected? Justify your answer. **[1½]**

41. (i) Draw a ray diagram to show image formation when the concave mirror produces a real, inverted and magnified image of the object. **[2½]**

(ii) Obtain the mirror formula and write the expression for the linear magnification. **[2½]**

42. State and derive mirror formula for a concave mirror. State the sign convention used.

43. Answer the following questions

(i) An object subtends an angle at the eye which is equal to the angle subtended at the eye by the virtual image that is produced by a magnifying glass, Does the magnifying glass provide angular magnification? Explain. **[1]**

(ii) A person's eyes are very close to the lens when he is viewing through a magnifying glass. Does angular magnification change if the eye is moved back? **[1]**

(iii) The focal length of the lens is inversely proportional to the magnifying power of a simple microscope. Why don't we achieve greater and greater magnifying power by using a convex lens of smaller and smaller focal length? **[1]**

(iv) Why must both the objective and the eyepiece of a compound microscope have short focal lengths? **[1]**

(v) Our eyes should be positioned not on the eyepiece but a short distance away from it for best viewing, when viewing from a compound microscope. Explain why? How much should be that short distance between the eye and eyepiece? **[1]**

44. (i) When a parallel beam of light enters water surface obliquely at some angle, what is the effect on the width of the beam? **[2]**

(ii) With the help of a ray diagram, show that a straw appears bent when it is partly dipped in water and explain it. **[1½]**

(iii) Explain the transmission of optical signal through an optical fibre by a diagram. **CBSE 2025 [1½]**

45. Explain the phenomenon of total internal reflection. Describe how TIR takes place in optical fibre. State any two uses of it.

46. Define power of a lens. Write its units. Deduce the relation $\frac{1}{f} = \frac{1}{f_1} + \frac{1}{f_2}$ for two thin lenses kept in contact coaxially.

Numerical Questions

Mirror Formula and Magnification

47. (i) Draw a ray diagram showing the formation of a real image of an object placed at a distance u in front of a convex mirror of radius of curvature R. Hence, obtain the relation for the image distance v in terms of u and R.

(ii) A 1.8 m tall person stands in front of a convex lens of focal length 1 m, at a distance of 5 m. Find the position and height of the image formed. **CBSE 2023**

48. A container is filled with water ($\mu = 1.33$) upto a height of 33.25 cm. A concave mirror is placed 15 cm above the water level and the image of an object placed at the bottom is formed 25 cm below the water level. What will be the focal length?

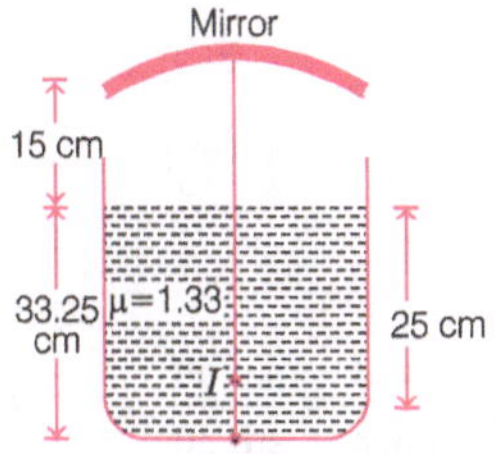

49. A concave mirror and a convex mirror of focal lengths 10 cm and 20 cm respectively are placed coaxially as shown. The distance of separation between the two mirrors is 40 cm.

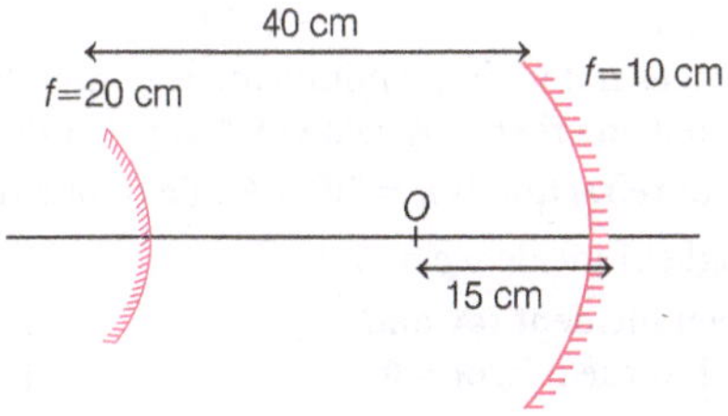

If an object O is placed in between them as shown, at a distance of 15 cm from the concave mirror, find the position of final image that is formed by two successive reflections, **Competency Based Que**

(i) by concave mirror and

(ii) by convex mirror.

Lens Formula and Magnification

50. Two concave lenses A and B, each of focal length 8.0 cm are arranged co-axially 16 cm apart as shown in figure. An object P is placed at a distance of 4.0 cm from A. Find the position and nature of the final image formed. **CBSE 2025**

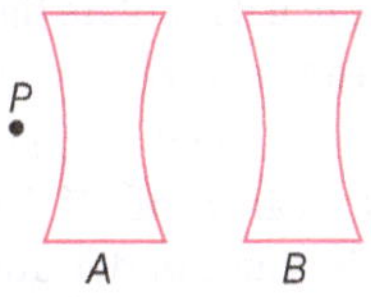

51. Two convex lenses A and B, each of focal length 10.0 cm, are mounted on an optical bench at 50.0 cm and 70.0 cm, respectively. An object is mounted at 20.0 cm. Find the nature and position of the final image formed by the combination. **CBSE 2025**

52. A tank is filled with water to a height of 12.5 cm. The apparenet depth of a needle lying at the bottom of the tank is measured by a microscope to be 9.4 cm. What is the refractive index of water? If water is replaced by a liquid of refractive index 1.63 upto the same height, then by what distance would the microscope have to be moved to focus on the needle again? **NCERT**

53. Double convex lenses are to be manufactured from a glass of refractive index 1.55, with both faces of the same radius of curvature. What is the radius of curvature required, if the focal length is to be 20 cm? **NCERT**

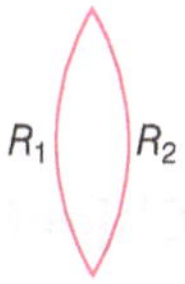

54. You are given three lenses L_1, L_2 and L_3 each of focal length 10 cm. An object is kept at 15 cm in front of L_1, as shown in figure. The final real image is formed at the focus of L_3. Find the separation between L_1, L_2 and L_3.

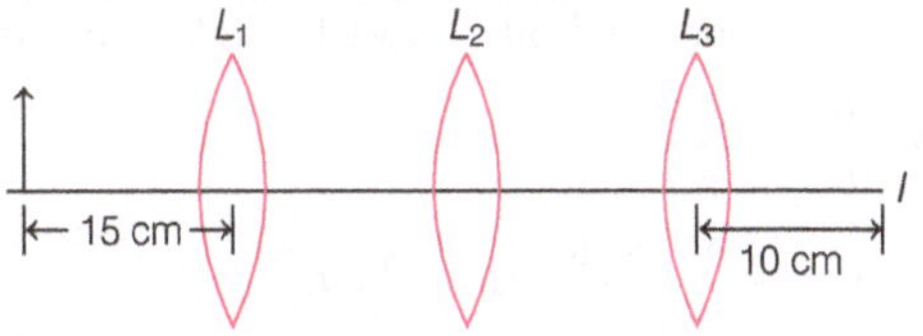

Prism

55. (i) Deduce the expression by drawing a suitable ray diagram for the refractive index of a triangular glass prism in terms of the angle of minimum deviation (D) and the angle of prism (A).

Draw a plot showing the variation of the angle of deviation with the angle of incidence.

(ii) Calculate the value of the angle of incidence when a ray of light incident on one face of an equilateral glass prism produces the emergent ray, which just grazes along the adjacent face. Refractive index of the prism is $\sqrt{2}$.

56. (i) A thin pencil of length $(f/4)$ is placed coinciding with the principal axis of a mirror of focal length f. The image of the pencil is real and enlarged, just touches the pencil. Calculate the magnification produced by the mirror.

(ii) A ray of light is incident on a refracting face AB of a prism ABC at an angle of 45°. The ray emerges from face AC and the angle of deviation is 15°. The angle of prism is 30°. Show that the emergent ray is normal to the face AC from which it emerges out. Find the refraction index of the material of the prism. **CBSE 2025**

Telescope

57. A small telescope has an objective lens of focal length 144 cm and an eyepiece of focal length 6 cm. What is the magnifying power of the telescope? What is the separation between the objective and the eyepiece? **NCERT**

58. A telescope consists of two thin lenses of focal lengths 0.3 m and 3 cm, respectively. It is focused on moon which subtends an angle of 0.5° at the objective, then what will be the angle subtended at the eye by the final image?

59. A small telescope has an objective lens of focal length 150 cm and eyepiece of focal length 5 cm. What is the magnifying power of the telescope for viewing distant objects in normal adjustments?
If this telescope is used to view a 100 m tall tower 3 km away, then what is the height of the tower formed by the objective lens?

60. (i) A giant reflecting telescope at an observatory has an objective lens of focal length 15 m. If an eyepiece lens of focal length 1.0 cm is used, find the angular magnification of the telescope.

(ii) If this telescope is used to view the moon, what is the diameter of the image of the moon formed by the objective lens? The diameter of the moon is 3.48×10^6 m and the radius of the lunar orbit is 3.8×10^8 m. **NCERT**

Hints & Solutions

Objective Type Questions

1. (c)	2. (b)	3. (b)	4. (b)	5. (c)
6. (c)	7. (c)	8. (c)	10. (c)	11. (d)
12. (c)	13. (c)	14. (b)	15. (d)	16. (b)
18. (c)	19. (c)	20. (b)	26. (a)	27. (a)

9. (a) $\text{RI} = \dfrac{\text{Real depth}}{\text{Apparent depth}} = \dfrac{\text{Speed of light in vaccum}}{\text{Speed of light in medium}}$

$$\Rightarrow \frac{30}{16} = \frac{3 \times 10^8}{v}$$

$$\Rightarrow v = \frac{3 \times 10^8 \times 16}{30} = 1.6 \times 10^8 \text{ m/s}$$

17. (b)

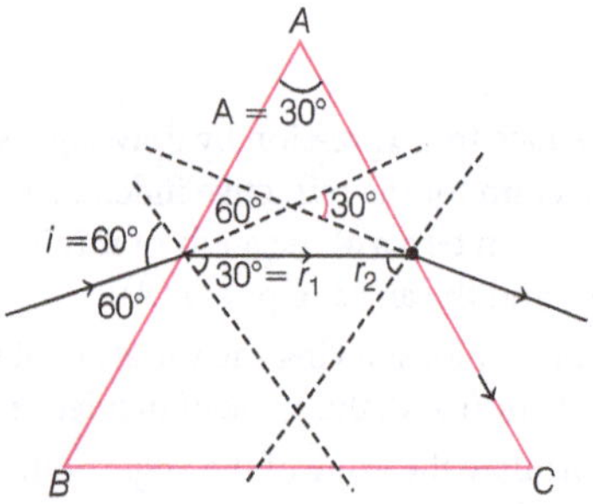

At the interface AB,

$$1 \times \sin i = \mu \times \sin r_1$$

$$\mu = \frac{\sin i}{\sin r_1} = \frac{\sin 60°}{\sin 30°} = \frac{\frac{\sqrt{3}}{2}}{\frac{1}{2}} = \sqrt{3}$$

For minimum deviation, $r_1 = r_2$

$\Rightarrow \quad A = r_1 + r_2$

$\Rightarrow \quad r_2 = A - r_1 = 30 - 30 = 0$

$= r_1 \neq r_2,$

Light does not undergo minimum deviation through the prism and emergent ray makes 90° angle at the AB face. Angle of refraction is $r_1 = 30° =$ Angle of prism.

21. (c) Angle of incidence = Angle between incident ray and normal to the mirror = 0°

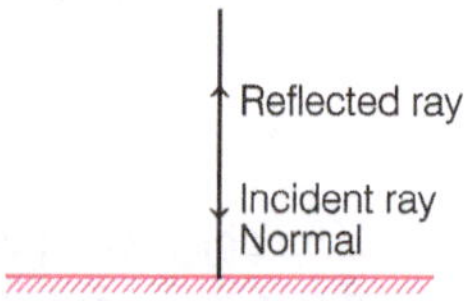

$\Rightarrow$ Angle of reflection = 0° (from laws of reflection)

Hence, the reflected ray retraces its path along the normal at an angle 0° with normal.

22. (b) Convex mirror always forms virtual image, so that Asseration is true. Parallel rays incident on convex mirror do not actually meet.

23. (b) Optical fibre communication is based on the phenomenon of total internal reflection at core-clade interface.

The refractive index of core is higher than that of the cladding .Hence light striking at core-cladding interface gets totally internally reflected. The light undergoes and reaches the other end of the fibre.

24. (*d*) In air or water, a convex lens made of glass behaves as a convergent lens but when it is placed in carbon disulfide, it behaves as a divergent lens. Therefore, when a convergent lens is placed inside a transparent medium having refractive index greater than that of material of lens, it behaves as a divergent lens.

25. (*d*) Focal length of the spherical mirror does not depend on the medium in which it is placed.

28. (*c*) Shining of bubble is due to total internal reflection of light.

29. (*d*) By interchanging objective and eyepiece, the microscope cannot be changed to the telescope because the focal length of the objective of the microscope is very small as compared to the telescope and the telescope has a large aperture.

30. (i) (*d*) Refraction does not change the frequency of light.

(ii) (*d*) From Snell's law of refraction,

$$^{a}\mu_{g} = \frac{\sin i}{\sin r} = \text{constant} \quad \text{...(i)}$$

Since, angle of incidence increase, the angle of refraction has to increase. So, that the ratio $\left(\frac{\sin i}{\sin r}\right)$ is a constant according to Eq. (i).

(iii) (*a*) When an object lying in a denser medium is observed from rarer medium, then real depth of object is more than that observed depth.

(iv) (*c*) As, $\mu = \frac{\sin i}{\sin r}$ ...(i)

or $\mu \propto \frac{1}{\sin r}$

$\Rightarrow$ Since, r is minimum and hence $\sin r$ is minimum.

Also, $\mu = \frac{c}{v}$ ...(ii)

Therefore, if μ is maximum, v is minimum, i.e. velocity of light is minimum in medium R and order of velocity will be $v_P > v_Q > v_R$.

(v) (*a*) When a ray arrives from medium A, it moves towards normal in medium B. So, medium B has a higher optical density than medium A. This indicate that the refractive index of medium B relative to medium A's refractive index will be higher than 1.

31. (i) (*b*) Given, focal length of thin converging lens,

$$f_c = 20 \text{ cm} = f_1$$

Focal length of thin diverging lens,

$$f_d = -15 \text{ cm} = f_2$$

Power of the combination, $P = ?$.

By using the formula, $\frac{1}{f} = \frac{1}{f_1} + \frac{1}{f_2}$

$$\frac{1}{f} = \frac{1}{20} - \frac{1}{15} = \frac{3-4}{60} = \frac{-1}{60}$$

$\therefore$ $f = -60$

Power of lenses, $P = \frac{100}{f} = \frac{100}{-60} = -\frac{5}{3}\text{D}$

(ii) (*c*) Given, radii of curvature of two surfaces of convex lens are R and $2R$.

Focal length of the lens,

$$f = \frac{4}{3}R$$

$$\mu = ?$$

We know that, $\frac{1}{f} = (\mu - 1)\left[\frac{1}{R_1} - \frac{1}{R_2}\right]$

$$\frac{3}{4R} = (\mu - 1)\left(\frac{1}{R} + \frac{1}{2R}\right)$$

$$3 = (\mu - 1)4R\left(\frac{3}{2R}\right)$$

$$3 = 6\mu - 6$$

$$-6\mu = -6 - 3 = -9$$

Refractive index, $\mu = \frac{3}{2}$

(iii) (*a*) The focal length of an equiconvex lens increases when the lens is dipped in water because the value of refractive index decreases.

(iv) (*a*)

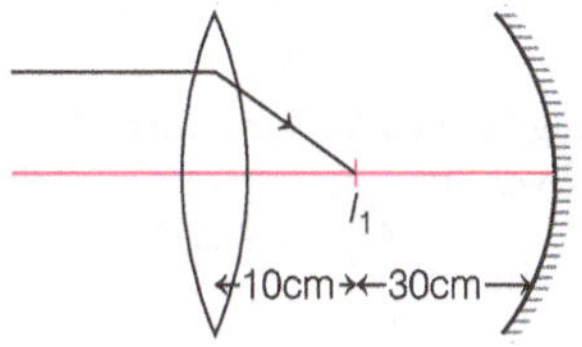

For convex lens, $u = \infty$, $f = 10$ cm

$$\frac{1}{f} = \frac{1}{v} - \frac{1}{u} \Rightarrow \frac{1}{10} = \frac{1}{v} - \frac{1}{\infty}$$

$$v = 10 \text{ cm}$$

The image I_1 is formed in front of the mirror, so this image acts as object for a concave mirror.

For concave mirror, $u = -30$ cm

$$f = -15 \text{ cm}$$

$$\frac{1}{f} = \frac{1}{v} - \frac{1}{u}$$

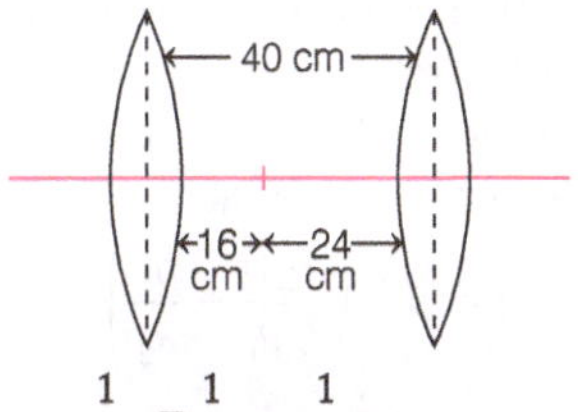

$$\Rightarrow \quad \frac{1}{-15} = \frac{1}{v} - \frac{1}{(-30)}$$

$$\frac{1}{v}=\frac{-3}{30} \Rightarrow v=-10 \text{ cm}$$

Or

(a) Focal length of convex lens L_1, $f_1 = 16$ cm

Focal length of convex lens L_2, $f_2 = 12$ cm

The coaxially distance, $d = 40$ cm

We know that, combined focal length,

$$\frac{1}{v}-\frac{1}{u}=\frac{1}{f}$$

$$\frac{1}{v}=\frac{1}{f}+\frac{1}{u}$$

$$\frac{1}{v}=\frac{1}{16}+\frac{1}{-\infty}$$

$$v = 16 \text{ cm}$$

Positive sign shows that the image is formed to the right of the lens,

So, this image acts as object for a convex lens L_2.

For this, $f = 12$ cm

$\therefore$ $u = (40-16)$ cm $= 24$ cm

u will take with negative sign.

$$\frac{1}{f}=\frac{1}{v}-\frac{1}{u}$$

$$\frac{1}{v}=\frac{1}{f}+\frac{1}{u}$$

$$\frac{1}{v}=+\frac{1}{12}-\frac{1}{24}$$

$\Rightarrow$ $v = +24$ cm (real)

32. (i) According to lens Maker's formula, focal length of a lens is given by

$$\frac{1}{f}=(\mu-1)\left(\frac{1}{R_1}-\frac{1}{R_2}\right)$$

Since, $\frac{1}{f}=P$ (Power of lens)

$$\therefore \quad P=(\mu-1)\left(\frac{1}{R_1}-\frac{1}{R_2}\right)$$

$\Rightarrow$ $P \propto \mu$ ...(i)

Since, refractive index (μ) of the medium decreases with increase of wavelength (λ) of light. Hence, from Eq. (i),

$$P \propto \mu \propto \frac{1}{\lambda}$$

Hence, with increase of wavelength of light, power of lens decreases.

(ii) For convex lens, $R_1 = R$ and $R_2 = -R$

$\therefore$ By lens Maker's formula,

$$\frac{1}{f}=(\mu-1)\left(\frac{1}{R_1}-\frac{1}{R_2}\right)$$

$$\Rightarrow \quad \frac{1}{R}=(\mu-1)\left(\frac{1}{R}-\frac{1}{-R}\right)$$

$$\Rightarrow \quad \frac{1}{R}=(\mu-1)\left(\frac{2}{R}\right)$$

$$\Rightarrow \quad \mu-1=\frac{1}{2} \Rightarrow \mu=\frac{3}{2}$$

(iii) Given, $f_{air} = -20$ cm

(focal length of concave lens is negative)

$\mu_g = 1.5$, $\mu_w = 4/3$

By using lens Maker's formula,

$$\frac{1}{f_{air}}=(\mu_g-1)\left(\frac{1}{R_1}-\frac{1}{R_2}\right)$$

$$\frac{1}{-20}=(1.5-1)\left(\frac{1}{R_1}-\frac{1}{R_2}\right)$$

$$\left(\frac{1}{R_1}-\frac{1}{R_2}\right)=-\frac{1}{10} \quad \text{...(i)}$$

When the lens is completely immersed in water, then focal length of lens in water is given by

$$\frac{1}{f_w}=({}^w\mu_g-1)\left(\frac{1}{R_1}-\frac{1}{R_2}\right)$$

$$f_w=\left(\frac{\mu_g}{\mu_w}-1\right)\left(-\frac{1}{10}\right) \quad \text{[from Eq. (i)]}$$

$$=\left(\frac{1.5}{4/3}-1\right)\left(-\frac{1}{10}\right)=\left(\frac{4.5-4}{4}\right)\left(-\frac{1}{10}\right)=-\frac{1}{80}$$

$\Rightarrow$ $f_w = -80$ cm

(iv) Given, magnification, $m = 3$

Since, $m=\frac{v}{u}=3 \Rightarrow v=3u$ ... (i)

Power, $P = 5$ D

$$\therefore \quad f=\frac{1}{5}=0.2=20 \text{ cm}$$

Now, by lens formula, $\frac{1}{f}=\frac{1}{v}-\frac{1}{u}$

$$\frac{1}{20}=\frac{1}{3u}-\frac{1}{4}$$

$$\Rightarrow u=-\frac{40}{3} \text{ cm}=-13.33 \text{ cm}$$

$\therefore$ Distance of the image, $v = 34 = 3(-13.3) = -40$ cm

33. (i) The refractive index of glass with respect to water is

$${}_w n_g=\frac{{}_a n_g}{{}_a n_w}=\frac{3/2}{4/3}=9/8$$

Let i be the angle of incidence in water and r the angle of refraction in glass. Then, by Snell's law, we have

$$\frac{\sin i}{\sin r}={}_w n_g=9/8$$

or $\quad \sin r = \dfrac{\sin 45^\circ}{9/8} = \dfrac{0.707}{9/8} = 0.6284$

or $\quad r = \sin^{-1}(0.6284) = 38.9^\circ$

(ii) Given, $\lambda = 589$ nm

and $\quad n = 4/3$

Frequency, $\nu' = \dfrac{c}{\lambda} = \dfrac{3\times10^8}{589\times10^{-9}} = 5.093\times10^{14}$ Hz

When light travels from air to water, its frequency remains unchanged.

Wavelength of light in water,

$$\lambda' = \frac{\lambda}{n} = \frac{589\times10^{-9}\text{ m}}{4/3}$$

$$= 441.75\times10^{-9}\text{ m} = 441.75\text{ nm}$$

Refractive index of water, $n = \dfrac{c}{v}$

or $\quad v = \dfrac{c}{n} = \dfrac{3\times10^8}{4/3} = 2.25\times10^8$ m/s

(iii) Let d be the distance by which the pin would appear to be raised due to refraction of light. Then,

d = real thickness of slab − apparent thickness of slab

$$= t - t/n = 15 - \frac{15}{1.5} = 5.0\text{ cm}$$

(iv) $i_c = \sin^{-1}\left(\dfrac{1}{{}_w{}^n g}\right) = \sin^{-1}\left(\dfrac{1}{{}_a{}^n g / {}_a{}^n w}\right)$

But $\dfrac{{}_a{}^n g}{{}_a{}^n w} = \dfrac{3/2}{4/3} = 9/8$

$\therefore \quad i_c = \sin^{-1}\left(\dfrac{1}{9/8}\right) = \sin^{-1}(8/9)$

Subjective Questions

1. Refer to text on page 279.

2. Slope = $\tan 60^\circ = \dfrac{\sin i}{\sin r}$

From Snell's law, $\dfrac{\sin i}{\sin r} = \mu$, $\mu = \sqrt{3} = \dfrac{c}{v}$

3.

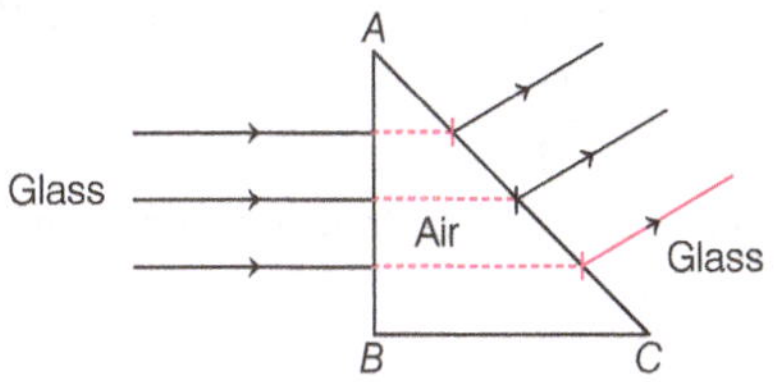

4. When refractive index of lens is equal to the refractive index of liquid, it will behave like plane glass sheet.

5. Given, focal length of convex lens $f_1 = 30$ cm

Focal length of concave lens $f_2 = -20$ cm

Using the formula of combination of lenses,

$$\frac{1}{f} = \frac{1}{f_1} + \frac{1}{f_2} = \frac{1}{30} - \frac{1}{20} = \frac{2-3}{60} = -\frac{1}{60}$$

$$f = -60\text{ cm}$$

Since, the focal length of combination is negative in nature. So the combination behaves like a diverging lens, *i.e.* as a concave lens.

6. When object is placed at the centre of curvature of convex lens, then size of image is equal to the size of object. It does not arise for the concave lens because it always forms diminished image.

7. The ability of lens to converge or diverge the rays of incident light on it. It is called the power of lens. Its SI unit is dioptre (D) or m^{-1}.

8. Since, the objective lens has large aperture and focal length, hence the lens having large focal length i.e., 50 cm will be used as objective lens.

9. Magnification of telescope is given by

$$m = \frac{f_o}{f_e} = \frac{100}{1} = -100$$

10. Given, focal length of objective lens $f_o = 144$ cm

Focal length of eyepiece $\quad f_e = 6$ cm

Magnifying power of the telescope in normal adjustment, when the final image is formed at ∞),

$$m = -\frac{f_o}{f_e} = -\frac{144}{6} = -24$$

$\therefore$ Separation between lenses,

$$L = f_o + f_e = 144 + 6 = 150\text{ cm}$$

11. Refer to text on page 283.

12. Here, $\mu = \dfrac{\mu_g}{\mu_c} = \dfrac{1.5}{1.65} < 1$

$\therefore \quad \dfrac{1}{f} = (\mu - 1)\left(\dfrac{1}{R_1} - \dfrac{1}{R_2}\right)$

Hence, it becomes negative, so it behaves like a diverging lens.

13. Any ray entering at an angle i shall be guided along AC, if the ray makes an angle with the face AC is greater than the critical angle as per the principle of total internal reflection, $\phi + r = 90^\circ$, therefore $\sin\phi = \cos r$

$\Rightarrow \quad \sin\phi \geq \dfrac{1}{\mu} \quad \Rightarrow \cos r \geq \dfrac{1}{\mu}$

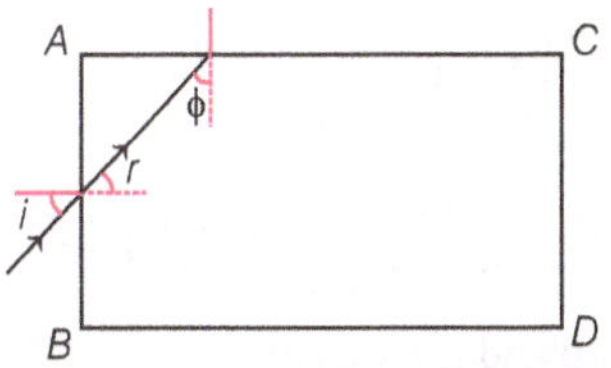

or $\quad 1 - \cos^2 r \leq 1 - \dfrac{1}{\mu^2} \Rightarrow \sin^2 r \leq \dfrac{1}{\mu^2} \quad \left[\because 1 - \cos^2 r = \sin^2 r\right]$

Since, $\sin i = \mu \sin r \quad \frac{1}{\mu_2}\sin^2 i \le 1 - \frac{1}{\mu^2}$

or $\quad \sin^2 i \le \mu^2 - 1$

When $i = \frac{\pi}{2}$, then we have smallest angle ϕ.

If the angle ϕ is greater than the critical angle, then all other angles of incidence shall be more than the critical angle.

Thus, $\quad 1 \le \mu^2 - 1 \text{ or } \mu^2 \ge 2 \Rightarrow \mu \ge \sqrt{2}$

This is the required result.

14. Light travels faster in medium *B*,

$$\mu_1 = \frac{\sin i}{\sin r_1}$$

$$\mu_2 = \frac{\sin i}{\sin r_2}$$

$$\therefore \quad \frac{\mu_1}{\mu_2} = \frac{\sin r_2}{\sin r_1} = \frac{\sin 35^\circ}{\sin 30^\circ} \Rightarrow \frac{\mu_1}{\mu_2} = \frac{v_2}{v_1} > 1$$

$$\therefore \quad v_2 > v_1$$

15. Refer to text on page 293.

16. Refer to text on pages 285 and 286.

17. Refer to text on pages 294 and 295.

18. Power of thin lens, $P = +5\text{ D}$

$$\mu_g = 1.5$$

$\therefore$ Focal length of thin lens in air,

$$f_{\text{air}} = \frac{1}{P} = \frac{1}{5} = 0.2\text{ m} = 20\text{ cm}$$

By using lens Maker formula,

$$\frac{1}{f_{\text{air}}} = (\mu_g - 1)\left(\frac{1}{R_1} - \frac{1}{R_2}\right)$$

$$= (1.5 - 1)\left(\frac{1}{R_1} - \frac{1}{R_2}\right)$$

$$\frac{1}{f_{\text{air}}} = \left(\frac{1}{R_1} - \frac{1}{R_2}\right) \quad \text{... (i)}$$

when lens is dipped in liquid, then focal length in liquid.

$$f_l = -100\text{ cm} \quad \text{(concave lens)}$$

Using lens Maker's formula,

$$\frac{1}{f_l} = ({}^l\mu_g - 1)\left(\frac{1}{R_1} - \frac{1}{R_2}\right)$$

$$= \left(\frac{\mu_g}{\mu_l} - 1\right)\left(\frac{1}{R_1} - \frac{1}{R_2}\right)$$

$$\frac{1}{100} = \left(\frac{1.5 - \mu_l}{\mu_l}\right) \cdot \frac{2}{f_{\text{air}}} \text{[from Eq. (i)]} \quad \text{...(ii)}$$

From Eqs. (i) and (ii), we get

$$\mu_l = \frac{15}{9} = \frac{5}{3}$$

19.

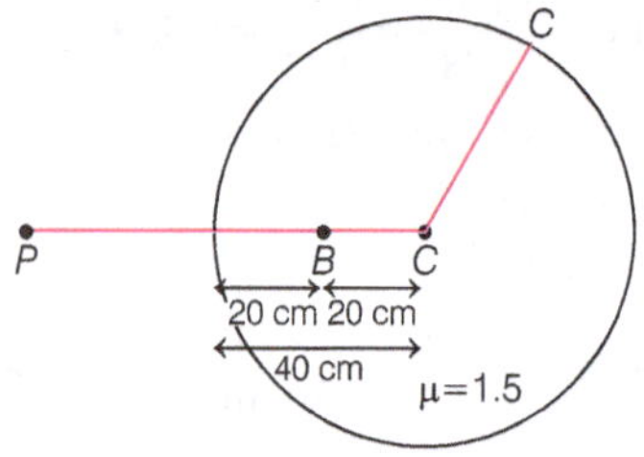

Radius of the glass sphere, $R = 40$ cm

Refractive index, $\mu_1 = 1.5$ of glass

Distance of the bubble from the centre of the sphere = 20 cm

Refractive index of air = 1

$$\frac{\mu_2}{v} - \frac{\mu_1}{u} = \frac{(\mu_2 - \mu_1)}{R}$$

$$\frac{1}{v} - \frac{1.5}{-20} = \frac{1 - 1.5}{-40}$$

$$\frac{1}{v} = \frac{0.5}{40} - \frac{1.5}{20} = \frac{1}{80} - \frac{15}{200}$$

$$\frac{1}{v} = \frac{5 - 30}{400} = -\frac{25}{400}$$

$$v = -\frac{400}{25} = -16\text{ cm}$$

Thus, image formed is at $v = -16$ cm to the right of the left surface.

20. By Snell's law,

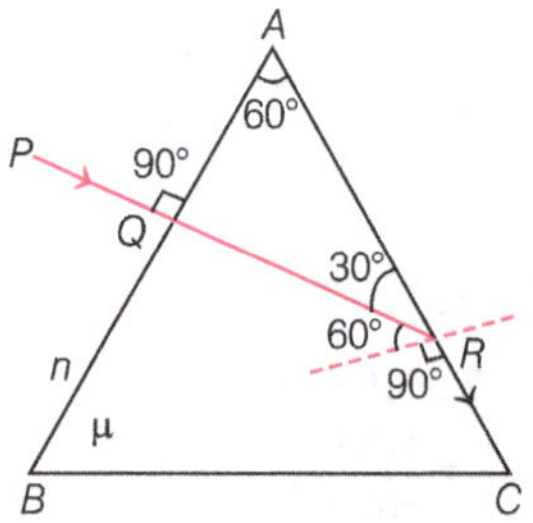

$$\frac{\sin i}{\sin r} = \frac{n}{\mu} \Rightarrow \frac{\sin 60^\circ}{\sin 90^\circ} = \frac{n}{\mu}$$

$$n = \mu \sin 60^\circ \quad [\because \sin 90^\circ = 1]$$

$$n = \frac{\sqrt{3}\mu}{2}$$

Thus, refractive index of the transparent medium is $n = \frac{\sqrt{3}\mu}{2}$.

21. (i) **Large focal length** To increasing magnifying power.

As, $\quad m = \frac{f_o}{f_e}$

and hence $\quad m_l = \pm f_o$

Large aperture To increase resolving power.

As, $\text{RP} = \dfrac{2a}{1.22\lambda}$

and, hence $\text{RP}_I \pm a$

(ii) Resolving power of a telescope is given by

$$\text{RP} = \frac{A}{1.22\lambda}$$

From the given condition, the ratio of resolving power of two astronomical telescopes will be

$$\frac{\text{Resolving power of 1}}{\text{Resolving power } 2v} = \frac{A_1}{A_2} \quad (\text{as, } \lambda \text{ is same})$$

Telescope with large aperture (A_1) should be preferred as it increases the resolution by collecting more light.

22. (i) Refer to diagram on page 299.

I. It has mirror objective, which is free from chromatic and spherical aberrations.

II. It can gather more light as objectives can be made larger, hence images can be brighter.

23. Uses of Spherical Mirrors

(i) Convex mirror is used as a reflector in street lamps to diverge the light over a large area.

(ii) Convex mirror is used as rear view mirror (or driver's mirror) in vehicles, because it has a wider field of view.

(iii) Concave mirror is used as a reflector in search light, head lights of vehicles, etc.

(iv) Concave mirror is also used as face looking mirror because it forms the erect and magnified image.

(v) Spherical mirrors are also used as trick mirrors.

24. Since, the object distance is u. Let us consider the two ends of the object be at distance $u_1 = u - L/2$ and $u_2 = u + L/2$ respectively, so that $|u_1 - u_2| = L$. Let the image of the two ends be formed at v_1 and v_2 respectively, so that the image length would be

$$L' = |v_1 - v_2| \quad \ldots\text{(i)}$$

Applying mirror formula, we have

$$\frac{1}{u} + \frac{1}{v} = \frac{1}{f} \text{ or } v = \frac{fu}{u-f}$$

On solving, the positions of two images are given by

$$v_1 = \frac{f(u - L/2)}{u - f - L/2},\; v_2 = \frac{f(u + L/2)}{u - f + L/2}$$

For length, substituting these values in Eq. (i), we get

$$L' = |v_1 - v_2| = \frac{f^2 L}{(u-f)^2 - L^2/4}$$

Since, the object is short and kept away from focus, we have

$$L^2/4 << (u-f)^2$$

Hence, finally, $L' = \dfrac{f^2}{(u-f)^2} L$

This is the required expression of length of an image.

25.

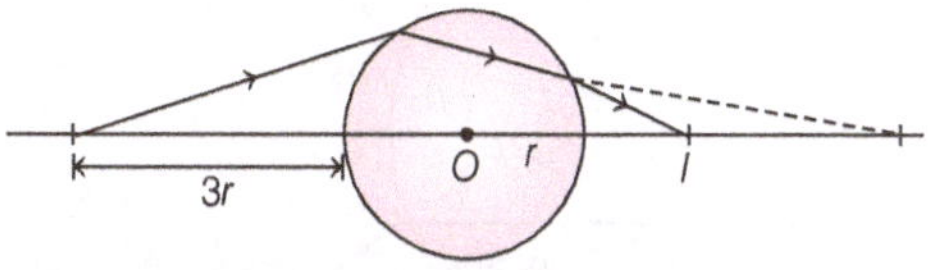

26. Characteristics of the images formed

(i) Virtual and enlarged image

(ii) Same side of the object

We know that, $\dfrac{1}{v} - \dfrac{1}{u} = \dfrac{1}{f}$

As both image and object lie on the same side, both v and u are negative,

$$\frac{-1}{v} + \frac{1}{u} = \frac{1}{f} \text{ or } \frac{1}{v} = \frac{-1}{f} + \frac{1}{u} = \frac{1}{u} - \frac{1}{f}$$

Comparing with $y = mx + c$, the graph is shown.

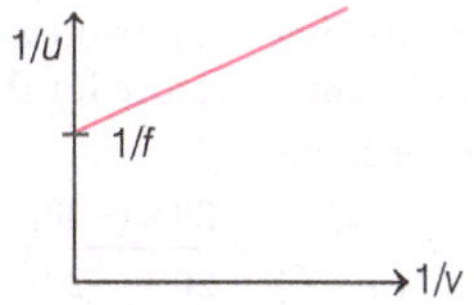

27. From lens Maker's formula, $\dfrac{1}{f} = \left(\dfrac{n_1}{n_2} - 1\right)\left(-\dfrac{1}{R_2} - \dfrac{1}{R_2}\right)$

(i) for $n_1 = n_2 \Rightarrow f = \infty$

(ii) for $n_1 < n_2 \Rightarrow f > 0$

(iii) for $n_1 > n_2 \Rightarrow f < 0$

The path of rays in three cases is shown in fig.

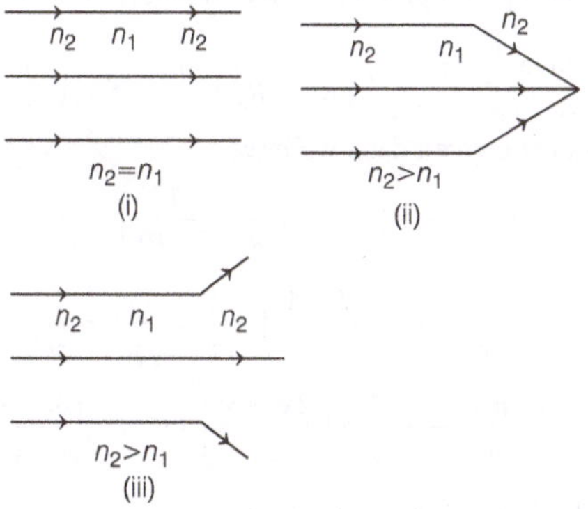

28. From lens maker's formula, $\dfrac{1}{f} = \left(\dfrac{n_1}{n_2} - 1\right)\left(\dfrac{1}{R_2} + \dfrac{1}{R_2}\right)$

In case (i) $n_1 > n_2$, the lens behaves as convergent lens.

In case (ii) $n_1 = n_2$ the lens behaves as a plane plate.

In case (iii) $n_1 < n_2$ the lens behaves as a divergent lens.

The path of rays in all the three cases is shown in figure.

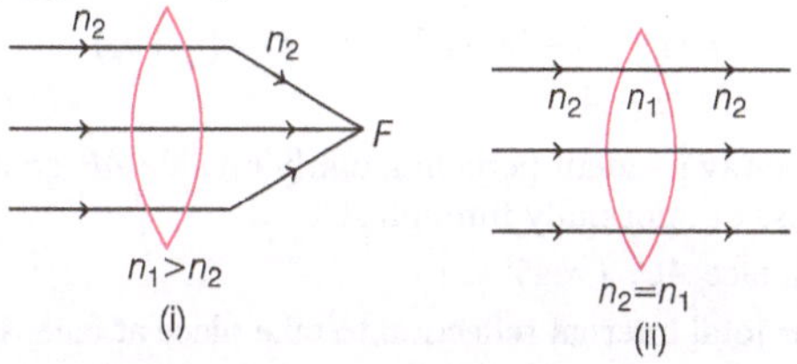

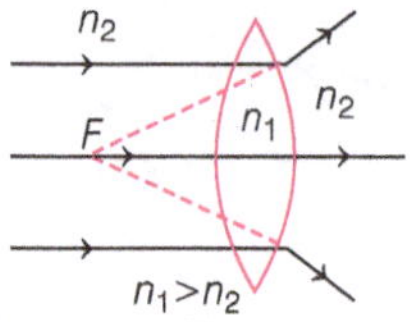

(iii)

29. The focal length of the plano-convex lens is

$$\frac{1}{f} = (1.5-1)\left(\frac{1}{(+15)} - \frac{1}{\infty}\right) = \frac{1}{30}$$

The focal length of plano-concave lens is

$$\frac{1}{f} = (1.5-1)\left(\frac{1}{\infty} - \frac{1}{15}\right) = -\frac{1}{30}$$

Since, parallel beams are incident on the lens, its image forms plano-concave lens will be formed at +30 cm from it (at the focus) and will act as an object for plano-concave lens. Since, the two lenses are separated by a distance of 20 cm, therefore for the next lens.

$$u = +20 \text{ cm}$$

$$v = \frac{uf}{(u+f)} = \frac{20\times(-30)}{20+(-30)} = \frac{600}{10}$$

$v = 60$ cm (Final position of the image formed).

30. Let n_l denotes the refractive index of the liquid. When the image of the needle coincides with the lens itself, its distance from the lens, equals the relevant focal length. With liquid layer present, the given set up, is equivalent to a combination of the given (convex) lens and a concave plane/plano concave 'liquid lens'.

We have $\frac{1}{f} = (n-1)\left(\frac{1}{R_1} - \frac{1}{R_2}\right)$ and $\frac{1}{f} = \left(\frac{1}{f_1} + \frac{1}{f_2}\right)$

As per the given data, we have

$$\frac{1}{f_2} = \frac{1}{y} = (1.5-1)\left(\frac{1}{R} - \frac{1}{(-R)}\right) = \frac{1}{R}$$

$$\therefore \quad \frac{1}{x} = (n_l - 1)\left(-\frac{1}{R}\right) + \frac{1}{y} = \frac{-n_1}{y} + \frac{2}{y}$$

$$\therefore \quad \frac{n_l}{y} = \frac{2}{y} - \frac{1}{x} = \left(\frac{2x-y}{xy}\right) \text{ or } n_l = \left(\frac{2x-y}{x}\right)$$

31. (i) We know that, $r_1 + r_2 = A$

Since QR is parallel to BC

So, $\quad r_1 = r_2$ and $i = e$

Therefore, $2r_1$ or $2r_2 = A \Rightarrow r_1 = r_2 = \frac{A}{2}$

(ii) D_m = Deviation at the first face + Deviation of the second face

$$= (i - r_1) + (e - r_2) = (i + e) - (r_1 + r_2)$$

$$= 2i - A \qquad (\because i = e)$$

32. The ray incident perpendicularly on side AB, so it will pass out normally through AB.

On face AC, $i = 45°$

For total internal reflection to take place at face AC,

Angle of incidence > critical angle

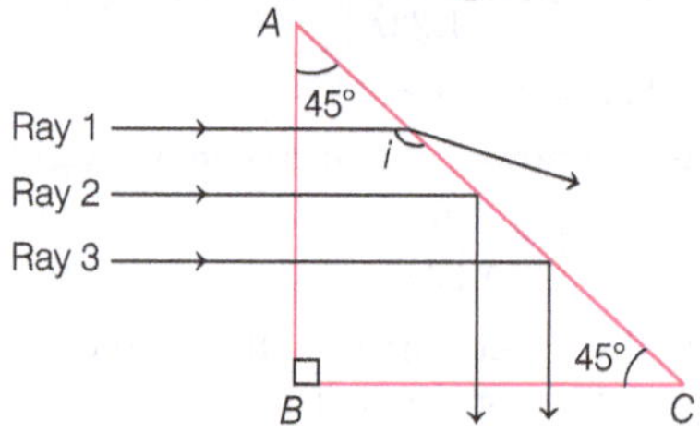

$$45° > i_c$$

$$\sin 45° > \sin i_c \Rightarrow \frac{1}{\sqrt{2}} > \frac{1}{n} \quad \left[\because i_c = \sin^{-1}\left(\frac{1}{n}\right)\right]$$

$$\Rightarrow \quad \sqrt{2} > n \Rightarrow 1.414 < n$$

Hence, rays 2, 3 will undergo TIR and path of ray will be as shown.

Ray 1 is refracted from AC.

33. Refer to text on pages 294 and 295.

34. (i) The mirror equation formula $\frac{1}{v} + \frac{1}{u} = \frac{1}{f}$

For concave mirror $f < 0$, as object always placed on the left side of mirror, so $u < 0$. According to question, $f < u < 2f$ (Object lies between f and $2f$)

$$\frac{1}{2f} > \frac{1}{u} > \frac{1}{f} \text{ or } -\frac{1}{2f} < -\frac{1}{u} < -\frac{1}{f}$$

Add $\frac{1}{f}$ on both sides, we get

$$\frac{1}{f} - \frac{1}{2f} < \frac{1}{f} - \frac{1}{u} < 0 \qquad \text{...(i)}$$

From lens formula, $\frac{1}{f} - \frac{1}{u} = \frac{1}{v}$, so from Eq. (i), we get

$$\frac{1}{f} - \frac{1}{2f} < \frac{1}{v}, \quad \frac{1}{2f} < \frac{1}{v} \text{ or } v > 2f$$

As, f is negative, $2f$ is also negative and hence v will be also negative. So, the image formed is real and image lies beyond $2f$.

(ii) For convex mirror f is always positive $f > 0$. As object always placed on left side of mirror $u < 0$.

From lens formula, $\frac{1}{v} = \frac{1}{f} - \frac{1}{u}$ as $f > 0$, and $u < 0$

The value of $\frac{1}{v} > 0$, or $v > 0$ or v is always positive.

The image formed is virtual. It does not depends on the location of object.

(iii) For convex mirror $\quad f > 0, u < 0$

From lens formula, $\frac{1}{v} = \frac{1}{f} - \frac{1}{u}$ so $\frac{1}{v} > \frac{1}{f}$ or $v < f$

Thus, image always located between pole and focus of the mirror, as $v < |u|$. So the image is always diminished in size.

(iv) For concave mirror $f < 0$.

As object is placed between pole and focus.

$\therefore \quad f < u < 0$

$\therefore \quad \frac{1}{f} - \frac{1}{u} > 0$

From Lens formula,

$$\frac{1}{f} - \frac{1}{u} = \frac{1}{v} > 0 \Rightarrow v > 0$$

It means that v is positive, image formed on right and virtual.

$$\frac{1}{v} < \frac{1}{u}$$

$v > |u|$ so image is enlarged.

35. Refer to text on pages 284 and 285.

36. Refer to text on pages 285 and 286.

37. (i)

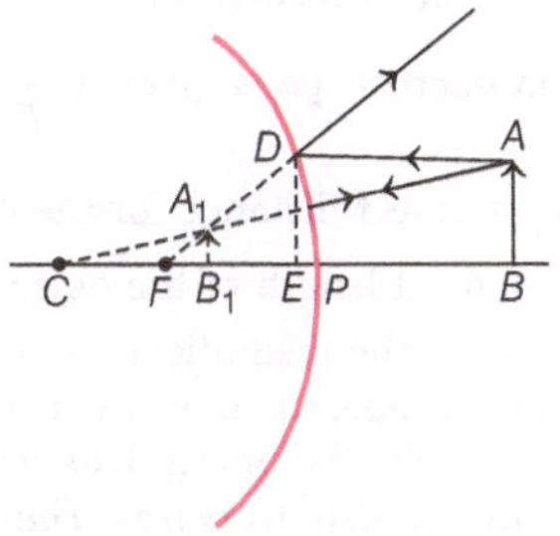

Let, AB be an object placed on the principal axis of a convex mirror of focal length f, u is the distance between the object and the mirror and v is the distance between the image and mirror.

In ΔABC and ΔA_1B_1C,

$\angle ABC = \angle A_1B_1C$ (right angles)

$\angle ACB = \angle A_1CB_1$ (common angle)

$\therefore \quad \angle CAB = \angle CA_1B$

$\therefore \Delta ABC$ is similar to ΔA_1B_1C

$$\therefore \quad \frac{AB}{A_1B_1} = \frac{BC}{B_1C} \quad \text{...(i)}$$

Similarly, ΔDEF is similar to ΔA_1B_1F

$$\therefore \quad \frac{DE}{A_1B_1} = \frac{EF}{B_1F} \quad \text{...(ii)}$$

But $DE = AB$ and when the aperture is very small $= EF = PF$

Eq. (ii) becomes

$$\frac{AB}{A_1B_1} = \frac{PF}{B_1F} \quad \text{...(iii)}$$

From Eqs. (i) and (iii), we get

$$\frac{PF}{B_1F} = \frac{BC}{B_1C} = \frac{PF}{PF - PB_1} = \frac{PB + BC}{PC - PB_1}$$

$$= \frac{f}{f - v} = \frac{-u + 2f}{2f - v}$$

Since, $PF = F$, $PB_1 = v$,

$PB = u$, $PC = 2f$

$\Rightarrow 2(2f - v) = (f - v)(2f - u)$

$\Rightarrow 2f^2 - vf = 2f^2 - uf - 2fv + uv = 0$

$\Rightarrow 2f^2 - vf - 2f^2 + uf + 2fv - uv = 0$

$\Rightarrow \quad -vf + uf + 2fv - vu = 0$

$$fv + uf - vu = 0 \quad \text{...(iv)}$$

Dividing both sides of the Eq. (iv) by uvf, we get

$$\Rightarrow \quad \frac{fv}{uvf} + \frac{uf}{uvf} - \frac{vu}{uvf} = 0$$

$$\Rightarrow \quad \frac{1}{v} + \frac{1}{u} = \frac{1}{f}$$

(ii) The multi-component lenses are used for both objective and the eye-piece to improve image quality by minimising various optical aberrations in lenses.

(iii) Magnification $\quad M = m_o m_e$

Magnification by objective, $m_o = \frac{M}{m_e}$

We have $\quad m_e = 1 + \frac{D}{f_e} = 1 + \frac{25}{2}$

$$m_e = \frac{27}{2}$$

$$\therefore \quad m_o = \frac{200}{\frac{27}{2}}$$

$$m_o = 14.8$$

38. Refer to text on pages 297 and 298.

39. Refer to text on pages 298 and 299.

Magnifying power (in normal adjustment) of a reflecting telescope is the ratio of the focal length of concave reflector and the focal length of eyepiece.

$$m = \frac{f}{f_e} = \frac{R/2}{f_e}$$

Limitations of refracting telescope over a reflecting type telescope

(i) Refracting telescope suffers from chromatic aberration as it uses large sized lenses.

(ii) It is also difficult and expensive to make such large sized lenses.

40. (i) (a) Refer to text on pages 298

(b) Given, focal length of lens $L_1, f_1 = 24$ cm

Focal length of lens $L_2, f_2 = -18$ cm

Separation between lens L_1 and $L_2, d = 45$ cm

Focal length of combined lens is given by

$$\frac{1}{f} = \frac{1}{f_1} + \frac{1}{f_2} - \frac{d}{f_1 f_2} = \frac{1}{24} + \frac{1}{-18} - \frac{45}{24 \times (-18)}$$

$$= \frac{1}{24} - \frac{1}{18} + \frac{5}{48} = \frac{6 - 8 + 15}{144} = \frac{13}{144}$$

$$\Rightarrow \quad f = \frac{144}{13} \text{ cm}$$

Distance of object, $u = -36$ cm

If v be the position of image, then using lens formula, we have $\frac{1}{v}-\frac{1}{u}=\frac{1}{f}$

$$\Rightarrow \frac{1}{v}=\frac{1}{u}+\frac{1}{f}=\frac{1}{-36}+\frac{1}{144/13}$$

$$=-\frac{1}{36}+\frac{13}{144}=\frac{9}{144}$$

$$\Rightarrow v=\frac{144}{9}=16 \text{ cm}$$

(ii) (a) Refer the text on page 286.

(b) Given, $i = 60°$, $A = 60°$

$$\therefore \quad i=\frac{A+\delta_m}{2}$$

$$\Rightarrow 60°=\frac{60°+\delta_m}{2} \Rightarrow \delta_m = 60°$$

$$\therefore \quad \mu=\frac{\sin\left(\frac{A+\delta_m}{2}\right)}{\sin A/2}$$

$$=\frac{\sin\left(\frac{60°+60°}{2}\right)}{\sin\frac{60°}{2}}=\frac{\sin 60°}{\sin 30°}=\frac{\sqrt{3}/2}{1/2}$$

$$\Rightarrow \mu=\sqrt{3}$$

If the prism is immersed in water, then relative refractive index decreases, hence angle of minimum deviation (δ_m) also decreases.

41. (i) Concave mirror form real, inverted and magnified image of an object, when it is placed between C and F. The ray diagram is given as

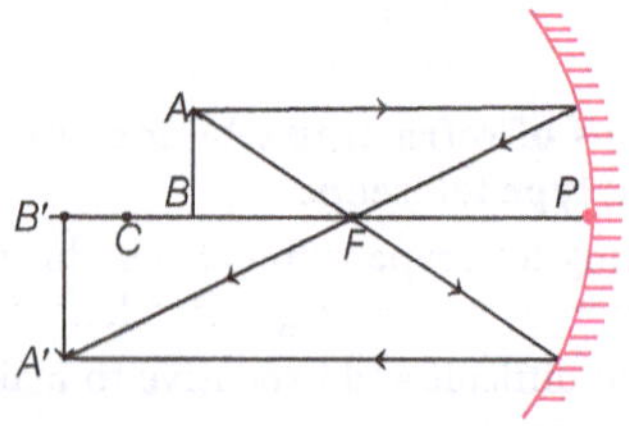

(ii) Refer to text on page 280 and 281.

42. Refer to the text on pages 280 and 281.

43. (i) The angular size of the image and of the object are equal. When the objects are placed at the least distance of distinct vision, they can be viewed with the help of magnifying glass. As the object gets closer, the angular size increases. A magnifying glass is used because it provides an angular magnification. Without magnification, it is difficult to place an object closer to the eye.

(ii) Yes, the angular magnification changes. As the distance between the eye and the magnifying glass increases, the angular magnification decreases. This is because the angle subtended by the eye is less than that of the angle subtended by the lens. Angular magnification is independent of the image distance.

(iii) Manufacturing lenses with small focal length is difficult. When the focal length is small, there are chances of production of spherical and chromatic aberrations. Therefore, there is no such reduction in the focal length of a convex lens.

(iv) A compound microscope produces an angular magnification of $\left[\left(\frac{25}{f_e}\right)+1\right]$

where, f_e = focal length of the eyepiece.

It can be inferred that if f, is small, then angular magnification of the eyepiece will be large.

The angular magnification of the objective lens of a compound microscope is given as $\frac{1}{(|\mu_0| f_0)}$

where, u_O = object distance for the objective lens

f_O = focal length of the objective

When $u_O > f_O$, the magnification is large. While using a microscope, the object is kept closer to the objective lens. So, the object distance is very less. As u_0 decreases, f_O also decreases. Therefore, in the given situation, both f_e and f_O are small.

(v) We are unable to collect much-refracted light when we place our eyes too close to the eyepiece of a compound microscope. As a result, there is substantial decrements in the field of view. Hence, the clarity of the image gets blurred. The eye-ring attached to the eyepiece gives the best position for viewing through a compound microscope. The precise location of the eye depends on the separation between the objective lens and the eyepiece.

44. (i)

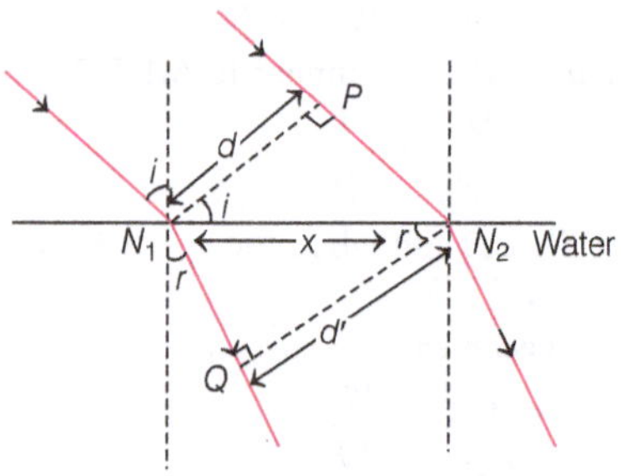

Let us consider a parallel beam of light entering water from air at an angle of incidence i and let the angle of refraction be r.

Let us draw perpendiculars N_1P and N_2Q on the incident beam and refracted beam respectively.

$\angle PN_1N_2 = i$ and $\angle QN_2N_1 = r$

Let $N_1N_2 = x$, $N_1P = d$ and $N_2Q = d'$.

$\therefore \quad \cos i = \frac{d}{x}$ and $\cos r = \frac{d'}{x}$.

$\therefore \quad \frac{\cos i}{\cos r} = \frac{d}{d'}$

Now, $i > r$ since light travels from rarer to denser medium.

$\therefore \quad \cos i < \cos r \Rightarrow d' > d$

$\therefore$ The width of the beam will increase after refraction.

(ii)

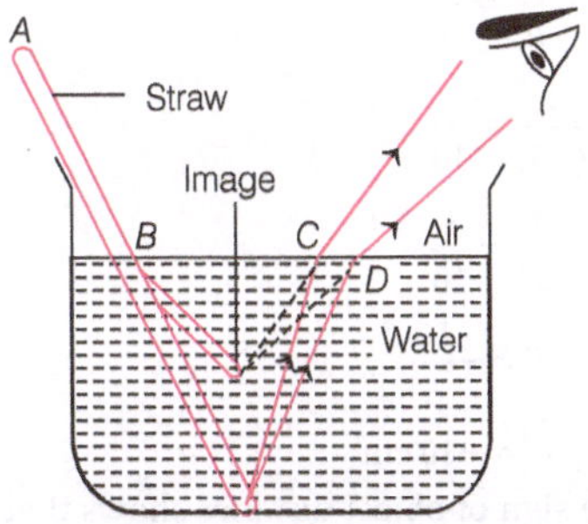

So, it can be seen from the above diagram that the light rays from the end of the straw which is dipped in water bends away from the normal as it is refracted from the surface of the water. When those rays are extended back so that it appears to meet at a point, the straw seems to be bent as one looks at it.

(iii) Refer to theory on page 286 (TIR in Nature and its technological Applications : Optical Fibres).

45. Refer to text on Pages 286.

46. Refer to text on Pages 292 and 293.

47. (i) From ray diagram,

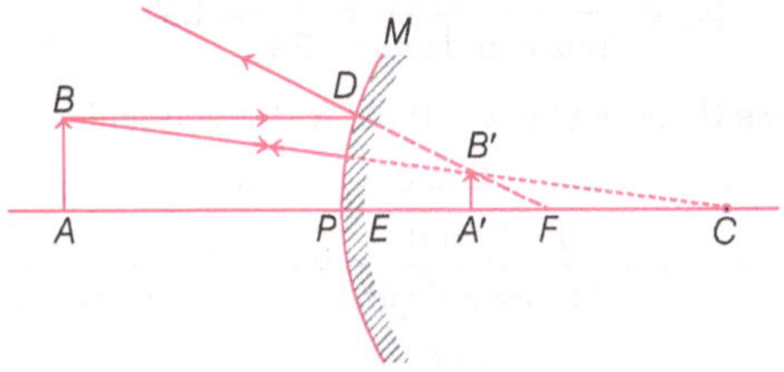

Now consider ΔABC and $\Delta A'B'C$

$\angle BAC = \angle B'A'C = 90°$

$\angle ACB = \angle A'CB'$

$\angle CAB = \angle CB'A'$ (common angle)

Therefore, we could say that, they are similar triangles.

$$\frac{AB}{A'B'} = \frac{AC}{A'C} \quad \text{...(i)}$$

Similarly, $\Delta DEF \sim \Delta A'B'F$

$$\frac{DE}{A'B'} = \frac{EF}{A'F} \quad \text{...(ii)}$$

We have convex mirror of small aperture

$\therefore \quad EF = FP$

From Eq. (ii), $\frac{AB}{A'B'} = \frac{PF}{A'F}$ ...(iii)

From Eqs. (i) and (iii), we get

$$\frac{PF}{A'F} = \frac{AC}{A'C} \Rightarrow \frac{PF}{PF - PA'} = \frac{PA + PC}{PC - PA'}$$

Now, $PF = f$, $PA = u$, $PA' = v$, $PC = 2f$

$$\frac{f}{f - v} = \frac{-u + 2f}{2f - v}$$

$$2f^2 - vf = 2f^2 - uf - 2fv + uv$$

$$fv + uf - vu = 0 \quad \text{...(iv)}$$

Dividing each term by uvf,

$$\frac{1}{u} + \frac{1}{v} - \frac{1}{f} = 0$$

$$\frac{1}{f} = \frac{1}{v} + \frac{1}{u}$$

$$\Rightarrow \quad \frac{1}{R/2} = \frac{1}{v} + \frac{1}{u} \quad (\because f = R/2)$$

$$\Rightarrow \quad \frac{2}{R} = \frac{1}{v} + \frac{1}{u}$$

(ii) Object height, $h = 1.8$ m

Focal length, $f = +1$ m

Object distance, $u = -5$ cm

Lens formula, $\frac{1}{v} - \frac{1}{u} = \frac{1}{f} \Rightarrow \frac{1}{v} - \frac{1}{(-5)} = \frac{1}{1}$

$$\frac{1}{v} = 1 - \frac{1}{5} = \frac{4}{5}$$

$$\frac{1}{v} = \frac{4}{5} = v = \frac{5}{4} = 1.2$$

Image is formed at distance of 1.2 m from the convex lens.

Image is formed on the right side of the lens.

48. Distance of object from mirror $= 15 + \frac{33.25}{4} \times 3 = 39.93$ cm

Distance of image from the mirror

$$= 15 + \frac{25}{4} \times 3 = 33.75 \text{ cm}$$

Using mirror formula, $\frac{1}{v} + \frac{1}{u} = \frac{1}{f} \Rightarrow \frac{1}{-33.75} - \frac{1}{39.93} = \frac{1}{f}$

$\therefore \quad f = -18.3$ cm

49. (i) First by concave mirror

$u = -15$ cm, $f = -10$ cm

Using mirror formula, $\frac{1}{f} = \frac{1}{v} + \frac{1}{u}$

Substituting and calculating, $v = -30$ cm

Image is real

This image I_1 formed by concave mirror acts as an object

(ii) Image formation by convex mirror, $u = +10$ cm

$$f = -20 \text{ cm}$$

Using mirror formula and substituing $v = \frac{-20}{3}$. Final image I_2 is formed behind the convex mirror at a distance of $\frac{20}{3} = 6.66$ cm.

50.

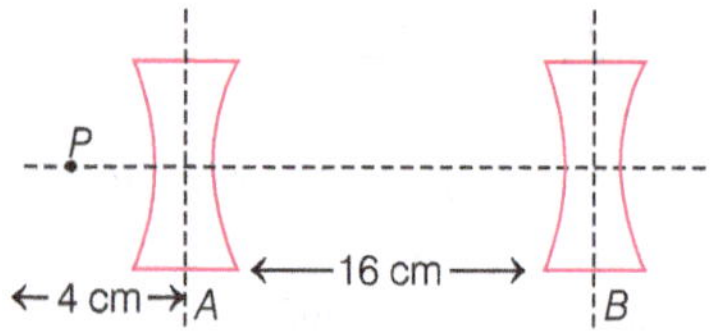

Let us first consider lens A.

Focal length of lens $A = 8$ cm.

Let the image distance be v_1.

$\therefore$ By lens formula, $\frac{1}{f} = \frac{1}{v_1} - \frac{1}{u}$

Here, $u = 4$ cm.

$$\therefore \quad \frac{1}{-8} = \frac{1}{v_1} - \frac{1}{(-4)}$$

$$\Rightarrow \quad \frac{1}{v_1} = \frac{-1}{8} - \frac{1}{4} = \frac{-3}{8} \text{ cm}$$

$$\Rightarrow \quad v_1 = \frac{-8}{3}$$

$\therefore$ The image for lens A is formed at a distance of $\frac{8}{3}$ cm at the left of A.

Now, this image acts as an object for lens B.

Lens B also has the focal length of 8 cm.

Let the final image be formed at a distance v from lens B.

The object distance is equal to $\frac{8}{3} + 16 = \frac{56}{3}$ cm to the left of lens B.

$$\therefore \quad u_B = \frac{-56}{3} \text{ cm}$$

$\therefore$ From lens formula,

$$\frac{1}{f} = \frac{1}{v} - \frac{1}{u_B} \Rightarrow \frac{1}{-8} = \frac{1}{v} + \frac{3}{56}$$

$$\Rightarrow \quad v = -5.6 \text{ cm}$$

$\therefore$ The final image is formed at a distance of 5.6 cm to the left of lens B.

51. Object distance from the first lens, $u = -30$ cm

Distance between both lenses, $d = 20$ cm

Focal length of both lenses, $f = 10$ cm

Use lens formula,

$$\frac{1}{v} - \frac{1}{u} = \frac{1}{f}$$

$$\frac{1}{v} - \frac{1}{(-30)} = \frac{1}{10}$$

$$V = \frac{300}{20} = 15 \text{ cm}$$

The image is inverted and formed at right side of the lens A.

Distance from the second lens B,

$$u' = d - v = 20 - 15 = 5 \text{ cm}$$

where, u' is the object distance for the lens B.

Use lens formula,

$$\frac{1}{v'} - \frac{1}{u'} = \frac{1}{f}$$

$$\frac{1}{v'} - \frac{1}{(-5)} = \frac{1}{10}$$

$$\frac{1}{v'} = \frac{1}{10} - \frac{1}{5}$$

$$v' = -\frac{50}{5}$$

$$v' = -10 \text{ cm}$$

Negative sign of object distance shows that object is located left side of the lens.

The image is located at 10 cm left to the lens B.

Nature of the image Virtual and inverted.

The position of the final image on the optical bench at 60 cm.

52. ***Case* I** When tank is filled with the water.

Given, the apparent depth = 9.4 cm

Height of water, $t = 12.5$ cm

So, real depth = 12.5 cm

Refractive index of water,

$$\mu_w = \frac{\text{Real depth}}{\text{Apparent depth}} = \frac{12.5}{9.4} = 1.33$$

***Case* II** When tank is filled with the liquid.

Refractive index of liquid, $\mu_l = 1.63$

$$\text{Again, } \mu_l = \frac{\text{Real depth}}{\text{Apparent depth}} \Rightarrow 1.63 = \frac{12.5}{\text{Apparent depth}}$$

$$\text{Apparent depth} = \frac{12.5}{1.63} = 7.67 \text{ cm}$$

$\therefore$ The microscope is shifted by $9.4 - 7.67 = 1.73$ cm

53. Given, the refractive index of glass with respect to air,

$${}^a\mu_g = 1.55$$

For double convex lenses, $R_1 = R$, $R_2 = -R$

[$\because$ both faces have same radius of curvature, but for double convex lens, one radius is taken as positive and other negative]

Focal length of lens, $f = +20$ cm

Using the lens Maker's formula,

$$\frac{1}{f} = ({}^a\mu_g - 1)\left(\frac{1}{R_1} - \frac{1}{R_2}\right)$$

$$\Rightarrow \quad \frac{1}{20} = (1.55-1)\left(\frac{1}{R}+\frac{1}{R}\right)$$

$$\Rightarrow \quad \frac{1}{20} = 0.55 \times \frac{2}{R} \Rightarrow R = 0.55 \times 2 \times 20 = 22 \text{ cm}$$

Thus, the required radius of curvature is 22 cm.

54. For lens L_1, $\frac{1}{f} = \frac{1}{v} - \frac{1}{u}$

Given, $u = -15$ cm, $f = +10$ cm, $v = ?$

$$\therefore \quad \frac{1}{10} = \frac{1}{v} + \frac{1}{15} \Rightarrow \frac{1}{v} = \frac{1}{10} - \frac{1}{15} \Rightarrow \frac{1}{v} = \frac{1}{30}$$

Distance of image from lens L_1, $v = 30$ cm

For lens L_3, $\frac{1}{f''} = \frac{1}{v''} - \frac{1}{u''}$

Distance of image from lens L_3, $v'' = 10$ cm

$$\therefore \quad \frac{1}{10} = \frac{1}{10} - \frac{1}{u''} \Rightarrow \frac{1}{u''} = 0 \Rightarrow \quad u'' = \infty$$

The refracted rays from lens L_2 becomes parallel to principal axis. It is possible only when image formed by L_1 lies at first focus of L_2, i.e. at a distance of 10 cm from L_2.

$\therefore$ Separation between L_1 and $L_2 = 30 + 10 = 40$ cm

The distance between L_2 and L_3 may take any value.

55. (i)

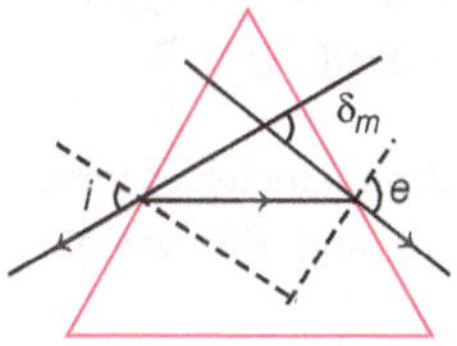

At a minimum angle of deviation, $i = e$, $r_1 = r_2$

$$\therefore \; \delta_m = i + e - A = 2i - A$$

$$i = \frac{A + \delta m}{2}$$

By Snell's law,

$$n_1 \sin i = n_2 \sin r = n_1 \sin\left(\frac{A+\delta_m}{2}\right) = n_2 \sin\left(\frac{A}{2}\right)$$

$$\frac{n_2}{n_1} = \frac{\sin(A+\delta_m)}{\sin\left(\frac{A}{2}\right)}$$

(ii) Given, the emergent ray grazes along the face AC,

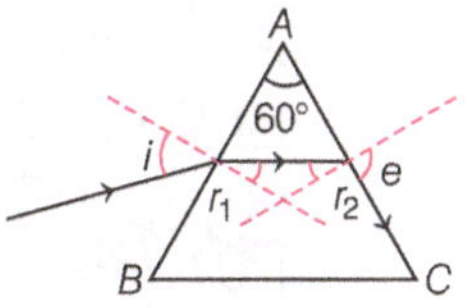

$$e = 90^\circ$$

$$\mu = \sqrt{2}$$

$$\frac{\sin i}{\sin r_1} = \mu = \frac{\sin e}{\sin r_2}$$

$$\frac{\sin 90^\circ}{\sin r_2} = \sqrt{2}$$

i.e. $\quad \sin r_2 = \frac{1}{\sqrt{2}}$ or $r_2 = 45^\circ$

$$\Rightarrow \quad r_1 + r_2 = \angle A = 60^\circ$$

$$r_1 = 60^\circ - r_2 = 15^\circ$$

$$\Rightarrow \quad \frac{\sin i}{\sin 15^\circ} = \sqrt{2} \Rightarrow i = 21.47^\circ$$

56. (i) Let us draw the ray diagram of the situation. Since, the mirror produces an enlarged and real image, so the mirror used must be concave. The image is also inverted since it is real in nature. From the above understanding and the provided data, the ray diagram is as follows.

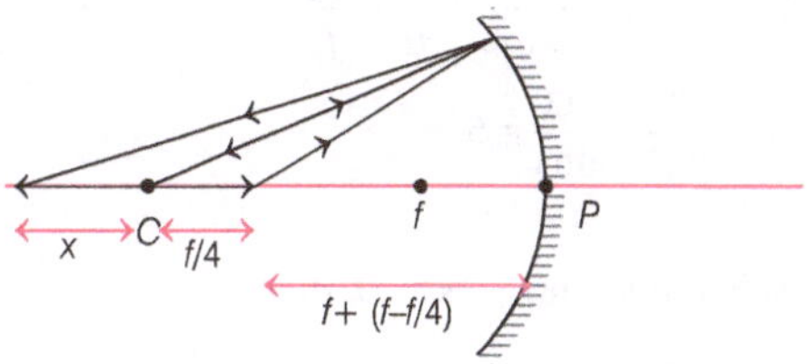

Let the length of the image be x.

The pencil is kept with the edge coinciding with the centre of curvature and the tip facing the concave mirror.

Considering the tip of the pencil, the distance from the principal axis at which it is placed is

$$u = -\left[f + \left(f - \frac{f}{4}\right)\right] = \frac{-7f}{4}.$$

The image distance of the tip of the pencil from

$$P = v = -(2f + x)$$

We know that,

$$m = \frac{h_I}{h_o} = \frac{-v}{u}$$

$$\Rightarrow \quad \frac{x}{\frac{f}{4}} = \frac{-\{-(2f+x)\}}{\frac{-7f}{4}}$$

$$\Rightarrow \quad -7x = 2f + x$$

$$\Rightarrow \quad -6x = 2f$$

$$\Rightarrow \quad x = \frac{-f}{3}$$

$$\therefore \text{ Magnification, } m = \frac{x}{\frac{f}{4}} = \frac{\frac{-f}{3}}{\frac{f}{4}} = \frac{-4}{3}$$

$\therefore$ The magnification produced is $\frac{-4}{3}$.

(ii) The angle of incidence $i = 45^\circ$, let the angle of emergence be e, the angle of prism $A = 30^\circ$ and the angle of deviation $\delta = 15^\circ$.

We know that,

$$\delta = i + e - A$$

$$\Rightarrow \quad 15^\circ = 45^\circ + e - 30^\circ \Rightarrow e = 0^\circ$$

$\therefore$ The ray emerges out normal to the surface AC.

57. Given, focal length of objective lens, $f_o = 144$ cm

Focal length of eyepiece, $f_e = 6$ cm

Magnifying power of the telescope in normal adjustment (i.e. when the final image is formed at ∞),

$$m = -\frac{f_o}{f_e} = -\frac{144}{6} = -24$$

$\therefore$ Separation between lenses,

$$L = f_o + f_e = 144 + 6 = 150 \text{ cm}$$

58. Since, $m = \dfrac{\tan\beta}{\tan\alpha} \approx \dfrac{\beta}{\alpha} = \dfrac{f_o}{f_e}$

$$\therefore \quad \frac{\beta}{0.5^\circ} = \frac{0.3}{0.03} = 5^\circ$$

59. When final image is at D, then

magnifying power, $m = \dfrac{-f_o}{f_e}\left(1 + \dfrac{f_e}{D}\right)$

In normal adjustment, $m = \dfrac{-f_o}{f_e}$

For telescope, focal length of objective lens,

$$f_o = 150 \text{ cm}$$

Focal length of eye lens, $f_e = 5$ cm

When final image forms at D, i.e. 25 cm, then

magnification, $m = \dfrac{-f_o}{f_e}\left(1 + \dfrac{f_e}{D}\right)$

$$= \frac{-150}{5}\left(1 + \frac{5}{25}\right) = \frac{-150}{5} \times \frac{6}{5} \Rightarrow m = -36$$

Let height of final image be h cm.

$$\Rightarrow \quad \tan\beta = \frac{h}{25} \text{ and } \tan\alpha = \frac{100\text{m}}{3000\text{m}} = \frac{1}{30}$$

where, β = visual angle formed by final image at eye and α = visual angle subtended by object at objective.

But $\quad m = \dfrac{\tan\beta}{\tan\alpha} \Rightarrow -36 = \dfrac{\left(\frac{h}{25}\right)}{\left(\frac{1}{30}\right)}$

$$\Rightarrow \quad -36 = \frac{h}{25} \times 30 \Rightarrow -36 = \frac{6h}{5}$$

$$\Rightarrow \quad h = \frac{-36 \times 5}{6} \Rightarrow h = -30 \text{ cm}$$

Negative sign indicates inverted image.

60. (i) For astronomical telescope,

$$f_o = 15 \text{ m} = 1500 \text{ cm}, \; f_e = 1 \text{ cm}$$

Angular magnification, $m = -\dfrac{f_o}{f_e} = -\dfrac{15 \times 100 \text{ cm}}{1 \text{ cm}}$

$$= -1500$$

(ii) Given diameter, $D = 3.48 \times 10^6$ m, $f_o = 3.8 \times 10^8$ m

Let α be the angle subtended by the moon at objective.

$$\therefore \quad \alpha = \frac{D}{\text{Radius of lunar orbit}}$$

$$\alpha = \frac{3.48 \times 10^6 \text{ m}}{3.8 \times 10^8 \text{ m}} \quad \text{...(i)}$$

Also, then angle subtended by image formed by objective on itself, $\alpha = \dfrac{d}{f_o}$ ...(ii)

where, d = diameter of image.

From Eqs. (i) and (ii), we get

$$\frac{3.48 \times 10^6}{3.8 \times 10^8} = \frac{d}{1500} \quad \text{[given]}$$

$$\therefore \quad d = \frac{1500 \times 3.48 \times 10^6}{3.8 \times 10^8}$$

$$= 13.7 \text{ cm}$$

QR Code for Quick Test 1	QR Code for Quick Test 2	QR Code for Quick Test 3	QR Code for Quick Test 4

SELF ASSESSMENT TEST

Multiple Choice Questions (MCQs)

1. For a concave mirror of focal length f, the minimum distance between the object and its real image is

(a) zero (b) f

(c) $2f$ (d) $4f$

2. A converging lens is used to focus the image of an object on a screen. If the object is placed at a distance of 10 cm from the lens and the screen is 20 cm away, what is the focal length of the lens?

(a) 6.67 cm (b) 7.5 cm

(c) 10 cm (d) 12 cm

3. Two thin lenses of focal lengths +15 cm and −10 cm are placed in contact. The combination behaves as a

(a) converging lens with focal length 6 cm

(b) converging lens with focal length 10 cm

(c) diverging lens with focal length 6 cm

(d) diverging lens with focal length 30 cm

4. A plane mirror is inclined at 30° to the horizontal. A ray of light strikes the mirror at an angle of 90° with the horizontal. What is the angle of reflection?

(a) 90° (b) 45° (c) 30" (d) 60°

5. A light ray is incident at an angle of 45° on the surface of a glass slab of refractive index 1.5. The thickness of the slab is 10 cm. What is the lateral displacement of the light ray?

(a) 6.6 cm (b) 4.33 cm

(c) 3.3 cm (d) 7.07 cm

Assertion-Reason

Directions *(Q. Nos. 6-8) In the following questions, two statements are given- one labeled Assertion (A) and the other labelled Reason (R). Select the correct answer to these questions from the codes (a), (b), (c) and (d) as given below.*

(a) Both Assertion and Reason are true and Reason is the correct explanation of Assertion.

(b) Both Assertion and Reason are true but Reason is not the correct explanation of Assertion.

(c) Assertion is true but Reason is false.

(d) Assertion is false but Reason is true.

6. **Assertion (A)** When a ray of light passes through a prism, the angle of deviation decreases with an increase in the wavelength of the incident light.

Reason (R) The refractive index of a material decreases with increasing wavelength of light.

7. **Assertion (A)** A convex lens of focal length 10 cm forms a virtual image when the object is placed at a distance of 5 cm from the lens.

Reason (R) A convex lens always forms a real image when the object is placed in front of it.

8. **Assertion (A)** A ray of light passing through the center of curvature of a concave mirror retraces its path after reflection.

Reason (R) The angle of incidence is equal to the angle of reflection for any ray of light falling on a mirror.

Case Based Question

Directions *(Q. Nos. 9) This question is case study based question. Read the following paragraph and answer the questions on the basis of same.*

9. An astronomical telescope has an objective lens of focal length 100 cm and an eyepiece of focal length 10 cm. The telescope is adjusted for normal vision (the final image is at infinity), and the object observed is at a large distance. The lenses are separated by the appropriate distance.

(i) What is the magnifying power of the telescope?

(ii) If the distance between the objective and the eyepiece is decreased by 1 cm, where is the final image formed?

(iii) If the eyepiece is replaced with a lens of focal length 15 cm, how will the magnifying power change?

(iv) Explain how the resolving power of the telescope depends on the diameter of the objective lens.

(v) What are the conditions required to achieve maximum magnification using this telescope?

Very Short Answer Type Questions

10. Explain why a diamond sparkles more than a piece of glass of the same shape.

11. Discuss the principle of reversibility of light and provide an example where this principle is applicable.

12. A convex lens of focal length 10 cm is placed in front of a plane mirror. An object is placed 30 cm in front of the lens. Find the position of the final image and the magnification of the system.

Short Answer Type Questions

13. A thin lens has a focal length of 15 cm. A point object is placed at a distance of 10 cm from the lens. Calculate the position and magnification of the image formed by the lens.

14. An object is placed 40 cm from a convex lens of focal length 30 cm. If a concave lens of focal length 50 cm is introduced between the convex lens and the image formed such that it is 20cm from the convex lens. Find the change in the position of the image.

15. A ray of light is incident at an angle of 30° on one of the faces of an equilateral prism 15 (refractive index $\mu = \mu = 1.5$). Calculate the angle of deviation for the ray passing through the prism.

Long Answer Type Question

16. (i) Draw a ray diagram of compound microscope for the final image formed at least distance of distinct vision.

(ii) An angular magnification of $30X$ is desired using an objective of focal length 1.25 cm and an eyepiece of focal length 5 cm. How will you set-up the compound microscope for the final image formed at least distance of distinct vision?

Answers

1. (a)	*2.* (b)	*3.* (c)	*4.* (d)	*5.* (c)
6. (a)	*7.* (c)	*8.* (a)		

10

CHAPTER

Wave Optics

Wave theory fundamentally changed our understanding of light. Initially, light was thought to be a particle, but experiments, like Thomas Young's double slit experiment in 1801, demonstrated that light behaves as a wave. This wave behaviour explains phenomena such as interference and diffraction, leading to the development of the wave theory of light which becomes the base of quantum mechanics.

YOUR STUDY GOALS

YOUR PRACTICE GOAL

- Objective Type Questions (32 Qs ; MCQs, A-R, Matching)
- Case Based Questions-2
- Subjective Questions (7 VSAs, 8 SAs, 9 LAs)
- Numerical Problems-9

10.1 Wavefront

The locus of all the particle, which oscillate in same phase is called **wavefront.**

- A line perpendicular at any point an wavefront represent the direction of propagation.
- This perpendicular line is called a **ray.**

The wavefront can be of different shapes, depending on the shape of source of light wavefront can be of three types, which are given below.

(i) **Spherical wavefront** When the source of light is a **point source,** the wavefront is **spherical.**

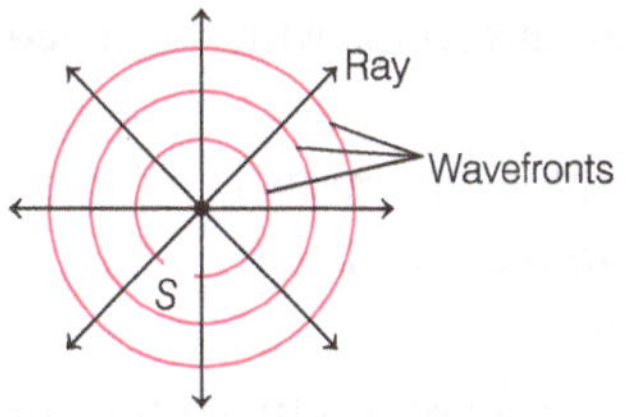

(ii) **Cylindrical wavefront** When the source of light is **linear,** e.g. a straight line source, slit etc. as shown in the figure.

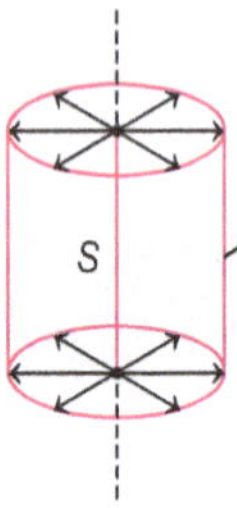

All the points equidistant from the source lie on a cylinder. Therefore, the wavefront is produced cylindrical in shape.

(iii) **Plane wavefront** When the point source or linear source of light is at very large distance, the wavefront appears to be plane, known as a **plane wavefront.**

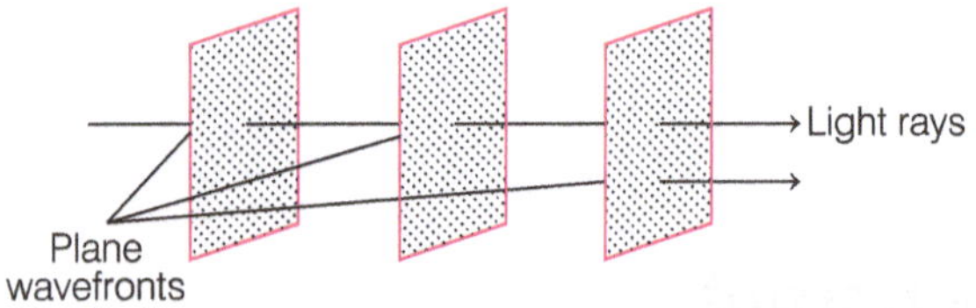

10.2 Huygens' Principle

In order to explain how a wavefront is propagated forwards and to construct the position of a wavefront at any instant of time, Huygens has given following two assumptions.

According to Huygens' principle,

(i) Each point of the wavefront is the source of a secondary disturbance (called **secondary wavelets**) and the wavelets emanating from these points spread out in all directions with the **speed of the wave.**

The energy of the wave travels in a direction perpendicular to the wavefront.

(ii) A surface touching these secondary wavelets, tangentially in the forward direction at any instant of time gives the new wavefront at that instant. This is called **secondary wavefront.**

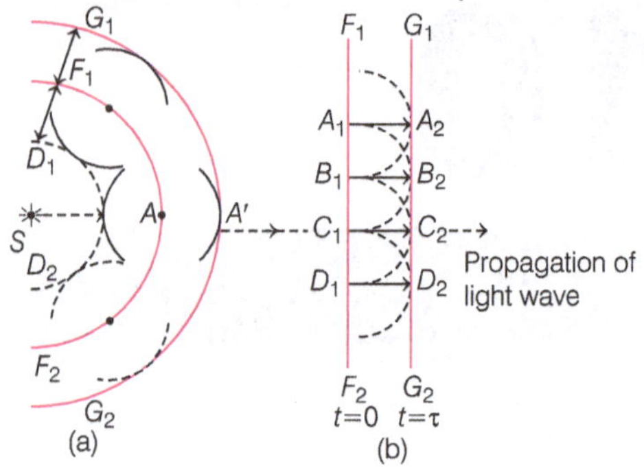

In Fig.(a), $F_1 F_2$ is the section of the given spherical wavefront and $G_1 G_2$ is the new wavefront in the forward direction. In Fig.(b), $F_1 F_2$ is the section of the given plane wavefront and G_1G_2 is the new wavefront in the forward direction.

TEACHER TIP

The amplitude of the secondary wavelets is maximum in the forward direction and zero in the backward direction. Hence, the backward secondary wavefront is absent.

10.3 Reflection and Refraction of Plane Waves at a Plane Surface using Huygens' Principle

Huygens' principle can be used to explain the phenomena of reflection and refraction of light on the basis of wave theory of light.

Reflection of Plane Waves at a Plane Surface

Let 1, 2, 3 be the incident rays and 1′, 2′, 3′ be the corresponding reflected rays.

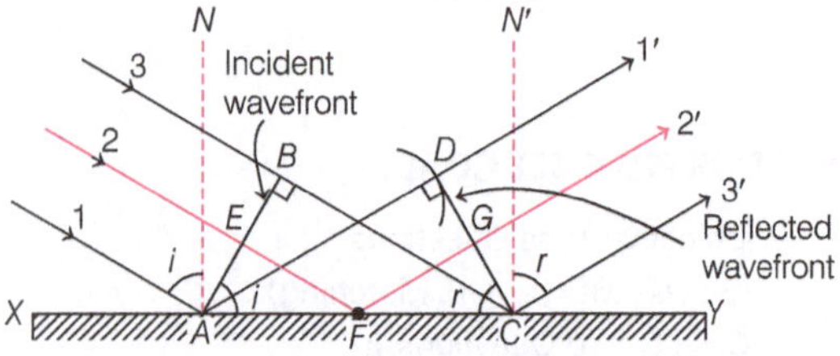

Reflection of plane wave

If c is the speed of the light, t is the time taken by light to go from B to C or A to D or E to G through F, then

$$t = \frac{EF}{c} + \frac{FG}{c} \qquad \ldots\text{(i)}$$

In ΔAEF, $\sin i = \frac{EF}{AF}$

In ΔFGC, $\sin r = \frac{FG}{FC}$

or $$t = \frac{AF \sin i}{c} + \frac{FC \sin r}{c}$$

$$\Rightarrow \quad t = \frac{AC \sin r + AF(\sin i - \sin r)}{c}$$

$[\because FC = AC - AF]$

For rays of light from different parts on the incident wavefront, the values of AF are different. But light from different points of the incident wavefront should take the same time to reach the corresponding points on the reflected wavefront.

So, t should not depend upon AF.This is possible only, if

$$\sin i - \sin r = 0$$

i.e. $$\sin i = \sin r$$

or $$\boxed{\angle i = \angle r} \qquad \ldots\text{(ii)}$$

which is the **first law of reflection.**

Further, the incident wavefront AB, the reflecting surface XY and the reflected wavefront CD are all perpendicular to the plane of the paper.

Therefore, incident ray, normal to the mirror XY and reflected ray all lie in the same plane. This proves the **second law of reflection.**

Refraction of plane wave (Snell's Law) at a Plane Surface

Let 1, 2, 3 be the incident rays and 1′, 2′, 3′ be the corresponding refracted rays.

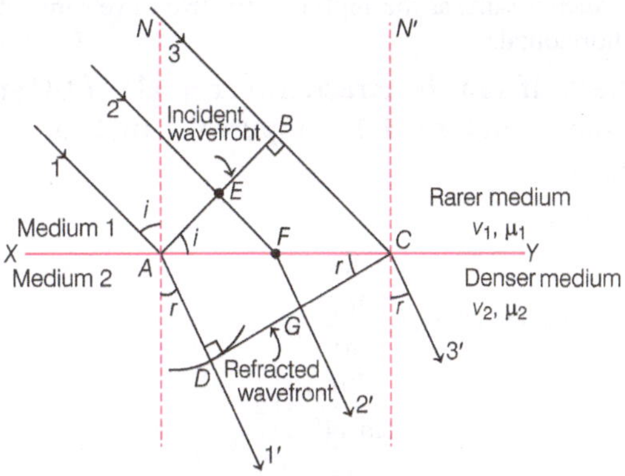

Refraction of a plane wave

If v_1 and v_2 are the speeds of light in the two media and t is the time taken by light to go from B to C or A to D or E to G through F, then $$t = \frac{EF}{v_1} + \frac{FG}{v_2}$$

In ΔAFE, $\sin i = \frac{EF}{AF}$

In ΔFGC, $\sin r = \frac{FG}{FC}$

$$\Rightarrow \quad t = \frac{AF \sin i}{v_1} + \frac{FC \sin r}{v_2} \qquad \ldots\text{(iii)}$$

$$\Rightarrow \quad t = \frac{AC \sin r}{v_2} + AF\left(\frac{\sin i}{v_1} - \frac{\sin r}{v_2}\right)$$

For rays of light from different parts on the incident wavefront, the values of AF are different. But it take the same time to reach the corresponding points on the refracted wavefront. So, t should not depend upon AF. This is possible only, if

$$\frac{\sin i}{v_1} - \frac{\sin r}{v_2} = 0 \Rightarrow \frac{\sin i}{\sin r} = \frac{v_1}{v_2} \qquad \ldots\text{(iv)}$$

Now, if c represents the speed of light in vacuum, then $\mu_1 = \frac{c}{v_1}$ and $\mu_2 = \frac{c}{v_2}$ are known as the **refractive indices** of medium 1 and medium 2, respectively.

In terms of refractive indices, Eq. (iv) can be written as

$$\mu_1 \sin i = \mu_2 \sin r$$

$$\Rightarrow \quad \boxed{\frac{\mu_2}{\mu_1} = \frac{\sin i}{\sin r}}$$

This is known as **Snell's law of refraction.**

Further, if λ_1 and λ_2 denote the wavelengths of light in medium 1 and medium 2, respectively and if the distance BC is equal to λ_1, then the distance AD will be equal to λ_2, thus

$$\frac{\lambda_1}{\lambda_2} = \frac{BC}{AD} = \frac{v_1}{v_2} \quad \text{or} \quad \frac{v_1}{\lambda_1} = \frac{v_2}{\lambda_2}$$

$$\Rightarrow \quad \boxed{\nu_1 = \nu_2} \qquad \left[\because \frac{v}{\lambda} = \nu\right]$$

Hence, **the frequency does not change on refraction.** It remains the same as light travels from one medium to another.

Since, the velocity of light v_1 and v_2 are different in different medium, the wavelengths λ and λ' are also different.

Also, **wavelength is directly proportional to the phase velocity and inversely proportional to refractive index.**

$$\therefore \quad \lambda' = \frac{\lambda}{\mu}, \ \mu = \frac{\lambda}{\lambda'} = \frac{c\lambda}{v\lambda} = \frac{c}{v}$$

- When the plane wave undergoes refraction from denser to rarer medium, all conditions remain same except that **angle of refraction is greater than the angle of incidence and $v_2 > v_1$.**
- Also, when $i = i_c$ (critical angle), then $r = 90°$. (so, for all angles of incidence greater than cirtical angle, no wave is refracted and it undergo total internal reflection).

Behaviour of Prism, Lens and Spherical Mirror towards Plane Wavefront

(i) **Behaviour of a prism** The speed of light waves are less in glass, so the lower portion of the incoming wavefront (which travels through the greatest thickness of glass prism) will get delayed resulting in a tilt in the emerging wavefront.

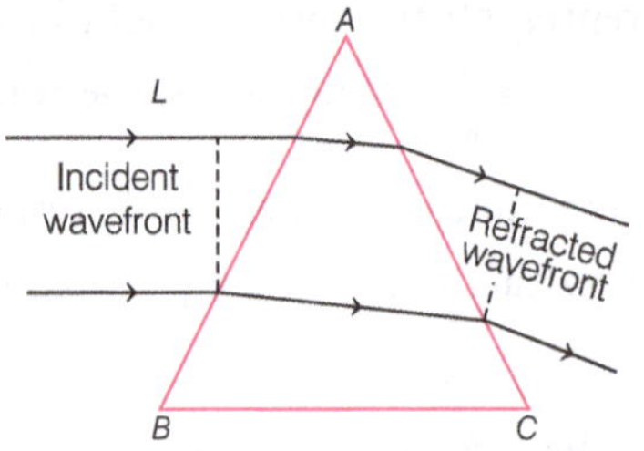

Refraction of plane wave by a thin prism

(ii) **Behaviour of a lens** The central part of the incident plane wave moves through the thickest portion of the lens and is delayed the most.

Due to this, the emerging wavefront has a depression at the centre. Therefore, the wavefront becomes spherical and converges to the point F which is known as the **focus.**

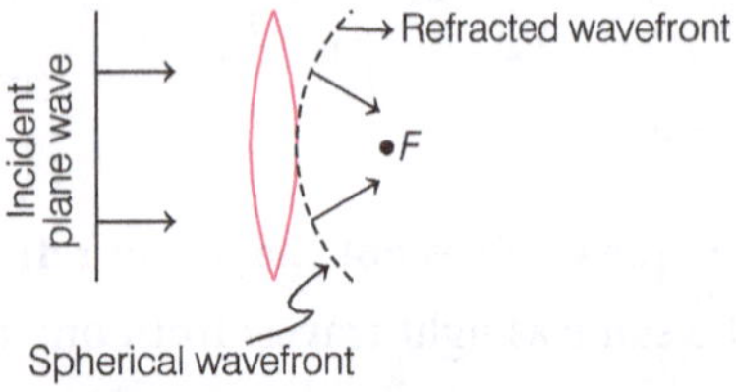

Refraction of plane wave by convex lens

(iii) **Behaviour of a spherical mirror** The central part of the incident wavefront travels the largest distance before reflection from the concave mirror.

Hence, gets delayed, as a result the reflected wavefront is spherical which converges at F.

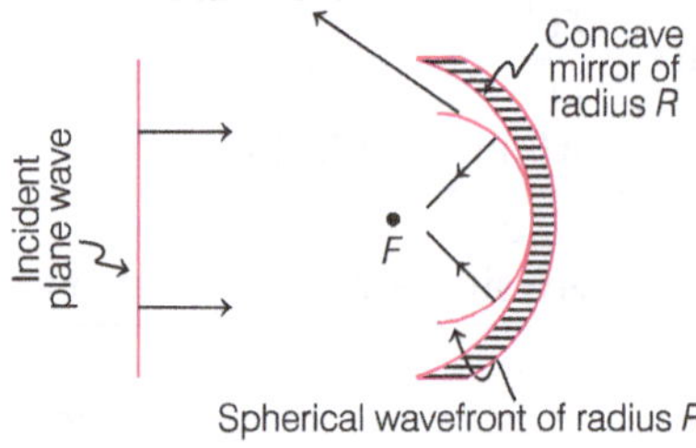

Reflection of plane wave by concave mirror

Example 1. **A plane wavefront is incident from air ($\mu = 1$) at an angle of 37° with a horizontal boundary of a refractive medium from air of refractive index $\mu = \frac{3}{2}$. Find the angle of refracted wavefront with the horizontal boundary.**

Sol. It has been given that incident wavefront makes 37° with horizontal. Hence, incident ray makes 53° with normal as the ray is perpendicular to the wavefront.

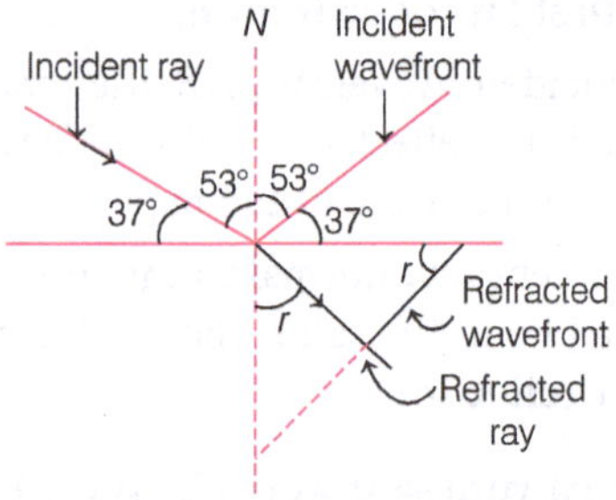

Now, by Snell's law, $\frac{\sin 53°}{\sin r} = \frac{3}{2} \Rightarrow \sin r = \frac{2}{3} \times \sin 53°$

$\therefore \quad r = \sin^{-1}(0.66 \times 0.79) = 31.43°$

which is same as the angle of refractive wavefront with horizontal.

Example 2. **If a ray is refracted at an angle of 14° and the refractive index is 1.2, compute the angle of incidence**

Sol. Given, $r = 14°$

$\mu = 1.2$

By using Snell 's law $\frac{\sin i}{\sin r} = \mu$

$$\frac{\sin i}{\sin 14°} = 1.2$$

then $\sin i = 1.2 \times \sin 14° = 1.2 \times 0.2419$

$i = \sin^{-1}(0.288) \Rightarrow 16.9$

Quick Test 1

Conceptual Questions

1. In the given figure, there are two points P and Q, what is the phase difference between them?

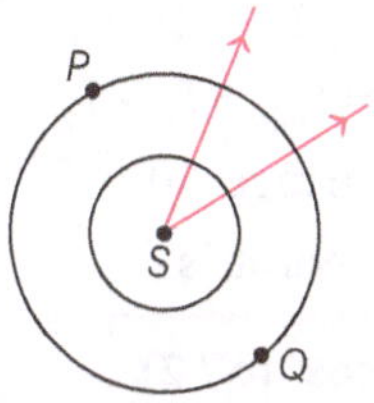

2. (i) Differentiate between a ray and a wavefront.
   (ii) What is the phase difference between any two points on a wavefront?
3. What is the shape of the wavefront on earth for sunlight? *NCERT Exemplar*
4. State Huygens' principles of secondary wavelets.
5. Using Huygens' principle, verify the laws of reflection at a plane surface.
6. Consider a point at the focal point of convergent lens. Another convergent lens of short focal length is placed on the other side. What is the nature of the wavefronts emerging from the final image? *NCERT Exemplar*
7. Light of wavelength 5000 Å propagating in air gets partly reflected from the surface of water. How will the wavelengths and frequencies of the reflected and refracted light be affected?

Numerical Questions

8. Light of wavelength 5000 Å falls on a plane reflecting surface. What are the wavelength and frequency of the reflected light? For what angle of incidence is the reflected ray normal to the incident ray?
9. (i) The refractive index of glass is 1.5. What is the speed of light in glass? (Speed of light in vacuum is 3×10^8 ms^{-1})
   (ii) Is the speed of light in glass independent of the colour of light? If not, which of the two colours red and violet travels slower in a glass prism? *NCERT*

Answers

8. 5000Å, 6×10^{14}Hz, 45° 9. (i) 2×10^8 ms^{-1} (ii) No

For Solutions, See QR Code on Pg. 347

10.4 Interference of Light

Coherent and Incoherent Sources

- Light sources are of two types, i.e. coherent and non-coherent light sources.
- The sources of light which emit light waves of same wavelength, same frequency and are in same phase or having constant phase difference are known as **coherent sources.**
- Two such source of light, which do not emit light waves with constant phase difference are called **incoherent sources.**

Condition for interference

As discussed earlier, when two independent sources of light emits monochromatic waves of intensities I_1, I_2 and phase difference ϕ meet at a point, then the resultant intensity is given by

$$I = I_1 + I_2 + 2\sqrt{I_1 I_2}\cos\phi$$

Here, the term $2\sqrt{I_1 I_2}\cos\phi$ is called **interference term.** There are two possibilities.

(i) If $\cos\phi$ remains constant with time, then the total intensity at any point will be constant.
The intensity will be **maximum** $(\sqrt{I_1}+\sqrt{I_2})^2$ at points, where $\cos\phi$ is 1 and **minimum** $(\sqrt{I_1}-\sqrt{I_2})^2$ at point, where $\cos\phi$ is -1.
Hence, **to obtain interference,we need two sources with same frequency and with a constant phase difference.**
The two sources in this case are coherent sources.

(ii) If $\cos\phi$ varies continuously with time assuming both positive and negative value, then the average value of $\cos\phi$ over a full cycle will be zero.
The interference term averages to zero. There will be same intensity, $I = I_1 + I_2$ at every point.
Hence, the two sources in this case are **incoherent sources.**

Conditions for Obtaining Two Coherent Sources of Light

Following are the requirements (conditions) for obtaining two coherent sources of light

(i) Coherent sources of light should be obtained from a single source.
(ii) Source should be monochromatic.
(iii) Path difference should be small.

Young's Double Slit Experiment

Young in 1802, experimentally demonstrated the phenomenon of interference of light.

The set-up is shown in figure given below

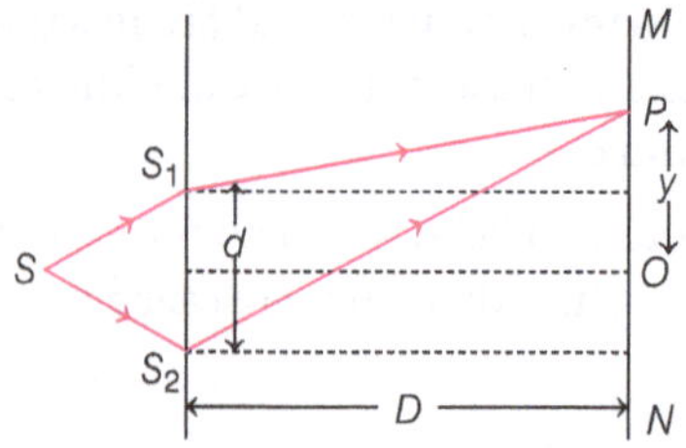

Young's double slit arrangement to produce interference pattern

Suppose S_1 and S_2 are two fine slits, a small distance d apart. They are illuminated by a strong source S of monochromatic light of wavelength λ. MN is a screen at a distance D from the slits.

For constructive interference (Bright fringes)

The distance of nth **bright fringe** from point O is

$$\therefore \quad y = \frac{nD\lambda}{d} \quad \text{[where, } n = 0, 1, 2, 3, \ldots]$$

Hence, for $n = 0$, $y_0 = 0$ at O central bright fringe

for $n = 1$, $y_1 = \frac{D\lambda}{d}$ for 1st bright fringe

for $n = 2$, $y_2 = \frac{2D\lambda}{d}$ for 2nd bright fringe

for $n = n$, $y_n = \frac{nD\lambda}{d}$ for nth bright fringe

For destructive interference (Dark fringes)

The distance of nth **dark fringe** from point O is,

$$\text{or} \quad y = (2n-1)\frac{D\lambda}{2d}, \quad \text{[where, } n = 1, 2, 3, \ldots]$$

Hence, for $n = 1$, $y'_1 = \frac{D\lambda}{2d}$ for 1st dark fringe

for $n = 2$, $y'_2 = \frac{3D\lambda}{2d}$ for 2nd dark fringe

for $n = n$, $y'_n = (2n-1)\frac{D\lambda}{2d}$ for nth dark fringe

Fringe width The separation between any two consecutive bright or dark fringes is called fringe width. It is given by

$$\beta = \frac{D\lambda}{d}$$

Intensity of the Fringes

For a bright fringe, $\phi = 2n\pi$

and $\cos\phi = \cos 2n\pi = 1$

So, $I_R = I_{max} = I_1 + I_2 + 2\sqrt{I_1 I_2} = 4I_0$

[as, $I_1 = I_2 = I_0$ in YDSE]

$\therefore$ Intensity of a bright fringe $= 4I_0 =$ constant

For a dark fringe, $\phi = (2n-1)\pi$

$\Rightarrow \quad \cos\phi = -1$

So, $I_R = I_{min} = I_1 + I_2 - 2\sqrt{I_1 I_2} = 0$

$\therefore$ Intensity of a dark fringe $= 0$

The intensity at any point is

$$I = 4I_0 \cos^2(\phi/2)$$

Note Fringe width in medium, $\beta_m = \frac{D\lambda}{d\mu}$

Example 3. **Two slits are made one millimetre apart and the screen is placed one metre away. What is the fringe separation when blue-green light of wavelength 500 nm is used ?**

Sol. Here, $d = 1\text{mm} = 1 \times 10^{-3}\text{m}$, $D = 1$ m,

$$\lambda = 500 \text{ nm} = 500 \times 10^{-9}\text{m} = 5 \times 10^{-7}\text{m}$$

As, fringe width, $\beta = \frac{D\lambda}{d}$

$$\therefore \quad \beta = \frac{1 \times 5 \times 10^{-7}}{1 \times 10^{-3}} = 5 \times 10^{-4}\text{m}$$

$$= 0.5 \text{ mm}$$

Example 4. **In Young's experiment, the width of the fringes obtained with light of wavelength 6000 Å is 2 mm. What will be the fringe width, if the entire apparatus is immersed in a liquid of refractive index 1.33?**

Sol. As, $\beta = \frac{D\lambda}{d}$ and $\beta_1 = \frac{D\lambda_1}{d}$

$$\therefore \quad \frac{\beta_1}{\beta} = \frac{\frac{D\lambda_1}{d}}{\frac{D\lambda}{d}} = \frac{\lambda_1}{\lambda} = \frac{1}{\mu} \quad \text{or} \quad \beta_1 = \frac{\beta}{\mu} = \frac{2}{1.33} = 1.5 \text{ mm}$$

Example 5. **Distance between the slits, in YDSE, shown in figure is $d = 20\,\lambda$, where λ is the wavelength of light used. Find the angle θ, where**

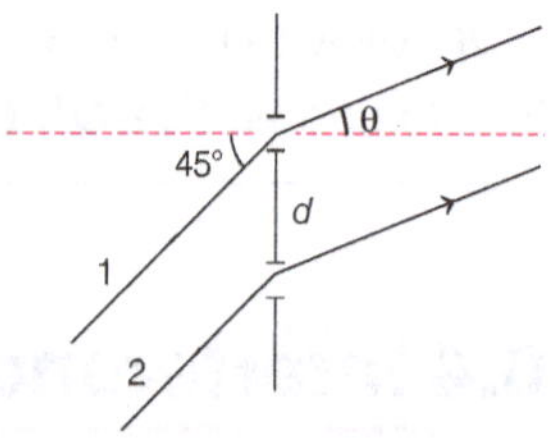

(i) central maxima (where path difference is zero) is obtained.

(ii) third order maxima is obtained.

Sol. Ray 1 has a longer path than that of ray 2 by a distance $d \sin 45°$, before reaching the slits. Afterwards ray 2 has a path longer than ray 1 by a distance $d \sin\theta$. The net path difference is therefore, $d \sin\theta - d \sin 45°$.

(i) Central maxima is obtained where net path difference is zero.

$\therefore \quad d \sin\theta - d \sin 45° = 0 \Rightarrow \quad \theta = 45°$

(ii) Third order maxima is obtained, where net path difference is 3 λ, i.e.

$$d \sin\theta - d\sin 45° = 3\lambda \Rightarrow \quad \sin\theta = \sin 45° + \frac{3\lambda}{d}$$

Putting $d = 20\lambda$, we have

$$\sin\theta = \sin 45° + \frac{3\lambda}{20\lambda}$$

$\therefore \quad \theta \approx 59°$

Conditions for Sustained Interference

In order to obtain a well defined observable interference pattern, following conditions must be satisfied

(i) The two sources of light must be coherent.

(ii) The two sources must be very close to each other and the pattern must be observed at a larger distance to have sufficient width of the fringe $\left(\frac{D\lambda}{d}\right)$.

(iii) The sources must be monochromatic.

(iv) The two waves must be having same amplitude for better contrast between bright and dark fringes.

Quick Test 2

Conceptual Questions

1. Define the term "coherent sources" which are required to produce interference pattern in Young's double slit experiment.

2. What are the conditions for obtaining two coherent sources of light?

3. Why we cannot obtain interference using two independent sources of light?

4. Write the conditions on path difference under which (a) constructive and (b) destructive interference occur in Young's double slit experiment. *Delhi 2020*

5. How will the fringe pattern change, if the screen is moved away from the slits?

6. In Young's double slit experiment, the intensity of central maxima is I. What will be the intensity at the same place, if one slit is closed?

Numerical Questions

7. The intensity at the central maxima O in a Young's double slit experiment is I_0. If the distance OP equals one-third of the fringe width of the pattern, the intensity at point P would be ....

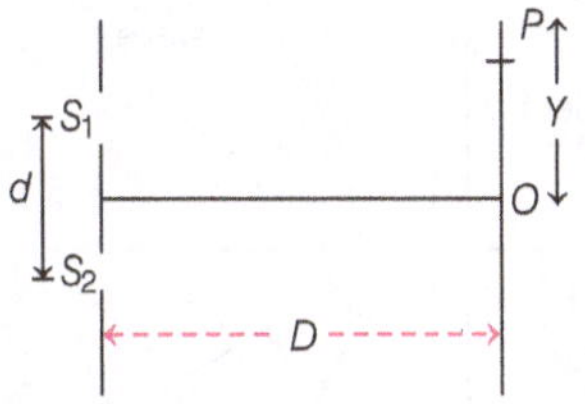

NCERT Exemplar

8. In Young's double slit experiment, two coherent sources S_1 and S_2 are placed at a distance D from screen, such that a bright fringe is obtained at a distance x from the centre line of screen. Give the value of x for which there is a bright fringe.

9. Light waves from coherent sources arrive at two points on a screen with path difference of 0 and λ. Find the ratio of intensities at the points.

10. In Young's double slit experiment, the slits are separated by 0.28 mm and the screen is placed 1.4 m away. The distance between the central bright fringe and the fourth bright fringe is measured to be 1.2 cm, determine the wavelength of light used in the experiment. *NCERT*

Answers

7. $\frac{I_0}{4}$ *9.* 1   *10.* 6×10^{-7} m

For Solutions, See QR Code on Pg. 347

10.5 Diffraction of Light

The phenomenon of bending of light around the sharp corners and the spreading of light within the geometrical shadow of the opaque obstacles is called **diffraction of light.** In result light deviates from its linear path. The deviation becomes much more pronounced, when the dimensions of the aperture or the obstacle are comparable to the **wavelength** of light.

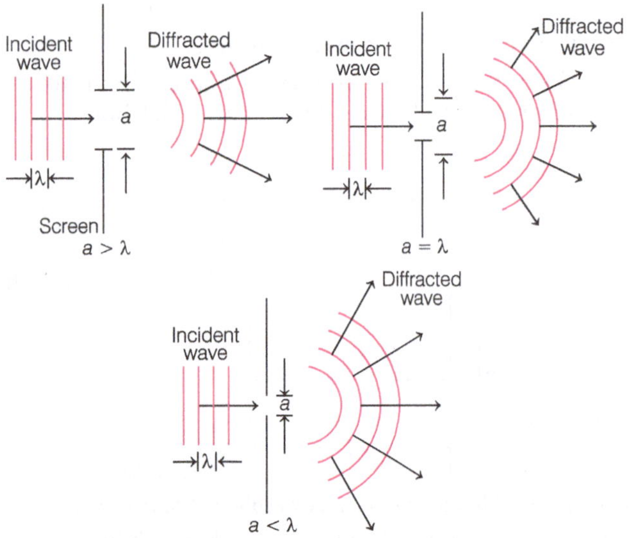

Diffraction of waves for slits of different width

Diffraction of Light at a Single Slit

A parallel beam of light with a plane wavefront is made to fall on a single slit LN. As width of the slit $LN = a$ is of the order of wavelength of light, therefore diffraction occurs when beam of light passes through the slit.

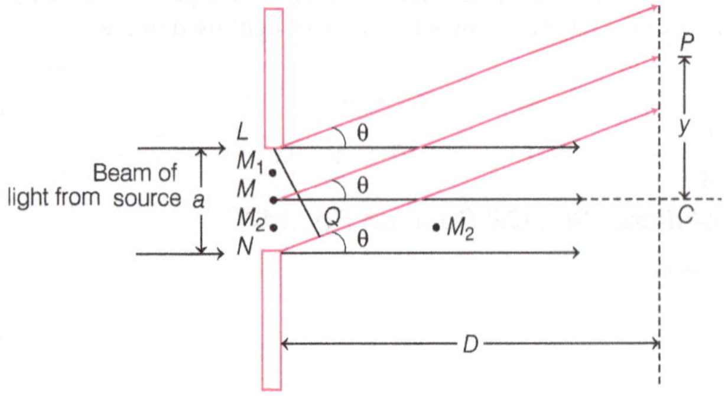

Geometry of single slit diffraction

The wavelets from the single wavefront reach the centre C on the screen in same phase. Hence, interfere constructively to give central maximum (bright fringe).

The diffraction pattern obtained on the screen consists of a central bright band, having alternate dark and weak bright bands of decreasing intensity on both sides.

for ***n*th secondary minima**, the slit can be divided into $2n$ equal parts.

Hence, for nth secondary minima,

$$\text{Path difference} = \frac{a}{2}\sin\theta = \frac{\lambda}{2} \qquad \ldots\text{(i)}$$

or

$$\boxed{\sin\theta_n = \frac{n\lambda}{a}, \ (n = 1, 2, 3, \ldots)}$$

for ***n*th secondary maxima**, the slit can be divided into $(2n+1)$ equal parts.

Hence, for nth secondary maxima,

$$a\sin\theta_n = (2n+1)\frac{\lambda}{2} \qquad [n = 1, 2, 3, \ldots]$$

or

$$\boxed{\sin\theta_n = (2n+1)\frac{\lambda}{2a}}$$

Graphical representation of diffraction pattern

The diffraction pattern can be graphically shown as below

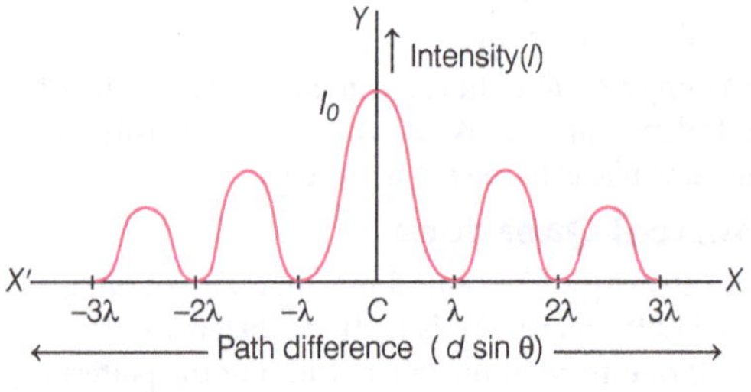

The point C corresponds to the position of central maxima and the position $-3\lambda, -2\lambda, -\lambda, \lambda, 2\lambda, 3\lambda \ldots$ are secondary minima. The above conditions for diffraction maxima and minima are exactly reverse of mathematical conditions for interference maxima and minima.

Width of Central Maximum

It is the distance between first secondary minimum on either side of the central bright fringe C.

For first secondary minimum, from (i)

$$a \sin\theta = \lambda \quad \text{or} \quad \sin\theta = \frac{\lambda}{a} \quad \text{...(ii)}$$

If θ is small, $\sin\theta \approx \theta = \frac{y}{D}$ ...(iii)

From Eqs. (ii) and (iii), we get

$$\frac{y}{D} = \frac{\lambda}{a} \quad \text{or} \quad y = \frac{D\lambda}{a}$$

$$\text{Width of central maximum} = 2y = \frac{2D\lambda}{a}$$

As, the slit width a increases, width of central maximum decreases.

$$\therefore \quad \text{Angular width of central maxima, } 2\theta = \frac{2\lambda}{a}$$

Difference Between Interference and Diffraction

The some important points of difference is given below in table.

Interference	Diffraction
Width of fringes in equal in interference	Width of fringes is unequal in diffraction
The intensity of all bright fringes is same interference	Intensity of fringes is not same in diffraction
The direction of wave propagation does not change in diffraction	There is change in direction of propagation of wave in diffraction.

Diffraction is a general characteristic exhibited by all types of wave. For visible light λ is very small ($\approx 10^{-6}$ m), therefore, **diffraction of visible light is not so common as obstacles/ apertures of this size are hardly available.**

TEACHER TIP

In interference and diffraction, light energy is redistributed. If it reduces in one region, producing a dark fringe, it increases in another region, producing a bright fringe. There is no gain or loss of energy, which is consistent with the principle of conservation of energy.

Quick Test 3

1. Why is the diffraction of sound waves more evident in daily experience than that of light wave? *NCERT Exemplar*
2. Explain how the intensity of diffraction pattern changes as the order(n) of the diffraction band varies?
3. In a single slit diffraction experiment, the width of the slit is decreased. How will the (a) size and (b) intensity of the central bright band be affected? Justify your answer. *Delhi 2020*
4. What should be the width of each slit to obtain n-maxima of double slit pattern within the central maxima of single slit pattern? *CBSE SQP 2023*
5. In double slit experiment SS_2 is greater than SS_1 by 0.25 λ. Calculate the path difference between two interfering beam from S_1 and S_2 for minima and maxima on the point P as shown in figure.

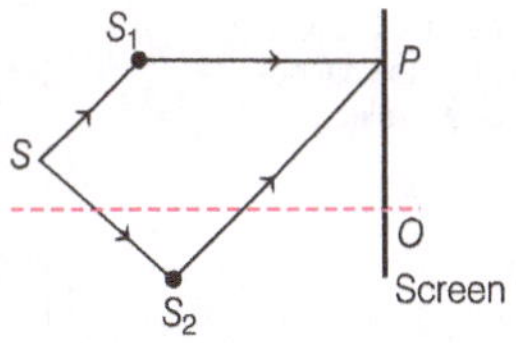

For Solutions, See QR Code on Pg. 347

Mind Map

Wave Optics

Wavefront

It is the continuous locus of all such particles of the medium which are vibrating in the same phase at any instant.

- **Spherical Wavefront**
  In case of waves travelling in all directions from a point source, the wavefronts are spherical in shape.

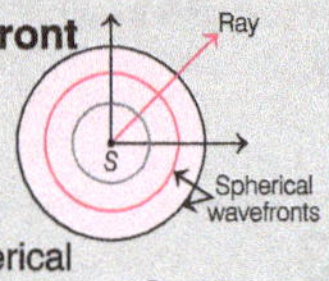

- **Cylindrical Wavefront**
  When the source of light is linear in shape, the wavefronts are cylindrical.

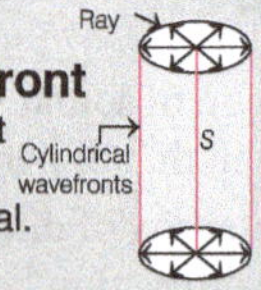

- **Plane Wavefront**
  At very large distances from the source, a portion of spherical or cylindrical wavefront is plane wavefront.

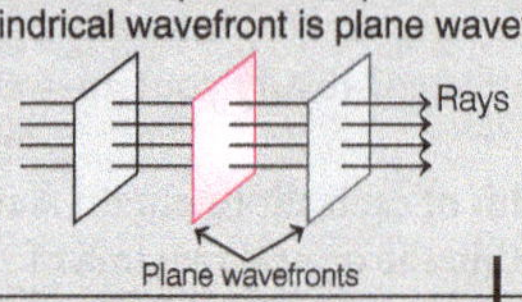

Huygen's Principle

The wave theory of light tells how a wavefront propagates through a medium.

Assumptions

(i) Each point on a wavefront acts as a source of new disturbance called secondary waves or wavelets.

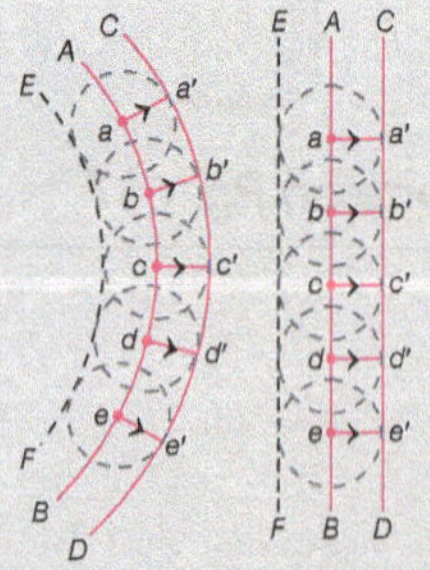

(ii) The secondary wavelets spread out in all directions with the speed of wave in the given medium.

(iii) The wavefront at any later time is given by the forward envelope of the secondary wavelets at that time.

Interference of Light

The superposition of two coherent waves resulting in a pattern of alternating dark and bright fringes of equal width.

When two independent monochromatic waves of intensities I_1 and I_2 and phase difference ϕ meet at a point, then the resultant intensity is given as

$$I = I_1 + I_2 + 2\sqrt{I_1 + I_2}\cos\phi$$

The term $2\sqrt{I_1 + I_2}\cos\phi = 1$ is called the interference term.

For maximum intensity, $\cos\phi = 1$

$$I_{max} = (\sqrt{I_1} + \sqrt{I_2})^2$$

For minimum intensity, $\cos\phi = -1$

$$I_{min} = (\sqrt{I_1} - \sqrt{I_2})^2$$

Young's Double Slit Experiment

Two identical narrow slits S_1 and S_2 are placed symmetrically with respect to narrow slit S illuminated with monochromatic light. The interference pattern is obtained on an observation screen placed at large distance D from S_1 and S_2.

The position of nth bright fringe from the centre of screen is $x_n = n\dfrac{D\lambda}{d}$

The position of nth dark fringe from the centre of the screen is $x'_n = (2n-1)\dfrac{D\lambda}{2d}$

Expression for Fringe Width

Fringe width is the separation between two successive bright or dark fringes and is given by $\beta = \dfrac{D\lambda}{d}$

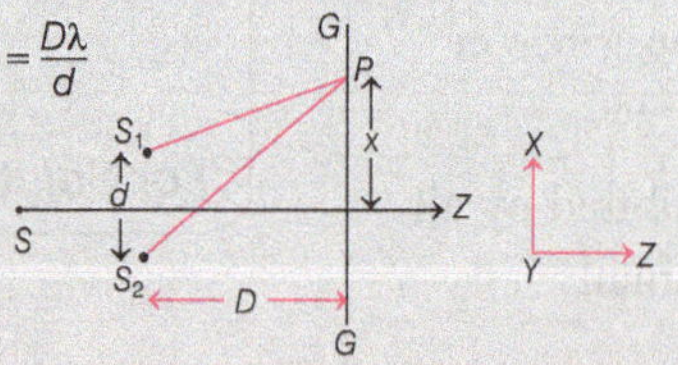

Coherent and Incoherent Sources

Coherent sources are light sources that emit waves with a constant phase relationship and the same frequency, leading to stable interference patterns (e.g., lasers).

Incoherent sources emit waves with random phase relationships and varying frequencies, resulting in unstable interference patterns (e.g., sunlight, incandescent bulbs).

Diffraction of Light

The phenomenon of bending of light around the corners of small obstacles or apertures and their consequent spreading into the regions of geometrical shadow is called diffraction of light.

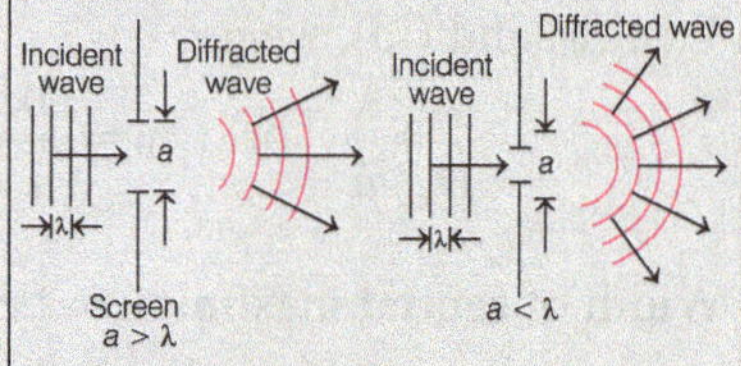

Diffraction of waves for slits of different width

Diffraction due to Single slit

A parallel beam of light with a plane wavefront is made to fall on a single slit LN. As width of the slit $LN = a$ is of the order of wavelength of light, therefore diffraction occurs when beam of light passes through the slit.

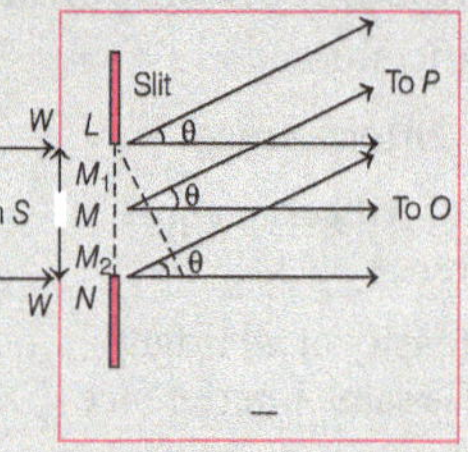

- **For nth minimum**
  $a\sin\theta_n = n\lambda$, where $n = 1, 2, 3, \ldots$
- **For nth secondary maximum**
  $a\sin\theta_n = (2n-1)\dfrac{\lambda}{2}$, where $n = 1, 2, 3, \ldots$
- **Width of a secondary maximum**
- **Width of central maximum** $\beta = \dfrac{D\lambda}{a}$,

$$\beta_0 = 2\beta = \frac{2D\lambda}{a}$$

Conditions for Sustained Interference

- The sources must be coherent.
- The light sources must emit light of a single wavelength (monochromatic).
- The path difference between the two waves must remain constant.

EXAM PATTERN QUESTIONS

Objective Type Questions

Multiple Choice Questions (MCQs)

1. Spherical wavefronts, emanating from a point source, strike a plane reflecting surface. Will there be any change in the shape of wavefronts, immediately after reflection? **Competency Based Que.**

(a) They will remain spherical will the same curvature and same direction of propagation.
(b) They will become plane wave fronts.
(c) They will remain spherical, with the same curvature, but direction of propagation is reversed.
(d) They will remain spherical, but with different curvature and different direction of propagation.

2. A plane wavefront is incident on a concave mirror of radius of curvature *R*. The radius of the reflected wavefront will be **CBSE 2023**

(a) $2R$ (b) R
(c) $\frac{R}{2}$ (d) $\frac{R}{4}$

3. In the wave picture of light, the intensity *I* of light is related to the amplitude *A* of the wave as **CBSE 2023**

(a) $I \propto \sqrt{A}$
(b) $I \propto A$
(c) $I \propto A^2$
(d) $I \propto \frac{1}{A^2}$

4. According to Huygens' principle, the amplitude of secondary wavelets is **CBSE 2023**

(a) equal in both the forward and the backward directions
(b) maximum in the forward direction and zero in the backward direction
(c) large in the forward direction and small in the backward direction
(d) small in the forward direction and large in the backward direction

5. Huygen assumed that light waves are

(a) transverse waves and require a medium to travel.
(b) longitudinal waves and require a medium to travel.
(c) longitudinal waves and require no medium to travel.
(d) transverse waves and require no medium to travel

6. Figure shows a standard two slit arrangement with slits S_1, S_2, P_1, P_2 are the two minima points on either side of *P* (figure).

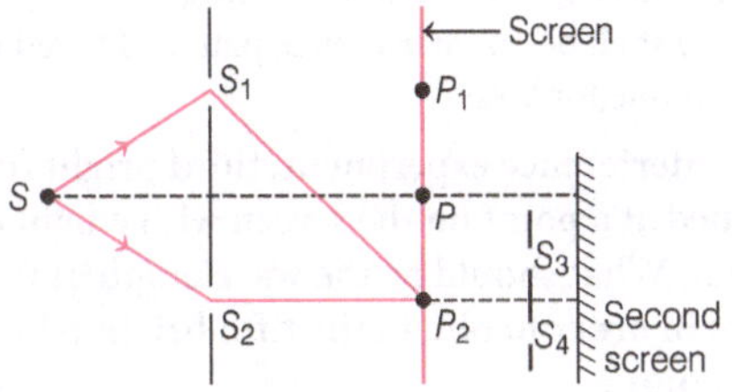

At P_2 on the screen, there is a hole and behind P_2 is a second 2-slit arrangement with slits S_3, S_4 and a second screen behind them.

(a) There would be no interference pattern on the second screen but it would be lighted.
(b) The second screen would be totally dark .
(c) There would be a single bright point on the second screen.
(d) There would be a regular two slit pattern on the second screen.

7. When a wave undergoes reflection at an interface from rarer to denser medium, then change in its phase is **All India 2020**

(a) $\frac{\pi}{2}$ (b) zer (c) π (d) $\frac{\pi}{4}$

8. Consider a ray of light incident from air onto a slab of glass (refractive index *n*) of width *d*, at an angle θ. The phase difference between the ray reflected by the top surface of the glass and the bottom surface is **NCERT Exemplar**

(a) $\frac{4\pi d}{\lambda}\left(1-\frac{1}{n^2}\sin^2\theta\right)^{1/2}+\pi$
(b) $\frac{4\pi d}{\lambda}\left(1-\frac{1}{n^2}\sin^2\theta\right)^{1/2}$
(c) $\frac{4\pi d}{\lambda}\left(1-\frac{1}{n^2}\sin^2\theta\right)^{1/2}+\frac{\pi}{2}$
(d) $\frac{4\pi d}{\lambda}\left(1-\frac{1}{n^2}\sin^2\theta\right)^{1/2}+2\pi$

9. A magician puts some glass object into a liquid, the object gets disappeared. Then,

(a) the refractive index of object is more than that of liquid
(b) the refractive index of object is less than that of liquid
(c) the refractive index of object is equal to that of liquid
(d) Data insufficient

10. **In a Young's double slit experiment, the source is white light. One of the holes is covered by a red filter and another by a blue filter. In this case,** NCERT Exemplar

(a) there shall be alternate interference patterns of red and blue
(b) there shall be an interference pattern for red distinct from that for blue
(c) there shall be no interference fringes
(d) there shall be an interference pattern for red mixing with one for blue

11. **In an interference experiment, third bright fringe is obtained at a point on the screen with a light of 700 nm. What should be the wavelength of the light source in order to obtain the fifth bright fringe at the same point ?** CBSE 2023

(a) 420 nm (b) 750 nm
(c) 630 nm (d) 500 nm

12. **In a Young's double slit experiment, the path difference at a certain point on the screen between two interfering waves is $\frac{1}{8}$th of the wavelength. The ratio of intensity at this point to that at the centre of a bright fringe is close to** CBSE 2023

(a) 0.80 (b) 0.74 (c) 0.94 (d) 0.85

13. **The diffraction effect can be observed in** CBSE SQP 2024-25

(a) sound waves only
(b) light waves only
(c) ultrasonic waves only
(d) sound waves as well as light waves

14. **In Young's double slit experiment using sodium light ($\lambda = 5898Å$), 92 fringes are seen. If greenish colour (5480Å) is used, how many fringes will be seen?** Competency Based Que.

(a) 62 (b) 99
(c) 67 (d) 85

15. **The fringe width in YDSE is β. If the whole set-up is immersed in a liquid of refractive index μ, then the new fringe width will be**

(a) β (b) β / μ
(c) $\beta\mu$ (d) β / μ^2

16. **Consider sunlight incident on a slit of width 10^4 Å. The image seen through the slit shall** NCERT Exemplar

(a) be a fine sharp slit white in colour at the centre
(b) a bright slit white at the centre diffusing to zero intensities at the edges
(c) a bright slit white at the centre diffusing to regions of different colours
(d) only be a diffused slit white in colour

17. **A light wave of wavelength λ, frequency ν and velocity v enters in oil (refractive index μ) from air. The frequency, wavelength and velocity in the oil will be respectively.**

(a) $\frac{2\nu}{\mu}, \frac{\lambda}{\mu}$ and v
(b) $\nu, 2\lambda$ and $\frac{v}{\mu}$
(c) $\frac{\nu}{\mu}, \frac{\lambda}{\mu}$ and $\frac{v}{\mu}$
(d) $\nu, \frac{\lambda}{\mu}$ and $\frac{v}{\mu}$

18. **The Young's double slit experiment is performed with blue light (4360Å) and then with green light (5460Å). If x is the distance of 4th maxima from the central one, the observations say that**

(a) $x_{\text{blue}} > x_{\text{green}}$ (b) $\frac{x_{\text{blue}}}{x_{\text{green}}} = \frac{5460}{4360}$
(c) $x_{\text{blue}} < x_{\text{green}}$ (d) $x_{\text{blue}} = x_{\text{green}}$

19. **The slits are moved toward the source of light in Young's double slit experiment. What changes will you see in (i) angular reparation of fringes and (ii) fringe-width.** Competency Based Que.

(a) Both (i) and (ii) remain constant
(b) (i) remains constant but (ii) increases
(c) (i) remains constant but (ii) decreases
(d) Both (i) and (ii) increases

20. **A third slit's introduced in between the double slits of Young's double slit experiment, then** Competency Based Que.

(a) intensity of fringes totally disappears
(b) contrast between bright and dark fringes is reduced.
(c) Only bright light is observed.
(d) fringes of unequal width are formed.

21. **Nishchay performs YDSE by using yellow, blue and red lights in turn. If the fringe width measures in three cases are x_1, x_2 and x_3, respectively then which of the following is correct?**

(a) $x_1 > x_2 > x_3$
(b) $x_3 > x_1 > x_2$
(c) $x_2 > x_1 > x_3$
(d) $x_1 < x_2 < x_3$

22. **When monochromatic light is replaced by white light in a single slit experiment, then**

(a) the diffraction pattern disappears
(b) the diffraction band becomes circular
(c) a white band is formed at the centre and coloured bands are formed at both its sides
(d) only a white band is formed at the centre

23. Consider a light beam incident from air to a glass slab at Brewster's angle as shown in figure.

A polaroid is placed in the path of the emergent ray at point *P* and rotated about an axis passing through the centre and perpendicular to the plane of the polaroid.

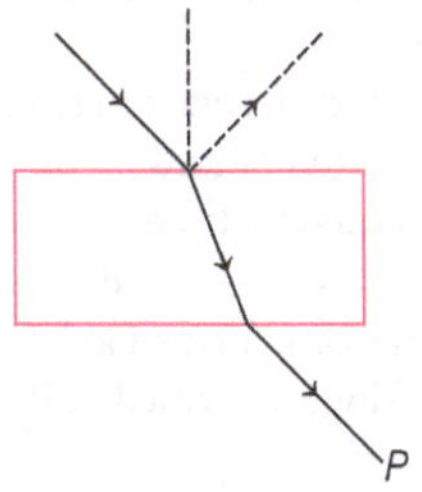

(a) For a particular orientation, there shall be darkness as observed through the polaroid
(b) The intensity of light as seen through the polaroid shall be independent of the rotation
(c) The intensity of light as seen through the polaroid shall go through a minimum but not zero for two orientations of the polaroid
(d) The intensity of light as seen through the polaroid shall go through a minimum for four orientations of the polaroid

24. Match the Column I with Column II.

Column I	Column II
A. Coherent sources	1. $n\lambda$ path difference
B. Condition for constructive interference	2. Distance between adjecent slits in YDSE
C. Fring width Competency Based	3. Monochromatic, constant phase difference
D. Condition for minima in single slit diffraction	4. $\lambda/2$
E. Path difference in distructive interference	5. $a \sin\theta = n\lambda$

(a) A-2, B-3, C-1, D-4, E-5 (b) A-3, B-2, C-5, D-4, E-1
(c) A-3, B-1, C-2, D-5, E-4 (d) A-1, B-2, C-3, D-4, E-5

25. Match the Column I with Column II.

Column I	Column II
A. When width of one slit is slightly increased	1. fringe width will increase.
B. When wavelength of light increased (in YDSE)	2. fringe width will decrease.
C. When distance between slits and screen incereased	3. fringe width will increase.
D. In YDSE appratus immersed in liquid	4. maximum intensity will decrease.

(a) A-4, B-1, C-3, D-2 (b) A-1, B-2, C-3, D-4
(c) A-2, B-1, C-4, D-3 (d) A-3, B-4, C-2, D-1

Assertion-Reason

Directions *(Q. Nos. 26-32) In the following questions, two statements are given- one labelled Assertion (A) and the other labelled Reason (R). Select the correct answer to these questions from the codes (a), (b), (c) and (d) as given below.*

(a) Both A and R are true and R is the correct explanation of A.
(b) Both A and R are true but R is not the correct explanation of A.
(c) A is true but R is false.
(d) A is false but R is true.

26. **Assertion (A)** In the field of geometrical optics, light can be assumed to approximately travel in straight line.

Reason (R) The wavelength of visible light is very small in comparison to the dimensions of typical mirrors and lenses, then light can be assumed to approximately travel in straight line.

Competency Based Que.

27. **Assertion (A)** When monochromatic light is incident on a surface separating two media, the reflected and refracted lights both have the same frequency as the incident frequency.

Reason (R) Speed of light and wavelength of light both changes in refraction and hence, the ratio $v = c/\lambda$ is a constant. **Competency Based Que.**

28. **Assertion (A)** The emergent plane wavefront is tilted on refraction of a plane wave by a thin prism.

Reasons (R) The speed of light waves is more in glass and the base of the prism is thicker than the top.

Competency Based Que.

29. **Assertion (A)** Interference pattern is made by using blue light instead of red light, the fringes becomes narrower.

Reason (R) In Young's double slit experiment, fringe width is given by relation.

$$\beta = \frac{\lambda D}{d}$$

CBSE 2024

30. **Assertion (A)** In Young's double slit experiment, the fringe width for dark fringes is same as that for white fringes.

Reason (R) In Young's double slit experiment, when the fringes are performed with a source of white light, then only dark and bright fringes are observed.

31. **Assertion (A)** In an interference pattern observed in Young's double slit experiment, if the separation (d) between coherent sources as well as the distance (D) of the screen from the coherent sources both are reduced to 1/3rd, then new fringe width remains the same.

Reason (R) Fringe width is proportional to (d/D).

CBSE 2023

32. **Assertion (A)** To observe diffraction of light the size of obstacle aperture should be of the order of 10^{-7} m.

Reason (R) 10^{-7} m is the order of wavelength of visible light.

Case Based Questions

Directions *(Q.Nos. 33-34) These questions are case study based questions. Read the following paragraph and answer the questions on the basis of same.*

33. **The British physicist Thomas Young explained the interference of light using the principle of superposition of waves. He observed the interference pattern on the screen, in his experimental set-up, now as known Young's double slit experiment.**

The two slits S_1 and S_2 were illuminated by light from a slit S. The interference pattern consists of dark and bright bands of light. Such bands are called fringes. The distance between two consecutive bright and dark fringes is called fringe width. **CBSE 2022 (Term-II)**

(i) What will happen to the pattern on the screen, when the two slits S_1 and S_2 are replaced by two independent but identical sources?
   (a) The intensity of pattern will increase.
   (b) The intensity of pattern will decrease
   (c) The number of fringes will become double
   (d) No pattern will be observed on the screen

(ii) Two sources of light are said to be coherent, when both emit light waves of
   (a) same amplitude and have a varying phase difference
   (b) same wavelength and a constant phase difference
   (c) different wavelengths and same intensity
   (d) different wavelengths and a constant phase difference

(iii) The total path difference between two waves meeting at points P_1 and P_2 on the screen are $(3\lambda/2)$ and 2λ respectively, then
   (a) bright fringes are formed at both points
   (b) dark fringes are formed at both points
   (c) a bright fringe is formed at P_1 and a dark fringe is formed at P_2
   (d) a bright fringe is formed at P_2 and a dark fringe is formed at P_1

34. **In 1802, Young experimentally demonstrated the phenomenon of interference of light. The intensity distribution takes place such that at some point maximum intensity is observed known as constructive interference, and some other points minimum intensity is observed known as destructive interference.**

(i) What will be the phase difference in case of constructive interference?

(ii) What will be the interference pattern when one slit is covered with red glass and another slit is covered with green glass?

(iii) What is the interference pattern, if slits are situated at larger distance.

(iv) Why a thin film of oil on the surface of water appears coloured?

Subjective Questions

Very Short Answer Type Questions

1. Show the refraction of light wave at a plane interface using Huygens' principle and prove Snell's law. **CBSE 2025**

2. State two condition for two lights to be coherent. **CBSE 2022**

3. In a wave picture of light, intensity of light is determined by the square of the amplitude of the wave. What determines the intensity of light in the photon picture of light? **Competency Based Que.**

4. What is the effect on the interference pattern in Young double slit experiment when **Competency Based Que.**

(i) the screen is moved closer to the slit? **[1]**

(ii) the separation between slits is increased? **[1]**

5. Why is interference pattern is not detected when two coherent sources are

(i) far apart **[1]**

(ii) infinitely close to each other. **[1]**

6. What is the effect on the interference fringes in a Young's double slit experiment, if the monochromatic source S is replaced by a source of white light? **CBSE 2023**

7. How does the fringe width of interference fringes changes, when the whole apparatus of Young's experiment is kept in a liquid of refractive index 1.3? **Competency Based Que.**

Short Answer Type Questions

8. State Huygen's principle. With the help of a diagram show how a plane wave is reflected from a surface? Hence, verify the law of reflection. **CBSE 2023**

9. A plane wavefront is propagating from a rarer into a denser medium. Use Huygens principle to show the refracted wavefront and verify Snell's law. **CBSE 2022, Term-II**

10. Write two points of difference between an interference pattern and a diffraction pattern. **CBSE SQP 2023**

11. In Young's double slit experiment using monochromatic light of wavelength λ, the intensities of two sources is I. What is the intensity of light at a point where path difference between wavefront is $\lambda/4$? **CBSE SQP 2024-25**

12. (i) The interference pattern is not observed in Young's double slit experiment when the two sources S_1 and S_2 are far apart. Explain. **[1]**

(ii) Mention the conditions for the two sources to be coherent. **[1]**

(iii) What is the effect on the interference pattern in a Young's double slit experiment, if the source of wavelength λ is replaced by another source of wavelength 1.5 λ, with interference pattern still observable? **CBSE 2022, Term-II** **[1]**

13. In a Young's double slit experiment $SS_2 - SS_1 = \frac{\lambda}{4}$, where S_1 and S_2 are the two slits as shown in the figure. Find the path difference $(S_2P - S_1P)$ for constructive and destructive interference at P. **CBSE 2023**

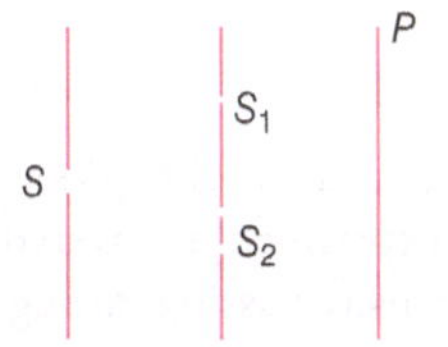

14. The intensity of the two interfering waves in Young's double slit experiment is I_0 each. Find the intensity at a point on the screen, where path difference between the interfering waves in (a) $\frac{\lambda}{2}$ and (b) $\frac{\lambda}{3}$ **CBSE 2024C**

15. In the experiment on diffraction due to a single slit, show that

(i) the intensity of diffraction fringes decreases as the order increases **[1½]**

(ii) angular width of the central miximum is twice that of the first order secondary maximum. **[1½]**

Long Answer Type Questions

16. Define the following terms and give its source of origin.

(i) Spherical wavefront **[1]**

(ii) Plane wavefront **[2]**

(iii) Cylindrical wavefront **[2]**

17. What is the shape of the wavefront in each of the following cases?

(i) Light diverging from point source. **[1]**

(ii) Light emerging out of a convex lens when a point source is placed at its focus. **[2]**

(iii) The portion of the wavefront of light from a distant star intercepted by the earth. **NCERT** **[2]**

18. (i) Differentiate between a wavefront and a ray. **[1]**

(ii) State Huygens' principle and verify laws of reflection using suitable diagram. **[2]**

(iii) In Young's double slit experiment, the slits S_1 and S_2 are 3 mm apart and the screen is placed 1.0 m away from the slits. It is observed that the fourth bright fringe is at a distance of 5 mm from the second dark fringe. Find the wavelength of light used. **CBSE 2024** **[2]**

19. (i) Define a wavefront. **[1]**

(ii) Draw the diagram to show the shape of plane wavefront as they pass through

(a) a thin prism and

(b) a thin convex lens. State the nature of refracted wavefront. **[2]**

(iii) Verify Snell's law of refraction using Huygens' principle. **CBSE SQP 2023** **[2]**

20. Define the term refractive index of a medium. Verify Snell's law of refraction when a plane wavefront is propagating from a denser to a rarer medium. **Delhi 2019**

21. (i) What is the effect on the interference fringes to a Young's double slit experiment when **[3]**

(a) the width of the source slit is increased?

(b) the monochromatic source is replaced by a source of white light? Justify your answer in each case.

(ii) The intensity at the central maxima in Young's double slit experiment set-up is I_0. Show that the intensity at a point, where the path difference is $\lambda/3$ is $I_0/4$. **Competency Based Que.** **[2]**

22. Four identical monochromatic sources A, B, C and D as shown in the figure produce waves of the same wavelength λ and are coherent. Two receivers R_1 and R_2 are at great but equal distances from B.

(i) Which of the two receivers picks up the larger signal with B is turned off? **[2]**

(ii) Which of the two receivers picks up the larger signal when D is turned off? **[3]**

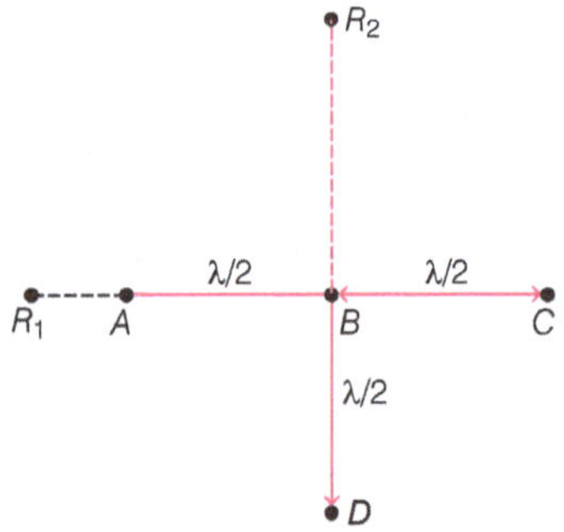

$$R_1B = d = R_2\ B$$
$$AB = BC = BD = \lambda/2$$

23. The refractive index is defined as $\sqrt{\mu_r \varepsilon_r} = n$. For ordinary material, $\varepsilon_r > 0$ and $\mu_r > 0$ and the positive sign is taken for the square root.

In 1964, a Russian scientist V. Veselago postulated the existence of material with $\varepsilon_r < 0$ and $\mu_r < 0$.

(i) According to the description above show that, if rays of light enter such a medium from air (refractive index = 1) at an angle θ in 2nd quadrant, then the refracted beam is in the 3rd quadrant. **[2]**

(ii) Prove that Snell's law holds for such a medium. **[3]**

24. (i) In a Young's double slit experiment the separation between the two slits is d and distance of the screen from the slits is $1000\,d$. If the first minima falls at a distance d from the central maximum. Obtain the relation between d and λ. **[2½]**

(ii) When a tiny circular obstacle is placed in the path of light from a distant source, a bright spot is seen at the centre of the obstacle. Explain, why? **CBSE 2023** **[2½]**

Numerical Problems

Young's Double Slit Experiment (YDSE)

25. A beam of light consisting of two wavelengths 4000Å and 6000Å, is used to obtain interference fringes in a Young's double slit experiment. What is the least distance from the central maximum, where the dark fringe is obtained? **CBSE SQP 2024-25**

26. Monochromatic light of wavelength 589 nm is incident from air on a water surface. What are the wavelength, frequency and speed of

(i) reflected and

(ii) refracted light? (μ of water is 1.33) **NCERT**

27. A beam of light consisting of two wavelengths 650 nm and 520 nm, is used to obtain interference fringes in a Young's double slit experiment.

(i) Find the distance of the third bright fringe on the screen from the central maximum for wavelength 650 nm.

(ii) What is the least distance from the central maximum, where the bright fringes due to both the wavelengths coincide? **NCERT**

28. Laser light of wavelength 630 nm incident on a pair of slits produces an interference pattern in which the bright fringes are separated by 7.2 mm. Calculate the wavelength of another source of laser light which produce interference fringes separated by 8.1 mm using same pair of slits.

29. In a double-slit experiment, 6th dark fringe is observed at a certain point of the screen. A transparent sheet of thickness t and refractive index n is now introduced in the path of one of the two interfering waves to increase its phase by $2\pi(n-1)t/\lambda$. The pattern is shifted and 8th bright fringe is observed at the same point. Find the relation for thickness t in terms of n and λ? **CBSE 2025**

30. Consider a two slit interference arrangements (figure) such that the distance of the screen from the slits is half the distance between the slits. Obtain the value of D in terms of λ such that the first minima on the screen falls at a distance D from the centre O. **NCERT Exemplar**

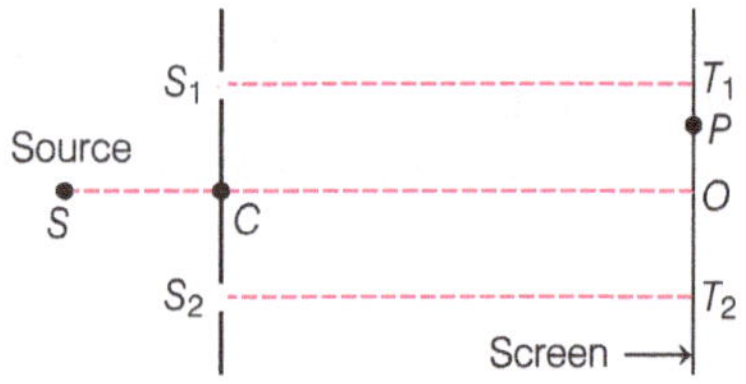

31. (i) If one of two identical slits producing interference in Young's experiment is covered with glass, so that the light intensity passing through it is reduced to 50%. Find the ratio of the maximum and minimum intensity of the fringe in the interference pattern.

(ii) What kind of fringes do you expect to observe, if white light is used instead of monochromatic light?

Diffraction at Single Slit

32. (i) Why cannot the phenomenon of interference be observed by illuminating two pin holes with two sodium lamps? **[2]**

(ii) Two wavelengths of sodium light of 590 nm and 596 nm are used in turn to study the diffraction taking place at a single slit of aperture 2×10^{-6} m. If the distance between the slit and the screen is 1.5 m, calculate the separation between the positions of the second maxima of diffraction pattern obtained in the two cases. **All India 2019** [3]

33. (i) Light consisting of two wavelengths 600 nm and 480 nm is used to obtain interference fringes in a double slit experiment. The screen is placed 1.0 m away from slits which are 1.0 nm apart.

(a) Calculate the distance of the third bright fringe on the screen from the central maximum for wavelength 600 nm. [3]

(b) Find the least distance from the central maximum where the bright fringes due to both the wavelengths coincide.

(ii) (a) Draw the variation of intensity with angle of diffraction in single slit diffraction pattern. Write the expression for value of angle corresponding to zero intensity locations.

(b) In what way diffraction of light waves differs from diffraction of sound waves? **CBSE 2025** [2]

Hints & Solutions

Objective Type Questions

1. (c)	3. (c)	4. (b)	5. (b)	7. (c)
9. (c)	13. (d)	14. (b)	15. (b)	17. (d)
18. (c)	20. (b)	21. (c)	22. (c)	24. (c)
25. (a)	26. (a)	27. (b)	28. (c)	29. (a)
30. (a)	31. (c)	32. (a)		

2. (c) After reflection all waves will meet at focus hence, radius of reflected wavefront will be half of radius of curvature.

6. (d) According to question, there is a hole at point P_2. From Huygen's principle, wave will propagate from the sources S_1 and S_2. Each point on the screen will act as secondary sources of wavelets.

Now, there is a hole at point P_2 (minima). The hole will act as a source of fresh light for the slits S_3 and S_4.

Therefore, there will be a regular two slit pattern on the second screen.

8. (a) Consider the diagram, the ray P is incident at an angle θ and gets reflected in the direction P' and refracted in the direction P''. Due to reflection from the glass medium, there is a phase change of π.

Time taken to travel along OP''

$$\Delta t = \frac{OP''}{v} = \frac{d/\cos r}{c/n} = \frac{nd}{c\cos r}$$

From Snell's law, $n = \dfrac{\sin\theta}{\sin r} \Rightarrow \sin r = \dfrac{\sin\theta}{n}$

$$\cos r = \sqrt{1-\sin^2 r} = \sqrt{1-\frac{\sin^2\theta}{n^2}}$$

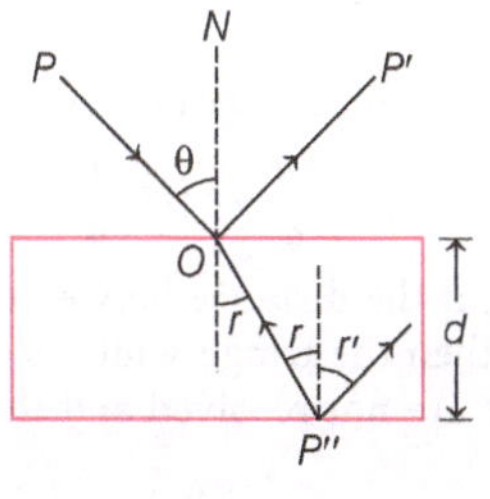

$$\therefore \Delta t = \frac{nd}{c\left(1-\dfrac{\sin^2\theta}{n^2}\right)^{1/2}} = \frac{n^2 d}{c}\left(1-\frac{\sin^2\theta}{n^2}\right)^{-1/2}$$

Phase difference $= \Delta\phi = \dfrac{2\pi}{T} \times \Delta t$

$$= \frac{2\pi nd}{\lambda}\left(1-\frac{\sin^2\theta}{n^2}\right)^{-1/2}$$

So, net phase difference $= \Delta\phi + \pi$

$$= \frac{4\pi d}{\lambda}\left(1-\frac{1}{n^2}\sin^2\theta\right)^{-1/2} + \pi$$

10. (c) There will be no interference because frequency of red and blue light is not same.

11. (a) At same spot, fringes coincide if $n_1\lambda_1 = n_2\lambda_2$

$\Rightarrow \quad 3 \times 700 = 5 \times \lambda_2 \Rightarrow \lambda_2 = 420$ nm

12. (d) Path difference, $\Delta x = \dfrac{\lambda}{8}$

Phase difference, $\Delta\phi = \dfrac{2\pi}{\lambda}\Delta x = \dfrac{\pi}{4}$

Intensity of fringe in terms of intensity of central maxima is given by

$$I = I_{max}\cos^2\left(\frac{\Delta\phi}{2}\right)$$

Now, $\dfrac{I}{I_{max}} = \cos^2\left(\dfrac{\pi}{8}\right) = 0.85$

16. (a) Given, width of the slit $= 10^4$ Å

$= 10^4 \times 10^{-10}$ m $= 10^{-6}$ m $= 1\,\mu$m

Wavelength of (visible) sunlight varies from 4000 Å to 8000 Å.

As the width of slit is comparable to that of wavelength, hence, diffraction occurs with maxima at centre. So, at the centre all colours appear *i.e.*, mixing of colours form white patch at the centre.

19. (b) On moving slits towards source, distance between screen and slit increases due to which fringe-width increase but angular separation remains constant.

23. (c) Consider the diagram the light beam incident from air to the glass slab at Brewster's angle (i_p). The incident ray is unpolarised and is represented by dot (.).

The reflected light is plane polarised represented by arrows.

As the emergent ray is unpolarised, hence intensity cannot be zero when passes through polaroid.

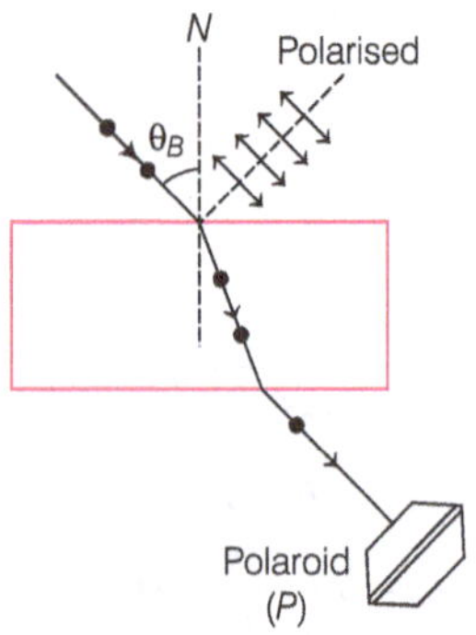

33. (i) (d) When two slits are replaced by two independent but identical sources, then no pattern will be observed on the screen as two identical sources cannot be coherent.

(ii) (b) Two sources of light are said to be coherent, when both emit light waves of same wavelength, same frequency and have a constant phase difference.

(iii) (d) Since at P_1, the path difference is of form $(2n-1)\frac{D\lambda}{2d}$, so a dark fringe is formed at P_1.

Similarly, at P_2, the path difference is form $\frac{nD\lambda}{d}$, so a bright fringe is formed at P_2.

34. (i) For constructive interference, $\cos\phi = +1$

$\Rightarrow \phi = 2n\pi,\ n = 0, 1, 2, \ldots$

$\therefore$ Phase difference is even multiple of π.

(ii) In the interference pattern, when one slit is covered with red glass and another slit is covered with green glass, then two monochromatic lights of different wavelengths are observed. It makes two incoherent sources of light. Hence, the interference pattern will not be observed.

(iii) The fringe width in interference pattern is given by

$$\beta = \frac{D\lambda}{d} \quad \Rightarrow \quad \beta \propto \frac{1}{d}$$

If the slits are situated at large distance, then the fringe width will be very small such that it will not resolved and the interference pattern is not detected.

(iv) A thin film of oil on the surface of water appears coloured due to interference.

Subjective Questions

1. Refer page no. 327 (Refraction (Snell's law) at a plane surface).

2. The condition must be satisfied for the source to be coherent are

(i) the two light waves should be of same wavelength.

(ii) the two light wave should be in same phase or zero phase difference.

3. For a given frequency, intensity of light in photon picture is determined by the number of photons crossing an unit area per unit time.

4. (i) When screen is moved away, D increases, therefore the width of the fringes increases.

(ii) As the source slit width increases, the fringe pattern gets less and less sharp. When the source slit is so wide the interference pattern disappears.

5. (i) We know $\beta \propto \frac{1}{d}$ Since d is very large β may reduce so much i.e, beyond visible region.

(ii) If d is too small, β becomes very large. It may be possible that the whole screen is occupied by only one fringe resulting no detection of pattern.

6. The central fringe will be white. The closest fringe on both sides of white fringe will be violet and the farthest fringe will be red.

7. The fringe width will decrease.

8. Refer to pages no. 326 and 327.

9. Refer to text on page 327.

10. Refer to text on Page. 333.

11. In Young's double slit experiment, if the intensity of the two sources are I and the path difference between the wave is $\frac{\lambda}{4}$.

$$\text{Phase difference} = \frac{2\pi\,(\text{Path difference})}{\lambda} = \frac{2\pi\left(\frac{\lambda}{4}\right)}{\lambda}$$

$$\Rightarrow \quad \phi = \frac{\pi}{2}$$

For monochromatic light,

$$I = I_1 + I_2 + 2\sqrt{I_1 I_2}\cos\phi$$

$$= 4I \quad \left(\because \cos\frac{\pi}{2} = 0 \text{ and } I_1 = I_2\right)$$

$\therefore$Intensity at point where path difference is $\frac{\lambda}{4}$ is $4I$.

12. (i) Fringe width of interference pattern is given by

$$\beta = \frac{D\lambda}{d} \Rightarrow \beta \propto \frac{1}{d}$$

Hence, if the distance between two slits d is very large, then the fringe width is so small that the fringes are not resolved and they do not appear separate. So, interference pattern is not detected for large separation of coherent sources.

(ii) Refer to text on Page. 329.

(iii) Fringe width in interference pattern is given by

$$\beta = \frac{D\lambda}{d}$$

At $\lambda' = 1.5\lambda$, $\beta' = \frac{D\lambda'}{d} = \frac{1.5\,D\lambda}{d} = 1.5\,\beta$

The interference pattern will be still observable with fringe width 1.5 times of the fringe width of previous case.

13. In YDSE,

Given, initial path difference $= SS_2 - SS_1 = \frac{\lambda}{4}$

Final path difference $= (S_2P - S_1P)$

$\therefore$ Total path difference,

$$\Delta x = \frac{\lambda}{4} + (S_2P - S_1P)$$

For constructive interference, $\Delta x = n\lambda = \frac{\lambda}{4} + (S_2P - S_1P)$

$$\therefore \quad (S_2P - S_1P) = \left(n - \frac{1}{4}\right)\lambda,$$

$$n = 0, 1, 2, \ldots\ldots$$

For destructive interference,

$$\Delta x = (2n-1)\cdot\frac{\lambda}{2} = \frac{\lambda}{4} + (S_2P - S_1P)$$

$$\therefore \quad (S_2P - S_1P) = \left(n - \frac{1}{2} - \frac{1}{4}\right)\lambda = \left(n - \frac{3}{4}\right)\lambda,\ n = 1, 2, 3, \ldots.$$

14. $I = 4I_0 \cos^2\frac{\phi}{2}$

(i) $\phi = \frac{2\pi}{\lambda} \times \frac{\lambda}{2} = \pi$

$$I = 4I_0\left(\cos\frac{\pi}{2}\right)^2 = 0$$

(ii) $\phi = \frac{2\pi}{\lambda} \times \frac{\lambda}{3} = \frac{2\pi}{3}$

$$I = 4I_0\left(\cos\frac{\pi}{3}\right)^2 \Rightarrow I = I_0$$

15. (i) The reason is that the intensity of central maximum is due to constructive interference of wavelets from all parts of slit, the first secondary maximum is due to contribution of wavelets from one third part of slit (wavelets from remaining two parts interfere destructively) the second secondary maximum is due to contribution of wavelets from one fifth part only and so on.

(ii) For 1st minima, $a\sin\theta = \lambda$ or $a\theta = \lambda$

Also, $\tan\theta = \frac{\lambda}{D}$ or $\theta = \frac{y_1}{D}$

$$\frac{ay_1}{D} = \lambda \text{ or } y_1 = \frac{\lambda D}{a} = y_2$$

where, y_1 and y_2 are distance of 1st minima on both side of central maxima.

Hence, the angular width of central maximum

$$= \frac{2\lambda D}{a}$$

width of secondary maxima = separation between nth and $(n+1)$ th minima

For minima $\theta_n = \frac{n\lambda}{d}$ and $\theta_{n+1} = \frac{(n+1)\lambda}{d}$

Now, angular width of secondary maxima = separation between nth and $(n+1)$th minima

Hence, β = Angular width $\times D = \frac{\lambda D}{d}$

Thus, central maxima has twice the angular width of secondary maxima.

16. Refer to text on pages 325 and 326.

17. (i) The geometrical shape of the wavefront would be diverging spherical front, as shown in figure.

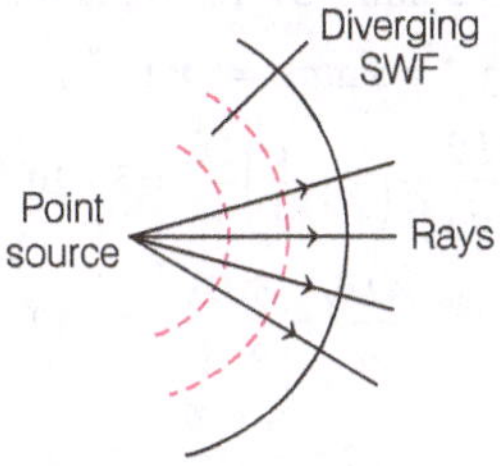

(ii) When a point source is placed at the focus of a convex lens, the rays emerging from the lens are parallel. Therefore, the wavefront must be plane, as shown in the figure.

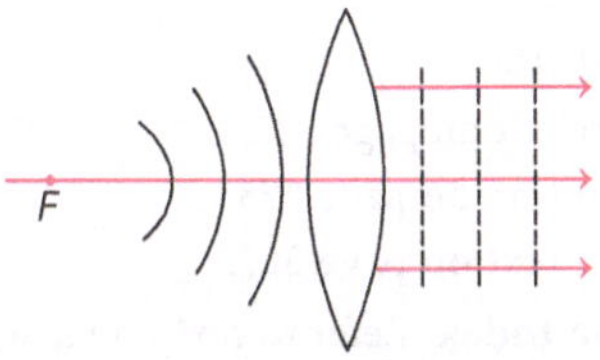

(iii) As the star (i.e. source of light) is very far off i.e. at infinity, the wavefront intercepted by earth must be a plane wavefront as shown in figure.

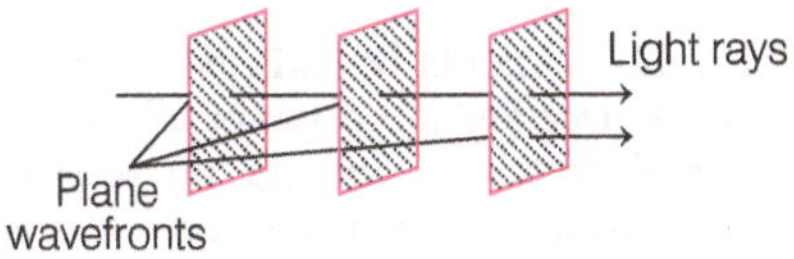

18. (i) A wavefront is defined as the locus of all the particles of a medium vibrating in the same phase at a given instant. The shape of a wavefront depends upon the shape of the source of disturbance and it is normal to the direction of propagation of wave.

A line drawn perpendicular to the plane wavefront gives the direction of propagation of a wave and is called ray of light.

(ii) According to Huygens' principle,

(a) Every point on a wavefront behaves like a light source and emits secondary wavelets. The secondary wavelets spread in all directions in space (or given medium) with the velocity of light.

(b) The envelope of wavefront of secondary wavelets, after a given time, along forward direction gives the new position of wavefront. The laws of reflection and refraction can be verified using Huygens' wave theory. Refer to text on page no. 326 (Reflection at a plane surface)

(iii) Position of nth maxima, $y_n = \frac{nD\lambda}{d}$ (Bright fringe) and

position of mth minima, $y_m = \left(m - \frac{1}{2}\right)\frac{D\lambda}{d}$ (Dark fringe)

Given, $d = 3\text{ mm} = 3 \times 10^{-3}\text{m}, D = 1\text{ m}$

and $y_4 - y_2' = 5\text{ mm} = 5 \times 10^{-3}\text{ m}$

Now, $\frac{4D\lambda}{d} - \left(2 - \frac{1}{2}\right)\frac{D\lambda}{d} = 5 \times 10^{-3}\text{ m}$

$\Rightarrow \quad \frac{4D\lambda}{d} - \frac{3}{2}\frac{D\lambda}{d} = 5 \times 10^{-3}$

$\Rightarrow \quad \left(4 - \frac{3}{2}\right)\frac{D\lambda}{d} = 5 \times 10^{-3}$

$\Rightarrow \quad \frac{5}{2}\left(\frac{(1)\lambda}{3 \times 10^{-3}}\right) = 5 \times 10^{-3}$

$\Rightarrow \lambda = 6 \times 10^{-6}\text{ m}$

$\Rightarrow \lambda = 6\ \mu\text{m}$

19. (i) Refer to text on page 325.

(ii) Refer to text on page 328.

(iii) Refer to text on page 327.

20. **Refractive index** Refer to text on page 327.

Law of refraction from Huygen's wave theory Refer to text on page 327.

21. (i) (a) For interference fringes to be seen, $\frac{s}{S} \le \frac{\lambda}{d}$ condition should be satisfied where, s = size of the source and d = distance of the source from the plane of two slits. As, the source slit width increases, fringe pattern gets less and less sharp. When the source slit is so wide, the above condition does not get satisfied and the interference pattern disappears.

(b) The interference pattern due to the different colour components of white light overlap. The central bright fringes for different colours are at the same position.

Therefore, central fringe is white and on the either side of the central fringe (i.e. central maxima), coloured bands will appear.The fringe closest on either side of central white fringe is blue and the farthest will be red. After a few fringes, no clear fringe pattern is seen.

(ii) Phase difference, $\phi = \frac{2\pi}{\lambda} \times$ path difference

$$= \frac{2\pi}{\lambda} \times \frac{\lambda}{3} = \frac{2\pi}{3}$$

Now, intensity at this point,

$$I = I_0 \cos^2 \frac{\phi}{2} = I_0\left(\cos\frac{\pi}{3}\right)^2$$

$$= \frac{I_0}{4}$$ **Hence proved**

22. Consider the disturbances at the receiver R_1 which is at a distance d from B.

Let the wave at R_1 because of A be $Y_A = a\cos\omega t$. The path difference of the signal from A with that from B is $\lambda/2$ and hence, the phase difference is π.

Thus, the wave at R_1 because of B is

$$y_B = a\cos(\omega t - \pi) = -a\cos\omega t.$$

The path difference of the signal from C with that from A is λ and hence the phase difference is 2π.

Thus, the wave at R_1 because of C is $Y_c = a\cos(\omega t - 2\pi) = a\cos\omega t$

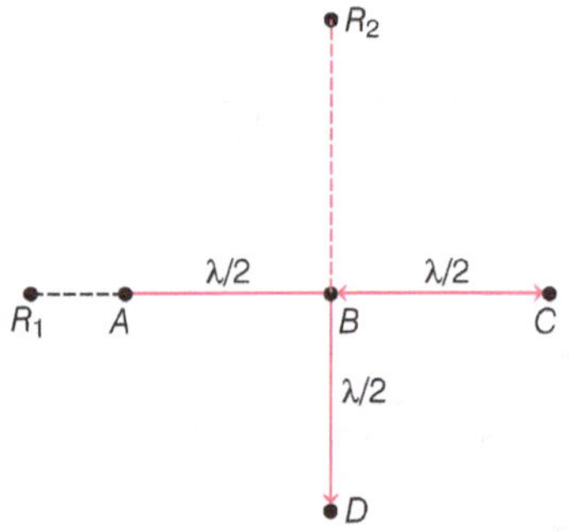

The path difference between the signal from D with that of A is

$$\sqrt{d^2 + \left(\frac{\lambda^2}{2}\right)} - \left(d - \frac{\lambda}{2}\right) = d\left(1 + \frac{\lambda}{4d^2}\right)^{1/2} - d + \frac{\lambda}{2}$$

$$= d\left(1 + \frac{\lambda}{4d^2}\right)^{1/2} - d + \frac{\lambda}{2} \approx \frac{\lambda}{2} \qquad (\because d >> \lambda)$$

Therefore, phase difference is π

$\therefore \quad Y_D = a\cos(\omega t - \pi) = -a\cos\omega t$

Thus, the signal picked up at R_1 from all the four sources is $Y_{R_1} = y_A + y_B + y_C + y_D$

$$= a\cos\omega t - a\cos\omega t + a\cos\omega t - a\cos\omega t = 0$$

(i) Let the signal picked up at R_2 from B be

$$y_B = a_1\cos\omega t$$

The path difference between signal at D and that at B is $\lambda/2$.

$$y_D = -a_1 \cos \omega t$$

The path differnce between signal at A and that at B is

$$\sqrt{d^2 + \left(\frac{\lambda^2}{2}\right)} - d = d\left(1 + \frac{\lambda^2}{4d^2}\right)^{12} \simeq d\frac{1\lambda^2}{8d^2}$$

As, $d > \lambda$, therefore this path difference $\to 0$

and phase difference $= \frac{2\pi}{\lambda}\left(\frac{1}{8}\frac{\lambda^2}{d^2}\right) \to 0$

Hence $y_A = a_1 \cos(\omega t - \phi)$

Similarly, $y_C = a_1 \cos(\omega t - \phi)$

$\therefore$ Signal picked up by R_2 is

$y_A + y_B + y_C + y_D = y = 2a_1 \cos(\omega t - \phi)$

$\therefore \quad |y|^2 = 4a_1^2 \cos^2(\omega t - \phi)$

$\therefore \quad < I > = 2a_1^2$

Thus, R_1 picks up the larger signal.

(ii) If B is switched off, R_1 picks up $y = a \cos \omega t$

$\therefore \quad I_{R_1} = \frac{1}{2}a^2$

R_2 picks up $= a \cos \omega t$

$\therefore \quad < I_{R_2} > = a^2 < \cos^2 \omega t > y = \frac{a^2}{2}$

23. Let us assume that the given postulate is true, then two parallel rays would proceed as shown in the figure below

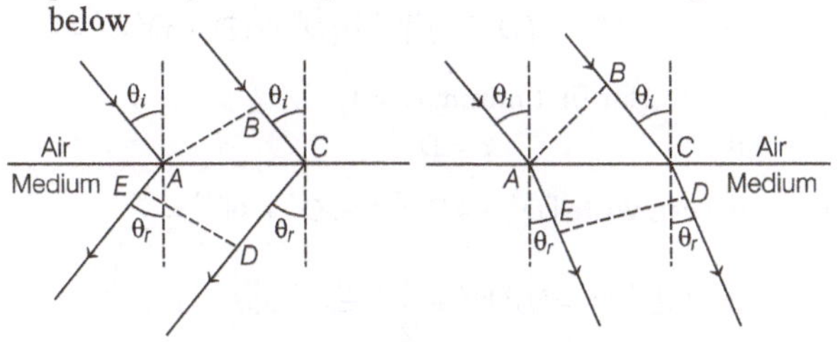

(i) (ii)

(i) Let AB represent the incident wavefront and DE represent the refracted wavefront. All points on a wavefront must be in same phase and in turn, must have the same optical path length.

Thus $-\sqrt{\varepsilon_r \mu_r}\ AE = BC - \sqrt{\varepsilon_r \mu_r}\ CD$

or $BC = \sqrt{\varepsilon_r \mu_r}\ (CD - AE)$

$$BC > 0,\ CD > AE$$

As showing that the postulate is reasonable. If however, the light proceeded in the sense it does for ordinary material (*viz.* in the fourth quadrant, Fig. 2)

Then, $-\sqrt{\varepsilon_r \mu_r}\ AE = BC - \sqrt{\varepsilon_r \mu_r}\ CD$

or $BC = \sqrt{\varepsilon_r \mu_r}\ (CD - AE)$

If $BC > 0$, then $CD > AE$

which is obvious from Fig (i).

Hence, the postulate reasonable.

However, if the light proceeded in the sense it does for ordinary material, (going from 2nd quadrant to 4th quadrant) as shown in Fig. (i)., then proceeding as above,

$$-\sqrt{\varepsilon_r \mu_r}\ AE = BC - \sqrt{\varepsilon_r \mu_r}\ CD$$

or $BC = \sqrt{\varepsilon_r \mu_r}\ (CD - AE)$

As $AE > CD$, therefore $BC < 0$ which is not possible. Hence, the given postulate is correct.

(ii) From Fig. (i),

$$BC = AC \sin \theta_i$$

and $CD - AE = AC \sin \theta_r$

As $\quad BC = \sqrt{\mu_r \varepsilon_r} \quad [CD - AE = BC]$

$\therefore \quad AC \sin \theta_i = \sqrt{\varepsilon_r \mu_r}\ AC \sin \theta_r$

or $\quad \frac{\sin \theta_i}{\sin \theta_r} = \sqrt{\varepsilon_r \mu_r} = n$

Which proves Snell's law.

24. (i) According to the question,

The separation between slits is d, and distance between screen and slits is $1000d$.

Since, we know, nth dark fringe,

$$Y_n = (2n - 1)\frac{D\lambda}{2d}$$

For Ist minima, $(n = 1)$

$$d = (2 \times 1 - 1)\cdot\frac{D\lambda}{2d}$$

$$d = 1 \times \frac{1000d\lambda}{2d} \quad \text{(putting, } D = 1000d\text{)}$$

$$d = 500\lambda$$

(ii) When a tiny circular obstacle is placed in the path of light from a distant source, a bright spot is seen at the centre of the obstacle because the waves diffracted from the edge of circular obstacle interfere constructively at the centre of the shadow resulting in the formation of a bright spot.

25. Given, $\lambda_1 = 4000\ \text{Å} = 4 \times 10^{-7}$ m

$$\lambda_2 = 6000\ \text{Å} = 6 \times 10^{-7}\ \text{m}$$

Distance at which dark fringe is observed,

$$x = \left(n + \frac{1}{2}\right)\frac{\lambda D}{d}$$

1st dark fringe for $\lambda_1 d_1 = \frac{1}{2} \times \frac{4 \times 10^{-7}}{10^{-2}}\ \text{m} = 2 \times 10^{-5}\ \text{m}$

2nd dark fringe for $\lambda_2 d_2 = \frac{1}{2} \times \frac{6 \times 10^{-7}}{10^{-2}}\ \text{m} = 3 \times 10^{-5}\ \text{m}$

The least distance from the central maxima where the dark fringe obtain is the distance where both dark fringes will coincide,

i.e. LCM of d_1 and $d_2 = 2 \times 3 \times 10^{-5}\text{m} = 6 \times 10^{-5}$ m

26. Here, wavelength, $\lambda = 589$ nm,

$$c = 3\times10^8 \text{m/s}, \; \mu = 1.33$$

(i) For reflected light,

Wavelength, $\lambda = 589 \text{ nm} = 589\times10^{-9}$ m

$$\Rightarrow \quad \nu = \frac{c}{\lambda} = \frac{3\times10^8}{589\times10^{-9}} = 5.09\times10^{14} \text{ Hz}$$

Speed, $v = c = 3\times10^8$ m/s

(ii) For refracted light,

$$\lambda' = \frac{\lambda}{\mu} = \frac{589\times10^{-9}}{1.33} = 4.42\times10^{-7} \text{ m}$$

As, frequency remains unaffected on entering another medium, therefore

$$\nu' = \nu = 5.09\times10^{14} \text{ Hz}$$

$$\therefore \text{Speed, } v' = \frac{c}{\mu} = \frac{3\times10^8}{1.33} = 2.25\times10^8 \text{ m/s}$$

27. Here, $\lambda_1 = 650 \text{ nm} = 650\times10^{-9}$ m,

$$\lambda_2 = 520 \text{ nm} = 520\times10^{-9} \text{ m}$$

Suppose, d = distance between two slits

D = distance of screen from the slits

(i) For third bright fringe, $n = 3$

$$\therefore \quad y = n\lambda_1\frac{D}{d} = 3\times650\frac{D}{d} \text{ nm} = 1950\frac{D}{d} \text{ nm}$$

(ii) Let n th order bright fringe of λ_1 coincides with $(n+1)$th order bright fringe of λ_2

$$\therefore \quad \frac{Dn\lambda_1}{d} = \frac{D(n+1)\lambda_2}{d}$$

$$\Rightarrow \quad \frac{n+1}{n} = \frac{\lambda_1}{\lambda_2} \Rightarrow 1+\frac{1}{n} = \frac{650}{520} \Rightarrow n = 4$$

Least distance from the central fringe where bright fringe of two wavelengths coincides

= distance of 4th order bright fringe of λ_1

$$\Rightarrow \quad y_n = \frac{4D\lambda_1}{d} = (4\times650 \text{ nm})\frac{D}{d} = 2600\frac{D}{d} \text{ nm}$$

28. According to the question, $\frac{\beta_1}{\beta_2} = \frac{\lambda_1}{\lambda_2}$ [$\because$ D and d are same]

Here, $\beta_1 = 7.2\times10^{-3}$ m,

$\beta_2 = 8.1\times10^{-3}$ m

and $\lambda_1 = 630\times10^{-9}$ m

Wavelength of another source of laser light,

$$\lambda_2 = \frac{\beta_2}{\beta_1}\times\lambda_1 = \frac{8.1\times10^{-3}}{7.2\times10^{-3}}\times630\times10^{-9} \text{ m}$$

$$\therefore \quad \lambda_2 = 708.75\times10^{-9} \text{ m} = 708.75 \text{ nm}$$

29. For destructive interference, the path difference x is given as

$$x = (2m-1)\frac{\lambda}{2}$$

For the 6th dark fringe, $x_6 = (2\times6-1)\frac{\lambda}{2} = \frac{11\lambda}{2}$

Now, when a sheet of thickness t and refractive index n is introduced, the path difference increases by $\frac{2\pi(n-1)t}{\lambda}$

Now, the 8th bright fringe is formed at the same place.

$$\therefore \quad x_8 = 8\lambda$$

Since, both the dark and the bright fringes are formed at the same place, so

$$x_6 + \frac{2\pi(n-1)t}{\lambda} = x_8 \Rightarrow \frac{11\lambda}{2} + \frac{2\pi(n-1)t}{\lambda} = 8\lambda$$

$$\Rightarrow \quad \frac{2\pi(n-1)}{\lambda} = 8\lambda - \frac{11\lambda}{2} = \frac{(16-11)}{2}\lambda$$

$$\Rightarrow \quad t = \frac{5\lambda^2}{4\pi(n-1)}$$

30. From the given figure of two slit interference arrangements, we can write

$$T_2P = T_2O + OP = D + x$$

and $$T_1P = T_1O - OP = D - x$$

$$S_1P = \sqrt{(S_1T_1)^2 + (PT_1)^2} = \sqrt{D^2 + (D-x)^2}$$

and $$S_2P = \sqrt{(S_2T_2)^2 + (T_2P)^2} = \sqrt{D^2 + (D+x)^2}$$

The minima will occur when $S_2P - S_1P = (2n-1)\frac{\lambda}{2}$

i.e., $$[D^2 + (D+x)^2]^{1/2} - [D^2 + (D-x)^2]^{1/2} = \frac{\lambda}{2}$$

[for first minima $n = 1$]

If $$x = D$$

we can write $[D^2 + 4D^2]^{1/2} - [D^2 + 0]^{1/2} = \frac{\lambda}{2}$

$$\Rightarrow \quad [5D^2]^{1/2} - [D^2]^{1/2} = \frac{\lambda}{2} \quad \Rightarrow \quad \sqrt{5}D - D = \frac{\lambda}{2}$$

$$\Rightarrow \quad D(\sqrt{5}-1) = \lambda/2 \text{ or } D = \frac{\lambda}{2(\sqrt{5}-1)}$$

Putting $\sqrt{5} = 2.236$

$$\Rightarrow \quad \sqrt{5} - 1 = 2.236 - 1 = 1.236$$

$$D = \frac{\lambda}{2(1.236)} = 0.404\,\lambda$$

31. (i) Given, $I_1 = I_0$ and $I_2 = 50\%$ of I_1 i.e., $I_2 = \frac{I_0}{2}$

Now, ratio of maximum and minimum intensity is given as

$$\frac{I_{max}}{I_{min}} = \left(\frac{\sqrt{I_1} + \sqrt{I_2}}{\sqrt{I_1} - \sqrt{I_2}}\right)^2$$

$$=\left(\frac{\sqrt{I_0}+\sqrt{I_0/2}}{\sqrt{I_0}-\sqrt{I_0/2}}\right)^2=\frac{(\sqrt{I_0}+\sqrt{I_0/2})^2}{(\sqrt{I_0}-\sqrt{I_0/2})^2}$$

$$=\frac{\left(1+\frac{1}{\sqrt{2}}\right)^2}{\left(1-\frac{1}{\sqrt{2}}\right)^2}=\left(\frac{\sqrt{2}+1}{\sqrt{2}-1}\right)^2=\frac{3+2\sqrt{2}}{3-2\sqrt{2}}$$

$$=\left(\frac{3+2\sqrt{2}}{3-2\sqrt{2}}\right)\times\left(\frac{3+2\sqrt{2}}{3+2\sqrt{2}}\right)$$

$$=\frac{(3+2\sqrt{2})^2}{(3)^2-(2\sqrt{2})^2}=17+12\sqrt{2}$$

(ii) When a white light source is used, the interference patterns due to different component of white light overlap incoherently. The central bright fringe for different colours is at centre. So, central bright fringe is white. As $\lambda_{blue} < \lambda_{red}$, fringe closest on either side of central bright fringe is blue and the farthest is red. After few fringes, no clear pattern of fringes will be visible.

32. (i) Two pin holes with two sodium lamps cannot produce coherent sources of light, so the phenomenon of interference cannot be observed.

(ii) Given, $\lambda_1 = 590\,\text{nm}, \lambda_2 = 596\,\text{nm}$.

$$d = 2\times10^{-6}\,\text{m}, D = 1.5\,\text{m}$$

Distance of secondary maxima from centre,

$$x=\frac{3}{2}\frac{D\lambda}{d}$$

Spacing between the first two maxima of sodium light

$$\Rightarrow \quad x_2 - x_1 = \frac{3D}{2d}(\lambda_2-\lambda_1)=\frac{3\times1.5}{2\times2\times10^{-6}}(596-590)\times10^{-9}$$

$$=6.75\times10^{-3}\,\text{m}=6.75\,\text{mm}$$

33. (i) Here, light of two different wavelengths are used.

(a) The distance for the mth bright fringe w.r.t the central bright fringe is given by $x_m=\frac{mD\lambda}{d}$.

Here, $m=3$, $D=1$ m, $d=1\times10^{-9}$ m,

$$\lambda=\lambda_1=600\times10^{-9}\text{ m}$$

$$\therefore \quad x_3=\frac{3\times1\times600\times10^{-9}}{1\times10^{-9}}=1.8\times10^3\text{m}$$

(b) Let the bright fringe for wavelength λ_1 coincide with the mth bright fringe of wavelength λ_2.

$$\therefore \quad x_n=\frac{n\times1\times600\times10^{-9}}{1\times10^{-3}}$$

$$y_m=\frac{m\times1\times480\times10^{-9}}{1\times10^{-3}}$$

Now, $x_n = y_m$

$$\Rightarrow \quad \frac{n\times1\times600\times10^{-9}}{1\times10^{-3}}=\frac{m\times1\times480\times10^{-9}}{1\times10^{-3}}$$

$$\Rightarrow \quad \frac{n}{m}=\frac{480}{600}=\frac{4}{5}\Rightarrow 5n=4m$$

$\therefore$ At the last, the 5th bright fringe of λ_1 will coincide with the 4th bright fringe of λ_2

$$\therefore \quad x_5=\frac{5\times1\times600\times10^{-9}}{10^{-9}}=3\times10^3\text{ m.}$$

$\therefore$ The last distance from the central maximum where the bright fringes due to both wavelengths coincide is 3×10^3 m.

(ii) (a) The variation of I with θ is given below

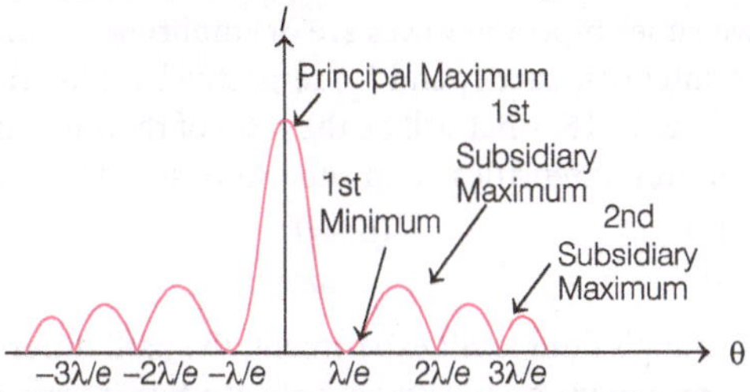

Angles corresponding to zero intensity locations are.

$$e\sin\theta=\pm m\lambda\,;\ m=1, 2, 3, ...$$

where, e is the slit width and λ is the wavelength of the light used.

(b) In case of sound waves, it is easier to observe diffraction because the wavelength of sound is comparable to the size of the obstacles which we encounter in our daily life whereas, the wavelength comparison to sound waves which makes it difficult for the observation of diffraction.

QR Code for Quick Test 1

QR Code for Quick Test 2

QR Code for Quick Test 3

SELF ASSESSMENT TEST

Multiple Choice Questions (MCQs)

1. Which of the following statements does not correctly comply with Huygens' principle of constructing a secondary wavefront from a primary wavefront?
   (a) After some time interval, the new position of the wavefront is the surface tangent to the secondary wavelets.
   (b) Secondary wavelets propagate outward through a medium with speeds characteristic of waves in that medium.
   (c) A secondary wavefront is always a plane wavefront irrespective of whether the primary wavefront is plane or spherical.
   (d) All points on a given primary wavefront are taken as point sources for the production of spherical secondary waves, called wavelets.

2. Two superimposing waves are of amplitudes a_1 and a_2 and intensities are I_1 and I_2, respectively. If the ratio $I_1 : I_2$ is 1 : 16, what will be the ratio of their maximum to minimum intensities upon superimposition?
   (a) 1/4 (b) 4/1
   (c) 25/9 (d) 9/25

3. In Young's double slit experiment, the path difference at a certain point on the screen between two interfering waves is $\left(\frac{1}{8}\right)$th of wavelength. The ratio of the intensity at this point to that at the centre of a bright fringe is close to
   (a) 0.80 (b) 0.94
   (c) 0.85 (d) 0.74

4. What happens to the interference pattern when the two slits S_1 and S_2 in Young's double slit experiment are illuminated by two independent sources as shown?

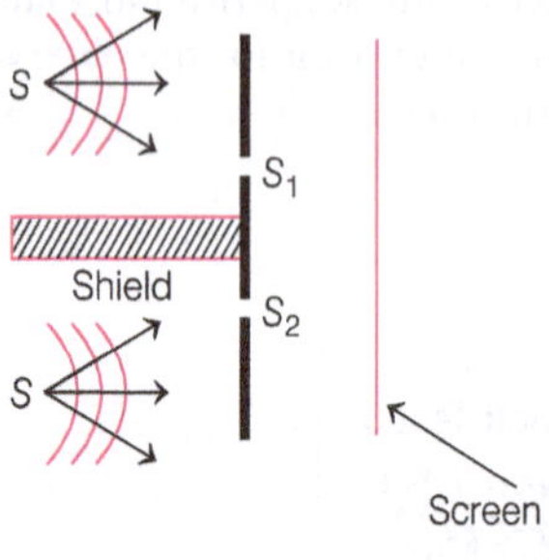

   (a) The intensity of the bright fringes gets doubled
   (b) The intensity of the bright fringes becomes four times
   (c) Two sets of interference fringes overlap
   (d) No interference pattern is observed

5. In diffraction from a single slit the angular width of the central maxima does not depends on
   (a) λ of light used
   (b) width of slit
   (c) distance of slits from the screen D
   (d) ratio of λ and slit width

Assertion-Reason

Directions *(Q.No. 6-8) In the following questions, two statements are given- one labelled Assertion (A) and the other labelled Reason (R). Select the correct answer to these questions from the codes (a), (b), (c) and (d) as given below.*

(a) Both Assertion and Reason are true and Reason is the correct explanation of Assertion.
(b) Both Assertion and Reason are true but Reason is not the correct explanation of Assertion.
(c) Assertion is true but Reason is false.
(d) Assertion is false but Reason is true.

6. **Assertion (A)** In Young's double slit experiment, if the distance between the slits is halved, the fringe width will double.
   Reason (R) Fringe width in Young's double slit experiment is directly proportional to the wavelength of the light used.

7. **Assertion** (A) When light passes through a single slit, the central maxima is twice as wide as the other maxima.
   Reason (R) The intensity of the central maxima is greater than the intensity of the other maxima.

8. **Assertion** (A) The fringe visibility in Young's double slit experiment decreases if one slit is covered with a transparent medium of higher refractive index.
   Reason (R) The optical path difference between the two slits increases if one slit is covered with a medium of higher refractive index.

Case Based Questions

Directions *(Q.No. 9) This questions is a case study based read the following paragraph and answer the questions on the basis of same.*

9. When an opaque object is placed in the path of light rays, we see a shadow of object on a screen under some specific conditions, we see a bright spot at the centre of geometrical shadow region. This happens due to a phenomenon called diffraction. Diffraction is a characteristic shown by all types of waves. When the double slit in Young's experiment is replaced by a single narrow slits (illuminated by a monochromatic source), a broad pattern with a central bright region is seen, on either sides, there are alternate dark and bright regions?

(i) The size of an opaque object is 0.5 μm. Which of the following waves would exhibit diffraction pattern on the screen?

(a) Red light (b) Yellow light
(c) Green light (d) Orange light

(ii) Which of the following statements is incorrect.

(a) In YDSE light waves from two different wavefronts superposed on each other to produce interference pattern.
(b) In single slit experiment light wave from different parts of same wavefront superposed to produce different patterns.
(c) The intensity of bright bands in YDSE is same for all
(d) The intensity of a maxima's single slit experiment is same

(iii) In a single slit experiment, the screen is moved away from the plane of slits such that distance between screen and slit is doubled. The angular width of central maxima would

(a) become 4 times (b) remain uncharged
(c) become 2 times (d) become $\frac{1}{2}$ times

(iv) Which the following can be explained by both wave nature and particle nature of light?

(a) Diffraction
(b) Reflection of light
(c) Refraction of light
(d) Both reflection and refraction of light

Very Short Answer type Questions

10. State two conditions for sustained interference of light.

11. Light of wavelength 600 nm is incident on a single slit of width 0.5 mm at normal incidence. Calculate the separation between two dark bands on either side of the central maximum, if the diffraction pattern is observed on a screen placed at 2 m from the slit.

Short Answer Type Questions

12. What will be the effect on the interference fringes in a Young's double slit experiment, if
(i) monochromatic source is replaced by a source of white light,
(ii) the screen is moved away from the slit? Justify your answer.

13. Two independent sources of light cannot be coherent, Why? Can two identical and independent sodium lamps acts as coherent sources?

14. State Huygen's postulates of wave theory. Sketch the wavefront emerging from a (i) point source of light and (ii) linear source of light like a slit.

Long Answer type Question

15. Define the term wavefront of light. A plane wavefront *AB* propagating from denser medium (1) into a rarer medium (2) is incident on the surface P_1P_2 separating the two media as shown in figure.

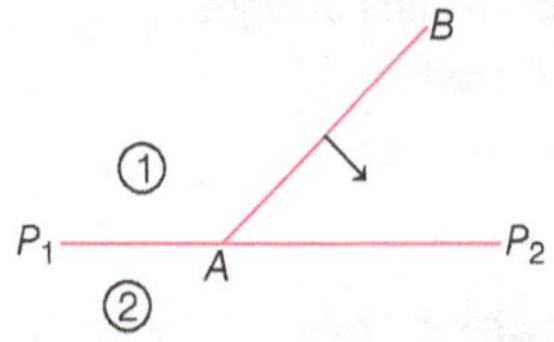

Using Huygens' principle, draw the secondary wavelet and obtain the refracted wavefront in the diagram and verify Snell's law.

Answers

1. (c) 2. (c) 3. (c) 4. (d) 5. (c) 6. (b) 7. (b)
8. (a) 9. (i) (c), (ii) (d), (iii) (b) (iv) (d) 11. 4.8 mm

11
CHAPTER

The Maxwell's equations of electromagnetism and Hertz experiments on generation and detection of electromagnetic waves established the wave nature of light in 1887. But the discoveries of photoelectric effect by Hertz, Compton effect by Compton, established the particle nature of light. Hence, it was concluded that **light has dual nature.**

YOUR STUDY GOALS

YOUR PRACTICE GOAL

- Objective Type Questions (32 Qs ; MCQs, A-R, Matching)
- Case Based Questions-3
- Subjective Questions (10 VSAs, 9 SAs, 14 LAs)
- Numerical Problems-14

Dual Nature of Radiation and Matter

Electron Emission

The phenomenon of emission of electrons from the surface of a metal by applying required energy to overcome the attractive force of positive ion is called **electron emission**.

The minimum energy required for the electron emission from the metal surface can be supplied to the free electrons by anyone of the following physical processes

(i) **Thermionic Emission** Sufficient thermal energy can be imparted to the free electrons by suitable heating, so that they can come out of the metal.

This process of emission of electrons is known as thermionic emission and the emitted electrons are known as **thermions**. The number of thermions emitted depends upon the nature of the metal.

(ii) **Field Emission or Cold Cathode Emission** It is the phenomenon of emission of electrons from the surface of a metal by applying a very strong electric field ($\sim 10^8\ \text{Vm}^{-1}$) to a metal.

One of the examples of cold emission is spark plug.

(iii) **Photoelectric Emission** It is the phenomenon of emission of electrons from the surface of metal when light radiations of suitable frequency fall on it, the energy required to the free electrons for their emission is being supplied by the photons.

The emitted electrons are called **photoelectrons.** The number of photoelectrons emitted depends on the intensity of the incident light.

Work Function

A minimum amount of energy is required to pull out a free electron from the surface of the metal. This minimum energy is called as the work function of the metal.

It is generally denoted by ϕ_0 or W_0 and measured in **eV (electron volt).**

- It depends on the properties of the metal and the nature of its surface.
- It decreases with the increase in temperature.
- **One electron volt** (1 eV) is the energy gained by an electron when it has been accelerated by a potential difference of one volt (1 V), so that $1\,\text{eV} = 1.602 \times 10^{-19}$ J.
- Work function of **platinum is the highest** ($\phi_0 = 5.65$ eV), while it is the **lowest for caesium** ($\phi_0 = 2.14$ eV).

11.1 Photoelectric Effect

The phenomenon of emission of electrons from the surface of metal, when radiations of suitable frequency fall on it, is called photoelectric effect.

The emitted electrons are called **photoelectrons** and the current, produced by these electrons is called **photoelectric current.**

Alkali metals like lithium, sodium, etc., show photoelectric effect with visible light, whereas the metals like zinc, cadmium and caesium etc., are sensitive only to ultraviolet light.

- Non-metals also show photoelectric effect. Liquids and gases show this effect too but upto the limited extent.

Hertz's Observations

- In 1887, Heinrich Hertz discovered the phenomenon of photoelectric emission while working with his electromagnetic wave experiment, by means of spark discharge.
- He observed that high voltage sparks across the detector loop were enhanced when the emitter plate was illuminated by ultraviolet light from an arc lamp.
- When suitable radiations fall on a metal surface, some electrons near the surface absorb enough energy, to overcome the attraction of the positive ions in the material of the surface. This helps them to escape from the surface of the material to the surrounding space.
- Hertz could not explain his observation.

Hallwachs' and Lenard's Observations

- During 1886 -1902, Wilhelm Hallwach's and Philipp Lenard made a detailed study of photoelectric effect.
- Lenard observed that, if a potential difference is applied across the tube, then there is no flow of current in the circuit, when emitter plate, kept at negative potential is exposed with ultraviolet radiations, the current begins to flow in the circuit as shown in figure.

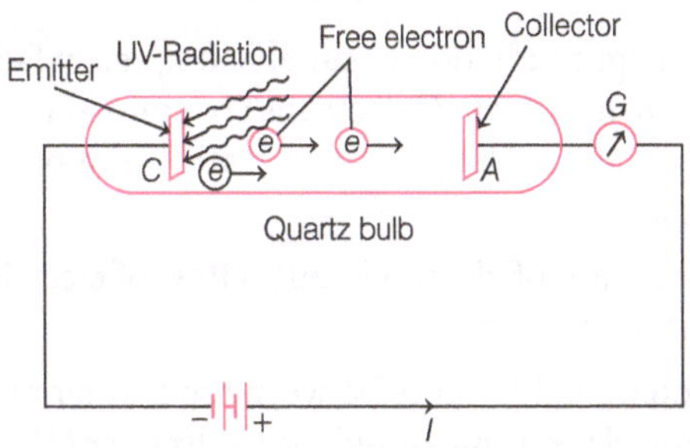

Some key observations from the experiment are given below

- Incident light causes electron to move out from the metal.
- Hallwach's and Lenard also observed that when UV light falls on the emitter plate, no electrons were emitted, until the frequency of incident light was smaller than a certain minimum value, called the threshold frequency. This minimum frequency depends on the nature of the material of the emitter plate.

Experimental Study of Photoelectric Effect

The given figure shows the experimental set-up for the study of photoelectric effect.

The set-up consists of an evacuated glass or quartz tube which encloses a photosensitive plate C (called **emitter**) and a metal plate A (called **collector**).

- A transparent quartz window is sealed onto the glass tube which permits ultraviolet radiation to pass through it and irradiate the photosensitive plate C.

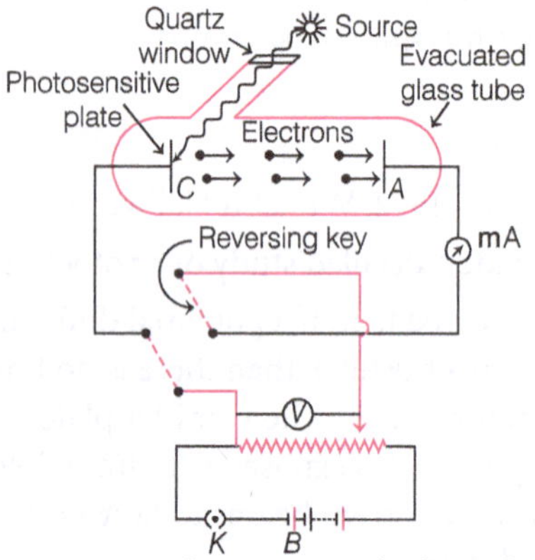

Experimental arrangement for the study of photoelectric effect

- When a light radiation of suitable frequency fall on the photosensitive plate C electrons are emitted by plate C and are collected by plate A, as plate A is at positive potential.
- This emission of electrons causes flow of electric current in the circuit.
- The potential difference between the emitter and collector plates is measured by a voltmeter (V), and photocurrent is measured by a microammeter (μA).

The above experimental arrangement is used to study the variations of photocurrent with different parameters which are given below.

Effect of Intensity of Light on Photoelectric Current

- For a fixed frequency of incident radiation and accelerating potential, the photoelectric current increases linearly with increase in intensity of incident light.
- As, the photoelectric current is directly proportional to the number of photoelectrons emitted per second and the number of photoelectrons emitted per second is directly proportional to the intensity of the incident so, **the photoelectric current is directly proportional to intensity of light.**

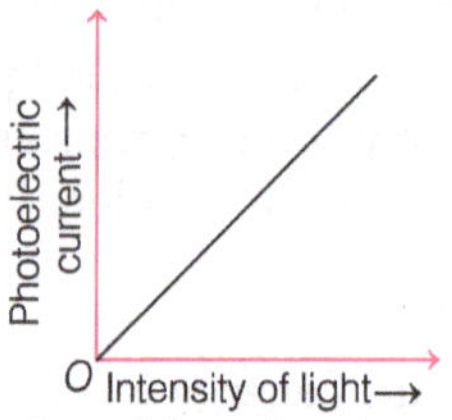

Variation of photoelectric current with intensity of light

Effect of Potential on Photoelectric Current

For a fixed frequency and intensity of incident light, **photoelectric current increases with increase in potential applied to the collector** till the current reaches a saturation value, as shown in the graph.

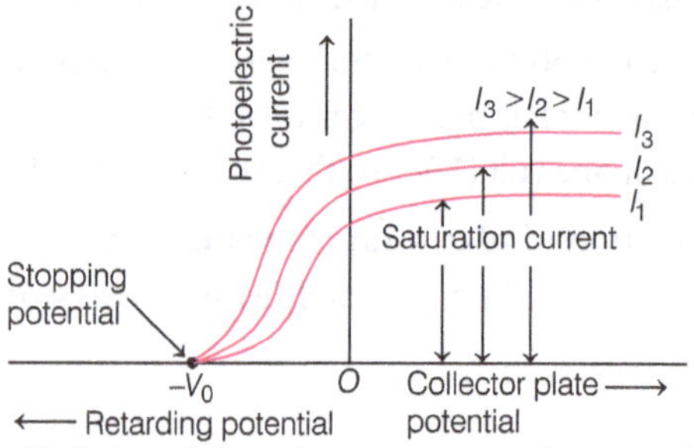

Variation of photoelectric current with potential for different intensities but constant frequency

From the above graph, we can observe that,

(i) On increasing the value of accelerating potential, there is no change in photocurrent and this maximum value of photoelectric current is called **saturation current.**

(ii) When the potential is decreased, the current decreases but does not become zero at zero potential. This shows that even in the absence of accelerating potential, few photoelectrons manages to reach the plate A on their own due to their kinetic energy.

(iii) The minimum negative (retarding) potential V_0 given at collector plate A for which photoelectric current becomes zero at that particular value of negative potential, V_0 is called **stopping potential** or **cut-off potential**.

The photoelectric current becomes zero whenever no electron or even the fastest photoelectron cannot reach the plate *A*. Hence, maximum kinetic energy is given as

$$K_{max} = eV_0 = \frac{1}{2}mv^2_{max}$$

where, *m* is the mass of photoelectron and v_{max} is the maximum velocity of emitted photoelectron.

The maximum kinetic energy of emitted photoelectron depends on the frequency of light source and the emitter plate material but is independent of intensity of incident radiation.

Example 1 **In a photoelectric experiment, the potential required to stop the ejection of electrons from cathode is 4 V. What is the value of maximum kinetic energy of emitted photoelectrons?**

Sol. The maximum kinetic energy of emitted electron (KE_{max}) is given by

$$KE_{max} = \frac{1}{2}Mv^2{}_{max} = eV_0$$

We have given data

i.e $V_0 = 4V$

Putting the value in above expression, we get

$$KE_{max} = eV_0 = 4eV$$

This is the maximum kinetic energy of emitted photoelectron.

Effect of Frequency of Incident Radiation on Stopping Potential

If we take radiations of different frequencies but of same intensity. For each radiation, the variation of photoelectric current against the potential difference between the plates as shown in the graph below.

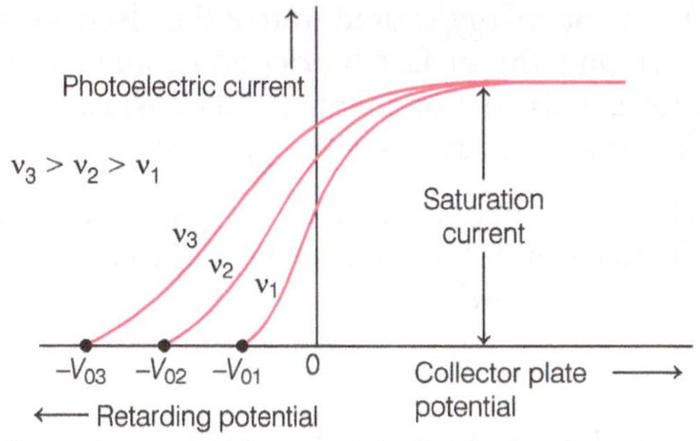

Variation of photoelectric current with potential for different frequencies but constant intensity of incident radiation

From the given graph, we observe that

(i) the value of stopping potential is different for radiation of different frequencies but the value of saturation current (for given intensity) remains constant.

(ii) the value of stopping potential is more negative for incident radiation of higher frequency. This means that the energy of the emitted electrons depends on the frequency of incident radiations. **Greater the frequency of incident radiation, greater is the maximum kinetic energy of photoelectrons, consequently greater retarding potential or stopping potential is required to stop them completely.**

(iii) the value of saturation current depends upon the intensity of incident radiation but independent of the frequency of the incident radiation.

If we plot a graph between stopping potential and the frequency of the incident radiation for two different metals *A* and *B*, we get the graph as shown below.

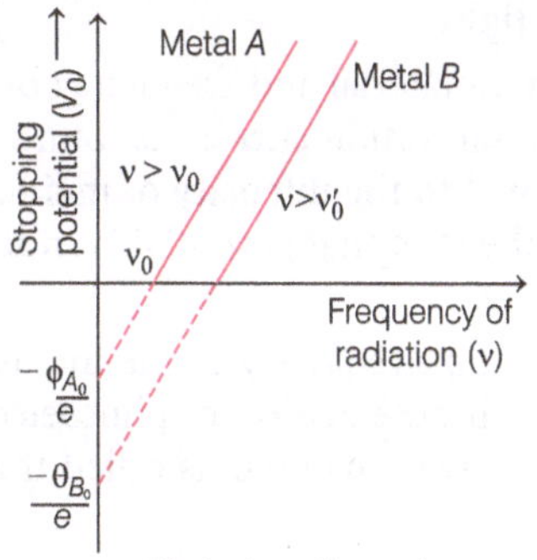

Variation of stopping potential with frequency of

From the graph, we observed that

(i) the stopping potential V_0 varies linearly with the frequency of incident radiation for a given photosensitive material.

(ii) there exists a certain minimum cut-off frequency ν_0 for which the stopping potential is zero. This frequency is called **threshold frequency**.

The minimum frequency of light which can emit photoelectrons from a material is called **threshold frequency or cut-off frequency** of that material. It is a characteristic property of material.

The slope of the graph is equal to $\left(\frac{h}{e}\right)$. Therefore, the slope does not depend an any factor and the intercept $\frac{\phi}{e}$ of the line depends on the work function of the metal.

For a frequency lower than cut-off frequency, no photoelectric emission is possible even if the intensity is large. If frequency of incident radiation is more than the threshold frequency, the photoelectric emission starts instantaneously without any apparent time lag (-10^{-9} s or less) even when the incident radiation is very dim.

Laws of Photoelectric Emission

The laws of photoelectric emission are as follows

(i) For a given material and a given frequency of incident radiation, the photoelectric current or **number of photoelectrons ejected per second is directly proportional to the intensity of the incident light.**

(ii) For a given material and frequency of incident radiation, saturation current is found to be proportional to the intensity of incident radiation, whereas the stopping potential is independent of its intensity.

(iii) The minimum frequency of the incident radiation below which no emission of photoelectrons takes place for a given material, is called threshold frequency.

Above the threshold frequency, the K_{max} of the emitted photoelectrons or equivalent stopping potential is independent of the intensity of the incident light but depends only upon the frequency (or wavelength) of the incident light.

(iv) The photoelectric emission is an instantaneous process. **The time lag between the incidence of radiations and emission of photoelectrons is very small, less than even 10^{-9} s.**

Photoelectric Effect and Wave Theory of Light

Huygens' wave theory of light could not explain the photoelectric emission due to the following main reasons

The **major drawbacks of wave theory** are given below.

(i) Photoelectric emission is not instantaneous.

(ii) Maximum kinetic energy of photoelectron on the surface should increase with increase in intensity.

(iii) No concept of threshold frequency was introduced.

There are the major drawbacks of Huygens' wave theory of light.

Einstein's Photoelectric Equation

- In 1905, Albert Einstein explained the various laws of photoelectric emission on the basis of Planck's quantum theory.
- According to the theory, electromagnetic waves consist of discrete packet or bundles of energy called **quanta of energy of radiation.** It is also called as **photon** which travels with the speed of light, having energy.

$$\boxed{E = h\nu}$$

where, h is **Planck's constant** and ν is the frequency of light radiation.

- When a quantum of light radiation of energy $h\nu$ falls on a metal surface, then this energy is absorbed by the electron and is used in following two ways

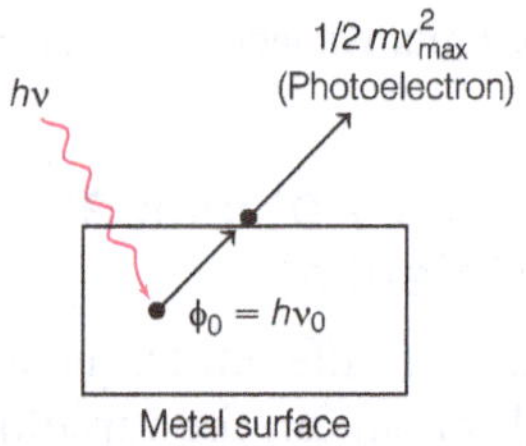

Emission of photoelectron by a metal surface when a quanta of light is absorbed by it

(i) A part of energy is used to free the electron to overcome the surface barrier and come out of the metal. This part of energy is called **work function.** It is expressed as $\phi_0 = h\nu_0$.

(ii) The remaining part of the energy is used in giving the maximum kinetic energy (K_{max}) to the emitted photoelectron

$$K_{max} = \frac{1}{2}mv_{max}^2$$

According to the law of conservation of energy,

$$h\nu = \phi_0 + \frac{1}{2}mv_{max}^2$$

$$\therefore \quad \frac{1}{2}mv_{max}^2 = h\nu - \phi_0 \quad \text{or} \quad \boxed{K_{max} = h\nu - \phi_0}$$

This equation is called **Einstein's photoelectric equation.**

It can also be written as

$$K_{max} = h(\nu - \nu_0) \qquad [\because \phi_0 = h\nu_0)$$

where, ν_0 is threshold frequency.

Relation between Stopping Potential (V_0) and Threshold Frequency (ν_0)

Maximum kinetic energy is given by

$$K_{max} = h(\nu - \nu_0)$$

Also, $K_{max} = eV_0$

$$\therefore \quad \boxed{eV_0 = h(\nu - \nu_0)} \qquad \ldots(i)$$

If λ = wavelength of the incident radiation,

λ_0 = threshold wavelength of the metal surface and

c = velocity of light, then

$$\nu = \frac{c}{\lambda} \text{ and } \nu_0 = \frac{c}{\lambda_0}$$

Putting these values in Eq. (i), we get

$$eV_0 = h\left(\frac{c}{\lambda} - \frac{c}{\lambda_0}\right)$$

$$\therefore \quad \boxed{eV_0 = hc\left(\frac{1}{\lambda} - \frac{1}{\lambda_0}\right)}$$

Example 2. The electric field associated with a monochromatic beam of light becomes zero, with frequency 2.4 × 10¹⁵ times per second. Find the maximum kinetic energy of the photoelectrons when this light falls on a metal surface whose work function is 2.0 eV.

Sol. Given, $\phi_0 = 2.0$ eV, $h = 6.63 \times 10^{-34}$ J - s, $KE_{max} = ?$

In one complete vibration twice a the electric field becomes zero, so the frequency of incident light is given by

$$\nu = \frac{1}{2} \times 2.4 \times 10^{15}$$

$$= 1.2 \times 10^{15} \text{ Hz}$$

Hence, maximum kinetic energy,

$$KE_{max} = h\nu - \phi_0$$

$$= \frac{6.63 \times 10^{-34} \times 1.2 \times 10^{15}}{1.6 \times 10^{-19}} - 2 = 2.97 \text{ eV}$$

Example 3. The work function of caesium is 2.14 eV. Calculate

(i) the threshold frequency for caesium and

(ii) the wavelength of the incident light, if the photocurrent is brought to zero by a stopping potential of 0.60 V. Given, $h = 6.63 \times 10^{-34}$ J-s.

Sol. Here, $V_0 = 0.60$ V, $\phi_0 = 2.14$ eV

$$= 2.14 \times 1.6 \times 10^{-19} \text{ J}$$

(i) Threshold frequency, $\nu_0 = \dfrac{\phi_0}{h}$ $\qquad [\because \phi_0 = h\nu_0]$

$$= \frac{2.14 \times 1.6 \times 10^{-19}}{6.63 \times 10^{-34}} = 5.16 \times 10^{14} \text{ Hz}$$

(ii) We have, $eV_0 = \dfrac{hc}{\lambda} - \phi_0 \Rightarrow \lambda = \dfrac{hc}{(eV_0 + \phi_0)}$

$$= \frac{6.63 \times 10^{-34} \times 3 \times 10^{8}}{(1.6 \times 10^{-19} \times 0.60 + 2.14 \times 1.6 \times 10^{-19})}$$

$$\approx 454 \times 10^{-9} \text{ m} = 454 \text{ nm}$$

Verification of Laws of Photoelectric Emission Based on Einstein's Photoelectric Equation

Einstein's photoelectric equations is

$$K_{max} = \frac{1}{2}mv_{max}^2 = h(\nu - \nu_0)$$

This equation successfully explains the laws of photoelectric emission. These are as follows

(i) If $\nu < \nu_0$, then $\frac{1}{2}mv_{max}^2$ is negative, that implies the photoelectric emission will not take place. Therefore, for photoelectric emission to take place, $\nu > \nu_0$.

(ii) Since, one photon emits one electron, so the number of photoelectrons emitted per second is directly proportional to the intensity of incident light.

(iii) It is clear that $\frac{1}{2}mv_{max}^2 \propto \nu$, as h and ν_0 are constants. This shows that kinetic energy of the photoelectrons is directly proportional to the frequency of the incident light.

(iv) Photoelectric emission is due to elastic collisions between a photon and an electron. As such there cannot be any significant time lag between the incidence of photon and emission of photoelectron.

Graphs Related to Photoelectric Effect from Einstein Photoelectric Equation

The important graphs related to photoelectric effect are as follows

(i) Frequency (ν) and stopping potential (V_0) graph

We know that, $eV_0 = h\nu - \phi_0$

$$\Rightarrow \quad V_0 = \frac{h\nu}{e} - \frac{\phi_0}{e}$$

So, $\boxed{V_0 \propto \nu}$

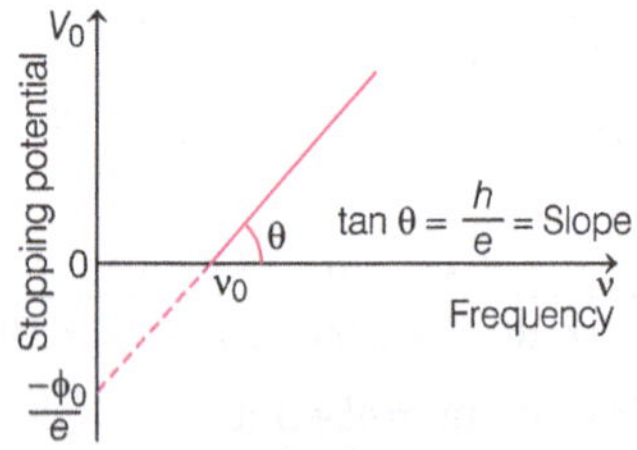

Graph of V_0 *versus* ν

It could be seen that, **V_0 *versus* ν curve is a straight line with slope = (h/e) and is independent of the nature of material.**

(ii) Frequency (ν) and maximum kinetic energy (K_{max}) graph

As, $K_{max} = h\nu - \phi_0$ ...(i)

$$\Rightarrow \quad \boxed{K_{max} \propto \nu}$$

From Eq. (i), we noted that slope of the graph is h, and ν intercept is ν_0 and KE_{max} = intercept is $-\phi_0$.

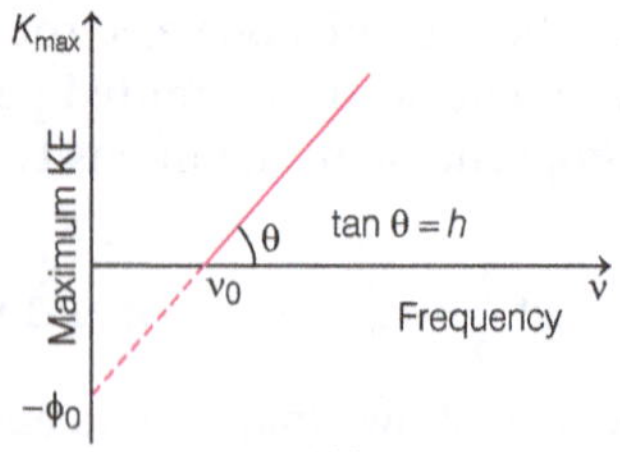

Graph of K_{max} *versus* ν

(iii) Frequency (ν) and photoelectric current (I) graph

The given graph shows that, the photoelectric current I is independent of frequency of the incident light, till intensity remains constant.

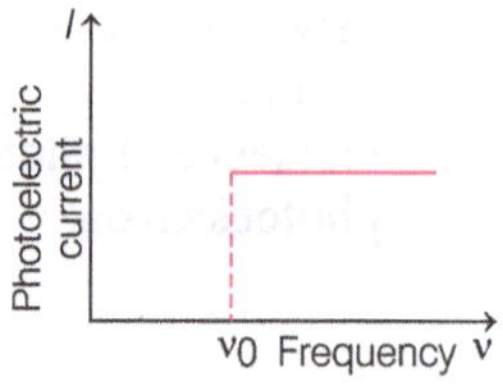

(iv) Intensity and stopping potential (V_0) graph

Stopping potential is independent of the intensity of incident light.

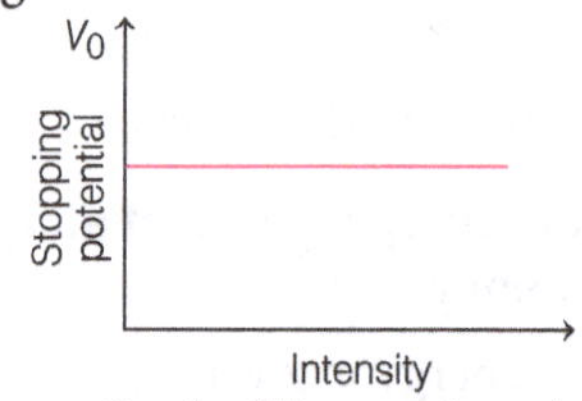

Graph of V_0 *versus* intensity

(v) Photoelectric current (I) and time lag (t) graph

The photoelectric current attains the saturation value in 10^{-9} s from the start of radiation falling.

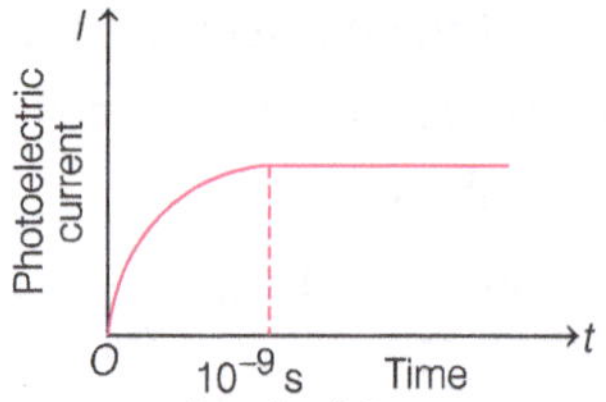

Graph of I *versus* t

11.2 Particle Nature of Light : The Photon

Photoelectric effect gave evidence that light consists of packets of energy. These packets of energy were called **light quanta** that are associated with particles named as **photons**. So, photons confirm the particle nature of light.

Energy of a photon is given by

$$\boxed{E = h\nu = \frac{hc}{\lambda}} \qquad \left[\nu = \frac{c}{\lambda}\right]$$

where, h is the Planck's constant, ν is the frequency of radiation or photon, c is the speed of light in vacuum and λ is the wavelength of photon.

The **momentum of photon** is given by

$$\boxed{p = \frac{E}{c} = \frac{h\nu}{c} = \frac{h}{\lambda} \text{ kgms}^{-1}}$$

Example 4. The momentum of photon of electro magnetic radiation is 3.3×10^{-29} kg-ms^{-1}. Find out the frequency and wavelength of the wave associated with it.

Sol. Given, $p = 3.3 \times 10^{-29}$ kg-ms^{-1}, $h = 6.63 \times 10^{-34}$ J-s
$c = 3 \times 10^8$ m/s, $\nu = ?$ and $\lambda = ?$

Since, $E = h\nu = mc^2 = mc \times c = p \times c$

$$\therefore \quad \nu = \frac{pc}{h} = \frac{3.3 \times 10^{-29} \times 3 \times 10^8}{6.63 \times 10^{-34}} = 1.5 \times 10^{13} \text{ Hz}$$

and $$\lambda = \frac{c}{\nu} = \frac{3 \times 10^8}{1.5 \times 10^{13}} = 2 \times 10^{-5} \text{m}$$

Characteristic Properties of Photons

Different characteristic properties of photons are given below

(i) In interaction of radiation with matter, radiation behaves as if it is made up of particles called photons.

(ii) A photon travels at a speed of light c in vacuum (i.e. 3×10^8 m / s), in a straight line.

(iii) The inertial mass of a photon is given by

$$m = \frac{E}{c^2} = \frac{h}{c\lambda} = \frac{h\nu}{c^2}$$

(iv) Irrespective of the intensity of radiation, all the photons of a particular frequency ν or wavelength λ have the same energy E and momentum, $\left(p = \frac{h}{\lambda}\right)$.

(v) Energy of a photon depends upon its frequency, so the energy of the photon does not change when photon travels from one medium to another.

(vi) Wavelength of the photon changes in different media, so velocity of a photon is different in different media.

(vii) Photons are not deflected by electric and magnetic fields. This shows that photons are electrically neutral.

(viii) In a photon-particle collision (such as photoelectron collision), the energy and momentum are conserved. However, the number of photons may not be conserved in a collision.

TEACHER TIP

According to the theory of relativity, the mass m of a particle moving with velocity v, comparable with the speed of light c is given by

$$m = \frac{m_0}{\sqrt{1 - \frac{v^2}{c^2}}} \Rightarrow m_0 = m\sqrt{1 - \frac{v^2}{c^2}}$$

where, m_0 is the mass of the particle at rest.

As, a photon moves with the speed of light, i.e. $v = c$, hence $m_0 = 0$. So, **rest mass of photon is zero.**

Example 5. **Monochromatic light of wavelength 632.8 nm is produced by a helium-neon laser. The power emitted is 9.42 mW.**

(i) Find the energy and momentum of each photon in the light beam.

(ii) How many photons per second, on the average, arrive at a target irradiated by this beam? (Assume the beam to have uniform cross-section, which is less than the target area.)

(iii) How fast does a hydrogen atom have to travel in order to have the same momentum as that of the photon? NCERT

Sol. Given, wavelength of monochromatic light,

$$\lambda = 632.8 \text{ nm} = 632.8 \times 10^{-9} \text{ m}$$

Power = 9.42 mW = 9.42×10^{-3} W

(i) Energy of each photon,

$$E = \frac{hc}{\lambda} = \frac{6.63 \times 10^{-34} \times 3 \times 10^8}{632.8 \times 10^{-9}} = 3.14 \times 10^{-19} \text{ J}$$

We know that, momentum of each photon,

$$p = \frac{h}{\lambda}$$

$$p = \frac{6.63 \times 10^{-34}}{632.8 \times 10^{-9}} = 1.05 \times 10^{-27} \text{ kg-m/s}$$

(ii) Let n be the number of photons per second, so

$$n = \frac{\text{Power}}{\text{Energy of each photon}} = \frac{9.42 \times 10^{-3}}{3.14 \times 10^{-19}} = 3 \times 10^{16} \text{ photons / s}$$

(iii) Momentum,

$$p = mv,$$

$$m = 1.66 \times 10^{-27} \text{ kg (mass of proton)}$$

$\therefore$ Velocity of hydrogen atom,

$$v = \frac{p}{m} = \frac{1.05 \times 10^{-27}}{1.66 \times 10^{-27}} = 0.63 \text{ m/s}$$

Quick Test 1

Conceptual Questions

1. Define the term threshold frequency, in the context of photoelectric emission. Delhi 2019
2. The given graph shows the variation of photoelectric current I *versus* applied voltage V for two different photosensitive materials and for two different intensities of the incident radiations. Identify the pairs of curves that correspond to different materials but same intensity of incident radiation.

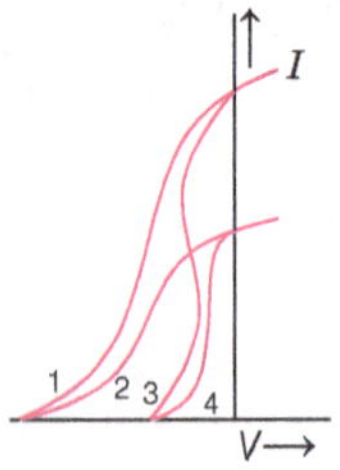

3. Two monochromatic beams A and B of equal intensity I, hit a screen. The number of photons hitting the screen by beam A is twice that by beam B, then what inference can you make about their frequencies? NCERT Exemplar
4. In case of photoelectric effect experiment, explain the following facts, giving reasons.
   (i) The wave theory of light could not explain the existence of the threshold frequency.
   (ii) The photoelectric current increases with increase of intensity of incident light.
5. All the photoelectrons are not emitted with same energy. The energies of photoelectrons are distributed over a certain range. Why?

Numerical Questions

6. In a photoelectric experiment, the potential required to stop the ejection of electrons from cathode is 4 V. What is the value of maximum kinetic energy of emitted photoelectrons?
7. The work function for a certain metal is 4.2 eV. Will this metal give photoelectric emission for incident radiation of wavelength 330 nm? NCERT
8. The maximum kinetic energy of photoelectrons emitted from a surface, when photons of energy 6 eV fall on it is 4 eV. What is the stopping potential (in V) for the fastest photoelectrons?
9. In an experiment on photoelectric effect, the slope of the cut-off voltage *versus* frequency of incident light is found to be 4.12×10^{-15} V-s. Calculate the value of Planck's constant. NCERT

Answers

6. 4eV 8. 4 V 9. 6.592×10^{-34} J-s

For Solutions, See QR Code on Pg. 378

11. 3 Matter Waves

- Wave theory of electromagnetic radiations explained the phenomenon of interference, diffraction and polarisation of light.
- On the other hand, quantum theory of electromagnetic radiations successfully explained the photoelectric effect, Compton effect, black body radiation, X-rays spectra, etc.
  From photoelectric and Compton effects, it was concluded that the **radiation possesses particle nature**.
- It means radiation sometimes behaves as a wave and sometimes as a particle. Therefore, Louis Victor de-Broglie suggested that **the particles like electrons, protons, neutrons, etc., have dual nature, i.e. they can have particle as well as wave nature.**

Note Matter cannot exist both as a particle and as a wave simultaneously. At a particular instant of time, it is either the one or the other aspect, i.e. the two aspects are complementary to each other.

Wave Nature of Particles: (de-Broglie Hypothesis)

According to de-Broglie, a wave is associated with moving material particle which controls the particle in every aspect. The wave associated with moving particle of matter is called **matter wave** or **de-Broglie wave** whose wavelength is called **de-Broglie wavelength,**

which is given by $\boxed{\lambda = \frac{h}{mv}}$

where, m and v are the mass and velocity of the particle and h is Planck's constant.

According to de-Broglie hypothesis, the wavelength of wave associated with moving material particle becomes

$$\boxed{\lambda = \frac{h}{p} = \frac{h}{mv}}$$

which is the expression for de-Broglie wavelength.

From the above expression, following observations we made

(i) The de-Broglie wavelength $\lambda \propto \frac{1}{v}$. If the particle moves faster, then the wavelength will be smaller and *vice-versa*.

(ii) If the particle is at rest ($v = 0$), then the de-Broglie wavelength is infinite ($\lambda = \infty$). Such a wave cannot be visualised.

(iii) The de-Broglie waves cannot be electromagnetic in nature because electromagnetic waves are produced by accelerating charged particles.

(iv) Matter waves can travel in vacuum and hence, they are not mechanical waves.

(v) The wavelength of a wave associated with moving particle defines a region of uncertainty, within which the information about the particle are unknown.
i.e. The position and momentum of a particle (like electron) cannot be determine simultaneously. This is called **Heisenberg uncertainty principle.**

TEACHER TIP
Matter waves are probability waves, their amplitude gives the probability of existence of the particle at that point.
If at a point, the amplitude of the wave is A, then probability of the particle being found in a small volume dV around that point is $|A|^2\,dV$.

Wavelength of Electron Wave

The kinetic energy of particle of mass having momentum p is given by

$$K = \frac{p^2}{2m} \Rightarrow p = \sqrt{2mK} \quad \ldots\text{(i)}$$

Putting the value of p in de-Broglie wavelength equation,

$$\lambda = \frac{h}{\sqrt{2mK}} \Rightarrow \lambda_e = \frac{h}{\sqrt{2meV}} \quad \ldots\text{(ii)}$$

[$\because$ In photoelectric equation, kinetic energy of electron at potential V is $K = eV$

By putting the value of mass of electron, its charge and Planck's constant in Eq.(ii), we get

$$\boxed{\lambda_e = \frac{1.227}{\sqrt{V}}\ \text{nm}}$$

Note
- Wavelength associated with the charge particle accelerated through a potential of V volt,
$$\lambda = \frac{h}{\sqrt{2mqV}}$$
- Matter wave is a third type of wave as it is different from mechanical and electromagnetic waves.

Example 6. **An electron and a photon each have a wavelength 1.00 nm. Calculate** *NCERT*
(i) their momenta, (ii) the energy of the photon and (iii) the kinetic energy of electron.

Sol. Given, $\lambda = 1\,\text{nm} = 1\times 10^{-9}\,\text{m}$,
$h = 6.63\times 10^{-34}$ J-s
$c = 3\times 10^8$ m/s,
$p = ?, E = ?, K = ?$

(i) Momentum of the photon, $p_p = \dfrac{h}{\lambda}$

$$= \frac{6.63 \times 10^{-34}}{1\times 10^{-9}}$$
$$= 6.63 \times 10^{-25}\ \text{kg-m/s}$$

Momentum of the electron, $p_e = \dfrac{h}{\lambda}$

$$= \frac{6.63 \times 10^{-34}}{1 \times 10^{-9}}$$
$$= 6.63 \times 10^{-25}\ \text{kg-m/s}$$

(ii) Energy of the photon,

$$E = \frac{hc}{\lambda} = \frac{6.63 \times 10^{-34} \times 3 \times 10^8}{1 \times 10^{-9}} = 1.99\times 10^{-16}\,\text{J}$$

(iii) Kinetic energy of the electron,

$$K = \frac{p^2}{2m_e}$$
$$= \frac{(6.63\times 10^{-25})^2}{2\times 9.1\times 10^{-31}} = 2.41\times 10^{-19}\ \text{J}$$

Example 7. **A proton and an electron have same de-Broglie wavelength. Which of them moves fast and which possesses more kinetic energy? Justify your answer.**

Sol. Kinetic energy of particle of mass m having momentum p is given by $K = \dfrac{p^2}{2m}$

$\Rightarrow \quad p = \sqrt{2mK}$

The de-Broglie wavelength, $\lambda = \dfrac{h}{p} = \dfrac{h}{\sqrt{2mK}}$

$$\therefore \quad p = \frac{h}{\lambda} \quad \ldots\text{(i)}$$

$$\text{and} \quad K = \frac{h^2}{2m\lambda^2} \quad \ldots\text{(ii)}$$

If λ is constant, then from Eq. (i), we get

$p = \text{constant}$, i.e. $m_p v_p = m_e v_e$

or $\quad \dfrac{v_p}{v_e} = \dfrac{m_e}{m_p} < 1$ or $v_p < v_e$

If λ is constant, then from Eq. (ii), $K \propto \frac{1}{m}$

$$\therefore \quad \frac{K_p}{K_e} = \frac{m_e}{m_p} < 1 \quad \text{or} \quad K_p < K_e$$

It means that the velocity of electron is greater than that of proton. Hence, kinetic energy of electron is greater than that of proton.

Example 8. **Find de-Broglie wavelength of neutron at 127 °C. Given, mass of neutron = 1.66×10^{-27} kg, Boltzmann constant, $k = 1.38 \times 10^{-23}$ J mol^{-1} K^{-1}, and Planck's constant, $h = 6.63 \times 10^{-34}$ J-s.**

Sol. Here, $T = 127\,°C = 127 + 273 = 400$ K

Energy of neutron at 127° C,

$$E = \frac{3}{2}kT = \frac{3}{2} \times 1.38 \times 10^{-23} \times 400$$

$$= 8.28 \times 10^{-21} \text{ J}$$

$$\therefore \quad \lambda = \frac{h}{\sqrt{2mE}}$$

$$= \frac{6.63 \times 10^{-34}}{\sqrt{2 \times 1.66 \times 10^{-27} \times 8.28 \times 10^{-21}}}$$

$$= 1.264 \times 10^{-10} \text{ m}$$

$$= 1.264 \text{ Å}$$

Quick Test 2

Conceptual Questions

1. What consideration led de-Broglie to suggest that material particles can also show wave property?
2. Are the matter waves electromagnetic in nature?
3. Show that the wavelength of electromagnetic wave is equal to the de-Broglie wavelength of its quantum (photon). NCERT
4. A particle with rest mass m_0 is moving with velocity c. What is the de-Broglie wavelength associated with it?
5. A photon and an electron have the same de-Broglie wavelength, which one has higher total energy?
6. A proton and an α-particle are accelerated through the same potential. Which one of the two has
   (i) greater value of de-Broglie wavelength associated with it and
   (ii) less kinetic energy? Give reason to justify your answer.
7. Plot a graph showing variation of de-Broglie wavelength λ associated with a charged particle of mass m *versus* $\frac{1}{\sqrt{V}}$ where V is the potential difference through which the particle is accelerated. How does this graph give us the information regarding the magnitude of the charge of the particle?
8. (i) Plot a graph showing variation of de-Broglie wavelength λ associated with a charged particle of mass m *versus* $\sqrt{V}$, where V is the accelerating potential.
   (ii) An electron, a proton and an alpha particle have the same kinetic energy. Which one has the shortest wavelength?
9. A photon and a proton have the same de-Broglie wavelength λ. Prove that the energy of the photon is $(2m\lambda c/h)$ times the kinetic energy of the proton.

Numerical Questions

10. A particle is moving three times as fast as an electron. The ratio of the de-Broglie wavelength of the particle to that of the electron is 1.813×10^{-4}. Calculate the particle's mass and identify the particle.

Answers

10. 1.673×10^{-27} kg, proton or neutron

For Solutions, See QR Code on Pg. 378

Mind Map

Dual Nature of Radiation and Matter

Wave Nature of Radiation
The wave nature of light is demonstrated through phenomena like
- **Interference** Light waves superpose to form patterns of constructive and destructive interference.
- **Diffraction** Light bends around obstacles or openings, spreading out and forming patterns.
- **Polarisation** Light waves can oscillate in specific directions, indicating its transverse nature.

de-Broglie hypothesis (Matter wave)
Louis de-Broglie proposed that particles, like electrons and protons, also exhibit wave like behavior under certain conditions. This wave like nature of matter is referred to as matter waves.

de-Broglie Relation

$$\lambda = \frac{h}{p}$$

For a particle with kinetic energy K,

$$\lambda = \frac{h}{\sqrt{2mK}}$$

de-Broglie Wavelength of Electron
Consider an electron of mass m and charge e. Let v be the final velocity attained by the electron when it is accelerated from rest through the potential difference of V volts.

$$\lambda = \frac{h}{p} = \frac{h}{\sqrt{2mK}} = \frac{h}{\sqrt{2meV}}$$

Radiation, such as light, exhibits dual nature. It behaves as both a wave and a particle, depending on the phenomenon being observed.

Wave-Particle Duality Radiation has a dual nature with wave like properties evident in propagation and particle like properties in interaction with matter.

Hertz's and Lenard's Observations
Hallwach connected a zinc plate to an electroscope. He allowed ultraviolet light to fall on a zinc plate. He observed that the zinc plate became
(i) uncharged if initially negatively charged.
(ii) positively charged if initially uncharged.
(iii) more positively charged if initially positively charged.

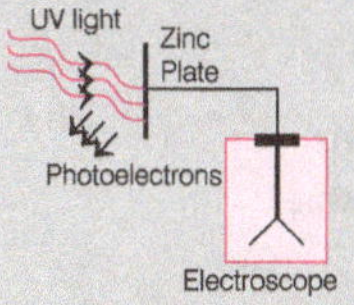

Hertz initial discovery and Lenard's detailed experiments provided crucial experimental evidence that light could interact with matter to release electrons.
These observations could not be explained by classical wave theories of light.
They paved the way for Albert Einstein's explanation of the photoelectric effect in 1905, which introduced the concept of light quanta (photons) and supported the emerging quantum theory.

Particle Nature of Radiation
The particle nature of radiation is demonstrated by phenomena like
- **Photoelectric Effect** Light ejects electrons from a metal surface when it shines on it, showing that light transfers energy in discrete packets called photons.

Experimental Setup of Photoelectric Effect

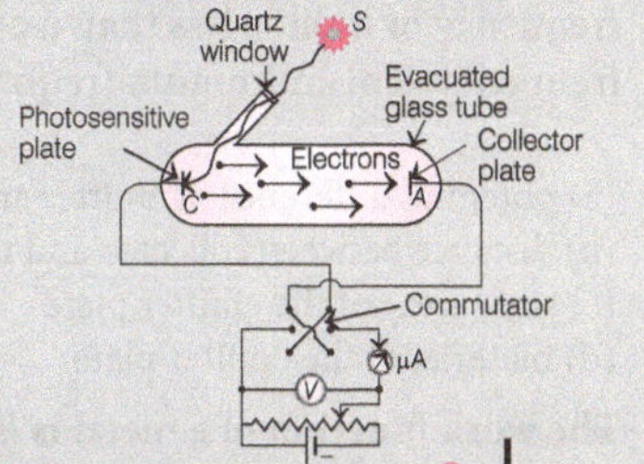

Photoelectric Effect
The photoelectric effect is the phenomenon in which electrons are ejected from the surface of a metal when light of sufficient frequency shines on it.

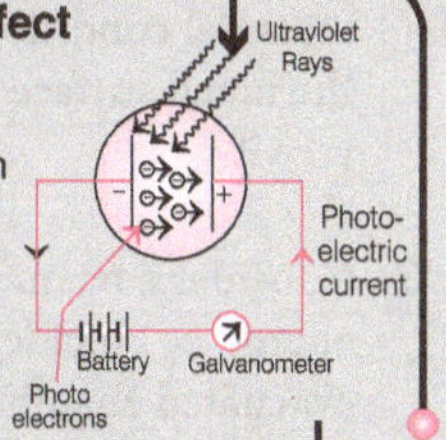

Key Observations from Photoelectric Effect
- **Threshold Frequency (f_o)** Photoemission occurs only if the frequency of the incident light is above a certain minimum, called the threshold frequency.
- **Instantaneous Emission** The ejection of electrons happens almost instantly after light falls on the metal surface.

Einstein's Photoelectric Equation
effect by proposing that light consists of particles called photons.
The energy of each photon is given by
$E = h\nu$, $\quad KE_{max} = h\nu - \phi$

Stopping Potential
It is the minimum reverse voltage needed to stop the most energetic photoelectrons emitted from a metal surface during the photoelectric effect.
Relation between stopping potential (V_s) and threshold frequency (f_o) is derived from the Einstein's photoelectric equation:

$$eV_o = h(\nu - \nu_o)$$

Effect of Different Parameters on Photoelectric Current

Effect of Frequency on Incident Radiation and Stopping Potential
The greater the frequency of the incident radiation, greater is the maximum kinetic energy of the photoelectrons and hence, greater is the retarding potential required to stop such electrons completely.

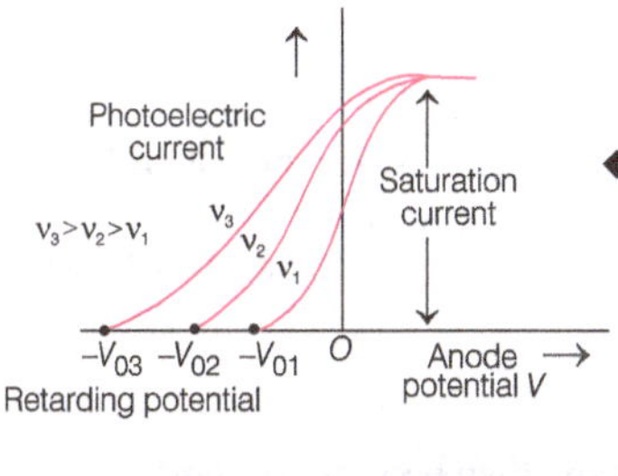

Effect of Intensity
The number of photoelectrons emitted per second is proportional to the intensity of incident radiation.

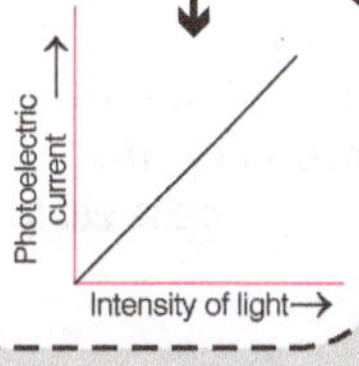

Effect of Potential
For a fixed frequency and intensity of incident light, photoelectric current increases with increase in potential applied to the collector.

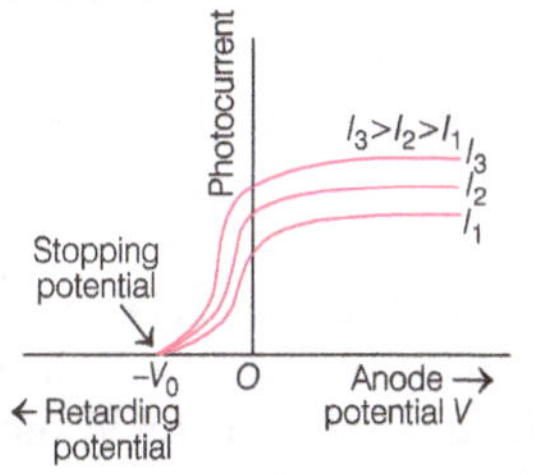

$$K_{max} = \frac{1}{2}mv_{max}^2 = eV_0$$

EXAM PATTERN QUESTIONS

Objective Type Questions

Multiple Choice Questions (MCQs)

1. Lenard observed that no electrons are emitted when frequency of light is less than a certain minimum frequency. This minimum frequency depends on **Competency Based Que.**

(a) potential difference of emitter and collector plates
(b) distance between collector and the emitter plate
(c) size (area) of the emitter plate
(d) material of the emitter plate

2. The work function of a metal is hc/λ_0. If light of wavelength λ is incident on its surface, then the essential condition for the electron to come out from the metal surface is **Competency Based Que.**

(a) $\lambda \geq \lambda_0$ (b) $\lambda \geq 2\lambda_0$
(c) $\lambda \leq \lambda_0$ (d) $\lambda \leq \lambda_0/2$

3. Consider a beam of electrons (each electron with energy E_0) incident on a metal surface kept in an evacuated chamber, then **NCERT Exemplar**

(a) no electrons will be emitted as only photons can emit electrons
(b) electrons can be emitted but all with an energy, E_0
(c) electrons can be emitted with any energy, with a maximum of $E_0 - \phi$ (ϕ is the work function)
(d) electrons can be emitted with any energy, with a maximum of E_0

4. The wavelength of a photon needed to remove a proton from a nucleus which is bound to the nucleus with 1 MeV energy is nearly **NCERT Exemplar**

(a) 1.2 nm (b) 1.2×10^{-3} nm
(c) 1.2×10^{-6} nm (d) 1.2×10^{-2} nm

5. If photons of frequency ν are incident on the surfaces of metals A and B of threshold frequencies $\frac{\nu}{2}$ and $\frac{\nu}{3}$ respectively, the ratio of the maximum kinetic energy of electrons emitted from A to that from B is **Delhi 2020**

(a) 2:3 (b) 3:4 (c) 1:3 (d) $\sqrt{3}:\sqrt{2}$

6. Photons of energy 3.2 eV are incident on a photosensitive surface. If the stopping potential for the emitted electrons is 1.5 V, the work function for the surface is **CBSE 2023**

(a) 1.5 eV (b) 1.7 eV
(c) 3.2 eV (d) 4.7 eV

7. A particle is dropped from a height H. The de-Broglie wavelength of the particle as a function of height is proportional to

(a) H (b) $H^{1/2}$
(c) H^0 (d) $H^{-1/2}$

8. Figure shows a plot of stopping potential (V_0) *versus* $\frac{1}{\lambda}$, where λ is the wavelength of the radiation causing photoelectric emission from a surface. The slope of the line is equal to **CBSE 2023**

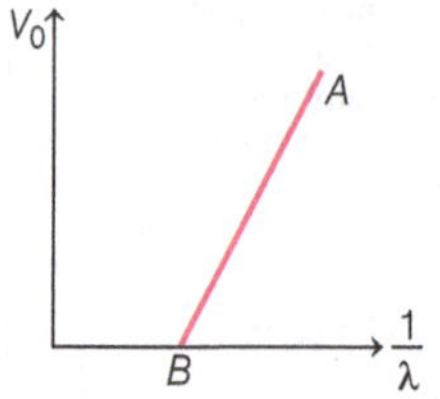

(a) ϕ_0 (b) $\frac{h}{e}$
(c) $\frac{hc}{e}$ (d) $\frac{h^2c}{e^2}$

9. The de-Broglie wavelength of a particle of K is λ. What will be the wavelength of the particle, if its' kinetic energy is $\frac{K}{9}$?

(a) λ (b) 2λ
(c) 3λ (d) 4λ

10. Light of frequency 6.4×10^{14} Hz is incident on a metal of work function 2.14 eV. The maximum kinetic energy of the emitted electrons is about **CBSE 2023**

(a) 0.25 eV (b) 0.51 eV
(c) 1.02 eV (d) 0.10 eV

11. The work function for a metal surface is 4.14 eV. The threshold wavelength for this metal surface is **CBSE SQP 2022-23**

(a) 4125 Å (b) 2062.5 Å
(c) 3000 Å (d) 6000 Å

12. With the increase in potential difference of emitter and collector, the photoelectric current **Competency Based Que.**

(a) increases
(b) decreases
(c) remains constant
(d) increases initially and then become constant

13. The quantum nature of light explains the observations on photoelectric effect as **CBSE 2024**

(a) there is a minimum frequency of incident radiation below which no electrons are emitted
(b) the maximum kinetic energy of photoelectrons depends only on the frequency of incident radiation
(c) when the metal surface is illuminated, electrons are ejected from the surface after sometime
(d) the photoelectric current is independent of the intensity of incident radiation

14. Light of wavelengths λ_A and λ_B falls on two identical metal plates A and B, respectively. The maximum kinetic energy of photoelectrons is K_A and K_B respectively, then which one of the following relations is true? ($\lambda_A = 2\lambda_B$)

(a) $K_A < \frac{K_B}{2}$ (b) $2K_A = K_B$
(c) $K_A = 2K_B$ (d) $K_A > 2K_B$

15. All photons present in a light beam of single frequency have **Competency Based Que.**

(a) same frequency but different momentum
(b) same momentum but different frequency
(c) different frequency and different momentum
(d) same frequency and same momentum

16. The linear momentum of a 6 MeV photon is

(a) 0.01 eV-s m^{-1} (b) 0.02 eV-s m^{-1}
(c) 0.03 eV-s m^{-1} (d) 0.04 eV-s m^{-1}

17. Given below are two charged subatomic particles P and Q, that are accelerated through same potential difference V.

Here, masses, $m_P = m_Q$ and charges, $\frac{q_P}{2} = q_Q$

Which of the two sub-atomic particles will have longer de-Broglie wavelength? **Competency Based Que.**

(a) Particle P, because it has the greater momentum
(b) Particle Q, because it has the greater momentum
(c) Particle P, because it has the smaller momentum
(d) Particle Q, because it has the smaller momentum

18. The energy of a photon of wavelength 663 nm is **CBSE 2023**

(a) 6.64×10^{-20} J (b) 5.18×10^{-10} J
(c) 3.0×10^{-19} J (d) 2.0×10^{-20} J

19. The energy of a photon of wavelength λ is **CBSE 2023**

(a) $hc\lambda$ (b) hc / λ
(c) λ / hc (d) $\lambda h / c$

20. A photon of wavelength 663 nm is incident on a metal surface. The work function of the metal is 1.50 eV. The maximum kinetic energy of the emitted photon electrons is **CBSE 2023**

(a) 3.0×10^{-20} J (b) 6.0×10^{-20} J
(c) 4.5×10^{-20} J (d) 9.0×10^{-20} J

21. A proton and an alpha particle have the same kinetic energy. The ratio of de-Broglie wavelengths associated with the proton to that with the alpha particle is **CBSE 2023**

(a) 1 (b) 2 (c) $2\sqrt{2}$ (d) $\frac{1}{2}$

22. The graph showing the correct variation of linear momentum p of a charge particle with its de-Broglie wavelength λ is **Delhi 2020**

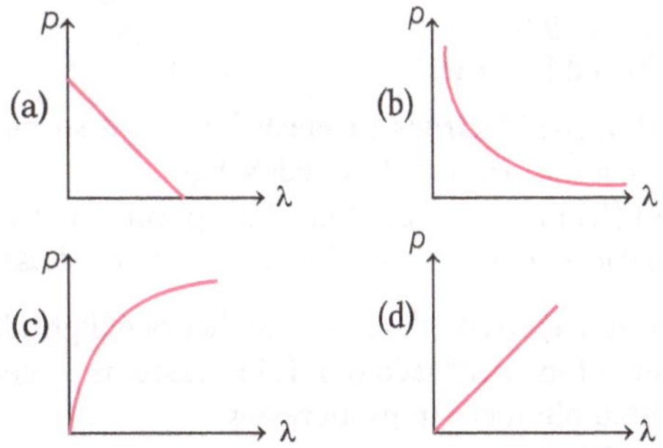

23. Match the Column I with Column II and choose the correct option.

	Column I		Column II
A.	Work function	1.	$E = h\nu - \phi$
B.	Threshold frequency	2.	Energy require to remove an electron from metal surface
C.	Stopping potential	3.	Momentum associated with matter wave
D.	Wave-particle duality	4.	Minimum frequency to eject electron
D.	Einstein's photoelectric equation	5.	Negative potential required to stop photoelectrons

(a) A-2, B-1, C-3, D-5, E-4 (b) A-2, B-4, C-5, D-3, E-1
(c) A-1, B-2, C-4, D-3, E-5 (d) A-4, B-3, C-5, D-1, E-2

24. Match the Column I with Column II and choose the correct option.

	Column I		Column II
A.	de-Broglie wavelength	1.	Emission of electrons from metal surface
B.	Photoelectric effect	2.	$\frac{h}{mv}$
C.	Kinetic energy of photoelectron	3,	Proportional to the intensity of incident light
D.	Photocurrent	4.	Depends on light frequency

(a) A-2, B-1, C-4, D-3 (b) A-1, B-2, C-3, D-4
(c) A-4, B-1, C-2, D-3 (d) A-3, B-2, C-4, D-1

Assertion-Reason

Directions *(Q. Nos. 25-32) In the following questions, two statements are given- one labelled Assertion (A) and the other labelled Reason (R). Select the correct answer to these questions from the codes (a), (b), (c) and (d) as given below.*

(a) Both A and R are true and R is the correct explanation of A.
(b) Both A and R are true but R is not the correct explanation of A.
(c) A is true but R is false.
(d) A is false but R is true.

25. **Assertion** (A) Electrons are ejected from the surface of zinc when it is irradiated by yellow light.
Reason (R) Energy associated with a photon of yellow light is more than the work function of zinc. **CBSE 2024**

26. **Assertion (A)** According to wave theory of light, if intensity of incident radiation is increased, then energy of emitted photoelectrons increases.
Reason (R) Energy of a wave is proportional to its intensity.

27. **Assertion (A)** Photoelectric current depends on the intensity of incident light.
Reason (R) Number of photoelectrons emitted per second is directly proportional to the intensity of incident radiation.

28. **Assertion (A)** Photosensitivity of a metal is high, if its work function is small.
Reason (R) Work function $= h\nu_0$, where ν_0 is the threshold frequency.

29. **Assertion (A)** In photon-particle collision, the total energy and total momentum are conserved.
Reason (R) The number of photons are conserved in a collision.

30. **Assertion** (A) The photoelectrons produced by a monochromatic light beam incident on a metal surface have a spread in their kinetic energies.
Reason (R) The energy of electrons emitted from inside the metal surface, is lost in collision with the other atoms in the metal. **CBSE SQP 2022-23**

31. **Assertion (A)** The photoelectrons produced by a monochromatic light beam incident on a metal surface have a spread in their kinetic energies.
Reason (R) The energy of electrons emitted from inside the metal surface, is lost in collision with the other atoms in the metal. **CBSE SQP 23**

32. **Assertion** (A) de-Broglie's wavelength of a freely falling body keeps decreasing with time.
Reason (R) The momentum of the freely falling body increases with time.

Case Based Question

Directions *(Q.Nos. 33) This question is case study based question. Read the following paragraph and answer the questions on the basis of same.*

33. **It is the phenomenon of emission of electrons from a metallic surface when light of a suitable frequency is incident on it. The emitted electrons are called photoelectrons.**
Nearly all metals exhibit this effect with ultraviolet light but alkali metals like lithium, sodium, potassium, cesium etc. Show this effect even with visible light. It is an instantaneous process, i.e. photoelectrons are emitted as soon as the light is incident on the metal surface. The number of photoelectrons emitted per second is directly proportional to the intensity of the incident radiation.
The maximum kinetic energy of the photoelectrons emitted from a given metal surface is independent of the intensity of the incident light and depends only on the frequency of the incident light. For a given metal surface, there is a certain minimum value of the frequency of the incident light below which emission of photoelectrons does not occur.

(i) In a photoelectric experiment, plate current is plotted against a node potential.

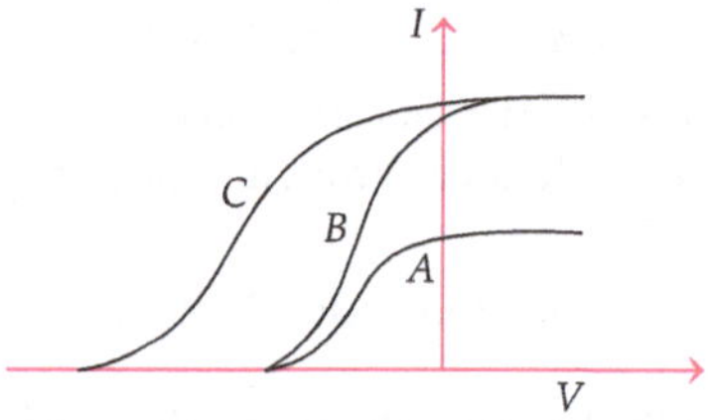

(a) A and B will have same intensities while B and C will have different frequencies.
(b) B and C will have different intensities while A and B will have different frequencies.
(c) A and B will have different intensities while B and C will have equal frequencies.
(d) B and C will have equal intensities while A and B will have same frequencies.

(ii) Photoelectrons are emitted when a zinc plate is
(a) heated
(b) hammered
(c) irradiated by ultraviolet light
(d) subjected to a high pressure

(iii) The threshold frequency for photoelectric effect on sodium corresponds to a wavelength of 500 nm. Its work function is about
(a) 4×10^{-19} J (b) 1 J
(c) 2×10^{-19} J (d) 3×10^{-19} J

(iv) The maximum kinetic energy of photoelectrons emitted from a surface when photons of energy 6 eV fall on it is 4 eV. The stopping potential is

(a) 2 V (b) 4 V
(c) 6 V (d) 10 V

Or

(iv) The minimum energy required to remove an electron from a substance is called its

(a) work function (b) kinetic energy
(c) stopping potential (d) potential energy

34. **Light from a lamp is incident on a vacuum tube containing two electrodes *A* and *B* made from same metal. These electrodes are connected to a very sensitive ammeter and a variable voltage power supply (figure). Near electrode *A* is a transparent window, so that light from the lamp can reach this electrode only. A succession of filters can be placed between the lamp and the window, so that light of specific wavelengths is transmitted to the electrode.**

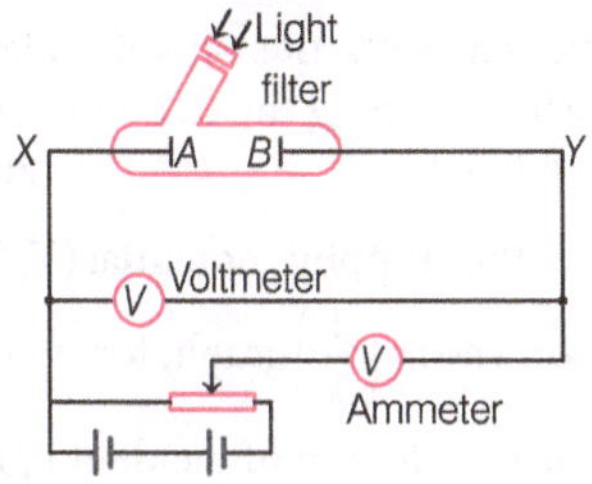

(i) Explain in terms of photons of light, why a current may be expected to flow through this tube for only certain wavelengths of the incoming light?

(ii) Why must a negative potential be applied to electrode *B* to stop the flow of electrical current?

(iii) When the ammeter reads zero, what is the relationship between the potential difference across the electrodes and the kinetic energy of the electrons leaving electrode *A*? If ϕ is the minimum energy required to remove an electron from the metal as used for electrodes *A* and *B*, obtain a relationship between the wavelength λ of the light hitting an electrode, the potential difference *V* across the tube and ϕ

(iv) The data below has been obtained from such an experiment.

Wavelength (nm)	589	552	330	285
Potential difference (V)	−0.246	−0.367	−1.870	−2.463

Plot a suitable graph to determine Planck's constant *h* and the minimum energy ϕ in SI units.

Competency Based Que

35. **When a photon of suitable frequency is incident on a metal surface, photoelectron is emitted from it. If the frequency is below a threshold frequency (ν_0) for the surface, no photoelectron is emitted. For a photon of frequency $\nu(\nu > \nu_0)$ the kinetic energy of the emitted photoelectrons is $h(\nu - \nu_0)$. The photocurrent can be stopped by applying a potential V_0 called stopping potential on the anode. Thus maximum kinetic energy of photoelectrons $K_m = eV_0 = h(\nu - \nu_0)$. The experimental graph between V_0 and ν for a metal is shown in figure. This is a straight line of slope *m*.**

CBSE 2025

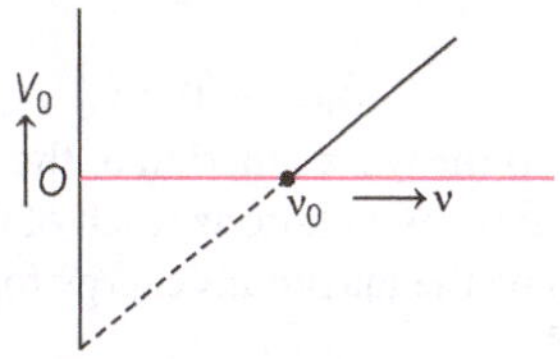

(i) The straight line graphs obtained for two metals

(a) coincide each other.
(b) are parallel to each other.
(c) are not parallel to each other and cross at a point on ν-axis.
(d) are not parallel to each other and do not cross at a point on ν-axis.

(ii) The value of Planck's constant for this metal is

(a) $\frac{e}{m}$ (b) $\frac{1}{me}$
(c) me (d) $\frac{m}{e}$

(iii) The intercepts on ν-axis and V_0-axis of the graph are respectively

(a) $\nu_0, \frac{h\nu_0}{e}$ (b) $\nu_0, h\nu_0$
(c) $\frac{h\nu_0}{e}, \nu_0$ (d) $h\nu_0, \nu_0$

Or

(iii) When the wavelength of a photon is doubled, how many times its wave number and frequency become, respectively?

(a) $2, \frac{1}{2}$ (b) $\frac{1}{2}, \frac{1}{2}$
(c) $\frac{1}{2}, 2$ (d) 2, 2

(iv) The momentum of a photon is 5.0×10^{-29} kg m/s. Ignoring relativistic effects (if any), the wavelength of the photon is

(a) 1.33 μm (b) 3.3 μm
(c) 16.6 μm (d) 13.3 μm

Subjective Questions

Very Short Answer Type Questions

1. Work function of sodium is 2.75 eV. What will be the KE of emitted electron when photon of energy 3.54 eV is incident on the surface of sodium? **CBSE SQP 2019-20**

2. (i) In the explanation of photoeletric effect, we assume one photon of frequency ν collides with an electron and transfers its energy. This leads to the equation for the maximum energy E_{max} of the emitted electron as

$$E_{max} = h\nu - \phi_0$$

where ϕ_0 is the work function of the metal. If an electron absorbs 2 photons (each of frequency ν), what will be the maximum energy for the emitted electron? **[1]**

(ii) Why is this fact (two photon absorption) not taken into consideration in our discussion of the stopping potential? **NCERT Exemplar [1]**

3. Two metals A and B have work functions 2 eV and 4 eV, respectively. Which metal has lower threshold wavelength for photoelectric effect? **Competency Based Que**

4. Do all the electrons that absorb a photon come out as photoelectrons? **NCERT Exemplar**

5. (i) When radiations of frequency 10^{14} Hz is incident on certain surface, no photoemission takes place. What does this statement mean? **Competency Based Que. [1]**

(ii) For a given photosensitive material and with a source of constant frequency of incident radiation, how does the photocurrent vary with the intensity of incident light? **[1]**

6. Define the term intensity in photon picture of electromagnetic radiation.

7. There are materials which absorb photons of shorter wavelength and emit photons of longer wavelength. Can there be stable substances which absorb photons of larger wavelength and emit light of shorter wavelength? **NCERT Exemplar**

8. A proton and an α-particle are accelerated, using the same potential difference. How are the de-Broglie wavelengths λ_p and λ_α related to each other? **NCERT Exemplar**

9. Write the expression for the de-Broglie wavelength associated with a charged particle having charge q and mass m, when it is accelerated by a potential V.

10. Why is the wave nature of matter not more apparent to our daily observations?

Short Answer Type Questions

11. A platinum surface having work function 5.63 eV is illuminated by a monochromatic source of 1.6×10^{15} Hz. what will be the minimum wavelength associated with the ejected electron. **SQP 2024-25**

12. Explain how does (i) photoelectric current and (ii) kinetic energy of the photoelectrons emitted in a photocell vary, if the frequency of incident radiation is doubled but keeping the intensity same? Show the graphical variation in the above two cases.

13. In photoelectric effect experiment, show the variation of

(i) photocurrent with collector plate potential for a given surface for different intensities of incident radiation. Do the curves meet at any point? If so, why? **[1½]**

(ii) photocurrent with intensity of radiation incident on a surface keeping the frequency and plate potential fixed. **CBSE 2024C [1½]**

14. Figure shows the stopping potential (V_0) for the photoelectron *versus* $\left(\frac{1}{\lambda}\right)$ graph, for two metals A and B, λ being the wavelength of incident light.

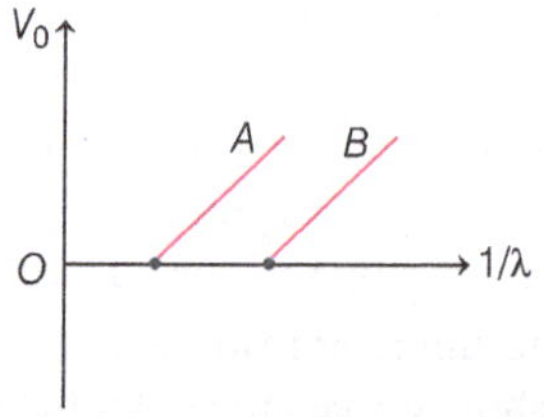

(i) How is the value of Planck's constant determined from the graph? **[1½]**

(ii) If the distance between the light source and the surface of metal A is increased, how will the stopping potential for the electrons emitted from it be effected? Justify your answer. **[1½]**

15. The following graph shows the variation of stopping potential V_0 with the frequency f for the two photosensitive materials A and B.

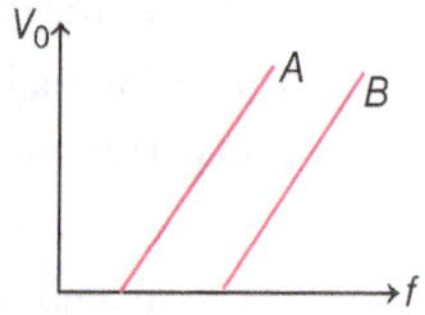

(i) Why is the slope same for both the lines? **[1½]**

(ii) For which material will the emitted electrons have greater kinetic energy, for the incident radiation of the same frequency? Justify your answer. **[1½]**

16. A particle A with a mass m_A is moving with a velocity v and hits a particle B (mass m_B) at rest (one dimensional motion). Find the change in the de-Broglie wavelength of the particle A. Treat the collision as elastic. **NCERT Exemplar**

17. The de-Broglie wavelength of a particle of kinetic energy K is λ. What would be the wavelength of the particle, if its kinetic energy were $\frac{K}{4}$?

18. What are matter waves ? A proton and an alpha particle are accelerated through the same potential difference. Find the ratio of the de-Broglie wavelength associated with the proton to that with the alpha particle. **CBSE 2022, Term-II**

19. The wavelength of the waves associated with a particle having kinetic energy E, is λ. How and by what factor should its kinetic energy be changed, so that the wavelength becomes half ? Also, find the ratio of the final to the initial velocity of the particle. **CBSE 2022, Term-II**

Long Answer Type Questions

20. Light of wavelength 2000 Å falls on a metal surface of work function 4.2 eV.

(i) What is the kinetic energy (in eV) of the fastest electrons emitted from the surface? **[2]**

(ii) What will be the change in the energy of the emitted electrons, if the intensity of light with same wavelength is doubled? **[2]**

(iii) If the same light falls on another surface of work function 6.5 eV, what will be the energy of emitted electrons? **CBSE SQP 2021-22 (Term-II)** **[1]**

21. (i) Figure shows the variation of photoelectric current measured in a photocell circuit as a function of the potential difference between the plates of the photocell when light beams A, B, C and D of different wavelengths are incident on the photocell. Examine the given figure and answer the following questions.

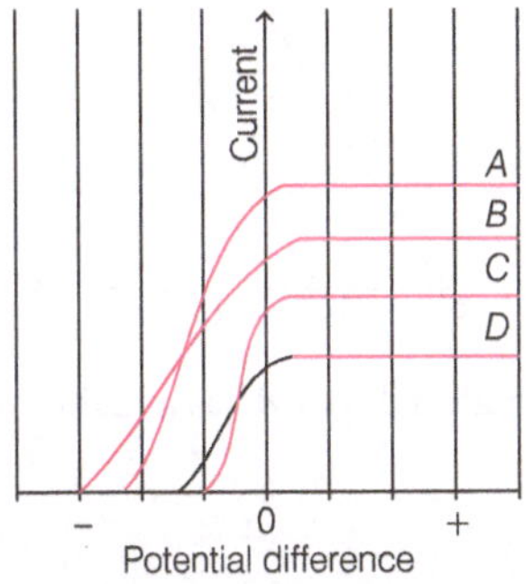

(a) Which light beam has the highest frequency and why? **[2]**

(b) Which light beam has the longest wavelength and why? **[1]**

(c) Which light beam ejects photoelectrons with maximum momentum and why? **Competency Based Que.** **[2]**

Or

(ii) What is the effect on threshold frequency and stopping potential on increasing the frequency of incident beam of light? Justify your answer. **CBSE 2023**

22. Write Einstein's photoelectric equation relating the maximum kinetic energy of the emitted electron to the frequency of the radiation incident on a photosensitive surface. State clearly, the basic elementary process involved in photoelectric effect.

23. (i) Increase in the intensity of the radiation causing photoelectric emission from a surface does not affect the maximum KE of the photoelectrons. Explain. **[2½]**

(ii) The photon emitted during the de-excitation from the first excited level to the ground state of hydrogen atom is used to irradiate a photocathode in which stopping potential is 5 V. Calculate the work function of the cathode used. **CBSE 2023** **[2½]**

24. Radiation of frequency 10^{15} Hz is incident on three photosensitive surfaces A, B and C. Following observations are recorded:

(i) **Surface A** no photoemission occurs **[2]**

(ii) **Surface B** photoemission occurs but the photoelectrons have zero kinetic energy. **[2]**

(iii) **Surface C** photoemission occurs and photoelectrons have some kinetic energy. Using Einstein's photoelectric equation, explain the three observations. **CBSE SQP 2023** **[1]**

Or

The graph shows the variation of photocurrent for a photosensitive metal

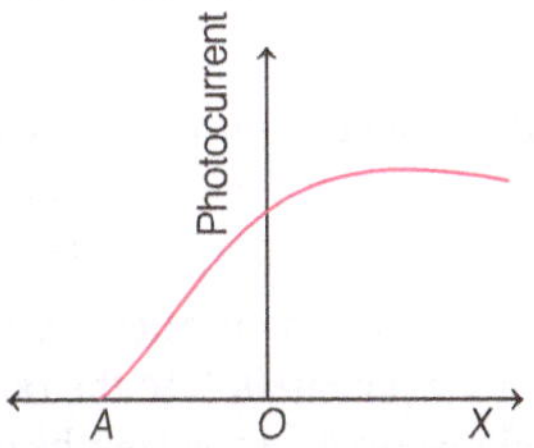

(i) What does X and A on the horizontal axis represent? **[2]**

(ii) Draw this graph for three different values of frequencies of incident radiation ν_1, ν_2 and ν_3 $(\nu_3 > \nu_2 > \nu_1)$ for the same intensity. **[2]**

(iii) Draw this graph for three different values of intensities of incident radiation I_1, I_2 and I_3 $(I_3 > I_2 > I_1)$ having the same frequency. **[1]**

25. Sketch the graphs showing variation of stopping potential with frequencies of incident radiations for two photosensitive materials A and B having threshold frequencies $\nu_A > \nu_B$.

(i) In which case is the stopping potential more and why? **[2½]**

(ii) Does the slope of the graph depend on the nature of the material used? Explain. **[2½]**

26. Define the terms cut-off voltage and threshold frequency in relation to the phenomenon of photoelectric effect. Using Einstein's photoelectric equation, show how the cut-off voltage and threshold frequency for a given photosensitive material can be determined with the help of a suitable plot/graph.

27. Define the terms threshold frequency and stopping potential in the study of photoelectric emission. Explain briefly the reasons, why wave theory of light is not able to explain the observed features in photoelectric effect?

28. (i) Write the important properties of photons which are used to establish Einstein's photoelectric equation. **[3]**

(ii) Use this equation to explain the concept of

(a) threshold frequency and **[1]**

(b) stopping potential. **[1]**

29. (i) What are matter waves? A particle of mass m and charge q is accelerated from rest through a potential difference V. Obtain an expression for de-Broglie wavelength associated with the particle. **[2]**

(ii) Monochromatic light of frequency 5.0×10^{14} Hz is produced by a source of power output 3.315 mW. Calculate

(a) energy of the photon in the beam and **[2]**

(b) number of photons emitted per second by the source. **CBSE 2024C** **[1]**

30. (i) Explain de-Broglie argument to propose his hypothesis. Show that de-Broglie wavelength of photon equals electromagnetic radiation. **[2½]**

(ii) If deuterons and alpha particles are accelerated through same potential, find the ratio of the associated de-Broglie wavelengths of two. **[2½]**

31. (i) Determine the de-Broglie wavelength of a proton whose kinetic energy is equal to the rest mass energy of an electron. Mass of proton is 1836 times that of electron. **[2½]**

(ii) In which region of electromagnetic spectrum does this wavelength lie? **[2½]**

32. An electron, α-particle and a proton have the same de-Broglie wavelengths. Which of these particle has

(i) minimum kinetic energy? **[2½]**

(ii) maximum kinetic energy and why? **[2½]**

In what way has the wave nature of electron beam exploited in electron microscope?

33. Electrons are emitted from the cathode of a photocell of negligible work function, when photons of wavelength λ are incident on it. Derive the expression for the de-Broglie wavelength of the electrons emitted in terms of the wavelength of the incident light.

Numerical Problems

Photoelectric Effect

34. A light of wavelength 400 nm is incident on metal surface whose work function is 3.0×10^{-19} J. Calculate the speed of the fastest photoelectrons emitted. **CBSE 2025**

35. Light of frequency 7.21×10^{14} Hz is incident on a metal surface. Electrons with a maximum speed of 6×10^5 m/s are ejected from the surface. What is the threshold frequency for photoemission of electrons? **NCERT**

36. Consider a metal exposed to light of wavelength 600 nm. The maximum energy of the electron doubles when light of wavelength 400 nm is used. Find the work function in eV. **NCERT Exemplar**

37. A student performs an experiment on photoelectric effect, using two materials A and B. A plot of V_{stop} *versus* ν is given in the figure.

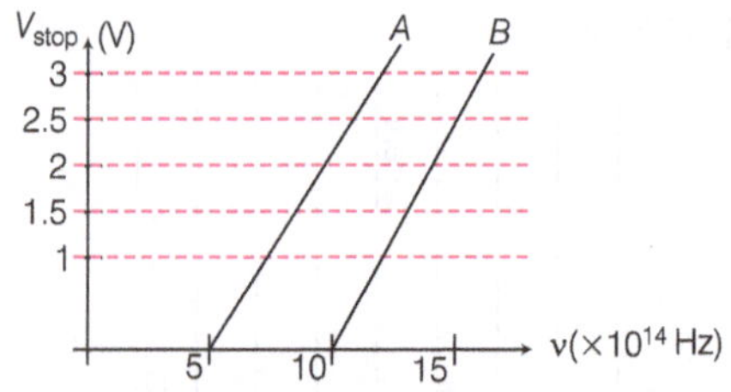

(i) Which material A or B has a higher work function? **[2½]**

(ii) Given the electric charge of an electron = 1.6×10^{-19} C, find the value of h obtained from the experiment for both A and B. Comment on whether it is consistent with the Einstein's theory. **NCERT Exemplar [2½]**

38. Radiations of frequency 3.0×10^{15} Hz are incident on a photosensitive surface of threshold frequency 1.0×10^{15} Hz. Calculate

(i) work function of the surface **[1]**

(ii) maximum kinetic energy of photoelectrons **CBSE 2024C [1]**

39. Radiations of two frequencies are incident on a metal surface of work function 2.0 eV one by one. The energies of their photons are 2.5 eV and 4.5 eV respectively. Find the ratio of the maximum speed of the electrons emitted in the two cases. **CBSE 2025**

Einstein Photoelectric Equation and Stopping Potential

40. Ultraviolet light of wavelength 200 nm is incident on polished surface of iron. Work function of the surface is 4.71 eV. Calculate its stopping potential.

41. In the study of a photoelectric effect, the graph between the stopping potential V and frequency ν of the incident radiation on two different metals P and Q is shown below. **Competency Based Que.**

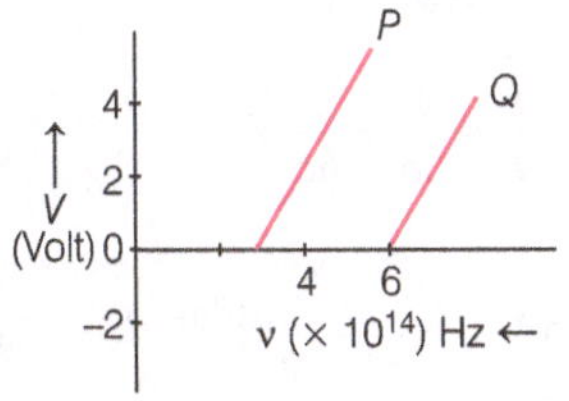

(i) Which one of the two metals has higher threshold frequency?

(ii) Determine the work function of the metal which has greater value.

(iii) Find the maximum kinetic energy of electron emitted by light of frequency 8×10^{14} Hz for this metal.

Matter Wave and de-Broglie Wavelength

42. The work function of cesium metal is 2.14 eV. When light of frequency 6×10^{14} Hz is incident on the metal surface, photoemission of electrons occurs. What is the

(i) maximum kinetic energy of the emitted electrons,

(ii) stopping potential and

(iii) maximum speed of the emitted photoelectrons?

43. Calculate the wavelength of de-Broglie waves associated with a proton having $\left(\frac{500}{1.673}\right)$eV energy. How will the wavelength be affected for an alpha particle having the same energy? **CBSE 2023**

44. There are two sources of light, each emitting with a power of 100 W. One emits X-rays of wavelength 1 nm and the other visible light at 500 nm. Find the ratio of number of photons of X-rays to the photons of visible light of the given wavelength. **NCERT Exemplar**

45. A proton and α-particle are accelerated through different potentials V_1 and V_2 respectively, so that they have the same de-Broglie wavelengths. Find $\frac{V_1}{V_2}$. **CBSE 2024**

46. What are matter waves? A proton, an electron and an α-particle have the same kinetic energy. Write the de-Broglie wavelengths associated with them in increasing order. **CBSE 2024**

47. The ratio of de-Broglie wavelengths of a proton and a deuteron accelerated by potential V_p and V_d respectively, $\left(\frac{\lambda_p}{\lambda_d}\right)$ is $\frac{1}{2}$. Find $\frac{V_p}{V_d}$. **CBSE 2024**

Hints & Solutions

Objective Type Questions

1. (d)	2. (c)	3. (d)	6. (b)	7. (d)
8. (c)	9. (c)	10. (b)	11. (c)	12. (d)
13. (a)	14. (a)	15. (d)	17. (d)	19. (b)
21. (b)	22. (b)	23. (b)	24. (a)	25. (c)
26. (a)	27. (a)	28. (b)	29. (c)	30. (a)
31. (a)	32. (a)			

4. (*b*) Here, $E = 1$ MeV $= 10^6$eV, $h = 6.63\times 10^{-34}$ Js

$c = 3\times 10^8$ ms^{-1}

$$\therefore\ hc = \frac{6.63\times 10^{-34}\times 3\times 10^8}{1.6\times 10^{-19}} \approx 1240 \text{ eVnm}$$

As $E = \dfrac{hc}{\lambda}$

$$\text{or}\quad \lambda = \frac{hc}{E} = \frac{1240 \text{ eVnm}}{10^6\text{eV}} = 1.2\times 10^{-3}\text{nm}$$

5. (*b*) Maximum kinetic energy of electron for metal *A*

$$K_A = h\nu - h\frac{\nu}{2} = \frac{h\nu}{2}$$

Maximum kinetic energy of electron for metal *B*

$$K_B = h\nu - \frac{h\nu}{3} = \frac{2h\nu}{3}$$

Ratio of maximum kinetic energies,

$$\frac{K_A}{K_B} = \frac{\frac{h\nu}{2}}{\frac{2h\nu}{3}} = 3:4$$

16. (*b*) Energy of a photon,

$$E = 6 \text{ MeV} = 6\times 10^6 \text{ eV}$$

Linear momentum of the photon

$$p = \frac{E}{c}$$

$$p = \frac{6\times 10^6\text{eV}}{3\times 10^8\text{ms}^{-1}}$$

$$= 2\times 10^{-2}\text{ eVsm}^{-1}$$

$$= 0.02 \text{ eV sm}^{-1}$$

18. (*c*) The energy of a photon of wavelength 66 nm can be calculated using the formula $E = \dfrac{hc}{\lambda}$, where E is the energy of the photon, h is the Planck's constant, c is the speed of light in vacuum and λ is the wavelength of the photon. Plugging in the value, we get

$$E = \frac{(6.62\times 10^{-34}\times 3\times 10^8)}{663\times 10^{-9}}$$

$$= 3\times 10^{-19}\text{J}$$

20. (*b*) Given, $\lambda = 663$ nm, $\phi_0 = 1.5$ eV

We know that, KE $= hf - \phi_0$

$$\text{KE} = \frac{hc}{\lambda} - \phi_0$$

$$\text{KE} = \frac{(6.62\times 10^{-34}\times 3\times 10^8)}{(663\times 10^{-9})} - 1.5\times 1.6\times 10^{-19}$$

$$\text{KE} = 6\times 10^{-20}\text{ J}$$

33. (i) (*d*) (ii) (*c*) (iii) (*a*) (iv) (*b*) or (iv) (*a*)

34. (i) Energy of photons hitting electrode must be greater than minimum energy to release electrons from electrode. Released electrons moving across tube constitute the current.

$$\frac{hc}{\lambda} > \text{work function}$$

(ii) If the electrons leave the electrode with kinetic energy and other electrode is positive, electrons will be accelerated.

If other electrode is sufficiently negative, then even electrons with greatest kinetic energy will not have energy sufficient to reach electrode. Therefore, current will be zero.

(iii) eV = maximum kinetic energy of electrons

Relation between wavelength of light hitting the electrode and potential difference.

$$\frac{hc}{\lambda} = \phi + eV$$

$$\frac{1}{\lambda} = \frac{\phi}{hc} + \frac{e}{hc}V \qquad \text{...(i)}$$

(iv)

λ (nm)	$\frac{1}{\lambda}(10^6\text{m}^{-1})$	Potential Difference (V)
589	1.70	–0.246
552	1.81	–0.367
330	3.03	–1.870
285	3.51	–2.463

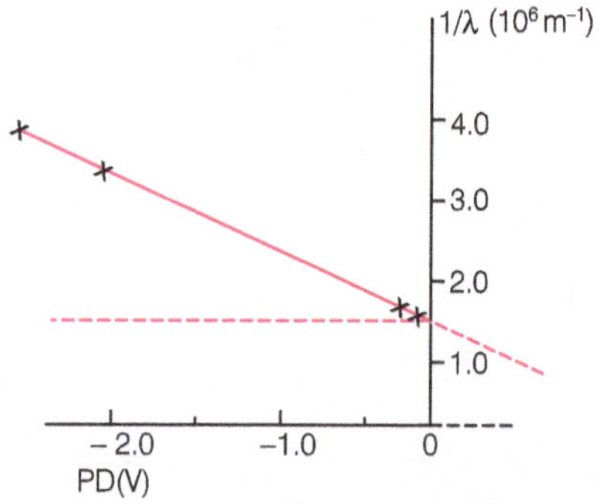

$$\text{Gradient} = \frac{e}{hc} = \frac{3.51}{-2.463} \times 10^6$$

(from Eq. (i) and graph)

$$h = \frac{1.60 \times 10^{-19} \times 3.51}{3 \times 10^8 \times 2.463 \times 10^6} = 7.6 \times 10^{-34} \text{ Js}$$

Intercept = ϕ/hc

$$\phi = 7.6 \times 10^{-34} \times 3 \times 10^8 \times 1.55 \times 10^6$$
$$= 3.5 \times 10^{-19} \text{ J}$$

35. (i) (*b*) They are parallel to each other because the work function might differ depending on the material.

(ii) (*c*) Slope, $m = \frac{\Delta V_0}{\Delta \nu_0} = \frac{h(\Delta \nu_0)}{\varepsilon(\Delta \nu_0)}$

$\Rightarrow \quad h = me$

(iii) (*a*)

Or

(*c*) When wavelength is doubled, wave number becomes $\frac{1}{2}$ time and frequency becomes 2 times.

(iv) (*d*) $p = \frac{h}{\lambda} \Rightarrow \lambda = \frac{6.63 \times 10^{-34}}{5 \times 10^{-29}} = 1.33 \times 10^{-5} \text{m} = 13.3 \ \mu\text{m}$

Subjective Questions

1. Given, $\phi_0 = 2.75$ eV, $\phi = 3.54$ eV

From Einstein's photoelectric equation,

$$\text{KE} = \phi - \phi_0 = 3.54 - 2.75 = 0.79 \text{ eV}$$

2. (i) Here it is given that, an electron absorbs 2 photons each of frequency ν then $\nu' = 2\nu$ where, ν' is the frequency of emitted electron.

Given, $\quad E_{max} = h\nu - \phi_0$

Now, maximum energy for emitted electrons is

$$E'_{max} = h(2\nu) - \phi_0 = 2h\nu - \phi_0$$

(ii) The probability of absorbing 2 photons by the same electron is very low. Hence, such emission will be negligible.

3. We know that, $\lambda_0 = \frac{hc}{\phi_0}$ $\quad \left[\because \phi_0 = \frac{hc}{\lambda_0}\right]$

$\Rightarrow \quad \lambda_0 \propto \frac{1}{\phi_0}$

Hence, metal *B* has lower threshold wavelength for photelectric effect.

4. In photoelectric effect, we can observe that most electrons get scattered into the metal by absorbing a photon.
Thus, all the electrons that absorb a photon doesn't come out as photoelectron. Only a few come out of metal whose energy becomes greater than the work function of metal.

5. (i) The value of threshold frequency is more than 10^{14} Hz.

(ii) The photocurrent increases linearly with the intensity of incident radiation.

6. It is the number of photons passing through an area in a given interval of time. Its SI unit is watt/steradian.

7. According to first statement, when the materials which absorb photons of shorter wavelength has high energy of the incident photon on the material and low energy of emitted photon of longer wavelength. But in second statement, the energy of the incident photon is low for the substances which has to absorb photons of larger wavelength and energy of emitted photon is high to emit light of shorter wavelength. This means in this statement material has to supply the energy for the emission of photons. But this is not possible for a stable substances.

8. As, $\quad \lambda = \frac{h}{\sqrt{2mqv}}$

$\therefore \quad \lambda \propto \frac{1}{\sqrt{mq}}$

$$\frac{\lambda_p}{\lambda_\alpha} = \frac{\sqrt{m_\alpha q_\alpha}}{\sqrt{m_p q_p}} = \frac{\sqrt{4m_p \times 2e}}{\sqrt{m_p \times e}} = \sqrt{8}$$

$\therefore \quad \lambda_p = \sqrt{8}\lambda_\alpha$

i.e., wavelength of proton is $\sqrt{8}$ times wavelength of α-particle.

9. de Broglie wavelength,

$$\lambda = \frac{h}{p} = \frac{h}{\sqrt{2mqV}}$$

where, h = Planck's constant and p = momentum of charged particle.

10. The de-Broglie wavelength associated with a body of mass m, moving with velocity v is given by $\lambda = \frac{h}{mv}$.

Since, the mass of the objects used in our daily life is very large, hence the de-Broglie wavelength associated with them is quite small and is not visible. Hence, the wave nature of matter is not more apparent to our daily observations.

11. Given, $\phi = 5.63 \text{ eV} = 5.63 \times 1.6 \times 10^{-19}$ J

$$\nu = 1.6 \times 10^{15} \text{ Hz}$$

$$\text{KE} = h\nu - \phi_0 = \frac{hc}{\lambda} \Rightarrow \lambda = \frac{hc}{h\nu - \phi_0}$$

On putting the values, we get

$$\lambda = \frac{6.63 \times 10^{-34} \times 3 \times 10^8}{6.63 \times 10^{-34} \times 1.6 \times 10^{15} - 5.63 \times 1.6 \times 10^{-19}}$$

$$\Rightarrow \quad \frac{19.89 \times 10^{-26}}{1.6 \times 10^{-19}(6.63 - 5.63)} = \frac{19.89 \times 10^{-26}}{1.6 \times 10^{-19}}$$

$\lambda = 12.4 \times 10^{-7}$ m

This is the minimum wavelength associated with the ejected electron.

12. (i) Since, photoelectric current depends on intensity of incident radiation and does not depend on the frequency of incident radiation. Therefore, when frequency of incident radiation is increased to double, then photoelectric current remains same. This is shown in the following graph.

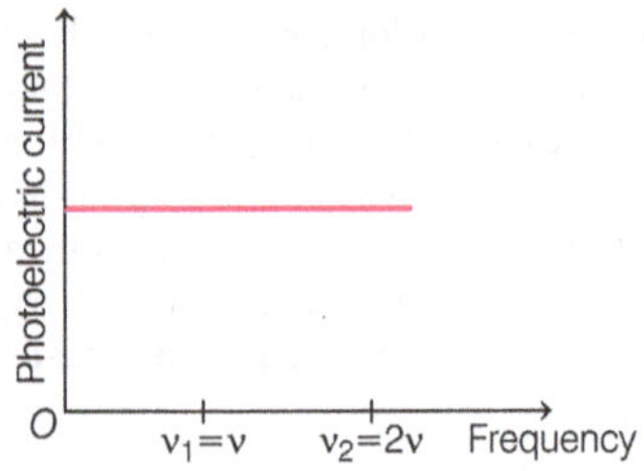

(ii) Kinetic energy of emitted photoelectrons,

$$K = \frac{1}{2} m v_{max}^2 = h\nu \Rightarrow K \propto \nu$$

Hence, on increasing the frequency of incident radiation to double, kinetic energy of emitted photoelectrons also will increase to double. This is shown below

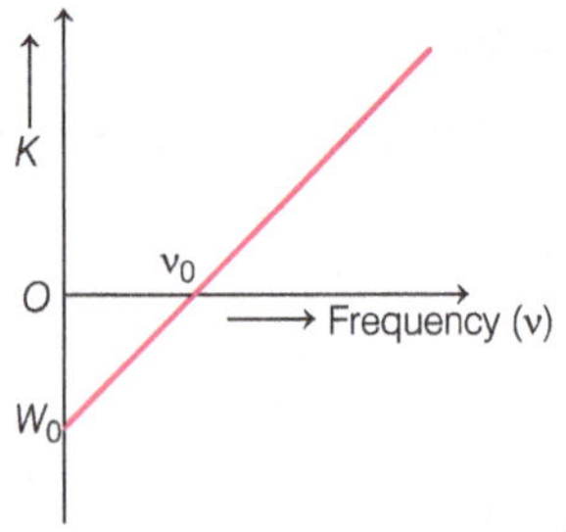

where, ν_0 = threshold wavelength.

13. (i) Yes, these curves meet at stopping potential for any surface, as the energy of photons does not depend upon intensity of light, at the stopping potential current reduce to zero.

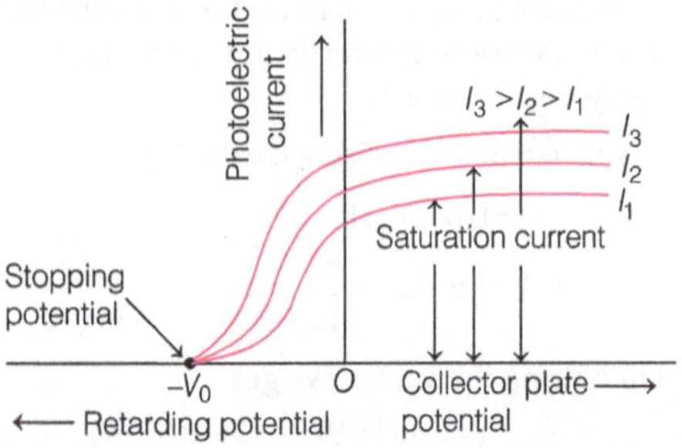

(ii) If intensity of incident light is O, then photocurrent becomes 0. As intensity increases, number of photoelectrons increases and hence photocurrent also increases.

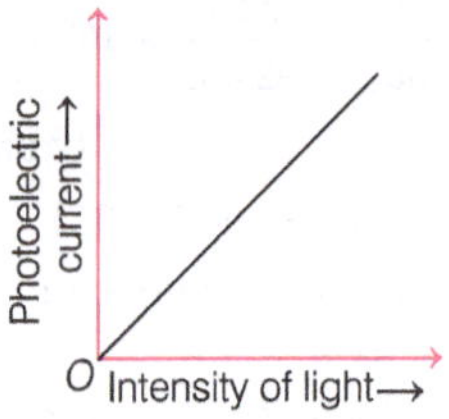

14. (i) The variation of stopping potential (V_0) for the photoelectron *versus* $\left(\frac{1}{\lambda}\right)$ graph is as shown below

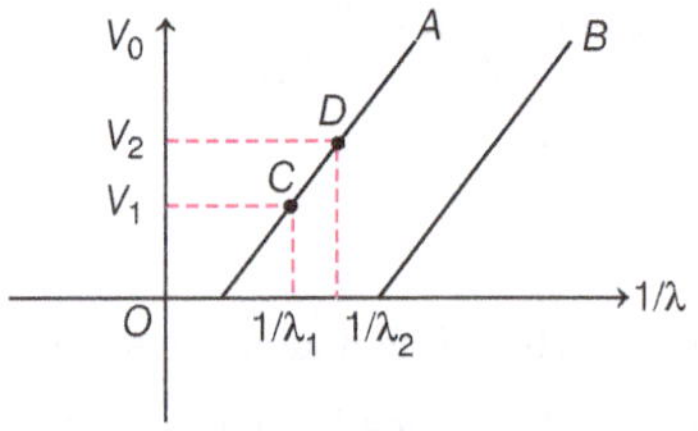

Take any two points C and D on the graph as shown above.

According to Einstein's photoelectric equation, we can write,

$$eV_1 = \frac{hc}{\lambda_1} - \phi_0 \qquad \text{...(i)}$$

and $$eV_2 = \frac{hc}{\lambda_2} - \phi_0 \qquad \text{...(ii)}$$

Subtracting Eq. (i) from Eq. (ii), we get

$$\Rightarrow \quad e(V_2 - V_1) = hc\left(\frac{1}{\lambda_2} - \frac{1}{\lambda_1}\right)$$

or $$h = \frac{e(V_2 - V_1)}{c\left(\frac{1}{\lambda_2} - \frac{1}{\lambda_1}\right)} = \frac{e(V_2 - V_1)\lambda_1\lambda_2}{c(\lambda_1 - \lambda_2)}$$

Thus, Planck's constant can be determined from graph.

Note Since, h is a constant, so it will be same for both metals A and B.

(ii) Stopping potential V_0 for the electrons emitted will not be affected by the increase in distance between light source and the metal surface A. This is because V_0 is independent of the intensity of the incident light but depends only upon the frequency (or wavelength) of incident light. So, increase in the given distance affects only the intensity of the light but not the frequency. Thus, V_0 remains same.

15. (i) The slope of the graph gives the value of h/e. Which is same for both the materials A and B.

(ii) The material A has lower value of threshold frequency. So, A will emit photoelectron of greater kinetic energy.

16. As collision is elastic, hence laws of conservation of momentum and kinetic energy are obeyed.

According to law of conservation of momentum,

$$m_A v + m_B 0 = m_A v_1 + m_B v_2$$

$$\Rightarrow \quad m_A(v - v_1) = m_B v_2$$

According to law of conservation of kinetic energy,

$$\frac{1}{2}m_A v^2 = \frac{1}{2}m_A v_1^2 + \frac{1}{2}m_B v_2^2 \quad \text{...(i)}$$

$$\Rightarrow \quad m_A(v - v_1^2) = m_B v_2^2$$

$$\Rightarrow \quad m_A(v - v_1)(v + v_1) = m_B {v_2}^2 \quad \text{... ()ii}$$

Dividing Eq. (ii) by Eq. (i),

we get, $v + v_1 = v_2$ or $v = v_2 - v_1$ ...(iii)

Solving Eqs. (i) and (iii), we get

$$v_1 = \left(\frac{m_A - m_B}{m_A + m_B}\right)v \text{ and } v_2 = \left(\frac{2m_A}{m_A + m_B}\right)v$$

$$\lambda_{\text{initial}} = \frac{h}{m_A v}$$

$$\lambda_{\text{final}} = \frac{h}{m_A v_1} = \frac{h(m_A + m_B)}{m_A(m_A - m_B)v}$$

$$\Delta\lambda = \lambda_{\text{final}} - \lambda_{\text{initial}} = \frac{h}{m_A v}\left[\frac{m_A + m_B}{m_A - m_B} - 1\right]$$

17. As we know, de-Broglie wavelength,

$$\lambda = \frac{h}{p} = \frac{h}{\sqrt{2mK}}$$

Hence, $K_1 = \frac{h^2}{2m\lambda_1^2}$ ...(i)

According to the question, $K_2 = \frac{K_1}{4}$

$$K_2 = \frac{h^2}{2m\lambda_2^2}$$

$$\frac{K_1}{4} = \frac{h^2}{2m\lambda_2^2} \quad \text{..(ii)}$$

From Eqs. (i) and (ii), we get

$$\frac{\frac{K_1}{4}}{K_1} = \frac{h^2}{2m\lambda_2^2} \times \frac{2m\lambda_1^2}{h^2}$$

$$\frac{1}{4} = \frac{\lambda_1^2}{\lambda_2^2} \Rightarrow \frac{\lambda_1}{\lambda_2} = \frac{1}{2}$$

Hence, wavelength of the particle will be doubled when kinetic energy becomes $\frac{1}{4}$ th.

18. For matter wave, Refer to text on page 348

$$V_\alpha = V_p = V$$

$$\therefore \quad \frac{\lambda_p}{\lambda_\alpha} = \frac{\sqrt{2meV_\alpha}}{\sqrt{2meV_p}} = \sqrt{\frac{V_\alpha}{V_p}} = 1$$

$$\therefore \quad \lambda_p : \lambda_\alpha = 1:1$$

19. As, $\lambda = \frac{h}{\sqrt{2mE}}$ ...(i)

$\therefore$ At $\lambda' = \frac{\lambda}{2}, E' = ?$

$$\therefore \quad \lambda' = \frac{h}{\sqrt{2mE'}}$$

$$\Rightarrow \quad \frac{\lambda}{2} = \frac{h}{\sqrt{2mE'}}$$

$$\therefore \quad \lambda = \frac{2h}{\sqrt{2mE'}} \quad \text{...(ii)}$$

From Eqs. (i) and (ii), we get

$$\frac{h}{\sqrt{2mE}} = \frac{2h}{\sqrt{2mE'}}$$

$$\therefore \quad E' = 4E$$

$$\text{Also, } \frac{v'}{v} = \frac{\frac{1}{2}mv'^2}{\frac{1}{2}mv^2} = \frac{E'}{E} = 4$$

20. Wavelength of light,

$$\lambda = 2000 \text{ Å}$$
$$= 2 \times 10^{-7} \text{ m}$$

Work function, $\phi_0 = 4.2$ eV

$$h = 6.63 \times 10^{-34} \text{ J-s}$$

(i) Using Einstein's photoelectric equation, kinetic energy of fastest electron,

$$K_{\max} = hv - \phi_0 = h\frac{c}{\lambda} - \phi_0$$

$$= \left(\frac{6.63 \times 10^{-34} \times 3 \times 10^8}{2 \times 10^{-7} \times 1.6 \times 10^{-19}} - 4.2\right) \text{eV}$$

$$= 6.2 \text{ eV} - 4.2 \text{ eV}$$
$$= 2.0 \text{ eV}$$

(ii) Since, the energy of emitted electron does not depend upon intensity of incident light, hence the energy of emitted electrons remains unchanged.

(iii) For this surface, electrons will not be emitted as the energy of incident light (6.2 eV) is less than the work function ($\phi' = 6.5$ eV) of the surface.

21. (i) (a) As, the frequency of incident radiation is directly proportional to stopping potential. Hence, the light beam *B* has highest stopping potential and hence highest frequency.

(b) As, the frequency is inversely proportional to the wavelength. Hence, the light beam *C* has smallest stopping potential or frequency and the longest wavelength.

(c) As, momentum $\propto \text{KE}_{\max} \propto$ stopping potential. The light beam *B* has highest stopping potential and hence, it ejects photoelectrons with maximum momentum.

Or

(ii) Stopping potential is directly proportional to the frequency of incident beam of light. So, on increasing the frequency, the stopping potential increases.

Threshold frequency is the property of the metal. It is independent of the frequency of the incident beam of light. So, on increasing the frequency does not affect the threshold frequency the metal.

22. Refer to the text on pages 352 and 353.

23. (i) Einstein's photoelectric equation is

$$KE_{max} = h\nu - \phi_0 \quad ...(i)$$

From Eq. (i), as the maximum kinetic energy of the photoelectrons only depends on the frequency of the incident light and is independent of its intensity. Hence, by changing, intensity does not affect the KE_{max}.

(ii) The energy of photon in various states of hydrogen atom is

In ground state, $E_1 = -13.6$ eV

In first excited state, $E_2 = -3.4$ eV

$\therefore$ Energy of photon,

$$\Delta E = E_2 - E_1$$
$$= -3.4 - (-13.6) = 10.2 \text{ eV}$$

Stopping potential, $V_0 = 5$ V

From Einstein's photoelectric equation,

$$eV_0 = \Delta E - \phi_0$$
$$\therefore \quad \phi_0 = \Delta E - eV_0$$
$$= 10.2 - 5 = 5.2 \text{ eV}$$

$\therefore$ Work function, $\phi_0 = 5.2$ eV

24. The three observations for surfaces *A*, *B* and *C* are as follow

(i) For surface *A*,

Frequency of incident radiation,

$$\nu = 10^{15} \text{ Hz}$$

As, there is no photoemission occurs

$\therefore$ Threshold frequency $(\nu_0) > 10^{15}$ Hz

(ii) For surface *B*, $\nu = 10^{15}$ Hz

As, $KE_{max} = 0$, but photoemission occurs.

$\therefore$ from Einstein's photoelectric equation,

$$KE_{max} = h\nu - h\nu_0$$

$\therefore$ Threshold frequency $(\nu_0) = \nu = 10^{15}$ Hz

(iii) For surface *C*, $\nu = 10^{15}$ Hz

As, photoemission occurs and photoelectrons have some KE.

$\therefore$ From Einstein's photoelectric equation,

$$h\nu = h\nu_0 + KE$$
$$\therefore \quad h\nu > h\nu_0$$

Threshold frequency $(\nu_0) < 10^{15}$ Hz

Or

(i) On the horizontal axis, *A* represents cut-off or stopping potential and *X* represents anode potential.

(ii) The photocurrent *versus* anode potential graph for different frequencies and same intensity is given below

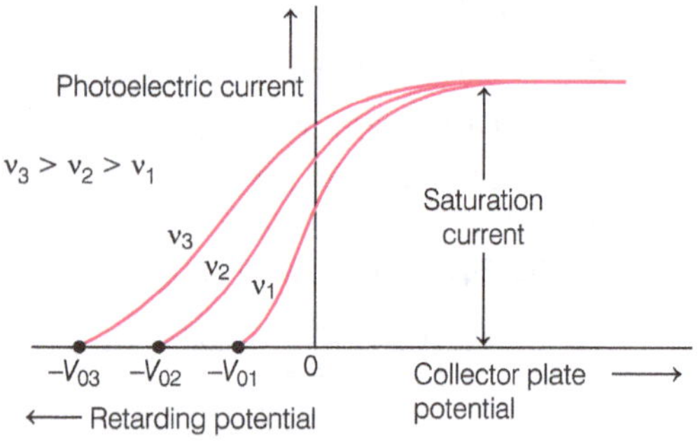

(iii) The photocurrent *versus* anode potential graph for different intensities and same frequency is given below

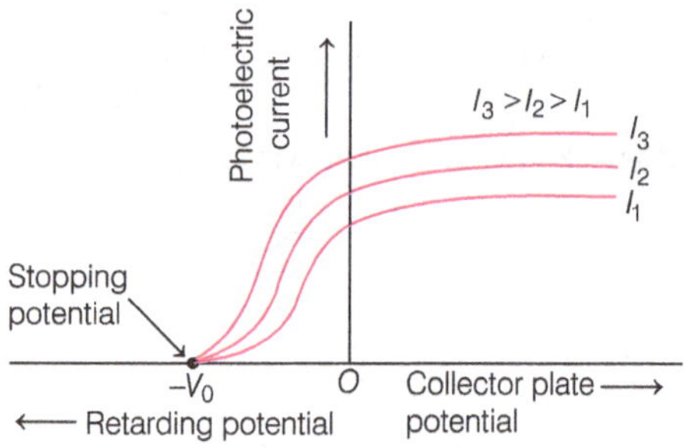

25. For the graph, refer to text on page 356.

(i) From the graph for the same value of ν, stopping potential is more for material *B*.

As, $$V = \frac{h}{e}(\nu - \nu_0)$$

$\therefore$ *V* is higher for lower value of ν_0. Here $\nu_B < \nu_A$, so $V_B > V_A$.

(ii) Slope of the graph is given by $\frac{h}{e}$ which is constant for all the materials. Hence, slope of the graph does not depend on the nature of the material used.

26. Cut-off voltage and threshold frequency

Refer to text on page 353.

Graph between stopping potential V_0 and frequency ν.

Refer to text on page 356.

27. Refer to the text on pages 352 and 353.

28. (i) Refer to text on page 357.

(ii) Since, Einstein's photoelectric equation is given by

$$KE_{max} = \frac{1}{2}mv^2_{max} = h\nu - h\nu_0 = eV_0$$

(a) For a given material, there exist a certain minimum frequency of the incident radiation, below which no emission of photoelectron takes place. This frequency is called threshold frequency ν_0. Above threshold frequency, the maximum kinetic energy of the emitted photoelectron or equivalent stopping potential is independent of the intensity of the incident light but depends only upon the frequency of the incident light.

(b) If the collecting plate in the photoelectric apparatus is made at high negative potential, then most of the high energetic electrons get repelled back along the same path and the photoelectric current in the circuit becomes zero. So, for a particular frequency of incident radiation, the minimum negative potential for which the electric current becomes zero is called cut-off or stopping potential V_0.

29. (i) Waves associated with a mass in motion is called matter waves. Particle of mass m and charge q gains energy in the form of kinetic energy.

$$\frac{1}{2}mv^2 = qV$$

$$(mv)^2 = 2qVm$$

$$mv = \sqrt{2mqV}$$

According to de-Brogile relation,

$$\lambda = \frac{h}{mv}$$

$$\lambda = \frac{h}{\sqrt{2mqV}}$$

(ii) (a) $E = h\nu$

$$= 6.63 \times 10^{-34} \times 5 \times 10^{14}$$

$$= 3.315 \times 10^{-19} \text{ J}$$

(b) $n = \frac{P}{E} = \frac{3.315 \times 10^{-3}}{3.315 \times 10^{-19}} = 10^6 \text{s}^{-1}$

30. (i) **de-Broglie Hypothesis** According to de-Broglie, a wave is associated with moving material particle which controls the particle in every respect. The wave associated with moving material particle is called matter wave or de-Broglie wave whose wavelength is called **de-Broglie wavelength** which is given by

$$\lambda = \frac{h}{mv}$$

where, m is mass of the particle, v is velocity of the particle and h is Planck's constant.

This means the mass and radiation are symmetrical in nature.

According to de-Broglie equation, wavelength,

$$\lambda = \frac{h}{p}$$

where, p = momentum of photon

$$= mc = \frac{h\nu}{c}$$

$$\therefore \quad \lambda = \frac{hc}{h\nu} = \frac{c}{\nu}$$

which is equal to the wavelength of an electromagnetic radiation.

(ii) The de-Broglie wavelength of a particle is given by

$$\lambda = \frac{h}{\sqrt{2mV_0 q}}$$

Since, V_0 is same, so $\lambda \propto \frac{1}{\sqrt{mq}}$

For deuteron, $q_d = +e$, $m_d = 2m_p$

For α-particle, $q_\alpha = +2e$, $m_\alpha = 4m_p$

$$\therefore \quad \frac{\lambda_d}{\lambda_\alpha} = \sqrt{\frac{m_\alpha q_\alpha}{q_d m_d}} = \sqrt{\frac{4m_p \times 2e}{e \times 2m_p}} = 2:1$$

31. (i) de-Broglie matter wave equation is given by

$$\lambda = \frac{h}{p} = \frac{h}{\sqrt{2mK}} \qquad (\because p = \sqrt{2mK})$$

where, m = mass of proton

and K = kinetic energy of proton.

According to the question, kinetic energy of proton,

$$K = m_e c^2$$

[using Einstein's mass-energy relation]

$$\Rightarrow \quad \lambda = \frac{h}{\sqrt{2m(m_e c^2)}} = \frac{h}{\sqrt{2}c \cdot \sqrt{m \cdot m_e}}$$

$$= \frac{h}{\sqrt{2}\,c \cdot m_e \sqrt{1836}} \qquad [\because m = 1836\, m_e]$$

$$= \frac{6.63 \times 10^{-34}}{1.414 \times (3 \times 10^8) \times 9.1 \times 10^{-31} \times 42.8}$$

$$= 4 \times 10^{-14} \text{ m}$$

(ii) The region of electromagnetic spectrum is γ-ray.

32. de-Broglie matter wave equation,

$$\lambda = \frac{h}{p} = \frac{h}{\sqrt{2mK}} \qquad \left[\because K = \frac{p^2}{2m}\right]$$

where, K is kinetic energy and m is mass of particle.

$$K = \frac{h^2}{2m\lambda^2} \qquad \text{[for same wavelength } \lambda]$$

$$\Rightarrow \quad K \propto \frac{1}{m} \Rightarrow K_e : K_\alpha : K_p = \frac{1}{m_e} : \frac{1}{m_\alpha} : \frac{1}{m_p}$$

where, m_e, m_p and m_α are masses of electron, proton and α-particle, respectively.

Also, K_e, K_p and K_α are their respective kinetic energies.

$\because \quad m_\alpha > m_p > m_e \Rightarrow m_\alpha m_p > m_e m_\alpha > m_e m_p$

$\Rightarrow \quad K_e > K_p > K_\alpha$

(i) α-particle possesses minimum kinetic energy.

(ii) Electron has maximum kinetic energy.

The magnifying power of an electron microscope is inversely related to wavelength of radiation used. Smaller wavelength of electron beam in comparison to visible light increases the magnifying power of microscope.

33. We know that, $\dfrac{hc}{\lambda} = \dfrac{hc}{\lambda_0} + \dfrac{1}{2}mv^2$

Neglecting the work function, we get

$$\frac{hc}{\lambda} = \frac{1}{2}mv^2 \Rightarrow v = \sqrt{\frac{2hc}{m\lambda}}$$

de-Broglie wavelength is given by, $\lambda_e = \dfrac{h}{mv}$

$$\Rightarrow \quad \lambda_e = \frac{h\sqrt{m\lambda}}{m\sqrt{2hc}} = \sqrt{\frac{h\lambda}{2mc}}$$

34. The wavelength of the light wave is

$$\lambda = 400 \times 10^{-9} \text{ m}$$

$\therefore$ Frequency, $\nu = \dfrac{c}{\lambda} = \dfrac{3 \times 10^8}{400 \times 10^{-9}} \text{ s}^{-1}$

$$\Rightarrow \quad h\nu = \frac{6.63 \times 10^{-34} \times 3 \times 10^8}{400 \times 10^{-9}} = 0.05 \times 10^{-17} \text{ J}$$

$$= 5 \times 10^{-19} \text{ J}$$

From Einstein's photoelectric equation, we know that if the maximum velocity of the emitted photoelectron is v_{max}, then

$$\frac{1}{2} m_e v_{max}^2 = h\nu - h\nu_0$$

Where $h\nu_0$ is the work function given as 3×10^{-19} J and m_e is the mass of the electron.

$$\Rightarrow \quad \frac{1}{2} m_e v_{max}^2 = (5-3) \times 10^{-19} \text{ J}$$

$$\Rightarrow \quad v_{max}^2 = \frac{4 \times 10^{-19}}{9.1 \times 10^{-31}}$$

$$\Rightarrow \quad v_{max}^2 = \frac{4}{9.1} \times 10^{12}$$

$$\Rightarrow \quad v_{max} = 0.663 \times 10^6 = 6.63 \times 10^5 \text{ m/s}$$

$\therefore$ The maximum velocity of the electron ejected in 6.63×10^5 m/s

35. Given, $\nu = 7.21 \times 10^{14}$ Hz, $m = 9.1 \times 10^{-31}$ kg

$v_{max} = 6 \times 10^5$ m/s

Let ν_0 be the threshold frequency.

Use the formula for kinetic energy,

$$\text{KE} = \frac{1}{2} mv_{max}^2 = h\nu - h\nu_0$$

$$\Rightarrow \quad \frac{1}{2} \times 9.1 \times 10^{-31} \times (6 \times 10^5)^2 = 6.63 \times 10^{-34} (\nu - \nu_0)$$

$$\text{or} \quad \nu - \nu_0 = \frac{36 \times 9.1 \times 10^{-21}}{2 \times 6.63 \times 10^{-34}}$$

$$= 2.47 \times 10^{14} \text{ Hz}$$

$$\therefore \quad \nu_0 = 4.74 \times 10^{14} \text{ Hz}$$

36 Given, for the first condition, $\lambda = 600$ nm

For the second condition, $\lambda' = 400$ nm

$$K'_{max} = 2K_{max}$$

Here, $K'_{max} = \dfrac{hc}{\lambda} - \phi_0 \Rightarrow 2K_{max} = \dfrac{hc}{\lambda'} - \phi_0$

$$\Rightarrow \quad 2\left(\frac{1240}{600} - \phi_0\right) \approx \left(\frac{1240}{400} - \phi_0\right)$$

[$\because hc \approx 1240$ eV-nm]

$$\Rightarrow \quad \phi_0 = \frac{1240}{1200} = 1.03 \text{ eV}$$

37. (i) We know that $\phi = h\nu_0$, where ν_0 = threshold frequency

$$\frac{\phi_{OA}}{\phi_{OB}} = \frac{h_A}{h_B} = \frac{5 \times 10^{14}}{10 \times 10^{14}} = \frac{1}{2}$$

Thus, work function of B is higher than A.

(ii) For metal A, slope $= \dfrac{h}{e} = \dfrac{2}{(10-5) \times 10^{14}}$

$$\text{or} \quad h = \frac{2 \times e}{5 \times 10^{14}} = \frac{2 \times 1.6 \times 10^{-19}}{5 \times 10^{14}}$$

$$= 6.4 \times 10^{-34} \text{ J-s}$$

For metal B, slope $= \dfrac{h}{e} = \dfrac{2.5}{(15-10) \times 10^{14}}$

$$\text{or} \quad h = \frac{2.5 \times e}{5 \times 10^{14}} = \frac{2.5 \times 1.6 \times 10^{-19}}{5 \times 10^{14}}$$

$$= 8 \times 10^{-34} \text{ J-s}$$

Since, the value of h from experiment for metals A and B is different. Hence, experiment is not consistent with theory.

38. (i) $\phi = h\nu_0 = 6.63 \times 10^{-34} \times 1.0 \times 10^{15}$

$$= 6.63 \times 10^{-19} \text{ J}$$

$$= 4.14 \text{ eV}$$

(ii) $\text{KE}_{max} = h(\nu - \nu_0)$

$$= 6.63 \times 10^{-34} [3.0 \times 10^{15} - 1.0 \times 10^{15}]$$

$$= 13.26 \times 10^{-19} \text{ J}$$

$$= 8.29 \text{ V}$$

39. Energy of the first photon, $E_1 = 2.5$ eV

Energy of the second photon, $E_2 = 4.5$ eV

The work function of metal, $W = 2$ eV

Mass of the electron, $m = 9.1 \times 10^{-31}$ kg

Use the photoelectric equation,

$$KE = E - W$$
$$KE_1 = E_1 - W$$
$$KE_1 = 2.5 - 2$$
$$KE_1 = 0.5 \text{ eV}$$

or $KE_1 = 0.5 \times 1.6 \times 10^{-19} \text{J}$

$$KE_1 = 0.8 \times 10^{-19} \text{ J} \quad \text{...(i)}$$

For the second photon

$$KE_2 = E_2 - W$$
$$KE_2 = 4.5 - 2$$
$$KE_2 = 2.5 \text{ eV}$$

or $KE_2 = 2.5 \times 1.6 \times 10^{-19} \text{ J}$

$$KE_2 = 4 \times 10^{-19} \text{ J} \quad \text{...(ii)}$$

Dividing Eq. (i) by Eq. (ii)

$$\frac{KE_1}{KE_2} = \frac{0.8 \times 10^{-19}}{4 \times 10^{-19}}$$

$$\frac{\frac{1}{2}m_e v_1^2}{\frac{1}{2}m_e v_2^2} = \frac{1}{5}$$

$$\frac{v_1^2}{v_2^2} = \frac{1}{\sqrt{5}}$$

$$v_1 : v_2 = 1 : \sqrt{5}$$

40. Given, $\lambda = 200 \text{ nm} = 200 \times 10^{-9} \text{m}$

$$KE_{max} = h\nu - \phi$$
$$KE_{max} = eV_0$$
$$eV_0 = h\nu - \phi$$
$$eV_0 = \frac{hc}{\lambda} - \phi$$

$$\therefore 1.6 \times 10^{-19} V_0 = \frac{6.6 \times 10^{-34} \times 3 \times 10^8}{200 \times 10^{-9}} - 4.71 \times 1.6 \times 10^{-19}$$

$$V_0 = 6.19 - 4.71 = 1.48 \approx 1.50 \text{ V}$$

41. (i) Since, Q has greater negative intercept, it will have greater ϕ (work function) and hence higher threshold frequency.

(ii) To know work function of Q, we put $V = 0$ in the following equation.

$$V = \frac{h\nu}{e} - \frac{\phi}{e} \Rightarrow 0 = \frac{h\nu}{e} - \frac{\phi}{e} \Rightarrow \phi = h\nu$$

$$\therefore \quad \phi = 6.6 \times 10^{-34} \times 6 \times 10^{14} \text{ J}$$

$$= \frac{6.6 \times 6 \times 10^{-20}}{1.6 \times 10^{-19}} = 2.5 \text{ eV}$$

(iii) From the equation, $\nu\lambda = c$

$$\Rightarrow \lambda = \frac{c}{\nu} = \frac{3 \times 10^8}{8 \times 10^{14}} = \frac{30}{8} \times 10^{-7} \text{m}$$

$$= \frac{30}{8} \times 10^3 \times 10^{-10} \text{m}$$

$$= \frac{30}{8} \times 10^3 \text{ Å} = 3750 \text{ Å}$$

$$\text{Energy} = \frac{12375}{\lambda(\text{Å})} \text{eV} = \frac{12375}{3750} \text{ eV}$$

$$= 3.3 \text{ eV}$$

$\therefore$ Maximum KE of emitted electron $= (3.3 - 2.5)$ eV

$$= 0.8 \text{ eV}$$

42. Given, work function of cesium metal,

$$\phi_0 = 2.14 \text{ eV}$$

Frequency of light, $\nu = 6 \times 10^{14}$ Hz

(i) $\therefore K_{max} = h\nu - \phi_0$

$$= 6.63 \times 10^{-34} \times 6 \times 10^{14} - 2.14$$

$$= \frac{6.63 \times 6 \times 10^{-20}}{1.6 \times 10^{-19}} \text{eV} - 2.14$$

$$= 2.48 - 2.14 = 0.34 \text{ eV}$$

(ii) Let stopping potential be V_0.

We know that, $KE_{max} = eV_0$

$\Rightarrow$ $0.35 \text{ eV} = eV_0$

$\therefore$ $V_0 = 0.35$ V

(iii) Maximum kinetic energy, $KE_{max} = \frac{1}{2}mv_{max}^2$

$$0.35 \text{ eV} = \frac{1}{2}mv_{max}^2$$

(where, v_{max} is the maximum speed and m is the mass of electron)

$$\frac{0.35 \times 2 \times 1.6 \times 10^{-19}}{9.1 \times 10^{-31}} = v_{max}^2 \quad [\because e = 1.6 \times 10^{-19}]$$

$$\Rightarrow \quad v_{max}^2 = 0.123 \times 10^{12}$$

$$\Rightarrow \quad v_{max} = 350713.55 \text{ m/s}$$

$$= 350.7 \text{ km/s}$$

43. de-Broglie wavelength of a particle,

$$\lambda = \frac{h}{p}, \text{ where } h = \text{Planck's constant}$$

and p = momentum of particle

$$E = \frac{p^2}{2m} \Rightarrow p = \sqrt{2mE}$$

Mass of proton $= 1.679 \times 10^{-27}$ kg

$$\text{Energy of proton, } E = \frac{500}{1.673} \text{ eV}$$

$$\Rightarrow \quad E = \frac{500}{1.679} \times 1.602 \times 10^{-19} \text{J}$$

$$= 0.477 \times 10^{-16} \text{ J}$$

Now, $p = \sqrt{2mE}$

$$= \sqrt{2 \times 1.679 \times 10^{-27} \times 0.477 \times 10^{-16}}$$

$$\approx 4 \times 10^{-22} \text{ kg m/s}$$

$\therefore$ de-Broglie wavelength of proton,

$$\lambda = \frac{h}{p} = \frac{6.626 \times 10^{-34} \text{ Js}}{4 \times 10^{-22} \text{ kg - m/s}} = 1.6565 \times 10^{-12} \text{ m}$$

Alpha particle (which has a mass of approximately 4 times that of proton), with same energy,

Momentum, $p = \sqrt{2mE}$

$$= \sqrt{2 \times 4 \times 1.673 \times 10^{-27} \times 0.477 \times 10^{-16}}$$

$$p = 8 \times 10^{-22} \text{ kg m/s}$$

$\therefore$ de-Broglie wavelength of alpha particle.

$$\lambda = \frac{h}{p} = \frac{6.626 \times 10^{-34} \text{ Js}}{8 \times 10^{-22} \text{ kg- m/s}} = 8.28 \times 10^{-11} \text{ m}$$

So, we can see that de-Broglie wavelength of the alpha particle is shorter than that of proton, because the alpha particle has a higher momentum due to its greater mass.

44. Suppose wavelength of X-rays is λ_1 and the wavelength of visible light is λ_2.

Given, $P = 100$ W, $\lambda_1 = 1$ nm, $\lambda_2 = 500$ nm

Also, n_1 and n_2 represent number of photons of X-rays and visible light emitted from the two sources per second.

So, $$\frac{E}{t} = P = n_1 \frac{hc}{\lambda_1} = n_2 \frac{hc}{\lambda_2}$$

$$\Rightarrow \frac{n_1}{\lambda_1} = \frac{n_2}{\lambda_2} \Rightarrow \frac{n_1}{n_2} = \frac{\lambda_1}{\lambda_2} = \frac{1}{500}$$

45. de-Broglie wavelength is given as $\lambda = \frac{h}{p} = \frac{h}{\sqrt{2mqV}}$

where, m is the mass of particle,

q is the charge of particle

and V is the accelerating voltage.

de-Broglie wavelength of proton and α-particle is same but different accelerating voltage.

$$\Rightarrow \lambda_p = \lambda_\alpha \Rightarrow \frac{h}{\sqrt{2m_p q_p V_1}} = \frac{h}{\sqrt{2m_\alpha q_\alpha V_2}}$$

$$\Rightarrow \frac{V_1}{V_2} = \frac{m_\alpha q_\alpha}{m_p q_p} = \frac{4m_p \cdot 2q_p}{m_p \cdot q_p} = 8 \quad \left[\because \begin{matrix} m_\alpha = 4m_p \\ q_\alpha = 2q_p \end{matrix}\right]$$

Hence, $\frac{V_1}{V_2} = \frac{8}{1}$

46. The matter wave is also called as de-Broglie wave. The matter wave describes the relationship between momentum and wavelength.

We know that, de-Broglie's wavelength is given by

$$\lambda = \frac{h}{p} = \frac{h}{mv} = \frac{h}{\sqrt{2m\text{KE}}}$$

where, $h =$ Planck's constant,

$m =$ mass of particle

and $v =$ velocity of particle.

If KE same, then $\lambda \propto \frac{1}{\sqrt{m}}$.

The order of mass of electron, proton and alpha particle is $m_\alpha > m_p > m_{e^-}$, hence order of de-Broglie wavelength is $\lambda_\alpha < \lambda_p < \lambda_{e^-}$.

47. The de-Broglie wavelength of a particle is given by

$$\lambda \propto \frac{1}{\sqrt{mq}}$$

Thus, $\lambda_p = \lambda_d$

For accelerating potential,

$$\lambda = \frac{12.27}{\sqrt{V}}$$

or $$V_p = \left(\frac{12.27}{\lambda_p}\right)^2$$

Now, $$\frac{V_p}{V_d} = \frac{(12.27/\lambda_p)^2}{(12.27/\lambda_d)^2}$$

$$\frac{V_p}{V_d} = \left(\frac{\lambda_d}{\lambda_p}\right)^2 \quad (\because \lambda_p = \lambda_d)$$

$$V_p : V_d = 4$$

QR Code for Quick Test 1

QR Code for Quick Test 2

SELF ASSESSMENT TEST

Multiple Choice Questions (MCQs)

1. When UV-rays are incident on metal plate, photoelectric effect does not occur.
It occurs by incidence of
(a) infrared rays (b) X-rays
(c) radio waves (d) microwaves

2. The difference between threshold wavelengths for two metal surfaces A and B having work function $\phi_A = 9$ eV and $\phi_B = 4.5$ eV (in nm) is (Given, $hc = 1242$ eV-nm)
(a) 540 (b) 276 (c) 264 (d) 138

3. A radiation of energy E falls normally on a perfectly reflecting surface. The momentum transferred to the surface is
(a) $\frac{E}{c}$ (b) $\frac{2E}{c}$
(c) Ec (d) $\frac{E}{c^2}$

4. Two beams, one of red light and the other of blue light having the same intensity are incident on a metallic surface to emit photoelectrons. Which emits electrons of greater frequency?
(a) Red light (b) Blue light
(c) Both red and blue light (d) None of these

5. If the maximum kinetic energy of emitted photoelectrons from a metal surface of work function 2.5 eV is 1.7 eV. If wavelength of incident radiation is halved, then stopping potential will be
(a) 2.5 V (b) 6.7 V (c) 5 V (d) 1.1 V

Assertion-Reason

Directions *(Q. Nos. 6-8) In the following questions, two statements are given- one labelled Assertion (A) and the other labelled Reason (R). Select the correct answer to these questions from the codes (a), (b), (c) and (d) as given below.*

(a) Both A and R are true and R is the correct explanation of A.
(b) Both A and R are true but R is not the correct explanation of A.
(c) A is true but R is false.
(d) A is false but R is true.

6. **Assertion** (A) For $\nu > \nu_0$ (threshold frequency), photoelectric current is proportional to intensity.
Reason (R) Greater the number of energy quanta available, greater is the number of electrons absorbing the energy quanta and greater is the number of electrons coming out of the metal.

7. **Assertion** (A) The kinetic energy of photoelectrons emitted from metal surface does not depend on the intensity of incident photon.
Reason (R) The ejection of electrons from metallic surface is not possible with frequency of incident photons below the threshold frequency.

8. **Assertion** (A) If distance of the point source is increased from the photoelectric plate, then stopping potential will remain unchanged.
Reason (R) Saturation current will decrease.

Case Based Question

Directions *(Q. No. 9) This question is case study based question. Read the following paragraph and answers the questions on the basis of same.*

9. We know that metals have free electrons, which contribute towards conduction of electricity and heat. The electrons cannot normally escape from the metal surface.
When an electron escapes from the metal surface, it is quite likely to be quickly absorbed back as the metal becomes positive. One can thus understand that it is captive within the metal even though it can freely move within the metal. A certain minimum (external) energy is required to be given to an electron for it to escape a given metal surface. This is known as the work function for that metal. It is denoted by ϕ and is measured in electron volt (eV).

1 eV is the energy gained by an electron when it is accelerated by a potential difference of 1 V.

(i) Does the size of the atom affects the value of work function?
(a) Yes (b) No
(c) Sometimes (d) Remains same

(ii) From which type of metal, electron emission would be easier?

(a) Caesium
(b) Potassium
(c) Sodium
(d) Calcium

(iii) The work function would depend upon which of the following ?
(a) Material of the metal
(b) Temperature
(c) The nature of its surface
(d) All of the above

(iv) Work function of platinum is the highest (=5.65 eV) and least for caesium (=2.1 eV). If energy equal to the work function is required by electrons to escape, which of the two will need lesser energy?
(a) Caesium
(b) Platinum
(c) Same for both
(d) Can't be calculated

Very Short Answer Type Questions

10. When radiation of frequency 10^{14} Hz is incident on certain surface, no photoemission takes place. What does this statement means ?

11. Define the term intensity in photon picture of electromagnetic radiation.

Short Answer Type Questions

12. Write two characteristic features observed in photoelectric effect which supports the photon pictures of electromagnetic radiation.

13. Why photoelectric effect cannot be explained on the basis of wave nature of light? Give reason.

14. A light of wavelength 3000 Å emits photoelectrons of maximum KE of 0.5 eV. What will be the maximum KE of photoelectrons, if the wavelength is changed to 2000 Å ? (Take, $hc = 12400$ eV-Å)

Long Answer Type Question

15. Consider a thin target (10^{-2} m square, 10^{-3} m thickness) of sodium, which produces a photocurrent of 100 μA when a light of intensity 100 W/m^2 ($\lambda = 660$ nm) falls on it. Find the probability that a photoelectron is produced when a photon strikes a sodium atom.
[Take, density of Na = 0.97 kg/m^3]

Answers

1. (b)	2. (d)	3. (b)	4. (b)	5. (b)	6. (a)
7. (b)	8. (b)	9. (i) (a), (ii) (a), (iii) (d), (iv) (a)			
14. 2.57 V					

12

CHAPTER

The first model of atom was proposed by JJ Thomson in 1898 called **plum pudding model** of the atom. Later, Rutherford worked on it and named this model as **Rutherford's planetary model** of atom in 1911. In 1913, Niels Bohr worked on the model named as

Atoms

YOUR STUDY GOALS

12.1 α-Particles Scattering Experiment by Rutherford
12.2 Rutherford's Model of Atom
12.3 Electron Orbits
12.4 Bohr's Model of Hydrogen Atom
12.5 Hydrogen Spectrum or Line Spectra of Hydrogen Atom

YOUR PRACTICE GOAL

- Objective Type Questions (28 Qs ; MCQs, A-R, Matching)
- Case Based Questions-2
- Subjective Questions (6 VSAs, 7 SAs, 6 LAs)
- Numerical Problems-10

12.1 α-Particles Scattering Experiment by Rutherford

This experiment was suggested by Rutherford in 1911 as given in the figure below

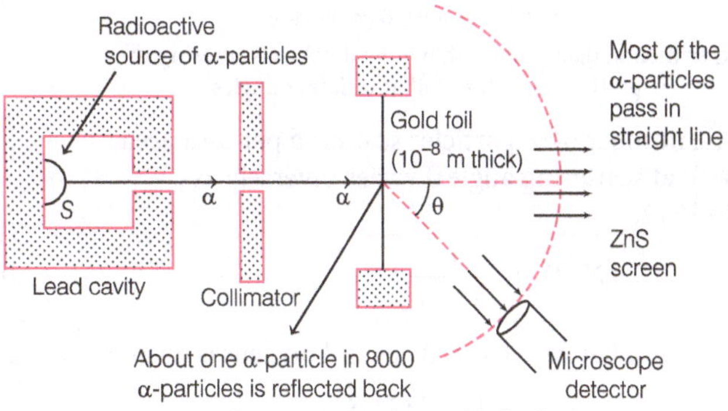

Experimental arrangement for Rutherford's theory

In this experiment, H.Geiger and E.Marsden took $^{214}_{83}$**Bi as a source for α-particles.** A collimated beam of α-particles of energy **5.5 MeV** was allowed to fall on 2.1×10^{-7} m thick gold foil.

The α-particles were observed by a rotatable detector consisting of a zinc sulphide screen and microscope, it was found that α-particles got scattered and produced bright **flashes or scintillations** on the zinc sulphide screen, these scintillations were counted at different angles from the direction of incident beam.

Note Gold is preferred in this experiment due to its malleable properties.

Observations

Rutherford made the following observations from his experiment :

(i) Most of the α-particles passed through the gold foil, it means they do not suffer any collision.

(ii) Only about 0.14% of the incident α-particles scattered by more than 1°.

(iii) About one α-particle in every 8000 α-particles deflected by more than 90°.

The total number of α-particles (N) scattered through an angle (θ) is as shown in the figure below

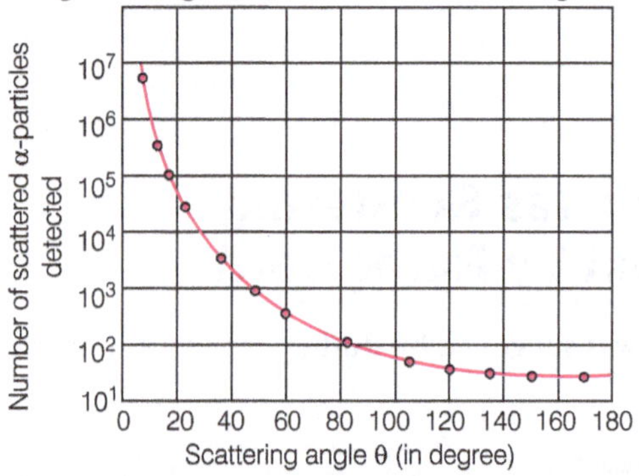

Experimental data points (shown by dots) on scattering of α-particles by a thin foil at different angles

(iv) The number of α-particles scattered per unit area $N(\theta)$ at scattering angle θ varies inversely as $\sin^4 \theta/2$.

$$N(\theta) \propto \frac{1}{\sin^4 \theta/2}$$

(v) The force between α-particles and nucleus is given by

$$F = \frac{1}{4\pi\varepsilon_0} \cdot \frac{(2e)(Ze)}{r^2}$$

where, r is the distance between the α-particles and the nucleus. This force is directed along the line joining the α-particle and the nucleus. The magnitude and direction of this force on α-particle continuously changes as it approaches the nucleus and recedes away from it.

Conclusions

On the basis of his experiment, Rutherford concluded that

(i) Atom has a lot of empty space and practically the entire mass of the atom is confined at extremely small central core called **nucleus,** whose size is of the order from 10^{-15} m to 10^{-14} m.

(ii) Scattering of α-particles (positively charged) is due to the Coulomb's law of electrostatic force of repulsion between the positive charge of nucleus and α-particles.

(iii) Distance between electron and nucleus is from 10^4 to 10^5 times the size of the nucleus itself.

(iv) The α-particles that pass at a large distance from the nucleus go almost undeviated.

α-Particle Trajectory

The α-particle experiences deflection due to repulsive electrostatic force of nucleus when passes through the atom.

- **deflection is very large** when α-particle passes close to the nucleus
- **deflection is very small** when α-particle passes far away from the nucleus.

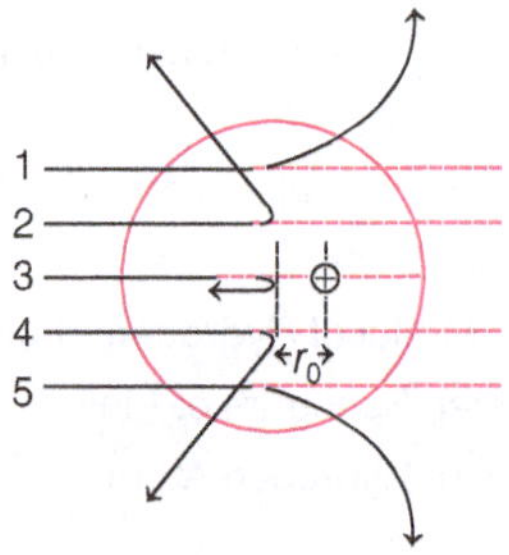

Trajectory of α-particles close to an atom

The α-particles which travel towards the nucleus directly, slow down, comes to rest and ultimately repelled back and retrace their path at 180°.

Distance of Closest Approach

At a certain distance r_0 from the nucleus, KE of α-particle reduces to zero. The particle stops and cannot go further close to the nucleus due to the strong repulsive force of nucleus. This distance r_0 is known as the **distance of closest approach** and it can be define as

The distance of charged particle from the centre of the nucleus (r_0) at which complete kinetic energy of

the charged particle gets converted into the electric potential energy of the system.

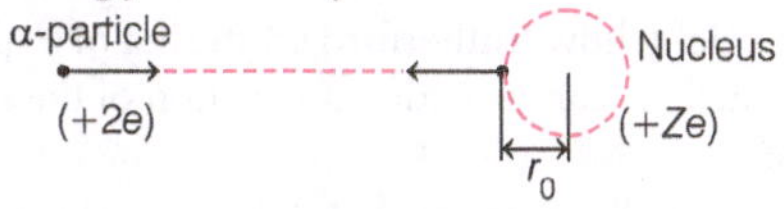

The force between α-particles and nucleus is given by

$$F = \frac{1}{4\pi\varepsilon_0} \cdot \frac{(2e)(Ze)}{r^2}$$

where, r is the distance between the α-particles and the nucleus. **The magnitude and direction of this force on α-particle continuously changes as it approaches the nucleus and recedes away from it.**

At the distance of closest approach,

KE of α-particle = Electrostatic potential energy

$$K = \frac{1}{4\pi\varepsilon_0} \cdot \frac{(Ze)(2e)}{r_0}$$

[∵ charge on α-particle is $+2e$ and charge on nucleus is Ze, where Z is atomic number]

$$\therefore \quad r_0 = \frac{1}{4\pi\varepsilon_0} \cdot \frac{2Ze^2}{K}$$

or

$$r_0 = \frac{1}{4\pi\varepsilon_0} \cdot \frac{2Ze^2}{\left(\frac{1}{2}mv^2\right)}$$

where, m = mass of α-particle and v = initial velocity of α-particle.

From the formula, **it is clear that distance of closest approach of α-particle to the nucleus depends on the kinetic energy of α-particle.**

Example 1. **The number of α-particles scattered at an angle of 90° is 100 per minute. What will be the number of α-particles, when it is scattered at an angle of 60°?**

Sol. Number of α-particles scattered at an angle of θ is given by

$$N \propto \frac{1}{\sin^4 \theta/2} \Rightarrow \frac{N_1}{N_2} = \left(\frac{\sin\frac{\theta_2}{2}}{\sin\frac{\theta_1}{2}}\right)^4$$

$$\Rightarrow \quad \frac{100}{N_2} = \left(\frac{\sin 30^\circ}{\sin 45^\circ}\right)^4$$

$$\Rightarrow \quad \frac{100}{N_2} = \frac{4}{16} \Rightarrow N_2 = 400$$

Example 2. **In a head-on collision between an α-particle and gold nucleus, the closest distance of approach is 4×10^{-14} m. Calculate the initial kinetic energy of α-particle.**

Sol. Here, closest distance of approach, $r_0 = 4 \times 10^{-14}$ m

Atomic number, $Z = 79$, $KE_i = ?$

$$\therefore \; KE_i \text{ of α-particle} = \frac{Ze(2e)}{4\pi\varepsilon_0 r_0} = \frac{2Ze^2}{4\pi\varepsilon_0 r_0}$$

$$= \frac{2 \times 79 \times (1.6 \times 10^{-19})^2 \times 9 \times 10^9}{4 \times 10^{-14}}$$

$$= 9.1 \times 10^{-13} \text{ J}$$

Angle of Scattering (θ)

Angle by which α-particle gets deviated from its original path around the nucleus is called angle of scattering.

Impact Parameter (*b*)

Perpendicular distance of the velocity vector of α-particle from the central line of the nucleus of the atom is called impact parameter. Mathematically, it is expressed as

$$b = \frac{1}{4\pi\varepsilon_0} \cdot \frac{Ze^2 \cot\frac{\theta}{2}}{KE}$$

where, b = impact parameter,

θ = angle of scattering

and KE = kinetic energy of α-particle $= \frac{1}{2}mv^2$.

In case of head-on collision with nucleus, the impact parameter is minimum and the α-particle rebounds back, i.e. (θ = π). For a large impact parameter, the α-particle goes nearly undeviated and has a small deflection, i.e., (θ = 0°).

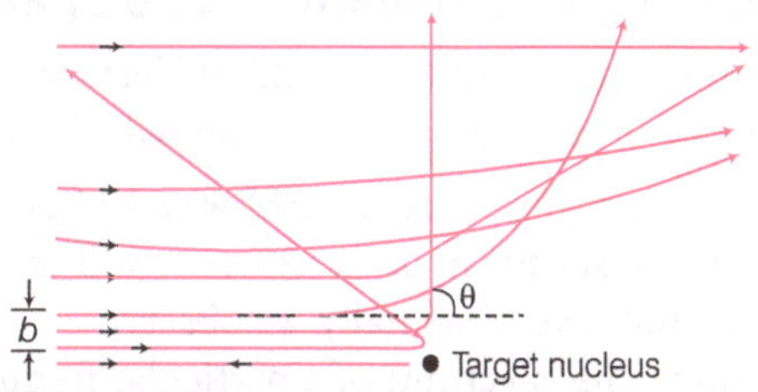

Trajectory of α-particles in the Coulombic field of a target nucleus. The impact parameter b and scattering angle θ are also depicted

12.2 Rutherford's Model of Atom

The essential features of Rutherford's nuclear model of the atom are as follows

(i) Every atom consists of a central core, called the **atomic nucleus**, in which the entire positive charge and almost entire mass of the atom is concentrated.

(ii) The size of nucleus is of the order of 10^{-15}m, which is very small as compared to the size of the atom which is of the order of 10^{-10}m.

(iii) The atomic nucleus is surrounded by certain number of electrons which is equal to the total positive charge in the nucleus. Thus, atom becomes electrically neutral.

(iv) These electrons revolve around the nucleus in various circular orbits as same as the planets revolve around the sun.

The centripetal force required by electrons for revolution is provided by the electrostatic force of attraction between the electrons and nucleus.

Drawbacks of Rutherford's Model

Rutherford's model suffers two major drawbacks

(i) Regarding Stability of Atom

Electrons revolving around the nucleus have centripetal acceleration. According to classical electromagnetic theory, **the electrons must radiate energy in the form of electromagnetic wave.**

Due to this continuous loss of energy, the electrons should fall in the nucleus. Thus, atom cannot remain stable.

(ii) Regarding Explanation of Line Spectrum

Due to continuous decrease in radii of electron's orbit, the frequency of revolution of electron will also change.

As a result, electron will radiate EM waves of all frequencies and spectrum of these waves will be continuous. But, experimentally we observe discontinuous line spectrum of a particular frequency. Thus, **Rutherford model was unable to explain line spectrum.**

Quick Test 1

1. Explain briefly how Rutherford scattering of α-particle by a target nucleus can provide information of the size of the nucleus?
2. An α-particle of kinetic energy K is bombarded on a thin gold foil. The distance of the closest approach is r. What will be the distance of closest approach for an α-particle of double the kinetic energy?
3. What is the impact parameter for scattering of α-particle by 180°?
4. What is the ratio of mass of an α-particle to that of an electron?
5. Why is the classical (Rutherford) model for an atom of electron orbiting around the nucleus not able to explain the atomic structure?
6. The number of α-particles scattered at 90° is 50 per minute. What will be the number of α-particles, when it is scattered at an angle of 120°?

Answers

3. 0 *4.* 7341

For Solutions, See QR Code on Pg. 401

12.3 Electron Orbits

A positively charged nucleus at the centre of atom is surrounded by the revolving electrons in their respective dynamically stable orbits.

The electrostatic force of attraction (F_e) between the revolving electrons and the nucleus provides the requisite centripetal force (F_c) to keep them in their orbits. Thus, for a dynamically stable orbit in a H-atom,

$$F_c = F_e \Rightarrow \frac{mv^2}{r} = \frac{1}{4\pi\varepsilon_0} \cdot \frac{e^2}{r^2} \qquad [\because Z = 1]$$

Thus, the relation between the orbit radius and the electron velocity is $r = \dfrac{e^2}{4\pi\varepsilon_0 mv^2}$

The kinetic energy (K) and electrostatic potential energy (U) of the electron in H-atom are

$$K = \frac{1}{2}mv^2 = \frac{e^2}{8\pi\varepsilon_0 r} \qquad \left[\because mv^2 = \frac{e^2}{4\pi\varepsilon_0 r}\right]$$

and $$U = -\frac{e^2}{4\pi\varepsilon_0 r}$$

(the negative sign in U signifies that the electrostatic force is attractive in nature).

Thus, the total mechanical energy (E) of the electron in a H-atom is

$$E = K + U = \frac{e^2}{8\pi\varepsilon_0 r} - \frac{e^2}{4\pi\varepsilon_0 r}$$

$$\boxed{E = -\frac{e^2}{8\pi\varepsilon_0 r}}$$

The total energy of the electron is negative. This implies the fact that the electron is bound to the nucleus. If E is positive, then any electron will not follow a closed orbit around the nucleus and it would leave the atom.

Example 3. **It is found experimentally that energy 13.6 eV is required to separate a ground state H-atom into a proton and an electron. Compute the orbital radius and velocity of the electron in a H-atom.**

Sol. Total energy of the electron in H-atom,

$$\text{TE} = -13.6 \text{ eV} = -13.6 \times 1.6 \times 10^{-19} \text{ J}$$
$$= -2.2 \times 10^{-18} \text{ J}$$

We know that, total energy, $\text{TE} = \frac{-e^2}{8\pi\varepsilon_0 r}$

$$\Rightarrow \quad r = \frac{-e^2}{8\pi\varepsilon_0(\text{TE})} = \frac{-9 \times 10^9 \times (1.6 \times 10^{-19})^2}{2 \times (-2.2 \times 10^{-18})}$$
$$= 5.3 \times 10^{-11} \text{ m}$$

$\therefore$ Velocity of the revolving electron,

$$v = \frac{e}{\sqrt{4\pi\varepsilon_0 mr}}$$
$$= \frac{1.6 \times 10^{-19}}{\sqrt{4 \times 3.14 \times 8.85 \times 10^{-12} \times 9.1 \times 10^{-31} \times 5.3 \times 10^{-11}}}$$
$$= 2.2 \times 10^6 \text{ m/s}$$

12.4 Bohr's Model of Hydrogen Atom

Bohr combined **classical** and early **quantum concepts** and gave his theory in the form of three postulates.

These three postulates are as follows

(i) **Bohr's first postulate** was that an electron in an atom revolves in certain **stable orbits** without the emission of radiant energy, i.e. each atom has certain definite stable states in which it can exist and each possible state has **definite total energy.** These are called the **stationary states** of the atom.

(ii) **Bohr's second postulate** states that the electron revolves around the nucleus only in those orbits for which the **angular momentum is integral multiple of $h/2\pi$,** where h is the Planck's constant ($h = 6.63 \times 10^{-34}$ J-s).

Thus, the angular momentum (L) of the orbiting electron is quantised,

i.e. $\quad L = \frac{nh}{2\pi}$

As, angular momentum of electron $= mvr$

$\therefore$ For any permitted (stationary) orbit,

$$\boxed{mvr = \frac{nh}{2\pi}}$$

where, n = any positive integer 1, 2, 3, ...

It is also called **principal quantum number.**

(iii) **Bohr's third postulate** states that an electron might make a **transition** from one of its specified orbits to another of lower energy orbit. When it does so, a photon is emitted having energy equal to the energy difference between the initial and final states,

i.e. $\quad E = h\nu = E_i - E_f$

where, E_i and E_f are the energies of the initial and final states, ν is frequency and $E_i > E_f$.

Bohr's Radius of Hydrogen Atom

According to Niels Bohr, electron revolves around nucleus in stationary orbits. In these orbits, angular momentum of electron is quantised.

The radius of nth orbit of the H-atom,

$$\boxed{r_n = \frac{\varepsilon_0 h^2}{\pi m_e \cdot e^2} n^2} \text{ or } \boxed{r_n \propto n^2}$$

where, ε_0 = permittivity of vacuum

h = Planck's constant

m_e = mass of electron and

n is also known as **principal quantum number.**

For $n = 1$ and putting values of constants, we get

$$r_0 = \frac{8.85 \times 10^{-12} \times (6.63 \times 10^{-34})^2}{3.14 \times 9.1 \times 10^{-31} \times (1.6 \times 10^{-19})^2} \text{ m}$$
$$= 5.29 \times 10^{-11} \text{ m} \approx 0.53 \text{ Å}$$

$$\boxed{r_0 = 0.53 \text{ Å}}$$

This is called **Bohr radius.**

Since, $r_n = 0.53 \times n^2$ Å, the radius of the second orbit of H-atom will be (4×0.53) Å and that of the third orbit (9×0.53) Å.

Note Velocity and energy of electron in stationary orbits of hydrogen atoms are given by

$$v_n = \frac{e^2}{2h\varepsilon_0 n} \text{ and } E_n = -\frac{me^4}{8\varepsilon_0^2 n^2 h^2}$$

Example 4. **In Bohr's model of H-atom, the radius of the first electron orbit is 0.53 Å. What will be the radius of the third orbit and the first orbit of singly ionised helium atom?**

Sol. Radius of the nth Bohr orbit, $r = \frac{n^2 h^2 \varepsilon_0}{\pi m Z e^2}$

Again, $r \propto \frac{1}{Z}$

$\therefore \quad \frac{r_{He^+}}{r_H} = \frac{Z_H}{Z_{He^+}}$

For hydrogen, $Z = 1$ and for helium, $Z = 2$

$\therefore \quad \frac{r_{He^+}}{r_H} = \frac{1}{2} \Rightarrow r_{He^+} = \frac{1}{2} r_H = \frac{0.53}{2} = 0.265$ Å

For radius of third orbit, i.e. for $n = 3$,

$$r_3 = (3)^2 \times 0.265 \text{ Å} = 9 \times 0.265 \text{ Å} = 2.38 \text{ Å}$$

Energy Levels

The energy of an atom is the least, when its electron is revolving in an orbit closest to the nucleus, i.e. for which $n = 1$, so **the energy is progressively larger in outer orbits.**

The energy of the electron in the nth orbit is

$$E_n = -\frac{13.6}{n^2} \text{ eV}$$

The lowest state of the atom is called the **ground state.** The energy of this state is -13.6 eV. Therefore, the **minimum energy required to free the electron from the ground state of the H-atom is 13.6 eV. It is called ionisation energy of the H-atom.**

At room temperature, most of the H-atoms are in ground state. When an atom receives some energy (i.e. by electron collisions), the atom may acquire sufficient energy to raise electron to higher energy state. In this condition, the atom is said to be in **excited state.**

From the excited state, the electron can fall back to lower energy state by emitting a photon equal to the energy difference of the energy states.

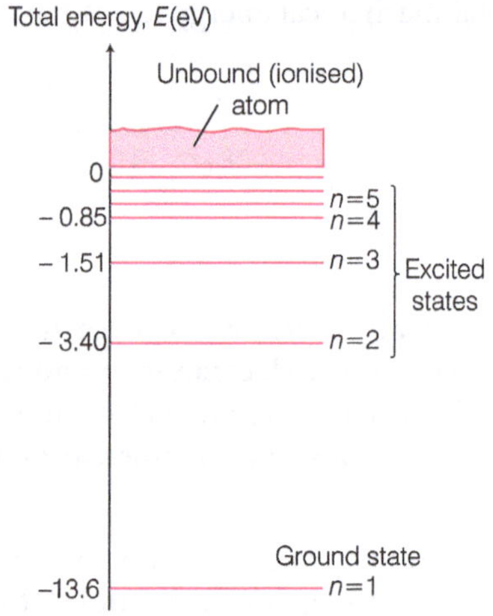

Energy level diagram for hydrogen atom

Suppose, an electron jumps from some higher energy state n_2 to a lower energy state n_1.

The energy difference between these states is the energy of radiation emitted and is given by

$$E_2 - E_1 = 13.6\left[\frac{1}{n_1^2} - \frac{1}{n_2^2}\right] \text{eV}$$

According to Bohr's third postulate, the frequency ν of the emitted electromagnetic wave (photon) is

$$\nu = \frac{E_2 - E_1}{h} = \frac{13.6}{h}\left(\frac{1}{n_1^2} - \frac{1}{n_2^2}\right)$$

The corresponding wavelength λ of the emitted radiation is given by

$$\frac{1}{\lambda} = \frac{\nu}{c} = \frac{13.6}{hc}\left(\frac{1}{n_1^2} - \frac{1}{n_2^2}\right)$$

$\frac{1}{\lambda}$ is called **wave number** (number of waves per unit length).

Note $hc = 12400$ eV in the above expression.

TEACHER TIP

Johannes Rydberg noted that all series of lines in the hydrogen spectrum could be described by the following expression :

$$\frac{1}{\lambda} = R\left(\frac{1}{n_1^2} - \frac{1}{n_2^2}\right)$$

where, $R = 109677 \text{ cm}^{-1}$ called the **Rydberg constant** for hydrogen and $n_1 = 1, 2 \ldots$

$n_2 = n + 1, n + 2 \ldots\ldots$

Example 5. **In the ground state of H-atom, its Bohr radius is given as 5.3×10^{-11} m. The atom is excited such that the radius becomes 21.2×10^{-11} m. Find (i) the value of the principal quantum number and (ii) the total energy of the atom in this excited state.**

Sol. (i) We know that, $r \propto n^2$

$$\frac{r_1}{r_2} = \frac{n_1^2}{n_2^2}$$

$$\Rightarrow \quad \frac{1}{n_2^2} = \frac{5.3 \times 10^{-11}}{21.2 \times 10^{-11}}$$

$$n_2^2 = 4$$

$$n_2 = 2$$

(ii) We know that, $E = \frac{-13.6}{n^2} = \frac{-13.6}{4}$

$$= -3.4 \text{ eV}$$

Example 6. **A H-atom initially in the ground level absorbs a photon, which excites it to the $n = 4$ level. Determine the wavelength and frequency of photon.** *NCERT*

Sol. To find the wavelength and frequency of photon, use the relation of energy of electron in hydrogen atom.

$$E_n = -\frac{13.6}{n^2} \text{ eV}$$

$$\Rightarrow \quad E_1 = \frac{-13.6}{1^2} \text{ eV} = -13.6 \text{ eV}$$

$$E_4 = \frac{-13.6}{4^2} \text{ eV} = -\frac{13.6}{16} \text{ eV} = -0.85 \text{ eV}$$

$$\Delta E = E_4 - E_1 = -0.85 - (-13.6) = 12.75 \text{ eV}$$

$$= 12.75 \times 1.6 \times 10^{-19} = 20.4 \times 10^{-19} \text{ J}$$

$$\because \quad \Delta E = h\nu$$

$$\Rightarrow \quad \nu = \frac{\Delta E}{h} = \frac{20.4 \times 10^{-19}}{6.63 \times 10^{-34}} = 3.1 \times 10^{15} \text{ Hz}$$

Wavelength of photon,

$$\lambda = \frac{c}{\nu} = \frac{3 \times 10^8}{3.1 \times 10^{15}}$$

$$= 9.67 \times 10^{-8} \text{ m}$$

Thus, the wavelength is 9.67×10^{-8} m and frequency is 3.1×10^{15} Hz.

12.5 Hydrogen Spectrum or Line Spectra of Hydrogen Atom

Hydrogen spectrum consists of discrete bright lines in a dark background and it is specifically known as **hydrogen emission spectrum.** There is one more type of hydrogen spectrum that exists where we get **dark lines on the bright background**, it is known as **absorption spectrum.**

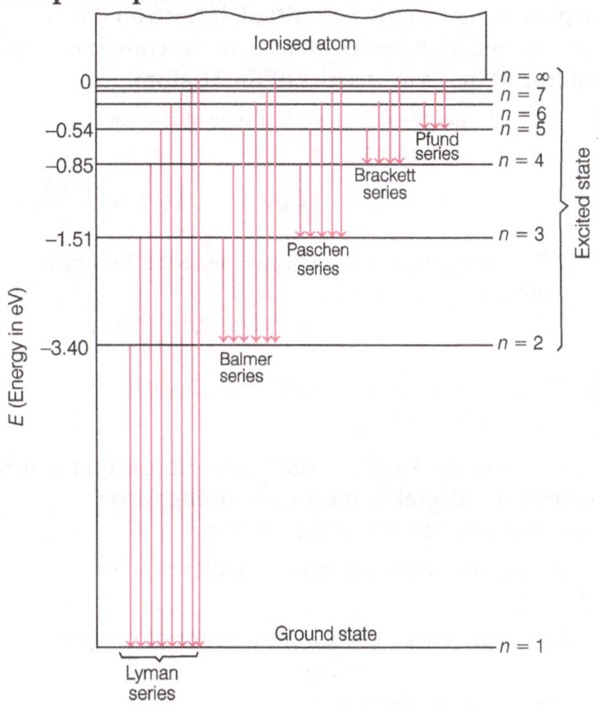

Line spectra of the H-atom

When an electron jumps from excited state to ground state in hydrogen atom, it emits electromagnetic radiation known as hydrogen spectrum or line spectrum of hydrogen atom. It is also known as **emission spectrum of hydrogen atom.**

- Balmer was the first who found emission spectrum of hydrogen atom in **visible region** known as **Balmer series.**
- Other series of spectra for hydrogen were subsequently discovered and known by the name of their discoverers. These series were found in the **invisible parts** of the spectrum, i.e. **Lyman series** in the **ultraviolet region** and **Paschen, Brackett** and **Pfund** in the **infrared region.**
- If value of n increases progressively, E_n becomes less negative. At $n = \infty$, $E_n = 0$.

Balmer Series in Emission Spectrum of Hydrogen

In Balmer series, the spectral line with the longest wavelength (656.3 nm) in red region is called H_α.

Next line with wavelength 486.1 nm in blue-green region is called H_β; the third line with 434.1 nm in violet region and is called H_γ and so on. **As the wavelength decreases, the lines are weaker in intensity and appear closer together.**

Example 7. **The energy of the electron in the ground state of hydrogen is – 13.6 eV. Calculate the energy of the photon that would be emitted, if electron was to make a transition corresponding to the emission of the first line of the Lyman series of the H-atom.**

Sol. Given, energy of e^- in ground state of H-atom,

$$E_1 = -13.6 \text{ eV}$$

For $n = 2, E_2 = -3.4$ eV $\left[\because E_n = -\frac{13.6}{n^2} \text{ eV}\right]$

The energy of photon corresponding to the first line is given by $E = E_2 - E_1$

$\therefore$ $E = [-3.4 - (-13.6)]$ eV $= 10.2$ eV

de-Broglie's Comment on Bohr's Second Postulate

According to de-Broglie, a stationary orbit is that which contains an integral number of **standing waves** associated with the revolving electron.

For an electron revolving in nth circular orbit of radius r_n,

Total distance covered = Circumference of the orbit $= 2\pi r_n$

$\therefore$ For the permissible orbit,

$$2\pi r_n = n\lambda$$

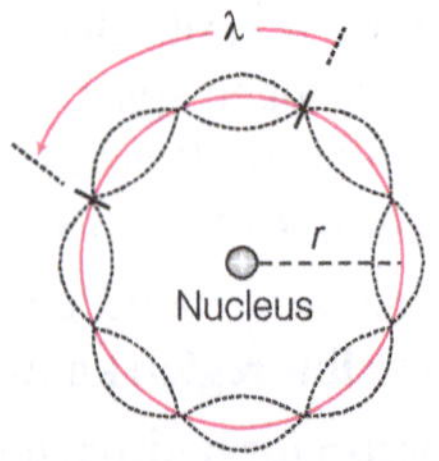

A standing wave is shown on a circular orbit

According to de-Broglie wavelength, $\lambda = \frac{h}{mv_n}$

where, v_n is speed of electron revolving in nth orbit.

$\therefore$ $$2\pi r_n = \frac{nh}{mv_n}$$

or $$mv_n r_n = \frac{nh}{2\pi} = n(h/2\pi)$$

i.e. **angular momentum of electron revolving in nth orbit must be an integral multiple of $h/2\pi$,** which is the quantum condition proposed by Bohr in his second postulate.

> **Orbital Picture of Electron in an Atom**
>
> With the development of quantum mechanics, we have a better understanding of structure of atom. The **Schrodinger wave equation** gives information about the probability of finding an electron in various regions around the nucleus, which is known as **orbital**.

Example 8. **When an electron in hydrogen atom jumps from the third excited state to the ground state, how would the de-Broglie wavelength associated with the electron change? Justify your answer.**

Sol. We know that, $\lambda = \frac{h}{p} = \frac{h}{mv}$ or $mv = \frac{h}{\lambda}$

or $mvr = \frac{hr}{\lambda} = \frac{nh}{2\pi}$ or $\lambda = \frac{2\pi}{nh} \times hr = \frac{2\pi r}{n}$

As, $r \propto n^2 \Rightarrow \lambda \propto \frac{1}{n}(n^2) = n$

Thus, we can say that, $\frac{\lambda_3}{\lambda_1} = \frac{4}{1}$ or $\lambda_1 = \frac{\lambda_3}{4}$

Thus, wavelength decreases 4 times as an electron jumps from third excited state to the ground state.

Quick Test 2

Conceptual Questions

1. What is the value of angular momentum of electron in the second orbit of Bohr's model of hydrogen atom?
2. Write shortcomings of Rutherford atomic model. Explain how these were overcome by the postulates of Bohr's atomic model? *Delhi 2020*
3. Show that the radius of the orbit in hydrogen atom varies as n^2, where n is the principal quantum number of the atom.
4. Positronium is just like a H-atom with the proton replaced by the positively charged anti-particle of the electron (called the positron which is as massive as the electron). What would be the ground state energy of positronium? *NCERT Exemplar*

Numerical Questions

5. The gravitational attraction between electron and proton in a H-atom is weaker than the Coulombic attraction by a factor of about 10^{-40}. Estimate the radius of the first Bohr orbit of a H-atom, if the electron and proton were bound by gravitational attraction.
6. A difference of 2.3 eV separates two energy levels in an atom. What is the frequency of radiation emitted when the atom makes a transition from the upper level to the lower level? *NCERT*

Answers

4. -6.8 eV 5. 1.2×10^{29} m 6. 5.6×10^{14} Hz

For Solutions, See QR Code on Pg. 401

Mind Map

Atom

Alpha-Particle Scattering Experiment

This experiment was a groundbreaking experiment conducted by **Ernest Rutherford** and his team in 1909.

Rutherford Model

(i) Most of the α-particles pass straight through the gold foil or suffer only small deflection.

(ii) A few α-particles, about 1 in 8000, get deflected through 90° or more.

(iii) Occasionally, an α-particle gets rebounded from the gold foil, suffering a deflection of nearly 180°.

Distance of Closest Approach

When an α-particle of mass m and velocity v moves directly towards a nucleus of atomic number Z, its distance of closest approach is given by

$$r_0 = \frac{2kZe^2}{E} = \frac{4kZe^2}{mv^2}$$

where, $E = \frac{1}{2}mv^2$

and $k = \frac{1}{4\pi\varepsilon_0} = 9 \times 10^9\ \text{Nm}^2\text{C}^{-2}$

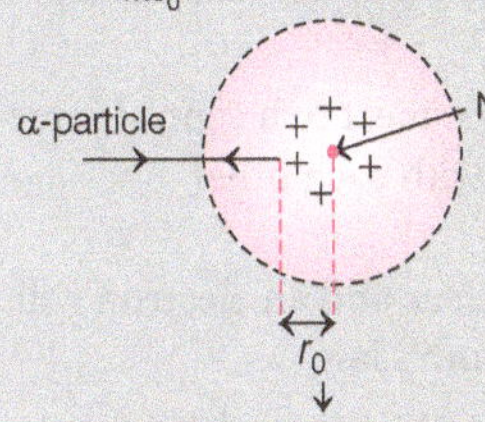

Impact Parameter

The perpendicular distance of the velocity vector of the α-particle from the centre of the nucleus, when it is far away from the atom.

$$b = \frac{1}{4\pi\varepsilon_0} \cdot \frac{Ze^2 \cot\frac{\theta}{2}}{E} = \frac{1}{4\pi\varepsilon_0} \cdot \frac{Ze^2 \cot\frac{\theta}{2}}{\frac{1}{2}mv^2}$$

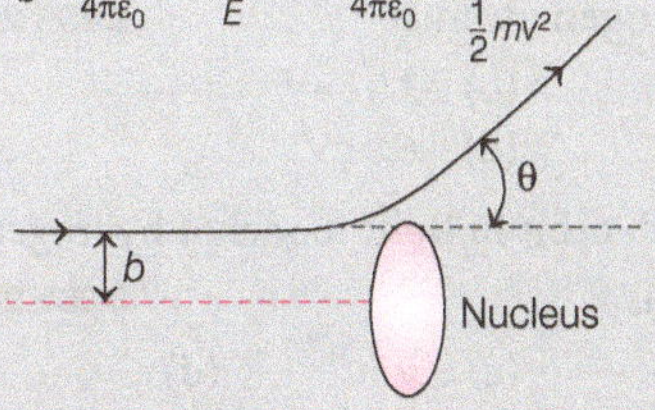

Limitation of Rutherford's Model

- Inability to explain atomic stability.
- No explanation of atomic spectra.
- Violation of energy conservation for orbiting electrons.

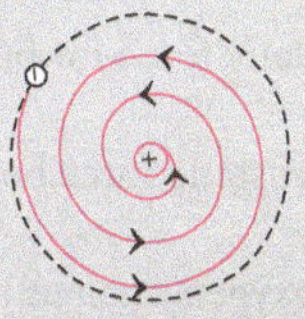

Rutherford orbit of electron

Bohr's Model of Hydrogen Atom

Niels Bohr in 1913 successfully explained the spectral lines of hydrogen and resolved some limitations of Rutherford's atomic model.

Bohr's Radius of Hydrogen Atom

$$r_n = \frac{\varepsilon_0 h^2}{\pi m_e e^2} n^2 \quad \text{or} \quad r_n \propto n^2$$

Total energy of electrons in Bohr's stationary orbits

$$E = \frac{-me^4Z^2}{8n^2\varepsilon_0^2 h^2}$$

Bohr radius, velocity and energy of nth orbit is given in table.

Quantity	Expression	Simplified form
Radius, r_n	$r_n = n^2 \cdot \frac{h^2}{ke^2m_e}$	$r_n = n^2 \cdot 0.529\text{Å}$
Velocity, v_n	$v_n = \frac{e^2}{2\varepsilon_0 hn}$	$v_n = \frac{2.18 \times 10^6}{n}$ m/s
Energy, E_n	$E_n = \frac{ke^4m_e}{2h^2n^2}$	$E_n = \frac{13.6}{n^2}$ eV

Postslates of Bohr Model

- **Quantised Orbits** Electrons revolve around the nucleus in specific, quantised circular paths or orbits without emitting radiation.
- **Angular Momentum Quantisation** The angular momentum of an electron in a permitted orbit is quantised and given by

$$L = \frac{nh}{2\pi}$$

- **Energy Transitions and Photon Emission** Electrons can transit between these quantised orbits by absorbing or emitting photons. With

$$E = E_I - E_F = h\nu$$

Each orbit corresponds to a fixed energy level, electrons remain in their orbits unless disturbed.

Hydrogen Line Spectrum

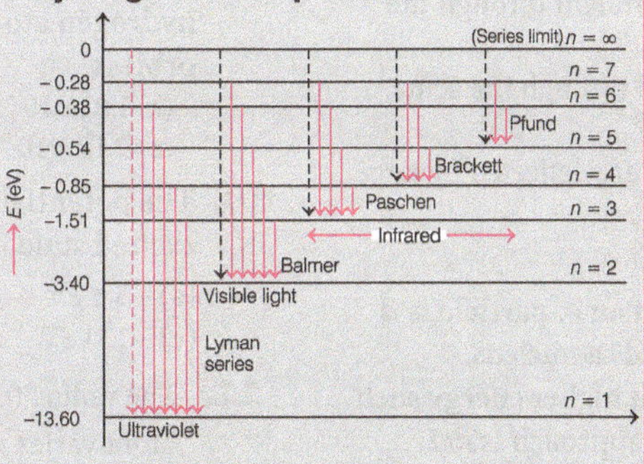

$$E_n = \frac{E_1}{n^2} = -\frac{13.6}{n^2}\ \text{eV}$$

Spectral Series of Hydrogen Atom

The transitions corresponding to maximum energy or smallest wavelength of a given series of hydrogen spectrum is called series limit.

To calculate wavelength corresponding to a series limit, we use $n_2 = \infty$.

$$\bar{\nu} = \frac{1}{\lambda} = \frac{13.6}{hc}\left(\frac{1}{n_1^2} - \frac{1}{n_2^2}\right)\ \text{cm}^{-1}$$

Series	n_1	n_2	Region of Spectrum
Lyman	1	2, 3, 4, ...	Ultraviolet
Balmer	2	3, 4, 5, ...	Visible
Paschen	3	4, 5, 6, ...	Near Infrared
Brackett	4	5, 6, 7, ...	Infrared
Pfund	5	6, 7, 8, ...	Far Infrared

de-Broglie Conclusion on Bohr's Second Postulate

- Electrons exhibit wave like behavior, Bohr's 2nd postulate can be explained by treating the electron as a standing wave around the nucleus.

Total distance covered = Circumference of the orbit = $2\pi r_n$

$\therefore$ For the permissible orbit, $2\pi r_n = n\lambda$.

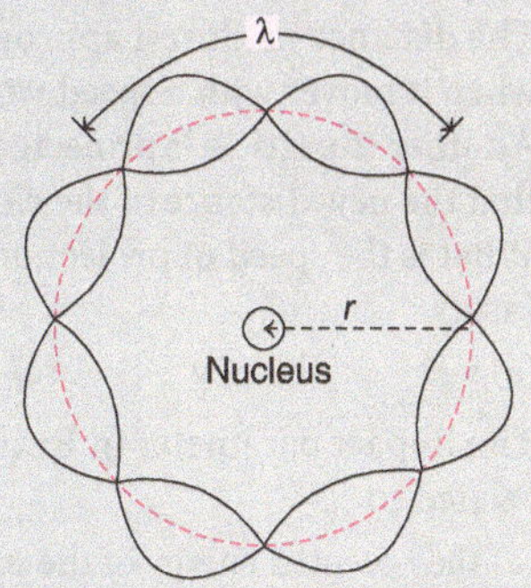

A standing wave is shown on a circular orbit

According to de-Broglie wavelength,

$$\lambda = \frac{h}{mv_n}$$

- de-Broglie's wave theory linked Bohr's quantum condition to the fundamental nature of matter waves.

EXAM PATTERN QUESTIONS

Objective Type Questions

Multiple Choice Questions (MCQs)

1. For scattering of α-particles, Rutherford suggested that

(a) mass of atom and its positive charge were concentrated at centre of atom
(b) only mass of atom is concentrated at centre of atom
(c) only positive charge of atom is concentrated at centre of atom
(d) mass of atom is uniformly distributed throughout its volume

2. In the α-particle scattering experiment, the shape of the trajectory of the scattered α-particles depend upon

(a) only on impact parameter **All India 2020**
(b) only on the source of α-particles
(c) Both impact parameter and source of α-particles
(d) impact parameter and the screen material of the detector

3. Atoms consist of a positively charged nucleus is obvious from the following observation of Geiger-Marsden experiment

(a) most of α-particles do not pass straight through the gold foil
(b) many of α-particles are scattered through the acute angles
(c) very large number of α-particles are deflected by large angles
(d) None of the above

4. The distance of closest approach of an α-particle is d when it moves with a speed v towards a nucleus. Another α-particle is projected with higher energy such that the new distance of the closest approach is $d/2$. What is the speed of projection of the α-particle in this case?

(a) $v/2$ (b) $\sqrt{2}v$ (c) $2v$ (d) $4v$

5. The impact parameter in Rutherford's scattering is related to **Competency Based Que**

(a) the potential energy of the incoming particle
(b) the angle of scattering
(c) the total energy of the system
(d) Both (a) and (b)

6. The de-Broglie wavelength of an electron in first Bohr's orbit is

(a) equal to $\frac{1}{4}$ of circumference of orbit
(b) equal to $\frac{1}{2}$ of circumference of orbit
(c) equal to twice of circumference of orbit
(d) equal to the circumference of orbit

7. The energy of an electron in a hydrogen atom in ground state is – 13.6 eV. Its energy in an orbit corresponding to quantum number n is – 0.544 V. The value of n is **CBSE 2025**

(a) 2 (b) 3 (c) 4 (d) 5

8. The simple Bohr model cannot be directly applied to calculate the energy levels of an atom with many electrons. This is because

(a) of the electrons not being subject to a central force
(b) of the electrons colliding with each other
(c) of screening effects
(d) the force between the nucleus and an electron will no longer be given by Coulomb's law

9. The radius of the innermost electron orbit of a hydrogen atom is 5.3×10^{-11} m. The radius of the $n=3$ orbit is **CBSE 2023, SQP**

(a) 1.01×10^{-10} m (b) 1.59×10^{-10} m
(c) 2.12×10^{-10} m (d) 4.77×10^{-10} m

10. The potential energy of an electron in the second excited state in hydrogen atom is **CBSE 2023**

(a) –3.4 eV (b) –3.02 eV
(c) –1.51 eV (d) –6.8 eV

11. The radius (r_n) of n th orbit in Bohr model of hydrogen atom varies with n as **CBSE 2024**

(a) $r_n \propto n$ (b) $r_n \propto \frac{1}{n}$ (c) $r_n \propto n^2$ (d) $r_n \propto \frac{1}{n^2}$

12. O_2 molecule consists of two oxygen atoms. In the molecule, nuclear force between the nuclei of the two atoms **Competency Based Que**

(a) is not important because nuclear forces are short-ranged
(b) is as important as electrostatic force for binding the two atoms
(c) cancels the repulsive electrostatic force between the nuclei
(d) is not important because oxygen nucleus have equal number of neutrons and protons

13. **In Balmer series of hydrogen atom, as the wavelength of spectral lines decreases, they appear** **CBSE 2024**

(a) equally spaced and equally intense
(b) further apart and stronger in intensity
(c) closer together and stronger in intensity
(d) closer together and weaker in intensity

14. **The wavelength limits of Lyman, Balmer and Paschen series are λ_L, λ_B and λ_P respectively. Wavelength increasing order can be written as**

(a) $\lambda_P < \lambda_B < \lambda_L$
(b) $\lambda_P > \lambda_B > \lambda_L$
(c) $\lambda_P = \lambda_B = \lambda_L$
(d) $\lambda_L > \lambda_B > \lambda_P$

15. **A photon beam of energy 12.1 eV is incident on a hydrogen atom. The orbit to which electron of H-atom be excited is** **CBSE SQP 2019-20**

(a) 2nd (b) 3rd (c) 4th (d) 5th

16. **Angular momentum of an electron in the second orbit of an atom is**

(a) 5×10^{-31} Js (b) 2.1×10^{-34} Js
(c) 5×10^{-9} Js (d) 2.1×10^{-9} Js

17. **The diagram shows four energy levels of an electron in Bohr model of hydrogen atom. Identify the transition in which the emitted photon will have the highest energy.** **CBSE 2023**

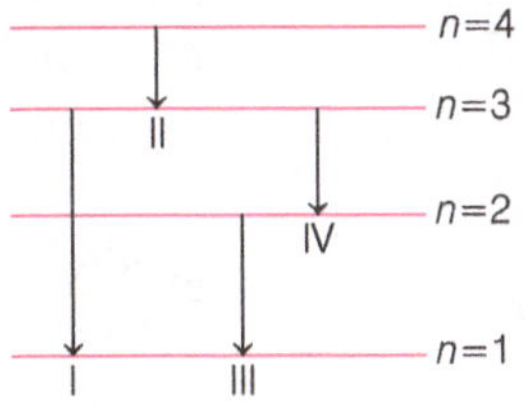

(a) I (b) II
(c) III (d) IV

18. **An electron makes a transition from orbit $n = 2$ to $n = 1$, in Bohr's model of hydrogen atom. Consider change in magnitudes of its kientic energy (K) and potential energy (U).** **CBSE 2024C**

(a) K increases and U decreases
(b) K decreases and U increases
(c) Both K and U decrease
(d) Both K and U increase

19. **Atomic spectral emission lines of hydrogen atom are incident on a zinc surface. The lines which can emit photoelectrons from the surface are members of** **CBSE 2025**

(a) Balmer series
(b) Paschen series
(c) Lyman series
(d) Neither Balmer, nor Paschen nor Lyman series

20. **Match the Column I with Column II.**

	Column I		Column II
A.	Energy level of hydrogen atom	1.	1.097×10^7 m^{-1}
B.	Bohr's first postulate	2.	$E_n = \frac{13.6}{n^2}$ eV
C.	Value of Rydberg constant (R)	3.	Electron revolve in certain stable orbit
D.	Ground state energy of hydrogen atom	4.	Balmer series
E.	Series corresponding to visible spectrum	5.	13.6 eV

(a) A-2, B-3, C-1, D-5, E-4 (b) A-4, B-5, C-1, D-2, E-3
(c) A-2, B-3, C-4, D-5, E-1 (d) A-1, B-2, C-3, D-4, E-5

21. **Match the Column I with Column II.**

	Column I		Column II
A.	Bohr's atomic model	1.	Discovery of the nucleus and dense core of the atom
B.	Rutherford's gold foil experiment	2.	Explain discrete spectral lines in hydrogen atom
C.	de-Broglie hypothesis	3.	Define the unique state of an electron in an atom
D.	Emission spectrum	4.	Concept of matter waves and wave particle duality
E.	Quantum number	5.	Energy emitted when electron transition between orbitals

(a) A-2, B-1, C-4, D-5, E-3
(b) A-4, B-1, C-5, D-2, E-3
(c) A-2, B-1, C-5, D-4, E-3
(d) A-1, B-2, C-3, D-4, E-5

Assertion-Reason

Directions *(Q. Nos. 22-28) In the following questions, two statements are given- one labelled Assertion (A) and the other labelled Reason (R). Select the correct answer to these questions from the codes (a), (b), (c) and (d) as given below.*

(a) Both Assertion and Reason are true and Reason is the correct explanation of Assertion.
(b) Both Assertion and Reason are true but Reason is not the correct explanation of Assertion.
(c) Assertion is true but Reason is false.
(d) Assertion is false but Reason is true.

22. **Assertion (A)** Large angle of scattering of alpha particles led to the discovery of atomic nucleus.
Reason (R) Entire positive charge of atom is concentrated in the central core.

23. **Assertion (A)** Atom as a whole is electrically neutral.
Reason (R) Atom contains equal amount of positive and negative charges.

24. **Assertion** (A) If the electrons in an atom were stationary, then they would fall into the nucleus.
Reason (R) Electrostatic force of attraction acts between negatively charged electrons and positive nucleus.

25. **Assertion (A)** Angular momentum of single electron in any orbit of hydrogen type atoms is independent of the atomic number of the element. **Competency Based Que**
Reason (R) In ground state, angular momentum is minimum.

26. **Assertion** (A) In a hydrogen atom, there is only one electron but its emission spectrum shows many lines.
Reason (R) In a given sample of hydrogen, there are many atoms each containing one electron, hence many electrons in different atoms may be in different orbits, so many transitions from higher to lower orbits are possible. **Competency Based Que**

27. **Assertion (A)** The ionisation energy of an atom is the energy required to remove an electron from the atom in its ground state.
Reason (R) Ionisation energy is a measure of the binding energy of the electron in the ground state. **Competency Based Que**

28. **Assertion (A)** In Bohr model of hydrogen atom, the angular momentum of an electron in nth orbit is proportional to the square root of its orbit radius r_n.
Reason (R) According to Bohr's model, electron can jump to its nearest orbits only. **CBSE 2025**

Case Based Questions

Directions *(Q.Nos. 29-30) These questions are case study based questions. Read the following paragraph and answer the questions on the basis of same.*

29. **At room temperature, most of the H-atoms are in ground state. When an atom receives some energy (i.e. by electron collisions), the atom may acquire sufficient energy to raise electron to higher energy state. In this condition, the atom is said to be in excited state. From the excited state, the electron can fall back to a state of lower energy, emitting a photon equal to the energy difference of the orbit.** **Competency Based Que**

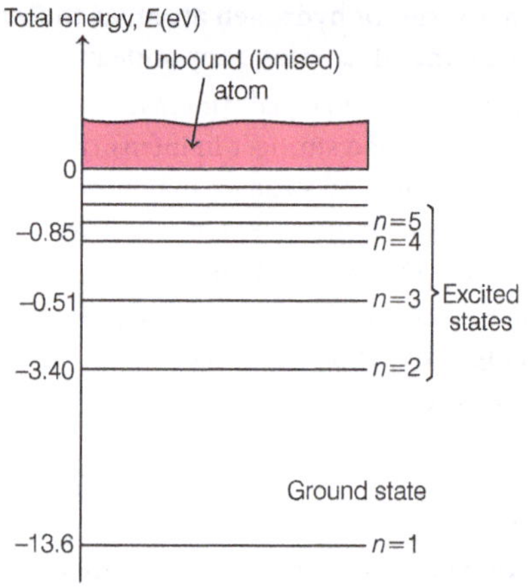

In a mixture of H—He^+ gas (He^+ is single ionised He atom), H-atoms and He^+ ions are excited to their respective first excited states. Subsequently, H atoms transfer their total excitation energy to He^+ ions (by collisions).

(i) The quantum number n of the state finally populated in He^+ ions is
(a) 2 (b) 3
(c) 4 (d) 5

(ii) The wavelength of light emitted in the visible region by He^+ ions after collisions with H-atoms is
(a) 6.5×10^{-7} m (b) 5.6×10^{-7} m
(c) 4.8×10^{-7} m (d) 4.0×10^{-7} m

(iii) The radius of the ground state orbit of H- atom is
(a) $\frac{\varepsilon_0}{h\pi me^2}$ (b) $\frac{h^2\varepsilon_0}{\pi me^2}$
(c) $\frac{\pi me^2}{h}$ (d) $\frac{2\pi h\varepsilon_0}{me^2}$

30. **In this experiment, H. Geiger and E. Marsden took radioactive source ($^{214}_{83}$Bi) for α-particles. A collimated beam of α-particles of energy 5.5 MeV was allowed to fall on 2.1×10^{-7} m thick gold foil. The α-particles were observed through a rotatable detector consisting of a zinc sulphide screen & microscope and it was found that α-particles got scattered. These scattered α-particles produced scintillations on the zinc sulphide screen.** **Competency Based Que**

Observations of this experiment are as follows
I. Many of the α-particles pass through the foil without deflection.
II. Only about 0.14% of the incident α-particles scattered by more than 1°.
III. Only about one α-particle in every 8000 α-particles deflected by more than 90°.

Based on these observations, they were able to propose a nuclear model of atom, called planetary model, in which entire positive charge and most of the mass of atom is concentrated in a small volume called the nucleus with electron revolving around it as planets revolve around the sun.

(i) Rutherford's atomic model can be visualised as

(a) 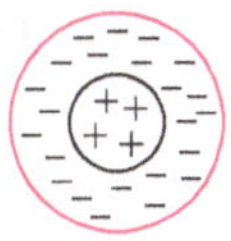

(b) 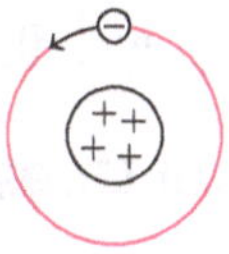

(c) 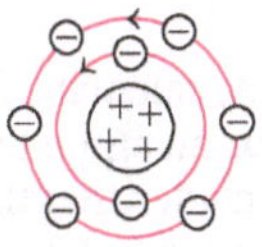

(d) 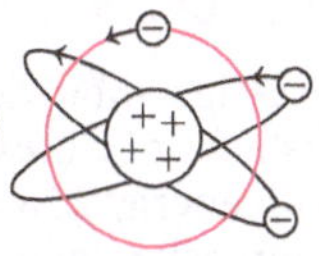

(ii) Gold foil used in Geiger-Marsden experiment is about 10^{-8} m thick. This ensures
- (a) gold foil's gravitational pull is small as possible
- (b) gold foil is deflected when α-particle stream is not incident centrally over it
- (c) gold foil provides no resistance to passage of α-particles
- (d) most α-particles will not suffer more than 1° scattering during passage through gold foil

(iii) In Geiger-Marsden experiment, detection of α-particles scattered at a particular angle is done by
- (a) counting flashes produced by α-particles on a ZnS coated screen
- (b) counting spots produced on a photographic film
- (c) using a galvanometer detector
- (d) using a Geiger-counter

(iv) Atoms consist of a positively charged nucleus is obvious from which of the following observation of Geiger-Marsden experiment?
- (a) Most of α-particles pass straight through the gold foil
- (b) Many of α-particles are scattered through the acute angles
- (c) Very large number of α-particles are deflected by large angles
- (d) None of the above

Or (iv) The fact that only a small fraction of the number of incident particles rebound back in Rutherford scattering indicates that
- (a) number of α-particles undergoing head-on collision is small
- (b) mass of the atom is concentrated in a small volume
- (c) mass of the atom is concentrated in a large volume
- (d) Both (a) and (b)

Subjective Questions

Very Short Answer Type Questions

1. What will be the distance of closest approach for an α-particle of double the kinetic energy?

2. Using Rutherford's model of the atom, derive the expression for the total energy of the electron in H-atom. What is the significance of total negative energy possessed by the electron?

3. Consider two different hydrogen atoms. The electron in each atom is in an excited state. Is it possible for the electrons to have different energies but the same orbital angular momentum according to the Bohr's model? **CBSE SQP 2021-22**

4. What is the ratio of radii of the orbits corresponding to first excited state and ground state in a hydrogen atom?

5. When an electron falls from a higher energy level to a lower energy level, the difference in the energies appears in the form of electromagnetic radiation. Why cannot it be emitted as other forms of energy? **Competency Based Que**

6. Calculate energy required to excite an electron from ground state to second excited state.

Short Answer Type Questions

7. Calculate the impact parameter of 6 MeV particle scattered by 90° when it approaches a gold nucleus. **Diksha Question**

8. (i) Differentiate between distance of closest approach and impact parameter. **[1½]**

(ii) Determine the distance of closest approach when an α-particle of kinetic energy 3.95 MeV approaches a nucleus of $Z = 79$ stops and reverses i **CBSE 2023** **[1½]**

9. Energy of electron in first excited state in hydrogen atom is -3.4 eV. Find KE and PE of electron in the ground state. **CBSE SQP 2019-20**

10. (i) Calculate the radius of the first orbit of H-atom. Also, find out the ratio of $\frac{r_1}{r_4}$? **[1½]**

(ii) Explain, why scattering of α-particles in Rutherford's experiment is not affected by the mass of the nucleons? [1½]

11. (i) Find out the wavelength of the electron orbiting in the ground state of hydrogen atom. [1½]

(ii) What is the minimum energy that must be given to a H-atom in ground state so that it can emit an H_γ line in Balmer series? If the angular momentum of the system is conserved, what would be the angular momentum of such H_γ photon? [1½]

12. Show that the first few frequencies of light that is emitted when electrons fall to *n*th level from levels higher than *n*, arc approximate harmonics (*i.e.*, in the ratio $1:2:3\ldots$) when $n >> 1$. **CBSE SQP 2021-22 (Term-II)**

13. Obtain the expression for the ratio of the de-Broglie wavelengths associated with the electron orbiting in the second and third excited states of hydrogen atom. **Delhi 2019**

Long Answer Type Questions

14. Define the distance of closest approach. An α-particle of kinetic energy K is bombarded on a thin gold foil. The distance of the closest approach is r. What will be the distance of closest approach for an α-particle of double the kinetic energy? Write two important limitations of Rutherford nuclear model of the atom.

15. State the basic assumption of the Rutherford's model of an atom. Explain in brief, why this model cannot account for the stability of an atom?

16. Draw the graph showing variation of scattered particles detected (N) with the scattering angle (θ) in Geiger-Marsden experiment. Write two conclusions that you can draw from this graph. Obtain the expression for the distance of closest approach in this experiment. **CBSE 2024**

17. (i) Define the terms impact parameter and distance of closest approach for an α-particle in Geiger-Marsden scattering experiment. [2½]

(ii) What will be the value of the impact parameter for scattering angle (a) $\theta = 0°$ and (b) $\theta = 180°$? **CBSE 2022 (Term-II)** [2½]

18. Prove that the magnetic moment of the electron revolving around a nucleus in an orbit of radius r with orbital speed v is equal to $evr/2$. Hence, using Bohr's postulate of quantisation of angular momentum, deduce the expression for the magnetic moment of hydrogen atom in the ground state. **All India 2019**

19. (i) State Bohr's postulates and derive an expression for the energy of electron in *n*th orbit in Bohr's model of hydrogen atom. [2½]

(ii) Calculate binding energy per nucleon (in MeV) of C_6^{12} [2½]

Given, $m\,({}^{12}_{6}\text{C}) = 12.000000$ u

$m\,({}^{1}_{0}n) = 1.008665$ u

$m\,({}^{1}_{1}\text{H}) = 1.007825$ u **CBSE 2024C**

Numerical Questions

α-Particles Scattering

20. (i) In Geiger-Marsden experiment, calculate the distance of closest approach for an alpha particle with energy 2.56×10^{-12} J. Consider that the particle approaches gold nucleus ($Z = 79$) in head-on position. [2]

(ii) If the above experiment is repeated with a proton of the same energy, then what will be the value of the distance of closest approach? **CBSE 2022, Term-II** [1]

21. A narrow beam of protons, each having 4.1 MeV energy is approaching sheet of lead ($Z = 82$). Calculate

(i) the speed of a proton in the beam and [1½]

(ii) the distance of its closest approach. **CBSE 2022 (Term-II)** [1½]

22. In Rutherford's α-particle scattering experiment with their gold foil 8100 scintillation per minute are observed at an angle of 60°. What will be the number of scintillations per minute at 120°?

Bohr's Model of Hydrogen Atom

23. Obtain the first Bohr's radius and the ground state energy of a muonic hydrogen atom. i.e., an atom where the electron is replaced by a negatively charged muon (μ^-) of mass about 207 m_e that orbits around a proton. (Given for hydrogen atom, radius of first orbit and ground state energy are 0.53×10^{-10} m and -13.6 eV respectively).

24. The radius of the innermost electron orbit of a H-atom is 5.3×10^{-11} m. What are the radii of $n = 2$ and $n = 3$ orbits? **NCERT**

Energy Level and Line Spectra of Hydrogen Atom

25. The ground state energy of a H-atom is -13.6 eV. If an electron makes a transition from an energy level -0.85 eV to -1.51 eV, then calculate the wavelength of the spectral line emitted. To which series of hydrogen spectrum, does this wavelength belong?

26. The first four spectral lines in the Lyman series of a H-atom are $\lambda = 1218\text{Å}$, 1028Å, 974.3Å and 951.4Å. If instead of hydrogen, we consider deuterium, calculate the shift in the wavelength of these lines.

Competency Based Que

27. A hydrogen atom in the ground state is excited by an electron beam of 12.5 eV energy. Find out the maximum number of lines emitted by the atom from its excited state.

28. The ground state energy of hydrogen atom is −13.6 eV. If an electron makes a transition from an energy level −1.51 eV to −3.4 eV, then calculate the wavelength of the spectral line emitted and name the series of hydrogen spectrum to which it belongs.

29. What is the minimum energy that must be given to a H-atom in ground state, so that it can emit an H_γ-line in Balmer series? If the angular momentum of the system is conserved, what would be the angular momentum of such H_γ photon? **NCERT Exemplar**

Hints & Solutions

Objective Type Questions

1. (a)	2. (a)	3. (b)	4. (b)	5. (d)
6. (d)	8. (a)	10. (a)	11. (c)	12. (a)
13. (d)	14. (b)	16. (b)	18. (a)	19. (c)
20. (a)	21. (a)	23. (a)	27 (a)	

7. (*d*) Here, $E_0 = -13.6\text{ eV}$, $E_n = -0.544\text{ eV}$

$$E_n = \frac{E_0}{n^2} \Rightarrow n^2 = \frac{-13.6}{-0.544} = 25$$

$\therefore \quad n = 5$

9. (*d*) The radius of an atom whose principal quantum number is *n*, is given by $r = n^2 r_0$

where, r_0 = radius of innermost electon orbit for hydrogen atom and

$$r_0 = 5.3 \times 10^{-11}\text{ m}$$

For the second excited state, $n = 3$

$\therefore \quad r = 3^2 \times r_0 = 9 \times 5.3 \times 10^{-11}$

$$r = 4.77 \times 10^{-10}\text{ m}$$

15. (*b*) The energy of electron in *n*th orbit of hydrogen atom is given by $E_n = -\frac{13.6}{n^2}\text{ eV}$

$\therefore$ According to the question,

$$E_n - E_1 = 12.1\text{ eV}$$

$$\Rightarrow \quad -\frac{13.6}{n^2} - (-13.6) = 12.1$$

$\therefore \quad n = 33$

Hence, the electron of hydrogen atom is excited to 3rd orbit.

17. (a) The energy of electron in *n*th orbit in H-atom is

$$E_n = -\frac{13.6}{n^2} = -\frac{K}{n^2}$$

From the given diagram,

$$E_3 - E_1 = -\frac{K}{9} - (-K) = \frac{8K}{9} = 0.88K$$

$$E_4 - E_3 = -\frac{K}{16} - \left(-\frac{K}{9}\right) = \frac{7K}{144} = 0.04\,K$$

$$E_2 - E_1 = -\frac{K}{4} + K = \frac{3K}{4} = 0.77K$$

$$E_3 - E_2 = -\frac{K}{9} - \left(-\frac{K}{4}\right) = \frac{5K}{36} = 0.13K$$

Hence, the transition $(E_3 - E_1)$ i.e. I has the highest energy.

22. (*a*) As, α-particle is positively charged, and the large angle of scattering of α-particle shows that the nucleus is positively charged and concentrated in the central core.

24. (*a*) In an atom, electron revolves around nucleus. For this, required centripetal force is provided by electrostatic force of attraction between negatively charged electron and positive nucleus.

If the electrons were stationary, then the electrostatic force will remain unbalanced, which leads to the electron to fall into the nucleus.

25. (*b*) From, $L = n\left(\frac{h}{2\pi}\right)$, i.e. $L \propto n$.

In ground state, $n = 1$, so L = minimum.

26. (*a*) The Assertion is true. Even though a hydrogen atom contains only one electron, the emission spectrum shows many lines because the electron can transit between various energy levels, leading to different

wavelengths of emitted radiation.The Reason is also true and correctly explains the Assertion. In a sample of hydrogen, there are numerous hydrogen atoms. While each atom has only one electron, these electrons are in different energy states. Therefore, multiple transitions and hence, multiple spectral lines are observed.

28. (*d*) In Bohr's model of hydrogen atom, the angular momentum L is given as

$$L = mvr_n = \frac{nh}{2\pi}$$

$$\Rightarrow \quad L \propto r_n$$

According to Bohr's third postulate, electrons can make a transition from any fixed orbit to another by emitting photons of a particular frequency, $\nu = E_i - E_f$.

29. (i) (*c*) $E_n = \frac{-13.6}{n^2}(Z^2)$

In first excited state, $E_{H_2} = 3.4$ eV

and $E_{He} = -13.6$ eV

So, H_2 atom gives excitation energy ($13.6 - 3.4 = 10.2$ eV) to helium atom.

Now, energy of He ion $= -13.6 + 10.2 = -3.4$ eV

Again, $E = \frac{-13.6}{n^2} \times Z^2$

$$\Rightarrow \quad -3.4 = \frac{-13.6}{n^2} \times (2)^2 \Rightarrow n = 4$$

(ii) (*c*) $\frac{1}{\lambda} = \frac{13.6\, Z^2}{hc}\left[\frac{1}{n_1^2} - \frac{1}{n_2^2}\right]$

Here $n_1 = 3$ and $n_2 = 4$

$$\Rightarrow \quad \lambda = 4.8 \times 10^{-7} \text{ m}$$

(iii) (*b*) Radius of the permitted orbit,

$$r = \frac{n^2 h^2 \varepsilon_0}{\pi\, mZe^2}$$

For hydrogen atom in ground state, i.e.

$$n = 1, Z = 1$$

$$\Rightarrow \quad r = \frac{h^2 \varepsilon_0}{\pi m e^2}$$

30. (i) (*d*) Rutherford's atom had a positively charged centre and electrons were revolving outside it. It is also called the planetary model of the atom as in option (d).

(ii) (*d*) As the gold foil is very thin, it can be assumed that α-particles will suffer not more than one scattering during their passage through it. Therefore, computation of the trajectory of an α-particle scattered by a single nucleus is enough.

(iii) (*a*) The scattered α-particles were observed through a rotatable detector consisting of zinc sulphide (ZnS) screen and a microscope. The scattered α-particles on striking the screen produced bright light flashes or scintillations. These flashes may be viewed through a microscope and the distribution of the number of scattered particles may be studied as a function of angle of scattering.

(iv) (*a*) In Rutherford's nuclear model of the atom, the entire positive charge and most of the mass of the atom are concentrated in the nucleus with the electrons some distance away. It is obvious from the observation of Geiger-Marsden experiment that most of the α-particles pass straight through the gold foil.

Or

(iv) (*d*) In case of head-on collision, the impact parameter is minimum and the α-particle rebounds back. So, the fact that only a small fraction of the number of incident particles rebound back indicates that the number of α-particles undergoing head-on collision is small.

This in turn implies that the mass of the atom is concentrated in a small volume.

Subjective Questions

1. We know that distance of closest approach,

$$r_e = \frac{1}{4\pi\varepsilon_0} \cdot \frac{2Ze^2}{K}$$

r_e is inversely proportional to K. Thus, if K is doubled, distance of closest approach becomes half, i.e. $\frac{r_e}{2}$.

2. Refer to text on page 384 (Electron orbits)

3. According to Bohr's model, electrons having different energies belong to different levels having different values of n. So, their angular momenta will be different, as

$$L = \frac{nh}{2\pi}$$

or $\quad L \propto n$

Now, angular momentum in 2nd orbit is

$$L_2 = \frac{2h}{2\pi} = \frac{h}{\pi}$$

4. For 1st excited state, $n = 2$

Ground state occurs for $n = 1$

We know, $\quad r \propto n^2$

Hence, $\frac{r_1}{r_2} = \left(\frac{n_1}{n_2}\right)^2 = \left(\frac{2}{1}\right)^2 = r_1 : r_2 = 4:1$

5. The electrons are charged particles. When an electron falls from a higher energy level to a lower energy level, it accelerates. We know, accelerating charged particles radiates energy in the form of electromagnetic radiation.

6. Energy in ground state $(n = 1)$,

$$E_1 = \frac{-13.6}{1^2} = 13.6 \text{eV}$$

Energy in second excited state $(n = 3)$

$$E_3 = \frac{-13.6}{3^2} = 1.51\,\text{eV}$$

Required energy $= E_3 - E_1 = 12.09\,\text{eV}$

7. Here, KE $= 6$ MeV

$$= 6 \times 1.6 \times 10^{-3}\ \text{J}$$

and $\theta = 90°$, $Z = 79$ for gold

We know that impact parameter is

$$b = \frac{k.Ze^2 \cot\frac{\theta}{2}}{\text{KE}}$$

$$b = \frac{9 \times 10^9 \times 79 \times (1.6 \times 10^{-19})^2 \cot 45°}{6 \times 1.6 \times 10^{-13}} = 1.89 \times 10^{-14}\ \text{m}$$

8. (i) Refer to text on pages 382 and 383.

(ii) $Z = 79$

$$e = 1.6 \times 10^{-19}\text{C}$$

$$\text{KE} = 3.95\ \text{MeV} = 6.329 \times 10^{-13}\text{J}$$

$$6.329 \times 10^{-13} = \frac{79 \times 2(1.6 \times 10^{-19})^2 \times 9 \times 10^9}{r_0}$$

$$r_0 = \frac{158 \times 1.6 \times 1.6 \times 10^{-38} \times 9 \times 10^9 \times 10^{13}}{6.329}$$

$$r_0 = 575.18 \times 10^{-16}\ \text{m}$$

9. Given, $E_2 = -3.4$ eV (For first excited state in H-atom)

For ground state, $n = 1$

So, $E_1 = 4E_2 = 4 \times (-3.4\ \text{eV}) = -13.6$ eV

Now, kinetic energy in ground state is

KE $= -$(Total energy) $= -(-13.6) = 13.6$ eV

and potential energy in ground state is

PE $= 2$ (Total energy) $= 2 \times (-13.6) = -27.2$ eV

10. (i) We have, radius of nth orbit,

$$r_n = \frac{n^2 h^2 \varepsilon_0}{\pi m e^2} \quad \text{...(i)}$$

For $n = 1$,

$$r_1 = \frac{h^2 \varepsilon_0}{\pi m e^2} = \frac{(6.63 \times 10^{-34})^2 \times (8.85 \times 10^{-12})}{(3.14)(9.1 \times 10^{-31})(1.6 \times 10^{-19})^2} = 0.53\text{Å}$$

From Eq. (i), we get

$$r_n \propto n^2$$

$$\Rightarrow \quad \frac{r_1}{r_4} = \frac{n_1^2}{n_4^2} = \frac{1}{(4)^2}$$

$$\therefore \quad \frac{r_1}{r_4} = \frac{1}{16}$$

(ii) The scattering of alpha particles in Rutherford's experiment is unaffected by the mass of the nucleus because the deflection is caused by Coulomb force (electrostatic repulsion) between the alpha particles and the nucleus. This force depends on the charge of the nucleus, not its mass. Since, the nucleus is much heavier than the α-particles, it remains nearly stationary during the interaction and only the charges influence the scattering pattern.

11. (i) For an electron revolving in nth orbit of radius r_0,

$$n\lambda = 2\pi r_0$$

For electron orbiting in ground state, i.e. $n = 1$,

$$1 \times \lambda = 2\pi r_0 = 2\pi \times 0.5\text{Å} \qquad [\because r_0 = 0.5\ \text{Å}]$$

$$= \pi\text{Å}$$

or $\lambda = 3.14$ Å

(ii) H_γ in Balmer series corresponds to transition $n = 5$ to $n = 2$. So, the electron in ground state, i.e., from $n = 1$, must first be placed in state $n = 5$.

Energy required for the transition from $n = 2$ to $n = 5$ is given by

$$= E_1 - E_5 = 13.6 - 0.54 = 13.06\ \text{eV}$$

Since, angular momentum is conserved,

$\therefore$ angular momentum corresponding to $H\lambda$ photon

= change in angular momentum of electron

$= L_5 - L_2 = 5h - 2h = 3h = 3 \times 1.06 \times 10^{-34}$

$= 3.18 \times 10^{-34}$ kg-m^2 /s

12. The frequency of any line in a series in the spectrum of hydrogen like atoms corresponding to the transition of electrons from $(n + p)$ level to nth level can be expressed as a difference of two terms;

$$v_{mn} = cRZ^2\left[\frac{1}{(n+p)^2} - \frac{1}{n^2}\right]$$

where, $m = n + p$, $(p = 1, 2, 3, \ldots)$ and R is Rydberg constant.

For $p << n$

$$v_{mn} = cRZ^2\left[\frac{1}{n^2}\left(1 + \frac{p}{n}\right)^{-2} - \frac{1}{n^2}\right]$$

$$v_{mn} = cRZ^2\left[\frac{1}{n^2} - \frac{2p}{n^3} - \frac{1}{n^2}\right]$$

[By binomial theorem $(1 + x)^n = 1 + nx$ if $|x| < 1$]

$$v_{mn} = cRZ^2\,\frac{2p}{n^3} \simeq \left(\frac{2cRZ^2}{n^3}\right)p$$

Thus, the first few frequencies of light that is emitted when electrons fall to the nth level from levels higher than n, are approximate harmonic (*i.e.*, in the ratio 1 : 2 : 3 ...) when $n >> 1$.

13. We know that, $\lambda = \frac{h}{p} = \frac{h}{mv} \Rightarrow mv = \frac{h}{\lambda}$

$$\Rightarrow \quad mvr = \frac{hr}{\lambda} = \frac{nh}{2\pi}$$

$$\Rightarrow \quad \lambda = \frac{2\pi}{nh} \times hr = \frac{2\pi r}{n}$$

As, $\quad r \propto n^2$

$$\Rightarrow \quad \lambda \propto \frac{1}{n}(n^2) = n$$

Thus, we can say that, $\frac{\lambda_3}{\lambda_1} = \frac{3}{1}$

$$\Rightarrow \quad \lambda_1 = \frac{\lambda_3}{3}$$

Thus, wavelength decreases 3 times as an electron jumps from third excited state to the ground state.

14. When an α-particle is bombarded over a gold nucleus, it is repelled by electrostatic repulsion. As a result KE of α-particle is converted into electrostatic PE. At a certain distance between the α-particle and nucleus at which the moving charge loses all its kinetic energy and becomes stationary momentarily. This distance (r) is known as distance of closest approach.

In this process, all the kinetic energy (K) of moving particle is converted into potential energy.

From the given data,

Initially, $$\frac{1}{4\pi\varepsilon_0} \cdot \frac{2e \times Ze}{r} = K \quad \ldots\text{(i)}$$

Let r_0 be the new distance of closest approach for a twice energetic α-particle. Then, we have,

$$\frac{1}{4\pi\varepsilon_0} \times \frac{2e \times Ze}{r_0} = 2K \quad \ldots\text{(ii)}$$

On dividing Eq. (i) by Eq. (ii), we get

$$\frac{r_0}{r} = \frac{1}{2}$$

$$\Rightarrow \quad r_0 = \frac{r}{2}$$

Refer to text on page 384 (Drawbacks of Rutherford's model).

15. Refer to the text on pagea 381 and 382.

16. Refer to text on pages 381 and 382 (α-particles scattering experiment by Rutherford observations).

Distance of closest approach

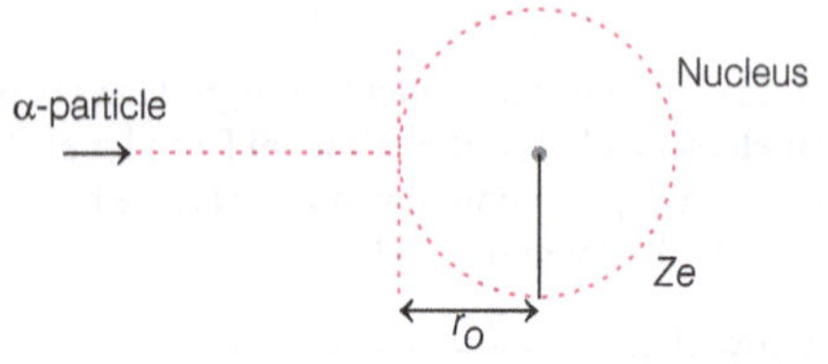

Distance of closest approach,

Kinetic energy = Electrostatic potential energy

$$K = \frac{1}{4\pi\varepsilon_0} \frac{(Ze)(2e)}{r_0}$$

$$\therefore \quad r_0 = \frac{1}{4\pi\varepsilon_0} \cdot \frac{2Ze^2}{K} = \frac{1}{4\pi\varepsilon_0}\left(\frac{2Ze^2}{\frac{1}{2}mv^2}\right)$$

17. (i) Refer to text on pages 382 and 383 (Impact parameter and distance of closest approach)

(ii) (a) For $\theta = 0°$, the impact parameter is

$$b = \frac{KZe^2 \cot\frac{\theta}{2}}{\left(\frac{1}{2}mv^2\right)} = \frac{KZe^2 \cot 0°}{\left(\frac{1}{2}mv^2\right)} = \infty \text{ (infinity)}$$

(b) For $\theta = 180°$, the impact parameter is

$$b = \frac{KZe^2 \cot\left(\frac{180°}{2}\right)}{\left(\frac{1}{2}mv^2\right)} = 0$$

18. According to Bohr's model of atom, negatively charged electron revolves around the positively charged nucleus. This is same as that of a current loop of dipole moment $= IA$. Let the electron is moving in a circle with speed v in anti-clockwise direction of radius r and time period T.

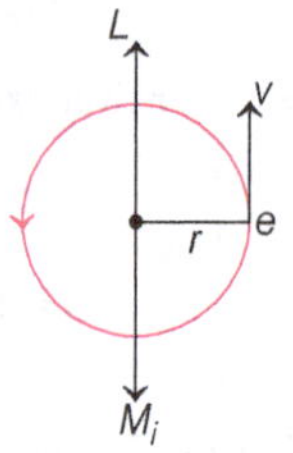

Current, $\quad I = \frac{e}{T} = \frac{e}{2\pi r / v} = \frac{ev}{2\pi r}$

Area of loop $= \pi r^2$

$\therefore$ Orbital magnetic moment of electron is

$$M_i = IA = \frac{ev}{2\pi r} \times \pi r^2 = \frac{evr}{2}$$

The angular momentum of electron due to orbital motion is $\quad L = m_e vr$

It is directed unwond in perpendicular direction to the plane.

$$\frac{M_i}{L} = \frac{evr/2}{m_e vr} = \frac{e}{2m_e}$$

This ratio is constant called gyromagnetic ratio. Its value is $8.8 \times 10^{10}\text{C kg}^{-1}$, so $\mu_i = \frac{e}{2m_e} L$

The vector form $\mu_i = -\frac{e}{2m_e} L$

The negative sign shows that the direction of L is opposite to μ_i. According to Bohr's quantisation condition, the angular momentum of an electron is an integral multiple of $\frac{h}{2\pi}$.

$$\therefore \quad L = \frac{nh}{2\pi}$$

$$\Rightarrow \quad \mu_l = n\left(\frac{eh}{4\pi m_e}\right)$$

This is the equation of magnetic moment of an electron revolving in nth orbit.

19. (i) **Bohr's postulates** Refer to text page no 385.

Derivation Total energy of electron in the stationary state of hydrogen atom is

$$E = \frac{e^2}{8\pi\varepsilon_0 r_n} \qquad \text{...(i)}$$

where, r_n is radius of nth orbit

$$r_n = \frac{n^2 h^2 \varepsilon_0}{\pi m e^2} \qquad \text{... (ii)}$$

Substituting Eqs. (ii) in Eq. (i), we get

$$E_n = \frac{me^4}{8n^2\varepsilon_0^2 h^2}$$

(ii) Mass defect,

$$\Delta m = [6m({}_0^1 n) + 6m({}_1^1\text{H})] - m({}_6^{12}\text{C})$$

$$\Delta m = (6 \times 1.008665 + 6 \times 1.007825) - 12.000000$$

$$\Delta m = 0.09894 \text{ u}$$

$$\text{BE} = \Delta m \times 931.5 \text{ MeV}$$

$$= 92.16 \text{ MeV}$$

Binding energy per nucleon,

$$E_{\text{bn}} = \frac{E_b}{A} = \frac{92.16}{12} = 7.68 \text{ MeV}$$

20. Given, $E = 2.56 \times 10^{-12}$ J,

$$Z = 79, e = 1.6 \times 10^{-19} \text{ C}$$

(i) For α-particle (He^{2+}),

Distance of closest approach,

$$r_0 = \frac{1}{4\pi\varepsilon_0} \cdot \frac{2Ze^2}{E}$$

$$= \frac{9 \times 10^9 \times 2 \times 79 \times (1.6 \times 10^{-19})^2}{2.56 \times 10^{-12}}$$

$$= 14.22 \times 10^{-15} \text{ m}$$

(ii) For proton,

Distance of closest approach,

$$r_0 = \frac{1}{4\pi\varepsilon_0} \cdot \frac{Ze^2}{E}$$

$$= \frac{9 \times 10^9 \times 79 \times (1.6 \times 10^{-19})^2}{2.56 \times 10^{-12}}$$

$$= 7.11 \times 10^{-15} \text{m}$$

21. (i) KE of 4.1 MeV proton

$$= 4.1 \times 10^6 \times 1.6 \times 10^{-19} \text{ J}$$

Mass of proton $= 1.67 \times 10^{-27}$ kg

$$v^2 = \frac{2\text{KE}}{m}$$

$$\text{or } v^2 = \frac{2 \times 4.1 \times 10^6 \times 1.6 \times 10^{19}}{1.67 \times 10^{-27}}$$

$$\text{or } v^2 = 7.85 \times 10^{14}$$

$$\therefore v = 2.8 \times 10^7 \text{MeV}$$

(ii) Energy of proton = 4.1 MeV

Atomic number (Z) of lead = 82

When the proton is at the distance of the closest appraoch (r) then,

$$\text{KE of the system} = \frac{KZe^2}{r}$$

So, from the conservation of principle,

$$4.1 \text{ MeV} = 0 + \frac{KZe^2}{r}$$

$$r_0 = \frac{KZe^2}{(4.1 \times 10^6 e)}$$

$$\text{or} \quad r_0 = \frac{9 \times 10^9 \times 82 \times e^2}{4.1 \times 10^6 e}$$

$$\therefore \quad r_0 = 288 \times 10^{-16}$$

$$r_0 = 2.88 \times 10^{-14} \text{ m}$$

22. The number of α-particles scattered at an angle θ is given by

$$N = \frac{\theta_n t Z^2 e^4}{8\pi\varepsilon_0^2 r^2 E^2 (\sin\theta/2)^4}; \; N \propto \frac{1}{\sin^4\frac{\theta}{2}}$$

$$\Rightarrow \quad \frac{N_1}{N_2} = \frac{\sin^4\frac{\theta_2}{2}}{\sin^4\frac{\theta_1}{2}}$$

$$\Rightarrow \quad \frac{8100}{N_2} = \frac{\sin^4\frac{120°}{2}}{\sin^4\frac{60°}{2}} = \frac{\sin^4(60°)}{\sin^4(30°)}$$

$$\therefore \quad N_2 = \frac{8100}{9} = 900$$

23. In Bohr's model of hydrogen atom, the radius of nth orbit is given by

$$r_n = \frac{n^2h^2}{4\pi^2e^2m_e}$$

$$r_1 \propto \frac{1}{m_e} \qquad (\because n=1)$$

Similarly, $r_\mu \propto \dfrac{1}{m_\mu}$

$$\frac{r_\mu}{r_e} = \frac{m_e}{m_\mu} = \frac{1}{207}$$

$$\Rightarrow \quad r_\mu = \frac{1}{207}r_e = \frac{0.53\times10^{-10}}{207} = 2.56\times10^{-13}\text{ m}$$

24. 2.12×10^{-10} m and 4.47×10^{-10} m; Refer to Example 5 on page 387.

25. 18751 Å; Refer to Example 7 on page 388 and $\lambda = \dfrac{hc}{\Delta E}$.

The wavelength belongs to Paschen series of hydrogen spectrum.

26. The total energy of the electron in the stationary states of the hydrogen atom is given by

$$E_n = -\frac{me^4}{8n^2\varepsilon_0^2h^2}$$

where signs are as usual and the m that occurs in the Bohr formula is the reduced mass of electron and proton in hydrogen atom.

By Bohr's model,

$$h\nu_{if} = E_{n_i} - E_{n_f}$$

On simplifying,

$$\nu_{if} = \frac{me^4}{8\varepsilon_0^2h^3}\left(\frac{1}{n_f^2} - \frac{1}{n_i^2}\right)$$

Since, $\lambda \propto \dfrac{1}{\mu}$

Thus, $\lambda_{if} \propto \dfrac{1}{\mu}$ ...(i)

where, μ is the reduced mass. (Here, μ is used in place of m).

Reduced mass for $H = \mu_H = \dfrac{m_e}{1+\dfrac{m_e}{M}} \approx m_e\left(1-\dfrac{m_e}{M}\right)$

Reduced mass for $D = \mu_D \approx m_e\left(1-\dfrac{m_e}{2M}\right)$

Now, $\dfrac{\mu_H}{\mu_D} = \left(1-\dfrac{m_e}{2M}\right)\left(1+\dfrac{m_e}{2M}\right)$

$$\approx 1-\frac{m_e}{2M}$$

For hydrogen and deuterium, the wavelength is $\dfrac{\lambda_H}{\lambda_D}$

$$\frac{\lambda_D}{\lambda_H} = \frac{\mu_H}{\mu_D} \simeq \left(1-\frac{m_e}{2M}\right)$$

$$\simeq \left(1-\frac{1}{2\times1840}\right)$$

$$\lambda_D = \lambda_H\times(0.99973)$$

On substituting the values,

lines are 1217.7Å, 1027.7Å, 974.04Å, 951.143Å.

Thus, shift in wavelength $(\lambda_0 - \lambda_H) = 0.3$ Å

27. The energy absorbed by it is

$-13.6 + 12.5 = -1.1$ eV

Energy, $E_n = -\dfrac{13.6}{n^2}$

$$\Rightarrow \quad n^2 = \frac{-13.6}{-1.1} = 12.36$$

$$\Rightarrow \quad n \simeq 3$$

Thus, number of transitions = 3

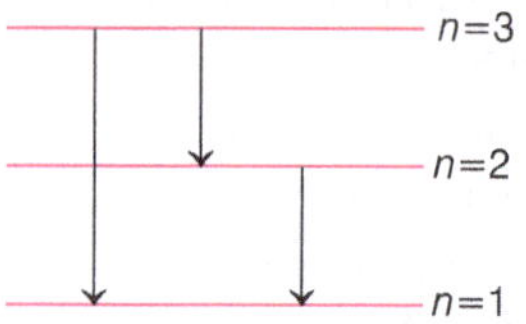

28. Energy levels of H-atom are as shown below

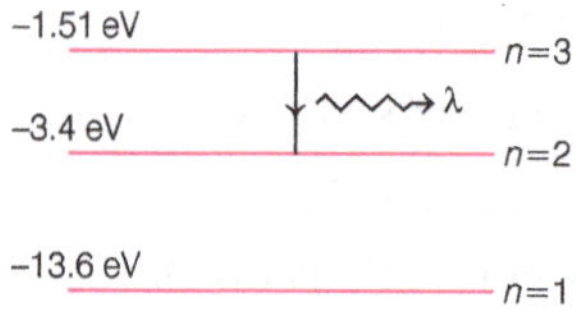

Wavelength of spectral line emitted, $\lambda = \dfrac{hc}{\Delta E}$

Taking $hc = 1240$ eV-nm, we have

$$\Delta E = -1.51 - (-3.4) = 1.89\text{ eV}$$

$$\therefore \quad \lambda = \frac{1240}{1.89} \approx 656\text{ nm}$$

This belongs to Balmer spectral series.

29. The third line in Balmer series in the spectrum of hydrogen atom is H_γ. H_γ in Balmer series corresponds to transition $n=5$ to $n=2$, so the electron in ground state, i.e. from $n=1$ must first be placed in state $n=5$.

Energy required for the transition from $n=1$ to $n=5$ is given by

$$= E_5 - E_1$$
$$= 13.6 - 0.54$$
$$= 13.06 \text{ eV}$$

Since, angular momentum is conserved.

Angular momentum corresponding to H_γ photon
= Change in angular momentum of electron

$$= L_5 - L_2 = \frac{5h}{2\pi} - \frac{2h}{2\pi} = \frac{3h}{2\pi}$$
$$= 3 \times 1.06 \times 10^{-34}$$
$$= 3.18 \times 10^{-34} \text{ kg-m}^2/\text{s}$$

QR Code for Quick Test 1

QR Code for Quick Test 2

SELF ASSESSMENT TEST

Multiple Choice Questions (MCQs)

1. In Bohr's model of the atom, the angular momentum of an electron in the nth orbit is proportional to

(a) n (b) n^2

(c) $\frac{1}{n}$ (d) $\sqrt{n}$

2. The wavelength of the first line of the Lyman series (in hydrogen atom) is approximately

(a) 121.6 nm

(b) 91.2 nm

(c) 102.5 nm

(d) 656.3 nm

3. According to Heisenberg's uncertainty principle, which of the following cannot be precisely determined simultaneously?

(a) Energy and time

(b) Position and momentum

(c) Angular momentum and radius

(d) Charge and mass

4. The total energy of an electron in the hydrogen atom in the nth energy level is given by

(a) $E_n = -\frac{13.6}{n^2}$ eV (b) $E_n = -\frac{13.6}{n}$ eV

(c) $E_n = 13.6n$ eV (d) $E_n = 13.6n^2$ eV

Assertion-Reason

Directions (Q. Nos. 6-7) *In the following questions, two statements are given- one labelled Assertion (A) and the other labelled Reason (R). Select the correct answer to these questions from the codes (a), (b), (c) and (d) as given below*

(a) Both Assertion and Reason are true and Reason is the correct explanation of Assertion.

(b) Both Assertion and Reason are true but Reason is not the correct explanation of Assertion.

(c) Assertion is true but Reason is false.

(d) Assertion is false but Reason is true.

5. Assertion (A) The energy of an electron in the n th orbit of hydrogen atom is inversely proportional to n^2.
Reason (R) The energy of an electron is quantised and can have only certain specific values.

6. Assertion (A) The electron in the ground state of a hydrogen atom does not radiate energy.
Reason (R) The electron in the ground state of an atom has zero kinetic energy.

7. Assertion (A) The radius of the first orbit of hydrogen atom is 0.529 Å.
Reason (R) The radius of an orbit is directly proportional to the square of the principal quantum number.

Case Based Questions

Directions *(Q. Nos. 8) This question is case study based question. Read the following paragraph and answer the questions on the basis of same.*

8. In a laboratory, a hydrogen atom is placed in an excited state, where the electron is in the $n=4$ energy level. It is known that when the electron transitions to a lower energy level, it emits photons with specific energies. The energy of an electron in a particular level n for a hydrogen atom is given by the formula, $E_n = -\frac{13.6}{n^2}$ eV

where, n is the principal quantum number and E_n is the energy of the electron in that state. The electron can transition to any of the lower energy levels, emitting a photon whose energy corresponds to the difference between the initial and final energy levels.
Consider the following transitions of the electron from

1. $n=4$ to $n=3$ 2. $n=4$ to $n=2$ 3. $n=4$ to $n=1$

(i) Calculate the energy of the photon emitted when the electron transitions from $n=4$ to $n=2$.

(ii) Determine the wavelength of the photon emitted in the transition from $n=4$ to $n=2$.
(Use, $hc = 1240$ eV/nm)

(iii) Which transition from $n=4$ results in the emission of the highest energy photon? Justify your answer with calculations.

(iv) What is the shortest wavelength of Lyman series ?

Very Short Answer Type Question

9. In what way does the emission spectrum of hydrogen provide experimental verification of Bohr's theory?

10. (i) In accordance with the Bohr's model find the quantum number that characteristics the earth's revolution around the sun in the orbit of radius 1.5×10^{11} m with orbital speed 3×10^4 m/s. (Mass of earth $= 6.0 \times 10^{24}$ kg)

(ii) A difference of 2.3 eV separate two energy levels in an atom. What is the frequency of radiation emitted when the atom makes a transition from the upper level to the lower level?

Short Answer Type Questions

11. Explain how the de-Broglie hypothesis leads to Bohr's quantisation condition for angular momentum?

12. Calculate the radius of the second orbit ($n = 2$) of a hydrogen atom according to Bohr's theory.
(Given: $\varepsilon_0 = 8.85 \times 10^{-12}\, C^2/Nm^2$, $e = 1.6 \times 10^{-19}$ C, $m_e = 9.1 \times 10^{-31}$ kg, $h = 6.63 \times 10^{-34}$ Js)

13. Determine the energy difference between the $n = 3$ and $n = 2$ energy levels of a hydrogen atom and hence determine the wavelength of photon emitted by an electron when it jumps from $n = 3$ to $n = 2$.

Long Answer Type Questions

14. If a proton had a radius R and the charge was uniformly distributed, calculate using Bohr theory, the ground state energy of H-atom when
(i) $R = 0.1$ Å and (ii) $R = 10$ Å

Answers

1. (a) *2.* (b) *3.* (b) *4.* (a) *5.* (a)
6. (c) *7.* (a)
10. (i) 2.57×10^{14} (ii) 5.58×10^{14} Hz
12. 2.12×10^{-10} m *13.* 6561 Å *14.* (i) 13.6 eV (ii) – 3.83 eV

13 CHAPTER

In every atom, the positive charge and mass are densely concentrated at the centre of the atom forming its nucleus. The radius of the nucleus is smaller than the radius of an atom by a factor of 10^4. This means **the volume of a nucleus is about 10^{-12} times the volume of the atom.**

YOUR STUDY GOALS

13.1 Composition of Nucleus
13.2 Classification of Nuclei
13.3 Mass-Energy and Nuclear Binding Energy
13.4 Nuclear Energy

YOUR PRACTICE GOAL

- Objective Type Questions (28 Qs ; MCQs, A-R, Matching)
- Case Based Questions-4
- Subjective Questions (5 VSAs, 8 SAs, 6 LAs)
- Numerical Problems-4

Nuclei

13.1 Composition of Nucleus

The nucleus was first discovered in 1911 by Lord Rutherford and his associates in experiment on scattering of α-particles.

The outcomes of his experimental observations are

- **Atom** consists of a small, central, massive and positive core surrounded by orbiting electrons.
- The size of the nucleus is of the order of 10^{-15} m, thus it is 10000 times smaller than the size of atom.
- Nucleus is not a composite body, it is made of nucleons (proton and neutron).
- The positive charge of the nucleus is due to the protons present in the nucleus.

Atomic Mass Unit

The mass of an atom is measured by a unit called **atomic mass unit** (amu). It is denoted by u.

It is defined as $\frac{1}{12}$th of the masses of an atom of ${}^{12}_{6}\text{C}$.

i.e. $$1\,\text{u} = \frac{\text{mass of one } {}^{12}\text{C atom}}{12} = \frac{1.992647 \times 10^{-26}\ \text{kg}}{12}$$

$$\boxed{1\,\text{u} = 1.660539 \times 10^{-27}\ \text{kg}}$$

- Atomic masses are measured by an instrument called **mass spectrometer.**

Discovery of Neutron

The nuclei of atoms contain neutral particles. This hypothesis was verified in 1932 by James Chadwick. Chadwick observed that when beryllium was bombarded with α-particles, some neutral radiations were emitted, which could knockout protons from lighter nuclei such as those of helium, carbon and nitrogen.

Application of the principles of conservation of energy and momentum showed that these neutral radiations could not be photons.

Chadwick assume that the neutral radiation consists of a new type of neutral particles called **neutrons.**

He estimated the **mass of a neutron being roughly equal to mass of a proton.** However, **unlike a free proton, a free neutron is unstable.**

The composition of a nucleus can be described by using the following terms and symbols.

Atomic Number (Z)

It is the number of protons present inside the nucleus of an atom of the element. It is also equal to the number of electrons revolving in various orbits around the nucleus of the neutral atom and denoted by Z.

Atomic number, Z = Number of protons
= Number of electrons (in a neutral atom)

Mass Number (A)

It is the total number of protons and neutrons inside the atomic nucleus of the element and denoted by A.

Mass number, A = Number of protons
+Number of neutrons

= Number of electrons (in a neutral atom)
+ Number of neutrons

= Atomic number + Number of neutrons = $Z + n$

- The term **nucleon** is also used for neutron and proton. Thus, **the number of nucleons in an atom is its mass number *A*.**
- Nuclear species or nuclides are shown by the notation ${}^{A}_{Z}X$, where X is the chemical symbol of the species.

13.2 Classification of Nuclei

Nuclei are classified on the basis of number of protons and number of nucleons present inside the nucleus as given below.

1. Isotopes

The atoms of same elements having the same number of protons but different number of neutrons are called isotopes.

e.g. The isotopes of hydrogen, oxygen and chlorine are
${}_1H^1, {}_1H^2, {}_1H^3$; ${}_8O^{16}$, ${}_8O^{17}$, ${}_8O^{18}$; ${}_{17}Cl^{35}, {}_{17}Cl^{37}$

Properties of Isotopes

The main properties of isotopes are as follows

(i) All isotopes of an element have same atomic numbers, hence these are located at single place in periodic table.

(ii) Mass numbers of all isotoes of an element are different.

(iii) All isotopes of an element have same chemical properties due to same electronic configuration.

(iv) The physical properties of all isotopes of an element are different due to different number of neutrons in nucleus.

(v) Due to same chemical properties, isotopes of an element cannot be separated by chemical process.

2. Isobars

The atoms of different elements having the same mass number (A) but different atomic number (Z) are called isobars. ${}_1H^3$ and ${}_2He^3$, ${}_8O^{17}$ and ${}_9F^{17}$ are examples of isobars.

Properties of Isobars

The main properties of isobars are as follows

(i) Isobars are placed at different positions in periodic table because they have different atomic numbers.

(ii) Isobars have different chemical properties because they have different atomic numbers.

3. Isotones

The atoms of different elements having equal number of neutrons ($A - Z$) but different number of protons are called isotones.

${}_3Li^7$ and ${}_4Be^8$, ${}_1H^3$ and ${}_2He^4$ are examples of isotones.

Example 1. **In a nucleus of $_{92}U^{238}$, find the number of protons and the number of neutrons.**

Sol. Number of protons, $Z = 92$

$\therefore$ Number of neutrons, $n = A - Z = 238 - 92 = 146$

Size of Nucleus

From the various experiments performed on atom and nucleus, it was observed that the volume of the nucleus is directly proportional to the number of nucleons (mass number) constituting nucleus.

If R is the radius of the nucleus having mass number A,

then $$\frac{4}{3}\pi R^3 \propto A \Rightarrow R \propto A^{1/3}$$

$$\Rightarrow \boxed{R = R_0 A^{1/3}}$$

where, $R_0 = 1.2 \times 10^{-15}$ m is the range of nuclear size.

It is also known as **nuclear unit radius.**

A is different for different elements, therefore atomic nuclei of different element have different size.

Note Fermi (fm) is found to be a convenient unit of length in nuclear physics. It is given as, 1 fermi (fm) = 10^{-15} m.

Nuclear Density

It is the ratio of mass of nucleus to its volume.

If m is the average mass of a nucleon and A is the mass number of element, then the mass of nucleus $= mA$. If R is the nuclear radius, then

$$\text{volume of nucleus} = \frac{4}{3}\pi R^3 = \frac{4}{3}\pi (R_0 A^{1/3})^3 = \frac{4}{3}\pi R_0^3 A$$

As, density of nuclear matter $= \dfrac{\text{Mass of nucleus}}{\text{Volume of nucleus}}$

$$\therefore \quad \boxed{\rho = \frac{mA}{\frac{4}{3}\pi R_0^3 A}} \quad \text{or} \quad \boxed{\rho = \frac{3m}{4\pi R_0^3}}$$

Thus, the density of nucleus is a **constant, independent of A**, for all nuclei.

The density of nuclear matter is approximately 2.3×10^{17} kg/m^3. This density is very large as compared to an ordinary matter.

Example 2. **Obtain the approximate value of the radius of a nucleus $_{92}U^{238}$. (Take, $R_0 = 1.2 \times 10^{-15}$ m)**

Sol. Given, $A = 238$, $R_0 = 1.2 \times 10^{-15}$ m

As, $R = R_0 A^{1/3} = 1.2 \times 10^{-15} (238)^{1/3}$

$\therefore$ $R = 7.437 \times 10^{-15}$ m

Example 3. **Find the ratio of radii of two nuclei of mass number 27 and 64, respectively.**

Sol. The radius (R) of nucleus of an atom depends on the mass number (A) as $R = R_0 A^{1/3}$, where R_0 is constant for all nuclei.

$$\therefore \quad R \propto A^{1/3} \Rightarrow \frac{R_1}{R_2} = \left(\frac{A_1}{A_2}\right)^{1/3}$$

Here, $A_1 = 27$ and $A_2 = 64$

$$\therefore \quad \frac{R_1}{R_2} = \left(\frac{27}{64}\right)^{1/3} = \left[\left(\frac{3}{4}\right)^3\right]^{1/3} = \frac{3}{4} \Rightarrow R_1 : R_2 = 3:4$$

Example 4. **Given the mass of iron nucleus as 55.85 u and $A = 56$. Find the nuclear density.** *(NCERT)*

Sol. Given, mass, $m = 55.85\text{ u} = 55.85 \times 1.67 \times 10^{-27}$ kg

Volume, $V = \frac{4}{3}\pi R^3 = \frac{4}{3}\pi (R_0 A^{1/3})^3 = \frac{4}{3}\pi R_0^3 \times A$

$$\therefore \text{ Nuclear density, } \rho = \frac{3m}{4\pi R_0^3 \times A}$$

$$= \frac{3 \times 55.85 \times 1.67 \times 10^{-27}}{4 \times \frac{22}{7} \times (1.2 \times 10^{-15})^3 \times 56}$$

$$= 2.29 \times 10^{17} \text{ kg/m}^3$$

13.3 Mass-Energy and Nuclear Binding Energy

Mass-Energy Relation

Einstein showed that mass and energy are equivalent. i.e., mass can be converted into energy and *vice-versa*. Einstein's mass-energy equivalence equation is

$$\boxed{E = mc^2}$$

where, E is the energy, m is the mass and c is the velocity of light in vacuum (approximately equal to 3×10^8 m/s).

Rest Mass and Effective Mass

The mass of a particle measured in a frame of reference in which the particle is at rest is called its rest mass, usually denoted by m_0. The rest mass-energy of a particle would be $m_0 c^2$, which is enormously large on account of large value of c.

If K is kinetic energy of the particle, then its total energy, $$E = mc^2$$

$$\boxed{E = \text{Rest mass-energy} + \text{KE} = m_0 c^2 + K}$$

where, m is called effective mass of the particle, when it is moving. Clearly, $m > m_0$.

The conservation law of energy states that the initial energy and final energy are equal, provided the energy associated with mass is also included.

Mass Defect and Binding Energy of Nucleus

The mass of nucleus is little less than the sum of masses of individual neutrons and protons. This missing mass is known as the **mass defect.** It can be defined as the difference in masses of nucleus and neucleons is called as mass defect. It is denoted by Δm.

i.e. $$\Delta m = (Zm_p + Nm_n) - M_N$$

where, Zm_p, Nm_p and M_N are the masses of proton, neutrons and nucleus of an atom, respectively.

Mass defect represents the binding energy of the nucleus, i.e. the binding energy of a nucleus is equivalent to the mass defect, which is liberated during the formation of nucleus. From Einstein's equation,

$$E_b = \Delta mc^2$$

where, E_b is the binding energy of nucleus to separate a nucleus into its component (proton and neutron) we would have to supply a energy equal to the binding of energy (E_b). It can be defined as

The amount of external energy of Δmc^2 is required to break the nucleus into its constituent particles is called binding energy.

Average Binding Energy Per Nucleon of a Nucleus

It is the average energy spent to remove a nucleon from the nucleus to infinite distance. It is given by total binding energy divided by the mass number of the nucleus.

Binding energy per nucleon

$$= \frac{\text{Total binding energy}}{\text{Number of nucleons}} \quad \text{or} \quad \boxed{E_{bn} = \frac{E_b}{A}}$$

Example 5. **A given coin has a mass of 3.0 g. Calculate the nuclear energy that would be required to separate all the neutrons and protons from each other. For simplicity assume that the coin is entirely made of $^{63}_{29}$Cu atoms (of mass 62.92960 u).** *NCERT*

Sol. Given, mass of coin = 3 g

Atomic mass of Cu, $A = 63$

Atomic number of Cu, $Z = 29$

Mass of $^{63}_{29}$Cu, $m_N = 62.92960$ u

Avogadro's number $= 6.023 \times 10^{23}$

Mass of proton, $m_p = 1.007825$ u

Mass of neutron, $m_n = 1.008665$ u

Nuclear energy required to separate neutrons and protons, $E_b = ?$

Each atom of copper contains 29 protons and 34 neutrons. Therefore, mass defect of each atom using the relation,

$$\Delta m = [Zm_p + (A - Z)m_n] - m \text{ or } m_N$$

$$\Delta m = [29 \times 1.007825 + 34 \times 1.008665] - 62.92960$$

$$= 0.591935 \text{ u}$$

Number of atoms in 3 g coin

$$= \frac{6.023 \times 10^{23} \times 3}{63} = 2.868 \times 10^{22}$$

Total mass defect of all atoms,

$$(\Delta m)_{\text{total}} = 0.591935 \times 2.868 \times 10^{22} = 1.6977 \times 10^{22}$$

The nuclear energy required (E_b) to separate all the neutrons and protons from each other and can be calculated by using the relation,

$$E_b = (\Delta m)_{\text{total}} \times c^2 = (\Delta m)_{\text{total}}\, c^2 \times \frac{931}{c^2} \text{MeV}$$

$$[\because 1 \text{ u} = 931 \text{ MeV}]$$

$$= 1.6977 \times 10^{22} \times 931 = 1.58 \times 10^{25} \text{ MeV}$$

Example 6. **Find the binding energy per nucleon of $_{20}Ca^{40}$ nucleus. Given, $m_N\ (_{20}Ca^{40}) = 39.962589$ u, $m_n = 1.008665$ u and $m_p = 1.007825$ u. (Take, 1 amu $= \frac{931}{c^2}$ MeV)**

Sol. In a nucleus of $_{20}Ca^{40}$,

Number of protons = 20

Number of neutrons = 40 − 20 = 20

Total mass of 20 protons and 20 neutrons

$$= 20m_p + 20m_n = 20(m_p + m_n)$$

$$= 20(1.007825 + 1.008665)$$

$$= 40.3298 \text{ u}$$

Mass defect, $\Delta m = 40.3298 - 39.962589$

$$= 0.367211\, u$$

$$\text{Total binding energy} = \Delta m \times c^2 \times \frac{931}{c^2} \text{MeV}$$

$$= \Delta m \times 931 \text{MeV}$$

$$= 0.367211 \times 931$$

$$= 341.873441 \text{ MeV}$$

$$E_b \text{ per nucleon, } E_{bn} = \frac{341.873441}{40}$$

$$= 8.547 \text{ MeV/nucleon}$$

Binding Energy Curve

It is a plot of the binding energy per nucleon E_{bn} *versus* the mass number A for a large number of nuclei.

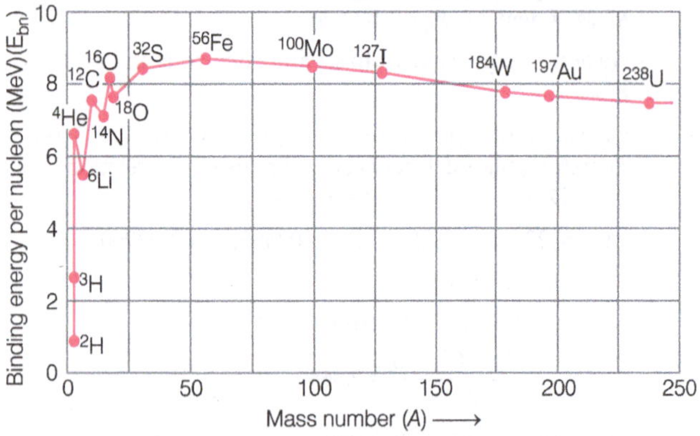

Binding energy per nucleon as a function of mass number

The following are the features of the plot

(i) Average BE/nucleon for lighter nuclei like $_1H^1$, $_1H^2$, $_1H^3$ is small.

(ii) For mass numbers ranging from 2 to 20, there are sharply defined peaks corresponding to $_2He^4$, $_6C^{12}$, $_8O^{16}$, etc. These peaks indicate that these nuclei are relatively more stable than the other nuclei in their neighbourhood.

(iii) The BE curve has a broad maximum peak in the range $A = 30$ to $A = 120$. It is practically constant corresponding to average binding energy per nucleon as 8.5 MeV. The peak value for the above given range is 8.8 MeV per nucleon for $_{26}Fe^{56}$.

(iv) As the mass number increases, the BE/nucleon decreases gradually falling to about 7.6 MeV per nucleon for $_{92}U^{238}$, due to coulomb repulsion between the protons. Therefore, heavy nuclei are relatively less stable.

Conclusions

Following conclusions are obtain from the graph

(i) A very heavy nuclei having lower E_{bn} are unstable in nature, to become more stable it break into two smaller nuclei and energy is released. This process is known as nuclear fission.
e.g. A nucleus $A = 240$ breaks into two $A = 120$ nuclei having higher E_{bn} and more stable than $A = 240$.

(ii) Two light nuclei ($A \leq 10$) fuse to form a heavier nucleus to become more stable by releasing energy in this process, such process is called as **nuclear fusion.**

Nuclear Stability

- The stability of a nucleus is determined by the value of its binding energy per nucleon. Higher the binding energy of nucleon, more stable is the nucleus.
- The stability of a nucleus is also determined by its neutron to proton ratio. A plot of number of neutrons and number of protons is shown in the figure below.
- The solid line shows the nuclei with equal number of protons and neutrons. Only light nuclei are on this line, i.e. they are stable, if they contain approximately same number of protons and neutrons.

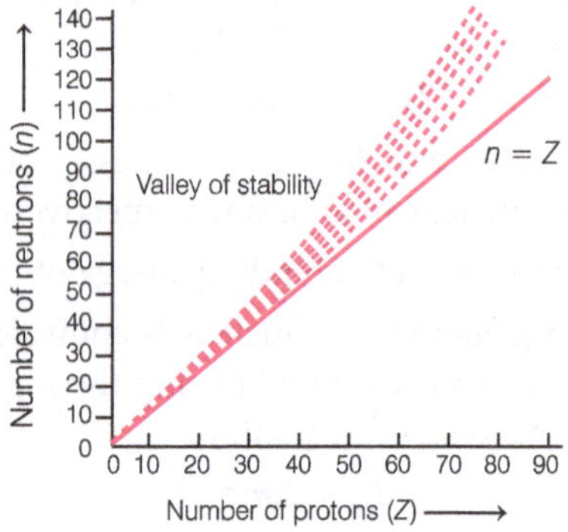

Graphical representation of number of neutrons *versus* number of protons

- The long narrow region shown in the figure which contains the cluster of dotted lines representing stable nuclei is referred to as the **valley of stability**.
- Heavy nuclei are stable only when they have more neutrons than protons.
- Experimental study shows that the more stable nuclei contain even number of protons or neutrons or both.

Nuclear Force

- Nuclear forces are the strongest attractive forces between nucleons. They hold nucleons together in the tiny nucleus, inspite of strong electrostatic forces of repulsion between them.

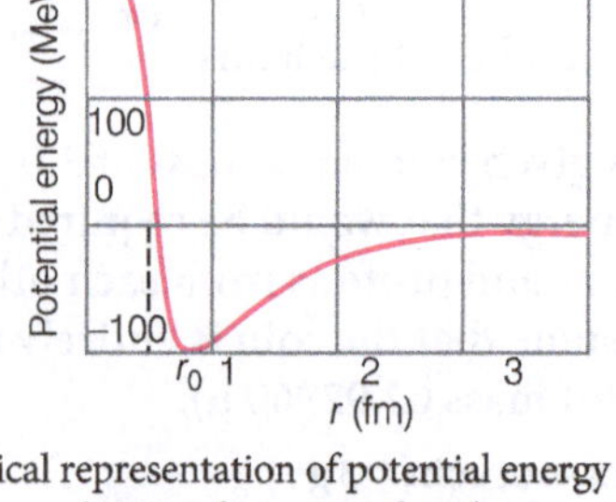

Graphical representation of potential energy *versus* distance for a pair of nucleon.

- Nuclear force is non-conservative and does not obey inverse square law. It is non-central force.
- The constancy of the binding energy in the range $30 < A < 170$ is a consequence of the fact that the **nuclear force is short-ranged.**
- From the plot, it is concluded that potential energy is minimum at a distance $r_0 (\approx 0.8$ fm) which means, the force is attractive for distances larger than 0.8 fm and repulsive for the distances less than 0.8 fm between nucleons.

Some of the important characteristics of these forces are as given below.

(i) Nuclear force among a pair of neutrons, a pair of protons and neutron-proton pair, is approximately the same. This shows that **nuclear force is independent of charge.**

(ii) The nuclear forces are very short range forces.

(iii) The nuclear force is strongest force in nature.

(iv) Nuclear force between two nucleons falls rapidly to zero as their distance is more than a few femtometres (fm). This leads to saturation of forces in a medium or large sized nucleus, i.e. each nucleon interacts with its immediate neighbours only, rather than with all the other nucleons in the nucleus.

(v) The nuclear forces are dependent on spin or angular momentum of nuclei.

Quick Test 1

Conceptual Questions

1. Does the radius of nucleus depends on its mass number ?

2. The mass of a nucleus is less than the sum of the masses of constituent neutrons and protons. Comment.

3. ${}_2^3\text{He}$ and ${}_1^3\text{He}$ nuclei have the same mass number. Do they have same binding energy? *NCERT Exemplar*

4. Why do stable nuclei never have more protons than neutrons? *NCERT Exemplar*

5. Proton and neutron exist together in an extremely small space within the nucleus. How is this possible, while protons repel each other?

6. What is the significance of nuclear binding energy per nucleon in nuclear stability?

7. Which property of nuclear forces is responsible for constancy of E_b per nucleon? Comment.

Numerical Questions

8. (i) What is the nuclear density of ${}_{90}^{228}\text{Th}$?

(ii) Is the nuclear density of an α-particle (${}_2^4\text{He}$) to be greater than, less than or equal to ${}_{90}^{228}\text{Th}$? Explain.

(iii) Determine the nuclear density of an α-particle.

9. Calculate the energy equivalent of 2 g of substance.

10. Obtain the binding energy (in MeV) of a nitrogen nucleus (${}_7^{14}\text{N}$), given m (${}_7^{14}\text{N}$) = 14.00307 u. *NCERT*

Answers

8. (i) 2.3×10^{17} kg/m^3 (iii) 2.3×10^{17} kg/m^3

9. 1.8×10^{14} J *10.* 104.67 MeV

For Solutions, See QR Code on Pg. 423

13.4 Nuclear Energy

Nuclear energy is the energy released during the transformation of nuclei with less total binding energy to the nuclei with greater binding energy.

Two distinct ways of obtaining energy from nucleus are as follows:

1. Nuclear fission 2. Nuclear fusion

Nuclear Fission

Nuclear fission is the phenomenon of splitting of a heavy nucleus (usually A > 230) into two or more lighter nuclei by the bombardment of proton, neutron, α-particle, etc. **Energies associated with nuclear processes are about a million times larger than chemical process.**

In fission, a heavy nucleus like ${}_{92}^{235}\text{U}$ breaks into two smaller fragments by the bombardment of thermal neutron (low energy or slow moving).

$$\text{e.g. } {}_{92}^{235}\text{U} + {}_0^1n \longrightarrow {}_{56}^{141}\text{Ba} + {}_{36}^{92}\text{Kr} + 3\,{}_0n^1 + Q$$

(Energy released)

Q-value here refer to the energy released in the nuclear process, which can be determined using Einstein's mass-energy relation, $E = mc^2$.

- The Q-value is equal to the difference of mass of products and reactants multiplied by square of velocity of light. Energy released per fission of ${}_{92}^{235}\text{U}$ is 200.4 MeV.

- The fragment nuclei produced in fission are highly unstable. They are highly radioactive and emit β-particles in succession until each reaches to a stable end product.

Nuclear Chain Reaction

In the nuclear fission reaction, there is a release of extra neutrons. The extra neutrons bring about the fission of three more nuclei and produce nine neutrons, which in turn can bring about the fission of nine nuclei and so on. Thus, **a continuous chain of nuclear fission is set-up called nuclear chain reaction.** It starts a huge amount of energy release in short time (in few microseconds).
The chain reactions may be of two types

(i) **Uncontrolled Chain Reaction** During fission reaction, released neutrons causes further fissions, then number of fissions increase rapidly with time. So, the reaction becomes very fast and huge amount of energy is liberated in each fission with violent explosion. The cycle repeats to give a **self-sustaining chain reaction and gives off energy at a rate that increases rapidly with time.** This is called uncontrolled chain reaction. It is used in nuclear bomb.

(ii) **Controlled Chain Reaction** By some means, the reaction is controlled in such a way that only one of the neutrons emitted in a fission causes another fission, then **the fission rate remains constant and the energy is released steadily.** Such a chain reaction is called a controlled chain reaction.

- It is used in a nuclear reactor.
  The sustained feasibility of nuclear chain reaction depends on the multiplication factor or reproduction factor K.

$$K = \frac{\text{Rate of production of neutrons}}{\text{Rate of loss of neutrons}}$$

- If $K = 1$, the operation of reactor is said to be critical. It is what we wish to be for steady power operation.
- If $K > 1$, the reaction rate and reactor power increases exponentially. In this case, reaction is super-critical and can even explode.
- If $K < 1$, the reaction gradually stops, and the condition is called sub-critical.

Nuclear Fusion

Nuclear fusion is the phenomenon of fusing of two or more lighter nuclei forming a single heavy nucleus.

For fusion to take place, the two nuclei must come close enough so that nuclear force is able to affect them. Since both the nuclei experience coulomb's repulsion. Therefore, they must have enough energy to overcome this coulomb barrier.

e.g.
$${}_1H^1 + {}_1H^1 \longrightarrow {}_1H^2 + {}_1e^+ + \nu + 0.42 \text{ MeV}$$
$${}_1H^2 + {}_1H^2 \longrightarrow {}_2He^3 + {}_0n^1 + 3.27 \text{ MeV}$$
$${}_1H^2 + {}_1H^2 \longrightarrow {}_1H^3 + {}_1H^1 + 4.03 \text{ MeV}$$

- Fusion of hydrogen nuclei into helium nuclei is the source of energy of most of the stars including the sun.

TEACHER TIP

- Unstable nucleus undergoes a decay, this is referred to as radioactive decay. Three types of radioactive decay occur in nature
- **α-decay** in which a helium nucleus He is emitted.
- **β-decay** in which electrons or positrons are emitted.
- **γ-decay** in which high energy photons are emitted.

Energy Generation in Stars

Thermonuclear fusion is the source of energy in the stars. The interior of the sun has a temperature of 1.5×10^7 K, which is considerably less than the estimated temperature required for fusion of particles of average energy. Fusion in the sun involves protons whose energies are much above the average energy.

When fusion is achieved by raising the temperature of the system, so that particles have enough KE to overcome the coulomb repulsive behaviour. It is called thermonuclear fusion.

The fusion reaction in the sun is a multi-step process in which the hydrogen is fused into helium. The proton-proton (p, p) cycle by which this occurs is represented by the following sets of reactions:

$${}_1^1H + {}_1^1H \rightarrow {}_1^2H + e^+ + \nu + 0.42 \text{ MeV} \quad \text{...(i)}$$
$$e^+ + e^- \rightarrow \gamma + \gamma + 1.02 \text{ MeV} \quad \text{...(ii)}$$
$${}_1^2H + {}_1^1H \rightarrow {}_2^3He + \gamma + 5.49 \text{ MeV} \quad \text{...(iii)}$$
$${}_2^3He + {}_2^3He \rightarrow {}_2^4He + {}_1^1H + {}_1^1H + 12.86 \text{ MeV} \quad \text{...(iv)}$$

For the fourth reaction to occur, the first three reactions must occur twice, in case two light helium nuclei unite to form ordinary helium nucleus. If we consider the combination 2(i) + 2(ii) + 2(iii) + (iv), the net effect is

$$4{}_1^1H + 2e^- \rightarrow {}_2^4He + 2\nu + 6\gamma + 26.7 \text{ MeV}$$

or $(4{}_1^1H + 4e^-) \rightarrow ({}_2^4He + 2e^-) + 2\nu + 6\gamma + 26.7$ MeV

Thus, **four hydrogen atoms combine to form ${}_2^4$He atom with a release of 26.7 MeV of energy.**

- As the hydrogen in the core gets depleted and becomes helium, the core starts to cool. The star begins to collapse under its own gravity, which increases the temperature of the core.
- The age of the sun is about 5×10^9 yr and it is estimated that there is enough hydrogen in the sun to keep it going for another 5 billion years.

Controlled Thermonuclear Fusion

The natural thermonuclear fusion in a star is replicated in a thermonuclear fusion device. The aim of controlled thermonuclear fusion is to generate the steady power by heating the nuclear fuel to a temperature in the range of 10^8K. At these temperature, the fuel is a mixture of positive ions and electrons (plasma).

The challenge is to confine this plasma, since no container can stand such a high temperature. Several countries around the world including India are developing techniques in this connection. If successful, fusion reactors will hopefully, supply almost unlimited power to humanity.

Example 7. **How long can an electric lamp of 100 W be kept glowing by fusion of 2 kg of deuterium? Take, the fusion reaction as**

$$ {}_1^2H + {}_1^2H \longrightarrow {}_2^3H + n + 3.27 \text{ MeV} $$

Sol. Given, $P = 100$ W

According to question, fusion reaction is given as

$$ {}_1^2H + {}_1^2H \longrightarrow {}_2^3He + n + 3.27 \text{ MeV} $$

$\therefore$ Energy released in fusion of 2 deuterium atoms,

$E_1 = 3.27$ MeV

Number of atoms present in 2 g of deuterium

$= 6 \times 10^{23}$

Number of atoms present in 2 kg of deuterium

$= 6 \times 10^{23} \times 10^3 = 6 \times 10^{26}$

$\therefore$ Energy released in fusion of 2 kg of deuterium atoms

$$ = \frac{E_1}{2} \times 6 \times 10^{26} \text{ MeV} $$

$$ = \frac{3.27}{2} \times 6 \times 10^{26} \text{ MeV} $$

$$ = 9.81 \times 10^{26} \text{ MeV} $$

$$ = 9.81 \times 10^{26} \times 10^6 \times 1.6 \times 10^{-19} $$

$$ = 15.696 \times 10^{13} \text{ J} $$

$\therefore$ Energy consumed by bulb per second

$$ E = \frac{P}{t} = \frac{100}{1} = 100 \text{ J} $$

$\therefore$ Time for which bulb will glow

$$ = \frac{15.696 \times 10^{13}}{100} \text{ s} = 4.97 \times 10^4 \text{ year} $$

Difference between Nuclear Fission and Nuclear Fusion

Nuclear Fission	Nuclear Fusion
Fission is the splitting of a large nucleus into two or more smaller ones.	Fusion is the combining of two or more lighter nuclei.
Fission does not normally occur in nature.	Fusion occurs in star such as the sun.
Fission can often be initiated with little or no energy input.	Fusion requires extremely high temperature and pressure to overcome electrostatic repulsion of nucleons.
Energy release during fission is less than the energy release in fusion.	Energy release is greater than the energy release in fission.
Uranium is the primary fuel for fission reaction.	Hydrogen isotopes are the primary fuel in nuclear fusion reaction.

Quick Test 2

Conceptual Questions

1. Mention the two distinct ways to obtain energy from nucleus.
2. What is the significance of multiplication factor (K), when (i) $K = 1$ and (ii) $K > 1$?
3. Complete the following fission reaction and calculate the amount of energy it releases.

$$ {}_0^1n + {}_{92}^{235}U \longrightarrow {}_{38}^{88}Sr + {}_{54}^{136}Xe + (?) $$

Numerical Questions

4. Determine the energy released in the following fusion reaction.

$$ {}_1^1H + {}_1^2H \longrightarrow {}_2^3He + \gamma $$

5. The sun is believed to be getting its energy from the fusion of four protons to form a helium nucleus and a pair of positrons. Calculate the release of energy per fusion in MeV.
Mass of proton = 1.007825 amu, mass of positron = 0.000549 amu and mass of helium nucleus = 4.002603 amu.
(Take, 1 amu = 931.5 MeV)
6. An unstable heavy nucleus at rest breaks into two nuclei which move away with velocities in the ratio of 8 : 27. What is the ratio of the radii of the nuclei? *NCERT*

Answers

4. 5.94 MeV 5. 25.7MeV 6. 3 : 2

For Solutions, See QR Code on Pg. 423

Mind Map

Nuclei

Composition of the Nucleus
Its composition includes protons (positive) and neutrons (neutral).

Size $R = R_O \cdot A^{1/3}$

$R = 1.2.\ A^{1/3}$ fm, very small compared to the overall atom ($\approx 10^{-10}$ m).

Density Extremely high, approximately 2.3×10^{17} kg/m^3.

Nuclear Stability
It refers to the ability of a nucleus to remain intact without undergoing radioactive decay.

- Nuclear stability depends on the balance of the neutron to proton (n/p) ratio, strong nuclear force and binding energy with stable nuclei often exhibiting even nucleon numbers or magic numbers.

Nuclear Force
It is one of the strongest force in nature.
It acts only in the range of the order of few fermi metres ($\approx 4.2 \times 10^{-15}$m)
It balances the electrostatic force between protons in the nucleus.

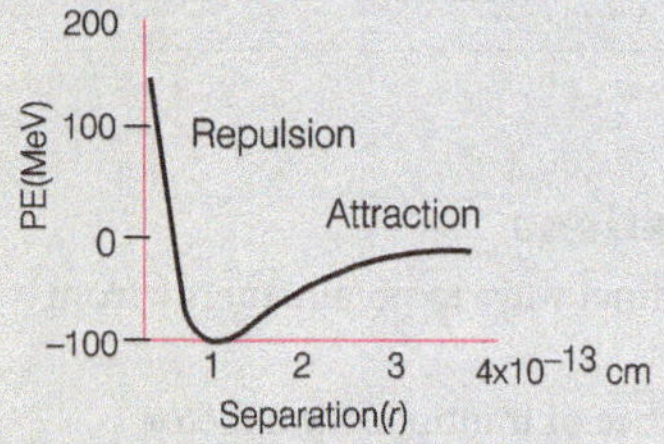

Binding Energy
The energy required to break up a nucleus into its constituent protons and neutrons and to separate them to such a large distance that they may not interact with each other.
The binding energy of a nucleus ${}_Z^AX$ is given by $\Delta E_b = [Zm_H + (A - Z)m_n - m_N]c^2$

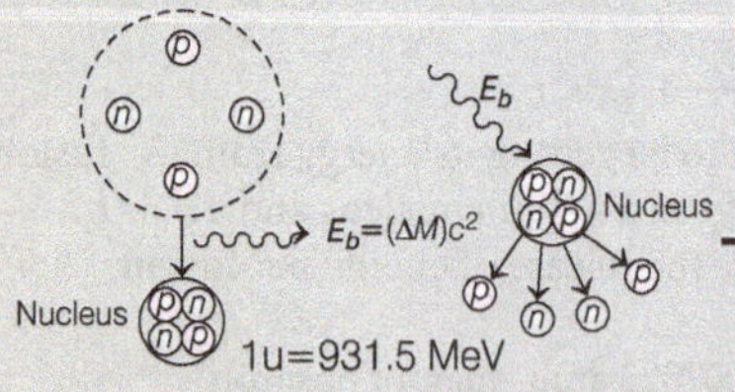

Nuclear Binding Energy per Nucleon
Average energy required to extract one nucleon from the nucleus. It is obtained by dividing the binding energy of a nucleus by its mass number.

$$\Delta E_{bn} \text{ or } \bar{B} = \frac{BE}{A}$$

$$= \frac{[Zm_H + (A - Z)M_n - m]\,c^2}{A}$$

Concept related to Nucleus
- **Nucleons** Protons and neutrons present in the nuclei of atoms are collectively known as nucleons.
- **Atomic Number** The number of protons in the nucleus is called the atomic number of the element. It is denoted by Z.
- **Mass Number** The total number of protons and neutrons present in a nucleus is called the mass number of the element. It is denoted by A.
- **Nuclear Mass** The total mass of the protons and neutrons present in a nucleus is called the nuclear mass.
- **Nuclide** A nuclide is a specific nucleus of an atom characterised by its atomic number Z and mass number A, represented as ${}_Z^AX$.

Isotopes, isobars and Isotones
- **Isotopes** The atoms of an element, which have the same atomic number but different mass number are called isotopes.
  Example ${}_{17}Cl^{35}$ and ${}_{17}Cl^{37}$ have same number of protons.
- **Isobars** The atoms of different elements (different atomic number) but having the same mass number are called isobars.
  Example ${}_1^3H$ and ${}_2^3He$, as both have same A=3.
- **Isotones** The nuclides having the same number of neutrons are called isotones.
  Example ${}_{17}^{37}Cl$ and ${}_{19}^{39}K$ are isotones, as both contain the same number of neutrons,

Binding Energy Curve
The value of binding energy per nucleon of a nucleus gives a measure of the stability of that nucleus. Greater is the binding energy per nucleon of a nucleus, more stable is the nucleus.

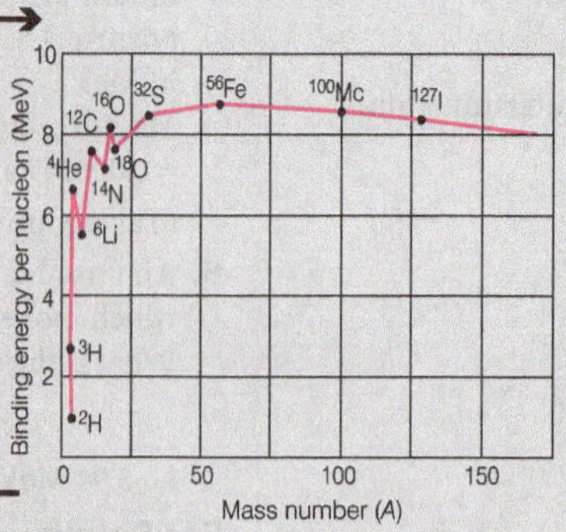

Mass-energy relation
Mass-energy relation introduced by Albert Einstein, is expressed as $E = mc^2$. This equation signifies that mass and energy are interchangable.

Mass Defect
The difference between the rest mass of a nucleus and the sum of the rest masses of its constituent nucleons.

$$\Delta m = Zm_p + (A - Z)m_n - m$$

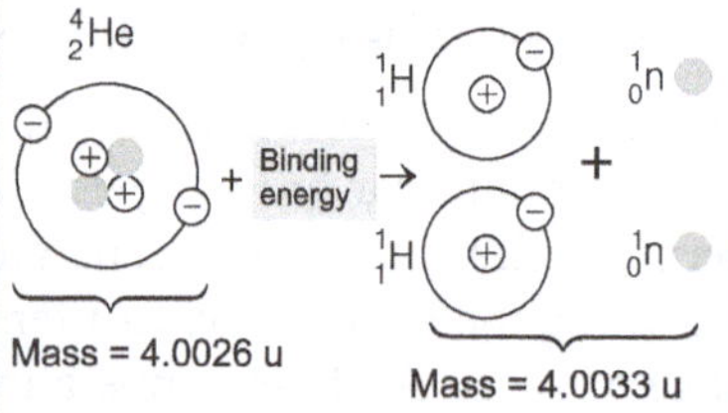

Nuclear Fusion
It is the process of fusion of two smaller nuclei into a heavier nucleus with the liberation of large amount of energy.
Example

$${}_1^2H + {}_1^3H \longrightarrow {}_2^4He + 24\text{MeV}$$

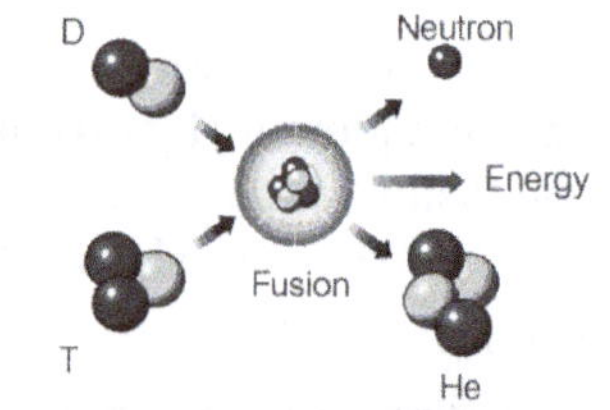

Nuclear Fission
It is the process in which a heavy nucleus ($A > 230$), when hit by a proton, neutron or an α-particle, gets split up into two smaller nuclei of nearly comparable masses.
Example

$${}_{92}^{235}U + {}_0^1n \longrightarrow {}_{56}^{144}Ba + {}_{36}^{89}Kr + 3\,{}_0^1n + Q$$

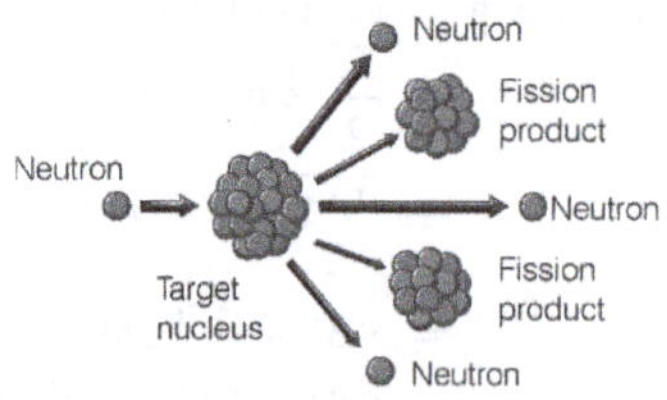

EXAM PATTERN QUESTIONS

Objective Type Questions

Multiple Choice Questions (MCQs)

1. **Atomic mass unit (1 u) is** **Competency Based Que.**

(a) 1/12 of mass of ^{12}C atom
(b) 1/14 of mass of ^{14}C atom
(c) 1/12 of mass of ^{14}C atom
(d) 1/6 of mass of ^{12}C atom

2. **Ratio of radius of an atom to the radius of its nucleus is around** **Competency Based Que.**

(a) 10^{-2} (b) 10^4
(c) 10^{12} (d) 10^{15}

3. **The radius of $^{27}_{13}X$ nucleus is R. The radius of $^{125}_{53}Y$ nucleus will be** **CBSE 2023**

(a) $\frac{5}{3}R$ (b) $\left(\frac{13}{53}\right)^{1/3} R$
(c) $\left(\frac{5}{3}R\right)^{1/3}$ (d) $\left(\frac{13}{53}R\right)^{1/3}$

4. **If the nuclear radius of ^{27}Al is 3.6 fm, the approximate nuclear radius of ^{64}Cu (in fm) is** **Competency Based Que.**

(a) 2.4 (b) 1.2 (c) 4.8 (d) 3.6

5. **The ratio of the nuclear densities of two nuclei having mass numbers 64 and 125 is** **CBSE 2023**

(a) $\frac{64}{125}$ (b) $\frac{4}{5}$ (c) $\frac{5}{4}$ (d) 1

6. **The gravitational force between a H-atom and another particle of mass m will be given by Newton's law $F = G\frac{M \cdot m}{r^2}$, where r is in km and**

(a) $M = m_{\text{proton}} + m_{\text{electron}}$
(b) $M = m_{\text{proton}} + m_{\text{electron}} - \frac{B}{c^2}$ ($B = 13.6$ eV).
(c) M is not relate to the mass of the hydrogen atom.
(d) $M = m_{\text{proton}} + m_{\text{electron}} - \frac{|V|}{c^2}$ ($|V|$ = magnitude of the potential energy of electron in the H-atom.

7. **M_x and M_y denote the atomic masses of the parent and the daughter nuclei respectively in radioactive decay. The Q-value for a β^- decay is Q_1 and that for a β^+ decay is Q_2. If m_e denotes the mass of an electron, then which of the following statements is correct?**

(a) $Q_1 = (M_x - M_y)c^2$ and $Q_2 = (M_x - M_y - 2m_e)c^2$
(b) $Q_1 = (M_x - M_y)c^2$ and $Q_2 = (M_x - M_y)c^2$
(c) $Q_1 = (M_x - M_y - 2m_e)c^2$ and $Q_2 = (M_x - M_y + 2c_e)c^2$
(d) $Q_1 = (M_x - M_y + 2m_e)c^2$ and $Q_2 = (M_x - m_y + 2m_e)c^2$

8. **The difference in mass of ^7X nucleus and total mass of its constituent nucleons is 21.00 u. The binding energy per nucleon for this nucleus is equal to the energy equivalent of** **CBSE 2023**

(a) 3 u (b) 3.5 u (c) 7 u (d) 21 u

9. **The curve of binding energy per nucleon as a function of atomic mass number has a sharp peak for helium nucleus. This implies that helium nucleus is** **CBSE 2023**

(a) radioactive
(b) unstable
(c) easily fissionable
(d) more stable nucleus than its neighbours

10. **Which of the following statements about nuclear forces is not true?** **CBSE SQP 2023**

(a) The nuclear force between two nucleons falls rapidly to zero as their distance is more than a few femtometres.
(b) The nuclear force is much weaker than the Coulomb force.
(c) The force is attractive for distances larger than 0.8 fm and repulsive if they are separated by distances less than 0.8 fm.
(d) The nuclear force between neutron-neutron, proton-neutron and proton-proton is approximately the same.

11. **When a nucleus in an atom undergoes a radioactive decay, the electronic energy levels of the atom**

(a) do not change for any type of radioactivity
(b) change for α and β-radioactivity but not for γ-radioactivity
(c) change for α-radioactivity but not for others
(d) change for β-radioactivity but not for others

12. **Tritium is an isotope of hydrogen whose nucleus triton contains 2 neutrons and 1 proton. Free neutrons are decay into $p + \bar{e} + \bar{\nu}$. If one of the neutrons in triton decays, then it would transform into He^3 nucleus. This does not happen, because**

(a) triton energy is less than that of a He^3 nucleus
(b) the electron created in the beta decay process cannot remain in the nucleus

(c) both the neutrons in triton have to decay simultaneously resulting in a nucleus with 3 protons, which is not a He^3 nucleus.
(d) free neutrons decay due to external perturbations which is absent in triton nucleus

13. Heavy stable nuclei have more neutrons than protons. This is because of the fact that
(a) neutrons are heavier than protons
(b) electrostatic force between protons are repulsive
(c) neutrons decay into protons through beta decay
(d) nuclear forces between neutrons are weaker than that between protons

14. In a nuclear reactor , moderators slow down the neutrons which come out in a fission process. The moderator used have light nuclei. Heavy nuclei will not serve the purpose, because
(a) they will break up
(b) elastic collision of neutrons with heavy nuclei will not slow them down
(c) the net weight of the reactor would be unbearably high
(d) substances with heavy nuclei do not occur in liquid or gaseous state at room temperatur

15. In a nuclear reaction $^{238}_{92}U \rightarrow ^{A}_{Z}Th + ^{4}_{2}He$, the value of *A* and *Z* are
(a) $A = 234, Z = 94$ (b) $A = 238, Z = 94$
(c) $A = 234, Z = 90$ (d) $A = 238, Z = 90$

16. In fusion reaction occurring in the sun,
(a) hydrogen is converted into carbon
(b) hydrogen and helium are converted into carbon and other heavier metals/elements
(c) helium is converted into hydrogen
(d) hydrogen is converted into helium

17. Fusion process, like combining two deuterons of form a He nucleus are impossible at ordinary temperatures and pressure. The reason for this can be traced to the fact
(a) nuclear forces have short range
(b) nuclear density is very high
(c) the original nuclei must be completely ionized before fusion can take place
(d) the original nuclei must first break up before combining with each other.

18. Match the Column I with Column II.

	Column I (Concept)		Column II (Expression)
A.	Size of nucleus	1.	$E = \frac{E_b}{A}$
B.	Nuclear density	2.	$E = \Delta mc^2$
C.	Mass-energy relation	3.	$\rho = 3m / 4\pi R_0^3$
D.	Mass defect	4.	$R = R_0 A^{1/3}$
E.	Average binding energy	5.	$E = mc^2$

(a) A-4, B-3, C-5, D-2, E-1 (b) A-1, B-2, C-3, D-4, E-5
(c) A-4, B-3, C-2, D-5, E-1 (d) A-2, B-4, C-3, D-1, E-5

19. Match the Column I with Column II.

	Column I (Term)		Column II (Explanation)
A.	Binding energy per nucleon	1.	Process in which light nuclei combine
B.	Nuclear fission	2.	Energy requires to separate nucleons
C.	Nuclear fusion	3.	Emission of two protons and two neutrons
D.	Alpha decay	4.	Process in which reaction products cause further reaction
E.	Chain reaction	5.	The process of splitting a heavy nucleus

(a) A-1, B-2, C-3, D-4, E-5 (b) A-2, B-3, C-5, D-4, E-1
(c) A-2, B-5, C-1, D-3, E-4 (d) A-4, B-3, C-2, D-1, E-5

Assertion-Reason

Directions *(Q. Nos. 20-29) In the following questions, two statements are given- one labelled Assertion (A) and the other labelled Reason (R). Select the correct answer to these questions from the codes (a), (b), (c) and (d) as given below.*

(a) Both Assertion and Reason are true and Reason is the correct explanation of Assertion.
(b) Both Assertion and Reason are true but Reason is not the correct explanation of Assertion.
(c) Assertion is true but Reason is false.
(d) Assertion is false but Reason is true.

20. Assertion (A) Nuclear density is very large as compared to ordinary matter.
Reason (R) Nuclear density increases with the increase of mass number. **Competency Based Que.**

21. Assertion (A) The curve between the binding energy per nucleon *versus* mass number drops at high mass numbers ($30 < A < 170$) as well as at low mass numbers ($A < 30$).
Reason (R) Nuclei with middle mass numbers ($30 < A < 170$) have higher binding energy per nucleon.
Competency Based Que.

22. Assertion (A) Nuclear force between neutron-neutron, proton-neutron and proton-proton is approximately the same.
Reason (R) The nuclear force does not depend on the electric charge.

23. **Assertion (A)** Nuclei having mass number about 60 are least stable.

Reason (R) When two or more light nuclei are combined into a heavier nucleus, then the binding energy per nucleon will decrease. **SQP 2024-25**

24. **Assertion (A)** The nucleus $_{7}^{3}X$ is more stable than the nucleus $_{3}^{4}Y$.

Reason (R) $_{3}^{7}X$ contains more number of protons.

Competency Based Que.

25. **Assertion (A)** Naturally, thermonuclear fusion reaction is not possible on earth.

Reason (R) For thermonuclear fusion to take place, extreme condition of temperature and pressure are required. **Competency Based Que.**

26. **Assertion (A)** In radioactive decay an electron is emitted by the nucleus.

Reason (R) Electrons are present inside the nucleus.

27. **Assertion (A)** Nuclear force acting between proton-proton is less than force acting between proton-neutron inside a nucleus.

Reason (R) Proton being positively charged, repel each other by coulombian force.

28. **Assertion (A)** Higher the binding energy of nucleon, more stable is the nucleus.

Reason (R) The stability of nucleus is determined by the value of its binding energy per nucleon

Case Based Questions

Directions *(Q.Nos. 29-32) These questions are case study based questions. Read the following paragraph and answer the questions on the basis of same.*

29. **The nucleus was first discovered in 1911 by Lord Rutherford and his associates by experiments on scattering of α-particles by atoms. He found that the scattering results could be explained, if atoms consist of a small, central, massive and positive core surrounded by orbiting electrons.The experimental results indicated that the size of the nucleus is of the order of 10^{-14} m and is thus 10000 times smaller than the size of atom.**

Competency Based Que.

(i) Ratio of mass of nucleus with mass of atom is approximately

(a) 1 (b) 10

(c) 10^{3} (d) 10^{10}

(ii) Masses of nuclei of hydrogen, deuterium and tritium are in ratio

(a) 1 : 2 : 3 (b) 1 : 1 : 1

(c) 1 : 1 : 2 (d) 1 : 2 : 4

(iii) Density of a nucleus is

(a) more for lighter elements and less for heavier elements

(b) more for heavier elements and less for lighter elements

(c) very less compared to ordinary matter

(d) a constant

(iv) If R is the radius and A is the mass number, then log R *versus* log A graph will be

(a) a straight line (b) a parabola

(c) an ellipse (d) None of the above

Or

The ratio of the nuclear radii of the gold isotope $_{79}^{197}$Au and silver isotope $_{47}^{107}$ Au is

(a) 1.23 (b) 0.216

(c) 2.13 (d) 3.46

30. **In the year 1939, German scientist Otto Hahn and Strassmann discovered that when a uranium isotope was bombarded with a neutron, it breaks into two intermediate mass fragments. It was observed that, the sum of the masses of new fragments formed were less than the mass of the original nuclei. This difference in the mass appeared as the energy released in the process.**

Thus, the phenomenon of splitting of a heavy nucleus (usually $A > 230$) into two or more lighter nuclei by the bombardment of proton, neutron, α-particle, etc., with liberation of energy is called nuclear fission.

Fission reaction resulting from the absorption of neutron is known as induced fission.

$$_{92}U^{235} + _{0}n^{1} \rightarrow \underset{\text{Unstable nucleus}}{_{92}U^{236}} \rightarrow _{56}Ba^{144} + _{36}Kr^{89} + 3\,_{0}n^{1} + Q$$

(i) Fission of nuclei is possible because the binding energy per nucleon in them

(a) increases with mass number at high mass numbers

(b) decreases with mass number at high mass numbers

(c) increases with mass number at low mass number

(d) decreases with mass number at low mass number

(ii) For sustaining the nuclear fission chain reaction in a sample (of small size) of $_{92}^{235}$U, it is desirable to slow down fast neutrons by

(a) friction

(b) elastic damping/scattering

(c) absorption

(d) None of the above

(iii) Which of the following is/are fission reaction(s)?

I. ${}_0^1n + {}_{92}^{235}U \rightarrow {}_{92}^{236}U \rightarrow {}_{51}^{133}Sb + {}_{41}^{99}Nb + 4{}_0^1n$

II. ${}_0^1n + {}_{92}^{235}U \rightarrow {}_{54}^{1.40}Xe + {}_{38}^{94}Sr + 2{}_0^1n$

III. ${}_1^2H + {}_1^2H \rightarrow {}_2^3He + {}_0^1n$

(a) Both II and III (b) Both I and III
(c) Only II (d) Both I and II

(iv) If a nucleus with mass number $A = 240$ with $E_{bn} = 7.6$ MeV breaks into two fragments of $A = 120$ and $E_{bn} = 8.5$ MeV, then released energy is around

(a) 216 MeV (b) 200 MeV
(c) 100 MeV
(d) Cannot be estimated from given data

Or

In any fission process, ratio of mass of daughter nucleus to mass of parent nucleus is

(a) less than 1
(b) greater than 1
(c) equal to 1
(d) depends on the mass of parent nucleus

31. **Nuclear forces are the strong forces of attraction which hold together the nucleons (neutrons and protons) in the tiny nucleus of atom, inspite of strong electrostatic forces of repulsion between protons. Nuclear force is strongest force. It is 100 times that of electrostatic forces and 10^{38} times that of gravitational forces between nucleons. It is independent of charge, short range, non-conservative force and not obeying inverse-square law.**

(i) If the nuclear force between two neutrons is F, then what will be the nuclear force between a proton and a neutron?

(ii) If the electrostatic force between nucleons is F_e, then what is the nuclear force of nucleons?

(iii) Out of nuclear force, electrostatic force and gravitational force, which one is not obeying inverse-square law.

(iv) Which force is responsible to hold all the nucleons in an atom?

32. **The density of nuclear matter is the ratio of the mass of the nucleus to its volume. As the volume of a nucleus is directly proportional to its mass number A, so the density of nuclear matter is independent of the size of the nucleus.**

$$\therefore \text{Nuclear density, } \rho = \frac{\text{Mass of nucleus}}{\text{Volume of nucleus}} = \frac{mA}{\frac{4}{3}\pi (R_0 A^{1/3})^3} = \frac{3m}{4\pi R_0^3}$$

where, m = average mass of a nucleon.

Clearly, nuclear density is independent of mass number (A) for all nuclei. The nuclear mass density is of the order of 10^{17} kg/m^3.

(i) If nuclear radius of O^{16} is 3×10^{-15} m, then what will be the density of nuclear matter?

(ii) If $R_0 = 1.2$ fm, $m_p = 1.007825$ u, then what will be the density of hydrogen nucleus in SI units?

(iii) If the nuclear density of a matter X (mass number = A) is 2×10^{15} kg/m^3, then what will be the nuclear density of matter Y (mass number = $2A$)?

(iv) Draw a graph between the nuclear density of a matter *versus* its mass number (A).

Subjective Questions

Very Short Answer Type Questions

1. (i) Distinguish between isotopes and isobars. [1]

(ii) Two nuclei have different mass numbers A_1 and A_2. Are these nuclei necessarily the isotopes of the same element ? Explain. **CBSE 2022 (Term-II)** [1]

2. Select the pairs of isotopes and isotones from the following nuclei ${}_{11}^{22}Na$, ${}_{12}^{24}Mg$, ${}_{11}^{24}Na$, ${}_{10}^{23}Na$

3. The carbon-13 nucleus has one additional neutron as compared to nucleus of carbon-12. The difference in the BE of these two nuclei is approx. 5 MeV. Take, mass of neutron = 1.0086 u.

Using this information, determine the difference in the atomic masses of these two nuclei.

4. Define the term mass defect. How is it related to stability of the nucleus? **CBSE 2023**

5. Which physical quantity in a nuclear reaction is considered equivalent to the Q value of the reaction? **CBSE SQP 2020**

Short Answer Type Questions

6. What is the nuclear radius of ^{125}Fe, if that of ^{27}Al is 3.6 fm?. **CBSE SQP 2023**

7. Given below are two probable nuclear reactions

$${}_Z^AX \longrightarrow {}_Z^{A-1}X + {}_0^1n$$

$${}_Z^AY \longrightarrow {}_{Z-1}^{A-1}Z + {}_1^1p$$

(i) State the condition under which nuclear reactions can occur spontaneously without any external energy input. **[1½]**

(ii) Using the following data of nuclear masses, identify which of the given reactions can occur spontaneously without any external energy input.

Mass of $^{A}_{Z}X = 230.033927$ u

Mass of proton = 1.0078 u

Mass of neutron = 1.0087 u

Mass of $^{A-1}_{Z}X = 229.033496$ u

Mass of $^{A}_{Z}Y = 230.049289$ u

Mass of $^{A-1}_{Z-1}Z = 229.032089$ u **[1½]**

8. (i) Show the variation of binding energy per nucleon with mass number. Write the significance of binding energy curve. **[1½]**

(ii) Two nuclei with lower binding energy per nucleon form a nuclei with more binding energy per nucleon. **CBSE 2025**

(a) What type of nuclear reaction is it?

(b) Whether the total mass of nuclei increases, decreases or remains unchanged? **[1½]**

(c) Does the process require energy or produce energy?

9. Draw a graph showing the variation of binding energy per nucleon as a function of mass number A. The binding energy per nucleon for heavy nuclei ($A > 170$) decreases with the increase in mass number. Explain. **CBSE 2023**

10. Draw a graph showing the variation of potential energy of a pair of nucleons as a function of their separation. Indicate the region in which the nuclear force is (i) attractive and (ii) repulsive. **CBSE 2023**

11. Binding energy per nucleon *versus* mass number curve for nuclei is as shown in the figure. W, X, Y and Z are four nuclei indicated on the curve. Indentify which of the following nuclei is most likely to undergo

(i) nuclear fission **[1½]**

(ii) nuclear fusion **[1½]**

Justify your answer.

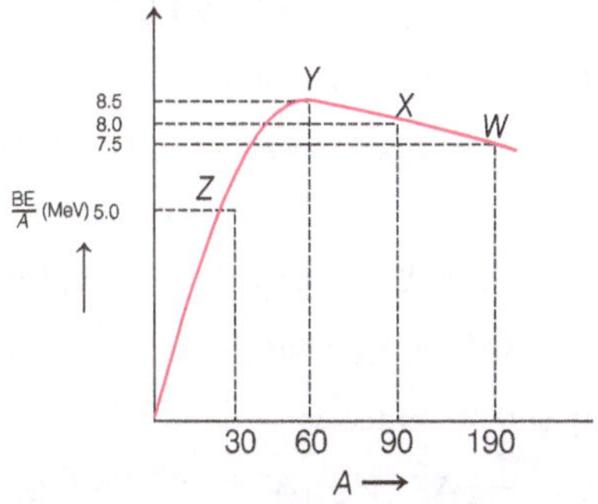

12. (i) Distinguish between nuclear fission and fusion giving an example of each. **[1½]**

(ii) Explain the release of energy in nuclear fission and fusion on the basis of binding energy per nuclear curve. **CBSE 2023** **[1½]**

13. (i) In a typical nuclear reaction e.g., $^{2}_{1}H + ^{2}_{1}H \rightarrow + ^{3}_{2}He + ^{1}_{0}n + 3.27$ MeV, although number of nucleons is conserved, yet energy is released. How? Explain. **[1½]**

(ii) Deuterium undergoes fusion as per the reaction

$$^{2}_{1}H + ^{2}_{1}H \longrightarrow ^{3}_{2}He + ^{1}_{0}n + 3.27 \text{ MeV}$$

Find the duration for which an electric bulb of 500 W can be kept glowing by the fusion of 100 g of deuterium. **[1½]**

Long Answer Type Questions

14. Deuteron is a bound state of a neutron and a proton with a binding energy $B = 2.2$ MeV.

A γ-ray of energy E is aimed at a deuteron nucleus to try to break it into a (neutron + proton), such that the n and p move in the direction of the incident γ-ray. If $E = B$, show that this cannot happen. Hence, calculate how much bigger than B must be E for such a process to happen? **NCERT Exemplar**

15. Nuclei with magic number of protons $Z = 2, 8, 20, 28, 50, 52$ and magic number of neutrons $N = 2, 8, 20, 28, 50, 82$ and 126 are found to be very stable.

(i) Verify this by calculating the proton separation energy S_p for ^{120}Sn ($Z = 50$) and ^{121}Sb ($Z = 551$). The proton separation energy for a nuclide is the minimum energy required to separate the least tightly bound proton from a nucleus of that nuclide. It is given by **[3]**

$$S_p = (M_{Z-1,N} + M_H - M_{Z,N})c^2$$

Given, $^{119}In = 118.9058$ u,

$^{120}Sn = 119.902199$ u

$^{121}Sb = 120.903822$ u,

$^{1}H = 1.0078252$ u

(ii) What does the existence of magic number indicate? **NCERT Exemplar** **[2]**

16. Define the Q-value of a nuclear process. When can a nuclear process not proceed spontaneously? If both the number of protons and the number of neutrons are conserved in a nuclear reaction, in what way is mass converted into energy (or *vice-versa*) in the nuclear reaction?

17. The Q-value of a nuclear reaction $A+b \longrightarrow C+d$ is defined by $Q=[m_A+m_b-m_C-m_d]c^2$, where the masses refer to the respective nuclei. Determine from the given data, the Q-value of the following reactions and state whether the reactions are exothermic or endothermic.

(i) ${}_1^1\text{H}+{}_1^3\text{H} \longrightarrow {}_1^2\text{H}+{}_1^2\text{H}$ **[2½]**

(ii) ${}_6^{12}\text{C}+{}_6^{12}\text{C} \longrightarrow {}_{10}^{20}\text{Ne}+{}_2^4\text{He}$ **[2½]**

Atomic masses are given to be

$m({}_1\text{H}^1)=1.007825\text{ u},\ m({}_1^2\text{H})=2.014102\text{ u},$

$m({}_1^3\text{H})=3.016049\text{ u},\ m({}_6^{12}\text{C})=12.000000\text{ u}$

$m({}_{10}^{20}\text{Ne})=19.992439\text{ u}$ **NCERT**

18. A 1000 MW fission reactor consumes half of its fuel in 5 yr. How much ${}_{92}^{235}\text{U}$ did it contain initially? Assume that the reactor operates 80% of the time that all the energy generated arises from the fission of ${}_{92}^{235}\text{U}$ and that this nuclide is consumed only by the fission process.

19. (i) Write two characteristics of nuclear force. **[2]**

(ii) Suppose we consider fission of a ${}_{26}^{56}\text{Fe}$ into two equal fragments of ${}_{13}^{28}\text{Al}$ nucleus. Is the fission energetically possible? Justify your answer by working out Q-value of the process.

Given $(m)\ {}_{26}^{56}\text{Fe}=55.93494\text{ u}$

and $(m)\ {}_{13}^{28}\text{Al}=27.98191$ **[3]**

Numerical Problems

20. Obtain approximately the ratio of the nuclear radii of the gold isotope ${}_{79}^{197}\text{Au}$ and the silver isotope ${}_{47}^{107}\text{Ag}$. **NCERT**

21. The fission properties of ${}_{94}^{239}\text{Pu}$ are very similar to those of ${}_{92}^{235}\text{U}$. The average energy released per fission is 180 MeV. How much energy in MeV, is released if all the atoms in 1 kg of pure ${}_{94}^{239}\text{Pu}$ undergo fission? **NCERT**

22. Before the neutrino hypothesis, the beta decay process was throught to be the transition.

$$n \longrightarrow p+\bar{e}$$

If this was true, show that if the neutron was at rest, the proton and electron would emerge with fixed energies and calculate them. Experimentally, the electron energy was found to have a large range.

23. How long can an electric lamp of 100 W be kept glowing by fusion of 2 kg of deuterium? Take the fusion reaction as **CBSE 2022 Term-II**

$${}_1^2\text{H}+{}_1^2\text{H} \rightarrow {}_2^3\text{He}+n+3.27\text{ MeV}$$

Hints & Solutions

Objective Type Questions

4. (c) 9. (d) 10. (b) 16. (d) 18. (a)
19. (c) 22. (a) 24. (c) 25. (a) 27. (b)
28. (a)

1. (a) Atomic mass unit (1 u) is defined as

$$1\text{ u}=\frac{\text{Mass of }{}^{12}\text{C atom}}{12}$$

2. (b) Radius of atom $\simeq 10^{-10}$

Radius of nucleus $\simeq 10^{-14}$

$$\therefore \frac{\text{Radius of atom}}{\text{Radius of nucleus}}=\frac{10^{-10}}{10^{-14}}\simeq 10^4$$

3. (a) $\dfrac{R_X}{R_Y}=\dfrac{R_0(27)^{1/3}}{R_0(125)^{1/3}}=\dfrac{3}{5}$

$$R_Y=\frac{5}{3}R_X$$

$$R_Y=\frac{5}{3}R \qquad (\because R_X=R)$$

5. (d) Nuclear density of two nuclei is independent of mass number.

6. (b) Given, $F=\dfrac{GMm}{r^2}$

M = effective mass of hydrogen atom

= mass of electron + mass of proton $-\dfrac{B}{c^2}$

where B is BE of hydrogen atom = 13.6 eV.

7. (a) Let the nucleus is ${}_ZX^A$. β^+ decay is represented as

$${}_zX^A \rightarrow {}_{z-1}y^A+{}_{+1}e^0+\nu+Q_2$$

$$\therefore \quad Q_2=[m_n({}_ZX^A)-m_n({}_{z-1}y^A)-m_e]c^2$$

$$=[m_n({}_zX^A)+zm_e-m_n({}_{Z-1}Y^A)-(Z-1)m_e-2m_e]c^2$$

$$=[m({}_zX^A)-m({}_{Z-1}Y^A)-2m_e]c^2$$

$$=(M_x-M_y-2m_e)c^2$$

β^- decay is represented as

$$={}_ZX^A \rightarrow {}_{Z+1}A^Y+{}_{-1}e^0+\bar{\nu}+Q_1$$

$$Q_1 = [\, m_n\,({}_Z X^A) - m_n\,({}_{Z+1} Y^A) - m_e\,]\,c^2$$
$$= [m_n\,({}_Z X^A) + Zm_e - m_n\,({}_{Z+1}Y^A) - (Z+1)\,me\,]c^2$$
$$= [m\,({}_Z X^A) - m({}_{Z-1}Y^A)]c^2$$
$$= (\,M_x - M_y\,)\,c^2$$

8. (*a*) Binding energy per nucleus

$$= \frac{\text{Total Binding Energy}}{\text{Number of Nucleus}} = \frac{21}{7} = 3\,\text{u}$$

11. (*b*) α and β particles carries one unit of negative charge, an α-particle carries 2 units of positive charge and γ particle carries no charge, therefore electronic energy levels of the atom changes for α and β decay, but not for γ-decay.

12. (*a*) Tritium (${}_1H^3$) contains 1 proton and 2 neutrons. A neutron decays as $n \longrightarrow p + \bar{e} + \bar{\nu}$, the nucleus may have 2 protons and 1 neutron, i.e. tritium will transform into $2He^3$ (2 protons and 1 neutron).

Triton energy is less than that of $2He^3$ nucleus, i.e., transformation is not allowed energetically.

13. (*b*) Stable heavy nuclei have more neutrons than protons. This is because electrostatic force between protons is repulsive , which may reduce stability.

14. (*b*) According to the question, the moderator used have light nuclei (like proton). When protons undergo perfectly elastic collision with the neutron emitted their velocities are exchanged, i.e. neutrons come to rest and protons move with the velocity of neutrons.

Heavy nuclei will not serve the purpose because elastic collisions of neutrons with heavy nuclei will not slow them down.

15. (*c*) ${}^{238}_{92}U \rightarrow {}^{234}_{90}Th + {}^{4}_{2}He$

When an α-particle is emittted mass number decreases by 4 and atomic number by 2.

17. (*a*) Nuclear forces are short range that's why nuclear force can act between two nucleus if they are very close. On the other hand electrostatic force repel two nuclei if they are brought close.

20. (*c*) Nuclear density is extremely equal to 2.3×10^{17} kg/m^3 which is much greater than density of ordinary matter. Nuclear density is independent of mass number.

21. (*b*) The binding energy per nucleon of range $30 < A < 170$ is close to its maximum value.

So, the nucleus belongs to this region is highly stable.

23. (*d*) Nuclei having mass number 60 are most stable.

26. (*c*) Electrons are not present inside the nucleus but they are produced while nuclear decay takes place.

29. (i) (*a*) As nearly 99.9% mass of atom is in nucleus.

$$\therefore \quad \frac{\text{Mass of nucleus}}{\text{Mass of atom}} = \frac{99.9}{100} = 0.99 \approx 1$$

(ii) (*a*) Since, the nuclei of deuterium and tritium are isotopes of hydrogen, they must contain only one proton each. But the masses of the nuclei of hydrogen, deuterium and tritium are in the ratio of 1 : 2 : 3, because of presence of 1 neutron in deuterium and 2 neutron tritium nuclei.

(iii) (*d*) Density $= \dfrac{\text{Mass}}{\text{Volume}} = \dfrac{mA}{\frac{4}{3}\pi R_0^3 A} = \dfrac{3m}{4\pi R_0^3}$

As, $m = m_P = m_N$

$= 2.3 \times 10^{17}$ kgm^{-3}, which is a constant.

(iv) (*a*) $R = R_0 A^{1/3}$, $\log R = \log R_0 + \frac{1}{3} \log A$

On comparing the above equation of straight line $y = mx + c$. So, the graph between log A and log R is a straight line.

Or

(*a*) Here $A_1 = 197$ and $A_2 = 107$

$$\therefore \quad \frac{R_1}{R_2} = \left(\frac{A_1}{A_2}\right)^{1/3} = \left(\frac{197}{107}\right)^{1/3} = 1.225 \simeq 1.23$$

30. (i) (*b*)

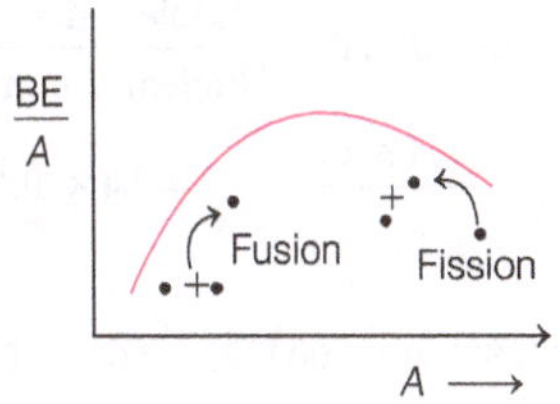

So, from graph, it is clear that binding energy per nucleon decreases with mass number at high mass numbers.

(ii) (*b*) Fast neutrons are slowed down by elastic scattering with light nuclei as each collision takes away nearly 50% of energy.

(iii) (*d*) Reactions I and II represent fission of uranium isotope ${}^{235}_{92}U$, when bombarded with neutrons that breaks it into two intermediate mass nuclear fragments. However, reaction III represents that two deuterons fuse together to form the light isotope of helium.

(iv) (*a*) The energy released (i.e. Q-value) in the fission reaction of nuclei like uranium is of the order of 200 MeV per fissioning nucleus. This is estimated as follows

Let us take a nucleus with $A = 240$ breaking into two fragments each of $A = 120$, then

E_{bn} for $A = 240$ nucleus is about 7.6 MeV.

E_{bn} for the two $A = 120$ fragment nuclei is about 8.5 MeV.

So, gain in binding energy for nucleon is about 0.9 MeV.

Hence, the total gain in binding energy is 240×0.9 or 216 MeV.

Or

(*a*) In fission process, when a parent nucleus breaks into daughter products, then some mass is lost in the form of energy. Thus, mass of fission products < mass of parent nucleus.

$$\Rightarrow \quad \frac{\text{Mass of fission products}}{\text{Mass of parent nucleus}} < 1$$

31. (i) The nuclear force acting between a pair of neutrons, a pair of protons and also between a neutron-proton pair will be of same strength.

$\therefore$ If nuclear force between two neutrons = F

$\therefore$ Nuclear force between a proton and a neutron = F

(ii) If electrostatic force between nucleons = F_e

$\therefore$ Nuclear force between nucleons = $100\ F_e$

(iii) The nuclear force does not follow the inverse square law.

(iv) The nuclear force is responsible to hold all the nucleons in an atom.

32. (i) Given, $R = 3 \times 10^{-15}$ m

Nuclear mass, $M = 16$ amu $= 16 \times 1.66 \times 10^{-27}$ kg

$$\therefore \text{Nuclear density, } \rho = \frac{\text{Nuclear mass}}{\text{Nuclear volume}}$$

$$\therefore \quad \rho = \frac{16 \times 1.66 \times 10^{-27}}{\frac{4}{3}\pi \times (3 \times 10^{-15})^3} = 2.4 \times 10^{17} \text{ kg/m}^3$$

(ii) $m_p = 1.007825$ u $= 1.007825 \times 1.66 \times 10^{-27}$kg,

$R_0 = 1.1$ fm

$$\text{Nuclear density, } \rho = \frac{3m_p}{4\pi R_0^3}$$

$$= \frac{3 \times 1.007825 \times 1.66 \times 10^{-27}}{4\pi \times (1.2 \times 10^{-15})^3}$$

$$= 2.3 \times 10^{17} \text{ kg/m}^2$$

(iii) The nuclear density of a matter,

$\rho = \frac{3m}{4\pi R_0^3}$, which is independent of mass number (A).

$$\therefore \quad \rho_X = 2 \times 10^{15} \text{ kg/m}^3$$

$$\Rightarrow \quad \rho_Y = 2 \times 10^{15} \text{ kg/m}^3$$

(iv) The graph of nuclear density *versus* mass number is

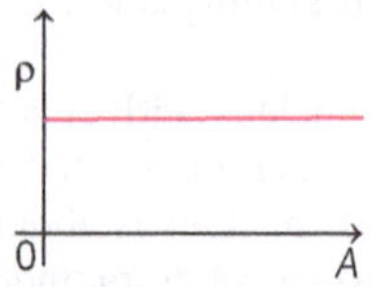

Subjective Questions

1. (i) Nuclides of an element having same atomic number but different mass number called isotopes, while isobars are the nuclides with same mass number but different atomic number.

(ii) No, the difference in mass number may be due to different atomic number, so these cannot be necessarily isotopes of same element. For isotopes, their atomic number must be same.

2. Isotopes = $^{22}_{11}\text{Na}, ^{24}_{11}\text{Na}$

(both have same atomic number, i.e. 11)

Isotones = $^{24}_{11}\text{Na}, ^{23}_{10}\text{Na}$

(both have same number of neutrons, i.e. 13)

3. Difference in BE of ^{12}C and ^{13}C is 5 MeV.

The corresponding mass defect that resulted in the above difference in BE = 5 / 931 = 0.0054 u

Since, ^{13}C nucleus has one extra neutron of mass 1.0086 u as compared to ^{12}C nucleus, the difference in atomic masses between ^{12}C and ^{13}C is given as

$$1.0086 \text{ u} - 0.0054 \text{ u} = 1.0032 \text{ u}$$

4. Refer to text on Pg. 407 (Mass defect)

Stability of nucleus $\propto$ BE/nucleon

Also, BE/nucleon $\propto$ Mass defect

Hence the stability of the nucleus is directly proportional to its mass defect.

5. The nuclear reaction is represented by

$$X \longrightarrow Y + Z + Q$$

$\therefore$ Q-value of reaction $= (m_X - m_Y - m_Z)c^2$, which is equivalent to kinetic energy.

6. Given, nuclear radius of ^{27}Al, $R_1 = 3.6$ fm

Nuclear radius of ^{125}Fe, R_2 =?

$$A_1 = 27, A_2 = 125$$

The nuclear radius is given by

$$R = R_0 A^{\frac{1}{3}} \Rightarrow R \propto A^{\frac{1}{3}}$$

$$\therefore \quad \frac{R_2}{R_1} = \left(\frac{A_2}{A_1}\right)^{\frac{1}{3}} = \left(\frac{125}{27}\right)^{\frac{1}{3}} = \frac{5}{3}$$

$$\therefore \quad R_2 = \frac{5}{3}R_1 = \frac{5}{3} \times 3.6 = 6 \text{ fm}$$

$$\therefore \quad R_2 = 6 \text{ fm}$$

7. (i) The nuclear reaction that occur spontaneously without any external energy input, if the Q value of the reaction is positive.

Alternatively, sum of the reactant masses exceeds the sum of product masses.

(ii) Reaction (a) $^{A}_{Z}X \rightarrow ^{A-1}_{Z}X + ^{1}_{0}n$

Mass of the reactant $^{A}_{Z}X$: 230.033927 u

Sum of the masses of the products

$= 229.032089$ u $+ 1.0078 = 230.03869$

Mass of reactant $^{A}_{Z}$Y : 230.0492894

$= 229.032089$u $+ 1.0078 = 230.039889$u

Since, the sum of product masses exceeds the mass of the reactant, reaction a is not possible.

Reaction (b) ${}^{A}_{Z}Y \rightarrow {}^{A-1}_{Z-1}Z + {}^{1}_{1}p$

Sum of the masses of the products

$= 229.032089 \text{ u} + 1.0078 = 230.039889$

Mass of the reactant ${}^{A}_{Z}Y$: 230.049289 u

Since, the sum of product masses is less than the mass of the reactant, reaction (b) is possible.

8. (i) Refer to the graph on page 408 (Binding energy per nucleon as a function of mass number).
Refer to theory on page 408
(Binding energy curve : Conclusions).

(ii) (a) The process is known as nuclear fusion.
(b) After nuclear fusion, the total mass of the nuclei decreases as compared to the individual masses of the nuclei before the fusion.

(iii) The process produces a large amount of energy.

9. Refer to graph on page 408 (Binding energy curve). For the heavy nuclei ($A > 170$), as we go rightward with increasing mass number, the graph gradually becomes downward. This shows the BE/nucleon of the heavy nuclei decreases as the mass number increases.

10. Refer to text on page no. 408 and 409.

11. (i) Nuclei with higher binding energy per nucleon are more stable.
From the curve, nucleus W has the highest mass number and relatively low binding energy per nucleon as compared to Y and X. Thus, nucleus W is most liekly to undergo nuclear fission.

(ii) From the curve, nucleus Z has the lowest mass number and also a relative low binding energy per nucleon. Therefore, nucleus Z is most likely undergo nuclear fusion.

12. (i) Refer to text on page 409 and 410.
(ii) Refer to text on page no. 408.

13. (i) In a nuclear reaction, the sum of the masses of the target nucleus (${}^{2}_{1}$H) and the bombarding particle (${}^{2}_{1}$H) may be greater than the product nucleus (${}^{3}_{2}$He) and the outgoing neutron ${}^{1}_{0}n$. So, from the law of conservation of mass-energy some energy (3.27 MeV) is evolved due to mass defect in the nuclear reaction. This energy is called Q-value of the nuclear reaction.

(ii) Number of atoms in 100 g deuterium,

$$\frac{100}{2} \times 6.023 \times 10^{-23}$$

Energy released, $\frac{3.27}{2} \times 1.6 \times 10^{-13}$ J

Time required = Total energy (E)/Power of lamp (P)

$500 \times 60 \times 60 \times 24 \times 365$

$t = 1.5768 \times 10^{10}$ yrs

14. Apply conservation of energy as well as conservation of momentum.
Given, binding energy, $B = 2.2$ MeV
From the energy conservation law,

$$E - B = K_n + K_p = \frac{p_n^2}{2m} + \frac{p_p^2}{2m} \quad \text{...(i)}$$

From conservation of momentum,

$$p_n + p_p = \frac{E}{c} \quad \text{...(ii)}$$

As, $E = B$

Eq. (i) becomes, $p_n^2 + p_p^2 = 0$

It only happen, if $p_n = p_p = 0$

So, the Eq.(ii) cannot be satisfied and the process cannot take place.

Let $E = B + X$, where $X << B$ for the process to take place.

Put the value of p_n from Eq. (ii) in Eq. (i), we get

$$\Rightarrow \quad X = \frac{\left(\frac{E}{c} - p_p\right)^2}{2m} + \frac{p_p^2}{2m}$$

$$\Rightarrow \quad 2p_p^2 - \frac{2Ep_p}{c} + \frac{E^2}{c^2} - 2mX = 0$$

Using the formula of quadratic equation, we get

$$p_p = \frac{\frac{2E}{c} \pm \sqrt{\frac{4E^2}{c^2} - 8\left(\frac{E^2}{c^2} - 2mX\right)}}{4}$$

For the real value p_p, the determinant is positive

$$\frac{4E^2}{c^2} = 8\left(\frac{E^2}{c^2} - 2mX\right) \Rightarrow 16mX = \frac{4E^2}{c^2}$$

$$\therefore \quad X = \frac{E^2}{4mc^2} = \frac{B^2}{4mc^2} \quad [\because X << B \Rightarrow E \cong B]$$

15. (i) The proton separation energy is given by

$$S_{p\,(\text{Sn})} = (M_{119,70} + M_H - M_{120,70})\, c^2$$
$$= (118.9058 + 1.0078252 - 119.902199)c^2$$
$$= 0.0114262\, c^2$$

Similarly, $S_{p\,(\text{Sb})} = (M_{120,70} + M_H - M_{121,70})\, c^2$
$$= (119.902199 + 1.0078252 - 120.903822)c^2$$
$$= 0.006202\, c^2$$

Since, $S_{p\,(\text{Sn})} > S_{p\,(\text{Sb})}$, Sn nucleus is more stable than Sb nucleus.

(ii) The existence of magic numbers indicates that the shell structure of nucleus is similar to the shell structure of an atom. This also explains the peaks in binding energy/nucleon curve.

16. The Q-value of a nuclear process refers the energy release in the nuclear process which can be determined using Einstein's mass-energy relation, $E = mc^2$. The

Q-value is equal to the difference of mass of products and reactant nuclei multiplied by square of velocity of light.

$$Q = [m_x - m_\pi - m_{He}]\, c^2$$

The nuclear process does not proceed spontaneously when Q-value of a process is negative or sum of masses of product is greater than sum of masses of reactant.

The sum of masses of nuclei of product element is less than sum of masses of reactants and hence, loss of mass takes place during the reaction.

The difference of mass of product element and reactant convert into energy and liberated in the form of heat.

17. (i) The given reaction, ${}_1^1\text{H} + {}_1^3\text{H} \longrightarrow {}_1^2\text{H} + {}_1^2\text{H}$

Mass defect, $\Delta m = m\,({}_1^1\text{H}) + m\,({}_1^3\text{H}) - 2m\,({}_1^2\text{H})$

$$= 1.007825 + 3.016049 - 2(2.014102)$$
$$= -0.00433 \text{ u}$$

Q-value of the reaction,

$$Q = \Delta m \times 931 \text{ MeV} = -0.00433 \times 931 \text{ MeV}$$
$$Q = -4.031 \text{ MeV}$$

As, the energy is negative, so the reaction is endothermic.

(ii) The given reaction,

$${}_6^{12}\text{C} + {}_6^{12}\text{C} \longrightarrow {}_{10}^{20}\text{Ne} + {}_2^4\text{He}$$

Mass defect, $\Delta m = 2\,m\,({}_6^{12}\text{C}) - m\,({}_{10}^{20}\text{Ne}) - m\,({}_2^4\text{He})$

$$= 2 \times 12 - 19.992439 - 4.002603$$
$$\Delta m = 0.00495 \text{ u}$$

Q-value of the reaction,

$$Q = \Delta m \times 931 \text{ MeV} = 0.00495 \times 931 \text{ meV}$$
$$= 4.62 \text{ MeV}$$

Since, the energy is positive, thus the reaction is exothermic.

18. Given, power of reactor, $P = 1000$ MW

We will use concept that the energy generated in one fission of ${}_{92}^{235}\text{U}$ is 200 MeV.

Number of ${}_{92}^{235}\text{U}$ atoms in 1 g $= \dfrac{1}{235} \times 6.023 \times 10^{23}$

$\therefore$ Energy generated per gram of ${}_{92}^{235}\text{U}$

$$= \left(\frac{1}{235} \times 6.023 \times 10^{23} \times 200 \times 1.6 \times 10^{-13}\right)$$

Total energy generated in 5 yr with 80% of the time

$$= 1000 \times 10^6 \times 5 \times 365 \times 24 \times 60 \times 60 \times \frac{80}{100}$$

[as $E = Pt$]

$\therefore$ Mass of ${}_{92}^{235}\text{U}$ consumed in 5 yr,

$$m = \frac{\text{Total energy}}{\text{Energy consumed per gram}}$$

$$= \frac{1000 \times 10^6 \times 5 \times 365 \times 24 \times 60 \times 60 \times 0.8}{\left(\frac{1}{235}\right) \times 6.023 \times 10^{23} \times 200 \times 1.6 \times 10^{-13}}$$

$$= 1.538 \times 10^6 \text{ g}$$
$$= 1538 \text{ kg}$$

$\therefore$ Initial amount of ${}_{92}^{235}\text{U} = (1544 \times 2)\text{ kg} = 3076 \text{ kg}$

19. (i) Two characteristics of nuclear force are given as

(a) These are short range forces.

(b) These are strongest force of attractive nature upto certain distances.

(ii) The given reaction for decay process,

$${}_{26}^{56}\text{Fe} \longrightarrow 2\,{}_{13}^{28}\text{Al}$$

Mass defect, $\Delta m = m\,({}_{26}^{56}\text{Fe}) - 2m\,({}_{13}^{28}\text{Al})$

$$= 55.93494 - 2(27.98191)$$
$$= -0.02888 \text{ u}$$

$\Rightarrow$ $Q = \Delta m \times 931$ MeV

$$= -0.02888 \times 931 \text{ MeV}$$
$$= -26.88728 \text{ MeV}$$

Because the energy is negative, so the fission is not possible energetically.

20. Radius of nuclei, $R = R_0\, A^{1/3}$

where A is the mass number of nucleus and R_0 is an empirical constant.

$$\therefore \quad R \propto A^{1/3}$$

$$\therefore \quad \frac{R_{Au}}{R_{Ag}} = \left(\frac{A_{Au}}{A_{Ag}}\right)^{1/3} = \left(\frac{197}{107}\right)^{13} = 1.225 = 1.23$$

21. Number of atoms in 1 kg of pure Pu

$$= \frac{6.023 \times 10^{23}}{239} \times 1000 = 2.52 \times 10^{24}$$

As average energy released in fission is 180 MeV, the total energy released

$$= 2.52 \times 10^{24} \times 180 \text{ MeV}$$
$$= 4.53 \times 10^{26} \text{ MeV}$$

22. Before β-decay, neutron is at rest.

Hence, $E_n = m_n c^2$, $p_n = 0$,

$$p_n = p_p + p_e$$

or $\quad p_p + p_e = 0 \Rightarrow |p_p| = |p_e| = p$

Also, $\quad E_p = (m_p^2 c^4 + p_p^2 c^2)^{\frac{1}{2}}$,

$$E_e = (m_e^2 c^4 + p_p^2 c^2)^{\frac{1}{2}}$$
$$= (m_e^2 c^4 + p_e^2 c^2)^{\frac{1}{2}}$$

From conservation of energy,

$$(m_p^2 c^4 + p^2c^2)^{\frac{1}{2}} = (m_e^2 c^4 + p^2c^2)^{\frac{1}{2}} = m_n c^2$$

$$m_p c^2 \approx 936 \text{ MeV}, m_n c^2 \approx 938 \text{ MeV}$$

$$m_e c^2 = 0.51 \text{ MeV}$$

Since, the energy difference between n and p is small, pc will be small, $pc <<< m_p c^2$, while pc may be greater than $m_e c^2$.

$$\Rightarrow \qquad m_p c^2 + \frac{p^2c^2}{2m_p^2 c^4} \simeq m_n c^2 - pc$$

To first order,

$$pc \simeq m_n c^2 - m_p c^2 = 938 \text{MeV} - 936 \text{ MeV} = 2\text{MeV}$$

This gives the momentum of proton or neutron. Then,

$$E_p = (m_p^2 c^4 + p^2c^2)^{\frac{1}{2}} = \sqrt{936^2 + 2^2} \simeq 936 \text{ MeV}$$

$$E_e = (m_e^2 c^4 + p^2c^2)^{\frac{1}{2}} = \sqrt{(0.51)^2 + 2^2}$$

$$\simeq 2.06 \text{MeV}$$

23. Number of atoms present in 2g of deuterium

$$= 6.023 \times 10^{23}$$

Total number of atoms present in 2000g of deuterium

$$= \frac{6.023 \times 10^{23} \times 2000}{2} = 6.023 \times 10^{26}$$

Energy released in the fusion of 2 deuterium atoms

$$= 3.27 \text{ MeV}$$

Total energy released in the fusion of 2.0 kg of deuterium atoms

$$E = \frac{3.27}{2} \times 6.023 \times 10^{26}$$

$$= 9.81 \times 10^{26} \text{ MeV}$$

$$= 15.696 \times 10^{13} \text{ J}$$

Energy consumed by the bulb per second = 100 J

Time for which the bulb will glow,

$$t = \frac{15.69 \times 10^{13}}{100} \text{ s}$$

$$\text{or} \qquad t = \frac{15.69 \times 10^{11}}{3.15 \times 107} \text{ years}$$

$$= 4.9 \times 10^4 \text{ years}$$

QR Code for Quick Test 1

QR Code for Quick Test 2

SELF ASSESSMENT TEST

Multiple Choice Questions (MCQs)

1. Which of the following statements is correct about nuclear forces?
   (a) Nuclear forces are charge independent.
   (b) Nuclear forces are long-range forces.
   (c) Nuclear forces decrease with an increase in distance beyond 10^{-15} m.
   (d) Nuclear forces are weaker than electromagnetic forces.
2. The mass defect in a nucleus is due to
   (a) proton-proton repulsion
   (b) loss of energy as radiation
   (c) binding energy
   (d) neutron decay
3. Which of the following processes converts a proton into a neutron?
   (a) α-decay
   (b) β^- decay
   (c) β^+ decay
   (d) γ-decay
4. What factor primarily determines the stability of a nucleus?
   (a) Number of neutrons
   (b) Number of protons
   (c) Ratio of neutrons to protons
   (d) Total mass
5. In a nuclear fission reaction, which of the following occurs?
   (a) A heavy nucleus splits into lighter nuclei.
   (b) Light nuclei combine to form a heavier nucleus.
   (c) Energy is absorbed.
   (d) Electrons are emitted.

Assertion-Reason

Directions (Q. Nos. 6-8) *In the following questions, two statements are given- one labelled Assertion (A) and the other labelled Reason (R). Select the correct answer to these questions from the codes (a), (b), (c) and (d) as given below.*

(a) Both Assertion and Reason are true and Reason is the correct explanation of Assertion.
(b) Both Assertion and Reason are true but Reason is not the correct explanation of Assertion.
(c) Assertion is true but Reason is false.
(d) Assertion is false but Reason is true.

6. **Assertion (A)** A nucleus with high binding energy per nucleon is more stable.
   Reason (R) Binding energy per nucleon decreases as mass number increases beyond iron ($A \approx 56$).
7. **Assertion (A)** During alpha decay, the mass number of the parent nucleus decreases by 4 and atomic number decreases by 2.
   Reason (R) Alpha particles consist of 2 protons and 2 neutrons.
8. **Assertion (A)** In the process of nuclear fission, energy is released because the sum of the masses of the products is less than the mass of the original nucleus.
   Reason (R) The mass defect in a fission process is converted into energy according to Einstein's equation, $E = mc^2$.

Case Based Question

Directions (Q. No. 9) *This question is case study based question. Read the following paragraph and answer the questions on the basis of same.*

9. A nucleus of uranium isotope ${}^{235}_{92}\text{U}$ is bombarded with a slow neutron and undergoes nuclear fission. One of the possible fission reaction is given as

$$ {}^{235}_{92}\text{U} + {}^{1}_{0}n \rightarrow {}^{141}_{56}\text{Ba} + {}^{92}_{36}\text{Kr} + 3\,{}^{1}_{0}n + \text{Energy} $$

The binding energy per nucleon for ${}^{235}_{92}\text{U}$, ${}^{141}_{56}\text{Ba}$ and ${}^{92}_{36}\text{Kr}$ are approximately 7.6 MeV, 8.3 MeV and 8.5 MeV, respectively.

Given that the mass of a neutron is 1.008665 u and the unified atomic mass unit (u) corresponds to 931.5 MeV/c^2.

(i) Calculate the mass defect for the above fission reaction (You can neglect the mass of the emitted neutrons in this calculation).

(ii) Using the mass defect, calculate the total energy released in this fission reaction in MeV.

(iii) Compare the total binding energy of the products with the binding energy of the parent uranium nucleus. Explain how this difference contributes to the energy release during fission?

Very Short Answer Type Questions

10. How does the presence of neutrons in the nucleus contribute to the stability of heavier elements?

11. Calculate the energy released when 1 u (unified atomic mass unit) of mass is completely converted into energy.

12. Why are neutrons more effective than protons in causing nuclear fission?

Short Answer Type Questions

13. Why is energy released in both nuclear fusion and nuclear fission, even though they involve opposite processes?

14. Why is the binding energy per nucleon not constant for all nuclei and why does it show a peak around iron (Fe)?

15. A heavy nucleus splits into two lighter nuclei. Explain why this process is energetically favorable in terms of binding energy.

Long Answer Type Question

16. The binding energy per nucleon of a uranium nucleus $^{235}_{92}U$ is approximately 7.6 MeV, while that of an iron nucleus $^{56}_{26}Fe$ is approximately 8.8 MeV. Explain why, despite having a higher mass, the uranium nucleus is less stable compared to the iron nucleus ?

Answers

1. (a)	*2.* (c)	*3.* (c)	*4.* (c)	*5.* (a)
6. (b)	*7.* (a)	*8.* (a)	*11.* 931.5 MeV	

14

CHAPTER

In this chapter, we will discuss the concept of semiconductor physics and some semiconductor device along with their working and application.

YOUR STUDY GOALS

YOUR PRACTICE GOAL

- Objective Type Questions (26 Qs ; MCQs, A-R, Matching)
- Case Based Questions-3
- Subjective Questions (6 VSAs, 12 SAs, 3 LAs)
- Numerical Problems-4

Semiconductor Electronics : Materials, Devices and Simple Circuits

14.1 Classifications of Metals, Conductors and Semiconductors

On the basis of the relative values of electrical conductivity (σ) or resistivity ($\rho = 1/\sigma$), the solids are broadly classified as

(i) **Metals** They possess very low resistivity **or high conductivity**. For example, Al, Cu, Ag, Au, etc.

$$\rho \sim 10^{-2}\text{-}10^{-8}\,\Omega\text{m},\quad \sigma \sim 10^{2}\text{-}10^{8}\ \text{Sm}^{-1}$$

Silver (Ag) is the best metal conductor.

(ii) **Semiconductors** They have **conductivity intermediate to metals and insulators.**

$$\rho \sim 10^{-5}\text{-}10^{6}\,\Omega\text{m},\ \sigma \sim 10^{+5}\text{-}10^{-6}\text{Sm}^{-1}$$

(iii) **Insulators** They have **high resistivity** and **low conductivity**.

For example, rubber, plastic, putty, etc.

$$\rho \sim 10^{11}\text{-}10^{19}\Omega\text{m}, \sigma \sim 10^{-11}\text{-}10^{-19}\ \text{Sm}^{-1}$$

The values of ρ and σ given above are indicative of magnitude and could well go outside the ranges as well.

Semiconductor can be of the following types

(i) **Element semiconductors** These semiconductors are available in natural form.

e.g. Silicon (Si) and germanium (Ge).

(ii) **Compound semiconductors** These semiconductors are made by compounding the metals. e.g.
   (a) Inorganic semiconductors are CdS, GaAs, CdSe, InP, etc.
   (b) Organic semiconductors are anthracene, doped pthalocyanines, etc.
   (c) Organic polymer semiconductors are polypyrrole, polyaniline, polythiophene, etc.

14.2 Energy Bands in Solids

According to Bohr's atomic model and concept of electronic configuration in an isolated atom, the electrons have definite discrete amounts of energy corresponding to different shells and subshells, i.e. there are well-defined energy levels of electrons in an isolated atom.

But in a crystal due to interatomic interaction, valence electrons are shared by more than one atom. Due to this, splitting of energy level takes place. The collection of these closely spaced energy levels is called an **energy band.** These bands are formed due to the continuous energy variation in different energy levels.

These different energy levels for different electrons are formed because inside the crystal, each electron has a unique position and no two electrons are exactly at the same pattern of surrounding charges.

Valence Band

The energy band which includes the energy levels of the valence electrons is called valence band or **the range of energies possessed by the valence electrons is called valence band.**

This band may be partially or completely filled with electrons but is never empty. In this band, electrons are not capable of gaining energy from external electric field. So, **it does not contribute to electric current.**

Conduction Band

The energy band above the valence band is called conduction band or **the range of energies possessed by the conduction electrons is called conduction band.**

At room temperature, this band is either empty or partially filled with electrons. Electrons can gain energy from external electric field, then jump from valence to conduction band and **contribute to the electric current.**

Energy Band Gap

The minimum energy required for shifting electrons from valence band to conduction band is called **energy band gap(E_g).**

- It is the gap between the top of the valence band and bottom of the conduction band.
- It can be zero, small or large depending upon the material.
- If λ is the wavelength of radiation used in shifting the electron from valence band to conduction band, then energy band gap is

$$E_g = h\nu = hc/\lambda$$

where, h is called Planck's constant and c is the velocity of light.

Fermi Energy

It is the maximum possible energy possessed by free electrons of a material at absolute zero temperature (i.e. 0 K).

- **The value of fermi energy is different for different materials.**

14.3 Semiconductors

The materials whose conductivity lie between metals and insulators are known as semiconductors. They are characterised by narrow energy gap (less than 3eV) between the valence band and conduction band.

At low temperatures, pure semiconductors behave like insulators.

Electrons and Holes in Semiconductors

At room temperature, however some of the valence electrons acquire thermal energy greater than E_g and move into conduction band.

A vacancy is created in the valence band at each place where an electron was present before moving into conduction band. This vacancy is called hole.

It is a seat of positive charge of magnitude equal to the charge of an electron. Thus, free electrons in the conduction band and the holes are created in the valence band, which can move even under a small applied field. Thus, conduction in semiconductor material occurs due to electrons and holes.

Difference between Conductor, Insulator and Semiconductor on the basis of Energy Bands

Conductor (Metal)	Insulator	Semiconductor
In conductor, either there is no energy gap between the conduction band and valence band or both the bands overlap each other. Thus, many electrons shift to higher energy levels, i.e., above the **fermi level** in the conduction band and behave as free electrons by acquiring a little more energy from any other sources.	In insulator, the valence band is completely filled, the conduction band is completely empty and **energy gap is quite large** due to which energy from any other sources cannot help electrons to overcome it. Thus, electrons are bound to valence band and are not free to move. Hence, **electric conduction** is not possible in this type of material.	In semiconductor, the valence band is completely filled and the conduction band is empty but the energy gap between conduction band and valence band, is very small. Thus, at room temperature, some electrons in the **valence band** acquire thermal **energy greater than energy band gap** and jump over to the conduction band where they are free to move under the influence of even a small electric field and acquire small conductivity.
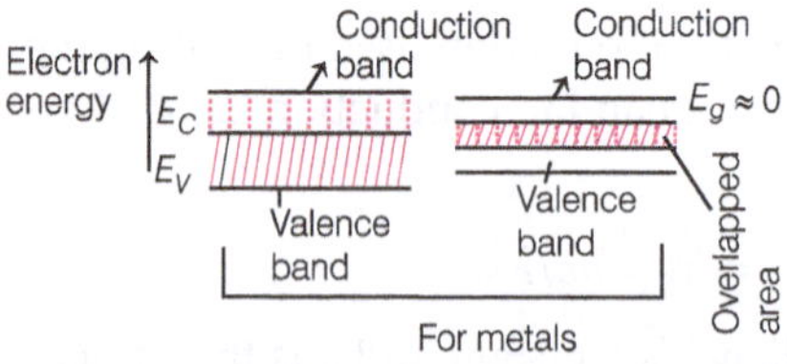	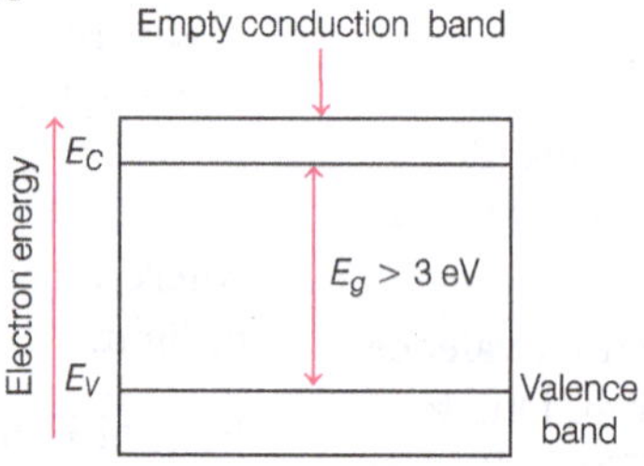	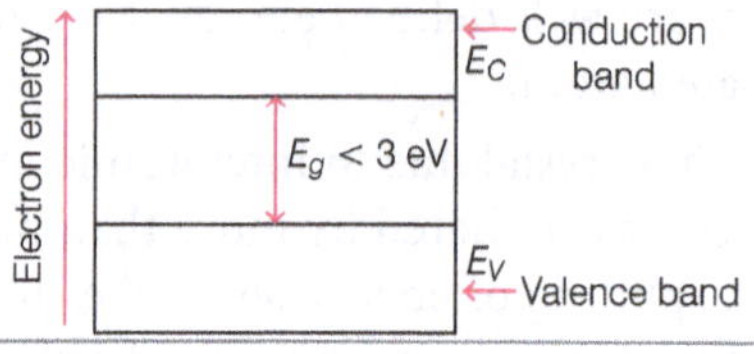

On the basis of purity, semiconductors are of two types

Intrinsic Semiconductors

This type of semiconductor is also called an **undoped semiconductor** or ***i*-type semiconductor**. It is a pure semiconductor without any significant presence of dopant species.

In intrinsic semiconductors, the number of excited electrons is equal to number of holes, i.e. $n_h = n_i$. where n_i is called intrinsic carrier concentration.

Under the action of an electric field, electrons move towards the positive potential and holes move towards negative potential giving hole current I_h. The total current I is the sum of the electron current I_e and the hole current I_h, i.e.

$$I = I_e + I_h.$$

It may be noted that a simultaneous process of recombination occurs in which the electrons recombine with the holes. **At equilibrium, the rate of generation is equal to rate of recombination of charge carriers.** The recombination occurs due to an electron colliding with a hole as shown in Figs. (a) and (b).

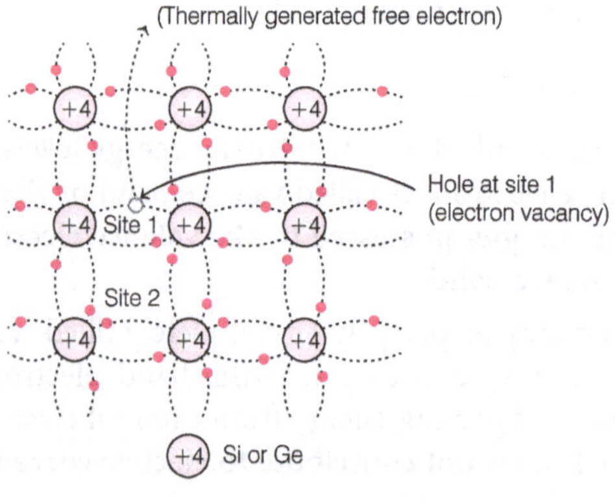

Fig. (a) is representing the generation of hole at site 1 and conduction electron due to thermal energy at moderate temperature

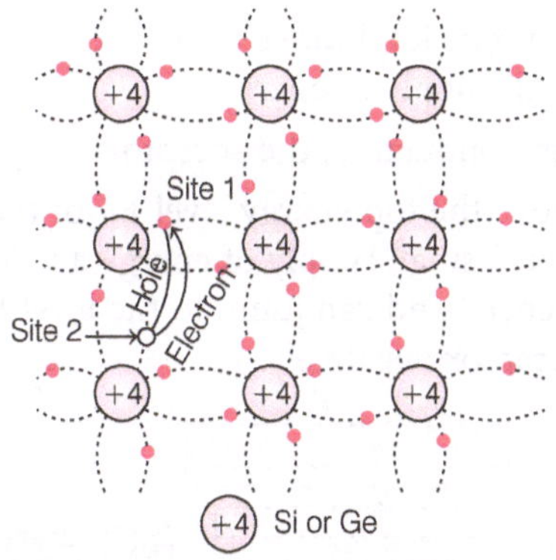

Fig. (b) is representing possible thermal motion of a hole. The electron from the lower left hand covalent bond (site 2) goes to the earlier hole site 1, leaving a hole at its site indicating an apparent movement of the hole from site 1 to site 2.

An intrinsic semiconductor behaves like an insulator at $T = 0\,K$. These thermally excited electrons at $T > 0\,K$ partially occupy the conduction band.

They come from the valence band leaving equal number of holes there as shown below in figure.

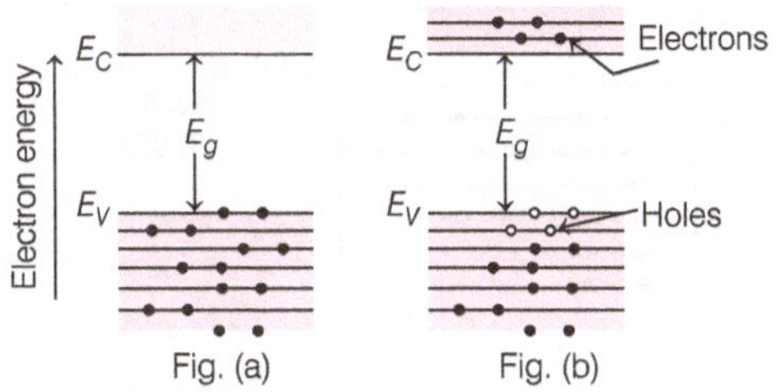

Fig. (a) an intrinsic semiconductor at $T > 0\,K$ behaves like an insulator. Fig. (b) is representing four thermally generated electron-hole pairs at $T > 0\,K$

Extrinsic Semiconductors

A semiconductor in which some impurity are embedded are known as extrinsic or impure semiconductors.

The process of adding impurity to an intrinsic semiconductor in a controlled manner is called **doping** and impurity which is added is called **dopant.**

There are two types of dopants used in doping.

(i) **Trivalent** (valency 3) atoms: e.g., Indium (In), Boron (B), aluminium (Al), etc.

(ii) **Pentavalent** (valency 5) atoms: e.g., Arsenic (As), Antimony (Sb), Phosphorous (P), etc.

Extrinsic semiconductors are basically of two types

(i) *n*-type semiconductors

(ii) *p*-type semiconductors

n-Type Semiconductors

This type of semiconductor is obtained when pentavalent impurity is added to Si or Ge. The four electrons of pentavalent element bond with the four silicon neighbours while fifth remains very weakly bound to its parent atom and are almost free to move. These electrons are donated by the impurity atoms, also known as **donor atoms.**

The conduction inside such type of semiconductor will take place with the help of the negatively charged electrons and hence it is called as ***n*-type semiconductors.**

When semiconductor are placed at room temperature, some of its covalent bonds break and free electrons are generated. As a result, same number of holes are also created.

Due to the presence of donated electron, number of holes are comparatively less compare to free electron.

i.e. $n_e >> n_h$

Therefore, major conduction in *n*-type semiconductors is due to electrons. So, electrons are known as **majority, carriers** and the holes are known as the **minority carriers.**

This means, $n_e >> n_h$; $I_e >> I_h$

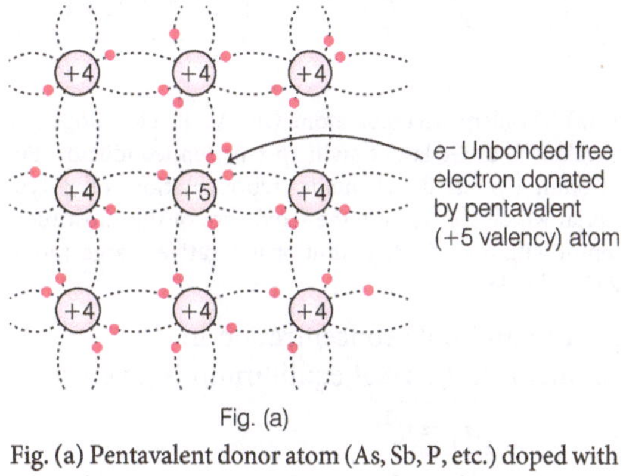

Fig. (a) Pentavalent donor atom (As, Sb, P, etc.) doped with tetravalent Si or Ge giving *n*-type semiconductor

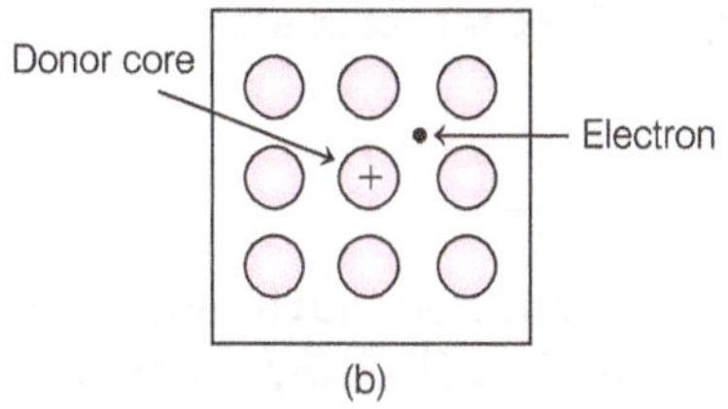

Fig. (b) Commonly used schematic representation for *n*-type material which shows only the fixed cores of the semiconductor material.

p-Type Semiconductors

This type of semiconductor is obtained when a trivalent impurity is added to Si or Ge. So, the three valence electron of the impurity atom will form covalent bonds with the adjoining three atoms of germanium (Ge), while there will be one incomplete covalent bond with a neighbouring Ge atom, this deficiency of an electron creates a hole.

- These trivalent atoms are called **acceptor atoms** and the conduction of current occurs due to motion of holes.
- This means, in this type of semiconductor, majority charge carriers are holes and minority charge carries are electrons.
  i.e. $n_h >> n_e$

$\therefore$ $I_h >> I_e$, hence these conductors are known as ***p*-type semiconductor or acceptor type semiconductor.**

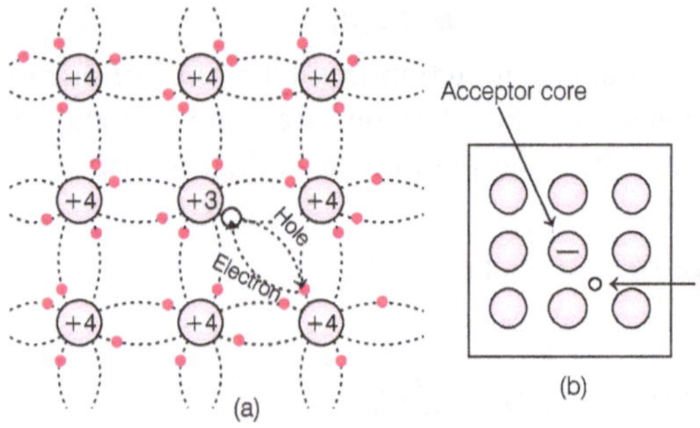

Fig. (a) Trivalent acceptor atom (In, Al, B, etc.) doped in tetravalent Si or Ge lattice giving *p*-type semiconductor. Fig. (b) Commonly used schematic representation of *p*-type material which shows only the fixed core of the substituent acceptor with one effective additional negative charge and its associated hole.

The electron and hole concentration in a semiconductor in thermal equilibrium is given by

$$n_e n_h = n_i^2$$

Note The energy gaps of C, Si and Ge are 5.4 eV, 1.1 eV and 0.7 eV, respectively.
Sn is a group IV element as its energy gaps is zero.

Energy Band in Extrinsic Semiconductors

In extrinsic semiconductors, additional energy states due to donor impurities (E_D) and acceptor impurities (E_A) also exist. In the energy band diagram of *n*-type semiconductor, the donor energy level E_D is slightly below the bottom E_C of conduction band and the electrons from this level move into conduction band with very small supply of energy.

In *p*-type semiconductors, the acceptor energy level E_A is slightly above the top energy level E_V of the valence band. With very small supply of energy an electron from the valence band can jump to the level E_A and ionise the acceptor negatively.

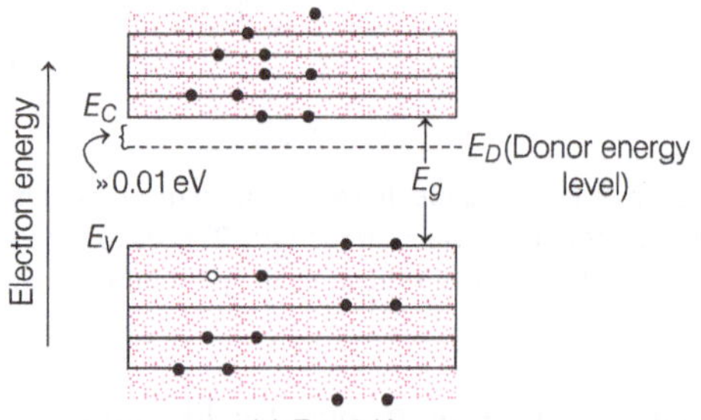

(a) $T > 0$ K
one thermally generated electron-hole pair +9 electrons from donor atoms

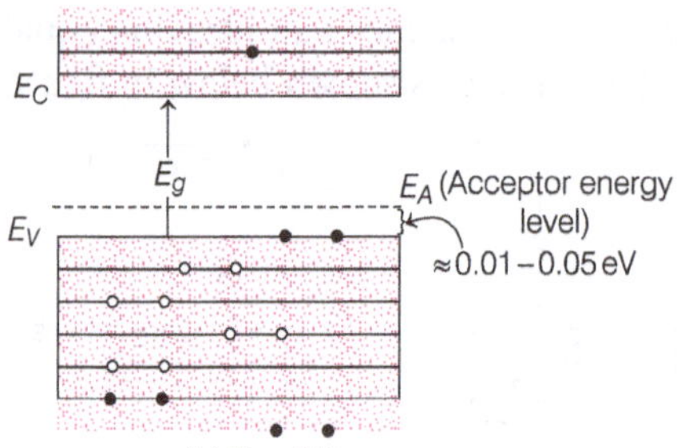

(b) $T > 0$ K

Energy bands of (a) *n*-type semiconductor at $T > 0$ K,
(b) *p*-type semiconductor at $T > 0$ K

Example 1. **A semiconductor material has equal hole and electron concentration of $6 \times 10^{10}\ m^{-3}$. On doping with certain impurity the electron concentration increases to $12 \times 10^{12}\ m^{-3}$. Find the new hole concentration in the semiconductor.**

Sol. Here,
$$n_i = 6 \times 10^{10}\ m^{-3}$$
$$n_e = 12 \times 10^{12}\ m^{-3}$$

We know that $n_e \cdot n_h = n_i^2$

$$\Rightarrow \quad n_h = \frac{n_i^2}{n_e} = \frac{(6 \times 10^{10})^2}{12 \times 10^{12}}$$
$$= 3 \times 10^8\ m^{-3}$$

Example 2. **The number of silicon atoms per m^3 is 5×10^{28}. This is doped simultaneously with 5×10^{22} atoms per m^3 of arsenic and 5×10^{20} atoms per m^3 of indium. Calculate the number of electrons and holes. Given that, $n_i = 1.5 \times 10^{16}\ m^{-3}$. Is the material *n*-type or *p*-type?**

Sol. For each atom doped with arsenic, one free electron is received. Similarly, for each atom doped of indium, a vacancy is created. So, number of free electrons introduced by pentavalent impurity is

$$N_{As} = 5\times 10^{22}\ m^{-3}$$

The number of holes introduced by trivalent impurity added is $N_I = 5\times 10^{20}\ m^{-3}$

So, net number of electrons added is

$$n_e = N_{As} - N_I = 5\times10^{22} - 5\times10^{20}$$
$$= 4.95\times10^{22}\ m^{-3}$$

We know that, $n_e n_h = n_i^2$

So, $$n_h = \frac{n_i^2}{n_e} = \frac{(1.5\times10^{16})^2}{4.95\times10^{22}} = 4.54\times10^9\ m^{-3}$$

As, $n_e > n_h$ (number of holes). So, the material is n-type semiconductor.

Quick Test 1

Conceptual Questions

1. Write any two distinguishing features between conductors, semiconductors and insulators on the basis of energy band diagrams.
2. Sn, C and Si, Ge are all group XIV elements. Yet, Sn is a conductor, C is an insulator while Si and Ge are semiconductors. Why? NCERT Exemplar
3. In a pure semiconductor crystal of Si, if antimony is added, then what type of extrinsic semiconductor is obtained? Draw the energy band diagram of this extrinsic semiconductor so formed.

Numerical Questions

4. A non-ideal diode causes a voltage drop of 0.2 V when in forward bias. The diode burns out, if the current through it exceeds 8 mA through it.
   In which of the following instances will this diode run the risk of burning out? Show the working.
   (i) A battery of 4.2 V and resistor of 1 kΩ connected in series to the diode.
   (ii) A battery of 6.2 V and a resistor of 0.6 kΩ connected in series to the diode.
5. The impurity levels of doped semiconductor are 30 meV below the conduction band. Determine whether the semiconductor is n-type or p-type. At the room temperature, thermal collisions occur as a result of which, the extra electron loosely bound to the impurity ion gets an amount of energy kT and hence this electron can jump into conduction band. What is the value of T ?
   (Take, k is Boltzmann constant $= 8.62\times10^{-5}$ eV/K.)

Answers

5. 348.02 K

For Solutions, See QR Code on Pg. 448

14.4 *p-n* Junction

It is an arrangement made by a close contact of n-type semiconductor and p-type semiconductor. There are various methods of forming p-n junction.

Formation of *p-n* Junction

In one method, an n-type germanium crystal is cut into thin slices called **wafers.** An aluminium film is laid on an n-type wafer, which is then heated in an oven at a temperature of about 600° C. Aluminium then diffuses into the surface of wafer. In this way, a p-n junction is formed.

Formation of Depletion Region in *p-n* Junction

In an n-type semiconductor, the concentration of electrons is more than that of holes.
Similarly, in a p-type semiconductor, the concentration of holes is more than that of electrons.

During the formation of p-n junction and due to the concentration gradient across p and n-sides, holes diffuse from p-side to n-side ($p \rightarrow n$) and electrons diffuse from n-side to p-side ($n \rightarrow p$).

The diffused charge carriers combine with their counterparts in the immediate vicinity of the junction and neutralise each other.

Thus, positive charge is built on n-side and negative charge on p-side near the junction.

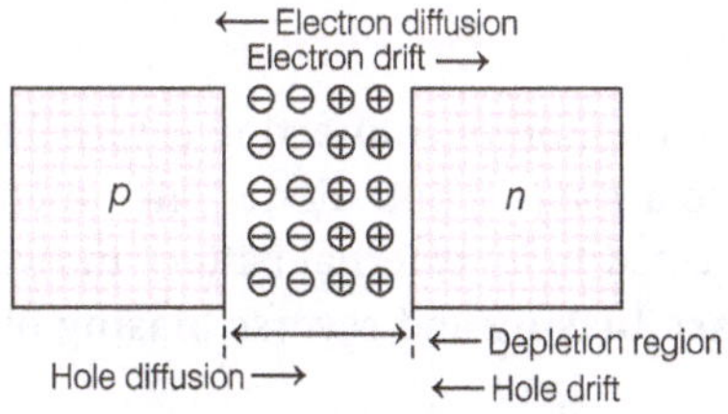

p-n junction formation process

This sets up potential difference across the junction and an internal electric field E_i directed from n-side to p-side.

- The equilibrium is established when the field E_i becomes strong enough to stop further diffusion of the majority charge carriers (however, it helps the minority charge carriers to diffuse across the junction).
- The region on either side of the junction which becomes depleted (free) from the mobile charge carriers is called **depletion region** or **depletion layer.**

The width of depletion region is of the order of 10^{-6} m.

- The potential difference developed across the depletion region is called the **potential barrier** (V_B). It depends on dopant concentration in the semiconductor and temperature of the junction.

TEACHER TIP

- Due to the diffusion of holes from p-side to n-side and electrons from n-side to p-side at the junction, a current rises from p-side to n-side, which is called **diffusion current.**
- If an electron-hole pair is created on the depletion region due to thermal collision, the electrons are pushed by the electric field towards the n-side and the holes towards the p-side, which gives rise to a current from n-side to p-side known as **drift current.**
- In steady state, diffusion current = drift current.

14.5 Semiconductor Diode or *p-n* Junction Diode

It is basically a p-n junction with metallic contacts provided at the ends for the application of an external voltage. It is a two terminal device.

- It is represented by the symbol 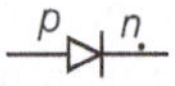

- The **direction of arrow indicates the conventional direction of current.**

Forward Biasing and Reverse Biasing of Junction Diode

Biasing is the method of connecting external battery or emf source to a p-n junction diode. The junction diode can be connected to an external battery in two ways, called **forward biasing** and **reverse biasing** of the junction.

Forward Biasing

A junction diode is said to be forward biased when the positive terminal of the external battery is connected to the p-side and negative terminal to the n-side of the diode.

Flow of Current in Forward Biasing

In this situation, the forward voltage opposes the potential barrier, due to which both the potential barrier and **width of the depletion layer decreases.** Under the effect of external electric field, holes in the p-region and electrons in the n-region, both move towards the junction.

For each electron-hole combination, a covalent bond breaks up in the p-region near the positive terminal of the battery.

Out of the hole and electron so produced, the hole moves towards the junction, while the electron enters the positive terminal of the battery through the connecting wire.

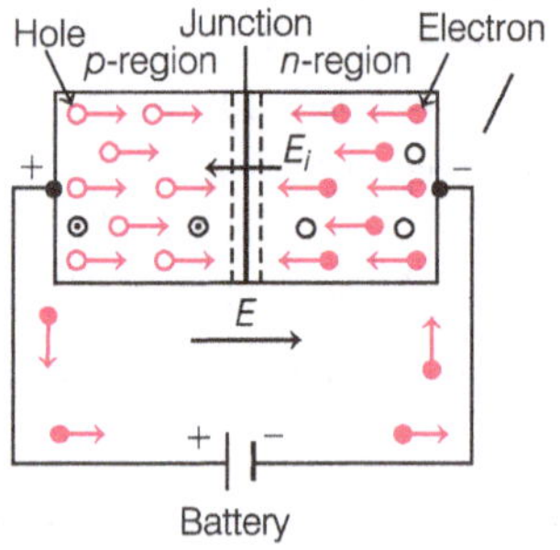

Forward biasing of junction diode

Just at this moment, an electron is released from the negative terminal of the battery which enters the n-region to replace the electron lost by combining with a hole at the junction. Thus, a current called **forward current** is constituted by the motion of majority charge carriers across the junction.

In forward bias, the junction diode offers low resistance.

Reverse Biasing

A junction diode is said to be reverse biased when the positive terminal of the external battery is connected to the n-side and negative terminal to the p-side of the diode.

Flow of Current in Reverse Biasing

In this situation, the reverse voltage supports the potential barrier, due to which both the potential barrier and **width of the depletion layer increases.**

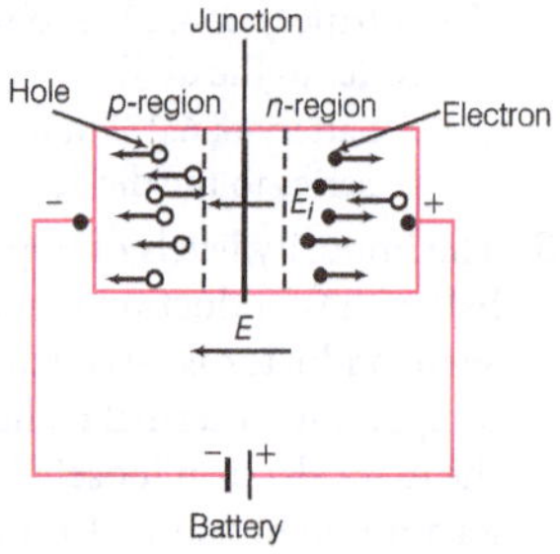

Reverse biasing of junction diode

Under the effect of external electric field, holes in the p-region and electrons in the n-region are pushed away from the junction i.e. they cannot be combined at the junction. So, **there is almost no flow of current due to majority charge carriers.**

However, a very small current due to minority charge carriers flows across the junction. This current is called **reverse current.**

I-V Characteristics of p-n Junction Diode

The graphical relations between voltage applied across *p-n* junction and current flowing through the junction are called ***I-V* characteristics of junction diode.**

Forward Biased Characteristics

The circuit diagram for studying forward biased characteristics is shown in the figure (a). Starting from a low value, forward bias voltage is increased step by step (measured by voltmeter) and forward current is noted (by ammeter). A graph is plotted between voltage and current is shown in figure (b).

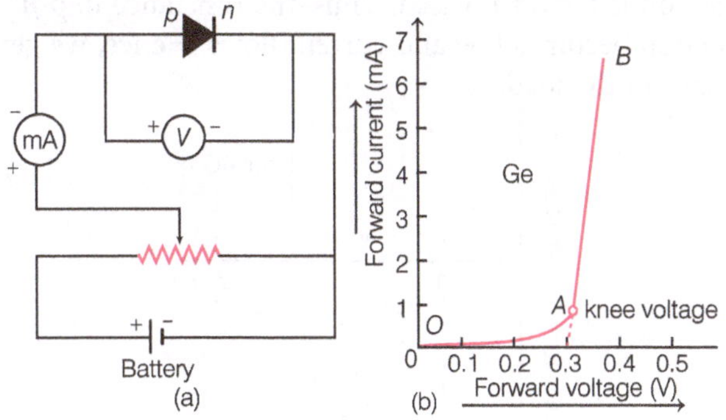

Forward biased characteristic of a diode

- The current through the diode is almost zero at low voltage, due to the potential barrier, which oppose the applied voltage.
- When applied voltage exceeds the potential barrier, the current starts increasing slowly. Further, increase in applied voltage, the current increases very rapidly (*AB* portion of the graph).
- The forward voltage beyond which the current through the junction starts increasing rapidly with voltage is called **knee voltage** or **threshold voltage** which is 0.3 V for Ge and 0.7 for Si.

Reverse Biased Characteristics

The circuit diagram for studying reverse biased characteristics is shown in the figure (a).

- In reverse bias, a very small current flows across the junction due to minority charge carriers. Motion of minority charge carriers is also supported by internal potential barrier.
- Therefore, **the small reverse current remains almost constant over a sufficiently long range of reverse bias,** increasing very little with increasing voltage (*OC* portion of the graph).

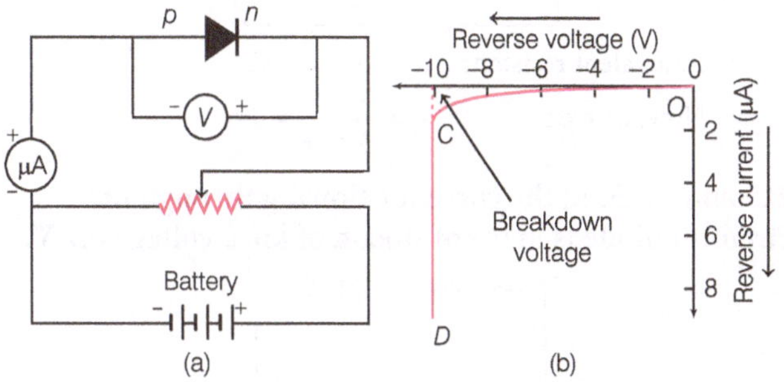

Reverse biased characteristic of a diode

- This reverse current is voltage independent upto certain voltage known as **breakdown voltage** and this voltage independent current is called **reverse saturation current.**

Avalanche Breakdown

If the reverse bias is equal to the breakdown voltage, then the reverse current through the junction increases very rapidly (*CD* portion of the graph), this situation is called **avalanche breakdown** and the junction may get damaged due to excessive heating if this current exceeds the rated value of *p-n* junction.

Dynamic Resistance

In diodes, a resistance is offered by the function which depends on the applied voltage, which is called **dynamic resistance.** It is the ratio of small change in voltage to the small change in current produced.

Dynamic resistance, $r_d = \dfrac{\Delta V}{\Delta I}$.

Example 3. Find the current I_1 and I_2 shown below if diodes D_1 and D_2 are ideal.

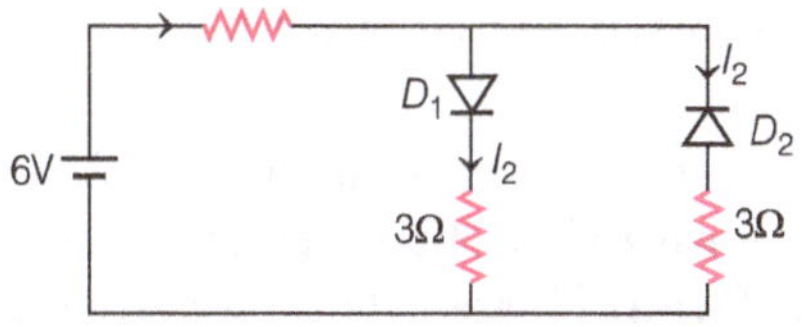

Sol. From the given circuit diagram, diode D_1 is in forward bias whereas diode D_2 is in reverse bias. Hence, no current will flow through diode D_2.

$\therefore \quad I_2 = 0$

Now, circuit diagram is reduced as

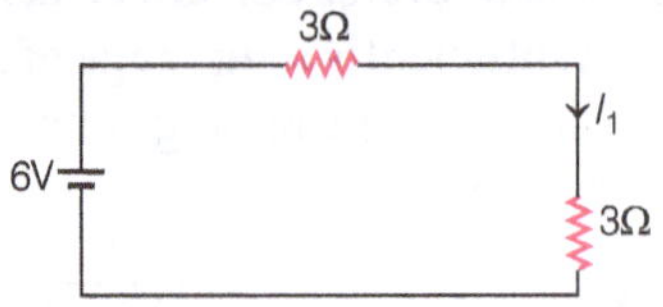

∴ Equivalent resistance, $R = 3 + 3 = 6\,\Omega$

Now, Current $I_1 = \frac{V}{R} = \frac{6}{6} = 1\text{ A}$

Example 4. **Find the current I flowing through the circuit if diode is made of silicon of knee voltage 0.7 V.**

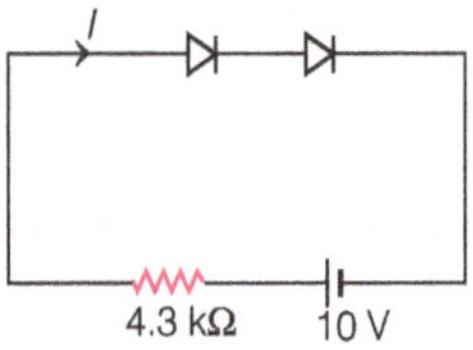

Sol. Given, knee voltage of silicon diode $V_1 = V_2 = 0.7$ V

Since, both diodes are connected in forward bias, hence circuit diagram is redrawn as

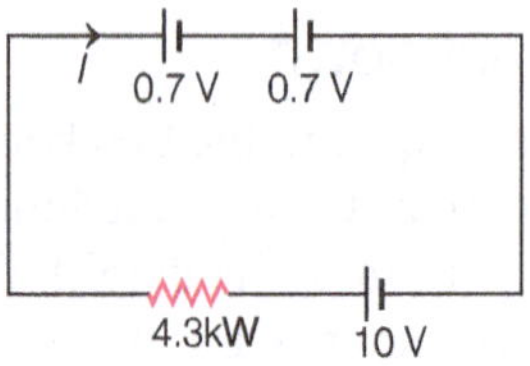

Applying KVL in the loop,

$$-10 + 4.3 \times 10^3 I + 0.7 + 0.7 = 0$$

$$\Rightarrow \quad I = \frac{8.6}{4.3 \times 10^3} = 2 \times 10^{-3}\text{ A} = 2\text{ mA}$$

14.6 Diode as a Rectifier

The process of converting alternating voltage/current into direct voltage/current is called **rectification**. Diode is used as a rectifier for converting alternating current/voltage into direct current/voltage.

Principle

From the V-I characteristic of a junction diode, we see that it allows current to pass only when it is forward biased.

So, if an alternating voltage is applied across a diode, the **current flows only in that part of the cycle when the diode is forward biased.** This property is used to rectify the current/voltage.

There are two ways of using a diode as a rectifier, i.e.

(i) Diode as a half-wave rectifier

(ii) Diode as a full wave rectifier

Diode as a Half-Wave Rectifier

In this, the AC voltage to be rectified is connected to the primary coil of a step-down transformer and secondary coil is connected to the diode through resistor R_L across which output is obtained.

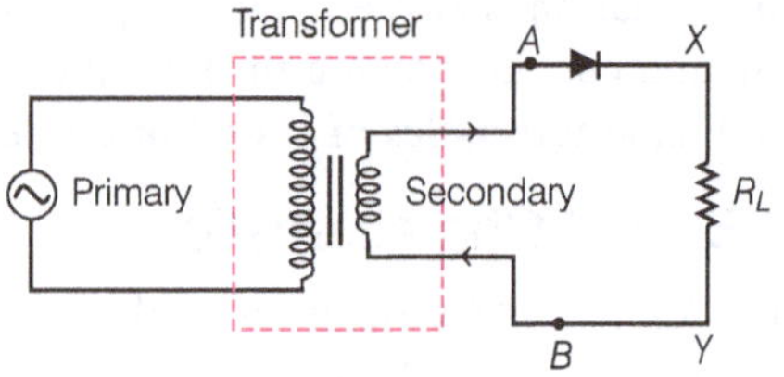

Circuit diagram of half-wave rectifier

Working

During positive half cycle of the input AC, the p-n junction is forward biased. Thus, the resistance in p-n junction becomes low and current flows. Hence, we get output in the load.

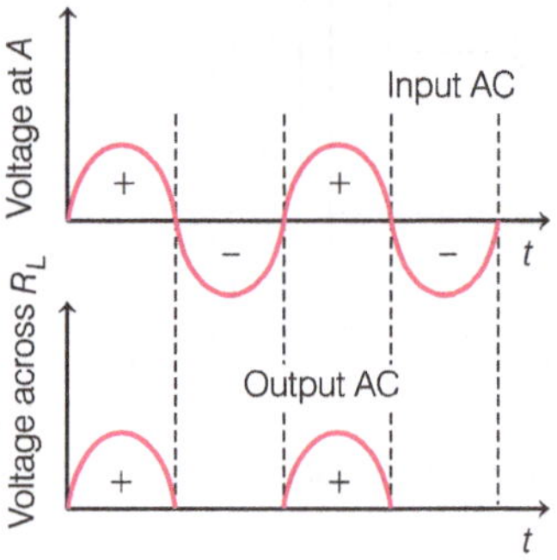

Input and output waveforms

During negative half cycle of the input AC, the p-n junction is reverse biased. Thus, the resistance of p-n junction is high and current does not flow. Hence, no output is in the load.

Diode as a Full Wave Rectifier

In the full wave rectifier, two p-n junction diodes, D_1 and D_2 are used. This arrangement is shown in the diagram below.

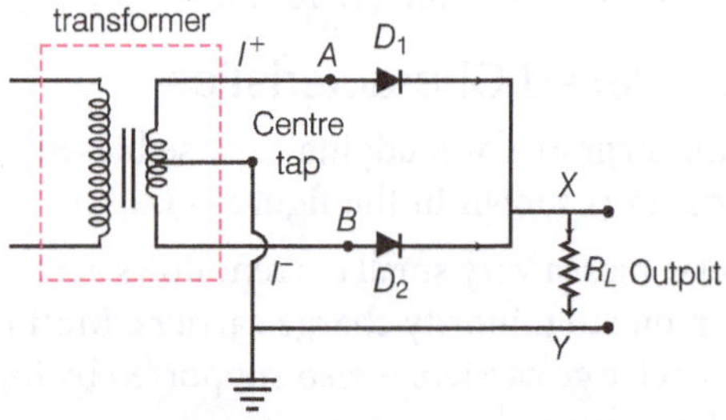

Circuit diagram of full wave rectifier

Working

During the positive half cycle of the input AC, the diode D_1 is forward biased and the diode D_2 is reverse biased. The forward current flows through diode D_1.

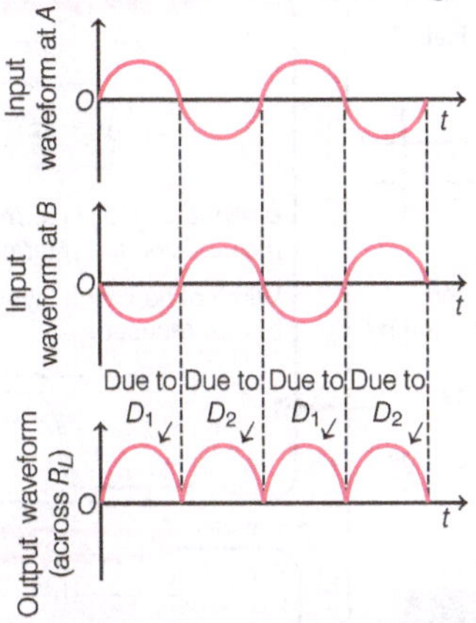

Input and output waveforms

During the negative half cycle of the input AC, the diode D_1 is reverse biased and diode D_2 is forward biased. Hence, current flows through diode D_2. Hence, we find that during both the halves, current flows in the same direction.

Role of Filters

In order to get the steady DC output from the pulsating voltage normally, a capacitor is connected across the output terminals (parallel to load R_L). An inductor can also be used in series for the same purpose.

As these additional circuits appear to filter out the AC ripple and provide a pure DC voltage, so they are called **filters**.

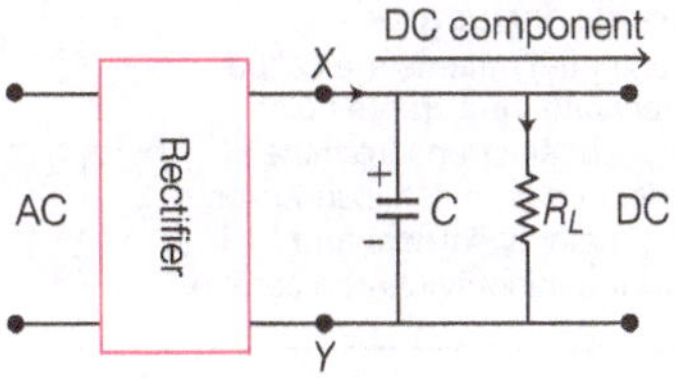

Fig. (a)

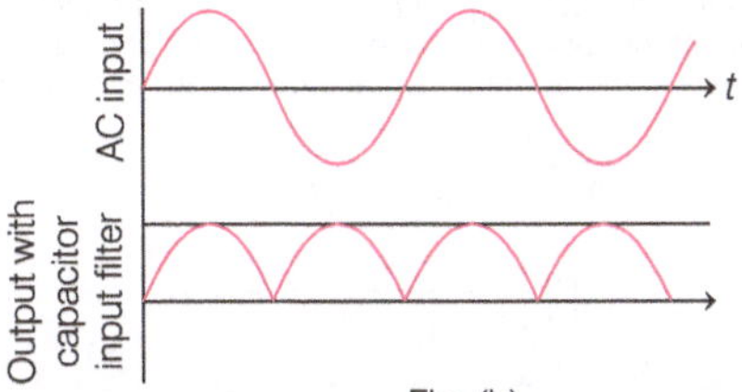

Fig. (b)

A full wave rectifier with capacitor filter Fig. (a) and input and output voltage of rectifier in Fig. (b).

Role of Capacitor in Filtering

The capacitor offers high resistance to low frequency signal and low resistance to high frequency signal.

Using the formula, $X_e = \frac{1}{2\pi f_e}$. Due to this, the 'AC' component is bypassed or filtered out.

It produces a voltage drop across load resistance R_L as a filtered DC output.

Quick Test 2

1. How does the width of a depletion region of a p-n junction vary, if doping concentration is increased?
2. Briefly explain how a potential barrier is set up across a p-n junction as a result of diffusion and drift of the charge carriers. *All India 2020*
3. Explain the formation of potential barrier and depletion region in a p-n junction diode. What is effect of applying forward bias on the width of depletion region? *Delhi 2020*
4. Define the following terms used in electronic devices.
   (i) Reverse breakdown voltage
   (ii) I-V characteristic of forward biased diode
5. Write the two processes that take place in the formation of a p-n junction. Explain with the help of a diagram, the formation of depletion region and barrier potential in a p-n junction.
6. (i) In the following diagram, is the junction diode forward biased or reverse biased?

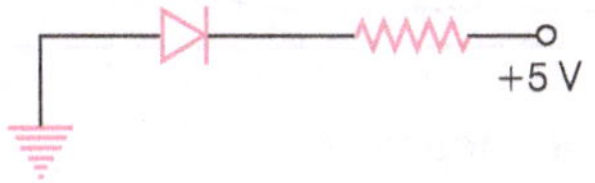

   (ii) Draw the circuit diagram of a full wave rectifier and state how it works?
7. Explain with the help of a circuit diagram, the working of a p-n junction diode as a half-wave rectifier.
8. Assuming an ideal diode, draw the output waveform for the circuit given in the figure, explain the waveform. *NCERT Exemplar*

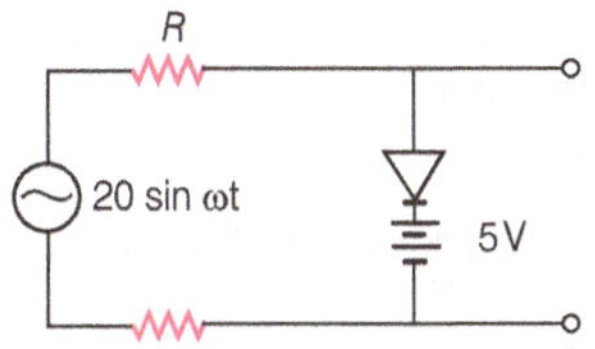

9. A student wants to use two p-n junction diodes to convert alternating current into direct current. Draw the labelled circuit diagram she would use and explain, how it works?

For Solutions, See QR Code on Pg. 448

Mind Map

Semiconductor Electronics

Classification of Solids on the Basis of their Electrical Properties

(i) Metals have very low resistivity or high conductivity.

$\rho \approx 10^{-2}\text{-}10^{-8}\ \Omega m$
$\sigma \approx 10^{2}\text{-}10^{8}\ Sm^{-1}$

(ii) Insulators have high resistivity or low conductivity.

$\rho \approx 10^{11} - 10^{-18}\ \Omega m$
$\sigma \approx 10^{-11} - 10^{-19}\ Sm^{-1}$

(iii) Semiconductors possess resistivity or conductivity intermediate to metals and insulators.

$\rho \approx 10^{-5}\text{-}10^{+6}\ \Omega m$
$\sigma \approx 10^{5}\text{-}10^{-6}\ Sm^{-1}$

Energy Bands in Solids

- **Valence Band (VB)**
  It is the range of energies of valence electron.
- **Conduction Band (CB)**
  It is the range of energies of conduction electron.

(a) For insulators $E_g \approx 15$ eV
(b) For conductors $E_g \approx 0$
(c) For semiconductor $E_g \approx 1$ eV

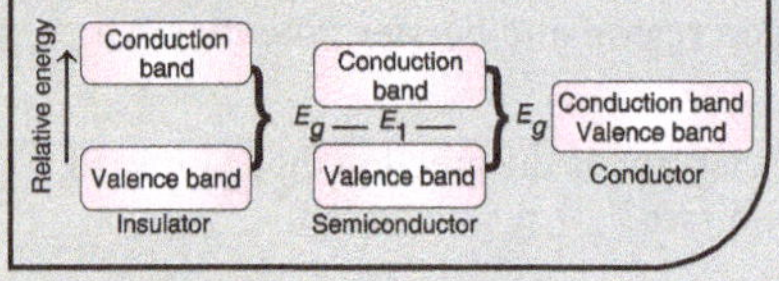

Semiconductor is a material whose electrical conductivity lies between that of a conductor (like metals) and an insulator (like glass).

Semiconductor Diode

It is a material that allows current to flow in one direction while blocking it in the opposite direction.
A diode consists of a ***p-n* junction**, which is formed by joining
***p*-type material** Contains holes (positive charge carriers).
***n*-type material** Contains electrons (negative charge carriers).

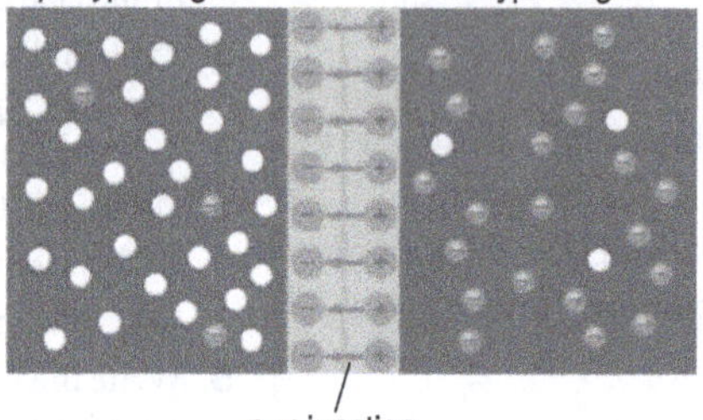

Forward Biasing

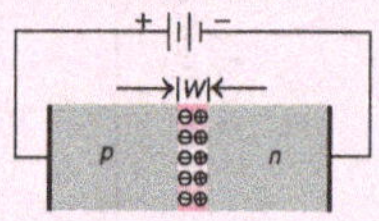

p connected to (+) terminal of battery.
n connected to (–) terminal of battery.

Width of depletion layer and potential barrier reduced.

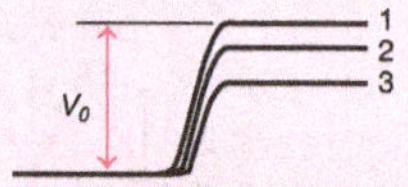

Reverse Biasing

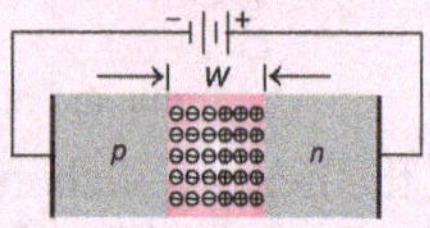

p connected to (–) terminal of battery.
n connected to (+) terminal of battery.

Width of depletion layer and potential barrier increases.

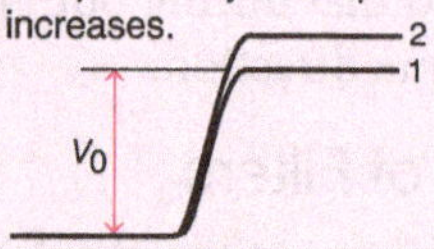

Intrinsic Semiconductors

Pure materials like silicon (Si) and germanium (Ge) that exhibit semiconducting properties naturally.

Extrinsic Semiconductors Doped materials where impurities are added to enhance conductivity.

- ***n*-type** Doped with elements that add extra electrons (negative charge carriers).
- ***p*-type** Doped with elements that create holes or a lack of electrons (positive charge carriers).

Types of Extrinsic Semiconductor

- ***n*-type semiconductors**
  The pentavalent impurity is used in this type of semiconductor.
  In *n*-type semiconductors, electrons are the majority charge carriers and holes are the minority charge carriers.

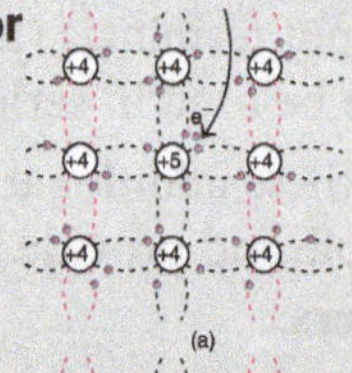

- ***p*-type semiconductors**
  The trivalent impurity atoms are called acceptors because they create holes which can accept electrons from the nearby bonds. In *p*-type semiconductor, holes are the majority carriers and electrons are the minority charge carriers.

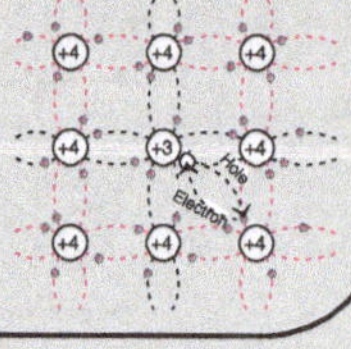

Diode as a Rectifier

A device which rectifies AC to DC.

- **Half-wave rectifier**
  During positive half cycle of input AC, the diode is reverse biased, hence current doesn't flow.

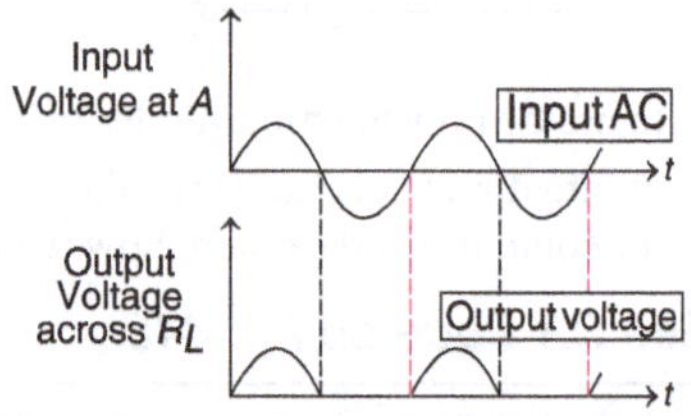

- **Full wave rectifier**
  During positive half cycle diode D_1 is forward biased and D_2 reverse biased and during the negative half cycle D_2 is forward biased and D_1 is reverse biased. Hence, current flows throughout the full cycle of AC.

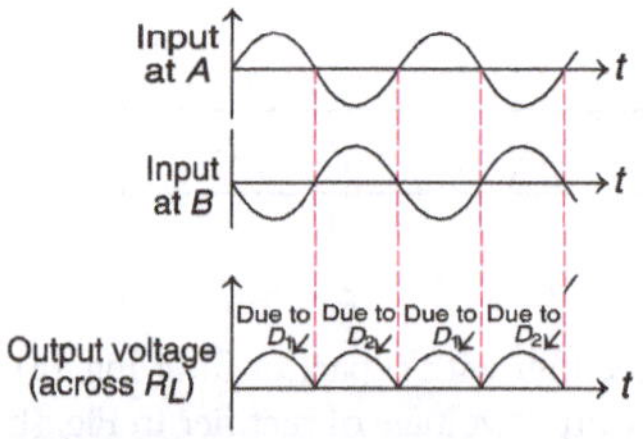

EXAM PATTERN QUESTIONS

Objective Type Questions

Multiple Choice Questions (MCQs)

1. The conductivity of a semiconductor increases with increase in temperature, because **NCERT Exemplar**

(a) number density of free current carriers increases
(b) relaxation time increases
(c) both number density of carriers and relaxation time increase
(d) number density current of carriers increases, relaxation time decreases but effect of decrease in relaxation time is much less than increase in number density

2. The number of electrons made available for conduction by dopant atoms depends strongly upon **SQP 2024-25**

(a) doping level
(b) increase in ambient temperature
(c) energy gap
(d) Both (a) and (b)

3. In figure given below, V_0 is the potential barrier across a *p-n* junction, when no battery is connected across the junction. **Competency Based Que**

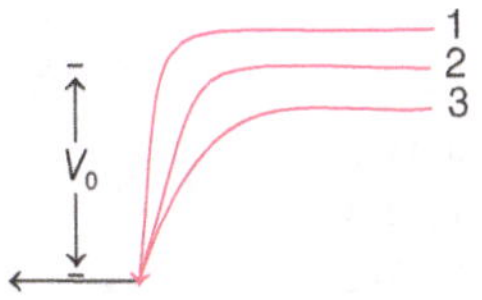

Choose the correct statement.

(a) 1 and 3 both correspond to forward bias of junction
(b) 3 corresponds to forward bias of junction and 1 corresponds to reverse bias of junction
(c) 1 corresponds to forward bias and 3 corresponds to reverse bias of junction
(d) 3 and 1 both correspond to reverse bias of junction

4. At a certain temperature in an intrinsic semiconductor, the electrons and holes concentration is $1.5 \times 10^{16}\ m^{-3}$. When it is doped with a trivalent dopant, hole concentration increases to $4.5 \times 10^{22}\ m^{-3}$. In the doped semiconductor, the concentration of electrons (n_e) will be **CBSE 2023**

(a) $3 \times 10^{6}\ m^{-3}$ (b) $5 \times 10^{7}\ m^{-3}$
(c) $5 \times 10^{9}\ m^{-3}$ (d) $6.75 \times 10^{38}\ m^{-3}$

5. If a *p-n* junction diode is reverse biased. **CBSE 2023**

(a) the potential barrier is lowered.
(b) the potential barrier remains unaffected.
(c) the potential barrier is raised
(d) the current is mainly due to majority charge carriers.

6. During the formation of a *p-n* junction **CBSE 2023**

(a) diffusion current keeps increasing
(b) drift current remains constant
(c) both the diffusion current and drift current remain constant.
(d) diffusion current remains almost constant but drift current increases till both currents-become equal

7. The formation of depletion region in a *p-n* junction diode is due to **CBSE 2023**

(a) movement of dopant atoms
(b) diffusion of the electrons and holes
(c) drift of electrons only
(d) drift of holes only

8. When the resistance measured between *p* and *n* ends of a *p-n* junction diode is high, it can act as a/an- **CBSE 2025**

(a) resistor (b) inductor (c) capacitor (d) switch

9. The energy gap is much more in silicon than in germanium because

(a) its crystal has much stronger bonds
(b) its valence electrons are more tightly bound to their parent nuclei
(c) it has high atomic mass number
(d) it has less number of electrons

10. The threshold voltage for a *p-n* junction diode used in the circuit is 0.7 V. The type of biasing and current in the circuit are **CBSE 2023**

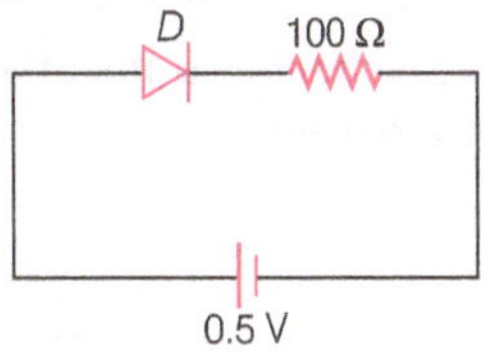

(a) forward biasing, 0 A (b) reverse biasing, 0 A
(c) forward biasing, 5 mA (d) reverse biasing, 2 mA

11. A 220 V AC supply is connected between points *A* and *B* (figure). What will be the potential difference *V* across the capacitor? **NCERT Exemplar**

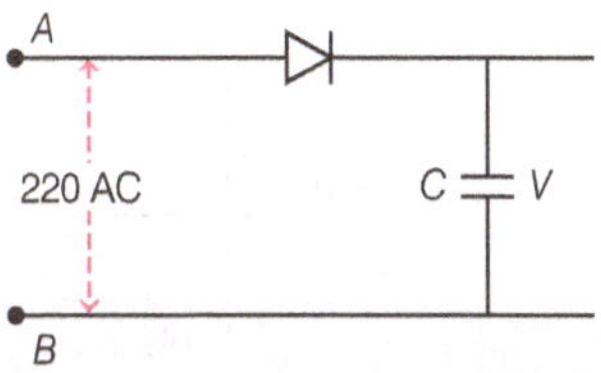

(a) 220V (b) 110 V
(c) 0 V (d) $220\sqrt{2}$V

12. **In an extrinsic semiconductor, the number density of holes is 4×10^{20} m^{-1}. If the number density of intrinsic carriers is 1.2×10^{15} m^{-3}, the number density of electrons in it is** CBSE 2023
(a) 1.8×10^{9} m^{-3}
(b) 2.4×10^{10} m^{-3}
(c) 3.6×10^{9} m^{-3}
(d) 3.2×10^{10} m^{-3}

13. **A semiconductor device is connected in series with a battery, an ammeter and a resistor. A current flows in the circuit. If the polarity of the battery is reversed, the current in the circuit almost becomes zero. The device is a/an** CBSE 2023
(a) intrinsic semiconductor
(b) *p*-type semiconductor
(c) *n*-type semiconductor (d) *p-n* junction diode

14. **In an unbiased *p-n* junction, holes diffuse from the *p*-region to *n*-region because**
(a) free electrons in the *n*-region attract them
(b) they move across the junction by the potential difference
(c) hole concentration in *p*-region is more as compared to *n*-region
(d) All of the above

15. **In an ON state, the individual Silicon and Germanium diodes, allow a voltage drop of 0.7 V and 0.3 V respectively across them. In the circuit shown, the Si and the Ge diode, are connected in a parallel combination to a voltage source of 10V.**

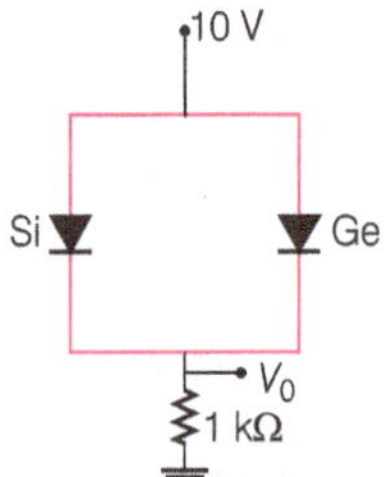

What is the voltage V_0 for the circuit network? Competency Based Que
(a) 0 V (b) 9.3 V
(c) 9.7 V (d) 10 V

16. **Which of these graphs shows potential difference between *p*-side and *n*-side of a *p-n* junction in equilibrium?**

(a)
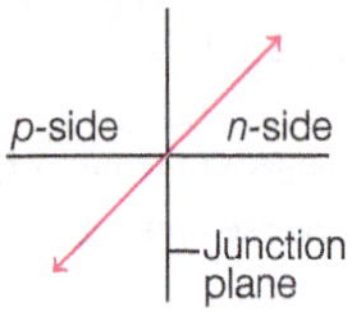

(b)
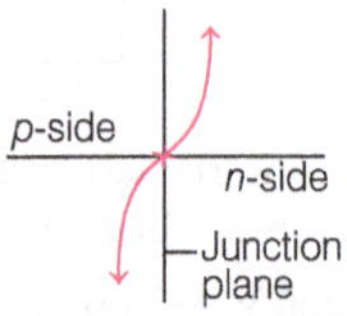

(c)
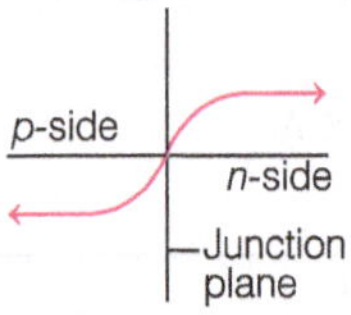

(d)
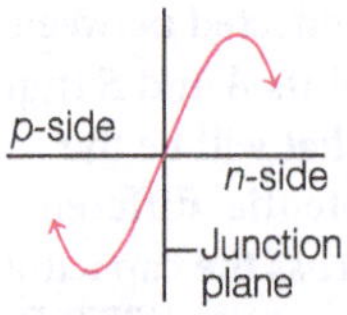

17. **Which is reverse biased diode?**

(a)
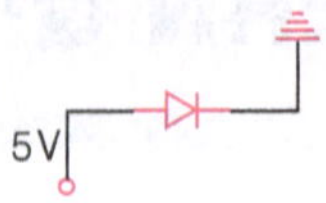

(b)
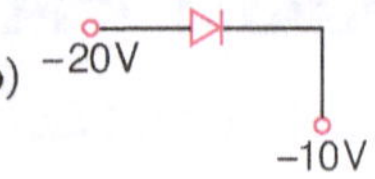

(c)
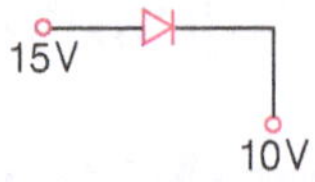

(d)
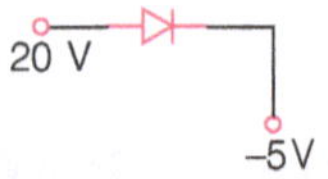

18. **The current through an ideal *p-n* junction shown in the following circuit diagram will be**

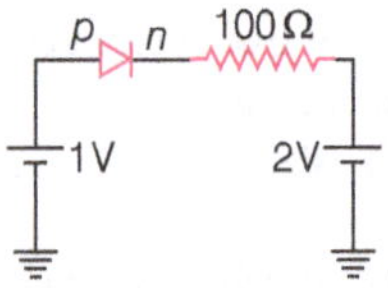

(a) Zero (b) 1 mA (c) 10 mA (d) 30 mA

19. **Match the Column I with Column II.**

Column I (Concept)		Column II (Related terms/Definition)	
A.	Intrinsic semiconductor	1.	Reduce the width of the depletion layer.
B.	Forward bias in diode	2.	Semiconductor with no doping.
C.	Doping	3.	Opposes the flow of majority carriers.
D.	Depletion region	4.	Process of adding impurities to increase conductivity.

(a) A-2, B-3, C-4, D-1
(b) A-2, B-1, C-4, D-3
(c) A-1, B-2, C-3, D-4
(d) A-3, B-4, C-2, D-1

20. **Match the Column I with Column II.**

Column I		Column II	
A.	Potential barrier (V_B)	1.	Minority charge carriers are electrons
B.	*n*-type semiconductor	2.	The potential difference developed across the depletion region.
C.	Energy band gap	3.	Majority charge carriers are electrons.
D.	*p*-type semiconductor	4.	$E = \frac{hc}{\lambda}$

(a) A-2, B-3, C-4, D-1
(b) A-2, B-3, C-1, D-4
(c) A-3, B-4, C-1, D-2
(d) A-1, B-2, C-3, D-4

Assertion-Reason

Directions *(Q. Nos. 21-26) In the following questions, two statements are given- one labelled Assertion (A) and the other labelled Reason (R). Select the correct answer to these questions from the codes (a), (b), (c) and (d) as given below.*

(a) Both Assertion and Reason are true and Reason is the correct explanation of Assertion.

(b) Both Assertion and Reason are true but Reason is not the correct explanation of Assertion.

(c) Assertion is true but Reason is false.

(d) Assertion is false but Reason is true.

21. **Assertion (A)** In insulators, the forbidden gap is very large.

Reason (R) The valence electrons in an atom of an insulator are very tightly bound to the nucleus. **CBSE 2023**

22. **Assertion (A)** The electrical conductivity of a semiconductor increases on doping.

Reason (R) Doping always increases the number of electrons in the semiconductor. **CBSE SQP 2022-23**

23. **Assertion (A)** The resistance of an intrinsic semiconductor decreases with increase in its temperature.

Reason (R) The number of conduction electrons as well as holes increase in an intrinsic semiconductor with rise in its temperature. **CBSE 2024**

24. **Assertion (A)** The temperature coefficient of resistance is positive for metals and negative for p-type semiconductors.

Reason (R) The charge carriers in metals are negatively charged whereas the majority charge carriers in p-type semiconductors are positively charged. **CBSE 2024**

25. **Assertion (A)** In n-type semiconductor, number density of electrons is greater than the number density of holes but the crystal maintains an overall charge neutrality.

Reason (R) The charge of electrons donated by donor atoms is just equal and opposite to that of the ionised donor. **CBSE 2023**

26. **Assertion (A)** In a semiconductor diode the thickness of depletion layer is not fixed.

Reason (R) Thickness of depletion layer in a semiconductor device depends upon many factors such as biasing of the semiconductor. **CBSE 2025**

Case Based Questions

Directions *(Q.Nos. 27-32) These questions are case study based questions. Read the following paragraph and answer the questions on the basis of same.*

27. **A semiconductor diode is basically a p-n junction with metallic contacts provided at the ends for the application of an external voltage. It is a two terminal device. When an external voltage is applied across a semiconductor diode, such that p-side is connected to the positive terminal of the battery and n-side to the negative terminal, it is said to be forward biased. When an external voltage is applied across the diode, such that n-side is positive and p-side is negative, it is said to be reverse biased. An ideal diode is one whose resistance in forward biasing is zero and the resistance is infinite in reverse biasing. When the diode is forward biased, it is found that beyond forward voltage called knee voltage, the conductivity is very high. When the biasing voltage is more than the knee voltage, the potential barrier is overcome and the current increases rapidly with increase in forward voltage. When the diode is reverse biased, the reverse bias voltage produces a very small current about a few microamperes which almost remains constant with bias. This small current is reverse saturation current.**

CBSE SQP 2023

(i) In the given figure, a diode D is connected to an external resistance $R = 100\ \Omega$ and an emf of 3.5 V. If the barrier potential developed across the diode is 0.5 V, the current in the circuit will be

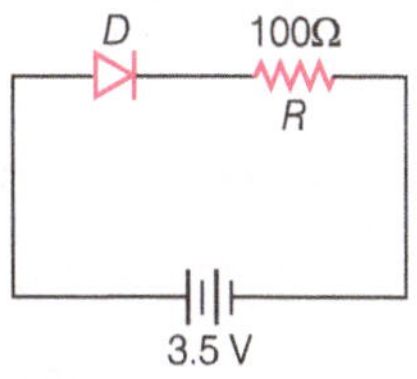

(a) 40 mA (b) 20 mA (c) 35 mA (d) 30 mA

(ii) In which of the following figures, the p-n diode is reverse biased?

(a)
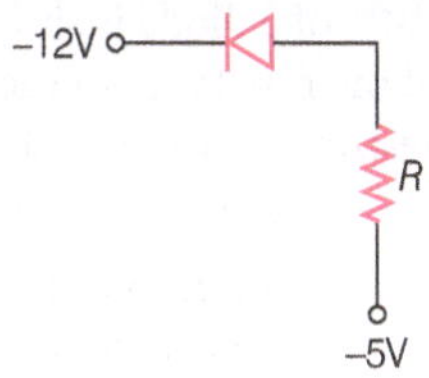

(b)
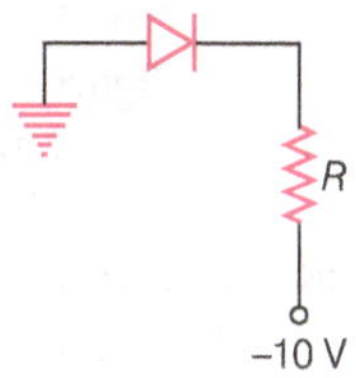

(c)
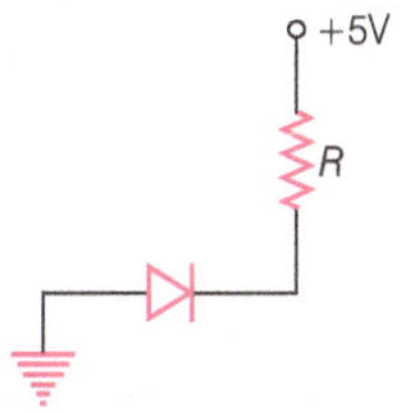

(d)
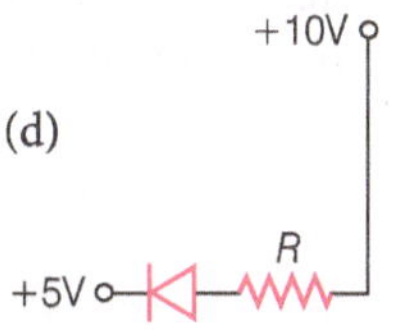

(iii) Based on the V-I characteristics of the diode, we can classify diode as
(a) bilateral device
(b) ohmic device
(c) non-ohmic device
(d) passive element

Or

Two identical p-n junctions can be connected in series by three different methods as shown in the figure. If the potential difference in the junctions is the same, then the correct connections will be

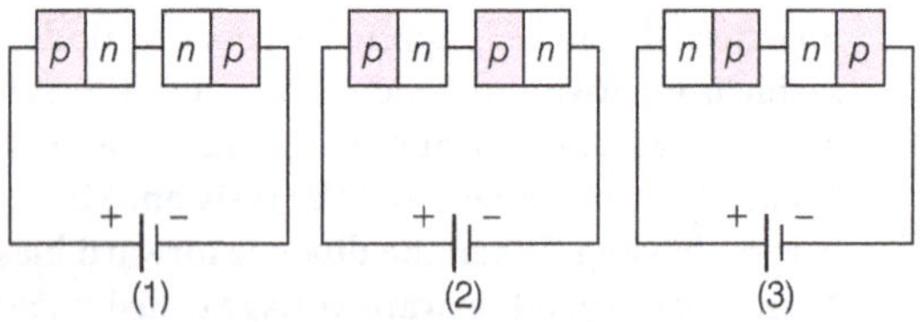

(a) in the circuits (1) and (2)
(b) in the circuits (2) and (3)
(c) in the circuits (1) and (3)
(d) only in the circuit (1)

(iv)

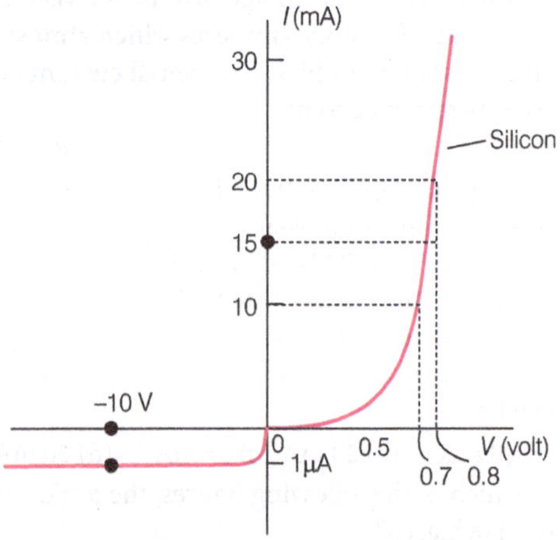

The V-I characteristic of a diode is shown in the figure. The ratio of the resistance of the diode at $I = 15$ mA to the resistance at $V = -10$ V is
(a) 100 (b) 10^6 (c) 10 (d) 10^{-6}

28. **According to Bohr's atomic model and the concept of electronic configuration of an isolated atom, the electrons have well defined energy levels in isolated atom. But, due to interatomic interaction in a crystal, the electrons of the outer shells are forced to have energies different from those in isolated atoms.**

Each energy level splits into a number of energy level splits into a number of energy levels forming a continuous band. The gap between top of valence band and bottom of conduction band in which electrons are not found is called energy gap (E_g).

(i) What is the order of energy band gap of an insulator?
(ii) A radiation of wavelength 300 nm is used to shift the electron from valence band to conduction band. What is the energy band gap of the material?
(iii) The separation between valence band and conduction band is 10 eV. Find the wavelength of the radiation used to transfer electron from valence band to conduction band.
(iv) Which band is responsible for current flow in a semiconductor in presence of external field?

29. **When some desirable impurity is added to intrinsic semiconductors deliberately, then this process is called doping and the impurity is called dopant. As a result of doping, the intrinsic semiconductors are converted to *p*-type or *n*-type based on the addition of trivalent or pentavalent impurities. The electrons are majority carrier in *n*-type semiconductors, whereas holes are majority carriers in *p*-type semiconductors.**
(i) What do you mean by intrinsic semiconductors?
(ii) Name the dopant which is used to make n-type semiconductor.
(iii) What will be the majority carrier in case of p-type semiconductors?
(iv) What is the charge on a n-type semiconductor?

Subjective Questions

Very Short Answer Type Questions

1. Two halves of a silicon crystal (A and B) are doped with arsenic and boron respectively, forming a p-n junction in it. A battery is connected arcoss it as shown in the figure.

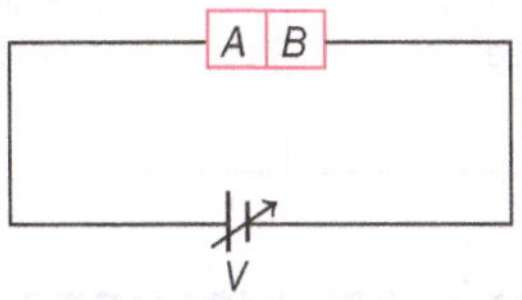

(i) Will the junction be forward biased or reverse biased? Give reason.

(ii) Draw V-I graph for this arrangement. **CBSE 2024**

2. Can the potential barrier across a p-n junction be measured by simply connecting a voltmeter across the junction? **Competency Based Que.**

3. As we know that, n-type semiconductor has large number of electron but it is still electrically neutral. Why? **Competency Based Que.**

4. How does the width of a depletion region of a p-n junction vary, if doping concentration is increased? **CBSE SQP 2020-21**

5. The threshold voltage of a silicon diode is 0.7 V. It is operated at this point by connecting the diode in series with a battery of V volt and a resistor of 1000 Ω. Find the value of V when the current drawn is 15 mA. **CBSE 2025**

6. Draw the output waveform across the resistor in the given figure. **Competency Based Que.**

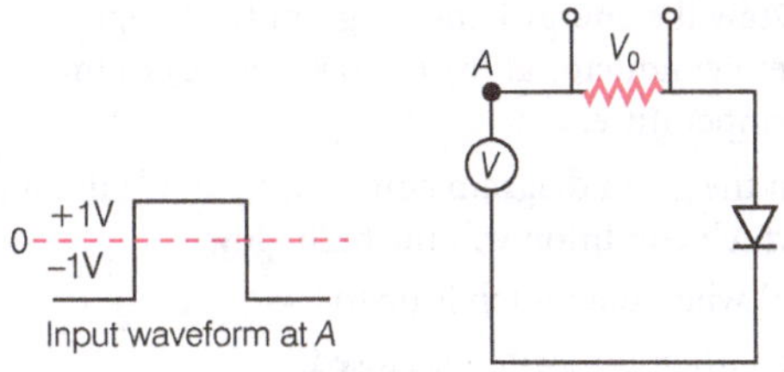

Short Answer Type Questions

7. (i) What are majority and minority charge carriers in an extrinsic semiconductor? **[1]**

(ii) A p-n junction is forward biased. Describe the movement of the charge carriers which produce current in it. **[1]**

(iii) The graph shows the variation of current with voltage for a p-n junction diode. **[1]**

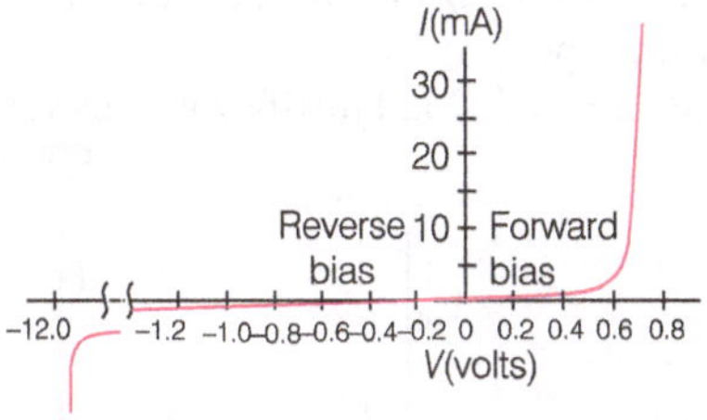

Estimate the dynamic resistance of diode at $V = -0.6$ volt. **CBSE 2025 [1]**

8. Draw energy band diagram for an n- type and p-type semiconductor at $T > 0$ K. **CBSE 2023**

9. Draw the circuit diagram of a p-n junction diode in (i) forward biasing and (ii) reverse biasing. Also, draw its I-V characteristics in the two cases. **CBSE 2024**

10. (i) Name the type of a diode whose characteristics are shown in figures. (a) and (b). **[1]**

(ii) What does the point P in fig. (a) represent? **[1]**

(iii) What does the points P and Q in fig. (b) represent? **[1]**

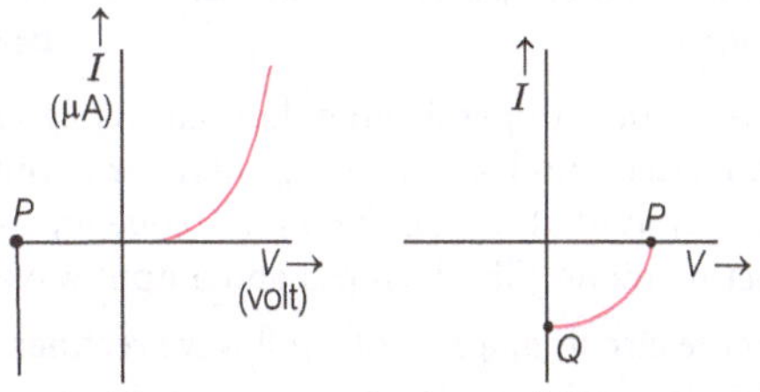

(a) (b)

11. What is meant by energy band gap in a solid ? Draw the energy band diagrams for a conductor, an insulator and a semiconductor. **CBSE 2022, Term-II**

12. Answer the following and giving reason.

(i) The resistance of a p-n junction is low when it is forward biased and is high when it is reversed biased. **[1½]**

(ii) Doping of intrinsic semiconductors is a necessity for making electronic devices. **CBSE 2022, Term-II [1½]**

13. The figure shows a piece of pure semiconductor S in series with a variable resistor R and a source of constant voltage V. Should the value of R be increased or decreased to keep the reading of the ammeter constant, when semiconductor S is heated? Justify your answer.

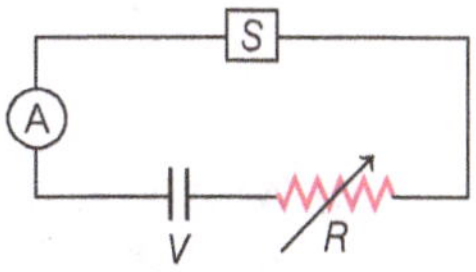

Or The graph of potential barrier *versus* width of depletion region for an unbiased diode is shown in graph *A*. In comparison to *A*, graphs *B* and *C* are obtained after biasing the diode in different ways. Identify the type of biasing in *B* and *C* and justify your answer. **CBSE SQP 2023**

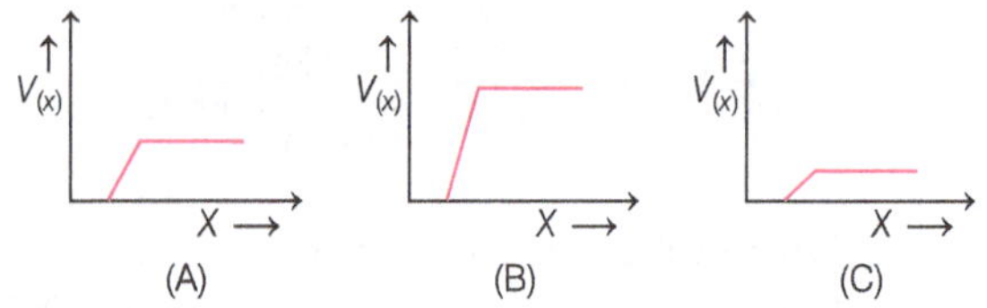

14. Name the device which converts an AC input signal into a DC output signal. Write the principle of working of the device. **CBSE 2022, Term-II**

15. Explain the property of a *p-n* junction which makes it suitable for rectifying alternating voltages. Differentiate between a half-wave and a full-wave rectifier. **CBSE 2023**

16. Draw the circuit diagram of a full wave rectifier and explain its working. Also, give the input and output waveforms. **Delhi 2019**

Or Explain with a proper diagram how an AC signal can be converted into DC (pulsating) signal with output frequency as double than the input frequency using *p-n* junction diode. Give its input and output waveforms.

Or Draw the circuit diagram of a full wave rectifier. Explain its working principle. Show the input waveforms given to the diodes D_1 and D_2 and the corresponding output waveforms obtained at the load connected to the circuit. **All India 2019**

17. In the circuit containing an ideal *p-n* junction diode *D* and a resistor *R* is given an input square wave as shown

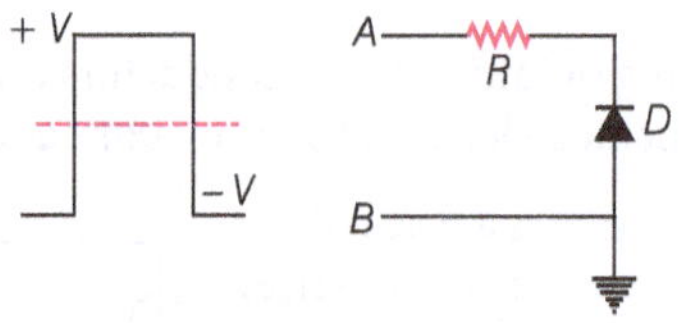

(i) What is the shape of the output waveform across diode *D*? **[1]**

(ii) Give an explanation for your answer in part (ii). **[2]**

18. A Zener of power rating 1 W is to be used as a voltage regulator. If Zener has a breakdown of 5 V and it has to regulate voltage which fluctuated between 3 V and 7 V, what should be the value of R_s for safe operation (see figure)?

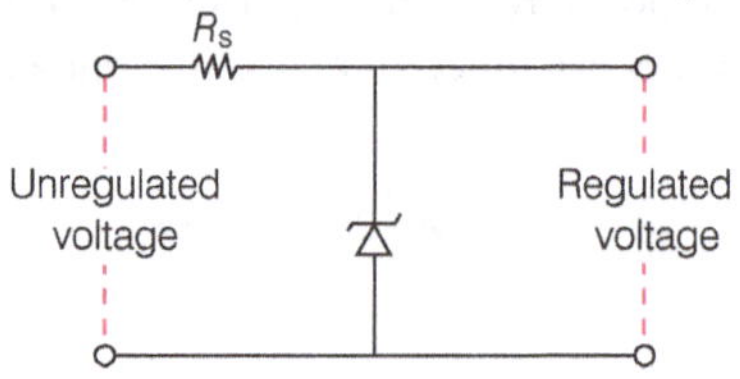

Long Answer Type Questions

19. (i) (a) A germanium crystal is doped with antimony. With the help of energy-band diagram, explain how the conductivity of the doped crystal is affected. **[1]**

(b) Briefly explain the two processes involved in the formation of a *p-n* junction. **[2]**

(c) What will the effect of (I) forward biasing, and (II) reverse biasing be on the width of depletion layer in a *p-n* junction diode? **CBSE 2023** **[2]**

Or

(ii) (a) In half-wave rectification, what is the output frequency, if input frequency is 25 Hz? **[1]**

(b) Draw *V-I* characteristics of a *p-n* junction diode. Explain how these characteristics make a diode suitable for rectification. **[2]**

(c) Carbon and silicon have the same lattice structure. Then, why is carbon an insulator but silicon a semiconductor? **[2]**

20. (i) Draw the energy band diagram for *p*-type semiconductor at (a) $T = 0$ K and (b) room temperature. **[2½]**

(ii) In the given diagram considering an ideal diode, in which condition will the bulb glow

(a) when the switch is open

(b) when the switch is closed

Justify your answer. **CBSE SQP 2024-25** **[2½]**

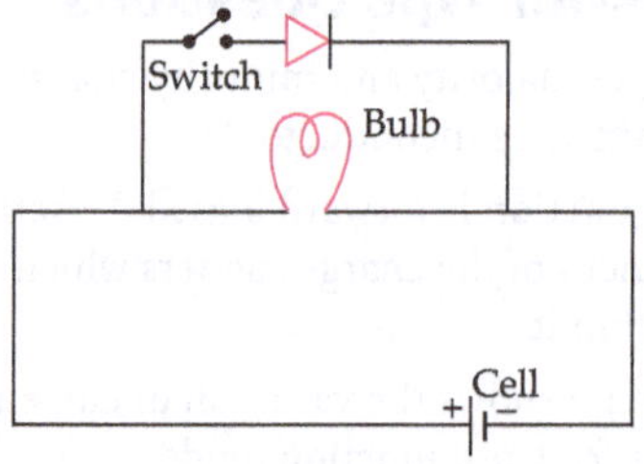

21. Name two important processes involved in the formation of a *p-n* junction diode. With the help of a circuit diagram, explain the working of junction diode as a full wave rectifier. Draw its input and output waveforms. State the characteristic property of a junction diode that makes it suitable for rectification. **CBSE 2023**

Numerical Problems

22. A potential barrier of 0.4 V exists across *p-n* junction.

(i) If the depletion region is 4.0×10^{-7} m wide, what is the intensity of the electric field in this region? **[1½]**

(ii) If an electron with speed 4×10^5 m/s approaches the *p-n* junction from the *n*-side, find the speed with which it will be *p*-side.

Competency Based Que. [1½]

23. In half-wave rectification, what is the output frequency, if the input frequency is 50 Hz? What is the output frequency of a full wave rectifier for the same input frequency? **NCERT**

24. If each diode in figure has a forward bias resistance of 25 Ω and infinite resistance in reverse bias, what will be the values of the currents I_1, I_2, I_3 and I_4?

Competency Based Que.

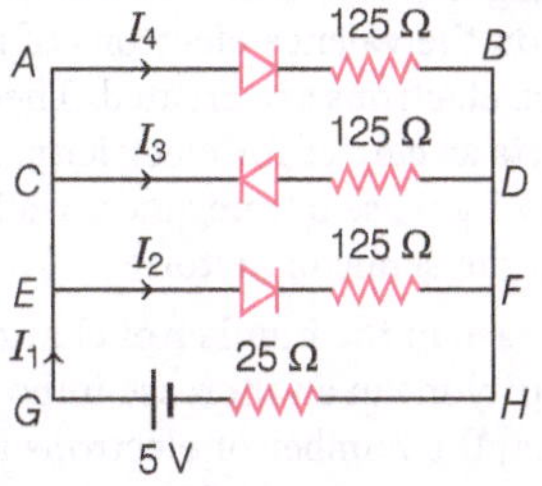

25. Assuming that the two diodes D_1 and D_2 used in the electric circuit as shown in the figure are ideal, find out the value of the current flowing through 1 Ω resistor.

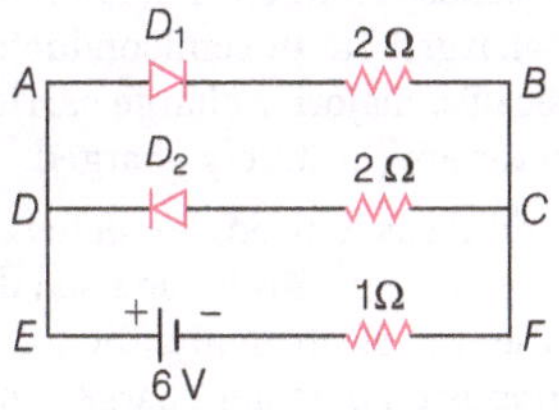

Hints & Solutions

Objective Type Questions

2. (*a*)	3. (*b*)	5. (*c*)	6. (*d*)	7. (*b*)
8. (*d*)	10. (*a*)	13. (*d*)	16. (*c*)	17. (*b*)
18. (*b*)	19. (*b*)	20. (a)	26. (a)	

1. (*d*) The conductivity of a semiconductor increases with increase in temperature, because the number density of current carriers increases, relaxation time decreases but effect of decrease in relaxation is much less than increase in number density.

4. (*c*)
$$n_i = 1.5 \times 10^{16}\,\text{m}^{-3}$$
$$n_h = 4.5 \times 10^{22}$$
$$n_e \cdot n_h = (n_i)^2$$
$$n_e = \frac{(n_i)^2}{n_h} = \frac{(1.5 \times 10^{16})^2}{4.5 \times 10^{22}} = \frac{1.5 \times 1.5 \times 10^{32}}{4.5 \times 10^{22}}$$

9. (*b*) Its valence electrons are more tightly bound to their parent nuclei.

11. (*d*) As *p-n* junction conducts during positive half cycle only, the diode connected here will work in positive half cycle. Potential difference across C = peak voltage of the given AC voltage $= V_0 = V_{\text{rms}}\sqrt{2} = 220\sqrt{2}$ V.

12. (c) Given that,
Number density of holes $= 4 \times 10^{20}\ \text{m}^{-1}$
Number density of intrinsic $= 1.2 \times 10^{15}\ \text{m}^{-3}$
Then, number density of electrons, $n_i^2 = p \times n$
where, p is the number density of holes and n is the number density of electrons.
$$4 \times 10^{20} \times n = (1.2 \times 10^{15})^2$$
We get, $$n = \frac{(1.2 \times 10^{15})^2}{4 \times 10^{20}} = 3.6 \times 10^9\ \text{m}^{-3}$$

14. (c) In an unbiased *p-n* junction, the diffusion of charge carriers across the junction takes place from higher concentration to lower concentration. Therefore, hole concentration in *p*-region is more as compared to *n*-region.

15. (c) Equivalent voltage drop across Si and Ge diode
$$= 0.3\text{V}$$
Current through 1 kΩ,
$$I = \frac{10 - 0.3}{1\,\text{k}\Omega} = 9.7\,\text{mA}$$
$$V_0 = IR = 9.7\,\text{mA} \times 1\,\text{k}\Omega = 9.7\ \text{V}$$

18. (*a*) Output frequency of full wave rectifier is twice the output frequency of half wave rectifier.
$$\therefore \quad \frac{f_{\text{half wave}}}{f_{\text{full wave}}} = \frac{1}{2}$$

21. (a) The forbidden gap between the valence band and conduction band is very large in insulator and valence electrons of an insulator are very tightly bound to the nucleus.

22. (c) By doping impurities into semiconductors, depending on the valence electrons of impurities, either holes or free electrons are created. These holes and electrons acts as carrier for electricity, hence conductivity increase but not increase in number of electrons in the semiconductor.

23. (c) The increase in the number of charge carriers does not necessarily mean an increase in both electrons and holes. In fact, the number of electrons and holes may increase or decrease depending on the material and the temperature range.

24. (a) For metal, the temperature coefficient of resistance is positive because charge carriers in metals are negatively charged but in semiconductor (p-type), it is negative because majority charge carriers in p-type semiconductor are positively charged.

25. (a) When a donor is ionised, it creates a free electron but it also creates a positively ionised donor atom. The charge on the free electron and the ionised donor are equal and opposite, thus net charge remain zero.

27. (i) (d) The circuit is represented by

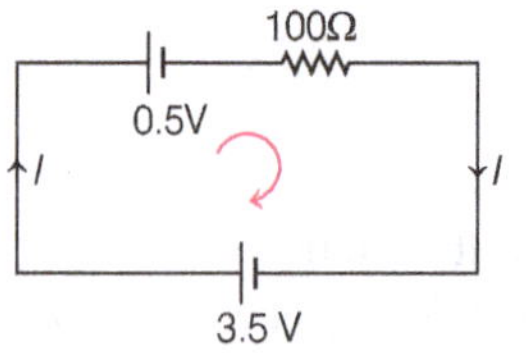

∴ Applying KVL in the loop,

$$3.5 - 0.5 - 100\, I = 0$$

∴ $$I = 30 \text{ mA}$$

(ii) (c) In Fig. (c), n-side terminal of the diode is connected to lower potential. So, it is reversed biased.

(iii) (c) Based on V-I characteristics, the diode is classified as non-ohmic device.

Or

(b) For series combination of diode, n-side of one diode is connected to p-side of other diode and *vice-versa*.

(iv) (d) R_f = Resistance of diode at

$$I = 15 \text{ mA} = \frac{V_f}{i_f} = \frac{(0.75 - 0.7)}{(15-10)\times 10^{-3}} = 10$$

R_b = Resistance of diode at $V = -10$ V

$$= \frac{V_b}{i_b} = \frac{10}{10^{-6}} = 10^7$$

$$\therefore \quad \frac{R_f}{R_b} = \frac{10}{10^7} = 10^{-6}$$

28. (i) The order of energy band gap (E_g) of an insulator is greater than 3 eV. Thus, more energy is required to move the electrons from valance band to conduction band.

(ii) Given $\lambda = 300$ nm

$= 300 \times 10^{-9}$ m

∴ Energy band gap, $E_g = \dfrac{hc}{\lambda}$

$$\therefore \quad E_g = \frac{6.63\times 10^{-34} \times 3\times 10^8}{300\times 10^{-9} \times 1.6\times 10^{-19}} = 4.14 \text{ eV}$$

(iii) Given, $E_g = 10$ eV, $\lambda = ?$

$$\therefore \quad E_g = \frac{hc}{\lambda}$$

$$\Rightarrow 10 \times 1.6 \times 10^{-19} = \frac{6.63\times 10^{-34} \times 3 \times 10^8}{\lambda}$$

$$\therefore \quad \lambda = 124.3 \text{ nm}$$

(iv) In the energy band diagram, conduction band is responsible for current flow in a semiconductor in presence of applied electric field.

29. (i) A pure semiconductor before dopping is called intrinsic semiconductor. It contains an equal number of excited electrons and holes.

(ii) When pentavalent impurities like phosphorous (P), arsenic (As), antimony (Sb) are added to Si or Ge, then n-type semiconductor is obtained.

(iii) Holes are the majority charge carriers in p-type semiconductors.

(iv) The dopped or extrinsic semiconductor (p-type or n-type) have no charge. They are electrically neutral

Subjective Questions

1. (i) p-n junction is reversed biased. Crystal A is doped with arsenic which is pentavalent. Hence, it is n-type. Crystal B is doped with boron which is trivalent.

Hence it is p-type.

(ii)

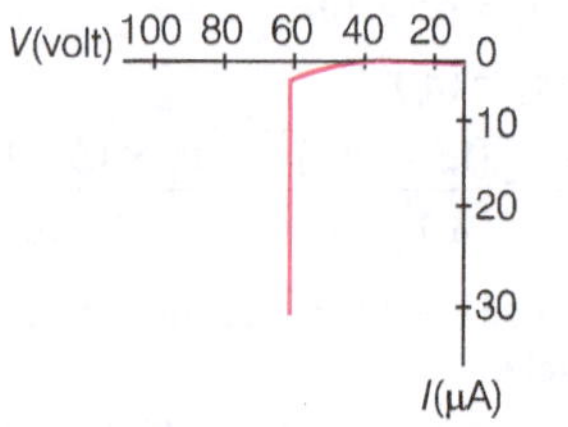

2. We cannot measure the potential barrier across a p-n junction by a voltmeter because the resistance of voltmeter is very high as compared to the junction resistance

3. n-type semiconductor is obtain when pentavalent impurities added to Si or Ge. All there material are electrically neutral, so n-type semiconductor is also neutral.

4. When doping concentration is increased or heavily doped, width of the depletion layer will decreases.

5. 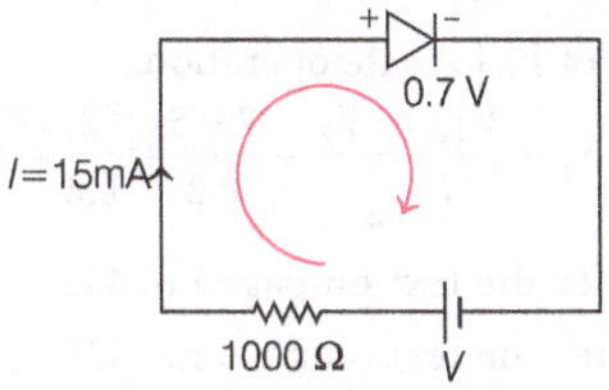

From the above circuit diagram, applying KVL, we get

$$V - 1000 \times 15 \times 10^{-3} - 0.7 = 0$$

$$\Rightarrow \quad V = (15 - 0.7)\ \text{V} = 14.3\ \text{V}$$

∴ The value of V is 14.3 V.

6. As we know that the diode only works in forward biased, so the output is obtained only when positive input is given, so the output waveform is

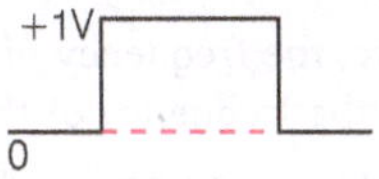

7. (i) Extrinsic semiconductors are of two types
   (a) n-type semiconductors
   (b) p-type semiconductors

   In n-type semiconductors, majority carriers are electrons and minority carriers are holes.

   In p-type semiconductors, majority carriers are holes whereas minority carriers are electrons.

   (ii) Refer to theory on page 432 (Flow of current in forward biasing)

   (iii) Dynamic voltage is given as $r_d = \frac{\Delta V}{\Delta I}$.

   Here, $\Delta V = -0.6$ V, $\Delta I = 0$

$$\therefore \quad r_d = \frac{-0.6}{0} = \infty$$

8. Refer to text on page no. 430.

9. Circuit diagram of a p-n junction diode in
   (i) Forward biasing

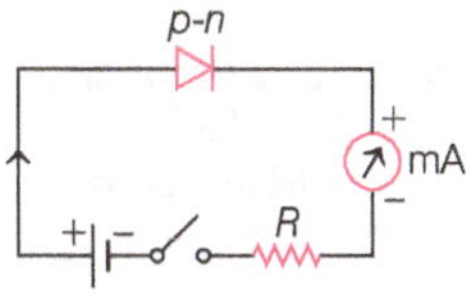

   (ii) Reverse biasing

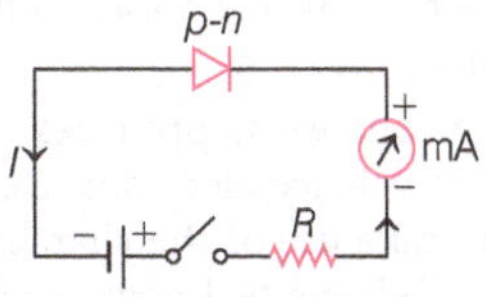

I-V characteristics of p-n junction diode

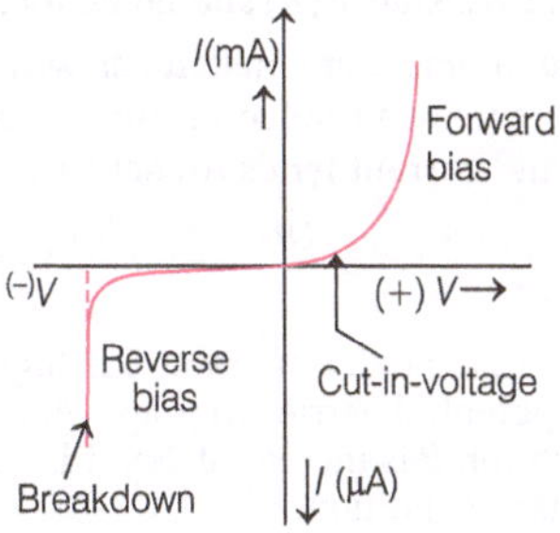

10. (i) The characteristic curve (a) is of Zener diode and curve (b) is of solar cell.

   (ii) The point P in fig. (a) represents Zener breakdown voltage.

   (iii) In fig. (b), the point Q represents zero voltage and negative current. It means light falling on solar cell with atleast minimum threshold frequency gives the current in opposite direction to that due to a battery connected to solar cell. But for the point Q, the battery is short circuited. Hence, represents the short circuit current.

   In fig. (b), the point P represents some positive voltage on solar cell with zero current through solar cell.

   It means, there is a battery connected to a solar cell which gives rise to the equal and opposite current to that in solar cell by virtue of light falling on it.

   As current is zero for point P, hence we say P represents open circuit voltage.

11. In the energy band diagram, energy band gap (E_g) is the separation between highest energy level of valance band and lowest energy level of conduction band. It is the minimum energy required for shifting electrons from valance band to conduction band.

   For energy band diagrams of conductor, insulator and semiconductor refer to text on page no. 428.

12. (i) Forwarding current increases significantly when the forwarding voltage across the p-n junction is just slightly increased. Because of this, a forward biased p-n junction has low resistance. (= voltage/current).

   Reverse current increases little as the reverse voltage across the p-n junction increases significantly. As a result, the *p-n* junction has a high resistance when reverse biased and low resistance in forward bias.

(ii) Doping semiconductors produces either an excess or a shortage of valence electrons. Doping enables scientists to take use of the characteristics of collections of elements, known as dopants, in order to modify a semiconductor's conductivity.

13. The value of resistance (R) should be increased to keep the reading of ammeter constant, as with the increase in the temperature of a semiconductor, its resistance decreases and current tends to increase.

Or

For graph B,

As the potential barrier in graph B is higher with respect to potential barrier in graph A, i.e. potential barrier in graph B is increased. So, it is the case of reverse biased condition.

For graph C,

As the potential barrier in graph C is decreased with respect to potential barrier in graph A. So, the graph C is the case of forward biased condition.

14. Diode is used as a rectifier to convert an AC input signal into a DC output signal.

For principle of working of rectifier refer to text on page 434.

15. The property of a *p-n* junction that makes it suitable for rectifying alternating voltages is its ability to act as a diode, allowing current flow in only one direction. This property is a result of the formations of a depletion region at the interface between the *p*-type and *n*-type semi-conductor which acts as a barrier for the flow of current in one direction making the *p-n* junction a useful device for rectifying AC signals.

For the difference between half wave and a full wave rectifier, refer the text on pages no. 434 and 435.

16. Refer text on page 434 and 435. (Principle, Diode as a Full Wave Rectifier).

17. (i)

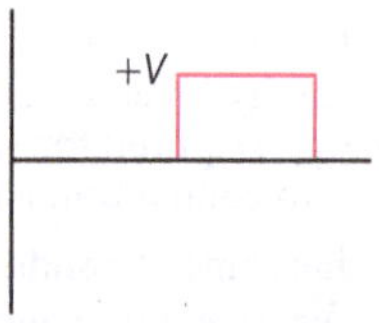

(ii) When the input voltage is negative, then it would be forward bias for diode. So, waveform would pass through the diode and we get no voltage on output. If input voltage is positive, then diode is in reverse bias and behaves as a open circuit. Now, input wave form is passed to the output terminals.

18. Given, power = 1 W

Zener breakdown, $V_z = 5\text{ V}$

Minimum voltage, $V_{\text{min}} = 3\text{ V}$

Maximum voltage, $V_{\text{max}} = 7\text{ V}$

Current, $I_{Z_{\text{max}}} = \dfrac{P}{V_Z} = \dfrac{1}{5} = 0.2\text{ A}$

The value of R_s for safe operation,

$$R_s = \frac{V_{\text{max}} - V_Z}{I_{Z_{\text{max}}}} = \frac{7-5}{0.2} = \frac{2}{0.2} = 10\ \Omega$$

19. (i) (a) Refer the text on page no. 430.

(b) Refer the text on page no. 431.

(c) Refer the text on page no. 432.

Or

(ii) (a) Given that, input frequency,

$\nu = 25\text{ Hz}$

Output frequency

$\nu_{\text{out}} = 25\text{ Hz}$

Hence, the output waveform completes one cycle at the same time that of the input.

Therefore, the frequency of the output wave is equal to the frequency of the input wave.

(b) Refer to text on pages no. 433 and 434.

(c) Carbon is an insulator because all of its valence electrons are used up in covalent bonding, while silicon is a semiconductor because some of its valence electrons are not involved in bonding, creating a small number of free electrons in the conduction band. This slight difference in electronic configuration results in a significant difference in their electrical properties, despite having the same lattice structure.

20. (i) (a) **At $T = 0$ K**

- The valence band is fully filled.
- The conduction band is empty.
- The fermi level is close to the valence band but below the acceptor levels.

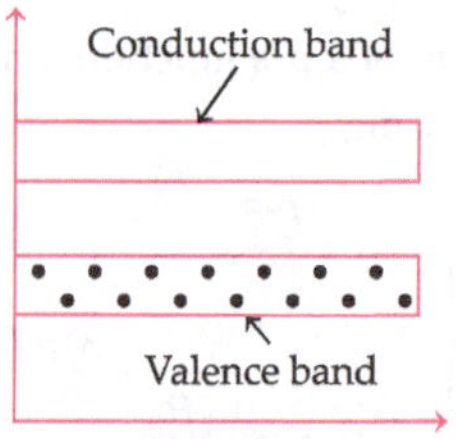

(b) **At room temperature**

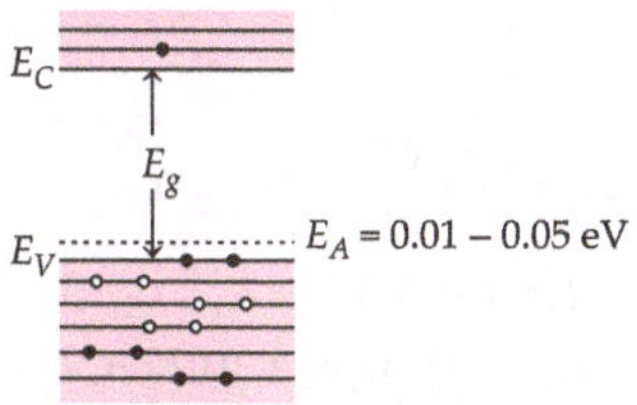

The valence band is partially filled with holes.

- The conduction band has a few electrons.
- The fermi level is still closer to the valence band, representing a higher probability of holes being the majority charge carrier.

(ii) (a) When the switch is open, the bulb will glows.

(b) When the switch is closed the diode will be forward biased and current will bypass the bulb.

21. Diffusion and drift are two processes that take places in the formation of p-n junction.

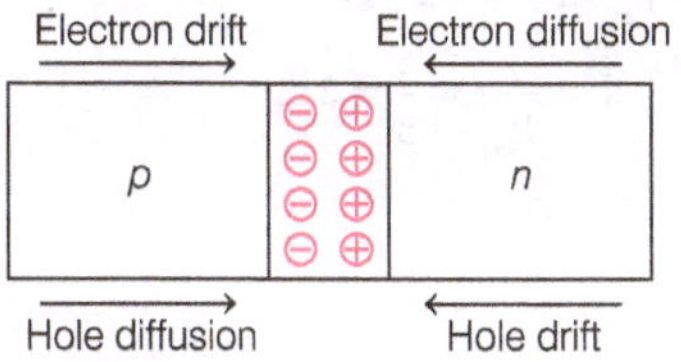

Diffusion is the process of movement of charge carrier due to concentration gradient along the semiconductor whereas drift is the process of movement of charge carriers due to the net electric field. In the full wave rectifier, two p-n junction diodes D_1 and D_2 are used. This arrangement is shown in the diagram below.

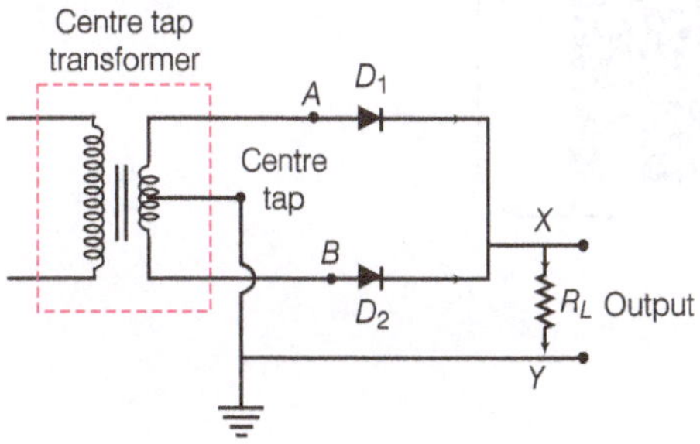

Working During positive half cycle of the input AC, the diode D_1 is forward biased and the the diode D_2 is reverse biased. The forward current flows through diode D_1.

During the negative half cycle of the input AC, the diode D_1 is reverse biased and diode D_2 is forward biased, so current flows through diode D_2. Hence, we find that during both the halves, current flows in the same direction.

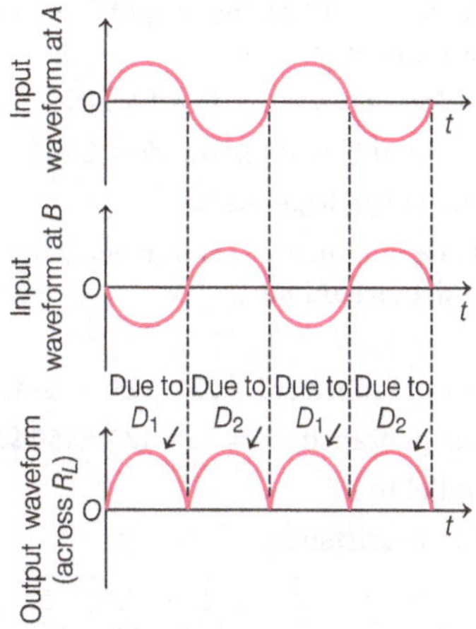

Characteristic property of junction diode

As an alternating voltage is applied across a junction diode, the current will only in the part where it is forward biased.

This property of junction diode can be used to rectify alternating current, so this circuit is used for rectification process.

22. Given, $V = 0.4$ V

(i) $d = 4 \times 10^{-7}$ m, $E = ?$

$$\text{Electric field, } E = \frac{V}{d} = \frac{0.4}{4\times 10^{-7}}$$

$$= 1\times 10^{6} \text{ V/m}$$

(ii) $v_1 = 4 \times 10^5$ m/s, $v_2 = ?$

Let v_1 be the speed of electron when it enters the depletion layer and v_2 be the speed when it comes out of the depletion layer.

According to principle of conservation of energy,

KE before entering the depletion layer = loss in PE + KE after crossing the depletion layer

$$\Rightarrow \quad \frac{1}{2}mv_1^2 = e \times V + \frac{1}{2}mv_2^2$$

$$\Rightarrow \quad \frac{1}{2} \times 9.1 \times 10^{-31} \times (4 \times 10^5)^2$$

$$= 1.6\times 10^{-19} \times 0.4 + \frac{1}{2} \times 9.1\times 10^{-31} \times v_2^2$$

$$\therefore \quad v_2 = 1.39\times 10^5 \text{ m/s}$$

23. Given, input frequency = 50 Hz

For a half-wave rectifier, the output frequency is equal to the input frequency.

$\therefore$ Output frequency = 50 Hz

For a full wave rectifier, the output frequency is twice the input frequency

$\therefore$ Output frequency $= 2 \times 50 = 100$ Hz.

24. Given, forward biased resistance = 25 Ω

Reverse biased resistance = ∞

As the diode in branch CD is in reverse biased which having resistance infinite,

So, $I_3 = 0$

Resistance in branch $AB = 25 + 125 = 150\ \Omega$ (say R_1)

Resistance in branch $EF = 25 + 125 = 150\ \Omega$ (say R_2)

AB is parallel to EF.

So, resultant resistance,

$$\frac{1}{R'} = \frac{1}{R_1} + \frac{1}{R_2} = \frac{1}{150} + \frac{1}{150} = \frac{2}{150}$$

$\Rightarrow$ $R' = 75\ \Omega$

Total resistance, $R = R' + 25 = 75 + 25 = 100\ \Omega$

Current, $I_1 = \frac{V}{R} = \frac{5}{100} = 0.05$ A

$I_1 = I_4 + I_2 + I_3$ [here, $I_3 = 0$]

So, $I_1 = I_4 + I_2$

Here, the resistances R_1 and R_2 are same.

i.e. $I_4 = I_2$

$\therefore$ $I_1 = 2I_2$

$\Rightarrow$ $I_2 = \frac{I_1}{2} = \frac{0.05}{2} = 0.025$ A

and $I_4 = 0.025$ A

Thus, $I_1 = 0.05$ A, $I_2 = 0.025$ A, $I_3 = 0$

and $I_4 = 0.025$ A

25. According to the question,

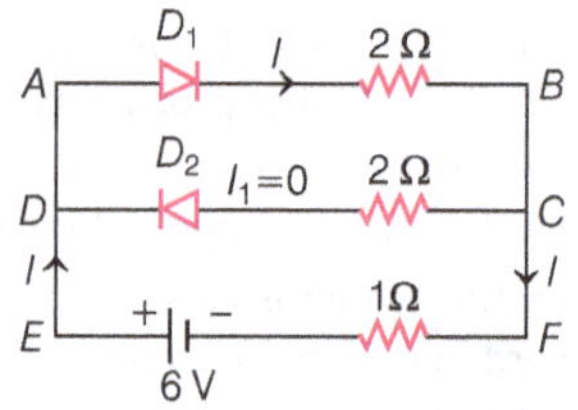

D_2 is in reverse bias, so it acts as open circuit.

$\therefore$ $R_{eq} = 2 + 1 = 3\Omega$

$$I = \frac{V}{R_{eq}} = \frac{6}{3} = 2\text{ A}$$

QR Code for Quick Test 1

QR Code for Quick Test 2

SELF ASSESSMENT TEST

Multiple Choice Questions (MCQs)

1. If a small amount of antimony is added to germanium crystal,
   (a) it becomes a *p*-type semiconductor
   (b) the antimony becomes an acceptor atom
   (c) there will be more free electrons than holes in the semiconductor
   (d) its resistance is increased
2. The electron concentration in an *n*-type semiconductor is the same as hole concentration in a *p*-type semiconductor. An external field (electric) is applied across each of them. Compare the currents in them.
   (a) Current in *n*-type = Current in *p*-type
   (b) Current in *p*-type > Current in *n*-type
   (c) Current in *n*-type > Current in *p*-type
   (d) No current will flow in *p*-type, current will only flow in *n*-type
3. The two ends of a *p*-*n* junction are joined by a wire,
   (a) there will not be a steady current in the circuit
   (b) there will be a steady current from the *n*-side to the *p*-side
   (c) there will be a steady current from the *p*-side to the *n*-side
   (d) there may or may not be a current depending upon the resistance of the connecting wire
4. At room temperature, the current carriers in an intrinsic semiconductor are
   (a) Holes only
   (b) electrons only
   (c) both electrons and holes
   (d) will act as an insulartor
5. When a forward bias is applied to a *p*-*n* junction, it
   (a) raises the potential barrier
   (b) reduces the majority carrier current to zero
   (c) lowers the potential barrier
   (d) None of the above

Assertion-Reason

Directions *(Q. Nos. 6-8) In the following questions, two statements are given- one labelled Assertion (A) and the other labelled Reason (R). Select the correct answer to these questions from the codes (a), (b), (c) and (d) as given below.*

(a) Both A and R are true and R is the correct explanation of A.
(b) Both A and R are true but R is not the correct explanation of A.
(c) A is true but R is false.
(d) A is false but R is true.

6. **Assertion (A)** Electron has higher mobility than hole in a semiconductor.
   Reason (R) The mass of electron is less than hole.
7. **Assertion (A)** The energy gap between the valance band and conduction band is greater in silicon than in germanium.
   Reason (R) Thermal energy produces fewer minority carriers in silicon than in germanium.
8. **Assertion (A)** When a p-n junction diode is reverse biased, a feeble reverse current flows known as reverse saturation current.
   Reason (R) In reverse bias condition, the minority carriers can cross the junction.

Case Based Question

Directions *(Q. No. 9) This question is case study based question. Read the following paragraph and answer the questions on the basis of same.*

9. When the diode is forward biased, it is found that beyond forward voltage $V = V_2$ called knee voltage, the conductivity is very high. At this value of battery biasing for *p*-*n* junction, the potential barrier is overcome and the current increases rapidly with increase in forward voltage.

When the diode is reverse biased, the reverse bias voltage produces a very small current about a few microamperes which almost remains constant with bias. This small current is reverse saturation current.

(i) In which of the following figures, the *p-n* diode is forward biased?

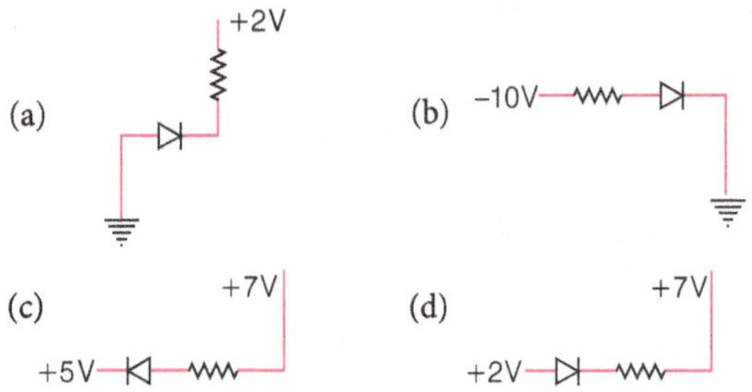

(ii) The *V-I* characteristic of a diode is shown in the figure. The ratio of forward to reverse bias resistance is

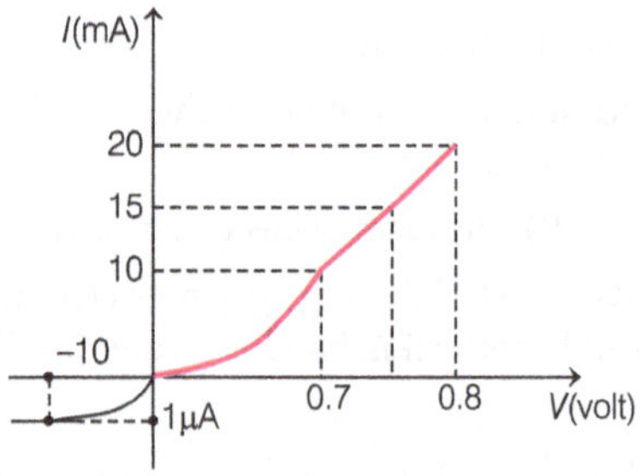

(a) 100
(b) 10^6
(c) 10
(d) 10^{-6}

(iii) In the case of forward biasing of a *p-n* junction diode, which one of the following figures correctly show the output direction of conventional current (indicated by an arrow mark)?

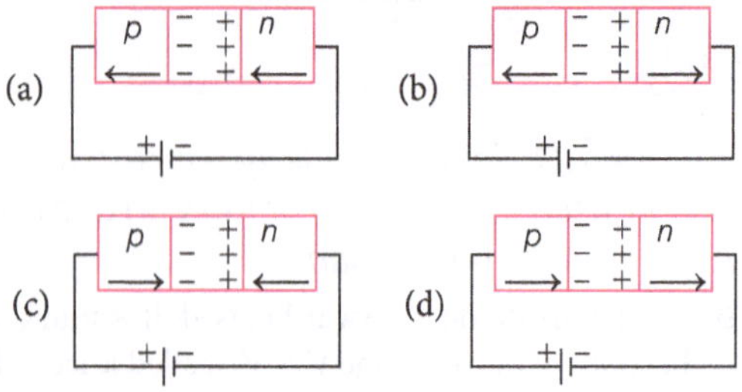

(iv) If an ideal junction diode is connected as shown, then the value of the current is

(a) 0.013 A
(b) 0.02 A
(c) 0.01 A
(d) 0.1 A

Very Short Answer Type Questions

10. In a *p-n* junction diode, the forward bias resistance is low as compared to the reverse bias resistance. Give reason. **All India 2020**

11. In half-wave rectification, what is the output frequency, if input frequency is 25 Hz? **CBSE SQP 2020-21**

Short Answer Type Questions

12. Answer the following and giving reasons.
(i) A *p-n* junction diode is damaged by a strong current.
(ii) Impurities are added in intrinsic semiconductors. **CBSE 2023**

13. Draw energy band diagram of *p* and *n* type semiconductors. Also, write two differences between *p* and *n* type semiconductors. **CBSE SQP 2020-21**

Long Answer Type Question

14. A *p-n* junction diode has a depletion layer of thickness 500 nm and an electric field 16×10^5 V/m.
(i) Find the potential barrier created.
(ii) Determine the minimum kinetic energy (in eV) that the conduction electrons must have so that they can diffuse from *n*-side onto *p*-side, in case of
(a) the junction is unbiased,
(b) the junction is forward biased at 0.5 V and
(c) the junction is reverse biased at 0.5 V. **CBSE 2023**

Answers

1. (c) 2. (c) 3. (a) 4. (c) 5. (c) 6. (a) 7. (b)
8. (a) 9. (i) (c) (ii) (d) (iii) (d) (iv) (c)

SAMPLE QUESTION PAPERS (1-3)

SAMPLE QUESTION PAPER 1

A Highly Simulated Sample Question Paper for CBSE Class XII Examination

PHYSICS

Time : 3 Hours **Max. Marks : 70**

General Instructions

1. There are 33 questions in all. All questions are compulsory.
2. This question paper has five sections : Section A, Section B, Section C, Section D and Section E.
3. All the sections are compulsory.
4. Section A contains sixteen questions, twelve MCQs and four Assertion Reasons based of 1 mark each, Section B contains five questions of two marks each, Section C contains seven questions of three marks each, Section D contains two case study based questions of four marks each and Section E contains three long answer questions of five marks each.
5. There is no overall choice. However, an internal choice has been provided in one question in Section B, one question in Section C, one question in each CBQ in Section D and all three questions in Section E. You have to attempt only one of the choices in such questions.
6. Use of calculators is not allowed.
7. You may use the following values of physical constants where ever necessary
   I. $c = 3 \times 10^8$ m/s
   II. $m_e = 9.1 \times 10^{-31}$ kg
   III. $e = 1.6 \times 10^{-19}$ C
   IV. $\mu_0 = 4\pi \times 10^{-7}$ T m A^{-1}
   V. $h = 6.63 \times 10^{-34}$ Js
   VI. $\varepsilon_0 = 8.854 \times 10^{-12} C^2 N^{-1} m^{-2}$
   VII. Avogadro's number = 6.023×10^{23} per gram mole

SECTION A

1. An electric dipole of moment 2×10^{-8} C-m is aligned in a uniform electric field of 2×10^4 N/C. The work done in rotating the dipole from 30° to 60° is

(a) 1.464×10^{-3} J (b) 1.464×10^{-4} J
(c) 4.164×10^{-3} J (d) 4.164×10^{-4} J

2. Equipotentials at a great distance from a collection of charges whose total sum is not zero are approximately

(a) spheres (b) planes
(c) paraboloids (d) ellipsoids

3. A photon of energy 3.4 eV is incident on a metal surface whose work function is 2 eV. Maximum kinetic energy of the photoelectron emitted by the metal surface will be

(a) 1.4 eV (b) 1.7 eV
(c) 5.4 eV (d) 6.8 eV

4. An electron of charge (e) is moving parallel to uniform magnetic field B with constant velocity v. The force acting on electron is

(a) Bev (b) Be/v
(c) B/ev (d) zero

5. Correct match of Column I with Column II is

	Column I		Column II
1.	Infrared waves	P.	to treat muscular strain
2.	Radio waves	Q.	for broadcasting
3.	X-rays	R.	to detect the fracture of bones
4.	Ultraviolet rays	S.	absorbed by the ozone layer of the atmosphere

(a) 1-Q, 2-R, 3-P, 4-S
(b) 1-R, 2-P, 3-Q, 4-S
(c) 1-P, 2-Q, 3-R, 4-S
(d) 1-S, 2-R, 3-P, 4-Q

6. **The self-inductance L of a solenoid of length l and area of cross-section A, with a fixed number of turns N increases when**
   (a) both l and A increase
   (b) l decreases and A increases
   (c) l increases and A decreases
   (d) both l and A decrease

7. **For scattering of α-particles, Rutherford suggested that**
   (a) mass of atom and its positive charge were concentrated at centre of atom
   (b) only mass of atom is concentrated at centre of atom
   (c) only positive charge of atom is concentrated at centre of atom
   (d) mass of atom is uniformly distributed throughout its volume

8. **The angular momentum of an electron in hydrogen atom in ground state is**
   (a) $\frac{h}{\pi}$ (b) $\frac{h}{2\pi}$
   (c) $\frac{2\pi}{h}$ (d) $\frac{\pi}{h}$

9. **An ammeter of resistance 0.81 Ω reads up to 1A. The value of the required shunt to increase the range to 10 A is**
   (a) 0.9 Ω (b) 0.09 Ω
   (c) 0.03 Ω (d) 0.30 Ω

10. **The relative permeability of a substance X is slightly less than unity and that of substance Y is slightly more than unity, then**
    (a) X is paramagnetic and Y is ferromagnetic
    (b) X is diamagnetic and Y is ferromagnetic
    (c) X and Y both are paramagnetic
    (d) X is diamagnetic and Y is paramagnetic

11. **An electron with angular momentum L moving around the nucleus has a magnetic moment given by**
    (a) $eL/2m$ (b) $eL/3m$
    (c) $eL/4m$ (d) eL/m

12. **The large scale transmission of electrical energy over long distances is done with the use of transformers. The voltage output of the generator is stepped-up because of**
    (a) reduction of current
    (b) reduction of current and voltage both
    (c) power loss is cut down
    (d) (a) and (c) both

For questions 13 to 16, two statements are given-one labelled Assertion (A) and the other labelled Reason (R). Select the correct answer to these questions from the options as given below.

(a) If both A and R are true and R is the correct explanation of A.
(b) If both A and R are true but R is not the correct explanation of A.
(c) If A is true but R is false.
(d) If both A and R are false.

13. **Assertion** A capacitor is connected to a direct current source. Its reactance is infinite.
    Reason Reactance of a capacitor is given by $X_C = \frac{1}{\omega C}$.

14. **Assertion** If a proton and an α-particle enter a uniform magnetic field perpendicularly with the same speed, then the time period of revolution of α-particle is double than that of proton.
    Reason In a magnetic field, the period of revolution at a charged particle is directly proportional to the mass of the particle and inversely proportional to the charge of particle.

15. **Assertion** If the inner solenoid was much shorter than (and placed well inside) the outer solenoid, then we could still have calculated the flux linkage $N_1\phi_1$.
    Reason The inner solenoid is effectively immersed in a uniform magnetic field due to the outer solenoid.

16. **Assertion** Propagation of light through an optical fibre is due to total internal reflection taking place at the core-clad interface.
    Reason Refractive index of the material of the core of the optical fibre is greater than that of air.

SECTION B

17. **A germanium *p-n* junction diode is connected to a battery with milliammeter in series.**
    (a) What should be the minimum voltage of battery, so that current may flow in the circuit?
    (b) What happens, if the diode is now made of silicon? Give reason for your answer.

18. **The wavelength λ of a photon and the de-Broglie wavelength of an electron of mass m have the same value. Show that the energy of the photon is $2\lambda mc/h$ times the kinetic energy of the electron, where c and h have their usual meanings.**

19. A ray of light is incident at a glass-water interface at an angle of i, it emerges finally parallel to the surface of water, then what will be the value of μ_g?

20. What is the difference between the values of potential difference across the two terminals of a cell in an open circuit and closed circuit?

21. I. "Mirrors used in search lights are parabolic but not concave spherical". Explain, why?

Or

II. Use the mirror equation to show that an object placed between f and $2f$ of a concave mirror produces a real image beyond $2f$.

SECTION C

22. I. Find the binding energy per nucleon of ${}_{20}\text{Ca}^{40}$ nucleus. Given,

$m({}_{20}\text{Ca}^{40}) = 39.962589$ u,

$m_n = 1.008665$ u and $m_p = 1.007825$ u.

Take, 1 amu $= 931\ \text{MeV}/c^2$.

Or

II. Draw a labelled diagram of a moving coil galvanometer and explain its working. What is the function of radial magnetic field inside the coil?

23. In an aluminium (Al) bar of square cross-section, a square hole is drilled and is filled with iron (Fe) as shown in the figure. The electrical resistivities of Al and Fe are $2.7 \times 10^{-8}\ \Omega$-m and $1.0 \times 10^{-7}\ \Omega$-m, respectively.

Calculate the electrical resistance between the two faces P and Q of the composite bar.

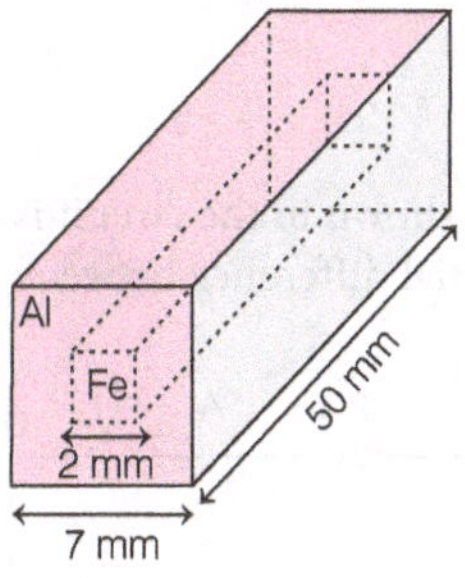

24. How are electromagnetic waves produced by oscillating charges? Draw a sketch of linearly polarised electromagnetic waves propagating in the z-direction. Indicate the directions of the oscillating electric and magnetic fields.

25. A straight wire carrying a current of 10 A is bent into a semi-circular arc of radius 2.0 cm as shown in the figure. What is the magnetic field at O due to

(i) straight segments

(ii) the semi-circular arc?

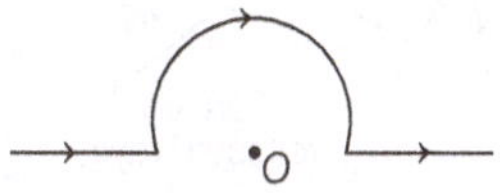

26. Three charges $-q, +Q$ and $-q$ are placed at equal distance on straight line. If the potential energy of the system of three charges is zero, then what is the value of ratio $Q:q$?

27. A circular coil of 200 turns and radius 10 cm is placed in a uniform magnetic field of 0.5 T, normal to the plane of the coil. If the current in the coil is 3 A, then calculate the

(i) total torque on the coil,

(ii) total force on the coil and

(iii) average force on each electron in the coil, due to the magnetic field.

Assume the area of cross-section of the wire to be 10 cm and the free electron density is 10^{29} m.

28. I. (a) Define self-inductance. Write its SI unit.

(b) Derive the expression for self-inductance of a long solenoid of length l and having cross-sectional area A, having N number of turns.

Or

II. A current carrying conductor, I be current in the conductor, dl be infinitesimal small element of the conductor, dB be the magnetic field at point Q, then what will be the magnetic field at given point Q. Write the vector form of this law.

SECTION D

(Case Study Based Questions)

29. *Read the following paragraph and answer the questions that follow*

Total internal reflection is the phenomenon of reflection of light into denser medium at the interface of denser medium with a rarer medium. Light must travel from denser to rarer medium and angle of incidence in denser medium must be greater than critical angle

(i_c) for the pair of media in contact, we can show

$$\mu = \frac{1}{\sin i_c}.$$

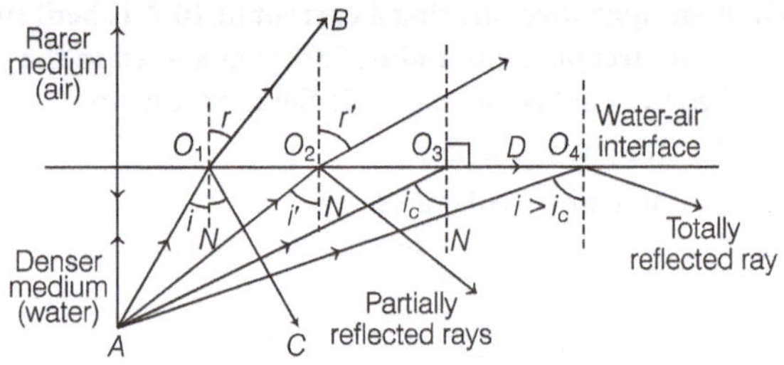

(i) In total internal reflection,
 (a) light ray travelling through a denser medium is completely reflected back to denser medium
 (b) light ray travelling through a denser medium is completely refracted to rarer medium
 (c) light ray is partially reflected back to denser medium and partially refracted to rarer medium
 (d) light ray is absorbed completely by denser medium

(ii) Total internal reflection of a light ray travelling from denser medium to rarer medium occurs only when angle of incidence is
 (a) 45°
 (b) 90°
 (c) acute
 (d) more than a certain value

(iii) Critical angle for water-air interface is 48.6°. What is the refractive index of water?
 (a) 1 (b) 3/2
 (c) 4/3 (d) 3/4

(iv) Light is travelling from air to water at $\angle i = 50°$, which is greater than critical angle for air-water interface. What fraction of light will be totally reflected?
 (a) 100% (b) 50%
 (c) 25% (d) None of these

Or

Critical angle for glass-air interface where refractive index μ of glass is 3/2, is
 (a) 41.8° (b) 60°
 (c) 30° (d) 44.3°

30. *Read the following paragraph and answer the questions that follow*

A semiconductor diode is basically a *p-n* junction with metallic contacts provided at the ends for the application of an external voltage. It is a two-terminal device. When an external voltage is applied across a semiconductor diode such that *p*-side is connected to the positive terminal of the battery and *n*-side to the negative terminal, it is said to be forward biased. When an external voltage is applied across the diode such that *n*-side is connected to positive terminal and *p*-side is connected to negative terminal, it is said to be reverse biased. An ideal diode is one whose resistance in forward biasing is zero and the resistance is infinite in reverse biasing. When the diode is forward biased, it is found that beyond forward voltage called knee voltage, the conductivity is very high. When the biasing voltage is more than the knee voltage, the potential barrier is overcome and the current increases rapidly with increase in forward voltage. When the diode is reverse biased, the reverse bias voltage produces a very small current about a few microamperes which almost remains constant with bias. This small current is reverse saturation current.

(i) If reverse biasing potential is increased beyond a certain critical (breakdown) value, then
 (a) diode gets destroyed due to overheating
 (b) no current flows through the diode
 (c) after breakdown a heavy current flows from *p* to *n*-side
 (d) potential barrier becomes zero

(ii) In which of the following figures, the *p-n* diode is reverse biased?

(a)
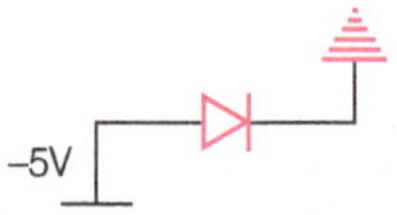

(b)
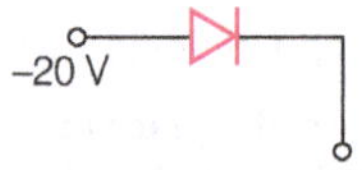

(c)
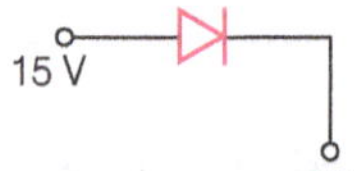

(d)
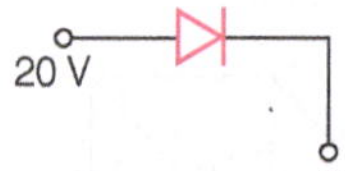

(iii) The diode shown in the circuit is a silicon diode. The potential difference between the points *A* and *B* will be

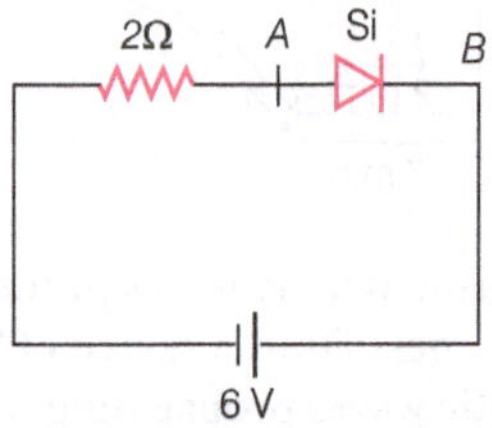

 (a) 6 V (b) 0.6 V
 (c) 0.7 V (d) 0 V

Or

Based on the *V-I* characteristics of the diode, we can classify diode as
 (a) bilateral device (b) ohmic device

(c) non-ohmic device (d) passive element

(iv) Which of these graphs shows potential difference between p-side and n-side of a p-n junction in equilibrium?

(a) 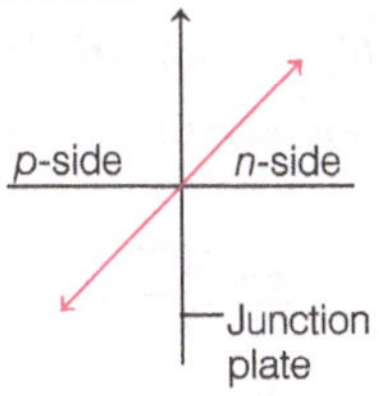

(b) 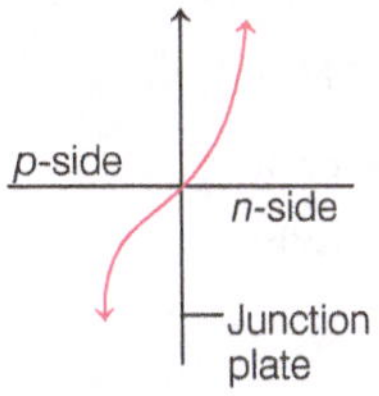

(c) 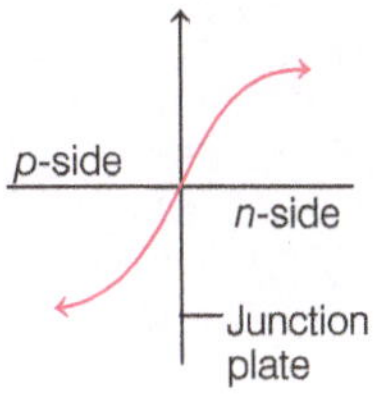

(d) 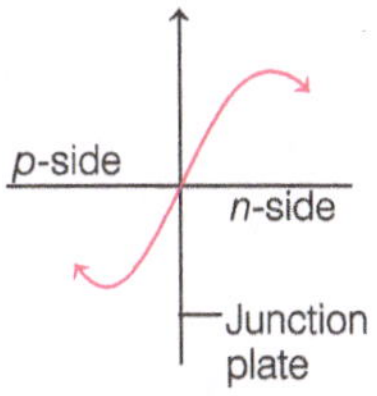

SECTION E

31. I. (a) Define a wavefront and how they are different from a ray?

(b) Using Huygens' construction of secondary wavelets, sketch a diagram showing the passage of a plane wavefont from a denser to a rarer medium and verify by using Snell's law.

(c) What is the shape of the wavefront on the earth for sunlight?

Or II. (a) Draw a ray diagram for the formation of image of a point object by a thin double convex lens having radii of curvature R_1 and R_2. Hence, derive lens Maker's formula.

(b) Light from a point source in air falls on a spherical glass surface ($n = 1.5$, radius of curvature = 20 cm). The distance of the light source from the glass surface is 100 cm. Calculate the image distance from the glass surface.

32. I. (a) Derive an expression for the capacitance of a parallel plate capacitor each of area A held parallel to each other at suitable distance d and there is vacuum between the plates.

(b) In the circuit shown in figure, find the equivalent capacitance and the charge stored in each capacitor.

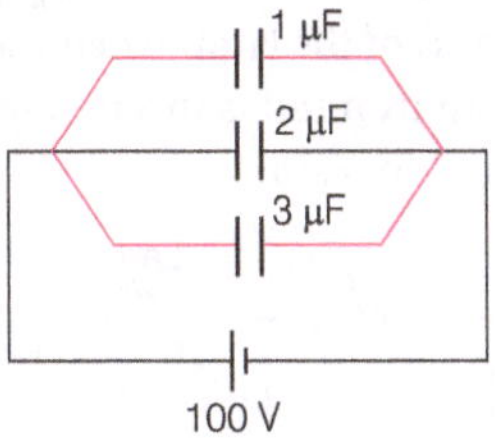

Or

II. (a) A slab of material of dielectric constant K has the same area as that of the plates of a parallel plate capacitor, but has the thickness $d/2$, where d is the separation between the plates. Find out the expression for its capacitance when the slab is inserted between the plates of the capacitor.

(b) A network of four capacitors each of $12\,\mu F$ capacitance is connected to a 500 V supply as shown in the figure.

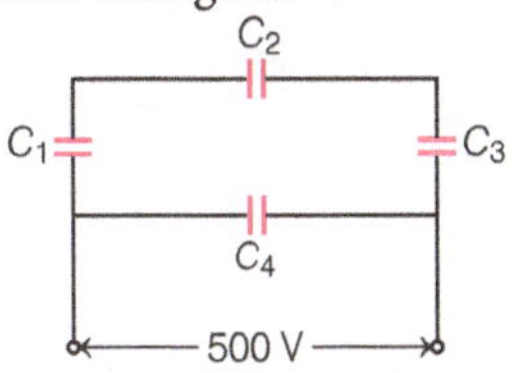

Determine the equivalent capacitance of the network and the charge on each capacitor.

33. I. (a) Draw graphs showing the variation of inductive reactance and capacitive reactance with frequency of applied AC source.

(b) Draw the phasor diagram of series L-R-C circuit connected to an AC source $E = E_0 \sin \omega t$.

(c) A device X is connected to an AC source $V = V_0 \sin \omega t$. The variation of voltage, current and power in one complete cycle is shown in the following figure.

(i) Which curve shows power consumption over a full cycle?

(ii) Identify the device X.

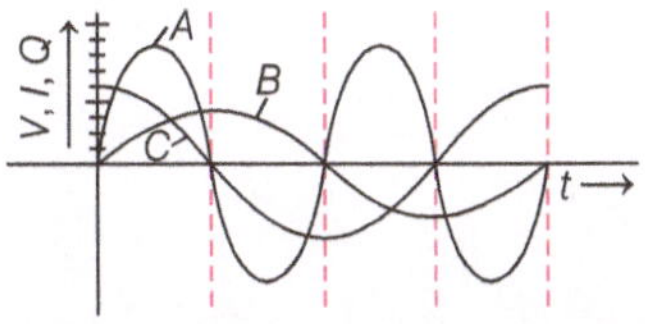

Or

II. (a) Draw a graph showing variation of amplitude of circuit current with changing frequency of applied voltage in a series *L-C-R* circuit for two different values of resistance R_1 and $R_2 (R_1 > R_2)$.

(b) A lamp is connected in series with an inductor and an AC source. What happens to the brightness of the lamp when the key is plugged in and an iron rod is inserted inside the inductor? Explain.

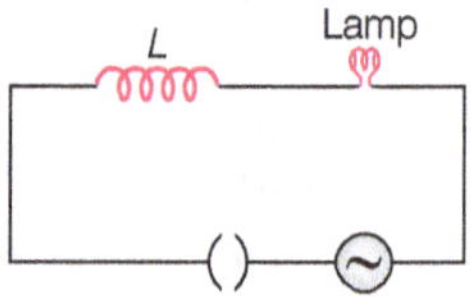

(c) An AC voltage $V = V_m \sin \omega t$ is applied across an inductor of inductance L. Find the instantaneous power P_i supplied to the inductor. Show graphically the variation of P_i with ωt.

Answers

1. (b) **2.** (a) **3.** (a) **4.** (d) **5.** (c) **6.** (b) **7.** (a) **8.** (b) **9.** (b) **10.** (d) **11.** (a) **12.** (d) **13.** (a) **14.** (b) **15.** (a) **16.** (c)

22. I. 8.55 MeV/nucleon **23.** $\frac{1875}{64} \mu\Omega$

25. (i) zero, (ii) $5\pi \times 10^{-5}$ T **26.** 1 : 4

27. (i) 0, (ii) 0, (iii) 1.5×10^{-24} N

29. (i)-c, (ii)-d, (iii)-c (iv)-a or a

30. (i)-a, (ii)-b, (iii)-a or c, (iv)-c

31. II. (b) 100 cm

32. II. (b) 16 μF and 8 μC

SAMPLE QUESTION PAPER 2

A Highly Simulated Sample Question Paper for CBSE Class XII Examination

PHYSICS

Time : 3 Hours **Max. Marks : 70**

General Instructions

1. There are 33 questions in all. All questions are compulsory.
2. This question paper has five sections : Section A, Section B, Section C, Section D and Section E.
3. All the sections are compulsory.
4. Section A contains sixteen questions, twelve MCQs and four Assertion Reasons based of 1 mark each, Section B contains five questions of two marks each, Section C contains seven questions of three marks each, Section D contains two case study based questions of four marks each and Section E contains three long answer questions of five marks each.
5. There is no overall choice. However, an internal choice has been provided in one question in Section B, one question in Section C, one question in each CBQ in Section D and all three questions in Section E. You have to attempt only one of the choices in such questions.
6. Use of calculators is not allowed.
7. You may use the following values of physical constants where ever necessary
   I. $c = 3 \times 10^8$ m/s
   II. $m_e = 9.1 \times 10^{-31}$ kg
   III. $e = 1.6 \times 10^{-19}$ C
   IV. $\mu_0 = 4\pi \times 10^{-7}$ T m A^{-1}
   V. $h = 6.63 \times 10^{-34}$ Js
   VI. $\varepsilon_0 = 8.854 \times 10^{-12}$ C^2 N^{-1}m^{-2}
   VII. Avogadro's number $= 6.023 \times 10^{23}$ per gram mole

SECTION A

1. If electrostatic potential at the surfce of a sphere of 5 cm radius is 50 V, then the potential at the centre of sphere will be

(a) 10 V (b) 50 V
(c) 250 V (d) zero

2. Work done by an external force in bringing a unit positive charge from infinity to a point is

(a) equal to the electrostatic potential (V) at that point
(b) equal to the negative of work done by electrostatic forces
(c) Both (a) and (b)
(d) Neither (a) nor (b)

3. If drift velocity of electron is v_d and intensity of electric field is E, then which of the following relations obeys the Ohm's law?

(a) $v_d =$ constant
(b) $v_d \propto E$
(c) $v_d = \sqrt{E}$
(d) $v_d \propto E^2$

4. If the velocity of charged particle is doubled and value of magnetic field is reduced to half, then the radius of path of charged particle will be

(a) 8 times (b) 4 times
(c) 3 times (d) 2 times

5. The current i is flowing in a coil of area A with the number of turns N, then the magnetic moment of the coil M will be

(a) NiA (b) Ni/A
(c) $Ni/\sqrt{A}$ (d) N^2Ai

6. A pure inductor of 25.0 mH is connected to a source of 220 V. Find the inductive reactance if the frequency of the source is 50 Hz.

(a) 785Ω (b) 6.50Ω

(c) 7.85Ω (d) 8.75Ω

7. Correct match of Column I with Column II is

Column I		Column II	
1.	p –type semiconductor	P.	Pure semiconductor
2.	Intrinsic semiconductor	Q.	Doped with impurity
3.	Extrinsic semiconductor	R.	Majority charge carriers are electrons
4.	n – type semiconductor	S.	Majority charge carriers are holes

(a) 1-R, 2-Q, 3-S, 4-P
(b) 1-P, 2-R, 3-Q, 4-S
(c) 1-Q, 2-P, 3-R, 4-S
(d) 1-S, 2-P, 3-Q, 4-R

8. Given, $m({}^{56}_{26}\text{Fe}) = 55.934939\,\text{u}$ and $m({}^{209}_{83}\text{Bi}) = 208.980388\,\text{u}$

$m_{\text{proton}} = 1.007825\,\text{u}, m_{\text{neutron}} = 1.008665\,\text{u}$.

Then, BE per nucleon of Fe is?

(a) 8.790 MeV (b) 7.75 MeV

(c) 7.5 MeV (d) Data insufficient

9. The substance which is doped in an intrinsic semiconductor to make p-type semiconductor is

(a) phosphorus (b) antimony

(c) aluminium (d) arsenic

10. The speed of electromagnetic wave in vacuum depends upon the source of radiation,

(a) increases as we move from γ-rays to radio waves

(b) decreases as we move from γ-rays to radio waves

(c) is same for all of them

(d) None of the above

11. Which one of the following phenomena is not explained by Huygens' construction of wavefront?

(a) Refraction (b) Reflection

(c) Diffraction (d) Origin of spectra

12. The work function of a metal is hc/λ_0. If light of wavelength λ is incident on its surface, then the essential condition for the electron to come out from the metal surface is

(a) $\lambda \geq \lambda_0$ (b) $\lambda \geq 2\lambda_0$

(c) $\lambda \leq \lambda_0$ (d) $\lambda \leq \lambda_0/2$

For questions 13 to 16 two statements are given-one labelled Assertion (A) and the other labelled Reason (R). Select the correct answer to these questions from the options as given below.

(a) If both A and R are true and R is the correct explanation of A.

(b) If both A and R are true but R is not the correct explanation of A.

(c) If A is true but R is false.

(d) If both A and R are false.

13. **Assertion** Magnetism is relativistic in nature, i.e. stationary charges do not produce magnetic field.

Reason When we move along the charge, i.e. there is no relative motion, then we find no magnetic field associated with the charge.

14. **Assertion** Inductance coils are made of copper.

Reason Induced current is more in wire having less resistance.

15. **Assertion** Atoms of each element are stable and emit characteristic spectrum.

Reason The spectrum provides useful information about the atomic structure.

16. **Assertion** The applied voltage (in forward bias of a p-n junction) mostly drops across the depletion region and the voltage drop across the p-side and n-side of the junction is negligible.

Reason Resistance of depletion region is large compared to resistance of n or p-side.

SECTION B

17. For spherically symmetrical charge distribution with charge density varying as $\rho(x) = \rho_0\left(\frac{5}{4} - \frac{x}{R}\right)$

where, $x < r$, upto $r = R$

The electric field at a distance $(r < R)$ comes out to be $E = \frac{\rho_0 r}{4\varepsilon_0}\left(\frac{5}{3} - \frac{r}{R}\right)$

Justify the relation obtained.

18. The bombardment of lithium with protons gives rise to the following reaction

$${}^{7}_{2}\text{Li} + {}^{1}_{1}\text{H} \longrightarrow {}^{4}_{2}\text{He} + {}^{4}_{2}\text{He} + \text{Energy}$$

The atomic masses of lithium, hydrogen and helium are 7.016 amu, 1.008 amu and 4.004 amu, respectively. Find the initial energy of each helium atom. (Take, 1 amu = 931 MeV/c^2)

19. The plot of the variation of potential difference across a combination of three identical cells in series *versus*

current is as shown in the figure. What is the emf of each cell?

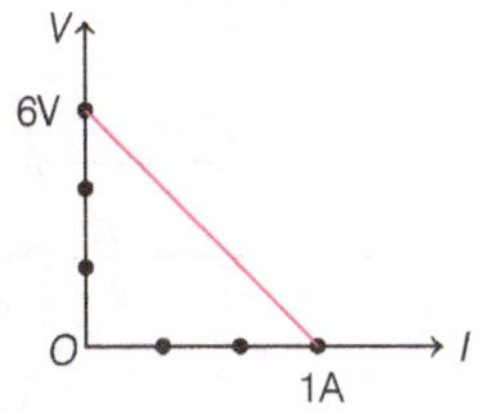

20. **What are extrinsic semiconductors? Write the names and types of dopants.**

21. I. The electric potential V as a function of distance x is shown in the figure. Construct a graph of the electric field strength E *versus* distance x.

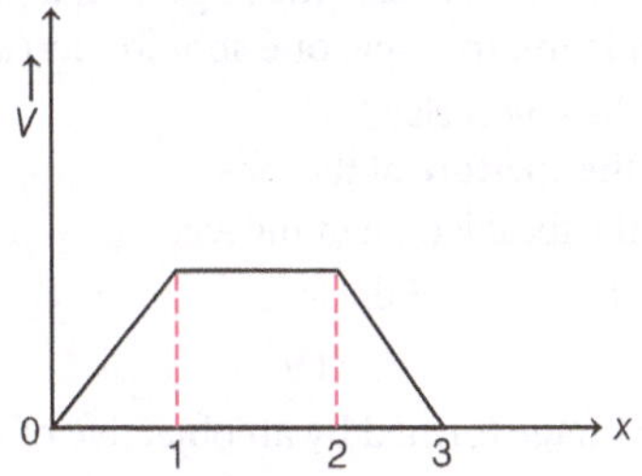

Or

II. The graph shows the variation of charge q *versus* potential difference V for two capacitors C_1 and C_2. The two capacitors have the same plate separation but the plate area of C_2 is double than that of C_1. Which of the lines in the graph corresponds to C_1 and C_2, and why?

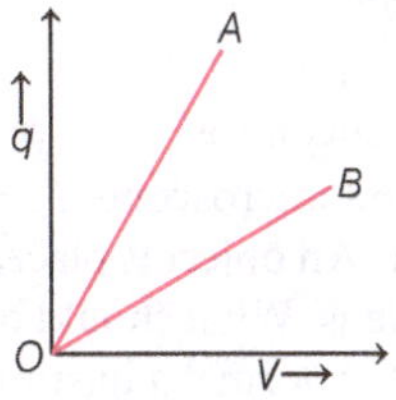

SECTION C

22. I. (a) Name the electromagnetic waves which

(a) maintain the earth's warmth and

(b) are used in aircraft navigation.

(b) To which regions of the electromagnetic spectrum do the following wavelengths belong

(a) 250 nm (b) 1500 nm

Show that the radiation pressure exerted by an EM wave of intensity I on a surface kept in vacuum is $\frac{I}{c}$.

Or

II. (a) Write two characteristic features of nuclear force.

(b) Draw a plot of potential energy of a pair of nucleons as a function of their separation.

23. **A metallic rod of length l and resistance R is rotated with a frequency ν, with one end hinged at the centre and the other end at the circumference of a circular metallic ring of radius l, about an axis passing through the centre and perpendicular to the plane of the ring. A constant and uniform magnetic field B parallel to the axis is present everywhere.**

(i) Derive the expression for the induced emf and the current in the rod.

(ii) Due to the presence of the current in the rod and of the magnetic field, find the expression for the magnitude and direction of the force acting on this rod.

24. **Two convex lenses A and B of an astronomical telescope having focal lengths 5 cm and 20 cm respectively, are arranged as shown below**

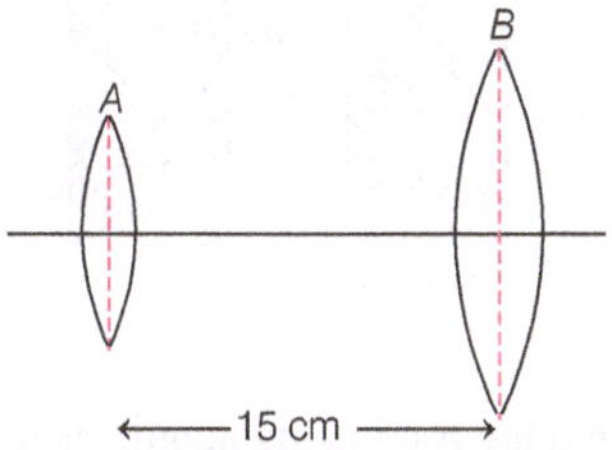

(i) Which one of the two lenses you will select as the objective lens and why?

(ii) What should be the change in the distance between the lenses to have the telescope in its normal adjustment position?

(iii) Calculate the magnitude of magnifying power of the telescope in the normal adjustment position.

25. I. The force experienced by a unit charge when placed at a distance of 0.10 m from the middle of an electric dipole on its axial line is 0.025 N and when it is placed at a distance of 0.2 m, the force is reduced to 0.002 N. Calculate the dipole length.

Or

II. A point charge causes an electric flux -3×10^{-14} N-m^2/C to pass through a spherical Gaussian surface.

(a) Calculate the value of the point charge.

(b) If the radius of the Gaussian surface is doubled, how much flux would pass through the surface?

26. **Two identical loops A and B each of radius 5 cm are lying in perpendicular planes such that they have a common centre as shown in the figure. Find the magnitude and direction of the net magnetic field at the common centre of the two coils A and B, if they carry currents equal to 3 A and 4 A, respectively.**

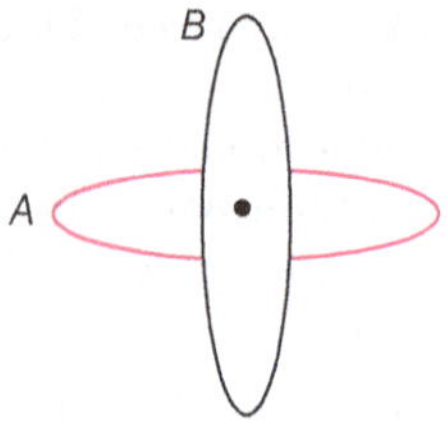

27. **Let two identical parallel plate (air) capacitors C_A and C_B have capacitance each. The space between their plates is now filled with dielectrics as shown in the figure. If the two capacitors still have equal capacitance, then obtain the relation between dielectric constants K, K_A and K_B.**

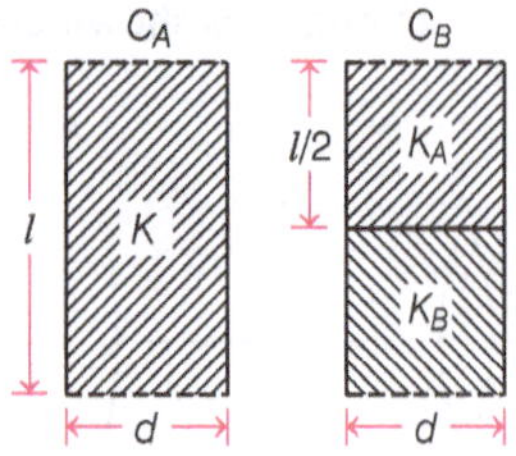

28. I. (a) A metallic rod having length l is moved perpendicular to its length with velocity v in a magnetic field **B** acting perpendicular to the plane in which rod moves. Derive the expression for the induced emf.

(b) State Lenz's law. When a metallic rod held horizontally along East-West direction, is allowed to fall under gravity, will there be an emf induced at its ends? Justify your answer.

SECTION D

(Case Study Based Questions)

29. *Read the following paragraph and answer the questions that follow*

Microscope is an optical instrument which forms large image of close and minute objects. A simple microscope is a converging lens of small focal length. When an object is at a distance less than the focal length of the lens, the image obtained is virtual, erect and magnified.

When the object is at a distance equal to the focal length of the lens, the image is formed at infinity.

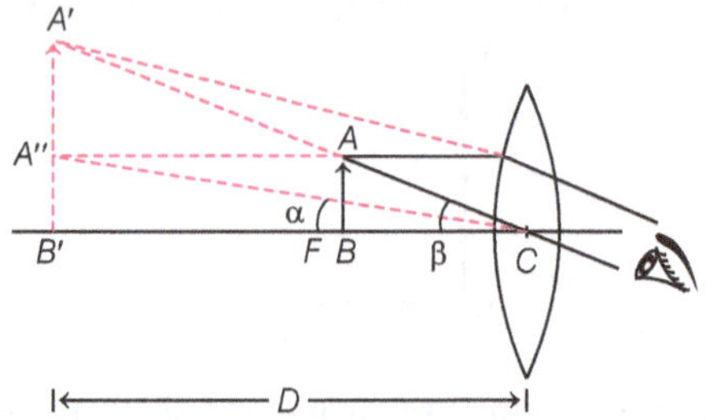

(i) A simple microscope has a limited maximum magnification

(a) greater than 9 (b) lesser than 9
(c) equal to 9 (d) Both (b) and (c)

(ii) In order to increase the angular magnification of a simple microscope, one should increase

(a) the object size
(b) the aperture of the lens
(c) the focal length of the lens
(d) the power of the lens

Or

The image formed by an objective of a compound microscope is

(a) virtual and diminished
(b) real and diminished
(c) real and enlarged
(d) virtual and enlarged

(iii) The distance between the second focal point of the objective f_o and first focal point of the eyepiece, i.e. f_e is called

(a) tube length
(b) focal length
(c) image distance
(d) radius of curvature

(iv) For compound microscope, $f_o = 1$ cm, $f_e = 2.5$ cm. An object is placed at distance 1.2 cm from object lens. What should be the length of microscope for normal adjustment?

(a) 8.5 cm (b) 8.3 cm
(c) 6.5 cm (d) 6.3 cm

30. *Read the following paragraph and answer the questions that follow*

Matter cannot exist both as a particle and as a wave simultaneously. At a particular instant of time, it is either the one or the other aspect, i.e. the two aspects are complementary to each other.

According to de-Broglie, a wave is associated with moving material particle which controls the particle in every respect. The wave associated with moving

material particle is called matter wave or de-Broglie wave whose wavelength is called de-Broglie wavelength.

(i) The de-Broglie wave of a moving particle does not depend on

(a) mass (b) charge
(c) velocity (d) momentum

(ii) The de-Broglie wavelength of a particle of kinetic energy, K is λ. What will be the wavelength of the particle, if its kinetic energy is $\frac{K}{9}$?

(a) λ (b) 2λ (c) 3λ (d) 4λ

(iii) Which of the following figures represents the variation of particle momentum and the associated de-Broglie wavelength?

(a)
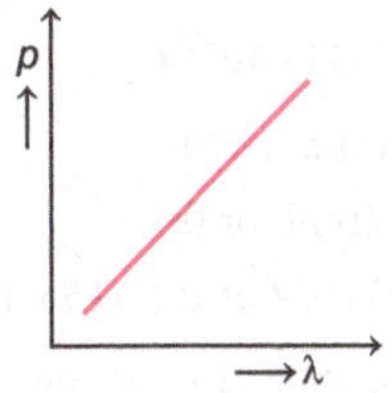

(b)
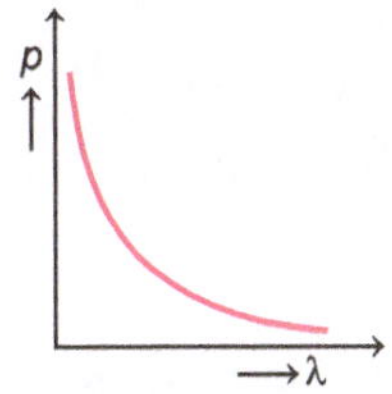

(c)
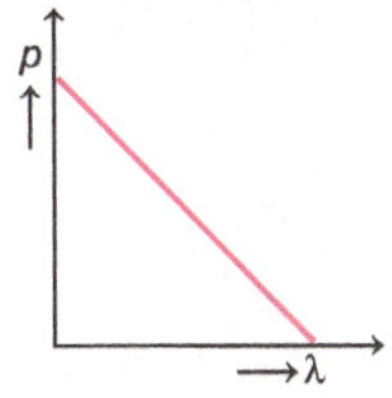

(d)
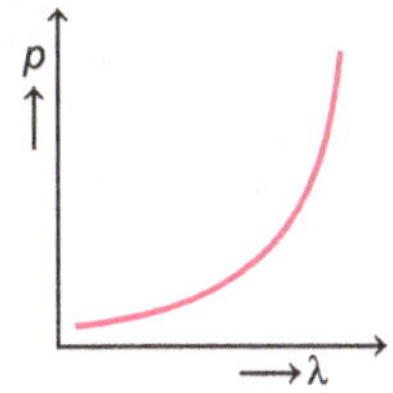

(iv) de-Broglie wavelength associated with an electron, accelerating through a potential difference of 100 V lies in the region of

(a) Gamma rays
(b) X-rays
(c) Ultraviolet rays
(d) Visible region

Or

A proton and an α-particle are accelerated through the same potential difference. The ratio of de-Broglie wavelength λ_p to that of λ_α is

(a) $\sqrt{2}:1$ (b) $\sqrt{4}:1$
(c) $\sqrt{6}:1$ (d) $\sqrt{8}:1$

SECTION E

31. I. (a) Show that the refractive index of the material of a prism is given by

$$\mu = \frac{\sin\frac{(A+\delta_m)}{2}}{\sin\left(\frac{A}{2}\right)}$$

where, symbols have their usual meanings.

(b) Show analytically from the lens equation that when the object is at the principal focus, the image is formed at infinity.

Or

II. (a) Construct secondary wavelets by using Huygens' principle and draw a diagram showing the passage of plane wavefront from an oil medium to air medium and verify Snell's law.

(b) Write three characteristic features to differentiate between diffraction and interference.

32. I. (a) The coil area of a galvanometer is $25 \times 10^{-4}\ m^2$. It consists of 150 turns of a wire and is in a magnetic field of 0.15 T. The restoring torque constant of the suspension fibre is 10^{-6} N-m per degree. Assuming the magnetic field to be radial, calculate the maximum current that can be measured by the galvanometer if the scale can accommodate 30° deflection.

(b) A proton and α-particle, accelerated through same potential difference, enter in a region of uniform magnetic field with their velocities perpendicular to the field. Compare the radii of circular path followed by them.

Or

II. (a) Write the four important properties of the magnetic field lines due to a bar magnet.

(b) A wire of length L is bent in the form of a circle of radius R and carries current I. What is its magnetic moment?

(c) A bar magnet of length 0.1 m and a pole strength 10^{-4} A-m is placed in a magnetic field of 30 Wb/m at an angle 30°. Determine the couple acting on it.

33. I. Figure shown below, shows how the reactance of a capacitor varies with frequency.

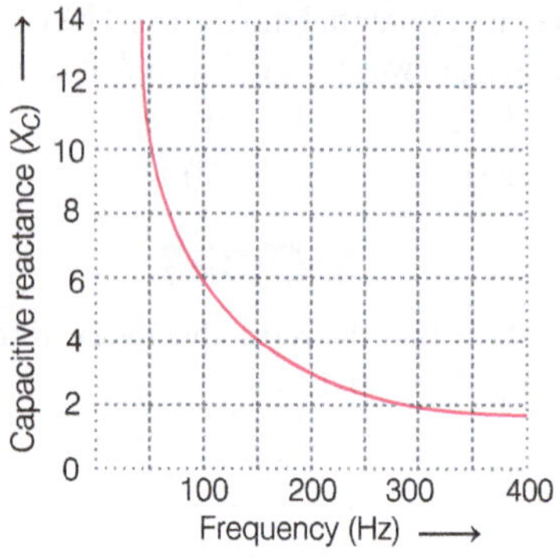

(a) Use the information of the graph to calculate the value of capacitance of capacitor.

(b) An inductor of inductance L has the same reactance as the capacitor at 100 Hz. Find the value of L.

(c) Using the same axes, draw a graph of reactance against the frequency for the inductor given in part (ii).

(d) If this capacitor and inductor were connected in series to a resistor of $10\,\Omega$, what would be the impedance of the combination at 300 Hz?

Or

II. Draw a labelled diagram of AC generator, explain its theory and working. An armature coil consists of 20 turns of wire, each of area, $A = 0.09\,\text{m}^2$ and total resistance $15\,\Omega$ rotates in a magnetic field of 0.5T at a constant frequency $(150/\pi)$ Hz.

Calculate the value of maximum emf produced in the coil.

Answers

1. (b) *2.* (c) *3.* (b) *4.* (b) *5.* (a) *6.* (c) *7.* (d)
8. (a) *9.* (c) *10.* (c) *11.* (d) *12.* (c) *13.* (a) *14.* (a)
15. (b) *16.* (a)

24. (ii) 10 cm (iii) 4

25. I. 0.1 m or II. (a) -2.655×10^{-25}C

29. (i)-d, (ii)-c or (c) (iii)-a (iv)-b

30. (i)-b, (ii)-c, (iii)-b (iv)-b or (b)

32. I. (a) 5.3×10^{-4}A, (b) $1/\sqrt{2}$ or II (c) 1.5×10^{-4} Nm

33. I. (a) 2.65×10^{-4}F, (b) 9.55×10^{-3} H or II. 270 V

SAMPLE QUESTION PAPER 3

A Highly Simulated Sample Question Paper for CBSE Class XII Examination

PHYSICS

Time : 3 Hours **Max. Marks : 70**

General Instructions

1. There are 33 questions in all. All questions are compulsory.
2. This question paper has five sections : Section A, Section B, Section C, Section D and Section E.
3. All the sections are compulsory.
4. Section A contains sixteen questions, twelve MCQs and four Assertion Reasons based of 1 mark each, Section B contains five questions of two marks each, Section C contains seven questions of three marks each, Section D contains two case study based questions of four marks each and Section E contains three long answer questions of five marks each.
5. There is no overall choice. However, an internal choice has been provided in one question in Section B, one question in Section C, one question in each CBQ in Section D and all three questions in Section E. You have to attempt only one of the choices in such questions.
6. Use of calculators is not allowed.
7. You may use the following values of physical constants where ever necessary
   I. $c = 3 \times 10^8$ m/s
   II. $m_e = 9.1 \times 10^{-31}$ kg
   III. $e = 1.6 \times 10^{-19}$ C
   IV. $\mu_0 = 4\pi \times 10^{-7}$ T m A^{-1}
   V. $h = 6.63 \times 10^{-34}$ Js
   VI. $\varepsilon_0 = 8.854 \times 10^{-12}$ $C^2 N^{-1} m^{-2}$
   VII. Avogadro's number $= 6.023 \times 10^{23}$ per gram mole

SECTION A

1. **As compared to ^{12}C atom, ^{14}C atom has**

(a) two extra protons and two extra electrons

(b) two extra protons but no extra electrons

(c) two extra neutrons and no extra electrons

(d) two extra neutrons and two extra electrons

2. **Density of a nucleus is**

(a) more for lighter elements and less for heavier elements

(b) more for heavier elements and less for lighter elements

(c) very less compared to ordinary matter

(d) a constant

3. **The conductivity of a semiconductor increases with increase in temperature, because**

(a) number density of free current carriers increases

(b) relaxation time increases

(c) both number density of carriers and relaxation time increase

(d) number density of carriers increases, relaxation time decreases but effect of decrease in relaxation time is much less than increase in number density

4. **According to Huygens' principle, each point of the wavefront is the source of**

(a) secondary disturbance

(b) primary disturbance

(c) third disturbance

(d) fourth disturbance

5. **The instantaneous magnetic flux linked with a coil is given by $\phi = (5t^3 - 100t + 300)$ Wb. The emf induced in the coil at time $t = 2$ s is**

(a) -40 V (b) 40 V (c) 140 V (d) 300 V

6. A magician during a show makes a glass lens with $n = 1.47$ disappear in a trough of liquid. Refractive index of the liquid is

(a) 1.47 (b) 1.33 (c) $\frac{4}{3}$ (d) $\frac{12}{5}$

7. If the orbital radius of the electron in a hydrogen atom is 4.7×10^{-11} m. Compute the kinetic energy of the electron in hydrogen atom.

(a) 15.3 eV (b) −15.3 eV (c) 13.6 eV (d) −13.6 eV

8. Two thin lenses are in contact and that combination has 15 cm focal length. If one lens has focal length 30 cm, then what is the second lens focal length?

(a) 15 cm (b) 25 cm (c) 20 cm (d) 30 cm

9. Correct match the Column I with Column II is

Column I	Column II
1. Torque on a dipole in unform electric field	P. $\frac{1}{4\pi\varepsilon_0}\int\frac{dq}{r^2}$
2. Electric field of a dipole at a point on the dipole axis	Q. $\frac{P}{4\pi\varepsilon_0 r^3}$
3. Electric field intensity at a point due to continuous charge distribution	R. $\frac{2P}{4\pi\varepsilon_0 r^3}$
4. Electric field of dipole at point on the equatorial plane	S. $2qaE\sin\theta$

(a) 1-S, 2-R, 3-P, 4-Q (b) 1-P, 2-Q, 3-R, 4-S
(c) 1-R, 2-P, 3-S, 4-Q (d) 1-Q, 2-R, 3-S, 4-P

10. Twenty million electrons reaches from point X to point Y in two micro second as shown in the figure. Direction and magnitude of the current is

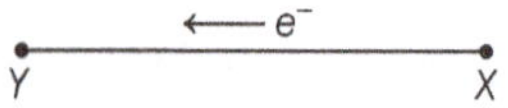

(a) 1.5×10^{-10} A from X to Y

(b) 1.6×10^{-6} A from Y to X

(c) 1.5×10^{-13} A from Y to X

(d) 1.6×10^{-4} A from X to Y

11. A charge q moving with velocity perpendicular to the magnetic field B will be

(a) $F = qvB$ (b) $F = \frac{qv}{B}$ (c) $F = \frac{qB}{v}$ (d) $F = \frac{Bv}{q}$

12. A resistance of 20Ω is connected to a source of an alternating potential, $V = 220\sin(100\pi t)$. The time taken by current to change from its peak value to rms value is

(a) 0.2 s (b) 0.25 s

(c) 25×10^{-3} s (d) 2.5×10^{-3} s

For questions 13 to 16 two statements are given-one labelled Assertion (A) and the other labelled Reason (R). Select the correct answer to these questions from the options as given below.

(a) If both A and R are true and R is the correct explanation of A.
(b) If both A and R are true but R is not the correct explanation of A.
(c) If A is true but R is false.
(d) If both A and R are false.

13. Assertion If Gaussian surface does not enclose any charge, then **E** at any point on the Gaussian surface must be zero.

Reason No net charge is enclosed by Gaussian surface, so net flux passing through the surface is non-zero.

14. Assertion Critical angle of light passing from glass to air is minimum for violet colour.

Reason The wavelength of violet light is greater than the light of other colours.

15. Assertion To observe diffraction of light, the size of obstacle aperture should be of the order of 10^{-7} m.

Reason 10^{-7} m is the order of wavelength of visible light.

16. Assertion When two long straight wires are connected to a battery, they may come close to each other.

Reason Force of attraction acts between two wires carrying current.

SECTION B

17. Why is it that while using a moving coil galvanometer as a voltmeter, a high resistance in series is required? Also draw the circuit diagram for a voltmeter.

18. Draw energy band diagrams for germanium and wood.

19. Four identical cells, each of emf 8 V and internal resistance 2.5Ω are connected in series and charged by a 100 V DC supply, using a 24Ω resistor in series.

Calculate

(i) charging current in the circuit
(ii) and potential difference across the cells during recharging.

20. Define the following terms and give their source of origin.

(i) Plane wavefront (ii) Cylindrical wavefront

21. I. Derive an expression for the force between two long parallel current carrying conductors.

Or II. State Biot-Savart's law and express this law in vector form. Among Biot-Savart's law and Coulomb's law which one is angle dependent?

SECTION C

22. I. (a) Assuming that protons and neutrons have equal masses. Calculate how many times nuclear matter is denser than water? Given, mass of a nucleon $=1.67\times10^{-27}$ kg and $R_0=1.2\times10^{-15}$ m.

(b) Why do stable nuclei never have more protons than neutrons?

Or

II. Derive the expression for an alpha particle approaches the nucleus and how kinetic energy of α-particle converts into potential energy.

23. A rectangular conducting loop *DEFG* in which arm *FG* of length *l* is movable. The loop is kept in a uniform magnetic field *B* directed downward perpendicular to the plane of the loop. The arm *FG* is moved with a uniform speed *v*.

Deduce the expression for

(i) the emf induced across the arm *FG*

(ii) the external force required to move the arm.

24. In a parallel plate capacitor with air between the plates, each plate has an area of 6×10^{-3} m^2 and the separation between the plates is 3 mm.

(i) Calculate the capacitance of the capacitor.

(ii) If this capacitor is connected to 100 V supply, calculate charge on each plate?

(iii) How would charge on the plates be affected if a 3×10^{-3} m thick mica sheet of $K=8$ is inserted between the plates while the voltage supply remains connected?

25. I. (a) Draw a plot of potential energy of a pair of nuclons as a function of their separation. Write two important conclusions that can be drawn from the graph.

(b) Write three characteristic properties of nuclear force.

26. Two long wires having currents I_1 and I_2 are arranged as shown in the figure. One carrying current I_1 is along the *X*-axis. The other carrying current I_2 is along a line parallel to *Y*-axis, given by $x=0$ and $z=d$. Determine the force exerted at point O_2 because of the wire along the *X*-axis.

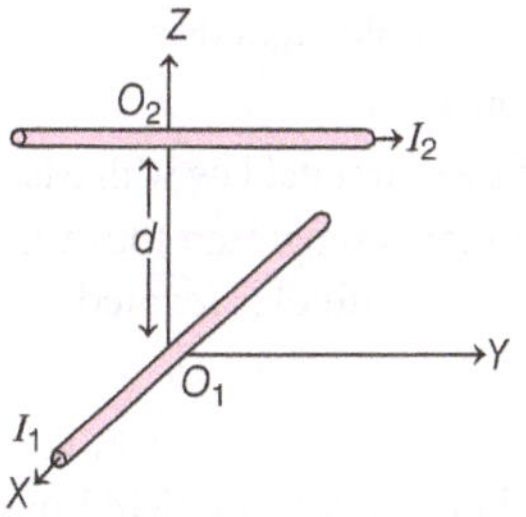

27. I. (a) Deduce the relation between current *I* flowing through a conductor and drift velocity v_d of the electrons.

(b) Why alloys like constantan and manganin are used for making standard resistors?

28. I. For a given lens, the magnification was found to be twice as large when the object was 0.15 m distant from it than when the distance was 0.2 m. What is the focal length of the lens?

Or

II. An astronomical telescope has objective and eyepiece of focal lengths 40 cm and 4 cm, respectively. Find the distance by which the lenses must be separated, so that image of an object 200 cm away from the objective can be seen at infinity. Also, draw the ray diagram.

SECTION D

(Case Study Based Questions)

29. *Read the following paragraph and answer the questions that follow*

We can write Gauss' law for magnetostatics as $\int \mathbf{B}\cdot d\mathbf{A}=\mu_0 m$, where $\int \mathbf{B}\cdot d\mathbf{A}$ is the magnetic flux and *m* is the net magnetic pole strength inside a closed surface.

It was found that magnetic flux through a closed surface is always zero. Thus, we reach at a conclusion that magnetic monopoles do not exist. A bar magnet always attains north-south poles no matter how many times it is cut into pieces.

(i) The net magnetic flux due to a bar magnet over a closed surface is

(a) zero (b) $\frac{\mu_0}{4\pi}$

(c) $4\pi\mu_0$ (d) $\frac{4\mu_0}{\pi}$

(ii) The presence of magnetic monopoles is ruled out by
(a) Gauss' law of electrostatics
(b) Gauss' law of magnetism
(c) Faraday's law
(d) Ampere's circuital law with Maxwell's addition

(iii) A bar magnet is separated four times, the number of monopoles and dipoles formed are
(a) 0, 8 (b) 0, 4
(c) 8, 2 (d) 8, 1

Or The number of magnetic field lines passing through a surface area normally is called
(a) magnetic field (b) electric field
(c) magnetic flux (d) electric flux

(iv) The dimensional representation of magnetic flux density is
(a) $[MLT^{-2}]$ (b) $[MLT^{-2}A^{-1}]$
(c) $[MT^{-2}A^{-1}]$ (d) $[MLT^{-2}A^{2}]$

30. ***Read the following paragraph and answer the questions that follow***

An oscillating charge is an example of accelerating charge. It produces an oscillating electric field in space, which produces an oscillating magnetic field, which in turn, produces an oscillating electric field and so on. The oscillating electric and magnetic fields regenerate each other as a wave which propagates through space.

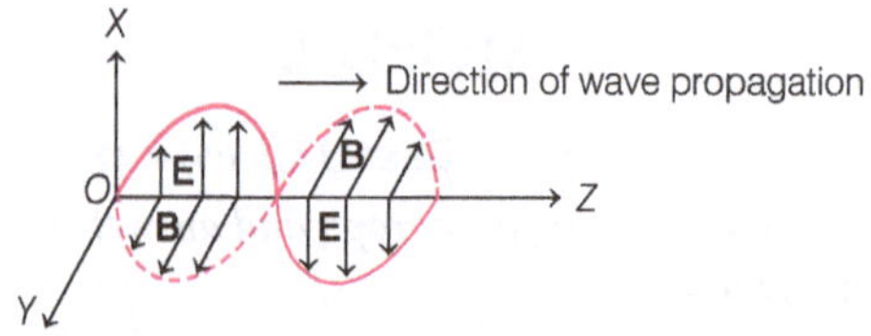

(i) Electromagnetic waves can be deflected by
(a) only electric field
(b) only magnetic field
(c) Both (a) and (b)
(d) None of the above

(ii) Total energy density of electromagnetic waves in vacuum is given by the relation
(a) $\frac{1}{2}\cdot\frac{E^2}{\varepsilon_0}+\frac{B^2}{2\mu_0}$ (b) $\frac{1}{2}\varepsilon_0 E^2+\frac{1}{2}\mu_0 B^2$
(c) $\frac{E^2+B^2}{c}$ (d) $\frac{1}{2}\varepsilon_0 E^2+\frac{B^2}{2\mu_0}$

(iii) The speed of electromagnetic wave in vacuum depends upon the source of radiation
(a) increases as we move from γ-rays to radio waves
(b) decreases as we move from γ-rays to radio waves
(c) is same for all of them
(d) None of the above

(iv) Solar radiation is
(a) transverse electromagnetic wave
(b) longitudinal electromagnetic wave
(c) stationary wave
(d) None of the above

Or

A plane electromagnetic wave of frequency 25 MHz travels in free space along the x-direction. At a particular point in space and time, $E = 6.3\,\hat{\mathbf{j}}\,\text{V/m}$. What is B at this point?
(a) $2.1\times10^{-8}\,\hat{\mathbf{k}}\text{T}$ (b) $2.1\times10^{8}\,\hat{\mathbf{k}}\text{T}$
(c) $3.5\times10^{6}\,\hat{\mathbf{k}}\text{T}$ (d) $3.0\times10^{5}\,\hat{\mathbf{k}}\text{T}$

SECTION E

31. I. (a) What is the focal length of the combination of a convex lens of focal length 30 cm in contact with a concave lens of focal length 20 cm? Is the system a converging or a diverging lens? Ignore thickness of the lenses.

(b) At what angle should a ray of light be incident on the face of a prism of refracting angle 60°, so that it just suffers total internal reflection at the other face? The refractive index of the material of the prism is 1.524.

Or

II. (a) Define the term wavefront. State Huygens' principle. Consider a plane wavefront incident on a thin convex lens. Draw a proper diagram to show how the incident wavefront traverses through the lens and after refraction focuses on the focal point of the lens, giving the shape of the emergent wavefront.

(b) Monochromatic light of wavelength 650 nm falls normally on a slit of width 1.3×10^{-4} cm and the resulting Fraunhofer diffraction is obtained on a screen. Find the angular width of the central maxima.

32. I. An AC source of voltage $V = V_0 \sin\omega t$ connected to a series combination of R, C and L. Use the phasor diagram to obtain expressions for impedance of the circuit and phase angle between voltage and current. Find the condition when current will be in phase with the voltage. What is the circuit in the condition called?

Or

II. (a) State the underlying principle of a transformer. How is the large scale transmission of electric energy over long distances done with the use of transformers?

(b) A step-down transformer operated on a 2.5 kV line. It supplies a load with 20 A. The ratio of the primary winding to the secondary is 10 : 1. If the transformer is 90% efficient, calculate

(i) the power output,

(ii) the voltage

(iii) and the current in the secondary coil.

33. I. Two charged conducting spheres of radii a and b are connected to each other by a wire. What is the ratio of electric fields at the surfaces of the two spheres? Use the result obtained to explain, why charge density on the sharp and pointed ends of a conductor is higher than on its flatter portions?

Or

II. (a) Intensity of electric field at a perpendicular distance of 0.5 m from an infinitely long line charge having linear charge density (λ) is 3.6×10^3 Vm^{-1}. Find the value of λ.

(b) Three equal charges of 5.0 μC each are placed at the three vertices of an equilateral triangle of side 5.0 cm each. Calculate the electrostatic potential energy of the system of charges.

(c) A hollow conducting sphere is placed in an electric field produced by a point placed at P as shown in figure.

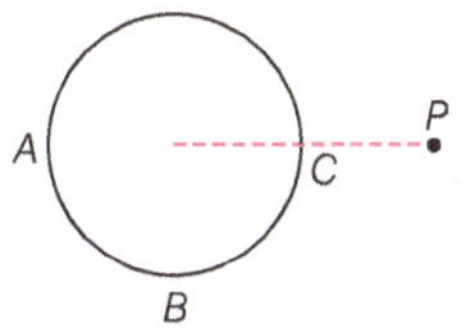

Let V_A, V_B and V_C be the potentials at points A, B and C respectively. Then, find out the relation between V_A, V_B and V_C.

Answers

1. (c) *2.* (d) *3.* (d) *4.* (a) *5.* (b) *6.* (a) *7.* (a) *8.* (d) *9.* (a) *10.* (b) *11.* (a) *12.* (d) *13.* (d) *14.* (b) *15.* (a) *16.* (d)

19. (i) 2 A, (ii) 52 V

24. (i) 17.7×10^{-12}F (ii) 17.7×10^{-10}C (iii) 1.416×10^{-8}C

28. I. 0.10 m or II. 54 cm

29. (i)-a, (ii)-b, (iii)-b or c (iv)-c

30. (i)-d, (ii)-d, (iii)-c, (iv)-(a) or (a)

31. I. (a) 60 cm, (b) 29°75' or II. (b) 1 rad

32. II. (b) (i) 4.5×10^4 W, (ii) 250 V and (iii) 180 A

33. II. (a) 10^{-7} cm^{-1}, (b) 13.5

CBSE
Examination Paper 2025

CBSE
EXAMINATION PAPERS 2025
PHYSICS

Time : **3 Hours** Max. Marks **: 70**

General Instructions

(i) This question paper contains 33 questions. All questions are compulsory.
(ii) This question paper is divided into five sections-Sections A, B, C, D and E.
(ii) In **Section A** Question numbers 1 to 16 are Multiple Choice type questions. Each question carries 1 mark.
(iv) In **Section B** Question numbers 17 to 21 are Very Short Answer type questions. Each question carries 2 marks.
(v) In **Section C** Question numbers 22 to 28 are Short Answer type questions. Each question carries 3 marks.
(vi) In **Section D** Question numbers 29 & 30 are Case Study Based questions. Each question carries 4 marks.
(vii) In **Section E** Question numbers 31 to 33 are Long Answer type questions. Each question carries 5 marks.
(viii) There is no overall choice given in the question paper. However, an internal choice has been provided in few questions in all the Sections except Section A.
(ix) Kindly note that there is a separate question paper for Visually Impaired candidates.
(x) Use of calculators is not allowed.

You may use the following values of physical constants wherever necessary:

$$c = 3 \times 10^8 \text{ m/s}, h = 6.63 \times 10^{-34} \text{ J-s}, e = 1.6 \times 10^{-19} \text{ C}, \mu_0 = 4\pi \times 10^{-7} \text{ T m A}^{-1}, \varepsilon_0 = 8.854 \times 10^{-12} \text{C}^2\text{N}^{-1}\text{m}^{-2}$$

$$\frac{1}{4\pi\varepsilon_0} = 9 \times 10^9 \text{ N m}^2 \text{ C}^{-2}$$

Mass of electron $(m_e) = 9.1 \times 10^{-31}$ kg, Mass of neutron $= 1.675 \times 10^{-27}$ kg, Mass of proton $= 1.673 \times 10^{-27}$ kg.
Avogadro's number $= 6.023 \times 10^{23}$ per gram mole, Boltzmann's constant $= 1.38 \times 10^{-23}$ JK^{-1}

SET - I (Code 55/2/1)

SECTION A

Directions (Q. Nos. 1-15) *Select the correct option out of the four given options.*

1. Two charges $-q$ each are placed at the vertices A and B of an equilateral triangle ABC. If M is the mid-point of AB, the net electric field at C will point along

(a) CA (b) CB (c) MC (d) CM

2. A student has three resistors, each of resistance R. To obtain a resistance of $\frac{2}{3}R$, she should connect

(a) all the three resistors in series.
(b) all the three resistors in parallel.
(c) two resistors in series and then this combination in parallel with the third resistor.
(d) two resistors in parallel and then this combination in series with the third resistor.

3. A 1 cm straight segment of a conductor carrying 1 A current in x-direction lies symmetrically at origin of Cartesian coordinate system. The magnetic field due to this segment at point (1m, 1m, 0) is

(a) $1.0 \times 10^{-9} \hat{k}$ T (b) $-1.0 \times 10^{-9} \hat{k}$ T
(c) $\frac{5.0}{\sqrt{2}} \times 10^{-10} \hat{k}$ T (d) $-\frac{5.0}{\sqrt{2}} \times 10^{-10} \hat{k}$ T

4. The magnetic field due to a small magnetic dipole of dipole moment M at a distance r from the centre along the axis of the dipole is given by

(a) $\frac{\mu_0}{4\pi} \times \frac{2M}{r^3}$ (b) $\frac{\mu_0}{4\pi} \times \frac{M}{r^3}$

(c) $\frac{\mu_0}{4\pi} \times \frac{M}{2r^3}$ (d) $\frac{\mu_0}{4\pi} \times \frac{2M}{r^2}$

5. In the figure, X is a coil wound over a hollow wooden pipe.

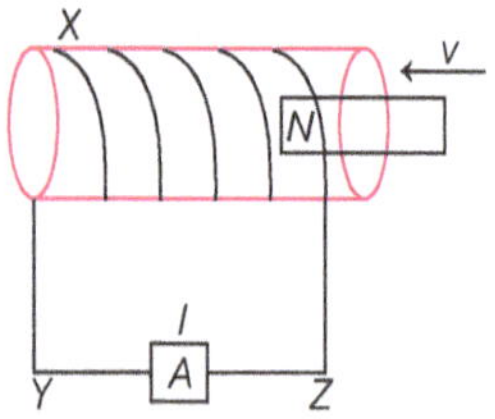

A permanent magnet is pushed at a constant speed v from the right into the pipe and it comes out at the left end of the pipe. During the entry and the exit of the magnet, the current in the wire YZ will be from

(a) Y to Z and then Y to Z

(b) Z to Y and then Y to Z

(c) Y to Z and then Z to Y

(d) Z to Y and then Z to Y

6. The alternating current I in an inductor is observed to vary with time t as shown in the graph for a cycle.

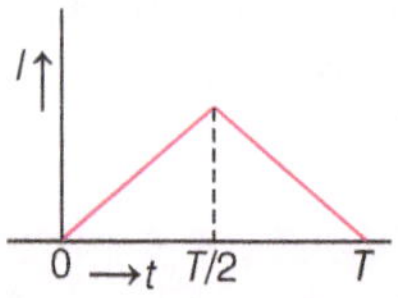

Which one of the following graphs is the correct representation of waveform of voltage V with time t?

(a)
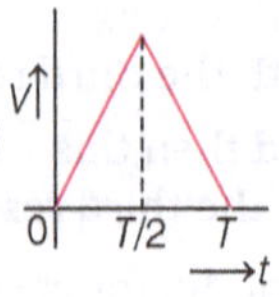

(b)
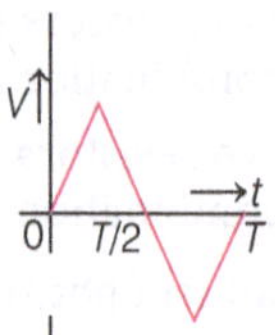

(c)
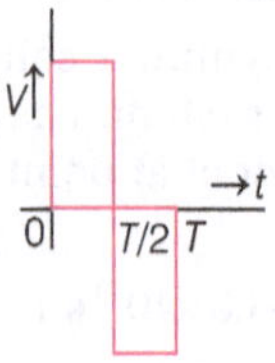

(d)
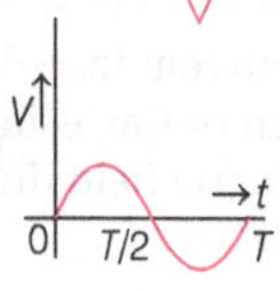

7. A transformer is connected to a 200 V AC source. The transformer supplies 3000 V to a device. If the number of turns in the primary coil is 450, then the number of turns in its secondary coil is

(a) 30 (b) 450 (c) 4500 (d) 6750

8. Which one of the following statements is correct?

Electric field due to static charges is

(a) conservative and field lines do not form closed loops.

(b) conservative and field lines form closed loops.

(c) non-conservative and field lines do not form closed loops.

(d) non-conservative and field lines form closed loops.

9. A tub is filled with a transparent liquid to a height of 30.0 cm. The apparent depth of a coin lying at the bottom of the tub is found to be 16.0 cm. The speed of light in the liquid will be

(a) 1.6×10^8 ms^{-1} (b) 2.0×10^8 ms^{-1}

(c) 3.0×10^8 ms^{-1} (d) 2.5×10^8 ms^{-1}

10. Atomic spectral emission lines of hydrogen atom are incident on a zinc surface. The lines which can emit photoelectrons from the surface are members of

(a) Balmer series

(b) Paschen series

(c) Lyman series

(d) Neither Balmer nor Paschen nor Lyman series

11. The energy of an electron in a hydrogen atom in ground state is – 13.6 eV. Its energy in an orbit corresponding to quantum number n is – 0.544 eV. The value of n is

(a) 2 (b) 3 (c) 4 (d) 5

12. When the resistance measured between p and n ends of a p-n junction diode is high, it can act as a/an

(a) resistor (b) inductor

(c) capacitor (d) switch

Directions (Q. Nos. 13-16) two statements are given-one labelled Assertion (A) and other labelled Reason (R). Select the correct answer to these questions from the codes (a), (b), (c) and (d) as given below:

(a) If both Assertion (A) and Reason (R) are true and Reason (R) is the correct explanation of Assertion (A).

(b) If both Assertion (A) and Reason (R) are true but Reason (R) is not the correct explanation of Assertion (A).

(c) If Assertion (A) is true but Reason (R) is false.

(d) If both Assertion (A) and Reason (R) are false.

13. **Assertion** (A) In a semiconductor diode, the thickness of depletion layer is not fixed.

Reason (R) Thickness of depletion layer in a semiconductor device depends upon many factors such as biasing of the semiconductor.

14. **Assertion** (A) In Bohr model of hydrogen atom, the angular momentum of an electron in nth orbit is proportional to the square root of its orbit radius r_n.

Reason (R) According to Bohr model, electron can jump to its nearest orbits only.

15. **Assertion** (A) Out of infrared and radio waves, the radio waves show more diffraction effect.

Reason (R) Radio waves have greater frequency than infrared waves.

16. **Assertion** (A) In an ideal step-down transformer, the electrical energy is not lost.

Reason (R) In a step-down transformer, voltage decreases but the current increases.

SECTION-B

17. (a) Two wires of the same material and the same radius have their lengths in the ratio 2: 3. They are connected in parallel to a battery which supplies a current of 15 A. Find the current through the wires.

Or

(b) In the circuit, three ideal cells of emf V, V and $2V$ are connected to a resistor of resistance R, a capacitor of capacitance C and another resistor of resistance $2R$ as shown in figure. In the steady state, find (i) the potential difference between P and Q and (ii) potential difference across capacitor C.

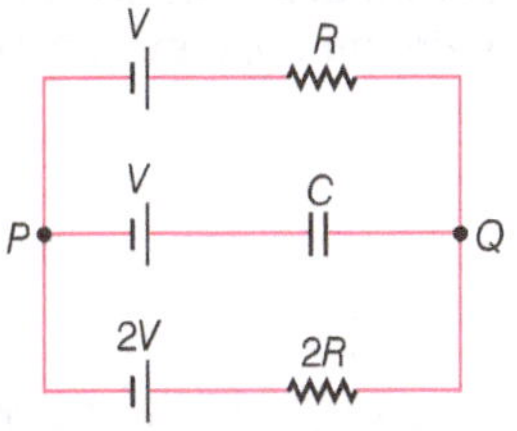

18. In a double-slit experiment, 6th dark fringe is observed at a certain point of the screen. A transparent sheet of thickness t and refractive index n is now introduced in the path of one of the two interfering waves to increase its phase by $2\pi(n-\lambda)t/\lambda$. The pattern is shifted and 8th bright fringe is observed at the same point. Find the relation for thickness t in terms of n and λ.

19. Two concave lenses A and B, each of focal length 8.0 cm are arranged coaxially 16 cm apart as shown in figure. An object P is placed at a distance of 4.0 cm from A. Find the position and nature of the final image formed.

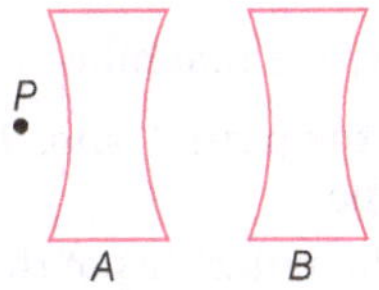

20. A light of wavelength 400 nm is incident on metal surface whose work function is 3.0×10^{-19} J. Calculate the speed of the fastest photoelectrons emitted.

21. The threshold voltage of a silicon diode is 0.7 V. It is operated at this point by connecting the diode in series with a battery of V volt and a resistor of 1000 Ω. Find the value of V when the current drawn is 15 mA.

SECTION-C

22. (a) A cell of emf E and internal resistance r is connected with a variable external resistance R and a voltmeter showing potential drop V across R. Obtain the relationship between V, E, R and r.

(b) Draw the shape of the graph showing the variation of terminal voltage V of the cell as a function of current I drawn from it. How one can determine the emf of the cell and its internal resistance from this graph?

23. (a) In a region of a uniform electric field $\mathbf{E}$, a negatively charged particle is moving with a constant velocity $\mathbf{v} = -v_0\hat{\mathbf{i}}$ near a long straight conductor coinciding with XX'-axis and carrying current I towards $-X$-axis. The particle remains at a distance d from the conductor.

(i) Draw diagram showing direction of electric and magnetic fields.

(ii) What are the various forces acting on the charged particle?

(iii) Find the value of v_0 in terms of E, d and I.

Or

(b) Two infinitely long conductors kept along XX' and YY' axes are carrying current I_1 and I_2 along $-X$-axis and $-Y$-axis respectively. Find the magnitude and direction of the net magnetic field produced at point $P(X,Y)$.

24. (a) State Lenz's law.
(b) In the given figure:

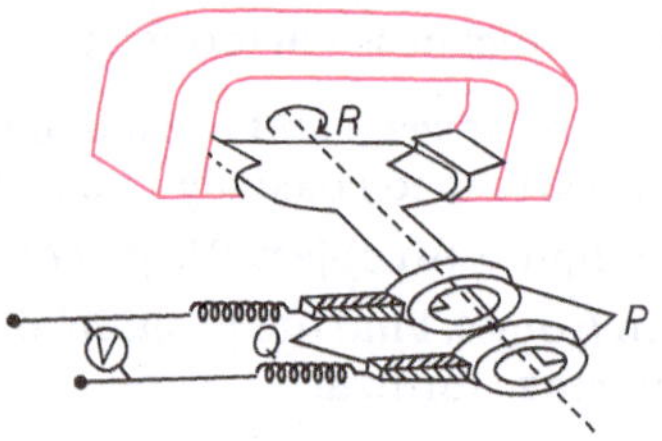

(i) Identify the machine.
(ii) Name the parts P and Q and R of the machine.
(iii) Give the polarities of the magnetic poles.
(iv) Write the two ways of increasing the output voltage.

25. (a) The electric field **E** of an electromagnetic wave propagating in north direction is oscillating in up and down direction. Describe the direction of magnetic field **B** of the wave.
(b) Are the wavelength of radio waves and microwaves longer or shorter than those detectable by human eyes?
(c) Write main use of each of the following in human life:
(i) Infrared waves (ii) Gamma rays

26. (a) When a parallel beam of light enters water surface obliquely at some angle, what is the effect on the width of the beam?
(b) With the help of a ray diagram, show that a straw appears bent when it is partly dipped in water and explain it.
(c) Explain the transmission of optical signal through an optical fibre by a diagram.

27. (a) Show the variation of binding energy per nucleon with mass number. Write the significance of the binding energy curve.
(b) Two nuclei with lower binding energy per nucleon form a nuclei with more binding energy per nucleon.
(i) What type of nuclear reaction is it?
(ii) Whether the total mass of nuclei increases, decreases or remains unchanged?
(iii) Does the process require energy or produce energy?

28. (a) What are majority and minority charge carriers in an extrinsic semiconductor?
(b) A p-n junction is forward biased. Describe the movement of the charge carriers which produce current in it.
(c) The graph shows the variation of current with voltage for a p-n junction diode.

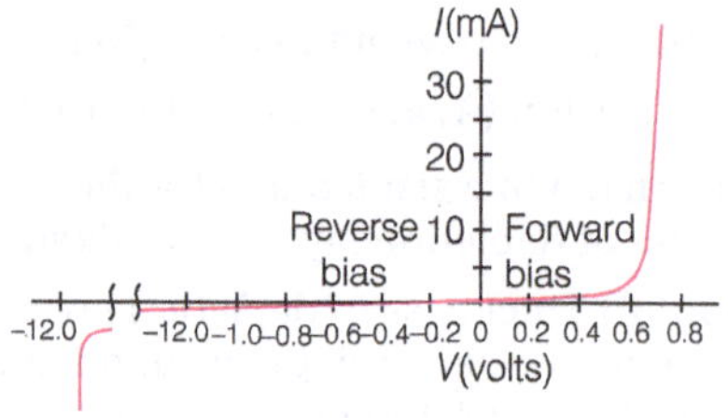

Estimate the dynamic resistance of diode at $V = -0.6$ volt.

SECTION-D

Directions (Q. Nos. 29-30) are case study based questions. Read the following paragraphs and answer the questions that follow.

29. A parallel plate capacitor has two parallel plates which are separated by an insulating medium like air, mica, etc. When the plates are connected to the terminals of a battery, they get equal and opposite charges and an electric field is set up in between them. This electric field between the two plates depends upon the potential difference applied, the separation of the plates and nature of the medium between the plates.

(i) The electric field between the plates of a parallel plate capacitor is E. Now the separation between the plates is doubled and simultaneously the applied potential difference between the plates is reduced to half of its initial value. The new value of the electric field between the plates will be
(a) E (b) $2E$ (c) $\frac{E}{4}$ (d) $\frac{E}{2}$

(ii) A constant electric field is to be maintained between the two plates of a capacitor whose separation d changes with time. Which of the graphs correctly depict the potential difference (V) to be applied between the plates as a function of separation between the plates (d) to maintain the constant electric field?

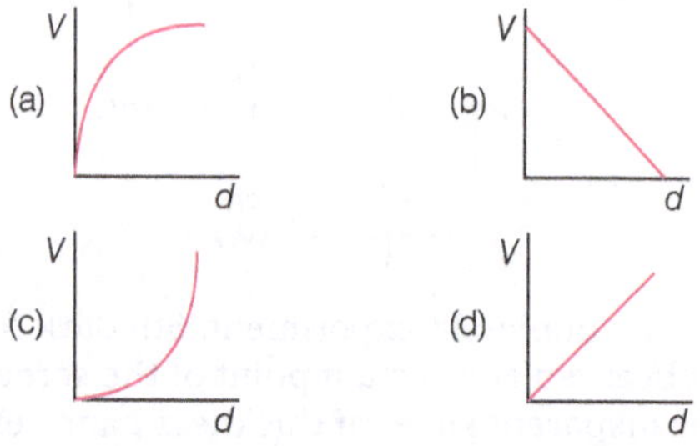

(iii)

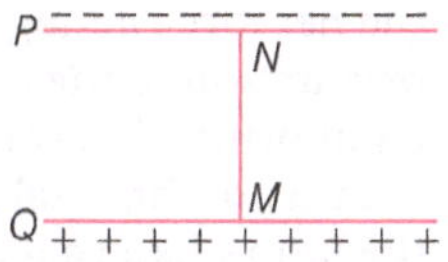

In the above figure *P*, *Q* are the two parallel plates of a capacitor. Plate Q is at positive potential with respect to plate *P*. *MN* is an imaginary line drawn perpendicular to the plates. Which of the graphs shows correctly the variations of the magnitude of electric field strength *E* along the line *MN*?

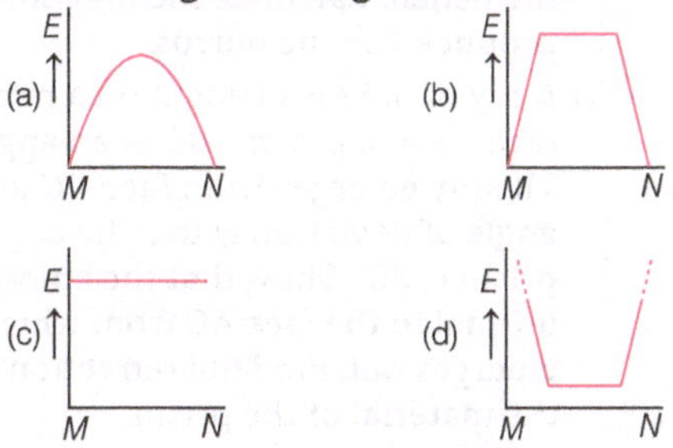

(iv) Three parallel plates are placed above each other with equal displacement **d** between neighbouring plates. The electric field between the first pair of the plates is $\mathbf{E}_1$ and the electric field between the second pair of the plates is $\mathbf{E}_2$. The potential difference between the third and the first plate is

(a) $(\mathbf{E}_1 + \mathbf{E}_2) \cdot \mathbf{d}$ (b) $(\mathbf{E}_1 - \mathbf{E}_2) \cdot \mathbf{d}$

(c) $(\mathbf{E}_2 + \mathbf{E}_1) \cdot \mathbf{d}$ (d) $\frac{d(E_1 + E_2)}{2}$

Or

(iv) A material of dielectric constant *K* is filled in a parallel plate capacitor of capacitance *C*. The new value of its capacitance becomes

(a) C (b) $\frac{C}{K}$

(c) CK (d) $C\left(1 + \frac{1}{K}\right)$

30. When a photon of suitable frequency is incident on a metal surface, photoelectron is emitted from it. If the frequency is below a threshold frequency (ν_0) for the surface, no photoelectron is emitted. For a photon of frequency $\nu(\nu > \nu_0)$, the kinetic energy of the emitted photoelectrons is $h(\nu - \nu_0)$. The photocurrent can be stopped by applying a potential V_0 called 'stopping potential' on the anode. Thus, maximum kinetic energy of photoelectrons $K_m = eV_0 = h(\nu - \nu_0)$.
The experimental graph between V_0 and ν for a metal is shown in figure. This is a straight line of slope *m*.

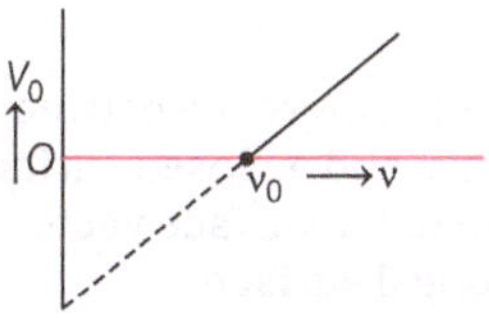

(i) The straight line graphs obtained for two metals

(a) coincide each other

(b) are parallel to each other

(c) are not parallel to each other and cross at a point on ν-axis

(d) are not parallel to each other and do not cross at a point on ν-axis

(ii) The value of Planck's constant for this metal is

(a) $\frac{e}{m}$ (b) $\frac{1}{me}$

(c) me (d) $\frac{m}{e}$

(iii) The intercepts on ν-axis and V_0-axis of the graph are respectively

(a) $\nu_0, \frac{h\nu_0}{e}$ (b) $\nu_0, h\nu_0$

(c) $\frac{h\nu_0}{e}, \nu_0$ (d) $h\nu_0, \nu_0$

Or

(iii) When the wavelength of a photon is doubled, how many times its wave number and frequency become, respectively?

(a) $2, \frac{1}{2}$ (b) $\frac{1}{2}, \frac{1}{2}$

(c) $\frac{1}{2}, 2$ (d) $2, 2$

(iv) The momentum of a photon is 5.0×10^{-29} kg m/s. Ignoring relativistic effects (if any), the wavelength of the photon is

(a) 1.33 μm (b) 3.3 μm

(c) 16.6 μm (d) 13.3 μm

SECTION - E

31. (a) (i) A small conducting sphere *A* of radius *r* charged to a potential *V*, is enclosed by a spherical conducting shell *B* of radius *R*. If *A* and *B* are connected by a thin wire, calculate the final potential on sphere *A* and shell *B*.

(ii) Write two characteristics of equipotential surfaces. A uniform electric field of 50 NC^{-1} is set up in a region along +*X*-axis. If the potential at the origin (0, 0) is 220 V, find the potential at a point (4m, 3m).

Or

(b) (i) What is difference between an open surface and a closed surface? Draw elementary surface vector $d\mathbf{S}$ for a spherical surface S.

(ii) Define electric flux through a surface. Give the significance of a Gaussian surface. A charge outside a Gaussian surface does not contribute to total electric flux through the surface. Why?

(iii) A small spherical shell S_1 has point charges $q_1 = -3\ \mu C$, $q_2 = -2\ \mu C$ and $q_3 = 9\ \mu C$ inside it. This shell is enclosed by another big spherical S_2. A point charge Q is placed in between the two surfaces S_1 and S_2. If the electric flux through the surface S_2 is four times the flux through surface S_1, find charge Q.

32. (a) (i) What is the source of force acting on a current-carrying conductor placed in a magnetic field? Obtain the expression for force acting between two long straight parallel conductors carrying steady currents and hence define 'ampere'.

(ii) A point charge q is moving with velocity V in a uniform magnetic field B. Find the work done by the magnetic force on the charge.

(iii) Explain the necessary conditions in which the trajectory of a charged particle is helical in a uniform magnetic field.

Or

(b) (i) A current carrying loop can be considered as a magnetic dipole placed along its axis. Explain.

(ii) Obtain the relation for magnetic dipole moment M of current carrying coil. Give the direction of M.

(iii) A current carrying coil is placed in an external uniform magnetic field. The coil is free to turn in the magnetic field. What is the net force acting on the coil? Obtain the orientation of the coil in stable equilibrium. Show that in this orientation the flux of the total field (field produced by the loop + external field) through the coil is maximum.

33. (a) (i) A thin pencil of length $\left(\frac{f}{4}\right)$ is placed coinciding with the principal axis of a mirror of focal length f. The image of the pencil is real and enlarged, just touches the pencil. Calculate the magnification produced by the mirror.

(ii) A ray of light is incident on a refracting face AB of a prism ABC at an angle of 45°. The ray emerges from face AC and the angle of deviation is 15°. The angle of prism is 30°. Show that the emergent ray is normal to the face AC from which it emerges out. Find the refraction index of the material of the prism.

Or

(b) (i) Light consisting of two wavelengths 600 nm and 480 nm is used to obtain interference fringes in a double slit experiment. The screen is placed 1.0 m away from slits which are 1.0 nm apart.

(1) Calculate the distance of the third bright fringe on the screen from the central maximum for wavelength 600 nm.

(2) Find the least distance from the central maximum where the bright fringes due to both the wavelengths coincide.

(ii) (1) Draw the variation of intensity with angle of diffraction in single slit diffraction pattern. Write the expression for value of angle corresponding to zero intensity locations.

(2) In what way diffraction of light waves differs from diffraction of sound waves?

SET-II (Only Uncommon Questions from Set-I) (Code 55/2/2)

SECTION-A

1. Two identical point charges are placed at the two vertices A and B of an equilateral triangle of side l. The magnitude of the electric field at the third vertex P is E. If a hollow conducting sphere of radius $\left(\frac{l}{4}\right)$ is placed at P, the magnitude of the electric field at point P now becomes

(a) $> E$ (b) E (c) $\frac{E}{2}$ (d) zero

2. A battery of emf 12 V and internal resistance 0.5 Ω is connected to a 9.5 Ω resistor through a key. The ratio of potential difference between the two terminals of the battery, when the key is open to that when the key is closed, is

(a) 1.05 (b) 1 (c) 0.95 (d) 1.1

4. A diamagnetic substance is brought, one by one, near the north pole and the south pole of a bar magnet. It is

(a) repelled by north pole and attracted by south pole.
(b) attracted by north pole and repelled by south pole.
(c) attracted by north pole as well as by south pole.
(d) repelled by north pole as well as by south pole.

5. Two long solenoids of radii r_1 and $r_2 (> r_1)$ and number of turns per unit length n_1 and n_2 respectively are coaxially wrapped one over the other. The ratio of self-inductance of inner solenoid to their mutual inductance is

(a) $\frac{n_1}{n_2}$ (b) $\frac{n_2}{n_1}$ (c) $\frac{n_1 r_1^2}{n_2 r_2^2}$ (d) $\frac{n_2 r_1^2}{n_1 r_2^2}$

7. A coil of an AC generator, having 100 turns and area 0.1 m^2 each, rotates at half a rotation per second in a magnetic field of 0.02 T. The maximum emf generated in the coil is

(a) 0.31 V (b) 0.20 V
(c) 0.63 V (d) 0.10 V

9. The focal length of a concave mirror in air is f. When the mirror is immersed in a liquid of refractive index $\frac{5}{3}$, its focal length will become

(a) $\frac{5}{3}f$ (b) $\frac{3}{5}f$
(c) $\frac{2}{3}f$ (d) f

SECTION-B

18. Show the refraction of light wave at a plane interface using Huygens' principle and prove Snell's law.

19. Two convex lenses A and B, each of focal length 10.0 cm, are mounted on an optical bench at 50.0 cm and 70.0 cm respectively. An object is mounted at 20.0 cm. Find the nature and position of the final image formed by the combination.

20. Radiations of two frequencies are incident on a metal surface of work function 2.0 eV one by one. The energies of their photons are 2.5 eV and 4.5 eV respectively. Find the ratio of the maximum speed of the electrons emitted in the two cases.

SECTION-C

22. (a) Define resistivity of a conductor. Discuss its dependence on temperature of the conductor and draw a plot of resistivity of copper as a function of temperature.
(b) (i) A low voltage battery from which high current is required must have low internal resistance. Justify.
(ii) A high voltage battery must have a large internal resistance. Justify

24. Differentiate between the peak value and root mean square value of an alternating current. Derive the expression for the root mean square value of alternating current, in terms of its peak value.

25. (a) How is an electromagnetic wave produced?
(b) An electromagnetic wave is travelling in vertically upward direction. At an instant, its electric field vector points in west direction. In which direction does the magnetic field vector point at that instant?
(c) Estimate the ratio of shortest wavelength of radio waves to the longest wavelength of gamma waves.

SET - III (Only Uncommon Questions from Set-I & II) (Code 55/2/3)

SECTION - A

1. Consider two identical dipoles D_1 and D_2. Charges $-q$ and q of dipole D_1 are located at (0, 0) and $(a, 0)$ and that of dipole D_2 at $(0, a)$ and $(0, 2a)$ in XY-plane, respectively. The net dipole moment of the system is

(a) $qa(\hat{i} + \hat{j})$ (b) $-qa(\hat{i} + \hat{j})$

(c) $qa(\hat{i} - \hat{j})$ (d) $-qa(\hat{i} - \hat{j})$

2. Which pair of readings of ideal voltmeter and ideal ammeter in the given circuit is possible when a suitable power source of 3 Ω internal resistance is connected between P and Q?

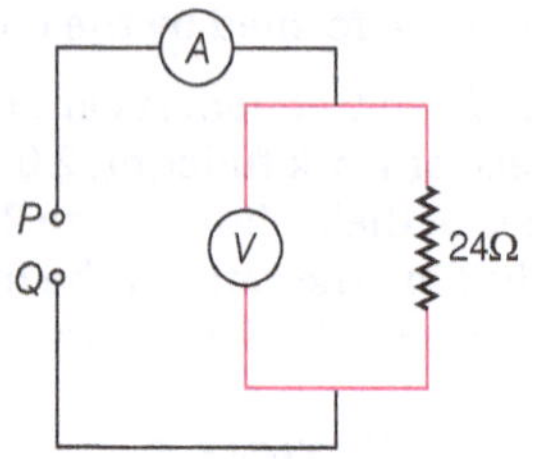

(a) 12.0 V, 2.0 A (b) 2.0 V, 0.5 A

(c) 6.0 V, 2.0 A (d) 12 V, 0.5 A

4. A material is pushed out when placed in a uniform magnetic field. The material is

(a) non-magnetic (b) diamagnetic

(c) paramagnetic (d) ferromagnetic

5. A soft iron rod X is allowed to fall on the two poles of a U shaped permanent magnet as shown in figure. A coil is wrapped over one arm of the U shaped magnet.

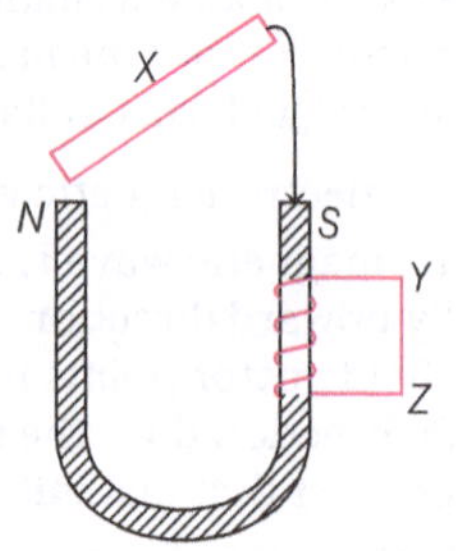

During fall of the rod, the current in the coil will be

(a) clockwise current

(b) anti-clockwise current

(c) alternating current

(d) zero

7. The number of turns between different terminals are shown for a step-up transformer.

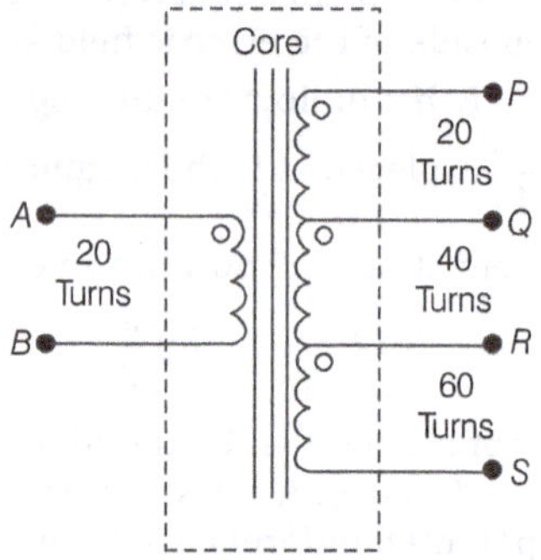

Input voltage of 20 V is applied between A and B. Between which two terminals will the output be 120 V ?

(a) P and Q (b) Q and S

(c) P and R (d) P and S

9. The plane face of a planoconvex lens is silvered. The refractive index of material and radius of curvature of the curved surface of the lens are n and R respectively. This lens will behave as a concave mirror of focal length

(a) $\frac{R}{n}$ (b) $\frac{R}{(n-1)}$ (c) nR (d) $\frac{R}{2(n-1)}$

SECTION-B

19. A light beam converges at a point O. In the path of this beam, a concave lens of focal length 15 cm is placed at a distance of 10 cm before point O. The beam now converges at a point O'. Find the magnitude and the direction of shift OO'.

20. The threshold wavelength of a metal is 450 nm. Calculate (i) the work function of the metal in eV and (ii) the maximum energy of the ejected photoelectrons in eV by incident radiation of 250 nm.

SECTION-C

24. (a) AC voltage of frequency ω is applied across a series L-C-R circuit. Draw the phasor diagram and obtain the impedance of the circuit.

(b) Discuss resonance in a series *L*-*C*-*R* circuit and write the expression for resonant frequency.

25. (a) The amplitude of a light wave becomes *n* times. This results in intensity of the wave becoming *m* times. What is the relation between *n* and *m*?

(b) White light is incident on three identical surfaces a black surface, a yellow surface and a white surface, one by one. For which surface, the pressure exerted on the surface by the incident light will be (i) maximum (ii) minimum? Justify your answer.

Solutions

Set-I

Section - A

1. Refer to solution 5 on page 27
2. Refer to solution 2 on page 115.
3. Refer to solution 4 on page 155.
4. Refer to solution 9 on page 188.
5. Refer to solution 12 on page 188.
6. Refer to solution 14 on page 247.
7. Refer to solution 25 on page 247.
8. Refer to solution 4 on page 27.
9. Refer to solution 9 on page 310.
10. Refer to solution 19 on page 395.
11. Refer to solution 7 on page 395.
12. Refer to solution 8 on page 443.
13. Refer to solution 26 on page 443.
14. Refer to solution 28 on page 396.
15. Refer to solution 26 on page 272.
16. Refer to solution 37 on page 247.

Section - B

17. (i) Refer to solution 2 on pages 117 and 118.

Or

(ii) Refer to solution 2 on page 118.

18. Refer to solution 29 on page 346.
19. Refer to solution 50 on page 320.
20. Refer to solution 34 on page 376.
21. Refer to solution 5 on page 445.

Section - C

22. (a) Refer to solution 13 (i) on page 119.

Or

(b) Refer to solution 13 (ii) on pages 119.

23. (a) Refer to solution 33 (i) on pages 161 and 162

Or

(b) Refer to solution 33 (ii) on page 162.

24. (a) Refer to solution 12 (i) on page 217.

Or (b) Refer to solution 12 (ii) on page 217.

25. (a) Refer to solution 16 (i) on page 273.
(b) Refer to solution 16 (ii) on page 273.
(c) Refer to solution 16 (iii) on page 273.

26. (a) Refer to solution 44 (i) on pages 318 and 319.
(b) Refer to solution 44 (ii) on page 319.
(c) Refer to solution 44 (iii) on page 319.

27. (a) Refer to solution 8 (i) on page 421.
(b) Refer to solution 8 (ii) on page 421.

28. (a) Refer to solution 7 (i) on page 445.
(b) Refer to solution 7 (ii) on page 445.
(c) Refer to solution 7 (iii) on page 445.

Section - D

29. Refer to solution 40 on page 73.
30. Refer to solution 35 on page 371.

Section - E

31. (a) Refer to solution 54 on pages 83 and 84.

Or (b) Refer to solution 35 on page 38.

32. (a) Refer to solution 37 on page 163.

Or

(b) Refer to solution 24 on pages 191.

33.

(a) Refer to solution 56 on page 321.

Or

(b) Refer to solution 33 on pages 347.

Set-II

Section - A

1. Refer to solution 3 on page 27.
2. Refer to solution 19 on page 116.
4. Refer to solution 11 on page 188.
5. Refer to solution 22 on page 215.

7. (c) Given $N = 10$, $A = 0.1\ m^2$, $B = 0.02$ T and $f = \frac{1}{2}$ Hz,
which means $\omega = 2\pi f = \pi$ rad/s
∴Maximum emf induced in the coil is
$$\varepsilon = NBA\omega = 100 \times 0.02 \times 0.1 \times 3.14 = 0.63\ V$$

9. (d) The focal length of the concave mirror will remain same because it is independent of the refractive index of the medium in which it is kept

Section - B

18. Refer to solution 1 on page 342.
19. Refer to solution 51 on page 320.
20. Refer to solution 39 on pages 376 and 377.
22. (a) Refer to solution 16 (i) on page 119.
(b) Refer to solution 16 (ii) on page 119.
24. Refer to solution 25 on page 251.
25. Refer to solution 14 on page 273.

Set - III

Section A

1. (a)

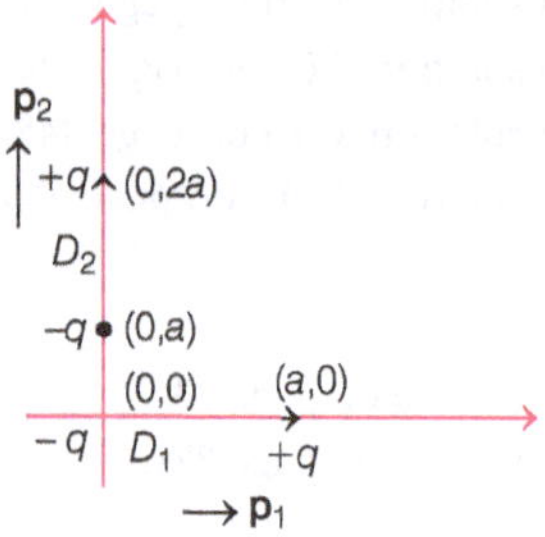

$$\mathbf{p}_1 = qa\hat{\mathbf{i}}\ ;\ \mathbf{p}_2 = qa\hat{\mathbf{j}}.$$
$$\therefore \quad \mathbf{p}_{net} = qa(\hat{\mathbf{i}} + \hat{\mathbf{j}})$$

2. Given,
External resistance, $R = 24\ \Omega$
Voltage drop across R,
$$V = IR$$
Let voltage drop is measured as 12V by ideal voltmeter.
$$12 = I \times 24$$
$$I = \frac{12}{24}$$
$$I = 0.5\ A$$
So, ideal ammeter will measure the current.
$$I = 0.5A$$

4. (b) diagmagnetic

5. (a) The magnetic flux intensity will increase due to the fall of soft iron and emf will induced in the coil. By Lenz's law, to oppose the magnetic flux, the induced magnetic field generated in the upward direction. Hence, from the right hand rule the direction of current is clockwise.

7. (d) Use formula,
$$N_S = \frac{N_P V_S}{V_P}$$
$$N_S = \frac{20 \times 120}{20}$$
$$N_S = 120$$
Since, the number of turns $N_S = 120$ is between P and S terminal.

9. (b) When plano-convex lens is converted into concave mirror.
Then, $R_1 = R$, $R_2 = \infty$, $\mu_g = n$, $\mu_a = 1$
Use Lens formula,
$$\frac{1}{f} = \left(\frac{\mu_g}{\mu_a} - 1\right)\left(\frac{1}{R_1} - \frac{1}{R_2}\right)$$
$$\frac{1}{f} = \left(\frac{n}{1} - 1\right)\left(\frac{1}{R} - \frac{1}{\infty}\right)$$
$$\frac{1}{f} = \frac{(n-1)}{R} \text{ or } f = \frac{R}{(n-1)}$$

19. Given, $u = +10$ cm, $f = -15$ cm
Use lens formula,
$$\frac{1}{v} - \frac{1}{u} = \frac{1}{f}$$
$$\frac{1}{v} = \frac{1}{f} + \frac{1}{u}$$
$$\frac{1}{v} = \frac{1}{(-15)} + \frac{1}{10}$$
$$\frac{1}{v} = \frac{15-10}{150}$$
$$v = \frac{150}{5}$$
$$v = +30\ \text{cm}$$
Magnitude of the shift,
$$v - u = 30 - 10$$
$$= 20\ \text{cm}$$
Direction of shift towards right.

20. (i) Work function, $\phi = \frac{hc}{\lambda_0}$
where,
$h = 6.626 \times 10^{-34}$ J-s
$c = 3.0 \times 10^8$ m/s
$\lambda_0 = 450$ nm
$= 450 \times 10^{-9}$m
$$\therefore \quad \phi = \frac{(6.626 \times 10^{-34}) \times (3.0 \times 10^8)}{450 \times 10^{-9}}$$
$$= 4.417 \times 10^{-19}\ J$$
Convert to electron volts (eV) using
$$1\ eV = 1.602 \times 10^{-19}\ J$$

$\therefore \quad \phi = \frac{4.417 \times 10^{-19}}{1.602 \times 10^{-19}} = 2.76\,\text{eV}$

(ii) Maximum kinetic energy (K_{max}),

$K_{max} = hf - \phi$

where, f = frequency of incident radiation $= \frac{c}{\lambda}$

We know that, $\lambda = 250\text{ nm} = 250 \times 10^{-9}$ m.

hf is the energy of the incident photon

$$E_{Photon} = \frac{(6.626 \times 10^{-34}) \times (3.0 \times 10^{8})}{250 \times 10^{-9}}$$

$$= 7.9512 \times 10^{-19}\text{ J}$$

Convert to eV,

$$E_{Photon} = \frac{7.9512 \times 10^{-19}}{1.602 \times 10^{-19}} = 4.96\text{ eV}$$

$\therefore \quad K_{max} = E_{Photon} - \phi = 4.96 - 2.76$

$= 2.20\,\text{eV}$

Therefore, the work function of the metal is 2.76 eV and the maximum energy of the ejected photoelectrons is 2.20 eV.

24. (a) Phasor diagram of series *L-C-R* circuit.

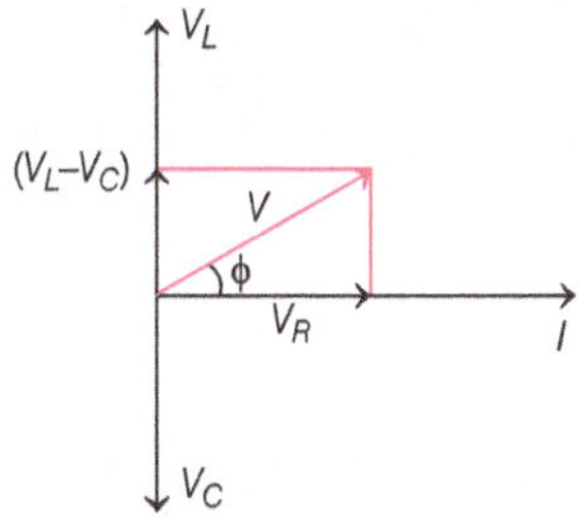

Expression for the impedance in circuit.

The same current I will flow in all the three components.

At any instant time, V_L, V_C and V_R are the potential differences across the components L, C, R, respectively.

Then,

$$V_L = IX_L,\ V_C = IX_C \text{ and } V_R = IR$$

The resultant voltage V,

$$V^2 = V_R^2 + (V_L - V_C)^2$$

$$V^2 = I^2[R^2 + (X_L - X_C)^2]$$

$$I = \frac{V}{\sqrt{R^2 + (X_L - X_C)^2}}$$

Applying Ohm's law, we see that $\sqrt{R^2 + (X_L - X_C)}$ is the effective resistance of the circuits and is called impedance.

i.e., $\quad Z = \sqrt{R^2 + (X_L - X_C)^2}$

(b) At resonance, the inductive reactance is equal to capacitive reactance. In this condition, the circuit becomes purely resistive and hence the current is maximum.

At resonance, $\quad X_L = X_C$

$$\omega L = \frac{1}{\omega C}$$

$$\omega^2 = \frac{1}{LC}$$

but $\quad \omega = 2\pi f$

Therefore, $\quad f = \frac{1}{2\pi\sqrt{LC}}$

25. (a) The intensity of wave is directly proportional to the square of amplitude.

$$I_0 \propto A_0^2$$

Since, $\quad I' = nI_0$ and $A' = mA_0$

Therefore, $\quad I' \propto A'^2$

$$nI_0 \propto (mA_0)^2$$

Hence, $\quad n \propto m^2$

(b) The pressure exerted by the incident light on the surface will be maximum for yellow and white surfaces. Since, both will reflect white light.

i.e. $\quad p_R = \frac{2I}{C}$

Expression for pressure exerted on the surface,

$$p = (1 + \sigma)\frac{I}{C}$$

where, σ is coefficient of reflection.

(i) For yellow and white surface the coefficient of reflection is high. So, the pressure exerted on the yellow and white surface is maximum.

(ii) For black surface the coefficient of reflection is low. So, the pressure exerted on the black surface is minimum.